DATE DUE

			PRINTED IN U.S.A.

THE CHINESE FILMOGRAPHY

THE
CHINESE
FILMOGRAPHY

*The 2444 Feature Films
Produced by Studios in the
People's Republic of China
from 1949 through 1995*

by DONALD J. MARION

McFarland & Company, Inc., Publishers

Jefferson, North Carolina, and London

British Library Cataloguing-in-Publication data are available

Library of Congress Cataloguing-in-Publication Data

Marion, Donald J.
    The Chinese filmography : the 2444 feature films produced by
studios in the People's Republic of China from 1949 through 1995 /
by Donald J. Marion.
      p.   cm.
    Includes bibliographical references and index.
    ISBN 0-7864-0305-5 (library binding : 50# alkaline paper) ∞
    1. Motion pictures — China — Catalogs. I. Title.
PN1993.5.C4M37   1997
016.79143'0951— dc21

                    96-49551
                    CIP

Manufactured in the United States of America

McFarland & Company, Inc., Publishers
  Box 611, Jefferson, North Carolina 28640

To Lynn,
who makes it all possible

Table of Contents

Acknowledgments

As this book is my own creation, responsibility for any shortcomings or errors herein are mine alone. Credit, on the other hand, must in this case be shared, and I wish to acknowledge the contributions of a few others. First, the University of Minnesota Libraries for granting me a leave to complete the project. Second, my former student Yi Li, who assisted me in locating some scarce resources. And finally my wife Lynn, who assisted in more ways than I could say. Her contributions ranged from helping me identify and track down sources in bookstores and libraries, through typing and proofreading, to listening patiently to countless drafts. But most of all for providing encouragement when I needed it, and for just being there.

Introduction

Anyone who becomes involved in research into any area of Chinese studies soon becomes aware of the impressive richness of the resources available. The Chinese scholarly tradition has amassed a vast and well organized literature in virtually every area of human endeavor. While this presents an intellectual banquet for the seeker of knowledge, without the requisite language capability the non–Chinese researcher is doomed to at best remain outside the banquet hall looking in, perhaps not even aware of the riches that do exist. Film studies are no exception. As cultural exchanges with China have expanded, so has awareness of China's motion picture output. Today, while many film scholars and foreign film buffs would immediately recognize such recent titles as *Raise the Red Lantern* and *Farewell to My Concubine*, or such contemporary artists as Gong Li, Zhang Yimou and Chen Kaige, few are familiar with their predecessors, although China's rich tradition of filmmaking extends back to 1905. (There are actually two Chinese traditions in this field, as the "left" and "right" split in China's 20th century politics was paralleled in its motion picture community.)

Since the founding of the People's Republic of China (PRC) in 1949, there have been several thousand films produced in that country, over 2,500 of them feature films ("story films" in Chinese). Many of these movies have been unabashedly politi-cal, often mirroring the political tides of their times and the various political policies and campaigns of the ruling Chinese Communist Party (CPC). Although the leftist sympathies of many Chinese artists had existed for many years, the use of their art as official political expression had its real gene-sis in two speeches made by CPC Chairman Mao Zedong in May, 1942 at the famous Yanan Forum on Art and Literature, a con-ference of cultural workers. In discussing various art-related issues and making clear the Party line, Mao set forth the dictum that "the purpose of art is to serve politics." With that pronouncement, the Chairman estab-lished the underlying principle that pro-duced for many years to come the basic didacticism of so much of modern Chinese literature and art, including cinema. So studies of the Chinese films of this era are really as much a topic for the student of political history as they are for the film his-torian. My hope is that this book will serve as a tool for both.

How well China's filmmakers accom-plished the entertainment half of their dual objective can of course be determined only by actually viewing the movies. While the restrictions of time and availability make this an impossible task outside of China, we are fortunate in that many of the best Chi-nese films of this era are now available in the West for purchase or rental. I leave it to stu-dents of Chinese political history to judge

1

the success of PRC filmmakers in carrying out the political half of their goal.

The objective of this work is to provide as detailed as possible a listing of the roughly 2500 feature films produced by studios in the People's Republic of China since that nation's founding in 1949. I have placed a few limitations on the coverage: the films included are those which the Chinese call *gushi pian* (literally, "story films"), the category which corresponds most closely to what are termed "feature films" in the West. I have excluded filmed operas, but have included feature films based on operas. While straight documentaries are excluded, the many docudramas produced in the PRC are included. The cutoff date for completion of a film is December 31, 1995. However, there were an undetermined number of films completed by that date which had not been released by mid–1996 when this book went into editing. These have not been included because of a lack of information about them.

Each entry in the filmography provides as much vital information concerning a film as is available, drawn either from Chinese sources or, when possible, from actual viewing of the film and recording of its credits. In a handful of cases, reference was made to reliable Western sources, but this was used as a last resort, usually for confirming questionable points, such as the actual title a film was released under in the west. While the entries are for the most part uniform, there has been some deviation when it seemed more informative to do so. In general, each listing contains the following information:

Title in English: In a great many cases these would appear to reflect the original Chinese title to little if any degree; this is because so many Chinese movies are released outside of Asia under a title more indicative of the film's content. If reliable sources indicated that a given film was released in the West under a particular English title, that is the one I have provided. If no such indication was found, the title given here is my own translation of the original.

Title in romanized Chinese: The title in each case is presented in *pinyin* romanization, the form used in the PRC. For clarity, I have noted each Chinese syllable separately.

Year: The year in which production of the film was completed, rather than the year of its release. (As noted, an exception was necessary for some 1995 productions.)

Studios: For PRC studio names, the standard English translation is given. In the case of co-productions with companies outside of China, the information is given as it appeared in the Chinese credits.

Technical Information: Color or black and white, letterboxed or wide screen (when applicable). I have also noted Dolby when that was the sound system employed.

Length: While the standard practice in the West is to indicate the length of films by their running time, usually in minutes, until very recently the Chinese practice has been to list only the number of reels. I have followed this, except in a handful of cases where a reliable source furnished the running time. I avoided, however, relying too heavily on these sources, especially if I suspected the provider of the information may have viewed an edited copy of the film, e.g., on television.

Technical Credits: At a minimum, these include direction, screenplay, cinematography, art direction, music and sound. For some films, information concerning costuming and makeup has been included as well. In most instances, the names are listed in *pinyin* romanization, with the exceptions noted below.

Literary Source: Like filmmakers everywhere, the Chinese have drawn heavily on literary properties as sources, and I have noted this where applicable. In addition, I have provided the dates for authors' lives when I was able to find the information. This was done in part to provide a temporal context for film scholars, and to increase this work's utility for the student of Chinese literature.

Cast: All names are listed in the Chinese fashion, i.e., with the surname or family name first, followed by the given name. As with technical credits, Chinese names are listed in their Mandarin Chinese form, in *pinyin* romanization. In addition, when a cast member in a co-production was recognized as a Hong Kong performer with an English name, that name is listed in addition to the Mandarin Chinese name, e.g., Zhang Guorong (Leslie Cheung), or Lin Qingxia (Brigitte Lin). Especially problematic was how to deal with non–Chinese names: Chinese film credits, either as presented on the screen or as listed in secondary compilations, have in most cases transliterated foreign names into Chinese. Such names are recognizable, but beyond an awareness that this person was not Chinese, there is very little way of distinguishing their real name. Some of these transliterated names are well known to students of the Chinese film, e.g., "Tan Ningban" is recognized as the 1950s American actor Gerald Tannebaum. But in the great majority of such cases, the only information available is the Chinese transliteration, so that is what is listed here. The same practice applies for non–Han Chinese ethnic minorities as well.

Plot Summary: These vary in length according to the amount of information available and the importance of the film. I have tried insofar as possible to provide more detailed summaries for the more significant films. For a small number of films, no plot information was available, and for these only the credits are provided.

Awards: In the entries, I have noted when a particular film or artist won one of China's two domestic film awards. The PRC has two sets of awards: the Golden Rooster and the Hundred Flowers. The more prestigious Golden Rooster has been awarded since 1981 by the Chinese Film Artists Association, with members voting for nominees in their individual membership categories, similar to the practice of film academies in other nations. The Hundred Flowers is a mass award comparable to the People's Choice awards in the United States, with the winners determined by a vote of the readers of *Popular Cinema*, the largest-circulation film magazine in the country. Hundred Flowers awards are confined to Best Picture and the four acting categories. I have also tried to cover awards presented to Chinese films at major foreign film competitions and festivals, but this too is selective.

Historical Overview

The founding of the People's Republic of China (PRC) in 1949 marked the closure of an old era in every aspect of Chinese life, including motion pictures. While the Chinese film industry had reached a high level of artistic and technical development during the 1930s, by 1949 the industry was just starting to get back to where it had been before the devastation of World War II. Development after 1949 was rapid but not always smooth, especially during the Cultural Revolution of 1966–1976, when the industry was nearly destroyed by malevolent political forces, notably that of Lin Biao and Jiang Qing (Madame Mao). It was not until 1979, after a series of major and far-reaching economic reforms were announced as public policy, that the film industry entered a new era of development, with a vitality previously unseen. Whenever the ruling Chinese Communist Party (CPC) has loosened controls and adopted policies encouraging art and culture, Chinese filmmaking has prospered; when policies have been otherwise, the industry has declined and even shut down altogether. In summary, it has been impossible to separate filmmaking from politics in the New China.

The PRC film industry from 1949 to today may be divided into three phases:

1949–1966: the 17 years before the Cultural Revolution; Chinese film journalists and scholars have given it the rather unimaginative label of the "17 Years";

1966–1976: the period of the Cultural Revolution, increasingly referred to by Chinese writers as the "period of political disturbance" or the "10 years of chaos";

1976–present: the "New Era."

CHINESE FILM IN THE "17 YEARS" (1949–1966)

Film creation during the "17 Years" traveled an intermittent developmental road, with four peaks in that development: the initial boom just after the CPC took control of the country; development around 1956; that decade's peak in 1959; and the first few years of the 1960s. These four are also called the "three-and-a-half" peaks, because the developmental phase of the early 1960s died just before reaching its zenith.

On October 1, 1946, exactly three years before the founding of the PRC, the Communist Party established the first film studio under public ownership — the Northeast China Film Studio (later renamed the Changchun Film Studio). This became the Party's first film production base. On November 26, 1949, the Shanghai Film Studio was established. In April of that year, the Northeast China Film Studio had completed its filming of *Bridge*, the first feature film produced by the People's Republic of China.

While *Bridge* is noteworthy only for its historical significance as the first PRC

5

feature film, there were some good films completed by the fledgling industry in the days immediately following the founding of the new nation, especially those produced by private film studios. In those first days, the Party's policies and principles regarding the film industry were appropriately loose, as rapid development was encouraged in everything. The film industry at this time was particularly well positioned for rapid development, because it already had a large pool of talented and experienced personnel to draw on. In the words of Chinese film theorist Zhong Dianfei, "New China's film industry has a high starting point."

This first peak ended somewhat abruptly in 1951, with the political attacks on *The Life of Wu Xun*, the epic historical biography from Kunlun, a privately operated studio. After that, film production dropped off markedly, and in some studios completely dried up. This state of affairs continued until May 2, 1956, when Chairman Mao Zedong announced publicly the new policy that would "let a hundred flowers bloom" in arts and letters and "a hundred schools of thought contend" in science. Since film production had slowed to a crawl after the 1951 attacks, the arrival of the "Two Hundreds" policy created a new situation and a new stage of development for the film industry. Films made during this new stage tended to be concerned with human nature and feelings; this was a return to pre-liberation concerns with the emotions and actions of people, rather than using art and film to explain political policies and strategies to the masses. With this return to human concerns, film again became a powerful force attracting audiences.

However, the "Two Hundreds" policy soon led to the anti-rightist campaign backlash. The aforementioned Zhong Dianfei, a prominent and respected film theorist, was labeled a rightist and attacked for having suggested that serving the working classes did not necessarily mean making working class movies. Following Zhong's downfall, many other talented and contributing film artists were similarly vilified and stripped of their right to make movies. The literature of this time is full of attacks on specific movies as well, for one perceived deviation or another.

Premier Zhou Enlai suggested that while Chinese filmmakers might not be able to produce feature films appropriate for the time, they could try making some quasi-documentary stories which would reflect the political realities of the day and still satisfy audiences. So 1958 saw the production of a great many such documentary style art films. During the Great Leap Forward campaign which began in 1958, film studios were established in each of China's 19 provinces, in the 3 municipalities directly under the central government and in 4 of the 5 autonomous regions, Tibet being the lone exception. Most of their production output consisted of the documentary style art films and filmed staged operas, so while there was indeed a "Great Leap" in Chinese motion pictures, it was in quantity only. None of the products of this time, represented by such films as *Bells Ring in Green County*, *A Thousand Miles a Day*, and *Young Masters of the Great Leap Forward*, while numerous, had any lasting value or interest.

No one involved with Chinese motion pictures was satisfied with the poor quality of 1958's output. An effort to rectify this began in the first half of 1959, with Zhou Enlai again taking the lead. Zhou was at the head of several major projects planned to celebrate the approaching 10th anniversary of the founding of the PRC and the 40th anniversary of the CPC, and suggested that one of these projects could be to make some good films as contributions to the celebrations. Many in the film community were still smarting from unfair political attacks, and naturally gun-shy about becoming involved again in anything that might be risky. Nevertheless, Zhou's campaign for good movies inspired an experienced group of film artists to organize for another attempt. The result was an excellent series of films such as *The Lin Family Shop, Lin Zexu,* and *Five Golden Flowers*. These constituted the best group of motion pictures produced in the first decade of the PRC, whether judged by their art, their technology or their content. New Chinese filmmaking was well on the road to maturity.

An Aborted New Peak
for Film Production
(June 1961–December 1963)

Following China's breakup with its former mentor the Soviet Union, China terminated nearly all cultural exchanges with foreign countries. In the early years of the 1960s, filmmakers concentrated on turning out film productions which reflected China's cultural traditions and national characteristics, with notable achievements. Some of the better films produced during this time, such as *Red Detachment of Women*, *Li Shuang-shuang*, *Early Spring in February*, and *Stage Sisters*, exemplify the vigorous development of Chinese film. Viewing them today makes it clear that if China's motion picture industry had not been devastated by the political storm which loomed just beyond the horizon, China's film industry today might be much closer to the level of the world's more developed nations. China certainly had hopes of joining the front ranks of advanced national film industries, but the arrival of the Cultural Revolution pushed it far to the rear.

Chinese Film During the
Cultural Revolution
(1966–1976)

The Cultural Revolution was a time without precedent in Chinese history. It inflicted massive chaos and destruction on the entire nation and its institutions, and arts and letters were certainly no exception. While the whole arts community came under attack and development ground to a halt, the film industry in particular was victimized.

The "Great Proletarian Cultural Revolution" was launched by Party Chairman Mao Zedong. His principal justification was that China was no longer "red" enough: to the Chairman, every institution in China, the Communist Party, the government, the military, educational and cultural circles, etc., had been infiltrated by counterrevolutionaries, figures representing capitalism, to the point where a great many sectors were no longer in the hands of dedicated Marxists. This signified a loss of control by the people.

All the political struggles of the past could not provide guidelines for resolving this problem; it was only through a "cultural revolution," in which the masses of people would expose and root out society's dark forces, that Communism would return to power. This exposure would be public, comprehensive and from top to bottom. It would be a major political revolution in that one class would overthrow another, and it would be repeated many times in the future, as a safeguard against inevitable complacency and diminished revolutionary fervor.

The film community was buffeted by attacks, with Mao's wife Jiang Qing spearheading the assault. Jiang, herself a 1930s film star, totally rejected all previous achievements of the "17 Years" period, calling instead for a complete reorganization of China's film community. She was personally responsible for driving many famous and accomplished film artists from Beijing, and many of them died during long prison terms or as the result of cruel persecution. Estimates of the number of film studio personnel sent down to labor in the countryside vary from one-third to as high as two-thirds of the total.

Jiang Qing also ordered the closing of the Beijing Film Academy (BFA), which was founded in 1956 and had more than 2,000 graduates by that time. The huge losses suffered by Chinese filmmaking during this decade really amounted to the comprehensive destruction of the industry. During the seven year period from June, 1966 to 1973, China did not produce a single feature film.

Jiang Qing's replacement for film and theater was the revolutionary opera. The directing principle of revolutionary opera would be the "three standouts," i.e., stand out (give prominence to) all positive figures, stand out heroic figures among the positive ones and stand out the major heroic figures among the heroic figures.

This absurd theory dominated the making of revolutionary opera. The revolutionary opera was derived from contemporary Beijing opera: after the birth of New China, opera circles had begun to experiment with reforming classical Beijing Opera, typically making Beijing opera fit contemporary reality. Eight such operas were adopted by Jiang Qing as revolutionary operas. Revolutionary operas were a unique cultural phenomenon of the Cultural Revolution period, the product of an extremely abnormal situation. As abnormal as the situation was, however, the people selected to make these revolutionary operas were all the top people in their fields.

CHINESE FILM IN THE NEW ERA (1976–   )

Mao Zedong died in September, 1976; Jiang Qing and her allies, collectively referred to as the "Gang of Four," were disgraced and arrested the following month. The period from that event until the 3rd Plenary Session of the 11th Party Congress in 1979 marked the ending of the Cultural Revolution and could be summarized as a "recovery time" for the Chinese film industry. This was a historic turning point from the past to the future, and while it was a time for correcting previous mistakes, film production was restricted by that specific situation. In neither content nor style were there any breakthroughs of significance.

FIRST NEW WAVE OF FILM PRODUCTION IN THE "NEW ERA"

The 3rd Plenary Session of the 11th Party Congress set out many far-reaching policies for China, generally summed up in the phrase "reform and opening." Again, the motion picture industry was carried along with the political tide, this time to its benefit. Great changes began to appear in the Chinese film industry in just a few years. Films made after 1979 were no longer tools in the direct service of politics, but were more personalized, a reflection of the artist's own understanding of life. While films such as *The Legend of Tianyun Mountain* and *A Corner Forsaken by Love* were imbued with a deep political sense, they were no longer tools of politics but rather reflected the filmmaker's personal view of politics.

The Fifth Generation has become a common expression among scholars of Chinese film in both China and the West, but it still might be beneficial to review briefly why this group of directors has been so labeled, who were the other four (now five) generations and what is their significance. In general, the term First Generation is applied to the founding fathers of Chinese film, exemplified by Zheng Zhengqiu and Zhang Shichuan; these people entered filmmaking in the years just before World War I, and were most active in the silent film era of the 1920s and 1930s. The Second Generation directors were the students of the First, represented by Cai Chusheng, Sun Yu, Wu Yonggang, Fei Mu and Shen Fu, among others; they were most active during the early sound era of the 1930s and 1940s. The Third Generation of directors was the student generation of the second, directors who were at their professional peak in the 1950s and 1960s, represented by such as Zheng Junli, Xie Jin, Shui Hua, Cheng Yin, Cui Wei and Ling Zifeng. The Fourth Generation were part of China's lost generation of intellectuals, people who had the misfortune to be completing their formal education or just starting their careers when the Cultural

Revolution uprooted them and sent them to the countryside. In the case of the Fourth Generation of filmmakers, they were on the verge of graduating from BFA when the Cultural Revolution forced its closure. These people had lengthy service as assistants to experienced directors, but it was not until the Gang of Four was brought down that they had the chance to direct their own films. Representative of this group are Xie Fei, Zheng Dongtian, Zhang Nuanqin and Huang Shuqin. The heralded Fifth Generation were mostly 1982 graduates of BFA, the first class to graduate after the film school resumed accepting enrollments. They soon received the opportunity to make films on their own, and displayed their talents. The Fifth Generation is the one most familiar to filmgoers in the West, represented by such directors as Chen Kaige, Tian Zhuangzhuang, Wu Ziniu, Zhang Junzhao and Zhang Yimou.

The first years of the New Era after the initial recovery phase, specifically 1979–1984, saw the by now middle-aged Fourth Generation at last getting their chance to mature as filmmakers. But filmmaking at this time actually cut across generation lines, with Third Generation veteran Xie Jin having the most noteworthy achievements during this period. In fact, at one time during the first decade of the "New Era," there were representatives of all five generations of directors active in production. Directors in this group largely reverted to China's tradition of film realism, and their films during that time concentrated on expressing the lives and feelings of ordinary people.

The year 1984 was important in contemporary Chinese film history, for that is when the young film workers who graduated from the BFA after the conclusion of the Cultural Revolution began to turn out their first film products. Zhang Junzhao's *One and Eight*, Chen Kaige's *Yellow Earth*, Tian Zhuangzhuang's *On the Hunting Ground* and Wu Ziniu's *Secret Decree* appeared on screens with an entirely different look from that of earlier Chinese films, startling the nation's filmgoers and critics. The greatest shock, however, was to the Fourth Generation of directors, whose just-established leadership status was already being challenged by a new generation. So these directors pushed on to discover their own advantages and strengths, continuing to make their contributions simultaneous with those of the Fifth. Wu Tianmin's *Old Well* is an example of their success, one of the first films which showed the world the quality that Chinese filmmakers were capable of achieving. By the early 1990s, BFA's Class of '89 was on the scene, the "Sixth Generation." Representative of this class are He Jianjun, director of *Red Beads* and *Postman*, Wang Xiaoshuai and Zhang Yuan, like Zhang Yimou a graduate of BFA's cinematography department.

The younger generation of filmmakers, those recent graduates of the Beijing Film Academy, absorbed both the positive and negative experiences of the previous generation while adding their own creation. Their films were most distinguished by the attention given to visual images and the expressive power of sound and language. All filmmakers, but especially the younger ones, brought massive changes to the worldwide image of Chinese film, and Chinese productions began showing up throughout the world, winning their share of awards at film festivals. Zhang Yimou's films in particular, e.g., *Red Sorghum*, the Oscar-nominated *Ju Dou, Raise the Red Lantern, The Story of Qiu Ju, To Live*, and *Shanghai Triad*, have all been presented worldwide, and have done much to heighten the world's awareness of Chinese motion pictures.

As economic reform and opening have continued and directed all aspects of Chinese life, there have been massive changes in the politics, economy and culture of this huge country. The suppression of the pro-democracy movement in 1989 and the resultant tightening of political controls have naturally had an impact on the motion picture industry, with several films banned and restrictions consequently placed on their creators. But there has been nothing comparable to the severe repression and persecution of artists that accompanied earlier political campaigns. Actually, the major outside influence on the Chinese film industry in recent years has been economics, and this situation will probably continue. Films of quality are still being produced, and the best of these are still finding an audience, but film attendance in China has in general fallen off sharply.

The Chinese economy is in a transitional stage from a planned to a market economy, and the majority of PRC motion pictures, especially if they deal with purely "Chinese" (as opposed to universal) themes, do not draw domestic audiences sufficient to offset their lack of appeal overseas. The Chinese government is well aware of this, and in early 1996 announced new measures intended to improve the quality and competitiveness of Chinese motion pictures in the marketplace. This last point is especially important, as the same year also saw an agreement with the United States to allow more foreign films into the Chinese domestic market and to clear the way for Sino-American joint venture filmmaking. If these measures result in a large group of superior motion pictures flooding the Chinese market, it will present a massive challenge to the Chinese film industry. Another event which will inevitably have its impact is the mid–1997 turnover of Hong Kong to PRC control. While the concept of "One Country, Two Systems" has been said to apply, an eventual merging of the HK and PRC motion picture industries would seem likely. Indeed, a look at the co-productions in this filmography, especially in the early 1990s, indicates that the trend is already well under way.

Whatever the immediate future may bring, the trends of recent years allow us to take a few points as certainties. Chinese films will no longer be tools of political struggles, but will be more reflective of worldwide trends in filmmaking and of the filmmakers' personalities. Chinese films no longer deal with single themes that reflect the politics of the day, but deal with a multiplicity of themes as varied as human nature. And finally, Chinese film artists realize as well as those in any industry that their products have a commercial aspect which must be taken into account along with their artistic aspect, and to survive they must satisfy their audiences' interests and needs.

The Films

1. *A Long's Revenge (A Long Yu Xue Ji)*

1986. Xi'an Film Studio. Color. 10 Reels. Direction: Zhang Yumin. Screenplay: Xiong Li, Liu Qin. Cinematography: Liu Cangxun. Art Direction: Yang Gang. Music: Li Yaoding. Sound: Chen Li. Cast: Guo Bichuan as A Long, Fu Yongcai as Yu Zhiqin, Chen Mingao as Liu Yunpu, Wu Lijie as A Yin, Zuo Ling as Liu Yaqing, Liu Jingyi as Liu Yabiao

In 1920s Shanghai, police move in to smash a workers' strike, and young worker Zhao Zhilong is shot and killed. His school friend and sworn brother A Long rushes back to Shanghai to avenge him. He asks another old friend, Liu Yunpu, to help. Liu says he will help, but then his son rapes and murders Zhao Zhilong's young widow A Ying. This alienates A Long from Liu Yunpu's daughter Yaqing, who loves him. In time, A Long himself is betrayed by his own people and killed. Yaqing takes A Long's orphaned son Xiao Long and leaves Shanghai.

2. *A Tan's Story (A Tan Nei Zhuan)*

1988. Fujian Film Studio. Color. 10 Reels. Direction: Yan Shunkai. Screenplay: Zhao Huanan, Yan Shunkai. Cinematography: Chen Zhengxiang, Li Min. Art Direction: Liu Nanyang. Music: He Zhanhao. Sound: Liu Weijie. Cast: Yan Shunkai as A Tan, Zhang Xiaomin as Xiuyun, Jia Meiying as Bilian, Ye Huixian as Haiyin

In Taiwan, pharmacist Si Renpu and his wife are very pleased with their son A Tan's success in business. A Tan's wife remained on the mainland, and he has remained true to her since their separation years before. His parents keep urging him to remarry so they may have a grandchild. The story relates how A Tan sneaks back to the mainland for a brief reunion with his wife Xiuyun, then returns to Taiwan. A year later she has a son, and the grandparents are overjoyed.

3. *A Yong (A Yong)*

1975. Xi'an Film Studio. Color. B & W. 9 Reels. Direction: Yan Xueshu, Sun Jing. Screenplay: Hu Huiyin. Cinematography: Wang Zhixiong, Ling Xuan. Art Direction: Hu Qiangsheng. Music: Li Yaodong, Wei Ruixiang. Sound: Che Zhiyuan. Cast: Liang Baoqin as A Yong, Li Qing as Li Wei, Bi Fusheng as Grandpa Hong, Jin Fuli as Gengsheng's mother, Zhang Shikun as Geng Sheng, Huang Wei as Little Brother, Gao Shuyi as Ling Jincai

Former landlord Ling Jincai wants to turn a nice profit through sale of some lost ducks, but is stopped by A Yong and other Young Pioneers. While they try to find the owners, the children temporarily house and care for the ducks. The story revolves their search for the owner and their struggles with Ling Jincai who keeps trying to get the ducks. Finally, the ducks are returned to their proper owner.

4. *Abandon Superstitions (Po Chu Mi Xing)*

1958. August First Film Studio. B & W. 8 Reels. Direction: Wang Bing. Cinematography: Chen Jun, Chen Zhiqiang. Art Direction: Mai Yi, Xu Run, Music: Li Weicai, Sound: Kou Shenkang

Two stories of the Great Leap Forward, "Homemade Cement" and "People Daring to Create":

11

"Homemade Cement" (Tu Yang Hui). Screenplay: Li Yang. Cast: Wang Xingang as Yang Fangzheng, Qian Shurong as Liu Yufang, Hu Xiaoguang as Yu Gui, Zhang Chi as the Director, Shi Chunyu as Li Shouyi, Ju Chunhua as Ernu. During the Great Leap Forward, a production group director makes cement using a homemade recipe. After many failures, he ultimately succeeds.

"People Daring to Create" (Yong Yu Ge Xin De Ren). Screenplay: Wang Bing, based on Zhang Feng's short story "24 Nights." Cast: Wang Yi as Chen Zhigao, Wu Fan as Yuan Ling, Wang Xinjian as Du Zhendong, Jin Xin as the director, Hu Xiaoguang as Master Worker Zhang. During the Great Leap Forward, three young people in a manufacturing plant abandon superstition, liberate their thinking, and after many failures succeed in producing a new type of bearing.

5. The Abandoned Boy (Bei Pao Qi De Ren)

1983. Pearl River Film Studio. Color. 10 Reels. Direction: Liu Xin. Screenplay: Zhou Jie. Cinematography: Yan Xuzhong. Art Direction: Huang Chaohui. Music: Zhang Jielin. Sound: Lu Minwen. Cast: Li Lan as Ren Shufeng, Hao Yibo as Xiaoyuan, Shen Guangwei as Xiao Bingcheng, Shi Ren as Shufeng's mother, Wang Shan as Xiao Shan

After his father abandons him on a train, six-year-old blind boy Xiaoyuan is found and taken home by Ren Shufeng, a young woman employed at the railway station. Not knowing he was abandoned, Shufeng and her mother decide they will locate the boy's parents. When Shufeng's new boy friend Xiao Bingcheng comes over, he turns out to be the boy's father who had abandoned him at the station. The father cooks up a pretense to get the boy out of the house, then takes him onto a ship and abandons him once more. This time, Xiaoyuan realizes he is deliberately being abandoned, and he is very unhappy, although he is able to get back home. In the meantime, Shufeng has learned the little boy's home address. When she gets there she sees a wedding picture and realizes what is going on. She and the boy's mother talk things over, then Shufeng angrily writes a letter to the father criticizing him. When Xiao Bingcheng returns home, he finds his son will not talk to him, and all the neighbors shun him.

6. Abduction (Bang Piao)

1987. Xiaoxiang Film Studio. Color. Letterboxed. 10 Reels. Direction: Jiang Weihe. Screenplay: Wang Dawei. Cinematography: Yang Wei. Art Direction: Na Shufeng. Music: Li Lifu. Sound: Huang Qizhi. Cast: Wang Zhengjun as Li Aqiang, Zhou Mei as Feng Peihua, Liu Yajun as Wang Cheng, Jiang Jun as Jin Changcheng, Hua Ronghua as Luo Feihu, Yuan Yuliang as Feng Zhentai, Li Nong as Feng Bingxiang, Lin Rongcai as Xi Gengsheng, Niu Qian as Zhu Dingshan

In 1949, on the eve of the final Communist victory, famous entrepreneur Feng Bingxiang is abducted in a large southeastern city. The news shocks the entire city. The Nationalist chief of police accuses the Communist Party of the crime. Li Aqiang, the ex-bodyguard of Feng Bingxiang's son, approaches the missing man's son and daughter with an offer to help. They think he is doing this from personal loyalty, but Li is actually a covert member of the CPC who knows this was not the Party's doing. The case is very complex, but as Li gains the family's trust and confidence he acquires more clues. At last he determines who kidnapped Feng Bingxiang and where he is being held. After a bloody shootout, Li Aqiang gets Feng Bingxiang out safely.

7. Abduction (Jie Chi)

1983. Liaoning Science Film Studio. Color. 9 Reels. Direction: Li Sibing, Liu Guoquan. Screenplay: Li Ning, Sun Maoqing, Liu Guoquan. Cinematography: Zhang Chi. Art Direction: Xun Zenhua. Music: Wang Ming. Sound: Xu Zhiping. Cast: Zhang Jie as Ouyang Yujie, Guo Yuxiang as Liu Lu, Guo Bichuan as Zhou Xiang, Li Xiaoli as Ouyang Xiaoping, Li Lin as Dong Xingzhai

In the city of Binghai, the Public Security Bureau gets a tip that an espionage ring is plotting to abduct famous Chinese physicist Professor Ouyang Yujie to an overseas country. The bureau assigns Detective Zhou Xiang as the scientist's driver and bodyguard. They know that someone close to the professor is working for the spy ring, but not who. It turns out to be his doctor, a woman named Liu Lu. But while Liu was recruited by the spies because of her professional relationship with Professor Ouyang, she has fallen in love with him and is torn by internal conflicts. She unfortunately commits suicide before revealing the abduction plan. When the abduction operation goes into action, Zhou Xiang and the other

PSB agents have to react with little advance information.

8. *Abductor of a Woman (Nu Bang Jia Zhe)*

1990. Inner Mongolia Film Studio. Color. Wide Screen. 9 Reels. Direction: Sun Zhiqiang. Screenplay: Zhang Shilu. Cinematography: Ge Lisheng. Art Direction: Tong Yonggang, Feng Yanqing. Music: Moer Jihu. Sound: Sangsi Erfu. Cast: Qiena Ritu as Zhang Sanjiang, Ai Liya as Wu Mengmeng, Huang Xiaoli as Aoqing

Zhang Sanjiang's gang massacres a rival organization in a gang war, then cleverly arranges the scene to appear that both sides were wiped out in the final battle. The police consider the case closed, but later, two reporters spot a passenger on a train who looks exactly like the supposedly dead Zhang Sanjiang. They secretly photograph the man, and turn this proof over to the police. This results in the case being reopened. Eventually Zhang, with a female geologist in tow as a hostage, is pursued to the border for a final battle with police.

9. *Absurd Adventure (Huang Tang Li Xian)*

1990. Changchun Film Studio. Color. Letterboxed. 9 Reels. Direction: Wang Wenzhi. Screenplay: Chen Aimin. Cinematography: Yu Bing. Art Direction: Ju Lutian, Liu Hong. Music: Lu Shilin. Sound: Liao Yongliang. Cast: Sun Yanjun as Luo Yiming, Song Jie as Xiao Diandian, Wang Baosheng as Kong Long, Shao Xiaowei as Song Binbin, Bi Hui as Kong Jiao, Huang ling as the boss's wife, Ye Lingliang as Song Binbin's mother

Writer Luo Yiming is asked by female reporter Xiao Diandian to travel to a certain city to investigate the Golden Dragon Company's involvement in illegal automobile dealing. Unfortunately, Luo is mistaken by police for an aircraft hijacker, setting off a wild chase by air, sea and land. At last, Luo and Xiao not only uncover evidence of Golden Dragon's illegal dealings, they solve a murder as well.

10. *Absurd Event (Huang Tang Shi Jian)*

1989. Beijing Film Studio. Color. Wide Screen. 9 Reels. Direction: Li Xin. Screenplay: Li Xing, Hua Xia. Cinematography: Zhu Chuanjia, Liu Jirui. Art Direction: Tu Juhua, Song Zhengshan. Music: Zhu Feng, Tang Yuanru. Sound: Zhang Baojian. Cast: Zhao Youliang as Zhao Youliang, Zhang Tianxi as Zhang Tianxi

Zhao Youliang, mayor of a north China city, becomes ill after eating food at a street stall. He is diagnosed as having appendicitis and hospitalized. The news that the mayor is one of their patients throws the hospital staff into a tizzy, with everyone wanting to attend to his needs. Various people from outside descend on the hospital as well, especially bureaucrats hoping to ingratiate themselves by visiting the mayor and bringing him gifts. All this attention becomes too much for Mayor Zhao to put up with, and he skillfully maneuvers these people into making fools of themselves.

11. *An Absurd Prank (Ming Yun Xi Huan Er Zuo Ju)*

1989. Beijing Film Studio. Color. 9 Reels. Letterboxed. Direction: Liu Shu'an. Screenplay: Wang Zunxi. Cinematography: Chen Youqun. Art Direction: Luo Yurong. Music: Weng Zhongjia. Sound: Li Bojiang. Cast: Chang Lantian as Rui Jiaju, Ning Haiqiang as Zhu Fusheng, Gao Fang as Mrs. Yuan, Ge Cunzhuang as Wu Youguang

A dark comedy. Middle-aged Rui Jiaju was at one time the top student in his university's computer science department, but now works as a flunky in a large, overstaffed organization, doing his best to keep his bosses happy and hold on to his job. One day, Rui feels ill and is diagnosed as having terminal stomach cancer. Hearing the news, he decides to live his remaining life to the fullest. Since he no longer cares if he gets fired, he starts doing inappropriate and for him bizarre things, such as insulting his superiors and taking liberties with female employees. The results turn out quite different from what he had expected: everyone begins to respect him for his arrogance and take him more seriously. He is promoted to deputy chief of the General Affairs Section, where he is an instant success. He even manages to allocate fairly the organization's housing, a difficult task in China. No matter what he tries to do to foul up the organization, the higher he rises up the corporate ladder. He soon finds himself back in the hospital from overwork. In the hospital, he realizes he must rethink his plans...

12. *The Accused (Bei Kong Gao De Ren)*

1983. Beijing Film Studio. Color. 10 Reels. Direction: Fu Jie. Screenplay: Li Hua.

Cinematography: Cao Zhuobing. Art Direction: Fu Delin. Music: Fu Gengcheng. Sound: Wei Xueyi. Cast: Li Fazen as Long Hansheng, Wang Huaiwen as Zeng Kun, Song Ge as Huang Xianda, Tang Jishen as Chen Lanxiang, Zhang Changshui as Zeng Xuemin

In a border town, Long Hansheng is an ordinary Party cadre in the customer service department of a branch office. He goes very strictly by the book in everything he does. One day, he is shocked to find clues indicating that a woman named Chen Lanxiang, director of the county commercial bureau and wife of the county Party Secretary, may be involved in smuggling. He begins an investigation of this on his own, and finds further evidence that Party Secretary Zeng Kun may himself be involved in this and other economic crimes. He decides for once in his career to take a chance and report the matter to the appropriate authorities at the provincial and central government levels. When the authorities investigate, Zeng Kun cleverly turns the evidence to throw suspicion on Long Hansheng. The investigative team at last determines that Zeng Kun and his wife are indeed the criminals.

13. The Accused Uncle Shangang (Bei Gao Shan Gang Ye)

1994. Emei Film Studio. Color. Letterboxed. 11 Reels. Direction: Fan Yuan. Screenplay: Bi Bicheng, Fan Yuan, based on Li Yiqing 's novel "Uncle Shangang." Art Direction: Tan Xiaolin. Music: Tang Qingshi. Sound: Tu Liuqing. Costume: Shuai Furong, Chen Jiying. Makeup: Zeng Xiaozhen, Liu Qingshu. Cast: Li Rentang, Yang Hua, Dong Danjun, Zhu Xiaodan, Min Jie, Bi Fu, Zhang Yanxia, Wang Chengjian, Zu Yimin, Zhang Yimei, Hao Shaoming, Li Meng

After village chief Shangang has a woman named Qiangying bound and exhibited in their village, she hangs herself. Her husband threatens to take Shangang to the authorities, but the old man is unafraid: he claims the woman had constantly beaten and otherwise abused her poor old mother-in-law, and the public humiliation merely served the interests of justice. He had criticized Shangang for her conduct, but she refused to change. After receiving an anonymous letter about the incident, prosecutors Su Qiang and Xiao Ding go to the village to investigate. They find that Shangang is a good man, but often practices the "law" as he understands it. Su Qiang is very upset that he has to inform Shangang that

tying the woman up and putting her on public exhibit was a violation of the law, and they have to take him away. All the villagers appeal on Shangang's behalf, but the old man tells them the law is the law, and he does not complain.

14. Ace! Soccer (Fei Ba, Zhu Qiu!)

1980. Shanghai Film Studio. Color. Wide Screen (Letterboxed) 9 Reels. Direction: Lu Ren. Screenplay: Zhou Kangyu, Da Shibiao, Lu Ren. Cinematography: Zhang Yuanmin, Ji Hongsheng. Art Direction: He Zhaojie. Music: Xu Jingxin. Sound: Feng Deyao. Cast: Sun Bing as Yang Bo, Ma Guanyin as Liu Gang, Zhao Jing as Luo Fang, Tan Pengfei as Zhang Wenbiao, Yang Degeng as Wu Zhongfa, Wun Xiying as Luo's father

In an international soccer contest, the Chinese Bodou team loses 0–3 to a European team when its best players like Liu Gang play to please the girls in the crowd. The athletic commission restores the team's former coach Yang Bo to his old job as head coach. Yang Bo decides that the team has the talent, what they need is stricter discipline and training. With the coach's help, Liu Gang comes to realize he is sacrificing professionalism, and vows to improve. When the European team tours China again, they are very arrogant. But the Bodou team is reorganized and united: Liu Gang and his teammates play as a close-knit unit, and the game ends in a 1–1 tie.

15. Across Ten Thousand Rivers and One Thousand Mountains (Wan Shui-Qian Shan)

1959. August First Film Studio. Color. Wide And Narrow Screen. 10 Reels. Direction: Cheng Yin, Hua Chun. Screenplay: Sun Qian and Cheng Yin, based on the stage play of the same title by Chen Qitong. Cinematography: Gao Hongtao. Art Direction: Zhang Zheng. Music: Shi Lemeng, Chen Geng. Sound: Wu Hanbiao. Cast: Lan Ma as Li Youguo, Huang Kai as Zhao Zhifang, Liang Yuru as Luo Shuncheng, Chen Huiliang as Company Commander Wang, Bai Erchun as Xiao Zhou, Li Meng as Li Fenglian

The title is an idiom for the trials of a long journey.

In 1935, the Chinese Workers and Peasants Red Army is retreating to the north. They battle their way over Luding bridge, fight across the Dadu River, and cross snowcapped mountains. All along, battalion political instructor

Li Youguo keeps up their spirits and resolve. When the army is crossing the grasslands, it must contend with gales and rain as well as hunger, at one point killing their horses for food, and cooking leather belts to fill their bellies. The valiant and inspirational Li Youguo is killed by enemy snipers. The army continues to move North, and after a battle at Lazhikou link up with the Red Army in North Shanxi province, completing the Chinese Communists' famous "Long March."

16. *The Acting Mayor (Dai Li Shi Zhang)*

1985. Beijing Film Studio. Color. 10 Reels. Direction: Yang Zaibao. Screenplay: Ou Weixiong, Yang Miaoqin, Qian Shicang, Yao Guilin. Cinematography: Huang Xinyi. Art Direction: Wang Jixian. Music: Lu Qimin. Sound: Liu Shida, Guan Shuxin. Cast: Yang Zaibao as Xiao Zhiyun, Xu Huanshan as Luo Ting, Pan Weixing as Liu Lixun, Feng Hanyuan as Li Huaxin, Sun Shaowei as Tian Luo, Chen Limin as Li Yufang, Lin Yu as Weihong

In the early 1980s, the south China city of Yingzhou is undergoing reform. Acting Mayor Xiao Zhiyun announces a list of "10 good things" he will do for the people during his 3-month term of office. But reforms always run counter to somebody's self-interest, and while everyone likes the majority of his list, no one supports him on all 10. Xiao's determination to fulfill all 10 items on the list caused his supporters to desert him one by one, with even local Party Secretary Luo Ting turning against him. Luo does not give up, and when his three months expire, he requests and is granted an extension of his term, so he can fulfill his promise of getting through the whole list.

Best Actor Yang Zaibao, 1986 Hundred Flowers Awards.

17. *Action Without a Mission (Wu Shi Ming Xing Dong)*

1992. Changchun Film Studio. Color. Letterboxed. 9 Reels. Direction: Qiao Kejie. Screenplay: Wang Dawei. Cinematography: Chen Chang'an, Wang Jian. Art Direction: Gao Tinglun. Music: Liu Kexin. Sound: Yang Yuedong, Meng Gang. Costume: Ouyang Yongkuan, Li Xiuzhi. Makeup: Jing Yichu. Cast: Chen Jianfei as Chen Derong, Chen Xiaoyi as Lin Jie, Shu Yaoxuan as Zhang Tianren, Li Ling as Gu Yaping, Wen Haitao as Li Fuxiang

On the eve of Shanghai's liberation, many in the local business community prepare to accept the Communist takeover and work with the new regime to clean up the corrupt and crime-ridden city. The local Communist underground organization knows that such people are likely targets for Nationalist agents and gangsters and try to offer protection. A prominent capitalist and his son are assassinated by an abduction ring, and his daughter flees. Reporter Chen Derong, a member of the Communist underground, takes protection of the girl as his unassigned mission.

18. *Adoptive Mother (Ye Ma Ma)*

1985. Xi'an Film Studio & Anhui Film Studio Co-Production. Color. 9 Reels. Direction: Yao Shougang. Screenplay: Fang Yihua, Yao Shougang. Cinematography: Zhi Lei. Art Direction: Zhang Lin. Music: Wei Ruixiang, Xiang Yin. Sound: Gu Changning. Cast: Chi Peng as Luo Bitao, Xu Weiping as Yusheng, Mi Diqi as Ge Yi, Jia Liu as Luo Ershu, Zhang Muqin as Goudan's mother, Wei Beiyuan as Gu Tiezheng

In the early 1970s, sweet and innocent country girl Luo Bitao meets technician Ge Yi who comes from an overseas Chinese background. Ge was recently widowed and left with a one-year-old son, Chengxiang. As if life as the single parent of an infant were not difficult enough, Ge Yi is soon arrested on political charges and sent to prison. Luo Bitao decides to adopt little Chengxiang despite the opposition of many, including her father Luo Ershu. People eventually come to understand her behavior, but when Chengxiang enters elementary school Luo is also sent to prison because of her connection to Ge Yi. Years later, Ge Yi is declared to be politically rehabilitated and released. The first thing he does is return to the village to thank Bitao, but learns she has died.

19. *Adventure on a Small Island (Xiao Dao Qing Shen)*

1994. Children's Film Studio. Color. Letterboxed. 9 Reels. Direction: Wang Xuexin. Screenplay: Li Yunliang. Cinematography: Ning Changcheng. Art Direction: Dong Xue, Gao Jianhua. Music: Guo Xiaotian. Sound: Zhang Hongguang. Makeup: Pan Li. Cast: Man Xuchun as Xiao Long, Wang Lei as Hai Liu, Lu Yinuo as Brigade Commander Peng, Li Ying as Bai Ying, Zhang Xianming as Staff Officer Li

During his summer vacation from school, Peng Xiaolong decides to travel by himself to visit his naval officer father so as not to disrupt his mother Bai Qing's work. On the train he meets Hai Liu, a girl traveling to the same destination. When he arrives, Xiaolong finds his father has just shipped out on a mission. So Xiaolong and Hai Liu decide to go out on the ocean by themselves. Their boat capsizes, and the two children take a life raft to an island. There, they must cope with a typhoon, snakes, and various other troubles. Their adventure ends when Xiaolong's parents and Hai Liu's grandfather find them on the beach.

20. *Adventures in Guangzhou (Yang Cheng Qi Yu Ji)*

1991. Pearl River Film Studio. Color. 10 Reels. Letterboxed. Direction: Cao Zheng. Screenplay: Liao Zhikai. Cinematography: Wu Benli. Art Direction: Zhang Jingwen, Tu Benyang. Music: Du Jiangang. Sound: Liu Haiyan. Cast: Lu Niu as A Chang, Zhang Yanli as A Qing, Kong Xianzhu as Uncle Fa, Wang Weibo as A Kun

A Chang, a rich fisherman from Hainan Island, comes to Guangzhou with his Uncle Fa to see his fiancee A Xiang, although Fa, her father, opposes their marriage. Angered at her father's stubbornness, A Xiang has left her hometown and gone to Guangzhou to find work there. Arriving in the bustling metropolis, A Chang and Uncle Fa encounter many problems. They find themselves cheated, their identity cards are stolen and they are detained and interrogated. But at the same time, they meet many kindly people who help them, such as taxi driver A Qing and her fiance, a fat policeman, and A Xiang, a fellow villager who has the same name and is the same age as his fiancee. They all become friends. Finally A Chang and his lover come together with their help.

21. *Adventures of a Panda (Xiong Mao Li Xian Ji)*

1983. Emei Film Studio & Hongkong Zhongyi Company Jointly. Color. 10 Reels. Direction: Guang Yuan. Screenplay: Ding Yuanting. Cinematography: Yang Minliang, Guang Yuan, Song Jianwen. Art Direction: Li Fan. Costume: Yuan Shuhua. Makeup: You Qingshu. Cast: Yu Xiaofeng as Xiao Feng, Gao Qun as Grandpa, Wu Xiaoping as Du Jiao, Zhou Fengshan as the Clan Head

A long, long time ago, little panda Pingping lived with his mother in a great forest.

Also living at a nearby mountain was a Tibetan doctor and his grandson Xiao Feng. One day, Pingping became caught in a trap set by a cruel hunter, but he was saved by Xiao Feng and his grandpa. The story tells how the little boy and the old man outwit the hunter and get Pingping home safely.

22. *Afanti (A Fanti)*

1980. Beijing Film Studio. Color. 10 Reels. Direction: Xiao Lang. Screenplay: Wang Yuhu, Xiao Lang. Cinematography: Wu Shenghan, Li Yuebing. Art Direction: Chen Xiaoxia, Yang Raolong. Music: Shao Guangsheng, Kuerban. Sound: Zhen Chunyu. Cast: Tuyigong as Afanti, Tuhadi as the headman, Abake as Laboke, Guzelinuer as Laili, Tuersong as Musha, Abulimiti as Kehan

Afanti is a legendary figure in the culture of the China Xinjiang Uygur nationality. He frequently goes abroad in the world in support of justice and fairness. The movie relates a few examples of this: helping a poor girl, punishing a greedy local resident administrator and rescuing Laili Guli, a beautiful girl given as compensation for taxes owed to Master Abu Laboke.

23. *Affection Between Father and Daughter (Fu Nu Qing)*

1983. Changchun Film Studio. Color. 9 Reels. Direction: Guangbudao Erji. Screenplay: Hu Su. Cinematography: Dan Sheng, Ni Ma. Art Direction: Liu Kai, Wei Hongyu. Music: Wang Furong. Sound: Yu Kaizhang. Cast: Zhao Fengxia as Fang Shanshan, Zhao Fan as Fang Yuting, Yi Da as Luo Yu, Ji Hengpu as Ding Shan, Yang Xiaodan as Yu Shaofan, Liao Jingfeng as Li Chunman

A young woman named Fang Shanshan is employed in the heavy machinery plant where her father Fang Yuting is Director and Party Secretary. When Personnel Director Ding Shan recruits six new workers in direct violation of current policy, she goes to her father and asks him to rescind the unauthorized hirings. To her surprise, her father confirms he personally approved the hirings and now refuses to reverse his action. They argue, and she leaves home. This deeply disturbs her father, who now realizes how important this matter is to her. He wonders if she will ever come home again. She does return after a while, and it turns out she has spent the time in Beijing, reporting the matter to the Central Party Disciplinary Examination Commission. From this incident, Fang Yuting decides to reform himself and regain his revolutionary attitude.

24. *Affection for Huangshan Mountain (Qing Man Huang Shan)*

1986. Changchun Film Studio. Color. 9 Reels. Direction: Wang Wenzhi. Screenplay: Jia Menglei. Cinematography: Jin Hengyi. Art Direction: Song Honghua. Music: Ye Zhigang. Sound: Wun Liangyu, Luo Huailun. Cast: Wang Wei as Shu Yin, Xue Bai as Shi Mei, Dong Wei as Gao Xiaofeng, Bi Hui as Xu Zhenhai

In the summer of 1983, young woman composer Su Yin returns to her native place on near Huangshan Mountain, now a popular resort, to compose a symphony entitled "Soul of Huangshan." There she meets her childhood friend Gao Xiaofeng. Gao tells her of his difficult past, including being jilted by the girl he loved. But now he has met someone who really loves him and is devoting himself to building the Huangshan area. Su Yin visits and gets to know other local people, and feels that through these people and their work she will capture the true soul of Huangshan.

25. *After Being Arrested (You Pu Zhi Hou)*

1982. Changchun Film Studio. Color. 10 Reels. Direction: Hua Ke. Screenplay: Jun Xiang, Hua Ke. Cinematography: Yan Xuzhong. Art Direction: Gao Guoliang. Music: Wang Liping. Sound: Wun Liangyu. Cast: Liang Tongyu as Xia Dongyue, Wang Huayin as Ding Jiantang, Jiang Lili as Ye Yuzhi, Li Lan as Su Ruijuan, Yu Liwen as Zhen Zhilong, Li Xiangang as Lu Chengshun

Just before the anti-Japanese war, Qingdao CPC undercover leader Zhen Zhilong is arrested while meeting with his intelligence source to receive some vital information. That same night the information comes into the possession of another undercover Party member, dentist Ding Jiantang. His bride, CPC liaison Ye Yuzhi, leaves to take the information to Party leaders, but she is unsuccessful. When a young man named Xia Dongyue shows up, he is assigned to purchase weapons for the anti-Japanese forces. When Ding Jiantand and Xia Dongyue discuss the arrest of Zhen Zhilong, Xia begins to suspect another Party liaison Lu Chengshun of being the one who betrayed Zhen. But it turns out that Ding Jiantang is the traitor. The CPC underground organization is contacted, the weapons are purchased and delivered to revolutionary forces, and Ding Jiantang is executed. Ye Yuzhi, who had gone through an ordeal, leaves the city with Xia Dongyue and heads for the revolutionary base.

26. *After Separation (Da Sha Ba)*

1992. Beijing Film Studio. Color. Letterboxed. 9 Reels. Direction: Xia Gang. Screenplay: Feng Xiaogang. Cinematography: Ma Xiaoming. Art Direction: Huo Jianqi. Music: Liang Gang. Sound: Li Bojiang. Costume: Chen Jidong. Makeup: Chen Jidong. Cast: Ge You as Gu Yan, Xu Fan as Lin Zhouyun, Zhang Huizhong as Yang Zhong, Liu Yi as Jin Ling, Li Ting as Yang Xu

At the Beijing airport, Gu Yan see his wife off for graduate study in Canada. After she leaves, he happens upon a woman fainting as her husband is leaving the country. The husband, rushing to catch his plane, prevails on Gu Yan to see to his wife. Afterwards, Gu Yan checks in on the woman, Lin Zhouyun, to see how she is doing. She has high hopes of joining her husband soon, but this never seems to materialize, and two years later she is still waiting for the visa. One New Year's Eve, the two decide that instead of spending the holiday season alone again, they will imitate family life; they spend five happy days together, and as another year passes they spend more time together and become close. Then Lin Zhouyun receives her visa and Gu Yan's wife sends a lawyer with divorce papers for him to sign. Gu takes Lin to the airport, and he holds her as she waits to board the plane. She wants him to ask her to stay, but he remains silent. We see the plane taking off; is she on it?

Best Director Xia Gang, 1993 Golden Rooster Awards.

Best Actor Ge You, 1993 Golden Rooster Awards.

27. *After the Blue Light Shines (Lan Guang Shan Guo Zhi Hou)*

1979. Shanghai Film Studio. Color. Direction: Fu Chaowu, Gao Zheng. Screenplay: Gao Xing, Meng Shenghui. Cinematographer: Peng Enli, Shen Miaorong. Art Direction: Huang Qiagui. Music: Lu Qiming. Sound: Huang Dongping. Cast: Zhao Lian as Xing Huimin, He Suohua as Zhuang Jingxian, Zhang Fa as Tang Hui, Feng Xiao as Shi Xin, Li Zhaiyang as Wang Wei, Li Baoluo as Li Shan

On a pleasant summer evening, nearly all the residents of a small city are enjoying an

After the Blue Light Shines. **Xing Huimin (Zhao Lian, right) establishes an orphanage school after losing his own daughter in an earthquake. 1979. Shanghai Film Studio.**

outdoor concert. As a little girl performs, her father Xing Huimin watches proudly from the audience. Many small children are in the audience, as well as a young doctor Zhuang Jingxian. But just as the concert ends, a massive earthquake hits the city. Xing Huimin's daughter is killed, but he is able to rescue others. Afterwards, seeking an outlet for his grief, Xing Huimin requests and is granted permission by the city's Party Secretary Tang Hui to open an orphanage to care for those many children who lost their parents in the quake. An orphanage school is also established, and Doctor Zhuang Jingxian is among those caring for its several hundred orphans who go there. The teachers understand the plight of the children, and try to care for them as if they were their own. Xing Huiming is particularly unselfish in his care, and some of the children begin to call him "Daddy."

28. *After the Final Battle (Parts 1 & 2) (Jue Zhan Zhi Hou)*

1991. Xi'an Film Studio. Color. 17 Reels. Letterboxed.

Direction: Li Qiankuan, Xiao Guiyun. Screenplay: Zheng Zhong. Cinematography: Ma Delin. Art Direction: Wang Ziwei, Wang Yingbing. Music: Shi Wanchun. Sound: Ma Delin. Cast: Gu Yue as Mao Zedong, Huang Kai as Zhou Enlai, Liu Xitian as Chen Yi, Di Guoqiang as Luo Ruiqin, Li Fazeng as Du Zhaoming, Zhen Danian as Director Li, Ge You as Wenqiang, Zhao Xiaorui as Qiu Xingxiang, Xu Shouqin as Huang Wei, Wang Zhaogui as Wang Shaoshan, Shu Yaoxuan as Yang Guangyu, Chen Shensheng as Yang Botao, Ma Xin as Zhang Gan

After the final Communist victory and the establishment of the People's Republic of China, the problem remains of what to do with captured war criminals. The Communist leadership decides to submit most of the former Nationalists to thought reform, and an ideological war begins. The battle of wits at Beijing's Gongdelin Prison is in some ways even more vehement than the civil war which preceded it. Each of the high-ranking Nationalist officers and officials has his own, differing mentality. Some refuse to cooperate, others are too depressed to do anything, still others vacillate. The process of mental remolding is long and arduous for both captor and captive alike.

29. *After the Harvest (Feng Shou Zhi Hou)*

1964. Haiyan Film Studio. B & W. 11 Reels. Direction: Xu Tao. Screenplay: Shen Fu and Xu Tao, based on the stage play of the same title. Cinematography: Xu Qi. Art Direction: Ding Cheng. Music: Wang Yunjie. Sound: Lu Zhongbo. Cast: Wang Yumei as Zhao Wusheng, Guo Diancang as Zhao Dachuan, Gao Ruping as Wang Baoshan, Yuan Yaodong as Uncle Xu, Liu Guifang as Wang Xiaomei, Jia Zhongqian as Wang Xuekong

In 1962, in the village of Kaoshan, in the Jiaodong Mountain area of Shandong province, it is harvest time. Village Party Secretary Shao Wusheng suggests selling surplus grain to the state to support socialist construction. But her husband, Director Zhao Dachuan, trades the surplus grain to broker Wang Laoshi in exchange for some livestock. Wusheng opposes her husband's selfishness and recovers the grain. She also exposes Wang Laoshi's speculative activities, and makes her husband sell the surplus grain to the state.

30. *After the Rain (Yu Hou)*

1982. Changchun Film Studio. Color. 10 Reels. Direction: Rong Lei. Screenplay: Si Minshan, Yang Shiwen, Zhou Yang, Wu Benwu. Cinematography: Li Chaoren. Art Direction: Yuan Dianmin, Wei Hongyu. Music: Lou Zhanghou, Fang Zhenxiang. Sound: Hong Di. Cast: Zhang Xianheng as Chen Hanru, Gu Yongfei as Fang Ming, Li Zhiyu as Bai Junmin, Zhen Kunfan as Meng Jian, Li Ying as Bai Shan

After the defeat of the Gang of Four, Judge Meng Jian is assigned to hear the divorce case of Chen Hanru and Fang Ming. Chen Hanru is a medical researcher and the couple were wed before the Cultural Revolution. But that period of social and political turbulence seriously damaged their relationship, as ideological and political oppression combined with a heavy family burden to cause Fang Ming to lose hope and ambition. Chen Hanru was so devoted to his research work he had no idea of his wife's unhappiness. Two years after the couple separated, Fang Ming met and fell in love with Doctor Bai Junmin, who was unaware the woman was not divorced. Bai Junmin is Meng Jian's brother-in-law. The judge talks to Bai and has him persuade Fang Ming to go back to her husband, now seriously ill from years of exposure to radiation. Fang Ming finally understands her husband's devotion to his career and goes back to him.

31. *After the Second Husband Died (Dou Hua Nu)*

1992. Emei Film Studio and Taiwan Hongqing Film Company Co-Production. Color. Letterboxed. 9 Reels. Direction: Chen Zhuhuang. Screenplay: Liu Zhengqian. Cinematography: Peng Dawei. Art Direction: Zhang Linwan. Music; Huang Zhengxiang. Sound: Tu Liuqing. Costume: Xu Yuqi. Makeup: Jiang Shufei. Cast: Di Ying as Jin Zhi, Li Xiaofei as Huang Tianzhu, Xia Xiaoyu as Huang Jinyu, Su Yuyun as Xiao Juan

Jin Zhi's husband is lost at sea, and in order to support herself and her daughter Xiaojuan, the widow starts a small business making and selling soy bean juice. She later remarries, to a widowed mine worker with a son. The boy, Xiao Yu, has serious behavioral problems, but Jin Zhi's patient kindness helps improve his attitude. But disaster strikes again when her second husband is killed in a mining accident. A few years later, in order that Xiao Yu can study abroad, Xiaojuan sacrifices the money she had been saving for marriage. They send Xiao Yu abroad for study, and he is very successful. But just when he is due to return home, a letter arrives informing them that Xiao Yu has been killed saving the lives of some classmates in a laboratory explosion.

32. *Against the Current (Tong Zai Lan Tian Xia)*

1987. Beijing Film Studio. Color. 10 Reels. Direction: Liu Shuan. Screenplay: Jiang Defu. Cinematography: Chen Youqun. Art Direction: Ma Gaiwa. Music: Wang Xiling. Sound: Li Bojiang, Zhen Chunyu. Cast: Wang Jiakui as Jin Kui, Yan Liqiu as Jin's mother, Jin Ping as Ouyang Zhen, Liu Jian as Xiao Jun

After losing his right leg as a child, Jin Kui has to live with his mother, who earns a living doing laundry for other families. Mother and son depend on each other for survival and suffer hardships and humiliation together. The Qingshui River is the only place Jin Kui can go to enjoy himself. He trains himself diligently at swimming, and becomes a strong swimmer. After he criticizes Ji Xiaojun, the son of a senior official, for being rude and unkind to a handicapped girl, Jin Kui is fired from his temporary job in a shoe factory. After that incident, he travels from village to village on a bicycle, earning his living by taking photos for farmers during the day and making shoes at night. Qu Yangzhen, a nursery school teacher, is strongly attracted to Jin Kui because of his drive and skill, and finally marries him. Soon after their wedding, Jin Ki is recruited by the Physical Education Committee assigned to train athletes for the International Handicapped Olympics. When Jin Kui hears that his old tormentor Ji Xiaojun has died in battle fighting for his country, Jin is deeply moved and decides he will train hard and strive to win honors for his motherland.

33. *Aggressively Moving Forward (Gao Ge Meng Jing)*

1950. Northeast Film Studio. B & W. 8 Reels. Direction: Wang Jiayi. Screenplay: Yu Ming. Cinematography: Nie Jin. Art Direction: Dong Ping. Music: Xu Xu. Sound: Jue Jingxiu. Costume: Xin Yulan. Makeup: Wang Fenrui. Cast: Pu Ke as Li Guangcai, Zhang Xiqi as Meng Kuiyuan, Qu Wei as Li Xiulan, Xu Liankai as Mr. Wei, Lu Fei as Head of the Labor Union, Zhang Yue as the Factory Director, Yin Yiqing as Qi Ziming.

Meng Kuiyuan, a young worker in the Songjiang Machine Plant, takes the lead in responding to the call from higher authorities to upgrade their plant's technology. Some of the workers are unhappy with the changes, most notably veteran technician Li Guangcai, a conservative, and Mr. Wei, a worker who believes the upgrading will result in staff cuts. Their doubts are exploited by Li's nephew Qi Ziming, a clever businessman who stands to profit if the upgrading fall through. He also hopes to marry Mr. Li's daughter Li Xiulan. Deceived by Qi, Mr. Li and Mr. Wei agree to the marriage. With the aid of technician Li, Meng Kuiyuan succeeds in upgrading the plant's technology. The others now see through Qi's deception, and withdraw their permission for the engagement. Finally, Meng Kuiyuan and Li Xiulan are happily married.

34. *Ai Zhu (Ai Zhu)*

1985. Changchun Film Studio. Color. 10 Reels. Direction: Ma Shida. Screenplay: Liu Jianan, Cheng Ming. Cinematography: Li Guanghui, Li Fengming. Art Direction: Liu Huanxing. Music: Lei Zhenbang. Sound: Dong Baosheng. Cast: Zhuang Peiyuan as Wen Jian, Gu Qian as Xi Die, Jin Liang as Niu Junqi

A south China TV station receives a questionable news report concerning the great success a man named Niu Junqi has had in leading the people of a particular commune to prosperity through pearl raising. To verify the truth of the story, the station director sends reporter Wen Jian to investigate. Wen had worked at the commune in question 10 years earlier. Wen Jian's probe of the matter uncovers the fact that the true factor behind the commune's success is a woman named Ai Zhu, a close friend of the reporter's during his commune days. Niu Junqi had actually stolen Ai Zhu's achievements from her. Wen Jian returns to his station to report the truth, but when he arrives finds the station director has received a letter accusing Wen Jian of conspiring with the woman.

35. *AIDS Victims (Ai Zi Bing Huan Zhe)*

1988. Youth Film Studio, Beijing Film Academy. Color. 9 Reels. Letterboxed. Direction: Xu Tongjun. Screenplay: Liu Yibing, Huang Dan. Cinematography: Liao Jiaxiang. Art Direction: Zhang Yafang. Music: Ma Ding. Sound: Zhang Yaling. Cast: Xiu Jian as Lin Zhigang, Zhang Anli as Song Ruming, Ma Lun as Zhang Sidong, Yan Qing as Ji Yin, Zhao Ying as Jiang Mingxia, Zuo Ling as Wang Xiaoyu, Kaiwen as Tony Pinkerton.

The World Health Organization notifies China's state epidemic control agency that Tony Pinkerton, a foreigner who had once taught in one of China's open coastal cities, has died of AIDS. Just before his death, the foreigner informed medical authorities that he had sex with three Chinese women while in that country. The Chinese agency dispatches PSB officers Lin Zhigang and Song Ruming to south China to locate the three women. The officers start their search at the university there. Assigned to assist them is Wang Xiaoyu, a woman official from the university's foreign liaison office, their investigation soon spreads beyond the school to uncover a local prostitution ring. At last, Lin and Song identify the three women involved. Ji Ying, an offbeat college student, attempts suicide when she learns the news. The second woman, Wang Mingxia, is a call girl who has since married a Japanese businessman and now lives in Japan. The third victim turns out to be Wang Xiaoyu herself; when the investigation starts getting close to her, she tries to burn records linking her to Tony, but dies in the fire.

36. *Ailipu and Sainaimu (Ai Li Pu Yu Sai Nai Mu)*

1981. Tianshan Film Studio. Color. 11 Reels. Direction: Fu Jie. Screenplay: Aili Aizezi, Zhunonghadier. Cinematography: Ding Zhenyu. Art Direction: Zhang Tiren, Ma Shaoxian. Music: Hao Yasi, Balati, etc., Sound: Zhang Xiceng, Zhang Baojian. Cast: Maimaitizhunong as Ailipu, Buweiguli Sainaimu, Abulimitishadike as Abasi

Ailipu, son of the former prime minister, and Sainaimu, daughter of the king, are in love. However, the current prime minister Xiawazi wants to marry his son Abudula to Sainaimu in order to seize power. He frames Ailipu and forces the king to break the engagement between Sainaimu and Ailipu and banish Ailipu's family from the kingdom. Later, Ailipu returns seeking to clear his name. Hasimu and other honest court officials work hard to get justice for Ailipu. They expose Xiawazi and his son's conspiracy to seize the throne, and also present evidence that they murdered Ailipu's father the former prime minister. The king wakes up to the facts and the lovers finally get together.

37. *Air Pirate on Emei Mountain (E Mei Fei Dao)*

1985. Emei Film Studio. Color. 9 Reels. Direction: Zhang Xihe. Screenplay: Zhou Gang, Qian Daoyuan. Cinematography: Song Jianwen. Art Direction: Lin Qi. Music: Tian Feng, Liu Qin. Sound: Zhang Jianping. Cast: Xia Zongyou as Lu Peimin, Ma Shuchao as Zhao Hai, Zhang Zhiqiang as Xu Wen, Li Dianfang as the robber, Tu Zhongru as a thug, Luo Yuncong as Wu Jiagui

One night, the Emei Mountain Museum is broken into and some priceless antique jewelry stolen. The local PSB's chief investigator and his staff soon apprehend the thief, who insists he was just following the orders of a local man named Wu Jiagui.

But when investigators arrive at Wu's home, they find him murdered. The case grows more complex. Investigators conclude the manner in which the jewels were taken points to a martial arts teacher, who helps them on the case. The culprit is at last determined to be a martial arts student known as the "air pirate."

38. *Alima (A Li Ma)*

1981. Inner Mongolia Film Studio. Color. 10 Reels. Direction: Ge Gengtana, Zhang Lun.

Screenplay; Yun Zhaoguang. Cinematography: Zhang Lun, Wulan Mulin. Art Direction: Zhang Guozhen. Music: Tuliguer, Bayin Manda. Sound: Li Yan. Cast: Sharen Gaowa as Alima, Siqin Gaowa as Nabuqi, Qina Ritu as Tala, Degeji as Bao Yin, Er Changlin as Qi Dalai, Gengdeng as Ren Qin

During the Second Civil War, a Mongolian nationality girl is sent by Party leaders to the Chagan prairie from Yanan on an important assignment. She is escorted by a Chinese liaison named Mr. Zhao. Unfortunately, Zhao is killed protecting her. On a Mongolian people's religious holiday, the Nationalist commander Qi Dalai holds a public execution of nine undercover Communist agents, including District Secretary Tegexi, Alima's father. Although grieving, Alima vows to fulfill her important assignment. She locates Tala, her contact, and with Tala's help she goes to the home of enemy deputy regimental commander Ren Qin with a letter of introduction from his daughter, for he is believed sympathetic to the Communists. However, things go badly when Bao Yin, a fellow Communist, betrays the revolution. Finally, Alima organizes a reliable group of cadres. By pretending to be a wedding party, they gain access to enemy headquarters and wipe them out.

All of My Life **see** *This Life of Mine*

39. *All Who Came Are Guests (Lai De Dou Shi Ke)*

1990. Emei Film Studio. Color. Wide Screen. 10 Reels. Direction: Ma Shaohui, Shen Rongji. Screenplay: Bi Bicheng. Cinematography: Rao Ren. Art Direction: Luo Guohua, Hua Yaozhu. Art Direction: Ao Cangqun. Sound: Luo Guohua, Hua Yaozhu. Cast: Zhao Bengshan as Xiao Wangfa

As the South China town of Zhulin prospers with its new bamboo products plant, it also becomes very crowded. An endless stream of inspectors, tourists, etc., comes and goes. The demands of these guests soon tires out the plant's dining hall manager Xiao Wangfa. When the deputy provincial Party Secretary comes on an inspection visit, some local leaders devour the banquet prepared for him before he arrives at the dining hall. The manager and his staff have only congee to serve the official, but much to everyone's surprise he praises this simple food highly, a model of conduct for the others to emulate.

40. *Alluring Engagement Gift (You Ren De Ding Qing Wu)*

1986. Xi'an Film Studio. Color. 9 Reels. Direction: Jin Jiwu. Screenplay: Yang Lie, Han Dong and Shi Yong, based on the novel "The Nine Dragon Jade." Cinematography: Chen Wancai. Art Direction: Wang Yingbing. Music: Xiang Yin. Sound: Dang Chunzhu. Cast: Pao Haiming as Jiang Menghua, Yang Xiaodan as Ding Jianhu, Wei Zongwan as Li Ruihan, Zhang Yin as Zhou Weiwei, Zhu Guizhen as Sheng Lan, Du Peng as Lin Tianchi, Wu Qi as He Ming, Wang Wenhong as Mi Aili

Wu Renfeng, a direct descendant of the Tang Empress Wu Zetian, is killed when a suspicious fire sweeps her home. Her husband Li Rui, rushes home from his business trip and finds the Wu family treasure the "Nine Dragon Jade" has disappeared. Chief of Detectives Jiang Menghua takes charge of the investigation, and soon identifies a possible suspect in neighbor Ding Jianhu. Further probing identifies a second suspect, family doctor Sheng Lan. At last, the complex case appears to be solved when Jiang finds the treasure. But the jade he finds turns out to be bogus, and the true location remains a Wu family secret.

41. *Along the Jialing River (Jia Ling Jiang Bian)*

1960. Emei Film Studio. B & W. 9 Reels. Direction: Wang Shaoyan and Zhao Qiang. Screenplay: Sha Ting. Cinematography: Liu Ying. Art Direction: Wang Wei. Music: Chang Sumin. Sound: Li Bojian. Cast: Wei Beiyuan as Ji Daming, Lei Nan as Wei Suzhen, Song Tao as Mr. Zhu, Tian Guangcai as Engineer Zhuang, Liu Xi as Master Worker Zhang, Li Shiling as the old man

Before liberation, technician Ji Daming is fired from his job at a Chongqing factory when he points out the mistakes made by a careless engineer. He is then forced to do hard manual labor at the Jialing River port to earn his living. On this job, he becomes acquainted with a Mr. Zhu, an underground Communist Party member. With Zhu's inspiration and teaching, he learns revolutionary theory, and later goes to work in the maintenance shop of a trucking company. Before the liberation of Chongqing, he participates in the protect factories movement led by the Party. After liberation, he is named Master Technician at a natural gas mine, and with the support of Mr. Zhu, now Party Secretary, is successful in upgrading the mine's technology.

42. *Aluohan Miraculous Animal (A Luo Han Shen Shou)*

1989. Pearl River Film Studio. Color. Letterboxed. 10 Reels. Direction: Liu Xin. Screenplay: Yu Li. Cinematography: Zhu Junheng. Art Direction: Li Xin. Music: Fang Xiaoming. Sound: Lu Minwen. Cast: Fu Zhonggui as Cheng Haiqing, Liu Wenzhi as Shi Lei, Zhang Jiping as Fang Sheng

Cheng Haiqing, general manager of a five-star hotel, has a nationwide reputation for his involvement in social reforms. But the local disciplinary committee begins receiving letters alleging Cheng is really engaged in economic crimes. The committee's chief investigator Shi Lei looks into the accusations, and at last finds sufficient evidence to bring Cheng Haiqing to trial.

43. *Am I Your Father? (Wo Shi Ni Ba Ba Ma?)*

1995. Beijing Shanhe Film & Television Art Co. Ltd. Color. Letterboxed. Direction: Wang Shuo. Screenplay: Wang Shuo, Feng Xiaogang, based on the novel by Wang Shuo (1958–). Cinematography: Yang Xiaoxiong. Art Direction: Collective. Music: Gao Erdi. Cast: Feng Xiaogang as Ma Linsheng, Hu Xiaopei as Ma Che, Xu Fan as Qi Huaiyuan

Like many teenagers, Ma Chen finds much in life unsatisfactory: school, home life, and most of all his relationship with his father Ma Linsheng, chairman of a factory labor union. His father is rude and domineering with Ma Chen, which the boy rejects. The father tries to get closer to his son, however, and as he comes to better understand his father, Ma Chen at last realizes his father needs a wife. He helps his father meet a woman named Qi Huaiyuan, and they get married. Ma Linsheng treats his son better after this, but the boy's behavior improves very little. Now, however, the father finds himself excusing or making apologies for Ma Chen's behavior; Ma Linsheng comments that he often feels more like the boy's grandfather than his father. By film's end, father and son have grown close.

44. *Amannisahan (A Man Ni Sha Han)*

1993. Tianshan Film Studio, Tianjin Film Studio, Xinjiang TV Station and Tianjin Film Studio. Co-Production. Color. Letterboxed. 10 Reels. Direction: Wang Yan, Wang Xingjun.

Screenplay: Saifuding Aizi and Wang Yan, based on the former's opera of the same title. Cinematography: Zhou Jixun. Art Direction: Gao Feng, A Dixia. Music: Ai Weixin. Sound: Ju Weijun, Bahetiguli Aken. Cast: Munire as Amannisahan, Mulading as Abudu Rexitihan, Tuerxunjiang as Wumaier, Huer Xide as Hanhou, Rejiepu as Yizhe

In mid-16th Century Xinjiang, Prince Abudu Rexitihan inherits the royal throne and the Uighur people begin a golden era of enlightened and cultured governance. Meanwhile, a girl named Amannisahan is gaining a reputation among the people for her beauty and musical talent. The king meets her and brings her to court. Amannisahan's life there is not an easy one: she encounters considerable persecution and discrimination, particularly from the queen. But the girl perseveres and continues her work of collecting and organizing folk music and songs, and makes great contributions to the classic music of the Uighur people. She dies of an illness while still a young woman, but her memory lives on through the 12-volume set of songs she collected and passed down. She remains a legendary figure among the Uighur people.

45. *Aman's Stories (Duo Guan Xian Shi)*

1991. Shanghai Film Studio. Color. 9 Reels. Letterboxed. Direction: Zhang Gang, Screenplay: Zhang Gang, Cinematography: Cheng Shiyu, Zhang Jian, Art Direction: Sun Weide, Wang Renchen, Music: Wang Ming, Sound: Liu Guangjie, Cast: Li Jianhui as Wei Aman, Tu Linghui as Tian Hong, Cheng Zhi as Zhong Youdde, Ni Yuanyuan as Tong An'an

Kindhearted social worker Wei Aman is always ready to help others. He tries to intervene to prevent a suicide but discovers that it was only an attempt by a retired old man to frighten his unfilial son and daughter into paying more attention to him. Aman fails, however, to persuade the children to keep their father at home rather than send him to a retirement home. Aman also takes care of an orphan, An'an, abandoned by her parents at the welfare house. The little girl regards Aman as her father. Aman has been so kind helping others that Tian Hong, who works with him, is thinking of introducing him to her widowed mother.

46. *An American in Shaolin (Hua Qi Xiao He Shang)*

1994. Changchun Film Studio, Hong Kong Siyan Film Company. Color. Letterboxed. 11 Reels. Direction: Lu Yuanming. Screenplay: Keith W. Strandberg. Cinematography: Zhao Weijian. Sound: Zhang Xiaonan. Cast: Lisa Madigan, Dannier Daijin, Billy Chang, Zhang Zhiren, Jin Lan, Jiang Xinai, Zhang Hong, Jiang Chuanrong, Liu Fei, Ni Yilin, Lu Tongsheng

Young American Dale Carson is badly beaten and humiliated by a rival. He vows to fulfill his kung fu instructor's dream by becoming a real Shaolin monk, so he travels to the Shaolin Temple in Henan Province. He is at first refused, but is later accepted for training and in time acquires super martial arts skills. In an international competition in Shanghai, Carson defeats his cruel and fierce old rival.

47. *An American Pilot (Yi Ge Mei Guo Fei Xing Yuan)*

1980. Pearl River Film Studio. Color. 9 Reels. Direction: Wang Weiyi, Wang Yi. Screenplay: Fan Ruoyou. Cinematography: Lu Dongqin. Art Direction: Ge Xinger, Qin Hongyi. Music: Che Min. Sound: Wang Zhongxuan, Wu Chengxin. Cast: Zhang Qingdao as Aipusitan, Liu Zhenguo as Zhao Dahai, Wu Jing as Chen Yindi, Li Shixi as Li Min, Du Wenhuan as Yang Debiao

A former American pilot who had served in China during World War II, is returning some 30 years later, hoping to find his old friends from those days. He recalls the events of the past: his plane is shot down, and after bailing out he makes his way to a Chinese village and asked the villagers to hide him from the Japanese soldiers searching for him. At the house he goes to, Mrs. Zhao and her daughter-in-law Chen Yingdi are at first very suspicious, but when they learn he is a foreigner helping the Chinese resist the Japanese invaders, they hide him and deliver him to the New Fourth Route Army. At that time, the American only trusts the Nationalists, and flees when he hears the Communists are also looking for him. He feels safe when he reaches the Nationalist Army, but is shocked when they turn him over to the Japanese for money. Suddenly he is a prisoner of war and subjected to torture. The Japanese are moving their American prisoner elsewhere when a Chinese guerrilla troop commanded by Li Min attacks the Japanese unit and rescues him. As the pilot recuperates at the guerrilla base, he becomes very friendly with the Zhao family. To try to recapture their lost prisoner, the Japanese abduct Chen Yingdi, then offer her in exchange for the American. Li Min devices a strategy which rescues the young woman while getting the American back to his own forces. In the operation, Mrs. Zhao is badly wounded. The American pilot is aroused from his reverie by his arrival at the Shanghai airport, where he has a joyous reunion with Zhao Dahai, Li Min and Chen Yingdi.

48. *An American Woman's Adventure (Yi Ge Mao Xian De Mei Guo Nu Ren)*

1989. August First Film Studio. Color. Letterboxed. Direction: Wang Jia, Yu Shishu. Screenplay: Bi Bicheng, based on an incident in the life of American writer Helen Foster Snow (1907–). Cinematography: Sang Hua, Yang Ke. Art Direction: Liu Jisheng. Music: Zhu Shirui. Sound: Zhang Lei. Cast: Debbie Gates as Helen Snow, Gao Fa as Ouyang Chuan, John Perry as Fei Qi, Kang Li as Manager Zhou, Li Yongtian as Whisker

In the late 1930s, the Chinese Communists are at their base camp at Yan'an in Northern Shaanxi province. Western journalists are unable to learn anything about the situation in the Communist-held areas, as the Nationalists have used a net of napalm and spies to seal off all roads leading into them. An adventuresome American woman writer living in China, Helen Snow, wife of *New York Times* correspondent Edgar Snow, determines to find some way into the Red area. She travels to the Northwest Chinese city of Xi'an, where she soon becomes aware of being closely watched and followed by government spies. Undeterred, Snow keeps trying, and with the help of some local people sympathetic to the Red cause, she at last succeeds in running a blockade during a curfew. She becomes one of the few Western journalists to tell the world what the Communists were doing in Northern China in the 1930s.

49. *Amid the Howling Wind (Luo Shan Feng)*

1990. Guangxi Film Studio and Hainan International Film and Television Corporation Co-Production. Color. 14 Reels. Wide Screen. Direction: Bai Chen. Screenplay: Zhao Lihong. Cinematography: Xiao Feng. Art Direction: Ge

Shicheng, Li Jiajun. Music: Jin Fuzai. Sound: Feng Deyao. Cast: Song Jia as Subi, Liu Xin as Lin Wenxiang, Tong Ruimin as Yan Shixiong

In Taiwan, Young Subi is abandoned by her husband's family because she fails to conceive a child. She loses her confidence and enters the Qingtuo Convent, where she becomes a nun. A young male student, Wenxiang, enters the convent on a study retreat. He meets Subi and the two fall in love. Subi becomes pregnant. This affair is revealed. She is driven out of the convent. Wenxiang returns to his original girlfriend, and Subu is left in despair.

Best Actress Song Jia, 1991 Hundred Flowers Awards.

50. *Amnesiac (Shi Qu Ji Yi De Ren)*

1978. Shanghai Film Studio. Color. 9 Reels. Direction: Huang Zuolin, Yan Bili. Screenplay: Yang Shiwen, Si Minsan. Cinematography: Ma Linfa, Yin Fukang. Art Direction: Han Shangyi, Dong Jingsheng. Cast: Wu Xiqian as Ye Chuan, Zhao Jiayan as A Geng, Ma Guanyin as Si Junsheng, Wei Qimin as Jing Zhou, Lin Lan as Liang Bing, Yang Hailian as Tang Minxiu, Xia Keqin as Lin Fan, Feng Chunzhao as Hu Yichuang.

Dongfeng Chemical Industry Equipment Plant Party Secretary Ye Chun conscientiously carries out instructions from the central government concerning the manufacture of large scale chemical industry equipment. But the plant's deputy Party Secretary Hu Yichuang and the city's Office Director Lin Fan accuse Ye Chun of being a "capitalist roader," and he is severely persecuted for this. Later, his enemies plan to cause a permanent memory loss in Ye Chun by having a secret lobotomy performed on him, but doctor Liang Bing does not perform the operation as per instructions. In time, Ye Chun meets his old army buddy Jing Zhou, now a writer. Jing Zhou had been assigned to write a public essay criticizing Ye, but when he discovers Ye is being framed he organizes other honest workers and cadres in uniting to smash the conspiracy.

51. *Anaerhan (Anaerhan)*

1962. Beijing Film Studio & Xinjiang Film Studio Co-production. Color. 11 Reels. Direction: Li Enjie. Screenplay: Lin Yi. Cinematography: Qian Jiang. Art Direction: Yang Yuhe and Yang Raolong. Music: Ge Guangrui. Sound: Fu Yingjie. Cast: Wulike as Anaerhan, Reheman as Kuerban, Maimaiti Yibulayinjiang as Wusiman,

Amid the Howling Wind. After becoming a nun when her husband divorces her for infertility, Subi (Song Jia, right) learns the conception problem was his. 1990. Guangxi Film Studio, Hainan International Film & Television Corporation Co-Production.

Tuhuti Aizemu as Maimaiti, Lu Fei as Zhang Jie, Roumu Yasheng as Simayi

In 1949 Xinjiang, Anaerhan, a Uighur nationality girl, is detained and confined by landlord Wusiman because she refuses to marry him. Shortly after, when he realizes that the advancing PLA will soon occupy Xinjiang, the landlord becomes very pious and correct as a cover. He agrees to drop his marriage suit and release the girl, but fires Kuerban, a servant in his household who had been sympathetic to her. Kuerban leaves town to find work elsewhere, and Anaerhan goes with him. The following year their hometown is liberated, and the young couple, now married, return. The angry and jealous Wusiman uses his new-found religion to persecute the two, forcing them to leave again. But when Kuerban joins a working group reducing the payments farmers must turn over to landowners, Anaerban is able to expose Wu's scheming, allowing she and Kuerban to live in their hometown once more.

52. *Ancient Hunting Song (Yuan Gu Lie Ge)*

1987. Shenzhen Film Studio. Color. 10 Reels. Direction: Xie Xiaojing. Screenplay: Huang Enda, Wu Qitai. Cinematography: Liang Min, Li Jianguo. Art Direction: Ma Yingbo. Music: Guo Wenjing. Sound: Yao Guoqiang. Cast: Tian Shouqing as the first warrior, Shi Yongyuan as the second warrior, Liu Baosheng as the third warrior

53. *An Ancient Tomb's Frightening Ghost (Gu Mu Jing Hun)*

1986. Inner Mongolia Film Studio. Color. 10 Reels. Direction: Dong Tao, Sun Zhiqiang. Screenplay: Jiang Ao. Cinematography: Na Risu. Art Direction: Shen Minquan. Music: Chulun Buhe. Sound: Bu Ren. Cast: Zhu Yanping as Wuyun Batu, Sharen Gaowa as Sha Runa, Li Hongwei as Deli Geer, Dong Tao as the bald man

Archaeology graduate students Sha Runa and Deli Geer are assigned to assist with an excavation seeking an ancient tomb of the Xiongnu (Huns) who terrorized China's frontiers for many years. Team leader Wuyun Batu was at one time a tomb robber, now he works hard to find ancient tombs for the nation. The female student, Sha Runa, and Wuyun Batu are initially hostile to each other, but gradually move to grudging respect, then understanding, and ultimately they fall in love. This greatly upsets Deli Geer, who has loved Sha Runa for some time. Later, Deli Geer is killed in a fight with tomb robbers. The others vow to carry on the work in his memory.

54. *Anecdotes of the Ancient Yue Kingdom (Gu Yue Yi Shi)*

1985. Emei Film Studio. Color. Letterboxed. 10 Reels. Direction: Yang Gansheng. Screenplay: Yan Yi. Cinematography: Cheng Zhaoxun, Zhang Wenzhu. Art Direction: Xia Zhengqiu. Music: Xie Gongcheng, Gao Hongxiang. Sound: Zhang Jianping. Cast: Xu Huanshan as Goujian, Wan Qiong as Yuenu, Lu Jinlong as Fan Rong, Wang Ruoli as the Queen, Qi Feng as Tian Sang, Tang Yuanzhi as Hai He

Around the middle of the Spring and Autumn Period in Chinese history (c6th Century B.C.), King Gou Jian of Yue has his general Zheng Wu put to death. Now the king realizes his error, as his country sorely needs the general's military talent. Court Administrator Fan Rong reports to the king that he has found an unusual woman with super skills at swordsmanship. The woman is called Yuenu, but is actually the late Zheng Wu's daughter. When she demonstrates her skills, the king and all his commanders are amazed. Yuenu has entered the king's service with a purpose: her goal is to find out who bore false witness against her father, and then avenge his death. She at last uncovers the villain, who commits suicide when trapped. At first the king wants to take Yuenu as a concubine, but at last agrees to marry her to her lover Tian Sang in gratitude for her service to the country.

55. *Angel and Devil (Tian Shi Yu Mo Gui)*

1987. Pearl River Film Studio. Color. 10 Reels. Direction: Ling Qiwei. Screenplay: Ling Qiwei, Peng Yun. Cinematography: Han Xingyuan. Art Direction: Tan Ancang. Music: Cheng Dazhao. Sound: Wu Muqin. Cast: Chen Baoguo as Zhen Tian, Li Yun as Bai Yun

Young worker Zhen Tian, hungry for the things that more money could buy, turns to crime. He is arrested but receives a relatively light sentence. After his release, he writes a screenplay about his experience, and is invited to play himself in the movie. He meets innocent and trusting young art student Bai Yun, who falls in love with him. She forgives his past, and he swears to her that is all behind him. But some of his old cronies show up, and intimidate Zhen into pulling another job with them. When he is caught this time, his sentence is a harsher one. In addition, Bai Yun is expelled from her school because she knew of the crime but failed to report it. She returns to her hometown, and becomes a nun in a temple. After Zhen is released from prison, he goes to visit her. Bai Yun tells him she plans to apply to a Buddhist research institute. They part in sorrow.

56. *Angry Airport (Feng Nu De Hang Kong Gang)*

1989. Emei Film Studio. Color. Letterboxed. 10 Reels. Direction: Li Baoping. Screenplay: Yu Ji. Cinematography: Du Xiaosi. Art Direction: Yan Dingfu. Music: Tang Qinshi. Sound: Wang Guangzhong. Cast: Feng Fusheng as Cheng Dong, Zhang Guomin as Kang Defa, Dai Ke as Mr. Mo, Liu Xi as Yang Wenguang, Lu Jun as Yu Xiaogang, Ge Yaming as Guo Shan, Zhang Yanqiu as Li Yuan, Zhang Lu as Shasha

Upon his release from prison, Kang Defa goes immediately to see his former partner Yu Xiaogang. Yu has in his possession a valuable national treasure the two had stolen years before, and Kang wants his cut. The two are under surveillance, for the "Golden Bell Theft" is the major unsolved case in the Jiangcheng City PSB files, and Chief Inspector Cheng Dong has always suspected that Kang and Yu were involved. The two thieves try to take the bell out of the country in order to sell it. When they realize the police are following them, Kang and Yu hijack a bus full of school children and a harrowing chase ensues which ends at the airport. Kang uses a hostage to force the PSB to let him board an airplane, but just as he starts to board the officers make their move and Kang is killed.

57. *Angry Lone Island (Feng Nu De Gu Dao)*

1989. Xiaoxiang Film Studio. Color. Wide screen. 10 Reels. Direction: Jiang Weihe. Screenplay: Wu Tiange. Cinematographer: Yan Yunzhao. Art Direction: Xie Wuqian, Zhang

Xingchuan. Music: Li Lifu. Sound: Huang Qizhi. Cast: Shi Zhaoqi as Xu Tianxiao, Liu Jiaoxin as Asi, Zhao Yang as Shi Dongying, Yan Xiang as Qin Zhixin

Early in the anti-Japanese War, occupied Shanghai becomes an "isolated island." Wounded army officer Xu Tianxiao is forced by his wounds to remain in the city, where he organizes an assassination squad to kill Japanese collaborators. Among his team is Shi Dongying, a patriotic Singapore Chinese. They have some success, but come to realize that this approach will not save China. Xu and Shi decide to leave Shanghai and join the anti-Japanese army, but are killed by the Japanese before they can do so.

58. *Angry Sea and Good Pirates (Xia Hai Nu Dao)*

1993. Emei Film Studio. Color. Letterboxed. Direction: Jiang Guoqin. Screenplay: Deng Jiahui. Cinematography: Zhang Hai, Song Jianwen. Art Direction: Chen Zhizhong, Zhang Xuezhong. Cast: Li Yuanba as Zhang Baozhai, Ye Tong as Zhen Yi's wife, Lu Huiguang as Guo Podai, Zhang Xueao as Lin Zexu

During the early 19th Century, foreigners begin selling opium to Chinese. When a South China pirate is killed, his friend Zhen Yi adopts the dead man's son Zhang Baozhai. He raises the boy in the spirit of his father, and when Baozhai grows up he begins waging an anti-opium campaign, attacking and hijacking drug ships at sea. His name comes to be hated by the foreigners. They petition Governor Lin Zexu to do something about it, but he always protects the pirates, who Lin and the ordinary Chinese people view as patriots. Eventually Lin and Zhang join forces in a major sea battle with British drug boats, and the Chinese win. At the post-victory celebration Lin praises Zhang highly and asks him to join the Chinese navy to protect the coast. Zhang Baozhai thanks the governor, but chooses to continue his life on the sea.

59. *An Angry Sword East of the Great Wall (Jian Hou Chang Cheng Dong)*

1990. Changchun Film Studio & Tianjin Film Studio. Color. 9 Reels. Direction: Fang Cheng, Ma Huiwu. Screenplay: Gui Yuqin. Cinematographer: Xing Shumin. Art Direction: Ma Huiwu. Music: Si Wanchun. Sound: Liu Xi-

aochuan. Cast: Liao Jingsheng as Pao Zhen, Sun Changjiang as Ma Tietui, Tan Tianqian as Jia Teng

In the fall of 1941, Pao Zhen, deputy commander of the Eighth Route Army's branch in East Hebei province, makes an alliance with local bandit Ma Tietui to make common cause against the Japanese. During a joint action, Ma has farmer Lao Mo and his grandson buried alive, mistakenly taking them for Japanese collaborators. Instead of executing Ma for murdering innocent civilians, Pao Zhen takes the bandit's contributions to the resistance into account, and lets him leave the military. In a decisive battle, Pao Zhen defeats the Japanese troops in the region by applying traditional Chinese military tactics. Pao is killed soon thereafter. One day in 1986, the Japanese commander lays a floral wreath at Pao Zhen's tomb to show his respect for his former rival.

60. *Annoying Marriage Event (Fan Nao De Xi Shi)*

1982. Shanghai Film Studio. Color. 10 Reels. Direction: Tian Ran. Screenplay: Yu Hongjun, Song Zhenguo. Cinematography: Gu Wunhou, Dai Qimin. Art Direction: Zhen Changfu. Music: Xiao Yan. Sound: Jin Fugeng. Cast: Cheng Suqing as Wei's wife, Ma Xiaowei as He Zhi, Chen Yanhua as Yuhua, Li Jianhua as Tian Jian, Xu Xin as Yuting,

Wei's two daughters are both engaged. However, Wei's wife demands their daughters' fiances own complete sets of expensive furniture and household electric appliances before the marriage can take place. Elder daughter Yuhua's boyfriend He Zi has to borrow money to get these things. Younger daughter Yuting and her boyfriend Tian Jian want to marry and then acquire such things as their financial ability grows, but Wei's wife refuses to accept this, insisting they have everything first. Tian Jian had some savings but lent it to his co-worker Big Li. When Tian Jian asks for repayment, it turns out Big Li has given the money to He Zhi, who has spent it all for his wedding and has no ability to repay the debt immediately. The men decide to move He Zhi's new wedding furniture to Tian Jian's home for inspection by Wei's wife. A series of comic incidents follow, which not only ends the lovers' wedding plans but causes them to break up as well. Wei's wife then decides to marry Yuhua to a man she hears has good housing and money. She finds out the man is Tian Jian. After considerable embarrassment, Wei's wife realizes her mistakes and with Yuting's help Yuhua and He Zhi are reconciled.

61. *Anonymous Phone Calls (Ni Ming Dian Hua)*

1987. Shanghai Film Studio. Color. 10 Reels. Direction: Jiang Haiyang. Screenplay: Li Xian. Cinematography: Liu Lihua. Art Direction: Chen Shaomian. Music: Yang Yu. Sound: Lu Jiajing. Cast: Wang Sihuai as Wen Xianyu, Lou Jicheng as Jin Chu, Hong Rong as Luo Wenjing, Xiao Xiong as Xiao Yi, Zhu Lei as Qu Shikui, Wu Jing as Rugui

Scientific researcher Wen Xianyu has made many outstanding contributions to the nation in astronomy and aeronautics, but finds himself feeling increasingly nervous and confused. Every night he hears the phone ring, but when he answers there is never anyone there. Are they crank calls? Or is he just imagining he hears the ring? He seeks psychiatric help, and tells Dr. Jin Chu that he knows he has been driving himself too hard, and that his behavior in many respects has lately deviated from his normal practice. He is also afraid of having his privacy violated. The personal secrets Wen divulges cause the doctor to think back over his own life, and a series of unhappy incidents in his past. Dr. Jin goes home, and that night his phone rings and there is nobody there...

62. *An Answer from Heaven (Tian Tang Hui Xing)*

1992. Beijing Film Studio. Color. Letterboxed. 9 Reels. Direction: Wang Junzheng. Screenplay: He Guopu. Cinematography: Yan Junsheng. Art Direction: Shao Ruigang, Yang Wan. Music: Zhang Qianyi. Costume: Chen Jidong. Makeup: Liu Qiuxiang, Yu Xiaoting. Cast: Shi Cheng as Chengcheng, Li Ding as Grandpa, Xiao Xiong mother

Chengcheng's parents are working overseas, but the boy is happy living with his grandfather in Beijing. When Chengcheng's mother returns, the boy and his mother have a communication problem and frequent misunderstandings occur between the two. They grow apart in affection, and the mother is very upset. Fearing that he may be causing the relationship problem, the grandfather moves back to his own place, in spite of the mother's pleading with him to stay. One day, Chengcheng and his mother take a birthday gift to the old man, but they find he has passed away. Sadly, Chengcheng talks to Heaven promising he will send grandfather a birthday card and wait for his reply.

63. *Anticipation (Wang Chuan Qiu Shui)*

1983. Color. Xi'an Film Studio. Color. 9 Reels. Direction: Liu Bing. Screenplay: Gao Shijie. Cinematography: Xu Deyun, Yan Zhijie. Art Direction: Wang Fei. Music: Li Yaodong. Sound: Dang Chunzhu. Cast: Cao Jingyang as Shi Boyan, Xin Jing as Shi Hailiang, Bao Ming as Ai Li, Han Bingjie as Huang Cang, Sun Jinglu as the mother

Former Nationalist general Shi Boyan finally returns for a visit to the Chinese mainland he left more than 30 years ago. In Nanjing, Shi Boyan, his daughter Ai Li and his son-in-law Huang Cang search in vain for the grave of Shi's mother. When they visit the tomb of Dr. Sun Yat-sen, he sees an old veteran soldier who he recognizes as his cousin Shi Hailiang. The two men had grown up together but later parted and fought on opposite sides in China's civil wars. So Shi Boyan is embarrassed to identify himself to his cousin. When the tourists arrive in Shi Boyan's hometown in rural Shanxi, he finds his mother there, still alive and well in her 80s. He is also surprised to learn that Shi Hailiang, who he thought would still regard his as an enemy, has actually been caring for Shi Boyan's mother for these 30 years. On Moon Festival night, Shi Hailiang and his daughter arrive in the old hometown, and he and Shi Boyan meet again at last.

64. *Antique Coin Disturbance (Gu Bi Feng Bo)*

1987. Shanghai Film Studio. Color. 10 Reels. Direction: Fu Jinggong. Screenplay: Liang Xingmin. Cinematography: Cha Xiangkang, Jing Shuzhen. Art Direction: Jin Qifeng. Music: Xu Jingxin. Sound: Dong Yan, Ni Zheng. Cast: He Wei as Xiao Mingda, Wang Su as Liu Azhen, Shu Shi as Huang Yifang, Wu Lijie as Xiao Mingjuan, Shen Xiaoqian as Zhang Delin, Wang Su as Liu Azhen

One day, Shuncang machine manufacturing plant worker Xiao Mingda finds an ancient coin at work. This coin is later identified by numismatic authority Huang Yifang as money from the Song Dynasty (10th-12th Centuries). This discovery gains Xiao Mingda considerable attention from the people around him, all hoping to share in the wealth they think will come to him. When the coin is later claimed to be bogus, their attitude toward Xiao changes immediately, and everyone treats him like a con man. Soon, however, the coin is confirmed as genuine, and everyone flocks around him once more. But this time Xiao Mingda wants no more disruptions in his quiet life, and throws the coin into a nearby river.

65. *Anxious to Return (Gui Xin Si Jian)*

1979. August First Film Studio. Color. 11 Reels. Direction: Li Jun. Screenplay: Li Keyi. Cinematography: Yang Guangyuan, Chen Zhenzhong. Art Direction: Kou Honglie. Music: Li Weicai. Sound: Zhen Mingzhe. Makeup: Yi Hui, Zhang Bangxian. Costume: Zhao Mei. Cast: Zhao Etai as Wei Desheng, Siqin Gaowa as Yu Zhen.

In Manchuria in the winter of 1939, Company Commander Wei Desheng is seriously injured in battle and becomes separated from his unit of the anti-Japanese forces. The movie follows his adventures as he struggles to get back to his company while dealing with danger and the constant threat of death from the Japanese military and Chinese collaborators, as well as the temptations of money and romance. He eventually locates and rejoins his military unit.

66. *Ao Jinma (Ao Jin Ma)*

1977. Xi'an Film Studio. Color. 11 Reels. Direction: Liu Baode, Zhang Qicang. Screenplay: Wu Yuxiao. Cinematography: Ling Xuan, Zhang Faliang. Art Direction: Zhang Zhien. Music: Han Zhongcai. Sound: Che Zhiyuan. Cast: Zhaxi Lamu as Ao Jinma, Deqin Zuoma as Old Auntie, Tie Duoji as Luo Buzang, Dao Lu as Qiang Ba, Ya Duoji as Baerdai, Gong Baocuo as Zuo Ma, Shen Ying as Dan Zeng

IN 1962, county administrator Dan Zeng arrives in the Xingke prairie region of Northwest China, an area peopled largely by ethnic Tibetans. His objective there is to implement the individual household method of production. Party Secretary Ao Jinma perceives this to be a "new trend in class struggle," so she resists Dan Zeng's efforts and goes on with her unit's water conservancy project. She also opposes his incorrect decision to cut off lumber for her project. At first she cannot understand why, but she gains her answer from Chairman Mao's instruction to "never forget the class struggle." Ao Jinma is at last victorious in this class struggle on the Xingke prairie.

67. *Aolei Yilan (Parts 1 and 2) (Ao Lei Yi Lan)*

1979. Shanghai Film Studio. Color. 20 Reels. Direction: Tang Xiaodan. Screenplay: Ye Nan. Cinematography: Luo Chongzhou. Art Direction: Ding Cheng, Wang Xingcang, Chen Chudian. Music: Wang Yunjie, Sound: Wu Jianghai, Li Bingkui. Cast: Zhang Yuhong as Yilan, Zhong Xinghuo as Xierqiyi, Tong Chiling as Andajin, Kou Zhenghai as Aobuku, Pang Wanlin as Habaluofu, Waersi as Sijiepannuofu

In the fall of 1643, in Northeast China's Heilongjiang province, two minority tribes hold a gala betrothal ceremony. The wedding, which will unite their tribes by marrying Aolei Yilan, daughter of one tribe's chief, to Aobuku, son of the other tribe's chief, is planned for that winter. But on the eve of the wedding, the Russians invade Heilongjiang, kill one of the chiefs, and abduct the bride-to-be as a hostage. Yilan is taken to Moscow and put in prison for steadfastly refusing to declare loyalty to the Czar. Later, thinking that she may change at home, the Russians bring Yilan back to Heilongjiang. where she again meets her aged mother, now blind. Bur the mother sacrifices herself by poisoning Yilan's guards, allowing her daughter to escape. Their captive flown, the Russians attempt to discredit Yilan by spreading the rumor that she has declared her loyalty to the Czar and returned to Moscow. This causes Aobuke to denounce his fiancee at first, but he later learns the truth of her courage in captivity, and the couple is at last reconciled. Aolei Yilan unites the several minority peoples of Northeast China into a joint anti-Russian effort. After the invaders are driven out, Aolei Yilan is honored.

68. *Apartment (Gong Yu)*

1985. Pearl River Film Studio. Color. 10 Reels. Direction: Liu Xin. Screenplay: Ling Qiwei, Zhen Binghui. Cinematography: Zhu Junheng. Art Direction: Li Wenguang. Music: Zhang Jielin. Sound: Jiang Shaoqi. Cast: Jin Ping as Liang Yufeng, He Qing as Xiao Qing, Xu Xin as Xiu Er, Xi Meijuan as Huifang, Zhang Tianxi as Ling Hui, Kang Tai as Ling Yunxuan, Zhu Manfang as Gu Xuanyan, Feng Qi as Doctor Xu, Liang Ming as Director Chen

Four girls come from the countryside to

Anxious to Return. Yu Zhen (Siqin Gaowa, center) takes wounded soldier Wei Desheng (Zhao Etai) into her home to recuperate. 1979. August First Film Studio.

work as housekeepers in a large, old-style apartment building. Their family backgrounds differ, as do their thoughts and life goals. They experience city life, and learn much about themselves in the process. In the end, two decide to return to the countryside while two remain.

69. *Apprehending Drug Smugglers (Qin Huai Da Ji Du)*

1993. Changchun Film Studio. Color. Letterboxed. 9 Reels. Direction: Luo Heling. Screenplay: Zhou Chunyuan, Huang Xianwu, Yi Menglin. Cinematography: Zhang Haimin. Art Direction: Gao Tinglun. Music: Fan Weiqiang. Sound: Luo Huailun, Gu Kejian. Costume: Ouyang Yongkuan, Wang Xiyou, Ouyang Chunyu, An Lixin. Makeup: Liang Ling, Zhao Liying. Cast: Ma Cangyu as Zhou Longshan, Cu Zhibo as Sun Dingyu, Zhou Ningchao as Chang Jiuheng

Just after the founding of the People's Republic in 1949, the former Nationalist capital of Nanjing is a hotbed of drugs and drug dealers. Zhou Longshan, the first Public Security Director appointed by the new regime, vows to stamp out the drug problem. Beginning by investigating some drug related killings, his officers led by Sun Dingyu focus on Hongda Company President Ding Jiaxian as the probable drug lord in Nanjing. In a raid on Ding's heavily fortified mansion, Sun is killed in the shootout, but Ding and his gunmen are wiped out.

70. *Apricot Blossom in March (Xing Hua San Yue Tian)*

1993. Youth Film Studio. Color. Letterboxed. 10 Reels. Direction: Yi Li. Screenplay: Shi Ling. Cinematography: Li Jianguo. Art Direction: Cui Junde. Music: Liu Weiguang. Sound: Yao Guoqiang. Costume: Zhao Hui. Makeup: Ma Hongyan. Cast: Jiang Wenli as Xinghua, Tian Shaojun as Fu Lin, Zhang Guoli as Wang Lai, Niu Xingli as Wan Shanye

For 5,000 yuan, prosperous Wang Lai buys himself a bride, sweet and pretty Xinghua (Apricot Blossom). But when they are still childless after five years of marriage, he becomes abusive to her, and throws himself into improving his business. Wang Lai grows rich by cheating in his business practices. When he

Aolei Yilan (Parts 1 & 2). **Daughter of a tribal chief, Aolei Yilan (Zhang Yuhong) unites the several minority peoples of Northeast China into a joint anti–Russian front. 1979. Shanghai Film Studio.**

enters into an affair with another woman, Xinghua turns for comfort to the arms of Fu Lin, a young man just starting out, and she soon becomes pregnant. When Wang Lai learns of her affair, he destroys Fu Lin's career. Fu Lin is too weak to fight back, and runs away. Wang Lai then sets out to hunt for a reported cache of gold, but is killed in the attempt. Xinghua leaves to start a new life elsewhere with her still unborn child.

71. *Arc Light (Hu Guang)*

1988. Guangxi Film Studio. Color. 11 Reels. Wide Screen. Direction: Zhang Junchao. Screenplay: Xu Xiaobin. Cinematography: Xiao Feng. Art Direction: Deng Jin. Music: Wan Xiaoyong. Sound: Yao Guoqiang, Li Ao. Cast: Bai Ling as Jing Huan, Zhang Guangbei as Liu Kai, Xiao Xiong as Xie Ni

Two psychology students, Liu Kai and his girlfriend Xie Ni, are interns in a psychiatric hospital. There they become interested in a female patient called Jing Huan. At Xie Ni's suggestion, Jing Huan is discharged from the hospital into her custody, where she hopes Liu Kai will succeed in curing the patient using treat-

ment methods based on friendship and caring. At Xie Ni's home, it becomes clear that although she is mentally ill Jing Huan is a woman of great intelligence. The students find that Jing Huan's instability seems to have been triggered by the recent death of her father. Touched by Liu Kai's caring treatment methods, Jing Huan cooperates, and during the therapy sessions she gives Liu Kai an insight into the fantasy world of freedom she has created for herself— an icy lake suffused with the glow of an arc lamp. As she reveals more of her innermost secrets to her therapist, Liu Kai finds himself falling in love with his patient. Soon he must choose between her and his colleague Xie Ni.

72. *Arise United Toward Tomorrow (Tuan Jie Qi Lai Dao Ming Tian)*

1951. Shanghai Film Studio. B & W. 10 Reels. Direction: Zhao Ming. Screenplay: Huang Gang. Cinematography: Li Shengwei. Fang Shugao. Set Design: Han Xin and Chen Bosheng. Music: Wang Yunjie. Sound: Wu Jianghai. Costume: Chen Junde. Makeup: Ni Yefei. Cast: Bai Yang as Peng Amei, Sun Zheng as Zhang Shifang, Zhou

Lai as the Committee Member, Tie Niu as Mr. Fang, Zhou Wei as Sister Yang Fa, Zhang Yan as Xiao Zhang.

On the eve of the liberation of Shanghai, the underground CPC organization leads cotton mill workers out on strike. Initial underestimation of the difficulties and the considerable violence that ensues, soon lead to a loss of zeal among the strikers. Zhang Shifang, a CPC Secretary working under cover in the cotton mill, is able to avoid large-scale bloodshed and keep his forces together. In order to have the votes to win the upcoming election, Zhou Gaoming, a Nationalist agent, collects all the workers' identity cards and causes the entire plant to go on strike. Agents of the plant owners carry out a bloody attack on the plant workers, but workers and students from throughout the city come to support the strikers, ensuring the strike's success. Soon afterwards, the PLA enters Shanghai, and Nationalist agents attempt to make off with all the goods from the plant and destroy its facilities, but Zhang organizes the workers in guarding the plant, and they smash the conspiracy.

73. *Armed Troops Behind Enemy Lines (Parts 1 & 2) (Di Hou Wu Gong Dui)*

1995. Changchun Film Studio. Color. Letterboxed. Direction: Lei Xianhe, Kang Ning. Screenplay: Han Jiangxue, Zhao Baohua, Guo Tiecheng, based on the novel of the same title by Feng Zhi. Cinematography: Zhang Haiming, Su Zaili. Art Direction: Gong Minghui. Music: Zhang Guangtian. Cast: Wu Jingan as Wei Qiang, Ru Ping as Wang Xia, Dong Ziwu as Liu Taisheng, Sun Chengxi as Jia Zheng, Wang Hui as Xin Fengming, Liu Zhibing as Ma Ming, He Saifei as Xiao Hongyun, Shu Yuexuan as Songtian, Ma Jie as Haba Gou, Ji Jun as Liu Kuisheng, Zhou Minghan as Xiao Man, Li Mingqi as Aunt Hetao

Chinese resistance fighters battle Japanese troops and collaborators on the Jizhong Plateau.

74. *An Army at an Impasse (Bing Lin Jue Jing)*

1990. Youth Film Studio. Color. 9 Reels. Wide Screen. Direction: Jin Jiwu. Screenplay: Zheng Dingyu, Jin Jiwu. Cinematography: Bao Xiaoyan. Art Direction: Chen Xiaoxia. Music: Jin Fuzai. Sound: Wang Junzhi, Huang Yingxia. Cast: Lou Jicheng as the Army Commander,

Shen Junyi as Bai Yunsen, Sun Yanjun as Liang Wanyu, Chu Zhibo as Zhou Hao

In the earliest days of China's anti-Japanese war, Japanese forces surround the ancient city of Lingcheng in Southern China. The newly-reorganized Nationalist 22nd Army is bottled up in the city and is suffering heavy casualties. The commander of the 22nd army is determined to fight to the end, but the reinforcements surrender one after another, so he finally loses confidence in his army's ability to withstand the Japanese. In order to preserve his army and save his troops, he issues an order to his army to surrender, after which he commits suicide. But Bai Yunsen, an obstinate division commander with a maverick's reputation, is unwilling to give up. He kills the deputy army commander who wants to surrender, and insists that the original surrender order was a forgery. The Japanese attack again, and are turned back by the Chinese, but at high cost to the defenders. Bai Yunsen now has control, and decides to reveal the truth about the surrender order, that it was not a forgery. His motive is to have his former commander discredited as a traitor. However, this puts him in conflict with the former commander's bodyguard. A new, internal struggle erupts.

75. *Army Commander He Long (He Long Jun Zhang)*

1983. Xiaoxiang Film Studio. Color. 10 Reels. Direction: Chen Xinzi, Shi Wenzhi. Screenplay: He Xingtong, Gu Xiaoyan. Cinematography: Yin Qiaofang, Teng Xihui. Art Direction: Ma Yibiao, Guo Dexiang. Music: Wei Jingshu. Sound: Li Yan, Ning Yuqin. Cast: Xia Zongyou as He Long, Ma Hongying as Wang Jingwei, Liu Yu as Bai Ying, Huang Kai as Zhou Enlai, Zhen Zaishi as Zhang Guotao

In July, 1927, the Northern Expeditionary Army under the command of General He Long defeats warlord General Zhang Zuolin (Chang Tsolin) in Henan. The Wuhan Government Chairman Wang Jingwei orders He Long to return to Wuhan, where the General is successful in blocking Wang's plan for rebellion, in spite of efforts to divide his army. General He's family is later persecuted by his political enemies. To this point the Communists and Nationalists were allied, but now Wang Jingwei and Chiang Kai-shek turn on the Communists and slaughter many of them. When He Long's 20th Army stops at Jiujiang, Zhou Enlai delivers a message from the Communists asking that He Long's army be the main force in a rebellion they plan to hold at Nanchang. Nationalist spy Bai Ying infiltrates He Long's headquarters and stirs up trouble between He Long and the Communists, trying to persuade the General to ally with Chiang Kai-shek. He Long at last decides to support the Communists, and participates in the "August 1st" rebellion at Nanchang, which marked the beginning of the People's Liberation Army.

76. *Army Nurse (Nu Er Lo)*

1985. August First Film Studio. Color. 9 Reels. Direction: Hu Mei, Li Xiaojun. Screenplay: Kang Liwen, Ding Xiaoqi. Cinematography: He Qin, Wu Fei. Art Direction: Yu Maiduo. Music: Sun Baolin. Sound: Tang Yuanping. Cast: Xu Ye as Qiao Xiaoyu, Hasi Bagen as Ding Zhe, Zhao Gang as Tu Jianli

During the Cultural Revolution, after her parents are sent to cadre school, Qiao Xiaoyu becomes an army nurse at the age of 15. When army transportation platoon leader Ding Zhe is brought to the hospital as a patient, she is assigned to care for him, and in time they fall in love. However, the strict military discipline of the time prevents the two young people from developing their relationship. Many years later, Qiao has risen to the rank of Chief Nurse, but while many of her girlfriends have husbands, Qiao seems to show little interest in marriage. The truth is, she cannot forget Ding Zhe. She is introduced to Chief of Staff Tu Jianli, a nice man who is also single. Tu later proposes, and while she at first agrees, Qiao decides to tell him her true feelings before the marriage. Tu respects her feelings, and the marriage is cancelled.

77. *An Arrest Order Will Be Issued Soon (Ji Jiang Fa Chu De Dai Bu Ling)*

1984. Xi'an Film Studio. Color. Letterboxed. 9 Reels. Direction: Yao Shougang. Screenplay: Lu Kejian, Liu Guangjie. Cinematography: Liu Cangxu. Art Direction: Dai Yuanzhong, Zhang Gong. Music: Li Yaodong. Sound: Hua Juan. Costume: Zhu Hong. Makeup: Yang Huaiyu. Cast: Sun Feihu as Feng Kun, Ma Chongle as Dong Fei, Li Jimin as Li Zhongchun, Han Bingjie as Hou Zhiliang, Mai Wenyan as A Fang, Wang Bingyan as Jiang Shaowu

A detective story centering around a precious jade item which mysteriously disappears from the Qing emperor's personal collection in the late 18th Century, then reappears just as mysteriously 200 years later in the South China city of Haiwan.

78. *As Both Sides' Wish (Liang Xiang Qing Yuan)*

1987. Inner Mongolia Film Studio. Color. 9 Reels. Direction: Chen Da, Qin Wubo. Screenplay: Lu Zhirong. Cinematography: Na Risu. Art Direction: Aori Lige. Music: Xia Zhongtang. Sound: Da Yin. Cast: Li Lingdi as Tian Xiuxiu, Wu Liping as Li Gougou, Kang Fulei as Youyou, Wulan Tuoya as Meimei

Widow Tian Xiuxiu has a bachelor neighbor Li Gougou. Both want to become prosperous, but while Xiuxiu makes it through hard work, Gougou always looks for the easy way, so he always loses money. Xiuxiu is sympathetic with Gougou's situation and leads him into the correct path. The two draw closer through their work, and at last, Gougou and Xiuxiu fall in love.

79. *As One Wishes (Ru Yi)*

1982. Beijing Film Studio. Color. 10 Reels. Direction: Huang Jianzhong. Screenplay: Liu Xinwu, Dai Zongan. Cinematography: Gao Lixian. Art Direction: Shao Ruigang. Music: Si Wanchun. Sound: Zhen Chunyu. Cast: Li Rentang as Shi Yihai, Zhen Zhenyao as Jin Qiwen, Tan Tianqian as Cheng Yu

While high school custodian Shi Yihai works very hard he is also somewhat eccentric, believing very firmly in ghosts. As he does his work every morning, he often relates to Cheng Yu and other teachers stories of ghosts in the school building. This quirk has caused people to leave him alone. During the Cultural Revolution years, he had mocked the absurd political views of that time, and helped those being criticized or persecuted in the movement. Even his love life was very unusual: although he was an uneducated man from a working class background, he had an affair with an aristocratic lady, Jin Qiwen. Criticism of their relationship by society and the media forced them to hide their love from the outside world. After Shi Yihai dies, people are at a loss to explain him. Just an ordinary man with no great contribution or honors, and yet many find they miss him although they had ignored his existence when he was alive.

80. *Ashes of Time (Dong Xie Xi Du)*

1994. Beijing Film Studio, Hongkong Zedong Film Production Company Co-production. Color. Letterboxed. 9 Reels. Direction: Wang Jiawei. Screenplay: Wang Jiawei, based on the novel by Jin Yong. Cinematography: Christopher Doyle. Art Direction: Zhang Shuping. Music: Chen Xunqi. Sound: Zhang Baojian. Cast: Leslie Cheung (Zhang Guorong) as Ouyang Feng, Tony Leung (Liang Jiahui) as Huang Yaoshi, Brigette Lin (Lin Qingxia) as Mu Rongyan, Zhang Xueyou as Master Hong 7, Tony Leung (Liang Chaohui) as the blind warrior

When his brother marries the girl he loves, Ouyang Feng leaves his hometown of Baituoshan and becomes a professional killer called "West Poison." He becomes good friends with another man called "East Evil." A woman named Mu Rongyan, gone mad after "East Evil" rejects her, asks Ouyang Feng to kill his friend for her. "East Evil" leaves. Later, Ouyang Feng hears his brother's wife has passed away, and he returns to Baituoshan.

81. *Ashima (Ashima)*

1964. Haiyan Film Studio. Color. Wide screen. 10 Reels. Direction: Liu Qiong. Screenplay: Ge Yan and Liu Qiong, based on an epic poem of the same title. Cinematography: Xu Qi. Art Direction: Ding Cheng. Music: Luo Zongxian, Ge Yan. Sound: Miao Zhengyu. Cast: Yang Likun as Ashima, Baosier as Ahei, Han Fei as Azhi, Cui Chaoming as Rebubala, Huang Qiongying as Azhi's mother, Liu Jie as Ashima's mother

In a place called Azhedi lived Ashima, a beautiful girl of the Bai nationality. She loved a hard-working and brave young man named Ahei. The son of the local headman admired Ashima's beauty and longed to possess her, but she rejected him. At a time when Ahei is away from the area, the headman's family abducts Ashima. The girl puts an engagement flower from Ahei in a stream, and the current carries to it Ahei, uses his miraculous arrow to cut through the mountains and rescue his beloved. As the two are happily going home, they stop to rest by the stream, attracted by the beautiful scenery of the area. But some of the headman's henchmen steal Ahei's miraculous arrow and dam up the stream, causing a flood which drowns Ashima. The heartbroken Ahei stands on the bank of the stream crying out her name, and suddenly Ashima appears as a stone image of herself.

Asian Car Rally (Ya Xi Ya Sai Che) **see** *Begin the "Pluto" Operation*

82. *Assassinating Wang Jingwei (Ci Sha Wang Jing Wei)*

1988. Guangxi Film Studio. Color. Letterboxed. 10 Reels. Direction: Ying Qi. Screenplay: Wang Shengrong, Jin Zhenzong, Song Chong. Cinematography: Yang Yuming, Mo Shaoxiong. Art Direction: Chen Yaogong. Music: Sun Chengye, Tao Siyao. Sound: Han Weijun. Cast: Wu Gang as Sun Fengming, Zhang Minliang as Zhang Songnan, Sun Yanjun as Wang Jingwei

Wang Jingwei signs a series of agreements with the Japanese that sell out China's interests, causing widespread anger among the Chinese people. At the Nanjing railway station, a train loaded with wounded soldiers of the Nationalist 19th Route Army pulls into the station. Suddenly a soldier draws a gun, aiming to shoot a man clad in a white suit. Just in time, the would-be assassin recognizes the man is not Wang Jingwei and puts the gun away. The soldier, Sun Fengming, wants to kill Wang in the name of his patriotic comrades-in-arms, many of whom have been killed and wounded in a cause their government has now abandoned. Sun tries a second time at the Jinling Woman's College where Wang is going to give a speech. However, this plan aborts when a group of people arrive to demonstrate against Wang, causing him to leave in a hurry. Sympathetic journalist Zhang Song arranges a press pass for Sun Fengmin, permitting him to attend the Nationalist Party Conference. There, Sun mingles with a group of reporters, and when he feels the time is ripe runs out of the group and fires three shots at Wang, all of which miss. Sun Fengming is fatally shot by bodyguards. This was the attempted assassination of Wang Jingwei, an event which shocked all China at the time.

83. *Assassination (Jue Sha)*

1993. Changchun Film Studio. Color. Letterboxed. 9 Reels. Direction: Zhang Zhongwei. Screenplay: Zhao Yansheng, Zhang Jiongqiang. Cinematography: Yan Kai. Art Direction: Wang Di. Music: Chen Chunguang. Sound: Cao Feng, Zhang Xiaonan. Costume: Hu Lianzhong. Makeup: Li Chunhai. Cast: Chen Baoguo as Ding Mang, Xu Xiaojian as Yan Qi, Wang Daming as Uncle Xia, Zhen Tianwei as Yun Lan, Lu Yi as Ye Zhuqing, Wang Gang as Chuanqi, Li Yuling as Songben, Zhen Tianyong as Uncle Hou

After the fall of Shanghai to the Japanese, the people of the city continue to resist. Patriotic businessman Xia draws up an "absolute killing" plan intended to kill all important Japanese officers, and thereby hamper plans to occupy more of China. To implement his plan, Xia hires a couple of young professional killers, Ding Man and Yan Qi. As a series of important figures begin turning up murdered, the Japanese deputy ambassador draws up a counter-plan. His agent for implementation is another professional killer, Ye Zhuqin, a man who had raped Xia's daughter Yunlan when the girl was only six. Ye traces the killings to Xia, and kills him, but Yunlan gains revenge by killing Ye. After the Nationalist government signs the "Song Hu Cease Fire Agreement," humiliating to China, the deputy ambassador and seven other high-ranking Japanese civilian and military officials are killed one after another.

84. *The Assembled Man (Bai Bian Jin Gang)*

1995. China Film Co-production Co., Hong Kong Yongsheng Entertainment Co. Ltd, Yunnan Nationalities Film Studio Co-production. Color. Letterboxed. Direction: Ye Weimin. Cast: Zhou Xingchi, Liang Yongqi, Wu Mengda, Sun Jiajun

A fantasy in which a wealthy Hong Kong man sends his son to study at the University of Hawaii where the boy becomes involved with a woman who turns out to the mistress of a crime boss. The jealous gangster has the student murdered. The father then approaches his son's professor, and begs him to restore his son to life. The professor does so, but insufficient funds lead him to use some cheap replacement parts, and this leads to some farcical situations. Finally, the professor obtains some quality body parts and the young man, restored to life, avenges himself on the killers.

85. *An Astonishing Dream While Visiting the Zoo (You Yuan Jin Meng)*

1956. Central Newsreel And Documentary Film Studio. B & W. 4 Reels. Direction: Shi Lan. Screenplay: Xie Tian, Shang Fu, Yu Yanfu. Cinematography: Zhang Zhaobing. Art Direction: Zhang Xiande, Tian Shizhen. Music: He Fang. Sound: Liu Zhao. Cast: Kou Baolin, Guo Qiru.

An instructional tale of a zoo visitor who ignores zoo rules. He plays with the animals, pets those he should not and scatters litter about the grounds. When he tires, he lays down in a prohibited spot and takes a nap. In his sleep, he dreams that various wild and fierce animals are chasing him. He awakens suddenly when someone touches him, and realizes it was just a dream.

86. *At Middle Age (Ren Dao Zhong Nian)*

1982. Changchun Film Studio. Color. 11 Reels. 110 min. Direction: Wang Qimin, Sun Yu. Screenplay: Shen Rong, based on her novel of the same title. Cinematography: Wang Qimin. Art Direction: Gao Tinglun. Music: Wu Damin. Sound: Chen Wenyuan. Cast: Pan Hong as Lu Wenting, Da Shichang as Fu Jiajie, Zhao Kuier as Jiang Yafeng, Zhen Qianlong as Liu Xuerao, Wu Zuang as Sun Yimin, Pu Ke as Jiao Shicheng

Ophthalmologist Lu Wenting has worked for 18 years at the same hospital. Year in and year out, she has worked incessantly to save or restore the sight of thousands of people. Although she is the mainstay of the optical department, she has never received a promotion. She and her husband Fu Jiajie, a researcher in a Metallurgical Institute, live with their two children in the same 12 square meter room she was assigned at the outset of her career. Overloaded with household responsibilities and professional work, Lu has a heart attack. She had actually performed three successful surgeries on the morning of the attack. Now, lying in her hospital bed, she thinks back over her life and realizes that although she has given everything to her patients, she feels guilty for neglecting her children. Lu Wenting's life is saved. Everyone realizes that while China's future may be with its young people, middle-aged people like Lu and her husband are the nation's backbone today.

Best Picture, 1983 Golden Rooster Awards.

Best Picture, 1983 Hundred Flowers Awards.

Best Actress Pan Hong, 1983 Golden Rooster Awards.

At the Age of 40 **see** *Family Portrait*

87. *At the Foot of Ice Mountain (Bing Shan Jiao Xia)*

1984. Tianshan Film Studio. Color. 10 Reels. Direction: Zhen Guoen, Tang Guangtao. Screenplay: Abudu Kadier, Zhu Make, Zhen Guoen.

Cinematography: Ai Lijiang. Art Direction: Zhang Shisheng. Music: Ma Shizen, Maxia Dadai. Sound: Jin Wenjiang. Cast: Talai Guli as Akelai, Yeerken as Baike Mulati

Akelai is a woman veterinarian among the Uighur people of Xinjiang. When an uncontrollable disease kills a group of sheep, local people turn on her, thinking it was her treatment of the sheep that was the cause. The arrival of another veterinarian, Baike Mulati, calms their anger, and in time Akelai and Baike Mulati fall in love. Her father opposes this, as he wants his daughter to marry someone else. The two young lovers continue working hard, and in time persevere in both work and romance.

88. *Attacking the Invaders (Da Ji Qin Lue Zhe)*

1965. August First Film Studio. B & W. 10 Reels. Direction: Hua Chun. Screenplay: Cao Xin and Zhen Hong, based on the stage play "Protecting Peace" by Song Zhi. Cinematography: Yang Zhaoren. Art Direction: Jiang Zhenkui. Music: Fu Gengcheng. Art Direction: Li Yan. Cast: Li Yan as Army Commander Li, Hu Xiaoguang as Political Commissar Fang, Yu Chunmian as Cui Kai, Zhang Liang as Ding Dayong, Huang Huanguang as Little Bean, Huang Bangrui as Big Zhou

In the summer of 1953, PLA Volunteer Army deputy regimental commander Cui Kai leads a contingent on a mission. With the help of North Korean spy Yi Yushan, they surprise and destroy the enemy's crack White Tiger regimental command post, then free some North Korean prisoners, including guerrilla chief Kim Zhekui. Pursued and trapped by the enemy regiment, the group is seriously decimated and Cui Kai is seriously wounded. Soon Ding Dayong, Yi Yushan and Kim Zhekui are left. But at the critical moment the main force of the North Korean People's Army arrives, and turns the tide of battle.

89. *Automobile Accident Story (Che Huo Yi Shi)*

1984. Liaoning Science Film Studio. Color. 9 Reels. Direction: Niu Lishan. Screenplay: Bai Hong, Li Xiaojun. Cinematography: Wang Weiguo. Art Direction: Chen Ke. Music: Qin Yongcheng. Sound: Zhang Baojian. Cast: Da Shichang as Bai Ping, Zhang Zhiqiang as Xu Datong, Chen Ao as Liu Min, Xie Wei as Xu Yan

News reporter Bai Ping receives an anony-

mous letter which calls upon his paper to look into an injustice being committed in connection with a recent accident. The reporter finds out that the case involves a young worker named Liu Min whose bicycle was involved in an accident in which an old lady was fatally injured. Although the accident was not Liu's fault, but that of a third party, the old woman's disabled son Xu Datong is now seeking compensation from Liu Min. The reporter's investigation at last determines that the writer of the letter was Xu Datong's sister Xu Yan, for as she says, "Mother never wanted to make trouble for others." Faced with these facts and Bai Ping's persuasion, Xu Datong withdraws his demands.

90. *Autumn Harvest Uprising (Qiu Shou Qi Yi)*

1993. Xiaoxiang Film Studio. Color. Wide Screen. 11 Reels. Direction: Zhou Kangyu. Screenplay: Luo Ju, Zhou Kangyu, Huang Demin. Cinematography: Zhang Jianzhong, Zhang Yuefu. Art Direction: Li Shu. Music: Xu Jingxin, Wei Jingshu. Sound: Huang Qizhi. Costume: Li Huimin, Liang Ting. Makeup: Zhang Jing, Jiang Chunyan. Cast: Wang Yin as Mao Zedong, Li Yongtian as Yu Shadu, Yao Gang as Lu Deming, Liu Falu as Zhang Guoping, Chen Kang as Wu Zhonghao, Wang Qian as Yan Lingzhi, Liu Ying as Su Xianjun

In 1927, Chiang Kaishek breaks the Nationalist-Communist collaboration, and begins a massacre of Communists in Shanghai. The Communist Party Central Committee holds an emergency meeting, at which the current leadership's political line is criticized and a new principal line established. As part of the new anti-Nationalist line, Mao Zedong is ordered to go down to the countryside and organize the peasants. The rest of the film details Mao's work in organizing what becomes known as the Autumn Harvest Uprising.

91. *Autumn Impressions (Qiu Tian De Yin Xiang)*

1983. Pearl River Film Studio. Color. 9 Reels. Direction: Duan Bing. Screenplay: Ou Weixiong, Yang Miaoqin, Yao Zhulin, Huang Yonghu. Cinematography: Wu Yukun. Art Direction: Ye Jialiang. Music: Zhang Hong. Sound: Li Dehua. Cast: Song Jia as Qiao Wanjun, Liu Wei as Su Chi, Xu Ruiping as Yang Xiaozhi

Qian Wanjun, a Chinese-American girl about to graduate from college in South

China, starts out on a bicycle trip to the North with a group of other students. The first day out, she becomes separated from the rest. One of the other girls, Yang Xiaozhi, is quite anxious and begins searching for her, enlisting the aid of an art institute graduate student named Su Chi. When they do find Qian Wanjun the next day, the rest of the group is too far ahead to for them to catch up. So the two young women and the young man they have just met decide to tour China on their own. They have a series of small adventures together, and Qian Wanjun discovers the sincere and unselfish nature of Su Chi. They become good friends, and when Qian compares the warmth of the Chinese people with those she had known in America, she knows that when she leaves she will carry with forever beautiful memories of China.

92. *Avenging Beauty (Nu Hai Hong Yan)*

1994. Beijing Film Studio. Color. Letterboxed. 9 Reels. Direction: Xu Qingdong. Screenplay: Ma Junxiang. Cinematography: Hua Qing, Xu Hongbing. Art Direction: Song Jun. Music: Gao Erdi. Sound: Liu Xiaodong. Costume: Hu Fuhua, Liu Weifeng, Xia Hongbing. Makeup: Ma Shuangying, Zhao Zhiping. Cast: Wang Xi as Songben Chuanzi, Yi Fang as Xiuchun, Chen Guodian as Sha Kun, Zhang Yi as Duan Xiaorong, Chong Zhijun as Lin Da, Yao Erga as Duan Dacheng, Fu Xiaodong as Liu the thief

When Shanghai elementary school principal Lin De learns of a secret Japanese plot to abduct 50 Chinese children and send them to Japan for training as future spies, he tries to block the scheme and threatens to take his story to the newspapers. As a result, he and his wife are murdered before the plot becomes public knowledge. Their daughter Lin Ruolan believes her parents were killed by triad boss Sha Kun, whose organization had been criticized by Lin's father. She vows to have her revenge on Sha, despite warnings from her boyfriend, police officer Long Er, that killing innocent citizens is not Sha Kun's style, and that Long believes the killer was a Japanese. As part of her vengeance scheme, Lin Ruolan marries Duan Xiaorong, head of a rival triad. Then she learns the truth about her parents' deaths. Meanwhile, Long Er learns of the Japanese plot, and he and Lin Ruolan free the 50 children. But in the bitter battle that follows, Lin and Long are both killed by Japanese agents.

93. *Avenging Gun (Shen Qiang Xue Hen) (aka: Hold On His Gun)*

1993. Xiaoxiang Film Studio. Color. Letterboxed. 9 Reels. Direction: Tu Jiakuan. Screenplay: Zhao Qihe. Cinematography: Tu Jiakuan, Liu Weiwei. Art Direction: Zhang Wenqi, Zhu Lin. Music: Guan Xia, Luo Xiaojian. Sound: Yu Xiaoli. Costume: Liu Nian, Pang Yan. Makeup: Guo Dali, Yi Xiaoxiao. Cast: Huang Guoqiang as Shitou, Aixin Jueluo as Mangmei, Yu Shaokang as Zhao Jinchuan, Sun Chengxi as Ma Liuzi, Wei Luping as Shitou's mother, Cao Xiaowen as Peach, Hou Yueqiu as Housan, Wang Xiyuan as Chen Shan

In Fengshu Village in the 1930s, laborer Shitou and village girl Mangmei are lovers. But Shitou's employer, local despot Zhao Jinchuan, wants the girl to marry his retarded son. She refuses, so Zhao forces Shitou to flee for his life. Five years pass, and Shitou is now a greenwoods bandit and an expert gunman. Back at the village, Zhao Jinchuan buries a national treasure, a white gold monkey, to hide it from the Japanese invaders. The Japanese know of the treasure, but Zhao refuses to divulge its hiding place. Because of Zhao's patriotic resistance to the Japanese, Shitou decides to rescue his old adversary. He then has Zhao take the treasure away, while he and Mangmei fight a delaying action to cover Zhao's escape. The reunited lovers die together.

94. *Awakening (Su Xing)*

1981. Xi'an Film Studio. Color. 10 Reels. Direction: Teng Wenji. Screenplay: Xu Qingdong, Teng Wenji. Cinematography: Song Dingyu. Art Direction: Liu Xinghou. Music: Wang Ming. Sound: Chen Yudan. Cast: Chen Chong as Su Xiaomei, Gao Fei as Tian Dan, Xu Huanshan as Tian Zhonghua, Zhi Yitong as Song Qi, Zhang Xiaolin as Li Fei, Tu Ruyin as Peng Fang

A contemporary love story. Tian Dan, employed by a foreign trade company, by chance runs into Su Xiaomei, a young woman he has not seen in years. Her appearance brings hope again to Tian's quiet and lonely life. As they have many conversations about their beliefs, lives and careers, Tian Dan is impressed by her attitude of facing reality and continuing to forge ahead. Su Xiaomei admires his ambitions and desire to make the most of his life.

95. *Awakening from a Dream (Mi Meng Chu Xing)*

1987. Beijing Film Studio. Color. 3-D. 7 Reels. Direction: Zhang Zhucheng, Zhang Shichun. Screenplay: Zhang Zhucheng, Zhang Shichun. Cinematography: Zhang Zhucheng, Hou Yuzhi. Art Direction: Ma Zhoren. Music: Lu Yuan, Cheng Kai. Sound: Lan Fan, Sun Xiuyun. Cast: Tong Jiaqi as Zhen Xin, Xu Mingyong as Chen Youan, Liu Jun as Li Yeqiu

In a south China city, a government bureaucrat starts a newspaper in his spare time, employing young people who have finished school but are awaiting work assignments. Instead of a regular newspaper, he publishes a quasi-pornographic "scandal sheet" in order to make more money. Although sales are brisk at first, he soon encounters trouble from readers, who flood the paper with critical letters. At last, he sees his own children are being negatively influenced by the paper's unwholesome content. With criticism and education from Party leaders, he sees his errors and determines to reform the newspaper.

96. *Awakening from a Nightmare at Dawn (Er Meng Xing Lai Shi Zhao Cheng)*

1980. Pearl River Film Studio. Color. 9 Reels. Direction: Wang Ti. Screenplay: Wang Pei. Cinematography: Shi Fengqi, Xia Lixing. Art Direction: Li Pingye. Music: Yang Shuzheng. Sound: Deng Qinhua, Le Dehua. Cast: Yu Ping as Chen Jinglan, Ma Yi as Zhou Chuan, Bai Li as Jianfang

During the years that the Gang of Four dominate China, the family of shipyard manager Zhou Chuan is subjected to considerable public humiliation and persecution. He is sent to jail, and his wife, public security cadre Jian Fang, disappears. Although presumed dead, her body is never found. The couple's daughter Juanjuan is bullied by other children and is very lonely. Also persecuted is Juanjuan's teacher Chen Jinglan: an honest and kindly woman, sympathetic to the family's suffering, she gives Juanjuan some of the motherly care the child needs after her mother's death. For this the teacher is labeled a criminal and is forced out of the teaching job she loves so dearly. After Zhou Chuan is released, he and Chen are drawn together in mutual suffering and comfort. The two eventually fall in love, marry, and in time have a baby boy. After the Gang of Four is defeated, Chen Jinglan learns

quite accidentally that Zhou Chuan's first wife who had disappeared is not dead after all. Although greatly pained and distressed by this news, Chen keeps it all inside her. She decides to go away to where she is most needed for national modernization, and leaves before daybreak, in the red dawn.

97. *Axing Axin (A Xing A Xin)*

1987. Shanghai Film Studio. Color. 3-D. 8 Reels. Direction: Yu Jie. Screenplay: Cheng Zhi, Liang Zhen. Cinematography: Xie Guojie. Art Direction: Cai Lu, Gao Yinghua. Music: Zhang Kanger, Hui Juanyan. Sound: Zhao Xianrui. Cast: Zhang Li as Ann, Shi Shugui as Grandma, Zhang Kanger as Axing, Zhang Kanger as Axin, Lu Ying as Jimei

Axin, a young man working as part of a TV series film crew, returns to the scenic area where he grew up. His fiancee Meiyi still lives there in their old home town. Axing, a Chinese-American young man taken overseas as a child by his father, returns with his fiancee Ann to seek his grandmother and his twin brother. A comedy of errors ensues, built around misidentifications of the two identical twins, particularly by their fiancees. At last, all the confusion is straightened out, and Axing also finds his grandmother.

98. *Azalea (Du Juan Ti Xue)*

1984. Emei Film Studio. Color. 10 Reels. Direction: Zhang Fengxiang. Screenplay: Jiang Sheng. Cinematography: Sun Guoliang. Art Direction: Luo Zhicheng, Cheng Jinyong. Music: Zhang Peiji. Sound: Zhang Jianping. Cast: Sharen Gaowa as Juanzi, Zhang Yi as Chunyyou, Yu Xiuchun as Mother-in-Law, Zhao Chunmin as Xu Qiang, Xie Chengxin as Old Man Lin

When Juanzi's husband Xu Qiang joins the Red Army, Juanzi moves in with her mother-in-law. Life is very hard for them. A kindly man named Chunyou helps the two women, and in time he and Juanzi become very close. When word comes that Xu Qiang is dead, the mother-in-law asks Juanzi and Chunyou to marry before the older woman dies. They marry, and are happy together. But then Xu Qiang turns up alive and well. When he finds his wife married to another man, and they explain the story to him, Xu Qiang understands and leaves to rejoin his military unit. Later, Juanzi and Chunyou learn that an enemy force is moving into the area and Xu Qiang's unit will be in danger. They go to warn him and his colleagues, but are killed on the way.

99. *"Baby" Pickpocket and Grafter (Bao Bei Xiao Tou Yu Da Dao)*

1991. Beijing Film Studio. Color. 9 Reels. Direction: Chen Guojun. Screenplay: Wang Zhunxi. Cinematography: Zhen Yiyuan. Li Jianxin. Art Direction: Ning Lanxin, Qin Duo. Music: Lu Yuan. Sound: Guan Shuxin. Cast: Shi Guoqing, Wang Yin, Shi Lan, Wang Qinshan

A satire, in which two people find a gold case and make every attempt to find the owner. In the process of their search, many corrupt contemporary social phenomena are lampooned, while also expressing people's longing for clean and honest government.

100. *Back to the Jail (Xue Qiu)*

1994. Shanghai Film Studio. Color. Letterboxed. 10 Reels. Direction: Wu Tiange. Screenplay: Lan Zhiguang, Fu Xing, Wu Tiange, based on a true story. Cinematography: Gao Ziyi, Wang Guofu. Art Direction: Zhou Xinren. Music: Yang Mao. Sound: Qian Ping. Costume: Zhang Ming. Makeup: Zhang Zhen. Cast: Ding Jiayuan as Kong Guoying, Meng Jun as Fan Jiajun, Zhou Guobing as Li Qiang, He Min as Wang Shuilai, Zhu Yin as woman wife of boss, Hai Da as Yang Muwan, Yang Yetian as Shen Yiqing, Hu Ronghua as Lu Kang, Bi Yuanjin as Luo Zhanjun, Zhou Bo as Qin Hongchang, Zhang Yuan as Gu Denian

Based on a true incident. A bus transporting prisoners to a clinic for health checks crashes in the mountains, and some are killed. The uninjured survivors are faced with the choice of fleeing or staying behind to help the injured ones. As they debate this, some old hostilities come to the surface and some fight among themselves. At last they decide to get down from the mountain, and take the injured with them. After much hardship, they reach a resort, and medical assistance is found for the injured. The prisoners are told their good moral conduct will work in their favor with the authorities.

101. *The Bad Girl (Wei Qing Shao Nu)*

1994. Shanghai Film Studio, Hong Kong Longwei Film Company. Color. Letterboxed. 10 Reels. Direction: Lou Ye. Screenplay: Tao Lingfeng, Wu Zhennian, Song Jigao. Cinematography: Zhang Xigui. Art Direction: Ji Jixian. Music: Pan Guoxing, Li Jie. Sound: Lu Jiajing. Costume: Feng Jianmin. Makeup: Yin Lihua.

Cast: Ju Ying, You Yong, Nai An, Zhang Xiansheng, Wu Wenlun, Li Jie, Gu Yanqin

After her mother dies, Wang Lan lives alone in the large mansion her mother left her. Wang Lan is continually harassed and threatened by what seem to be ghosts in the house. Her skeptical boy friend Lu Mang decides to investigate. He at last travels to visit Wang Lan's father, divorced from her mother some years earlier. There, he finds that the mother had been married once before, to a man named Wang Jing, and that this man had at one time made claims on the mother's property. He realizes that the mysterious ex-husband is the likely "ghost," and that Wang Lan's life may really be in danger. He hurries back to her. In the end, Wang Lan is saved by her father and the father's lady friend.

102. *Bahe Town (Ba He Zhen)*

1985. Emei Film Studio. Color. Letterboxed. 10 Reels. Direction: Li Yalin. Screenplay: Chen Ke, Cai Jiangang. Cinematography: Li Baoqi. Art Direction: Li Fan. Music: Su Hanxing, Liu Zhupei. Sound: Zhang Jianping. Cast: Ma Xiaomao as Dong Kang, Zhang Qingchun as Tonghua, Ma Ning as Ding Lanxiang, Li Xiangang as Xue Laoer, Xie Jiarong as Xia Shihua, Qin Fang as Liu Xiaoqing, Xu Zhongru as Li Wenchun, Liu Hanpu as Pockmarked Wu.

After graduating from agricultural machinery college, Dong Kang returns to his hometown to improve its backwardness and poverty. He contracts to operate the commune's farm machine plant which is slated for shutdown, but soon finds himself embroiled in a battle with rampant local corruption. Two of his opponents who especially want to get rid of him are the commune director Xia Shihua and commune store director Li Wenchun. But with the support of County Director Jin and Dong's former classmate Liu Xiaoqing, he turns the tables and exposes Xia and Li's economic crimes. Although they are brought to justice, the struggle continues to achieve economic justice and root out the old traditional ways of doing things.

103. *Baige (Bai Ge)*

1982. Beijing Film Studio. Color. 5 Reels. Direction: Li Wenhua, Dudu. Screenplay: Hua Yulin. Cinematography: Xu Xiaoxian. Music: Chen Xiaoxia. Music: Huang Xiaofei. Sound: Zhang Baojian. Cast: Hong Xueming as Wu Baige, Zhang Tianxi as Xu Li, Zhang Ping as Secretary Wu

Wu Baige is the daughter of a certain city's Party Committee secretary, and an outstanding worker at a power station. She falls in love with a young man named Xu Li who works as a barber and hair stylist. But one day she gets word that her lover has been arrested for taking pictures of young girls in a park, which leads to a misunderstanding between the two young people. It turns out that Xu Li has been building up a reference collection of attractive hair styles, and that while he had been taking his pictures, some police officers had come to take him to cut the hair of prisoners in the local jail. Xu Li and Wu Baige now have a better understanding of each other.

104. *The Baise Uprising (Bai Se Qi Yi)*

1989. Guangxi Film Studio. Color. 11 Reels. Wide Screen. Direction: Chen Jialin. Screenplay: Zhu Xuming, Hou Yuzhong. Cinematography: Liu Jiankui, Cai Xiaopeng. Art Direction: Lu Qi. Music: Jin Fuuzai. Sound: Han Weijun. Cast: Lu Qi as Deng Bin, Tang Tangmin as Li Mingrui, Guo Shaoxiong as Yu Zuobo, Cheng Wenkuan as Zhang Yunyi, Xu Daolin as Chiang Kaishek

During the Chinese civil war of the late 1920s, Deng Xiaoping, using the alias Deng Bin, works with Guangxi Provincial Party Chairman Yu Zuobo to unite anti-Chiang Kaishek forces in south China, a united front of armed fighters and the peasant movement. After forming the united force, they attack Chiang's forces in Guangxi. The attempt fails and Yu escapes to Hong Kong. With the situation changed so suddenly, Deng Bin makes a snap decision to move the remaining Communist troops as quickly as possible to Baise, a strategically important town in western Guangxi. Deng Bin operates a revolutionary base from there, sending Red troops and cadres into every county to develop the peasant movement and launch guerrilla strikes against Chiang's civilian and military supporters in the area. Revolutionary fervor sweeps the region and at last leads to the Baise Uprising on December 11, 1929 by troops designated as the 7th Red Army.

105. *Bald-cop and Girl Student (Tu Tan Yu Qiao Niu)*

1994. Changchun Film Studio. Color. Letterboxed. 9 Reels. Direction: Lei Xianhe, Li Jun. Screenplay: Sheng Manmei, Jia Lixian, based on

the novel by Huang Huizhong. Cinematography: Zhang Haiming, Su Zaili. Art Direction: Wang Di. Music: Gao Erdi. Sound: Cao Feng, Zhang Xiaonan. Costume: Liang Xuejie. Makeup: Zhao Li, Dan Xiangsuo. Cast: Lu Liang as Cheng Chang, Li Ting as Liu Bingbing, Li Yongtian as Zhou Tianpeng, Liu Changwei as Haozhi, Wang Weiyan as Mimi, Wu Kejian as A Long, Chen Jiming as Xuedao, Zhao Hengxuan as Yu Lei, Di Jianqing as Director Wei

Hong Kong police detective Cheng Cang, known among police and the underworld for his bald head, travels to the mainland on vacation. He is also supposed to be introduced to a girl while there, but the girl he is supposed to meet doesn't show up. So he goes to visit the China Police University, and there meets Liu Bingbing, a pretty student in the school's detection department. While in China, Cheng is called upon to investigate some suspicious circumstances connected with a bankruptcy case, and Liu assists. They find that there is indeed a crime involved, and the man behind it is Zhou Tianpeng, the organized crime boss in Hong Kong. With the help of mainland police, they catch the criminals, and although Cheng Cang is badly wounded, he wins the love of Liu Bingbing.

106. *Bald Head (Tu Tu Fa Xing)*

1991. Emei Film Studio and Heilongjiang Film Studio Co-Production. Color. Letterboxed. 9 Reels. Direction: Zhou Wei. Screenplay: Wang Lixiong, Liu Ling and Hou Ruoxuan. Cinematography: Liu Jiankui. Art Direction: Li Deyu and Wang Di. Music: Meng Qinyun, Jin Wei and Jiang Han. Sound: Li Zhenduo, Gu Xiaolian. Costume: Ji Xiuping. Makeup: Zhao Li. Cast: Zhang Ren as Bai Lu, Shi Lei as Lanhua, Wu Li as Ge Dai, Du Yuan as Lanhua's father, Liu Boyin as Bailu's father, Xu Jinghua as Bai Lu's mother.

High school student Bao Lu is a slave of fashion, blindly following whatever is the current trend. He wears his hair long, takes a casual approach to everything, and organizes several of his friends into a rock band. When his father returns home from the U.S., he is very angry with his son's behavior and sends him to the countryside where he was born. There, the simple village people such as the girl Lanhua and her parents help him to see what is real in this world. He leaves the village a considerably changed young man.

107. *Ballad of the Yellow River (Huang He Yao)*

1989. Xi'an Film Studio With the assistance of Hong Kong Tian He Film Corporation & China Film Corporation Co-Production. Color. 11 Reels. Wide screen. Direction: Teng Wenji. Screenplay: Lu Wei, Zhu Xiaoping. Cinematography: Zhi Lei. Art Direction: Yang Gang, Chen Xin. Music: Chang Yuhong. Sound: Xiong Huajuan. Cast: Yu Lin as Dang Gui, Duan You as Hong Hua, Chi Peng as Liu Lan, Ge You as Hei Gutou

In the loess plateau of Northwest China, penniless drifter Dang Gui sympathizes with the plight of child-widow Wu Wei and tries to elope with her. But their attempt fails and they are cruelly separated. Dang Gui later becomes a porter in a caravan. One day the caravan arrives at a remote village upriver, where he meets another girl named Hong Hua. They fall in love, but Hong Hua's uncle sells her to someone with money. Dang Gui spends his youth in a long and arduous journey. At last, in middle age, he rescues a woman, Liu Lan, and her daughter who are fleeing the woman's abusive husband Hei Gutou. Dang Gui and Liu Lan move in together, but not long after that, Liu Lan again falls back into the hands of Hei Gutou.

Best Director (Teng Wenji), 14th Montreal World Film Festival.

108. *Bamboo (Zhu)*

1980. Emei Film Studio. Color. 9 Reels. Direction: Wang Shuihan, Situ Zhaodun. Screenplay: Wang Shuihan, Situ Zhaodun. Cinematography: Liang Jiaxiang, Yu Defu. Art Direction: Wang Shuwei. Music: Yan Fei. Sound: Sui Xizhong, Zhang Ruikun. Cast: Cui Xinqing as Zhuzhi, Li Lan as Zhuhua, Zhao Chunmin as A Fu, Li Yulong as Xiao Guan, Liu Zhongyuan as Uncle

Taking her mother Zhuzhi's advice, Zhuhua returns from school to her hometown of Zhushan to work. There she meets a young male teacher named Xiao Guan, an encounter which reminds her of her parents' story. When Zhuzhi was young, she and a Communist undercover liaison named A Fu fell in love and were married. A Fu was arrested soon after, and Zhuzhi took over his work. She too was soon arrested. Their captors unsuccessfully tried every means to get information from the couple. A Fu and Zhuzhi dug a tunnel to escape, but A Fu was killed just before it was completed. Zhuzhi continued digging alone and escaped. The story moves to the present and Zhuzhi is falsely accused of treason, which reflects negatively on her daughter Zhuhua. The girl studies and works hard, meanwhile developing a true love relationship with Xiao Guan, but she still cannot avoid the brand of a "traitor's daughter." Later, Zhuhua is taken to the home of an elderly veteran for protection. A few years later, the Gang of Four is defeated and Zhuhua is happily reunited with her mother and Xiao Guan.

109. *The Bandit and the Black Swan (Qiang Dao Yu He Tian Er)*

1988. Guangxi Film Studio. Color. Wide Screen. 11 Reels. Direction: Wu Yingxun. Screenplay: Li Hun. Cinematography: Zhu Dingyuan. Art Direction: Chen Yaogong. Music: Nusi Leti. Sound: Han Weijun. Cast: Tuyigong as Rexiti, Luxiou as Gina, Yusupu as Hasimu, Zhang Shan as Company Commander Zhang

A commercial delegation is to be sent abroad on business. Some members of the delegation, led by Feng Zhiqiao, illegally gain possession of a national treasure. The see the trip as an opportunity to smuggle the treasure out of China and sell it abroad. The team's guide is a young man named Rexiti. A rumor spreads that the treasure may be with the delegation, and this attracts the attention of people of every sort: Italian Gina tells her Russian Army officer lover Vassily, who wants it badly; a landowner sends his agent Haenmu to follow the commercial team, and PLA company commander Zhang has orders to stop the delegation and protect the national treasure. In the midst of all the intrigue, the guide Rexiti recognizes the true natures of Feng Zhiqiao, Vassily, and others, and at the critical moment, he bravely assists Zhang in stopping the delegation and recovering the treasure.

110. *Bandits in the Capital (Jing Cheng Jie Dao)*

1992. Tianshan Film Studio & China Film Release Import And Export Company Co-Production. Color. Letterboxed. 10 Reels. Direction: Li Wenhua. Screenplay: Chen Wenmin, Ke Zhanghe. Cinematography: Zhao Peng, Liu Weiwei. Art Direction: Zhen Huiwen, Liu Qin. Music: Guo Wenjing. Sound: Liu Xiaodong, Wun Gang. Costume: Cai Peixin, Lin Rong. Makeup: Mai Xin. Cast: Huang Guoqiang as Dai Ping, Liu Ningning as Yuan Jingwen, Zong Ping as Jiang Zhongjian, Xia Zongxue as Dai Muchun, Wang Hongtao as Dong Weida

In old Beijing, recent police academy graduate Dai Ping is unexpectedly set upon and beaten by thugs. He later finds this apparently random attack is connected to a rare and valuable set of jewelry owned by his family, a possession previously unknown to him. Fellow police officer Jiang Zhongjian involves himself in the case to help, and in the process wins the affection of Dai Ping's fiancee Yuan Jingwen. But Jiang turns out to be a would-be robber of the jewelry, a fact Dai Ping is eventually able to detect. Dai Ping recovers the jewelry, and in the fight Jiang is killed by Yuan Jingwen. She returns to Dai Ping, who truly loves her.

111. *The Banks of the Jinsha River (Jin Sha Jiang Pan)*

1963. Tianma Film Studio. B & W. 10 Reels. Direction: Fu Chaowu. Screenplay: Chen Jing, Li Bai, Fu Chaowu and Mu Hong. Cinematography: Cha Xiangkang. Art Direction: Ge Shicheng. Music: Ji Ming. Sound: Huang Dongping. Cast: Feng Ji as Jin Ming, Mu Hong as Tan Wensu, Zhang Fa as the Sangge village headman, Qi Heng as Jin Wande, Cao Lei as Zhuma, Cui Chaoming as Chou Wanli

In 1936, the Red Army on the Long March passes through the Jinsha River area on the Tibetan border. Their way is blocked by units of the Nationalist Army associated with powerful local landlord Chou Wanli. Some of Chou's thugs masquerade as Red Army soldiers to abduct Zhuma, the only daughter of the Sangge village headman, invoking the headman's hatred of the Red Army. The Red Army sticks to the Party's minority policy, and rescues Zhuma from Chou Wanli. They then drive the enemy back and cross the Jinsha River, reaching the Tibetan border. But Chou sneaks into the Sangge area ahead of the Red Army and reports Zhuma has been killed by the Red Army, further embittering the headman. Meanwhile, Zhuma has gradually gained understanding and trust of the Red Army, and sends her father a jewel he had once given her to show she is still alive. At a critical point, Zhuma guides the Red Army safely to the village and exposes Chou Wanli's plot to her father. Chou Wanli attempts to flee the area, but drowns attempting to cross the Jinsha River. The Red Army continues on its way north.

112. *Bao and Son (Bao Shi Fu Zi)*

1983. Beijing Film Studio. Color. 9 Reels. Direction: Xie Tieli. Screenplay: Xie Tieli. Cinematography: Huang Xinyi. Art Direction: Tu Juhua. Music: Wang Ming. Sound: Lu Xiancang. Cast: Guan Zongxiang as Father Bao, Liu Cangwei as Bao Guowei, Bao Xun as Guo Chun

In a small port city in South China, Mr. Bao works as a housekeeper in the Qin family mansion. He has a son, Bao Guowei, whose mother died when the boy was five. When his wife died, Old Mr. Bao moved to the city with his son, and saved for many years to send Guowei to school. Unfortunately, Guowei is a poor student, interested only in the lifestyle of his well-to-do fellow students and his own dreams of wealth. He is so ashamed of his hardworking father that he goes out of his way to prevent others from associating the two. When Old Bao's savings run out, he borrows money to pay his son's school expenses, and now at New Year's he worries how to repay the debt. Then he learns that his son has been fighting with others and has injured someone. Old Bao comes to the heartbreaking realization that his dreams for the boy will never come true.

113. *Battle at Baozi Bay (Bao Zi Wan Zhan Dou)*

1978. Changchun Film Studio. Color. 13 Reels. Direction: Wang Jiayi, Jiang Shusheng. Screenplay: Collective, recorded by Ma Jixing, based on the stage play of the same title. Cinematography: Wang Qimin, Li Huailu. Art Direction: Huang Chaohui, Sun Sixiang. Music: Liu Zhi. Sound: Yu Kaizhang, Dong Baosheng. Cast: Li Chengbing as Ding Yong, Liu Guifeng as Yang Hong, Yang Xiuzhang as the Regimental Commander, Wei Jian as the mess officer, Wang Yan as Wang Datie, Ren Shiyi as Gao Dali

An Eighth Route Army division is relocated from the front line battle zone to protect a liberated base area in northern Shanxi province. One of the division's companies which had served valiantly in battle, is assigned to work with a women's platoon, something both Company Commander Ding Yong and his troops have trouble dealing with. At first, the men's lack of understanding of the significance of production to the Communist movement results in their doing a poor job; later, they realize its importance to that phase of the revolution, so they volunteer for assignment to textile work, and realize a series of

Battle at Baozi Bay. **When his company is assigned to work with a women's platoon, Commander Ding Yong (Li Chengbing, second left) and his men at first have trouble dealing with it. 1978. Changchun Film Studio.**

production successes. Four years later, with the enemy's plan to block the Communist liberation bases completely defeated, the PLA's border defense troops have plenty of food and clothing. When China enters the Korean War, the company is once again called to battle.

114. *Battle at No–Name River (Jizhan Wuming Chuan)*

1975. August First Film Studio. Color. 10 Reels. Direction: Hua Chun, Wang Shaoyan. Screenplay: Zhen Zhi and Huang Zongjiang, based on the novel of the same title. Cinematography: Kou Jiwen, Yin Xiufang. Art Direction: Zhen Ta. Music: Li Weicai, Zhu Renyu. Sound: He Baoding. Casting: Guan Changzhu as Guo Tie, Huo Deji as Wang Shigui, Yu Chunmian as Division Commander, Zhang Lianfu as the Political Commissar, Zhang Jinsheng as Liu Xi, Peng Guozhong as Wu Xingliang

In Korea in the winter of 1951, Chinese Volunteer Army Engineer Company No. 9 takes on the assignment of repairing the bridge over No-Name River, key to the Chinese position. Company Commander Guo Tie leads his soldiers in overcoming the vast difficulties, and

with the help of North Korean support units, they at last complete the repairs ahead of schedule, guaranteeing Chinese supplies can get through to the troops at the front.

115. *The Battle at the Lake (Hushang De Douzheng)*

1955. Shanghai Film Studio. B & W. 10 Reels. Direction: Gao Heng. Screenplay: Yang Cunbing and Wang Yuanmei. Cinematography: Li Shengwei. Art Direction: Zhang Hanchen. Music: Xiang Yi and Gao Tian. Sound: Zhu Weigang. Cast: Xiang Lei as "Young Iron" (Shi Chunlai), Shi Lianxing as Wu Fengtai, Qi Heng as Ma Fucang, Bu Jiali as Sister Shen, Li Yong as Li Sanyang, Kang Tai as Zhao Guanghong.

In 1946, the Nationalist-Communist cease-fire breaks down, and Chiang Kaishek launches an all-out attack on Communist-held areas. In Zhaojiatan, a liberated village in Northern Jiangsu province, the farmers arm themselves for defense under the leadership of the district Party committee. A deposed landlord named Zhao returns to the village with the Nationalist army, hoping to regain his power. District Party Secretary Wu Fengtai and Civil Guard Commander Shi Chunlai organize the locals into an army and carry on the resistance around the area of Zhaojiatan. By relying on the masses of the people, Shi Chunlai drives the enemy out of the village. In 1948, the PLA begins its final big counterattack to destroy the Nationalist forces, and the Zhaojiatan civil guard is part of it. In the Nationalist retreat, the landlord Zhao is captured, but Wu Fengtai is killed during the last battle.

116. *Battle Between Humans and Evil (Ren Gui Zhi Zhan)*

1994. Changchun Film Studio. Color. Letterboxed. 9 Reels. Direction: Hao Bing, Luo Liang. Screenplay: Li Honglin. Cinematography: Yan Songyan. Art Direction: Zhang Yan. Music: Wang Meng. Sound: Zhang Hongguang. Costume: Ma Jun. Makeup: Wang Xiaoling. Cast: Shen Junyi as Fan Dabao, Wang Ningsheng as Huang Zhiqiang, Xin Xin as Ji Li, Li Yongtian as Fan Ercai, Gao Aijun as Fan Sanxi, Liu Jinbin as Director Fei

Based on a true case. In Northeast China, a legal technicality allows violent and ruthless criminal Fan Laoda to be released from prison after serving only three years of his long sentence. This infuriates Huang Zhiqiang, deputy chief of police in the town of Funeng where Fan committed his crimes, which included multiple rapes, assaults, extortion, blackmail and embezzlement, as well as unproven suspicions of murder. At the same time, local prosecutors Jin Ling and Xing Liang determine to keep a close watch on Fan, but soon realize the criminal must have allies in the local police department as important documents are missing from his file. The prosecutors at last locate a vital witness in Ma Lian, although she at first declines to cooperate because she believes the law cannot touch the criminal or protect her from him. The chief prosecutor decides to throw out the original case and start all over again. It is a long, difficult struggle between humanity and evil, but at last the gang led by Fan and his brothers is smashed, and the Fan brothers are punished to the full extent of the law.

117. *The Battle for Nan Island (Nan Dao Feng Yun)*

1955. Shanghai Film Studio. B & W. 10 Reels. Direction: Bai Cheng. Screenplay: Li Yingmin, Cinematography: Zhu Jing. Art Direction: Wang Yuebai and Hu Dengren. Music: Zhang Linyi. Sound: Li Liehong. Cast: Shangguan Yunzhu as Fu Luohua, Sun Daolin as Han Chengguang, Mu Hong as Chief of Affairs, Hu Xiaohan as Xiao Chun, Zhong Xinghuo as Zhang Qiang, Sun Yongping as Xiao Yang, Li Wei as Lin Dong.

In 1943, the anti-Japanese resistance forces on Hainan Island move out to conduct a "mopping up" operation. When the main force leaves the mountainous area, they leave behind 18 recovering wounded, with just Fu Luohua, a female nurse, to care for them. They are isolated in the mountains, lacking food and medicine. The chief of affairs leaves the mountain in search of food but is killed. One of the wounded, Lin Dong, turns traitor and attempts to betray their location to the Japanese, but Fu Luohua kills him before he succeeds. Political Instructor Han Chengguang dies from his wounds, and Fu Luohua becomes the branch Party Secretary. She and the others uncover and capture a Japanese spy in their midst, after which Fu Luohua is able to obtain some food and medicine from helpful villagers. Eventually the main force returns to the mountains, and Fu and the others rejoin the army.

The Battle of Huai-Hai **see** *The Decisive Engagement, Part 2*

118. *The Battle of Jinan (Ji Nan Zhan Yi)*

1979. Changchun Film Studio. Wide Screen. Color. 12 Reels. Direction: Zhu Wenshun. Screenplay: Li Hongyu. Cinematography: Zhang Songping, Zhong Wenmin. Art Direction: Tong Jingwen, Wu Qiwen. Music: Zhang Jingyuan. Sound: Liu Jingui, Liu Yushan. Cast: Guo Zhengqin as Ding Yaodong, Chen Mu as Wang Yaowu, Liu Runcheng as Cui Tiezhu, Xiao Zhenghua as Meng Dalong, Shi Kefu as He Bing, Shao Chongfei as Liu Chi

In September 1948, the PLA launches a massive attack on the city of Jinan, Chiang Kaishek's main defense base in Northeast China. By exploiting the errors of judgment of Nationalist 2nd Army Commander Wang Yaowu, the Taishan troops led by Commander Ding Yaodong are able to mislead the commander of the Nationalists' 19th Army, in control of the airport, to defect to the Communist side. In the end, General Wang Yaowu is captured and the Battle of Jinan ends with a Communist victory.

The Battle for Nan Island. When resistance fighters are forced to evacuate Hainan, nurse Fu Luohua (Shangguan Yunzhu, left) is left behind to care alone for 18 wounded, including Han Chengguang (Sun Daolin). 1955. Shanghai Film Studio.

The Battle of Liao-Shen **see** *The Decisive Engagement, Part 1*

119. *The Battle of Luohun Bridge (Xue Zhan Luo Hun Qiao)*

1991. Shanghai Film Studio. Color. Letterboxed. 9 Reels. Direction: Hu Lide. Screenplay: Wu Tianci, Gong Nan, Xu Weiguang. Cinematography: Liu Lihua. Art Direction: Mei Kunping. Music: Xu Jingxin. Sound (Dolby): Dong Yan. Cast: He Ling as Cao Weilong, Hong Zugeng as Huzhi, Wei Zongwan as Zen Titou, Xu Shouqin as Zhang Pingshan, Shi Ge as Chunlan, Fang Zhoubo as Chen Zhimin, Zhou Guobing as Du Lazhi

In the early days of the People's Republic, Nationalist Army stragglers link up with some local gangsters to carry out sabotage and organize anti-Communist rebellion by exploiting the fact the new regime has not yet consolidated its hold on China. They are at last defeated at Luohun Bridge.

120. *The Battle of Mount Changpai (Chang Pai Shan Zhi Zhan)*

1981. August First Film Studio. Color. 6 Reels. Direction: Tian Yonggui. Screenplay: Xia Yan, Huang Jianmin. Cinematography: Jiang Xiande. Art Direction: Chen Mugu. Music: Yi Yi. Sound: Shen Guorui. Cast: Ji Hongjun as Song Botao, Jin Shisheng as the political instructor

During the Sino-Vietnamese border war, a Chinese company is ordered to take Mount Changpai. They first try a direct assault, but suffer serious losses from the Vietnamese dug in on the mountain. The company commander is among those killed. After assuming command, the company political instructor decides to try a new approach, with one platoon waging a direct assault while the second climbs up the back of the mountain during the night. This works, and after two days of fierce fighting, the Chinese take Mount Changpai.

The Battle of Ping-Jun **see** *The Decisive Engagement, Part 3*

121. *The Battle of Sangkumryung Ridge (Shang Gan Ling)*

1956. Changchun Film Studio. B & W. 14 Reels. Direction: Sha Meng, Lin Shan. Screenplay: Lin Shan, Cao Xin, Sha Meng, Xiao Mao. Cinematography: Zhou Daming. Art Direction: Liu Xueyao. Music: Liu Zhi. Sound: Chen Wenyuan. Cast: Gao Baocheng as Zhang Zhongfa, Xu Linge as Meng Degui, Zhang Liang as Yang Decai, Li Shukai as the Division Commander, Liu Lei as Chen Dehou, Liu Yuru as Wang Lan.

After the Panmunjom Peace Talks break down in the fall of 1952, U.S. forces launch a large scale attack on Chinese forces near the 38th Parallel. Their objective is to take from the Chinese the strategically important Sangkumryung Ridge (called "Heartbreak Ridge" by the Americans) and thereby gain militarily what could not be achieved at the negotiating table. The Chinese Volunteer Army's Eighth Division is assigned to defend the ridge. The fierce and bloody fighting is viewed through the eyes of one company commanded by Zhang Zhongfa. The Chinese turn back repeated U.S. assaults. At last the defenders are ordered to pull back into a mountain tunnel and hold off the attackers from there. Later, their communications and supply links with headquarters are cut off, and the Chinese begin running low on food and ammunition. Although their position is perilous, the Chinese hold the tunnel for 24 days, largely by sheer force of will. At last the Americans stop the assaults on the ridge, and the Panmunjom talks resume. In Chinese views of the Korean War, the Battle of Sangkumryung Ridge is regarded as a major victory, for it convinced American commanders the war could not be won, and a negotiated peace was the only option.

122. *The Battle of Shanghai (Zhan Shang Hai)*

1959. August First Film Studio. Color. 11 Reels. Direction: Wang Bing. Screenplay: Qun Li. Cinematography: Chen Jun. Art Direction: Xu Run. Music: Li Weicai. Sound: Hou Shenkang. Cast: Ding Ni as the Army Commander, Gao Yan as Political Commissar Zhang, Li Shutian as Division Commander Xiao, Li Changhua as the Company 3 Commander, Zhang Chongyun as Regimental Commander Yao, Wang Runsheng as Zhao Yongsheng, Zhang Liang as Xiao Ma, Hu Xiaoguang as Lin Fan

In the spring of 1949, the PLA approaches Shanghai. The commanders of Chiang Kaishek's 300,000-man army defending the city are certain that they can hold it, given their favorable location and U.S. equipment. While his forces have little trouble overwhelming the Nationalist troops outside of the city, Commander Fang of the PLA's 3rd Field Army hopes to avoid the destruction of China's largest city and its civilian population of 6 million. So he decides to wage political warfare, exploiting the dissension among Chiang's troops inside the city. Nationalist General Tang orders subordinate commander Liu Yi to hold the downtown area of Shanghai at all costs. The Nationalist command also assigns agents to commit acts of sabotage should Shanghai fall to the PLA, but the Communist underground intercepts and kills them all. At last the PLA surrounds the city, while continuing their unrelenting propaganda barrage. His military position untenable and his troops demoralized, Liu Yi leads his army in rebelling and defecting to the side of Communists, saving the city.

123. *Battlefield Stars (Zhan Di Zhi Xing)*

1983. August First Film Studio. Color. 10 Reels. Direction: Wei Long. Screenplay: Zhang Chongyou. Cinematography: Chen Zhenzhong. Art Direction: Liu Yushu. Music: Fu Gengcheng. Sound: Guo Yisheng. Cast: Gai Xiaoling as Bai Lu, Ji Ping as Niu Qiang, Feng Enhe as Yang Fusheng, Zhang Shan as Platoon Leader, Sun Jitang as the Political Supervisor

In the spring of 1952, woman college graduate Bai Lu goes to the Korean front as an English language radio announcer. Her station's programs, aimed at American soldiers, tell the Chinese side of the conflict. The broadcasts also foster homesickness in some U.S. soldiers, and so outrages their commander he orders the station bombed. Bai Lu and her colleagues risk their lives to continue their broadcasts.

124. *Battling the Drought Song (Kang Han Qu)*

1960. Xi'an Film Studio. B & W. 7 Reels. Direction: Wu Cun, Liu Bing and Zhang Ruoping. Screenplay, cinematography and art direction by the crew of "Battling the Drought Song" crew collectively. Music: Wei Ruixiang. Sound: Hong Jiahui. Cast: Wang Yutang as Yao Baocheng, Wu Binghui as Zhao Xiulan, Cheng Yi as Uncle Zhao, Hou Zhengmin as Zhao Dalong, Ma Huiying as Uncle Bai, Yi Donglin as Party Secretary Yang

The Battle of Sangkumryung Ridge. **In Korea, Chinese troops prepare to defend Heartbreak Ridge from American attack. 1956. Changchun Film Studio.**

Early in 1960, the Guanzhong plain is hit with a severe drought. Commune member Yao Baocheng brings young people Xiulan and Dalong to repair the water pumps. They work day and night, forgetting to eat and sleep. At the time, it happened that Yao's wife was having a baby, but Yao is so dedicated to fighting the drought he does not enter his home although he passes it often. Finally, he resolves the technical problems and, drawing water to the plateau from the Wei River, saves the dying wheat seedlings.

125. *Battling the Flood (Zhan Hong Tu)*

1973. Changchun Film Studio. Color. 10 Reels. Direction: Su Li, Yuan Naicheng. Screenplay: Hebei Province Stage Drama Troupe Collectively, recorded by Lu Shu. Cinematography: Li Guanghui. Art Direction: Wang Xingwen. Music: Lei Zhengbang. Casting: Lu Shu as Ding Zhenghong, Chun Li as Dayong, Cai Songling as Grandma Laogeng, Sun Guolu as Xiuhua, Liu Shilong as Ding Shenghe, Jiang Jianming as Tiecheng

Although floods are rare in the Haihe area of North China, there is a major one in 1963, seriously endangering the lives and property of the people of Jingjia Village. The production unit's Party branch secretary Ding Zhenghong twice leads commune members in turning back the flood tide and repairing the dam. Just as they have finished repairs, higher authorities decide to blow up the dam in order to spread out the flood waters and protect the city of Tianjin and the critical Jinpu Railway. Ding Zhenghong resolutely carries out the order based on his belief in doing what is best overall, and helps the other villagers come to terms with their anger at the decision. After the flood recedes, the people return to their work and realize a bumper harvest the following year.

126. *Be Proud, Mother! (Zihao Ba, Muqin!)*

1980. Changchun Film Studio. Color. 11 Reels. Direction: Li Guanghui, Bai Dezhang. Screenplay: Zhang Tianmin. Cinematography: Li Guanghui, Li Fengming. Art Direction: Ye Jiren. Music: Gao Feng. Sound: Yuan Minda. Cast: Wang Baosheng as Hou Fang, Gong Xibing as Wei Jiangbo, Gong Jianhua as Liang Qinqin,

Zhang Baishuang as Liang Shanshan, Zuang Peiyuan as Xiao Wang, Ren Yi as Hou Mangzhong

In early 1979, when the China-Vietnam border war begins, the wife of government bureau chief Hou Mangzhong learns that their soldier son Hou Fang is at the frontlines. Worried about his safety, she persuades her husband to call his former army commander Zhao, now the border military commander, and request an early discharge for his son, whose term of service is about to expire. Zhao's response is to harshly criticize the official for attempting to use his influence in this way. Meanwhile, Hou Fang himself applies for an extension of his service, as he does not want to leave while a war is going on. Later, Hou Fang's squad is assigned to clear out land mines, and his squad leader Liang Qinqin is killed on one of their clearing missions. Hou Fang and one of his close comrades Wei Jiangbo are wounded and hospitalized, Wei suffering permanent loss of one eye. When Hou Fang is released from the hospital, he volunteers to return to combat. He conducts himself bravely in battle, and once more is wounded and returned to the army hospital. When the border war ends, Liang Qinqin's former colleagues gather once more at his tomb in a ceremony to display their respect and affection for their old leader.

127. *Beach (Hai Tan)*

1984. Xi'an Film Studio. Color. Letterboxed. 10 Reels. Direction: Teng Wenji. Screenplay: Qin Peichun, Ma Zhongjun. Cinematography: Gu Changwei, Zhi Lei. Art Direction: Yang Gang. Music: Tan Dun. Sound: Li Lanhua, Hui Dongzhi. Costume: Ma Liping, Makeup: Li Xiaofang. Cast: Gao Jian as Mugeng, Liu Wei as Xu Yan, Zhu Yin as Fu Youru, Li Xiajin as Juhua, Zhao Xiaorui as Jin Geng, Wei Zongwan as Old Manli

The area around a beach is a study in contrasts one summer: on the one hand, we see people still practicing old, traditional marriage customs; on the other, a new type of satellite town is being built nearby. Through the stories of a young girl and a master worker and his girl friend, the film shows the confrontation between civilization and foolishness. The beach bears silent witness to the progress of history.

128. *Bear Tracks (Xiong Ji)*

1977. Changchun Film Studio. Color. 13 Reels. Direction: Zhao Xinshui. Screenplay: Gong Zuo. Cinematography: Chen Chang'an, Gao Hongbao. Art Direction: Shi Weijun. Music: Li Yuqiu. Sound: Tong Zongde. Cast: Shi Weijian as Li Xin, Li Muran as Zhang Jian, Deng Shutian as Master Worker Wei, Gu Lan as Xia Minfei, Pu Ke as Yan Zhizheng, Da Qi as Old Wei, Tang Ke as Yao Bingzhang

In 1971, two agents employed by the Soviets attempt to cross the Chinese border. One is killed, but the other, Zhou Yingjie, makes it to the city of Jiangcheng, where he contacts another agent code-named "Sable." Li Xin, an investigator for the local Public Security Bureau (PSB), learns that "Sable" is the head of a spy ring in the area, and that the agents have learned the content of a high-level defense conference. Through further investigation he determines that "Sable" is Yao Bingzhang, the head of an office which had in the past supplied special materials to the PSB. Acting on this information, Li Xin and his men set up a sting operation to catch Yao Bingzhang. In addition to "Sable," their trap nabs Zhou Yingjie and two Soviet spies in China under diplomatic cover. However, the Soviets refuse to give up, and make plans for another spy operation in China.

129. *Beautiful Night (Ye Se Duo Mei Hao)*

1983. Changchun Film Studio. Color. 10 Reels. Direction: Lin Ke. Screenplay: Gao Shiguo, Si Yigong. Cinematography: Sun Hui. Art Direction: Hu Pei. Music: Fan Weiqiang. Sound: Hong Di, Wang Lin. Cast: Tie Niu as Director Niu, Liu Zhao as Factory Director Hu, Hu Lepei as Fei Jin, Fu Yiwei as Hu Ping, Hong Xia as Ou Guizhi, Mo Yuanji as Big Guy Li

A workers' sparetime music troupe gives lovely evening concerts which attract sizable audiences at every performance. Some of the workers such as Liu Hu had been pretty rough individuals before, but participation in cultural events has polished them considerably. When textile plant Director Hu approaches Youth Secretary Gao about a problem employee called Big Guy Li, Gao suggest that Cultural Palace Director Niu take the young man into his music troupe, figuring it should work for him as well. At first, Director Hu disparages using cultural activities for this purpose, but decides to give it a try. A subplot relates how

Director Niu helps Big Guy Li and his wife re-solve a specific problem in their personal lives. Finally, Director Hu comes around and even wants to join in the cultural activities himself. The film ends with an outdoor concert, every-one enjoying the night and the music.

130. *A Beautiful Pair of Butterflies (Cai Feng Shuang Fei)*

1951. Da Tong Film Company. B & W. 10 Reels. Direction: Pan Jienong. Screenplay: Zhu Ruijun, Pan Jienong and Hu Daozha. Cine-matography: Luo Chongzhou. Set Design: Zhang Xibai. Music: Huang Yijun. Sound: Yao Shou-qing. Costume: Jin Heliang. Makeup: Chen Yan. Cast: Wang Danfeng as Jin Xiaofeng, Li Wei as Zhou Caigen, Chen Xu as Jin Sanbao, Wang Luxi as Shen Zigui, Zhou Chu as County Chair-man Wu, Yu Cong as Wang Shou, Wei Houling as Shen Lian, Lu Shan as Mrs. Shen.

Near the end of the Ming Dynasty (c1640) in Zhejiang province, a country girl named Jin Xiaofeng and a young carpenter named Zhou Caigen fall in love. At the Yuanxiao festival of lights, Xiaofeng and her father Jin Sanbao go into town to see the lights, where she attracts the eye of Shen Zigui, the only son of Shen Lian, the Deputy Prosecutor of the county court. When the light festival is over, Zigui follows Xiaofeng home, then waits till that night when she goes to see Caigen. He at-tempts to rape her, but Caigen arrives in time, and in the struggle kills Zigui. The two lovers put his body in a bag and throw it into the river. Not long after, Zigui's body floats to the river surface, and since the bag holding the body has Jin Sanbao's name on it, Jin and his daughter Xiaofeng are arrested. When it is dis-covered that Xiaofeng is pregnant, Shen Lian's buffoonish County Chairman Wu believes it is Zigui's child and orders that Xiaofeng be mar-ried into Shen's family so that the family line may continue. Xiaofeng is forced into the Shen household where she is treated like a prisoner. Sanbao dies from longing for his daughter. Later, Caigen goes to the Shen family home as a carpenter and sees Xiaofeng. Xiaofeng gives birth to a son, after which Shen Lian and his wife plot to kill Xiaofeng and announce that she committed suicide out of devotion to her late husband, thereby preserving the family's feudal reputation. But Cai Gen rescues Xiao Feng and the two flee from the Shen home as a pair of butterflies.

131. *Beautiful Phoenix and Sun (Dan Feng Chao Yang)*

1980. Changchun Film Studio. Color. 11 Reels. Direction: Liu Wenyu. Screenplay: Wang Yiping. Cinematography: Zhong Wenmin. Art Direction: Wu Qiwen, Lu Jun. Music: Qu Rufeng. Sound: Liu Yushan. Cast: Chen Ye as Wenfeng, Shi Zhongling as Zhou Lian, Gu Wei as Lu Yuanfeng, Pu Ke as the doctor, He Yani as Xiaofeng, Huang Bangrui as Zhao Cheng, Wang Renwu as Zhu Bai

Central Art Institute Professor Zhou Lian visits a Suzhou embroidery institution to select one product for commemoration of the Chi-nese Communist Party's 30th anniversary. There, he sees an unfinished embroidery called "Beautiful Phoenix and Sun" which takes his thoughts back more than 20 years. As a young man he had taken a teaching job in Suzhou, and one of his students there was Lu Wenfeng, the younger sister of Lu Yuanfeng, who had inherited their mother's famous style. The two sisters lived a very hard life, so in order that more than one of them would know the unique Lu style, the elder sister decided to let Wenfeng study at the South Jiangsu School of Art, where Zhou Lian happened to teach. The two fell in love. Later, the elder sister died from persecution by local despot Zhao Cheng, forcing Lu Wenfeng to leave school and live in the countryside with her sister's daughter. Zhou found Lu Wenfeng there, however, and later he arranges for Zhou Lian to be arrested and imprisoned. After that, the two lovers lost contact. In her despair, Lu Wenfeng poured herself into her work, but goes blind. Now, so many years later, Zhou Lian learns that Lu Wenfeng lives in a hospital. He rushes to see her, and when the sightless Lu learns it is Zhou Lian who has come to visit her she is so excited she finishes the "Beautiful Phoenix and Sun" embroidery overnight just through touching it. In the end, doctors are able to help Lu regain her vision. The two graying lovers leave together, finally able to start their new life.

132. *Beautiful Prisoner (Mei Li De Qiu Tu)*

1986. Changchun Film Studio. Color. 10 Reels. Direction: Yu Zhongxiao, Lu Jianhua. Screenplay: Guan Shouzhong. Cinematography: Wang Qimin, Li Junyan. Art Direction: Gao Guoliang. Music: Wu Damin, Yang Yilun. Sound: Dong Baosheng. Cast: Tao Huiming as

Ying Hong, Wang Fuyou as Lu Yuliang, Cui Muyan as Jin Zhiwei, Niu Piao as Shi Yong, Pan Shaquan as Bai Yueer, Tian Jihai as Yin Zuolei

In Harbin at the time of the Japanese invasion, and with the official Chinese government position being one of collaboration, Ying Hong is the beautiful daughter of a famous Chinese army general. She has many admirers, including Lu Yiliang, a dashing young naval officer. One day while she is out for a walk, a strange young man saves her from an attempted sexual assault. They become acquainted, and she finds out he is Shi Yong, an underground worker for the CPC. Another time, some Japanese soldiers try to abduct Ying Hong, and a kind woman named Bai Yuer intervenes to save her, but sacrifices her own life in doing so. After this, Ying Hong's has a change in attitude about collaboration, and provides a recommendation for Shi Yong to work near her father. She helps the young man in his intelligence work but in time Chinese Captain Zhao Yuxi discovers her intelligence activities. He demands she become his mistress in return for his silence. When she refuses, he tries to rape her and in the struggle she kills him. Ying Hong is arrested and naval officer Lu Yiliang is assigned to investigate the case. When Lu learns the truth, he shields Ying Hong's escape, but he is killed in the process.

133. *A Beautiful Woman's Head in the House of Murder (Xiong Zai Mei Ren Tou)*

1989. Xi'an Film Studio. Color. Letterboxed. 9 Reels. Direction: Hu Qingshi, Liu Yichuan. Screenplay: Shang Junxue, Xin Sheng. Cinematography: Zhao Fei. Art Direction: Xing Guozhen. Music: Xu Youfu. Sound: Li Ping, Hong Jiahui. Cast: Xu Ping as Shang Hua, Wang Yanmei as Luo Funa, Li Xiaobo as Wang Shanshou, Lei Ming as Ke Keer

A horror film revolving around a medical school graduate who goes to work for a scientific researcher involved in head transplants.

134. *Beautiful Youth (Hua Zhi Qiao)*

1980. August First Film Studio. Color. 10 Reels. Direction: Jing Mukui. Screenplay: Lu Zhuguo. Cinematography: Yang Guangyuan. Art Direction: Li Jian. Music: Wang Xiren. Sound: Yan Birong. Cast: Bao Xun as Huang Yongliang, Mu Huaihu as Luo Dajiang, Zhao Na as Yuehua, Wang Chong as Father

New PLA recruit Huang Yongliang takes a very casual approach to training and to military discipline. His father had been a military commander, and had always been very strict with his son. With help from his father and his company commander Luo Dajiang, Huang Yongliang decides to correct his mistakes, and makes rapid progress. When the border war with Vietnam starts, Huang Yongliang and his fellow soldiers are sent to the frontlines. Huang has a series of encounters with the enemy which he handles with intelligence and courage. Just on the point of victory, he is shot and killed by a sniper.

135. *Before the New Director Arrives (Xin Ju Zhang Dao Lai Zhi Qian)*

1956. Changchun Film Studio. B & W. 5 Reels. Direction: Lu Ban. Screenplay: Yu Yanfu, based on the stage play by He Qiu. Cinematography: Wang Chunquan. Art Direction: Wang Tao, Music: Li Jida. Sound: Sui Xizhong. Cast: Li Jingbo as division head Niu, Pu Ke as Director Zhang, Chen Guangting as Cui Shuwu, Su Jianfeng as Su Lin, Han Yan as Mr. Li, Zhang Hui as Mr. Zhong

Division Head Niu is a stereotypical bureaucrat, always ready to flatter his superiors and make sure they know of his achievements, but actually avoiding as much responsibility as he can. When word comes that a new director will be arriving soon, he regards it as imperative to make a great impression on the new boss. Assembling all his division's personnel, he mobilizes them for the "central work" of welcoming the new director. They put up many posters with slogans such as "Welcome Director Zhang! You have worked hard and your achievements are great!" He also dips into public funds to set up a plush office for the new boss. When heavy rains damage the building and the staff dormitory starts leaking water, he disregards it so that the "central work" can go forward. Unknown to Niu, the new director has made an unannounced early arrival and observed it all. Niu's actions and his misuse of public funds have exposed him as an incompetent, and in the end the staff votes him out of his position.

136. *Before the Storm (Lei Yu Zhi Qian)*

1975. August First Film Studio. Color. 6 Reels. Direction: Li Wenhu. Screenplay: Gao Hong, Sang Ping. Cinematography: Zhu Lutong. Art Direction: Liu Qian, Jiang Zhenkui. Music: Gong Zhiwei. Sound: Wu Hanbiao. Cast: Wang Baokun as Zhang Lihua, Wang Li as Jin Xia, Li Shixi as Xiao Qi, Zhao Yijun as Xiao Han, Shi Chunyu as Uncle Li, Wang Shaowen as the Station Director.

PLA weather station workers Zhang Lihua and Jin Xia argue over inaccurate weather reports. To improve forecasting accuracy, Zhang Lihua goes into the mountains to learn weather lore from the people. Jin Xia, however, only trusts what is in books. Later, Jin Xia provides erroneous information for an emergency flight, but Zhang Lihua uses the information he has gained in the field to successfully guide the aircraft around the mountains. Confronted with the realities, Jin Xia realizes the importance of the practical over the theoretical.

137. *Begin the "Pluto Operation" ("Ming Wang Xing" Xing Dong)*

1992. Youth Film Studio. Color. Letterboxed. 9 Reels. Direction: Qi Jian. Screenplay: Zi Feng, Li Baolin. Cinematography: Zhang Minqin. Music: Zhang Weida. Art Direction: Han Yuanfeng. Music: Zhang Weijing. Sound: Hu Bin. Costume: Zhen Wei. Makeup: Mu Yu. Cast: Zhou Lijing as Chen Xiaoxuan, Chang Rong as Liang Nianhao, Zuo Ling as Xin Xin, Ji Yemu as Kaluo, Chen Wei as Yang Qiong

An international drug cartel devises a scheme to create a new trafficking route called the "Pluto Channel" for smuggling drugs out of Asia. After their first shipment is intercepted and destroyed by the Pakistani Air Force, with over a billion dollars in drugs lost, the organization's New York kingpin decides their next attempt will take advantage of a Hong Kong automobile race scheduled to pass right by the route of the Pluto Channel. Through cosmetic surgery, one of the gang members is made to look like race participant Chen Xiaoxuan and then substituted for the real driver. At the race, mainland driver Liang Nianhao, an ex-cop, realizes something is not right about Chen, his old friend from police academy. Woman reporter Xin Xin takes a great interest in Liang, and helps him investigate. In the end, the smuggling plot is foiled, and the seemingly-helpful Xin Xin turns out to be head of the cartel's operations in Hong Kong.

138. *The Beginning of Life (Ren Zhi Chu)*

1992. Children's Film Studio. Color. Letterboxed. 10 Reels. Direction: Zhen Dongtian. Screenplay: Gu Yin. Cinematography: Sun Yongtian, Xie Ping. Art Direction: Yang Qinsheng. Music: Guo Wenjing. Sound: Feng Deyao. Costume: Du Jinghai, Ding Li. Makeup: Li Li. Cast: Ge Lin as Xinger, Zhang Liwei as Mother, Jia Yonghong as Sister, Chen Jianjun as Second Brother, Ren Lei as Third Brother, Zhou Jichuan as Quer, Meng Nan as Que Cai

Xinger is the youngest of his widowed mother's four children. They live in the back of their tiny drug store on a small street in Kunming City. Xinger loves music, and even when the family must sell personal possessions to make ends meet, he begs his mother not to sell his beloved music box. In elementary school, Xinger first experiences the pain of loss when his close playmate Quer dies in a boating accident. Life becomes even harder for his family, and his overworked mother falls seriously ill. This time, Xinger determines to assume more of the family's burden; he sells the music box and saves his mother's life. Although he earns the top grades in his class, he chooses to go to a cheap school where expenses will be less. The little boy is very proud of himself. These were the early years of the great Chinese musician Nie Erh, composer of China's national anthem.

Best Supporting Actress Zhang Liwei, 1993 Golden Rooster Awards.

139. *Behind the Defendant (Zhai Bei Gao Bei Hou)*

1983. Changchun Film Studio. Color. 11 Reels. Direction: Chang Yan. Screenplay: Shi Chao, Li Pingfeng. Cinematography: Gao Hongbao. Art Direction: Ye Jiren. Music: Zhang Hong. Sound: Tong Zongde. Cast: Si Xilai as Li Jiangchuan, Zhou Zheng as Shao Yan, Liao Youliang as Hao Baosheng

A certain province's Party Committee receives an anonymous letter alleging there are serious irregularities in the operations of the Zhonghua Machine Manufacturing Plant. The letter hints that Li Jiangchuan, the plant's director and Party Secretary, may be at the heart of the problem. The committee assigns Shao Yan to investigate, but he finds that no one will cooperate with him: everyone he talks to is very defensive, wanting to protect Li Jiangchuan. It turns out that Li himself wrote the letter, because he felt it was the only way he

The Beginning of the Life. **As one of four children of a poor widow, bright little Xinger (Ge Lin), appears to have little hope of fulfilling his dreams of a musical career. 1992. Children's Film Studio.**

could bring the irregular operations there to the attention of higher authority. Shao Yan realizes Li's motivation, and as he gathers all his data together he sees his role has changed from Li's prosecution to his defense.

140. *Behind the Gold Banner (Jin Bian Bei Hou)*

1988. Beijing Film Studio. Color. 10 Reels. Direction: Direction: Wang Haowei. Screenplay: Xi Fu, Yi Fu. Cinematography: Li Chengsheng, Zhang Bing. Art Direction: Shao Ruigang, Yi Hongyuan. Music: Zhang Peiji. Sound: Zhang Baojian, Li Fu. Cast: Ma Enran as Wan Manxi, Mi Tiezen as Jia Huairen, Liang Guanhua as Ying Long, Ma Dongju as Li Huihui

The Qinghe town government decides to send banners inscribed with the words "10,000 yuan household" to the town's most prosperous households, to honor their achievements under economic reforms. Township Enterprise Office Director Jia Huairen is sent to examine the "10,000 yuan household" situation in Qilipu Village. Wang Manfu has earned more than that in conventional farming, but he is reluctant to let others know that, so he refuses to display the banner. Wang Manfu's younger brother Wang Manxi is capable, but too greedy to let prosperity come naturally, so he has grown rich selling phony rat poison, as well as engaging in other types of illegal activities. The film tells how Manxi keeps trying to get the banner and celebrate, but all he really accomplishes is to make everyone angry and resentful. Eventually the town sends people over to take away the banner.

141. *Behind the Screen (Ying Mu Hou Mian)*

1984. Xiaoxiang Film Studio. Color. Letterboxed. 9 Reels. Direction: Pan Xianghe, Chen Lu. Screenplay: Kong Du, Yang Tao. Cinematography: Ding Xiaodong, Yu Yejiang. Art Direction: Li Jingjing, Li Yongqi. Music: Tan Dun. Sound: Huang Shiye. Cast: Shen Danping as Lu Xiaoyu, Ma Jing as Lin Xiaolan, Wang Yongge as Zhou Yi, Yang Huai as Xiao Tao, Liu Lijun as Qu Ping, Li Tiehan as Secretary Xu

A graduating class at a film academy is making a movie called "Sister Lan," set in a textile mill and based on an actual incident. A dispute arises between leading lady Lu Xiaoyu and director Zhou Yi: Lu Xiaoyu believes the character she portrays is considerably less selfless than written. When the two cannot reach an agreement, the director decides to drop Lu Xiaoyu and replace her in the role with another actress, Qu Ping. At this point the academy leaders bring the entire cast to the textile mill where the story is set, giving Lu Xiaoyu the opportunity to talk with Lin Xiaolan, the real-life model for the lead role. From the interview, Lu gains a new understanding of her character's motivations. When the cast returns to the set, it soon becomes obvious that Qu Ping is not right for the role. Lu Xiaoyu is reinstated to the lead, and this time does fine.

142. *Behold This Family (Qiao Zhe Yi Jiazi)*

1979. Beijing Film Studio. Color. 9 Reels. Direction: Wang Haowei. Screenplay: Lin Li. Cinematography: Li Chengsheng. Art Direction: Hao Jingyuan. Music: Wang Ming. Sound: Gui Zhilin. Cast: Chen Qiang as Mr. Hu, Zhang Jinling as Jiayin, Liu Xiaoqing as Zhang Lan, Wang Yongheng as Yu Lin, Chen Peisi as Jiaqi, Fang Shu as Xiao Hong

Mr. Hu heads the workshop at the Shuguang Textile Plant. All his life he has worked very hard and been as strict with others as with himself. His daughter Jiayin, a worker at the same workshop, is in love with her father's apprentice Yu Lin. Yu Lin, Jiayin and other young workers want to renovate the machinery to improve product quality and workload, but Mr. Hu opposes this. He also orders them to stop experimenting with workshop practice. But under the pressure of mass sentiment for reform in China, Mr. Hu cannot completely ignore their suggestions any more. Finally, their experiments succeed, and on China's National Day, Yu Lin and Jiayin are married. Mr. Hu's family decides things are pretty good after all.

Best Supporting Actress Liu Xiaoqing, 1980 Hundred Flowers Awards.

143. *Beijing Girl (Beijing Xiao Niu)*

1991. Children's Film Studio. Color. 9 Reels. Direction: . Screenplay: Zhang Aimin. Cinematography: Tian Jianmin. Art Direction: Guo Chenmei. Music: Li Dingyi. Sound: Guo Yingjiang and Zhao Zhiwei. Cast: Ma Shu as Jin Jing, Sun Jiaxing as Bai Yueyue, Hou Yaohua as Jin's father, Gao Fang as Jin Tian, Ling Yuan as Yueyue's grandma

A fantasy in which a timid girl tries to stand up for her rights, but is bullied by some toughs. A mysterious old man helps her, and she obtains super kung fu skills, which she uses to punish wrongdoers and mete out justice.

144. *Beijing Kebabs (Hei! Ge Meng Er)*

1987. Changchun Film Studio. Color. 10 Reels. Direction: Wang Fengkui. Screenplay: Peng Mingyan. Art Direction: Lu qi. Music: Hou Muren. Sound: Kang Ruixin. Cast: Lu Liang as Haizi, Zhou Lijing as Xiao Biao, Zhong Xinghuo as Geng Genghu, Lu Liping as Dongjia, Li Wanfeng as Mother

Haizi is a young man who just can't seem to get anything right. Always a failure in school, he messes up his job as a postman because he cannot read the names and addresses correctly. Meanwhile, his parents are pressuring him to better himself by learning Japanese. While making his rounds one day, Haizi meets his old schoolfriend Xiao Biao. Xiao Biao is making a good living selling kebabs from a street stand, and Haizi begins to think that would suit him too. Xiao Biao, on the other hand, harbors a secret desire for the culture and learning Haizi would rather do without.

145. *Beijing Soccer Heroes (Jing Du Qiu Xia)*

1987. Emei Film Studio. Color. 11 Reels. Direction: Xie Hong. Screenplay: Cao Hongxiang, Li Xin. Cinematography: Hou Yong. Art Direction: Xia Zhengqiu. Music: Xie Jun. Sound: Peng Wenguang. Cast: Zhang Fengyi as Zhou Tian, Sun Ming as Cripple Fei, Chen Peisi as Zhao Huli, Yu Shaokang as Hao Baozhi, Gao Qiang as Tiezhuang Li

Towards the end of the 19th Century, the champion of the European soccer clubs tours Asia putting on exhibition matches with a European all-star team. While the teams are in Beijing, the club team's coach issues a challenge, that his team will play any Chinese team. The Qing government orders its army to meet the challenge. As the soldiers have no concept of the game, everyone knows that China will be humiliated in the game, which is the European coach's intention. Zhou Tian, a young Chinese who had learned to play well while a student in Britain, forms his own team of volunteers from the local people. Their efforts are opposed by the army, which dislikes the local people. Zhou Tian wins out, however, and his volunteers are the ones taking on the Europeans. The match is hard fought and close, but the Chinese team wins. However, the corrupt and ruthless Empress has all of the Chinese team executed for embarrassing her army and angering foreigners, in violation of her policy of appeasement.

Best Supporting Actor Chen Peisi, 1988 Hundred Flowers Awards.

146. *Beijing Story (Bei Jing Gu Shi) (U.S. title: A Great Wall)*

1987. Nanhai Film Studio. Color. 10 Reels. Direction: Wang Zhengfang. Screenplay: Wang Zhengfang, Sun Xiaoling. Art Direction: Li Wen, Feng Yuan. Music: Ming Yue, Ge Ganru. Cast: Wang Zhengfang as Fang Liqun, Li Qingqing as Lili, Wang Lei as the son, Hu Xiaoguang as Mr. Zhao, Shen Guanglan as Fang Liming

Fang Liqun immigrated to America when very young, and more than 30 years of hard work there have made him a big success. He misses China and his relatives there very much, so returns to his hometown of Beijing, accompanied by his wife and son. The family is warmly welcomed by Fang's sister, but differing lifestyles and customs lead to many funny incidents. But the visit is a success, and Fang

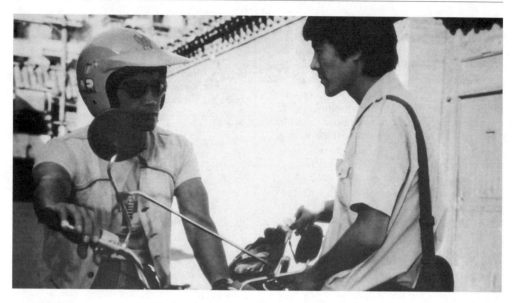

Beijing Kebabs. Haizi (Lu Liang, right) by chance meets his old schoolfriend Xiao Biao (Zhou Lijing). 1987. Changchun Film Studio.

Liqun and his family return to America full of happy memories they will cherish always.

147. *The Bell of Purity Temple (Qing Liang Si Zhong Sheng)*

1991. Shanghai Film Studio, the Shanghai Super Star Film Company & Hong Kong Haocheng Film Company Co-Production, with the assistance of the China Film Export & Import Corporation & the Japanese Daiei Co. Ltd. Color. 12 Reels. Wide Screen. Direction: Xie Jin. Screenplay: Li Zhun and Li Che. Cinematography: Lu Junfu. Art Direction: Chen Shaomian. Music: Jin Fuzai. Sound (Dolby): Ge Weijia. Cast: Ding Yi as Aunty Yangjiao, Kurihara Komaki as Oshima Kazuko, Pu Cunxi as Master Mingjing, You Yong as Kang Hulu, Li Ting as Xiuxiu

In 1945, as Japanese military personnel and civilians in China retreat in panic, a Japanese baby is abandoned in Hanjia Village near Luoyang, Henan Province. Aunty Yangjiao, a midwife, takes the baby in and names him Gouwa. Gouwa grows up with Aunty Yangjiao amid poverty. Thirty years later, Gouwa becomes an eminent monk called Master Mingjing. During a visit to Japan, Mingjing meets his mother Oshima Kazuko. Aged and weak, Oshima Kazuko strongly urges him to stay, but his love for the land where Aunty Yangjiao and his other kinsmen are buried compels him to say good-bye to his mother and return to China.

Best Music Jin Fuzai, 1992 Golden Rooster Awards.

148. *The Bell Tolls in Cold Mountain Temple (Zhong Ming Han Shan Shi)*

1991. Beijing Film Studio. Color. Letterboxed. 10 Reels. Direction: Tang Yanlin. Screenplay: Jiang Dian. Cinematography: Sun Cangyi, Xing Peixiu. Art Direction: Zhang Xiande, Yi Hongyuan. Music: Wang Ming. Sound: Liu Shida. Cast: Wang Zhongliang as Fan Juan (Lu Tianlong), Lu Yan as Hou Mengqin, Huang Weiqin as Xingmei (Xueyuan), Gong Lifeng as the first teenage boy, Liu Jingjing as the second teenage boy, Zhang Shuyu as Huiwu

In the early 17th Century, county magistrate Yu Weimin governs his people cruelly. When he learns that a merchant named Fan and his family will be traveling to meet their son's future in-laws, he has the party attacked and killed in order to gain the sizable dowry they were carrying. The son, Fan Juan, survives. He devotes his days to his studies, pursuing his own dream of becoming a government official. Meanwhile, his fiancee Mengqin devotes her time to studying kung fu, with revenge her sole motivation. A decade passes, and Fan Juan has a new name, Lu Tianlong, and an official position as magistrate of another county. He has long forgotten any thoughts of revenge. When Mengqin sees the change in him, she herself kills Yu Weimin and leaves their hometown. In the end, Lu has a falling out with his superior, which effectively terminates his career. He enters a nearby temple to become a monk.

149. *Bells Ring (Zhong Sheng)*

1981. Beijing Film Studio. Color. 10 Reels. Direction: Ma Erlu, Wen Yan. Screenplay: Zhang Yaojun, Jiang Zhilong. Cinematography: Hu Jihe. Art Direction: Fu Delin. Music: Zhang Peiji. Sound: Sun Yumin. Cast: Chen Yin as Qiao Guangpu, Wei Jian as Shi Gan, Shen Liang as Ji Shen, Jin Qi as Huo Dadao, gao Fang as Tong Zhen

In the second spring after the defeat of the Gang of Four, all industrial enterprises are being reorganized by their workers. In one city, the Hongguang Electronic Machine Plant had been so badly damaged during the Cultural Revolution that it faces closure. Former plant manager Qiao Guangpu had suffered humiliation and false accusations at the plant in the past. Now he volunteers to oversee the plant's refurbishing and brings along as assistant his old partner Shi Gan, the plant's former Party Secretary. When Qiao arrives however, he finds everything much worse than he expected: all is in chaos, with disorderly production management, no discipline, many personnel conflicts. Even more serious is that Ji Shen, a "political director in industrial circles" is trying to halt the refurbishing efforts for he is determined to shut the plant down. Qiao does not back off in the face of so much difficulty. With full support from the director of the Bureau of Electronic Machinery Huo Dadao, Qiao quickly reorganizes the plant, reinstilling discipline and management order, complete regulations and better living arrangements for the employees. He also finds romance with woman engineer Tong Zhen. After just one year's work, the plant survives and is thriving. Qian Guangpu proves himself to be a good manager who can attract people's support.

150. *Bells Ring at Hongshi (Hongshi Zhong Sheng)*

1966. Beijing Film Studio. B & W. 11 Reels. Direction: Fu Jie. Screenplay: Fang Chunru, Yang Shuhui. Cinematography: Nie Jing. Art Direction: Qin Wei. Music: Qin Yongcheng. Sound: Wang Yunhua. Casting: Tian Dan as Guo Changqin, Yu Shaokang as Che Fu, Lu Fei as the commune secretary, Qi Guirong as Che Feng, Huang Kui as Xiao Kui, Kang Guiqiu as Guo's wife

In the five years that Guo Changqin has been assigned as its leader, Fu Village has truly prospered, while neighboring Hongshi Village has shown no progress under the leadership of Director Che Fu, who feels the status quo is satisfactory. So the Party Committee sends Guo Changqin back to his home town of Hongshi as Party Secretary. Guo Changqin and Che Fu are long time friends and colleagues, and Changqin's son is engaged to Che Fu's daughter Che Feng, so they will soon be relatives as well. But the two men fall out over Guo's plan to build a reservoir, and Che Fu's daughter Che Feng supports Guo. With Guo Changqin's sincere help, Che Fu and Guo Changqin together devote themselves to building the reservoir.

151. *Bells Ring in Green Valley (Cui Gu Zhong Sheng)*

1958. Haiyan Film Studio. B & W. 9 Reels. Direction: Liu Qiong. Screenplay: Gao Xing. Cinematography: Shen Weikang. Art Direction: Wu Qiwen. Music: Chen Minjian. Sound: Miao Zhenyu. Cast: Ye Xiangyun as Ke Liaoxiang, Tian Jian as Xia Chong, Su Ge as Secretary Yao, Pao Xunrui as Political Commissar Wang, Liu Yongying as Li Feifan, Li Tan as Commissioner Yan

During the Great Leap Forward, the members of Green Valley Wenjiang Village's agricultural commune set production target of more than 500 kg of grain per plot of land. Most regard this as an impossible goal, but some, led by young member Li Feifan and old farmer Ke Laoxiang, are very confident. In addition to careful planning and hard work, they make artificial fertilizer and upgrade the commune's farm implements. Finally, the commune not only surpasses the original goal, it produces more than 1,000 kg per plot.

152. *Beneath the Yanhong Mountain Range (Yan Hong Ling Xia)*

1966. Changchun Film Studio. B & W. 8 Reels. Direction: Chang Zhenhua. Screenplay: Yang Peijing. Cinematography: Chang Yan. Art Direction: Wang Chong, Wang Jixian. Music: Quan Rufeng. Cast: Shi Jian as Yang Qinhu, Zhao Wenyu as Teacher Xu, Bai Dezhang as Qinhu's father, Zhang Yuan as Qinhu's mother

Fifth grade student Yang Qinhu, the son of a railway employee in the Yanhong Mountain, dreams of being a swashbuckling hero like those in his books, so he has little interest in ordinary work. Teacher Hu encourages him to begin helping his mother serve passengers. The teachers also helps Qinhu understand the relationship between doing one's daily tasks and learning from heroes. After his understanding improves, Qinhu enthusiastically participates in the railway station's junior service team, and does many good things for passengers.

153. *Between Life and Death (Shi Qu Huo Lai)*

1987. Beijing Film Studio. Color. 9 Reels. Direction: Li Xin. Screenplay: Xu Zhiheng, Li Xin. Cinematography: Liang Zhiyong. Art Direction: Yang Wan. Music: Li Lifu. Sound: Liu Shida. Cast: Fang Zhige as Li Qingyuan, Chen Xiaoyi as Yan Fang, Ren You as Zhou Jie, Zhen Baomin as Jin Bo, Zhan Pingping as Fang Liming

Li Qingyuan, chief engineer with a solar energy equipment company, is designated his city's new vice mayor because of his contributions and achievements in making the company profitable. Then Li is believed to have been killed in an industrial accident. Everything changes dramatically: his wife and child are evicted from their home, and no one seems to care about them at all. When Li suddenly turns up alive, everyone is shocked and baffled as to what they can do, since the city has already replaced him in his former post. They finally assign Li to direct a birth control project, a position more suitable to his rank.

154. *Between Life and Death (Sheng Si Zhi Jian)*

1988. Shanghai Film Studio. Color. 10 Reels. Direction: Shen Xiyuan, Can Jingwen. Screenplay: Shen Yaoting, Jin Zhaoqu. Cinematography: Peng Enli. Art Direction: Ju Ransheng. Music: Xu Jingxin. Sound: Feng Deyao, Qian Ping. Cast: Zhang Xiaolin as Du Du, Cui Jie as Da Chuan, He Ling as the boss

Young policeman Du Du and pretty flight attendant Yayuan are lovers, but as much as Yayuan admires Du Du she dislikes his work. Du Du and his partner Da Chuan are assigned to investigate the theft of two extremely valuable diamonds, a theft tied in to the operations of a smuggling ring. In the course of their investigation, a rookie policeman helping them is killed, and Da Chuan narrowly escapes with his life. The smuggling ring exploits a weakness in Yayuan to plant the diamonds on her.

When she discovers this, she is so fearful of telling Du Du that she takes poison. Fortunately the police arrive in time to save her and capture the criminals.

155. *Between the Two of Us (Wo Men Fu Fu Zhi Jian)*

1951. Kunlun Film Studio. B & W. 10 Reels. Direction: Zhen Junli. Screenplay: Zhen Junli. Cinematography: Hu Zhenhua. Art Direction: Ding Bing. Cast: Zhao Dan as Li Ke, Jiang Tianliu as Zhang Ying, Wu Yin as Qing Feng, Liu Xiaohu as Xiao Juan, Wen Ming as Zhang Ying's mother, Wang Guiling as Xiao Juan's father.

In the autumn of 1947, intellectual cadre Li Ke, a native of Shanghai working in a liberated rural area, falls in love with Zhang Ying, a girl from a poor rural family. They marry, and all goes well at first, but after the liberation of Shanghai, both are assigned to work there, Li in the archives office of a textile company, and Zhang in a cotton mill. Zhang, used to a rigorous rural lifestyle, finds it hard to adjust immediately to city life, while Li gradually loses the taste for simple farm life he developed while working in the countryside. The two begin to grow apart and eventually separate. But, through criticism from their old rural team leader Qing Feng, and aided by contact with other workers, Zhang acquires a new awareness, while Li writes a letter to his wife criticizing himself. The two eventually reconcile.

156. *Beyond the Horizon (Parts 1 & 2) (Zou Chu Di Pingxian)*

1992. Shanghai Film Studio. Color. Wide Screen. 17 Reels. Direction: Yu Bengzheng. Screenplay: Lu Tianmin. Cinematography: Gao Zhiyi. Art Direction: Wu Tianci. Music: Pan Guoxing. Costume: Zhang Xuelin, Luo Taojuan. Makeup: Shen Dongsheng, Zhang Zhen. Cast: Gao Qiang as Qu Manman, Xiao Rongsheng as Qin Jianjiu, Zhang Tieyuan as Qu Jiancheng, Ao Wenbing as Fang Zhaozhang, Jiang Baoyin as Fang Huiming

During an exceptionally cold winter at the end of the 1970s, the mountain village of Qugong is extremely poor, so much so that women of the village are selling themselves to strangers as a way out. No one sees any point in working hard, as it gets them nowhere. Party Secretary Qu Manman is so ashamed of the situation that he asks Qin Jianjiu to replace him in his post. Qin decides desperate

Beyond the Horizon (Parts 1 & 2). **Desperately poor farmers call for radical measures to help them, resulting in the rural contracting system. 1992. Shanghai Film Studio.**

measures are necessary, so he immediately begins contracting land, which gives the people an unprecedented enthusiasm for work. However, word of his unauthorized contracting reaches higher echelons of government, and Qin is called on the carpet for it. He defends his actions and takes full responsibility, gambling that the farmers will prosper under the contract system. This is the start of land reform in the countryside.

157. *Beyond the Red Wall (Hong Qiang Wai)*

1989. Beijing Film Studio. Color. Letterboxed. 9 Reels. Direction: Shi Xian. Screenplay: Xie Fengsong. Cinematography: Ru Shuiren. Art Direction: Fu Delin. Music: Zhang Peiji. Sound: Wan Dawen. Cast: Bai Zhidi as Zhong Dake, Xia Jing as Yangyang

After Zhong Dake retires, he goes to live with his daughter's family in a mountainous region. Although his family is very kind to him, he still feels very lonely and useless without work to do. One day when out for a walk, Zhong meets Duoduo, an orphan boy, and the two become good friends. He brings the little

boy home to visit his family, and soon Duoduo and his friends come over regularly to play there. As he gets to know these children, Zhong Dake encourages them to make the most of their educational opportunities. He also decides that while they are bright and good students, they require more revolutionary education. He gets the idea of starting a revolutionary school in the area, and his idea is supported by teachers at the regular school.

158/159. *Bi Sheng (Bi Sheng)*

1981. Pearl River Film Studio. Color. 10 Reels. Direction: Yu Deshui. Screenplay: Liang Gongxuan, Dai Minxian. Cinematography: Wang Yunhui, Ye Weimin. Art Direction: Wang Huisun. Music: Ge Guangrui. Sound: Lin Guoqiang. Cast: Ru Xuhua as Bi Sheng, Liu Guanxiong as Pi Zhilong, Lin Shujing as Wang Tianshu, Pu Chaoyin as A Xiang, Jin Limin as Chen Daliang

During the Northern Song Dynasty (960-1127), scholar Bi Sheng is hired by businessman Pi Zhilong, head of the "Baowentang" Publishing House in Hangzhou. Bi Sheng's dream is to publish and widely disseminate

"Agricultural Knowledge." Bi Sheng experiences various hardships at the Baowentang, but he masters the necessary publishing skills. He recognize that the traditional method of sculpting Chinese characters presents the greatest barrier to mass publishing, so he keeps on thinking and inventing, and in time invents a single character movable printing technology. Bi Sheng later leaves the Baowentang and establishes his own printing company. However, the corrupt feudal society of the time subjects him to harassment from rival businessmen and government officials. In the end, he and his wife A Xiang commit suicide together to escape harassment, but the printing technology he invented becomes widespread.

A Big Character Poster **see** *A Thousand Miles a Day*

160. *Big Li, Little Li and Old Li (Da Li, Xiao Li He Lao Li)*

1962. Tianma Film Studio. B & W. 10 Reels. Direction: Xie Jin. Screenplay: Yu Ling, Ye Ming, Xie Jin, Liang Yanqing, Wu Li and Jiang Rongquan. Cinematography: Lu Junfu. Art Direction: Wang Yuebai. Music: Wu Yinju. Sound: Gong Jianqing. Cast: Liu Xiasheng as Big Li, Yao Debing as Little Li, Fan Haha as Old Li, Guan Hongda as the big strong guy, Wen Bingbing as the barber, Yu Xiangming as the doctor, Zhang Xiaoling as Miaoyun, You Jia as Little Braids

Meat processing plant workers' unit chairman Big Li and workshop director Old Li dislike sports, but Old Li's son, young worker Little Li is more fond of sports than work. After Big Li is elected chair of the athletic association, he also becomes an enthusiastic advocate of sports and exercise. Old Li is upset to see them engaged in athletic activities, because he regards sports as play. Later, through the sports association, Old Li became a lover of taiqi exercise, and during an athletic contest wins a bicycle race. From that day on, sports became the passion of everyone in the plant.

161. *The Big Mill (Da Mo Fang)*

1990. Xiaoxiang Film Studio and Hong Kong Sil-Metropole Organization Ltd.,. Co-Production. Color. 9 Reels. Wide Screen. Direction: Wu Ziniu. Screenplay: Qiao Liang, Wu Ziniu. Cinematography: Yang Wei. Art Direction: Na Shufeng. Music: Yang Qing. Sound: Huang Qizi. Cast: Li Yusheng as Young Qingguo, Liu Zhongyuan as Old Qingguo, Shen Danping as Jiucui, Tao Zeru as Liao Baijun

By chance, a man called Old Qingguo encounters a group of people carrying a coffin to a cemetery. When he learns that the body in the coffin is that of his former lover, he recalls his early life, romantic yet bitter and violent. Over half a century before, Qingguo and beautiful Jiucui were very much in love. But an ill fate obliged Jiucui to live instead with a cruel and ugly cripple, Liao Baijun, shattering Qingguo's cherished dream of a happy family life with his beloved. He sadly follows the course of her life from afar, and finds that in her despair she makes some bad decisions.

162. *The Big Parade (Da Yue Bing)*

1986. Guangxi Film Studio. Color. 10 Reels. Direction: Chen Kaige. Screenplay: Gao Lili. Cinematography: Zhang Yimou. Art Direction: He Qun. Music: Zhao Jiping, Ju Xiaosong. Sound: Lin Lin. Cast: Wang Xueqin as Li Weicheng, Sun Chun as Sun Fang, Wu Ruopu as Lu Chun, Lu Lei as Jiang Junbiao

A PLA unit, 25 men in all, are selected to march in the National Holiday parade at Beijing's Tiananmen Square. We follow the officers and men as they prepare for the parade. On October 1st, they proudly march into the square.

163. *Big Star (Da Ming Xing)*

1985. Shenzhen Film Studio. Color. 9 Reels. Direction: Teng Wenji. Screenplay: Teng Wenji, A Cheng, Xiao Yu. Cinematography: Gu Changji. Art Direction: Yao Qin, A Cheng. Music: Guo Feng, Liu Suola, Qi Yunfei. Sound: Gu Changning. Cast: Ying Tingru as Tingting, Zhang Tianxi as Xizi

Bright and beautiful Tingting is an ordinary worker in a theater, but dreams of someday becoming an actress. One day, an assistant cinematographer at a local film studio attends a performance at the theater, a young man named Xizi, and he gets her an audition at the studio. He also falls in love with her. Tingting becomes a big star and Xizi advances in cinematography. They help and encourage each other and their future looks bright.

164. *Big Victory (Da Jie)*

1995. Shanghai Film Studio. Color. Letterboxed. Direction: Wu Tiange. Screenplay: Wu Yigong, based on the novel by Zhou Meishen.

The Big Mill. **Cruel and lustful Liao Baijun (Tao Zeru, top), shatters the dreams of two young lovers. 1990. Xi-aoxiang Film Studio, Sil-Metropole Organization Ltd. Co-Production.**

Cinematography: Pan Feng. Art Direction: Xue Jiangang. Music: Su Junjie. Cast: Lei Luosheng, Yuan Yuan, Zhao Shengsheng, Zhao Jun

The newly organized 3rd Regiment of the Nationalist Chinese 23rd Army consists largely of untrained recruits from various walks of Chinese life, so they naturally suffer massive losses in their first exposure to combat. Since they receive practically no support from other Nationalist forces, their commander Fang Xi-anggong realizes they have been sold out as cannon fodder. The 3rd Regiment tries to withdraw, but another regiment, the 1761st, turns its guns on the 3rd and stops them. Between the Japanese and the 1761st, the 3rd Regiment is virtually wiped out. Several of the survivors of the 3rd at last succeed in abducting the 1761st's commander Han Peige, after which they hold a "court martial" and execute him by firing squad.

165. *Birds Bring the Spring (Bu Gu Cui Chun)*

1982. August First Film Studio. Color. 10 Reels. Jia Shihong. Screenplay: You Fengwei. Cinematography: Gao Jiuling. Art Direction:

Zhao Changsheng. Music: Li Weicai. Sound: Song Tianpei. Cast: Jin Xin as Zhao Dongsheng, Wang Fang as Laifu's wife, Zhang Yin as Minyue, Liu Jizhong as Huzhi, Liu Fang as Zhenzhen

After his discharge from the Air Force, Zhao Dongsheng excitedly returns to his native village. He finds the situation there quite grim: many of the town's young bachelors are in such extreme poverty they have no hopes of finding wives. Zhao vows to change the situation, and gets himself elected director of the production team. Once in the job, he implements various kinds of management reforms, especially the contract responsibility system for production and the formation of contracted special production teams. Production takes a strong turn for the better, but the reforms go against commune policy, and when his superiors find out what Zhao has done he is ordered to submit himself for self-criticism. Fortunately, the spirit of the 3rd Plenary Session of the 11th Party Congress arrives in the village, and Zhao Dongsheng's work is now official policy. When the harvest season arrives, the village is prosperous and many young couples get together, including Zhao Dongsheng and Minyue.

166. *Bit by Bit (Dian Dian Di Di)*

1987. China City and Town Water Supply Association. Color. 9 Reels. Direction: Liu Guoquan. Screenplay: Chong Zhejia, Xiao Wei. Cinematography: Ma Liguo, Zhang Jingning. Art Direction: Zhang Yafang. Music: Wang Ming. Sound: Zhu Qijian, Wang Chunbao. Cast: Chen Qiang as Old Mr. Y, Ling Yuan as Old Mrs. Fang, Wan Qiong as Fang Mei, Li Xiangang as Daquan, Mi Tiezen as Liu Wu

Severe drought in a coastal city forces the authorities to strictly limit each resident's water supply. The story follows the varying responses to this from eight households in a neighborhood. It also shows the efforts people make to improve the situation. At last, a major water project is completed which resolves the city's water supply problem, although one of the project workers is killed during the final stage of construction.

167. *Bitter Cauliflower (Ku Cai Hua)*

1965. August First Film Studio. Direction: Li Ang. Screenplay: Feng Deying (1935–   ), based on his novel of the same title. Cinematography: Wei Linyue. Art Direction: Kou Honglie. Music: Xiao Yan. Sound: He Baoding. Cast: Qu Yun as Mother Feng, Yuan Xia as Xingmei, Wang Zhigang as Jiang Yongquan, Yang Yaqing as Juanzhi, Wan Cang as Deqiang, Tao Shan as Xiuzhi

In 1937, landlord Wang Weiyi mercilessly persecutes Mother Feng's poor farmer husband to death. Her eldest son Degang is forced to leave home. In 1940, an armed peasant rebellion sets up an anti-Japanese democratic government, and Mother Feng's eldest daughter Juanzhi participates, greatly worrying her mother. But when the Japanese invaders reach their area, Mother Feng not only supports her daughter's joining the militia, she also encourages her second son Deqiang to join the Eighth Route Army. When word reaches her that her eldest son has died, she becomes even more firmly devoted to the struggle and joins in the battle on the frontier. Later, Degang's fiancee is betrayed by a traitor, arrested and executed. Mother Feng is also arrested. She bears up bravely under the massive sorrow of seeing so many of her loved ones perish, and perseveres, eventually finding and killing the traitor.

168. *Bitter Fruit (Ku Guo)*

1981. Xi'an Film Studio. Color. 10 Reels. Direction: Liu Bing. Screenplay: Wang Lian, Li Yunliang, Liang Jianduo. Cinematography: Liu Cangxi, Wang Hui. Art Direction: Ai Nong. Music: Wei Ruixiang. Sound: Dang Chunzhu. Cast: Xiao Xiong as Lin Qiang, Huang Zhongqiu as Shangguan Jian, Bao Xun as Lin Rao, Shi Zhongqi as Xiao Xiang, Han Bingjie as Fan Zhu

In a post office, a young girl is found lying unconscious and bloodied, and cash is missing. Public Security Officers Shangguan Jian, Feng Yan and A Shu are assigned to investigate. The victim is identified as bus conductor Lin Qiang. However, when she comes to, she refuses to tell the officers anything. They look into the victim's background, and find that Lin Qiang has a younger brother, Lin Rao, a spoiled young man with a history of getting into trouble, progressively more serious, from which his sister would extricate him. Although employed, the brother had taken to serious gambling, and was getting increasingly out of his sister's control. It turns out that Lin Rao had robbed the post office, and his sister was injured trying to stop him. Lin Qiang breaks down when she realizes that it was her spoiling him which brought her brother to this end.

169. *A Black and White World (Hei Bai Ren Jian)*

1992. Beijing Film Studio and the Hainan Silver City Film Development Corporation Co-Production. Color. Letterboxed. 10 Reels. Direction: Wang Binglin. Screenplay: Wang Binglin. Cinematography: Guan Wu. Art Direction: Zhang Xiande. Music: Gao Erdi. Sound: Li Bojiang. Costume: Gong Zhanjing, Zhao Wenxiu. Makeup: Wang Xiufeng, Gao Lanying. Cast: Wu Weidong as Sun Liu, Qu Yan as Li Shuxian, Tan Zongrao as Boss Gu, Tian Chunkui as Boss Liu, Han Shanxu as Niu Erye, Liang Qingang as Bean Juice Sun, Huang Zongluo as Master, Du Zhengxi as Police Officer Feng

Niu Erye heads a gang of Beijing toughs. One day, Niu bullies a timid and honest man named Sun. The man's son, a hotheaded youngster named Sun Liu, becomes head of another gang in order to protect himself and avenge his father. But Sun Liu's involvement in gang activity estranges him from both his father and his sister. Sun Liu later marries a gang girl, and over the years his criminal activities grow. Boss Gu, head of a rival criminal organization, has Sun Liu framed for a capital crime, and Sun Liu is executed. His widow waits until Boss Gu's 50th birthday, then blows up the store where the celebration is taking place.

170. *Black Bandits (Hei Dao)*

1989. Changchun Film Studio. Color. 9 Reels. Direction: Li Yan. Screenplay: Xue Yandong. Cinematography: Feng Bingyong. Art Direction: Liang Shukui. Music: Tang Jianping. Sound: Liu Jingui. Cast: A Yunga as Li Xiao, Bi Hui as Hei Zhihu

As China's economy develops rapidly in the 1980s, so does its rail transport system. A gang calling itself the "Railway Guerrilla Troop" begins holding up trains, inflicting huge economic damage on the nation. PSB investigator Li Xiao infiltrates the gang, and after gaining their trust coordinates several police agencies in rounding up the gang. But Li Xiao's triumph ultimately ends in frustration, as he realizes that the top man in the gang is a government official operating behind the scenes, and untouchable.

171. *Black Butterfly (You Xia Hei Hu Die)*

1988. Changchun Film Studio. Color. 15 Reels. Direction: Lu Jianhua, Yu Zhongxiao. Screenplay: Xie Wenli, Han Qipeng. Cinematography: An Zhiguo. Art Direction: Sui Zuangji. Sound: Huang Lijia, Shi Lin. Music: Wang Ming. Cast: Zhen Shuang as Black Butterfly, Chen Peisi as Zhang Hu, Fang Xinmin as Zhang Long

In legend, a young woman called Black Butterfly traveled around Qing Dynasty China doing good. At a festival, an unusually strong man named Zhang Hu begins making trouble. Black Butterfly happens to be passing by, and kicks Zhang Hu to the ground. But later she and Zhang Hu become friends. Black Butterfly then catches a desert bandit called Black Bear who was a source of suffering for many. Her next exploit is to go to the famine-stricken area of Jiayuguan, where a local tyrant named Wei Sheng has appropriated all the emergency grain sent by the government. She sneaks into Wei Sheng's home and kills him, after which she opens the grain storehouse and feeds the hungry. Black Butterfly then resumes her nomadic existence.

172. *Black Cannon Incident (Hei Pao Shi Jian)*

1985. Xi'an Film Studio. Color. Letterboxed. 9 Reels. Direction: Huang Jianxin. Screenplay: Li Wei, based on Zhang Xianliang's novel "Romance of the Black Cannon." Cinematography: Wang Xinsheng, Feng Wei. Art Direction: Liu Yichuan. Music: Zhu Shirui. Sound: Li Lanhua. Cast: Liu Zifeng as Zhao Shuxing, Gao Min as Manager Li Renzhong, Gerhard Olschewski as Hans Schmidt, Wang Yi as Deputy Party Secretary Zhou Yuzhen, Yang Yazhou as Feng Liangcai, Ge Hui as Party Secretary Wu Kegong, Zhao Xiuling as Chen Shuzhen, Wang Beilong as Wang Hongye

One rainy night, engineer Zhao Shuxing braves the storm to go to the post office, where he hurriedly sends a telegram. The postal clerk notes the cryptic message "Lost black cannon, search in 301 for Zhao." Her suspicions aroused, she reports the matter to the Public Security Bureau. Quietly, officials launch an investigation of what appears to be a serious case of espionage. They soon affirm that Zhao is a middle-aged bachelor, a hard worker and a Christian. They decide to keep Zhao under surveillance. The engineer had earlier worked closely with a visiting German expert, Hans Schmidt, and had been his interpreter. Now Schmidt is back in China to assist on a project, but when he requests to work with Zhao again, the leaders of the unit send Zhao to work elsewhere temporarily and assign another interpreter Feng Liangcai to work with the German. The incompetent Feng makes so many errors it results in a million yuan loss for China. Finally, a package arrives, and when Party officials secretly intercept and open it, it contains only a single chesspiece—a black cannon. It turns out that while he was on a business trip, Zhao Shuxing played chess with his hotel roommate, and left behind the black cannon from his chess set. The telegram was a request that the hotel find the piece and return it to him. This was the cause of a major investigation behind the scenes. Zhao is reinstated to the project, but he cannot believe that the organization would suspect him and conduct so extensive an investigation.

Best Actor Liu Zifeng, 1986 Golden Rooster Awards.

173. *The Black Corridor (Hei Se Zou Lang)*

1990. Beijing Film Studio. Color. Wide screen. 9 Reels. Direction: Lu Xiaolong. Screenplay: Wang Shengrong. Cinematography: Guan Qingwu. Art Direction: Hao Jingyuan. Sound: Zhang Hua. Cast: Lu Xiaolong as Wang Long, Luoxiou Bading as Luo Na, Andeliegu as director Gu, Yidifei Landu as Dang Make,

Fengni Mainilu as Fengni, Liu Dong as Director Liu, Pan Jie as Ma Nao, Xu Zhiqun as Helen, Mu Tiezhu as Gao Lao, Liu Xiaoning as Kun Sha

A rehabilitated drug dealer is released from prison when he agrees to return to his former life, this time as an undercover narcotics agent. He first goes to Taiwan, where he rejoins his old mob. His first assignment is to open a new drug smuggling channel called "The Black Corridor." He goes to the Golden Triangle and locates the drug manufacturing site. Working with an undercover mainland Chinese policeman, he at last coordinates the Chinese PSB and an international agency in smashing the ring.

174. *Black Dragonfly (Hei Qin Ting)*

1984. Shanghai Film Studio. Color. Letterboxed. 10 Reels. Direction: Bao Zhifang. Screenplay: Wang Lian, Chen Wenyuan, Li Wen. Cinematography: Zhang Er. Art Direction: Wu Tianci. Music: Liu Yanxi. Sound: Ren Xinliang. Cast: Lu Jun as Yang Tianping, Chen Ye as Ye Hongye, Wu Gang as Cui Yong, Yu Daiqing as Director Wei, Li Jiayao as Mr. Cui

Qiuhua Textile Plant Director Wei wants to establish a fashion team to model the plant's line of clothing. Chief designer Cui Yong supports the idea. One who is particularly excited about it is young designer Yang Tianping, who wants his girlfriend Ye Hongye to apply for one of the modeling jobs. The only one opposed is Ye Hongye's mother. There are many mishaps at the first show, including Ye falling down, and the show is jeered by those attending. But the designers and models are determined the idea will succeed. A few days later, Ye Hongye's uncle arrives from Shenzhen on business, and when he learns his niece's boyfriend is a top designer he is very impressed. Eager to push their relationship, he starts to work on convincing Ye's mother. At last, the fashion team puts on a successful show, and even the mother is impressed with the beauty of it.

175. *Black Faced Person (Hei Mian Ren)*

1980. Xi'an Film Studio. Color. 10 Reels. Direction: Zhang Jingren, Shi Daqian. Screenplay: Zhao Donghui, Wu Shuang. Cinematography: Chen Wancai, Niu Han. Art Direction: Lu

Guangcai, Li Zhengxin. Music: Zhang Nan. Sound: Xiong Huajuan. Cast: Liu Jia as Zong Ni, Wei Ke as Ge Luo, Li Xiuwu as the local headman, Li Guilin as Yige's wife, Yan Wanzhong as Dahai

In the fall of 1948, soon after the PLA arrives in the mountainous region peopled by the Hani minority, the troops happen upon a person with a black face stealing the local headman's horse. He runs off, and the headman tells the soldiers that most of the local bandits have long fled across the border, and the only one still around is one they call the "black face bandit." But the local people say that the bandit never bothers them; he only steals from the headman and is probably the former bandit chief Ma Peng. Galuo, one of the soldiers who is also of the Hani nationality, goes to the village looking for someone he had once known, a girl named Zong Ni. He learns that Zong Ni had been abducted by Ma Peng and sold into prostitution abroad. But he investigates further and at last learns that the there are really more than 10 "black face bandits," all women. Three years earlier, Ma Peng had tried to sell them all, but Zong Ni in particular had led a resistance, killing the bandit chief and fleeing into the mountains with the other girls. From then on, they have been painting their faces and hiding in the forest. Galuo goes into the mountains and succeeds in persuading the young women to remove the paint and come back. Meanwhile the PLA has determined that the headman has been in league with Ma Peng, so they detain him when he tries to leave the country. Filled with hatred, Ma Peng ambushes the women on their way back to the village, hoping to kill Zong Ni. He misses and mortally wounds Galuo instead. Zong Ni then kills Ma Peng with an arrow.

176. *Black-Faced Son-in-Law (Hei Lian Niu Xu)*

1988. August First Film Studio. Color. 10 Reels. Direction: Wang Mengyuan, Yu Suping. Screenplay: Mo Yan. Cinematography: Gao Jiuling. Art Direction: Tang Shiyun. Music: Fang Xiacan. Sound: Zhu Junshan. Cast: Ma Jun as Long Zehai, Han Yueqiao as Fang Mengzhen

The reform atmosphere sweeping China arrives at Longjiazhuang Village, and Fang Mengzhen invites Long Zehai to be director of the local lace mill. Long Zehai, a military retiree, decides to establish the "Dragon Pearl Agriculture, Industry and Commerce Joint

Company" to help the village people get out of poverty. He also hires young widow Gong Yueer, a woman of low social status, to be a technician in the lace mill. It takes three years of hard work, but at last the company begins to boom. The mixture of Long Zehai's enthusiasm and the villagers' misunderstanding of reform means things do not always go smoothly. The story ends as their products sell overseas and Gong Yueer is invited by a foreign businessman to give an overseas demonstration of their lacemaking techniques.

177. *Black Fire (Hei Huo) (alternate title: Shuang Qiang Qing)*

1993. Tianshan Film Studio. Color. Letterboxed. 9 Reels. Direction: Li Ni. Screenplay: Li Ni, Yi Bai. Cinematography: He Qing. Art Direction: Li Daochu. Music: Guo Wenjing. Sound: Gu Yu, Wu Ling. Costume: Zhang Xiaojing. Makeup: Wang Yanxia. Cast: Jia Hongsheng as Zhao Mengyu, Hu Jun as Zhang Wu, Zou Yitian as Little Sister, Pao Lie as Zhao Huaizhong, Shen Lizi as Zhao Mengyun.

In 1940, triad boss Zhao Huaizhong, wealthy from drug dealing and gun running, holds a gala wedding for his son Mengyu. One of Zhao's partners in crime is a corrupt police captain, Zhang Wu. Zhang desires Zhao's daughter Mengyun, but she does not like him. Zhang Wu, frustrated at being turned down by, begins blackmailing Zhao and making troubles for his legal business interests. Zhao dies, and his son Mengyu, encouraged by his bride Xiaomei, decides he only wants to pursue legal business after this. But his business is destroyed by Zhang, causing the weak Mengyu to revert to his father's old ways, reinstating the drug business and co-operating with Zhang. At last, the desperate Mengyun kills the evil captain, and he and Xiaomei commit suicide.

178. *Black Flag's Special Representative (Hei Qi Te Shi)*

1988. Changchun Film Studio. Color. 9 Reels. Direction: Xue Yandong, Zhao Weiheng. Screenplay: Ning Xuancheng, Fu Sheng, Wang Tingjun. Cinematography: Liu Fengdi. Art Direction: Ju Lutian. Music: Xu Shuya. Sound: Liu Jingui. Cast: Ren Naichang as Duan Wenjing, Jing Feng as Bai Qiling, Zhang Lun as Pu Geng, Hu Yingjie as Sun Keyin

In 1867, the Qing government ruthlessly suppresses the Taiping Rebellion. The King of Liang and the commander of the Black Flag group, a part of the Taiping alliance, send Duan Wenjing to Daming City as their representative, where he tries to get the Black Flag Brigade there to rescue another brigade in Shandong province. The enemies order Sun Keyin to capture Duan Wenjing. Heroic Duan Wenjing avoids capture through his courage and intelligence, and in the final life and death struggle kills Sun Keyin.

179. *The Black Flower Killer (Hei Hua Sha Shou)*

1993. Changchun Film Studio. Color. Letterboxed. 9 Reels. Direction: Zhu Decheng. Screenplay: Chen Jiangong, Su Wenyang. Guo Baocang. Cinematography: Wu Wen. Art Direction: Wang Zhiwei. Music: Ren Zhang. Sound: Jiang Yan, Gu Xiaolian. Costume: Zhang Shufang, Liu Tao. Makeup: Liu Xiaona, Yan Zhenrong. Cast: Xu Chenglin as Qu Jingzhi, Liu Zhibing as Chen Min, Li Daqiang as Shi Xin, Li Ting as Su Jia, Hou Yansong as Liu Zheng, Guo Baocang as Shen Zhongyuan, Jiang Yining as Hao Maofu

During the Chinese Civil War of the late 1940s, Northeast China Communist liaison Liu Zheng works with Qu Jingzhi, an agent who has infiltrated Nationalist headquarters. Their objective is to obtain a secret plan of their enemy's defensive posture in the Northeast. In the final battle, Liu is sacrificed, and Qu escapes to Communist-held territory with the plans.

180. *Black Horse (Hei Ma)*

1989. Xiaoxiang Film Studio. Color. Letterboxed. 9 Reels. Direction: Luo Zheng, Hua Yongzuang. Screenplay: Hua Yongzuang, Huang Xufu. Cinematography: Li Xiaoping. Art Direction: Jin Bohao. Music: Wei Jingshu. Sound: Liu Jingfang. Cast: Wang Lei as Hulu, Peng Bing as Tianxing

Orphan children Tianxing and Hulu adopt a stray dog they call Black Horse. One day, the two boys come upon a wounded soldier from the New Fourth Army, Company Commander Fang Gang. They save his life and help him recover. After he recovers, Fang takes the boys and the dog back with him to rejoin the New Fourth Army, giving them a start on a new life.

181. *Black Horse (Hei Jun Ma)*

1995. Hong Kong Huanya Film Corp. Ltd., Youth Film Studio Co-Production. Color.

Direction: Xie Fei. Screenplay: Zhang Chengzhi, based on original novel of same title by Zhang Chengzhi. Cinematography: Fu Jingsheng. Art Direction: Li Yongxin, Na Yintai. Music: Teng Ge'er. Cast: Teng Ge'er as Baiyin Baolige, Na Renhua as Suomiya, Daolige'er Surong as grandma

When Baiyin Baolige's mother dies, his father sends him to live on the prairie with his great aunt. There, the little boy meets six-year-old Suomiya, his great aunt's granddaughter. The old woman engages the two children to marry when they became adults and when they grow up, the two young people do plan to marry after Baiyin returns from veterinary school. But when comes back he finds Suomiya pregnant by another man, Xila. Baiyin leaves, not to return for more than a decade. When he does return on a visit, he finds that Suomiya is now married to Dawacang, a man who helped her a lot when her grandmother was dying. He also meets her daughter, who has never seen her father Xila, who abandoned Suomiya soon after Baiyin left.

182. *Black Lightning (Hei Se Shan Dian)*

1992. Changchun Film Studio. Color. Letterboxed. 9 Reels. Direction: Zhao Weiheng. Screenplay: Zhen Qin. Cinematography: Su Zaidong. Art Direction: Ju Lutian. Music: Chen Chunguang. Sound: Sheng Hongtao. Costume: Zhao Jing. Makeup: Liu Jiao, Tan Shumei. Cast: Yu Xiaohui as Qin Jiao, Robert (American) as Sitelang, Wang Xinjian as Tie Gong, Hou Tianlai as Chen Ao, Shu Yaoxuan as Ji Yehong, Xu Wuyin as Gongqi Xiaonan, Liang Xueqiu as Ding Hui, Zhang Ke as Gao Keming

Two World War II intelligence agents, one American and one Nationalist Chinese, fail in their effort to obtain the plans for a secret Japanese base code-named the "Shenfeng Commando Base." They survive the botched attempt, and link up with a unit of the Communist New Fourth Army. They are ordered to change to the "Black Lightning Plan," which is to abduct the designer of the base instead. Their efforts are hampered by a Japanese woman spy, but at last they succeed in accomplishing their mission.

183. *Black Lion Action (Hei Shi Xing Dong)*

1993. Shanghai Film Studio. Color. 10 Reels. Direction: Zhuang Hongsheng. Screenplay:

Sima, Zhuge. Cinematography: Dan Lianguo. Art Direction: Shen Huizhong. Music: Liu Yanxi. Sound: Ge Fujia. Costume: Wang Youlong. Makeup: Zuang Yazhen. Cast: He Ling as Languang, Sun Jihong as Lin Ping and Lin Li, Kang Zhengda as Dan Hao, Zhang Xiaoqin as Song Jian, Tang Han as Jiajia, Zhu Yin as Liu Na

In 1988, the suburbs of a certain city are rocked by a series of murders and armed robberies. The chief of police personally undertakes the investigation, with a task force composed of his best officers. By painstakingly tracing the circumstances surrounding one of the murders, the officers at last determine that the crime wave is actually part of a plan designed to distract the police from another crime: the assassination of a high-ranking politician from another country, due to visit their city soon. The officers move in and smash the conspiracy.

184. *Black Mountain Blockade (Hei Shan Zu Ji Zhan)*

1958. August First Film Studio. B & W. 10 Reels. Direction: Liu Peiran, Hao Guang. Screenplay: Mao Feng, Lu Zhuguo. Cinematography: Xue Boqing. Art Direction: Wang Wei. Music: Gao Liang. Sound: Guo Dazhen. Cast: Zhang Shikai as the Column Commander, Bai Ping as the Column Political Commissar, Xing Jitian as Division Commander Lei, Su Youlin as Division Commander Lu, An Boyin as the Logistics Director, Jing Mukui as the Battle Section Chief.

In 1948, the PLA's Northeastern field army launches an autumn offensive against the Nationalists. Chiang Kaishek rushes five divisions to the area as reinforcements for the Nationalist troops blockaded in Northeast China. One PLA column holds its blockade despite being outnumbered five to one and faced with freezing temperatures and inadequate food and weapons. During the fiercest fighting, even the column's headquarters personnel take up weapons and fight. The column commander goes to the front lines to command his troops, where he is severely wounded and his guards killed. The column's political commissar takes command of the troops, and the enemy reinforcements' attack is finally turned back. In the end, all the Nationalist forces are either wiped out or driven from Northeast China.

185. *Black Rose (Xia Nu Hei Mei Gui)*

1991. Guangxi Film Studio. Color. Letterboxed. 9 Reels. Direction and Screenplay: Wang

Wenzhi. Cinematography: Lu Dongqing. Art Direction: Tang Xinghua. Music: Lu Shilin. Sound: Liao Yongliang. Cast: Chen Qi as Black Rose, Wang Xiaozhong as Ding Jingbao, Liu Weihua as Tian Xiongnan, Gao Lianna as Sun Cuihuan, Wang Baosheng as Niu Wu

During the early period of Japan's invasion of China, a woman singer who calls herself Black Rose finds the Japanese occupation and the Chinese government's official collaboration unbearable. She organizes a "Civilian Attacking Japanese Devils Brigade" to carry out underground resistance. Japanese intelligence sends two Chinese collaborators to infiltrate the resistance and try to take it over. At the same time, the Chinese Communist underground sends an agent to assist and keep an eye out for Japanese spies. He eventually exposes the infiltrators, smashes their plot and turns Black Rose's group in a more revolutionary direction.

186. *Black Snow (Ben Ming Nian)*

1989. Youth Film Studio. Color. 9 Reels. Direction: Xie Fei. Screenplay: Liu Heng. Cinematography: Xiao Feng. Art Direction: Li Yongxin. Music: Xuan Qu. Sound: Wu Ling. Cast: Jiang Wen as Li Huiquan, Cheng Lin as Zhao Yaqiu, Yue Hong as Luo Xiaofen, Liu Xiaoning as Chazi, Cai Hongxiang as Cui Yongli, Liu Bin as Liu Baotie

On a cold winter's day, 24-year-old Li Huiquan returns to his hometown after being released from prison, determined to go straight and begin a new life. However, he finds the town as cold as the weather. None of his relatives is still living, so he is truly alone. Kindly neighbor Mrs. Luo helps Li set up a small business, selling clothing at a street stall, but customers shun him, so-called friends lie to him, and profiteers cheat him. Lonely and fed up with everything around him, Li Huiquan begins spending all his spare time drinking. Then he meets an amateur singer, a pure and lovely girl named Zhao Yaqiu who restores his zest for living for a time. Li idolizes her, and looks forward to escorting her home every night when she gets off work. But as her singing career takes off, she has her pick of boy friends, and quietly drops him. Then Chazi, an old friend from his criminal past, comes to Li's home after escaping from prison. Li lets Chazi stay for a while, but after the escapee leaves Li is racked with despair and anxiety, for despite his vow to go straight he has harbored

Black Snow. **Li Huiquan (Jiang Wen) returns to his hometown after being released from prison on a cold winter day. 1989. Youth Film Studio.**

a fugitive. To calm his fears, Li starts drinking again and decides to confess everything to the police. As he staggers to the police station he is attacked and killed by two teenage hoods.

Best Picture, 1990 Hundred Flowers Awards.

Awarded Silver Bear for Outstanding Individual Achievement, 1990 Berlin International Film Festival.

187. *Black Snow (Hei Xue)*

1992. Beijing Film Studio. Color. Letterboxed. Direction: Li Wenhua, Li Ni, Screenplay: Zhang Yiping, Cinematography: Tu Jiakuan, Art Direction: Chen Xiaoxia, Music: Guo Wenjing, Cast: Shen Junyi as Zhou Tian, Jia Hongsheng as Xu Shanyuan, Zhang Hong as Xiao Cui, Yan Bide as Director Li, Hu Jun as Lu Liang

188. *Black Temptation (Hei Se De You Huo)*

1986. Pearl River Film Studio. Color. 10 Reels. Direction: Ling Qiwei. Screenplay: Ling Qiwei, Peng Yun. Cinematography: Wu Yukun. Art Direction: Tan Ancang. Music: Zhang Hong. Sound: Lin Guang. Cast: Zhang Xiaomin as Huang Qiuli, Du Xiongwen as Lin Kehan, Li Shujun as Sun Li, Li Zhiqiang as Xiao Zhang, Zhang Xiaolin as Tang Yun, Yu Haiyang as Huang Yu

Counterfeit bills turn up at the industrial and commercial bank in the city of Guangzhou. The case is assigned to veteran detective Sun Li and his assistant Xiao Zhang. They track the bogus bills to a counterfeiting ring in Guangdong province. The film traces their dogged investigation, which finally leads them to the head of the ring, Lin Kehan. Before the police can close in, Lin prepares to flee across the border to safety. His girl friend, nightclub singer Huang Qili, realizes she has just been Lin's stooge and he has no intention of taking her when he flees across the border. In her anger and despair she kills Lin and then herself. The police close in, round up the rest of the ring and recover all the bogus currency.

189. *The Black Triangles (Hei San-jiao)*

1977. Beijing Film Studio. Color. 10 Reels. Direction: Liu Chunlin, Chen Fangqian. Screenplay: Li Yinjie. Cinematography: Zhou Jixun, Yun Wenyao. Art Direction: Zhang Jinbiao. Music: Wang Biao. Sound: Zhang Jiake. Cast: Lei Min as Shi Yan, Zhang Ping as Bureau Director Hong, Ling Yuan as Yu Huangshi, Bi Jiancang as Lu Deqin, Liu Jia as Yu Qiulan, Qin Wen as Party Secretary Liu

Enemy spies steal secret information concerning the city of Songbing's "No. 110 defense project." The city's Public Security Bureau intercepts a telegram instructing one of the spies on the route to take to smuggle the information out of China. Chief Inspector Shi Yan and officer Li Hu pursue the spy, Xing Xiang, to the Chinese border. They catch up with and kill Xing, and while it turns out he does not have the stolen information, they do obtain clues pointing to Yu Huangshi, a seemingly innocuous ice cream salesman, as the spymaster. The officers win over Yu Qiulan, the suspect's adopted daughter, and in the end secret document "110" is recovered.

190. *Black 25 (Hei Se 25)*

1992. Changchun Film Studio. Color. Letterboxed. 9 Reels. Direction: Yi Aiqun. Screenplay: Jia Ruo, Sheng Manzhu. Cinematography: Xu Shouzen, Zhan Hongshun. Art Direction: Liu Zhongren, Zhang Hui. Music: Yang yilun. Sound: Cao Feng, Zhang Xiaonan. Costume: Zhang Renchun, Ouyang Chunyu. Makeup: Wang Zhaofeng, Tan Shumei. Cast: Wang Hongwu as Gao Tianye, Shen Junyi as "Wind," Luo Gang as Gao Han, Tian Min as Ma Erjie, Li Jianyi as Sang Zhe

Three years earlier, drug dealer Zong Yanfeng and his sister were involved in a shootout with police, and the sister was killed by officer Gao Tianye. Now, as the 25th of June approaches, Zong's family asks him to kill Gao to avenge their daughter before the police officer

retires. Zong shadows Gao, and decides the officer's greatest vulnerability is his retarded son Gao Han. The drug dealer kidnaps the boy, ties a time bomb to his body, and puts the child in a theater crowded with more than a thousand people. Gao Han is unable to follow police instructions to deactivate the bomb, so to save the lives of the other innocent people in the theater, Gao Tianye shoots his son.

191. *Blackmail (Qing Die)*

1994. Fujian Film Studio. Color. Letterboxed. 9 Reels. Direction: Liu Baolin. Screenplay: Wei Yanqun. Cinematography: Li Ming. Art Direction: Lin Zhixi. Music: Liu Yanxi. Sound: Zhu Wenzhong. Costume: Zang Weimin. Makeup: Zhou Qin. Cast: Li Qiang as Gao Da, Liu Wei as Boss Liao, Ju Xue as Xia Yi, Cao Peixi as Ye Zhi'nu, Er Yang as "Code 137," Xu Zhicheng as Li Guang, Zhou Jianjun as Director Wang, Wei Dong as Xiao Yu, Chen Hong as Xiao Fang

Xia Yi, a scientific researcher in a South China city, makes great strides in her research into magnetic resonance. Her husband Guo Da is an executive for a Chinese company in Hong Kong. One day, Guo Da is visited by a man named Ye, who tells Gao Da that he once had an affair with Gao's wife. Ye works for a foreign government which is very interested in his wife's research, and unless Gao cooperates with him, Ye will inform Chinese security forces of the past affair with a foreign agent. To protect his wife's career, Gao agrees to cooperate with the spy, and after he receives some intelligence training the two men cross into China. The plan is to obtain the information on Xia Yi's current research, then recruit her for future intelligence. At the critical moment, the Chinese PSB intervenes to arrest the spies.

192. *The Blank Letter (Mei You Zi De Xin)*

1981. Changchun Film Studio. Color. 10 Reels. Direction: Li Geng, Bei Zhaocheng. Screenplay: Liu Guohua, Mu Er. Cinematography: Cao Zhuobing. Art Direction: Hu Pei, Zhong Quan. Music: Tian Feng. Sound: Xing Guocang. Cast: Li Tie as Jin Hua, Ma Xiaoqing as the girl, Xiao Zhu as Father, Zhang Guixing as Zhou Laoda, Zhao Yong as Zhiping

Because he finds summer camp too arduous, junior high school student Jin Hua slips away and goes to the port of Yunhai where his father works. When he gets there, his father urges him to return to the camp and participate in their airplane model competition. He gives his son a silver coin with a hole in it and tells Jin Hua he may stop at a few places on the way back, and one should be the home of his Grandma Tie. When Jin Hua arrives at his grandmother's home, she welcomes him warmly and tells him the story behind the coin: Grandpa Tie had been a member of a guerrilla unit during the war, and the coin was used by the guerrillas as a means of identification. On the rest of the way back to camp, Jin Hua has a variety of experiences and learns much from them. Jin Hua's team wins the model airplane competition, his souvenir silver coin giving them inspiration.

193. *Bless the Children (Wei Hai Zi Men Zhu Fu)*

1953. Changjiang, Kunlun Associated Film Company. B & W. 9 Reels. Direction: Zhao Dan. Screenplay: Bao Shi, based on a novel by Qin Zhaoyang. Cinematography: Miao Zhushan and Yao Shiquan. Set Design: Ding Cheng. Music: Chen Gexin, Sound: Li Liehong. Costume: Jin Ke. Makeup: Yao Yongfu. Cast: Huang Zongyin as Wang Min, Wang Longji as Zhang Huaguo, Jiang Tianliu as Zhang's mother, Li Jinkang as Zhao Zengrong, Su Man as a collaborationist supervisor, Xie Yibing as a collaborationist girls' school principal, Qi Mengshi as the principal, Fu Botang as Wei Mazi.

Wang Min, a newly hired woman elementary school teacher, discovers a boy student named Zhang Huaguo crying in class. She learns that before liberation, the child's father was persecuted to death by a landlord and his mother abducted by Wei Mazi, a Nationalist agent. At home, Zhang is mistreated by his stepfather, while everyone at school looks down on him, some of the students bully him and a supervisor accuses him of theft when someone loses something. In his pain, the child becomes increasingly lonely and withdrawn. Shortly afterwards, Zhang's mother exposes Wei's criminal record as an enemy agent, leading to his arrest. After that, the school establishes a Young Pioneers' troop, and through their educational activities such as field trips and group travel, Zhang starts to become brighter and more energetic, which influences some of the former bullies to behave better.

194. *Blood Connection (Qin Yuan)*

1980. Xi'an Film Studio. Color. 10 Reels. Direction: Wu Tianmin, Teng Wenjing. Screenplay: Guo Qilong. Cinematography: Zhu Dingyu, Liu Cangxu. Art Direction: Zhang Zhien. Music: Xu Youfu. Sound: Chen Yudan. Cast: Liu Dong as Xiujuan, Xu Ming as Fang Jie, Li Weixin as Chen Yunxuan

In 1949, as China falls to the Communists, Chen Yunxuan and his pregnant wife prepare to flee to Taiwan with their daughter Xiujuan. But the wife goes into labor unexpectedly, and father and daughter leave alone. Over the years they comfort each other but cannot control the emotion of missing their relatives on the mainland. As an adult, Chen Xiujuan is a member of an oceangoing biological exploration ship. At sea, the ship is attacked by pirates, and Xiujuan escapes by jumping into the ocean. She is rescued by a young man named Fang Jie. He takes her in his boat to a mainland hospital where she is startled to find the mother she was separated from 30 years earlier and the younger brother she had never known. While they enjoy their reunion, mother, daughter and brother all worry about their upcoming separation. At last Xiujuan must return to Taiwan, leaving her mother, brother and Fang Jie, of whom she has become quite fond. Back in Taiwan, she and her elderly father call to her mother across the Taiwan Strait...

195. *Blood for Blood (Yi Xue Huan Xue)*

1991. Changchun Film Studio. Color. Letterboxed. 9 Reels. Direction: Zhang Hui, Screenplay: Xue Shouxian, Xue Cheng, Cinematography: Zhang Changan, Wang Jian, Art Direction: Yang Baocheng, Music: Yang Yilun, Sound: Wang Baosheng, Cast: Lin Qiang, An Zhimin, Gao Qiang, Chen Xiaolei, Song Shuangyue

In the Northeast Chinese city of Jinan in 1928, business tycoon Li Huating and all his family are murdered after Li refuses to sign a statement of support for the Japanese government. A young man who had been engaged to Li's daughter vows to avenge the family, and carries out a one-man campaign against the Japanese.

196. *Blood from Heaven (Tian Chu Xue)*

1991. Shenzhen Film Company. Color. Wide Screen. 9 Reels. Direction: Hou Yong.

Screenplay: Wu Qitai. Art Direction: Li Hong. Music: Zhao Jiping. Sound: Zhao Jun. Cast: Chang Rong as Wen Jiu, Ge Lili as Xiuxiu, Yu Shaokang as Grandpa, Yang Zhaoquan as Uncle 4, Hong Tao as Boss Zhang, Hong Yuzhou as White Face Wolf

197. *Blood in Hong Kong (Xiang Gang Yu Xue)*

1992. Shanghai Film Studio. Color. Letterboxed. 9 Reels. Stereo. Direction: Yao Shoukang. Screenplay: Sun Ganlu, Lan Zhiguang. Cinematography: Yin Fukang. Art Direction: Sun Weide. Music: Pan Guoxing. Sound: Ni Zheng. Costume: Ding Shulan, Zhang Fuzhen. Makeup: Mi Yude, Zhang Zhen. Cast: He Ling as Gai Jianzhong, Xia Jing as Ma Ning, Zhang Kanger as Hong Rongzhen, Wang Weiping as Liang Yincai, Li Ying as Luo Na

Two police detectives, Gai Jianzhong and his female partner Ma Ning, are sent from the mainland to work with drug enforcement authorities in Hong Kong. After they arrive, however, Ma Ning seems to betray the mission: claiming she wants freedom, she goes to drug lord Hong Rongzhen and offers her services. Ma Ning gradually gains Hong's trust, but her former partner Gai Jianzhong is killed in a gun battle. At last, Ma Ning kills the drug lord Hong and fulfills her true, covert mission of destroying the gang from within.

198. *The Blood Is Always Hot (Xue, Zhong Shi Re De)*

1983. Beijing Film Studio. Color. 10 Reels. Direction: Wen Yan. Screenplay: Zong Fuxian, He Guopu. Cinematography: Ru Shiren. Art Direction: Shao Ruigang. Music: Zhang Peiji. Sound: Fu Yinjie. Cast: Yang Zaibao as Luo Xingang, Liu Xingyi as Shen Hua, Yin Xin as Song Qiaozhen, Chen Guodian as Li zhiliang, Jin Kangning as Fang Ying

When Luo Xingang arrives at his new job as manager of a silk printing plant in Jiangnan, he finds the plant's most famous product is now going nowhere on the market. Luo decides the problem has been the past management's stress on filling production quotas at the expense of economic efficiency. His solution is to return to producing handmade silk handkerchiefs for the overseas market. He runs into all sorts of bureaucratic and systematic obstacles from those in the plant who resist change. In the end he is successful and even more determined to carry out reform.

Best Actor Yang Zaibao, 1984 Golden Rooster Awards.

Best Actor Yang Zaibao, 1984 Hundred Flowers Awards.

199. *Blood of the Leopard (aka True Colors of a Hero) (Ying Xiong Ben Se)*

1993. Pearl River Film Studio & Hong Kong Entertainment Film Company Co-Production. Color. Letterboxed. 10 Reels. Direction: Chen Huiyi. Screenplay: Li Jiangkai, from a story in the classic Chinese novel "Shui Hu Zhuan" (All Men Are Brothers, aka Outlaws of the Marsh) by Shi Naian (c1290-c1365). Cinematography: Chen Guanghong. Art Direction: Zhong Yifeng. Music: Hu Weili. Sound: Teyi Recording Studio. Cast: Liang Jiahui (Tony Leung) as Lin Chong, Wang Zuxian (Joey Wang) as Lin's wife, Xu Jingjiang as Lu Zhishen, Liu Qingyun as Chou Wu, Lin Wei as Lu Qian, Wu Ma as the Prime Minister

In the year 965, Gao Qiu's son Gao Yanei is abducted by bandits. Martial arts instructor Lin Chong goes to the bandits and they release the young man out of respect for Lin. But Gao Qiu repays Lin by insulting him at Gao's gala birthday celebration; in addition, Gao Yanei assaults Lin's wife. Monk-turned-greenwoods bandit Lu Zhishen rescues the woman, and he and Lin Chong become sworn blood brothers. Lin declines Lu's invitation to join him as a bandit, however, as he insists on remaining loyal to the imperial court. But the Gaos' persecution of Lin and his wife continue, including framing him for someone else's crime. When Gao Yanei's harassment pushes his wife to suicide, Lin Chong at last rebels.

200. *Blood Rose (Xue Se Mei Gui)*

1993. Changchun Film Studio. Color. Letterboxed. 9 Reels. Direction: Song Jiangbo. Screenplay: Li Jian. Cinematography: Zhang Songping, Ma Weiye. Art Direction: Qi Min, Zhang Ming. Music: Fan Weiqiang. Sound: Jiang Yan. Costume: Ge Junjie. Makeup: Liang Ling, Dan Jing. Cast: Lu Liang as Liu Gang, Song Yining as Feng Xiaoyue, Xia Jing as Gu Xiaolan, Yang Kun as Yu Fang, Zhou Guobing as Xu Zhou, Hu Ronghua as Ertiao, Yu Luosheng as the public security bureau director

One night, chief of detectives Liu Gang leads a raid on a building used for drug transactions. He learns the drugs there came from a man named Shanping. Through Shanping, the trail leads to Gu Xiaolan. At that point, Liu Gang's businesswoman ex-wife enters the case. To obtain her own goals, she sets the detective up. He later finds her murdered. Suspicion begins to point to Liu Gang himself, but he perseveres and smashes the drug organization in his city.

201. *Bloodshed at Dusk (Di Xue Huang Hun)*

1989. Xi'an Film Studio. Color. 9 Reels. Direction: Sun Zhou, Screenplay: Sun Yi'an. Cinematography: Zhao Lei. Art Direction: Dou Guoxiang, Shen Qin. Music: Guo Wenjing. Sound: Gu Changning. Cast: Shen Junyi as Lu Ye, Zhou Min as Lu Yi, Ge Lili as Xi Juan, Liu Xiaoning as Shi Wei

Lu Ye and Xi Juan are a divorced couple but their clever son Lu Yi is working hard to bring them together again. Ex-convict Wei Wenbin kidnaps the boy, thinking he is the son of Lu Jianguo, a local Nike manager who used to be Wei's accomplice. The two boys have the same name, they're best friends and often play together. The search for their son brings Lu Ye and Xi Juan closer. Lu Jianguo wants to make a private deal with Wei to keep his family out of trouble. Lu Ye sets out alone to look for his son, but disrupts the police's plan, and Xi Juan and Wei are killed. Father and son are reunited, but it's now a family without a mother.

202. *Bloodshed at Jialaman (Xue Jian Jia La Man)*

1988. Tianshan Film Studio. Color. Letterboxed. 9 Reels. Direction: Jin Suqi. Screenplay: Fu Bo, Jin Suqi, Zhao Zhiqiang. Cinematography: Zhang Jiwu. Art Direction: Ma Shaoxian. Music: Zhou Ji. Sound: Liu Honggang. Cast: Liu Diankun as Luo Ganzhi, Wang Hua as Zhang Lu, Huang Jiancheng as Li Xiaozhu, Li Xinmin as Liu Shandan, Ge Yi as Chen Guaizhi, Yang Chaocheng as Zhong Weiqiang

When a prison bus is overturned by a mudslide in the Tianshan Mountains, five desperate criminals escape and go on a crime spree. The story tracks their pursuit and eventual recapture by the PSB.

203. *Bloodshed at Luohuapo (Luo Hua Po Qing Chou)*

1991. Tianshan Film Studio. Color. 9 Reels. Letterboxed. Direction: Li Wenhua and Li Ni. Screenplay: Zhao Shunqi and Ke Zhanghe. Cinematography: Tu Jiakuan. Art Direction: Ning Lanxin. Music: Fu Lin. Sound: Chen Binglian and Liu Xiaodong. Cast: Gao Fa as Pei Ying, Huang Guoqiang as Yan Pengwei, Liu Hongmei as Sai Hua, Zhou Zhou as Bai Fei, Wang Wensheng as Xing Rulong, Guo Yulin as Ji Zhongliang.

During the 11th Century, women in one area are terrorized by a series of rape-murders. The perpetrator calls himself the "Mist Stalker." To get rid of this villain, itinerant hero Pei Ying comes to the area, where he meets his old friend Yan Pengwei and their mutual friend Xing Rulong. The three work together and catch the culprit. But not long after their captive is executed, the killings start again. By some brilliant detection, Pei Ying gets to the bottom of the matter when he learns that Yan is the son of Ji Zhongliang, master of the Zhenshan Martial Arts Academy, from whom he became estranged 20 years before. Yan fell in with bad elements and in time became the real Mist Stalker. Suddenly, old friends become enemies. At Luohuapo, the climactic battle begins between justice and evil…

204. *Bloodshed at Widow Village (Xue Ran Tao Hua Shui)*

1993. Changchun Film Studio. Color. Letterboxed. 9 Reels. Direction: Lei Xianhe, Zhao Lijun. Screenplay: Shao Hongda, Wang Yizhuo. Cinematography: Meng Xiandi, Wun Jiwu. Art Direction: Liu Huanxing. Music: Zou Ye. Sound: Cao Feng, Zhang Xiaonan. Costume: Zhang Xiaodong, Zhang Renchun. Makeup: Wang Keguang, Tan Shumei. Cast: Yu Hui as A Suya, Zhao Hengxuan as Lei Zhenshan, Zhang Guangbei as Lao Da, Yu Xiaohui as Zhuo Luowa, Bai Dezhang as Jiangda Mazang, Xie Lan as Aunt Xiu

A village deep in the snow-covered Xiaoxingyan Mountains is called Widow Village because all the male inhabitants were killed during World War II. The town has recovered some since then, and now Asuya, the fiancee of the present village chief, leads a group searching for a cache of gold believed hidden somewhere in the mountains by the Japanese. Bandit chieftain Jiang, also after the gold, sends his scout Ada to the village to find a map to where the gold is hidden. They wage a constant running battle over the gold, and at last Ada, Jiang and Asuya are all killed.

205. *Bloodshed in a Remote Place (Xue Sha Tian Ya)*

1988. Pearl River Film Studio. Color. Letterboxed. 9 Reels. Direction: Xing Jitian, Wang Wei. Screenplay: Shi Biao. Cinematography: Han Dongxia. Art Direction: Li Xin, Wang Jiufang. Music: Zhang Jielin. Sound: Lu Minwen. Cast: Hong Tao as Xu Yuan, Wang Lisha as Wang Qingfeng, Xu Zhaoyang as Yang Guanyu

After betraying his commander, anti-Qing General Zhang Huangyan, to the Qing government, Xu Yuan disguises himself as a monk and hides at a temple on Mount Putao. Learning that General Zhang is hiding on a nearby island, he goes to the island to seek a chance to capture the general and turn him over to the government. Xu succeeds in taking Zhang Huangyan captive, but two of Zhang's companions, his student Wang Qingfeng and his servant Yang Guanyi, are rescued by anti-Qing warrior Shi Bing. Shi Bing and Wang Qingfeng attack Xu Yan on the road, and a bloody battle ensues. Shi Bing is killed, but before he dies he tells Wang Qingfeng to seek help from a man named Luo, a hermit warrior on Mount Hengshan. Wang Qingfeng goes through many hardships to get to Mount Hengshan, and his dedication at last moves Luo to help. Luo fights Xu Yuan and forces him into flight and at last suicide.

206. *Bloodshed on the Yellow Desert (Xue Ji Huang Sha Zhen)*

1993. Nanhai Film Company. Color. Letterboxed. 9 Reels. Direction: Liu Guoquan. Screenplay: Yu Yonghe, Wu Bing, Liu Yiran. Cinematography: Li Dawei, Lin Jinggang. Art Direction: Zhang Yafang. Sound: Wang Yingang. Costume: Yi Shenglin, Dai Lingling. Makeup: Zhao Zhiming. Cast: Zhou Lijing as Wang Xiaotian, Sun Song as Ma Yijian, Wang Hong as Hua Erhong, Hao Yan as Ma Feihong, Jiang Gengcheng as Ma Tianba, Yu Ping as the West Nurse, Xu Yuanqi as Yang Zhenyuan

A town on the Yellow Desert is run with an iron fist by despot Ma Tianba. When local businessman Yang Zhenyuan dares to stand up to him, Ma kills Yang and his two employees, Li and Wang. Then, having no children of his own, Ma adopts Yang's small son and Li's daughter and renames them Ma Yijian and Ma Feihong, respectively. More than a decade later, the two young people are totally under Ma Tianba's control. One day, two strangers come to town. They turn out to be the son of the murdered Wang and the daughter of Yang Zhenyuan, seeking to avenge their fathers. At last, Ma Feihong learns the truth of her background, and helps the two newcomers kill the evil Ma Tianba.

207. *The Bloodstained Screen (Xue Jian Hua Ping)*

1986. Xi'an Film Studio. Color. 10 Reels. Direction: Zhang Qicang. Screenplay: Shao Licheng and Zhang Qicang, based on the novel "The Lacquer Screen" by Robert van Gulik (1910-1967). Cinematography: Ma Shusheng. Art Direction: Hu Qiangsheng and Li Yongqi. Music: Han Zhongcai. Sound: Xiong Huajuan. Cast: Sun Chongliang as Di Renjie, Wun Qian as Teng Kan, Zhang Jiumei as Yanxiang, Wang Wensheng as Qiao Tai, Wang Shuqing as Lady Ke, Dong Shaoming as Xiao Liang

Two apparently unrelated tragedies occur on the same night: the wife of Yunzhou City official Teng Kan is raped and murdered, and a local silk merchant drowns himself in the river. Pengcheng County magistrate Di Renjie happens to be passing through the area, and is troubled by Teng Kan's handling of these cases, which leave too many questions unanswered. Judge Di conducts his own investigation and proves that Teng was the perpetrator of a double murder.

208. *A Blood-Stained Sword (Bi Xue Bao Dao)*

1991. Beijing Film Studio. Color. 9 Reels. Direction: Yang Qitian. Screenplay: Meng Zhu, Xia Gang. Cinematography: Li Shen. Art Direction: Yu Yiru, Yang Baigui. Music: Meng Xianbing. Sound: Ke Hu, Lan Fan. Cast: Zhao Changjun as Qiu Wenhuan, Li Yan as Gen Chunxiong, Xia as Peony, Hou Yueqiu as Black Zhang

During the Qing dynasty, the Emperor Daoguang is angered with his highest ranking concubine, and orders imperial guard Wang Debao to kill her with the emperor's own sword. Daoguang later regrets his rash decision and banishes Wang and the sword from the court to a remote part of China. Meanwhile, martial arts master Zhen Luoyang takes his favorite disciple Qiu Wenhuan to pursue and apprehend a lecher preying on local women, only to be killed himself. To avenge his master, Qiu sets out to find Wang Debao and his legendary sword, believed to be magic. With the help of itinerant hero Black Zhang, he finally locates Wang. Wang tells Qiu there is no sword that can cut iron like clay. He says the skill lies in the swordsman. He gives Qiu the imperial sword sent by the emperor to kill the concubine and teaches him the "gale-force sword technique." Using his superb martial arts, Qiu finally kills the lecher with the sword, rids the people of an evil and avenges his master's death.

209. *Bloody Autumn at Wind Palace (Xue Jian Qiu Feng Liu)*

1989. Changchun Film Studio. Color. Letterboxed. 10 Reels. Direction: Xu Shutian. Screenplay: Yuan Lang. Cinematography: Meng Xiandi. Art Direction: Tian Feng. Music: Chen Shouqian. Sound: Fu Linge, Jiang Yan. Cast: Wang Chunyuan as Bentian, Zhang Qiqing as Yiteng, Zhongjie as Meiyu, Li Baocheng as Li Tietou, Wang Zhicheng as Xiao Langjiao, Zhang Jibo as Yun Zhongyan, Wang Yan as Qiong Yu.

Japanese army officer Yiteng brings karate expert Bentian from Japan to challenge Chinese kongfu fighters in Shandong Province. The challenge is that if a Chinese can win in a one-on-one match, they can pull down the Japanese Rising Sun flag which flies over Wind Palace, the Japanese headquarters. A man named Yun Zhongyan accepts the challenge, and three other kongfu fighters help him train for the match: Xiao Langjiao, Meiyu and Qiongyu, the latter two of them women. Yun Zhongyan defeats Bentian, but is shot to death when he attempts to claim the flag. Yiteng lusts for Qiongyu, and has her persecuted when she rejects him. She is arrested, but Xiao Langjiao and Meiyu rescue her and take revenge on the Japanese for Yun's death and Qiongyu's mistreatment. At last, Meiyu decides to become a nun, while Xiao Langjiao and the badly injured Qiongyu flee the area.

210. *Bloody Battle at Jialing River (Die Xue Jia Ling Jiang)*

1992. Emei Film Studio. Color. Letterboxed. 9 Reels. Direction: Xue Yandong, Huang Lijia. Screenplay: Zhao Xuebing. Cinematography: Liu Jiankui, Liu Taitian. Art Direction: Lu Qi. Music: Yang Yilun. Sound: Liao Yongliang. Costume: Liu Changxiu, Li Xuehong. Makeup: Niu Yongling, Liao Yongguang. Cast: Xu Ling as Wu Ling, Liu Pei as Wu Pei, Huang Xiaoying as Liu Zhen, Zhang Xin as An Jing, Pao Bei as Mo Ruide, Jiang Yishou as Xiao Chun

A traitor's betrayal leads to Wu Pei's mother and fiancé being killed by the Japanese.

Wu Pei and her sister Wu Ling kill the traitor, but are then captured by the enemy. Three years later, Wu Ling's husband is a Chinese intelligence agent in Chongqing (Chungking) working with the U.S. Air Force. Word arrives that the Japanese have devised a strategy to sabotage all American aircraft, and a spy has been sent out from Hong Kong to carry out the plan.

211. *Bloody Battle at Kunlun Pass (Tie Xue Kun Lun Guan)*

1994. Guangxi Film Studio. Color. Wide Screen. 14 Reels. Direction: Yang Guangyuan. Screenplay: Wang Tianyun, Li Jianchen, based on the novel "The Soul of Kunlun Pass" by Chen Dunde. Cinematography: Liu Baogui. Art Direction: Chen Yaogong, Lei Xiaolan. Music: Zhao Jiping. Sound: Lin Lin, Ma Ting. Costume: Yang Zhenhai. Makeup: Yang Shuoling, He Hong, Shen Yueying. Cast: Gao Zhang as Dong Yanguan, Liu Dawei as Tian Shiyuan, Tan Feng as Li Aniu, Liu Yingtao as Du Zhaoming, Zhen Yu as Dai Anlan

In 1939, at the most difficult time for China in its resistance of the Japanese invaders, the Japanese attack pushes into South China and directly menace the wartime capital of Chongqing. China's First Mechanized Military Division under General Du Zhaoming and the Guilin troops of Bai Chongxi amass a force of 150,000 into the battle of Kunlunguan. With additional support from the local people, the Chinese turn back the Japanese attack in January of 1940, after a battle which cost the Chinese over 10,000 men. From that point on, the Chinese anti-Japanese war enters a new period of stalemate.

212. *Bloody Battle in a Border Town (Yu Xue Jiang Cheng)*

1990. Inner Mongolia Film Studio. Color. Wide Screen. 10 Reels. Direction: Abuer. Screenplay: Cheng Zhong. Cinematography: Narisu, Zhao Ping. Art Direction: Du Changshun. Music: Moer Jihu. Sound: Bu Ren. Cast: Lu Yi as Huang Laopiao, Chen Yi as Feng Ya, Ma Shixiang as Yan Sipeng

In the early days of China's anti-Japanese war, General Fu Zuoyi allocates a supply of weapons for shipment to the Chinese 526th Regiment in Inner Mongolia. A corrupt county official involved in drug trafficking puts a shipment of drugs in with weapons, so the army will unknowingly transport the drugs for him. On the road, bandit Huang Laopiao intercepts the shipment, and finds the drugs in with the guns. In time, Communist guerrillas get involved, and appeal to Huang to turn in the drugs and weapons. Responding to patriotic appeals, Huang decides to help the Chinese war effort. When 526th Regiment commander Yan Sipeng commits to holding out until the end against the Japanese, Huang Laopiao comes with the guerrillas to help. The bandit dies a hero.

213. *The Bloody Battle of Taierzhuang (Xue Zhan Tai Er Zhuang)*

1986. Guangxi Film Studio. Color. 14 Reels. Direction: Yang Guangyuan, Zhai Junjie. Screenplay: Tian Junli, Huang Linjun. Cinematography: Ju Feng, Lei Jiaming. Art Direction: Wu Zhaohua, Chen Yaogong. Music: Su Tie. Sound: Han Weijun, Li Zhuwen. Makeup: Yan Bijun, Zhao Zhiming. Cast: Shao Honglai as Li Zongren, Jiang Hualing as Chi Fengcheng, Zhai Junjie as Wang Mingzhang, Zhao Hengduo as Chiang Kaishek, Zhang Mingyu as Tang Enbo, Ge Yamin as Zhang Jingbo, Qi Chunxiang as Han Fuqu, Li Jingye as Pang Bingbiao

In 1938, the Japanese army pushes further into east China, with the city of Suzhou their obvious goal. To the Chinese army, the Japanese must be stopped at all costs to prevent a repetition of the previous year's "Rape of Nanking," with similar devastation and slaughter in Suzhou, a city beloved by the Chinese people for its scenic beauty and cultural significance. The Nationalist army commanders determine to make a stand at Taierzhuang, a village that stands as the gateway to Suzhou. Told in semi-documentary style, the movie traces the historical events leading up to the battle, and the battle itself. In the end, the seemingly invincible Japanese army was stopped, forcing its high command to change its strategy. More than 10,000 of the invaders were killed in the Chinese victory, but at a fearsome cost to the victors.

Best Screenplay Tian Junli and Jia Linjun, 1987 Golden Rooster Awards.

Best Makeup Yan Bijun and Zhao Zhiming, 1987 Golden Rooster Awards.

214. *Bloody Dust (Ru Xue Huang Hun)*

1995. Changchun Film Studio. Color. Letter-boxed. Direction: Cheng Ke. Screenplay: Du Lijuan. Cinematography: Gao Hongbao. Art Direction: Zhu Jiaxin. Music: Yang Yilun. Cast: Xu Yang as Ying Chan, An Yaping as Qiu Jian, Ge Yunping as Huang Yishan, Guan Xiwei as Jiang Linda, Zhao Fan as Huang Zhongde, Liu Fan as Liu Suxian

In the 1930s, after her father is killed, pretty young Yingchan goes to live with the wealthy and powerful family of her aunt Liu Suxian. Liu's daughter Huang Yishan is very jealous of Yingchan's beauty, and well she might be, as Yishan's husband Jiang Linda lusts for the newcomer. One day, Jiang seduces young Yingchan and gets her pregnant. Liu Suxian's husband Master Huang wants to sell Yingchan while Jiang Linda, driven by his ambitious wife, wants to replace Master Huang as master of the mansion. Before she can be sold, however, a young worker on the family's estate takes Yangchan away. Many years later, her daughter Taoer is 15 years old, and Jiang Dalin controls the family mansion and money. He sends one of his men, Ashan, to abduct Taoer. His unexpected motive is to acknowledge his daughter and raise her as the eventual heiress to the family fortune. But while she is happy for her daughter, Yingchan never forgets her personal grudge against Jiang. When she is finally in a position to save his life, she lets him die, despite Taoer's pleas.

215. *Bloody Fight on Tianshi (Xue Zhan Tian Shi Hao)*

1991. Youth Film Studio and Pearl River Film Studio. Color. Letterboxed. 9 Reels. Direction: Wang Hengli. Screenplay: Wang Hengli and Wang Rui. Cinematography: Zhang Guoqing. Art Direction: Song Qiang. Music: Fang Xiaomin. Sound: Liu Haiyan. Cast: Liao Jingsheng as Li Zhen, Xu Ling as Lin Yuer, Wang Ping as Li Zhilong, Xu An as Gao Yehan, Li Yongtian as Zhou Zhifang, Wang Yunting as Jian Yingliang, Liu Yan as the PSB Director, Cao Zhong as He Li, Jiang Wei as Puladuo, Shang Baolin as Shi Tianlong

International drug enforcement authorities inform China that a cargo ship will soon be arriving at a Chinese port from Macao, carrying a huge quantity of drugs. Meanwhile, the PSB learns that someone has targeted woman ship owner Lin Yuer for assassination. Lin's parents had been killed more than a decade ago by drug kingpin Jian Yingliang, who then took their ship to make his drug deliveries. Lin wants to implicate Jian in the present drug shipment in order to avenge her parents, so she works with the Chinese police. After a series of battles, the drug dealers are killed or captured, and Jian Yingliang is put on trial in Macao.

216. *Bloody Gambling Hell (Sheng Si Du Men)*

1992. Emei Film Studio. Color. Letterboxed. 9 Reels. Direction: Li Xian. Screenplay: Li Xian, He Yulan, based on Lin Xi's original novel. Cinematography: Luo Xun. Art Direction: Lin Qi. Music: Duan Yongsheng. Sound: Lin Guang. Costume: Cai Peiqiong, Xie Huizhen. Makeup: He Ziyun, Zhao Liyang. Cast: Lei han as Hou Xuemeng, Yang Chiyu as Hou Qinyu, Qu Guoqiang as Ma Zhanshan, Liu Deyi as Wu Taizhi, Zhang He as Hou Xuekong

In pre-liberation Tianjin, three friends, Hou, Meng and Wu grow up together. After they reach adulthood, Meng becomes addicted to gambling, and is financially ruined. He asks Hou to adopt his son, then commits suicide. Twenty years later, Hou is the wealthy owner of a gambling hall, but when he finds his own son addicted to gambling, he drives him out of his home. The adopted son then takes over management of the hall. Wu has saved a good deal of money over the years, but loses it all gambling. He instigates trouble between Hou and his adopted son, which results in the son losing everything. When the elder Hou realizes his old friend's trickery, he kills Wu and then takes his own life.

217. *Bloody Poppy Flower (Lie Xue Ying Shu Hua)*

1993. Pearl River Film Studio. Color. Letterboxed. 9 Reels. Direction: Wang Lianping. Screenplay: Liang Husheng. Cinematography: Zhang Fengquan, Ning Jiashen. Art Direction: Xu Shaojun. Music: Cheng Dazhao, Shen Nalin. Sound: Liu Haiyan, Zhang Handong. Costume: Fu Ping. Makeup: Wang Yuanjian. Cast: Zhao Yang as Chou Fei, Liu Yi as Long Xinru, Guao Jianguo as He Mangzi, Cui Xiaoping as Yu Zikui, Wu Dongming as Long Haiqing, Chen Aiyu as Hui Hong

In Heiniu, a small town on China's southwestern border, the farmers' principal crop is opium. Chou, the town's lone police officer, argues that this an evil, and tries to have the practice banned. When he seems to be having some effect, a local drug gang kills him. Years later, his son Chou Fei grows up to become the town's mayor. Like his father before him, he also advocates stamping out opium, with the same tragic outcome.

218. *Bloody Red Carriage (Yu Xue Hong Ma Che)*

1991. Youth Film Studio. Color. 9 Reels. Direction: Sun Sha. Screenplay: Zhu Zi. Cinematography: Meng Xiandi. Art Direction: Yang Yucheng. Sound: Yang Qun. Costume: Qi Chunzhi, Li Lei. Makeup: Ji Weihua, Wang Zhaofeng. Cast: Jing Gangshan as Gu Jie, Zhang Jing as Guan Bao, Fan Zhaiqi as Wang Zilong, Dongfang Wenying as Jiyong Meihuizi, Li Xida as the mute, Wang Runshen as Ouyang Qun, Zhang Lin as Hu Lian

In Northeast China during World War II, young student Gu Jian is forced to witness his brother being killed by the Japanese. Before his death, the brother passes on to Gu Jian a package of drugs which he says is evidence the Japanese are trafficking drugs in China. Gu Jian flees for his life with the drugs, and with the help of the Communist underground and patriotic guerrillas, he finally succeeds in blowing up a warehouse in which the Japanese have stored both drugs and weapons.

219. *Bloody Soul (Xue Hun)*

1988. Emei Film Studio. Color. Letterboxed. 9 Reels. Direction: Wang Jixing. Screenplay: Liu Ping, Ji Wen. Cinematography: Li Dagui. Art Direction: Xie Huibing. Music: Ao Cangqun. Sound: Wang Guangzhong. Cast: Zhang Fengyi as Baibing, Sun Ming as Xue Fei

In the fall of 1948, the Nationalist government implements its secret "Project 07," against Communists in southwest China. To counter this move, CPC headquarters sends veteran officer Bai Bing and communications specialist Xue Fei to the area to contact Red guerrillas there. They are captured, however, and sent to Nationalist headquarters for interrogation. On the way there, their driver kills the guards escorting them. He introduces himself as an undercover CPC liaison, and takes Bai Bing and Xue Fei to guerrilla headquarters. Once they are there, a series of suspicious occurrences casts a cloud of suspicion over Bai Bing. He flees guerrilla headquarters and goes to enemy intelligence to obtain the documents describing "Project 07." He succeeds in this mission, and in doing so unmasks Xue Fei as the real traitor.

220. *The Bloody Tablet (Xue Bei)*

1964. Tianma Film Studio. B & W. 10 Reels. Direction: Gao Heng. Screenplay: collectively written, recorded by Li Hongxin, and based on the opera "Yang Libei." Cinematography: Cao Weiye. Art Direction: Wang Yuebai. Music: Ji Ming. Sound: Wu Hua. Cast: Wei Heling as Lin Youshan, Shangguan Yunzhu as Lin Youshan's wife, Zhen Jiasheng as Lin Zhigang, Wu Yewen as Juying, Li Baoluo as Old Wang, Liang Ming as Grandma Jiang, Mu Hong as Wu Zhancheng, Han Fei as Wu Tianbao

In the 1930, in mountainous western Zhejiang province, poor tenant farmer Lin Youshan works a small piece of government-owned land. After three years of hard work, the government grants him ownership of the land, but landlord Wu Zhancheng's son Wu Tianbao wants it for himself. When Lin and his wife oppose his efforts to take over their land, Wu has thugs attack their farm, destroying their crops and their ownership certificate. In the fight, the Lins' baby is killed. Putting his trust in the Nationalist government, Lin goes to the local court but is himself jailed. Lin's wife goes to the provincial court, but Wu has her murdered. When Lin is released from jail he returns home to find his wife dead and his son Zhigang evicted from their home. Lin's daughter Juying travels to Nanjing to petition the national court, but is forcibly committed to an asylum. Ten years later, Lin returns to his hometown and sets up a stone tablet on which he records the entire affair, so that future generations will know what happened. He then commits suicide by hurling himself against the tablet. In 1949, Lin Youshan's hometown is liberated. His son Lin Zhigang, now a PLA soldier, returns and has landlord Wu Tianbao put on public trial. The injustices to Lin Youshan are finally avenged.

221. *Bloody Wine Erdek (E De Ke Xue Jiu)*

1992. Changchun Film Studio. Color. Letterboxed. 9 Reels. Direction: Zhou Wei, Zhao Lijun. Screenplay: Liang Guowei. Cinematography: Zhong Wenmin, Yang Kai. Art Direction: Li Baoshu. Music: Wang Meng. Sound: Zeng Feng, Zhang Xiaonan. Costume: Wang Chunfeng, Guo Xiuying. Makeup: Wang Keguang, Hanyi. Cast: Li Dongbing as Liu Hanwu, Xin Ying as Lin Cuiyun, Hou Zhengmu as Sun Deshun, Xie Yan as Wang Fengju

In 1940, in the Northeast China city of Harbin, Volunteer Army soldier Liu Hanwu sneaks into the city to obtain medical supplies donated by an international aid society for Chinese war relief. When he arrives at the rendezvous point, however, he finds his contact has been murdered by a Japanese agent. Liu kills the Japanese, and sets off a cross-city chase involving spies, Japanese soldiers and Chinese collaborators. In the end, Liu secures the supplies and returns to his army unit.

222. *Blooming Flowers and a Full Moon (Hua Hao Yue Yuan)*

1958. Changchun Film Studio. Color. 11 Reels. Direction: Guo Wei. Screenplay: Guo Wei, based on the novel, "Three Mile Bend" by Zhao Shuli (1905–) Cinematography: Ge Weiqin. Art Direction: Wang Xingwen. Music: Lei Zhenbang. Sound: Shen Guli. Cast: Wang Qiuyin as Fan Denggao, Qing Han as Wang Yusheng, Wang Jingfang as Wang Jinsheng, Xu Liankai as Zhang Leyi, Guo Jun as Little Confusion, Kuo Ke as Chang Youli, Yang Qitian as Ma Youyi, Tian Hua as Fan Linzhi, Chen Lin as Wang Yumei.

During the transition from mutual assistance groups to communization, a north China village called Three Mile Bend plans to dig a canal and expand the village commune. The Party branch secretary directs village head Fan Denggao to encourage prosperous farmer "Little Confusion" to turn his family's inherited land over to the commune. Fan refuses to do so, as he still adheres to the idea of people seeking individual wealth. Fan Denggao's daughter Linzhi and Little Confusion's son Youyi, the village's only two high school students, loathe their reactionary families. But while Linzhi, an avid Communist Youth League member, argues with her father about this and his plans to marry her to someone other than Yusheng, the boy she loves, Youyi is weak and backs down before his strong-willed father on everything. The story continues this line as the background for the two young people's differing love stories. Finally, with the help of Yumei, the girl he loves, Youyi stands up to his father, rejects the marriage his parents have arranged for him, gives his own land to the commune and urges his family to join. Through the young people's efforts, Three Mile Bend digs its canal and expands the commune as planned. All the young people of the village are allowed to marry whomever they choose.

223. *Blossoms Bloom and Fall (Hua Kai Hua Luo)*

1980. Changchun Film Studio. Color. 9 Reels. Direction: Sun Yu. Screenplay: Xiao Yixian, Sun Yu. Cinematography: Han Dongxia. Art Direction: Liu Jinnai. Music: Zhang Junqin. Sound: Chen Wenyuan. Cast: Lin Qiang as Luo Xiaoshan, Zhao Fengxia as Liu Huiling, Xu Meina as Kang Xiuyun, Wei Bingzhe as Kang Shourong, Zheng Hua as Liu Shan, Zhang Baishang as Zhen Yonghong

Young farmer Luo Xiaoshan bears a heavy class burden: his father had been a landlord in the old days. He comes to the village of Yanluo Tan, hoping he can find a suitable wife there. Liu Huiling, daughter of rich farmer Liu San, feels that her class status is unfavorable, and hopes to change it by marrying into a better class family. She hopes to marry Kang Wenbing, son of the village's Party secretary, but Kang's family will not accept someone who comes from a background like hers. Luo Xiaoshan works hard in Yanlou Tan, and Liu soon becomes interested in him even though he is poor and she is unaware of his class background. They fall in love, and even after Liu learns the young man's father had been a landlord she still finds him suitable. For political reasons, they are unable to marry, and two years later, Luo Xiaoshan is still a single man. One day, a mountain flood sweeps a girl into the river, and Luo saves her life even though he cannot swim. This heroic action impresses the Party secretary's daughter Kang Xiuyun, and she sets her sights on Xiaoshan. They fall in love, but Kang Xiuyun's father Kang Shourong will not allow his daughter to get involved with Luo Xiaoshan. He announces that Luo Xiaoshan is not welcome in Yanluo Tan. Luo Xiaoshan leaves angrily, and Kang Xiuyun goes chasing after him.

224. *The Blue Dossier (Lan Se Dang An)*

1980. Shanghai Film Studio. Color. 10 Reels. Direction: Liang Tingduo. Screenplay: Hua Yongzheng, Meng Shenghui, Shi Yong. Cinematography: Chen Ling, Cai Guangeng. Art Direction: Li Jinggui, Zhen Changfu. Music: Yang Mao. Sound: Lin Bingsheng. Cast: Xiang Mei as Shen Yaqi, Liang Boluo as Li Hua, Tang Ke as Wang Zhou, Li Wei as Zhao Kang, Shen Guangwei as Wang Zhankui, Feng Qi as Gang Tian, Yu Fei as Tang Muxun

The time is 1948, in an area of Northeast China still controlled by the Nationalists. Prior to the Japanese surrender, a spy for the Japanese named Gang Tian had compiled a "blue dossier" which was a list of spies who would stay in China for the long term. The Nationalist government in Nanjing orders local military intelligence chiefs Wang Zhou and Zhao Kang to get this dossier. US intelligence is anxious to obtain it as well, and arranges for one of their own spies, Tang Muxun, to work as a secretary to Zhao Kang. The Communist Party assigns female agent Shen Yaqi to infiltrate enemy headquarters and get the blue dossier. She struggles with the various foes, and with the help of her assistant Li Hua, under cover as a bank officer, finally obtains the real blue dossier. But Zhao Kang learns her identity and sends troops to pursue her. At the critical moment, Shen Yaqi lets her colleague take the blue dossier, while she leads the enemy to a dead end cliff, sacrificing herself.

225. *Blue Evil (Lan Sha Xing)*

1989. Xi'an Film Studio. Color. 9 Reels. Direction: Li Yucai. Screenplay: Gao Jianjun. Cinematographer: Feng Wei. Art Direction: Yan Pingxiao. Music: Tao Long. Sound: Gu Changning. Cast: Chen Xi as Wang Zhichuan, Xu Huanshan as Zhao Yinglong, Zhi Yitong as Chen Mingjiang, Gan Yingsa as the mysterious nurse.

In a Southeast Asian city, banker Wang Zhichuan receives a threatening letter informing him his entire family will be killed as revenge for something that happened 30 years before. Wang is totally in the dark as to the cause, but his family members begin to die one by one, and even private detective Zhao Yinglong is unable to stop it. Another private detective, Chen Mingjiang, digs back into the past and concludes that 30 years ago, Wang Zhichuan's father killed a man and his wife, but their small son and daughter survived. Now adults, the brother and sister are avenging their parents. When the killers are trapped, they commit suicide.

226. *Blue Flower (Lan Se De Hua)*

1984. Beijing Film Studio. Color. 10 Reels. Direction: Shui Hua, Ma Bingyu. Screenplay: Li Guowen, Feng Jifu, Wang Baoshan. Cinematography: Zhou Jixun. Art Direction: Yang Yuhe, Fu Delin. Music: Qin Yongcheng, Li Lifu. Sound: Chen Yanxi. Cast: Guo Kaiming as Yi Ru, Shen Danping as Niuniu, Li Rentang as Bi Jing, Su Zhen as Old Mrs. Zhao

During wartime, young Eighth Route Army soldier Yi Ru meets a country girl named Niuniu, and they become lovers. After the founding of the PRC, Yi Ru becomes a provincial newspaper reporter, Niuniu is employed in agrarian reform, and the two are finally married. Later, Yi Ru is falsely labeled as a rightist and sent to work in the harsh environment of West China's Qinghai province. In order to protect Niuniu and their baby daughter, Yi Ru says goodbye to them and severs all connections with his family members. Twenty-two years later, the Party corrects the mislabeling of many, including Yi Ru, and he anxiously returns to his hometown in hopes of reuniting with Niuniu. He worries about what reception lies ahead, but he finds Niuniu and their daughter waiting for him.

227. *The Blue Kite (Lan Feng Zheng)*

1993. Hong Kong Longwick, Beijing Film Studio Co-Production. Color. 139 minutes. Direction: Tian Zhuangzhuang. Screenplay: Xiao Mao. Cinematography: Hou Yang. Art Direction: Zhang Xiande. Music: Yoshihide Otomo. Sound (Dolby): Wu Ling and Yoshiaki Kondo. Cast: Yi Tian as Tietou (as an adolescent), Lu Liping as Mama (Chen Shujuan), Li Xuejian as Dad (Lin Shaolong) and as Uncle Li (Li Guodong), Guo Baochang as Stepfather, Zhong Ping as Chen Shusheng, Chu Quanzhong as Chen Shuyuan, Song Xiaoying as Sister, Zhang Hong as Zhu Ying, Liu Yanjin as Shuyuan's mother, Li Bin as Grandma, Yi Tian as Tietou (as an infant), Zhang Wenyao as Tietou (as a child), Lu Zhong as Mrs. Lau, Guo Donglin as Liu Yunwei, Wu Shumin as the Street Committee Officer, Zhang Fengyi as a street performer.

In Beijing in 1953, librarian Lin Shaolong and his bride, teacher Chen Shujuan, move into a home they share with some of her family. Not long afterwards, they have a baby son, Tietou. The backlash from the Hundred Flowers campaign of 1957 results in a demand for political scapegoats, and Shaolong is the one sacrificed by his library colleagues. He is sent to a labor camp in the forests, and the rigorous life soon leads to his death. A family friend, Li Guodong, cares for Shujuan and her son, and in a few years he marries the widow, although he is not in very good health. Before long, he also dies. Shujuan marries for a third time, to an older man with good Party connections. Tietou, now a teenager, resents his new step-father, although the latter is very patient with the rebellious youth. One evening the stepfather calls the family together and explains the arrangements he has made for their care during the dark years of chaos he knows are coming, a time when his Party connections will not help them. The Cultural Revolution begins in 1966, and suddenly Tietou finds himself on his own, his life changed again by still another political campaign.

Tokyo Film Festival, 1994: Grand Prix Award.

228. *Blue Love (Lan Se De Ai)*

1986. Changchun Film Studio. Color. 9 Reels. Direction: Xu Shutian. Screenplay: Wang Shicang, Zhao Xishun. Cinematography: Dansheng Nima. Art Direction: Liu Sheng. Music: Yang Yang. Sound: Fu Linge. Cast: Liang Tongyu as Ouyang Juntao, Guan Shouyi as Feng Wei, Li Qiulun as Lin Xiaobing, Zhang Yanli as Xu Liping

Ouyang Juntao is the captain of naval warship No. 1101. In his spare time he writes poetry about the sea which his sailors urge be set to music. Through an advertisement he locates a composer, a female college graduate named Lin Xiaobing. Working by correspondence, she composes music for all of his poems. In time they meet, and fall in love. But Ouyang decides they have no future together because of his sea-going lifestyle. He does not realize that she has loved the navy from childhood, when a sailor sacrificed his own life to rescue her father. The two lovers at last work it out.

229. *Blue Ocean Bay (Lan Se De Hai Wan)*

1978. Xi'an Film Studio. Color. 11 Reels. Direction: Yan Xuezhe, Ai Shui. Screenplay: Wu Yingxun, Zhou Minzheng. Cinematography: Zhang Faliang, Chen Wancai. Art Direction: Zhang Zhien, Hu Qiangsheng. Music: Li Yaodong. Sound: Hong Jiahui. Cast: Xin Jing as Ling Yong, Cao Jingyang as Wen Minhong, Wang Yixiang as Chief Engineer Du, Chen Minggao as Liao Chuyang, Chen Xingzhong as Chen Jinwang, Di Xin as Mama Ling, Zhi Yitong as Zhen Shikui.

In 1974, following Premier Zhou Enlai's instructions, Langwan port construction site chief commander Ling Yong and his workers build two 10,000-ton class ports. Officer Manager Wen Minhong tries to hamper port construction by attacking deputy commander Liao

Chuyang. He is helped in this by Zhen Shikui, editor-in-chief of a major newspaper and follower of the "Gang of Four." When Ling Yong resists the conspiracy, Zhen tries to have him killed. But just at that time, Ling Yong is called to Beijing, where he meets Premier Zhou. When Ling Yong returns, he reports to everyone the good news of Premier Zhou's speech at the Fourth People's Congress.

230. *Blue Shield Strongbox (Lan Dun Bao Xian Xiang)*

1983. Nanjing Film Studio. Color. 9 Reels. Direction: Luo Guanqun, Qiu Zhongyi. Screenplay: Xie Guangning, Yu Yuxing. Cinematography: Wang Ruobai, Zhang Pingqiang. Art Direction: Guo Dongcang, Liu Jiajing, Xiao Feng. Music: Xu Jingxin, Liu Yanxi. Sound: Qian Youshan. Cast: Ma Cangyu as Lu Hong, Chen Xu as Pang Chaoli, Wang Qingbao as Jin Mei, Hua Yin as Ding Rui, Zhang Yunian as Xiao Lin

Shortly after the Communists take Nanjing in 1949, a gang holds up a foreign ambassador and steals from him the "Blue Shield Strongbox," containing precious diamonds. Public Security investigators led by Lu Hong soon discover this to be no ordinary theft, but really a case of international espionage designed to harm the reputation of the new People's government. The Nationalists still hold Shanghai, and a Nationalist agent in Nanjing keeps hindering the investigation. Lu Hong and his men must crack the spy ring and uphold the fledgling government's reputation.

231. *Blue Sword's Duty (Lan Jian De Shi Ming)*

1987. Longjiang Film Studio. Color. 10 Reels. Direction: Wang Lei, Zhang Ping. Screenplay: Hou Xinzhi, Du Minxian. Cinematography: Wang Lei, Sun Fumao. Art Direction: Li Deyu. Music: Wang Ming. Sound: Wang Zhongshan, Wang Lianfang. Cast: Hao Yiping as Lu Peng, Ye Qinnan as Tang's wife, Zhang Yuhong as Wu Meng, Wang Ruiyun as Long Xiang, Ma Chunguang as Zhang Xing, Zhang Rongzhi as Lu Tieshan

Professor Tang Sihua fled mainland China for Taiwan just before it fell to the Communists. Now he accepts an invitation to deliver a scholarly paper there, and brings along his daughter Miss Tang on his visit. He has another purpose for making the trip: he wants to find his old friend Lu Tieshan, who had saved the life of Tang's wife Aiyun before they left.

But the PSB has information that the Tang family is being followed by some sort of criminal element, so they assign detective Lu Peng to protect them. After the case is cleared up and the criminal arrested, it turns out that detective Lu Peng is the son of Lu Tieshan. Professor Tang gets to see his old friend at last.

232. *Blue Whale's Emergency Action (Lan Jing Jing Ji Chu Dong)*

1985. Changchun Film Studio. Color. 10 Reels. Direction: Hua Ke. Screenplay: Zhou Zhentian. Cinematography: Yang Penghui, Liu Fengdi. Art Direction: Song Honghua, Liu Sheng. Music: Jin Fuzhai. Sound: Liu Xingfu. Cast: Zhu Shimao as Wu Zhongyi, Long Liling as Zhu Yuping, Hao Zhiben as Zhou Qun, Zhao Fuyu as Yu Zeliang, Ge Jianjun as Tao Wufu

As Chinese submarine No. 980 is conducting training exercises at sea, it is suddenly ordered to keep alert for unauthorized foreign observers in the area where Chinese missile launching is taking place. The film focuses on the hard work of the sailors in making the launching a success, despite an accident which kills one of the crew and badly injures another.

233. *Blush (Hongfen)*

1994. Beijing Film Studio, Ocean Film Co. (Hong Kong) Co-Production. Color. Letterboxed. 12 Reels. Direction: Li Shaohong. Screenplay: Ni Zhen, Li Shaohong, based on the novel by Su Tong (1963-). Cinematography: Zeng Nianping. Art Direction: Wang Zesheng, Xie Xinsheng. Music: Guo Wenjing. Sound (Dolby): Wu Ling. Costume: Liu Jianhua. Makeup: Sun Hongkui, Sun Bing. Cast: Wang Ji as Qiu Yi, He Saifei as Xiao'e, Wang Zhiwen as Lao Pu, Zhang Liwei as Liu Qing, Wang Ruoli as Mrs. Pu, Song Xiuling as Ruifeng, Xing Yanchun as Mr. Zhang, Zhou Jianying as Mr. Zhang, Cao Lei as Narrator

Qiu Yi and Xiao'e are prostitutes in the city of Suzhou in the early 1950s. When the Communist government outlaws their trade, immature and coquettish Xiao'e is caught and sent for re-education, while the older and more mature Qiu Yi escapes to the home of an old client, Lao Pu, who takes her in. But Lao Pu's mother resents Qiu Yi's presence in their home, and eventually drives her out. Qiu Yi finds sanctuary in a convent, but as she is now pregnant this is also just a temporary arrangement. Xiao'e has in the meantime completed her re-education, and is an ordinary worker.

One of her co-workers is Lao Pu, and they get married. Qiu Yi shows up at the wedding to wish them well and tell Xiao'e to take care of her husband. The couple have a baby boy, but the marriage does not turn out well: Xiao'e wants a better lifestyle than they can afford, and Lao Pu embezzles funds from his work unit to get them for her. He is caught, tried and sentenced to death. Xiao'e finds Qiu Yi, now unhappily married to a wealthy man, turns her son over to her old girlfriend, and then departs for the north.

Awarded Silver Bear for Visual Effects at the 1995 Berlin International Film Festival.

234. *A Boatswain's Story (Shui Shou Zhang De Gu Shi)*

1963. Haiyan Film Studio. B & W. 11 Reels. Executive director: Tang Xiaodan. Direction: Qiang Ming. Screenplay: Gao Xing and Qiang Ming, based on the novel of the same title by Gao Yuan. Cinematography: Zhu Jing, Cao Weiye. Art Direction: Zhong Yongqing. Music: Gao Tian. Sound: Zhou Hengliang. Cast: Meng Qingliang as Chen Fuhai, Zhao Mao as Li Zhengliang, Gu Xiaoshuang as Yuan Guoxing, Shi Jipu as Zhang Yuquan, Qu Lili as Chen Yuehua, Xu Junjie as the Captain

New naval recruit Li Zhengliang is unhappy with the new boatswain Chen Fuhai, thinking Chen pays too much attention to details. When the two go to an enemy occupied island on a scouting mission, Li's lack of experience leads to the enemy discovering and surrounding them. To save Li Zhengliang and protecting his safe return to ship, Chen exposes himself to draw the enemy's fire. Li Zhengliang is deeply moved by this. He gets to know Chen better, and meets and falls in love with the boatswain's sister Chen Yuehua, a navy nurse. Later, Chen and Li reconnoiter the enemy naval base, and by chance discover an enemy plan to attack the Chinese base. They make it back to their own ship and report the plot, allowing the Chinese to launch a preemptive strike on the enemy's flagship.

235. *The Bodyguard (Biao Wang)*

1986. Changchun Film Studio. Color. 10 Reels. Direction: Li Qimin. Screenplay: Xie Wenli, Han Qipeng. Cinematography: Sun Hui. Art Direction: Yuan Dianmin, Du Wencheng. Music: Chen Shouqian. Sound: Liu Wenzhang. Cast: An Yaping as Wang Zhaxi, Lu Jun as Jin Lei, Ma Junqing as Cui Hua, Zhang Yanli as Zuo Ma, Liu Tingrao as the church manager, Long Wei as Tom

In the early years of the Republic of China (c.1915), kung fu expert Wang Zhaxi is hired as bodyguard for a British businessman named Tom. Wang observes the businessman is being followed by someone he assumes is a potential kidnapper or assassin. Actually, the person shadowing Tom is Jin Lei, a Chinese customs officer gathering evidence on the Englishman's opium smuggling activities. After newspapers disclose that a large quantity of opium was hidden in a church with connections to Tom, the businessman frames Zhaxi by having the local police arrest his bodyguard as the one involved in the smuggling. Wang Zhaxi is sent to prison for a time, but after the customs agents secure his release, he is recruited to help them in their ongoing surveillance of Tom. But in spite of the efforts of Wang and others to rid China of the evils of opium, some giving their lives in the attempt, Tom eludes capture and gets his opium out by other delivery channels.

236. *Bodyguard Hasier (Bao Biao Ha Si Er)*

1992. Fujian Film Studio. Color. Letterboxed. 9 Reels. Direction: Liu Yunzhou. Screenplay: Huang Yazhou. Cinematography: Yang Ming. Art Direction: Zhao Shaoping. Music: Chen Yongtie. Sound: Zhu Wenzhong. Costume: Liu Huifang. Makeup: Yang Maorong. Cast: Zhao Liang as Hasier, Zhu Zhenzhen as Sha Nuo, Shi Lanya as Liu Ermei, Ji Chunhua as Dageda, Xu Zhongquan as Manager Sha

Shipping company boss Sha hires Mongolian kung fu expert Hasier as his bodyguard. Haiser accompanies Sha to a North China port, where Sha wants to purchase a ship. There, Hasier has a series of battles with thugs, sometimes protecting his boss, sometimes to guard the ship from smugglers who want it. On the trip, Hasier also falls in love with Liu Ermei, a woman being harassed by the smugglers.

237. *Boluo the Clown (Chou Jiao Bo Luo)*

1988. Inner Mongolia Film Studio. Color. 9 Reels. Direction: Chen Da, Wu Lansheng. Screenplay: Zhao Jingchao. Cinematography: Xiao Guoli. Art Direction: Du Changshun. Music: Guo Zhijie. Sound: Hu Bing. Cast: Dong Yong as Lu Xin, Gao Lingwei as Wang Jiajia, Wu Liping as Wang Hu

Lu Xin is a comic acrobat. He greatly admires Poro, a famous Brazilian detective, and like to refer to himself as Poro the 2nd. His talents as an amateur often help the police in criminal investigations. On one case, Lu disguises himself as the head of a small gang in order to conduct his own investigation. During his investigation, Lu Xin finds that a man called "Old K" controls all the gang activity in his city, and when Lu gets too close, the crime boss issues orders to have Lu Xin killed. Fortunately the real police are ready for this, and arrive in time to save Lu Xin and round up the criminals.

238. *Border Town (Bian Cheng)*

1984. Beijing Film Studio. Color. Wide Screen. 10 Reels. Direction: Ling Zifeng. Screenplay: Yao Yun, Li Junpei. Cinematography: Liang Zhiyong. Art Direction: Xia Rujin. Music: Liu Zhuang. Sound: Chen Yanxi, Sun Xiuyun. Cast: Feng Hanyuan as the boatman, Dai Na as Cuicui, Liu Kui as You Dalao, Shi Lei as Erlao, Li Hanpu as Shunshun, Jin Feng as Yang Mabing

In the early years of the Republic of China, a boatman and his granddaughter Cuicui live in a small river port town. Cuicui is a beautiful girl of 15, and her grandfather hopes to marry her into a good family someday. A prominent local boat owner has two sons who both love Cuicui, but she cares only for the younger son, Erlao. Unhappy that his younger brother has won out, elder brother Daluo decides it would be best if he left town. He leaves, but in traveling down the river he falls in and drowns. Erluo feels so guilty about his brother's death he begins avoiding Cuicui, and at last he too leaves home. The old boatman loses all hope of finding a good marriage for his granddaughter, and one night he dies. Now, only Cuicui is left alone to carry on the river transport business. She quietly works and waits...

Best Director Ling Zifeng, 1985 Golden Rooster Awards.

239. *Border Town Romance (Bian Xiang Qing)*

1983. Tianshan Film Studio. Color. 9 Reels. Direction: Zhang Cangyuan, An Haiping. Screenplay: Zhu Guanghua. Art Direction: Zhong Tong. Music: Rexiti, Yu Tianfu, Lu Guang. Sound: Tu Minde. Cast: Abudu Renyimu as Abulaiti, Shadaiti Kelimu as Baitiman, Abudu Rexiti as Naman, Xilinguli Maitiniyazi as Heiliqihan

A young man of the Xinjiang Uighur nationality, Abulaiti, is in love with a girl named Baitiman, but her father disapproves because the young man is so poor. Abulaiti despairs of ever getting out of poverty. But after the 3rd Plenary Session of the 11th Party Congress arrives in his village, he takes the lead in implementing the contracted production responsibility system. His chief opposition comes from production unit director Naman, who fears losing power. In the end, Abulaiti and his unit achieve a large harvest, and he and Baitiman are married.

240. *A Born Coward (Tian Sheng Dan Xiao) (alternate title: Sheng Ming Zhi Xia)*

1994. Youth Film Studio, Beijing Haolaixi Film & Television Company Co-Production. Color. Letterboxed. 9 Reels. Direction: Yan Xiaozhui. Screenplay: Feng Xiaogang. Cinematography: Zhang Huijun. Art Direction: Huang Jiaxiong. Music: Zang Tianshuo. Sound: Zhao Jun. Costume: Qiao Qingling. Makeup: Mu Yu. Cast: Liang Tian as Wu Xiaohui, Ge You as Director Guan, Xie Yuan as Ma Qiang, Li Yuanyuan as Liu Yu, Ma Ling as Yao Lan, Niu Xingli as Uncle Cao

A loss by the Chinese soccer team in an international match sends mobs of angry fans into the streets of Beijing. Director Guan, chief of a small branch precinct, and his officer Wu Xiaohui go into the street to try to calm things. The rioters throw rocks at the police, striking Wu in the head and knocking him unconscious. When he recovers, Wu asks Guan for a job transfer. Guan agrees, but says Wu has to solve three pending cases before he can leave. Wu Xiaohui works hard to solve the three so he can leave, but on the third case he realizes he really loves police work, and decides to stay.

241. *Bosimao Is in Action (Bo Si Mao Zhai Xing Dong)*

1986. Changchun Film Studio. Color. 9 Reels. Direction: Xing Jie. Screenplay: Li Zhengjia, Liu Xinping. Cinematography: Liu Yongzhen. Art Direction: Xu Zhengpeng. Music: Deng Erbo. Sound: Hong Bo. Cast: Xu Fucang as Chen Yi, Liu Jian as Hu Tiexiong, Xu Yuanqi as Lu Jun, Li Lingjun as Mother Liu, Tan Yuanyuan as Zhen Feifei

In the days just after the liberation of

Shanghai, many Nationalist agents still remain in the city. Mao Renfeng, their chief, learns that the PLA plans to move next on Zhoushan, a small nearby island. He orders that "Plan Bosimao" be put in action, a plan to assassinate Shanghai Mayor Chen Yi, figuring this will delay the military action long enough to permit evacuation of the Nationalist troops on the island. PSB investigator Li Jun is put in charge of protecting the mayor, and the film deals with that effort.

242. *Boss and Servant's Adventure (Zhu Pu Li Xian Ji)*

1995. Changchun Film Studio. Color. Direction: Sun Qingguo. Screenplay: Zhao Yansheng. Cinematography: Sun Guangwen, Lu Beiyu. Art Direction: Wang Chong. Music: Liang Qing. Cast: Chen Weirong as Boss Jia, Liu Liu as A San, Yu Xiaohui as Luo Na, Pan Jie as Miss Xue, Zhang Jibo as Mr. Hong

During World War II, the Singapore Chinese Commerce Committee entrusts one of their number, a jeweler named Jia, to transport to Shanghai a sizable amount of money the committee has raised for the anti-Japanese effort. Jia is to contact the Communist Party underground and turn the funds over to them. The mission is a risky one, for he must keep the funds out of the hands of the Japanese, the Nationalist collaborationist government and Shanghai triads. As a decoy, Jia and his servant A San switch clothes on the ship; after their arrival, A San is pursued by various enemies who think he is the jeweler. After many difficulties, Jia and A San accomplish their mission with the help of a Communist agent named Hong.

243. *Boxer (Quan Ji Shou)*

1988. Xiaoxiang Film Studio. Color. Letterboxed. 9 Reels. Direction: Liu Miaomiao. Screenplay: Liu Fangwei. Cinematography: Liu Yuefei. Art Direction: Yang Li. Music: Wun Zhongjia. Sound: Huang Siye. Cast: Liu Yan as Sima Lixiong, Liu Shangxian as Zhang Xiaowei, Zhang Zhongchao as Chen Dong, Xu Zhiqun as Nanni

Famous Chinese boxer Sima Lixiong accidentally kills his old friend and competitor Chen Weidong in a bout in the 1950s, which results in his being imprisoned for more than 10 years. After Sima is released, he becomes coach at a sports institute. He visits his former friend's widow Zhang Xiaowei, and Zhang

tells him her son Chen Dong loves boxing. With Sima's help, Chen Dong becomes a member of the sports institute. The film relates how Chen Dong overcomes various emotional disturbances revolving around the circumstances of his father's death, how he learns to concentrate on training, and how he is at last selected to participate in international boxing matches.

244. *A Boy in the Flames of War (Feng Huo Shao Nian)*

1975. Beijing Film Studio. B & W. Direction: Dong Kena. Screenplay: Yan Yiyan. Cinematography: Zhu Jinmin, Wun Zhixian. Art Direction: Zhang Jinbiao. Music: Cheng Geng, Wang Zhulin. Sound: Wang Yunhua. Cast: Qiu Yinshan as the political supervisor, Wang Jingchun as Xiao Song, Ma Jingwu as the director, Song Ge as the cook, Niu Shijun as the squad leader, Ma Fang as Xiao Lizhi, Lu Wenzhao as Xiao Hai

In 1943, Chinese guerrillas rescue orphan Xiao Song after he is wounded by the Japanese in an attack that kills his parents, and the group's political supervisor sends him to Zhen Daniang's home to recover. Xiao Song vows to become a soldier and avenge his parents. After joining the army, with the help of the political supervisor and his comrades, he grows up quickly. A strictly-disciplined soldier, he carries out his assignments and moves on with the army to greater victories.

245. *Boys and Girls (Shao Nan Shao Nu Men)*

1987. Children's Film Studio. Color. 9 Reels. Direction: Luo Xiaoling. Screenplay: Ye Xiaoshen, Zhou Jianxin. Cinematography: Li Yanzheng. Art Direction: Zhang Chongxiang. Music: Yang Shaolu. Sound: Ren Daming. Cast: Chen Rong as Liu Shu, Yu Meng as Hu Shuxian, Liu Yu as Yi Lianlian, Ying Meifang as Zhong Meiwen, Zhang Xiaolin as Sheng Li, Wang Weizhong as Gao Weiyi

Sheng Li is assigned as a teaching intern at his old high school. His class starts a fund for feeding the hungry in Africa, but the money is stolen. For various reasons, Sheng Li's supervisor Teacher Zhong suspects that a girl student named Hu Shuxian is the thief, and more things happen to cast suspicion on her. Sheng Li is at last able to prove the girl's innocence, but the pressure has affected her psychologically. In the end, the true thief is proven to be a student that Teacher Zhong had trusted completely.

246. *A Brave and Successful Ocean Troop (Nu Hai Qing Qi)*

1955. Changchun Film Studio. B & W. 11 Reels. Directions: Wang Bing and Tang Xiaodan. Screenplay: Collective work of the Naval Political Division, Cultural Department Writing Group. Cinematography: Wang Chunquan and Zhang Jun. Art Direction: Wang Tao. Music: Zhang Guocang. Sound: Sui Xizhong. Cast: Guo Yuntai as Commander Li, Gao Bo as the Political Commissar, Wei Rong as the Base Commander, Zhang Fengxiang as the Chief of Staff, Liu Chunlin as Regimental Commander Zhou, Jing Mukui as Staff Officer Dong.

In preparation for the liberation of Woyushan Island, a naval base command assigns Commander Li Longjiang's 3rd Gunboat Brigade to gather intelligence concerning the location of the enemy's artillery emplacements there. They dock at the port of Longmen on nearby Gao Island, and with the assistance of local fishermen, wipe out an enemy intelligence unit there. But another intelligence unit hidden on the island reports their presence to the enemy commander on Woyushan Island. Although they come under attack, Commander Li's gunboat penetrates deep into the enemy port on Woyushan, and by drawing fire expose the enemy's gun emplacements. After the successful accomplishment of this mission, the PLA with its naval and air forces invade and liberate Woyushan island.

247. *Brave Dragons of the Border (Bian Chui Wei Long) (original title: Chinese Special Police/Hua Xia Te Jing)*

1993. Pearl River Film Studio and Hong Kong Luo's Film Company Co-Production. Color. Letterboxed. Direction: Luo Lie. Screenplay: Luo Lie, Yang Zesheng, Liao Xiaoqi. Cinematography: Wang Yonglong. Art Direction: Du Xiufeng. Music: Nie Jianxin. Costume: Fan Shunhua. Makeup: Fu Liling. Cast: Mai Deluo as Chen De, Zhuang Li as Ai Ni, Luo Lie as Luo Zhiqiang, Chen Guantai as Liang Bide, Wu Ma as Ang Ji, Zhang Wulang as Huang Lang, Gan Shan as Rong Da

A special policeman is sent to Yunnan province to coordinate the anti-drug activities of local police.

248. *A Brave Eagle at Sea (Hai Shang Sheng Ying)*

1959. Changchun Film Studio. B & W. 10 Reels. Direction: Yin Yiqing. Screenplay: Sun Mu. Cinematography: Li Guanghui, Art Direction: Tong Jingwen. Music: Quan Rufeng, Bai Chongyan. Sound: Hong Bo. Cast: Liang Yin as Platoon Leader Liu, Liu Zhenzhong as Ma Hai, Liu Shilong as Private Yang, Yang Huang as Hong Xiugu, Zhao Baohua as Old Hong, Jin Li as Hong Dashui, Zhou Ke as Gao Zhiyang.

In 1954, in a battle to liberate a island on the Southeast China coast, PLA platoon leader Liu along with scouts Ma Hai and Private Yang cross the straits and land on the island to reconnoiter. They capture enemy staff officer Gao Zhiyang. When the enemy discovers that Gao has vanished, they launch an exhaustive search for him. Liu and his men disguise themselves as enemy soldiers, and with the help of the Hongs, a family of fishermen, escape and bring Gao to the mainland. Later the PLA force returns and wipes out the enemy on the island.

249. *Brave Eagles in the Vast Sky (Chang Kong Xiong Ying)*

1976. Changchun Film Studio. Color. B & W. 10 Reels. Direction: Wang Feng, Wang Yabiao. Screenplay: Chen Lide. Cinematography: Yi Zhi, Wu Bengli. Art Direction: Wang Xingwen, Cui Yongquan. Music: Lin Xuesong, Cao Shuzhuang. Casting: Li Tiejun as Gao Juntao, Wang Xiyan as Political Commissar Qi, Jin Zhengyuan as the regimental commander, Xu Guangmin as deputy regimental commander Meng, Yang Shujun as Gong Wancang, Wang Baosheng as Cheng Shuanghu

In the Korean war, the Americans plan to destroy the Jinchunali Bridge, thereby cutting off the Chinese forces' principal supply line. They are beaten back and the bridge saved by Chinese aviators led by Gao Juntao, although Gao must contend with opposition to his plans by Meng, the deputy regimental commander, who continually overestimates U.S. power.

250. *Brave the Wind and Waves (Cheng Feng Po Lang)*

1957. Jiangnan Film Studio. Color. 11 Reels. Direction: Sun Yu, Jiang Junchao. Screenplay: Sun Yu. Cinematography: Li Shengwei. Art Direction: Zhang Xibai and Fu Shuzhen. Music: Lu Qiming. Sound: Chen Jingrong. Makeup: Jiang Yongchang. Cast: Zhong Shuhuang as Ma Jun, Jin Chuan as You Renjie, Cao Duo as Mr. Wu, Cheng Zhi as Doctor Niu, Zhang Yi as Captain Zhao, Huang Yin as Liang Yin, Wang Yi as

Huang Liuhua, Er Lin as Yuan Pujun, Su Hui as Political Commissar Li.

Three female graduates of the Caoshan Advanced Commercial Ship Technology School, Liang Yin, Huang Liuhua and Yuan Pujun, are assigned to a seagoing internship. Conservative Captain Zhao has abundant shipping experience but is conservative and looks down upon women. He cautiously assigns his first mate You Renjie and boatswain Ma Jun to oversee the young women's practice assignment. With the support of Political Commissar Li, the three study hard and accomplish the assignment ahead of schedule. Not long after, Huang Liuhua and Yuan Pujun are relocated to another ship to practice ship operation. Liang Yin remains on the original ship, where she is subjected to constant harassment: Captain Zhao makes it plain he has no confidence in her; boatswain Ma Jun treats her rudely; and first mate You Renjie makes repeated unwelcome advances. But Liang Yin overcomes these difficulties and finally gets Captain Zhao to change his opinion of her. One year later, Liang Yin, Huang Liuhua and Yuan Pujun are all made third mates; meanwhile, Liang Yin and Ma Jun have fallen in love. After more training, Liang Yin is promoted to second mate.

251. *Break Through the Siege (Jun Lie Sha Chu Zhong Wei)*

1993. Changchun Film Studio. Color. Letterboxed. 9 Reels. Direction: Cheng Ke, Leng Shan. Screenplay: Zhou Xinde. Cinematography: Ning Changcheng. Art Direction: Zhu Jiaxin, Li Taiyang. Music: Guo Xiaotian. Sound: Cheng Xianbo. Costume: An Lixin. Makeup: Ji Weihua, Dan Xiangsuo. Cast: Liu Weihua as Yao Donglin, Su Ying as Shanmao, Wang Qing as Da Zhixiang, Jia Liyin as Little Widow

In Northeast China late in World War II, Japanese troops surround a Chinese unit. Yao Donglin is ordered to lead a group of Chinese soldiers attempting to break out of the encirclement with a trainload of arms obtained from a Japanese armory. They make it out through heavy fighting, but many of them are killed in the effort.

252. *Breaking (Jue Lie)*

1975. Beijing Film Studio. Color. 12 Reels. Direction: Li Wenhua. Screenplay: Chun Chao, Zhou Jie. Cinematography: Zhen Yuyuan, Luo Dean. Art Direction: Zhang Jinbiao. Music: Lu Yuan, Tang Ke. Sound: Fu Yinjie. Cast: Guo Zhenqin as Long Guozheng, Wang Suya as Li Jinfeng, Wun Xiying as Deputy Secretary Tang, Zhang Zheng as the old representative, Xu Zhan as Xu Niuzai, Li Shijiang as Jiang Danian

A party committee decides to operate an agricultural college, one that will practice true socialism. Long Guozheng, a graduate of the Yan'an Anti-Japanese University, is named the college's Party Secretary and President. The school staff are in conflict from the start. Academic Affairs Director Sun Zhiqin aims for high academic standards, so he refuses to accept working class students who lack a high school education. Long Guozheng advocates taking the classes into the mountains and letting in as students working class people who may lack formal education but have considerable real world experience. After the school is started, Long Guozheng urges that all teachers and students carry out an "educational revolution." In the end, the chairman approves this educational direction for the school. Long Guozheng reminds everyone that the struggle will not be over until everyone has broken completely with traditional thinking.

253. *Breaking Through the Gates (Unreleased) (Chuang Guan)*

1960. Haiyan Film Studio. B & W. 8 Reels. Direction: Xu Suling. Screenplay: Li Tianji. No record of other credits.

Production team Party Secretary Peng Aqiu leads farmers in developing their pig raising business despite being mocked by his conservative father-in-law and others. With the support of the commune secretary, he is eventually successful both in raising pig production and in educating the backward people who initially opposed him.

254. *Breathing Hard (Da Chuan Qi)*

1988. Shenzhen Film Studio. Color. 9 Reels. Direction: Ye Daying. Screenplay: Ye Daying, Zhang Qian, Wang Suo. Cinematography: Zhang Li, Zhong Dalu. Art Direction: Tan Xiaogang. Music: Li Lifu. Sound: Liu Haiyan. Cast: Xie Yuan as Ding Jian, Qi Ping as Li Bailing

Ding Jian, optimistic about life and personally ambitious, arrives in Guangzhou to seek his fortune. In this southern metropolis, he witnesses a series of unfortunate events and experiences a number of personal setbacks. He gradually comes to realize that big city life is not for him, and the once outgoing and optimistic young man becomes enured to everything going on around him.

Best Actor Xie Yuan, 1989 Golden Rooster Awards.

255. *The Bride (Xin Niang)*

1993. Xi'an Film Studio. Color. Letterboxed. 9 Reels. Direction and screenplay: Zhang Gang. Cinematography: Zhang Jian. Art Direction: Wang Renchen. Music: Dong Weijie. Sound: Liu Yunjie. Costume: Zhang Heru, Dai Yili. Makeup: Yin Fang, Zhou Liangeng. Cast: Zhuang Li as Wang Caijuan, Wu Gang as Liang Han, Tao Yuling as Ye Ganniang, Zhang Ziqiang as old man Bazi, Liu Shulin as the old political commissar, Tu Linghui as Yang Yunjiao, Cheng Pang as Tu Erbao, Wei Zhiyuan as Da Jinya, Qian Ruhe as Chunwang

During the Chinese Civil War of the late 1940s, a girl named Caijun marries guerrilla chief Liang Han, but three days later her uncle sells her to a businessman to be his wife. She escapes, and on the road her cousin Yuanjiao and the cousin's lover Zhang Yunxiang. Zhang is really a supporter of the Nationalists, so he pretends to help her in order to find out where the guerrillas are. When Caijun locates her husband, Liang Han sees the enemy following her. Everyone believe she has betrayed them. The enemy captures Liang Han, but Caijun proves her devotion by sacrificing herself so that he may escape.

256. *The Bridge (Qiao)*

1949. Northeast Film Studio. B&W. 10 reels. Direction: Wang Bin. Cinematography: Bao Jie. Screenplay: Yu Min. Art Direction: Liu Xueyao. Music: He Shide. Sound: Lu Xianchang. Costume: Mu Hua, Lin Na. Makeup: Bi Zepu. Principal Cast: Wang Jiayi as Liang Risheng, Lu Ban as the Factory Director, Jiang Hao as the Chief Engineer, Chen Qiang as Hou Zhanxi, Du Defu as Xi Buxiang, Yu Yang as Wu Yizhu.

In the winter of 1947, a railroad factory in Northeast China is given the assignment of repairing a bridge over the Song Hua River, vital to the Communist forces. The Chief Engineer doubts that the task can be successful. Most of the workers see it as a job and nothing more. But Liang Risheng, a worker-hero, is fired with enthusiasm for the mission, and devises a series of innovations which overcome some of the obstacles, such as a shortage of materials.

His zeal spreads to the others, they begin to see the project's feasibility, and with everyone pitching in, the bridge is repaired and opened before the river thaws.

257. *Bright Moon on the Sea (Hai Shang Sheng Ming Yue)*

1983. Shanghai Film Studio. Color. 11 Reels. Direction: Liu Qiong, Sha Jie, Deng Yimin. Screenplay: Ai Minzhi. Cinematography: Lu Junfu. Art Direction: Lin Guoliang. Music: Si Guangnan. Sound: Ren Daming. Cast: Guan Muchun as Li Yan, Wang Suya as Ye Zhi, Ling Zhiao as Lin Deping, Ji Ping as Xiao Lingtong, Niu Xinrong as Li's brother, Wang Xinjun as Ouyang Fu

When a provincial operatic company makes a tour appearance in a fishing village, their leading female singer Ye Zhi by chance overhears a young village girl singing. The girl is named Li Yan, and Ye Zhi is so impressed with the girl's voice and natural talent that she recruits her for the company. This is controversial, as the company usually employs only music academy graduates, but Ye Zhi is determined, and says she will train Li Yan herself. Li Yan makes significant progress, but when it comes time to perform in public she suffers a massive case of stage fright. Her confidence shattered, she runs away and returns to her village. Her brother strongly criticizes her actions, and with his prodding she starts singing again. Meanwhile, Ye Zhi contacts her, and with Ye's encouragement Li Yan returns to the opera company. Composer Lin Deping has prepared a special performance for Ye Zhi, but she unselfishly gives it to Li Yan for her debut presentation. With support from her teacher and her hometown people, Li Yan devotes herself to rehearsals. When the time comes, she gives a brilliant and flawless performance.

258. *Bright Ocean Pearl (Hai Shang Ming Zhu)*

1976. Beijing Film Studio. Color. 10 Reels. Direction: Lin Yang, Wang Haowei. Screenplay: Zhang Xianglin. Cinematography: Wang Zhaoling. Art Direction: Xiao Xia. Music: Li Yinhai. Sound: Zhen Chunyu. Casting: Wang Suya as Ling Yanzi, Chen Qiang as Guo Laoda, Pao Huiping as Cai Xia, Ma Ling as Dali's wife, Ding Shaokang as Uncle Hai, Chang Wenzhi as Dali

In the spring of 1974, Ling Yanzi travels to her wedding to the son of a Shandong coastal fishing village's Party secretary. On the way,

Bridge. **Opening ceremony for the finally completed bridge. 1949. Northeast Film Studio.**

she witnesses Cui Min, director of the village's by-product unit illegally using a commune fishing boat to do commercial shipping. But although she catches him red-handed, her prospective father-in-law Guo Laoda wrongly supported Cui Min. After she arrives in the village, Ling Yanzi gains the support of commune secretary Zhao in securing the job of directing the commune's aquatic products unit. When Cui Min continues his illegal activities, Yanzi posts big character posters exposing Cui's crimes. Stressing that this is a class struggle issue, she educates her father-in-law through the evidence and saves some good people who had been deceived by Cui Min. In the end, Cui is completely criticized for his actions, and labeled a "newly born capitalist."

259. *Bright Road (Part One)* (*Jin Guang Da Dao*)

1975. Changchun Film Studio. Color. 13 Reels. Direction: Lin Nong, Sun Yu. Screenplay: Collective, based on the novel of the same title by Hao Ran. Cinematography: Meng Xiandi. Art Direction: Liu Jinnai, Jin Bohao. Music: Zhang Dicang. Cast: Zhang Guomin as Gao Daquan, Zhu Decheng as Zhu Tiehan, Wang Fuli as Lu

Ruifeng, Gu Zhi as Liu Xiang, Pu Ke as Zhou Zhong, Miao Zuang as Gao Erlin

After land reform, the liberated farmers of Fangchao establish a mutual aid team to struggle with village chief Zhang Jinfa's erroneous policy of "seeking household prosperity" and with rich farmer Feng Shaohuai. To destroy this team, Feng Shaohuai and hidden counter-revolutionaries Fan Kemin and Zhang Jinfa tries to create disruption in the village. However, Gao Daquan and other team members deal strong setbacks to these class enemies. With the support of the county Party committee, Gao Daquan organizes the masses of poor and lower class peasants in accusing and criticizing the "seeking household prosperity" line and establish the first agricultural commune in the Tianmen area.

260. *Bright Road (Part Two)* (*Jin Guang Da Dao*)

1976. Changchun Film Studio. Color. 11 Reels. Direction: Sun Yu. Screenplay: Collective, recorded by Xiao Yixian, based on the novel "Bright Road, Part Three" by Hao Ran. Cinematography: Meng Xiandi. Art Direction: Liu Jinnai. Music: Gao Feng. Cast: Zhang Guomin as Gao Daquan, Zhu Decheng as Zhu Tiehan, Pu Ke as Zhou Zhong, Miao Zuang as Gao Erlin, Pan Demin as Qin Fu, Pan Shulan as Zhao Yuer, Ma Jingwu as Zhang Jinfa, Xu Zhongquan as Feng Shaohuai, Zhang Bolin as Fang Keming, Ge Cunzhuang as Gu Xinmin, Wu Bike as "Rolling Knife."

In the spring of 1953, under the leadership of village Party secretary and commune director Gao Daquan, the newly established "progressive production cooperative union" sets out to improve flood control. Their opposition comes from rich farmers Zhang Jinfa and Feng Shaohuai and covert counterrevolutionary Fan Keming. They create all sorts of problems for Gao Daquan, including manipulating grain prices at harvest time. Gao Daquan ships extra grain to the market, stabilizing prices. But when Fan Keming murders his hired thug "Rolling Knife" to keep him quiet, Gao Daquan is able to expose Zhang and Feng's crimes, and with them and Fan out of the way, the "progressive union" develops and expands.

261. *Bright Stream (Ming Liang De Xiao Xi)*

1984. Children's Film Studio. Color. 8 Reels. Direction: Lu Gang. Screenplay: Zhang Yuanzhong. Cinematography: Liu Huizhong. Art Direction: Yi Li. Music: Liu Weiguang. Sound: Ren Shanpu. Cast: Liu Zhaohui as Xiao Dou, Wang Feng as Stepgrandpa, Zhang Zhiyong as Xiao Min, He Minlan as Mother, Zhang Wenxue as Lin Quan

Xiao Dou is a 12-year-old student in the Chuandong Mountain area. He and his 6-year-old brother Xiao Min live with their widowed mother. When his mother marries boatman Lin Quan to reorganize a family, Xiao Dou is excited to learn that he now gains a stepgrandfather as well. But he soon becomes resentful of his mysterious stepgrandfather, a sad and lonely man who lives on the mountain and disdains contacts with others, especially children. The boy persists, and in time the old man warms up to him. Xiao Dou learns the old man once had a granddaughter Yuxiang, who he loved dearly. The little girl drowned years before while trying to catch a fish for her grandfather. Xiao Dou understands the old man, and wants to take Yuxiang's place in his heart. The old man and the boy become very close.

262. *Bright Sunny Skies (Yan Yang Tian)*

1973. Changchun Film Studio. Color. 10 Reels. Direction: Lin Nong. Screenplay: Collective, based on the novel of the same title by Ao Ran. Cinematography: Wang Qimin. Art Direction: Liu Jinnai. Music: Qu Rufeng, Zhang Dicang. Cast: Zhang Lianwen as Xiao Changchun, Ma Jingwu as Ma Laoshi, Guo Zhengqin as Han Baizhong, Shi Kefu as Secretary Wang, Yan Fei as Xiao Laoda, Zhang Mingzhi as Jiao Shuhong

In the fall of 1956, Dongshanwu Cooperative's militia platoon leader Xiao Changchun leads the people in dealing with disaster and helping themselves. But Ma Zhiyue, party branch secretary and the co-op's director, uses state loans to engage in business, abandoning farming. Xiao Changchun struggles with him, and through a party and commune Ma was demoted and Xiao named to replace him. Under Xiao's leadership, the commune produces at a high level and has a bumper harvest. In the 1957 reorganization campaign, Ma Zhiyue ties to disrupt the campaign as well as destroy the commune, and even tries to murder Xiao's only son. With the support of the district party committee, Xiao Changchun finally rids the Party and the country of the counter-revolutionary Ma Zhiyue once and for all.

263. *Bring Her to Justice (Ji Na "Xiao Hun Xiao Huang Hou")*

1992. Youth Film Studio. Color. Letterboxed. 9 Reels. Direction: Shao Xuehai. Screenplay: Kong Liang. Cinematography: Pu Songlian. Art Direction: Song Weidong. Music: Du Jiangang. Sound: Liu Haiyan. Costume: Sui Xiaomei, Liang Lijuan. Makeup: Chen Dong. Cast: Li Tie as A Kun, Fu Weixing as Chen Bo, Sui Keming as Mei Jie, Li Li as Lin Sisi, Zhang Yuekai as Chao Bo

Pornographic videos begin flooding Northwest China. Police learn the head of the ring distributing the tapes is a mysterious figure called "Charming Little Queen." Police follow the clues and crack the case.

264. *Bring Them to Justice (Tian Wang Xing Dong)*

1994. Beijing Film Studio & Hong Kong Anle Film Company Co-Production. Color. 9 Reels. Direction: Wang Biao, Jiang Yang. Screenplay: Liu Hanming. Cinematography: Zhang Zhongping. Art Direction: Duan Zhengzhong.

Sound: Zhang Zhizhong. Costume: Liu Fang. Makeup: Yu Baozhong. Cast: Wu Yijiang as Lin Xiao, Guo Xiuyun as Guo Xiaoyun, Huang Jiada as Police Officer Huang, Tang Zhenzong as Police Officer Tang, Zhen Shuang as Shen Lizhu, Chen Baolian as Mr. Chen

The Hong Kong police send an urgent message to a special economic zone in Guangdong that a drug ring is infiltrating the mainland from Hong Kong. In the zone, chief of detectives Lin Xiao and his assistants cooperate with Macao and Hong Kong police to stop the drug dealers.

265. *The Broad Road (Kang Zhuang Da Dao)*

1959. Changchun Film Studio. B & W. 9 Reels. Direction: Wang Yan. Screenplay: Xing Derun, Wang Gengzhu, Fan Qiuzhong. Cinematography: Yin Zhi. Art Direction: Li Fan. Music: Li Jida, Gao Hongliang. Cast: Wu Bike as Secretary Yuan, Ren Yi as Cheng Shan, Bai Yinkuan as Zhao Ming, Zhao Baohua as the Old Treasurer, Ayan as "Little Cannon"'s father, Zhang Guilan as Xiao Ying, Wang Chunying as "Little Cannon."

During the Great Leap Forward campaign in 1959, the Chaoying ("Surpass England") agricultural commune brings in the county's biggest harvest, for which they are highly praised by county Party Secretary Yuan. The neighboring Qianjin ("Progress") commune, meanwhile, lags far behind and is criticized. Hoping to learn from the more successful commune, Secretary Zhao of Qianjin suggests the two communes work together to build a reservoir. Unfortunately, all the praise has given Secretary Cheng of Chaoying something of a swelled head, and he rejects the suggestion. Even his own commune's Youth League Secretary Xiao Ying urges cooperation between the two, but Secretary Cheng turns him down as well. There is no progress until Party Secretary Yuan directs the merger of the two communes into one. After this is accomplished, with coordinated planning and a joint labor force, the reservoir and a power station are built ahead of schedule.

266. *Broken Dreams (Xia Ri De Qi Dai)*

1988. Shanghai Film Studio. Color. 9 Reels. Direction: Shi Shujun. Screenplay: Shi Shujun, Dong Jingsheng. Cinematography: Zhao Junhong. Art Direction: Dong Jingsheng. Music: Lu Qimin. Sound: Zhan Xin. Cast: Jia Hongsheng as Su Wei, Xiang Mei as Mother, Zhang Jie as Coach Wei

On the eve of college entrance examinations, recent high school graduate Su Wei breaks his foot, which prevents him from taking the exam. Even with his classmates' support and his mother's helpful advice, Su is so devastated by the lost opportunity that he feels his life has been ruined and even contemplates suicide. In his depression over the turn of events, Su goes to a disco to vent his frustration. He has some bad experiences there, but through them he learns how better to deal with life's setbacks.

267. *The Broken Promise (Shi Xin De Cun Zhuang)*

1986. Beijing film Studio. Color. Widescreen. 9 Reels. Direction: Wang Haowei. Screenplay: Li Chen, based on an original story by Li Zhun. Cinematography: Li Chensheng. Art Direction: Shao Ruigang. Music: Zhang Peiji. Sound: Zhang Baojian. Cast: Yu Shaokang as Ding Yunhe, Yang Zichun as the Party Secretary, Cheng Xuebing as Xin Laoling, Li Guangfu as Muquan, Chutai Renhui as Zhen Xiannu

Ding Yunhe, an elderly retired railway worker, now makes a tidy profit growing and selling watermelons. Impressed by his success, friends persuade him to move to their village and help them transform the local economy. The local Party Secretary is jealous of the respect accorded Ding, and approves Ding's contract only after repeated petitioning by the villagers. The first melon harvest under Ding's tutelage delights the villagers, but only upsets the Party Secretary even more. He determines to find a way to break the contract. Whenever he meets with Ding, the Secretary is courteous and charming, but behinds his back he stirs up rumors and gossip, even starting a rumor that the old man has been having illicit relations with women. Eventually Ding can bear it no longer and leaves the village.

When the next planting season arrives, the villagers realize what they have lost. Desperately, they set out to find him.

268. *Bronze Devil (Qing Tong Kuang Mo)*

1994. Changchun Film Studio. Color. Letterboxed. 9 Reels. Direction: Gu Jing. Screenplay: Mao Jie, Mao Xiaofeng. Cinematography: Shu

Li, Ba Te. Art Direction: Qi Ming, Yang Guomin. Music: Zou Ye. Sound: Cao Feng, Zhang Xiaonan. Costume: Qi Chunzhi, Tao Ni. Makeup: Ji Weihua, Liu Xiaohong. Cast: Chu Zhibo as Qu Zhisong, Dongfang Wenying as Deng Hong, Liu Zhibing as Zhou Runbing, Chen Mu as Li Zien, Zhang Jing as Maimai, Sun Yanjun as Director Leng, Chen Jian as Duan Minghai

Bihai City policewoman Deng Hong and her partner Duan Minhai are assigned to investigate a string of killing connected to the illegal trade in antiques. They begin their investigation at the local museum, and follow clues through a maze of antique dealing, both lawful and illicit. The trail at last leads to a worker at the museum, Qu Zhigong: he had lost a leg four years before in a fight at an archeological site with tomb robbers; now he hates both tomb robbers and antique dealers. Qu resists arrest and is killed. But another museum worker, who Deng Hong has met and fallen for during the course of the investigation, is also killed when he takes a bullet meant for her.

269. *Brother and Sister (Ge Ge He Mei Mei)*

1956. Changchun Film Studio. B & W. 8 Reels. Direction: Su Li, Screenplay: Yan Gong, based on the novel "Lu Xiaogang and His Sister" by Ren Daxing. Cinematography: Li Guanghui. Art Direction: Tong Jinwen. Music: Quan Rufeng. Sound: Jue Jinxiu. Cast: Su Liqun as Lu Xiaogang, Liu Nanlin as Lu Xiaoduo, Xiong Saisheng as Grandma, Qing Yi as Mother, Li Dongdong as Teacher Yang, Wang Bing as Sister Maomao

Lu Xiaogang is a 4th Grade student in a Beijing elementary school. Because of their grandmother's spoiling her, his younger sister Xiaoduo is lazy, interested only in playing. Xiaogang determines to correct his sister's shortcomings, but his direct approach and rudeness to her do not work. One Sunday, Xiaogang prepares to help his sister study, but Xiaoduo goes instead to the zoo with her neighbor Maomao. They get caught in a rainstorm and Xiaoduo unselfishly shields the smaller Maomao from the rain with her own body, resulting in Xiaoduo herself getting sick. Xiaogang feels guilty as he recalls his earlier rudeness to his sister, and he changes his approach, helping her study but also taking breaks to play with her. He loses his patience when he finds his

sister cannot perform even the simplest calculations, so he does her homework for her. When Teacher Yang discovers this she takes Xiaoduo through the problems step by step, and in time the little girl becomes an excellent student.

270. *Brother and Sister Exploring for Treasure (Xiong Mei Tan Bao)*

1963. Haiyan Film Studio. B & W. 8 Reels. Direction: Gao Zheng. Screenplay: Chen Bojun, Gao Zheng. Cinematography: Wang Zhichu. Art Direction: Xie Muqian. Music: Zhang Linyi. Sound: Wu Ying. Casting: Wang Shaoping as Little Yong, Li Daojun as Big Yong, Zhou Yiqing as Cai Hua, Deng Nan as Uncle Xu, Zhi Shiming as Mother, Wu Yuewen as Sister Black

Three Young Pioneer members, Big Yong, his brother Little Yong, and their sister Cai Hua, want to do something good for society during their summer vacation. One day, when visiting their Uncle Xu's home, they find a rare piece of ore their late father had once given the uncle. They determine to find the source of this ore, and armed with some information their uncle gives them, go to search for the mine on an island on Lake Tai deep in the mountains. They experience various difficulties and dangers, and finally find a place where their father had once been a guerrilla fighter. With the help of a kindly old man and his granddaughter Sister Black, they at last locate the mine that was the ore's source.

271. *Brothers (Ge Lia Hao)*

1962. August First Film Studio. B & W. 9 Reels. Direction: Yan Jizhou. Screenplay: Shuo Yunping and Bai Wen, based on the stage play "I Am a Soldier" by Shuo Yunping. Cinematography: Zhang Dongliang and Chen Ruijun. Art Direction: Zhang Zheng. Music: Li Weicai. Sound: He Baoding. Cast: Zhang Liang as Chen Dahu, Zhang Liang as Chen Erhu, Zhang Yongshou as the second squad leader, Xing Jitian as Army Commander Hong, Wang Xingang as the Political Commissar, Jia Shihong as Xiaowen

Twin brothers Chen Dahu and Chen Erhu join the army together and are assigned to the same company. Erhu is an undisciplined free spirit, while Dahu becomes an expert marksman. When some new recruits approach Dahu to learn shooting, they mistake Erhua for Dahu, which produces some humorous situations. Later, with patient inspiration and education from the political commissar and their

Building Industry. Zhou Tingbing (Zhang Lianwen) conducts oil explorations on the North China prairie. 1974. Changchun Film Studio.

commander, Erhu at last overcomes his shortcomings. The twin brothers both receive awards for outstanding performance.

Best Actor Zhang Liang, 1963 Hundred Flowers Awards.

272. *Bubbling Spring (Quan Shui Ding Dong)*

1982. Shanghai Film Studio. Color. 9 Reels. 97 min. Direction: Shi Xiaohua. Screenplay: Wu Jianxin. Cinematography: Yu Shishan. Art Direction: Xue Jianna. Music: Liu Yanxi. Sound: Zhuang Yongnan. Cast: Zhang Ruifang as Grandma Tao, Zhang Xiangfei as Xueli, Niu Beng as Big Liu, Wang Jiaying as Xiyan

Retired kindergarten teacher Grandma Tao moves to a new neighborhood with her niece

Xueli, a music student. Soon after their arrival, Tao is invited to a beach resort. This makes Xueli very happy, for she feels the beach will be the perfect spot to compose the music that will be her graduation project. When Grandma Tao learns that delays in residential construction have resulted in there being no kindergarten in the area, she cancels the trip to the resort and opens a temporary day care center in her apartment. The prospect of small children disrupting her work upsets Xueli and she moves out. Grandma Tao encounters considerable difficulty in her new work, but she soon wins the respect and affection of the children and their parents. When Tao becomes ill from overwork, all the children come to visit her. Xueli is persuaded by the neighborhood committee director to return home, and when she sees the heartfelt affection the children have for Grandma Tao she understands the innate goodness of the older woman. Xueli writes her graduation composition "Bubbling Spring," telling the story of Grandma Tao's contributions to society and comparing them to the pure waters of a bubbling spring.

273. *Building Industry (Chuang Ye)*

1974. Changchun Film Studio. Color. 15 Reels. Direction: Yu Yanfu. Screenplay: Collective, written by Zhang Tianming, Cinematography: Wang Lei. Art Direction: Wang Chong. Music: Qin Yongcheng. Cast: Zhang Lianwen as Zhou Tingbing, Li Rentang as Hua Cheng, Chen Yin as Zhang Yizhi, Zhu Decheng as Youwa, Gong Xibing as Qin Fafeng, Zhang Jie as Xu Guangfa

In 1949, educated by Party member Hua Cheng, Yuming Oil Field worker Zhou Tingbing is deeply involved in smashing the U.S. economic embargo of China, and its theory that "China has no oil." Ten years later, China still has not found oil. Specialist Feng Chao is a blind admirer of Western theories. so adopts the wrong line; chief geologist Zhang Yizhi also adheres to the "no oil" theory. Zhou Tingbing struggles against the incorrect theory that China does not have any major oil fields. Zhou Tingbing goes to participate in oil explorations on the North China prairie, working closely with Hua Cheng, now a political commissar. However, Feng Chao and Zhang Yizhi still insist in the old methods, and try to make trouble for Zhou. Finally, when Feng Chao's history of counter-revolution and his current counter-revolutionary crimes are disclosed, Zhang Yizhi learns a lesson from the reality. Zhou Yibing and the others discover a major oil field with high production capacity. This becomes the start of China's oil industry.

274. *Bullets from His Gun (Sha Ji Si Fu)*

1994. Changchun Film Studio. Color. Letterboxed. 9 Reels. Direction: Qiao Keji. Screenplay: Ding Mu. Cinematography: Chen Chang'an, Wang Jian, Sun Shengyun. Art Direction: Shen Huimin. Music: Liu Kexin. Sound: Wang Baosheng. Costume: Guo Xiuying. Makeup: Han Yi. Cast: Li Youbin as Yang Zijiang, Yu Yankai as Nan Tianyun, Dongfang Wenying as Nan Tianyan, Chen Meidong as Lan Feng, Du Song as Leng Ren, Li Xida as Yuwen Changcheng, Wu Kejian as Hei Dahan

At the end of World War II, when the city of Jiangcheng reverts to Chinese hands, senior detective Yang Zhigang is sent to investigate a murder case in which an important government official was found dead in a brothel. He unravels a tangled web of wartime collaboration and Nationalist-Communist political rivalries.

275. *Buluotuo River (Bu Luo Tuo He)*

1989. Guangxi Film Studio. Color. Letterboxed. 9 Reels. Direction: Tan Yijian. Screenplay: Chen Yufan, Mo Fei. Cinematography: Ye Ruiwei. Art Direction: Ni Shaohua. Music: Yang Xiwu. Sound: Wang Lewen. Cast: Lu Ling as Danian, Liu Kui as Guluo, Ma Jie as Tekang, Zhang Jing as Li Shijiao

When China enters its era of reform and opening during the early 1980s, young Zhuang minority girl Danian leaves her mountain village to pursue a fashion designing career in the city. Her designing talents attract the attention of Xinxin Clothing Company designer Tekang and company manager Li Shijiao. Adding her designs to their offerings enables the company to land a contract with overseas companies. At last, Danian wins a minority clothing award for her designs.

276. *Burning Flames in a Steel Window (Tie Chuang Lie Huo)*

1958. Tianma Film Studio. B & W. 10 Reels. Direction: Wang Weiyi. Screenplay: Ke Lan. Cinematography: Shen Xilin. Art Direction: Wang Yuebai. Music: Lu Qiming. Sound: Yuan

Qingyu. Makeup: Wang Tiebin. Cast: Zhang Hui as Zhang Shaohua, Zhang Yi as Mr. Shen, Qi Heng as Tang Yanjing, Feng Ji as Ma Jun, Wang Xin as Li Aqing, Jiang Shan as Mr. Wang

On the eve of liberation, Shanghai power plant worker Zhang Shaohua, a CPC member, infiltrates the company's yellow dog union in order to battle its reactionary leadership. But he soon arouses suspicions, and various stratagems are employed against him. These are at first attempts to discredit him with the union rank-and-file, and then later arrest and torture. The police finally forge a letter from Zhang claiming to have committed various crimes, and affix his fingerprint to the document while he is unconscious. While awaiting trial, Zhang's wife Aqing visits him, and seeing how she has grown politically under the Party's tutelage bolsters his confidence and resolve. In court, he deftly exposes the government conspiracy for all to see, but is killed at his moment of triumph.

277. *The Burning of Yuan Ming Yuan (Huo Shao Yuan Ming Yuan)*

1983. China Film Cooperation Company & Hong Kong New Kunlun Company Co-Production. 9 Reels. Direction: Li Hanxiang. Screenplay: Yang Chunbing, Cinematography: Yang Guanling, Tang Musheng. Art Direction: Song Hongrong. Music: Ye Chunzhi. Cast: Liang Jiahui (Tony Leung) as Xian Feng, Liu Xiaoqing as Yulan, Chen Ye as Cian, Xiang Lei as Shu Shun, Zhou Jie as the Concubine Li, Zhang Tielin as Yi Qing

In 1852, Yulan, daughter of a senior official at the Manchu court, is chosen at the age of 17 to serve the Imperial family in the Forbidden City. For some time she attracts no attention from the Emperor Xian Feng, until one day he chances to hear her singing. From that day on she becomes one of the Emperor's favorites, with the title the Concubine Yi. A year later she gives birth to a son Zhai Chun, which solidifies her status in the Forbidden City. When a British and French allied force attacks Beijing, Xian Feng takes his family and entourage and flees to the emperor's retreat at Rehe.

Sequel: "The Reign Behind the Curtain."

278. *Busy Metropolis (Che Shui Ma Long)*

1981. Shanghai Film Studio. Color. 10 Reels. Direction: Lu Ren. Screenplay: Zhao Danian. Cinematography: Zhang Yuanmin, Ji Hongsheng.

Art Direction: Zhang Chongxiang. Music: Yang Mao. Sound: Feng Deyao. Cast: Xu Zhongquan as Ma Dache, Zhao Jing as Ai Jinghua, Lei Zhongqian as Ma Luotuo, Ju Naishe as Ma Shanbei

A horsedrawn wagon loaded with fertilizer for a commune ties up traffic on a busy roadway in a Beijing suburb. An argument ensues between the wagon driver, Ma Dache, and a woman truck driver named Ai Jinghua. Although the two do not know each other, she is engaged to a soldier who happens to be Ma Dache's son. When the commune converts to delivering its vegetables to the city by truck, Ai Jinghua is assigned to supervise the changeover, and the commune arranges for her to stay in Ma Dache's home. The two former antagonists are shocked when they are first introduced, but they have no choice but to go along with the arrangement. The commune members welcome Ai Jinghua's arrival, and rush to sign up for driver training. Not so enthusiastic are the wagon drivers such as Ma Dache, who bitterly resent Ai Jinghua and try to block her work. When Ma Dache's son Ma Sanbei is released from the army, he stands by his fiancee, which makes his father very angry. They go ahead with wedding plans anyway, aided by the groom's Grandfather Ma Luotuo. At their wedding banquet, the father shows up unexpectedly to give the couple his blessing and apologize to his new daughter-in-law. It turns out that Ma Dache's beloved horse and wagon will have a new and important role, making deliveries to the many places that still cannot be reached by trucks.

279. *By the Lakeside (Hu Pan)*

1981. Shanghai Film Studio. Color. 5 Reels. Direction: Wu Zhennian. Screenplay: Lu Ping. Cinematography: Wang Yi. Art Direction: Yao Wei. Music: Yang Shaolu. Sound: Xu Xilin. Cast: Wang Weiping as Ke Ting, Liu Jia as Yuan Xia, Xu Jinjin as Li Lu, Lu Qin as the gossip, Cheng Zhi as Father, Zhang Ying as Mother

The Xinghuo Chemical Plant, a small street operation, determines to expand production, and technician Ke Ting is most anxious to have a larger furnace installed. One day, at a lake side bicycle repairing shop, Ke Ting meets Wan Xia, a girl who is also there for bicycle repairs. She has heard of the Xinghuo plant's urgent need for a bigger furnace, and offers to help Ke Ting buy one, for which he is very grateful. Ke Ting and Wan Xia are very at-

tracted to each other, and she later invites him to her home to talk about the furnace, although she really wants him to meet her parents. Wan Xia's father looks down upon Ke Ting because the young man works in a small street plant. His feelings hurt, Ke Ting misunderstands Wan Xia's intentions and leaves angrily. Wan Xia later goes to Ke Ting to apologize, and they also get the furnace situation resolved. Ke Ting and Wan Xia reconcile.

280. *Cai Yue and Her Lover (Cai Yue He Ta De Qing Ren)*

1992. Yunnan Minority Film Studio. Color. Letterboxed. 9 Reels. Direction: Yu Jie, Wu Kuangwen. Screenplay: Fang Yihua. Cinematography: Si Yongmin. Art Direction: Wang Binghui. Music: Xu Jingxin. Sound: Ou Lifeng. Costume: Jiang Xiaoyun, Zhao Qiongxian. Makeup: Yang Meixin. Cast: Wu Jing as Cai Yue, Lu Xiaohe as Che Zhao, Yang Jing as Qiao Hua, Zhang Shaojun as A Sheng

Middle-aged widow Cai Yue operates a store on Gold Jade Island. Also living on the island is Che Zhao, who had been her lover years before. Since he is also widowed, the two rekindle their old relationship, but encounter strong opposition from the adult children on both sides. Cai Yue patiently wins over Che Zhao's children, and buys a tourism boat to expand her business. At last, the two are married with the blessings of all.

281. *The Cailang Plan (Cai Lang Ji Hua)*

1989. Pearl River Film Studio. Color. 9 Reels. Direction: Xu Xiaoxing, Huo Zhuang. Screenplay: Zhao Danian, Huo Zhuang. Cinematography: Zhang Zhongping. Art Direction: Liu Changbao. Music: Zhang Qianyi. Sound: Li Jingcheng, Zhang Baojian. Cast: Wu Gang as Xiao Cai, Zhao Xiaorui as Liang Rong, Liang Danni as Lin Meishan, Sun Haiying as Qi Yuping, Ren Shen as Director Wang, Wang Wei as Xiao Wang, Li Yan as Xiao Li, Sun Benhou as Qi Jincai, Zou Jianzhong as Zhou Jianjun, Yu Zhijie as A Liu

282. *Camel Grass (Luo Tuo Cao)*

1983. August First Film Studio. Color. 10 Reels. Direction: Jing Mukui, Zhao Jilie. Screenplay: Wang Shuzen. Cinematographer: Yu Chengzhi, Yang Xiuqin. Art Direction: Cui Qinsheng. Music: Fu Gengcheng. Sound: Yu

Chengzhi, Yang Xiuqin. Cast: Zhu Lin as Liu Ying, Zhao Xiaomin as Ye Zhifeng, Sun Jitang as Ke Daguang

At the end of the 1950s, college graduate Liu Ying and some of her classmates have the opportunity to work in the desert of Northwest China as a part of China's missile research team under the command of PLA Captain Ke Daguang. Her boyfriend tries to persuade her to stay, but when he sees she is determined to go, they break up. At the desert outpost, her classmate Ye Zhifeng professes his love for Liu Ying, and although Ke Daguang has fallen for her too, he helps the two classmates get together and marry. But when China later enters a period of severe economic difficulties, Ye abandons the pregnant Liu Ying and returns to his hometown. They divorce, and Liu Ying gives birth to a little girl. Later, during the Cultural Revolution, she and Ke Daguang are married. All goes well until the early 1980s, when Ke Daguang is reassigned back to a military post deep in the desert. Ke and his unit disappear in a sandstorm. Fortunately they are found, and Liu Ying and her daughter rush to join him.

283. *Camel Xiangzi (Luo Tuo Xiang Zi)*

1982. Beijing Film Studio. Color. Wide Screen. 12 Reels. Direction: Ling Zhifeng. Screenplay: Ling Zhifeng, based on the novel of the same title by Lao She (1899-1966). Cinematographer: Wu Shenghan and Liang Zhiyong. Art Direction: Yu Yiru. Music: Ju Xixian. Sound: Wang Zemin. Cast: Zhang Fengyi as Xiangzi, Siqin Gaowa as Huniu, Yin Xin as Xiao Fuzhi, Yan Bide as Liu Shi, Liang Tang as Mr. Cao

A farm boy named Xiangzi comes to old Beijing from his rural home with dreams of controlling and mastering his own fate. He finds work pulling a rickshaw, but plans to become a "free and independent rickshaw puller," so that he does have to take the bullying these workers usually receive when working for rickshaw owners. He bears humiliation, hunger, and extremely hard labor to save enough for his own rickshaw. However, "camels" like Xiangzi never make it in old China. His boss's daughter is very attracted to him. Although she is unattractive, lazy and much older than Xiangzi, she is successful at seducing him, and when she gets pregnant he is forced to marry her. However, she dies in labor. Xiangzi finally loses his confidence and

hopes in his struggle to get ahead in life. At last he winds up a suicide.

Best Picture, 1983 Golden Rooster Awards.

Best Picture, 1983 Hundred Flowers Awards.

Best Actress Siqin Gaowa, 1983 Golden Rooster Awards.

Best Actress Siqin Gaowa, 1983 Hundred Flowers Awards.

Best Art Direction Yu Yiru, 1983 Golden Rooster Awards.

284. *Can Do Well Anyplace (He Chu Bu Feng Liu)*

1983. Zhejiang Film Studio. Color. 10 Reels. Direction: Zhu Wenshun, Chen Xianyu. Screenplay: Ma Sichong, Hu Yuewei. Cinematographer: Zhou Rongzheng, Zhou Ping. Art Direction: Lu Jun, Li Shuqi. Music: Lu Enlai. Sound: Dong Fuliang. Cast: Zhao Na as Zhuang Li, Pang Ming as Ai Na, Jin Kangmin as Old Uncle Fang, Wang Fuyou as Yang Guang, Song Yinqiu as Fan Xia

In 1969, Zhuang Li was sent to work in the countryside after graduating from high school. Now, 10 years later, she is permitted to return to her hometown where she moves in temporarily with her old classmate Fan Xia. Fan is 30 and still single, although she loves a man named Ai Hu. Zhuang Li has problems finding a worthwhile job, so she decides to take advantage of the growing tourist trade in the area by starting a snack food service in partnership with Ai Hu's younger sister. One day, Zhuang Li unexpectedly meets her old boy friend Yang Guang, who now works for a foreign trade company. He still cares for her, but looks down on her present work. He uses his connections to find her a cushy job in his company. But Zhuang Li soon finds her new job is really meaningless, created simply as a favor for Yang. In addition, she finds his values have changed for the worse, so she leaves the company and goes back to selling snack food. The young women's business flourishes and soon expands to a multiple service company. Fan Xia and Ai Hu marry and start a family. At last, Yang Guang sees the better lives the others lead, and begins to change for the good.

285. *Cannot Be Closed (Guan Bu Zhu)*

1956. Changchun Film Studio. B & W. 7 Reels. Directors: Zhang Xinshi and Liu Guoquan.

Screenplay uncredited, but based on the stage play of the same title by Zhao Yuxiang. Cinematographer: Wang Qiming. Set Design: Shi Weijun, Music: Che Ming. Sound: Shen Guli. Cast: Li Shugu as Secretary Fan, Tian Jihai as Lu Changqing, Wang Yuzhu as Zhou Gang, Zhang Yun as Old Mr. Liu, Wu Guilin as Jiangfa, Wu Zhende as Director Zhao

The farmers of Xinle Village in Northeast China request the establishment of an agricultural cooperative. Instead of conducting a study of the matter, District Secretary Fan just listens to the opinions of prosperous farmer Jiang Fa. Noting there would be some problems involved in organization, he unilaterally declares the conditions are not ripe, particularly the financial conditions, and rejects the proposal. He also criticizes Xinle Village Branch Secretary Lu Changqing for raising the topic in the first place. But Lu does not give up easily. He brings the local people together to figure out various ways of resolving the capital shortage. Then, when Director Zhao of the county work department arrives on an inspection visit, he persuades Secretary Fan, and approves the village's establishment of a co-op. Even comparatively prosperous Jiang Fa decides to join.

286. *Cannot Forget You (Wang Bu Liao Ni)*

1982. Shanghai Film Studio. Color. 6 Reels. Direction: Zhang Huijun. Screenplay: Zhao Jiadi, Xu Canglin, Zhang Huijun. Cinematographer: Shen Miaorong. Art Direction: Wu Weifei. Music: Yang Zhulu. Sound: Dong Juqing. Cast: Zhang Yanping as Fu Jiang, Qi Ping as Huang Li, Zhang Zhihua as Yang Xiu, Zhang Xiaorong as Wu Liang, Yan Yongxuan as Director, Liu Fei as Director Tian

A boy named Fu Jiang and a girl named Huang Liandi are sent to work in the same rural village during the Cultural Revolution. Huang Liandi's mother is sick and alone in the city, so when Fu Jiang is later offered a reassignment back to the city he unselfishly relinquishes it so that she may return. A few years later, Fu gets another chance to return to the city and becomes a street cleaner. One day by chance he meets Huang, now an actress. Huang had always been very grateful to Fu for his earlier help, and she is delighted to see him again. The two fall in love, but Huang looks down upon Fu's work and tries everything she can to get him out of his job. But Fu is de-

voted to his work, which he considers important to the environment. They eventually have a big argument and break up. Although Fu Jiang deeply loves Huang, he doesn't want to quit his job. Through a series of stories which illustrate Fu's sweet nature, Huang finally is moved to reconcile with him.

287. *Cannot Take Care of Everything (Gu Ci Shi Bi)*

1981. Guangxi Film Studio. Color. 9 Reels. Direction: Wu Yinxun. Screenplay: Zhou Minzheng. Cinematographer: Liao Fan, Sun Lixian. Art Direction: Lao Guanneng. Music: Yang Shaoyi. Sound: Li Zhuwen. Cast: Li Ding as Zhou Ding, Chi Zhiqiang as Guo Yunpeng, Jin Yi as Meiyan, Mei Zhaohua as Du Hai, Chen Zhonghe as Liao Liping, Li Tan as Director Lin

Although Zhou Ming, the new deputy director of the Qinshan County Bureau of Commerce, knows nothing of business, his massive ego keeps him from even trying to learn. As the Spring Festival approaches with a shortage of chickens in the markets, Zhou Ming urges getting chickens by any means possible. Bureau of Commerce cadre Guo Yunpeng, who is after Zhou's daughter Mei Yan, pleases his boss by proposing a plan to exchange the County's supply of sewing machines for chickens from another county. Although the markets wind up with a plentiful supply of chickens at the Festival, when it is over they are now out of sewing machines, presenting an entirely new problem. In contrast with Guo Yunpeng, the County department store manager Du Hai correctly points out the errors Zhou and Guo committed. This makes Zhou Ming angry, so he raises objections to his daughter's relationship with Du Hai. At last, Zhou Hai finally realizes the main problem is he does not know business. Meiyan and Du Hai are married.

288. *The Capable Brother (Qiao Ge Er)*

1983. Xi'an Film Studio. Color. 9 Reels. Direction: Yi Donglin, Zhang Yumin. Screenplay: Can Xuepeng. Cinematographer: Zhu Kongyang. Art Direction: Yang Gang, Dai Yuanzhong. Music: Xie Tiyin. Sound: Chen Yudan, Chen Chenli. Cast: Liao Jingsheng as Erzhu the capable brother, Li Baoan as Sun Xingguang, Fu Lili as Qiao Geer, Zhao Zhuguo as Liu's wife, Wang Lina as Xing's wife, Yan Cheng as Erzhu's mother, Fu Lin as Qiao Geer's mother

Erzhu is not only poor, he has to support and care for his ailing mother as well. Although 30, he is still single. His neighbor Xing's wife wants to help him find a mate, so she introduces him to Qiao Geer, who he finds very attractive. She likes Erzhu, but she is also being courted by another neighbor Sun Xingguang. Sun is making a lot of money, and this gives him an advantage in that Qiao Geer's mother dreams of wealth. She is adamantly opposed to poor Erzhu as a son-in-law. Qiao really admires Erzhu, for she remembers how some years ago he had saved the life of her father. So she devises a plan for Erzhu to become prosperous by making and selling handicrafts. With her help, his financial outlook turns around completely, and now Qiao Geer's mother welcomes Erzhu as her daughter's fiancee.

289. *A Capable Wife (Nei Dang Jia)*

1982. Emei Film Studio. Color. 9 Reels. Direction: Teng Jingxian. Screenplay: Wang Runzi. Cinematographer: Feng Shilin. Art Direction: Wang Yongkang. Music: Gao Chao. Sound: Zhang Jianping. Cast: Wang Yumei as Li Qiulan, Gao Baocheng as Shuocheng, Wang Qiuying as Liu Jingui, Zhao Shoukai as Director Sun, Zhou Hong as Xinni, Teng Jingxian as the county director

In a North China village, Party cadre Li Qiulan learns that former landlord Liu Jingui, now a successful overseas businessman, will soon visit his old hometown. She is even more upset when she is asked by county director Sun to be Liu's official greeter and host during his visit. She goes to the county to appeal this, for Liu had treated her and her family very badly when he lived there. But the county officials patiently explain to her the Party's new policy of opening and reform, so she must accept the assignment. Qiulan receives Liu and his granddaughter as a new society host. Her forgiving spirit deeply moves Liu, and brings out his love for his motherland.

290. *Capture by Stratagem of Mount Hua (Zhi Qu Hua Shan)*

1953. Beijing Film Studio. B & W. 12 Reels. Direction: Guo Wei. Screenplay: Guo Wei, Ji Ye and Dong Fang, from a novel by Ren Ping and Wang Zongyuan. Cinematography: Chen Minhun. Set Design: Qin Wei. Music: Chen Di and Li Jida. Sound: Cai Jun. Costume: Wang Feng. Makeup: Li Ende. Cast: Li Jinbang as the Commander, Xu Youxin as the Political Supervisor, Yang Qingwei as the Chief of Staff, Guo Yuntai as Li Minji, Tian Dan as Lu Deliang, Yan Zhenhe as Meng Shijun, Liu Qing as Chang Shenglin

In 1949, the PLA launches a massive attack aimed at liberating China's vast northwest. As a division of Hu Zongnan's Nationalist warlord army retreats southward, its commander decides to resist the Communist advance by digging in on treacherous Mount Hua. Liu Mingji, a scout in one PLA unit, aided by a local herb farmer named Chang Shenglin, cracks the riddle "since ancient times, there has been only one road to Mount Hua." They scale the north peak from a small back road and occupy the highest, controlling point, then send the farmer for help. The enemy commander desperately organizes an attack on them, but at this critical point, Chang Shenglin returns with the main PLA force, and the Nationalists are wiped out.

291. *Carefree Grass (Wang You Cao)*

1982. Changchun Film Studio. Color. 9 Reels. Direction: Ke Ren. Screenplay: An Zhi. Cinematographer: Liu Yongzhen. Art Direction: Xu Zhenou. Music: Gao Feng. Sound: Yuan Minda. Cast: Zhou Lina as Hua Gu, Li Shixi as Guan Fuxing, Li Ying as Lan, Ma Loufu as Mr. Qin, Shao Xicheng as Cheng Kun, Li Wei as Shu Kui

In 1934, the main force of the Red Army retreats from a Communist-held area, and their former base is taken over by the Nationalist Army. The local county CPC committee is wiped out when one of their members Cheng Run betrays the rest. The Party sends Hua Gu as a liaison to the county to locate members gone underground, organize a new Party committee and execute the traitor. With the help of some local people and the local Red Army regimental commander Guan Fuxing, he is initially successful. Then a Nationalist spy in the organization spreads a rumor that Hua Gu himself is a traitor, which deters his progress. Later, Hua is shot and killed in a gun battle with enemy agents, but the struggle goes on, and the new revolutionary organization continues to expand. In 1937, when the Nationalists and Communists establish an anti-Japanese alliance, Guan leads his army against the Japanese.

***Capture by Stratagem of Mount Hua.* 1953. Beijing Film Studio.**

292. *Careless Wife (Mao Jiao Xi Fu)*

1984. Shanghai Film Studio. Color. Letter-boxed. 10 Reels. Direction: Lu Ping. Screenplay: Qiang Fanjun, Gao Zhongxin, Gao Xiang. Cinematographer: Wun Sijie. Art Direction: Wu Weifei. Music: Yang Shaolu. Sound: Wang Shu. Cast: Qian Yinmei as Jia Yuezhen, Gao Zhongxin as He Yimin

Elementary school teacher Jia Yuezhen's family busily prepares for the first visit of their son's fiancee. When she arrives, however, a dispute occurs because the prospective daughter-in-law considers their "first meeting gift" to her too extravagant and their wedding plans too lavish. At last, they all agree to keep it simple, as she desires. At the home of Jia Yuezhen's brother, however, the reverse is true: their prospective daughter-in-law has the whole family upset with her continually escalating demands for her wedding.

293. *Case 405: Murder (405 Mou Sha An)*

1980. Shanghai Film Studio. B & W. 10 Reels. Direction: Shen Yaoting. Screenplay: Yu Bengzheng, Shen Yaoting. Cinematographer:

Zhang Guifu, Zhao Junhong. Art Direction: Li Huazhong, Wang Xingcang. Music: Xu Jingxin. Sound: Tu Minde. Cast: Zhong Xinghuo as Chen Minhui, Xu Ming as Qian Kai, Yan Xiang as Fang Minshan, Shi Jiufeng as Xu Yibing, Wu Xiqian as Lu Ao, Li Lanfa as Liu Guoqiang, Zhang Yan as Ding Juan

Donghai City PSB investigators Qian Kai and Chen Minhui are sent to investigate the murder of Li Liang, a young man found dead in his home by his girl friend Ding Juan. In the victim's bathroom, they find two V-shaped clumps of mud, and a vague reference in his notebook concerning someone named A San. The evidence leads the investigators to two A Sans, but Qian Kai gradually comes to realize this is no ordinary criminal case, but something much more complex. Qian Kai persuades Chen Minhui to stop investigating it as such, and with the support of Lu Ao, a consultant to the PSB, Chen broadens the investigation. He finds himself in danger: an attempt is made to steal the evidence, and later he is attacked, with only the timely arrival of his partner Qian Kai saving him. Knowing he is getting close to the truth, Chen doggedly moves forward with his investigation, and at last finds the truth, a conspiracy which reaches into the highest level of the PSB itself.

294. *Case 508 (Wu Ling Ba Yi An)*

1984. Guangxi Film Studio. Color. 9 Reels. Direction: Wu Tianren. Screenplay: Li Baolin. Cinematographer: Meng Xiongqiang. Art Direction: Lao Guanneng. Music: Li Yanlin. Sound: Li Zhuwen. Cast: Ma Guanyin as Yan Dun, Yang Baolong as Lu Tie, Ma Ning as Long Chengdi, Yin Shiqing as Song Yamei, Gao Bo as Su Yi

In 1981, steel mill worker Cai Ping falls from a platform and is killed. The suspicious circumstances surrounding the incident lead the PSB to detain workshop head Lu Tie for questioning as a possible murder suspect. Lu is soon released, however, for lack of evidence. Young PSB officer Yan Dun continues the investigation, and various clues point to the involvement of the son of the city's Party Secretary, the mill's chief of security and one of Yan Dun's close personal friends. Yan's investigation finally proves the Party Secretary's son was the killer.

295. *A Case of Economic Crime (Jin Yuan Da Jie An)*

1990. Shanghai Film Studio. Color. Wide Screen. 10 Reels. Direction: Zhuang Hongsheng. Screenplay: Zen Zhaohong. Cinematography: Shen Miaorong. Art Direction: Wang Xingcang. Music: Lu Qimin. Sound: Ren Daming. Cast: Wu Gang as Zhong Cheng, Zhu Lei as Guo Chao, Zhen Shuang as Ling Yun, Yu Fei as Moersi

A Chinese import-export company loses US$5 million when a shipment of tobacco it brings in turns out to be of poor quality. Detectives Zhong Cheng and Guo Chao find that the firm's contact, a Hong Kong businessman, has fled, as has one of the company's department directors. The director is later murdered by a mysterious woman, and later his wife is also found dead. Zhong Cheng's investigation is complicated when his former lover, fashion model Ling Yun, turns up and appears to be somehow involved. The case turns out to be involved with an international crime ring. Zhong Cheng is killed when rescuing a hostage, but the police at last smash the crime ring's operations in China. Ling Yun turns out to be an undercover policewoman who had infiltrated the ring.

296. *The Case of the Buddha (Fo Guang Xia Ying)*

1990. Shanghai Film Studio. Color. Letterboxed. 10 Reels. Direction: Bao Qicheng. Screenplay: Gong Nan. Cinematographer: Dan Lianguo. Art Direction: Wu Tianci. Music: Yang Mao. Sound: Tu Mingde. Cast: Li Wei as Yu Guiqin, Yan Xiang as Han Xiyuan, Nai She as Ouyang Xiong, Wang Zhihua as Shen Jianzhong, Huang Shoukang as Jiang Yijian and Liu Xuzhong, Wun Guojun as Qian Afa, Wang Shaoguang as Secretary Wang, Yu Guichun as Huang Jingeng

During World War II, the head of a clan entrusts one of his followers with a valuable 11th Century statuette of Buddha, instructing him to take it to Hong Kong, away from the fighting. This sets off a complex three-way struggle for the Buddha, between clan members, government police collaborating with the Japanese, and shady Shanghai businessmen.

297. *The Case of Xu Qiuying (Xu Qiu Ying An Jian)*

1958. Changchun Film Studio. B & W. 9 Reels. Direction: Yu Yanfu. Screenplay: Cong Chen, Li Chi. Cinematographer: Yi Zhi. Art Direction: Wang Xingwen. Music: Lei Zhenbang. Sound: Chen Yudan. Cast: Shen Bingning as Xu Qiuying, Liu Zenqing as He Bing, Pu Ke as Du Yongkai, Li Yalin as Wang Liang, Wang Chunying as Sui Fu, Qu Wei as Qi Lujun.

Xu Qiuying, an officer in the Civil Affairs Bureau's security department, is murdered on the eve of her marriage to coworker He Bing. When investigators Wang Liang and Du Yongkai search the murder scene, they find a military uniform button and a shell case which point them to Xu Qiuying's former lover, ex-soldier Peng Fang, who had been seen in the area on the night of the murder. At Peng's home, they find the button is from one of his old uniforms, and his service weapon matches the bullet used. From this evidence, Du Yongkai concludes Peng is the killer, but Wang Liang is unconvinced. After many days of intense investigation, he finds the truth: the murdered woman had been a Nationalist agent before Liberation, a fact she kept secret. Two of her former colleagues, still spying for Taiwan, had approached her and demanded she collect defense secrets for them. When she refused, threatening to turn them in, they killed her and planted evidence to frame Peng Fang. When arrested, the two spies implicate others, and the spy ring is destroyed.

298. *Casting Swords (Zhu Jian)*

1994. Beijing Film Studio, Hong Kong Film Work Studio Co-Production. Color. Letterboxed. 9 Reels. Direction: Zhang Huaxun. Screenplay: Zhang Yang, Yang Chongjie, based on the story of the same title by Lu Xun (1881–1936). Cinematography: Liu Xiaoming, Sun Xiaoguang. Art Direction: Liu Changbao, Qin Duo. Costume: Liu Fang. Makeup: Fang Yiping, Wang Wanbin, Ma Shuying. Cast: Gao Fa as Yan Zhiao, Ma Jingwu as the King of Chu, Ruan Xun as Mei Jianchi, Ma Chongle as Ganjiang, Yang Qing as Mo Xie

The King of Chu orders master sword-smith Gan Jiang and his wife Mo Xie to make a sword for him, a weapon superior to any other in the land. The couple labor for three years to produce such a sword, but when they present it to the king, he promptly kills Gan Jiang with it, to prevent anyone ever obtaining its equal. Over the next 16 years, Mo Xie raises the couple's son to be a master swordsman and swordsmith. He at last confronts and kills the evil king.

299. *Catch Them in Their Dens (Hu Xue Zhui Zong)*

1956. Changchun Film Studio. B & W. 9 Reels. Direction: Huang Shu. Screenplay: Yin Chi, Ren Guilin, Wang Yutang. Cinematographer: Nie Jing. Set Design: Dong Ping. Music: Wang Bo, Lou Zhanghou. Sound: Yuan Mingda. Cast: Ying Zhiming as Chen Huiyuan, Zhao Lian as Li Yonghe, Liu Zhenqin as Liu Ming, Li Yunong as Mr. Qian, Xu Shiyan as Fu Ke, Zhang Fengxiang as Xia Yunwu

Shortly after the establishment of the PRC, Nationalist spy master Cui Xizheng goes underground in a certain city in the cover of manager of a large grocery store. From there he commands a network of spies and a gang supporting them, in both the city and the surrounding countryside. They engage in acts of robbery and sabotage, and also assign woman agent Zhi Liping to infiltrate the industrial and commercial community to gather information. Officer Li Yonghe infiltrates the gang and gains their trust. Cui exploits the carelessness of the city's Bureau of Commerce director by having Zhi Liping hide a list of the spies in the director's home. Li Yonghe eventually obtains this list through some dangerous inside work, but has a very close call when Sun Shigao, a spy just arrived from Taiwan, tests him by pretending to be a PSB officer. Li skillfully evades the trap and uses the name list he obtains to help the real PSB officers capture all the spies and members of the gang.

300. *Catching Bandits in the Desert (Da Mo Qian Fei)*

1994. August First Film Studio. Color. Letterboxed. 9 Reels. Direction: Jiang Ge. Screenplay: Zhao Yuying. Cinematography: Wang Jianguo. Art Direction: Quan Rongzhe. Music: Xu Zhijun. Sound: Wang Yingang. Costume: Liang Ying. Makeup: Yang Shuoling. Cast: Feng Guoqiang as Zhang Junyao, Chang Xiaoyang as Zhang Fan, Qi Rong as Xiao Feng, Zhao Yuanyu as Yao Bing, Yang Haiquan as Xing Ge, Shi Ke as Yang Chunhua, Wang Xinghai as Ma Cheng, Wang Liangbo as Lao Jia, Yang Heizi as Zhao Zhonghua

A PLA camel transport team crossing the desert takes time out from its mission to battle a group of escaped prisoners planning to steal a gold Buddha from an ancient tomb. The army group wins out in the end, after which they resume their trek across the desert.

301. *Catching Folk (Lie Hu)*

1995. Beijing Xin Jiyuan Film Development Company, China Film Company, Youth Film Studio Co-Production. Color. Letterboxed. Direction: Dong Wei. Screenplay: Dong Wei, Jiang Dahai. Cinematography: Yan Weilun. Cast: Liang Zheng, Chen Xiaochun, Yu Rongguang

Hong Kong policewoman Yang Ling goes under cover as a barmaid to obtain evidence on crime boss Ruan Dong. When the police make their move to arrest Ruan, he flees and vengefully attacks Yang Ling's home, killing her beloved Uncle Zhang. Ruan flees to the mainland, with Yang in pursuit. The mainland police assign officers to assist Yang and follow Ruan. The joint operation at last brings Ruan Dong to bay.

302. *The Category 10 Storm (Shi Ji Lang)*

1960. Changchun Film Studio. B & W. 10 Reels. Direction: Zhang Qi. Screenplay: The East Sea Warships 307 and 314 Collective Writing Team. Cinematographer: Zhang Yi. Art Direction: Shi Weijun, Music: Li Yaodong, Bai Chongyan, Sound: Yan Jin. Cast: Zhang Fengxiang as the Political Commissar, Zhang Hui as the ship's captain, Liu Zhenqin as Deng Baocheng, Yang Qitian as Lin Xiaohu, Jin Li as Guan Tongzhang, Sun Xiaofei as Yie Kangling

A naval warship accepts the emergency mission of shipping a load of large furnaces to Qingdao from Shanghai. On the way, they run into a Category 10 storm, which destroys their navigation instruments and knocks out the radio communication with naval headquarters. Moreover, the cargo hold begins to leak. Led by their captain and political commissar, the entire crew rises to the task and overcomes one difficulty after another, finally getting the furnaces safely to their destination.

303. *Celebration (Zhang Deng Jie Cai)*

1982. Pearl River Film Studio. Color. Direction: Cao Zheng, Cai Yuanyuan. Screenplay: Song Fengyi, Song Yinjie. Cinematographer: Li Zhexian. Art Direction: Zhang Zhichu. Music: Liu Zuang. Sound: Li Dehua. Cast: Mu Huaihu as Dalu, Jin Yi as Qian Tieyin, Ma Zhigang as Uncle Li, Zhang Xiaochun as Erlu, Yan Lina as Wu Fengyin, Ma Qian as Huo Baosheng

Uncle Li lives with his two younger cousins in a mountain village. One of these, Li Dalu, has reached marriageable age, and Uncle Li sets out to find a wife for him through a matchmaker. He collects the demanded sum of money and makes all the wedding preparations. But on the day of the wedding, the bride-to-be attempts suicide. It turns out that she has a lover, but her parents are forcing her to marry Dalu because the boy she wants has too little money to satisfy them. Li Dalu is a kindly man, and since he refuses to make others unhappy, insists the wedding be cancelled. Uncle Li sets out to find others, but each time the monetary demands of prospective in-laws bring negotiations to a halt. In time, new customs replace the old traditional way of doing things, and the two younger cousins both find brides on their own.

304. *Challenge to Battle (Tiao Zhan)*

1990. Shanghai Film Studio. Color. Letterboxed. 9 Reels. Direction: Zhang Jianya. Screenplay: Zhang Xian and Mu Jiang. Cinematography: Huang Baohua. Art Direction: Zhou Xinren. Music: Xia Liang. Sound: Zhan Xin. Costume: Zhang Gengbao. Makeup: Yin Lihua. Cast: Zhang Kanger as Liu Gengquan, Ge Lili as Juzi, Liu Hongkun as Ma Wenguang, Cui Jie as Fang Hu, Wang Hui as He Da, Ye Xiaokeng as Manager Gao

305. *Changbai Mountain Heroes (Bai Shan Ying Xiong Han)*

1992. Children's Film Studio. Color. Letterboxed. 9 Reels. Direction: Wang Xuexin. Screenplay: Zhang Zhengqin. Cinematography: Ning Changcheng. Art Direction: Qi Ming. Music: Guo Xiaotian. Sound: Zhang Hongguang. Costume: Su Pengling. Makeup: Wang Xiaoling. Cast: Zhang Yan as Hou Xing, Huang Bo as Erniu, Guo Hongfei as Dagou

During the anti-Japanese War, an opera troupe is active in the Changbai Mountain area. Three young opera performers are also secret guerrilla fighters with excellent kung fu skills. The three teenagers steal a map of the Japanese defense layout for the area. Afterwards, on orders from the area Communist commander, they work with the Volunteer Army to blow up a Japanese train loaded with armaments. They also expose and kill a traitor and kill the Japanese commander in the area.

306. *Changed Lives (Huan Le Ren Jian)*

1959. Changchun Film Studio. Color. 11 Reels. Direction: Wu Tian. Screenplay: Hu Su, Wang Bing and Wu Tian, based on the stage play, "Two Marriages" by Ke Fu). Cinematography: Fang Weiche, Ge Weiqing. Art Direction: Wang Guizhi. Music: Jiang Wei. Sound: Hong Di. Cast: Guo Yiwen as Wei Xiulan, Guo Zhenqing as Lu Wanchun, Bai Dezhang as Jiangming, Guo Qi as He Sufang, Tian Lie as Old Mr. Wei, Liu Zhenzhong as He Ping, Liang Yin as Zhang Yuren, Zhao Yuhua as Wang Shouren, Ma Shida as He Zhenggang

Old Mr. Wei comes to Northeast China and works in a coal mine under the Japanese collaborationist government. Wei's daughter Xiulan marries young mine worker Xiao Wang, but he is killed on their wedding day in a gas explosion in the mine. In time, Xiulan marries mine worker He Zhengang, and has a daughter Sufang. But He Zhenggang also dies in a gas explosion not long after. Mine worker Lu Wanchun helps Xiulan's family, and the two gradually fall in love. But Xiulan believes she would be a burden to Lu, so she takes her daughter and returns to her native village in Shandong province. After liberation, Xiulan goes to Northeast China to seek her father, and finds that he and Lu Wanchun have both become model workers. Lu Wanchun leads the workers in controlling gas explosions, and Xiulan also works in the mines. She and Wanchun get married, and Sufang also marries, to Wangchun's adopted son Jiangming.

307. *Chase Foes to the Death (Xun Chou Yin Yang Jie)*

1994. Xi'an Film Studio. Color. Letterboxed. 9 Reels. Direction: Li Yucai, Lu Feng. Screenplay: Li Xingjie. Art Direction: Yan Pingxiao, Chen Zheying. Music: Tao Long. Sound: Guo Chao. Cast: Sun Feihu as Li Baxian, Guo Jinghua as old man, Liao Xueqiu as widow, Zhao Chunming as Shi Hang

At the end of the 19th Century, in a remote mountain village called Yinyangjie, there stands a large house, the finest in the village. Living there are a well-to-do old man and his adopted daughter Xinger. Xinger has just started seeing a young man of the village, Zhama, and one evening after a date with him she suddenly disappears. She is found later, murdered. Everyone is shocked to think that such a nice young man could commit such a crime, but if not him, who? A stranger named Li Baxian comes to the village and tells the story. Eighteen years before, the owner of the mansion, the old man, took Li Baxian's wife for his own and had Li put in prison. When the wife died, the old man took their daughter Xinger for his mistress, and lived with her for years pretending she was his daughter. When Xinger met Zhama, she rejected the old man, who then killed her. The people of the village, furious, march on the mansion to confront the evil old man, but find he has hanged himself.

308. *Chase in Manila (Xing Zhen Feng Yun)*

1994. Emei Film Studio. Color. Letterboxed. 9 Reels. Direction: Gao Fei, Yuan Fang. Screenplay: Li Xiaojun. Cinematography: Du Xiaosi. Art Direction: Li Xinzhong. Music: Zhou Furong. Sound: Shen Guli. Costume: Miao Yi. Makeup: Huang Hua. Cast: You Jiali as Li Liya, Yang Panpan as Yang Na, Gao Fei as Huang Hengli, Zhang Wulang as Hong Ben, Tu Zhongru as bureau director Liu

After robbing a jewelry store, Huang Hengli flees from Hong Kong to the mainland. He hides out in Shekou, but is forced to go on the run again when police track him there. He makes it out of China and heads for Manila, where he can link up with a gang there. The Chinese police send detective Yang Lina to the Philippines, where he coordinates police actions against Huang and the gang harboring him.

309. *Chasing the Devil (Di Yu Zhui Zong)*

1992. Tianshan Film Studio. Color. Letterboxed. 9 Reels. Direction: Liu Zhongmin, Liu Gongwei. Screenplay: Xu Guangshun. Cinematography: Yu Tian. Art Direction: Ma Shaoxian. Music: Chen Chunguang. Sound: Liu Hongming. Costume: Jiang Yanen. Makeup: Wang Mana. Cast: Shen Junyi as Xu Tianhua, Kou Zhenghai as Xiao Yan, Dong Zhizhi as Xiao Nan, Hou Yongsheng as Director He, Hao Tienan as Chen Dahe, Chen Qi as Li Mei

In Luozhou City, TV reporter Xiao Nan witnesses a killing across the street from her home. She quickly takes some pictures of the killer, but police officer Yang Jian confiscates them. He then sends her out to the suburbs, supposedly to identify the criminal. Actually, Yang is involved in the murder, and plans to kill the young woman after she is safely out of the way. Meanwhile, police detective Xu Tianhua is on the case, and is excited to find that the chief witness is Xiao Nan, for her brother Xiao Yan is an old friend of his he has not seen for years. It turns out that Xiao Yan is the real criminal, and when Xiao Yan tries to kill Xu Tianhua, Xiao Nan protects the detective and shoots her brother dead.

310. *Chasing the Enemy Through the Desert (Sha Mo Zhui Fei Ji)*

1959. Tianma Film Studio. B & W. 8 Reels. Direction: Ge Xin. Screenplay: Ge Xin and Feng Ji, based on an original work by Yang Shangwu. Cinematographer: Lu Junfu. Art Direction: Cai Xileng. Music: Shen Tiekou. Sound: Lu Jinsong. Cast: Zhang Wenjia as the company commander, Feng Ji as Zhong Yongming, Niu Beng as Xiao Jiang, Yu Mingde as Li Yugeng, Cheng Zhi as Jin Zhizhong, Zhu Jun as an enemy agent

In the Northwest China desert in 1951, a PLA cavalry unit is engaged in mopping up elements of the now-defeated Nationalist army. Three Nationalist special agents led by Jin Zhizhong break away and try to escape to the border. Although he is wounded, cavalry officer Zhong Yongming leads soldiers Li Yugeng and Xiao Jiang in pursuit. The enemy disappears in a sandstorm. They split up to search, but only Xiao Jiang finds the agents. In the ensuing gunfight, he kills one agent and Jin Zhizhong's horse. When Li Yugeng arrives to help, Jin kills Li's horse, leaving only one horse. They continue the pursuit toward the border, with Zhong Yongming at last dying of his wounds. Li Yugeng and Xiao Jiang finally catch up Jin Zhizhong, and capture him after a fierce battle.

311. *Chen Geng's Arrest (Chen Geng Meng Nan)*

1984. August First Film Studio. Color. Wide Screen. 9 Reels. Direction: Yan Jizhou. Screenplay: Wang Jun. Cinematographer: Huang Fuxiang. Art Direction: Jiang Zhenkui. Sound: Shi Pingyi. Cast: Yang Shaolin as Chen Geng, Zhao Hengduo as Chiang Kaishek, Zhu Kexin as Song Meiling (Madame Chiang), Xu Jinjin as Mary, Xiao Huifang as Song Qingling (Madame Sun Yatsen)

In 1933, Red Army division commander Chen Geng is in Shanghai, where he has gone on his own to seek medical aid for battlefield wounds. When Chen has recovered and is about to return, betrayal by a traitor results in his arrest in the British Concession. Nationalist commander Chiang Kaishek is very excited to hear of Chen's arrest, for the two are old comrades from the Whampoa Military Academy, and Chen had saved Chiang's life in 1925. Chiang relies heavily on Whampoa graduates as his subordinate officers, and is certain he can persuade Chen to defect to the Nationalist side. But all his persuasion and incentives are fruitless, as Chen adamantly refuses to go against the Communist cause. At last, Chiang decides that Chen must just disappear, which he does. But Chiang's sister-in-law, the politically progressive and influential Madame Sun Yatsen, determines that Chen must be found before harm comes to him.

312. *Chen Geng's Release (Chen Geng Tuo Xian)*

1984. August First Film Studio. Color. Wide Screen. 10 Reels. Direction: Yan Jizhou. Screenplay: Wang Jun. Cinematographer: Huang Fuxiang. Art Direction: Jiang Zhenkui. Sound: Shi Pingyi. Cast: Yang Shaolin as Chen Geng, Ren Guangzhi as Lu Xun (Lu Hsun), Zhao Hengduo as Chiang Kaishek, Zhu Kexin as Song Meiling (Madame Chiang), Xu Jinjin as Mary, Xiao Huifang as Song Qingling (Madame Sun Yatsen)

Chen Geng is secretly taken to Nanchang, where Chiang Kaishek is busy fighting. They meet, and Chiang again attempts his utmost to persuade Chen to defect. Chen continues to refuse. Meanwhile, Madame Sun Yatsen continues her efforts to determines Chen's whereabouts. Through a foreign college student named Mary, Madame Sun and Chinese writer Lu Hsun learn where Chen is being held and start a campaign to have him released. This puts considerable pressure on Chiang Kaishek, concerned that Chen's further detention could cost him support among Whampoa graduates. Chen Geng is released and returns to his troops.

313. *Chen Huansheng Visits the City (Chen Huan Sheng Shang Cheng)*

1982. Xiaoxiang Film Studio. Color. 10 Reels. Direction: Wang Xinyu. Screenplay: Wang Xinyu, Gao Xiaosheng. Cinematographer: Liu Yongshi. Art Direction: Li Jushan. Music: Xu Jingxin. Sound: Ding Baihe. Cast: Chun Li as Chen Huansheng, Wang Shuqing as the wife, Tian Yin as Lin Zhenhe, Song Chunling as Wu Chu, Qi Guirong as Liu Yumei, Li Xiaoli as Liu Xiaoyin

Honest and hardworking, Chen Huansheng leads a pretty comfortable life after the Party implements its new economic policy. This changes when the factory his village operates suddenly chooses him as their new marketing head. Chen realizes he has no sales or purchasing talent, and he does not want to change jobs. It turns out that the real reason for his selection is his close friendship with the current prefectural Party Secretary. When Chen does take the job, he is shocked to witness so much corruption and unfairness, and knows there is much he does not understand.

314. *Chen Sanliang (Chen San Liang)*

1959. Changchun Film Studio. B & W. 12 Reels. Direction: Wang Lan. Based on a traditional Yuan opera. Cinematography: Wang Lei. Art Direction: Liu Jinnai. Music: Zhang Yutian. Sound: Tong Zongde. Cast: Zhang Xinfang as Chen Sanliang, Liu Dedao as Li Fengming, Zhao Zhian as Chen Kui, Zhang Fengwu as the store owner, Bai Yaquan as Zhang Zichun, Gong Mingyi as Zhang Qi, Dong Zhangming as He Shang, Han Fenglan as Li Fengming (as a child), Liu Shuyun as Chen Kui (as a child)

Elderly jeweler Zhang Zichun buys popular courtesan Chen Sanliang as a concubine, but she rejects him, so he bribes county magistrate Li Fengming to threaten her. Li learns that her resistance to Zhang is because she is waiting for Chen Kui, once a poor scholar but now a success. He also discovers that Chen Sanliang is his biological sister, although neither is willing to acknowledge the fact, Li because his sister's status is inappropriate to his position as a magistrate, and she because he is a corrupt official. Just then, court inspector Chen Kui arrives on the scene, and he and Chen Sanliang meet. Seeing the close feelings between the two, Li hastens to ingratiate himself with his sister, but she is adamant that Chen Kui judge the case on its merits. The result is that Li Fengming is removed from his administrative post and reduced to the status of ordinary citizen.

315. *Chen Zhen* (*Jing Wu Ying Xiong*)

1994. Beijing Film Studio, Zhengdong Film Corp. Ltd. Color. Letterboxed. 9 Reels. Direction: Chen Jiashang. Screenplay: Chen Jiashang. Cinematography: Wun Wenjie. Art Direction: Ma Guangrong. Music: Ma Guangrong. Sound: Gu Xihui. Cast: Jet Li as Chen Zhen, Zhong Shanren as Tianshan Guangzi, Qian Xiaohao, Cai Shaofeng, Zhou Bili, Qin Pei

In the late 1920s, kung fu expert Chen Zhen is a Chinese student studying in Japan. When word arrives that his former martial arts instructor has died, he immediately returns to China. There, he learns the teacher was murdered. Because of Chen Zhen's influence with other students at the martial arts institute, the teacher's son, Huo Tingen, resents Chen Zhen's return. He challenges Chen to a contest, the loser to leave the school. Chen wins the contest, but voluntarily leaves anyway, so the school will stay united. Huo Tingen, depressed about not being as respected as Chen, turns to drugs. The school goes into decline. The Japanese want the school closed altogether to eliminate a potential source of opposition and send their best fighter in China for a challenge match. Huo swallows his pride and asks Chen to represent them. Chen Zhen wins, but the school remains closed. Huo decides to reopen in a new location, and Chen Zhen also leaves to make a fresh start.

316. *Cherries* (*Ying*)

1979. Youth Film Studio. Color. 10 Reels. Direction: Zhan Xiangchi, Han Xiaolei. Screenplay: Zhan Xiangchi. Cinematographer: Cao Zhuobing. Art Direction: Lu Zhicang, Wang Yanjin. Music: Wang Ming. Sound: Cao Zhuobing.

Cast: Xu Huanshan as Chen Jianhua, Cheng Xiaoying as Morimoto Koko, Ouyang Ruqiu as Mrs. Chen, Shi Yu as Director Yang, Du Bengzhen as He Yuliang, Jiang Yungui as Takachi Yoko, Li Lin as Xiulan (Koko as a child), Xu Bin as Chen Jianhua (as a child), Gao Wei as Xiao Mei

In 1945, after the Japanese are defeated, a group of Japanese refugees leave China. A Japanese woman leaves her infant girl, Koko, with a Chinese woman, Mrs. Chen. After the founding of the PRC, with the help of the government, Koko is returned to Japan. In 1975, when Koko visits Beijing as a foreign expert, Chinese engineer Chen Jianhua guesses that she is the Japanese sister his family called Xiulan, and he looks forward to a reunion. However, his wife advises him not to see Koko again because he had suffered much in the past for having a Japanese sister. Chen Jianhua therefore avoids seeing Koko, and she understands the reason why not. She returns to Japan so as not to bring trouble to the family. After the Gang of Four is smashed, Koko comes to China again, but this time her Chinese mother and brother come to welcome her in a joyous reunion.

317. *Chess King* (*Qi Wang*)

1988. Xi'an Film Studio. Color. 10 Reels. Wide Screen. Direction: Teng Wenji. Screenplay: Teng Wenji and Zhang Xinxin, from an original story by A Cheng. Cinematography: Wang Xinsheng. Art Direction: Cao Jiuping. Music: Guo Wenjing. Sound: Hua Juan. Cast: Xie Yuan as Wang Yisheng, Liu Hui as A Zhong, Duan Xiu as Xiao Ying, Ren Ming as Ni Bin, Niu Ben as the Secretary, Zhao Liang as Tiehan

While he does not appear to possess much intelligence, Wang Yisheng has from childhood made the study of Chinese chess his obsession. He comes from a poor Beijing family, but gains the attention of a chess master, and under the latter's tutelage Wang becomes a very skilled player. During the Cultural Revolution, Wang is sent to the Chinese border to work on a farm, where life is hard and often lonely. Chess is his escape, and he roams the hills looking for chess partners. As he becomes more physically hardened, his chess skills increase. An almost legendary figure among the area's players is "King Li," from a long line of chess players. The "King" lives like a hermit and spends all of his time playing chess. When he plays, it seems as if the chess piece called the "king" is nailed to the board. "King Li" has made a public vow that if he is ever forced to move the "king" even once, he will admit defeat. During a tournament, Wang Yisheng defeats eight players in a row and finally meets "King Li" in a showdown final. As most of the villagers look on and make side bets on the result, Wang and the "King" play late into the night by lamplight...

Best Actor Xie Yuan, 1989 Golden Rooster Awards.

318. *Child Violinist (Qing Tong)*

1980. Shanghai Film Studio. Color. 9 Reels. Direction: Fan Lai. Screenplay: Zhao Danian. Cinematographer: Li Chongjun, Wangyi. Art Direction: Guo Dongcang. Music: Liu Yanxi. Sound: Ren Xinliang. Cast: Xiang Mei as Yu Ping, Wu Cihua as Liu Xin, Gao Yang as Jingjing, Ding Yi as Jingjing, Mao Weiyu as Li Duohou

Woman singer Yu Ping and conductor Liu Xin have a son Jingjing, who already shows musical talent at the age of one. When the Cultural Revolution begins, Liu Xin is persecuted by a former classmate Fang Wei, who had long been jealous of Liu for marrying Yu Ping. When he is sent away, Liu Xin tells his wife not to let their son go into music. Later, Yu Ping is forced to go work in the countryside, where the local orchestra's chief violinist Li Dunhou discovers Jingjing's talent, and is able to persuade Yu Ping to let him teach Jingjing to play the violin. In 1977, Jingjing's sister Xiao Ming also learns to play the zheng, an ancient Chinese musical instrument. Unfortunately, when brother and sister go to take exams for music school, the director of admissions is Fang Wei, and when he learns who are the children's parents, he bars their admission. Later, the admissions committee adopts the principle of admission on merit. An investigation reveals that Fang Wei was the person responsible for the persecution of the music school.

319. *Childhood Friends (Tong Nian De Peng You)*

1984. Shanghai Film Studio. Color. Letterboxed. 10 Reels. Direction: Huang Shuqin. Screenplay: Liu Zhaolan. Cinematographer: Xia Lixing. Art Direction: Chen Chudian. Music: Yang Mao. Sound: Dong Jujing. Cast: Guo Kaimin as Squad Leader, Lu Liping as Sister Luo, Wang Yan as Tian Xiujuan (as a young woman), Lin Bing as Tian Xiujuan, Yang Yanqiang as Hou Zhi (as a boy), Wei Qiming as Hou Zhi

An inspection trip to Yan'an brings back childhood memories for Hou Zhi, a high-ranking government official. He recalls being assigned at the age of 12 to a Yan'an high school during the time the city served as Communist headquarters. His father was soon killed in battle. Hou Zhi became very ill and his sister donated her own blood to save his life. During the transfusion, she was fatally infected with the disease. At Yan'an, the adult Hou Zhi stops to visit Tian Xiujuan, a former nurse who is now the national kindergarten director. Tian and Hou reminisce together about old acquaintances who were killed in the war. Inspired by the stories of these fallen comrades, the two vow to work and live as these others did.

320. *Childhood in Ruijin (Tong Nian Zai Rui Jin)*

1989. Jiangxi Film Studio and Xi'an Film Studio Co-Production. Color. 9 Reels. Letterboxed. Direction: Huang Jun. Screenplay: Huang Jun. Cinematographer: Jin Guirong, Liu Chifeng. Art Direction: Wei Zhonghua, Gao Xixi. Music: Wen Deqing. Sound: Yu Meiqiang. Cast: Li Zhe as Pingping, Xiao Tie as Xiaohong, Xu Ke as Guigui, Ai Changqiang as Ganggang, Zeng Qiao as Qiaoqiao

A poignant tale, set several decades ago, of a group of children growing up in the South China village of Ruijin. The children all belong to the same clan. The film traces their idyllic school days. But real life shatters their dreams, as hardship forces the children to quit school one by one and bid farewell to the little attic where they do their homework and recite texts together. In the last scene, little Huang Pingping, the last of the six childhood friends, walks alone to the county middle school down the road she had so often traveled with her friends.

321. *Children of Sichuan (Ba Shan Er Nu)*

1984. August First Film Studio. Color. Wide Screen. 10 Reels. director: Wei Jia. Screenplay: Yang Xingyi, Wu Jinxian. Cinematographer: Jiang Xiande. Art Direction: Fang Xuzhi. Music: Li Weicai. Sound: Song Tianpei. Cast: Yan Shikui as Luo Jieshan, Shen Huifang as Li Cuizhu, Wu Jinhua as Cheng Jianyun, Wang Gang as Yu Mengshi, Xu Ming as Shangguan Tongchuan

In 1942, Luo Jieshan leads the Red Army's

Pioneer 4th Division into the Bashan Mountains of Sichuan to establish a revolutionary base there. When Jiang Guotao's incorrect leftist line is implemented, many Red Army officers and men come under political attacks, which greatly weakens the Communist cause militarily. Luo Jieshan angrily opposes this unjust treatment of his forces. Later, when the Nationalist army attempts its encirclement, the 4th Division is instrumental in leading a breakout.

322. *Child's Song in War (Zhan Zheng Tong Yao)*

1994. Children's Film Studio. Color. Letterboxed. 9 Reels. Direction: Chen Li. Screenplay: Gu Bai. Cinematography: Cheng Shengsheng. Art Direction: Chen Xianzhong, Jiao Zhenqi. Music: Wang Ming. Sound: Su Xiaorui, Liu Shida. Costume: Jia Xiangju. Makeup: Cheng Rong, Yuan Lin. Cast: Zhou Minghan as Xiaochao, Chen Si as Chang Shou, Zhang Liwei as Erhuo's mother, Zhang Qin as Fugui, Niu Yan as Erhuo, Si Weizheng as Li'er, Ma Lianxiang as Man Ji

When her parents are killed during the Japanese invasion, Xiaochao swears to avenge them. But the child comes in time to understand that the future of an entire nation is more important than one person's revenge. So when some Japanese soldiers arrive in her village scouting for the Eighth Route Army, Xiaochao leads them in the wrong direction.

323. *Chilly Night (Han Ye)*

1984. Beijing Film Studio. Color. Wide Screen. 10 Reels. Direction: Jue Wen. Screenplay: Jue Wen, Lin Hongtong. Cinematographer: Luo Dan. Art Direction: Xiao Bing, Ma Gaiwa. Music: Lu Qimin. Sound: Lai Qizhen. Cast: Xu Huanshan as Wang Wenxuan, Pan Hong as Zeng Zhusheng, Lin Muyu as Wang's mother

After the Nationalist government has moved to Chongqing (Chungking) in 1944, the daily lives of the city's residents are filled with poverty, fear and despair. Wang Wenxuan is a poorly paid proofreader at a publishing house, but jobs of any kind are precious so he hangs on to it. His wife Zeng Zhusheng wants to help the family out of poverty, so she uses her physical attractiveness to land a job in a bank. Wang's mother disapproves of her daughter-in-law's behavior, and the two argue. Zeng is unhappy because she feels no one in the family understands or appreciates her mo-

tivation in going to work to help the family. The family arguments get so bad that Zeng Zhusheng at last leaves home and runs off with the bank director. Wang Wenxuan later dies of overwork. Zeng Zhusheng comes to miss her family very much, and longs for the day of victory, when she can go back. At last, the Japanese surrender and Zeng returns home. But she finds no one there.

324. *China Heat (Zhong Hua Jing Hua)*

1991. Shanghai Film Studio. Color. Letterboxed. 10 Reels. Direction: Zhang Qi, Yang Yang. Screenplay: Gu Xiaoyan, Nan Feng, Zhang Qi. Cinematography: Li Pingbing, Zhang Qi, Zhang Hai. Art Direction: Wu Weifei. Music: Xi Yulong. Cast: Hu Huizhong as Tie Hua, Michael De Pasquale as Mike, Han Yongqing as Ruo Nan, Meng Xiangli as Meng Li, Guo Weiping as Jian Fei, Lan Haihan as Hong Gang, Li Zhiping as Li Xun, Jia Jiacun as Wang Li, Fred Bralas as Tony, Roosevelt Jackson as the Chief of Detectives

An American drug ring uses a Chinese-American, Hong Gang, to ship drugs to the U.S. from Asia. A woman special police unit led by Tie Hua struggles with the drug dealers, chasing Hong Gang from Asia to New York. Working with New York detectives, they at last kill all the drug dealers, and bring Hong Gang back to China for trial.

325. *China's "Little Emperors" (Zhong Guo De "Xiao Huang di")*

1987. Changchun Film Studio. Color. 9 Reels. Direction: Yu Yanfu, Zhang Yuan. Screenplay: Xiao Yixian, Zhang Yuhui, Yu Yanfu. Cinematography: Wang Jishun. Art Direction: Shi Weijun. Music: Wu Damin. Sound: Huang Lijia. Cast: Zhang Yuyu as Ma Qi, Pu Ke as Grandpa, Tang Guoqiang as Ma Qi's husband, Ding Yi as Grandma, Gu Lan as Gao Xiaoxing, Tian Tian as Yuanyuan

Elementary school teacher Ma Qi worries about the effect the one-child per family policy is having on education. She sees that even her own daughter Yuanyuan is very spoiled by her Grandparents. One of Ma Qi's pupils, Gao Xiaoxing, is growing up without his irresponsible parents instilling in him any sense of discipline, and he starts taking revenge on anyone who dares to oppose him on anything. Athletic Peng Lili's parents are blue collar workers who force her to learn the piano. Ling Mingming lives in the home of his grandparents, who treat him like an emperor. Eventually Peng Lili leaves home out of frustration with her parents not understanding her and Gao Xiaoxing is picked up by the police. These events shock many of the parents into an awareness of their parenting shortcomings.

326. *Chinese King of Gamblers (Zhong Guo Du Wang)*

1993. Xi'an Film Studio & China Film Release Import And Export Company Co-Production. Color. Letterboxed. Direction: Li Yunle. Screenplay: Wang Sheng. Cinematography: Wen Shibing. Art Direction: Dai Yunzhong. Cinematography: Wen Shibing. Cast: Zhou Lijing as the King of Gamblers, Zhen Tianyong as Gui Tian, Gao Min as Quan Shaoguang, Gong Youchun as Ling Lan, Tian Mo as Lian Xin

A master gamester known as the King of Gamblers takes his nephew and distant cousin to the "Gold Hook Gambling Hall," where he proceeds to win all the money of two Japanese. A detective tips off the King that the hall is really a cover for the activities of the "Black Dragon Society," a Japanese spy agency. But the King decides to become involved with the place anyway. He has a personal motive: these same Japanese killed a friend of his and took all the money he had painstakingly collected to buy medical supplies for the anti-Japanese resistance. In the end, the King of Gamblers kills the head of the Black Dragons and destroys the gambling hall.

327. *A Chinese Medical Doctor in an Era of Chaos (Ruan Shi Lang Zhong)*

1984. Xiaoxiang Film Studio. Color. Letterboxed. Direction: Hua Yongzhuang, Luo Zhen. Screenplay: Li Linmu. Cinematographer: Zhao Zelin. Art Direction: Wang Jixia, Yang Li. Music: Li Hangtao, Zhe Tinggui. Sound: Liu Yishen. Cast: Zhang Xianheng as Xu Hancheng, Li Lanfa as Ma Cang, Huo Xiu as Li Lanyin, Xu Caigeng as Zhang Laoshan, Xu Lei as Chen Yugu, Liu Guanxiong as Li Jiqiu

Xu Hancheng is a Taoist physician in the early years of the Republic of China. He develops "bai yao," an herbal medicine which is used to this day. After marrying Li Lanying, Xu sets up a practice in a rural area of Yunnan province, and uses the considerable income from his sale of bai yao to the wealthy to establish a free clinic for the poor. But the chaotic times lead to his downfall: China is racked by civil war and lawlessness, and Xu is thrown into prison, where he dies.

328. *Chinese Mother (Zhong Guo Ma Ma)*

1995. Liaoning Film Studio. Color. Direction: Huang Jianzhong. Screenplay: Liu Zhiqing, Xu Enzhi. Cinematography: Yun Wenyao. Art Direction: Zhao Zhenxue. Cast: Li Kechun as Wang Xiuqin

Nine-year-old Geng Hui and his mother live by themselves in a Northeast China city, while the father lives and works in another city. The boy suddenly loses his hearing, and improper medical care results in the loss being permanent. His mother tries everything, and is at last forced to take over her son's education herself. She takes the doctor to court for malpractice and wins. With his mother's support and encouragement, Geng Hui graduates from middle school. When he fails to qualify for college admission, she registers him in extension classes. He at last graduates, ready to start a new life.

329. *A Chinese Odyssey (Parts 1 & 2) (Da Hua Dong You)*

1994. Xi'an Film Studio, Hong Kong Caixing Film Company Co-Production. Color. Letterboxed. 9 Reels. Direction: Liu Zhenwei. Screenplay: An Zhi. Cinematography: Pan Hengsheng. Art Direction: Liang Huasheng. Music: Zhao Jiping. Costume: Yao Xiaohong, Ding Ni, Xiong Kai, Liu Yi. Makeup: Lu Yinchun, Wang Ping, Chen Xiaomei. Cast: Zhou Xingchi as Sun Wukong, Wu Mengda as Zhu Bajie, Zhu Yin as Zixia Xianzi, Lan Jieying as Chun Shisan Niang, Mo Wenwei as Bai Jingjing

A farce, intended as a satire on the classical Chinese novel "Xi You Ji" ("Voyage to the West") by Shi Naian (ca1290–ca1365). All the major characters so familiar in the novel, such as the Monkey King, Pigsy, etc., are given different and often bizarre interpretations.

330. *The Chinese Olive-Green Roof (Gan Lan Lu Wu Ding)*

1987. Changchun Film Studio. Color. 10 Reels. Direction: Sun Sha. Screenplay: Du Lijuan. Cinematography: Zhang Songping. Art Direction: Liu Huanxing. Music: Fan Weiqiang. Sound: Yi Wenyu. Cast: Xu Songzi as Ma Tiange, Zhen Zheng as Wang Qinguo

Five job-seeking young women operate a small book stall together. One day they see a job posting, with interviews held at a hotel. The film tells how each of the five girls uses her own method to compete for the job. Lin Rongrong goes to a Frenchman she knows who has connections with the employing company, but he declines to help her. Ma Tiange enlists the aid of Xia Cheng, a powerful businessman who turns out to be sexually very demanding as well. Wang Qinguo has cancer, and works very hard to succeed in the last part of her life. At last, Ma Tiange gets the job, but she realizes she will face more competition and challenges in the days to come.

331. *Chinese Policewomen (Zhong Guo Ba Wang Hua)*

1990. August First Film Studio. Color. Wide Screen. 9 Reels. Direction: Gong Yiqun, Wang Xiaomin. Screenplay: Yang Ying. Cinematography: Cai Shunan, Wang Weidong. Art Direction: Liu Jisheng. Music: Yang Xiwu. Sound: Shen Guorui. Cast: Zhou Yitian as Ou Xia, Zhang Jing as Wenli, Min Zhaohui as Xie Rongrong, Li Xia as Wen Huaqiang, Xing Minhua as Wu Ge

A group of wide-eyed and innocent young women join the police force and go through rigorous training together, bonding and helping each other overcome their shortcomings. After graduation, they are assigned to a major robbery case, and succeed in tracking down the criminals.

332. *Chivalrous Heroine (Qi Xia Qiao Mei Nao Re He)*

1993. Guangxi Film Studio. Color. Letterboxed. 9 Reels. Direction: Qiu Lili. Screenplay: Gu Jianzhong, Gu Zemin. Cinematography: Ru Shuiren, Ning Jiakun. Art Direction: Chen Xiaoxia, Wang Xinguo. Music: Gao Wendi. Sound: Wang Yunhua. Costume: Zhang Dezhong. Makeup: Guanjun. Cast: Sun Chengxi as Zhang Fengwu, Wang Limin as Fu Yulun, Wang Yan as sister happiness, Wang Zhigang as Tu Baer, Mi Li as Huiying, Dong Ping as Huiming

An action film set in the mid-19th Century. Pretty Xi Meizi and kung fu expert Zhang Fengwu risk their lives to protect a national treasure. They become lovers, and leave to join the Taiping Rebellion.

333. *The Chongqing Negotiations (Parts 1 & 2) (Chong Qing Tan Pan)*

1993. Changchun Film Studio. Color. Letterboxed. Stereo. 16 Reels. Direction: Li Qiankuan, Xiao Guiyun, Zhang Yifei. Screenplay: Zhang Xiaotian. Cinematography: Li Li. Art Direction: Lu Zhichang, Yang Baocheng. Music: Si Wanchun. Sound: Zhang Wen. Costume: Li Jingping, Zhao Huijie, Ma Jun. Makeup: Liu Xiaohong, Liu Huan, Jin Wansheng. Cast: Gu Yue as Mao Zedong, Sun Feihu as Chiang Kaishek, Huang Kai as Zhou Enlai, Li Fazen as Zhang Zhizhong, Hu Huizhong as Tong Xin, G. De Niro as Patrick Hurley, Dong Yugang as Wang Ruofei

After the Japanese surrender in August, 1945, Chiang Kaishek calls for peace negotiations to be held at his wartime capital of Chongqing, the aim being to prevent a reoccurrence of the Chinese Civil War. To everyone's surprise, he invites Communist leader Mao Zedong to attend. Chiang believes he has nothing to lose, as Mao is unlikely to show up in a place where he could be in personal danger. Mao in turn surprises everyone by attending, under a guarantee of safe passage from the U.S. The negotiations begin on August 29. During his stay in Chongqing, Mao conducts extensive social activities, and expands the Communists' influence, impressing foreign journalists, etc. After 40 days of negotiations, an agreement is reached and signed on October 10.

Best Art Direction Lu Zhichang and Yang Baocheng, 1994 Golden Rooster Awards.

Best Picture, 1994 Hundred Flowers Awards.

Best Supporting Actor Sun Feihu, 1994 Hundred Flowers Awards.

334. *Chrysanthemums (Shan Ju Hua)*

1982. Pearl River Film Studio. Color. 11 Reels. Direction: Chen Ying, Xing Jitian. Screenplay: Li Pingfeng, Chen Ying, Lin Hangsheng, Xing Jitian, Lu Wei. Cinematographer: Xie Yongyi. Art Direction: Huang Tongrong. Music: Zhu Zhengben, Zhang Jun. Sound: Wang Zhongxuan. Cast: Ni Ping as Taozhi, Li Chaoyou as Yu Zhenghai, Li Zhenfang as Chizhi, Liu Zhiyun as Zhang Laoshan, Gao Ruping as Kong Xiucai, Xu Wei as Jin Gui

In 1933, a peasant woman named Taozhi marries stonesmith Yu Zhenghai. All Taozhi wants from life is marriage to a good, reliable man, and the security she believes will come with it. So she is quite worried when she learns her new husband is a Communist. Later, government agents raid Communist Party headquarters and slaughter many of the Party's members. Yu Zhenghai is ordered to move to another area for his safety. Shocked and radicalized by the killings, Taozhi comes to realize that the only way to freedom for China's peasants is through revolution. She suffers considerable pain and humiliation, but endures through strength of will. Several years later, when her husband returns to their home to organize armed, violent struggle, she joins him in his work.

335. *Chrysanthemums Deep in the Mountains (Shen Shan Li De Ju Hua)*

1958. Haiyan Film Studio. B & W. 9 Reels. Direction: Ling Zifeng. Screenplay: Hai Mu. Cinematographer: Zhu Jing. Art Direction: Zong Yongqing. Music: Xu Xu. Sound: Shao Zihe. Makeup: Kong Lingqi. Cast: Tian Fang as Commander Yang, Chen Lizhong as Old Grandma, Hu Peng as Li Guirong, Song Xingnan as Zhang Meng, Che Yi as Song Yin, Wu Qi as Yang Wen

Young student Yang Wen goes to the countryside to work at a certain old revolutionary base in the place where he was born and spent his childhood. When he sees the chrysanthemums he planted 15 years before, he recalls growing up in a foster family during World War II, after his army parents' unit was shipped out. He recalls his playmates, and how they grew up against the background of war.

336. *Chunmiao (Chun Miao)*

1975. Shanghai Film Studio. Color. 12 Reels. Direction: Xie Jin, Yan Bili, Liang Tingduo. Screenplay: Collective, recorded by Yang Shiwen, Cao Lei. Cinematographer: Lu Junfu. Art Direction: Ge Sicheng. Music: Huang Zhun, Xu Jingxin. Cast: Li Xiuming as Chun Miao, Gao Baocheng as Uncle Shuicang, Da Shichang as Fang Ming, Liu Zinong as Li Aqiang, Li Lingjun as Sister Afang, Zhang Yu as Lian Lian, Bai Mu as Du Wenjie, Feng Qi as Doctor Qian Jiren

In 1965, certain events in a Southeast China village convince woman work team director Tian Chunmiao that Qian Jiren, doctor at the commune's aid station, really cares very little about the welfare of his farmer patients. So Chunmiao determines she will learn medicine by regularly observing the activities at the clinic. Chunmiao meets with hostility from both Doctor Qian and the clinic's director Du Wenjie. They subject her to constant criticisms and harassment, and spread rumors about her among the patients. Chunmiao perseveres in her studies in spite of all this. When the Cultural Revolution begins, Chun Miao becomes a rebel and attacks the "capitalist health care line." She also takes a farmer Uncle Shuichang to the country hospital when she suspects the treatment he is receiving at the aid station, and uncovers a plot by Du and Qian to poison the farmer. With Du and Qian removed, Chunmiao and other farmer doctors firmly control rural medicine.

337. *Circus Kid (Ma Xi Qing Wei Liao)*

1994. Pearl River Film Company, Hong Kong Dongrong Film Corp. Ltd. Co-production. Color. Letterboxed. 9 Reels. Direction: Wu Ma. Screenplay: Wu Ma. Cinematography: Yang Aochang, Zhu Junheng, Chen Lie. Art Direction: Lin Zhongcai. Music: Lu Guanting. Cast: Wu Ma as Shen Yiting, Yuan Biao as Yidong, Zhen Zidan as Tang Fa, Wun Bixia as Ding Lan, Lin Wei as Yitian, Li Lili as Ding Mei, Zhen Shuang as Mary, Hu Yingwen as Ding Ju

When Japanese planes bomb Shanghai, they destroy the Changfu Acrobatic Troupe's performing site and facilities. So troupe owner Shen leads the company to Guangzhou to seek work. There, Shen meets again his former lover Lu Cuiyu, and she helps the troupe members find jobs in a tobacco factory. After the factory is taken over by some foreigners, it becomes a secret drug factory as well. When Shen and the others discover this, the foreigners persecute them. But at last the circus performers turn on the drug producers, and burn down the factory.

338. *The Circus Troupe's New Programs (Ma Xi Tuan De Xin Jie Mu)*

1961. Changchun Film Studio. B & W. 11 Reels. Direction: Zhu Wenshun and Yin Yiqing. Screenplay: Jiang Xuren and Chong Sheng. Cinematography: Li Xiqian. Art Direction: Tong Jingwen and Li Wenguang. Music: Che Ming. Sound: Jue Jingxiu. Cast: Guo Suqing as Zhang Jinzhu, Guo Sulan as Zhang Yingzhu, Bai Mei as Zhou Ruilian, Bi Fu as Yu Lianfu, Wang Wenlin as Secretary Zhang, Wang Zhenrong as Lu Hongxiang

During the Great Leap Forward, an urban circus troupe enthusiastically develops new programs to serve the people under the policy of "a hundred flowers bloom, replacing old things with new." Two sisters, actress Zhang Jinzhu and acrobat Zhang Yingzhu plan new acts, but are opposed by their conservative mother, veteran actress Zhou Ruilian. With support from Secretary Zhang, the sisters convince their mother by comparing the old society with the new. Once she changes her thinking, Zhou Ruilian enthusiastically helps her daughters prepare their acts, and suggests some new ones.

339. *A Citizen Born Here (Gong Min Cong Zhe Li Dan Sheng)*

1987. Youth Film Studio. Color. 9 Reels. Direction: Wang Shuihan. Screenplay: Cheng Jingkai, Gu Yihan. Cinematography: Wang Zhaoling. Art Direction: Shi Jianquan. Music: Guo Xiaodi. Sound: Zhang Ruikun. Cast: Yu Ping as Han Qiong, Lin Yin as Liu Yemei, Yu Butao as Wu Dawei, Zhu Yi as Wang Haiyang, Huang Jing as Liang Shanshan, Ma Chi as Xiao Lu

In a port city on the east China coast, high school principal Han Qiong gathers all the "backward" students from the six classes of second year junior high, and puts them together in a special "Class Number 7," assigning her son Lin Meng as the new class's teacher. Principal Han believes this will improve their grades, but a series of unexpected events take place which at last force her to admit the experiment is a failure. She disbands the class and realizes that the school has a mission to produce good citizens as well as scholars.

340. *City Detective (Du Shi Xing Jing)*

1990. Shanghai Film Studio. Color. 9 Reels. Wide Screen. Direction: Sha Jie. Screenplay: Dongfang Xiao. Cinematography: Zhang Er. Art Direction: Zhao Xianrui. Music: Liu Yanxi. Sound: Qian Ping. Cast: Zhang Xiaolin as Zhang Xiaofeng, Li Hui as Sheng Ming, Chen Hong as Gu Ying, Liang Boluo as Qian Keqiang

In Jinggang City, young detectives Zhang Xiaofeng and Sheng Ming are getting nowhere in their investigation of a major case of antique theft, so they are taken off the case and reassigned to what appears to be a routine case of petty theft at Jinggang Normal University. Girl student Gu Ying tells them that one of the things lost in the theft did not belong to her: a box delivered to her roommate by a man in a car. The roommate, Wen Lihua, left the campus shortly thereafter and had not returned. Wen Lihua had a lover in Hong Kong businessman Qian Keqiang. Shortly after this, Wen is found murdered in a suburb. Various clues lead Zhang Xiaofeng to conclude that this case is somehow linked to the antiques case. At last, the clues lead Zhang to a major crime ring. He solves the case, and along the way he and Gu Ying fall in love.

341. *City Under Siege (Bing Lin Cheng Xia)*

1964. Changchun Film Studio. B & W. 10 Reels. Direction: Lin Nong. Screenplay: Bai Ren and Lin Nong, based on the stage play of the same title by Bai Ren. Cinematographer: Wang Qiming, Meng Xiandi. Art Direction: Wang Xingwen. Music: Liu Zhi. Sound: Chen Wenyuan. Cast: Hao Haiquan as Zhao Chongwu, Zhong Shuhuang as Zhen Hancheng, Zhang Ran as Qian Xiaozheng, Pang Xueqing as Li Zhongming, Li Muran as Minister Jiang, Chen Rubing as Fan Guoliang

During the Second Chinese Civil War. PLA forces surround a certain Northeast China city occupied by the Nationalist Army's 369th Division. The Communists know that Zhen Hancheng, a regimental commander in the 369th, is not particularly close to Chiang Kaishek. In order to lure him to defect to their side, the PLA grant safe passage out of the city to Zhen and his wife so that they may locate their children, separated from their parents earlier. Zhen is deeply moved by this. After he returns, he is suspected by Chiang's agents, and internal conflicts arise. Their suspicions aroused, Chiang's agents test division commander Zhao Chongwu by sending an agent in the guise of a Communist to persuade him to defect. Zhao is noncommittal, but when he learns of the ruse, he realizes that given Chiang's distrust of him and the realities of his military position, he has no choice but to go over to the Communists. His division then forces the surrender of the Nationalists' 203rd Division.

342. *Clash of the Warlords (Parts 1 & 2) (Zhi Feng Da Zhan)*

1986. Changchun Film Studio. Wide-screen. Color. 19 Reels. Direction: Zhou Yu, Wu Qiufang. Screenplay: Xiao Bo. Cinematography:

Wang Jishun, Yu Bin. Art Direction: Liu Xuerao. Music: Wang Liping, Zhan Qianyi. Sound: Yu Kaizhang. Cast: Wang Shangxin as Feng Yuxiang, He Haiuan as Cao Kun, Cao Jiechen as Wu Peifu, Hu Ao as Jiang Hongyu, Bi Yanjun as Lu Zhongling, Guo Yuntai as Sun Yue

Although China in the 1920s is officially a democratic republic, the country is in fact divided up among several mutually competing warlords, generals whose private armies control entire provinces or regions. Their perpetually shifting alliances and rivalries keep China in a state of almost constant civil war. Cao Kun, leader of the Chihli clique based in the Beijing area buys himself the Presidential election of 1922 by paying 5,000 silver dollars a vote. This does not go over at all well with his rivals, in particular Wu Peifu, leader of the Northeast China Fengtian warlord clique. It is Wu's ambition to use his military strength to unite China under his own control.

In 1924, war breaks out between the Chihli and the Fengtien warlords. One of the Chihli army leaders is patriotic warlord Feng Yuxiang, known and admired in the West as the "Christian General." Disgusted with the corrupt political machinations going on, Feng reorganizes his troops into a separate army and leads them back to Beijing, carrying out what comes to be known as the "Capital Revolution."

The film focuses on General Feng Yuxiang's exploits, both military and political. Feng overthrows the government which had come to power through bribery, and imprisons Cao Kun. He then expels deposed Emperor Puyi from his residence in the Forbidden City and welcomes to Beijing the man with the most legitimate claim to Chinese leadership, Dr. Sun Yatsen.

343. *Clear Earth (Ying Tu)*

1985. Longjiang Film Studio & Hong Kong Feifeng Film Company Co-Production. Color. 9 Reels. Direction: Huangpu Kerenj. Screenplay: Huangpu Keren. Cinematographer: Zhang Li, Lu Le, Zhou Xiaoping. Art Direction: Feng Yuan, Hao Bing. Music: Li Lifu. Sound: Feng Lingling. Cast: Wang Xueqin as Guan Shanfu, Xiao Xiong as Ding Sha, Li Qingqing as Yijinna, Liu Xin as Yijinna's father

Surgeon Guan Shanfu is released from prison after serving eight years for having botched an operation. He runs into his old girl friend Ding Sha, also a medical worker, and having no other options he follows her into a totally new world: a leper colony. He soon develops a feeling of sympathy for the lepers, people shunned by society for something that is no fault of theirs. Guan sees the devotion Ding Sha feels for her patients, and, expressing his love for her, he tells her wants to stay with her forever at the colony. Ding Sha rejects him, for since the tragic accident eight years earlier, with its consequences for any life together they might have had, she has totally devoted herself to her work. Although Guan realizes she no longer loves him, he understands her noble devotion to her patients.

344. *Clear Water Bay, Fresh Water Bay (Qing Shui Wan, Dan Shui Wan)*

1984. Beijing Film Studio. Color. Letterboxed. 11 Reels. Direction: Xie Tieli. Screenplay: Xie Tieli. Cinematographer: Huang Xinyi. Art Direction: Tu Juhua. Music: Wang Ming. Sound: Huang Xinyi. Cast: Zhang Yu as Gu Tingting, Xie Fang as Xiang Ping, Cui Yuemin as Sister Feng, Lu Shan as Grandma Du, Zhang Jinling as Sister Tong, Zhu Sha as Auntie

A disputed inheritance case is brought before woman judge Xiang Ping. The heiress is Gu Tingting, a girl adopted in childhood by a wealthy woman she called "Auntie," but her right to inherit is challenged by the deceased's Sister Feng. The judge's questioning brings out the facts that Sister Feng offered no support to Tingting after Auntie's death; rather, ordinary people in the neighborhood provided the girl with comfort and support. It also comes out that Tingting sees the admirable nature of working class people. Judge Xiang Ping rules that the entire 180,000 yuan estate should go to Gu Tingting, but the girl decides she can live on her own, and donates the entire fortune to the nation.

345. *The Clear Water Restaurant (Qing Shui Dian)*

1983. Shanghai Film Studio. Color. 6 Reels. Direction: Wang Xiuwen. Screenplay: Wei Shuhai, Jin Zhaoyuan, Lu Ping. Cinematographer: Wang Yi. Art Direction: Chen Fuxing. Music: Yang Mao. Sound: Zuang Yongnan. Cast: Sun Jinglu as Auntie Xu, Ma Guanyin as Tian Shuangxi, Zhang Zhihua as Xiulan

At a crossroads in a small town in the Yimeng Mountains is an old restaurant, the "Clear Water." Its owner Auntie Xu is renowned for her noodle dishes, and the restaurant never lacks for customers. Auntie finds a young man named Tian Shuangxi as a husband for her daughter Xiulan, and he marries into their family. Tian is a bright and capable young businessman, and Auntie likes him very much. But Tian is not at all happy with Auntie Xu's traditional business methods, and conflict erupts when he tries to get her to change. So the young couple move out and start their own restaurant, also called the "Clear Water." The two compete directly, and soon Tian's way of being more customer-oriented wins all of Auntie's customers. Tian Shuangxi takes the initiative in patching things up, and with a new understanding the new "Clear Water" and the old "Clear Water" merge.

346. *Clear Water Two Souls (Bi Shui Shuang Hun)*

1986. Shanghai Film Studio, Central Film Company Co-Production. Color. Wide Screen. 9 Reels. Direction: Chen Fan. Screenplay: Yu Mei, based on the story "Sunlight Before Dark" in the "Liao Zhai Zhi Yi" collection. Cinematography: Chen Zhengxiang, Zhang Yongzheng. Art Direction: Huang Qiagui, Yao Wei. Music: Xu Jingxin. Sound: Liu Guangjie. Cast: Zhang Xiaoqing as A Rui, He Qing as Wan Xia

In the Fuyang River area, Wan Xia is famed for her dancing talent. She is sold into the household of a wealthy landlord, where she is severely mistreated. Unable to bear her life, Wan Xia escapes from the mansion, jumps into the river and drowns herself. A traveling acrobatic troupe comes to the area and gives a demanding performance at the mansion, and afterwards one of the acrobats goes for a walk along the river. He falls into the river from exhaustion, and also drowns. The rest of the story relates how the two ghosts fall in love and wage a successful campaign to come back to life.

347. *Cleverly Defeating a Woman Spy (Zhi Dou Mei Nu She)*

1984. Changchun Film Studio. Color. Letterboxed. 10 Reels. Direction: Liu Zhongmin. Screenplay: Xu Jinyan, Peng Zhaoping, Peng Jiangliu. Cinematographer: Tang Yunsheng. Art Direction: Liu Jinnai, Song Honghua. Music: Wu Damin. Sound: Zhang Fenglu. Cast: Kou Zhenhai as Zheng Qian, Yu Li as Zhao Qiuyuan, Hong Guoli as Wang Songya, Hua Xiaoqing as Hu Xiuyin, Wang Zhongchao as Huang Kaitai,

Jin Weimin as Commander He, Huang Bangrui as Zhao Baojin, Sun Yanyan as Li Mengwen, Liu Tingrao as Hu Baotang, Di Jianqing as Captain Wang, Liu Junsheng as Wei Mingliang, Li Wei as Zeng Ming

In the fall of 1928, the Nationalist Army is ruthlessly finding and annihilating Communists. The Red Army retreats to a base in the Jinggangshan area to regroup, but soon faces a severe shortage of medical supplies. Agent Zheng Qian is ordered to find a source of supplies and build a line of communication between the city and the Communist base. Zheng soon finds out he has a Nationalist counterpart, a master spy called the "Beautiful Snake Lady." Zheng Qian struggles with the clever and mysterious "Snake," who seems to know his every move ahead of time. He at last gets the supplies through, and succeeds in unmasking drug seller Hu Baotang as the "Snake."

348. *Clown's Adventure (Xiao Chou Li Xian Ji)*

1990. Shanghai Film Studio. Color. Wide Screen. 10 Reels. Direction: Yu Jie. Screenplay: Wang Yonggang. Cinematographer: Liu Lihua. Art Direction: Qin Baisong. Music: Cai Lu. Sound: Xie Guojie. Cast: Mao Yongmin as Wan Xiaoxiao, Zhou Zhiqin as Da Huzhi, Cui Jie as Fatty, Zhang Yuan as Skinny

Beijing opera clown Wan Xiaoxiao is so busy with rehearsals that he tends to be a bit negligent about things. This gets him into considerable trouble when he chances to pick up the wrong briefcase, one that is filled with the tools for printing counterfeit money. He finds himself chased by the police, who think he is a criminal, and the real counterfeiters, who want the briefcase back. After a series of adventures, sometimes absurd, he is returned to his home and wife safely.

349. *Cockfighting (Dou Ji)*

1990. Beijing Film Studio. Color. Wide Screen. 10 Reels. Direction: Wang Binglin. Screenplay: Wang Binglin. Cinematographer: Huang Xinyi. Art Direction: Hao Jingyuan. Music: Zhang Qianyi. Sound: Zhang Baojian. Cast: Liang Tian as Tian Laifu, Fu Yiwei as Sun Chunxi, Ding Yi as Mrs. Sun, Chen Yude as Liu Laojue

In some areas of China, betting on cockfighting is still a popular form of gambling. Young farmer Tian Laifu loves Sun

Chunxi, a girl in his village, but Chunxi's mother insists her daughter will only marry a man of means. She agrees that she will give her daughter's hand to her first suitor to raise 10,000 yuan (about US$1,000). By chance, Tian comes into possession of a brave and fierce rooster, and begins entering it in cock fights, which earns him a tidy income in side bets. When his winnings reach the required 10,000, he goes to claim his bride. But another suitor shows up at the same time, with 10,000 yuan he has earned through hard work. Tian challenges the newcomer to a betting competition, which Tian wins handily. But the angry and disgusted Sun Chunxi rejects being a gambling prize and leaves. Tian Laifu loses his mind.

Best Supporting Actor Chen Yude, 1991 Hundred Flowers Awards.

350. *Coconut Town Story (Ye Cheng Gu Shi)*

1986. China Disabled People's Welfare Fund. Color. 10 Reels. Direction: Xu Qindong. Screenplay: Xu Qindong. Cinematography: Xiao Feng. Art Direction: Tang Shiyun. Music: Wang Ming. Sound: Zhao Zhiwei. Cast: Cheng Fangyuan as Lu Di, Liu Xuling as Li Ming, Sun Guoqin as Lu Xiaoke, Li Xiaohu as A Cheng

351. *Coconut Tree Song (Ye Lin Qu)*

1957. Tianma Film Studio. B & W. 10 Reels. Direction: Wang Weiyi. Screenplay: Chen Canyun and Li Yingming. Cinematography: Gu Wunhou. Art Direction: Hu Dengren. Music: Zhang Linyi. Sound: Li Liehong. Makeup: Yao Yongfu. Cast: Gao Bo as Tan Zhen, Shi Jiufeng as Zhang Ling, Li Yong as the radio repairman, Cui Chaoming as Hong Fei, Ye Ye as Lin Xiumei, Xu Wei as Wang's wife

During World War Two, a Red Army unit on Hainan Island loses contact with Party headquarters at Yan'an. The Party military organization sends staff officer Tan Zhen and squad leader Zhang Ling across the water to the Leizhou peninsula to obtain a radio transmitter. On their first attempt, Tan Zhen is injured, and on the second try Zhang Ling's boat is fired on and sunk. The third attempt is made by Zhang Ling's wife Lin Xiumei with assistance from veteran boatman Chen Ergong. They succeed in evading Japanese patrol boats and at last arrive on the peninsula. There they unexpectedly find Zhang Ling alive. He has also been able to contact the undercover Party organization on the peninsula. That same night, Lin Xiumei, Zhang Ling and Mr. Wang of the Party organization take the transmitter back to Hainan island. Chen Ergong gives his life protecting the others. Tan Zhen and Lin Xiumei's mother are to meet them at a prearranged spot, but are forced to change the rendezvous site when they learn a traitor has tipped off the Japanese. Covered by Mr. Wang and Tan Zhen, they get the transmitter to the base safely. Afterwards, they discover that Mr. Wang is really Xiumei's father Lin Hai, a military commander sent by the central Party from Yan'an. Lin Xiumei's family has a joyous reunion.

352. *Code Name "Cougar" (aka The Puma Action) (Dai Hao Mei Zhou Bao)*

1988. Xi'an Film Studio. Color. 9 Reels. Wide Screen. Direction: Zhang Yimou and Yang Fengliang. Screenplay: Cheng Shiqing. Cinematography: Gu Changwei, Yang Lun. Art Direction: Cao Jiuping, Dong Huamiao. Music: Guo Feng. Sound: Gu Changning. Cast: Liu Xiaoning as Liang Zhuang, Wang Yueqi as Huang Jingru, Ge You as Zheng Xianping, Gong Li as A Li

A routine commercial flight from Taibei to Seoul is hijacked by a terrorist group calling itself the Asian Black Commandos, who force the plane to land on the Chinese mainland. This forces the rival Beijing and Taibei governments to join together in a secret cooperative effort to smash the plot and rescue the hijacked hostages. They succeed but at a high price...

Best Supporting Actress Gong Li, 1989 Hundred Flowers Awards.

353. *Code Name "213" (Dai Hao "Er Yi San")*

1984. Shanghai Film Studio. Color. Letterboxed. 10 Reels. Direction: Tian Ran. Screenplay: Liu Quan, Liu Qiong, Shi Yong. Cinematographer: Cao Weiye. Art Direction: Zhen Changfu. Music: Xiang Yi. Sound: Li Bingkui. Cast: Ma Xiaowei as Xiao Jianfeng, Chen Xiaoyi as Xia Xuelan, Tan Feiling as Chief of Staff Lu, Guo Ao as Director Wei, Yao Keqing as Director Wu, Yao Debing as Lin Ji'en, Shi Shugui as Sister Zhang

At a border inspection station, Nationalist troops detain a man named Lin Ji'en. Under interrogation, he freely confesses to being a PLA liaison assigned to contact someone code-named "213." The troops begin a wide-ranging search for "213," but actually their intelligence director Wei and staff officers Xiao Jianfeng and Xia Xuelan are undercover Communist agents. In the end, Wei and Xiao kill the traitor but sacrifice their own lives. Before he dies, Wei passes the "213" designation to Xue, who will carry on as the Party's "mole" at Nationalist headquarters.

354. *Cold-Blooded Eagles (aka 13 Cold-Blooded Eagles) (Xin Leng Xue Shi San Ying)*

1993. Guangxi Film Studio. Color. Letter-boxed. 9 Reels. Direction: Xu Fa, Lu Dongqin. Cinematography: Ma Jinxiang, Chen Shenkai. Art Direction: Li Qining. Costume: Lu Shuping, Zhen Jiaxiong. Makeup: Shen Yueying, Huang Bingjin. Cast: Yang Liqing (Cynthia Khan) as the Kuihua girl, Liu Ziwei as Qi Yinmin, Li Zixiong (Waise Lee) as Lai Rufeng, Ren Shiguan as Yue Xihong, Zhong Fa as Xingshu Laoying

A martial arts movie, in which 13 orphans called the "Cold-Blooded Eagles" are trained by an evil man as kung fu experts and sent out to kill evildoers wherever they may appear. He sets them on the trail of a supposed "monster" who is really an ordinary man. When they learn the truth, they find themselves pitted against a new set of "Eagles" trained to kill the original 13.

355. *Collecting Able-bodied Men (Zhua Zhuang Ding)*

1963. August First Film Studio. B & W. 10 Reels. Direction: Chen Ge, Shen Dan. Screenplay: Chen Ge and Wu Xue, based on their stage play of the same title. Cinematographer: Chen Jun. Art Direction: Jiang Zhengkui. Music: Liu Wenjing, Zhang Chun. Sound: Li Yan. Cast: Wu Xue as Li Laoshuang, Chen Ge as residential manager Wang, Yin Wenyuan as Li's wife, Lei Ping as a housewife, Zhang Yisheng as Director Lu, Jin Tao as the big kid, Shao Hua as Jiang Guofu, Zhu Weiwei as Jiang Sun, Wang Zhigang as Jiang Zi

At the outset of World War Two, in a village in Sichuan province, the Nationalists begin collecting able-bodied men to fight the Japanese, and there are many corrupt practices. In one area under Nationalist administration, Director Lu, in charge of rounding up the able-bodied, demands them from local resident manager Wang. Wang in turn approaches landlord Li Laoshuang for money, and the landlord then turns to farmer Jiang Guofu. They obtain the money and then take Jiang's son as an able-bodied man, driving the elder Jiang to suicide. Shortly after, Li Laoshuang's son returns home, and the officials band together to blackmail the farmers, wildly collecting able-bodied men. Pushed to the limit and having lost everything, the farmers have no choice but to rebel and overthrow the corrupt officials.

Collective Honor **see** *Vast Oceans and Skies*

356. *College in Exile (Liu Wang Da Xue)*

1985. Shanghai Film Studio. Color. Wide Screen. 10 Reels. Direction: Wu Yigong. Screenplay: Tong Tingmiao, Fang Zhi. Cinematographer: Qiu Yiren. Art Direction: Chen Shaomian, Pu Jingsun. Music: Lu Qimin. Sound: Xie Guojie. Cast: Zhi Yitong as Jiang Weicheng, Xiang Mei as Tian Wan, Gao Bo as Gu Xiangping, Liu, Zifeng as Lu Zhonghan, Qi Minyuan as Fu Mengqi

In 1937, the Japanese invaders have occupied over half of China. Led by the school's President Jiang Weicheng, Southeast China Qianjiang University starts to move west, to avoid the war and continue the school's educational mission. As World War II develops further, Qianjiang University's faculty and students move a total of three times, but all are determined the university will carry on, preserving China's educational heritage. They overcome many difficulties, and graduate a class during the war. Their devotion to Chinese education and the widespread support they get from the people pressures Chiang Kai-shek into rescinding his order that the school be closed for the duration.

357. *College Students' Story (Da Xue Sheng Yi Shi)*

1987. Beijing Film Studio. Color. 9 Reels. Direction: Du Min. Screenplay: Wu Gu, Wang Junli. Cinematography: Huang Xinyi. Art Direction: Tu Juhua, Huo Jianqi. Music: Zhang Peiji. Sound: Lan Fuan. Cast: Zhou Sheng as the reporter, Zhi Yitong as the college president, Chi Peng as Xiao Sun

A reporter for the New China News Agency, China's official news agency, is invited by authorities in a certain city to do an article profiling the city's progress and attractiveness. She finds that graduates of the university there cannot find jobs because they finance their own educations, with no government guarantees of employment. The movie shows how the reporter works with faculty and students to gain recognition for the school in society. At last, all the graduates find jobs through ads in the news agency's leading business newspaper.

358. *Color Bridge (Cai Qiao)*

1982. Xi'an Film Studio. Color. 13 Reels. Direction: Jin Yin, Li Yucai. Screenplay: Zhou Zhengmin. Cinematographer: Niu Han. Art Direction: Yan Pingxiao. Music: Wei Ruixiang. Sound: Che Zhiyuan. Cast: Gao Yin as Huang Yan, Chi Zhiqiang as Wen Kecheng, Li Ping as Liu Qing, Yao Jun as Lin Hong, Bao Min as Ye Feng

Construction bureau employee Wen Kecheng meets and falls for Huang Yen, a girl temporarily working in a candy factory while waiting for permanent job assignment. When it comes, her assignment is to the office of a dating service, where she meets many eligible young bachelors who cannot find girlfriends because their jobs are too low in status. She finds herself very sympathetic to their plight, and works hard at arranging introductions for them. Wen Kecheng and his mother are both very upset with Huang Yen's work, thinking it improper for a young lady. The young couple's relationship is hurt for a time, but at last Wen changes in the face of reality and the couple reconcile.

359. *Colorful Morning (Duo Cai De Chen Guang)*

1984. Shanghai Film Studio. Color. 10 Reels. Letterboxed. Direction: Jiang Yusheng. Screenplay: Wu Jianxin. Cinematographer: Chen Ling, Cai Guangeng. Art Direction: Zhao Xianrui. Music: Lu Qimin. Sound: Wang Huimin. Cast: Gong Xue as He Yanling, Zhang Tielin as Lin Lishuang, Wang Sihuai as Shuiheng, Li Kechun as Ding Langmei

He Yanling, only daughter of Puquan City's education bureau director, falls in love with her education college classmate Lin Lishuang, who comes from a fishing village. When her father learns of this, he determines to break the relationship by assigning them to different areas after graduation. He sends his daughter to teach on the remotest island in his jurisdiction, while Lishuang is assigned to an inner city high school. Adjustment is particularly difficult for Yanling, but after overcoming the initial mutual unfamiliarity, she and the island people soon become close and she is fully accepted. She dedicates herself to the island's children. Lishuang, on the other hand, quickly adjusts to the comfortable urban lifestyle, and devotes himself to pleasing Yanling's parents, even helping her father cover up some corruption in his office. The father soon accepts Lishuang. When the young man proudly tells Yanling how he has succeeded in getting close to her father, Yanling realizes Lishuang has become a stranger to her, and their romance is ended.

360. *Colorful Night (Cai Se De Ye)*

1982. August First Film Studio. Color. Letterboxed Wide Screen. 9 Reels. Direction: Zhang Yongshou. Screenplay: Wang Qunsheng. Cinematographer: Yin Qiaofang. Art Direction: Zhang Guozhen. Music: Si Guangnan. Sound: Xiang Zhiliang. Cast: Li Guohua as Deputy Director Li, Wang Limin as Director Liu, Zhou Ling as Li Li, Chen Jianfei as Li Tao, Wang Anli as Wang Jing

Deputy Director Li of the Tibetan Transportation Bureau is a by-the-book manager, and very strict with the people he supervises. When driver Li Tao has an accident, the deputy director suspends the young man's license, although it is by no means clear whose fault it was. Many of the young people in the bureau question his action, including his own daughter Li Li, the driver's girlfriend. Director Liu, the head of the bureau, gathers the young people together and tells them a story from his experience which explains why the deputy director is so strict with them. After this, Li Tao and Li Li have a deeper understanding, respect and affection for her father.

361. *Combat at Heaven Gate (Jue Zhan Tian Men)*

1993. Xi'an Film Studio & Hong Kong Weiyi Company Co-Production. Color. Letterboxed. 9 Reels. Direction: Yu Jilian. Screenplay: Yuzen Huimei. Cinematography: Mo Zeren. Art Direction: Lu Guangcai. Music: Tao Long. Cast: Hu Huizhong as Fang Zhizhen, Wang Aishun as Chuan Duomo, Zhen Yuemin as Lin Lin, Long Fang as Gaocheng Zhanger, Zhang Xiaoyan as

Xixie Meizhizhi, Wang Zhigang as Lan Tian, Ma Ji as Gan Ge

362. *Come On, Team China! (Jia You, Zhong Guo Dui!)*

1985. Guangxi Film Studio. Color. Wide Screen. 10 Reels. Direction: Zhang Junzhao. Screenplay: Zhang Junzhao, Song Yijiang. Cinematographer: Xiao Feng. Art Direction: Yi Li. Music: Jin Wei. Sound: Zhang Yu. Costume: Dang Dongdong. Makeup: Zhu Xiaoling. Cast: Ma Zheng as Yang Shun, Rong Zhixing as Ji Cheng, Chi Shangbing as Mei Hai, Cai Jingbiao as Liu Gang, Wang Feng as Wei Jian, Yang Sanmin as Zhao Li, Wang Jianying as Xiao Ning, Yuan Qiming as Fan Zhong.

When the Asian soccer championship tournament is held in Beijing, China fields a strong team, with quality players. The movie follows their preparation for the big tournament. In the end, Team China loses, but the players are proud and happy that they have so improved the level of Chinese soccer in international competition.

363. *A Comedy of Divorce (Li Hun Xi Ju)*

1992. Changchun Film Studio. Color. Letterboxed. 10 Reels. Direction: Song Jiangbo. Screenplay: Xiao Mao, Li Shaohong. Cinematography: Wang Changning, Yan Songyan. Art Direction: Liu Huanxing. Music: Liu Xijing. Sound: Zhang Qingjiang. Costume: Chen Xiaoling. Makeup: Liang Ling. Cast: Lu Liang as Wu Fei, Wang Hui as Zhao Hong, Tao Huiming as Lin Xiaomei, Meng Qinbao as Yongsheng, Chang Lantian as Manager Chen, Sun Peijun as Manager Wu, Liang Tian as Third Brother

Wu Fei, a hard-working executive, is in the process of being divorced by his wife Zhao Hong, a fitness instructor. One day, he accidentally meets Lin Xiaomei, a girl from the countryside. She is pregnant, but her father wants her to marry someone other than her lover. She has been searching unsuccessfully for her lover in the city, and now has nowhere to stay. The kindly Wu Fei takes her home with him, and the next morning his estranged wife shows up, leading to misunderstanding concerning the girl's being there. After explanations, Zhao Hong offers to help Wu Fei and Xiaomei find the girl's boyfriend. In the process, the estranged older couple discover things about each other they had not realized before, and when they finally get the young lovers together, they reconcile as well.

364. *Comedy Star (Xi Ju Ming Xing)*

1991. Beijing Film Studio. Color. Letterboxed. 9 Reels. Direction: Liu Guoquan. Screenplay: Zhan Rong. Cinematography: Guan Qingwu, Cai Huimin. Art Direction: Tu Juhua, Zhang Wenqi. Music: Su Yue. Sound: Wang Dawen. Cast: Liang Tian as Liang Zhi, Ge You as Teacher Ge, Xie Yuan as Director Xie, Ma Xiaoqing as Xiao Qing, Ling Yuan as Grandma, Zhu Jinghong as Zhang Lingling

Clothing salesman Liang Zhi dreams of becoming an actor. After completing a quick spare-time session in acting techniques, he lands a part as an understudy, but his brief moment is cut out of the film's final version. He works hard to get more parts, spending so much time at it he is fired from his day job. He takes a job at the studio as part of a cleanup crew, and tries out for any roles he can get, usually as extras or walk-ons. Eventually, his appearances in tiny roles are so frequent that audiences begin to recognize him and he is cast in a significant role in a major film. Unfortunately, he falls from a tree and breaks a leg, forcing the director to replace him. His one chance at potential stardom gone, Liang sadly resigns himself to being a perennial bit player, although a popular one.

365. *Command Flags Flapping in the Wind (Shuai Qi Piao Piao)*

1958. Changchun Film Studio. B & W. 7 Reels. Direction: Yan Gong. Screenplay: Jia Ke. Cinematographer: Liu Yongzhen. Art Direction: Jin Bohao. Music: Quan Rufeng. Sound: Jue Jingxiu. Cast: Yan Fei as Secretary Zhang, Li Tiefeng as Director Song of the town, Chen Xizhen as Plant Director Lin, Ren Dao as Engineer Yang, Zhao Baohua as an older citizen, Li Wancheng as the old secretary

Basically an instructional film, this is the story of one Chinese county's success at backyard steel production during the Great Leap Forward campaign, beginning with finding and exploiting raw materials, then building the mill and producing the steel, and finally building a railway line to transport the steel.

366. *Commercial Circles (Parts 1 & 2) (Shang Jie)*

1989. Pearl River Film Studio. Color. Letterboxed. Direction: Hu Bingliu. Screenplay: Miao

Yue, Hu Bingliu. Cinematographer: Zhen Hua, Wang Huiguang. Art Direction: Zhang Zhichun. Music: Cheng Dazhao. Sound: Feng Lunsheng. Cast: Zhang Fengyi as Zhang Hanchi, Chen Baoguo as Liao Zuquan, Wang Wei as Qin Yueshuang, Lin Xiaojie as Liang Yiyun, Zhao Yue as Tao Lijin

Three stories of urban life in Guangzhou, where the policy of opening and reform has really taken hold. Zhang Hangchi is pushed into business much against his will, and becomes a company general manager. Despite his lack of enthusiasm, he makes money although he doesn't know why. Only when he is with his wife Qin Shuangyue, can he find peace and comfort. Liao Zuquan, a manager in a smaller company, dreams of owning his own tavern. He manages to raise the funds for it, but his girlfriend Liang Yiyun emigrates to the United States. Zeng Guangrong is self-employed, and while he is very good at making money he devotes so much time to it he neglects his fiancee, who breaks off with him. Through the stories of these three couples, the film examines how contemporary people can still be saddled with traditional conventions while seeking new ways of making a living.

Commissioner Lin **see** *Lin Zexu*

367. *Composite Man (He Cheng Ren)*

1988. Changchun Film Studio. Color. 10 Reels. Direction: Wang Yabiao, Yi Aiqun. Screenplay: Chu Liang, Wang Yabiao. Cinematography: Lei Xianhe. Art Direction: Yang Baocheng. Music: Li Bingyang. Sound: Cao Feng. Cast: Zhao Baocai as Wu Ao and the Composite Man, Du Shuang as the Professor, Liu Jun as Wang Yalan, Huang Ailing as Aunt Chun, Lei Guangying as Deputy CEO Zhang, Fang Yan as Secretary Chen, Li Yang as Li Yue, Li Xiaodong as Wu Feng

When Huaxia Trading Company CEO Wu Ao is on the verge of death from a brain disease, a medical school professor transplants into his body the brain of a farmer who has just died in an auto accident. The resultant composite man behaves strangely, as he now has an executive's image combined with a farmer's thinking. After a series of bizarre incidents involving Wu, his family and colleagues, Wu's deputy and his secretary are bribed by a foreign businessman to have Wu Ao sign a contract that in effect gives the company away. The conspirators flee with a huge amount of cash, the Huaxia Company declares bankruptcy and Wu Ao is put on trial for violating economic laws. In court, the professor shocks everyone when he relates Wu Ao's medical history. The question now becomes, who is guilty?

368. *Condemned to Death (Huan Qi Zhi Xing)*

1985. Inner Mongolia Film Studio. Color. 9 Reels. Direction: Liu Guoquan. Screenplay: Lin Hongtong. Cinematographer: Sun Xingyuan. Art Direction: Feng Yuan. Music: Wang Ming. Sound: Zhang Zhian. Cast: Zhao Youliang as Xing Dan, Yang Liping as Fang Hui, Xu Zhan as Wang Ruifeng, Jiang Gengcheng as Jiang Shaopeng

During the Cultural Revolution, medical school research assistant Xing Dan steals the cancer research papers of the professor he works for, then arranges for the professor to be persecuted to death. Years pass, and Xing Dan has become a top researcher. But when his girl friend Fang Hui stumbles across evidence of his past crime and urges him to go to the authorities and confess, he kills her. When a coworker happens to walk in on the murder, Xing Dan kills him as well. Xing Dan is arrested and sentenced to death, but the relevant government ministry intervenes and gets him a stay of execution so he can finish his cancer research. During his last days, Xing Dan finally is remorseful, but it is too late.

369. *Confession of Love (Zi Shou De Ai)*

1994. Beijing Film Studio. Color. Letterboxed. 9 Reels. Direction: Xu Qingdong. Screenplay: Lin Yueru, Xu Qing. Cinematography: Geritu. Art Direction: Song Jun. Music: Gao Erdi. Sound: Liu Xiaodong. Costume: Chen Yulian. Makeup: Xue Yuanyuan. Cast: Ma Xiaoqing as Su Ming, Ma Ling as Zhou Mei, Chen Baoguo as Xiao Jian, Tao Qiupu as Zhang Changfu, Qi Kejian as Wu Chaohui, Wang Xi as Qi Zhao, Zhao Zeren as the director, Jin Shunzi as Peng Ming, Xing Yuguo as Xiao Wang

Based on a true story. Just as her career is really taking off, singer Zhou Mei is raped one night in her Beijing apartment. She reports the incident to the police, but the next day returns to recant the whole story. It turns out that a decade earlier Zhou had a lover named Wu Zhaohui. They had consensual sex, but Zhou Mei's ignorance of legal terminology led her to tell others he had "raped" her. The confusion resulted in Wu's being sentenced to 10 years in prison. Upon his release, Wu returned to Zhou and this time really assaulted her out of revenge.

370. *Confident Man (Zi Xin De Nan Zi Han)*

1985. Xiaoxiang Film Studio. Color. 9 Reels. Direction: Xia Gang, Jiang Weihe. Screenplay: Shui Yunxian. Cinematographer: Wang Kekuan. Art Direction: Rao Weiquan. Music: Yang Yong. Sound: Ning Yuqin. Cast: Sun Min as Ding Zhuangzhuang, Hu Zongqi as Hu Yongsheng, Liu Qing as Luo Mingyan, Zhang Guixing as Liao Shantian

In a south China province, the Party Committee decides to use a city-owned vegetable company as a test site for reform measures, in the hope this will alleviate the province's vegetable shortage. College-trained Hu Yongsheng is named manager of the company. Hu changes some things for the better, but conflicts soon arise with his employees. One particular competitor of Hu is Ding Zhuangzhuang, who draws up his own proposals for reform. They eventually work out their differences and cooperate. Hu Yongsheng announces a new reform plan as a joint preparation. The employees all support the new plan, and the reform moves ahead.

371. *Conflicts in a Remote Village (Huang Huo)*

1988. Yunnan Minority Film Studio. Color. Letterboxed. 10 Reels. Direction: Wang Yan. Screenplay: Lian Zhi. Cinematography: Pao Xiaoran. Art Direction: Zhang Hongqi. Music: Cao Xuean. Cast: Zhang Fengyi as Lei Yingshan, Lu Liping as Mujing

The forested areas of western Yunnan province are inhabited primarily by people of the Jingpo nationality. One day, young village health care worker Mujing is injured in a forest fire, and young cadre Lei Yingshan carries her back to the village, an act of kindness that sets village gossips' tongues wagging. Lei Yingshan is later named head of the village, and tries to implement reforms despite considerable opposition. In addition, Mujing has conflicts with her conservative father. At last, Mujing leaves

to study in Hainan, and Lei Yingshan sees her off.

372. *A Confucius Family (Que Li Ren Jia)*

1992. Shanghai Film Studio. Color. Letterboxed. 10 Reels. Direction: Wu Yigong. Screenplay: Qiao Jian, Zhou Meisheng, Yua Aiping, Yang Jiang. Cinematography: Shen Miaorong. Art Direction: Xue Jianna. Music: Yang Mao. Sound: Zhan Xin. Costume: Zhang Chunzhong. Makeup: Xu Peijun. Cast: Zhu Xu as Kong Lingtan, Zhao Erkang as Kong Dexian, Zhang Wenrong as Jin Lan, Ning Li as Kong Weiben, Geng Ge as Yumei, Wei Zongwan as Kong Lingran, Yuan Zhiyuan as Kong Xiangbi

In China, people surnamed Kong are considered to be direct descendants of Confucius. This is the story of one family named Kong, and how traditional clan and family rules act as a restraint on them. When family patriarch Kong Lingtan, now a high official in Beijing, returns on a visit to his native place, the various members of his family react in widely different ways to his return. His son Dexian, an orthodox Confucian, cannot forgive the older man for having left his now-deceased wife many years earlier to pursue dreams of a political career. Grandson Weiben, on the other hand, admires how Lingtan took his own fate in hand; he himself thinks only of going abroad, and regards Confucian traditions and ethics as relics. A series of family conflicts unfolds.

Best Sound Zhan Xin, 1993 Golden Rooster Awards.

373. *Conspiracy for Death (Si Wang Yu Mou)*

1994. Xi'an Film Studio. Color. Letterboxed. 9 Reels. Direction: Li Yundong. Screenplay: Zhu Zhaobing. Cinematography: Song Chao, Cheng Yuandong. Art Direction: Ge Leye. Music: Xu Youfu. Sound: Ji Changhua. Costume: Su Jianjun, Kang Weijun. Makeup: An Hong, Chen Xiaochun. Cast: Zhou Lijing as Lu Yuanyue, Gong Youcun as Chen Mei, Wang Yanmei as Zuo Wei, Shi Xiaohong as Yu Xiaogang, Ma Kun as Chu Keyi, Yi Jiuxi as Su Rui, Chen Shuqing as public security bureau director

A West Asian republic decides to construct a nuclear power station, and invites bids on it from every major company in the world. The competition is very tough, but two leaders emerge: China's 702 Company and the Haitong Company from country D. The

Haitong Company contacts a criminal syndicate with a request they kill China's nuclear expert, a woman named Zuo Wei. The syndicate assigns the hit to Chen Mei, a woman in their organization who is an old friend of Zuo Wei's. Chinese public security officers protect Zuo Wei, and the plot is smashed. The 702 Corporation wins the bid.

374. *Contemporary King of Fire (Dang Dai Huo Shen)*

1986. Xiaoxiang Film Studio. Color. 9 Reels. Direction: Pan Xianghe. Screenplay: Luo Zhijun. Cinematography: Zhao Peng, Liu Yuefei. Art Direction: Rao Weiquan. Music: Liu Qi. Sound: Huang Shiye. Cast: Wang Runting as Jin Chao, Huang Ailing as Li Fengzhu

375. *Contemporary Style (Dang Dai Feng Ge)*

1984. Changchun Film Studio. Color. Letterboxed. 10 reels. Direction: Sun Sha. Screenplay: Sun Sha. Cinematographer: Han Dongxia. Art Direction: Gong Minhui. Music: Fan Weiqiang, Zhang Like. Sound: Yi Wenyu. Cast: Zhu Manfang as Shu Rong, Wang Huayin as Jiang Zhiyang, Lin Qiang as Gu Quan, Fu Hengzhi as Song Shouren, Mao Yiwen as Jiang Yue, Xi Junyi as Song Song

As two small children play in a road, a large truck bears down on them. A young worker named Gu Quan sees the impending disaster and saves the children, but is himself critically injured and rushed to the local hospital. Shu Rong, mother of one of the children, arrives at the hospital where she finds that Doctor Song Shouren, father of the other child, is incapable of treating the type of injuries the young worker has suffered. Shu Rong tries to get her husband, Doctor Jiang Zhiyang, to leave the academic conference he is attending and come to the hospital. He fails to do so and Gu Quan dies. When Jiang Zhiyang refuses to accept any blame in the matter, his wife angrily leaves him. The film relates how Jiang Zhiyang over time comes to realize the affection and respect that he has lost by not helping. When he is at last repentant, his wife Shu Rong returns to him.

376. *Contemporary Young Hero (Dang Dai Xiao Xia)*

1990. Shanghai Film Studio. Color. Wide Screen. 9 Reels. Direction: Yu Mei, Yang Jing.

Screenplay: Liu Ling, Yu Mei. Cinematography: Zhong Wenmin, Yang Kai. Art Direction: Zhen Changfu. Music: Xu Jingxin, Chen Xinxian. Sound: Ying Zhiping. Cast: Zhang Jing as Jin Baoguang, Liu Junjun as Xuefeng

377. *Contracted Couple (He Tong Fu Qi)*

1988. Xiaoxiang Film Studio And Jiangxi Film Studio Jointly. Color. Letterboxed. 9 Reels. Direction: Liang Zhiyong. Screenplay: Lu Nan. Cinematography: Liang Zhiyong, Meng Fanjun. Art Direction: Zhao Zhenxue. Music: Wang Ming. Sound: Wang Yunhua. Cast: Shi Xiaojie as Qiao Dexi, Wu Yufang as Huimei, Liang Qinggang as Yang Donggeng

Clothing store manager Qiao Dexi has prospered under reform, but is still not totally satisfied: he has two daughters but no son. While he and his wife Huimei are visiting Qiao's native home in the countryside, he finds she is pregnant. In order to avoid being punished for violating the one-child policy, Qiao decides to have his wife marry another man, then have the child. Therefore, they find a farmer called Yang Donggeng, honest and kind, but still unmarried though nearly 40. They sign a marriage agreement. But it turns out that Huimei is not pregnant after all. From the experience, Huimei begins to look at her husband differently, and at last decides to leave home, taking the children with her. As Qiao Dexi sits in his lonely home wondering what happened to him, Yang Dongcheng shows up to return the "marriage contract" and the 1,500 yuan cash payment Qiao had given him. Qiao Dexi is very ashamed and regretful.

378. *Contributing Everything to the Communist Party (Ba Yi Qie Xian Gei Dang)*

1992. Emei Film Studio. Color. Letterboxed. Direction: Mao Yuqing, Li Ling, Screenplay: Mao Mao, Liang Husheng, Cinematography: Sun Guoliang, Zhang Wenzhong, Art Direction: Luo Zhicheng, Cast: Zhang Guangbei as Wu Yunduo, Si Xiaohong as the military worker department director, He Yu as the female nurse

This is the story of Wu Yundao, a famous Chinese gunsmith during World War II. In 1941, Wu researches and develops his own weapons manufacturing facility under conditions of extreme shortages. He narrowly escapes death several times, as he makes major contributions to the eventual victory.

379. *Cops and Desperados (Feng Liu Jing Cha Wang Ming Fei)*

1988. Pearl River Film Studio. Color. 9 Reels. Letterboxed. Direction: Zheng Hua. Screenplay: Wang Zhonggang. Cinematography: Wang Suiguang. Art Direction: Feng Fang. Music: Zhou Xiaoyuan. Sound: Feng Lunsheng, Lu Hong. Cast: Li Xida as Zong Min, Lin Xiaojie as Mei Rong, Sun Lijun as the Boss, Dong Honglin as Ma Xiaolong, Wang Ping as Hu Fei

Along the Beijing-Guangzhou railway line, a bandit gang operates with seeming impunity. Ma Xiaolong, a young police chief, boards the train heading south to Guangzhou to try and catch the bandits should they raid the train again. Veteran policeman Zong Min, escorting his wife to Shenzhen for medical treatment, is ordered to help Ma on the case. On the train, Zong Min and his wife meet their cousin Mei Rong, a businesswoman also traveling south. When the bandits attack the train, Zong Min and Ma Xiaolong get off to chase them, leaving Zong's wife with Mei Rong, unaware the cousin is actually the bandit chief. After a breathtaking chase, the police succeed in capturing all the criminals including Mei Rong. But Zong Min loses his beloved wife.

380. *A Corner Forsaken by Love (Bei Ai Qing Yi Wang De Jiao Luo)*

1981. Emei Film Studio. Color. 10 Reels. Direction: Zhang Qi, Li Yalin. Screenplay: Zhang Xuan. Cinematography: Mai Shuhuan. Art Direction: Chen Desheng, Wu Xujing. Music: Wang Ming, Sound: Shen Guli. Cast: Shen Danping as Huangmei, He Xiaoshu as Linghua, Yang Hailian as Chunni, Zhang Shihui as Xu Rongshu, Li Guohua as Shen Shanwang, Zhang Chao as Little Leopard

Shen Shanwang's family lives in an isolated and extremely poor mountain village, a village in both physical and spiritual poverty, a village forgotten by love. When Shen Shanwang's daughter Chunni is 19, she falls in love with a young man called "Little Leopard." Tragically, some village people catch the young couple making love and under the feudal traditions of the village subject them to harsh public criticism. Chunni cannot bear the public humiliation and commits suicide, after which Little Leopard is jailed on the charge of driving a woman to suicide by raping her. Chunni's

tragedy casts a shadow over her younger sister Huangmei, who now thinks love is shameful. After the Gang of Four is deposed, Huangmei's childhood playmate Xu Rongshu returns to his native village from his army service. Rongshu, a bright and ambitious young man, decides to rid the village of its backward customs and thinking. His courage attracts Huangmei's feelings for him, but her sister's experience worries her. Huangmei's girlfriend Yingdi loves a boy named Erhui, but her mother and the village Party Secretary oppose the match and arrange for her to marry a man she has never met. To avoid the unhappy fates of her sister and friend Yingdi, Huangmei gathers strength and pursues true love. She runs away to her beloved Xu Rongshu and to a new life.

Best Screenplay Zhang Xuan, 1982 Golden Rooster Awards.

Best Supporting Actress He Xiaoshu, 1982 Golden Rooster Awards.

381. *The Corpse in the Canyon (Sheng Gu Si Bian)*

1985. Emei Film Studio. Color. Letterboxed. 9 Reels. Direction: Hao Weiguang. Screenplay: Wang Jiaming. Cinematographer: Mai Shuhuan. Art Direction: Li Fan. Music: Zhao Yulong. Sound: Shen Guli. Cast: Ye Erken as Du Weibing, Yang Xingyi as Fang Wen, Wang Hui as Chun Yan, Wu Nanshan as Pu Ping, Li Dapeng as Luo Yongsheng

In Yunnan province along China's south border, word comes of the tragic death of one of the area's most respected citizens. The county hospital's deputy director Pu Ping, a noted practitioner of traditional Chinese herbal medicine, has fallen into a canyon while he and his son-in-law Doctor Fang Wen were searching for a rare plant. The death is treated like a normal accident. But one night a month later, Pu Ping suddenly returns home. His frightened daughter goes to find her husband, but when Doctor Fang arrives he finds the old man dead by poisoning, apparently self-inflicted. The subsequent evidence uncovers evidence that Doctor Fang had pushed his father-in-law into the chasm, in order to take over the older man's research. Then when his victim turned up alive, Fang had given him the poison.

382. *Corruption (Fu Shi)*

1950. Wenhua Film Company. B & W. 17

Cops and Desperados. **Police officer Ma Xiaolong (Dong Honglin) is briefed on his coming mission. 1988. Pearl River Film Studio.**

Reels. Direction: Zuo Lin. Screenplay: Ke Ling, based on the novel of the same title by Mao Dun (1896–). Cinematographer: Xu Qi. Set Design: Wang Yuebai. Music: Huang Yijun. Sound: Shen Yimin. Costume: Qi Qiuming. Makeup: Ni Yifei. Cast: Dan Ni as Zhao Huiming, Shi Hui as Zhang Xiaozhao, Cui Chaoming as Xi Qiang, Yu Zhongying as Little Fu, Cheng Zhi as Section Chief Qi, Hong Xia as An Lan

In World War II Shanghai, a young woman named Zhao Huiming cares only for the pursuit of pleasure, which leads to a separation from her husband Zhang Xiaozhao. She meets and begins an affair with a man named Xi Qiang, but later discovers that he is an enemy agent. He soon dumps her, but not before trapping her into becoming a part of his undercover organization. After she carries out a series of operations for them, she is informed that the organization has arrested her estranged husband, now a Communist Party member. She is ordered to effect a reconciliation, then woo him to their side. But when she meets with Zhang in prison, she is moved by his spirit, and determines to help him escape. Her intentions are discovered, however, and she is demoted to doing clerical tasks. She also has a surprising encounter with a girl she had known

in school, now also trapped into working for the enemy. Zhang Xiaozhao is finally killed, but first writes his wife a letter pleading with her to change her life and become a new person. This jolts Zhao Huiming into a conversion, and she and her old schoolmate flee together to their hometown, now liberated.

383. *The Counter (Gui Tai)*

1965. Tianma Film Studio. B & W. 8 Reels. Direction: Yin Zhi. Screenplay: Collectively, recorded by Zhuang Xinru, based on the stage play of the same title by Gao Shiguo. Cinematographer: Cao Weiye. Art Direction: Xu Keji. Music: Zhang Linyi. Sound: Zhou Yunling. Cast: Da Shichang as Zhou Jinshan, Wei Heling as Han Zhonglin, Zhang Xiaoling as Yang Guixiang, Cui Yueming as Li Huiping, Feng Qi as Yang Zhenglin, Liu Jie as Mrs. Yang

Yang Guixiang, a young female high school graduate, is assigned to work in a department store. She looks down upon sales work, and her reluctance to work at the counter soon shows in her work. She is rude to Zhou Jinshan, a radio store salesman who comes in to buy a lock just before closing time; when two of her girlfriends come in to shop, she is ashamed to see them; after she is reassigned to work at the shoe and hat counter, she sells Zhou Jinshan an unmatched pair of shoes. Guixiang's father Han Zhonglin helps her correct her attitude, and she also learns a good lesson from Zhou Jinshan, who detected a quality problem in an item his shop was selling and thereby promoted quality improvement. Yang Guixiang comes to realize her errors.

384. *Counter Underground Crime Action (Fan Hei Xing Dong)*

1990. Pearl River Film Studio. Color. Wide Screen. 9 Reels. Direction: Yu Shibing. Screenplay: Li Yanxiong. Cinematographer: Yu Xiaoqun. Art Direction: Guan Yu. Music: Du Jiangang. Sound: Feng Lunsheng. Cast: Shen Junyi as Ling Gang, Yuan Xingzhe as Zhen Fei

A police procedural focused on the search for bank robbers, a Hong Kong-based gang called the "5-9-K."

385. *Counterattack (Fan Ji)*

1976, unreleased. Beijing Film Studio. Color. 13 Reels. Direction: Li Wenhua. Screenplay: Collective, recorded by Mao Feng. Cinematographer: Zhen Yuyuan. Art Direction: Zhang Jinbiao, Song Hongrong. Music: Luo Weilun. Sound: Fu Yinjie. Cast: Yu Yang as Jiang Tao, Hu Peng as Director Zhao, Liu Jizhong as Jiang Tao (as a child), Liang Yuru as Old Geng, Ding Yihong as Wang Jian, Kang Zuang as Old Mrs. Tian, Han Haiquan as Han Ling

Provincial Party secretary Han Ling, sent to the countryside during the Cultural Revolution, is restored to his position and returns to Beijing. His first action is to conduct a comprehensive reorganization of units under his control, including pushing through the provincial committee a resolution opposing Yellow River University's "no exam" system for selecting new students, promoting an examination system instead. Han Ling's committee is criticized by the University's Party secretary Jiang Tao and provincial committee Director Zhao, who call Han's action "reversing a verdict." Even though he is jailed, Jiang Tao persists in his views, and the struggle continues. Shortly afterwards, the Central government issues two decisions supporting Jiang Tao and ordering his release, and the "counterattack rightist reversal of verdicts campaign" begins.

386. *Counterattack (Po Xi Zhan)*

1986. August Film Studio. Color. Wide Screen. 10 Reels. Direction: Zhen Zhiguo, Yu Yehua. Screenplay: Xu Guoteng. Cinematography: Chen Yuanliang, Bao Shengjun. Art Direction: Sun Guoqin, Chen Bugu. Music: Yang Xiwu. Sound: Guo Yisheng. Cast: Wang Qinxiang as Liang Zhenshan, Mu Ning as Lu Chunxiu, Wang Futang as Song Fu, Da Li as Lang Youren, Dan Ningjun as Qian Ba

In 1940, an armed civil militia brigade wages guerrilla warfare in a Japanese-occupied area. The group's leader Lu Chunxiu loses both her husband and mother-in-law in an enemy attack on their village. Eighth Route Army Regimental Commander Liang Zhenshan makes contact with the guerrillas and asks them to carry out future missions in concert with the regulars. The joint force dynamites a key Japanese transport route — the Pingguanyuan railway bridge. Their success emboldens them to totally cut off the enemy's supply line by blowing up the Pingguanyuan tunnel. Lu Chunxiu is killed in this effort, but the mission is successful.

387. *Countering Lights (Ni Guang)*

1982. Pearl River Film Studio. Color. 10 Reels. Direction: Ding Yinnan. Screenplay: Qin Peichun. Cinematographer: Wei Duo. Art Direction: Huang Tongrong. Music: Zhang Hong. Sound: Lin Guoqiang. Cast: Guo Kaimin as Liao Xingming, Si Xilai as Su Ping, Wu Yuhua as Xia Yinyin, Liu Xinyi as Huang Mao, Xiao Xiong as Xu Shanshan, Xu Sheshe as Liao Xiaoqing, Shi Zhongling as Jiang Wei

When screenwriter Su Ping returns for a visit to his old neighborhood, it brings back some memories of people he had once known there. One is Liao Xingming, a shipyard worker, who through reading acquires an appreciation of culture although his family and practically everyone else around him is backward and ignorant. When he meets and falls in love with Xia Yinyin, from a cadre background, the social customs of the era cannot accept their relationship and try to force them apart. They go against convention and marry anyway. Liao's younger sister Xiaoqing is quite different: she has ambitions beyond personal wealth, and gives up her true love Huang Mao for money. Another one taking a different path is shipyard electrician Jiang Wei: interested only in having a good time and caring only for external appearance, he misses out on a chance for true love.

Best Cinematographer Wei Duo, 1983 Golden Rooster Awards.

388. *Country People (Xiang Xia Ren)*

1989. Xi'an Film Studio. Color. Letterboxed. 9 Reels. Direction: Wang Zhijie. Screenplay: Yu Yunhe. Cinematographer: Ma Shusheng. Art Direction: Han Shihua. Music: Xiang Yin. Sound: Che Zhiyuan. Cast: Yu Yunhe as Ren Beihang, Yu Fuhui as Song Rui, Li Rui as Xiumei

In the bidding for a large construction project, Ren Beihang, manager of the Farmers' Construction Company, has to resort to trickery to get the project, mostly due to the reluctance of female engineer Song Rui and others to accept his bid. When the project starts, he has to revert to the same old tricks in order to keep supplies coming in. Soon, the project loans dry up, but this time Song Rui comes to his rescue. As the ceremony marking the project unveiling, Ren Beihang, disgusted at the dirty tricks and compromise required to accomplish the task, quietly slips away by himself.

389. *The Country Tailor and the Elegant Lady (Tu Cai Feng Yu Yang Xiao Jie)*

1987. Changchun Film Studio. Color. 10 Reels. Direction: Li Geng, Bei Zhaocheng. Screenplay: Mu Er. Cinematography: Yang Penghui. Art Direction: Sui Zuangji. Music: Zhou Huimin. Sound: Xing Guocang, Zhen Yunbao. Cast: Zhang Keqing as Chen Fenglin, Zheng Hong as Yang Lijuan

Young tailor Chen Fenglin leaves the countryside where he has grown and learned his trade, and goes to the city to replace his father as costumer for the city's song and dance troupe. Chen is very curious and everything is all new to him. The people in the troupe always mock his "rural characteristics." He does not like the troupe people much, but does not let it interfere with his career. He continues learning the world trends in fashion and puts these into his designs. In time, he receives a major award. Yang Lijuan, a star of the troupe, falls in love with the simple and honest tailor, and often helps and encourages him. Their relationship subjects the couple to many pressures and rumors, but the couple challenges traditional convention and finally gain the understanding and support of the rest.

390. *Country Teachers (Feng Huang Qing)*

1993. Tianjin Film Studio & Xiaoxiang Film Studio Jointly. Color. Letterboxed. 9 Reels. Direction: He Qun. Screenplay: Ju Sheng, Liu Xinglong, Pu Yangui, based on Liu Xinglong's original novel of the same title. Cinematography: Meng Weibing. Art Direction: Zhao Mei. Music: Zhang Shaotong. Sound: Zou Jian. Costume: Lu Yunying. Makeup: Huang Lu. Cast: Li Baotian as Principal Yu, Wang Xueqin as Sun Shihai, Ju Xue as Zhang Yingzi, Xiu Zongdi as Uncle, Sun Qian as Deng Youmei

After failing to qualify for university admission, young country girl Zhang Yingzi goes to teach at a primary school in a mountainous area. Everything at the school is old and broken down, and the principal and the few other teachers dream of gaining official teaching status which will qualify them for regular pay and the possibility of transfer. One teacher, the principal's wife, is so ill she has been unable to teach for months, but the others cover for her out of kindness. In order to obtain the funds for badly needed renovations, the teachers falsify a report regarding the number of pupils in the school. Zhang goes to the county authorities and swears to the falsity of the report, so the school does not receive the funds it needs. Unfortunately, her honesty was misplaced, as the county was aware of the true situation but had no other way of making the allocation. So no one is happy with the young teacher. She writes an article praising the teachers, which is published in a national newspaper and carried on radio. The good publicity results in the school getting the funding it needs. Zhang Yingzi is given the chance to become an official teacher, but she defers to the principal's wife. But the poor woman dies right after completing the necessary forms. Zhang Yingzi then leaves the primary school in the mountains.

Best Picture, 1994 Golden Rooster Awards.
Best Picture, 1994 Hundred Flowers Awards.
Best Screenplay Ju Sheng, Liu Xinglong and Pu Yangui, 1994 Golden Rooster Awards.
Best Actor Li Baotian, 1994 Golden Rooster Awards.
Best Actor Li Baotian, 1994 Hundred Flowers Awards.

391. *Court Chicken Fight (Gong Ting Dou Ji)*

1994. Beijing Film Studio. Color. Letterboxed. 9 Reels. Direction: Wang Binglin. Screenplay: Wang Binglin. Cinematography: Guan Qingwu, Wun Deguang. Art Direction: Song Zhenshan. Music: Sun Chuan. Sound: Wang Dawen. Costume: Liu Fang. Makeup: Wang Xiufeng, Zhao Fengling. Cast: Huang Zongluo as the Emperor, Ma Enran as Zhang Laosan, Zhao Liang as Xian Wang, Wu Weidong as Hui Wang, Xie Lan as Princess Yueyue, Zhao Ziyue as Niu Guogong, Fang Zige as Prime Minister Niu

Two kingdoms called Dragon Country and Chicken Country settle their disagreements through cockfights held at court, each country represented by a battling rooster. Dragon Country usually wins, and is very proud of its success. Chicken Country wants to take over Dragon Country, and makes an offer: the country winning the next fight will absorb the other into its own kingdom, putting an end to the long-running rivalry. Its very survival at stake, Dragon Country searches for the best fighter it can find, and comes up with a rooster as fierce as it is ugly. The ugly bird protects the country and its king by defeating Chicken Country's rooster.

392. *Covert Investigation (Mi Mi Cai Fang)*

1989. Emei Film Studio. Color. Wide screen. 9 Reels. Direction: Wang Jixing. Screenplay: Cai Jiangang. Cinematographer: Qiang Jun. Art Direction: Chen Desheng. Music: Si Wanchun, Yang Qin. Sound: Wang Guangzhong. Cast: Wang Zhiwen as Mike Feng, Zuo Lei as Tang Liyuan

One night in 1949, former Nationalist General Wang Yehan is murdered in his Hong Kong home, and the police profess to having no clues. In spite of this and his own editor's discouragement, Mike Feng, Chinese-American reporter for a Hong Kong newspaper, begins his own covert investigation. He finds a twisted tale of intrigue, involving key figures in the Nationalist government and military. Everyone involved is closemouthed and uncooperative, and at times it seems the only person he can rely on for help is his girlfriend Tang Liyuan, an employee at the newspaper's reference library. Just as he feels he is getting close to the truth of the matter, Feng is summarily dismissed from his job and his residence visa revoked. Having no choice but to go

home, Feng boards a plane for the U.S., accompanied by Tang Liyuan. In the U.S., they are just leaving the San Francisco airport when shots ring out and Feng falls to the ground, dead. Not even looking around, Tang silently continues walking ahead...

393. *The Cradle (A, Yao Lan)*

1979. Shanghai Film Studio. Color. 10 Reels. Direction: Xie Jin. Screenplay: Xu Qingdong, Liu Qin. Cinematographer: Chen Zhengxiang. Art Direction: He Ruiji. Music: Liang Hanguang. Sound: Feng Deyao. Cast: Zhu Xijuan as Li Nan, Zhang Yongshou as Xiao Hanping, Cun Li as Luo Guitian, Yang La as Liangliang, Ma Xiaoqing as Xiangzhu, Zhang Yu as Liang Yan, Zhang Lei as Dan Dan, Li Zhongwen as Dong Lai, Ni Yilan as Zhao Yuxia

In 1947, Li Nan, political instructor in a frontline unit, is assigned to escort some kindergarten children back to a safe area. Each child's background, none normal, is discussed in detail: Liangliang's father was killed and her mother badly wounded; Dan Dan is an orphan found on the road; little Yuansheng was born in the kindergarten after her mother was driven from home by his father; chubby Dong Lai's parents are both fighting at the front... Li Nan brings the children through many difficulties, finally getting them all safely out of harm's way.

394. *Cradle on Wheels (Dai Gu Lu De Yao Lan)*

1994. Emei Film Studio. Color. Letterboxed. 9 Reels. Direction: Mi Jiashan. Screenplay: Chen Jianyu. Cinematography: Qiang Jun. Art Direction: Chen Ruogang. Music: Liu Huan. Sound: Luo Guohua. Costume: Lin Ailian. Makeup: Wang Ping. Cast: Wang Xueqi as Qiangzi, Hao Yan as sister, Zhen Weiwei as abandoned infant, Ge Lili as mother of the abandoned infant, Liang Tian as Maozai, Yue Hong as wife of Maozai, Ding Jiali as woman driver

One winter night in Beijing, taxi driver Qiangzi finds someone has abandoned a 4- or 5-month-old infant in his cab. He winds up having to take the baby home to his bachelor apartment. Later, for various reasons, Qiangzi keeps the baby and raises it by himself, installing a small cradle in the back seat of his cab, so he can care for the child while working. Then the baby's mother shows up wanting the

The Cradle. Li Nan (Zhu Xijuan, second left) brings her kindergarten class to greet military leaders. 1979. Shanghai Film Studio.

child back. Qiangzi fights her in court, but the mother wins. Qiangzi, not really young but still single, decides that his taste of fatherhood makes marriage a more inviting prospect than it had been.

395. *The Crane Flying Back (Fei Lai De Nu Xu)*

1982. Shanghai Film Studio. Color. 10 Reels. Director: Zhong Shuhuang. Screenplay: Wu Zhongchuan, Hu Linsheng, Yang Shiwen. Cinematographer: Zhu Yongde. Art Direction: Wu Tianci. Music: Yang Shaolu. Sound: Lu Bingkui. Cast: Chen Xu as Gu Zhengmao, Li Lingjun as Xiaolan's mother, Zhu Shunliang as Liuchun, Chen Hongmei as Xiaolan, Gao Cui as Zhu Er's wife, Mao Yongmin as Zhu Xing

In the south China countryside, production unit deputy director Gu Zhengmao is obsessed with the application of scientific methods to farming. While both he and his daughter Xiaolan are devoted to it, Xiaolan's mother is more concerned with getting their daughter married. One day she meets Zhu Er's wife, who is also worried about finding a wife

for her son Liuchun, an agricultural technician who is also committed to scientific farming. The two mothers hit it off very well, so they arrange a date for their children. However, Xiaolan and Liuchun disapprove of such old-fashioned arrangements, and both refuse to keep the date. To get away from his mother's badgering him, Liu Chun comes to Xiaolan's home that day to discuss the application of technology to farming with Gu Zhengmao. Xiaolan and Liuchun get into a deep discussion of Pearl No. 74, a new rice variety, and agree to work on developing it together. The new variety is a complete success, and through working on it together the two young people fall in love. The two mothers have their own happy ending.

Agricultural Credit Bank Award, Alencon International Children's Film Festival.

396. *Crazed Woman Avenger (Wei Qing Kuang Die)*

1994. Xi'an Film Studio. Color. Letterboxed. 9 Reels. Direction: Qiang Xiaolu. Screenplay: Qiang Xiaolu. Art Direction: Liu Yichuan.

Music: Cui Bingyuan. Sound: Hui Dongzhi. Costume: Zhang Yaodong. Makeup: Li Lan. Cast: Han Qing as Lin Peng, Wang Yanmei as Mengyan, Wu Dan as Liu Lan, Hou Zi as Juanmao, Zhang De as Xiao San

Auto thief Meng Long is killed while trying to escape the police. His sister Meng Yan swears to avenge him, as she believes his death was caused by somebody setting him up to be caught. She also suspects Meng Long's old girl friend Liu Lan of having betrayed him. She asks her boy friend Lin Peng to get close to Liu Lan and help her learn the truth. But Lin finds he likes Liu, and their close relationship blossoms into love. Lin Peng also gradually comes to realize that Meng Yan is insane, obsessed with killing the other woman, not with finding the truth. In a final confrontation, Lin Peng rescues Liu Lan and kills the crazed Meng Yan.

397. *Crazy Dancers (Xi Bu Kuang Wu)*

1988. Tianshan Film Studio. Color. 9 Reels. Letterboxed. Direction: Guang Chunlan. Screenplay: Ran Hong, Maimaiti Tatilik, Guang Chunlan. Cinematography: Qi Xing. Art Direction: Xiang Shaowei. Music: Yikemu. Sound: Li Fu. Cast: Tu'erxun Nayi as Paxia, Asihar as Yasen, Zhoulaiti as Julaiti, Milading as Nijiati, Mihai Guli as Ayi Guli

Yasen, Paxia, Nijiati, Ayi Guli and Aishan are five young people of the Uighur minority living in a city in Xinjiang. Devoted to song and dance, the film shows their lives and loves against a backdrop of modern music and dancing, including break dancing. The film also underlines the conflict between old and new ideals in modern China.

398. *Crazy Dragon Becomes a Hero (Kuang Long Cheng Ying Hao)*

1994. Emei Film Studio. Color. Letterboxed. 9 Reels. Direction: Ni Feng. Screenplay: Ni Feng, Xu Xing. Cinematography: Ning Jiakun. Art Direction: Xu Shaojun. Music: Liu Zupei. Sound: Tu Liuqing. Costume: Fu Ping, Li Yuli. Makeup: Duan Hong. Cast: Liu Chengxi as Dong Dashao, Li Li as Shanmei, Huang Ling as Madame Long, Wu Lan as La Jie, Zhang Sheng as Shengkoumei

It is 1900, and the armies of eight foreign powers invade China to protect foreign legations during the Boxer Rebellion. A small county called Dragon Town has never had a hero in its entire history. Everyone, including the county's chief administrator, is afraid of foreigners. Some British and Japanese come to Dragon Town in search of antiques, and when they discern the residents' obvious fear, the foreigners bully and humiliate them. This at last converts the son of the county administrator from a lazy playboy to a brave, anti-foreign fighter. He inspires all the people of the county to rise up and defend their homes.

399. *Crazy Robber (Kuang Dao)*

1988. Inner Mongolia Film Studio. Color. 9 Reels. Direction: Abuer. Screenplay: Zhang Jiping. Cinematography: Narisu, Zhao Ping. Art Direction: Shen Minquan. Music: Guo Zhijie. Sound: Hu Bing. Cast: Wun Haitao as Angqing, Ren Naichang as Yu Ye, Zhu Huiguo as Maiwang, Zhao Guohua as Moergeng, Mai Xiaoqing as Tiandai

A Chinese–Hong Kong–Japanese joint venture movie crew is filming on location at an ancient tomb. In the course of their work, some golden statues dating from the 1st Century A.D. are removed from the tomb and replaced by fakes. Crew director Angqing suspects that someone from the film crew is guilty. He turns amateur detective and uncovers the thief.

400. *Crazy Small Town (Feng Kuang De Xiao Zhen)*

1987. Changchun Film Studio. Color. 9 Reels. Direction: Wang Fengkui. Screenplay: Qian Daoyuan. Cinematography: Xu Shouzen. Art Direction: Guo Yansheng. Music: Yang Yilun. Sound: Gu Xiaolian. Cast: Liu Yanguang as Salesman Yu, Ruan Furen as Fu Zhenfa, Zhao Dengfeng as Liu Zhenfu, Li Tingdong as Zhang Gongdian, Dong Zhiwu as Lei Dahan, Cui Muyan as Gan Guangbo

High school teacher Wang rushes to add a small room to his home so his daughter will have a place to stay during her summer break from school. But his explanation is interpreted by some people to mean that "there will be an earthquake early tomorrow morning." The rumor spreads rapidly, sending his panicky neighbors in a rush to buy emergency supplies. Soon the city government gets involved as well. The entire community passes a terrifying day and night of frantic preparation which costs nearly 100,000 yuan. The next morning there is of course no earthquake, and the community has spent as much as a real earthquake would have cost them. But when the county investigates, no one will claim responsibility.

401. *Creating a New World (Parts 1 & 2) (Kai Tian Pi Di)*

1991. Shanghai Film Studio. Stereo. Color. Wide Screen. 17 Reels. Direction: Li Xiepu, Screenplay: Huang Yazhou, Wang Tianyun, Cinematography: Shen Miaorong, Zhu Yongde, Art Direction: Ju Ransheng, Sun Weide, Music: Yang Mao, Sound: Ren Daming, Cast: Shao Honglai, Sun Jitang, Wang Dou

A historical drama tracing the founding of the Chinese Communist Party in 1921.

Best Screenplay Huang Yazhou and Wang Tianyun, 1992 Golden Rooster Awards.

402. *Crescent Moon (Yue Ya Er)*

1986. Beijing Film Studio. Color. 9 Reels. Direction: Huo Zuang, Xu Xiaoxing. Screenplay: Huo Zuang, Zhang Fan. Cinematography: Sun Cheng, Meng Fanjun. Art Direction: Yang Yuhe, Zhao Zhenxue. Music: Liu Zuang. Sound: Wang Yunhua, Wang Chunbao. Cast: Song Dandan as Han Yuerong, Siqin Gaowa as Mother, Liang Jingsheng as Gao Junsheng, Yuan Li as Meng Shuxian, Wang Xian as Mr. Kang, Bai Huiwen as the woman principal

In the early years after the founding of the Republic of China (c1920), eight-year-old Beijing girl Han Yuerong loses her father. Her mother remarries in order to support herself and the child, but when the stepfather also dies, financial reasons force the mother into prostitution. Unable to understand her mother's motives, the now-teenaged Han Yuerong moves out. She meets and has an affair with a man named Gao Junsheng, only to find he is already married. She finds a job as a waitress, which ends when she is raped by the boss, Mr. Kang. Eventually Yuerong also becomes a prostitute, always sending a part of her earnings to her aging mother. When she contracts a social disease, her mother comes to see her and the two have a heartbreaking reunion. A new district director starts a campaign to clean up prostitutes, and Yuerong is sent to a reformatory. Then she finds the new district director is the Mr. Kang who assaulted her before. Yuerong walks out into the cool night and gazes at the moon, feeling very lonely and helpless.

Silver Award, 41th Salerno International Film Festival.

403. *Crime Story Collection (Zui Er Jing Hun Lu)*

1987. Pearl River Film Studio. Color. 9 Reels. Direction: Li Yeyu. Screenplay: Du Jiafu. Cinematography: Yu Xiaoqun, Gang Yi. Art Direction: Li Xin, Guan Yu. Music: Wang Xiaoyong. Sound: Huang Minguang. Cast: Xue Shan as Wang Qiang, Wang Jiancheng as Erxiang, Xin Jing as the rich man, Xu Chengxian as Ji Chongguang, Gu Xiaokang as Gou Shener, Zhang Qing as Zhang Li, Wang Shanshu as Grandfather, Liu Xuling as the madwoman

Businessman Wang Qiang's partner threatens him because of the way Wang distributes their profits. To get away from the arguing for a while, he and his wife go to visit her grandparents in the countryside. There, the grandfather tells Wang Qiang a story from the Qing Dynasty, about a greedy man who secured some antiques he had no right to, and was then visited by a ghost. When he finishes the tale, the grandfather says that this story was meant for Wang Qiang in particular. After the couple returns to the city, Wang finds he cannot get it out of his mind, and he walks the streets alone, deep in thought.

404. *Critical Experience (Yan Jun De Li Cheng)*

1978. Changchun Film Studio. Color. 12 Reels. Direction: Su Li, Zhang Jianyou. Screenplay: Zhang Xiaotian, Shi Jiyu, Cinematographer: Wu Guojiang, Han Hanxia. Art Direction: Wang Xingwen, Du Xiufeng. Music: Gao Feng. Sound: Wang Fei. Cast: Guo Zhengqin as Cheng Wanpeng, Tian Chengren as Cheng Guanghan, Sun Guolu as Cheng Xiaoyue, Zhao Zhilian as Cheng Shaojie, Ma Qun as Xiao Qian, Zhen Zhaishi as Fang Lei

A provincial railway bureau requests the central government send them a "Long March" trouble-shooting team to resolve a major railway transport snag. But bureau chief Cheng Shaojie, acting on orders from the "Gang of Four," accuses bureau Party secretary Fang Lei of being a "capitalist roader," and setting up "illegal administration." When the "Long March" team led by Cheng Wanpeng arrives, the bureau chief tries to block their work. But with Fang Lei's help, the team resolves the snag, allowing relief supplies to get through to victims of the Tangshan earthquake. Cheng Shaojie accelerates his attempt to seize power by causing a railway accident, but Cheng Wanpeng bravely rescues the train and thwarts the conspiracy. At the critical moment that Cheng Shaojie plans to blow up the modernized railway station to cut off all north-south transportation, news comes from the Ministry of Railways in Beijing that the "Gang of Four" has been defeated.

405. *Critical Moment (Guan Jian Shi Ke)*

1984. Inner Mongolia Film Studio. Color. 9 Reels. Direction: Sun Tianxiang. Screenplay: Chen Beng, Xi Cheng, Bao Xiang. Cinematographer: Zhang Faliang. Art Direction: Shen Minquan. Music: Bing He, Liu Qin. Sound: Li Juncheng. Cast: Li Qide as Meng Chunyu, Xia Hui as He Yudan, Gu Zhi as He Sheng, Li Ming as Cheng Yuejing, Yu Zhongyuan as Song Jiabao, Er Changlin as Mr. Niu

Meng Chunyu is named director of a mine, replacing He Sheng, father of Meng's lover He Yudan. Most people are unhappy with Meng's appointment, but He Yudan continues to support him. The film follows the development of their relationship, but the ending is ambiguous as to whether they will stay together.

406. *Crossing Border Action (Chao Guo Jie Xing Dong)*

1986. Shanghai Film Studio. Color. 10 Reels. Direction: Huang Shuqin. Screenplay: Cheng Shiqin. Cinematography: Xia Lixing. Art Direction: Chen Chudian. Music: Liu Yanxi. Sound: Zhou Hengliang. Cast: Jin Xing as Qi Ye, Wu Junmei as Tong Nian, Xu Bu as Director Yan, Ye Hui as Lu Yuan, Zhang Zhijian as Li Qiang, Zhang Minghua as Wang Lan

Reliable intelligence sources report that the international terrorist organization "Black Storm" is sending agents to Beijing to assassinate a foreign general when he makes a visit to China. Chinese intelligence agencies start a counter-terrorist operation. The story follows the operation in parallel with the operation of two assassins, a man named Li Qiang and a woman named Wang Lan. At last, the plot is foiled and the assassins are killed. The general's important visit goes off smoothly.

407. *Crossing Camel Mountain Range by Night (Ye Zou Luo To Ling)*

1958. Haiyan Film Studio. B & W. 2 Reels. Direction: Xu Tao, Zhang Zheng. Screenplay: Li Zhun. Cinematographer: Qiu Yiren. Sound: Lu Zongbo. Art Direction: Yao Mingzhong. Cast: Li Huanqing as Liang Fengxian, Deng Nan as Yang Zhuang, Wun Xiying as Ma Wen, Xia Tian as Gao Tianbao

After the wheat harvest, in order to get their wheat to the nation as soon as possible, an agricultural commune holds a competition on getting the wheat delivered. Team No.1, led by Yang Zhuang, leaves at midnight to get a head start on the rest, but when they pass Team No.4's village — Camel Mountain Range — they find that No.4's director has already led his team out ahead of them. Team No.1 hurries to catch up, but cannot. Finally, Team No.4's leader Liang Fengxian modestly allows No.1 to catch up, so the two wheat delivery teams can arrive at their destination together.

408. *Crossing the Chishui River Four Times (Parts 1&2) (Si Du Chi Shui)*

1983. August First Film Studio. Color. 17 Reels. Direction: Cai Jiwei, Gu Dexian. Screenplay: Li Min, Wang Hao, Wang Yuanjian, Li Chuandi. Cinematographer: Cai Jiwei, Xu Lianqin. Art Direction: Ren Huixing, Fei Lansheng. Music: Yan ke. Sound: Wu Shibiao, Shen Guorui. Cast: Gu Yue as Mao Zedong, Fu Xuecheng as Liu Bocheng, Tang Guoqiang as Lu Qinsong, Zhao Hengduo as Chiang Kaishek, Jin Ange as Wang Daoyuan

In January, 1935, the 30,000-man Red Army arrives at the banks of the Chishui River where they are opposed by a much larger Nationalist force. The film tells how the Red Army under Commanders Mao Zedong and Zhou Enlai makes four attempts to cross the river, each time drawing out some of the opposing force and inflicting heavy casualties. At last, they succeed in crossing the river in May, and break through the Nationalist encirclement. The civil war enters a new phase.

409. *Crossing the Dragon River (Guo Jiang Long)*

1987. Emei Film Studio. Color. 9 Reels. Direction: Zhang Che. Screenplay: Zhang Che, Tan Su. Cinematography: Xie Erxiang. Art Direction: Li Fan. Music: Huang Dian. Sound: Zhang Jianping. Cast: Zhou Wenlin as Liu Shaoqi, Dong Zhihua as Mu Xiaolou, Xu Xiaojian as Cao Yukun, Sun Yiwen as Hua Yunfang, Jia Yongzhong as Shen Guisheng, Chen Ergang as Ding Chunhua

During the time in the mid–1930s that the Nationalist Army was collaborating with the Japanese invaders, the Chinese commander in Sichuan is General Liu Shaoqi. Liu lusts after famous opera star Hua Yunfang, a woman happily married to Cao Yukun. The general decides his own chances will improve with the husband out of the way, so he has Cao killed. With her husband dead, however, Hua Yunfang is offered comfort and protection by another actor, Mu Xiaolou, and eventually Hua and Mu fall in love. This results in the general having Mu killed as well. Realizing the general will never leave her alone if she stays, Hua Yunfang gives up her career and flees the region by river boat.

410. *Crossing the Wu River (Tu Po Wu Jiang)*

1961. August First Film Studio. B & W. 10 Reels. Direction: Li Shutian and Li Ang. Screenplay: Zhu Xin. Cinematography: Kou Jiwen and Ji Ming. Art Direction: Mai Yi. Music: Shi Feng. Sound: He Baoding. Cast: Li Jiufang as Regimental Commander Zhang, Zhou Zhengyu as Political Commissar Qing, Yu Chunmian as Company Commander Chen, Liu Bingzhang as Second Squad Leader, Lin Hongtong as Luo Xiaoguang, Zhu Qi as Li Biao

Late in 1934, a Red Army regiment on the Long March arrives at the south bank of the Wu River in Guizhou, and prepares to cross. Their first two efforts both fail, and by the third day their situation is almost desperate, for the pursuing government forces are drawing closer. They decide to make another try, but when the first boat arrives on the north bank they come under ferocious fire from an enemy force dug in there. At this critical juncture, a Red Army company in hiding on the north bank ambushes the government defenders and turns the tide, the regiment's first victory over a government force in three years. This breakthrough allows the rest of the regiment to cross the Wu River, called since ancient times "Heaven's peril," allowing them to continue the Long March.

411. *Crows and Sparrows (Wu Ya Yu Ma Que)*

1949. Shanghai Kunlun Film Studio. B&W. 12 reels. Direction: Zhen Junli. Screenplay: Chen Baicheng, Shen Fu, Wang Linggu, Xu Tao, Zhao Dan and Zhen Junli. Cinematography: Miao

Zhenhua, Hu Zhenhua. Music: Wang Yunjie. Sound: Li Liehong. Art Direction: Niu Baorong, Xu Zhicheng. Cast: Zhao Dan as Boss Xiao, Wei Helin as Kong Youwen, Sun Daolin as Hua Jiezhi, Li Tianji as Kou Yibo, Huang Zongying as Yu Xiaoyin, Wang Pei as Little Sister, Shangguan Yunzhu as Mrs. Hua, Wu Yin as Mrs. Xiao

In the winter of 1948, on the eve of Shanghai's fall to the Communists, corrupt Nationalist official Hou Yibo confiscates the home of Kong Youwen, an elderly newspaper proofreader, on grounds that Kong's son has joined a unit of the Communist armed forces. As the Nationalist regime is on the verge of collapse, Hou plans to sell the house in preparation for flight. Several others live there in addition to Kong, including high school teacher Hua Jiezhi and his wife, street vendors "Boss" Xiao and his wife, and others, but all are afraid to speak out. One by one they are victimized by Hou or by other Nationalist officials: Kong's sleeping room is trashed by gangsters in Hou's pay; for not siding with school officials during a student strike, Hua Jiezhi is denied housing at his school, then jailed for allegedly fomenting the students' action; Mrs. Hua is assaulted by Hou; Hou entices Boss Xiao and his wife to sink their savings in a business deal, then swindles them. Finally, unable to bear it any longer, the tenants join together to confront Hou, and he backs down. As the Nationalist government collapses, Hou and his wife flee the city. At New Year's Eve, the residents sit down to dinner together, and hearing the sound of fireworks and celebration in the streets, they begin to feel that an era of darkness has passed.

Best Recommendation, Coulommiers International Entertainment Film Festival.

412. *Crucial Summer (Can Ku De Xia Tian)*

1992. Xi'an Film Studio. Color. Letterboxed. 9 Reels. Direction: Jin Yin. Screenplay: Sun Yian. Cinematography: Zhang Faliang, Zhao Yimin. Art Direction: Cheng Minzhang, Li Zhengshen. Music: Zhang Dalong. Sound: Hong Jiahui, Yuan Xiaoyong. Costume: Du Longxi. Makeup: Liu Xiaoqiao, An Hong. Cast: Ju Naishe as Zhu Menglong, Qu Guoqiang as Zhu Mengfei, Wu Qianqian as Yu Shanshan, Zhang Xiaotong as Guorong, Yang Ping as Zhang Zhenbang

A policeman named Zhu, killed in the line of duty, left three sons, now adults: Mengfei, also a policeman; Menglong, a company

Crows and Sparrows. **Mrs. Hua (Shangguan Yunzhu, second left seated) and Yu Xiaoyin (third right, standing) play Majong. 1949. Kunlun Film Studio.**

executive; and Guorong, adopted by the Zhu family when his policeman father was killed rescuing the other two boys. A man named Zhang Zhenbang, sent to prison years before by the late policeman Zhu, is finally released. Although his enemy is now dead and he himself is old, he still plans vengeance on Zhu's family. He first approaches Guorong, whose morals are not the best, and gets him involved in drug dealing. When Menglong learns of his brother's involvement, he advises Guorong to turn himself in; but he is moved by Guorong's pleading, so does nothing. From then on, he is implicated as well. At last, the vengeful Zhang takes the young men's mother hostage, and in a bloody shootout the mother bravely sacrifices herself so that Zhang can be captured. Mengfei has to kill Guorong and arrest Menglong.

413. *Cry from the Heart (Xin Ling De Hu Sheng)*

1982. Fujian Film Studio. 5 Reels. Direction: Chen Lizhou. Screenplay: Chen Mobo. Cinematographer: Zhou Zhaiyuan. Art Direction: Shi Jiandu, Tang Peijun. Music: Zhang Shaotong. Sound: Wu Hua. Makeup: Chen Yun, Yang Maorong. Cast: Xie Yuan as Gao Liming, Wang Ye as Xu Tao, Liu Jia as Liu Wei, Ma Binbin as Xiao Yu, Zhang Wei as Xiao Wei, Chen Jiayuan as Yang Xiaole, Sun Xi as Director Wang

Two days before their wedding, young driver Xiao Gao and his fiancee Xiao Yu are busily preparing their new home. Meanwhile, Doctor Xu Tao prepares a fine dinner as he and his five-year-old daughter Weiwei await the arrival of their wife and mother Liu Wei, who works in another city and can only return home on weekends. The next day, Xiao Gao gives up his day off to work for fellow driver Xiao Le, but before starting his shift he accepts some friends' invitation to have a few celebratory drinks with them. That day, he is involved in a serious accident, and the victim is so badly injured as to be unrecognizable. Doctor Xu Tao performs emergency surgery but is unable to save the victim. Then he finds out the victim he did not recognize was his own wife. A little girl loses her mother and Xiao Gao goes to jail on what should have been his wedding day. Drinking and driving have caused a tragedy for all concerned.

414. *Crystal Stream (Qing Qing Xi Liu)*

1984. Emei Film Studio. Color. 10 Reels. Direction: Tai Gang. Screenplay: Wu Zeqian, Dai Zongan. Cinematographer: Cheng Zhaoxun. Art Direction: Lin Qi. Music: Mu Hong. Sound: Hua Yuezhu. Cast: Xu Jingzhi as Fang Xuemei, Li Yuan as Liu Juan, Xu Xing as Zhang Guigeng

After graduating from normal school, Fang Xuemei goes to the remote mountain village of Baiyunshan to teach in the elementary school there. She becomes acquainted with a young man who helps out around the school, Zhang Guigeng. She encourages and helps Guigeng to study and improve himself, and the two fall in love. In time Guigeng improves to the point he is admitted to college. While he is away at college, Xuemei sends him money every month as support, unaware that Guigeng is dating a professor's daughter, Liu Juan. When Liu Juan finds out about Guigeng's dual relationship, she breaks off with him and her father strongly criticizes the young man. Zhang Guigeng vows to devote himself to developing his native village and returns home. But when he gets there, he finds Xuemei refuses to take him back.

415. *Cuckoo Sings Again (Bu Gu Niao You Jiao Le)*

1958. Tianma Film Studio. Color. 10 Reels. Direction: Huang Zuolin. Screenplay: Yang Lufang, based on the stage play of the same name. Cinematographer: Xu Qi. Art Direction: Ding Cheng, He Ruiji. Music: Hu Dengtiao. Sound: Zhu Weigang. Cast: Xie Dehui as Tong Yaman, Zhou Zhijun as Wang Bihao, Liu Tongbiao as Shen Xiaojia, Wang Qi as Kong Yucheng, Tie Nu as Guo Jialin, Zhang Yan as Fang Baoshan

Tong Yaman, a girl member of a youth brigade in an agricultural commune, loves both work and singing, so everyone calls her "Cuckoo." She is loved by two young men named Wang Bihao and Shen Xiaojia, but when Shen learns that "Cuckoo" loves Wang Bihao, he decides to step aside and devote himself to making others happy by becoming the best tractor operator he can be. Wang Bihao is selfish, however, and begins putting restrictions on "Cuckoo," in particular preventing her from learning tractor operation. The girl realizes Wang's true nature, so she breaks the engagement and again becomes involved with Shen Xiaojia. Wang seeks revenge on "Cuckoo," but she stands up to him, and in the end Wang is punished. "Cuckoo" and Shen Xiaojia look forward to a happy life together.

Cultural Pioneers **see** *Young Masters of the Great Leap Forward*

416. *Da Hu (Da Hu)*

1981. Tianjin Film Studio. Color. 11 Reels. Direction: Guo Zhengqin, Yin Zhimin. Screenplay: Yuan Jing, Zhang Fuling. Cinematography: Wang Yizhi. Art Direction: Tong Jingwen. Music: Wang Ming. Sound: Xue Shenxing. Cast: Zhang Chi as Li Dahu, Zhang Tong as Tiantian, Si Jianlan as Chen Juan, Liu Xinmeng as Ai Qiang, Liang Zhinong as Xiao Wei, Qi Yinlai as Zhao Hua

Da Hu is a bright but very naughty child. He does not follow the rules, lacks a sense of discipline, and affects his whole class by his bad behavior. Da Hua's mother spoils her son, even protecting him when he makes friends with obviously bad influences and protecting him in front of Chen, his teacher. Later, Da Hu's "friends" take him to a cinema, where they plant on him a wallet they steal. Da Hu is caught with the wallet in his possession and sent to the police department. His teacher gets him out of jail, and Da Hu feels very ashamed of himself. Teacher Chen is glad to see Da Hu has a sense of honor and starting from that, the teacher's caring motivates Da Hu into making progress. He finally becomes a good student.

417. *Da Ze Dragon Snake (Da Ze Long She)*

1982. Shanghai Film Studio. Color. Wide Screen. Direction: Zhang Junxiang, Wang Jie, Li Xiepu. Screenplay: Li Hongxin, Peng Yonghui. Cinematography: Yin Fukang. Art Direction: Huang Qiagui, Zhu Jiancang. Music: Huang Zhun. Sound: Feng Deyao. Cast: Guo Bichuan as Yi Mengzhi, Wang Weiping as Chen Zhenyun, Siqin Gaowa as Zhang Ruonan, Zhen Shuzhi as Shunzhi's wife, Zhang Yan as Wang Liankui, Wun Guojun as Xu Jiawu, Kong Xiangyu as Lei Huanjue

In the fall of 1926, Ganxi Coal Mine labor union header Yi Mengzhi is happy to see his old friend Chen Zhenyun back to their hometown. The two had been comrades-in-arms during the Northern Expedition against the warlords. Yi is in the midst of a struggle with mine owners and wants the support of Chen, now the local CPC representative. County Director Xu Jiawu claims to be a revolutionary, but is really a tool of the government-backed mine owners. When the dispute between Xu Jiawu and Yi Mengzhi becomes sharp, though, Chen Zhenyun gives Yi no support at all. Yi does get support from Zhang Ruonan, a capitalist woman sympathetic to the workers but opposed to Chen Zhenyun. On April 12, 1927, there is a counterrevolution which turns the political confrontation violent: armed workers are forcibly disarmed; a key figure in the labor movement is murdered; Chen Zhenyun betrays the revolution; and Zhang Ruonan, unable to bear the political pressure, withdraws her support. Conditions in the Ganxi Coal Mine are miserable. After many hardships, Yi Mengzhi finally makes contact with Lei Huanjie, another CPC representative, who tells Yi to make contact with He Qinshan, one of the mine police, but really an undercover CPC member. He Qinshan helps Yi organize a farmer-worker rebellion. The rebellion succeeds, Xu Jiawu is forced out and Chen Zhenyun is killed. In the end, as government troops move in, Yi Mengzhi leads the armed miners to CPC headquarters in the Jinggangshan Mountains.

418. *Dad Would Be the Best (Wang Fu Cheng Long)*

1992. Nanchang Film & Television Creation Institution & Xi'an Film Studio Co-Production. Color. Letterboxed. 9 Reels. Direction and Screenplay: Zhang Gang. Cinematography: Zhang Jian. Art Direction: Wang Renchen. Music: Dong Weijie. Sound: Liu Guangjie. Costume: Dai Yili. Makeup: Zhou Liangeng. Cast: Ni Yuayuan as Yinyin, Zhang Le as Xiao Bao, Chang Lantian as Guan Aman, Wu Mian as Liu Meng, Dong Huaiwen as Zhong Ruojian, Zhang Haiyan as Gan Baomei

Guan Aman spends a lot of his time puttering around with various inventions, and one day he finally succeeds in creating a new type of machine for dispensing drinking water. However, his former schoolmate cheats him out of the invention and uses it to make a lot of money for himself. Guan Aman feels like a failure in life who has let down his family once again. Later, he goes to a special economic zone, and by taking advantage of the favorable policies there becomes rich. He returns home to his proud and happy family.

419. *Dadu River (Da Du He)*

1980. Changchun Film Studio. Color. 12 Reels. Direction: Lin Nong, Wang Yabiao. Screenplay: Lu Qi. Cinematography: Wang Qimin, Wei Tingting. Art Direction: Liu Xuerao. Music: Liu Zhi. Sound: Chen Wenyuan. Cast: Han Shi as Mao Zedong, Zhao Shenqiu as Zhou Enlai, Liu Huaizheng as Zhu De, Fu Xuecheng as Liu Bocheng, Zhao Hengduo as Chiang Kaishek

In May 1935, the Red Army is about to do battle with several hundred thousand of Chiang Kaishek's Nationalist troops, a battle which will decide whether the Red Army survives. As the Red Army moves between the Jingsha and Dadu Rivers, Communist commanders Mao Zedong, Zhou Enlai, Zhu De and Liu Bocheng devise a tactical plan of pretending to attack a place called Dashu Bao, while secretly crossing Anshun Chang. A scout troop rapidly takes over Anshun Chang, causing Chiang to quickly revise his strategy. The Nationalist forces remove all wood from the only bridge across the Dadu River, a matter of life or death for the Red Army. They finally cross the river by moving on the steel cords left over the river.

420. *A Dai Girl's Hatred (Dai Nu Qing Hen)*

1991. Yunnan Film Studio. Color. Letterboxed. 10 Reels. Direction: Yao Shoukang, Liu Huguang. Screenplay: Li Changxu. Cinematography: Yang Changsheng, Wang Jiangdong. Art Direction: Li Zhengxin. Music: Jin Fuzai. Sound: Ou Erfeng. Costume: Jiang Xiaoyun. Makeup: He Yaling. Cast: Can Xingmei as Nan Bo, Jia Ping as Yan Le, Wang Hua as Yanhan, Han Laoliu as Fan Hu, Yudan as Fan Jiao

In 1911, China is swept by anti–Qing revolutionary fervor. A group of overseas Chinese in Southeast Asia raises a fund to donate to the cause, and smuggles it across the Yunnan border into China. The Qing government learns of the fund, and sends agents to track it. The film relates the many risks, dangers and difficulties the revolutionaries go through to get the fund to its destination.

421. *Daji and Her Fathers (Da Ji He Ta De Fu Qin)*

1961. Emei Film Studio & Changchun Film Studio Co-Production. Color. 12 Reels. Direction: Wang Jiayi. Screenplay: Gao Ying. Cinematography: Wang Chunquan and Zhang Yi. Art

Daji and Her Fathers. **Young Daji (Chen Xueji) on the eve of her abduction by a slave trader. 1961. Emei Film Studio and Changchun Film Studio Co-Production.**

Direction: Li Junjie. Music: Lei Zhengbang and Ya Xin. Sound: Lin Bingcheng. Cast: Zhu Dannan as Ma He, Liu Lianchi as Ren Bingqing, Chen Xueji as Daji, Niu Qian as Mujia, Yi Haichi as Wu Zhihong, Zhou Shu as Jiajiamu

Daji, a Han Chinese girl abducted by a slave trader when she is very young, is raised by Ma He, a Yi nationality slave. After liberation, a Han Chinese worker named Ren Bingqing comes to help a commune with a water project, and there he finds that Daji is the daughter abducted from his home years before. However, he cannot bear to take her from her kindly stepfather. Although Ma is quite shocked by this fact, he insists Daji acknowledge her biological father. Daji is glad to be reunited with her father, but she is reluctant to leave her stepfather. Finally, Ren Bingqing moves into Ma He's home, and the three people live together happily.

422. *Dancing Flames (Tiao Dong De Huo Yan)*

1984. Changchun Film Studio. Color. Letterboxed. 9 Reels. Direction: Lin Nong. Screenplay: Li Xintian. Cinematography: Xing Eryou. Art

Direction: Liu Jinnai, Song Honghua. Music: Zhang Dicang. Sound: Liu Jingui. Cast: Liu Qin as Xiao Yu, Wang Lu as Er Ya, Cao Cuifen as Feng Min, Qi Guirong as Jin Guixiang, Liang Yin as Wang Qingshan, Li Lianyi as Wei Baolin, Kang Jingyu as Guo Huayu, Ji Hengpu as Department Head Shen, Wu Lilin as Shen's wife, Wang Gang as the enemy officer

On the eve of Chinese New Year 1948, in the Xingye Match Factory, the workers are close to rebellion from factory manager Guo Huayu's constant bullying. As PLA troops approach the city, CPC members working under cover in the factory make plans to ease the troops' entry into the city by exploiting this labor unrest. The CPC agents learn that Nationalist agents plan to use the factory's large supply of wood and combustibles to blow up the factory as the PLA enters the city, and the CPC determines to fight to protect the factory.

423. *Dangerous Deal (Wei Xian De Jiao Yi)*

1990. Changchun Film Studio & Nanjing Film Studio Co-Production. Color. Wide Screen. 9 Reels. Direction: Zhang Zheng, Wang Shuyan.

Screenplay: Li Yanxiong, Zen Xiangping. Cinematography: Liao Jiaxiang. Art Direction: Yang Yuhe, Yan Lijun. Music: Pan Hongmei. Sound: Wang Yunhua, Wang Yubing. Cast: Wang Biao as Chen Shihuai, Chen Shaoze as He Ping, Wang Chunren as Liang Gui, Wang Zhongxing as Liu Quan, Bai Ming as Cao Ying, Zhen Zhong as Guo Qingtian, Pang Hao as Chen Liming, Li Xiaoli as Liang Yun, Liu Jia as Lin Jianping, He Zhengqi as Yang Yilin

424. *Dangerous Honeymoon Trip (Wei Xian De Mi Yue Lu Xing)*

1987. Inner Mongolia Film Studio. Color. 9 Reels. Direction: Sai Fu. Screenplay: Zhao Yuheng. Cinematography: Na Risu. Art Direction: Wang Xiaohong. Music: Bayin Manda. Sound: Hu He. Cast: Lu Liping as Dalisha, Mandufu as Fu Jinbiao, Wuri Jitu as Haiqin, Zhao Qiansun as Ma Zhankui, Jia Ruixin as Feifei, Degeji as Luo Hua

Psychology graduate student Dalisha and public security officer Haiqin are two lovers who grew up on the prairie. After their marriage, they go on a honeymoon trip with several other newlywed couples. Haiqin is called back on emergency duty, but insists Dalisha remain, and he will rejoin the group later. After he leaves, one of the young couples dies suddenly at an outdoor party. Dalisha silently observes the other members of the tour group. Applying psychological analysis to each couple, Dalisha comes to a conclusion about the deaths, and when Haiqin returns he agrees totally. Dalisha proves the deaths were a case of murder, and exposes the killer. Although their honeymoon trip was a dangerous one, Dalisha and Haiqin still feel it has strengthened their feelings for each other.

425. *Dark Shadows (Hei Ying)*

1991. Emei Film Studio. Color. Wide Screen. 10 Reels. Director and Screenplay: Bai Song. Cinematography: Song Jianwen and Chen Ruogang. Art Direction: Gao Xinchun. Music: selected songs. Sound: Wang Guangzhong. Cast: Wang Zhenrong as Xie Xing, Xia Hui as Jiang Zizhu, Shi Zhaoqi as Bai Peng, Zhang Tianxi as Fan Yong, Chen Jing as Shantian Yangzi, Xie Xu as Yu Mei, Xiao Yunchun as woman, Yu Xianpeng as Zhang Dali

In July, 1985, nearly 50 years after the Nanjing Massacre, a series of murders take place in Nanjing. In a local hospital, one of the physicians is Jiang Zizhu, raped by a Japanese soldier when she was a young girl. One of her colleagues is a visiting Japanese whose father was the man who raped her, and one of the murder victims was another former Japanese soldier. According to a witness, the killer was a Japanese about 60 years old. The story unfolds as different people of different ages and backgrounds recall their own experiences so long ago.

426. *The Date of Death Has Arrived (Si Qi Ling Jin)*

1989. Emei Film Studio. Color. Letterboxed. 10 Reels. Direction: Xie Hong. Screenplay: Xie Hong. Cinematography: Li Zhao. Art Direction: Luo Zhicheng. Music: Xie Jun. Sound: Shen Jinghua. Cast: Li Wenqi as An Liang, Sun Chun as Wang Kewei, Lin Fangbing as Lu Jing

Chinese police detect a pattern to a series of murders, each in a different city but all happening on April 30th and similar in circumstances. As the fatal date nears, Chief Inspector An Liang makes plans to forestall a reoccurrence by feverishly trying to find a link between the murders. The date also happens to be the birthday of advertising executive Wang Kewei, and his wife Lu Jing plans a party for him on that date. It turns out that Wang himself is the mad killer, a man seething with hatred at having been publicly humiliated on that date years before, and now taking his revenge on those responsible. The detectives successfully trace the pattern to Wang, and arrive just in time to save his wife Lu Jing, the final target in Wang's mad quest for vengeance.

427. *Dating Under the Fengwei Bamboo Tree (Xiang Ye Zhai Feng Wei Zhu Xia)*

1984. Changchun Film Studio. Color. Letterboxed. 9 Reels. Direction: Wang Jiayi, Chen Xuejie, Zhou Wei. Screenplay: Sheng Manshu, Jia Lixian, Gan Zhaopei. Cinematography: Feng Bingyong. Art Direction: Shi Weijun. Music: He Zhanhao. Sound: Huang Lijia. Cast: Bao Ping as Han Muna, Yan Duan as Yan Han, Yi Die as Han Liang, Yan Wu as Tong Yiban, Meimeng as Yixiang, Sisang as Ensai

In a region of Southwest China peopled mostly by those of the Dai nationality, there has been marked improvement in the quality of life. A young man named Yan Han and a young woman named Han Muna are enthusiastic about life and work. Han Muna operates a successful chicken raising business, but Yan Han is one of a group of young men who think that men should do something much more important. They set off on a gold prospecting trip into the mountains, but return empty-handed. Later, Yan Han and his friends realize that such dreams are unrealistic without proper education. Han Muna and some others want to start a spare time school for workers and farmers, and Yan Han helps them find a facility and secure chairs and desks. The two young people find they share a mutual attraction and start to date.

428. *Datura (Man Tu Luo)*

1991. China Film Co-Production Corp. and Japan Kaomunaite Corp. Color. Letterboxed. 11 Reels. Direction: Teng Wenji. Screenplay: Yuan Yuanyi. Cinematography: Zhi Lei, Gangtian Cixiong. Art Direction: Muchun Weifu, Yang Gang. Music: Lichuan Zhishu. Sound: Honggu Shixuanyi. Makeup: Hengxian Zhenxin, Sun Wei and Li Yanping. Cast: Yongdao Mingxing, Hengtian Yingzhi, Shulin Jiaozi, Daqiao Wulang, Cao Jingyang, Zhang Fengyi, Jiang Lili

In the Tang Dynasty, a Japanese monk comes to China to study Buddhism. After many hardships, he is taken into the Green Dragon Temple by the Seventh Master of the temple. At last he masters the sutras and becomes the Eighth Master. He later returns to Japan to spread Buddhism there.

429. *Daughter of the Mountains (Shan De Nu Er)*

1985. Henan Film Studio. Color. 5 Reels. Direction: Chen Shengli. Screenplay: Chen Shengli, Lian Jing. Cinematography: Fu Dawei. Art Direction: Wang Hanjun. Music: Si Wanchun. Sound: Cui Weimin. Cast: Xu Jingzhi as Puxiao, Zhang Yi as Guan Yuxing, Ge You as Zhu Guangjin

Puxiao bears the burden of supporting her three children and her husband Zhu Guangjin, disabled in an industrial accident 10 years before. In town one day, she meets Guan Yuxing, a stonemason from her native village. Guan helps the family quite a bit, and they become friends. After the 11th Party Congress, Puxiao starts a stone business and invites Guan Yuxing to help. The business goes well, but rumors begin to spread about the stonemason's relationship with Puxiao. Her husband, formerly trusting and supportive, hears the rumors and begins to get jealous. Guan Yuxing and Puxiao

discuss the situation, and he confesses that he does indeed love her, but she refuses him. Guan decides to leave the family. Puxiao knows her life will not be easy, but she will not give up.

430. *Daughter of the Party (Dang De Nu Er)*

1958. Changchun Film Studio. Color. 10 Reels. Direction: Lin Nong. Screenplay: Lin Shan, based on the novel "Party Membership Dues" by Wang Yuanjian. Cinematography: Wang Qimin. Art Direction: Liu Xuerao. Music: Zhang Dicang. Sound: Chen Wenyuan. Cast: Tian Hua as Li Yumei, Chen Ge as Wang Jie, Li Lin as Ma Jiahui, Xia Peijie as Second Sister, Li Meng as Xiuying, Du Fengxia as Huizhen, Meng Xianying as Guiying

During the second Chinese Civil War, after the Red Army moves north from its old revolutionary base in Jiangxi province to resist the Japanese invasion, the town of Taohua is occupied by Nationalist forces, and the Communist Party organization there is destroyed. Li Yumei, a female Party member, escapes death in the purge, but is turned in by the traitor Ma Jiahui. She escapes again with the help of Ma's wife Guiying. Yumei then heads east, hoping to find another Party organization. On the way, she meets Xiuying and Huizhen, two other women. After initial mistrust, the three of them come to an understanding and establish a Party group to organize the people in the area. Shortly afterwards, a nearby guerrilla troop sends a messenger to collect the Party membership dues which support the guerrillas' activities, but he is arrested by the enemy. In helping him to escape, Yumei is also arrested and dies a martyr.

431. *Daughter of the Sun (Tai Yang De Nu Er)*

1982. Guangxi Film Studio. Color. 10 Reels. Direction: Zen Xueqiang. Screenplay: Chen Dunde, Zen Xueqiang. Cinematography: Meng Xiongqiang, Chen Shengkai. Art Direction: Li Runzhi. Music: Li Yanlin. Sound: Lin Lin. Cast: Zhang Yin as Xia Yin, Yang Fengliang as Lin Yuan, Li Xuehong as Li Wenling, Ma Qun as Professor Rong Guang, Teng Fang as Xiao Lan, Mai Xiaoqing as Xiao Yang

Although she is an orphan with but one year of senior high school, welder Xia Ying is ambitious and tries to improve herself through self-study. She is particularly interested in solar

Daughter of the Party. **Communist Party member Li Yumei (Tian Hua) is arrested and dies a martyr. 1958. Changchun Film Studio.**

energy, but when she mentions a "black spot on the sun" one day, woman factory director Li Wenling brands her a counterrevolutionary and downgrades her from welder to cleaning lady. Xia Ying still continues her individual scholarship, and learns enough that local university Professor Rong Guang agrees to advise her on a project, the design of a solar energy oven. With support and counsel from Rong and other teachers, the project is successful, but Li Wenying still uses her power to suppress Xia Ying. In the meantime, Li's son Lin Yuan has met and fallen for Xia Ying, but his mother opposes the relationship, and even wants to punish Xia Ying for having "lured" her son. All this stress makes Xia Ying sick. Then word comes that an uncle living overseas will give her the chance to study abroad, which gives the girl some very contradictory feelings. In the end, she decides to remain in China.

432. *Daughters of China (Zhong Hua Nu Er)*

1949. Northeast Film Studio. B&W. 10 reels. Co-Directors: Ling Zifeng and Zhai Qiang. Screenplay: Yan Yiyan, based on a historical incident. Cinematography: Qian Jiang. Set Design:

Zhu Ge. Music: Ge Yan. Sound: Lu Xianchang. Cast: Zhang Zheng as Hu Xiuzhih, Yue Shen as Leng Yun, Bo Li as Big Sister An, Qin Buhua as Yang Shuzhen, Xue Yan as Huang Guifen, Zhou Sufei as Little Wang, Sun Yuezhi as Little Jin, Jin Feng as Lieutenant Zhou, Du Defu as the old villager, Hua Yongzhuang as Shijiazhang, Wu Yu as the policeman, Wang Ying as Liu Chang

In 1936, the Japanese Kwantung Army occupies all of Northeast China, and sets up the puppet state of Manchukuo. Many people seek refuge with the Volunteer Army, Chinese allied forces waging guerrilla warfare against the invaders. A woman named Hu Xiuzhi joins the Chinese forces to avenge the death of her husband, murdered by the Japanese. Lieutenant Zhou, husband of a woman soldier, Leng Yun, is on a secret mission in enemy-occupied territory when he is captured and executed. Although grieving deeply, Leng Yun accepts a mission to blow up enemy vehicles. Returning to their unit after completing their mission, the women discover a large Japanese force moving into position to attack the allied forces' encampment. After dispatching someone to warn the camp, Leng Yun leads several dozen Chinese troops in luring the enemy forces to the bank of the Mudan River. During the ensuing battle, many of Leng Yun's troops are killed, until finally only eight women soldiers remain, including Leng Yun and Hu Xiuzhi. Running out of ammunition and food, they face death calmly and hurl themselves into the river. (Remade in 1987 as "Eight Women Fighters.")

433. *Daughters' Story (Nu Er Jing)*

1986. Shanghai Film Studio. Color. 10 Reels. Direction: Bao Qicheng. Screenplay: Ye Dan. Cinematography: Luo Zhensheng. Art Direction: Wu Tianci. Music: Lu Qimin. Sound: Tu Minde. Cast: Zhen Shuzhi as Mother, Zhao Ying as Pei Qing, Zhang Ming as Pei Qiong, Yan Xiaoping as Pei Ti, Jiao Huang as Ye Weiping, Wang Weiping as Tang Jialu, Zhang Xiaolin as Jian Xiong

In the Shen household, Mrs. Shen lavishes her love and caring on her three daughters. Her fondest dream is that they will do better in marriage than she did: a one-time campus beauty queen, she married a humble bank clerk and has lived ever since out of her native and beloved Shanghai. Eldest daughter Pei Qing is now over 30, a doctor at a local hospital; although beautiful, she has missed most of her marriage opportunities. She has been

Daughters of China. **Two of the eight surviving women soldiers face death calmly before committing mass suicide. 1949. Northeast Film Studio.**

involved with a married man seeking distraction from loneliness while his wife is in America, but now his wife is returning and it looks like the end of the affair is near. Second daughter Pei Qiong has been dating a boy named Tang Jialu, but when his family inherits a fortune, they start to drift apart and eventually break up. Youngest daughter Pei Ti is open and straightforward, very much like a boy; she rejects all third-party introductions, and insists she will choose her own man when she is ready. At last she connects with technical school graduate Jian Xiong. Mother Shen reflects that this whole daughter business is wearing her out.

434. *Dawn (Parts 1 & 2) (Shu Guang)*

1979. Shanghai Film Studio. Color. 17 Reels. Direction: Shen Fu, Tian Ran. Screenplay: Bai Hua, Wang Pei. Cinematography: Xu Qi. Art Direction: Ge Sicheng, Zhen Changfu. Music: He Luting, Wang Qiang. Sound: Liu Guangjie. Cast: Wang Tianpeng as He Long, Da Shichang as Yue Minghua, Ma Guanyin as Feng Dajian, Li Zhengtong as Lin Han, Guo Ao as Lan Jian

In the spring of 1930, when Nationalist troops attack the Communists in the Hong Lake area, the Red commander's adherence to the ideas of Communist Party theorist Wang Ming almost results in disaster. The day is saved by the arrival of the Red Third Army commanded by He Long, who promptly alters the battle plan to avert huge losses and win the battle. He Long sends his trusted lieutenant Feng Dajian into enemy territory on a scouting mission, and while there Feng learns there is an enemy spy at Third Army headquarters. The spy, Lan Jian, tries to kill Feng before the latter can identify the spy. When that is unsuccessful, Lan accuses Feng of being the spy. He is supported in this by another officer, Lin Han, a follower of Wang Ming. But He Long, his officers and men all resist Lin Han and uncover Lan Jian's treason. In the spring of 1935, a top-level Party meeting ends Wang Ming's leadership of the Party, and all those who had been persecuted for opposing his ideas are exonerated.

435. *Dawn (Shu Guang)*

1989. Inner Mongolia Film Studio. Color. Letterboxed. 10 Reels. Direction: Sai Fu. Screenplay: Zhao Yuheng, Sai Fu. Cinematography:

Geritu. Art Direction: Aogesu, Rihua, Liying. Music: Gude. Sound: Hu Linping. Cast: Deng Xiaoguang as Haiqin, Wu Lijie as Yalun, Ye Hui as Tenggeli

Photography shop owner Haiqin happens to meet Yalun, a young college graduate who works at a zoo. He helps her in a variety of ways, for which she is very grateful, but the strange young man wants her to show it by becoming his lover. Yalun already has a fiance, but Haiqin will not give up, obsessively stalking her everywhere. His insane pursuit makes Yalun's life a living hell, and even the police are unable to stop Haiqin. When the mental torment becomes too much for her to bear, Yalung and her fiance leave the city and move to the prairie, but Haiqin follows them. At last, the couple accidentally kill the stalker, setting up an inevitable tragedy.

436. *Daylight Valley (Ri Guang Xia Gu)*

1995. Huanya Film Corporation Ltd. Color. Stereo. Direction: He Ping. Screenplay: Ya Zhong, based on the novel by Zhang Rui. Cinematography: Yang Lun. Art Direction: Yang Gang. Sound: Ge Weijia. Cast: Zhang Fengyi as the Man, Yang Guimei as Hong Liu, Wang Xueqi as Hei Niu, Gu Feng as old man, Chen Yuan as Huang Mao

In the barren West China desert, widow Hong Liu runs a small hotel, living there with her little boy Shazhao. One morning, a man comes to the hotel. He is in the area searching for an old enemy. In time, he and the widow fall in love, but on the night they consummate their relationship, he discovers that the enemy he seeks is the woman's dead husband. The next morning, this man who had sworn he would find and kill the family of the man he hated, gets up and starts a normal work day for Hong Liu, his inner demons finally at rest.

The Dead and the Living (Yin Yang Jie) **see** *To Die Like a Man*

437. *Dead Light on Shanhu Island (Shan Hu Dao Shang De Shi Guang)*

1980. Shanghai Film Studio. Color. 9 Reels. Direction: Zhang Hongmei. Screenplay: Tong Enzheng, Shenji. Cinematography: Luo Zhengsheng, Sun Hualing. Art Direction: Dong Jingsheng. Music: Yang Shaolu, Zhou Yunlin. Cast:

Qiao Qi as Ma Tai, Ling Zhiao as Zhao Qian, Qiao Zhen as Chen Tianhong, Li Nong as A Mang

In a foreign country, Chinese scientist Professor Zhao Qian successfully designs a high efficiency atomic battery. He turns down many lucrative financial offers for the patent from foreign financial groups, for he intends to take the prototype and all documents back to China. One night, Professor Zhao is murdered. The professor's future son-in-law, young scientist Chen Tianhong, takes the battery prototype and professor's documents and flees before they can fall into the wrong hands. But his plane is shot down before it can reach China. Chen is rescued and taken to a mysterious island by an elderly doctor, Ma Tai, an old friend of the professor, and the doctor's mute manservant A Mang. The doctor tells him the conspirators seeking the battery are from the Weina Company, which intends to use it to create an ultimate weapon. They vow to prevent the Weina Company from getting it. The company sends armed men to the island, and a fierce battle ensues. The defenders blow up the island. Although the new invention is also destroyed, the defenders preserve world peace by sacrificing their blood and lives.

438. *Deadly Cliff (Zhi Ming De Shen Yuan)*

1989. Shanghai Film Studio. Color. Letterboxed. 19 Reels. Direction: Wu Tianren. Screenplay: Zong Fuxian. Cinematography: Yu Shishan. Art Direction: Guo Dongcang. Music: Xu Jingxin. Sound: Zhao Jianzhong. Cast: Ju Naishe as Tang Youliang, Zhou Guobing as Gao Di, Zhang Ming as Zhang Yaxin, Yang Kun as Lin Yifan, Lu Ling as Wei Weian, Cui Jie as Guo Zhiyi

After motorcycle plant manager Tang Youliang is killed in a race when his cycle goes off a cliff, TV reporter Gao Di notices a mysterious woman in attendance at Tang's funeral. He investigates and finds she is Wei Weian, a model who had been involved in an affair with Tang. Tang's wife Zhang Yaxin had supported her husband's career throughout their marriage, and now sees he betrayed her. In addition, there are signs that Tang's death was no accident. Gao Di, assisted by his wife Lin Yinfan, investigates further and turns up another suspect in Wei Weian's first husband, Guo Zhiyi. Guo readily confesses to having arranged Tang's death, but Gao and Lin believe he is just trying to protect Zhang Yanxin. At last the reporter and his wife clear everything up.

439. *The Deadly Dart (Suo Ming Fei Dao)*

1991. Changchun Film Studio. Color. Letterboxed. 9 Reels. Direction: Liu Zhongmin, Ji Shimin. Screenplay: Gao Weiren, Liu Tierong. Cinematography: Liu Jiankui, Lin Boquan. Art Direction: Gong Minhui. Music: Gao Feng. Sound: Zhang Qingjiang. Cast: Kou Zhenhai as Huang Tianba, Chen Qi as Dou Jinlian, Wang Gang as Hao Shanshi, Meng Xiangtai as Zhu Biaosi, Hou Shuang as Du Jinlian, Zhang Dehun as Fang Yong

In the late 17th century, greenwoods heroine Dou Jinlan tries repeatedly to kill a man who had betrayed her brother. Finally, with the help of some villagers also wronged by the traitor, she succeeds in her purpose.

440. *Deadly Melody (Liu Zhi Qin Mo)*

1993. Shanghai Film Studio, Hong Kong Huangpai Corp. Ltd. Co-Production. Color. Letterboxed. 10 Reels. Direction: Wu Mianqin. Screenplay: Chen Wenqiang, Li Mingcai, Li Jiongkai, based on the novel by Ni Kang. Cinematography: Guan Zhiqin, Wu Wending, Zhong Zhiwen, Zhang Jingnian. Art Direction: Chen Shaomian. Costume: Gao Peiyi, Zuang Peiling, Xu Laidi. Makeup: Ke Meihua, Gao Xiaoping, Mi Zide, Zhang Zhen. Cast: Lin Qingxia (Brigitte Lin) as Huang Xuemei, Yuan Biao as Lu Ling, Liu Jialing (Carina Lau) as Tan Yuehua, Zhen Shuang as Hao Xianghua

An action film set in the Ming Dynasty. When Huang Xuemei was just seven years old, an enemy named Dong Fangbai killed her parents and carried off her baby brother Lu Ling. Xuemei grows up preparing for revenge, but her brother has been raised to think Dong Fangbai is his father. Sister and brother become bitter combat opponents, until at last Lu Ling learns the truth.

441. *Deal Made Under a Noose (Jiao Suo Xia De Jiao Yi)*

1985. Shanghai Film Studio. Color. 10 Reels. Direction: Song Chong. Screenplay: Wang Shengrong, Song Chong. Cinematography: Zhang Yuanmin. Art Direction: Xue Jianna. Music:

Huang Zhun. Sound: Liu Guangjie. Cast: Ma Guanyin as Xu Zhijie, Mai Wenyan as Liu Xiangyun, Lu Qin as Liu Zhizhong, Huang Daliang as Hong Jinlong, Fu Lili as Lin Manli

In the early 1980s, China is shocked when several hundred ancient tombs are broken into in central China and more than 10,000 antiques stolen. Chinese Customs and the PSB move into action immediately. Meanwhile, the Hong Kong underworld sends its operatives to the mainland to link up with the thieves and smuggle the national treasures out of China. The movie relates the struggle between the Chinese law enforcement agencies and the smuggling ring.

442. *Dear Ones (Qing Ren)*

1960. Wuhan Film Studio. B & W. 10 Reels. Direction: Tao Jin, Xu Dan and Su Pu. Screenplay: Jiang Hongqi and Jin Feng. Cinematography: Yao Meisheng and Yang Zhixue. Art Direction: Cao Gengjun. Music: Wang Yi. Sound: Tang Rongchun. Cast: Li Xubing as Zhen Yulan, Hu Lingling as Gao Xiaoling, Zu Daobing as Qing Keming, Song Yingxue as Party Secretary Wang, Zhou Yuanbai as Zhang Zhengwu, Fu Botang as Gao Guangshan

During the Great Leap Forward, Wuhan resident Gao Guangshan's daughter-in-law Zhen Yulan and his daughter Gao Xiaoling take part in commercial work. Their activities are opposed by Gao Guangshan, who works in a capitalist's store, but after some persuasion he reluctantly approves. After the two women start their store work, Yulan progresses rapidly by hard study and work while Xiaoling, affected by her husband's capitalist ideas, concludes there is no future in sales work and wants to change her job. Yulan enthusiastically helps Xiaoling correct her wrong thoughts, and they progress together. Finally, Yulan becomes a "red flag" salesperson and joins the Party.

443. *Death and the Maiden (Si Shen Yu Shao Nu)*

1987. Youth Film Studio. Color. 10 Reels. Direction: Lin Hongtong. Screenplay: Shi Tiesheng, Lin Hongtong. Art Direction: Feng Yuan, Ma Yinbo. Music: Li Wanli. Sound: Wu Hao. Cast: Zuo Ling as Bei Fang, Liu Qiong as Tian Geng, Jiang Yunhui as Wang Wanyi

As doctors do their best to save him, an elderly man named Tian Geng lies in the hospital convinced his liver cancer is terminal and nothing can be done. One day on the hospital grounds he meets Bei Fang, a young woman whose illness has already cost her a leg. She is uncertain about what kind of future lies before her, and the prognosis for her illness. They talk, and become friends. Winter turns into spring, and as Tian Geng sinks further into depression over his condition, he refuses to eat. Bei Fang helps persuade him that dying earlier than necessary will serve no purpose. Tian Geng later learns that Bei Fang has her own problem: she has refused to let her boyfriend come and see her anymore, for she is afraid of becoming a burden to him. Tian Geng tries to make Bei Fang understand that if her boyfriend really loves her, her decision is as cruel for him as it is for her. Tian dies, leaving Bei Feng to come to a tough decision about the relationship with her boyfriend.

444. *Death Camp (Si Wang Ji Zhong Ying)*

1987. August First Film Studio. Color. 10 Reels. Direction: Yan Jizhou. Screenplay: Shen Mujun, Yan Jizhou. Cinematography: Zhu Lutong. Art Direction: Zhao Changsheng. Music: Yang Xiwu. Sound: Shen Guorui. Cast: Hao Zhibeng as Wu Xiao, A Tuyigong as Sikete, Jin Xing as Yedao, Shabier as Pannan Dika, Zhang Yulai as Hate, Zhen Chunpei as Bangeng

After occupying much of China, the Japanese invaders begin to plunder the country's natural resources such as minerals. A shipload of prisoners-of-war, including British and Indians as well as Chinese, are forced to do hard slave labor in the mines. At last unable to bear the brutality any longer, they stage a successful rebellion.

445. *Death Certificate (Si Zheng)*

1985. Changchun Film Studio. Color. 10 Reels. Direction: Ke Ren, Screenplay: Xu Ximei, Dong Yuzhen, Sheng Chunqin, Cinematography: Li Huailu, Art Direction: Yang Baocheng, Music: Gao Feng, Sound: Wang Lin, Cast: Li Youbing as Fang Shusheng, Zhang Xiaojun as Liu Yukang, Wu Mian as Chen Fang, Li Lei as Cai Zhiming, Di Jianqing as Mr. Hong

In 1937, China's most difficult period of the Anti-Japanese War, a Volunteer Army division fights for its life deep in a forested area. For pursuing an independent strategy, Division Commander Fang Shusheng is removed from his command and expelled from the Commu-

nist Party. Fang sets out to clear his name, and starts by secretly entering the enemy-held city of Harbin to contact the underground provincial Party Committee. After initial failure to find them, he at last makes contact but is later murdered by a traitor at Party headquarters. His death leads the local political commissar to renew his determination to resist the Japanese invaders. Under his command, the army destroys enemy headquarters and recruits larger numbers of volunteers.

446. *Death Chase (Si Wang Zui Zhong)*

1988. Inner Mongolia Film Studio. Color. 9 Reels. Direction: Sai Fu. Screenplay: Zhao Yuheng, Zuo Gehao. Cinematography: Ma Lie, Shen Tao, Yihu Hewula. Art Direction: Du Changshun. Music: Burigude. Sound: Da Ying. Cast: Zhao Na as Qidan, Wu Jingan as Ayingga

A truck is hijacked on a mountain highway, and a valuable antique jade horse is stolen. One of the robbers hides the horse, after which he goes home to lie low for a while. When his honest wife Qidan discovers his involvement, she pleads with him to turn himself in, but he refuses. So she drugs his drink, planning to search for the horse and return it while he sleeps. But after she recovers the horse, she returns home to find her husband dead. Thinking she was responsible for his death, Qidan flees, and finds herself pursued by two rival criminal gangs from China and Hong Kong, as well as the police who want her for murder. At last, it turns out the husband's death was unrelated to the drug she gave him, the police capture both gangs and rescue Qidan.

447. *Death Fight (Parts 1 & 2) (Si Ping)*

1990. Tianshan Film Studio. Color. Wide Screen. 17 Reels. Direction: Zhang Junzhao. Screenplay: Li Hun. Cinematography: Xiao Feng. Art Direction: Ma Shaoxian, Gao Feng. Music: Wang Xiaoyong, Zhou Yaping. Sound: Huang Yingxia, Liu Honggang. Cast: Li Yingjie as Master Qiu, Liang Baoxiang as Qiu Shuxiong, Zhang Shan as Sheng Shijun, Wang Yan as Lanlan

On the eve of liberation (1948), Xinjiang Governor Sheng Shicai is named a minister in the Nationalists' government-in-exile in Chongqing. His corrupt in-law Master Qiu takes this opportunity to relocate to Chongqing as well, taking with him a huge cache of treasures he has embezzled and stolen over the years. Along the way, several attempts are made to take the loot from Qiu, but his personal army of bodyguards repulses them all. At last, Qiu is killed by one of his guards, a woman kung fu expert named Lanlan.

448. *Death Hotel (Si Wang Ke Jian)*

1988. Shanghai Film Studio. Color. Letterboxed. 9 Reels. Direction: Xu Jihong. Screenplay: Gu Bai. Cinematography: Sun Guoliang. Art Direction: Zhang Chongxiang. Music: Lu Qimin. Sound: Jin Fugeng. Cast: He Ling as Duan Si, Huang Guoqiang as Zhang Longfei, Zhou Xiaofeng as Meng Yutang, Wang Qiang as Xue Cangzhou, Zhu Yongji as Boss Jin

Toward the end of the 1920s, a group of bandits and gangsters gathers at Jin's hotel in a small town in south China. All have come to seek a treasure chest supposedly buried somewhere on the hotel grounds. In the days that follow, provincial police bureau detective Xue Cangzhou's chief investigator is killed and the hotel's accountant is poisoned. Xue's prime suspect is woman bandit Meng Yutang. But the hotel murders continue, and at last the bandits kill each other off. The treasure chest winds up floating away down the river, with no one the winner.

449. *Death Is the Final Card to Play (Si Shen, Zui Hou Yi Zhang Wang Pai)*

1989. Changchun Film Studio. Color. Letterboxed. 10 Reels. Direction: Zhou Wei. Screenplay: Xu Guangshun. Cinematography: Li Junyan. Art Direction: Ding Laifu. Music: Liu Xijin. Sound: Gu Xiaolian. Cast: Zhang Zhizhong as Lu Shan and Xu Bowen

As high-level secret talks get under way between the Chinese government and a special emissary of the U.S. President, a terrorist organization called "Blue Hurricane" plans to destroy the negotiations by using a professional assassin named Lu Shan. Through plastic surgery, Lu's appearance has been altered to make him look like Chinese security officer Xu Bowen. The film traces the efforts of counter-intelligence officers to learn which of their people is really the assassin, and stop him.

450. *Death of a Woman Model (Nu Mo Te Zhi Shi)*

1987. Changchun Film Studio. Color. Direction: Guangbu Daoerji. Screenplay: Chen Fang. Cinematography: Liu Xing. Art Direction: Wei Hongyu. Music: Liu Xijin. Sound: Tong Zongde. Cast: Li Yuan as Shen Xiaoqing, Li Jingli as Liu Ping, Yang Juan as Lu Huanhuan, Liu Qiang as Zhen Feihong

A woman's body is discovered hidden in a valley. She is identified as Shen Xiaoqing, a beautiful fashion model with a fashion show company. Woman criminal investigator Liu Ping is put in charge of the investigation. As it develops, she has five suspects, including the dead woman's boyfriend. But further investigation eliminates each as a suspect. Liu Ping finally determines that the woman was driven to suicide by gossip and poor treatment by society.

451. *Death of a Beauty (Mei Ren Zhi Si)*

1986. Tianshan Film Studio. Color. 10 Reels. Direction: Guang Chunlan. Screenplay: Guang Chunlan and Duan Baoshan, based on Uighur folklore. Cinematography: Yu Shishan, Baihaiti. Art Direction: Gao Feng. Music: Zhou Guangsehng. Sound: Zhang Xicheng. Cast: Guzhalinu'er as Mariyam, Mulatin as Prince Kaisal, Meiliguli as the Maid, Hurxide as the Stepmother

On the eve of Prince Kaisal's departure on a long trip, he and Aishan Bayi's daughter Mariyam meet on the shore of Swan Lake. At their parting, the Prince promises they will marry upon his return. Tragically, Mariyam's stepmother burns and destroys the girl's beautiful face. After five years, Prince Kaisal returns and still seeks Mariyam's hand in marriage. The evil stepmother continues to intrigue against the young girl, bringing further tragedy.

452. *Death of the Marshal (Yuan Shuai Zhi Si)*

1980. Beijing Film Studio. Color. 10 Reels. Direction: Shi Yifu, Jue Wen. Cast: He Xingtong, Yu Li. Cinematography: Xu Xiaoxian, Tu Jiakuan. Art Direction: Hao Guoxin, Duan Zhengzhong. Music: Ju Xixian. Sound: Gui Zhilin. Cast: Li Rentang as Marshal He, Zhao Na as Wu Tonghua, Zhang Xian as Ma Yude, Zhu Yanping as Ma Honghu

In 1964, army officer Ma Honghu, son of high-ranking officer Ma Yude, falls in love with Wu Tonghua, a nurse whose father was killed in World War Two. She has been raised by Marshal He Long, a friend of her late father's, and both the lovers are deeply devoted to He Long. Shortly after the Cultural Revolution begins, Chairman Mao's deputy Lin Biao initiates political persecution of He Long. Ma Yude believes Lin Biao's charges, which affects his son Ma Honghu, who also becomes suspicious of He Long. Wu Tonghua continues to believe in her guardian, and tries to intercede on his behalf by using her position as a nurse to some government officials. Their disagreement over He Long causes the young couple to break up. He Long harshly criticizes Ma Yude for turning against him, which leads to still greater persecution, and a cutoff of his food and water supplies. However, many people with a sense of justice risk their lives to protect He Long, and when some die for doing so, Ma Honghu finally comes to his senses. He gives his life protecting Wu Tonghua in delivering a written defense of himself that He Long has written. On his prison deathbed, He Long is delirious, but continues to repeat over and over that "He Long will live for the Communist Party, He Long will follow the Communist Party forever..."

453. *The Decisive Engagement Part 1: The Battle of Liao-Shen (Da Jue Zhan; Diyibu: Liao-Shen Zhanyi; Part 2: The Battle of Huai-Hai (Da Jue Zhan; Dierbu: Huai-Hai Zhanyi); Part 3: The Battle of Ping-Jun (Da Jue Zhan; Disanbu: Ping-Jun Zhanyi)*

1991-92. August First Film Studio. Color. Wide Screen. 23 Reels. Direction: Li Jun, Wei Lian, Yang Guangyuan, Jing Mukui, Zhai Junjie and Cai Jiwei. Screenplay: Wang Jun, Shi Zhao, Li Pingfen. Cinematography: Xu Lianqin, Zhang Chi, Zhu Lutong, Yin Qiaofang, Jiang Jingde and Ye Naijun. Art Direction: Liu Fan, Liu Yushu, Zhao Changsheng, Cui Denggao and Ni Shaohua. Music: Wun Tao. Sound: Li Lin, Shi Pingyi (Director) and Sun Juzhen. Principal Cast: Gu Yue as Mao Zedong, Zhao Hengduo as Chiang Kaishek, Li Dingbao as Fu Zhuoyi, Su Lin as Zhou Enlai, Liu Huaizheng as Zhu De, Shi Chongren as Nie Rongzhen, Ma Shaoxing as Lin Biao, Lu Jixian as Luo Rongheng, Zhang Weiguo as Liu Yalou

A sweeping, epic docudrama, recounting the ultimate Communist-Nationalist confrontation of the Chinese Civil War. In the spring of 1948, the PLA and the KMT face off in a series of three battles: Liao-Shen, Huai-Hai and Ping-Jun.

Best Picture, 1992 Golden Rooster Awards.

Best Picture, 1992 Hundred Flowers Awards.

Best Direction (collective), 1992 Golden Rooster Awards.

Best Art Direction (collective), 1992 Golden Rooster Awards.

454. *Declawing the Devils (Zhan Duan Mo Zhao)*

1954. Shanghai Film Studio. B & W. 10 Reels. Direction: Shen Fu. Screenplay: Zhao Ming. Cinematography: Yao Shiquan. Set Design: Ding Chen. Music: Chen Gexin. Sound: Shao Zihe. Makeup: Wang Tiebin. Cast: Tao Jin as Zhou Changmin, Lin Zhihao as Plant Director Dong, Hu Shiqing as Pai Ke, Sun Baiqun as Secretary Yuan, Han Fei as Bai Bingzhong, Zhang Fa as Department Director Zhang

In 1950, during the War to Resist America and Aid North Korea, the U.S. sends Nationalist spy Bai Bingzhong into China from Hong Kong. Pretending to be the nephew of a defense plant's Chief Engineer Zhou Changmin, he hopes to obtain defense secrets from the plant, and for a while he fools Zhou Cangmin and Plant Director Dong. Also part of the spy ring are two Italian priests, who help Bai steal the key to a cabinet where the engineer keeps some important documents. An alert locksmith detects the key has been stolen, and reports it to the PSB. Bai steals the documents, then tries to use them to blackmail Zhou into defecting to Hong Kong, but the latter reports this to the plant director. It turns out the stolen papers are bogus, substituted for the real ones by the PSB. When the spy-priests see the plot has failed, and Bai Bingzhong is about to be arrested, they order Bai to murder Zhou, then order others to kill Bai after that to silence him. With the help of the plant workers, the security forces protect Zhou and round up all the spies.

455. *The Decorated Smuggler (Dai Xun Zhang De Zhou Si Fan)*

1988. Xi'an Film Studio. Color. Letterboxed. 9 Reels. Direction: Pan Peicheng, Zhu Dingyu. Screenplay: Li Xiaoning, Pan Peicheng. Cinematography: Wen Sibing, Zhu Dingyu. Art Direction: Ge Yue. Music: Mo Fan. Sound: Li Tie. Cast: Zhang Zhizhong as Dong Zhiming, Xie Wei as Fang Yi

Near the end of World War II, Nationalist Army company commander Dong Zhiming is ordered to escort a truckload of arms to Nanjing. After many difficulties on the road including the deaths of two of his men, the arms arrive safely and Dong is awarded a medal and promoted to Commandant of a military school. However, he gets an unexpected phone call accusing him of escorting a truckload of smuggled contraband rather than military supplies. In order to prove his innocence, Dong investigates, but many of his former colleagues die or disappear mysteriously, and his own life is threatened. At last, he discovers the truth, but this confronts him with a vital decision in his life.

456. *Dedicated Police and Crazy Criminal (Sheng Si Jing Tan Wang Ming Fei)*

1995. Changchun Film Studio. Color. Letterboxed. Direction: Liu Ewei. Screenplay: Liu Ewei. Cinematography: Wu Wen. Cast: Liu Changchun as Liu Hantao, Li Yinqiu as Wu Jie, Han Song as Hu Gang, Jiang Hongbo as Wild Rose

Criminals abduct a distinguished scientist to obtain information about a new energy resource of global significance, the critical data of which he has committed to memory then destroyed. Chief of detectives Li Hantao heads up the investigation team. At last, after a bloody gun battle, the police rescue the scientist and his family.

457. *Deep Emotions (Yi Zhong Qing Shen)*

1991. Inner Mongolia Film Studio. Color. 9 Reels. Direction: Bao Nayintai and Sun Tianxiang. Screenplay: Asichaolu, Wang Zhengping and Sun Tianxiang. Cinematography: Naersu. Art Direction: Alimusi and Mo Nayintai. Music: Yong Rubu. Sound: Buren Bayaer. Cast: Hasi Gaowa as Qimuge, Cheng Xiangying as Hude, Sun Weihua as Hude (as a child), Du Juan as Xiao Wen, Wu Rigeng as Gong Bu, Guan Qige as Party secretary Ba, Li Ying as teacher Xiao, Cao Lihua as Zhang Yiru, Yang Lihua as Sha Rula

A Mongolian herdsman's family adopts five orphans, four Chinese children from Shanghai and a Mongolian child. A touching tale of his wife's devotion to the children and her loving sacrifices for them.

458. *Deep Inside the Heart (Xin Ling Sheng Chu)*

1982. Changchun Film Studio. 11 Reels. Direction: Chang Yan. Screenplay: Chang Yan, Li Lingxiu. Cinematography: Gao Hongbao. Art Direction: Shi Weijun. Music: Wu Damin. Sound: Tong Zongde. Cast: Liu Xiaoqing as Ouyang Lan, Wang Zhihua as Huang Yisheng, Chen Guojun as Zhang Sheng, Yang Yaqing as Li Jian, Liu Tong as Weiwei, Xu Dahai as Chuanchuan

When the Korean War ends, Ouyang Lan, a woman doctor in the Chinese Volunteer Army, returns to her hometown of Shanghai to visit her parents and start planning her marriage to medical school professor Huang Yisheng. She also goes to visit the two children of Li Jian, a colleague of Ouyang's who died in the war. Ouyang Lan is shocked at the two orphaned children's reaction, as they have no memory of what their mother looked like, and take Ouyang Lan to be her. Ouyang Lan decides to adopt the two, and while her parents support her, her fiance cannot accept it and they break up. Later she is invited to a school to tell her story of the Korean War, and there she meets an ex-soldier named Zhang Sheng, who she had once met in Korea. They get married and look forward to a happy life with the two adopted children.

459. *Deep Love (Yi Wang Qing Sheng)*

1984. Pearl River Film Studio. Color. Letterboxed. 10 Reels. Direction: Wang Ti. Screenplay: Yao Xin. Cinematography: Zhu Junheng, Chen Xianghe. Art Direction: Huang Zhaohui. Music: Yang Shuzheng. Sound: Li Bojian. Cast: Huang Meiying as Yang Fangfei, Shen Guanchu as Liu Qin, Ma Xiaoqing as Yingying, Liu Yan as Mr. Zhou, Ye Jiangdong as Liu Qiang

The story of a woman who over a period of years keeps applying to join the Communist Party despite being rejected repeatedly for various reasons. After the 3rd Plenary Session of the 11th Party Congress, her hopes are born anew and she applies again.

460. *Deep Valley Love Story (You Gu Lian Ge)*

1981. Changchun Film Studio. Color. 10 Reels. Direction: Wu Guojiang, Huang Yanen. Screenplay: Su Fangxue, Zhou Xiao. Cinematography: Wu Guojiang, Zhao Yao. Art Direction: Wang Jiru, Jin Xiwu. Music: Lei Zhenbang, Cao Shuzuang. Sound: Han Weijun. Cast: Zhang Baishuang as A Ying, Lin Fangbing as Dali, Chen Baoguo as Teluo, Liu Huaizheng as Meng Bochao, Guo Qi as Badai

Shortly after the People's Republic is declared in 1949, the PLA arrives in Southwest China to liberate the many villages there. In an almost hidden valley, with considerable natural security on all sides, lies Jinfeng Village, where village head Meng Bochao is anxiously seeking a young man for his daughter Da Li. A handsome young man shows up unexpectedly, and Da Li falls for him on the spot. The unexpected guest is named A Ying, and he brings her a pearl, a family heirloom, as an engagement present. Da Li and her mother are very satisfied with A Ying, but Meng Bochao and village police director Guo Shanlong are very suspicious so they investigate. A Ying sees what they are up to, so under the guise of dating Da Li, he reconnoiters the terrain around the village and transmits the information to someone outside the village. With the help of Da Li and Te Luo, a young man of the village who A Ying befriends, the PLA liberates the village peacefully. It turns out that A Ying is a PLA woman soldier. A Ying apologizes profusely to the shocked and heartbroken Da Li, and eventually Da Li gets together with Te Luo, who has loved her since childhood.

461. *Deer Calls in Green Valley (Lu Ming Cui Gu)*

1981. Shanghai Film Studio. Color. 8 Reels. Direction: Hu Chengyi. Screenplay: Gu Xiaoyan, Zhao Xiaoya, He Xingtong. Cinematography: Li Kui. Art Direction: Wu Daci. Music: Xiang Yi. Sound: Li Bingkui. Cast: Zhu Jiwen as Tiezhi, Han Li as Yadan, Zhu Kexin as Wenwen

During the anti–Japanese war, the Volunteer Army in Northeast China is suddenly attacked and decimated by the Japanese. Tie Zhi, a 15-year-old soldier, finds a baby alive among the many dead bodies of soldiers. Call-

ing the baby Xiao Shitou ("Little Stone"), he carries the baby with him as he seeks the Chinese main force. On the way he meets Yadan, a 12-year-old girl, and Wenwen, an 11-year-old boy, both children of Volunteers. The three seek food for Xiao Shitou and make friends with a mother deer, whose milk is used to feed the baby. Finally, a Volunteer Army squad finds the children.

462. *Defense in the Sky (Lan Tian Fang Xian)*

1977. Pearl River Film Studio. Color. 11 Reels. Direction: Wang Weiyi. Screenplay: Lu Wei, Lin Hangsheng, Wang Peigong. Cinematography: Liu Hongming. Art Direction: Lin Guang. Music: Yang Hua. Sound: Lin Guang. Cast: Zhu Shimao as Yang Ping, Xia Zongyou as the Chief Staff Officer, Ning Xiaozhou as Lu Dali, Lin Shujing as Ding Aotian, Jin Jia as the major general, Huang Xiaomin as the adjutant

In the early 1970s, the Nationalists attempt to sabotage a PLA installation on Baisha Island, but they are thwarted by Yang Ping, the Lianghua Island political supervisor. with the help of local fishermen.

463. *Delta of Desire (Yu Wang San Jiao Zhou)*

1987. Changchun Film Studio. Color. 10 Reels. Direction: Rong Lei. Screenplay: Zhang Jianxing. Cinematography: Han Dongxia, Guo Lin. Art Direction: Liang Shukui. Music: Fan Weiqiang. Sound: Wang Fei, Liao Yongliang. Cast: Sun Delie as Yu Kejia, Wang Yanping as He Wei, Hua Mingwei as Ji Zongping

Under the reform measures of its new manager, college-trained Yu Kejia, the Xingguang Computer Factory is now showing a profit. Also benefiting from the improved situation is Ji Zongping, self-trained and awaiting a work assignment. Yu Kejia recruits Ji to help out while he awaits formal employment. As the factory continues to develop, Ji Zongping's reputation also grows among the employees, and this makes Yu Kejia jealous. He uses his influence to substitute another person's name for Ji's when a regular appointment comes in, and eventually he fires Ji Zongping. Ji Zongping has to sell his services on the free-lance labor market to make a living. The affair comes to the attention of a reporter who discloses the details in his column, bringing it to the attention of the city Party Committee. Ji is employed almost immediately. Meanwhile, strong societal and media disapproval, combined with new technological difficulties have placed Yu Kejia in a complex situation, one he does not understand.

464. *Democratic Youth on the March (Min Zhu Qing Nian Jin Xing Qu)*

1950. Beijing Film Studio. B & W. 10 Reels. Direction: Wang Yi. Screenplay: Jia Ke and Zhao Xun, based on the stage play of the same title. Cinematography: Lian Cheng. Set Design: Liu Rui. Music: Huang Zhun and Lei Zhengbang. Sound: Chen Yanxi. Costume: Ren Yanshu. Makeup: Zhang Jing, Li Ende. Cast: Sun Daolin as Fang Zheren, Yao Xiangli as Song Peihua, Sang Fu as He Mai, Xie Tian as Professor Song, Shi Lin as Elder Sister, Tong Chao as He Baili

Following victory over the Japanese, all-out civil war erupts between the Nationalists and Communists. While many of his college classmates join the CPC, one young Beijing student named Fang Zheren continues devoting himself to his studies, caring little for politics. This puts him in conflict with his activist sister. Two Nationalist secret agents are assigned to the campus to destroy the student movement. At first they are successful in using the apolitical Fang as a tool to splinter the student group. But Fang begins to undergo an ideological conversion when his sister is injured in a demonstration. Leadership and teaching from CPC underground leader He Mai completes the conversion. When the Nationalist government attempts to arrest He Mai, Fang joins his classmates in protecting the CPC leader, and exposes the Nationalist agents on campus. After the founding of New China, Fang eagerly accepts assignment in the new order.

465. *Desert Camel Bells Ring (Sha Mo Tuo Ling)*

1978. Shanghai Film Studio. Color. 10 Reels. Direction: Liu Qiong. Screenplay: Ye Dan and Li Weiliang. Cinematography: Shi Fengqi. Art Direction: Xue Jianna. Music: Gao Tian. Sound: Wang Huimin. Cast: Jiao Huang as Zhu Guanghan, Wang Hui as Qi Guodong, Liang Boluo as Fan Zhijie, Pan Hong as Yang Juan, Chen Hongmei as Liang Yin, Guo Kaiming as Xiao Wang, Maimaiti as Simayi, Xu Fu as Ma Huamin

In 1952, geologist Professor Zhu Guanghan leads a prospecting team to look for a lost mine . The team is stalked and surrounded by bandits, but a PLA detachment intervenes to save them. The elderly professor continues his search with aged local Simayi but 40 days of searching prove fruitless. This shakes the confidence of some team members, but Premier Zhou Enlai sends them a telegram of encouragement. The old professor finds the mine, but the team's driver Ma Huaming turns out to be an agent for a foreign country who tries to kidnap Professor Zhu and forcibly take him abroad. Ma Huamin is captured by the team's political supervisor who has been protecting the old professor. The team returns safely.

466. *Desert Combat (Sha Mo Li De Zhan Dou)*

1956. Shanghai Film Studio. B & W. 12 Reels. Direction: Tang Xiaodan. Screenplay: Wang Yuhu. Cinematography: Li Shengwei. Art Direction: Ge Shicheng, Music: Gao Tian, Sound: Wu Jianghai, Miao Zhenyu. Makeup: Jiang Youan. Cast: Wun Xiying as Yang Fa, Zhang Yuan as Zhang Zhen, Wei Yuping as Division Commander Chen, Gao Zheng as Li Hui, Mu Hong as Political Commissar Zhang, Niu Beng as Xiao Zhu

In 1951, a certain PLA division stationed in Xinjiang north of the Tian Mountains receives orders to assist in the construction and development of that remote area. Reconnaissance section chief Yang Fa leads a water conservancy team to prospect for water resources in a rocky area. They discover the ruins of an ancient city and a dried-up big river. Based on this, engineer Li Hui thinks the water resources are all gone, and that water cannot possibly be found in the area. But Yang Fa and woman technician Zhang Zhen still believe there must be water around. The team splits up into two groups, with Yang Fa taking Zhang Zhen and two others to look for a water source near the ice summit while Li Hui and the rest survey the land. Yang Fa's group encounters tremendous difficulties on the way. He and Zhang Zhen fall in love as well. Tragedy strikes when a flash flood hits, sweeping away Yang Fa and Xiao Zhu. Later, with help from a veteran hunter, the survivors finally find water resources at the ice summit. The division commander orders bombing which collapses the mountain blocking the water. The water problem is resolved, and this desolate, rocky region is transformed into good farmland.

467. *Desert Mission (Da Mo Zi Jing Ling)*

1986. Tianshan Film Studio & Taiwan Fangzhou (Hong Kong) Film Production Corp. Co-Production. Color. 10 Reels. Direction: Fang Xiang. Screenplay: Li Zhun. Cinematography: Yang Lin, Bao Xianran. Art Direction: Zhang Tiren, Qin Huilang, Music: Xiao Yan. Sound: Wang Huimin. Cast: Zhou Lijing as the Monk Wenhui, Zhu Wangyi as Shang Selan, Li Yan as Zhang Yichao, Cao Can as Bai Minzhong, Pu Cunxin as Li Shilang, Zhao Xiaoming as Geng Chao

The first PRC-Taiwan co-production, this film takes its story off the Dunhuang frescoes, and relates how the ancient Central Asian kingdom of Tuerfan (Turkistan) became a part of China.

During the reign of the Tang Emperor Xuanzong (847–860 A.D.), civil war erupts in the neighboring kingdom of Tuerfan following the death of its king. Zhang Yichao, leader of the Shazhou people, seeks the Emperor's help. Acting on advice from Prime Minister Bai Minzhong, the Emperor Xuanzong sends the Monk Wenhui to Shazhou to pacify the people. After an arduous journey, Wenhui finally arrives. He explains to Zhang Yichao the Tang policy of harmonious coexistence among the nationalities, puts down the Tuerfan civil war and brings the vast area of Shazhou into the Tang Empire.

468. *Desert Storm (Han Hai Chao)*

1985. Beijing Film Studio. Color. 10 Reels. Direction: Hua Xun. Screenplay: Wang Zequn. Cinematography: Yan Junsheng. Art Direction: Yu Fengming. Music: Li Fu. Sound: Wang Dawen, Ning Menghua. Cast: Bai Zhidi as Li Laoshan, Yuan Yuan as Han Xiaolong, Wang Qinxiang as Yan Jianping, Wu Ying as Deng Li, Yang Lishan as Huang Amin, Dong Lili as Li Xiaojuan

When a massive storm hits the Takeyili Desert, oil exploration team No. 205 loses contact with its command headquarters. Three members of the team disappear, including the team's guide. Death appears certain. After the storm passes, team leader Li Laoshen brings the rest of the team on a search mission. They finally find the new oil rig that had disappeared in the storm. A separate team led by the Commander finds the three missing people alive in the desert.

469. *Desire for Love in a Mountain Village (Shan Cun Feng Yue)*

1987. Guangxi Film Studio. Color. 9 Reels. Direction: Zhao Wen. Screenplay: Wang Yifei. Cinematography: Yang Yuming, Liu Baogui. Art Direction: Lao Guanneng. Music: Shao En. Sound: Lin Lin, Li Yunping. Cast: Han Xing as Guier, Ma Jun as Mangzi, Dong Ji as Wu Aba, Xu Yazhong as the old blind woman, Bai Ling as Dongsheng, Xiang Hong as Dongsheng's wife

In the lovely mountain village of Fengxiangxi, a man named Mangzi touches a woman named Guier while helping her do some work. In local custom this is very disgraceful behavior, so village chief Wu Aba sentences Mangzi to perform 15 days of labor at Guier's home. Wu Aba had also arranged Guier's marriage to Shusheng, although there was no affection at all between them. Shusheng never treated Guier as his wife, and soon left to work in the city. Now, spending every day with the hardworking Mangzi, Guier does fall in love. Her love is strong and pure, and Mangzi is torn between his desire for the woman and his fear of the consequences of such a romance. At last, the two enter into an affair.

470. *Desperate Songstress (Feng Kuang Ge Nu)*

1988. Inner Mongolia Film Studio. Color. 9 Reels. Direction: Liu Guoquan. Screenplay: Xiao Mao, Lin Hongtong. Cinematography: Zhang Zhongping, Ge Lisheng. Art Direction: Mo Nayintai, Zhang Yafang. Music: Li Lifu, Gu Jianfen, San Bao. Sound: Ao Si. Cast: Mao Amin as Wu Yani, Ma Chongle as the Adorer, Guo Xuxin as Li Wei

Wu Yani's pop singing performances are noted for the passion she puts into her song delivery. One evening, her performance is interrupted when the theater is rocked by an explosion which kills a man. Police investigator Li Wei determines that the explosion appears to have been set solely for the purpose of murdering the victim. He also learns the victim is none other than Wu Yani's husband Zhang Changshun, whom she had married during the years she was living in the countryside. Wu Yani becomes the prime suspect...

471. *Desperation (Zui Hou De Feng Kuang)*

1987. Xi'an Film Studio. Color. 10 Reels. Direction: Zhou Xiaowen, Shi Chengfeng.

Desperation. In prison, Song Ze (Zhang Jianmin, right), plans his escape. 1987. Xi'an Film Studio.

Screenplay: Zhou Xiaowen, Shi Chengfeng. Cinematography: Feng Wei. Art Direction: Liu Yichuan. Music: Guo Feng. Sound: Hui Fongzhi. Cast: Zhang Jianmin as Song Ze, Liu Ciaoning as He Lei, Jin Lili as Li Xiaohua, Zhu Lei as Zhu Fuxiang, Zhen Jianhua as Mr. Zhen

Escaped killer Song Ze continues to commit crimes while on the run. Young police officer He Lei is ordered to take him in. During the investigation, He Lei discovers Song's background is similar, almost a mirror of his own: both were raised by their fathers, served in the army, and display a streak of arrogance. Song's former girlfriend Li Xiaohua fails to persuade Song to turn himself in. Unknown to her, Song carries high-powered explosives and a detonator onto a train bound for Beijing. He Lei and several other policemen get on the train by helicopter, but find it difficult to draw Song's attention away from the briefcase containing the explosives. After several other plans fail, He Lei presents himself to the passengers as a filmmaker. As a joke he tells the passengers' fortunes by reading their palms. At last, Song Ze lets He Lei tell his fortune. If the explosives go off, the whole train will be in danger...

The film won an "Outstanding Feature Film" award in 1987 from the Ministry of Radio, Film and Television.

472. *Destiny (Gui Shu)*

1981. Beijing Film Studio. Color. 11 Reels. Direction: Dong Kena. Screenplay: Zhao Junfang. Cinematography: Zhang Shiwei. Art Direction: Hao Guoxin. Music: Hu Weili. Sound: Wang Dawen. Cast: Xu Huanshan as Yang Zhihe, Tao Yuling as Yang Xiumei, Zhao Ruping as Chang Laole, Wang Ruiyun as Zhao Feng, Qiu Yin as Gao Zhankui, Tan Tianqian as Li Niuhai

In 1949, a poor rural teacher named Yang Zhihe leaves his wife and newborn daughter to join the Nationalist Army in exchange for a bag of food and a few dollars. When the mainland falls to the Communists, he is part of the Nationalist forces evacuated to Taiwan. On the ship, he and fellow soldiers Chang Laole, Gao Zhankui and Li Niuhai become sworn brothers, vowing they will someday return to the mainland. As the years pass, their longing for their families grows. Li Niuhai and Gao Zhankui eventually die, and Chang Laole lives in a small restaurant he owns. Only Yang

Zhihe has remained in the army, although very old and lonely. To fulfill a promise to his two deceased blood brothers, Yang takes their ashes to the mainland. Yang Zhihe passes through Japan and gets to the mainland under the name Tian Fengren. There, he delivers the ashes to the dead men's families. He witnesses the huge changes in China, and how much better are the people's lives. At last he locates his wife and daughter, but they cannot unite yet. Tian Fengren has to leave but swears he will return again someday. His wife Yang Xiumei tearfully expresses her belief that China will someday be united.

473. *Destroy Them in Ice Town (Bing Cheng Qin Mo)*

1994. Pearl River Film Company. Color. Letterboxed. 9 Reels. Direction: Zhang Zhongwei. Screenplay: Li Zhen, Xu Luying. Cinematography: Yan Songyan, Li Dongbing. Art Direction: Gao Tinglun. Music: Wu Daming. Sound: Sheng Hongtao. Costume: Ouyang Yongkuan. Makeup: Zhao Li, Dan Xiangsuo. Cast: Wu Ruopu as Long Feng, Sun Han as Shang Wu, Xu Yang as Shen Yaping, Zhu Dexi as director, Zhen Aiping as Daban, Ma Xi as Dike, Bi Shaofu as manager Ruan, Wu Kejian as Lao Hei

A ruthless gang of drug dealers carry out a series of violent crimes in Hong Kong, including killing the city's chief customs official. The gang moves into North China, to a city called Ice Town. Chinese authorities send veteran officer Long Feng to investigate. Meanwhile, the murdered customs official's daughter Bai Li arrives on her own, and Long Feng takes on the added task of protecting her. This is not easy, for the lady has a penchant for getting into dangerous situations. Finally, the police win out, and Long Feng and Bai Li get together romantically.

474. *Destroying the Eagle's Tomb (Ping Ying Fen)*

1978. Shanghai Film Studio. B & W. 11 Reels. Direction: Fu Chaowu, Gao Zheng. Screenplay: Shandong Linqin Prefecture writing team collectively, written by Wang Huo, Zhu Mengmin, Cinematography: Peng Enli, Zuang Hongjun. Art Direction: Jin Qifeng. Music: Liu Yanxi. Sound: Zhou Hengliang. Cast: Zhang Fa as Lu Zhenshan, Deng xiaoling as Yan Yonghong, Qiao Qi as Zhang Wanqing, Wang Hui as Zhao Zhigang, Wang Yumei as Mrs. Hu, Wang Qi as Li Jiuzong, Zhou Guobin as Lu Mingsong

Despotic landlord Zhang Wanqing and his son Huo Yanwang train their eagle to kill stonemason Lu Zhenshan's chickens, so Lu's elder son Lu Mingsong kills the eagle. In retaliation, Huo Yanwang forces Lu's family to build a tomb for the dead eagle, appropriates Lu's land, and kills both Lu Mingsong and Lu Zhenshan's wife. Lu Zhenshan is forced to leave the area. Ten years later, he returns to his now liberated hometown and becomes chair of the farmers' association. The story centers around Lu Zhenshan's struggle with landlord Zhang Wanqing, symbolized by destruction of the eagle's tomb. Lu Zhenshan is at last successful in exposing the crimes of Zhang Wanqing and his son, and the two despots are executed according to law. The people of the town are truly liberated at last.

475. *Destruction (Da Hui Mie)*

1990. Inner Mongolia Film Studio & Hong Kong Shijia Film Company Co-Production. Color. 9 Reels. Direction: Mu Deyuan. Screenplay: Zhang Jiping. Cinematography: Lin Jian. Art Direction: Xing Zhen, Han Jingfeng, Yang Xiaowen. Music: Guo Wenjing. Sound: Huang Yingxia. Cast: Wang Xinhai as Zhang Yuanjie, Shen Junyi as Yuan Xiaoshun

In the 1930s, there is a repeated pattern of unidentified female murder victims floating in the river through the city of Tianjin. When Zhang Yuanjie is named Tianjin's chief of police, he determines to get to the bottom of these unexplained deaths. However, he soon finds his investigation blocked by Yuan Xiaoshun, relative of a powerful local businessman. In addition, his supervisor forbids him from going forward with the probe. Zhang continues anyway, and at last finds that the killings are tied in to a forced prostitution ring. All are killed in a final gun battle, including Chief Zhang.

476. *Devil's Hairpin (Mo Gui Fa Qia)*

1994. Beijing Film Studio. Color. Letterboxed. 8 Reels. Direction: Huo Zuang, Xu Xiaoxing. Screenplay: Huo Zuang, Xu Xiaoxing. Cinematography: Li Tingzhen. Art Direction: Hao Jingyuan. Music: Zhang Fuquan. Sound: Wang Dawen. Costume: Shang Liya. Cast: Liu Tong, Li Xia. Cast: Yue Wei as Wenwen, Shi Cheng as Qiangqiang, Li Longfei as Xio Lu, Lu Xiaoping as king of happiness, Juan Zi as queen of happiness, Li Li as Wenwen's mother, Chen Ke as Xiao Lu's mother

In a place called the Cave of Evil, wicked sorceress Huangzhen creates a magic pin with which she plans to lure children into rejecting their studies and just play. A masked stranger who had been one of her victims as a child now shows up to battle her and protect the children.

477. *Devil's House (Di Yu Shan Zhuang)*

1992. Guangxi Film Studio. Color. Letterboxed. 10 Reels. Direction: Zhao Wenqin. Screenplay: Lin Yuzhen. Cinematography: Ye Ruiwei, Xie Zhijun. Art Direction: Huang Shu. Music: Xian Zhengzhong, Xian Hua. Sound: Han Weijun. Costume: Qi Guishuang. Makeup: Yuan Chiling. Cast: Sun Feihu as Liu Xiongwu, Xia Jing as Xiao Juan, Wang Zhifei as Da Wen, Dong Ji as the housekeeper, Liu Yunhua as Yujie, Han Fei as Xiao Wu, Wang Xueqing as Madam Liu, Zhen Xiaoning as Doctor Li

In old China, a man named Fang owns two very valuable pieces of jade dating from the 3rd Century. While on a visit to the mountains, he casually mentions this to Liu Xiongwu, owner of the villa where he is staying. Liu arranges for Fang to be murdered and the jade stolen, only to discover he is too late: Fang had given one of the pieces to his sister and the other to his daughter Xiao Juan. So Liu courts and marries the victim's sister and thereby obtains one piece of the jade. He then arranges for Xiao Juan to be hired as teacher of Liu's younger son, planning to eventually get her jade as well. But after she arrives, Xiao Juan learns her aunt is kept in seclusion in the villa, and at last finds her. The two surmise what is going on and try to escape. In the climactic struggle, fire engulfs the villa, killing everyone but Xiao Juan and Liu's small son, who she carries to safety.

478. *Devotion to Martial Arts (Wu Lin Zhi)*

1983. Beijing Film Studio. Color. 10 Reels. Direction: Zhang Huaxun. Screenplay: Hua Xun, Xie Hong. Cinematography: Guan Qinwu. Art Direction: Zhang Xiande, Zhen Huiwen. Music: Wang Liping. Sound: Lai Qizhen. Cast: Li Junfeng as Dongfang Xu, Li Deyu as He Dahai, Zhang Yunxi as Magic Palm Li, Ge Yanchun as Ao Lianzhi, Aihati as Dadelov, Pang Wanlin as Tulayev

In the mid–17th century, a Russian strongman named Dadelov arrives in China challenging any and all Chinese willing to take him on. He humiliates every Chinese he faces, and the film shows the proud efforts of Chinese martial arts masters Dongfang Xu and He Dahai to defeat the Russian and preserve China's national self-respect. Before taking him on, He Dahai fights and wins a warmup match with Dadelov's main protégé, but He is mysteriously attacked and injured on the road back from that match. So his colleague Dongfang Xu signs up to replace his friend. To distract Xu from his training, Dadelov arranges for the abduction of Xu's daughter. Xu overcomes all the obstacles put in his path, and defeats the Russian with a traditional Chinese fighting method. Although the two national martial arts experts have won, the film ends with He Dahai dying, and Dongfang Xu having to flee.

479. *Devotion to Medicine (Dan Xin Pu)*

1980. Beijing Film Studio. Color. 11 Reels. Direction: Xie Tian, Zhen Guo Quan. Screenplay: Su Shuyang. Cinematography: Huang Xinyi. Art Direction: Chen Zhaomin, Zhou Dengfu. Music: Xu Jingqin, Zhang Zhian. Cast: Zhen Rong as Fang Lingxuan, Yu Shizhi as Ding Wenzhong, Xiu Zongdi as Zhuang Jisheng, Zhang Ping as Li Guang, Hu Zongwun as Fang's wife, Li Tingdong as Zhen Songnian

In 1973, Premier Zhou's speech at the Fourth National People's Congress brings renewed hope to a China which had passed through the Cultural Revolution and the Gang of Four's tyranny. Zhou stressed the need for research into heart disease, greatly inspiring elderly physician Fang Ling, a representative to the Congress. After returning home, he shares his excitement with his old friend Ding Wenzhong and they undertake experiments into a new medicine. However, Zhuang Jisheng, a zealous follower of the Gang of Four, orders a halt to their work. He also arranges a laboratory accident to cast doubt on the wisdom of the experiments. Fang Lingxuan realizes that the Gang's true objective in halting the experiments is to attack Premier Zhou, so he resists Zhuang. Party secretary Li Guang is also criticized for his support of Fang Lingxuan's experiment, and Fang's student Zhen Songnian is persecuted. During this difficult time, Premier Zhou calls Fang to express his concern for their progress and for Fang's family. With the Party's support and the trust of the people, the experimenters finally succeed. But just at that time, they learn that Premier Zhou has died. Fang Lingxuan and his colleagues decide to gain strength from their sorrow, and continue their struggle.

480. *Devotion to the Sky (Hun Ji Lan Tian)*

1982. Shanghai Film Studio. Color. 11 Reels. Direction: Yu Benzheng. Screenplay: Lu Wei, Lin Kangsheng, Li Pingfeng. Cinematography: Xia Lixing, Cheng Shiyu. Art Direction: Wang Xingcang. Music: Gao Tian. Sound: Lu Xuehan. Cast: Yu Ping as Fang Jie, Qian Yongfu as Gao Yang, Si Xilai as Liu Zhenmin, Wu Jing as Tao Tao, Li Lianyuan as Xiao Pan, He Ling as Xie Zhiao

An aviation institute designing a new model fighter plane receives a new test pilot. Gao Yang, the new pilot, is an active, enthusiastic man whose personality soon conflicts with that of chief designer Fang Jie, a woman he describes as a "dry piece of bread." Fang had once been as vibrant and active as he, but changed after her husband Xie Zhiao was killed testing the same "Blue Sky" model of fighter plane five years earlier. Since then she has withdrawn from the outside world and devoted herself totally to her work. At first, Fang Jie so dislikes Gao that she tries to block his being assigned the mission of testing the new fighter, but after he heroically handles a test flight accident, she gains new respect for him. Fang Jie and Gao Yang's grudging respect for each other eventually turns to love as they work together in getting the new plane ready. But her awareness of the dangers of his job, and the memories of her first husband's death makes Fang Jie so concerned about Gao Yang that if affects her own work. In the end, the couple overcomes this distraction and the "Blue Sky" model fighter plane successfully passes its test flight.

481. *Diamond Ring (Bao Shi Jie Zhi)*

1985. Inner Mongolia Film Studio. Color. 10 Reels. Direction: Shi Xian. Screenplay: Peng Mingyan, Bi Jiancang. Cinematography: Tu Jiakuan. Art Direction: Chen Yiyun. Music: Hu Weili. Sound: Zhang Zizhong. Cast: Xia Liyan as Wang Manyun, Xu Zhiqun as Yang Shan, Zhao Jianwen as Chen Agang, Guan Zongxiang as Zhong Xing, Duan Xin as Hui Feng, Bi Jiancang as Sun Biao, Sun Jianfei as Chen Atie, Libiyaengandu Kadiyata as Phillips

In 1946 Shanghai, Chinese boxer Chen Atie is killed during a bout with an American boxer named Phillips. Chen's brother Chen Agang is convinced his younger brother was intentionally and cruelly beaten to death. He signs a contract with female boxing promoter Wang Manyun, intending to seek a revenge bout with Phillips. Chen Agang later rescues the boss's daughter Yang Shan when an American soldier is attempting to assault her. The two become close, and Yang Shan tells Chen that her mother Wang Manyun is really a Japanese woman with a hatred of all Chinese people, and that his brother's death was the result of Wang having poisoned Chen Atie's prefight meal. With this information, Chen goes to Phillips, deeply troubled by the ring death, and tells him he was not responsible. Yang Shan tells her mother she can bear her no longer, and leaves for Japan by herself. The loss of her daughter drives Wang Manyun to suicide.

482. *Die All Together (Tong Gui Yu Jing)*

1993. Shanghai Film Studio. Color. Letterboxed. 10 Reels. Direction: Shen Yaoting. Screenplay: Shen Yaoting. Cinematography: Zhang Er. Art Direction: Zhang Wanhong. Music: Yang Shaolu, Su Junjie. Sound: Xu Xiushan. Costume: Zhang Fucai. Makeup: Zuang Yazhen. Cast: Wang Sihuai as Lin Mengshan, Zhou Xiaoli as Ma Xiuxiu, Peter Leigena as Badderly

In 1930s Shanghai, detective Lin Mengshan is investigating a woman's murder. It becomes more than just a routine case when he determines the killer was a foreigner named Badderly, protected by extraterritoriality. He requests permission to make an arrest, but his supervisor considers foreigners strictly off limits, and turns down the request. Lin's frustration turns to rage when his wife Ma Xiuxiu is killed. Finally, Lin takes things into his own hands and shoots Badderly just as the foreigner is about to leave China. The police come to surround Lin Mengshan, but he takes his own life.

483. *Digger-Dealer-Bodyguard (Jin Ke, Shang Ke, Biao Ke)*

1994. Changchun Film Studio. Color. Letterboxed. 9 Reels. Direction: Liu Zhongming, Li Shiming. Screenplay: Li Hun. Cinematography: Li Junyan, Lin Boquan. Art Direction: Liu

Sheng, Ji Shulin. Music: Wu Daming. Sound: Zhang Qingjiang. Costume: Qi Chunzhi, Ouyang Chunyu. Makeup: Li Yang, Sheng Libo. Cast: Wang Gang as Yang Liansheng, Zhao Mingming as Qiuhua, Chi Zhiqiang as boss Men, Sun Peijun as Yuegui, Wang Zhongxing as Jin Daya, Jin Weimin as Hei Shanbao, Zhang Guowen as Qiang Zi, Song Jing as Chun Hua

An action film set in the early years of the Republic of China. Yang Liansheng, a worker for Sun Yatsen's Revolutionary Party, comes to Northeast China to raise funds for Sun's challenge to Yuan Shikai. He has many confrontations and battles with local despots and others, but at last he accomplishes his mission.

484. *Dinglong Town (Ding Long Zhen)*

1978. Xi'an Film Studio. B & W. 9 Reels. Direction: Wei Rong. Screenplay: Tan Fuyong, Ren Qiguang. Cinematography: Cao Jinshan. Art Direction: Zhang Xiaohui, Ai Nong. Music: Xu Youfu, Xie Tiyin. Sound: Chen Yudan. Cast: Li Zhaomin as Zhong Cheng, Guan Changzhu as Lu Meng, Yan Bing as Liang Honglu, Zhi Yitong as Deputy District Director Gong, Han Bingjie as Da Kang, Chen Wanshun as Xiao Zhan, Zhang Chi as Yi Mu, Zhao Tao as Yuan Qing, Qiu Yuzhen as Sister Ku, Wang Yinglin as Grandma Kang, Zhang Ping as the commanding officer, Zheng Danian as the political commissar, Wang Chuanjiang as Battalion Commander Li, Jin Jiading as the Mayor, Zhang Muqin as the Mayor's wife, Sun Yuanxun as Tang Sijiu

After World War Two, Chiang Kaishek launches a wide scale attack on the areas under Communist control. Yang Wancai, a former spy for the Japanese who goes by the alias of Yi Mu, is sent to the town of Dinglong in a Communist-held area to try to take over its railway station. The objective is to allow military supplies for the Nationalist Army to get through Dinlong unimpeded. He locates Yuan Qing, the assistant district director, and threatens to expose Yuan's WWII pro-Japanese activities unless Yuan murders his boss, district director Zhong Cheng. Yuan's murder attempt is foiled by a local woman, Sister Ku. When a Nationalist Army supply train passes through Dinglong Town, Zhong Cheng stops it and alerts the PLA. The traitor Yuan Qing tries to deliver an order forged with Zhong Cheng's signature, trying to get the train started again. Zhong Cheng boards the train and kills the spies on board, then turns it back to Dinglong town.

485. *Dirty Men (Tou Fa Luan Le)*

1994. Inner Mongolian Film Studio, China Chemical Industry Import and Export General Corp. Co-Production. Color. Letterboxed. 9 Reels. Direction: Guan Hu. Screenplay: Guan Hu. Cinematography: Yao Xiaofeng, Wu Qiao. Art Direction: Wei Xinhua. Music: Guo Xiaohu, Gao Qi. Sound: Wu Gang. Costume: Zhao Hui. Makeup: Wang Liqiu. Cast: Kong Ling as Ye Tong, Zhang Xiaotong as Zhen Weidong, Geng Le as Peng Wei, Ding Jiali as Zhen Weiping, Yi Qiang as Lei Bing, Xie Kun as Chi Xuan, Li Mengrao as Zhen's father

The story of several children who grow up together in a simple courtyard in Beijing. The story follows what happens as they grow up and follow varied pursuits, a medical student, a policeman, a convict, a rock singer, etc.

486. *The Disappointed Lover (Shi Lian Zhe)*

1987. Beijing Film Studio. Color. 10 Reels. Direction: Qin Zhiyu. Screenplay: Zhang Xian, Qin Zhiyu, based on the novel "Geng Er in Beijing," by Chinese-Canadian author Chen Ruoxi (1938-). Cinematography: Zhang Shicheng. Art Direction: Huo Jianqi. Music: Wang Xiling. Sound: Sun Yumin. Cast: Liu Yan as Geng Er, Xu Lili as Xue Qing, Li Jing as Xiao Jin, Shen Chunxiang as Brother, Chang Lantian as Xiao Zhang, Li Keji as Ma Zhenguo

In the mid–1960s, Dr. Geng Er returns to China from studies in the United States, full of enthusiasm and resolved to devote his life to his country. In the turmoil of the Cultural Revolution, Geng's work seems meaningless and his patriotism in vain. But his love for his country never diminishes even though his heart is broken. In a simple yet melancholy style, the film's point is that there is more than one kind of love; Geng's patriotism is one of these, and makes his dignity and idealism easier to understand.

487. *Dislocation (Cuo Wei)*

1986. Xi'an Film Studio. Color. 10 Reels. Direction: Huang Jianxin. Screenplay: Li Wei. Cinematography: Wang Xinsheng, Feng Wei. Art Direction: Qian Yunxuan. Music: Han Yong. Sound: Gu Changning. Cast: Liu Zifeng as Zhao Shuxin & The Robot, Mu Hong as the secretary, Sun Feihu as the Director of Public Security, Yang Kun as Yang Lijuan

In this sequel to Huang Jianxi's successful first film, "Black Cannon Incident," Engineer

Dislocation. **In a rare moment of relaxation, Bureau Chief Zhao Shuxin (Liu Zifeng) tells his secretary (Mu Hong) of the frustrations of his job. 1986. Xi'an Film Studio.**

Zhao Shuxin has been promoted to Bureau Chief. To free himself from the bureaucratic tedium of shuffling piles of documents and attending countless meetings, he clones an intelligent robot in his own image to attend all those meetings for him. Unfortunately, the robot cannot avoid the pitfalls into which humans fall, and gets into a succession of hilarious situations. Finally, in desperation, Zhao Shuxin has to destroy his creation.

488. *The Dissolute Emperor (Feng Liu Qian Long)*

1991. Guangxi Film Studio and the Gold Island Film & TV Corporation. Color. 12 Reels. Letterboxed. Direction: Qiu Lili. Screenplay: Ni Feng. Cinematography: Ru Shuiren, Zhao Peng. Art Direction: Hao Jingyuan. Music: Li Wanli. Sound: Hao Jingyuan. Cast: Duo Fu as Qian-long, Dong Zhizhi as Xiao Ling, Wang Chen as Xi'er, Miao Fang as Mu Yan

The Golden Age of the Qing (Manchu) dynasty was the 60-year reign of the Emperor Qian Long. It is known that soon after ascending the throne in 1736, the young and intelligent emperor, who styled himself the "Solitary Gallant," made an incognito inspection tour of his realm. This is a fictional speculation of what might have happened on that trip. At the time of his trip, parts of China are troubled by a criminal organization called the "White Alliance." Qian Long starts his own investigation, and in the process he falls in love separately with three young women, each skilled in a different martial art. During the suppression of the alliance, the emperor repeatedly gets into trouble, but on every occasion one of the three women risks her life to save him. Eventually, all the members of the evil alliance are killed, but in the final battle with the alliance's mysterious leader, the three women give their own lives to save Qian Long.

489. *A Distant Spark (Yuan Fang Xing Huo)*

1961. Xinjiang Film Studio. B & W. 9 Reels. Direction: Ou Fan. Screenplay: Alehamu, Aetaimu, Kelimu, Haojieyefu, Judisheng and Liu Xiaowu. Cinematography: Liu Jingtang. Art Direction: Li Zhongzhi. Sound: Wang Lin. Cast: Aerkesai as Li Mutelifu, Huang Zhong as Director Yang, Tuerxun Aishan as Silamujiang,

Sulitang Mamuti as Aximu, Tuohuti Aizemu as the old artist, Wuliyate as Anaerhan

This is a film biography of Li Mutelifu, Uighur nationality poet and Communist Party activist.

In 1939, Li Mutelifu, then a student at Xinjiang Provincial Normal University, is influenced by the university director Yang, a covert member of the Communist Party. Li writes many poems which publicize the anti-Japanese campaign. After leaving school, he goes to work for the *Xinjiang Daily* while continuing to gain widespread notice for his literary creations. But in 1941, his mentor Director Yang is arrested, and Li moves to southern Xinjiang to continue his newspaper work, while writing revolutionary dramas. His poetry and drama are banned by the government, however, so he becomes more directly involved. In 1945, he organizes an anti–Nationalist political organization called the "Youth Star Association" which plots an armed rebellion. An undercover government agent in their midst betrays Li and the others, leading to their arrest and eventual execution.

490. *Distinguished Bureau Director (Feng Liu Ju Zhang)*

1985. Fujian Film Studio. Color. 10 Reels. Direction: Zhang Gang. Screenplay: Zhang Gang. Cinematography: Cai Zhengchang. Art Direction: Wang Renchen. Music: Wang Ming. Sound: Liu Jijie. Cast: Mao Yongmin as Liu Aman, Gu Ying as Luo Ling, Wei Huili as Bai Juan, Cheng Zhi as You Laoyun, Zhang Jiebing as Zhong Jian, Lu Lin as Xiang Liang

Actor Liu Aman is appointed director of a radio and TV bureau. He boldly implements reform, and appoints as his chief assistant You Laoyun, a former director who was unjustly ousted from his position during a political campaign. They decide to make a high quality TV series, and go against conventional thinking by casting restaurant worker Luo Ling in the lead female role. Liu Aman and Luo Ling start an affair at work, becoming the number one topic of gossip throughout the bureau. At last, their TV series begins, and is a hit.

491. *Disturbance (Yi Chang Feng Bo)*

1954. Shanghai Film Studio. B & W. 9 Reels. Direction: Lin Nong and Xie Jin. Screenplay: Yu Shan, from the novel of the same title by Shi Guo. Cinematography: Gu Wunhou. Set Design: Lin Lei. Music: Huang Yijun. Sound: Lu

Zhongbo. Cast: Shu Xiuwen as Lifu's wife, Fu Ke as Yang Yongcheng, She Wei as Yang Chunmei, Fu Huizhen as Rongshan's wife, Bai Mu as Yang Lihe, Feng Xiao as Zhu Xiaocang, Liu Wenhua as Wang Kai

In remote Yang Family Village, a widow called simply "Lifu's wife" lives with her only daughter Yang Chunmei, adhering to widowhood for more than 10 years under the Yang family's feudal clan law, which prohibits remarriage by a widow. A kindly bachelor farmer in the same village, Zhen Liangcheng, is sympathetic and helpful to the widow and her daughter. He and the widow gradually fall in love, but for years the two can only meet in secret. After liberation, they are able to be more open about their relationship. The daughter also falls in love with Zhu Xiaocan, a young man in their village. However, the clan elders consider the widow's relationship with Zhen Liangcheng to be something disgraceful, so they come up with a scheme to marry the daughter to the mother's lover, causing Lifu's widow to attempt suicide. But the daughter Yang Chunmei is firm in her opposition to the arrangement, and with the support of the Party organization and government she wins out. Wang, the district director, comes in to educate the people and awaken them to the harm caused by feudal thinking. Eventually, under the protection of the new marriage law, Lifu's widow and Zhen Liangcheng, Yang Chunmei and Zhu Xiaocang are married, and the disturbance has passed.

492. *Disturbance at Moon Bay (Yue Liang Wan De Feng Bo)*

1984. Shanghai Film Studio. Color. Letterboxed. 10 Reels. Direction: Zhong Shuhuang. Screenplay: Fang Yihua. Cinematography: Zhang Er. Art Direction: Wang Xingcang, Qin Bosong. Music: Xu Jingxin. Sound: Tu Minde. Cast: Zhang Yan as Uncle Mao Fu, Zhong Xinghuo as Qin Liang, Yu Guichun as Qiu Sheng, Fang Zhoubo as the militia battalion commander

Implementation of a new agricultural policy leads to prosperity for many in the countryside including Uncle Mao Fu, whose family becomes the first in their area to earn 10,000 yuan in a year. He soon finds, however, that wealth brings its own problems, as he is beset with would-be money borrowers. Some of those "borrowing" money from him are low-level Party cadres. Another of the newly rich is Qiu Sheng, who hides his income and constantly pleads poverty instead. The provincial Party Committee makes some policy adjustments to protect farmers' enthusiasm for achieving prosperity through hard work, and the situation improves. At last, the Party Secretary visits Uncle Mao and returns to him the various "loans" he had been intimidated into giving. Uncle Mao is so moved by this that he decides to put the money toward helping others in his village become wealthy.

493. *Disturbance on the Basketball Court (Qiu Chang Feng Bo)*

1957. Haiyan Film Studio. B & W. 9 Reels. Direction: Mao Yu. Screenplay: Tang Zhenchang. Cinematography: Luo Jizhi and Zhang Xiling. Art Direction: Lin Lei. Music: Li Yinhai. Sound: Huang Dongping. Makeup: Ni Yifei. Cast: Wun Xiying as Zhao Hui, Zhou Boxun as Zhang Renjie, Zhang Qian as Qian Zhenming, Gong Shihe as Lin Ruijuan, Cui Chaoming as Lin Yunwen, Guan Hongda as Zhen Xiaoxiu

Zhang Renjie, director of the Shanghai Medical Equipment Supply Bureau, opposes his staff's participation in athletics; he feels if they get sick they can take medicine. Young staff members Zhao Hui and Qian Zhenming love sports, and try to set up an intramural association in their work unit which will offer a variety of activities, but Director Zhang thwarts them at every turn. Zhao Hui does get up a basketball team which schedules a game with a local bank. In arranging the game, Zhao Hui becomes acquainted with Liu Ruijian, a woman on the bank's team, and the two fall in love, At last, Zhao Hui and Qian Zhenming place a call to Director Zhang ostensibly from a cabinet minister, who during the conversation mentions how he thinks staff sports programs are very progressive. The director suddenly changes his attitude and rushes to organize athletic activities. With coaching from Lin Ruijuan's father, a physical education professor, Zhao Hui and the others improve their skills, and the staff's health situation also improves. Following the example of his staff, Director Zhang also joins in various kinds of sports.

494. *Disturbances Around Women Models (Nu Mo Te De Feng Bo)*

1989. Beijing Film Studio. Color. Letterboxed. 9 Reels. Direction: Wang Binglin. Screenplay: Wang Binglin. Cinematography: Cai Rubing, Ma Ji. Art Direction: Hao Jingyuan. Music: Ma Ding. Sound: Li Bojiang. Cast: Chen Yude as Old Yu, Ma Ling as Yu Xiaoyan, Ding Yi as Yu's wife, Li Jing as Chunxing

To raise money for her ailing husband's medical treatment, country woman Chunxing finds work as a model at an art school. Humiliated that she would take such a job, her husband divorces her. Another model at the school, Yu Xiaoyan, has problems with her father Old Yu, who strongly opposes her doing modeling work. To add to the old man's worries, his son Dalong falls in love with Chunxing. Chunxing's relatives come from her village to take her back with them, as they feel disgraced by the work she does. Chunxing tries to commit suicide, but is rescued by Dalong and others.

495. *Disturbed Honeymoon (Feng Liu Mi Yue) (alternate title: Mi Yue You Xi)*

1994. Nanhai Film Company. Color. Letterboxed. 10 Reels. Direction: Wang Fengkui. Screenplay: Zhang Guanglie. Cinematography: Yan Songyan. Art Direction: Yang Baocheng. Music: Jiang Wantong. Sound: Jiang Yan. Costume: An Lixin. Makeup: Song Yingyuan. Cast: Ren Meng as Wenwen, Ren Mei as Meng Xia, Liu Zhibing as Su Peng, Wang Fengkui as Manager Wang, Wang Xiaowan as the secretary, Yan Shuqin as TV director, Ma Shuliang as assistant director, Li Xiaobo as the thief

Young worker Su Peng and his bride Wenwen arrive at a resort city to begin their honeymoon, but become separated at the train station. A series of funny things happen as the couple searches for each other, highlighted by Su Peng being used as an actor in a film and Wenwen substituting for her favorite singer when the latter fails to show up for a performance. It all ends happily when the couple at last find each other.

496. *Divorce (Li Hun)*

1992. Beijing Film Studio. Color. Letterboxed. 10 Reels. Direction: Wang Haowei. Screenplay: Li Chengsheng and Wang Haowei, from the novel of the same name by Lao She (1899-1966). Cinematography: Li Chengsheng. Art Direction: Hao Jingyuan. Music: Zhang Peiji. Sound: Liu Xiaodong. Costume: Feng Weijuan. Makeup: Ma Shuangying, Liu Li. Cast: Zhao Youliang as Old Li, Ding Jiali as Old Woman Li, Li Ding as Brother Zhang, Chen

***Divorce.* 1992. Beijing Film Studio.**

Xiaoyi as Madam Ma, Liu Peiqi as Xiao Zhao, Lu Qi as Wu Taiji, Tang Jishen as Madam Wu

In old Beijing, a group of low-ranking government officials in a financial bureau pass boring and at times sad lives. We meet several of them, including kindly Mr. Zhang, who loves to offer advice to everyone. One of his colleagues, Mr. Li, is unhappy with his marriage: his wife is a simple peasant from the countryside, and in the city her rural ways are even more prominent. He seriously contemplates divorcing her. Through the co-workers' relationships and the changing family relationships, the story focuses on how people felt about life and about each other in that time. In the end, Mr. Li decides to quit his job and take his whole family back to the countryside.

Best Cinematography Li Chengsheng, 1993 Golden Rooster Awards.

Best Supporting Actress Chen Xiaoyi, 1993 Hundred Flowers Awards.

497. *Divorce Contract (Li Hun He Tong)*

1990. Changchun Film Studio. Color. Wide Screen. 10 Reels. Direction: Song Jiangbo.

Screenplay: Jiang Nan, Jiang Yi. Cinematography: Niu Gang, Jiang Yi. Art Direction: Sui Zuangmu. Music: Li Lifu. Sound: Gu Xiaolian. Cast: Feng Gong as Liu Liu, Ren Meng as Ning Wa, Yan Qin as Yuerong

Dance hall band drummer Liu Liu and his wife, dance hall manager Ning Wa, get a divorce but are forced by the housing shortage to continue sharing an apartment. Yuerong, the band's singer, loves Liu Liu but the drummer still cares only for his wife, agreeing to the divorce only because his wife insisted on it. He at last returns Yuerong's affection, but just when it looks like they will get together, his wife asks for a reconciliation. Liu Liu confronts a dilemma.

498. *Divorce Wars (Li Hun Da Zhan)*

1992. Beijing Film Studio. Color. Letterboxed. 10 Reels. Direction: Chen Guoxing. Screenplay: Ma Junji, Chen Guoxing. Cinematography: Zhao Xiaoding. Art Direction: Song Zhenshan, Yang Hong. Music: Gao Erdi. Costume: Liu Huiping. Makeup: Cui Fa. Cast: Ge You as Da Ming, Ma Xiaoqing as Xiao Feng, Hou Yaohua as Liu Yishou, Cai Ming as Yinzi

Xiao Feng is a taxi driver, her husband Da Ming a trumpet player in a hotel's house band. Their relationship is quite amicable, but Xiao Feng has grown restless and dissatisfied with their marriage, craving more excitement. So she asks for a divorce. Because of a legal technicality, they cannot divorce easily and have to remain together indefinitely. This forces them to the realization that they still love each other and gives them a new understanding of their marriage and of life.

499. *Do You Love Me? (Ni Ai Wo Ma)*

1989. Changchun Film Studio and Nanjing Film Studio Co-Production. Color. Letterboxed. 10 Reels. Direction: Luo Guanqu. Screenplay: Chen Zhenan. Cinematography: Qiu Yiren, Zhang Pingqiang. Art Direction: Liu Jiajing. Music: Liu Yanxi. Sound: Feng Kaifa, Fu Ning. Cast: Zhao Jun as Huowang, Ma Xiaoqing as Shuihua, Hao Guang as Xiao Wang, Ma Jie as Erbao, Zhang Beizong as Grandpa Guang, Xie Dehui as Shuihua's mother, Zhou Zhijun as Mr. Zhou, Lu Yan as Ding Shuiyun, Zhang Qian as Lin Meimei

A young man named Huowang is dumped by his girlfriend Shuiyun, who decides she wants an urban lifestyle and would be better off looking for a husband in a bigger city. Her younger sister Shuihua, dismayed at her sister's behavior, determines to find a proper wife for poor Huowang. She starts by placing ads in the local newspaper, and several women apply, none of them appropriate. Shuihua keeps trying, and over time she falls for Huowang herself.

500. *Doctor Frog (Ha Mo Bo Shi)*

1984. Pearl River Film Studio. Color. Wide Screen. 10 Reels. Direction: Lin Lan. Screenplay: Li Daoji, Zhou Yuhe, Lu Yu, Lin Lan. Cinematography: Xie Yongyi, Liu Xinmin. Art Direction: Tu Benyang, Li Pingye. Music: Chen Qixiong. Sound: Deng Qinhua. Cast: Jin Naiqian as Jin Yuxin, Wang Ruoli as Ye Huizhen, Luo Qi as Wang Shuchao, Zhao Chunchang as Ye Jialin, Geng Xiaolu as Li Wan, Jin Kangmin as Chen Yi

In 1921, biologist Jin Yuxin receives his Ph.D. in France. He returns to China in 1931 to continue his research on achieving unisexual reproduction in frogs. His involvement in the anti-Japanese movement results in destruction of his laboratory. The underground Communist organizations help Jin and two students to continue their research in a mountain area. In 1948, he returns to Shanghai at a time when the city is in economic and political chaos, and shortly afterwards his wife dies. In 1949, after the liberation of Shanghai, Mayor Chen Yi nominates Jin as head of the Shanghai Biology Institute. In 1961, he finally succeeds in creating the first frog to have no grandfather. He dies shortly thereafter.

501. *Doctor Kotnis (Ke Di Hua Dai Fu)*

1982. Hebei Film Studio. Color. 10 Reels. Direction: Weijia, Su Fan, Jiang Xiangchen. Screenplay: Huang Zongjiang. Cinematography: Shi Fang. Art Direction: Fang Xuzhi. Music: Gong Zhiwei. Sound: Song Tianpei. Cast: Zhu Shimao as Kotnis, Niu Na as Huo Qinying, Wang Lihua as Wang Xiaohu, Li Changhua as Ma Hao, Jian Zhaoqiang as Doctor Chen

In 1940, Indian doctor Dwaranath S. Kotnis, part of the Indian medical mission to China, comes to the front lines to assist the Chinese fighting the Japanese invaders. Kotnis works day and night treating the wounded, while still teaching at the Norman Bethune School of Nursing and starting work on a textbook. He becomes the head of the Bethune School, and performs surgery under the poorest of conditions. When the Japanese launch a major attack on the Chinese forces, Kotnis often overworks himself and faints from hunger and fatigue. The Chinese people love and respect Kotnis and he returns their affection. On December 9th, 1942, Kotnis falls ill and dies from overwork at the age of 32.

502. *Doctor Norman Bethune (Bai Qiu En Dai Fu)*

1964. Haiyan Film Studio & August First Film Studio Co-Production. Color. 12 Reels. Chief Directors: Zhang Junxiang. Screenplay: Zhang Junxiang and Zhao Tuo, based on the book of the same title by Zhou Erfu. Chief Cinematographer: Wu Yinxian. Directors: Li Shutian, Gao Zheng. Cinematographers: Ma Linfa, Kou Jiwen. Art Direction: Han Shangyi. Music: Lu Qiming. Sound: Wu Jianghai. Cast: Gerald Tannebaum as Bethune, Chun Li as Fang Zhaoyuan, Yin Nuocheng as Secretary Tong, Xing Jitian as Minister Yu, Wu Xue as the commanding officer, Yang Zhaibao as Company Commander Xu

Canadian surgeon Norman Bethune travels to Yan'an, China, in 1938. In June he arrives at the Communists' Jincaiji base and sets to work

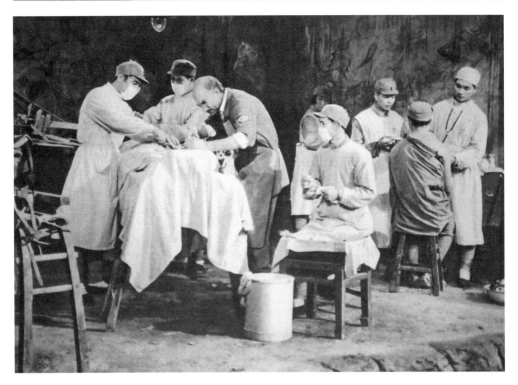

Doctor Norman Bethune. **Canadian surgeon Norman Bethune (Gerald Tannenbaum, center) performs frontline surgery on a Chinese soldier during World War II. 1964. Haiyan Film Studio, August First Film Studio Co-Production.**

in support of the Chinese people's anti–Japanese war effort. He organizes mobile medical teams to work in Shanxi and Hebei provinces. While he trains Eighth Route Army medical personnel, he always stays at the front lines himself, providing on-site surgery which greatly lowers the death rate. His work and his care for his coworkers gains him the respect and love of the Chinese people. One day he accidentally cuts his finger during surgery. It becomes infected and results in his death.

503. *Dr. Sun Yatsen (Parts 1&2) (Sun Zhong Shan)*

1986. Pearl River Film Studio. Color. Wide Screen. Direction: Ding Yinnan. Screenplay: He Mengfan, Zhang Lei. Cinematography: Wang Hengli, Hou Yong. Art Direction: Min Zongsi. Music: Si Wanchun. Sound: Deng Qinhua, Huang Minguang. Costume: Ren Fengyi, Wang Jizhu. Cast: Liu Wenzhi as Sun Zhongshan (Sun Yatsen), Liu Simin as Huang Xing, Zhang Yan as Song Qingling (Madame Sun), Xu Weihong as Lu Jiaodong, Ma Hongying as Wang Jingwei, Wang Sihuai as Chen Qimei

The story of Dr. Sun and his democratic revolution in China. After failed rebellions in Guangzhou in 1895 and Huizhou in 1900, Sun finally succeeds with the Wuhan Rebellion in 1911, which overthrows more than 2,000 years of feudal government in China. On December 29, 1911, Sun Yatsen is named Provisional President of the Republic of China. He marries Song Qingling, daughter of one of his closest friends, and she becomes his advisor and confidant in carrying out his revolutionary ideals. After the revolution is betrayed in June, 1920, Sun decides to reorganize the Nationalist Party he founded with help from its left wing, the Communists. Sun then establishes the Huangpu (Whampoa) Military Academy to train his own military force.

Best Picture, 1987 Golden Rooster Awards.

Best Director Ding Yinnan, 1987 Golden Rooster Awards.

Best Actor Liu Wenzhi, 1987 Golden Rooster Awards.

Best Cinematography Wang Hengli and Hou Yong, 1987 Golden Rooster Awards.

Best Art Direction Min Zongsi, 1987 Golden Rooster Awards.

Best Music Si Wanchun, 1987 Golden Rooster Awards.

Best Costume Ren Fengyi and Wang Jizhu, 1987 Golden Rooster Awards.

Best Picture, 1987 Hundred Flowers Awards.

504. *The Dog King (Quan Wang)*

1993. August First Film Studio. Color. Letterboxed. 9 Reels. Direction: Yao Shougang. Screenplay: Zhu Xiaocai, Yao Shougang. Cinematography: Cai Shunan, Song Chao, Dong Yachun. Art Direction: Zhang Lin, Li Jing. Music: Cui Bingyuan. Sound: Shen Guorui. Costume: Zhao Shunde. Makeup: Jin Ying. Cast: Hai Dun as Geng Erlin, Wun Yujuan as Dong Shaogu, He Yu as Guan Hanliang, Gao Fang as grandma, Lin Da as Xiao Shanzi, Lu Yiding as Xu Shaopu, Wang Chao as Shen Dashan

During World War II, Dashan and Erlin, hunters and brothers, raise a dog called Hailong. The dog mates with a wolf, and has two puppies, called Big Dragon and Little Dragon. A Japanese army officer and a dog trainer for anti-Japanese guerrillas both come separately looking for Hailong. Hailong is later killed protecting the brothers, after which they take its offspring to the guerrillas' dog training team. The dogs become fierce anti–Japanese fighters.

505. *Dong Fangjian (Dong Fang Jian)*

1982. Pearl River Film Studio. Color. 10 Reels. Direction: Wang Jing, Hu Bingliu. Screenplay: Fu Di, Wang Jing. Cinematography: Liang Xiongwei. Art Direction: Li Xin. Music: Yang Suzheng. Sound: Jiang Shaoqi. Cast: Yan Shikui as Dong Fangjian, Zhang Liwei as Shu Jing, Shi Jing as Xiong Xianyi, Song Dewang as Director Xiao, Xia Zongyou Mi Guoliang, Ding Tiebao as Lin Mengya

As part of its defense modernization, China in the late 1970s begins a naval buildup, including plans for testing a prototype submarine. A spy in the city of Lanling obtains critical intelligence on the project by bugging the conference room where the plans are discussed, but is temporarily unable to transmit the information overseas. PSB investigator Dong Fangjian is called back from his honeymoon to track down the spy. His bride, former singer Shu Jing, is understandably very disappointed.

The movie follows Dong's efforts to track down the spy. He at last flushes out the spy and recovers the information during a chase and battle at sea, but gives his life in the process. Shu Jing is devastated, but understands her husband's devotion to duty.

The Dongling Robbery (Part 1) **see** *Legend of the Cixi Tomb Treasure*

506. *The Dongling Robbery (Part 2) (Dong Ling Da Dao)*

1988. Xi'an Film Studio. Color. Wide Screen. 8 Reels. Direction: Li Yundong. Screenplay: Su Jinxing, Dou Bing. Cinematography: Yang Baoshi. Art Direction: Cheng Minzhang. Music: Guo Suying. Sound: Hong Jiahui, Li Ping. Cast: Ding Lan as Shen Zuohong, Zhao Mingjie as Shen Hui

After the treasure is stolen, Chiang Kaishek and Yan Xishan come to Beiping. Jiang orders Yan to finish this case as soon as possible but Yan deliberately postpones doing so in order to hold on to his military power. Qin Delu follows Shen Hui and finds the Nahe treasure. Taoist temple director Shen Jiu returns to the mountain, falsely accuses Na, and wants to kill him. Shen Jiu is killed in a fight over the treasure, after which Na persuades Shen Zhuohong to go to Beiping and negotiate terms for turning the treasure over to Chiang and Yan. Yan hosts an exhibition of the treasure, and Na is appointed associate director of the National Antique Protection League. When the exhibition ends, the treasures are scheduled to be sent to the association, and representatives from various cultural, political and business circles arrive to monitor the transfer. When a rumor circulates claiming the treasures are all gone, the boxes are opened and found to be empty.

507. *Dongmei (Dong Mei)*

1960. Changchun Film Studio. B & W. 8 Reels. Direction: Wang Yan. Screenplay: Lin Shan. Cinematography: Wang Qiming, Chang Yan. Art Direction: Wang Tao. Music: Zhang Decang. Sound: Chen Wenyuan. Cast: Bai Yang as Li Dongmei, Lu Guilan as Little Sister, Yang Qitian as Xiao Zhao, Ma Shida as Platoon Leader Chen, Bai Yingkuan as Squad Leader Zhang, Li Wancheng as Fourth Brother, Li Lin as Ma Jiahui, Zhou Wenlin as Commander Sun

In the fall of 1934, Regimental Commander

Wang Dadong goes north with the Red Army to resist the Japanese. His pregnant wife Dongmei (a Red Army political commissar) remains in their home area to continue her revolutionary work and await the arrival of the baby. When their contacts with the Communist Party organization are cut off, Dongmei and some wounded soldiers form a guerrilla band, carrying out raids and then finding and punishing a local traitor Ma Jiahui. When the Communists try to form an anti–Japanese alliance with the Nationalists, Dongmei is sent to negotiate as the CPC's military representative. However, she is arrested by enemy Commander Sun. But the masses of the people successfully pressure for her release, and when Wang Dadong arrives with the New Fourth Army, husband and wife are reunited.

508. *Don't Ask Where I Came From (Bu Yao Wen Wo Cong Na Li Lai)*

1991. Beijing Film Studio. Color. 9 Reels. Direction: Qiqing Gaowa. Screenplay: Wan Tianyun, Zhao Baohua. Cinematography: Huang Xinyi. Art Direction: Tu Juhua. Music: Liu Changyuan. Sound: Wang Yunhua. Cast: Sun Chun Ouyang Jie, Ju Ying as Zi Luolan, Niu Ben as Da Zhi, Zhao Liang as the chief detective, Fang Zige as person in blue clothes, Jiang Shan as woman police officer

A comedy in which a young woman about to graduate from police academy chooses a young economist as her investigative "target" in a mock counter-espionage training exercise, leading to many complications.

509. *Don't Call Me Scar (Bie Jiao Wo Ba Li)*

1987. Changchun Film Studio. Color. 10 Reels. Direction: Zhang Hui. Screenplay: Xu Shiyan, Liu Lin. Cinematography: Chen Chang'an. Art Direction: Li Junjie. Music: Chen Shouqian. Sound: Li Zhenduo. Cast: Li Baotian as Song Fuwang, Zhang Anli as Tian Hongxia, Zhan Jinbo as Wu Wencai, Song Yuxiang as Shi Liu

Song Fuwang is known through his country as its most prosperous person. One day, he makes a casual remark that everyone misunderstands, thinking Song will donate the funds to open and operate a "happy daycare center." An inspection team schedules a visit to see the new center, and he has to borrow some ele-mentary school students, a teacher and desks to please the team. This makes everybody look down upon him. Song Fuwang decides to regain his lost respect, so he really invests in a "happy daycare center." His entire family supports this action on his part, and is gradually understood by the rest of the villagers.

510. *Don't Cry, Mom (Bie Ku, Ma Ma)*

1990. Children's Film Studio. Color. 10 Reels. Wide Screen. Direction: Zhang Yuqiang. Screenplay: Yu Qiang, Wan Fang, Cheng Shijian. Cinematography: Sun Yongtian. Art Direction: Lin Chaoxiang. Music: Guan Xia. Sound: Zhen Chunyu. Cast: Tian Ye as Tongtong, Zhang Yan as Mom, Yu Shaokang as Grandpa Ma, Dong Ziwu as Father, Liu Zifeng as Lao Lin

Tongtong is a clever and sensible nine-year-old boy, but unlike most of his friends, his family life is unhappy. His parents are divorced, and his mother has become schizophrenic. This heavy burden casts a shadow over his life, but he carries on bravely. He cares for his mother with a selfless love and the support of their neighbors. Tongtong becomes a man in the face of hardship.

511. *Don't Disturb (Qing Wu Da Lao)*

1992. Inner Mongolia Film Studio. Color. Letterboxed. 9 Reels. Direction: Wang Fengkui. Screenplay: Zhang Guanglie. Cinematography: Gao Hongbao. Art Direction: Yi Zhenzhou. Music: Yu Baoshan. Sound: Wang Fuzhu. Costume: Cui Xiaohong. Makeup: Dong Weidong. Cast: Lu Liang as Fei Xiang, Song Yining as Can Dandan, Zhong Xinghuo as Fei's father

Nurse Can Dandan and her elementary school teacher husband Fei Xiang have a happy married life, although they are forced to share small, crowded living quarters with his parents. So to celebrate their fifth anniversary, Fei arranges for them to spend the night in a good hotel. Beginning with a suspicious hotel security officer who thinks they are an unmarried couple having an illicit rendezvous, the couple's night of romance turns out to be a series of comic interruptions. At last, when a foreign guest at the hotel has a medical emergency, Dandan saves his life. When the grateful hotel manager learns what happened to the couple that evening, he offers them a five night stay at the hotel.

512. *Don't Forget Me (Wu Wang Wo)*

1982. Changchun Film Studio. Color. 10 Reels. Direction: Yu Yanfu. Screenplay: Lu Qi, Liu Changyuan. Cinematography: Xu Shouzen. Art Direction: Huang Zhaohui. Music: Wu Damin. Sound: Kang Ruixin. Cast: Fang Shu as Wenwen, Li Zhiyu as Zhou Hong

In the early 1970s, Wenwen, a young city girl working in the countryside, has just lost her father. She goes to the provincial capital to claim his ashes, and on the way back is assaulted and beaten by some local thugs. With so many bad things happening to her, Wenwen loses all confidence and will to live. Fortunately, a middle-aged village doctor named Zhou Hong saves her life and nurses her back to health. After she recovers, Zhou Hong begins tutoring her and tells her of his own Cultural Revolution experience: the doctor was falsely accused of being a "rightist" for writing a book about health care in the north China countryside. Wenwen is very sympathetic with his bad experience. After the Gang of Four is defeated, Zhou encourages Wenwen to take college entrance exams, and she is admitted to a very good university. Wenwen then learns that Zhou's unfortunate life experiences prevented him from ever marrying. Wenwen tells him she loves him, but this makes the doctor uneasy, because he feels the age gap between them is too great, and believes his unfortunate past may affect the young girl's future. Wenwen boards the train for college. She looks out the window and knows she will miss this period of her life and him.

513. *Don't Forget That Time (Mou Wang Nei Duan Qing)*

1994. Guangxi Film Studio. Color. Letterboxed. 9 Reels. Direction: Lu Jianhua, Yu Zhongxiao. Screenplay: Xiao Yixian, Mou Jiaming. Cinematography: Xu Zengshou, Hu Xiaoping. Art Direction: Hua Ting. Music: Wu Daming, Wu Chaofan. Sound: Dong Baosheng. Costume: Qi Chunzhi. Makeup: Gan Jun. Cast: Guo Yuntai as Zhao Laohan, Lu Xiaohe as Zhao Yuxiang, Liu Lili as Da Feng, He Wei as Zhao Yufu, Wang Yuanqin as Erlan, Tian Ming as Aijuan, Chen Peng as Xin Shun, Li Shusheng as Tian Ming, Zhao Kuier as Du Zhi

During wartime, Old Zhao saved the life of a soldier named Feng, although he sacrificed his own son in doing so. Now, years later, Feng is still very close to Zhao's family, having been married to the older man's late daughter at one time. Now, remarried, and the local prefecture leader, Feng supports the building of a new insecticide plant. When the company's product fails to receive a license, Feng's wife accepts a bribe, and Feng lets the product go to market anyway. Zhao always defends Feng, and looks upon him as his second son. But when the defective insecticide brings disastrous economic losses to Zhao's village, he breaks off with Feng for good.

514. *Dragged In (Luo Shui Ji)*

1956. Shanghai Film Studio. B & W. 8 Reels. Direction: Zhou Feng. Screenplay: Li Tianji. Cinematography: Yao Meisheng, Ju Wei. Art Direction: Ge Xinger, Music: Jiang Yulin, Sound: Liu Guangjie, Cast: Zhang Qian as Tang Jin, Yang Hua as Zhang Shunfa, Bao Qi as Yao Yueyin, Liu Jie as Gu Azhu, Cui Wenshun as Chen Youbing, Liu Cang as Azhong

Tang Jin, a young member of the Guangming agricultural cooperative, loves to dress up. His fondest dream is to own a watch. This makes him an easy mark for wealthy farmer Zhang Shunfa. Zhang Shunfa pretends to be Tang Jin's uncle — the Guangming co-op's director Chen Youbing, and gets Tang Jin involved in cabbage speculation. They convince a member of the Red Flag co-op across the river, Yao Yueyin, and as a symbol of good will they sell her some cabbages at a very low price. Yao later sends over to Guangming three boatloads of cabbages as a symbol of her support for the other co-op. She also decides this would be a good opportunity to visit Guangming and learn its advanced pork-raising methods. When she arrives, she happens to run into Zhang Shunfa and Tang Jin. As Zhang Shunfa babbles about his great accomplishments as co-op director, the real director Chen Youbing arrives, and Zhang's pretense and speculating activities are immediately brought to light. Tang Jin is so embarrassed and regretful at having been taken in by Zhang that he smashes the cheap watch Zhang Shunfa had sent him.

515. *Dragon and Snake Battle for Dominance (Long She Zheng Ba)*

1990. Chinese Film Company & Hong Kong Changhe Film Company Co-Production. Color. Wide Screen. 9 Reels. Direction: Wu Yusheng, Wu Ma. Screenplay: Zhang Che. Cinematography:

Cao Huiqi, Er Dongsheng. Music: Huang Dian. Cast: Li Xiuqi as A Xiu, Chen Guantai as A Tai, Jiang Dawei as A Wei, Wu Ma as Ma Gong

Company manager Cao Laoda was once an underworld figure. Now he has gone straight, and raises his three adopted sons A Xiu, A Wei and A Tai to be law-abiding citizens. When someone kills their father, the three vow to avenge him regardless of the consequences. At last, the other two find that A Tai had actually planned the killing to gain his inheritance early. They fulfill their vow and kill A Tai.

516. *Dragon Beard Ditch (Long Xu Gou)*

1952. Beijing Film Studio. B&W. 11 Reels. Direction: Xian Qun. Screenplay: Xian Qun, adapted from the stage play by Lao She (1899-1966). Cinematography: Gao Hongtao. Set Design: Yu Yiru. Music: Su Min and Zhu Jianer. Sound: Chen Yanxi. Makeup: Sun Kuihong. Cast: Yu Shizhi as Cheng Baoqing ("Crazy Cheng"), Yu Lan as Mrs. Cheng, Zhang Fa as Ding Shi, Ye Zi as Sister Ding Shi, Liu Jie as Er Chun, Li Pin as Auntie Wang, Chen Shiwen as Little Girl

In the late 1940s, the people living in a squalid Beijing neighborhood called Dragon Beard Ditch lead a miserable existence. Their suffering stems from predatory gangs, persecution by the Nationalist government, and the bad environment of the polluted and odorous ditch. One of these unfortunates is Cheng Baoqing, a professional musician forced to flee to the area after having been severely beaten by a local gangster displeased with his performance. Cheng now earns his living operating a cigarette vending business with his wife. However, another gangster robs them of all their inventory. Another who suffers from the gangs is Ding Shi, who runs a bicycle repair service. Only Zhao, a neighborhood contractor, tries to stand up to the gangs, but he is ineffective. Their sufferings peak when Ding Shi's little daughter, a favorite of all the neighborhood people, falls in the polluted ditch and drowns. After Liberation, the People's Government arrests the gangsters and puts them on public trial. The Ditch is cleaned up, and the residents living along it have the promise of a better future.

517. *Dragon Chronicles, Part 1: Semi-Gods and Semi-Devils*

(Tian Long Ba Bu, Tian Shan Zhi Tong Lao)

1994. Shanghai Film Studio, Hong Kong Yongsheng Film Corp. Ltd. Co-Production. Color. Letterboxed. 10 Reels. Direction: Qian Yongqiang. Screenplay: Zhang Tan. Cinematography: Pan Hengsheng. Art Direction: Huang Ruimin, Guo Dongchang. Music: Lin Haiyi. Costume: Fang Ying. Cast: Lin Qingxia (Brigitte Lin) as Li Qiushui and Li Canghai, Gong Li as Wu Xingyun, Zhang Min (Cheung Man) as A Jin, Lin Wenlong as Xu Ju

Based on a story by Jin Yong. A supernatural action film set in the early 17th Century. Twin sisters Li Qiushui and Wu Xingyun were once very close, but become bitter enemies after falling for the same man. They fight. Also involved is a search for a magic scroll inscribed with kung fu secrets. In the end Wu Xingyun wins the battle for the man, but finds she cannot love anymore.

518. *Dragon of the Dragons (Long Zhong Long)*

1992. Pearl River Film Studio. Color. 70mm. 9 Reels. Direction: Gang Yi, Li Yaoguang. Screenplay: Deng Yuan, Li Yaoguang. Cinematography: Gang Yi. Art Direction: Zhou Weigong, Zhang Kai. Music: Zhang Xiaoming. Sound: Wu Hongtao. Costume: Liu Jian, Li Yuchang. Makeup: Gang Jian, Sun Bing. Cast: Mi Xuedong as Long Zhonglong, Xin Ying as Su Yun, Lu Yi as Long Anhai, Chen Liming as Madam Meizi

In 1915, revolutionary Long Anhai is on a mission to transport gold to the revolutionary army. Realizing his life is in danger, he asks his brother Long Zhonglong ("Dragon of Dragons") to complete the mission should anything happen to Anhai. When Anhai is murdered, Zhonglong sets out to complete the task, against Su Yun, a girl trained as an assassin by the Japanese. At last, Zhonglong turns Su Yun to his side, and together they kill the agents controlling the girl. Long Zhonglong continues on his dead brother's mission.

519. *Dragon Snakes of the Bund (Wai Tan Long She)*

1990. Changchun Film Studio. Color. Wide Screen. 10 Reels. Direction: Xue Yandong. Screenplay: Zhao Junmei, Li Yuchun. Cinematography: Yu Bing. Art Direction: Ju Lutian, Liu Hong. Music: Chen Shouqian. Sound: Liu

Jingui, Sheng Hongtao. Cast: Liu Weihua as You Tianhong, You Tianlang, Tian Chun as You Tianyun

In Shanghai in the late 1920s, triad head Bi Shixiao has silk plant owner You Xiang murdered so the triad can take over the plant. Later, You's son Tianlang returns to Shanghai from abroad to avenge his father, but the triad kills him first. You Xiang's adopted son Tianyun at last succeeds at killing the triad boss, but is upset when he finds that Bi was his biological father. To atone for his action, he decides to restore his father's gang to its former power. The other triads eventually kill him in the resulting gang war.

Dragon Year Cops see *Police in the Year of the Dragon*

520. *Dragons and Kites (Shen Feng Wei Long)*

1988. Xi'an Film Studio. Color. 10 Reels. Letterboxed. Direction: Zhang Zi'en. Screenplay: Han Zhongliang, Zhang Hongwei, Zhang Zi'en. Cinematography: Gan Quan. Art Direction: Yan Pingxiao. Music: Xu Youfu. Sound: Gu Changning. Cast: Chen Hong as Wang Minyue, Sun Song as Du Xichun, Li Nong as Chao Ran, Guo Jinghua as Min Desheng, Gao Baobao as Hong Suqing

During a Year of the Dragon in the 1930s, Wei County is under Japanese occupation. As the Japanese emperor's birthday approaches, a Japanese general interested in Chinese culture visits some Chinese folk artists. His aim is to find some outstanding local artworks to send as tributes to the emperor. He is particularly impressed with the work of one young unmarried couple who specialize in kite-making and embroidery. The general is unaware that traditional dragon dancing and kite flying are ways in which folk artists express their contempt for the Japanese. On New Year's Eve, the couple's preparations for the holiday are interrupted by the arrival of Chinese "puppet" soldiers with orders they make the dragon for a traditional dance to be performed on the emperor's birthday. The unwelcome assignment gives the artists an idea, and they devise a strategy to fight back through a complicated dragon dance.

521. *Dragons Leap Out of the Sea (Long Chu Hai)*

1992. Pearl River Film Studio. Color. Letter-boxed. 9 Reels. Direction: Zhang Liang. Screenplay: Wang Jingzhu, Zhang Liang. Cinematography: Wang Shuiguang. Art Direction: Guan Yu. Music: Zhen Qiufeng. Sound: Deng Qinghua, Dong Xiaozhi. Costume: Cheng Meizhi. Zhou Jianying. Cast: Liu Yan as Li Jingtian, Dai Yunxia as Ouyang Mei, Wang Jiancheng as Wang Zhiduan, Li Qiang as Cao Xin, Xia Zongyou as Secretary Zhou

Golden Dragon Village in the Pearl River delta has grown prosperous, but neighboring Silver Dragon Village remains in economic stagnation. Ouyang Mei, Silver Village's woman deputy director, is dating Cao Xin, a capable young man "brought in from the outside" (i.e., hired as a consultant) by Golden Dragon. The couple work together to design a new product for Silver Dragon, and this starts that village on the road to prosperity as well. The two villages at last decide to start a joint venture plant to manufacture refrigerators. After Cao Xin and Ouyang Mei are married, each is promoted to the post of chief executive of their respective village's technology development department.

522. *Drawing from the Yellow River (Huang He Fei Du)*

1959. Changchun Film Studio and Inner Mongolia Film Studio Co-Production. Color. 12 Reels. Direction: Liu Guoquan. Screenplay: Gansu Province Stage Drama Troupe Collective, Cinematography: Wang Lei. Art Direction: Liu Xuerao. Music: Lou Zhanghou. Sound: Tong Zongde. Cast: Feng Zhipeng as Wang Kai, Shi Kefu as Kou Jinbiao, Wang Yuanbiao as uncle He, Zhou Lei as Ertuzhi, Cheng Xiaoli as Ding Xiuer, Li Qiyuan as Ding Fugui

In a drought-ridden county in rural Gansu province, town leaders Wang Kai and Kou Jianbiao devise a plan to overcome the problem by drawing on the waters of the Yellow River. It develops that they need the help of the town on the opposite bank, but Ding Fugui, the leader of that town, is unenthusiastic, since his town has no water shortage. But with his daughter's urging, he changes his mind, and involves his entire community in the project, pushing it forward rapidly to a successful conclusion.

523. *The Dream Is Not a Dream (Meng Fei Meng)*

1993. Shanghai Film Studio. Color. Letter-boxed. 10 Reels. Direction: Chen Fan. Screenplay: Wang Zequn. Cinematography: Luo Chongzhou, Lu Junfu. Art Direction: Yao Mingzhong. Music: Chen Gang. Sound: Zhu Weigang, Li Bingkui. Costume: Zuang Peizhen, Xu Laidi. Cast: Qin Yi as Yan Wei, Liu Qiong as hospital director Sha, Du Fan as Yan Wei's mother, Zhen Shuzhi as Sha's wife, An Zhenji as Doctor Wang, Liu Haonan as Xia Ying

The setting is contemporary Shanghai. Xia Ying, daughter of famous opera actress Yan Wei, is suddenly stricken with mental illness and hospitalized. From then on, Yan Wei spends considerable time with her daughter, no matter how busy her own schedule. Hospital director Sha has a mentally ill wife at home, for whom he has cared for more than a decade, so he particularly sympathizes with Yan Wei's situation and with how painful the situation is for the victim's family. When Xia Ying's condition improves, she is allowed to leave the hospital and accompany her mother to visit the new Shanghai City Center. But the girl's condition suddenly deteriorates and she runs away. Her mother and Director Sha search for her everywhere, but cannot find her. Xia Ying makes her way to the roof of a 28-story building…

524. *The Dream of a Fairy (Shen Nu Meng)*

1989. Guangxi Film Studio. Color. 10 Reels. Letterboxed. Direction: Li Xiaolong. Screenplay: Wei Jiejing, Xu Xueda. Cinematography: Liu Baogui. Art Direction: Chen Yaogong, Liu Weixin, Huang Shu. Music: Li Yanlin, Chen Yuanlin. Sound: Liu Baogui. Cast: Cao Zhong as Gu Na, Li Baining as Lun Yan, Ma Yuqiu as mother, Sun Shaowei as Old Guizhu

This film is based on a folk tale of the Zhuang nationality people of Guangxi province. Gu Na, daughter of the King of Feathers, falls in love with Lun Yan, a Zhuang nationality youth. She descends to the human world wearing a gown of feathers. Various plot twists at last lead to she and Lun Yan getting married and spending their wedding night on a huge stone, in accordance with local custom. At daybreak, Lun Yan urges Gu Na to return to heaven, but she insists on staying with him. When the sun comes out, Gu Na, lying in Lun Yan's arms, has been transformed into a cascade of feathers.

525. *Dream of Becoming an Official (Wu Sha Meng)*

1984. Hebei Film Studio. Color. 10 Reels. Direction: Chen Fangqian. Screenplay: Han Weixin, Liu Zhiqin, Zhe Shuzhi, Chen Fangqian. Cinematography: Zhang Qinhua. Art Direction: Li Kangcheng. Music: Li Shitiao, Niu Beng. Sound: Liu Shida. Cast: Li Yongxin as Pan Zicai, Hu Jingying as Yuer, Fan Jianhui as Zhou Yanzhang, Deng Yinhe as the court official

In old China, years of study to become an official have proven fruitless for Pan Zicai. However, he still has hopes of attaining an appointment by getting his beautiful daughter Yuer married to someone with influence. Yuer, however, loves a young man named Zhou Yanzhang. When the son of a county-level official expresses his desire for Yuer, Pan Zicai hires some thugs to abduct Zhou Yanzhang and toss him into a river to get him out of the way once and for all. The young man survives the attempt on his life, however. But when the son of an even higher-ranking official becomes interested in Yuer, Pan cancels the first engagement. An official arrives from the imperial court on a routine inspection visit, and Zhou seizes the opportunity to petition the court concerning the attempt on his life. The court official criticizes Pan and tells him to go home and reflect on his transgressions. His hopes for an official career now shattered forever, Pan Zicai has no choice but to let his daughter marry Zhou Yanzhang as she wishes.

526. *A Dream of Red Mansions (Parts 1–6) (Hong Lou Meng)*

1988 (Parts 1–2) & 1989 (Parts 3–6). Beijing Film Studio. Color. 28 Reels. Direction: Xie Tieli and Zhao Yuan. Screenplay: Xie Tieli and Xie Fengsong, based on the classic Chinese novel by Cao Xueqin (1717–1763). Cinematography: Zhou Jixun (Parts 1–2) and Zou Yuan (Parts 3–6). Art Direction: Chen Yiyun and Yang Zhanjia. Music: Wang Ming. Sound: Liu Shida. Costume: Xia Yayi, Zhao Ruhua, Zhang Xuan, Hong Jun, Liu Huiping, Yu Meixian and Jiang Jingming. Cast: Xia Qin as Jia Baoyu, Tao Huiming as Lin Daiyu, Fu Yiwei as Xue Baochai, Liu Xiaoqing as Wang Xifeng, Lin Muyu as the Dowager, Zhang Jie as Jia Zheng, Li Xiumin as Yuanchun

The decline and fall of the Jia clan, a great family living in the imperial Chinese capital. Jia Zheng and his wife Lady Wang have a daughter, Jia Yuanchun, and a son, Jia Baoyu, the latter said to have been born with a piece of jade in his mouth. Jia Baoyu is handsome and bright, but an indifferent student. Jia Zheng's mother, the Dowager, is very fond of her grandson, although his father is very strict. Jia Baoyu grows up the only boy in a household filled with girls. He likes to play with them, and the servant girls in particular are fond of him.

Lin Daiyu, whose mother is Jia Zheng's sister, is very bright and beautiful, though fragile and in poor health. When her mother dies, she comes to live in her uncle's household. She and Jin Baoyu grow up together, and the two gradually become close friends.

Xue Baochai, whose mother is Lady Wang's sister, is one year older than Jia Baoyu. She is also elegant and educated. Since she has a golden locket which matches Jia Baoyu's jade, everyone believes they are a well-matched couple. But while Jia Baoyu gets along well with Xue Baochai, he does not love her.

The Jian clan's decline is related through a series of scenes which reflect the near-ritualistic manners of the time, such activities as attending a funeral or a bride visiting her parents. True love is ill-fated here: the Dowager contrives for Jia Baoyu to marry Xue Baochai instead of Lin Daiyu, and the latter dies in a fit of jealousy. Jia Baoyu breaks with his family and leaves home to become a monk. The Jia clan's declining fiscal and political status result in a search of their mansions by the authorities and confiscation of their property. Some of the girls die, some are married off, and some become nuns.

Best Director Xie Tieli and Zhao Yuan, 1990 Golden Rooster Awards.

Best Supporting Actress Lin Muyu, 1990 Golden Rooster Awards.

Best Supporting Actress Lin Muyu, 1990 Hundred Flowers Awards.

Best Art Direction Chen Yiyun and Yang Zhanjia, 1990 Golden Rooster Awards.

Best Costume Xia Yayi, Zhao Ruhua, Zhang Xuan, Hong Jun, Liu Huiping, Yu Meixian and Jiang Jingming, 1990 Golden Rooster Awards.

527. Dreamer (Meng Xiang Jia)

1987. Emei Film Studio. Color. 9 Reels. Direction: Chong Lianwen. Screenplay: Zhang Xiaoling. Cinematography: Li Erkang. Art Direction: Guan Xujing. Music: Tao Jiazhou. Sound: She Guli, Shen Jinghua. Cast: Hu Jian as Zhou Dawei, Wan Jun as Tian Xiaohuan, Tao Yuling as Teacher Wang, Chen Damin as Teacher Tang

In an elementary school in a certain city, second grade pupil Zhou Dawei does not do well in school. His father's philosophy of child-raising is to spare the rod and spoil the child. Another student, Tian Xiaohuan, is spoiled rotten by his grandmother. Dawei and Xiaohuan decide to do their best to be good students, but no one else recognizes their efforts. The situation in class makes Teacher Wang do some serious thinking, and he helps Teacher Tang alter her methods of dealing with these children, letting the pupils speak out about their hopes and dreams, and so build their confidence in life and learning.

528. The Dreaming Age (Duo Meng Shi Jie)

1988. Children's Film Studio. Color. 9 Reels. Direction: Lin Hongtong, Huang Xiaomo. Screenplay: Shi Tiesheng, Lin Hongtong. Cinematography: Sun Yongtian. Art Direction: Chen Zhuo. Music: Zhang Qianyi. Sound: Wu Ling. Cast: Wang Chunzhi as Luo Fei, Lou Jicheng as Father, Zhang Weixin as Mother

Luo Fei is a middle-school student of good character, but a girl who tends to daydream. She comes from a very close family, which includes her father, mother and grandmother. One day, their tranquil existence is disrupted by the arrival of Hua Guang, a cellist and her mother's old boyfriend. Luo works hard to restore her parents' loving relationship. The family becomes harmonious once again, but there are still many things that she can't understand, so she continues to daydream. Her parents say it is because she is at the dreaming age.

529. Drizzle in a Small Town (Xiao Cheng Xi Yu)

1983. Henan Film Studio. Color. 9 Reels. Direction: Jiang Shixiong. Screenplay: Tian Feng. Cinematography: Lu Zhenrong. Art Direction: Zhou Dengfu. Music: Tian Feng, Ma Jinggui. Sound: Lan Fuan. Cast: Han Guiju as Dai Yingtian, Zhang Xiaozhong as Shen Zhiliang, Liao Xueqiu as Shen Xiang

After Dai Yingtian loses her husband, she vows never to remarry unless her son and her mother-in-law can continue living with her. She meets and falls in love with Shen Zhiliang, a technician in her factory, but his sister and mother are adamantly opposed to the living arrangement Dai Yingtian wants. Shen has the courage to go against tradition, and at last he and Dai get together.

530. *Drowning (Yan Mo De Qing Chun) (alternate title: Yu Hai Wu Qing)*

1994. Shanghai Film Studio & Hainan Shifei Company Co-Production. Color. Letterboxed. 9 Reels. Direction: Hu Xueyang. Screenplay: Fang Jiajun, Xu Zhengqin. Cinematography: Hua Qin. Art Direction: Shen Lide. Sound: Ni Zheng. Costume: Zhao Baodi. Makeup: Zhu Peizhen. Cast: Sharen Gaowa as Mrs. Ou, Hu Xueyang as Luo Xiaoxu, Yu Luosheng as Mr. Ou, Yang Min as Brother, Yang Xiaowen as A Qin, Tan Tian as Mr. Tao

531. *Drug Enforcement Agents (Meng Jing Wei Long La Jiao Mei)*

1993. Beijing Film Studio, Beihai Siwei Culture Film and TV Corp. Ltd. Co-Production. Color. Letterboxed. 10 Reels. Direction: Xu Qingdong. Screenplay: Ma Junxiang, Chen Ming, Xu Qingdong. Cinematography: Hua Qin. Art Direction: Song Jun. Music: Gao Erdi. Sound: Liu Xiaodong. Costume: Dong Juying, Li Fengju. Makeup: Fan Qingshan. Cast: Zhao Liping as Li Huahua, Lu Jianmin as Wei Long, Shen Junyi as Liu Feng, Jia Ni as Li Nannan, Li Ping as Nina, Ren Zhigang as Ya Lun, Jiang Boping as Li Zheng, Dai Tongkun as Zhang Lan, Zhou Jingbo as Xiao Zhou

When drug dealers abduct Li Huahua, girl friend of narcotics agent Wei Long, they inject her with drugs then rape her. Wei Long rescues her before her attackers kill her, but he later misunderstands her entering drug treatment, and the couple break up. Five years later, Li Huahua is working in her father's factory. A man named Liu Feng gets a job in the plant, but is actually there to build up drug traffic among plant workers. When Li's father happens upon a drug deal in progress, Liu Feng kills him. Li Huahua finally realizes that Liu is one of the men who raped her five years before, she and her fellow employees help Wei Long battle the drug dealers in their midst, at last killing Liu Feng. Li Huahua and Wei Long get together again.

532. *The Drum Singers (Gu Shu Yi Ren)*

1987. Beijing Film Studio. Color. 11 Reels.

Direction: Tian Zhuangzhuang. Screenplay: Tian Zhuangzhuang, based on the novel of the same title by Lao She (1899–1966). Cinematography: Liang Zhiyong. Art Direction: Ning Lanxin. Music: Dai Yisheng. Sound: Wu Ling. Cast: Li Xuejian as Fang Baoqing, Tan Mindi as Xiu Lian, Chen Qin as Da Feng, Zhu Xu as Baosheng, Yang Haiying as Zhang Wen, Mo Qi as Meng Liang

Fang Baoqing, a street musician, escapes to Chongqing from Beiping (now Beijing) after the Japanese invasion. There he meets up with the Tang family and they start performing in the street as a team. Their make-shift stages are destroyed in an air raid so Fang opens a tea house where he performs while selling tea. A Commander-in-Chief Wang gets acquainted with Xiulian, Fang's adopted daughter, who is quite beautiful and wants to take her as a concubine. Fang is pushed to the limit by Wang and finally challenges him to a fight. Not long after, Fang's brother is killed in an air raid and his first daughter is deserted by her husband. Heartbroken, Fang spends a lot of time at his brother's grave. Xiulian grows up to be a bright and lovely young lady, dearly loved by her father. He sends Xiulian to school but she is rejected by the children of rich families. Fang hires a man named Zhang Wen as a bodyguard to look after Xiulian, but Zhang turns out to be a hypocrite and rapes her. Misfortune dominates Fang Baoqing's life. After the war against the Japanese, Fang bids his brother's grave farewell then boards a ship carrying himself and his family far away.

533. *Drumbeats in the Dark Forest (Hei Lin Gu Sheng)*

1985. Pearl River Film Studio. Color. Wide Screen. 9 Reels. Direction: Chen Ying. Screenplay: Wang Jing. Cinematography: Li Zhexian. Art Direction: Huang Tongrong. Music: Zhang Jun. Sound: Lu Minyi. Cast: Guo Jianguo as Zhageli, Cao Lu as Guolong, Liu Long as Wo Guli, Yang Xiuzhang as Du Ba, Zhang Xiaoling as Lanna, Cui Minli as Yemu

In early 1950, the Hani nationality people living on Yunnan's Wanni Mountain are liberated. Bandits who prey upon the people from their forest hideout try to break out. They engage in a decisive battle with the peaceful Wanni people and the "Red Chinese." Local militia leader Zhageli responds to a call from PLA platoon leader Xiao and leaves his wife and young son to go fight the bandits. He devises a plan to lure the remaining bandits out of the forest and into a trap. The film tells how eventually all of the bandits are caught by the PLA with the support of local people.

534. *The Drummer from Flame Mountain (Huo Yan Shan Lai De Gu Shou)*

1991. Children's Film Studio. Color. 9 Reels. Direction: Guang Chunlan. Screenplay: Ma Yan, Guang Chunlan. Cinematography: Qi Xing. Art Direction: Zhang Xiaochun. Music: Yikemu. Sound: Gu Jun. Costume: Tong Xiuhua. Makeup: Xiang Hong. Cast: Kuer Banjiang as Kulaixi, Ayi Nula as Xilin Nayi, Hanakezi as Lalaguli, Zhyinuer as Mayila, Gulisitan as Nana, Xiaogaiti as Mijiti

In a small village on the vast Gobi desert of West China lives a boy called Kulaixi. He is a drummer. His late mother had been an excellent dancer, and since her death he has lived with his grandparents in the village. One day, the "Little Moon" Children's Art Ensemble comes from the provincial capital to give a performance in the village. The troupe auditions village children, and its leaders are very impressed with Kulaixi's skills with the tambourine. The young woman leader of the troupe, Xilin Nayi, arranges for Kulaixi to join the ensemble, and to stay with her family after the troupe returns to the capital. Her stepfather turns out to be Kulaixi's real father. Xilin Nayi tries to keep the fact that Kulaixi is her elder brother separate from their work in the ensemble, but their close relationship and his obvious talent incur the other children's jealousy. Misunderstandings result, but eventually love and understanding prevail.

Best Children's Film Award, 42th Berlin International Film Festival.

535. *Drunkard Zhang San (Zui Gui Zhang San)*

1990. Youth Film Studio & Hong Kong Qimin Company Ltd. Co-Production. Color. Wide Screen. 9 Reels. Direction: Dai Baoshan. Screenplay: Zhang Baorui. Cinematography: Geritu. Art Direction: Ma Yingbo. Music: Ma Ding. Sound: Guan Shuxin. Cast: Xu Lingwei as Zhang San, Zhang Guoqiang as Wang Wu

Near the end of the Qing dynasty, a reform movement fails, and six reformers are executed in Beijing. Two heroes named Zhang San and Wang Wu devote themselves to helping rela-

tives of the executed men escape, which results in the Qing army chasing them as well. Zhang San is rescued by a young woman, who turns out to be Wang Liyuan, the fiancee he has never seen. When the expeditionary force of the eight Great Powers invades China to put down the Boxer Rebellion, Zhang and his fiancee ally themselves with the Boxers to oppose the invaders. They win a major battle, and the couple find they really love each other.

536. *Du Juan's Voice (Du Juan Sheng Sheng)*

1983. Guangxi Film Studio. Color. 10 Reels. Direction: Xu Sulin, Zhang Xiufang. Screenplay: Zhu Xumin. Cinematography: Gu Wunhou. Art Direction: Lao Guanneng. Music: Li Yanlin. Sound: Li Zhuwen. Cast: Liu Dong as Du Juan, Li Shaodan as Lu Chunyang, Xu Bu as Du Qiong, Liang Min as Mother, Zhang Xiaomin as Da Huan, Wu Baolin as Du Dexian

After Du Juan graduates from college in 1930, she returns with her mother to their home town in Guozhou County. Du Juan has been very confused and upset by the recent breakup of the Nationalist-Communist alliance. Her old friend Lu Chunyang, now a member of the Communist Party, returns to Guozhou to organize a Red Guard force, and Du Juan, fired with revolutionary enthusiasm, volunteers to assist him. She takes advantage of her father's position as county administrator to feed intelligence information to the Red Guard. During their revolutionary work together, Du Juan and Lu Chunyang fall in love. When he is killed by government agents, Du Juan leaves home to travel to a Communist-held area and carry on his work.

537. *Du Shiniang (Du Shi Niang)*

1981. Changchun Film Studio. Color. 13 Reels. Direction: Zhou Mao. Screenplay: Zhou Mao, Zhao Menghui. Cinematography: Wang Jishun. Art Direction: Wang Xingwen. Music: Huang Zhun, Lu Qimin. Sound: Wang Jishun. Cast: Pan Hong as Du Shiniang, Tong Ruiming as Li Jia, Lou Jicheng as Sun Fu, Jin Yaqing as the prostitute, Wu Cihua as Liu Yuchun

During the Ming dynasty, Du Shiniang is a well-known Beijing courtesan. Sold into prostitution as a girl, she has suffered humiliation and lack of respect for eight years while being a money machine for a brothel keeper. Although many men are crazy about her, true love is hard to find for one in her status. Young scholar Li Jia falls in love with Du Shiniang but he lacks the money to buy her out. His sincerity so impresses Du Shiniang that she herself gives him the money to pay off the brothel. The couple are married, and for the first time Du Shiniang experiences the pride and respect that comes with being the wife of a man with position. After the wedding, the couple leaves by boat for his family home in the south, but as they get close to Li's hometown he starts to become uneasy about the upcoming meeting with his family, for he knows they will be angry about his marriage. On the boat, Li Jia meets wealthy businessman Sun Fu, who greatly admires Du Shiniang's beauty. Wanting her for himself, Sun talks Li Jia out of having a serious relationship with a former prostitute, and bringing her home. They make a deal in which Li Jia sells Du Shiniang to Sun Fu for a thousand dollars. When Du Shiniang learns Li Jia has betrayed her, she loses all hope in life. Opening a chest she always has with her, she shows Li Jia that it is full of treasure. She jumps into the river with the treasure chest.

538. *Dumb Manager (Sha Mao Jing Li)*

1988. Shenzhen Film Studio. Color. 9 Reels. Direction: Duan Jishun. Screenplay: Wang Peigong. Cinematography: Xing Eryou. Art Direction: Liu Sheng. Music: Mao Shan. Sound: Fu Xu, Yu Xiaoli. Cast: Chen Qiang as Kuishu, Song Dandan as Yingzhi, Chen Peisi as Erzhi, Feng Yuanzheng as Magan, Song Xiaoying as the woman manager

Erzhi, manager of the Bijimei Hotel, recruits a bright group of young people to work for him, but he finds the woman manager of the nearby Jiuxiang Hotel is a tough competitor. In addition to being a poor manager, Erzhi loses business through his refusal to allow any of the hotel guests to engage in shady business dealings on the premises. He also has political problems with his neighborhood committee.

539. *Eagles Brave the Storm (Bao Feng Yu Zhong De Xiong Ying)*

1957. Changchun Film Studio. B & W. 11 Reels. Direction: Wang Yi. Screenplay: Shi Lu. Cinematography: Bao Jie. Art Direction: Wang Guizhi. Music: Xu Huicai. Sound: Lin Bingcheng. Cast: Bai Dezhang as Political Instructor

Liu, Sun Yu as Huo Wa, Liang Yin as Zhang Dashun, Song Baoyi as Zhou Heidan, Huo Deji as Xiao Wu, Jin Yan as Old Baer

In 1936, on the Long March, some Red Army soldiers fall behind and are captured by troops of warlord Ma Bufang. Some of the Red soldiers evade capture and are sheltered by an elderly Tibetan huntsman, Old Baer. But some in Old Baer's tribe want to turn the Red soldiers over to Ma Bufang's troops. The tribe headman sides with them, and the fugitive soldiers are ordered to leave. Just then an enemy patrol comes to search for the Red soldiers, and are killed by the Reds with the help of Old Baer. In retaliation, Ma's troops take several Tibetans prisoner, including Old Baer's son. The tribe blames Old Baer for its troubles. In order to get the tribe out of trouble, Political Instructor Liu and Huo Wa offer to exchange themselves for the Tibetans. The headman is deeply moved by this, and goes himself to negotiate with Ma, but he is so poorly treated that he decides his people should side with the Red Army. Led by Political Instructor Liu, Huo Wa and Zhang Dashun sneak into the enemy camp and free the Tibetan prisoners. But Ma Bufang's army surrounds the Tibetan camp and demands the Red soldiers surrender. The Tibetans and Red soldiers ally to resist, but are hopelessly outmanned and outgunned. The Red soldiers are all killed covering the Tibetans' safe withdrawal.

540. *Early Spring (Chu Chun)*

1982. Changchun Film Studio. Color. 10 Reels. Direction: Lu Shaolian. Screenplay: Cui Jingyuan. Cinematography: Meng Xiandi. Art Direction: Liu Xuerao. Music: Cui Shanmin. Sound: Liu Jingui. Cast: Li Dongfan as Jiang Zheyu, Gao Songji as Yushun, Li Yonggeng as Li Guinan, Xu Gaoji as Old Pu, Jiang Hengmo as Wanfu, Fang Meishan as Ji Shun

After the 3rd Plenary Session of the 11th Party Congress, Jiang Zeyu is pardoned and allowed to return to his hometown and his old job at the Nandaoguo plant. Several years before, Jiang had been falsely accused by Li Guinan, a man who seized power during the Cultural Revolution, and still follows the line of the Gang of Four. When Jiang Zeyu is elected production unit chief by his co-workers, Li refuses to relinquish power. Li goes to commune secretary Pu, an elderly man who does not understand the Party's new spirit, and accuses Jiang of wanting the job in order to

Early Spring in February. Tao Lan (Xie Fang) at last comes to understand her ex-lover's devotion to helping others. 1963. Beijing Film Studio.

engage in individual production to personal gain. Jiang also suffers from the rumors about his relationship with a woman worker named Yushun. Life at Nandaoguo is not easy. At last the secretary sees his mistakes, self-criticizes himself, and announces the county committee's decision to investigate Li Guinan for alleged crimes, including rape. Nandaoguo becomes prosperous.

541. *Early Spring in February (aka Early Spring) (Zao Chun Er Yue)*

1963. Beijing Film Studio. Color. 11 Reels. Direction: Xie Tieli. Screenplay: Xie Tieli, based on the novel "February," by Rou Shi. Cinematography: Li Wenhua. Art Direction: Ci Ning, Xiao Bing. Music: Jiang Dingxian. Sound: Fu Yingjie. Cast: Sun Daolin as Xiao Jianqiu, Xie Fang as Tao Lan, Shangguan Yunzhu as Mrs. Wen, Gao

Bo as Tao Mukan, Fan Xuepeng as Tao's mother, Wang Pei as Qian Zhengxing

In the mid–1920s, Xiao Jianqiu, a young teacher whose life has been disrupted by the chaotic conditions in China, takes a teaching job at a high school in Eastern Zhejiang province. He meets and is very sympathetic to Mrs. Wen, a poor widow in the town, tries to assist her financially. He also lets Mrs. Wen's little daughter attend the school for free, and escorts the little girl to and from school every day. Meanwhile, he also falls in love with a landlord's daughter, Miss Tao Lan. When Mrs. Wen's small son dies, Xiao decides to marry her out of sympathy, and decides to sacrifice his love for Tao Lan. His actions are strongly criticized and attacked by local people. The criticism so humiliates Mrs. Wen that she commits suicide by drowning herself. This shocks Xiao Jianqiu into some agonizing thought about the situation. He writes a farewell letter to Tao Lan, and leaves the town to devote himself to the social and political struggles going on in China. His letter deeply moves Tao Lan, and she rushes to follow him.

542. *Early Spring on China's South Border (Nan Jiang Zhao Chun)*

1978. Beijing Film Studio. Color. 10 Reels. Direction: Guo Jun, Xiao Lang. Screenplay: Zhu Xumin. Cinematography: Li Chengsheng. Art Direction: Tu Juhua. Music: Li Yanlin. Sound: Wang Zemin. Cast: Zhang Liwei as Chun Tao, Cui Hua as Fang Hua, Xu Xiaoyuan as Lu Yuan, Wang Limin as Ya Mang, Yang Hailian as Dafeng, Chou Hongwen as Yunshan, Zhao Chuan as Huang Deng

Under the control of its deputy director Huang Deng, Nanling Commune's farm machinery station is turned into a transportation station. Commune committee secretary Chun Tao requests an opinion on this from the local Party authorities, and when the commune's Party secretary investigates, he agrees that the machinery is not being used sufficiently for farming. Frightened, Huang Deng persuades county deputy secretary Lu Yuan to help in a coverup. Chun Tao realizes what is going on, and exposes Huang Deng's crime. With Huang replaced, agricultural production goes on with appropriate use of mechanization.

543. *Earth from Home (Lao Niang Tu)*

1992. Emei Film Studio. Color. Letterboxed. 10 Reels. Direction: Wang Jixing. Screenplay: Ji

***Earth from Home.* 1992. Emei Film Studio.**

Wen. Cinematography: Qiang Jun. Art Direction: Cheng Jinyong. Music: Zhao Jiping. Sound: Wang Guangzhong. Costume: Feng Guilan. Makeup: Xiao Guiyuan, He Yi. Cast: Hu Yajie as Zhiguo, Zhao Erkang as Lao Hei, Zhu Yanping as Big Wang, Dong Jie as Zhiguo (as a child), Geng Ge as Auntie Mei

A baby boy is found lying next to his mother's dead body. The infant is adopted and raised by a local couple, and grows up bright and diligent. The boy, named Zhiguo, gains entrance to the county high school by making excellent grades, and in time he becomes the commune's Party Secretary. He moves up steadily, and in the 1980s is named administrator of the area in which he was born. He always battles for the rights of the poor, and when there is a chance to get the railway run through their area, he even moves his nameless mother's tomb to help the cause. His unselfish actions move people deeply, and when he is at last promoted to administrator of a larger county, all the people of his area flock to bid him farewell.

544. *Earthquake (Zhen)*

1977, Unreleased. August First Film Studio.

B & W. 10 Reels. Direction: Shi Wenzhi. Screenplay: Shi Chao, Li Bai, Sang Ping, Zhang Yisheng. Cinematography: Chen Jun, Yin Qiaofang. Art Direction: Kou Honglie. Music: Ding Ping, Zhang Rui. Sound: Li Yan. Principal Cast: Li Changhua, Jiang Zeshan, Li Yan, Gao Baocheng, Wang Xiaotang, Ji Xiangrong, Li Tingxou

After a massive earthquake hits an industrial city, cadres, people and the PLA pull together in relief work, despite interference by the "Gang of Four" and their supporters.

545. *Eastward Marching Overture (Dong Jin Xuqu)*

1962. August First Film Studio. B & W. 10 Reels. Direction: Hua Chun. Screenplay: Gu Baozhang and Shuo Yunping, based on the stage play of the same title. Cinematography: Wei Linyue. Art Direction: Xu Run. Music: Shen Yawei and Zhang Mulu. Sound: He Baoding. Cast: Li Yan as Huang Bingguang, Zhang Zhongying as Meng Qiyu, Yu Chunmian as Deng Bing, Wang Linjia as Wang Yong, Zhou Zhengyu as Xu Yingping, Yang Zhaoquan as Xiao Liu

In 1940, on their eastward march to resist the Japanese, a column of the New Fourth

Army finds its progress blocked by Nationalist forces at the town of Qiaotou in northern Jiangsu. When the column's political director Huang Bingguang goes over to negotiate the impasse, he is arrested and detained. Meanwhile, one of the Nationalist companies attacks the Communist column and is totally routed. Zhou Mingzhe, commander of the other Nationalist company, not wanting to have Chinese fighting Chinese, rebels with his unit and allows the Communists' main column to cross the river successfully and continue on its way.

546. *Echo Brother (Yin Sheng A Ge)*

1982. Children's Film Studio. Color. 9 Reels. Direction: Wang Junzheng. Screenplay: Yan Tingting, Wang Junzheng. Cinematography: Ru Shuiren. Art Direction: Hao Jingyuan, Wu Yahua. Music: Wang Ming. Sound: Gui Zhilin. Cast: Ji Chengmu as Jingjing, Le Gang as Dirty Monkey, Li Shijiang as Uncle Meigan, Liu Xiaohua as Mother, Duan Hong as Grandma Mashuang

Jingjing, a six-year-old Beijing boy, arrives in the mysterious Jingpo Mountains with his Uncle Meigan to visit his mother who works there. At first, Jingjing is a very spoiled boy, not used to country life. He is also selfish, refusing to share his toys with other children. After a while, the Jingpo people's unselfish and caring help improves Jingjing: he becomes brave and willingly plays with the other children, sharing food and toys, etc. When the time comes for him to return to Beijing he gives his toys to his new friends and receives gifts from them. Rural living has greatly improved Jingjing.

547. *The Eerduosi Storm (E Er Duo Si Feng Bao)*

1962. August First Film Studio. B & W. 9 Reels. Direction: Hao Guang. Screenplay: Yun Zhaoguang. Cinematography: Kou Jiwen and Liu Ying. Art Direction: Fang Xuzi and Liu Jingsheng. Music: Tong Fu and Li Yaodong. Sound: Li Yan. Cast: Wen Xiying as Wuliji and Aoqier, Chang Wenzhi as Nayintai, Yang Wei as Liu Hongtai, Wang Xiaotang as Wuyunhua, Liu Jiyun as Bayaner, Han Mei as Fujin

In 1916, the governor of Inner Mongolia's Eerduosi prairie and his wife Fujin execute Aqqier, leader of the "Duguilong" farmers' movement. Ten years later, Aoqier's son Wuliji is grown, but is powerless to help when his sister Wuyunhua is forced to become a slave in the governor's household. Later, Wuliji leaves the prairie and meets undercover CPC agent Liu Hongtai. Wuliji returns to the prairie to lead a new "Duguilong" movement. Their inexperience results in initial failures, but afterwards, Wuliji and Liu organize a shepherd army, and through wise tactics seize and occupy the government building.

548. *Effects of Money (Jin Qian Da Lie Bian)*

1988. Changchun Film Studio. Color. 10 Reels. Direction: u Yanfu, Luo Heling. Screenplay: Yang Yingzhang. Cinematography: Wang Jishun. Art Direction: Shi Weijun. Music: Wu Damin. Sound: Tong Zongde. Cast: Tan Tianqian as Wang Xizhong

When honest high school teacher Wang Xizhong moves into his new home, he discovers 1,000 yuan hidden beneath the sofa. Since he plans to marry soon, this discovery excites him quite a bit at first. However, he overcomes the impulse and decides to return the money to its rightful owner. In his search for the money's owner, Wang Xizhong comes in contact with many different people, and a series of strange encounters demonstrate the varieties of people in modern Chinese society.

549. *Effendi II (A Fan Ti Er Shi)*

1991. Tianshan Film Studio. Color. Letterboxed. 9 Reels. Direction: Ye Yigong. Screenplay: Li Hun. Cinematography: Baihaiti and Mulati. Art Direction: Gao Feng. Music: Nusilati and Yikemu. Sound: Mayi Nuer. Cast: Aihemaiti as Malajuding, Tuyigong as Walihan, Guzhalinuer as Mayisha

The story of one of many legendary heroes among the Uighur people of Xinjiang. This one, Maolajuding, tricks corrupt government officials into helping him free his lover from the clutches of an evil landlord.

550. *Egg-Selling Team (Dao Dan Bu Dui)*

1990. Xi'an Film Studio. Color. Wide Screen. 9 Reels. Direction: Ge Xiaoying. Screenplay: Cui Jingsheng. Cinematography: Zhao Haifu. Art Direction: Liu Xinghou. Music: Xu Jingxin. Sound: Hui Dongzhi. Cast: Cai Min as Shuinu, Guo Da as Shuigou, Sun Xiangguang as Loudou

Shuiniu, Shuigou and Loudou are all ambitious young people from the countryside, but their goals vary. Shuiniu, a young woman, wants to assemble a group of young people to start a chicken farm together. Hard-working Loudou also wants to raise chickens, but he wants to do it on his own. Shuigou's principal talent is talking well; he admires Shuiniu's ability, and is convinced his glibness will make him her future husband as well as business partner. Little does he suspect that in spite of their many disagreements about business, Shuiniu and Loudou are in love.

551. *Eight Hundred Arhat (Ba Bai Luo Han)*

1985. Nanhai Film Studio and Hong Kong Crown Company, Ltd. Co-Production. Color. 9 Reels. Direction: Wang Xinglei. Screenplay: Chen Xi. Cinematography: Long Ying. Art Direction: Zhang Guozhen, Zhang Rongfa. Music: Wu Dajiang. Cast: Liu Zhenling as Zhixing, Gao Hongping as Zhao Xiang

In ancient China, the Kingdom of Jin invades, and a boy named Zhixing loses both his parents in the fighting. He is saved by a monk, and raised in the Baoguo Temple atop Mount Emei. Ten years later, he has mastered super martial arts skills. When the Jin attack the temple, Zhixing leads the monks in a counterattack which drive the Jin soldiers off the mountain.

552. *Eight Women's Suicide by Drowning (Ba Nu Tou Jiang)*

1987. August First Film Studio. Color. 10 Reels. Direction: Yang Guangyuan. Screenplay: Li Baolin. Cinematography: Yang Guangyuan, Sang Hua. Art Direction: Chen Bugu. Music: Li Weicai. Sound: Zhen Minzhe. Cast: Zhang Kaili as Leng Yun, Yue Hong as Yang Guizhen, Wang Lanyin as Hu Xiuzhi, Kou Qiaoling as An Shunfu, Chi Sujing as Guo Guiqin, Cai Ying as Wang Huimin

A remake of "Daughters of China" (Northeast Film Studio, 1949).

553. *Electronic Waves Never Disappear (Yong Bu Xiao Shi De Dian Bo)*

1958. August First Film Studio. B & W. 12 Reels. Direction: Wang Ping. Screenplay: Lin Jin. Cinematography: Xue Boqing. Art Direction: Wang Wei. Music: Li Weicai. Sound: He Baoding. Cast: Sun Daolin as Li Xia, Yuan Xia as He Lanfeng, Xing Jitian as Sun Mingren, Huang

Wansu as Bai Lijun, Lu Lizhu as Liu Nina, Wang Xingang as Yao Wei

In 1939, the low point for China in the anti–Japanese War, the central authorities of the Communist Party sends radio station political commissar Li Xia from Yan'an to Shanghai to strengthen the Party's undercover work in Shanghai. As a part of Li Xia's cover, the Shanghai underground branch assigns woman agent He Lanfeng to pretend she is his wife. During their work together, the two fall in love and are later approved as a couple by Party leaders. They start a family and continue their undercover work. When the Pacific war breaks out, Li Xia is arrested by the Japanese Army but released when the Japanese are convinced that he is really an agent for the Nationalist collaborationist government. Li Xia is able to penetrate enemy headquarters and obtains much important information, which he sends to Party headquarters in Yan'an from his underground radio station. But eventually his cover is compromised, and as the enemy searches desperately for Li's underground radio station, the Party orders him to shut down the station and flee Shanghai. But there are two emergency messages that should go out immediately, and Li Xia volunteers to implement this assignment after first assuring that his wife and son are evacuated. Just as he finishes sending the messages, he sees that the enemy has surrounded his house. He calmly sends a final farewell to Yan'an.

554. *Elopement (Si Beng)*

1988. Changchun Film Studio. Color. 10 Reels. Direction: Bei Zhaocheng, Li Geng. Screenplay: Jiao Shiyu. Cinematography: Yang Penghui. Art Direction: Liu Sheng. Music: Lu Yuan, Cheng Kai. Sound: Huang Yongqin. Cast: Cheng Mei as Liu Ye, Yii Ga as Yusheng, Zen Chunhui as Xiao Xue, Huo Qin as Tu Cai

While the policy of opening and reform has brought prosperity to farmers, the feudal practice of arranged marriages still persists. In the village of Taohuagou in the Zhongyuan Mountains, young Shiqiang and his girl Chunyan elope to avoid being forced to marry others; another couple, Yusheng and Xiaoxue elope for much the same reason. The young people's challenge to traditional customs at last liberates the thinking of their elders, and under the leadership of the village government the eloped young couples all return to their hometown. There, the village mayor hosts a joyous collective wedding for them.

555. Embarrassed Husband and Witty Wife (Lang Bei Zhang Fu Qiao Jiao Qi)

1993. Zhejiang Film Studio & Xi'an Film Studio Co-Production. Color. Letterboxed. 9 Reels. Direction: Zhang Zhien. Screenplay: Zhang Zhien, Chen Yutong. Cinematography: Wang Cai. Art Direction: Li Shuqi. Music: Xi Qimin. Sound: Guo Qiang. Costume: Wang Huijuan. Makeup: Zhang Shuguang. Cast: Chang Lantian as the Ph.D., Li Heling as the wife, Wei Yi as the son, Yu Wen as Doctor Zhang, Wei Zhengbai as Reporter Niu

A comedy about a Ph.D. bothered by his wife's shrewish nature. He invents a drug to make her sweet-tempered, but the results are not at all what he hoped for.

556. Embarrassing Man (Xian Shi Huo Bao)

1990. Beijing Film Studio. Color. Wide Screen. 9 Reels. Direction: Duan Jishun. Screenplay: Li Baoyuan, Lian Chunmin. Cinematographer: Gao Lixian. Art Direction: Liu Changbao. Music: Zhao Jiping, Wang Shi. Sound: Zhang Zhizhong. Cast: Shi Guoqing as Mudu, Zhao Bengshan as Bengshan

In a small county in the North China mountains, the "Shanmu Multi-functional Company, Ltd." opens for business, and soon does a bustling trade in giving massages, advising people on the best time to conceive a son, etc., really nothing of consequence. The company is really a sham, just a way to make money, run by a couple of broken-down actors. They leave the village people with nothing but embarrassment.

557. Emergency Alarm 333 (Te Ji Jing Bao 333)

1983. Emei Film Studio. Color. 9 Reels. Direction: Mao Yuqing. Screenplay: Guo Shaogui, Fan Yuan. Cinematography: Xie Erxiang. Art Direction: Lin Qi. Music: Tao Jiazhou. Sound: Shen Guli. Cast: Zhang Xian as Zhen Chi, Zhen Zhaishi as Fang Shengyu, Liu Yu as Yue Guang, Zhu Yanping as Chen Guang, Yang Muqin as Fang Shengyu's wife, Li Enqi as Fang's mother, Wang Yuzhen as Xiu Meizhi, Xia Hui as Deng Xiaoxian

In the summer of 1982, Jialing County is threatened by a massive flood. County Party Secretary Zhen Chi rushes back to the county from a provincial emergency flood control conference. Unfortunately, the flood hits some 10 hours earlier than expected, so the control measures are not in place. The story tells how Zhen Chi, County Administrator Fang Shengyu and PLA Captain Chen Guang organize rescue operations, restore power and help the people overcome panic. When they get the news that the flood will cover the entire county in two hours, they organize an evacuation in which Captain Guang sacrifices himself for the rest.

558. Emergency Brake (Jing Ji Sha Che)

1985. Emei Film Studio. Color. 9 Reels. Direction: Tai Gang. Screenplay: Si Jingyu, Fan Yuan. Cinematography: Hong Wenyuan. Art Direction: Luo Zhicheng. Music: Mu Hong. Sound: Hua Yuezhu. Cast: Cui Zhigang as Guo Yi, Yao Xiaoxia as Liang Xiaojuan, Zhang Danian as Fat Yang, Li Wenbing as Mr. Liang, Ma Weijun as Deputy Team Leader Luo

Liang Xiaojuan, daughter of a mountain region transport station director, has just graduated from medical school. Her fiance Guo Yi is a truck driver working for her father. Her father Mr. Liang clashes frequently with Guo over the younger man's speeding and other unsound driving practices. Xiaojuan's parents dislike her riding with Guo as a result. One day, when Liang Xiaojuan needs transportation to visit patients, she asks Guo to drive her. Unfortunately Guo Yi's truck blows a tire from the truck being overloaded. Another driver, Fat Yang, comes along and Guo lets Xiaojuan ride in Yang's truck. But Yang's attitude toward safety is no better than Guo Yi's: he drinks while he drives. About midnight, Xiaojuan falls asleep. She awakens just as the truck is going over a cliff. Guo Yi, following behind, sees the tragedy but is powerless to help.

559. An Emperor on the Run (Jiang Hu Ba Mian Feng)

1991. Youth Film Studio. Color. Wide Screen. 9 Reels. Direction: Hu Mei. Screenplay: Ni Feng. Cinematography: Sun Cheng. Art Direction: Zhang Zili. Music: Zhang Qianyi. Sound: Guan Shuxin. Costume: Liu Ying, Zhao Hui. Makeup: Wu Guihua. Cast: Che Yue as Zhu Youliang, Cheng Donghai as Zuo Mingyu, Hou Shuang as Hong Sumei, Hou Liansheng as Xia Laohu, Tao Qing as Ma Ying, Zhang Qihong as Hao Mu, Chen Xiaoyi as Long Zhumu, Yan Bide as father Long

In ancient China, the rightful heir to the throne is forced to flee to South China, pursued by troops of a usurper. Those tracking him soon grow in number, including revenge-seekers, bandits who wish to exploit the situation for their own gain, his own followers and minority people who want to help him. A series of fights surrounds the chase.

560. *The Emperor's Shadow (Qin Song)*

1995. Xi'an Film Studio and Hong Kong Ocean Film Co-Production. Color. 116 minutes. Direction: Zhou Xiaowen. Screenplay: Lu Wei. Cinematography: Lu Gengxin. Art Direction: Cao Jiuping. Music: Zhao Jiping. Sound (Dolby SR): Hong Yi. Costume: Tong Huamiao. Cast: Jiang Wen as Ying Zheng, Ge You as Gao Jianli, Xu Qing as Ying Yueyang. Also: Ge Zhijun, Wang Qingxiang, Di Guoqiang, Wang Ning, Shu Yaoxuan, Li Mengnan, Yuan Yuan

Set in the 3rd Century B.C., this is the story of two boys who grow up together. One of them, Ying Zheng, becomes a warrior, a king contending with other kings for ultimate supremacy; his childhood playmate Gao Jianli becomes a talented musician. Ying at last wins out over his rivals and unifies the kingdoms into the Chinese empire, with himself the first emperor of the Qin Dynasty. Gao, a musician in one of the defeated kingdoms, is captured and brought to the new emperor, who asks Gao to compose an anthem for the new dynasty. Gao refuses and starts a hunger strike. Ying Zheng's daughter tells her father she can convince Gao to write the anthem, in return for which the musician will become her "shadow," in effect her personal pet. Yueyang's obvious interest in the musician stirs the jealousy of one of the emperor's top generals, who expects Yueyang as his eventual prize for military success. A battle of wits ensues, as Gao avoids bending to Yueyang's will while frustrating the emperor by refusing to accede to his demand.

561. *Employee Representative (Zhi Gong Dai Biao)*

1983. Tianjin Film Studio. Color. 10 reels. Direction: Liu Qun, Gao Bu. Screenplay: Liu Qun, Gao Bu. Cinematography: Zhang Yong, Zuang Yongxing. Art Direction: Wang Zhongyu, Wang Tianshi. Music: Yan Fei. Sound: Xue Shenxing. Cast: Zhao Ruping as Yang Daliang, Jia Dongsuo as Hao Bohu, Li Xiaoli as Zhen

Zhu, Zhou Zhengyu as Bureau Director Jin, Yu Suping as Xin Lihua, Zhou Zongyin as Fang Jimin, Zhao Ruping as Lian Yiming

In 1976, a strong earthquake hits the Bohai Bay in North China. A certain city on the coast is particularly devastated, its industrial base in ruins and many of its people made homeless. The Haihe Electronic Supply Plant buys an apartment building to house its employees, and suddenly the building becomes the focus of attention. Workers' union chief Lian Yiming is especially busy with matters of housing, child care and other issues of importance to employees. An angry dispute erupts over who will get the available apartments. Lian Yiming and fellow workers' representative Hao Bohu put the interests of others ahead of their own, and at last those people who had the poorest housing before begin moving into the new building.

562. *Empress Dowager of Daliao (Da Liao Tai Hou)*

1995. Liaoning Film Studio. Color. Letterboxed. Direction: Xiang Dezhang, Huang Lijia. Screenplay: Wang Zhanjun. Cinematography: Zhang Chi, Xu Lianqing. Art Direction: Qi Zhenxue, Zhang Lei. Music: Chen Shouqian. Cast: Mu Qing as empress dowager, Yang Fan as Han Derang, Wang Zhihua as Jingzong, Ge Ren as King Qi, Gao Changli as King Song, Wei Ran as Xiao Susu, Zhang Qinming as Xiao Lili

In the mid–10th century, senior official Xiao Shiwen's third daughter Xiao Yanyan loves General Han Derang. But the situation is hopeless, since the emperor also has designs on her. The emperor's death does not resolve the situation, however: when Prince Xianwang inherits the throne he selects Yanyan as his empress. After years of power struggles and political maneuvering, Xiao Yanyan's son Yeliu Rongxu becomes emperor and Yanyan becomes the Dowager Empress. Once again she sees the only man she ever loved, Han Derang, and he helps her son Yeliu consolidate his power.

563. *The Empress of Flower Street (Hua Jie Huang Hou)*

1988. Pearl River Film Studio. Color. Letterboxed. 10 Reels. Direction: Cao Zheng. Screenplay: Liao Zhikai. Cinematography: Chen Xianghe. Art Direction: Zhang Jingwen. Music: Zhang Hong. Sound: Liu Haiyan. Cast: Zhang Tianxi as A Wei, Pu Chaoying as A Li, Zuo Ling as A Hao, Lu Niu as A Fa

The Emperior's Shadow. **Strong-willed court musician Gao Jianlin (Ge You, left) and Qin Emperor Ying Zheng (Jiang Wen). Once childhood playmates, now servant and master. 1995. Xi'an Film Studio and Hong Kong Ocean Film Co-Production.**

Taxi driver A Wei's rudeness to his customers is criticized by a newspaper, which holds him up as a bad example. His embarrassed girlfriend A Li breaks up with him over this. In a bad temper, A Wei gets drunk and drives under the influence. The police stop him and impound his car. Hearing it might turn his luck around, A Wei buys a beautiful peach blossom, and in the process gets to know florist A Hao. She employs A Wei in her shop and it does make a difference: in the new year, A Wei is ranked a good service worker. A Li returns to him, A Hao becomes the manager of a flower company, and her boyfriend, college student A Hui, is also hired by her company.

564. *Empty Position in the Manager's Office (Jing Li Shi De Kong Wei Zhi)*

1984. Lanzhou Film Studio. Color. 9 Reels. Direction: Xu Raoxian. Screenplay: Zhu Mingshen, Zhao Zhiqiang. Cinematography: Xu Raoxian, Ma Xuezhong. Art Direction: Luo Yurong, Li Bingguang. Music: Wang Ming. Sound: Gui Zhilin, Liu Deren. Cast: Zhang Jinling as He Yuying, Xu Ming as Zhao Qinghe, Wu Yi as Manager Fang, Wang Heming as Secretary Chen

When Chunguang Department Store manager Fang is about to retire, he recommends a young woman from outside, He Yuying, be appointed to the position of Deputy Manager of the store. Everyone welcomes her, including the other deputy manager Zhao Qinghe. The two deputies' differing approaches to management soon become evident, most notably in Zhao's approach.

Although he is bright and hard-working, Zhao tends to cheat customers, and has little sense of customer relations. At a criticism session, He Yuying criticizes herself, leading everyone on the staff to understand her better. Zhao is oblivious to his own shortcomings, and in time an inspection team suspends him so he can examine and reeducate himself. Later, He Yuying is named the manager to replace Mr. Fang.

565. *Enchanting Band (Mi Ren De Yue Dui)*

1985. Beijing Film Studio. Color. 10 Reels. Direction: Wang Haowei. Screenplay: Fang Chunru, Yang Shuhui. Cinematography: Li Chengsheng. Art Direction: Yang Zhanjia. Music: Jin Xiang. Sound: Li Bojiang. Cast: He Wei as Xin Tianxi, Mi Tiezen as Qu Lixin, Liang Guanhua as Zhang Kuiwu, Chen Qin as Li Sujing, Zhao Fan as Jin Sheng

In the 1980s, while the lives of Longgang Village's farmers have improved significantly, the village's People's Committee Director Xin Tianxi wants to bring a bit of culture and entertainment into their lives by establishing a band. Through his efforts, a farmers' band is finally set up, and many people are attracted to it, both as performers and as audience. Xin and some others travel to the city to invite Jin Sheng, a professional conductor, to join them. Jin is impressed with their sincerity, and agrees to supervise their band. The farmers' band grows rapidly, and their village gains a reputation for its contributions to building socialist culture.

566. *Encounter in Shanghai (Duo Ming Jing Hun Shang Hai Tan)*

1993. Shanghai Film Studio. Color. Letterboxed. 9 Reels. Direction: Jiang Haiyang. Screenplay: Wu Tiange and Yun Di. Cinematography: Huang Baohua. Art Direction: Shen Lide. Music: Pan Guoxing. Sound (Dolby): Qian Ping. Costume: Zhang Lifang. Makeup: Gui Shaolin. Cast: Yuan Yuan as Yuan Afa, Wei Guochun as Chitian Aoer, Ao Yaohong as Cha Yin, Cheng Xi as Xiao Hong, He Ling as Diao Deyi, Song Gangshen as Tanaka

In Shanghai in 1936, Japanese intelligence agency chief Tanaka receives a tip that a member of the Chinese Communist Party will soon arrive in the city. The information eventually proves false, but it sets off a series of personal tragedies for various Shanghai residents, including a young Japanese man, a Chinese girl just returned from study in Japan, a girl named Xiao Hong and a man named Afa, etc.

567. *The Endless Case (Qi An Wei Zhong Zhi)*

1992. Changchun Film Studio. Color. Letterboxed. 10 Reels. Direction: Li Qimin. Screenplay: Xu Guangshun. Cinematography: Han Dongxia. Art Direction: Wei Hongyu. Music: Wu Zhiyan. Costume: Chen Hua. Makeup: Yan Zhenrong. Cast: Zhang Jianmin as Fang Zhongjian, Ma Li as Lin Na, Zhang Jing as Xiao Ling, Wang Yuxiao as Zhang Yan, Xu Chenglin as Mei Shan

Two masked men hold up a jewelry store and kill a drunk who happens to be on the sidewalk outside. Policeman Fang Zhongjian is assigned to go under cover to investigate the case, but suffers a serious head injury and loses his memory. He is shocked back to normal when his girl friend, policewoman Lin Na is murdered investigating the same case. Outraged at her death, Fang kills a gangster who knows what happened. Fang and other police are tipped off to go to a certain spot, but what they find there are a Hong Kong jeweler and the owner of the local store that was held up. The case becomes more complex than they had thought.

568. *Enemies Meet (Bu Shi Yuan Jia Bu Peng Tou)*

1987. Shanghai Film Studio. Color. 9 Reels. Direction: Fu Jinggong. Screenplay: Shi Yong, Fu Jinggong. Cinematography: Cha Xiangkang. Art Direction: Zhong Yongqin. Music: Xu Jingxin. Sound: Ni Zheng, Dong Yan. Cast: Wu Shuangyi as Hong Yatian, Weng Shuangjie as Ding Yubai, Li Qing as Lin Ao, Lin Yanyu as Wang Sulan, Tao Zhuijuan as Li Juanjuan, Miao Jun as Ding Qing

Retired worker Ding Yubai and hospital physician Lin Ao live in the same building. Bad feelings arose between the two men during the Cultural Revolution, and their families have carried the arguing over to the present day. Neighborhood cadre Hong Yatian tries to get the two families to end their hostilities. In the end, all is well, with the two families actually becoming joined by marriage.

569. *Enigma at St. Paul's Hospital (Sheng Bao Luo Yi Yuan Zhi Mi)*

1990. Emei Film Studio. Color. 9 Reels. Wide Screen. Direction: Mi Jiashan. Screenplay: Zhao Erhuan. Cinematography: Li Erkang, Fu Wei. Art Direction: Gao Xinchun. Music: Xiao Gang, Li Xilin. Sound: Lin Bingcheng, Lin Xuede. Cast: Cai Hongxiang as Xiao Fan, Le Geng as Mr. Luo, Chen Maya as Yu Huiying

In early 1950, shortly after the liberation of the city of Chengdu in Sichuan, Nationalist spies blow up the city's power station, plunging half the city into darkness. Public Security

Chief Investigator Xiao Fan follows a new lead in the bomb case when he and his men begin to investigate the death of Yu Na, a nurse at St. Paul's Hospital. Yu's father, a chief engineer at the power station, also died in the hospital, shortly after designing the bomb. Xiao Fan's endeavors at St. Paul's finally pay off when he discovers the truth behind their deaths, and succeeds in smashing the terrorist group responsible for the power station explosions.

570. *An Era Aflame (Huo Hong De Nian Dai)*

1974. Shanghai Film Studio. Color. 11 Reels. Direction: Fu Chaowu, Sun Yongping, Yu Zhongying. Screenplay: Collective, recorded by Ye Dan and Fu Chaowu, and based on the stage play "Steel Storm." Cinematography: Luo Chongzhou, Cha Xiangkang. Art Direction: He Ruiji. Music: Lu Qiming. Cast: Yu Yang as Zhao Shihai, Zhen Danian as Wang Jian, Wen Xiying as Bai Xianzhou, Lou Jicheng as Mr. Tian, Liu Zhifeng as Chen Yougeng, Zhang Xiaoling as Xiang Zhihua, Zhang Yan as Ying Jiapei

In 1972, China's former ally the Soviet Union adopts an anti–China stand, breaking contracts and withdrawing its experts. Steel mill open hearth furnace director Zhao Shihai suggests using domestic materials in place of imported alloys, but the mill director wants to continue importing from the Soviet Union. Party Secretary Wang Jian and the millworkers all support Zhao Shihai, so the director has to go along. However, villainous Ying Jiapei deliberately messes up a test which results in the director punishing Zhao Shihai. Zhao continues testing anyway. Some of the workers are suspicious of Ying Jiapei, however, and when he makes a second attempt at sabotage, they nab him red-handed. The reality of the situation and the help of his comrades changes the director's thinking. With the plant finally united, everyone works together to successfully make alloy steel in strong support of China's effort to build a modern navy.

571. *Erhai Romance (Er Hai Qing Bo)*

1986. Yunnan Minority Film Studio. Color. 10 Reels. Direction: Zhong Shuhuang. Screenplay: Liang Zhen, Cheng Zhi. Cinematography: Si Yongmin. Art Direction: Qi Deyu. Music: Huang Xuean, Nie Lihua. Sound: Chen Baolin. Cast: Ji Haiyin as Wang Yanzhi, Ma Guanyin as Zhao Mutao, Xia Jin as Yang Haicui, Cui Yuemin as Haicui's mother, Zhou Guobing as A Zuo

In the small fishing village of Wanghai, a young carpenter named Zhao Mutao falls in love with Yang Haicui, a girl from the neighboring village of Erhai. Everyone including Haicui believes that Zhao is quite wealthy. In time, she learns that his savings are very modest, which disappoints her greatly. Meanwhile, another girl named Wang Yanzhi loves Zhao for himself, but she realizes he could never care for her as he does for Haicui, so she sets out to reconcile the two.

572. *Ermo (Er Mo)*

1994. Shanghai Film Studio, Hong Kong Dayang Film Corp. Ltd. Co-Production. Color. Letterboxed. 10 Reels. Direction: Zhou Xiaowen. Screenplay: Lang Yun, based on Xu Baoqi's original novel of the same title. Cinematography: Lu Gengxin. Art Direction: Zhang Daqian. Music: Zhou Xiaowen. Sound: Hong Yi. Costume: Liu Qingli. Makeup: Lu Yingchun. Cast: Ai Liya as Ermo, Liu Peiqi as "Blind Man," Ge Zhijun as the village chief, Zhang Haiyan as Xiuer's mother, Yan Zhenguo as Huzi, Yang Xiao as Xiuer, Yang Shengxia, Du Hui, Ren Fengwu, Li Guiming, Lu Yanyan

Ermo is a diligent and hardworking village woman, the sole support of her family after her husband dies in an accident. She becomes ambitious to buy the largest TV in the village for her son, so she works even harder. She has an affair with her neighbor "Blind Man," who runs a transport business. Ermo becomes obsessed with earning enough to buy the TV, even selling her blood. She also gets into trouble when her lover's unattractive and lazy wife learns of the affair. At last, Ermo buys her TV set, but there is not room for it in her cramped house; in addition, she finds herself unable to work due to overwork and loss of blood.

573. *Erzi Opens a Hotel (Er Zi Kai Dian)*

1987. Youth Film Studio. Color. 10 Reels. Direction: Wang Binglin. Screenplay: Wang Binglin. Cinematography: Liao Jiaxiang. Art Direction: Fu Delin. Music: Li Wanli. Sound: Li Bojiang. Cast: Chen Peisi as Erzi, Zhang Jinglin as Yingzi, Huang Ling as Erzi's mother, Cui Bing as Dahu, LI Nan as Xiao Dou (Little Bean), Jin Ping as Xinghua, Chen Qiang as Erzi's father

Erzi has failed to gain admission to college, and has grown bored awaiting an employment assignment. His friend Magan suggests the two of them contract to operate a small hotel. So Erzi and Magan pursue the idea, taking on as helpers: Yingzi, a girl who was dismissed from her job after becoming involved with a married man; Dahu, a homeless man; and Xiao Dou, a little girl fleeing an abusive stepfather. Erzi's father is persuaded to sponsor their business, and at last they get their business license. Business goes well until Yingzi professes her love for Erzi; the problem is that Erzi knows his friend Magan loves Yingzi. In addition, Erzi's father is adamantly opposed to his son getting involved with Yingzi. All this results in the hotel closing. After a while, all the young people return to the small hotel, which moves Erzi's parents to relent, and the hotel reopens.

574. *Escape from Church (Jiao Tang Tuo Xian)*

1992. Shanghai Film Studio. Color. Letterboxed. 10 Reels. Direction: Pao Zhifang. Screenplay: Zhang Laijun. Cinematography: Liu Lihua. Art Direction: Xue Jianna, Ye Jingmin. Music: Liu Yanxi. Sound: Lu Xuehan. Costume: Ye Gengsheng. Makeup: Zhou Meihua. Cast: Ding Xiaoqiu as Minister Wang, Wu Shanshan as Auntie Hong, Xie Yuanchao as Da Nian, Wang Kan as Hanyin, Ge Minmin as Nannan

In November, 1930, Mao Zedong's wife Yang Kaiwei is killed in the city of Changsha, Hunan by Nationalist government agents. The killers then set out to find the Communist leader's three children, Anying, Anqin and Anlong. The children are kept in hiding, then sent to Shanghai and given sanctuary in St. Peter's Church. The minister of the church, Wang, works very hard to protect the children and keep their presence a secret. But government suspicions are aroused, and Wang's task is increasingly difficult. Anlong falls ill and dies. At last, with the help of a woman called Auntie Hong, the children are smuggled aboard a ship and escape Shanghai for Europe.

575. *Escape to Hongkong (Tao Gang Zhe)*

1987. Pearl River Film Studio. Color. 10 Reels. Direction: Zhang Liang. Screenplay: Zhang Yiao. Cinematography: Wang Hengli. Art Direction: Zhang Jingwen. Music: Zhang Hong. Sound: Deng Qinhua. Cast: Zhu Lin as Liu Ying, Zhou Lijing as Ye Tao, Zhang Tianxi as Wang Sheng, Zhang Yanli as Ruohua, Xun Feng as A Cang, Xie Weixiong as Li Zhengguo

Several students are sent to do labor in the countryside during the Cultural Revolution. Unable to bear the poor living conditions and political turbulence of the times, they try to escape to Hong Kong via Shenzhen. One of the female students, Liu Ying, has to be left behind when she falls ill. Later, she hears that her lover Ye Tao is killed by sharks on the way to freedom. Some 15 years pass, and Liu Ying is now the manager of a Shenzhen hotel. She goes to Hong Kong on a business trip, and there she runs into A Cheng, a member of her old group of students. During their chat, A Cheng mentions that Ye Tao is still alive and living in Hong Kong. The next day she meets Ye Tao, but the former lovers find their reunion brings them mixed reactions of joy and sorrow. After 15 years of hard work, Ye has risen to be a company CEO, but admits he has not found happiness. Liu Ying's confidence in her career and hopes for the future bring back many memories and bitter nostalgia of home for Ye Tao.

576. *Eternal Friendship (Yong Heng De You Yi)*

1960. Xi'an Film Studio. B & W. 10 Reels. Also released as: "The Red Medal." Direction: Liu Baode. Screenplay: Lu Bingkun, Wang Guijun, Jiang Jicheng. Cinematography: Ling Xuan. Art Direction: Zhang Jingnan. Music: Xiang Yin. Sound: Hong Jiahui. Cast: Wang Zhijie as Li Qing, Ayixiamu as Meichekewa, Zhou Zheng as Tang Suhua, Zhao Zimin as Director Yang, Wang Jun as Zhang Zhiqiang, Fu Chengxun as Li Zeming

In the closing days of World War II, a Northeast China village is raided by the Japanese, with much bloodshed. Meishikewa, a Soviet Red Army nurse who was there in support of Chinese resistance, rescues a small Chinese boy called Little Tiger. The child's grateful parents give her a gift which traditionally means peace and happiness, and the nurse gives a pocket watch with her father's name on it to Little Tiger as a souvenir. When the war ends, the nurse returns to the Soviet Union and takes up the study of topology. Ten years later, she returns to Northeast China as an invited foreign expert. At this time, Little Tiger, under his real name of Li Qing, is working on the same prospecting team, although neither recognizes the other. On a prospecting expedition, the Soviet woman is stricken with an illness requiring hospitalization, and Li risks his life to get her to a hospital. Later, she finds the pocket watch Li carries on his person and realizes he is the boy she saved years before. After her recovery, the two resume their hard work.

577. *The Eve of a Fierce Battle (Ji Zhan Qian Ye)*

1957. August First Film Studio. B & W. 8 Reels. Direction: Wang Bing, Feng Yifu. Screenplay: Wang Jun, Zhang Rongjie, Xiang Zen. Cinematography: Xue Boqing. Music: Li Weicai. Sound: Guo Dazheng. Cast: Wang Runshen as Lu Weizhi, Yuan Xia as Zhou Jie, Wang Yong as Li Jian, Jiang Fang as Lin Meifang, Yu Shaokang as Sun Yamei, Yang Jiao as Chen Fengzhai.

In 1953, an anti–Communist spy ring along the coast of Fujian province is given the mission of coordinating a joint Chinese Nationalist–U.S. operation to seize control of strategic Haima Island, in the Taiwan straits. One of the spies is Lin Meifang, the wife of PLA staff officer Li Jian. After a series of suspicious incidents in the area, including the savage beating of a reporter and the murder of a fisherman, PLA counter-intelligence officer Lu Weizhi takes on the assignment of capturing the spies. With the aid of a coastal civil defense brigade, he figures out what the spies' plan must be and sets a trap for them. He first gains Lin Meifang's confidence with false pictures of the island's defense installations, then uses her to infiltrate the spy ring's headquarters, soon gaining the trust of spy chief Chen Fengzhai. Finally, the trap is sprung from both inside and outside of the spy organization, all the spies are rounded up, and the conspiracy is smashed.

578. *Evening at the Dream Bar ("Meng" Jiu Jia Zhi Ye)*

1992. Shanghai Film Studio. Color. Letterboxed. 10 Reels. Direction: Da Shibiao. Screenplay: Xu Shihua. Cinematography: Cheng Shiyu. Art Direction: Zhang Chongxiang. Music: Liu Yanxi. Sound: Gong Dejun. Costume: Zhang Fuzhen. Makeup: Yin Shangshan. Cast: Li Lina as Luo Ming, Zhang Yan as Li Zhigang, Ding Jiayuan as Song Siyuan, Zhang Zhihua as Lin Li, Xue Guoping as Wang Hui

Middle-aged accountant Luo Ming dislikes her job and wants to quit, but her husband Li Zhigang objects strongly. When she can bear it no longer, she quits and moves to South China, where she opens a "Dream Bar," a place where married couples can come to talk out their marital problems. Luo Ming counsels the couples, most of them young. Some marriages fail anyway, and some work things out, but Luo Ming starts feeling her own pressure after her husband shows up. At last, Luo Ming and Li Zhigang sign their own divorce agreement.

579. *Evening Bell (Wan Zhong)*

1988. August First Film Studio. Color. Wide Screen. 9 Reels. Direction: Wu Ziniu. Screenplay: Wu Zhiniu, Wang Yifei. Cinematography: Hou Yong. Art Direction: Na Shufeng. Music: Ma Jianfei. Sound: Wang Lewen, Zhang Lei. Cast: Tao Zeru as Platoon Leader, Lu Ruolei as Beard, Ge Yaming as Big Guy, Ye Nanqiu as Little Guy, Zhou Qi as Skinny, Sun Ming as the Japanese prisoner

In the fall of 1945, as the Japanese army faces defeat, more than 100,000 officers and men at a Japanese base in China decide to commit mass suicide. At one shabby ancient temple, soldiers of the Eighth Route Army find a Japanese soldier starving and near death. In a dark cave nearby, they also find hidden a store of weapons and 33 Japanese soldiers waiting the coming of death. The Eighth Route Army men negotiate with the Japanese to try to get them to surrender alive. At last, the soldiers agree to surrender, but their captain commits suicide.

Best Director Wu Ziniu, 1989 Golden Rooster Awards.

Best Actor Tao Zeru, 1989 Golden Rooster Awards.

Best Supporting Actor Sun Ming, 1989 Golden Rooster Awards.

Best Cinematography Hou Yong, 1989 Golden Rooster Awards.

Best Film, Best Director, Best Sound Effect, 7th Bogota Intl. Film Festival.

Silver Bear Award, 39th Berlin International Film Festival.

580. *Eventful Years (Zheng Rong Sui Yue)*

1978. August First Film Studio. Color. 11 Reels. Direction: Jing Mukui, Wang Feng. Screenplay: Gu Ertan, Fang Hongyou. Cinematography: Ding Shanfa. Art Direction: Fei Lanxin, Ren Huixing. Music: Li Weicai, Shi Feng. Sound: He Baoding. Cast: Zhang Hui as Gong Fang, Li Yan as Liao Pingshan, Tian Hua as Luo Xia, Gu Yongfei as Gong Lan, Ling Yuan as Grandma Gong, Wu Xun as Xue Cheng, Li Qing as Xu Xiu

In the fall of 1976, the "Gang of Four's" representative in the city of Pingyang, the city's Deputy Party Secretary Li Mengliang suddenly releases Gong Fang from jail. Gong Fang had been in charge of a project called "903," opposed by the Gang. When Party Secretary Liao Ping returns to the city, he meets with Gong and the two encourage each other to resist the Gang of Four and resume the project. The Gang sends their agent Kong Jing to Pingyang with instructions to destroy Project 903 and make it appear that it was Gong Fang's fault. But Gong Fang continues to resist despite persecution and personal attacks. Just before Chairman Mao's death, Gong and some of his supporters are illegally jailed, but Liao Ping brings masses of people to get them released. He also brings news that the Gang of Four has been defeated.

581. *Everybody's Happy (Jie Da Huan Xi)*

1981. Pearl River Film Studio. Color. 9 Reels. Direction: Luo Xiangchi. Screenplay: Zhan Xiangchi. Cinematography: Wei Duo. Art Direction: Li Pingye. Music: Yang Shuzheng. Sound: Li Xun. Cast: Wang Xiaozhong as Wei Jianmin, Li Weitian as Gao Liyan, Na Renhua as Wei Xiuming, Xing Mali as Li Xiaoling, Lu Yanfang as Liu Afang, Xu Ruiping as Gao Lan

Reporter Gao Liyan is given the assignment of reporting on the Jiankang Pharmaceutical Plant's environmental waste treatment problem. Although his girl friend Wei Xiuming is the daughter of Wei Jianmin, manager of the Jiankang Plant, he publishes an article critical of the plant. This causes a dispute between him and the Wei family, largely due to Wei Jianmin's ignorance of the problem of pollution. At last, the manager is educated as to the problem. He realizes he must learn something about science, then works hard with the plant's technicians and workers to resolve their problems while still keeping production high.

582. *Evidence of the Red Cross (Hong Shi Zi Zuo Zheng)*

1991. Emei Film Studio. Color. Letterboxed. 9 Reels. Direction: Jia Mu. Screenplay: Luo Xing, Xiong Yu. Cinematography: Jin Guirong. Art Direction: Chen Desheng. Music: He Xuntian. Sound: Shen Yihua. Costume: Shen Cheng. Makeup: Zhu Biaodi, Yao Xiaomiao. Cast: Sun Chun as Yu Xuecheng, Cheng Yuanli, Wu Qianqian as Wang Li, Wen Mingzhu as Chen Yuying, Sun Yushu as Professor Nie

A group of medical experts battles traditional prejudices while trying to gain acceptance for kidney transplants to save childrens' lives.

583. *Evil by Moonlight (Meng Long Zhong De Zui E)*

1991. Xiaoxiang Film Studio. Color. Letterboxed. 9 Reels. Director and Screenplay: Jiang Weiho. Cinematography: Xu Hongliang. Art Direction: Zhang Zili and Li Li. Music: Fang Xiaomin. Sound: Huang Qizhi. Cast: Zhang Jingsheng as Fang Kaiping, Wang Change as Su Ye, Tan Feiling as Mr. Luo, Huang Huiyi as Meng Lijun, Cao Zhong as Lu Yu, Li Bangyu as He Yu, Li Xiaohong as He Xiaoyang, Lin Rongcai as Zhao Xing, Lin Yizhen as Lin Haibo

Celebrated writer He Yu is found dead in his home, apparently a suicide by poisoning. Investigators set out to determine if the deceased had sufficient cause to take his own life. They learn that the dead man's daughter He Xiaoyang has been sent to reform school for involvement in prostitution, and the man's wife had recently divorced him. Further investigation at last discloses that He Yu was also a major pornographer under an assumed name, and that one of his sex novels had started the daughter into an active sexual life and eventually into prostitution. When He Yu refused to stop writing these books, his wife left him. Detectives conclude there was ample cause for suicide, and close the case.

584. *Evil Connection (Nie Yuan)*

1995. Tianshan Film Studio, Shanghai Film Technology Plant, Nantong Film Company Co-Production. Color. Letterboxed. Direction: Jin Lini. Cinematography: Lu Junfu. Art Direction: Zhang Xiaochun. Cast: Gao Baobao as Xiao Hong, Shi Ke as Li Biyun, Tong Fan as Qiu Jiping, Gao Wenjing as Tian Susu, Wang Yong as You Afu, Guo Gao as Zhou Yuming

Singing star Qiu Jiping seriously injures another person, and is sent to prison where he finds his former girlfriend Xiao Hong is the warden. Years before, Qiu had dumped her for a villainous woman, Li Biyun, now an inmate in the same prison. Shortly after this, Li's daughter Chen Xiaomei arrives, convicted of a crime committed under her mother's malevolent influence. Xiao Hong is able to disregard her personal feelings and help everyone get themselves straightened out. When Qiu Jiping is released, he believes he has learned much about life.

585. *Evil Queen (Yi Dai Yao Hou)*

1988. Pearl River Film Studio. Color. Letterboxed. 10 Reels. Direction: Li Hanxiang. Screenplay: Wang Shuyuan, Li Hanxiang. Cinematography: Zhao Yao, Zhao Xiaofeng. Art Direction: Mu Demin, Chen Yan. Music: Wang Xian. Sound: Huang Junshi. Cast: Liu Xiaoqing as Cixi, Chen Ye as Cian, Li Yan as An Dehai, Chen Daoming as the Emperor Tongzhi, Gong Li as Guilian

In 1864, after Dowager Empress Cixi suppresses the Taiping Rebellion, she obtains a huge amount of treasure from the Taiping leader's mansion headquarters. Cixi's trusted eunuch An Dehai comes to dominate the court and operate with a free hand, blackmailing official Zeng Guofan for silver and not even taking the Emperor Tongzhi seriously. One day, Tongzhi meets court servant girl Guilian and falls in love with her. An Dehai wants to control Guilian, so he sells her to a brothel. An Dehai is so bold that he leaves the court and makes an unauthorized visit to South China. Tongzhi learns this and orders Shandong Governor Ding Baozhen to assassinate the eunuch as he passes through Shandong. This worsens the already-bad relationship of Tongzhi and Cixi. Tongzhi later contracts a venereal disease which proves fatal. After his death, Cixi has her co-ruler Empress Cian killed, and from then on Cixi rules the Qing court unchallenged.

586. *Evil Star Over a Mansion (Bie Shu Zhai Xing)*

1991. Beijing Film Studio. Color. Letterboxed. 9 Reels. Direction: Yu Xiaoyang. Screenplay: Chen Keng. Cinematography: Li Sheng. Art Direction: Zhang Guojun. Music: Chen Wenqian. Sound: Zhang Zhizhong. Cast: Li Bo as Qi Ren, Gai Ke as An Ning, Song Ge as An Jide, Wang Weiguo as Zhang Qu, Yao Lu as Zhuge Zaimin, Yang Yang as Zhang Shen

Chinese business tycoon An Jide has withdrawn to his old mansion, passing his days as a virtual recluse from society. One of his few contacts is his daughter An Ning. One day, a young man is found murdered, and An Jide himself is kidnapped. Retired police detective Qi Ren is brought out of retirement to help

with the kidnapping case. His investigation at last links the murder with the kidnapping, when he discovers that the murder victim was An Jide's illegitimate son. It turns out the daughter An Ning arranged both the murder and the abduction after learning of the son's existence and of her father's plans to give the young man equal status in his will.

587. *Excitement in the Mountains (Fei Teng De Qun Shan)*

1976. Beijing Film Studio. Color. 11 Reels. Direction: Gan Xuewei, Li Wei, Chen Fangqian. Screenplay: Tao Zhonghua, Liu Zhongwei. Cinematography: Zhang Qinhua. Art Direction: Yang Yuhe. Music: Tang Ke, Lu Yuan. Sound: Wei Xueyi. Cast: Zhang Wen as Jiao Kun, Xu Changyou as Xue Hui, Shi Baoguang as Su Fushun, Zhao Yuxin as Xiao Zhao, Liang Zhipeng as Gu Shangqin, Jiang Gengcheng as Company Commander Xia

In the fall of 1948, Battalion Commander Jiao Kun leads his unit in liberating the mountainous Guyingling mining region of southern Liaoning province and supporting the people's efforts to restore the mines to full operation. For Jiao, this is a special mission since he comes from a mining family. Their efforts are hampered by guerrilla attacks by Nationalist bandits and covert saboteurs. Anti-Communist rumors spread and the saboteurs cause a mine collapse which stops construction temporarily. Jiao Kun repels every enemy attack, and captures the bandit chief and his agents. In less than one year, the mines are restored to full production in support of the ongoing military struggle to liberate all China.

588. *Exorcising Demons Through Courage (Yi Dan Chu Mo)*

1991. Emei Film Studio. Color. Letterboxed. 9 Reels. Direction: Ku Mei. Screenplay: Hu Bing. Cinematography: Li Erkang. Art Direction: Li Fan. Music: Ao Changqun. Sound: Lin Bingcheng, Qiu Shuchuan. Costume: Li Xuehong. Makeup: Cao Songlin and Zhong Li. Cast: Wen Haitao as Ye Feiyang, Yu Daijun as Nong Yu, Xu Ping as Ma Lihong, Chen Qi as Ye Xiaoye, Wu Likun as Huang Mianliang, Sun Fang as Cao Meimei, Li Jun as Sun Xiong, Zhang Li as Li Lichun, He Xiaole as Bureau Director Zhen

A gang comes to a Chinese coastal city from overseas and sets up a ring to abduct and sell girls. The public security forces smash the conspiracy.

589. *Experience at Happiness Island (Kuai Le Dao Qi Yu)*

1990. Pearl River Film Studio. Color. Wide Screen. 9 Reels. Direction: Wu Houxing. Screenplay: Lin Xiping, Xu Changbo. Cinematography: Wu Yukun. Art Direction: Zhu Jinhe. Music: Xu Zhaoji. Sound: Wu Hongtao. Cast: Xu Jianxiong as Gao Hai, Xu Jianying as Gao Hai, Liu Liang as Li Shuiman

Happiness Island Summer Camp receives a new group of campers, among who are two boys named Gao Hai, identical in appearance and unalike in personality. One is a rascal from a fishing village, the other a very well-behaved city boy. Many humorous incidents arise out of their identical looks and their counselors' confusion. When the first camp session ends, the teachers find their relief is short-lived: the second session campers are all sets of identical twins.

590. *Experiencing Prosperity (Ge Men Fa Cai Ji)*

1988. Changchun Film Studio. Color. 10 Reels. Direction: Cui Dongsheng. Screenplay: Zhong Jieyin, Cui Dongsheng. Cinematography: Xing Eryou. Art Direction: Sui Zuangji. Music: Tang Yuanru, Zhufeng. Sound: Tong Zongde. Cast: Chen Jianfei as Zhu Naigeng, Song Chunli as Du Lamei

When young electrician Zhu Naigeng starts work at a textile mill, he quickly identifies the mill's marketing problems as due to the outdated fashions it produces. He decides to get the mill out of its difficulties by designing a new, more fashionable men's tie style. However, after Zhu Naigeng's design is successful, mill director Wang Jiulu's ignorance of patent law results in his taking the new style ties to the market without Zhu's approval. At last, Zhu Naigeng and the mill reach a negotiated agreement, and Zhu turns patent rights over to the mill. Meanwhile, Zhu Naigeng's buddies who had originally cared only about money are now all on the road to prosperity through hard work.

591. *The Experimental Ship (Shi Hang)*

1959. Changchun Film Studio. Color. 9 Reels. Direction: Lin Nong. Screenplay: Liang Tianqing, Lin Shan. Cinematography: Wang Qimin. Art Direction: Sun Shixiang. Music: Zhang Dicang. Sound: Chen Wenyuan. Cast: Chen Ge as Liu Zhijian, Chen Qiang as Wang Wanshui, Zhang Fengxiang as the Chief Engineer, Song Xuejuan as Lanyin, Wang Chunyin as Xiaoli, Ye Linliang as Xiao Zhang

A manufacturer wants to import an internal-combustion engine for making a 10,000-ton ship, but is hampered by foreign businessmen. The plant's Party Secretary Liu Zhijian visits Chief Engineer Xing to seek his advice about such an engine. But Xing is a blind worshipper of all things foreign, and he believes that building even a 3,000-ton ship would be impossible. A Western European country offers to sell China the drawings for an internal-combustion engine, and Liu goes to Beijing for the negotiations. But the negotiations fail, due to the seller's too-high asking price. The ship plant's workers and technicians jointly vow to design a Chinese engine within a month. With the help of Soviet experts, they overcome many difficulties and succeed just before China's national holiday.

592. *Exploring a River Crossing (Du Jiang Tan Xian)*

1958. August First Film Studio. B & W. 9 Reels. Direction: Shi Wenzhi. Screenplay: Ma Jixing, Shi Daqian. Cinematography: Li Erkang, Chen Ruijun. Art Direction: Li Xinmao. Music: Jin Sha. Sound: Li Yan. Cast: Gao Baocheng as Li Yuming, Li Huijian as Yucai, Liu Lei as Wang Baocheng, Xing Jitian as the Political Commissar, Xie Wanhe as Chen Wenjian, Li Po as Tan Dashan

PLA platoon leader Li Yuming, just out of the hospital after being injured during construction of a major highway to Tibet, volunteers for a mission exploring a route to build a bridge to the Shizi Mountain peak. His lack of familiarity with the terrain and the inexperience of his troops results in several disasters along the way, resulting in the loss of their boat and the life of Deputy Platoon Leader Tan Dashan. Company Commander Chen Wenjian wants to wait for the river to recede before crossing the river, but Li Yuming insists on crossing by wooden raft. With support from the Youth League committee, Li is successful in getting his inexperienced troops to overcome their fear of the water, and they finally cross the river and find a route to Shizi Mountain.

593. *Exploring the Sun (Kai Cai Tai Yang)*

1992. Shanxi Film Studio & Youth Film

Studio Co-Production. Color. Letterboxed. 9 Reels. Direction: Sun Yu and Yao Xianling. Screenplay: Su Shuyang and Chen Yuancai. Cinematography: Zhang Songping and Bao Bo. Art Direction: Huang Chaohui. Music: Liu Yanxi. Sound: Ni Zheng, Li Liyi. Costume; Wang Ju, Li Li. Makeup: Jin Jinghua. Cast: Zhang Zhizhong as Wang Zhigang, Chen Dawei as Feng Xiaobao, Zhang Qi as Lin Dazhong, Zhang Guomin as Liang Jianxing, Duan You as Ma Lan

Although it is a good enterprise, the Yangcheng coal mine has never been able to resolve its coal dust problem. Wang Zhigang, professionally trained and experienced, is assigned to resolve the problem. He clashes often with mine manager Liang Jianxing, greedy and money-driven to the point of going outside of the law. At last, Wang finds his enemy is actually his long-lost brother. Wang cannot accept such a person, and refuses to acknowledge the relationship. At last, Wang's automatic equipment for controlling the coal dust is successful, and he leaves.

594. *Explosion Before Daybreak (Fu Xiao Qian De Bao Zha)*

1984. Changchun Film Studio. Color. Letterboxed. 10 Reels. Direction: Zhu Wenshun, Zhao Duanqi. Screenplay: Li Hongyu. Cinematography: Duan Zhenjiang. Art Direction: Liu Xuerao. Music: Zhang Jingyu. Sound: Liu Jingui, Shi Lin. Cast: Xu Yuanqi as Xie Yanfei, Pang Min as the girl tending geese, Yuan Yuping as Lu Guancheng, Bian Ju as Meijun, Pu Ke as Shen Jianqin, Zhao Yamin as Lou Amei

In the fall of 1948 on the eve of the Battle of Huaihai, which will be one of the three critical battles of the Second Chinese Civil War, Chiang Kai-shek orders a massive force moved to Xuzhou to stop the PLA from crossing the Yangtse into South China. At this time, PLA reconnaissance chief Xie Yanfei is sent to scout these troop movements. After he arrives in the city of Hekou, the disguised Xie looks for his Party contact there, but finds that the CPC underground in Hekou has been wiped out. Forced to work alone, Xie is successful at blowing up a just-completed bridge which the enemy had counted on as a troop withdrawal route. Blocking the withdrawal in this way buys time for the PLA.

595. *Extrordinary Era (Fei Chang Shui Yue)*

1983. Jiangxi Film Studio. Color. 9 Reels. Direction: Yuan Yuehua, Wu Anhua. Screenplay: Yang Peijing. Cinematography: Chen Youqun. Art Direction: Luo Yurong. Music: Wu Bingtong. Sound: Zhang Jiake. Cast: Ma Shuchao as Zhu Zhiyan, Luo Yan as Xu Chayin, Fang Hui as Xu Dengan, Xu Fuyin as Wen Dachui, Lei Ming as He Xingwu

After the Communist revolution fails in 1927, the Party comes under the domination of its right wing, headed by Chen Duxiu. The film tells how this affects the lives of two ordinary Chinese in Jiangxi province, Party volunteer Zhu Zhiyan and his girlfriend Xu Chaying. Later, after the CPC decides to reorganize and arm its people, they have many struggles but are reunited at last.

596. *Extraordinary Murder Case in the Republic of China (Min Guo Te Da Mou Sha An)*

1990. Changchun Film Studio. Color. Wide Screen. 10 Reels. Direction: Zhang Hui. Screenplay: Xue Shouxian. Cinematography: Chen Chang'an, Wang Jian. Art Direction: Xu Zhenkun. Music: Yang Yilun. Sound: Wang Baosheng. Cast: Du Lilu as Han Fuqu, Li Yunjuan as Luo Lan, Liu Tingrao as Zhang Shaotang, Liu Dianzhou as Yang Zhiyuan, Li Ying as Li Shuchun, Cao Jiecheng as Hua Gu, Guo Feng as deputy officer Zhou, Yang Juan as Xu Manhua

In 1929, warlord Feng Yuxiang's challenge to the Nanjing government is blunted when his ablest commander Han Fuju defects to Chiang Kai-shek, who makes Han the military governor of Shandong. Han retains the taxes raised in Shandong and uses them to expand his force, the 3rd Route Army. His frequent conflicts with Chiang leads the Generalissimo to send a spy, codenamed "Black Plum Blossom" to keep tabs on Han. Several attempts to kill Han are unsuccessful, due to his sophisticated security arrangements. When the Japanese invade Shandong, Han at first tries to defect, then retreats, taking the provincial treasury with him. At last the treacherous Han abandons his army and flees, but is caught, tried and sentenced to be executed. Late one night, the mysterious "Black Plum Blossom" enters Han Fuju's quarters to carry out the sentence. Just before shooting Han, the spy unmasks, revealing herself as his private secretary Luo Lan.

597. *Eyes of the People (Jiu Qian Liu Bai Wan Shuang Yan Jing)*

1990. Beijing Film Studio. Color. 9 Reels. Wide Screen. Direction: Liu Shu'an, Zheng Jianmin. Screenplay; Xie Haiwei, Li Baoqun. Cinematography: Chen Youqun, Zhang Jiang. Art Direction: Ma Gaiwa. Music: Xu Changjun. Sound: Lan Fuan, Wang Dawen. Cast: Wang Zhigang as Xiang Dake, Jiang Lili as Sha Feifei

As soon as Xiang Dake assumes his new position as head of a government oversight department, he gets a knotty case. Ni Dagong, a department director of the Taifeng Company, has been implicated in a case of fraud, but he is protected by his father, the provincial Deputy Governor Ni Dajiang. In addition, Gu Zhen, advisor and Party Secretary at the company, is responsible for an accident at the Children's Palace, but no charges were brought against her. After an investigation, Xiang decides the Taifeng Company has been profiteering in steel, and vows to put a stop to it. The crafty head of the company, Sha Feifei, tries to thwart his efforts, and Ni Dajiang tries to shield the Taifeng Company. Beset by corruption and influence on all sides, Xiang almost gives up but believes that the people all look to him. At last, the criminals are brought to justice.

598. *Facing the Red Cross (Mian Dui Hong Shi Zi)*

1992. Shanghai Film Studio. Color. Letterboxed. Direction: Shi Shujun. Screenplay: Dong Jingsheng, Lu Xinger, Shi Shujun. Cinematography: Zhao Junhong. Art Direction: Dong Jingsheng, Pu Jingsun. Music: Xi Qimin. Cast: Shen Chang as Zhou Yi, Ju Naishe as Mei's father, Ren Wei as Wang Jun, Lu Ling as Meizi, Wang Hongsheng as Director Feng, Song Yining as Ding Hong

Medical student Meizi is hospitalized with what at first appears a minor ailment, but by the next day her condition has deteriorated rapidly, and she dies early the following morning. One of Meizi's classmates learns that although the hospital has four doctors on its staff, all were absent from the hospital for the five hours preceding her death. Meizi's father and classmates believe the young woman's death was a gross injustice, but their attempts to get a formal investigation into the matter are met with a series of roadblocks thrown up by hospital administrators. At last the determined efforts of medical school representatives

brings the case to the attention of city political leaders, and justice is served.

599. *False Face (Jia Lian)*

1986. Xiaoxiang Film Studio. Color. 9 Reels. Direction: Zhang Jinbiao. Screenplay: Dai Peiling, Su Shuyang. Cinematography: Xu Hongliang, Liu Junyun. Art Direction: Bi Jianzhang. Music: Xian Hua. Sound: Liu Feng. Cast: Zhao Youliang as Zhang Youyan, Xu Lili as Fan Ruonan, Zhao Kuier as Gao Xiangyi, Zhang Da as Tong Boyi

When a certain city decides to hold an opera festival, the local bureau of culture invites Zhang Youyan, director of the county's opera company, to direct one of the performances. He is welcomed warmly by the bureau's deputy director Tong Boyi, who gives the director two scripts proposed for the festival. One of them, "Big Stream," Tong praises highly, while disparaging the other play, "Too Much Wine." When Zhang meets with the cast to discuss the plays before making a selection, he begins to find the bureaucrat has personal reasons for obviously wanting "Big Stream," and in time he finds that Tong's reasons are political. Zhang and the performers choose "Too Much Wine," and it is a great success. The deputy director still finds a way to take personal credit.

600. *False Faces (Mian Mu Quan Fei)*

1990. Emei Film Studio. Color. Wide Screen. 10 Reels. Direction: Zhang Gang. Screenplay: Zhang Gang. Cinematography: Zhang Jian. Art Direction: Wang Rencheng. Music: Wang Ming. Sound: Liu Guangjie. Cast: Zhang Gang as Xu Aman

In an urban company, manager Pan Zhinan is always angry and abrupt when dealing with Chinese citizens. The business department head always has a smile for everyone, but it is there only for business purposes. Kindly and congenial Xu Aman comes from the countryside to do some business with the company. In the process, he encounters all manner of trouble and unhappiness, and unfortunately acquires the false smile habit. He returns to the countryside with the false smile firmly implanted on his face, completely changed from the simple and pleasant man he was before.

601. *False Hero (Jia Da Xia)*

1989. Xiaoxiang Film Studio. Color. Letterboxed. 9 reels. Direction: Zhang Li. Screenplay: Jiang Qinmin, Luo Chengxing. Cinematographer: Lei Xinshi. Art Direction: Mao Shu. Music: Li Lifu. Sound: Huang Shiye. Cast: Niu Beng as Zhang Bihuo, Wei Wei as Huo Qingshan, Ji Ling as Xiao Cui

When the Allied Expeditionary Force occupies Tianjin as part of its suppression of the Boxer Rebellion, Boxer hero Huo Qingshan is rescued by Zhang Bihuo, a humble pancake vendor. By mistake, people come to think Zhang is the hero, so many people come to him demanding to learn his kongfu skills. Huo Qingshan sets Zhang up with a martial arts school which he uses to train rebel fighters. But they are beaten in a match with foreigners. Huo Qingshan is captured by Qing soldiers and sentenced to death. On the eve of his execution, Zhang Bihuo brings pancakes to the real hero.

602. *A False Woman's True Love (Jia Nu Zheng Qing)*

1990. Shanghai Film Studio & Zhejiang Film Studio Co-Production. Color. Wide Screen. 10 Reels. Direction: Wu Zhennian. Screenplay: Fang Youliang. Cinematography: Ju Jiazheng, Zhang Yongjiang. Art Direction: Luo Dejing, Qin Baisong. Art Direction: Xia Liang. Sound: Jn Fugeng. Cast: Xi Meijuan as Wang Yujuan, Zhong Xinghuo as Wang Fushou, Liu Zifeng as Mr. Ding

Middle-aged woman teacher Wang Yujuan accepts into her home an old man from Taiwan, Wang Fushou. Mr. Wang has arrived with the thought that Yujuan may be the daughter he had been forced to leave behind when he fled the mainland in 1949. She does nothing to dissuade him from the idea. The old man's visit disrupts the Wang family's normally tranquil life. Especially upset at first is Yujuan's engineer husband, Mr. Ding, who cannot understand what his wife is doing and argues with her about it. The Wang children also hope to get something from the old man. But later, the husband and children begin to see that Yujuan genuinely cares for Mr. Wang, and begin to understand her motivations. They also start to return his affection, making him truly feel like one of the family. Mr. Ding helps Wang Fushou reunite with his real daughter. The Wang family's life returns to normal, but now they feel something is missing.

Best Actress Xi Meijuan, 1991 Golden Rooster Awards.

603. *Family (Jia)*

1956. Shanghai Film Studio. B & W. 13 Reels. Direction: Chen Xihe, Ye Ming. Screenplay: Chen Xihe, based on the novel of the same title by Ba Jin (1905–). Cinematography: Xu Qi. Art Direction: Ding Cheng. Music: Huang Zhun, Lu Qiming. Sound: Lin Bingsheng. Cast: Wei Heling as Master Gao, Fu Huizhen as Concubine Chen, Jiang Rui as Mr. Gao, Han Tao as Gao Keming, Cheng Zhi as Gao Kean, Yang Hua as Gao Keding, Sun Daolin as Gao Juexin, Zhang Fei as Gao Juemin, Zhang Hui as Gao Juehui, Zhang Ruifang as Li Ruiyu, Huang Zongyin as Qian Meifeng, Wang Danfeng as Ming Feng, Wang Wei as Wan'er

The decline of a large, bourgeois family shortly after the overthrow of the Manchu Dynasty. Mr. Gao's three sons by his first wife are all oppressed by the feudal ethical code of the time. Eldest son Gao Juexin is an extremely weak man. Not daring to show displeasure or speak out, he gives in to his family's demands and agrees to marry Li Ruiyu, although he really loves a girl called Miss Mei. Ruiyu later dies as a result of the oppressive code. The family declines further. When progressive ideas begin to sweep China, Juexin finally begins to wake up. Second son Gao Juemin falls in love with a Miss Qing, but determines to follow his heart and marry who he chooses. He rejects a marriage arranged by his family and moves out. Third son Gao Juehui falls in love with family servant Ming Feng, and enthusiastically joins the student movement. When the local ethical association director wants to take Ming Feng as his concubine she chooses death by drowning herself. Juehui decides to disassociate himself from the family and devote himself to revolution.

604. *Family Dependence (Qi Er Lao Xiao)*

1984. Nanjing Film Studio. Color. 9 Reels. Direction: Luo Guanqun. Screenplay: Zhou Anhe. Cinematography: Qiao Jicang. Art Direction: Liu Jiajing. Music: Yi Bing, Chen Dawei. Sound: Qian Youshan. Cast: Jin Ange as Zhen Feng, Zhan Pingping as Li Lan, Chen Qi as Mother, Yuan Zongfu as Zhen Long, Cheng Mei as Geng Li, Zhu Sheng as Xiao Qin

In a dormitory for government workers and their families lives Bureau of Materials Director Wang and his family. In another wing lives the family of Zhen Feng, Deputy Secretary of the County's Party Disciplinary

Family. **Zhang Ruifang as Qian Meifeng (left) and Huang Zongyin as Li Ruiyu. 1956. Shanghai Film Studio.**

Inspection Committee. The Zhens are a happy family, but their troubles start when Zhen Feng begins investigating certain irregularities in Wang's office. First, Wang has Zhen Feng's brother dismissed from his job, then he arranges for Zhen Feng's wife to be sent to the countryside to teach. This causes great hardship for the Zhen family, but Zhen Feng perseveres and is at last triumphant and reconciled with his wife.

605. *Family Matters (Jia Ting Wen Ti)*

1964. Tianma Film Studio. B & W. 10 Reels. Direction: Fu Chaowu. Screenplay: Hu Wanchun and Fu Chaowu, based on the novel of the same title by Hu Wanchun. Cinematography: Lu Junfu. Art Direction: He Ruiji. Music: Xiao Yan. Sound: Gong Jianqin. Cast: Zhang Fa as Master Worker Du, Zhang Liang as Du Fuming, Zhao Lian as Du Fuxin, Xie Yibing as Mother, Hong Xia as Xiuying, Zhang Yi as Factory Director Li

Steel plant workshop director Du's younger son Fuming is assigned to work as a technician in his father's workshop after graduation from professional school. Du finds his son has little interest in physical labor, so he decides to let him become a worker and improve from work.

However, the son wants to become an engineer. Du's wife supports her son on this matter, and invites a group of relatives to their home to criticize her husband's decision. Finally, through a series of events and with the help of the father and coworkers, Fuming corrects his shortcoming and becomes a competent worker.

606. *Family Portrait (aka At the Age of 40) (Sishi Buhuo)*

1992. Beijing Film Studio. Color. Letterboxed. 9 Reels. Direction: Li Shaohong. Screenplay: Liu Heng. Cinematography: Cao Nieping. Art Direction: Lin Chaoxiang. Music: Hou Muren. Cast: Li Xuejian as Cao Depei, Song Dandan as Duan Jinghua, Ye Jing as Zhao Xiaomu, Ding Ding as Hanhan

Photojournalist Cao Depei, his young, pretty wife and their five-year-old son Hanhan have a happy life. One day, he receives a call from the Welfare Institute that a boy is waiting for him. It turns out that the boy, Xiaomu, is his son by his ex-wife in Northeast China, a child he has never seen. Now, his ex-wife has died and her recently remarried husband does not want the boy. The new arrival thoroughly disrupts the family's life, eventually leading to

Cao's wife and Hanhan leaving him. Xiaomu later leaves as well. Cao Depei sits at an exhibition devoted to his photographs, and reflects on what has happened to his life.

607. *Family Small Affairs Collection (Jia Ting Shuo Shi Lu)*

1984. Emei Film Studio. Color. 10 Reels. Direction: Zhang Qi. Screenplay: Wang Yimin. Cinematography: Li Erkang. Art Direction: Wu Qidi. Music: Si Wanchun. Sound: Lin Bingfa. Cast: Yu Xiuchun as Li Yuemei, Song Chunli as Chunxing, Ren Yexiang as Xuehua, Yang Guixiang as Juhua, Liu Linian as Jiaxing, Zhao Junkai as Jiaxi

Li Yuemei finds her otherwise comfortable life marred by a growing dispute among her four adult children. While her son Jiaxing has married a very nice girl named Chunxing, her daughter Xuehua bears a grudge against her mother for having terminated the daughter's formal education a year before. When Chunxing marries into the family, she suggests the family volunteer to run a home-operated library for the local people to use in self-education. She asks Xuehua to be the librarian. Li Yuemei is at first opposed, but finally agrees and all is tranquil again.

608. *Fang Shiyu (aka Legend of Fong Sai-yuk) (Fang Shi Yu)*

1993. Hong Kong Zhengdong Film Studio & Beijing Film Studio Co-Production. Color. Letterboxed. 10 Reels. Direction: Yuan Kui (Corey Yuan Kuai). Screenplay: Cai Kangyong. Cinematography: Ma Chucheng. Art Direction: Liu Mingxiong. Music: Huang Dian. Costume: Liu Weifeng, Wang Junying, Cai Jun, Jiang Jingming. Makeup: Cui Jie, Xu Qiuwen, Guo Jingxia. Cast: Li Lianjie (Jet Li) as Fang Shiyu, Li Jiaxin (Michelle Reis) as Lei Tingting, Xiao Fangfang (Josephine Siao) as Miao Cuihua, Hu Huizhong (Sibelle Hu) as Li Shaohuan, Zhen Shaoqiu (Adam Cheng) as Chen Jialuo

A tale about Fang Shiyu (Cantonese: Fong Sai Yuk), legendary folk hero of 19th Century South China. When the Red Flower Society led by Chen Jialuo launches the "down with the Qing, restore the Ming" rebellion, the Emperor Qianlong orders his generals to get him a list of the Red Flowers' membership. The one list in existence comes into the hands of Fang Shiyu's parents Fang De and Miao Cuihua, and the whole family battles fiercely to protect it. Between battles, Fang Shiyu finds time to romance Lei Tingting, daughter of wealthy Lei Laohu. Chen Jialuo appreciates the Fangs' assistance, and becomes so fond of Fang Shiyu he makes him his sworn son. Fang Shiyu and Lei Tingting say goodbye to their parents and leave to follow Chen Jialuo.

609. *Fang Zhenzhu (Fang Zhen Zhu)*

1952. Da Guang Ming Film Company. B & W. 11 Reels. Direction: Xu Cang Lin. Screenplay: Xu Canglin, based on the novel by Lao She (1899–1966). Cinematography: Chen Zhenxiang. Cast: Tao Jin, Little Wang Yurong, Sun Jinglu, Wei Xikui, Zhang Lide, Kou Baolin, Gao Zhanfei, Gu Eryi, Zhen Ming, Gu Yelu

When the Japanese Army moves into Beiping, Fang Zhenzhu, a performer called "Broken Kite," refuses to collaborate, and takes his wife and daughter to the Chinese interior, where he performs plays and musical numbers advocating resistance. As a result, his family is persecuted by the collaborationist government and its agents. When the war ends, the family returns to Beiping, hoping to settle back into a peaceful life. But the persecution by Nationalist government agents resumes. His family renews their friendship with a young art worker named Wang Li who had written many anti-Japanese scripts for "Broken Kite." With his help and much hard work, "Broken Kite" is finally able to organize a theater company and rent a theater for their performances. But on opening night, the theater is trashed by pro-government thugs. After the liberation of Beiping, "Broken Kite" becomes a respectable senior art worker, and begins a new life under the leadership of the people's government.

610. *The Fantastic Seedling Transplanter (Sheng Yang Shou)*

1960. Changchun Film Studio. B & W. 4 Reels. Direction: Huang Shu. Screenplay: Huang Shu. Cinematography: Wang Yizhi. Art Direction: Yun Liansheng. Music: Yan Shihua. Sound: Zhang Fenglu. Cast: Chen Hongsheng as Cao Shuncai, Lu Tinglan as Tian Xiaoqin, Ma Shida as Secretary Tian, He Zhongzhou as Cao Youwen, Duan Bing as Zhang Peng, Gao Fengxin as Li Jun

In the Spring of 1960, several young people from an agricultural commune of the banks of the Liao River are working hard to upgrade the commune's technology. With the support of Party Secretary Tian, they seek to replace manual rice transplanting with a transplanting machine. Old farmer Cao Shuncai is so experienced at transplanting rice seedlings he is called the "fantastic rice transplanter." However, he is conservative and distrusts machinery. He asks for a contest with the machine. In a tough rice transplanting contest between him and the transplanting machine operated by Tian Xiaoqin, one of the young people, the machine wins. Faced with the facts, Cao Shuncai finally overcomes his conservative thinking.

611. *Far East Espionage War (Yuan Dong Jian Die Zhan)*

1992. Emei Film Studio. Color. Letterboxed. 10 Reels. Direction: Jia Mu. Screenplay: Hu Yuewei. Cinematography: Li Erkang, Liang Baoqin. Art Direction: Wu Qidi. Music: Liu Zhupei. Sound: Shen Yihua. Cast: Paolisi Fulajimiweiqi Keliuyefu as Laisuo Tuofu, Sun Haiyin as Shenbeng Gongjie, Wu Jian as Shushoken, Si Tao as Gangbu Guowei, Wang Hui as Xiaoye Qianxiangzhi

One night in late 1937, a Soviet general flees from the army base where he is stationed and crosses the border into the Japanese puppet state of Manchukuo. When captured, he tells the Japanese commander that he has fled from Stalin's purge of the Soviet officer corps, and that he is willing to provide the Japanese with intelligence information if they in return will get his wife and daughter out of Russia. The Japanese decide he could be useful, especially if his information leads to Stalin's assassination, which the Japanese hope to accomplish somehow. They successfully get the Soviet general's family out for a happy holiday reunion. Afterwards, the Russian and a Japanese officer are assigned to lead a commando troop of mostly White Russian exiles back across the border to stage a raid on a Soviet position there. But they are trapped, obviously betrayed by someone, and wiped out. It is later learned that the Japanese officer was really a Chinese-Korean, a member of the Communist underground. The Russian general's true motivation for defecting remains a mystery to this day.

612. *Far Removed from War (Yuan Li Zhan Zheng De Nian Dai)*

1987. August First Film Studio. Color. 9

Reels. Direction: Hu Mei. Screenplay: Li Baolin. Cinematography: Zhang Li. Art Direction: Fang Xuzhi. Music: Zhen Qiufeng. Sound: Wang Defan, Huang Yinxia. Cast: Huang Zongluo as Gu Meng, Wang Xueqin as Gu Xiaozhou, Zhu Ling as Wenyan, Tao Yuling as Chen Yunhua

Eighth Route Army veteran Gu Meng is enjoying a peaceful retirement living with his son Xiao Zhou, a military school cadet, his son's wife and their child. Every once in a while Gu recognizes a familiar name or face in a magazine. As time goes by, he begins to reminisce more and more about his war years. One day, without telling his family, Gu leaves home to search for an old battlefield. It takes Xiao Zhou a long time to find his father, but when he does the generation gap between them is narrower because Xiao Zhou realizes that even though the war is ended, it still exerts a strong influence on the generation that fought it.

Second Prize, Silver Award, 10th Asian, African and Latin American Film Festival in Moscow.

Special Jury Award, 12th Salso International Film Festival.

613. *Faraway Star (Yuan Fang De Xing)*

1983. Xiaoxiang Film Studio. Color. 9 Reels. Direction: Wu Peimin. Screenplay: Bi Bicheng. Cinematography: Zhou Shengtong. Art Direction: Rao Weiquan. Music: Liu Qi. Sound: Huang Shiye. Cast: Gao Ying as Zhang Yunyun, Wang Yuzhang as Zhao Jianxin, Ma Jing as Danli, Kang Tai as Zhang Yuanxun, Shi Zhongling as Jiang Ruping, Zhou Liangliang as Zhou Shuyun

In 1977, young and inexperienced Shanghai girl Zhang Yunyun is assigned to work at the construction site of the Xingxing Dairy Products Plant. A year later, the plant is completed, and Zhang has become a veterinarian at the plant's cattle ranch. A new political line soon forces the plant to stop production, however, and when her father is restored to his position as director of the Steel Institute, he asks her to return to Shanghai. When Zhang Yunyun returns to Shanghai, she finds her father has made arrangements for her to work in the Institute's foreign documents office. Her former schoolmate Jiang Ruping begins to court her, and her father encourages Yunyun to marry him. Yunyun feels lost without the career she had chosen for herself, and finally she leaves Shanghai to return to the cattle ranch, working with her former colleagues in the career she loves.

614. *Farewell to My Concubine (Ba Wang Bie Ji)*

1993. Tomson (HK) Film Corp. Ltd., China Film Co-Production Corporation and Beijing Film Studio Co-Production. Color. Wide Screen. 16 reels. Direction: Chen Kaige. Screenplay: Li Bihua (Lillian Lee) and Lu Wei, based on the novel by Lillian Lee. Cinematography: Gu Changwei. Art Direction: Yang Zhanjia. Music: Zhao Jiping. Sound: Tao Jing. Costume: Jiang Jingming, Song Shangming, Huang Baorong, Wang Zhiming. Makeup: Fan Qingshan, Xu Guangrui. Cast: Zhang Guorong (Leslie Cheung) as Cheng Dieyi, Gong Li as Juxian, Zhang Fengyi as Duan Xiaolou, Lu Ji as opera school owner Guan , Ge You as Master Yuan, Ying Da as Na Kun, Li Chun as Xiao Si (as a teenager), Ma Mingwei as Douzi (as a child), Fei Yang as Shitou (as a child), Yin Zhi as Shitou (as a teenager), Jiang Wenli as Douzi's mother, Zhi Yitong as Aoki Saburo, David Wu as the Red Guard

In the 1920s, a prostitute brings her little boy Douzi to a school for training Beijing Opera performers, a regimen somewhat comparable to military boot camp. Douzi's slim figure and gentle features have fated him to always perform female roles, and he soon becomes close friends with Shitou, a boy being trained to portray masculine characters. The two are usually cast as the main characters in the historical tragedy "Farewell to My Concubine." They grow up to become major stars in Beijing, and Douzi (now called Cheng Dieyi) actually falls in love with Shitou, now called Duan Xiaolou. The two are close friends until Xiaolou becomes enamored of Juxian, a prostitute. He marries her, shattering Cheng Dieyi's dreams of a lifelong relationship with Duan Xiaolou. Their personal drama is played out against a background of a China in political turmoil, with World War II, Civil War and the Cultural Revolution all having an impact on the lives of these people and everyone around them. The last upheaval proves Juxian's undoing, as she commits suicide after Red Guards force her husband to declare publicly that he does not love her. In addition, both of the men are barred from performing, as their art is now considered a relic of feudalism. After the Cultural Revolution is over, the two aging actors prepare to resume performance of their classical roles. During a dress rehearsal of "Farewell to My Concubine" Dieyi kills himself in the manner of his character, his ultimate expression of love and loyalty to the king.

615. *Father and Son (Fu Yu Zhi)*

1986. Changlong Film & Television Company. Color. Letterboxed. 10 Reels. Direction: Wang Binglin. Screenplay: Li Baoyuan. Cinematography: Yang Wenqin. Art Direction: Cheng Rongyuan. Music: Ma Ding. Sound: Li Bojiang. Cast: Chen Qiang as Old Kui, Chen Peisi as Erzi, Huang Ling as Kui's wife, Liu Peiqi as Shunzi, Yu Li as Niuzi, Zhang Daizong as Shunzi's mother

First in a popular series of comedies featuring real-life father and son Chen Qiang and Chen Peisi.

616. *Father and Son Open a Bar (Ye Er Liang Kai Geting)*

1992. Liaoning Film Studio & Xi'an Film Studio Co-Production. Color. Letterboxed. 9 Reels. Direction: Chen Peisi and Ding Xuan. Screenplay: Gong Le. Cinematography: Zhang Zhongwei and Yu Changjiang. Art Direction: Zhang Lei. Music: Guo Xiaohu. Sound: Xiang Ziliang. Costume: Zhang Junlan. Makeup: Tian Xiaoxue. Cast: Chen Qiang as Old Kui, Chen Peisi as Erzi, Fu Yiwei as Lin Xiaoyi, Huang Ling as Kui's wife, Wang Zhongxing as Dakuan, Wang Xin as Mr. Wei

A sequel to the 1990 film, "Father and Son's Car."

Back from Shenzhen, Old Kui and his son Erzi open a karaoke singing hall and make pretty good money. Having some money for a change seems to change Old Kui a bit, and he is no longer satisfied with his previous style of eating and dressing. His wife soon has plastic surgery to keep up with him. Erzi falls for a singer working at the hall, but meanwhile she is also close to the old man. This sets up a confrontation between the two men which hurts business. Erzi eventually loses his temper and smashes the hall. He goes to the station and silently boards a train to leave home. Where will he go and what will he do?

617. *Father and Son's Car (Fu Zhi Lao Ye Che)*

1990. Shenzhen Film Corporation. Color. 9 Reels. Wide Screen. Direction: Liu Qingwu. Screenplay: Gong Le. Cinematography: Guan Qingwu. Art Direction: Chen Xiaoxia. Music: Fu Lin. Sound: Wang Yunhua. Cast: Chen Qiang as Old Kui, Chen Peisi as Erzi, Hao Yan as Shu Yin, Wang Bing as General Manager Ren

Old Kui buys an old, shabby 1940s automobile, with the idea of letting his son Erzi use it to do business. But father and son can't get the license they want, until they meet Mr. Ren, general manager of a local entertainment resort. In order to attract tourists with their car rental, Mr. Ren persuades them to work for his company. But he cheats them repeatedly. Their living quarters are inhumane, the car keeps breaking down, and they become a laughing stock everywhere they go. Their fortune changes when a visiting Japanese dignitary recognizes the car as his father's official car from the days he was a high-ranking official during the Japanese occupation of the area. The old jalopy suddenly becomes a much sought-after commodity.

618. *Favorite Piece of Music (Jue Xiang)*

1985. Pearl River Film Studio. Color. 10 Reels. Direction: Zhang Zeming. Screenplay: Zhang Zeming. Cinematography: Zhen Kangzhen, Zhao Xiaoshi. Art Direction: Zhang Jingwen, Peng Jun. Music: Zhou Xiaoyuan. Sound: Wu Muqin. Cast: Kong Xianzhu as Qu Laoshu, Feng Diqing as Guanzi, Li Jianjun as Huinu, Liu Qianyi as Huinu, Mao Shaoying as Hongmian

In the early 1960s, in a narrow old alley in Guangzhou's Xiguan area live elderly Qu Laoshu and his son. The older Qu had been an artist in the old society, and he loves Cantonese music very much. His greatest hope is to publish his own collected music compositions. His son Guanzi also loves music but the Cultural Revolution disturbs the peaceful life of the small alley, and the son is sent away to the countryside. When the Cultural Revolution ends, Guanzi returns to the small alley to find his old father still dreaming of assembling his music collection. After the old man's death, his favorite music is used as piano music and is played in music halls to great public acceptance. Guanzi eventually comes to realize the true value of his father's music, as well as his father's contributions to Cantonese music.

Best Cinematographer Zhen Kangzhen and Zhao Xiaoshi, 1986 Golden Rooster Awards.

Best Art Direction Zhang Jingwen and Peng Jun, 1986 Golden Rooster Awards.

619. *Feifei Becomes a Movie Actor (Fei Fei Cong Ying Ji)*

1986. Children's Film Studio. Color. 8 Reels. Direction: Lu Gang. Screenplay: Lu Gang. Cinematography: Sun Yongtian. Art Direction: Guo Juhai. Music: Lu Yuan, Yang Chunlin. Sound: Lan Fan. Cast: Ka Li as Feifei, Wu Peipei as He Ke, Wang Yunting as Ge Hua, Hu Wenbing as Laichun

Film director Ge Hua is preparing to make a children's movie called "Xiaolong Gaofei" ("Little Dragon Gaofei"). He is thrilled to find a boy named Feifei who seems ideal for the title role: he is bright, can swim, and knows some kongfu. Although he has no acting training or experience, Feifei arrives at the movie set with the idea that "acting is no different than playing," but he has many more difficulties than expected. But with the help of various members of the film crew, Feifei at last finishes the film successfully and acquires some new skills such as horse riding.

620. *Female Messenger (Nu Jiao Tong Yuan)*

1978. Changchun Film Studio. B & W. 10 Reels. Direction: Qin Basheng. Screenplay: Xue Shouxian. Cinematography: Wu Bengli. Art Direction: Gao Guoliang, Ju Lutian. Music: Cao Shuzuang. Sound: Liu Xingfu. Cast: Lu Guilan as the female messenger, Yi Da as Fang Zheng, Zhang Nan as Luo Xiaomin, Liu Hongkun as Fan Guoxiang, Ma Loufu as Uncle Song, Qu Yun as Old Mrs. Zhen

In 1947, the Nationalists launch a major assault on the Communist-held area of Shandong province, inflicting heavy losses. Communist Fang Zheng is ordered to Nationalist-occupied Fenghuoshan County to organize a new Party committee. The woman messenger accompanying him goes to the village of Hejiazhuang to contact the local liaison there, but finds the liaison, Old Mrs. Zhen, has been arrested and executed. She learns that before her death, Old Mrs. Zhen had left information at Huangshuling with a man named Fan Guoxiang. When she arrives there, the messenger learns that Fan has turned traitor and betrayed the Party, and that the Japanese searching for

Fang Zheng. To find and warn him, the messenger decides to go to Jiulonghe, where Mr. Zhao had worked before; when she arrives she instead finds Fan Guoxiang, and knowing that he is the traitor, kills him. Finally, after many difficulties, she finds Fang Zheng and gets him to a boat which will take him to safety. Before the boat can leave, however, the Japanese pursuing them arrive. The woman messenger at first surrenders to them, but then pulls the pin on a hand grenade, dying with her captors.

621. *Female Prisoners (Nu Qiu Da Dui)*

1992. Inner Mongolia Film Studio. Color. Letterboxed. 10 Reels. Direction: Wuer Shana. Screenplay: Lin Haiou. Cinematography: Ge Ritu. Art Direction: Dong Yonggang. Music: Guo Zhijie. Sound: Ao Si. Costume: Ta Na. Makeup: Su Bude. Cast: Song Chunli as Xiao Chun, Han Ying as Liu Lanxiang, A Lan as Li Yanan, Shen Yifeng as Zhang Chuyu, Zhou Hong as An Qi, Mi Jiazhai as Xiao Liuzhi, Gao Hong as Bai Yuping

Xiao Chun, cadre responsible for a team of women prisoners, begins to suspect that one of her charges was framed. The clues she finds point to the prisoner's lover and lawyer. At the same time, Xiao Chun helps in the adjustment of another prisoner who committed a crime so that her younger sister could go abroad for study, only to be rejected by her later.

622. *The Feng River Flows Far (Feng Shui Chang Liu)*

1963. Beijing Film Studio. B & W. 11 Reels. Direction: Sha Meng, Fu Jie. Screenplay: Hu Zheng and Sha Meng, based on the novel of the same title by Hu Zheng. Cinematography: Yang Jiming, Xu Xiaoxian. Art Direction: Yu Yiru, Mo Renji, Wu Shenghan. Music: Gao Ruxing. Sound: Cai Jun, Zhang Jiake. Cast: Gao Baocheng as Wang Liansheng, Wang Zhigang as Guo Chunhai, Zhang Ping as Zhou Fuyou, Li Renglin as Zhao Yucang, Guo Jun as Guo Shoucheng, Zhao Zhiyue as Xu Mingli

In 1954, the Xingyuanbao Agricultural Commune on the banks of the Feng River in Shanxi province suffers a series of natural disasters. Young Party Secretary Guo Chunhai leads the people in overcoming their difficulties. However, Deputy Commune Director Liu Yuanlu tries to thwart Guo's efforts, as he fears they will be an obstacle to his making personal profits from illegal grain sales. Guo's ideas are successful at overcoming drought and other natural disasters, and the commune realizes a bumper crop at the next harvest. However, Liu Yuanlu does nothing to help, even though the Party branch has helped him many times. In the end, Liu's plot to destroy the commune is exposed and he is dismissed from his position as deputy director.

623. *Fenshui Mountain Range (Fen Shui Ling)*

1964. August First Film Studio. B & W. 9 Reels. Direction: Li Jun. Screenplay: Li Yang and Lu Zhuguo. Cinematography: Chen Jun. Art Direction: Xu Run. Music: Gong Zhiwei. Sound: He Baoding. Cast: Zhang Yongshou as Li Yunhu, Zhou Zhengyu as the County Secretary, Liu Jiaoji as Li Yunlong, Gao Baocheng as Honest Zhang, An Qi as Sun Guilan, Liu Lei as Sun Qitang, Xin Xiaoming as Yan Wanshan

After he marries Sun Guilan, daughter of fugitive landlord Sun Qitang, Fengshui Mountain Range production team director Li Yunlong begins to lose his class awareness. He increasingly devotes himself to the road of "individual prosperity." After Yunlong's brother Yunhu returns home from army service, he criticizes Yunlong for in effect becoming the enemy. The two brothers quarrel. Some fertilizer is stolen, and, influenced by the words of Sun Qitang and former landlord Yan Wanshan, Yunlong accuses an innocent person of the crime. Sun Qitang also tries to falsely accuse Yunhu, but with the support of the county Party secretary and the local farmers, Yunhu is able to turn the tables and expose the true criminals. Sun Qitang and his daughter are arrested, and Yunlong is removed from his position as director.

624. *Fickle Changgeng (Nu Huang Ling Xia De Feng Liu Niang Men)*

1992. Xi'an Film Studio. Color. Letterboxed. 10 Reels. Direction: Dong Kena. Screenplay: Wang Baocheng. Cinematography: Mi Jiaqin, Song Zhaoguang. Art Direction: Wang Biao, Yu Shenglin. Music: Li Yaodong. Sound: Guo Chao. Costume: Zhang Ying. Makeup: Zhao Gang, Chen Ming. Cast: Li Lan as Wu Yueer, Lu Xiaohe as Sun Changqing, Xia Yonghua as "Naughty"

In a Northwest Chinese village, Sun Changqing has for more than a decade carried on an affair with his wife's best friend, nick-named "Naughty" for her flirtatious ways. But when his textile business makes him rich, Sun Changqing takes two more mistresses, which further alienates him from his wife and from Naughty. His long-suffering wife decides she needs a new life, so she leaves for the city, where she starts a business selling art objects to tourists. She also becomes successful. Back in the village, Sun is making lots of money, but finds himself shunned by other villagers disgusted with his treatment of his wife. At last he comes to his senses and goes to visit her. They reconcile and hold a new wedding to celebrate.

625. *Fierce Conflicts (Da Chong Zhuang)*

1992. Xi'an Film Studio. Color. Letterboxed. 10 Reels. Direction and Screenplay: Zhang Xiaomin, based on Shi Chengyuan's novel "Black Dream." Cinematography: Wang Dong. Art Direction: Li Xingzheng. Music: Liang Heping. Sound: Hua Juan, Ji Changhua. Costume: Liu Qingli. Makeup: Cheng Kelin, Chen Quan. Cast: Tian Jing as Zeng Jun, Zhang Xiaomin as Shen Li, Ju Yuguo as Song Youyou

Zeng Jun, Wang Haixiang and Che Tiao are members of an elite paramilitary task force assigned to combat drug traders along the Chinese border. In the fighting, Zeng suffers a serious head injury, Wang loses a leg, and Che is killed. The two survivors return to Beijing, and are shocked at how things have changed: Zeng's girlfriend Shen Li is now a celebrity pop singer, and their old friend Song Youyou is president and CEO of a luxury hotel. Zeng Jun and Shen Li are soon married. Wang Haixiang takes up with a girl who loves money, so to satisfy her demands he becomes involved in antique smuggling. He soon becomes a fugitive, and is abandoned by the girl. Zeng Jun becomes increasingly confused with how things in China have changed. One night at Song Youyou's hotel, Zeng intervenes to help a waitress being pawed by a foreigner, but finds himself accused of misconduct. In addition, his beating up the foreigner gets Song dismissed from his position. But the two men's friendship survives their troubles.

626. *Fight for the Right (Shu Yu Zheng Feng)*

1993. Inner Mongolia Film Studio, Beijing

Film Studio and Hong Kong Zhengdong Film Corp. Ltd. Co-Production. Color. Letterboxed. 10 Reels. Direction: Yuan Kui. Screenplay: Ji An, Chen Jianzhong. Cinematography: Li Pingbin. Art Direction: Fu Delin, Liang Huasheng. Costume: Li Jiqing, Li Xinyan, Li Weixian, Tang Baoli, Lu Baozhong. Makeup: Xu Qiuwen, Liu Jianping, Su Bao, Zhen Mengmeng, Guo Jingxia, Liu Li, Chou Ping, Lu Ruilian. Cast: Li Lianjie (Jet Li) as Fang Shiyu, Zhen Shaoqiu, Li Jiaxin, Guo Aiming, Yuan Kui, Ji Chunhua.

In the 18th Century, heroic Fang Shiyu (Cantonese: Fong Sai Yuk) is much admired by Red Flower Society head Chen Jialuo, which makes his second in command Yu Zhenhai very jealous. A Japanese agent finds a document indicating that Chen is really the brother of Emperor Qian Long, and is supplying the emperor with secret documents. This greatly worries Chen, for if this information were made public, no one in the anti–Qing movement would ever trust him again. So he asks Fang to retrieve the incriminating document. Fang succeeds, but is shocked at its content. To keep the organization intact, he keeps silent about it. Meanwhile, to take over the organization, Yu Zhenhai has Chen abducted, then replaces him at the top. Fang rescues Chen, killing Yu in the process. Chen Jialuo asks Fang to stay on and become his chief deputy, but Fang has had enough of fighting. He takes his mother and fiancee and returns to his hometown in search of a quiet life.

627. *Fighter in White (Bai Yi Zhan Shi)*

1949. Northeast Film Studio. B&W. 9 reels. Direction: Feng Bailu. Screenplay: Wang Zhenzhi. Cinematography: Ma Shouqing. Art Direction: Liu Xueyao. Music: Gao Tian. Sound: Zhao Hongjun. Set Design: Wang Yongrui. Cast: Yu Lan as Zhuang Yi, Huang Ling as Tang Weizhen, An Qi as Zhen Yuanping, Zhang Jingping as Da Long, Lu Fei as the Assistant, Chen Qiang as Yang Mingqing, Su Ling as Company Commander Zhu

During the War of Liberation, Zhuang Yi, an army nurse in a PLA medical unit, is transferring wounded soldiers to a hospital. En route, their convoy is attacked by enemy aircraft and she is herself wounded while protecting the soldiers in her care. However, she continues to care for the wounded soldiers and sees them safely to the hospital. Her courage moves hospital personnel to work feverishly to restore her to health. Eventually she rejoins her unit in the field, joyously reunited with old comrades.

628. *Fighting for the Gold Map (Ming Duo Huang Jin Tu)*

1990. Changchun Film Studio. Color. Wide Screen. 9 Reels. Direction: Zhao Weiheng. Screenplay: Yu Yanbing, Hou Ruoxuan. Cinematography: Xu Shouzen, Zhou Yu. Art Direction: Liu Zhongren, Min Jianguo. Music: Chen Shouqian. Sound: Huang Yongqing, Sheng Hongtao. Cast: Fu Yongcai as Jin Haiqin, Huang Chao as Yugu, Jing Zhengqi as Chu Yunlong

In the late 19th Century, various foreign imperialist nations exploit the weakness of the Qing dynasty to drain China of natural resources. Hearing reports of gold in Northeast China, the Chinese government sends an exploration team led by Jin Haiqin to check this out. The team finds the lode and draws a map of its location. But senior official Chu Yunlong, a traitor in the employ of the Japanese, tries to get the map away from them. Another who wants to obtain the map is Yugu, a woman "greenwoods bandit." Later, she is so impressed by Jin Haiqin's patriotism that she decides to join forces with him in protecting the map from the Japanese, but all the patriotic Chinese are killed in the struggle.

Fighting for Treasure at Pingjin see *Legend of the Cixi Tomb Treasure*

629. *Fighting for Power (Duo Yin)*

1963. August First Film Studio. B & W. 9 Reels. Direction: Wang Shaoyan. Screenplay: Wang Hong and Ding Yi, based on the stage play of the same title by Wang Hong. Cinematography: Chen Ruijun. Art Direction: Zhen Tuo. Music: Zhang Rui, Yu Ping. Sound: He Baoding. Cast: Li Yan as He Wenjin, Tian Hua as Hu Sufang, Gao Jialin as Chen Guangqing, Liu Lei as Chen Youcai, Li Huijian as Chen Guangyu, Shi Yan as Chunmei, Shi Cunyu as Yan Delin, Yan Xiaoming as Chen Dafu, Liu Jiyun as Chen Jingyi

In 1960, a counterrevolutionary family named Chen gains control of the Xiaochen Village production team in Northern Jiangsu. The local director Chen Guangqing provides a cover for his relatives' corrupt practices and economic crimes. When new Party secretary He Wenjin arrives, one of the Chens, Chen Jingyi, tries to win the newcomer over to their side. He Wenjin sees through Chen's efforts, and Chen begins to fear his crimes will be discovered. He goes to the production team's accountant to intimidate the latter into a cover-up. A power struggle breaks out in the village, with He Wenjin doggedly investigating. After he has gathered all his evidence, He brings in the militia to arrest Chen Jingyi and others involved. Power in the village is restored to the hands of the people.

630. *Fighting It Out at Huangqiao (Huang Qiao Jue Zhan)*

1985. August First Film Studio. Color. 10 Reels. Director: Yang Zhaoren. Screenplay: Shuo Yunping, Shi Chao. Cinematography: Yang Zhaoren. Art Direction: Ren Huixing. Music: Gong Zhiwei. Sound: Shen Guorui. Cast: Liu Xitian as Chen Yi, Xu Xing as Zhao Yong, Yang Chiyu as Han Deqing, Peng Qiyu as Li Shiyi, Jiang Hua as Lin Taiyuan

In 1940, the CPC advocates forming a united front with the Nationalist government to resist the Japanese invaders, but Chiang Kai-shek adheres to a policy of non-resistance while continuing his efforts to exterminate Chinese Communists. The CPC central command decides to link their bases in north and south China to present a stronger anti-Japanese force and has General Chen Yi lead the New Fourth Army north. When he learns of this move, Chiang orders Jiangsu's provincial governor Han Deqing to intercept Chen Yi in northern Jiangsu and wipe out his forces. To do this, Chiang gives Han a force that is 10 times larger than Chen's. The film relates how Chen Yi unites as many anti–Japanese forces as possible, brings some Nationalist troops over to the CPC's united front campaign, and in the end defeats the much larger Nationalist force at the famous and decisive battle of Huangqiao.

631. *Fighting North and South (Nan Zheng Bei Zhan)*

1952. Shanghai Film Studio. B & W. 13 Reels. Direction: Cheng Ying and Tang Xiaodan. Screenplay: Shen Ximeng, Shen Mujun and Gu Baozhang. Cinematography: Zhu Jinming and Gu Wunhou. Art Direction: Han Xin and Chen Bosheng. Music: Ge Yan. Sound: Miao Zhenyu. Costume: Zhi Guang. Makeup: Jiang Youan. Cast: Chen Ge as the Division Commander, Tang Huada as the Division Political Commissar, Wang Li as Regimental Commander Liu, Feng Ji

Fighting North and South. 1952. Shanghai Film Studio.

as Battalion Commander Gao, Pan Wengzhan as the Advisor, Liu Peiran as Company Commander Zhang

In the winter of 1947, the Nationalist Chinese Army launches a massive attack on Communist-held areas of Southeast China. Seven battles in the northern part of Jiangsu province result in seven Red Army victories. As a tactical move, the Communist forces began a rapid retreat, difficult for some of their troops to understand at first. Commander Gao's battalion moves into the Yimeng Mountain area of Shandong province to await further orders. The local villagers also question the order to withdraw, so in order to calm the rebellious mood of the troops and the villagers, Gao and village head Zhao Yuming explain the battle strategy of higher levels of command. The situation changes suddenly when the enemy, interpreting the Communist retreat as a sign of imminent collapse, masses a force of 300,000 in position to surround the Communists. But the attackers discover too late they have fallen into a trap, with Gao's unit blocking their retreat. In the battle, the Nationalist forces are annihilated.

632. *Fighting the Gunrunners (Ji Qiang Xing Dong)*

1991. Pearl River Film Studio. Color. Letterboxed. 9 Reels. Direction: Yu Shibing. Screenplay: Li Yanxiong. Cinematography: Yan Xuzhong and Wang Hongyan. Art Direction: Liang Guoxiong. Music: Cao Guangping. Sound: Li Dehua. Cast: Wang Jiancheng as Shang Yi, Lu Ying as Liu Yinyin, Feng Jinggao as Fang Yunsheng, Chen Jianjun as Old Scar, Wang Handong as Old Snake, Xi Xiaolu as Old Baldy

Police in Haidao City catch a man attempting to take guns across the border. Their investigation shows this to be part of a much larger effort by a Hong Kong triad to smuggle guns out of China. Chief detective Shang Yi infiltrates the triad and at last finds the guns are being smuggled out in disguised shipments of toy guns for the overseas market.

633. *Fighting the Power of Dongchang (Dong Chang Die Xue)*

1988. Changchun Film Studio. Color. 10 Reels. Direction: Ke Ren, Yu Mei. Screenplay: Wu Qitai, Lu Wenyu. Cinematography: Dansheng Nima. Art Direction: Wang Chong, Gan Jun. Music: Gao Feng. Sound: Zhang Fengxing.

Cast: Liang Boluo as Wei Zhongxian, Du Yulu as Yang Lian, Li Ying as Ke Shi

In the last years of his reign (ca1625), Ming Emperor Xi Zong has become so obsessed with collecting wood carvings that he has lost all interest in affairs of state. Eunuch Wei Zhongxian has moved into this vacuum to usurp de facto power, and plans to take over completely. Scholar Yang Lian undertakes the job of investigating Wei's conspiracy and other alleged crimes, and works with some loyal martial artists to gather evidence. Their efforts fail, however, as Yang Lian is falsely accused and then killed by Wei Zhongxian.

634. *Fighting the Sharks (Dou Sha)*

1978. Pearl River Film Studio. Color. 9 Reels. Direction: Tao Jin. Screenplay: Liu Xinping, Li Zhenjia. Cinematography: Liu Jingtang. Art Direction: Xu Peng, Ye Jialiang. Music: Tan Zhibing. Sound: Deng Qinhua. Cast: Zhang Guomin as Liang Feng, Zhang Liang as Guo Dongshan, Shi Jing as Qian Cangmao, Bai Li as Kang Manqian, Zhang Jianling as Hou Zupu, Hai Hong as Minister Hong

In 1949, it is learned that Nationalist agents plan to destroy the city of Binghai's water, gas and power supplies while the city is celebrating the founding of the PRC. Binghai city Military Administration Minister Hong assigns the case to a team of investigators headed by Liang Feng. They learn the code name for the spymaster is Jiang Sha, who is the former Nationalist Party Police Department Chief Hou Zupu. The investigators cast a wide net to wait for the enemy to make their move, and when they spring the trap the spies are all captured, guaranteeing the celebration will go unimpeded as planned.

635. *Filial Son and Filial Piety (Xiao Zi Xian Sun Ci Hou Zhe)*

1993. Youth Film Studio. Color. Letterboxed. 9 Reels. Direction: Chen Peisi, Zeng Jianfeng. Screenplay: Wang Peigong. Cinematography: Yang Ke. Art Direction: Yuan Chao. Music: Lei Lei. Sound: Li Bojiang. Costume: Zhen Wei, Liu Jianhua. Cast: Chen Peisi as Chen Erxiao, Zhao Lirong as Erxiao's mother, Wei Zongwan as old uncle, Ding Jiali as Erxiao's sister, Ni Dahong as husband of Erxiao's sister, Li Lina as Erxiao's wife

This comedy starts with Civil Affairs Department employee Mr. Chen urging his agency to implement funeral reform, which upsets his uncle, a provider of traditional funeral services. The uncle uses his sister, Chen's mother, to try and change his nephew's mind. So he convinces his elderly sister, who greatly fears cremation, to have her traditional funeral ahead of time, while she is still alive, with comic results.

636. *Fill the World with Love (Rang Shi Jie Chong Man Ai)*

1987. Xi'an Film Studio. Color. 10 Reels. Direction: Teng Wenji, Wen Luming. Screenplay: Qin Peichun, Teng Weiji. Cinematography: Mu Deyuan. Art Direction: Li Xingzheng, Feng Yuan. Music: Guo Feng. Sound: Hua Juan. Cast: Wang Xuehao as Zhao Wei, Yang Xiaojun as Lili, Li Xiaodong as Song Qi, Niu Beng as Director Ma

On a cold winter night, taxi driver Zhao Wei happens to see his girlfriend Lili coming out of a hotel on the arm of a foreigner. After she gets into his cab, Zhao angrily questions her. While they are quarreling, the car goes out of control and hits a motorcycle head on. Zhao Wei loads the two injured motorcyclists, a man and a woman, into his cab and rushes them through the deserted city streets to hospital. The woman, Song Qi, pulls through but the man, her brother, dies. When she recovers, Song Qi and her mother are very grateful to Zhao Wei for what they perceive as his Samaritan act, because they do not know he was responsible for the accident. Zhao Wei is so respectful and kind to them that gradually Song Qi falls in love with him. Tortured by mixed feelings of love and guilt, Zhao Wei confesses the truth to Song Qi just before the police arrive.

637. *The Filmmakers (Dian Ying Ren)*

1988. Pearl River Film Studio. Color. 9 Reels. Wide Screen. Direction: Ding Yinnan. Screenplay: Miao Yue, Ding Yinnan. Cinematography: Yu Xiaoqun. Art Direction: Fu Kai. Music: Dai Dawei. Sound: Huang Minguang. Cast: Xiong Yuanwei as Ge Yu, Siqin Gaowa as Shu Hua, Kuang Ping as Momo

A film crew on location is disrupted by constant squabbling between director Ge Yu and his cinematographer. Their quarreling extends even into the director's dreams. Shooting ceases while all await the arrival of Momo, the scenarist, but she is held up in another part of China trying to get a flight to the location site.

When she finally arrives and starts working on the screenplay, everything else seems to start breaking down. The lead actress, Shu Hua, feels mistreated because she has so little time for her young daughter. Egos clash, the best of intentions are misunderstood, etc. The director and the cinematographer at last work out an understanding, and the film within a film is finished. But the result is disappointing, and the director faces a career crisis…

638. *The Final Choice (Zui Hou De Xuan Ze)*

1983. Shanghai Film Studio. Color. 11 Reels. Direction: Song Chong. Screenplay: Zhang Qie, Gu Xiaoyan. Cinematography: Zhang Yuanmin. Art Direction: Xie Qiqian, Ye Jingmin. Music: Huang Zhun. Sound: Liu Guangjie. Cast: Li Yan as Chen Chunzhu, Tian Feiling as Wei Zhengguo, Xiang Mei as Chen Ying

In the fall of 1982, provincial Deputy Party Secretary Chen Chunzhu receives an anonymous letter alleging there are serious problems inside the Qinchuan City Party Committee. Since Qinchuan is his old hometown, he decides to make a personal investigation of the allegations. When he arrives he finds a series of irregular practices as well as many conflicts among the committee's members. The problems also have personal significance for Chen Chunzhu: at the center of the controversies is the Qinchuan Party Secretary Wei Zhenguo, Chen's old army buddy, and Chen's niece Chen Ying is Wei's wife. Chen at last finds the central problem to be that a "network" of "connections" has built up among the city's leadership like a spider's web, and this has become an obstacle to reform which he must break up if the city is to go forward.

639. *Final Clue of a Strange Global Case (Shi Jie Qi An De Zhui Hou Xian Suo)*

1985. Emei Film Studio. Color. 10 Reels. Direction: Bai Hong. Screenplay: Bai Hong. Cinematography: Wang Xiaochuan, Hou Yong. Art Direction: Jia Shiquan, Liu Yichun. Music: Zhou Long. Sound: Li Jian, Tu Liuqing. Cast: Liang Guoqing as Lin Fang, Shen Junyi as Wu Yuan, Cao Peng as Sun Xiu, Jia Yulan as Si Wen, Zhu Lei as Boss Wang, Liu Di as Shinko, Li Yue as Little Nan

In August, 1942, one of the world's most famous historical relics disappears: the skull of Peking Man. Even with Asia swept by war, the incident draws the attention of media worldwide, and a variety of people in China are concerned, including the invading Japanese Army and agents working for the U.S. Key to the search is Professor Si Xuzhi, an archaeologist: when Si and his daughter Wu Yuan show up in the north China area where Peking Man was found, all parties monitor their actions. Japanese collaborator Si Wen wants to abduct the two for he is certain they know where the skull is hidden. The professor is killed, but his documents are missing. Si Wen leaves town to search for where the professor might have hidden them, accompanied by Lin Fang, a covert agent for the CPC. Also pursuing them in their search is Sun Xiu, a spy for the Americans. In the end, the documents are discovered, but Si Wen and Lin Fang are killed fighting over them.

640. *A Fire Burns in the Furnace (Lu Huo Zheng Hong)*

1962. Changchun Film Studio. B & W. 10 Reels. Direction: Yan Gong. Screenplay: Yu Ming. Cinematography: Li Guanghui and Yin Zhi. Art Direction: Wang Xingwen and Jin Bohao. Music: Quan Rufeng. Sound: Jiang Junfeng. Cast: Pang Xueqing as Tian Hong, Zhang Juguang as Manager Wang, Ren Yi as Wu Shigang, Li Yalin as Zhu Quanzhong, Zhang Yuan as Nian Fengyi, Zhao Baohua as Qiao Yingmu

During the Great Leap Forward, Anshan steel workers propose building a furnace rapidly, so project director Wu Shigang advocates adoption of the "whole body installation" method to build it. Company manager Wang is adamantly opposed, for he believes that large-scale enterprises should not conduct mass movements. Party Secretary Tian Hong makes an on-site investigation, then enthusiastically supports the workers' suggestion and helps Manager Wang change his thinking. In the end, they adopt the "whole body installation" method and successfully accomplish their project on schedule.

641. *Fire in the Sky (Tian Huo)*

1991. Guangxi Film Studio. Color. Letterboxed. 9 Reels. Direction: Ying Qi. Screenplay: Ci Minhe. Cinematography: Jin Guirong. Art Direction: Huang Shu. Music: Zhao Jiping. Cast: Sun Feihu as Feng Shiguang, Xu Lei as Yan Yue, Ma Kun as Tang Rong, Rao Hongyi as Xing Zuo, Huang Minsheng as Zhao Erhong

The chief of a water conservancy project is under consideration for promotion to head of a provincial ministry. The provincial government sends two of its people to investigate the candidate. They find the man totally devoted to his work, a way to forget his pain over his estrangement from his daughter. At last, the candidate turns down the offer, preferring to remain at his present job.

642. *Fire Over the Yan River (Yan He Zhan Huo)*

1977. Changchun Film Studio. Color. 12 Reels. Direction: Lu Jianhua. Screenplay: Collective, recorded by Ji Ye. Cinematography: Wu Bengli. Art Direction: Liang Shukui. Music: He Yi. Sound: Huang Lijia, Liu Xinfu. Cast: Li Junhai as Regimental Commander Lu, Han Tao as Political Commissar Ding, Lu Jieren as Chief of Staff Zhou, Liu Xing as Staff Officer Liu, Du Tong as Battalion Commander Wu, Ye Zhikang as Company Commander Tong

In 1947, Chiang Kaishek concentrates forces to carry out a major attack on the area of Shandong province held by the Communists and on the Communist government in Yan'an. To protect the Communists' evacuation of the area, PLA Regimental Commander Lu Minyuan leads his forces in a strategic withdrawal which leads the enemy force away from Yan'an and to the west. This is the bait for the Nationalists to fall into a trap, which they do. The main part of the PLA forces wipe out the enemy after a major battle.

643. *Fire Sparks in a Mountain Village (Shan Zai Huo Zhong)*

1978. Changchun Film Studio. Color. 11 Reels. Direction: Liu Zhongming. Screenplay: Guiyang City Workers' Cultural Station Recreational Writing Team. Cinematography: An Zhiguo, Dansheng Nima. Art Direction: Wang Guizhi, Gao Tinglun. Music: Wu Damin. Sound: Xing Guocang. Cast: Zhao Yaming as Chi Li, Wang Yuning as Chi Li (as a child), Fang Hua as Bai Shanxiao, Li Wenwei as Ban Ergng, Wang Zhongchao as Niu Zai, Yi Fuwen as Wan Gang

In 1935, on the Red Army's Long March to the north, one company stops in a Buyi minority village. There, company commander Wan Gang rescues Chi Li, a girl being harassed by local strongman Bai Shanxiao, in close alliance with the Nationalist government. The Red Army educates Chi Li and others in the

class struggle, and then help the local minority people set up a self-defense militia. With Chi Li as their leader, the local people train to take up arms against Bai and the Nationalists. After the Red Army leaves, Bai Shanxiao returns, but Chi Li and her militia continue their struggle. Later, a Red Army troop returns to the area, and with their help the minority militia drives their enemies out once and for all. In the fighting, Chi Li kills Bai Shanxiao. The Red Army then resumes its march northward.

644. *Fire the Guns to Salute Him! (Kai Qiang, Wei Ta Song Xing!)*

1982. Shanghai Film Studio. Color. 10 Reels. Direction: Gao Zheng. Screenplay: Shen Ji, A Zhang. Cinematography: Shen Miaorong. Art Direction: Xie Muqian. Music: Yang Shaolu. Sound: Ren Xinliang. Cast: Ma Xiaowei as Mei Yukuan, Chen Shu as Songtian, Hui Juanyan as Zhang Xiaolan, Yu Guichun as Yang Ashi

In the fall of 1942, New Fourth Army guerrilla troop political supervisor Su Xin travels to Shanghai to purchase ammunition. On his arrival in Shanghai, he contacts the chief of the CPC's underground Mr. Zhao. But his arrival and the purpose of his visit are also known to Songtian, the head of Japanese intelligence in Shanghai, who orders his lieutenant Mei Yukuan to check it out. Mei Yukuan is an undercover CPC member, and he reports to Mr. Zhao that the Japanese must have a spy somewhere inside the guerrillas. The story evolves around Su Xin and Mei Yukuan's efforts to make the purchase and identify the spy, as well as continue protecting Mei Yukuan's cover. Eventually they buy the ammunition and deliver it to the guerrillas, and execute the traitor in their midst. They also arrange a ruse which restores Songtian's trust in Mei Yukuan, so that the Chinese agent remains firmly planted in the heart of the enemy.

645. *First Attraction (Di Yi You Huo)*

1993. Shanghai Film Studio. Color. Wide Screen. 10 Reels. Direction: Pao Zhifang. Screenplay: Wang Tianyun, Lu Shoujun. Cinematography: Ying Fukang. Art Direction: Zhou Xinren, Hu Zong. Music: Jin Fuzai. Sound: Feng Deyao. Costume: Zhang Gengbao. Makeup: Zhou Meihua. Cast: Xi Meijuan as Ye Ling, Zhen Qianlong as Zhou Wei, Jiao Huang as Ding Han, Xu Huanshan as Zhao Fengzhi, Da Shichang as Xu Gang, Ling Zhiao as Zhang Lao, Lu Yi as Xiao Ao, He Ling as Qingqing

An inspirational story of model worker Ye Ling, a senior engineer at a steel mill. After she and her husband divorce he departs for Singapore, leaving Ye to raise their teenage son alone. Ye Ling devotes her life to modernization of China's steel industry, and helps others overcome their difficulties, as well as coping with her own problems in life and work.

646. *The First Case in New China (Xin Zhong Guo Di Yi Da An)*

1992. Changchun Film Studio. Color. 10 Reels. Direction: Gao Tianhong. Screenplay: Lan Fu, Lu Bing, Xiao Yang, Shi Yuxin. Cinematography: An Zhiguo. Art Direction: Zhang Yan. Music: Qin Yongcheng, Lu Changwei. Sound: Gu Kejian, Zhang Fenglu. Costume: Ge Junjie. Makeup: Lu Huamin, Dan Xiangsuo. Cast: Li Guohua as Liu Qinshan, Li Yongtian as Zhang Zhishan, Du Yuan as Lin Kejian

In the summer of 1950, with the People's Republic less than a year old, Tianjin officials Liu Qinshan and Zhang Zhishan are lured into some corrupt business deals. They embezzle public funds to invest, even though thousands of ordinary people are going hungry. They are caught, tried and executed in February, 1952. This was a major scandal in China at the time, as both of the men had been respected veterans of the Long March.

647. *The First Gift (Jian Mian Li)*

1980. Shanghai Film Studio. Color. 4 Reels. Direction: Zhang Huijun, Chen Chan. Screenplay: Zhao Fujian, Li Tianji, Zhang Huijun, Chen Chan. Cinematography: Li Kui, Wang Tingshi. Art Direction: Zhao Yixuan. Music: Huang Zhun. Sound: Xie Guojie. Cast: Han Fei as Mr. Yang, Sun Jinglu as the old lady, Zhang Wenrong as Xiao Jing

Mr. Yang, Manager of the Qianjing Umbrella Factory, is very proud of his factory's output, but he ignores product quality. He selects and sends an umbrella as a gift for his fiancee's mother, but the woman is very embarrassed by the gift because it keeps opening unexpectedly and then is difficult to close again. On Yang's way to meet his future mother-in-law, it starts to rain and when using one of his own products, the dye is washed from the umbrella, staining his brand new white shirt. Yang's future in-laws realize the young man's ignorance of product quality, and decide to teach him a lesson. After returning to the factory, Mr. Yang devotes himself to improving product quality. Shortly after, the factory's products are welcomed by customers for their uniqueness and good quality. This time, Yang's future mother-in-law and his girl friend Xiao Jing both accept him.

648. *First Kiss (Chu Wen)*

1992. Beijing Film Studio, assisted by the China Zhongqiao Development Corporation. Color. Letterboxed. 9 Reels. Direction: Li Ni. Screenplay: Jiang Cheng, Chen Ding. Cinematography: He Qin. Art Direction: Yuan Chao. Music: Guo Wenjing. Sound: Wu Ling. Costume: Li Xinyan. Makeup: Liu Dan. Cast: Jiang Cheng as Chen Leping, Song Xiaoyin as Song Mumu, Zhang Li as Liu Tingting, Zhang Yan as Yuanyuan, Lin Hai as Luo Jing, Zhou Zhou as Yu Tian

A bachelor playwright falls for the woman director of his new play, "First Kiss." The director is still unmarried at middle age, and long ago gave up all thought or hope of ever getting married. Through their working together, the playwright is at last able to convince her they can find romance later in life.

649. *The First Sino-Japanese War (Jia Wu Feng Yun)*

1962. Changchun Film Studio. Color. 11 Reels. Direction: Lin Nong. Screenplay: Xi Nong, Ye Nan, Chen Ying, Li Xiongfei and Du Li. Cinematography: Wang Qimin. Art Direction: Lu Xin. Music: Zhang Dicang. Sound: Chen Wenyuan. Cast: Li Muran as Deng Shicang, Pu Ke as Ding Rucang, Wang Qiuying as Li Hongzhang, Zhou Wenbing as Fang Boqian, Li Jie as Liu Buchu, Pang Xueqing as Wang Guocheng

In 1894, in preparation for the invasion of China, the Japanese Imperial navy creates several provocative incidents designed to test Chinese naval defenses. Li Hongzhang, court minister in charge of North Sea defenses, supported by his chief ally at court, Fang Boqian, captain of the warship "Jiyuan," recommend China make concessions to the Japanese. At the same time, Deng Shichang, commander of the warship "Zhiyuan," and his officers and seamen demand China fight. His appeals are twice rejected by Li Hongzhang. When the Japanese invade China without warning, Li Hongzhang has to send Deng Shichang to resist them. In the ensuing naval battle, the chief military commander Liu Buchu deliberately hoists the wrong flag signals, causing the navy

The First Sino-Japanese War. **Li Muran as heroic naval commander Deng Shichang. 1962. Changchun Film Studio.**

to lose its advantageous position. When his flagship is hit and sunk, Deng Shichang transfers to another ship and continues his command from there. They fight bravely, sinking a Japanese warship, but at last they run out of cannonballs. At this point, Deng decides to ram the enemy, but the Chinese ship is hit by a torpedo and goes down with all hands.

650. *The First Spring of the Sixties (Liu Shi Nian Dai Di Yi Chun)*

1960. Haiyan Film Studio and Tianma Film Studio co-production. Color. 11 Reels. Direction: Shen Fu, Liu Qiong, Lin Yang. Screenplay: Zhang Junxiang, Shen Fu, Huang Zongying, Ding Ran, Sun Yongping, Wun Xiying, Han Fei, Liu Fei, Li Qizhen, Liang Boluo, Zhou Chong. Cinematography: Huang Shaofeng, Cao Weiye, Wang Zhichu. Art Direction: Zhong Yongqing. Music: Lu Qiming, Sound: Lu Zhongbo, Liu

Guangjie. Cast: Liu Hongsheng as Yang Guangpei, Deng Nan as Mr. Lei, Zhang Yan as Jin Hai, Liu Fei as Jin Afu, Wu Yunfang as Shen Hua, Li Qizhen as Li Huaikai

In the spring of 1960, Party Secretary Yang Guangpei leads the workers at a small steel plant in reforming their technology and fulfilling their mechanizations goals ahead of the target date assigned to them.

651. *The First Sword (Shen Zhou Di Yi Dao)*

1993. Changchun Film Studio and Hong Kong Wanli Film Corp. Ltd. Co-Production. Color. Letterboxed. 10 Reels. Direction: Hong Jinbao (Samo Hong). Screenplay: Zhang Tan, Situ Zuohan. Cinematography: Li Junyan, Lin Huitai. Art Direction: Ye Jiren, Huang Renkui. Music: Lu Guanting. Costume: Zhou Xingguo, Zhang Qixin, Sun Yujie. Makeup: Wang Meihua, Zhao Li, Song Yingyuan, Zhao Liying, Gao Shaoping. Cast: Di Long as Tan Citong, Yang Fan as Wang Wu, Yang Liqing (Cynthia Khan) as Jiujin, Guan Zhiling (Rosamund Kwan) as Yan Xi, Zhao Changjun as Yuan Shikai, Hong Jinbao (Samo Hong) as the prison worker, Ni Xing as Lu Xiaochuan, Liu Xun as Ao Bai

A story of Wang Wu and the legendary Black Flag swordsmen, told against the background of the Chinese revolution. Wang meets and is inspired by Tan Citong, who dreams of saving China through reforms. Wang returns with Tan to Beijing and works in his reform campaign. Then Tan makes the fatal error of trusting Yuan Shikai, and is betrayed. Tan is sentenced to death, but when Wang Wu breaks into the prison to free him, Tan insists on remaining, for he believes his martyrdom will better serve the revolutionary cause. After Tan is executed, Wang in an outrage invades Yuan's mansion with intent to kill the treacherous official. But Wang is surrounded by Qing soldiers and killed.

652. *The First Woman in the Forests (Shan Lin Zhong Tou Yi Ge Nu Ren)*

1986. Beijing Film Studio. Color. 10 Reels. Direction: Wang Junzheng. Screenplay: Qiao Xuezhu. Cinematography: Zhang Zhongping. Art Direction: Zhen Huiwen. Music: Zhang Qianyi. Sound: Lai Qizhen, Wu Ling. Cast: Li Xiuming as Lin Nan and White Shoe, Li Wei as Old Ni, Ding Jiali as Da Lishen, Lei Han as Xiao Bodai, Ji Ling as Xiunu, Zhu Decheng as the villain

Lin Nan, a modern female college student, travels into a forested area of Northeast China's Heilongjiang province to collect research materials, where she comes upon a story from the past. In the 1940s, eight brothers flee the famine and poverty of their native Hebei province, and travel to the virgin forests of Heilongjiang's Great Khing'an Mountains to seek a livelihood. They find work as lumberjacks, but the money they earn is only enough to buy them a little temporary warmth and tenderness from the prostitutes in the little town. Two of these relationships become more than casual: prostitute White Shoe's lover, Old Ni, develops a deep affection for the young woman and is determined to save her. However, White Shoe is exhausted and sick, and doesn't live to see that day. Old Ni's little brother Xiao Bodai has a wild and rough relationship with the prostitute Da Lishen, but they become the first couple to settle down and raise a family in the forests.

Best Supporting Actress Ding Jiali, 1987 Golden Rooster Awards.

Best Sound Lai Qizhen and Wu Ling, 1987 Golden Rooster Awards.

653. *Fish Poachers (Tou Yu Zei)*

1988. Shanghai Film Studio. Color. Letterboxed. 10 Reels. Direction: Shi Xiaohua. Screenplay: Liang Qinsheng. Cinematography: Luo Zhengsheng. Art Direction: Wu Tianci, Yao Wei. Music: Yang Mao. Sound: Dong Yan. Cast: Yu Lan as Bai Piaoer, Lu Yi as Da Bala, Xie Yan as Magan the fish poacher, Wei Guochun as Shui Yaozhi

A group of fish poachers led by Da Bala operate along the wild reaches of the Heishuiliu River. When rookie police officer Xiao Shuiyao decides to make a name for himself by apprehending the thieves, he lands himself in more trouble than he had anticipated. Fortunately he is rescued by Bai Piao'er, an attractive young widow who runs a local bar and also happens to be Da Bala's lover. Xiao Shuiyao later leads a group of police in an operation to seal off the Heishuiliu River. Things take a violent turn, and Da Bala is almost killed, but is saved by Xiao Shuiyao. Da Bala is finally captured, but his lover swears she will wait for him at the tavern.

654. *Fishing Island in a Fury (Yu Dao Nu Chao)*

1977. Xi'an Film Studio. B & W. 11 Reels.

Direction: Zhang Jingreng. Screenplay: Jiang Shumao, based on the novel of the same title. Cinematography: Ling Xuan. Art Direction: Wang Fei. Music: Wei Ruixiang, Wang Yan. Sound: Hua Juan. Cast: Da Qi as Wang Sijiang, Liu Jizhong as Wang Haisheng, Li Hui as Tie Dan, Guo Diancang as an old oil worker, Si Jianlan as Liu's wife, LI Xilian as Dagui's mother, Wang Qiuying as Chi Longzhang

In 1947, Nationalist military strength grows stronger in the area around Communist-held Longwang Island. After the PLA withdraws temporarily from the island, powerful landlord Chi Longzhang returns to the island he had controlled for so long. Wang Haisheng, leader of a gang of children who oppose Chi, is captured and imprisoned by the landlord but is rescued by another member Tie Dan. Instructed by the wife of Party member Liu, the young people post propaganda notices all over the island, and help the armed forces punish Chi and his supporters. In the end, the PLA retakes the Long Island with the help of its people.

655. *Fist from Shaolin (Shao Lin Hao Xia Zhuan)*

1993. Fujian Film Studio. Color. Letterboxed. 10 Reels. Direction: Zhang Xingyan. Screenplay: Si Yangping. Cinematography: Zhou Bailing, Li Min. Art Direction: Han Qinguo. Music: Yu Ling. Costume: Li Yanwen. Makeup: Li Yuping, Shen Keqiang. Cast: Wang Qun as Huang Feihong (Wong Fei Hung), Guo Xiuyun (Sharon Kwok) as Thirteenth Aunt, Ji Chunhua as Eleventh Shao, Huang Yishan as Ya Casu, Jin Demao as He Cang, Zhong Yumei as Xiao Lan

A story based on the exploits of legendary (but real) Chinese folk hero Huang Feihong (Cantonese: Wong Fei Hung). Towards the end of the Qing Dynasty, Huang and two of his acolytes travel to Guangzhou, where they open a martial arts academy. The city is a hotbed of revolutionary activity. Huang sympathizes with the revolutionaries, and uses his fighting skills to protect them. He later uncovers and helps common workers smash a government plot to sell Chinese laborers overseas.

Fist of Legend see *Chen Zhen*

656. *Five Color Road (Wu Cai Lu)*

1960. Beijing Film Studio. B & W. 10 Reels. Direction: Wei Rong. Screenplay: Hu Qi, based on the novel of the same title. Cinematography: Li Wenhua. Art Direction: Zhang Xiande. Music: Shi Lemeng. Sound: Lu Xiancang, Wang Zemin, Liu Shida. Cast: Li Mudan as Qula, Liu Pei as Danzhu, Yu Qiding as Sangdun, Hong Niuniu as Little Zhaxi, Guo Shanshan as Namu, Zhang Lingling as Zuoma, Zhao Ziyue as Master Ren, Zhou Ting as Mistress Ren

In Tibet, three poor children — Qula, Danzhu and Sangdun — live in a place called Snow Village. They hear that the PLA is building a road on the other side of the mountain, freeing the people there from ruling class oppression and giving them a better life. They decide to go look for that road. They encounter many difficulties on the way, but overcome them all. One day, they come upon the manor of Master Ren, a serf owner, and rescue Little Zhaxi, a serf being tortured there. They finally meet the PLA on the other side of the river and find the bright and hopeful road there.

657. *Five Golden Flowers (Wu Duo Jin Hua)*

1959. Changchun Film Studio. Color. 13 Reels. Direction: Wang Jiayi. Screenplay: Zhao Jikang, Wang Gongpu. Cinematography: Wang Chunquan. Art Direction: Lu Xin, Shi Weijun. Music: Lei Zhenbang. Sound: Lin Bingcheng. Cast: Yang Likun as the Deputy Commune Director Jinhua, Wang Suya as the steelworker Jinhua, Zhu Yijing as the tractor operator Jinhua, Tan Raozhong as the herdswoman Jinhua, Sun Jingzhen as the fertilizer maker Jinhua, Mo Zhijiang as A Peng

A young man named A Peng meets and falls for a girl called Jin Hua ("Golden Flower") at a Spring Festival celebration. The two agree to meet again at another festival the following year. The next year he goes to keep the appointment but the girl is not there. Unfortunately, he does not know her surname or address. He searches throughout the towns of Cangshan and Erhai, and finds four young women named Jin Hua, none of whom are the girl he loves. He finally finds the one: commune director Jinhua. A misunderstanding between the two causes him to think she has changed her mind, and the heartbroken young man prepares to leave. But others help him, and A Peng and his beloved "Golden Flower" are reunited and become engaged at the spot where they had first met.

658. *Five Heroes Go to Tianqiao (Wu Hu Chuang Tian Qiao)*

1990. Beijing Film Studio. Color. Wide Screen. 9 Reels. Direction: Tang Yanlin. Screenplay: Zhong Yuan. Cinematography: Xing Peixiu. Art Direction: Yu Jiru, Zhang Xiande, Yang Baigui. Music: Liu Shufang. Sound: Liu Shida. Cast: Wang Qun as Li Guangren, Gong Yuchun as Jinzhi, Dai Wenzhang as Ming Chengxiang

In the early years of the 20th Century, a dying revolutionary leader bequeaths two plates, decorated with a dragon and a phoenix, to his top two generals. He declares that whoever has the plates will be the revolutionary leader. Twenty years later, the generals' sons, the son of the plates' original owner, Japanese agents and a local warlord are all locked in a bloody battle for ownership.

659. *Five Heroes of Langya Mountain (Lang Ya Shan Wu Zhuang Shi)*

1958. August First Film Studio. B & W. 9 Reels. Direction: Shi Wenzhi. Screenplay: Xing Ye, Sun Futian, He Guyan. Cinematography: Xue Boqing, Li Erkang. Art Direction: Li Xinmao. Music: Gong Zhiwei. Sound: He Baodian. Makeup: Yan Bijun. Cast: Li Changhua as Ma Baoyu, Gao Baocheng as Ge Zhenlin, Li Li as Song Xueyi, Zhang Huaizhi as Hu Delin, Huo Deji as Hu Fucai, Wang Mu as the Regimental Commander

During the anti–Japanese war, five soldiers of the Eighth Route Army conduct a delaying action against the Japanese in the border area between Shanxi and Hebei provinces to cover the evacuation of local people and the withdrawal of the Chinese main force. Finally, their food and ammunition exhausted, they refuse to surrender and jump from a cliff to their deaths.

660. *Five Pictures (Wu Zhang Zhao Pian)*

1984. Inner Mongolia Film Studio. Color. 9 Reels. Direction: Dong Tao, Sun Zhiqiang. Screenplay: Wei Qinguo, Wang Zhengping, Ge Li. Cinematography: Sun Cheng. Art Direction: Mo Nayintai. Music: Xin Huguang. Sound: Bu Ren. Cast: Qina Ritu as Zhao Lu, Geng Xiaolu as Ling Jingjing, Li Shijiang as Bai Yun, Guan Zongxiang as the strange old man, Dong Tao as Yideer, Xie Shuhui as Li Li

PSB investigator Zhao Lu travels to Inner Mongolia to reopen a year-old robbery case.

Five Golden Flowers. **Deputy Commune Director Jinhua (Yang Likun, center) shares a laugh with her colleagues. 1959. Changchun Film Studio.**

The trail has grown cold, however, as one of the original suspects is now dead, and the other is insane. With tips from a strange old man, Zhao is able at last to solve the case.

661. *Five Tiger Generals (Wu Hu Jiang)*

1985. Children's Film Studio. Color. 8 Reels. Direction: Wang Yiwan. Screenplay: Guan Xizhi. Cinematography: Zuo Xinhui. Art Direction: Chen Zhuo. Music: Li Ning. Sound: Xun Xiuyun. Cast: Gao Lang as Coach Yang, Liang Geliang as Lin Cheng, Qi Yun as Kou Jingjing, Zhao Peng as Jin Shuisong, Li Qiang as Zhao Xinglin, Ka Yadong as Pao Yuan

When ill health forces her to retire from China's national table tennis team, a woman player named Yang is assigned to Haining City to coach five teenage table tennis players. Her young players are at first uncooperative, but she wins them over by her superior skill level and by showing she cares about them. She becomes their good friend, and the five players win the city table tennis championship. They vow to keep going for the world championship.

Public Sport Alliance Award (Five Tiger Generals) and Best Selection Award, 43th International Sport Film Festival.

662. *Flames of Desire (Yu Wang De Huo Yan)*

1988. Inner Mongolia Film Studio. Color. 9 Reels. Direction: Zhang Yuqiang. Screenplay: Zhong Yuan, Shu Ke. Cinematographer: Ge Lisheng, Li Yuebing. Art Direction: Tong Yonggang. Music: Moerjihu. Sound: Zhang Zhizhong. Cast: Du Yeqiu as Chen Ting, Zen Hongsheng as Song Bo

Clothing store manager Yang Xiaoli dies suddenly, and an autopsy shows she was poisoned. All indications are that the woman was a suicide, but chief investigator Chen Ting is not convinced. He probes further, and at last proves the woman was murdered by her husband Song Bo.

663. *Flames on the Border (Bian Zai Feng Huo)*

1957. Changchun Film Studio. Color. 10 Reels. Direction: Lin Nong. Screenplay: Lin Yu, Yao Leng and Peng Jingfeng. Cinematography: Nie Jing. Art Direction: Liu Xuerao. Music:

Zhang Dicang. Sound: Chen Wenyuan. Cast: Da Qi as Duorong, Wang Xiaotang as Manuo, Tian Lie as Meipu Shanguan, Li Renlin as Gedang, Pang Xueqing as the political instructor, Liu Huiming as Doctor Li

In the region along China's Southwestern border live the Jingpo nationality people. Because they have suffered for so long under Nationalist rule, they have a deep suspicion and hatred of all the majority Han Chinese, even after liberation. A PLA military company stationed along the border proposes building a water gate to help upgrade the Jingpo people's primitive cultivation methods. Nationalist agent Gedang inspires village headman Meipu Shanguan's son Duoren to engage in sabotage against the PLA company. To increase Duoren's hatred, Gedang poisons the medicine Chinese Doctor Li gives Duorong's ailing son. The boy's condition worsens, which so enrages Durong that he tries to kill the doctor. When that fails, he crosses the river to join a Nationalist army unit which had fled there at the end of the civil war. Doctor Li is able to save Duorong's son, for which his grandfather Meipu Shanguan is so grateful that he immediately gives his approval for local people to work with the PLA to build the water gate. When Duorong sneaks back into town to carry out some sabotage work, he learns the truth. He promises to render meritorious service while compensating for his crimes. When Gedang learns of Duorong's conversion, he tries to blow up the water gate. Meipu Shanguan thwarts his plot. Finally, Duorong lures the several hundred Nationalist troops there back across the river and into a PLA trap. The Nationalists are all wiped out.

664. *Fled Helter-Skelter (Qi San Yi Da Kui Tao)*

1992. Changchun Film Studio & the Hong Kong Yahui Investment Company Co-Production. Color. Letterboxed. Direction: Chang Yan. Screenplay: Xiao Yixian, Zhen Jingang. Cinematography: Gao Hongbao, Wu Fei. Music: Wu Damin. Makeup: Guo Zhen, Liu Xiaohong. Cast: Zhang Guowen as Qiushan Zhengfu, Mai Deluo as Shengdao Yilang, Wang Gang as Shijing Shiliang, Ou Ruiwei as Shan Tian Jiangshi, Han Yueqiao as Song Xiao, Zhu Gang as Gui Tian

In August, 1945, the Soviet Union declares war on Japan. The Japanese military command in China orders the evacuation of all Japanese personnel at their top-secret "731" laboratory in Xinjing before the Soviet forces reach them. The "731" project involved germ warfare experiments on human subjects. The Japanese destroy all laboratory equipment and records, and then pile onto a train to carry them to the coast for a ship to Japan. The killing continues on the train. Meanwhile, they find themselves followed closely by the Chinese Volunteer Army in Northeast China. When the Japanese emperor announces his nation's surrender, the fanatical "731" people refuse to surrender, and continue their flight to the coast.

665. *A Fledgling Gymnast (Ru Yan Fei)*

1979. Xi'an Film Studio. Color. 10 Reels. Direction: Sun Jing, Yao Shougang. Screenplay: Ang Jing, Guo Xuan, Mei Bing, Hai Yan. Cinematography: Wang Zhixiong, Wu Zheng. Art Direction: Zhang Jingnan. Music: Xu Youfu. Sound: Chen Yudan. Cast: Na Renhua as Shang Xiaoli, Chen Zhurong as Li Guifang, Tan Tiancai as Zhou Yiming

In the mid 1960s, gymnast Shang Xiaoli, winner of a national teenage gymnastics title, arrives in Beijing with her coach Li Guifang for intensive gymnastics team training. Li Guigang is very liberal about training methods, for she wants China to reach the world's most advanced level in the sport. Therefore, she devises a completely new training plan of high technical difficulty. She is opposed by the team director, her fiance Zhou Yimin. Li Guifang controls her personal feelings, relies on the Party, and puts all of her energy into training Shang Xiaoli, who finally achieves an excellent score at a world gymnastics meet. From this experience, Zhou Yimin comes to realize people must push forward and not be afraid of failure.

666. *Flier's Romance (Fei Ren Lang Man Qu)*

1985. Guangxi Film Studio. Color. 9 Reels. Direction: Zeng Xueqiang. Screenplay: Zhang Zhenqin, Chen Dunde. Cinematography: Meng Xiongqiang, Lei Jiaming. Art Direction: Chen Yaogong. Music: Xu Jingxin. Sound: Tu Mingde. Cast: Dai Zhaoan as Yang Xile, Kang Jingyu as Ye Shunan, Xia Jing as Xiao Huaiqing, Xue Guoping as Wu Chunsheng, Geng Tao as Can Qiong, Tan Pengfei as the old director

Yang Xile's talents as a clown have made him the hit of his acrobatic troupe's performances. He is loved by Xiao Huaiqing, a performer in the same troupe, but his single-minded devotion to his act causes him to ignore her. Then he meets and starts a romance with Ye Shunan, a sweet woman who works as a scientific researcher. Two things work against them: Yang Xile feels uncomfortable because of the wide gap in their respective educational backgrounds, while her colleagues all gossip about her affair with a clown actor. Later, Yang Xile is injured during a performance, and Xiao Huaiqing is the one who rushes to his side to care for him. Now Yang Xile is uncertain whom to choose.

667. *Flight from Death (Si Li Tao Sheng)*

1988. Xiaoxiang Film Studio. Color. Letterboxed. 9 Reels. Direction: Zhang Jinbiao. Screenplay: Guo Songyuan. Cinematography: Xu Hongliang. Art Direction: Xia Rujin. Music: Ma Jianping. Sound: Liu Feng. Cast: Hong Yuzhou as He Xiaoguang, Liang Guoqing as Pu Yaming, Zhang Jianwei as Niu Shiming, Wu Jianping as the big guy, Chu Jian as the little guy, Deng Youqing as Wang Ershun, Zhang Liping as Lin Li, Shu Yaoxuan as Wu Zhixiong, Liu Diancheng as Ni Fengtian

Shortly before the Communist victory in 1949, Nationalist agent Pu Yamin is given a secret assignment called the "devil plan," which involves escorting a truckload of silver coins into the mountains. The coins were withdrawn by the government from a storehouse guarded by an army unit. The commander of the unit, wanting to recover the coins for use in his own probable flight later, sends one of his best officers, Hu Xiaoguang, to go with the truck and recover the coins. Hu is actually an undercover agent for Communists, however, who ask him to clarify what is the "devil plan" and what role the coins will play in it. Hu's mission is a risky one, but he survives until the truck arrives at its destination, where it is surrounded by PLA troops. Hu "miraculously" breaks free through the ring surrounding them, bringing with him Pu Yamin who has by now come over to the Communist side. Pu then returns to Nationalist headquarters with a new assignment from the CPC.

668. *Flight No. 208 (Er Ling Ba Ke Ji)*

1984. Xiaoxiang Film Studio. Color. Wide Screen. 10 Reels. Direction: Zhou Kangyu.

Screenplay: Ji Hongshu. Cinematography: Wang Kekuan. Art Direction: Guo Dexiang. Music: Xu Jingxin. Sound: Liu Feng. Cast: Liu Falu as Gu Zhisong, Zhu Yanping as Long Fei, Liu Fei as Zhou Enlai, Mu Weihan as Su Quan, Zhao Xiuli as Qiao Xin, Wun Xiaoqiao as Li Rui

In 1965, Premier Zhou Enlai proposes that the General Administration of Civil Aviation of China (CAAC) begin planning for international flights. CAAC Director Gu Zhisong recognizes this assignment as a great honor, and involves all the airline's employees in preparing for it. But the Cultural Revolution intervenes, and Party left-wing extremism severely hampers progress. The CAAC's Party Secretary Su Quan is a particular obstacle to Gu and the others. However, with Premier Zhou's support, they overcome the political and other difficulties. On January 8, 1981, Flight 208, a Boeing 747 jumbo jet, takes off for the United States, history's first China to U.S. flight on a Chinese airline.

669. *Flirting Scholar (Tang Bo Hu Dian Qiu Xiang)*

1993. Hong Kong Yongsheng Film Company, Ltd., & the China Film Co-Production Corp. Co-Production. Color. Letterboxed. 9 Reels. Direction: Li Lichi. Screenplay: Chen Wenqiang, Gu Weimin. Cinematography: Zhong Zhiwen. Art Direction: Mo Shaoqi. Music: Hu Weili. Makeup: Wen Runling, Pan Minghua, Wun Weiming, Gu Yan. Cast: Zhou Xingchi (Stephen Chow) as Tang Bohu, Gong Li as Qiuxiang

A farcical and fanciful story about a real historical couple, the South China poet Tang Bohu and his lover Qiuxiang. Although Tang Bohu would seem to have a very comfortable life, what with an outstanding literary reputation and eight wives, he is still restless. One day he sees and is smitten by Qiuxiang, servant girl of a neighboring family. Unfortunately, an old feud between Tang's family and her employer prevents his approaching them for her hand. He enters their home with an assumed identity, and after a series of comic incidents wins the lady and settles the family feud.

670. *The Floating Bottle (Piao Liu Ping)*

1986. Shanghai Film Studio. Color. 10 Reels. Direction: Yao Shoukang. Screenplay: Deng Hainan. Cinematography: Shen Miaorong. Art Direction: Wu Tianci. Music: Liu Yanxi. Sound:

Feng Deyao. Cast: Wang Yuzhang as "Sailor," Xu Lili as Dandan, Lin Chunfang as Lin Aoran

Seven young people on a boat trip strike up shipboard acquaintances and by the end of the trip they are all friends. They make a promise to meet again on the same date three years later. Three years pass, and as they gather for their reunion, they are aware of the many changes which have occurred in their lives. One person is missing: the one they called "Sailor," the one who was most encouraging to the others about their futures. It turns out that "Sailor" has died of cancer, an illness of which he was aware at the same time he was encouraging the rest of them to make the most of their lives. In his memory, the others throw an empty "floating bottle" into the sea.

671. *Flowers and Flowers (Hua Er Duo Duo)*

1962. Beijing Film Studio. Color. 8 Reels. Direction: Xie Tie and Chen Fangqian. Screenplay: Xie Tie and Chen Fangqian. Cinematography: Li Wenhua and Chen Guoliang. Art Direction: Xiao Bing and Mo Renyi. Music: Tang Ke and Ding Ping. Sound: Cai Jun. Cast: Liu Pei as Fang Xiaohua, Wang Renmei as Fang Xiaohua's mother, Zhang Shipeng as the little backstage director, Hu Zhongtao as the little stage monitor, Cao Zhenggeng as Old Grandpa, Ling Yuan as the little backstage director's mother

On Children's Day, June 1st, Fang Xiaohua, the person in charge of a party goes to the suburbs to escort a model stock raising grandpa, but they do not get back on time. This unexpected event disrupts all the performance plans, since Xiaohua was scheduled to introduce all the initial acts. However, the little stage monitor and little backstage director rearrange the program, guaranteeing that all will go smoothly. When the party entertainment is almost finished, Xiaohua and Old Grandpa arrive. Old Grandpa immediately takes the stage and performs a program that relates Xiaohua's experience of rescuing a train, thereby being late to the party.

672. *Flowers Bloom in the Warmth of Spring (Chun Nuan Hua Kai)*

1960. Beijing Film Studio. B & W. 10 Reels. Direction: Xie Tie, Fu Jie. Screenplay: Xie Tie, Chen Fangqian. Cinematography: Chen Guoliang, Zhang Qinghua. Art Direction: Yu Yiru. Music: Li Ning. Sound: Wang Junhua, Zhang Jiake. Cast: Lin Dongsheng as Liu Guiying, Qing Wen as Peizhen, Ling Yuan as Lu's wife, Li Huan as Huang's wife, Wu Suqing as Wu Xiuying, Li Jian as Song's wife

Inspired by the Great Leap Forward, Beijing housewife Liu Guiying organizes the other women in her neighborhood to take part and do something to help the country. Their initial problems include their ignorance of technology, lack of raw materials and conservative thinking. In addition, each has problems at home which are distracting. Some want to quit, and at one point Liu's own confidence is shaken. With inspiration and help from Party Secretary Hong, they overcome the production problems and conservative thinking, and resolve their various personal problems as well. The women set up a factory to produce mousetraps, and in just one year expand to manufacturing springs. Liu becomes the plant director, and the plant successfully fulfills its first big order — 240,000 sofa springs for the Great Hall of the People — ahead of schedule.

673. *Flowers Bloom Toward the Sun (Xiang Yang Hua Kai)*

1960. Tianma Film Studio. B & W. 10 Reels. Direction: Wei Yuping. Screenplay: Zhao Qingge. Cinematography: Shen Xilin. Art Direction: Liu Fan. Music: Yang Jitao, Xiao Huang. Sound: Huang Donghai. Cast: Zhang Hongmei as Zhou Yuzhen, Wang Danfeng as Xie Jinfang, Cheng Zhi as Zhou Gengfa, Zhu Sha as Feng Axiang, Zhang Hongxing as Wang Guoping, Zhong Jingwen as Liu Xiaomei

To satisfy the growing demand for sewing machine needles, model factory worker Zhou Yuzhen requests reassignment to the new Yongxin needle manufacturing plant. After her arrival, she tries to lead and unite all the workers by her model behavior. She also visits and offers counsel to Jin Fang, a woman worker with low ideological sensibility. Jin Fang and her group go on to win Red Flag awards, and Zhou Yuzhen is awarded the title of Shanghai Red Flag Youth Worker.

Flowers Meet the Spring Rain **see** *Wreathed in Smiles*

674. *Flowers of the Motherland (Zuguo De Huaduo)*

1955. Changchun Film Studio. B & W. 9 Reels. Direction: Yan Gong. Screenplay: Lin Lan. Cinematography: Lian Cheng. Art Direction:

Flowers of the Motherland. 1955. Changchun Film Studio.

Tong Jingwen. Music: Liu Zhi. Sound: Hong Di. Casting: Zhao Weiqin as Liang Huiming, Li Xixiang as Jiang Lin, Zhang Junying as Yang Yongli, Zhang Yuan as Teacher Feng, Guo Yuntai as a volunteer soldier, Shi Lin as Yang's mother

Of the more than 40 students in Beijing Elementary School's Fifth Grade A Class, only Jiang Lin and Yang Yongli have still not qualified as members of the Young Pioneers. On the June 1st "Children's Day" holiday, the class is treated to an outing in a park with some volunteer soldiers. The soldiers tell many battle stories, and encourage the students to study hard, care for others and help those in need. After returning to the school, Liang Huiming, director of the school's Young Pioneer division, determines to apply their advice to help Jiang Lin and Yang Yongli. She encounters many problems at first, but her supervisor Mr. Feng teaches her and her students not to be too anxious, that a stress on methodology will bring the best results. When Yang Yongli suffers a leg injury and cannot come to school, her classmates help her make up the classes. When Jiang Lin's mother falls ill, they go to the Jiang home to do the housework. With the help of their teachers and the Young Pioneers, Jiang Lin and Yang Yongli make up their shortcom-

ings, and both happily become members of the Young Pioneers.

675. *Flowing Water's Joyous Song (Liu Shui Huan Ge)*

1959. Changchun Film Studio. B & W. 8 Reels. Direction: Lei Heng. Screenplay: Yan Zeming, Sun Mu. Cinematography: Guo Zhenting. Art Direction: Dong Ping. Music: Gao Hongliang. Sound: Jiang Junfeng. Cast: Han Deshan as Tian Youliang, Li Xida as Little Bean, Wu Yanshu as Gao Xiaoling, Guo Shutian as Old Gun, Zhang Jianyou as Erdan, Cheng Cheng as Tian's wife

Foothills Commune in rural Northeast China wants to build a hydropower station, but lacks the required technical expertise. Gao Xiaoling of the commune's water conservancy commission is in love with neighboring Shayuan commune's expert "Little Bean." She asks Shayuan commune to lend Little Bean to them as a technical consultant, but Shayuan's deputy director Tian Youliang turns her down. But the county commission sends Little Bean to Foothills Commune anyway. Little Bean decides that the way to overcome the large water level gap between the two communes is for the two communes to jointly build a reservoir and share the resulting power. His proposal is rejected by Tian Youliang, who wants Shayuan commune to do it alone. But with the persuasion of the Party organization and the people, Tian realizes his mistake, and the two communes jointly build the hydropower station.

676. *A Fluke (Wai Da Zheng Zhe)*

1993. Beijing Film Studio and Lanzhou Film Studio Co-Production. Color. Letterboxed. 9 Reels. Direction: Li Baoyuan, Ru Shuiren. Screenplay: Li Baoyuan, Lian Chunming. Cinematography: Ru Shuiren, Ma Ning. Art Direction: Ma Jiesheng. Music; Wu Jiaji. Sound: Liang Jiadong. Costume: He Li. Makeup: Ding Xiaoying. Cast: Chang Lantian as Ke Dao, Zhou Zhou as Sima Wen, Zhang Limei as Junzi, Liang Lansheng as Lao Xi, Wang Xiaolong as Zhugan, Liu Yaojun as the policeman

Ke Dao, editor of a mystery adventure magazine, feels the need for a break from his daily involvement with violence and murder. So he and his wife Junzi take a train trip. On the train, a salesman of prosthetic devices accidentally picks up the suitcase of a drug dealer, while Ke Dao picks up the salesman's case full of artificial limbs. Comic confusion arises, made worse when Ke's preoccupation with murder leads him to believe the suitcase contains real limbs.

677. *Flying Across the Pacific (Fei Xiang Tai Ping Yang)*

1982. Shanghai Film Studio. Color. 11 Reels. Direction: Zhang Hongmei. Screenplay: Ye Dan, Gao Xing. Cinematography: Luo Chongzhou, Wun Sijie. Art Direction: Dong Jingsheng. Music: yang Shaolu. Sound: Jin Fugeng. Cast: Xia Zongxue as Ouyang Guang, Gao Bao as Qi Rushan, Xiang Mei as Zhu Lan, Zhang Feijing as Ai Hua, Li Lanfa as Deputy Director Wang

Late in 1979, the government announces that China will launch an experimental incontinental missile in the South Pacific. The chief designer of the missile, Ouyang Guang, decides he will participate in the experiment despite his failing health. He feels that he can rely heavily on his female assistant Ai Hua for help. When he learns that the supervisory department has barred women from being on the ship taking them to target site, he sneaks the young woman on board disguised as a man. After she reveals herself as a woman, Ai Hua is either ignored or treated with contempt by the others, partly for her gender and partly for the

fact she is largely self-educated. The only ones encouraging her are Ouyang and a scientist named Qi Rushan. However, she proves herself by making a computer repair which saves the experiment. Qi Rushan, whose eldest son had been killed in the border war with Vietnam, worries about his younger son, also a missile crew member. When the mission is threatened with sabotage by a mysterious diver, the younger Qi successfully fights him and saves the mission. After the missile nose cone is located and a helicopter from the ship retrieves its instrument package, Ouyang collapses from overwork. To help speed his recovery, the Party reunites him with his wife, who had fled China when she was falsely accused during the Cultural Revolution and has been living in a foreign country. The research team is full of hope for the future of China.

678. *Flying Centipede (Fei Tian Wu Gong)*

1994. Changchun Film Studio. Color. Letterboxed. 9 Reels. Direction: Sun Qingguo. Screenplay: Qian Daoyuan. Cinematography: Sun Guangwen. Art Direction: Zhang Hui. Music: Yang Yilun. Sound: Meng Gang. Costume: Liu Tao, Su Pengling. Makeup: Wang Xiaoling. Cast: Ju Ying as Ailina, Wu Gang as Ouyang Long, Ge Sha as Aoersi, Guan Ying as Miqi, Fang Fang as A Hua, Xie Xu as black widow, Guo Kaixuan as Gao Fu

Chinese policeman Ouyang Long is assigned by his chief of detectives, a foreigner, to investigate a matter called the "American Centipede" case. During the investigation, Ouyang becomes aware of some sort of association between Interpol investigator Ailiya and himself, and at last he discovers they are brother and sister. But he also finds that his boss is the covert head of an international crime organization.

679. *Flying Golden Wings (Chan Dong De Jin Chi Bang)*

1986. Changchun Film Studio. Color. 10 Reels. Direction: Wang Xuexin. Screenplay: Wang Zequn. Cinematography: Xu Shouzen. Art Direction: Liu Huanxing, Ju Lutian. Music: Chen Shouqian. Sound: Xing Huanxing, Ju Lutian. Cast: Pang Ming as Mingyue, Zhu Xinyun as Tianbao, Shi Xiao as Manfeng, Liu Hanpu as Sixth Uncle, Wang Yanping as Weiwei, Liu Tongyan as Hu Lielie, Sun Li as Liu Fang, Jiang Yang as Chunsheng

In the Chinese coastal city of Dongfang, Mingyue, Manfeng and Tianbao are young women members of a forest products team. To combat the bugs that attack forest workers in the field, the young women spend their spare time working on a device to kill the pests. Veteran team leader Sixth Uncle is a kindly man, but very superstitious. He conducts a campaign to raise funds for restoring a local temple, in hopes the gods will keep the insects away. The movie tells how the young people at last convince Sixth Uncle to apply this fund to buying a small airplane which can be used in the effort to combat the bugs.

680. *Flying Knife Hua (Fei Dao Hua)*

1963. Haiyan Film Studio. B & W. 10 Reels. Direction: Xu Suling. Screenplay: Yan Li and Li Wei, based on the novel of the same title by Xiong Daba. Cinematography: Zhang Guifu. Art Direction: Huang Jianfeng, Zhang Wanhong. Music: Wang Yunjie. Sound: Liu Guangjie. Cast: Li Wei as Hua Shaojie, Wei Heling as Li Zhongyi, Wang Pei as Jin Sulan, Li Baoluo as Tan Zhiliu, Cheng Zhi as Li Zhongxia, Zhu Sha as Tian Yuzhen, Chen Shu as Niu Yaozhu

During World War Two, Hua Shaojie, who goes by the stage name of "Flying Knife Hua," is a top acrobat. Hua's troupe travels to the city of Hankou to perform, where Hua runs into an old enemy, Japanese collaborator Niu Yaozhu, now director of the "East Asian Japanese-Chinese Art Troupe." When Hua Shaojie refuses Niu's urgings to come over to the collaborationist group, Niu has Hua's troupe destroyed. Hua leaves Hankou, accompanied by female acrobat Jin Sulan, who is in love with him. They go to Sichuan province, controlled by the Nationalist government, where the new troupe they form is constantly intimidated by the police. When the war ends, the troupe once more goes to Hankou to perform, and Hua Shaojie and Jin Sulan are married. But they are still not free of Niu Yaozhu, now a Nationalist official. He orders the couple's arrest, but they are able to flee. No longer able to earn a living performing, Hua Shaojie becomes a dock worker. After liberation, they are once more permitted to practice their art, and create new programs for both domestic and foreign performance.

681. *Flying Over Natural Dangers (Fei Yue Tian Xian)*

1959. Beijing Film Studio. Color. 10 Reels. Direction: Li Enjie. Screenplay: Chen Ge. Cinematography: Zhu Jinming. Art Direction: Yu Yiru. Music: Li Weicai. Sound: Fu Yinjie. Cast: Zhang Aoran as the political commissar, Li Ziping as the regimental commander, Zhou Shengguan as the old mechanic, Shi Meifen as Zhao Mingyue, Yu Yang as Zhao Zhongkai, Zhao Lian as Zhang Qiliang, Qin Wen as Xu Rui

In the period just after liberation, a team of meteorologists led by Xu Rui is stranded in the Tibetan mountains by an avalanche. Xu Rui's wife, a pilot, is sent with her co-pilot Zhao Zhongkai to drop supplies to the stranded team. Their first attempt fails due to mechanical troubles, and the second flight is turned back by bad weather. On the third attempt they overcome the difficulties and succeed in the drop. But a shortage of oxygen endangers their return to base, and they are just able to make it back safely.

682. *Flying Shadow (Piao Hu De Ying Zi)*

1988. Changchun Film Studio. Color. 10 Reels. Direction: Zhu Wenshun. Screenplay: Du Lijuan. Cinematography: Duan Zhenjiang. Art Direction: Liu Xuerao. Music: Chen Shouqian. Sound: Kang Duanxin. Cast: Lu Xiaohe as Qiu Boxi, Pang Ming as Luo Su, Zhao Yamin as Yao Yuechan, Guan Xinwei as Ye Jingkui

City construction bureau director Ye Shuang accepts a large bribe from a Hong Kong businessman who wants to build a joint venture amusement park. Ye sends his female accountant Yao Yuechan on holiday at a resort city to pick up the money, followed by his son Ye Jingkui. The plan is to use the woman as a dupe, and to kill her after she gets the money. But Yao Yuechan's husband is actually police investigator Qiu Boxi; he pretends to be on vacation with his wife, but actually he has been assigned to keep an eye on Ye, father and son. At last, Qiu Boxi catches all the criminals in a coordinated PSB effort, and the bribe money is obtained as well.

683. *The Flying Swallow's Song (Fei Yan Qu)*

1981. Xi'an Film Studio. Color. 10 Reels. Direction: Guo Yangting. Screenplay: Zhao Zhiqiang, Wang Feng, Pan Beng, Wang Jie.

Cinematography: Zhang Faliang. Art Direction: Zhang Xiaohui. Music: Xie Tiyin. Sound: Che Zhiyuan. Cast: Pan Lianhua as Han Tianxiao, Tu Ruyin as Ling Yan, Liu Yuanyuan as Kang Di, Xue Weijun as Ai Qinbo, Yan Lirong as Man Tanghong, Jin Fuli as Hua Caiying

Through hard work, good coaching and the help of her performing partner Han Tianxiao, young female acrobat Ling Yan becomes one of China's top acrobats. Kang Di, the troupe's pianist, introduces her Ai Qinbo, Kang Di's boyfriend. Ai Qinbo is immediately taken with Ling Yan's beauty and performing skill. He drops Kang Di and turns his attention to Ling Yan. Ling Yan not only falls for the young man, she starts neglecting her training to spend more time with him. But when she falls and breaks a leg during a performance, Ain Qinbo drops her. Her partner Han Tianxiao, who has loved her for a long time, helps her and gives her the encouragement to come back. Liang Yan now sees the true nature of Ai Qinbo.

684. *Flying Symphony (Fei Xing Jiao Xiang Qu)*

1981. August First Film Studio. Color. Letterboxed. 10 Reels. Direction: Li Wenhu. Screenplay: Chen Lide. Cinematography: Huang Fuxiang, Wang Zhiqing. Art Direction: Wu Hanbiao. Music: Fu Gengcheng, Zhu Wanghua. Sound: Jiang Zhenkui. Cast: Zhu Shimao as Sun Jianhua, Ma Yaoyao as Zhou Wenjuan, Zhen Zhengyao as Ding Shuyun, Zhang Yongshou as Zhao Hui, Yu Yana as Su Manling, Zhang Lianwen as Zhou Shengbing

Flight squadron leader Sun Jianhua meets music school student Zhou Wenjuan and they fall in love. The romance is not smooth, however, because the nature of his work causes Sun Juanhua to break some dates with her, most notably missing her graduation recital. Wenjuan becomes very frustrated with Sun Jianhua's lack of time for her. Wenjuan's good friend, ballet dancer Su Manling, has a very smooth relationship with a friend of Jianhua's, which just frustrates Wenjuan all the more. As Jianhua and Wenjuan are on the point of breaking up, his commander Zhao Hui steps in to help, and with examples from their brave revolutionary ancestors, counsels them on balancing love and career. They give it another try.

685. *Flying Tiger Brigade (Fei Hu Dui)*

1995. Emei Film Studio, China Film Co-Pro-

duction Corporation Co-Production. Color. Letterboxed. Direction: Wang Jixing. Screenplay: Liang Husheng, Hu Jianxin, Wang Jixing, based on Liu Zhixia's novel. Producer: Shi Zhaoqi, Zhou Jun. Cinematography: Wang Xiaolie, Luo Xun. Art Direction: Wei Zhonghua. Music: Zhao Jiping. Sound: Wang Hui. Cast: Liu Wei as Liu Hong, Li Xuejian as Wang Qiang, Li Qiang as Li Zheng, Chen Xiaoyi as Fanglin's wife, Chang Rong as Peng Liang, Zhao Xiaorui as Lu Han, Cao Lian as Lin Zhong, Lei Han as Xia Po, Zhang Fengyi as Li Ji, Li Youbin as Qin Xiong, Wang Zhiwen as Zhang Lan, Lu Liang as Songwei, Pan Changjiang as Huang E

A remake of the 1956 Shanghai Film Studio's "Guerrillas on the Railway."

686. *Flying to the Future (Fei Xiang Wei Lai)*

1979. Emei Film Studio. Color. 9 Reels. Direction: Miao Ling, Lu Xiaoya. Screenplay: Qian Daoyuan. Cinematography: Shi Fengqi, Zhang Hongjun. Art Direction: Lin Qi. Sound: Zhang Jianping. Cast: Ju Jia as Han Xiaofei, Yan Yong as Pao Xiaomin, Luo Xuwu as Qin Daman

Xiaofei, a boy from Beijing, comes to South China to spend his school break with his grandfather Professor Zhong. There, he makes friends with other boys from the local elementary school's airplane modeling club. He joins their club, studying aviation and making models. But while Xiaofei is bright, he is also spoiled and arrogant: ignoring fundamental study, his models repeatedly fail to fly when tested. With guidance from Professor Zhong and Grandpa Pao, a local farmer, he learns that fundamental knowledge is vital to success. Xiaofei also learns to cooperate with the other club members. Finally, everyone's model airplane flies successfully.

687. *Fogbound (Wu Jie)*

1984. Guangxi Film Studio. Color. 9 Reels. Direction: Guo Baocang. Screenplay: Chen Dunde, Li Xiaolong, Gu Hua. Cinematography: Yang Yuming. Art Direction: Zhang Yafang. Music: Su Tie. Sound: Lin Lin. Cast: Milan as Jin Ye, Guo Yuntai as Zhao Shigu, Hasibageng as Zen Yushan

Yao nationality girl Jin Lan grows up in an undeveloped forest area, raised by her father Zhao Shigu. A young forester named Zen Yushan comes to the area looking for a rare tree, and stays at their home. His devotion to forest conservation appeals to Jin Lan, and she falls for Yushan. This troubles her father, for he recognizes the considerable gap in their backgrounds. Zen Yushan returns the girl's affection, but now he must make a choice between the forest and the realities of the situation. He at last leaves when he finishes his work. Jin Lan hopes he will return someday.

688. *Foggy City (Wu Du Mang Mang)*

1980. Pearl River Film Studio. Color. 10 Reels. Direction: Zhang Bo, Wang Jing. Screenplay: Kuang Aowen. Cinematography: Wei Duo. Art Direction: Li Xin. Music: Huang Zhun, Xiao Xi. Sound: Jiang Shaoqi. Cast: Yan Shikui as Shen Lan, Pang Ming as Lin Jing, Shi Jing as Lin Nanxuan, Wu Jing as Zhu Yuwan, Qian Yongfu as Chen Ao, Wang Chunhuai as Wu Meng

On the night that the Red Army occupies the city of Ruancheng, a murder takes place at the home of the Nationalist government's Ruancheng representative Lin Nanxuan. The victim is Lin's housekeeper, and a man and woman were seen running from the house. Just before the city had fallen to the Communists, Lin Nanxuan was ordered by Chiang Kaishek to implement "Plan C-3," which would totally destroy the city. But the city fell before the plan could be carried out, and Lin Nanxuan committed suicide. From Chief Inspector Shen Lan's recollection of past events and clues obtained from a telegram they find, the investigators conclude the killers had come to the house searching for "Plan C-3." They later find that the murderer was Chen Ao, Lin Nanxuan's former assistant, aided by a woman wearing embroidered shoes. The police realize that enemy agents throughout the city are preparing to launch the plan and blow up many public buildings. But just at the critical moment, the officers find and defuse the bombs in a secret tunnel beneath the city. Chen Ao and the other spies are caught. Meanwhile, a woman wearing embroidered shoes boards a ship. She is Lin Jing, daughter of Lin Nanxuan. When she turns and sees PLA soldiers approaching the ship, she sees it is all over and commits suicide by a poison pill hidden in her ring.

689. *A Foggy Night Voyage (Wu Hai Ye Hang)*

1957. Tianma Film Studio. B & W. 9 Reels.

Direction: Yu Tao. Screenplay: Yu Tao. Cinematography: Shen Xilin. Set Design: Zhang Hanchen. Music: Huang Zhun. Sound: Yuan Qingyu. Makeup: Wang Tiebin. Cast: Fan Xuepeng as the old lady, Zhang Ying as the bride, Wang Guilin as the old farmer, Wang Xin as the pregnant woman, Jin Naihua as the Lieutenant Commander, Guan Hongda as the fat man, Yu Fei as the photographer, Chen Bo as the photographer's assistant, Tie Niu as Platoon Leader Liu, Xiang Mei as He Meijuan, Wei Yuping as Professor Liu, Mu Hong as the ship's captain, Luo Qiyin as Zhou Dahai, Qi Heng as the political commissar

One morning in early spring, a passenger ship departs on a voyage down the East China coast from Shanghai to Ningbo, with over 1,300 people from various walks of life aboard. On the short trip, several stories are played out: a professor, depressed and suicidal over his impending blindness, regains his will to live after talking with a naval political commissar; navy lieutenant Zhou Dahai and girl student He Meijuan fall in love; a pregnant woman gives birth to twins, etc. At night, with the sea covered by a heavy blanket of fog, the ship strikes a reef and is in peril of sinking. The naval political commissar leads Zhou Dahai and a few soldiers on board in a desperate attempt to reach a nearby naval base by lifeboat. In the end, they succeed, and the ship's company is saved.

690. *Following the Bloody Case (Xue An Yi Zong)*

1986. Beijing Film Studio. Color. 10 Reels. Direction: Qiu Lili, Xiao Lang. Screenplay: Zhang Cuilan, Qiu Lili. Cinematography: Tu Jiakuan. Art Direction: Chen Xiaoxia. Music: Li Wanli. Sound: Wei Xueyi. Cast: Dou Bing as Qi Fan, Ma Tianfang as Lu Pingsheng, Fu Zhucheng as Xiao Cheng, Liang Yujing as Chu Ruiyuan, Shen Guanchu as Chen Hua, Liu Jiaoxin as Nie Jingyang

One night in late autumn, a young man named Chen Hua is badly beaten while returning from a date with his girlfriend Chu Ruiyuan. Meanwhile, Chu Ruiyuan is found murdered in the accounting office of a department store. Investigator Qi Fan and his assistant Lu Pingsheng at last establish a connection: although the murdered girl had nothing to do with the store, her father had owned it before liberation. The investigators push on to find that the killer is the store's Party Secretary Xiao Cheng and his wife: they found out that

Chu Ruiyuan's father had hidden a secret jewel box somewhere on the store's property, and killed her in the attempt to learn from her its location.

691. *Fools in Love (Ai Qing Sha Gua)*

1993. Beijing Film Studio, Beijing Film Distribution Company Co-Production. Color. Letterboxed. 9 Reels. Direction: Chen Guoxing. Screenplay: Li Xiaoming, Liu Shugang, Wang Zunxi. Cinematography: Zhao Xiaoding. Art Direction: Yang Hong. Music: Gao Erdi. Sound: Guan Jian. Costume: Liu Weifeng. Makeup: Xu Guangrui, Wang Yanxia. Cast: Xie Yuan as Xie You, He Hongqing as Tian Xi, Ju Ying as Xu Man, Qiu Yue as Cui Er, Ding Jiali as sister Ding, Liang Guanhua as big Liang, Han Qing as Xiao Lan, Zou Hewei as Xiao Lan's father, Li Wenling as Xiao Lan's mother, Fang Qingzuo as fat woman, Li Mingjun as Xie You's mother

Fleeing family opposition to their relationship, Tianxi and his lover Cuier leave their rural village and go to Beijing. There, Tianxi's strong resemblance to a famous comedy star combined with an impression that Cuier is pregnant creates a series of comic incidents. All ends happily.

692. *Footprints (Jiao Yin)*

1955. August First Film Studio. B & W. 4 Reels. Direction: Yan Jizhou. Screenplay: Yan Jizhou. Cinematography: Li Erkang. Set Design: Kou Honglie. Music: Gao Liang. Sound: Li Yan. Makeup: Fang Li. Cast: Ren Dongsheng as squad leader, Tang Deming as Qiao Qing, Li Zhiyuan as Tang Biao, Zhen Chunpei as Mu Jia, Zhou Qi as the platoon leader, Yang Jiao as the spy leader, Li Hongchang as the first spy, Ming Xuan as the second spy

Qiao Qing, a new recruit at a border patrol station in Yunnan province, finds his assignment boring. But when out on patrol, his squad discovers some suspicious footprints heading across the border into China. The squad leader orders Tang Biao to report this information to the base while he and Qiao Qing follow the suspicious prints and catch up to some spies who had snuck across the border. At that time, Tang Biao arrives with more soldiers, they kill two of the spies and capture their leader. From this Qiao Qing learns how important and interesting the work of a border patrol soldier can be.

693. *Footprints on the Beach (Liu Zhai Hai Bian De Jiao Yin)*

1986. Dalian Bohai Film & Television Company. Color. 10 Reels. Direction: Wu Peimin. Screenplay: Liu Zenqin, Yan Derong. Cinematography: Zhang Guifu. Art Direction: Zhang Zheng. Music: Liu Qi. Sound: Yang Liangkun. Cast: Wang Fuli, Shi Weijian, Zhong Xinghuo, Fan Yanhua

694. *Footsteps of Youth (Qing Chun De Jiao Bu)*

1957. Changchun Film Studio. B & W. 9 Reels. Direction: Yan Gong and Su Li. Screenplay: Xue Yandong. Cinematography: Li Guanghui. Art Direction: Tong Jingwen. Music: Quan Rufeng. Sound: Jue Jingxiu. Cast: Yuan Mei as Lin Meilan, Chen Ying as Peng Ke, Liu Zhenqing as Xiao Ping, Wang Renmei as Shu Fang, Zhao Shangyin as Peng's mother, Lin DongSheng as Chen Jingwen

Lin Meilan and Xiao Ping, two housing construction design technicians, are lovers, but have a falling out when they disagree over the design workers' housing. Xiao Ping's brother-in-law Peng Ke then declares his love to Meilan. She knows that he already has a wife and children, so she rejects Peng Ke and reconciles with Xiao Ping. However, Xiao Ping's criticism of her causes Lin Meilan to break off with him again. Peng Ke takes this opportunity to seduce Meilan and force his wife Shu Fang to grant him a divorce. Shortly after, Meilan gets pregnant. To protect his own reputation and social status and avoid responsibility for the child, Peng Ke gives Meilan a drug which aborts the baby but almost kills her. At last, Peng Ke's moral deterioration is punished by the authorities. Meilan realizes the capitalist nature of her thinking, and vows to correct her mistakes and redeem herself.

695. *For Friendship (Dan Yuan Ren Chang Jiu)*

1981. Changchun Film Studio. Color. 9 Reels. Direction: Bai Dezhang, Xu Xunxing. Screenplay: Zhang Tianmin. Cinematography: Tu Jiakuan. Art Direction: Wang Chong. Music: Gao Feng. Sound: Yuan Minda, Liu Wenzhang. Cast: Li Qiyuan as Huyan Ziqian, Gu Yongfei as Qiao Meng, Shi Jing as Luo Heng, Huang Daliang as Ou Yi, Gong Xibing as Luo Dachuan

After the Cultural Revolution is over, geologist Huyan Ziqian returns to his research work, where he learns that closest friend and colleague Ouyi died during those years of upheaval, leaving a widow Qiao Meng, a young daughter Ouxia and his father Luo Heng. Luo Heng likes Huyan Ziqian very much, and decides to make a match of Huyan, a middle-aged bachelor and Qiao Meng, the thirtyish widow who has been caring for him for years. Qiao Meng and Huyan meet, and his optimistic outlook on life so impresses her that they do decide to marry. By chance, Huyan Ziqian meets and adopts an orphan boy named Gu Li, and Qiao Meng prepares to take him into her new family as well. However, when Qiao Meng learns that Gu Li's father was Gu Jian, the man who had persecuted her husband to death, she refuses to become his stepmother. Gu Li hears their conversation and chooses to leave on his own, resuming his homeless wandering. Huyan Zhiqian persuades Qiao Meng that they must put the past behind them, and not blame the child for his father's acts. The new family is reunited.

696. *For Fun (Zhao Le)*

1992. Beijing Film Studio & Hong Kong Wanhe Film And Television Company Ltd. Co-Production. Color. 10 Reels. Direction: Ning Ying. Screenplay: Ning Dai, Ning Ying. Cinematography: Xiao Feng, Wu Di. Art Direction: Yang Xiaowen. Music: Meng Weidong. Sound: Chao Jun. Costume: Li Fengju. Makeup: Chao Ying. Cast: Huang Zongluo as Old Han, Huang Wenjie as Qiao Wanyou, He Min as He Min, Han Shanxu as Dong Tou, Yang Youtang as Mr. Yang

After retiring from his job as a theater doorman, Old Han feels unwanted and useless. One day while walking in the park, he chances upon a group of elderly people staging an amateur Beijing opera performance. This gives him an idea, and he opens a seniors activity center, at which many of his contemporaries have a great deal of fun. Although he is sometimes distressed at the arguments that pop up among the seniors now and then, he realizes that he cannot leave them.

697. *For Love (You Qing Ren)*

1991. Shanghai Film Studio. Color. Letterboxed. 10 Reels. Direction: Bao Qicheng. Screenplay: Chen Danlu. Cinematography: Peng Enli. Art Direction: Wang Xingcang. Music: Liu Yanxi. Sound: She Guojie. Cast: Li Tie as Gao Yibo, Zhong Xinghuo as Master Worker Aqi, Zhao Jing as Doctor Tong, Wang Zhihua as Guo Lufu

After her husband abandoned her to go abroad, clothing factory doctor Tong now lives with her son. The factory's chief designer Guo Lufu has been so devoted to his work for so long that he has passed the usual age of marriage. Factory labor union worker Gao Yibu and Master Worker Aqi decide to play matchmaker and get Tong and Guo together. After many humorous misfires, they at last succeed.

698. *For Love of an Orphan Girl (Gu Nu Lei)*

1986. Tianshan Film Studio. Color. 10 Reels. Direction: Guang Chunlan. Screenplay: Duan Baoshan, based on a legend. Cinematography: Yu Shishan, Bai Haiti. Art Direction: Gao Feng. Music: Zu Hengqian. Sound: Wang Huimin. Cast: Jhana as Haina, Ye Erken as Amman, Peierda Weisi as Sikai Deer

During fighting between Kazakh soldiers and bandits in the 1940s, orphan girl Haina flees to her mother's old friend Aunt Kamila for sanctuary. On the way, she meets Amman, Aunt Kamila's son, a local army platoon leader. Amman expresses his love for her, but to her great surprise and confusion, he leaves to join the bandits. After many adventures, Haina joins the army and learns that Amman was assigned the mission of infiltrating the bandits' lair. Disguising herself as a country girl, Haina joins Amman and his comrades to put down the bandits and punish a traitor.

699. *For Peace (Wei Le He Ping)*

1956. Shanghai Film Studio. B & W. 12 Reels. Direction: Zuo Lin. Screenplay: Ke Lin. Cinematography: Xu Qi. Art Direction: Ding Cheng. Music: Ju Xixian. Sound: Zhang Fubao. Cast: Zhao Dan as Jiang Ao, Bai Yang as Ding Menghui, Ren Shen as Jiang Shiling, Feng Xiao as Jiang Shiyuan, Xu Ming as Jiang Shixiu, Qi Heng as Yang Jian

In World War II Shanghai, East China University Professor Jiang Ao is jailed for encouraging students to resist the Japanese invaders. Released at war's end, he and his wife Ding Menghui look forward to some peaceful years together, but their dream is shattered by the outbreak of civil war. The school authorities exploit Jiang's admiration of America to counter the students' support of the Communist side. Faced with the reality of American support for the Nationalists, Jiang experiences

For Love of an Orphan Girl. **1986. Tianshan Film Studio.**

a conversion and enthusiastically throws his support to the Communists. For this, he is murdered by agents of the Nationalist government. Less than a year after the founding of the People's Republic, the Korean War starts. Ding Menghui, taking up her late husband's cause, sends their three children to fight in Korea. She is designated an "honorable mother," and is elected a people's representative.

700. *For 61 Brothers of the Same Class (Wei Le Liu Shi Yi Ge Jie Ji Xiong Di)*

1960. Beijing Film Studio. B & W. 6 Reels. Direction: Xie Tie, Chen Fangqian. Screenplay: Collectively written, based on news reports carried in the "People's Daily," "Shanxi Daily News," "China Youth Daily," "Beijing Evening News," and other papers, and recorded by Xie Tie and Chen Fangqian. Cinematography: Gao Hongtao. Sound: Zhang Jiake. No cast credits

In 1960, 61 highway construction workers in Pinglu County, Shanxi province, are stricken with food poisoning. County Party Secretary Hao heads up the rescue effort while sending the Public Security Bureau director

Yan to conduct an on-the-spot investigation. The urgency of the situation demands a large quantity of special medication unavailable in Shanxi. When the news reaches Beijing, the Ministry of Health, the Pharmacy Department of the Civil Aviation Bureau and the Chinese Air Force all make the rescue effort their highest priority. The Air Force delivers the medicine promptly to the county, and the workers are all saved. Investigation results in the arrest of two men for poisoning the food.

701. *For the Sake of Revolution (Yi Ge Ming De Ming Yi)*

1960. Beijing Film Studio. B & W. 16 Reels. Direction: Li Enjie, Shi Daqian. Screenplay adapted from the Soviet stage play "Lenin and the Second Generation," by Mi Shateluofu. Cinematography: Liu Hongming, Zhou Kun. Art Direction: Chi Ning, Yang Yuhe, Fan Shilian. Music: Du Mingxin, Wang Yefu. Sound: Lu Xiancang, Fu Yingjie, Chen Yanxi. Cast: Zhou Zheng as Lenin, Yu Shizhi as Kirensky, Tan Kun as Waxia, Fang Jufeng as Bijia, Tian Chong as Shaweiliefu, Wang Chengde as Gelubeifu

In 1918, shortly after the victory of the October Revolution, imperialists, capitalists and reactionaries begin the counter-revolution. After Waxia and Bijia's father is murdered by reactionaries, they and the young poet and singer Yacheka go to Moscow. Lenin and Kirensky view the work of rescuing and caring for children as a major part of the revolutionary struggle. The reactionaries try to destroy Lenin's work, but are unsuccessful. Many young people respond to Lenin's call to join the frontlines of battle. Waxia and Bijia stay on to study revolutionary theory, and become brave communist revolutionary soldiers.

702. *Forced to Marry (Hua Bi Lian Bi Hun)*

1993. Shanghai Film Studio. Color. Letterboxed. 9 Reels. Direction: Hu Lide. Screenplay: Jin Zhaoqu. Cinematography: Cheng Shiyu. Art Direction: Pu Jingsun. Music: Xu Jingxin. Sound: Dong Yan. Costume: Zhang Fuzhen, Zhang Chunzhong. Makeup: Xu Junpei, Ding Wei. Cast: Li Ling as Hua Bilian, Jia Ping as Luo Hongxun, Wang Xiangwei as Ruan Biao, Li Tie as Bajie, Sun Zhiqiang as Sun Tianpeng, Han Haihua as Yu Qian, Xu Ling as Jin Hua

Hua Village has a traditional practice in which the girls of the village choose their husbands through a kung fu contest. Since no one in the village has better skills in this than Hua Bilian, she decides to leave the village and look for someone she really likes. She meets and falls for a young man named Luo Hongxun, but he is already engaged to a Miss Gu in Yangzhou, and the couple will soon wed. But a man named Ruan Biao wants Miss Gu, and attacks her and Luo, injuring him and abducting his fiancee. When Hua Bilian hears of this, she goes to Luo and nurses him. When his recovery is assured, Bilian goes to Ruan's home to free Miss Gu, where she finds the unfortunate woman has committed suicide to avoid humiliation. After some misunderstandings between them are cleared up, Hua Bilian and Luo Hongxun are married.

703. *Foreign Girl Seeks Chinese Teacher (Yang Niu Xun Si)*

1987. Pearl River Film Studio. Color. 7 Reels. Direction: Zhang Rongren, Wang Wei. Screenplay: Kong Liang. Cinematography: Zhou Jianhui. Art Direction: Man Qinhai. Music: Zhen Qiufeng. Sound: Wu Chengxin. Cast: Falili as Katie, Lu Yongquan as Niu Guoqiang, Han Haihua as Zhu Zhongfa, Ju Yunkui as Chen Shangqing

A 17-year-old French girl, smitten with "kung fu fever," arrives in China by boat without even a passport. Her stated objective is to find an expert who will teach her the martial art. The girl is permitted to stay in China temporarily, with a policewoman assigned to keep an eye on her. She travels to a kung fu training camp and meets master Zhu Zhongfa. A series of humorous incidents follows, revolving largely around the girl's dogged persistence and the aging instructor's perplexed befuddlement about her. At last, the French girl's passport and visa problem is cleared up, she studies kung fu with another master Niu Guoqiang, and at last she prepares to make a Chinese kung fu film.

704. *Forever Young (Qing Chun Wan Sui)*

1983. Shanghai Film Studio. Color. 10 Reels. Direction: Huang Shuqin. Screenplay: Zhang Xuan. Cinematography: Can Lianguo. Art Direction: Chen Chudian. Music: Huang Zhun. Sound: Ni Zheng. Cast: Ren Yexiang as Yang Qiangyun, Zhang Ming as Zhen Bo, Liang Yan as Li Chun, Qin Ling as Su Ning, Si Tianyin as Humali, Zhang Haiyan as Wu Changfu

In a girls' high school in Beijing in 1952, Zhen Bo is a class leader. Zhen, an undercover Party member before liberation, uses her experience to help and guide her classmates in the right direction. Among these are: Yang Qiangyun, an energetic student with poor study habits; Li Chun, selfish and concerned only with personal ambition; unhappy Su Ning, who carries a heavy family burden dating from the old society; and orphan Humali, a Christian. The story tells of the young women's ambitions for China, and how they pull together to make contributions to building a new society.

705. *Four Buddies (Si Ge Xiao Huo Ban)*

1981. Children's Film Studio. Color. 9 Reels. Director: Qiqing Gaowa, Li Wei. Screenplay: Yao Yun, Tang Junhua. Cinematographer: Huang Xinyi. Art Direction: Duan Zhengzhong, Zhen Huiwen. Music: Jin Zhengping. Sound: Zhang Zhian. Cast: Yang Tong as Ding Xiaodong, Xiong Yifei as Chen Hui, Wang Suo as Wang Minmin, He Yong as Zhang Yong, Lu Guilan as Li Li

Chunjiang elementary school has a campaign called "everybody becomes a Red Flower

Child," which encourages children to do little things which are good deeds. However, four little playmates, Ding Xiaodong, Chen Hui, Wang Minmin and Zhang Ao are not interested in doing little things; they want some great accomplishment. As summer break approaches, and many students have already become Red Flower Children, the four become anxious, and make some humorous attempts at achieving greatness. Teacher Li patiently counsels them that they should start out by doing small things. The four children finally see the reasons behind this, and they too become Red Flower Children.

Honorary Award, 16th International Educational Film Festival.

706. *The Four Horsemen (Qi Shi Feng Yun)*

1990. Inner Mongolia Film Studio. Color. 9 Reels. Wide Screen. Direction: Saifu, Mailis. Screenplay: Mailis, Zhao Yuheng, Saifu. Cinematography: Yi Huhewula. Art Direction: Aori Lige. Music: Mor Jiling, Caodao Erji. Sound: Hu Linping. Cast: Bayin as Asir, Guli Zhar as the Princess, Erde Mutu as Masir, Dalie Lihan as Bosir, Bater as Gasir

In 1949, on the eve of the Communist takeover of China, the cultured and politically progressive Mongolian Prince of Turhut commissions his only daughter, Princess Nanselema, to carry a message to the revolutionary army urging them to move now and enter Xinjiang. Nationalist cavalrymen intercept the secret message and kidnap the princess. The Prince of Turhut asks four heroic horsemen to save the princess. They wage a struggle to the death against the cavalry.

Best Cinematographer Yi Huhewula, 1991 Golden Rooster Awards.

707. *Four Tyrants (Si Da Tian Wang)*

1994. Changchun Film Studio. Color. Letterboxed. 9 Reels. Direction: Yu Xiangyuan. Screenplay: Yu Xiangyuan. Cinematography: Song Dehua. Art Direction: Li Guo. Music: Fan Weiqiang. Sound: Meng Gang. Costume: Wu Boqiao. Makeup: Qiu Hong. Cast: Liu Zhibing as Sun Shaowu, Yu Xiaohui as Li Shuilian and Li Menglian, Chi Zhiqiang as the 4th King of Heaven

The city of Haicheng has four triad masters. One of these schemes to eliminate the other three by becoming a Japanese collabora-

tor. His uses his new allies to get rid of two of the rivals, then he sets out to eliminate his major police nemesis as well, detective Sun Shaowu. He sets up Sun in a situation that will lead the third rival to kill the detective, thereby getting rid of both of them. This will give Liu full control of the triad, free of police interference and with Japanese protection. Sun sees through the plot in time, and in the final confrontation kills both Liu and the Japanese agent working with the gangster.

708. *Fourth Class Small Station (Shi Deng Xiao Zhan)*

1984. Shanghai Film Studio. Color. Letterboxed. 9 Reels. Direction: Fu Jinggong. Screenplay: Wu Hongli, Yang Shiwen, Si Minshan. Cinematography: Cha Xiangkang. Art Direction: Zhu Jiancang. Music: Yang Mao. Sound: Ni Zheng. Cast: Guo Zhenqin as Station Director Pu, Wang Weiping as Ha Xiaole, Chen Xu as Quan Geng

After China implements its policies of openness and reform, the Fengting Railway Station in a remote mountainous region changes from a sleepy backwater to a bustling hub of activity, quadrupling its transport volume in just a few years. This worries Station Director Pu. While several local industries make demands on the little station's capacity, the greatest problems are created by Quan Geng, a farmer who specializes in raising ducks. As his business prospers, Pu's headaches mount as well. One of Pu's workers, Ha Xiaole, suggests a possible solution: establish a roast duck restaurant and takeout in the station. The food service facility attracts many passengers and resolves the transport problem. When Fengting is at last upgraded from a fourth to a third class station, the retiring Director Pu recommends that Ha Xiaole be promoted to succeed him as station head.

709. *The Fox Case (Hu Li Mi An)*

1988. Guangxi Film Studio. Color. Letterboxed. 10 Reels. Direction: Luo Yuzhong. Screenplay: Fang Ai. Cinematography: Feng Bingyong. Art Direction: Zhang Yafang. Music: Li Yanlin. Sound: Han Weijun. Cast: Jiang Jun as Zhou Zhean, Bai Mu as Ren Qianfan, Ren Weimin as Police Bureau Director Yang, Shen Jie as Hu Hong, Li Zhiyu as Zhao Jingbai

In the early years of the Republic of China, in a small town in Southeast China, a college student is bitten by a fox and dies. County

Director Ren Qianfan and Police Bureau Director Yang search the area with no results. On the night of the Moon Festival, Ren holds a banquet to which are invited many of the town notables, including "Little Peacock" the queen of the local dance hall, and Zhao Jingbai, who happens to be passing through on the way to assuming his new government post as Minister of Justice. During the evening, Little Peacock also dies of a fox bite. A third death follows the next night. But where is the murderous fox…?

710. *Fox Romance (Hu Yuan)*

1986. Xi'an Film Studio. Color. Letterboxed. 9 Reels. Direction: Sun Yuanxun. Screenplay: Fang Yihua. Cinematography: Zhao Zhiyu. Art Direction: Wang Fei. Music: Xiang Yin. Sound: Dang Chunzhu. Cast: Kong Aiping as Lady Xin 14, Lu Weiqiang as Feng Sheng, Zhao Mingjie as Mr. Chu, Zuo Ling as Liu Yuxiang

711. *Friends in Adversity (Huan Nan Zhi Jiao)*

1958. Changchun Film Studio. B & W. 10 Reels. Direction: Wang Yi. Screenplay: Wang Yi. Cinematography: Zhang Hui. Art Direction: Li Junjie. Music: Zhen Zhenyu. Sound: Yuan Mingda. Cast: Zhao Lian as Liu Jinbao, Han Yan as Liu's father, Bai Yinkuan as Jin Yongjun, Li Dade as Jin Huisu, Wang Jianhua as Jin's mother, Du Fengxia as Girl Sun

At the foot of Mount Changbai, in a village governed by Japanese collaborators, a Chinese man named Liu Jinbao and a Chinese-Korean man Jin Yongjun risk their lives to support their families by illegally harvesting ginseng from the mountain. One day they run into Japanese soldiers, and Youngjun is wounded and falls off a cliff while protecting Jinbao. Jinbao escapes, and gives all the money they earned from ginseng sales to Yongjun's family. He then takes on all the family's farm work. Youngjun's younger sister Huisu is at first grateful, the two become friends, then fall in love. Their fortunes turn for the worse, and just at that time, Yongjun returns; he had been rescued by anti–Japanese guerrillas after falling from the cliff. He is arrested, but Jinbao rescues him at night. Yongjun and Girl Sun, a former girlfriend of Jinbao's, decide to join the guerrillas, but in covering their escape, Jinbao and Huisu are captured by the Japanese. Yongjun and Girl Sun vow to join the guerrillas and seek revenge.

712. *Friendship (You Yi)*

1959. August Film Studio. B & W. 8 Reels. Direction: Li Jun. Screenplay: Li Jun, based on the stage play of the same title by Wang Ying. Cinematography: Zhang Dongliang. Art Direction: Ren Huixing. Music: Li Yuqiu. Sound: Li Yan. Cast: Li Jinming as Platoon Leader He, Wang Rui as Xiao Yang, Xu Yanming as Zhao Fa, Jiang Zeshan as the squad leader, Li Wanpeng as Wang Xi, Lin Lang as Liu Tian

During the Korean War, Volunteer Army platoon leader He rescues a Korean woman named Kim who is close to giving birth. The baby is born and named "Friendship." Platoon Leader He and scout Xiao Yang reconnoiter to determine the Americans' artillery deployment, but on their way back are discovered. Platoon Leader He is wounded, but rescued by Mrs. Kim's mother-in-law. Later, however, the Chinese officer is captured by the enemy who decide to shoot him as a spy. Just as he is about to be executed, Mrs. Kim arrives in time and helps him escape, although she loses her own life in doing so. After that, the volunteer soldiers give little "Friendship" to Mrs. Kim's mother-in-law to raise.

713. *From Slave to General (Parts 1 and 2) (Cong Nu Li Dao Jiang Jun)*

1979. Shanghai Film Studio. Color. 18 Reels. Direction: Wang Yan. Screenplay: Liang Xing. Art Direction: Han Shangyi, Yan Cangming, Chen Shaomian. Music: Ge Yan. Sound: Zhou Hengliang. Cast: Yang Zhaibao as "Little Basket," Zhang Jinling as Suoma, Feng Chunchao as Chen Yi, Si Xilai as Hao Jun, Wu Xiqian as Zhen Yi

The film biography of a Red Army commander. In 1915, Xiao Luo, a former slave, joins the army and rises through the ranks until 10 years later he is a deputy company commander. Inspired by Sun Yat-sen's teachings, Xiao Luo joins Sun's revolutionary movement and is assigned as an acting deputy regimental commander and sent to the front lines to "eradicate communism." But after he has some contacts with the Communists, he takes his army over to their side, becomes a Red Army division commander and changes his name to Luo Xiao. During a political struggle with the Communist Party, he stands with Mao Zedong, and when the Maoists are defeated, Luo Xiao is reduced to the ranks and assigned to tend horses. In 1934, when Mao takes command in the Party, Luo Xiao is restored to a divisional command post. After the Red Army sets up headquarters at Yanan in north Shanxi province, he accepts a frontline post in repelling the Japanese invasion, and becomes commander of the New Fourth Army. In the summer of 1947, General Luo Xiao takes on a major battle mission against the Nationalists. He dies at his post, his hands clutching binoculars as he looks at a map.

714. *From the Heart (Xin Quan)*

1982. Guangxi Film Studio. Color. 9 Reels. Direction: Wu Yingchun. Screenplay: Zhou Minzheng. Cinematography: Liao Fan, Sun Lixian. Art Direction: Lao Guanneng. Music: Yang Shaoyi. Sound: Li Zhuwen. Cast: Ouyang Ruqiu as Grandma, Gao Ying as Wen Ying, Bi Jiancang as Meng Yumin, Yang Xiaoning as Meng Xiaomin, Feng Jingbo as Kali, Zhang Lei as Xiao Yi, Wu Zhaolan as Lin Qing

Kali, a Miao nationality child, is invited to be a guest in the home of Meng Xiaomin, a Lijing City elementary school student. When they go with neighbor girl Xiao Yi to collect insect samples, Kali returns with a wonderful insect exhibit which draws high praise from the teacher. But Xiaomin's grandmother gives all the credit for the exhibit to her grandson, and as a result Xiaomin wins the city's first class award for best summer break science project. Xiaomin's mother Wen Ying is very upset to learn of her son's dishonesty, but decides not to make the truth public. As Xiaomin compounds his earlier mistake, she comes to realize he is a victim of some bad social customs and goes public with the story. This prompts her son to change his behavior for the better, and in the end Xiaomin, Kali and Xiao Yi go back together to collect samples for a group project.

715. *Frustrated Affection (Qing Tian Hen Hai)*

1980. Changchun Film Studio. Color. 12 Reels. Direction: Chang Yan. Screenplay: Li Dong, Chang Yan, Wang Yungao. Cinematography: Chang Yan, Gao Hongbao. Art Direction: Wang Guizhi, Shui Zhuangji. Music: Qin Yongcheng. Sound: Tong Zongde. Cast: Xia Zongxue as Wei Zhipu, Wu Xiqian as Zeng Geng, Zhang Ning as Zhong Lihan, Liang Tongyu as Zhu Fengyang, Zhang Xiaoming as Xiaozhen, Wang Baohua as Ren Jiuche

In 1949, when the defeated Nationalist government flees to Taiwan, former Nationalist senior military officer Wei Zhipu was at the time separated from his wife, and is tricked into going to Taiwan without her. In the 1970s, his godson Zhu Fengyang, the son of his former assistant back on the mainland, is arrested for trying to swim across the Taiwan Strait to the mainland. To be in a position to protect the young man, Wei has himself named to the government group involved with finding and arresting those who try to return to the mainland. Wei Zhipu by chance learns that his wife is still alive on the mainland. Wei Zhifu is finally able to get his godson and his niece Xiaozhen out of jeopardy. Together they look toward the mainland, hoping that the day of national reunification will come soon.

716. *Frustrated Childhood (Feng Yu Gu Yuan)*

1991. Children's Film Studio. Color. Letterboxed. 9 Reels. Direction: Xu Geng. Screenplay: Chen Shu, Wang Chuncan, Wang Yungeng. Cinematography: Xu Qi, Lu Li'an. Art Direction: Yao Mingzhong, Xia Nan. Music: Jin Fuzai. Sound: Du Xiaohua. Cast: Yang Yi as A Zhang, Jiao Tiyi as Zhou Boyi, Zhao Kuier as Lu Rui, Wang Zhiwen as Mr. Zhiling, Zhou Xuezheng as Aunt Cui, Zhang Zhaozong as Mr. Shou, Ye Meng as Mama Chang, Ding Yan as A Kui, Deng Xiyue as A Song, Feng Qi as Grandfather, Zhou Xianzhen as Grandmother, Yun Yuchun as Great Aunt Cui, Lu Zhirui as A Lin

The film relates the extraordinary childhood of the three Zhou brothers of Shaoxing (Zhou Shuren, Zhou Zuoren and Zhou Jianren), each of whom played important roles in the history of modern Chinese culture and ideology. The eldest, Zhou Shuren (called A Zhang in the film), went on to become China's greatest writer of the 20th Century under the pen name Lu Xun, and is the focus of the story.

Best Music Jin Fuzai, 1992 Golden Rooster Awards.

717. *The Fugitive (Tao Fan)*

1986. Changchun Film Studio. Color. 9 Reels. Direction: Li Qiankuan, Xiao Guiyun. Screenplay: Li Qiankuan, Chen Guidi, Wang Zequn. Cinematography: Han Dongcia. Art Direction: Wang Xingwen. Music: Jin Xiang. Sound: Yi Wenyu. Cast: Zhao Jun as Xin Dali, Wang Xiaowei as Xiao Yu, Zhao Zhiyin as the tailor, Zhang Wei as the stepmother

Fugitive from justice Xin Dali flees to an area of Yunnan province largely inhabited by people of the Dai nationality. He settles in a small town, and sets up a tailoring stall. Xin blends in well with the local people, and soon meets a girl named Xiao Yun. She and her family are very receptive to the young man, and the family's warmth and enthusiasm restores his own confidence in life. He in turn gives them business advice which turns around the fortunes of the family's unprofitable clothing business. He even designs styles which allow their business to enter the international market. He is successful, but increasingly regretful of his past. Xin Dali at last summons the courage to tell Xiao Yun the truth, which shocks and upsets her greatly. She runs away in tears. After thinking it over, she decides that together they can deal with this, and goes to find him. But when she arrives she finds him gone, with just a note to say he has returned to where he belongs.

718. *Full Moon (Shi Wu De Yue Liang)*

1986. Beijing Film Studio. Color. 10 Reels. Direction: Li Xin. Screenplay: Li Lin, Du Zhenyuan. Cinematography: Zhang Jiwu, Song Guanghua. Art Direction: Luo Yurong, Zhao Jinheng. Music: Li Lifu. Sound: Liu Shida, Qin Minde. Cast: Yu Li as Fang Xiaomei, Ma Shuchao as Yuan Shaolin, Sharen Gaowa as Tian Jing, Zhang Tianxi as Fang Hua, Sun Zhenhua as Director Sun, Guo Yuntai as Mayor Tian, Yang Guiquan as Ye Xiaomei

Army officers Yuan Shaolin and Fang Hua are comrades-in-arms. In addition, Yuan is the fiance of Fang's sister Fang Xiaomei. Fang Hua loves silk plant director Tian Jing, the only daughter of the city's mayor and his wife, city government office Director Ye Xiaomei. The two army officers are ordered to the battlefront. Director Ye decides she wants her daughter to marry the son of the provincial Party Secretary, a local TV station correspondent named Wu An. She arranges for the two to start dating, and Tian Jing soon writes Fang Hua a letter breaking off their relationship. Later, Wu An goes to the front lines to interview troops there, and learns for the first time the story of Fang Hua, and how he sacrificed himself in battle. Angry at Ye Xiaomei and Tian Jing's betrayal of the soldier, Wu An makes a TV program exposing them.

719. *Fun of Crosstalk (Xiao Po Qing Wang)*

1987. Xiaoxiang Film Studio. Color. 9 Reels. Direction: Hu Shue. Screenplay: Ma Ji, Wang Zhaoyuan, Yang Shanzhi. Cinematography: Hu Zhongqiu. Art Direction: Zhou Yi. Music: Gao Xiaobo. Sound: Liu Feng. Cast: Zhao Yan as Shu Huai, Ma Ji as Wen Shanfu, Liu Wei as Xiao Wen, Zhen Jian as Xie lin, Wang Jinbao as Xu Dafa, Feng Gong as Xiao Ma

"Crosstalk" (rapid-paced comedy dialogue) performer Su Huai and his partner Xie Lin, travel to the fishing village where Su lived 10 years before. They feel the experience will give them material for writing better crosstalk. They find that while the village has grown prosperous, the practice of gift-giving has become so dominant, and gotten so out of hand, that it has become a real burden. Su and Xie observe one family's wedding gifts and write a new routine based on this. The village people all find it hilarious, but it also makes them think afterwards.

720. *Gamblers (Du Ming Han)*

1989. Liaoning Film Studio and Changchun Film Studio Co-Production. Color. 9 Reels. Direction: Ding Xuan. Screenplay: Ding Xuan. Cinematography: Li Jun. Art Direction: Zhang Lei. Music: Li Yanzhong. Sound: Lin Zhi. Cast: Wu Jingan as Liu Yulin, Yuan Li as Yinzi

In a Northeast China village, young peasant Liu Yulin falls in love with Yinzi, a young widow. They agree to pool their resources and plan a new, happy life together. But Liu becomes addicted to gambling, and soon gambles away all their savings. He vows to change after they are married but does not, slipping away to gamble without telling his wife. Finally, however, he is involved in a fight in a gaming house, and arrested. Though greatly upset, Yinzi values their love so much that she determines to do everything necessary to save her husband. Her love and hard work finally force him to his senses. He vows anew to give up gambling, and this time everyone thinks he might make it.

721. *The Garden of Youth (Qing Chun De Yuan Di)*

1955. Shanghai Film Studio. B & W. 9 Reels. Direction: Wang Weiyi. Screenplay: Ren Deyao. Cinematography: Feng Sizhi. Art Direction: Huang Chong. Music: Wang Yunjie. Sound: Lu

Zhongbo. Cast: Su Manyi as Xiaohui's mother, Liu Jie as Mother Wang, Zhang Weina as Li Xiaohui, Gu Guoyi as Du Lihua, Jiang Ziqiang as Fang Xinghua, Chen Haigen as Zhao Dacheng, Fu Yanmin as Chen Yindi, Li Huanqing as Teacher Shi

Third-year junior high student Li Xiaohui is so devoted to the study of plants and plant implantation, she spends all her time in lab and declines to participate in group activities. Class chair Chen Yindi and Director Du Lihua suggest that her class develop a piece of uncultivated campus land as a graduation gift to the school. Virtually everyone in the school except Li Xiaohui is enthusiastic about the idea. She does offer a design for cultivating the garden, but when her classmates offer some criticisms of it, she leaves the collective. With the help of Chen Yingdi, Du Lihua and Teacher Shi, Xiaohui finally realizes she should stay with the collective, and she and her classmates devote themselves to the work. When the harvest season arrives, the garden yields many flowers and fruit. The students have enjoyed the physical labor, and thoughts of collective living is well-established in their minds.

722. *Garlands at the Foot of the Mountains (Gao Shan Xia De Hua Huan)*

1984. Shanghai Film Studio. Color. Wide Screen. 14 Reels. Direction: Xie Jin. Screenplay: Li Zhun, Li Cunbao. Cinematography: Lu Junfu, Shen Jie, Zhu Yongde. Art Direction: Zhong Yongqing. Music: Ge Yan. Sound: Zhu Weigang. Makeup: Shen Keqiang. Cast: Lu Xiaohe as Liang Shanxi, Tang Guoqiang as Zhao Mengsheng, He Wei as Jin Kailai, Ge Ke as Han Yuxiu, Wang Yumei as Liang's mother, Tong Chao as Lei Zheng

When the Sino-Vietnamese border war erupts in 1979, company commander Liang Shanxi cancels his planned leave home to visit his wife Han Yuxiu, soon to have a baby. A contrasting attitude is that of Zhao Mengsheng, son of a deceased high-ranking military officer, who tries to use his mother's connections to avoid going to the front. Liang Shanxi and another officer named Jin Kailai criticize him severely for this, pointing to the example of "Little Beijing," a young soldier who volunteered for combat to follow in the footsteps of his hero father Commander Lei. Zhao Mengsheng reluctantly changes his mind and goes with his unit to the front. In the fighting,

Liang, Jin and Little Beijing are all killed. The experience of combat and the sacrifices of others change Zhao Mengsheng completely; he becomes an outstanding soldier and serves valiantly. When he returns home, his new attitude and his guilt over his earlier behavior puzzles his mother. But she too has a change in attitude when the military base is visited by the mother and young widow of Liang Shanxi. It turns out that early in his military career the deceased commander had run up some debts to get his parents out of poverty, and his will stipulates these must be paid from his death compensation payments.

723. *Gate Number Six (Liu Hao Men)*

1952. Northeast Film Studio. B & W. 11 Reels. Direction: Lu Ban. Screenplay: Chen Ming, based on the stage play by Wang Xuebao and Zhang Xuexin. Cinematography: Du Yu. Art Direction: Zhang Hancheng. Music: Wang Yunjie. Sound: Sui Xizong. Cast: Guo Zhenqing as Hu Er, Li Zhiping as Ding Zhanyuan, Li Xiaogong as Hu's wife, Xie Tian as Ma Jinlong, Li Lin as Division Director Yu, Zhao Kuiyin as Zhao San

In a Northeast China city just prior to liberation, the Nationalists were shipping large quantities of goods and materials out of the country in preparation for flight to Taiwan. Ma Babei, supervisor of the city's freight yard, along with his son Ma Jinlong, also decided to exploit this opportunity by withholding the wages of workers at Gate Number 6. The workers oppose them with the help of the Communist Party underground. At Ma Babei's 70th birthday celebration, two workers named Hu Er and Ding Zhanyuan arrive to disrupt the banquet and force him to pay the workers' withheld wages. Ma not only refuses to pay, but also tries to force the workers to load more of the materials being shipped out by the Nationalists. The workers at Gate Number 6 unite with all of the city's deliverymen in a strike which wins the struggle. Ma Jinlong then sends special agents to put Hu Er in jail. After liberation, He Er gains his freedom and meets Ding Zhanyuan and others to plan what moves to take against their former oppressors. Ma Jinlong attempts to bribe Hu Er but is severely rebuked. Hu Er is elected director of the delivery service station, and Ding Zhanyuan becomes labor union chairman. Ma Babei attempts to destroy the delivery service station,

Garlands at the Foot of the Mountains. **Expectant parents Liang Shanxi (Lu Xiaohe) and his wife Han Yuxiu (Ge Ke) look forward to parenthood. 1984. Shanghai Film Studio.**

but is thwarted. In the end the two Mas, father and son, are put on trial for their crimes.

724. *The Geese Fly North (Da Yan Bei Fei)*

1985. Emei Film Studio. Color. 9 Reels. Direction: Zhang Lukun, Wang Kanghua. Screenplay: Hong Yi, Jin Di, Qi Li. Cinematography: Cui Yifeng, Shi Mu. Art Direction: Wang Yongkang. Music: Tian Feng, Chen Zhimei. Sound: Shen Guli. Cast: Jin Di as Cheng Yulan, Chen Shaoze as Qin Zhibing, Rui Xuhua as Zhong Ming, Hong Yi as Qin Youmei, Zhang Jie as Cheng Yu, Wu Gang as Pang Zizhang, Tan Meiying as Hua Beibei, Zhang Bei as Director Liang, Li Wei as Mother Zhong

In a part of south China which is the native place of many overseas Chinese, the Cuiling Rest Home admits Hong Kong businessman Qin Zhibing, who has a serious drug problem. Doctor Cheng Yulan recognizes Qin Zhibing as her old high school boy friend. Qin's sister Qin Youmei had called her brother back from Hong Kong when their father fell seriously ill. Qin Zhibing was persuaded to stay on for disposition of the family fortune after the father's death. He was then enticed by local villain Pang Zizhang to marry party girl Beibei, after which she and Pang got Qin Zhibing addicted to drugs, eventually taking the fortune. Under Cheng Yulan's treatment, Qin Zhibing's situation improves significantly, but he has lost everything to his wife and her fellow conspirator. In despair, Qin tries to take his own life, but Cheng Yulan's fiance Zhong Ming intervenes to save him. Zhong Ming's family takes Qin into their home and helps him regain his mental and spiritual health. When he is fully recovered, Qin vows that he will return to Hong Kong and build a new fortune, only this time he will make more contributions to China and his home town.

725. *The General and the Orphan Girls (Jiang Jun Yu Gu Nu)*

1984. August First Film studio. Color. Letterboxed. 10 Reels. Direction: Huang Fuxiang. Screenplay: Yao Yuanwen, Wang Gehong. Cinematography: Huang Fuxiang. Art Direction: Cui Denggao. Music: Liu Yanyu. Sound: Xiang Zhiliang. Cast: Lu Zhiqi as Xiao Gang, Cheng Anna as Xiuyun, Ren Guangzhi as Commander Nie

Rongzheng, Xing Long as Xiao Ma, Meng Weiran as Shuzi, Chen Jianfei as Zhongyuan

In 1940, Eighth Route Army soldier Xiao Gang finds two little Japanese girls whose parents have just been killed. The soldiers in his company take care of the orphans, and when he goes home on leave he takes them with him. His wife is delighted with the little girls until she finds out they are Japanese. Xiao Gang convinces her that children are innocents in war, and she becomes their surrogate mother. Shuzi, one of the girls, becomes ill, and Commander Nie sends an army doctor to treat her. At last, Commander Nie decides the children should be returned so they can go home to Japan. But while escorting them to the Japanese lines, Xiao Gang is killed. Forty years later, Shuzi returns to China and visits Nie Rongzheng and her surrogate mother, Xiao Gang's wife.

726. *General Peng Dehuai (Peng Da Jiang Jun)*

1988. Xi'an Film Studio. Color. Wide Screen. 16 Reels. Direction: Liu Bin, Li Yucai, Liu Haoxue. Screenplay: Zheng Zhong. Cinematography: Zhang Faliang, Liu Chengxu, Ma Delin. Art Direction: Wang Fei, Zhang Xiaohui, Zhao Jun. Music: Li Yaodong. Sound: Che Ziyuan. Cast: Ding Xiaoyi as Peng Dehuai, Gu Yue as Mao Zedong, Sun Feihu as Chiang Kaishek.

A film biography of one of the leading figures of modern Chinese history. In 1959, the long military career of General Peng Dehuai comes to an end when he is dismissed from his post as Defense Minister and evicted from Zhongnanhai, the residential compound adjacent to the Forbidden City reserved for senior Chinese officials. He moves to the Wujia Garden in Beijing's western suburbs. His fall from power is a direct result of his frequent expressions of concern for the direction in which China is going. These concerns had led him to write a personal letter to Chairman Mao Zedong, who promptly ordered Peng's dismissal. In the Wujia Garden, freed from the pressures of office, General Peng looks back at the highlights of his distinguished career. But he is not destined to live out his days in peace. The outbreak of the cataclysmic Cultural Revolution deals the final blow. General Peng prays for the nation as the chaos swirls around him.

727. *General with a Sword (Pei Jian Jiang Jun)*

1982. Changchun Film Studio. Color. 11 Reels. Direction: Xiao Guiyun and Li Qiankuan. Screenplay: Zhang Xiaotian, Shi Zhengxian. Cinematography: Wang Lei. Art Direction: Wang Xingwen. Music: Chen Min. Sound: Jue Jingxiu, Wang Wenfu. Cast: Wang Shangxing as He Jian, Xiang Lei as Yan Jun, Shen Liang as Gu Zhutong, Jiang Changhua as Shen Jiqin, Wang Shouquan as Gong Yinwei, You Lihua as Yang Cui.

On the eve of the Battle of Huaihai in the fall of 1948, Nationalist Army intelligence grows suspicious of two generals, Suijing area deputy commanders He Jian and Yan Jun. The two are close friends who have served together in many military campaigns. So Chief of Staff Shen Jiqin assigns a woman doctor named Yang Cui to He Jian's headquarters to keep an eye on the general. Gu Yiping, a Communist agent assigned to deliver the CPC's plans for a rebellion to He Jian, recognizes Yang Cui as his old girl friend from college. Unaware that Yang Cui is also a covert Communist agent, Gu hates her for being what she appears to be, an enemy officer spying on the general. In the end, He Jian and Yan Jun successfully bring their troops over to the Communist side, which contributes greatly to the Communist victory in the Battle of Huaihai. But Yang Cui sacrifices her own life for the rebellion's success. Gu Zhutong places a peach blossom on Yang Cui's grave. He has learned too late the woman he hated for 10 years was on his side all along.

728. *The General's Choice (Jiang Jun De Xuan Zhe)*

1984. Liaoning Science Film Studio. Color. Direction: Li Ning, Liu Guoquan. Screenplay: Mei Dai, Sun Xianzhi, Zhao Xianxun. Cinematography: Zhang Chi. Art Direction: Yao Mingzhong, Feng Yuan, Chen Bing. Music: Ma Ding. Sound: Lin Zhi. Cast: Hu Ao as Wu Fei, Xu Zhan as Yujian, Liu Dong as Yuzhen, Shen Guanglan as Jingyun, Xu Ming as Yu Maowen, Zhu Yurong as Qiuyue, Qina Ritu as Lu Ping, Li Ning as Director Luo.

The story takes place in 1947, and relates how a fictional Nationalist general named Wu Fei undergoes a conversion to Communism and works for the revolutionary cause while retaining the trust of Chiang Kaishek.

729. *Genghis Khan (Parts 1&2) (Cheng Ji Si Han)*

1986. Inner Mongolia Film Studio & Youth Film Studio Co-Production. Color. 20 Reels. Direction: Zhan Xiangchi. Screenplay: Chao Guangtu, Na Ren, Zhan Xiangchi. Cinematography: Gan Quan, Wulan Mulin. Art Direction: Song Hongrong. Music: Moer Jihu. Sound: Bu Ren. Cast: Siqing Gaowa as Keerlun, Enhesheng as Han, Chagan Chaolu as Shugai, Xurenhua as Boertie, Sharen Gaowa as Hedaan, Batuqinge as Chi Laowun, Deli Geer as Genghis Khan

Part 1: Genghis Khan is born in 1162 on the Mongolian prairie, the son of a chief. Growing up in an environment of almost constant warfare and bloodshed, he comes to realize the situation can be changed only by unifying the Mongolian people. When he becomes chief, he makes a temporary alliance with Zhamuhe and other chiefs, and together they launch a unification campaign with their combined force of several tens of thousand warriors. He is victorious in the final battle but Hedaan, the girl he loves, is killed.

Part 2: In 1189, the Mongolian prairie knows peace for the first time in many years. With high hopes that the peace will be a lasting one, the people choose Genghis Khan as their leader. He then allies with the Kingdom of Jin, and by taking advantage of its power he is able to defeat the Tartars, avenging his father. In 1206, Genghis Khan achieves unity among the Mongolian people at last, and becomes the Mongolian Emperor.

730. *Gentleman's Revenge (Jun Zi Fu Chou)*

1991. Tianshan Film Studio. Color. 9 Reels. Direction: Liu Guoquan. Screenplay: Li Mengxue. Cinematography: Guan Qingwu. Art Direction: Liu Zhangyu. Music: Fu Lin. Sound: Li Jingcheng. Cast: Zhou Lijing as Chen Ping, An Dong as Tian Fangfang, Zhang Xiao as Wang Daming, Liang Tian as bear, Zhang Guangbei as Lin Haibo, Zhu Shibin as Shi Tou, zhang Ying as Shi's wife, Li Dong as Wang Xiaomei, Gao Baoling as Lu Minhui, Li Hu as Li Zheng, Wang Bing as Cao Shan

A taxi driver sets out to avenge his mother, murdered in a robbery. The detectives on the case at last convince him to work with them, and they apprehend the robbers together.

731. *Getting Married (Jie Hun)*

1953. Northeast Film Studio. B & W. 8 Reels. Direction: Yan Gong. Screenplay: Ma Feng and Chen Ge, based on the novel of the same title by Ma Feng (1922–). Cinematography: Zhu Jinming and Bao Jie. Art Direction: Xu Wei. Music: Li Xi. Sound: Jue Jinxiu. Cast: Zhang Xiqi as Tian Chunsheng, Chen Qiang as Tian Gaohong, Di Li as Mother Tian, Ya Bin as Xiao Er, Wang Chunying as Li Donghe, Li Wancheng as the Village Head, Yang Jing as Yang Xiaoqing

Yang Xiaoqing, a girl from Liulin Village, and Tian Chunsheng, a young man from Qinshui Village, plan to marry right after the autumn harvest is in. The parents of both are anxious to have grandchildren, and can hardly wait for the wedding day to arrive. But two days before the wedding, Yang Xiaoqing goes to the county seat to learn a new method of child delivery, and after her return to the village she immediately starts work in maternity care. With Chunsheng's approval, they twice postpone their wedding. The following spring, Xiaoqing and Chunsheng at last make an appointment to finalize their marriage at the district government office. But on the way each is again diverted to help others, Chunsheng to push a broken cart then help mend a broken dam, Xiaoqing to assist someone having a baby. As a result, they arrive very late for their appointment, and both sets of parents are kept waiting.

732. *Getting Rich (Sheng Cai You Dao)*

1984. Beijing Film Studio. Color. Letterboxed. 10 Reels. Direction: Xie Tie. Screenplay: Wu Jiaxin, Wang Binglin. Cinematography: Tu Jiakuan. Art Direction: Zhang Xiande, Zhen Huiwen. Music: Jin Zhengping. Sound: Zhang Zhian. Cast: Zhao Zhiyue as Ren Laole, Chen Qiang as Li Laoda, Ling Yuan as Le's wife, Ma Shuchao as Li's son, Yu Li as Ren's daughter

At the party to announce the engagement of Ren Laole's daughter to Li Laoda's son, an argument breaks out between the parents over which of the two families the young couple will be marrying into, as each family wants an additional worker. The engagement is broken off the day it begins. Ren Laole decides to take the money he had been saving to buy the couple a house and use it to purchase a tractor and start a business instead. His wife objects at first, but when he starts making money, she agrees he was right. Li Laoda also wants to get rich, but his method is to marry his son to an unattractive rich girl. Nobody supports his plan, even his own family shuns him. At last, Li comes around and the young couple are reconciled.

733. *Ghost (Bai Ri Nu Gui)*

1994. Guangxi Film Studio. Color. Letterboxed. 9 Reels. Direction: Zhao Wenxin. Screenplay: Du Songzi. Cinematography: Cai Xiaopeng. Art Direction: Huang Shu. Art Direction: Xian Hua, Xia Zhenzhong. Sound: Han Weijun. Costume: Qi Guishuang. Makeup: Zhao Zhiming. Cast: Xu Wenguang as He Baigang, Dongfang Wenying as A Xue, Liu Yi as Lu Jiajia, Lei Wujia, Huang Mingsheng, Yang Aiming, Tang Xiaoling, Tan Yong, He Weian, Wang Jie

Company owner He Baigang is having an affair with Lu Jiajia, a woman in the same company. He decides to get rid of his wife Axue, so he drugs her with sleeping pills, then throws the unconscious woman into the sea. Axue survives however, and with her husband thinking her dead, she sets out for revenge. He Baigang and his love begin seeing signs they may be haunted by the wife's ghost. The guilty and terrified He Baigang begins losing his mind, and at last Axue appears before him. He flees from her and tries to hide. Axue sets a fire which kills her husband. But Lu Jiajia becomes the heiress to his company, and Axue is arrested.

734. *Ghost (You Ling)*

1980. Xiaoxiang Film Studio. Color. 10 Reels. Direction: Yun Wenyao. Screenplay: Chen Zhaomin, Zhang Jinbiao. Cinematography: Yun Wenyao. Art Direction: Zhang Jinbiao. Music: Si Guangnan. Sound: Lu Xichun. Cast: Shao Huifang as Xia Zhenglan, Wang Mincheng as Lu hanzhang, Yu Shaokang as Zhao Mingxiong, Ren Dao as Wu Sheng, Zhao Zhuguo as Wun Wanjun, Di Xiaohui as Xiao Xi

Just before the Gang of Four is forced from power, ballet dancer Xia Zhenlan and young doctor Lu Hanzhang are married in the city of Lugang. On their honeymoon, she gives him a bottle of water, which he drinks and then dies. Veteran public security officer Zhao Shuxiong comes with two assistants to investigate. They quickly eliminate Xia Zhenlan as a suspect, but they find poison in Doctor Lu's toothpaste. Suspicion soon turns to Wun Wanjun, a chief nurse at the hospital where the victim worked. It turns out that Wu Sheng, Deputy

Director of the city's revolutionary committee, was in league with Qi Feng, a key figure in the Gang of Four. When the former director of the Public Security Bureau learned that Qi had been a counterrevolutionary before 1949, Qi orders Wu Sheng to murder the policeman and dump his body into the sea. One of Doctor Lu's patients had witnessed the murder and informed the doctor. To silence the doctor, Wu had his mistress, Doctor Lu's nurse Wun Wanjun, poison the doctor. When Wu Sheng attempts to kill Wun Wanjun to silence her, she goes to the PSB and tells everything. But although Wu Sheng is arrested, supporters of the Gang of Four still control the city, so they suppress any further investigation of the case. When Xia Zhenglan learns that the Gang and its supporters have ordered her killed, she realizes they will never let her lead a normal life, so she commits suicide as an act of protest.

735. *The Ghost at Wild Hotel (Ye Dian You Ling)*

1990. Changchun Film Studio. Color. Wide Screen. 9 Reels. Direction: He Misheng. Screenplay: Xu Guangshun. Cinematography: Zhang Zhongnan. Art Direction: Zhang Yan. Music: Yang Yilun. Sound: Cao Feng. Cast: Yu Fuhui as Zhang Jiaping, Shen Guanchu as Luo Lin

Zhang Jiaping is a young and beautiful dancer who loves to read mystery stories. She worries about her sister Zhang Jiayi, who suffers from depression, and is engaged to her psychiatrist Luo Lin. The sister suddenly disappears. Then Jiaping receives a telephone call saying she can find her sister at a hotel in a mountain wilderness area. She goes to the sinister hotel, and finds Jiayi's body in the mountains. Later, the hotel owner dies mysteriously, and then Luo Lin. Jiaping pushes on with her investigation, and at last solves the mystery. She leaves the horrible hotel in a state of depression herself.

736. *Ghost Girls (Gui Mei)*

1985. Xi'an Film Studio. Color. 9 Reels. Direction: Sun Yuanxun. Screenplay: Fang Yihua, based on a story from the "Liao Zhai Zhi Yi" by Pu Songling (1640–1715). Cinematography: Chen Wancai, Zhao Zhiyu. Art Direction: Yan Pingxiao, Qian Yuanxuan. Music: Wei Ruixiang. Sound: Dang Chunzhu. Cast: Hao Jie as Tao Sheng, Wang Linghua as Ruan Xiaoxie, Zhang Jing as Qiao Qiurong

Scholar Tao Sheng is poor but honest and

helpful. To find a quiet place to study, he borrows from a friend a house believed to be haunted. Late each night, two beautiful girls appear to prepare food for Tao Sheng and do his housework. Tao Sheng knows they are ghosts but they do not frighten him, so Tao Sheng and the girls become sworn brother and sisters. It turns out the two girls had very unfortunate experiences in life and had died after unjust treatment. Tao Sheng is very sympathetic with their experience and decides to help them return to human society. At last, Tao Sheng finds a Taoist with magical powers who is so impressed with the scholar's determination that he helps the two girls return to life.

737. *Ghost Hunting Building (Gui Lou)*

1990. Changchun Film Studio. Color. Wide Screen. 10 Reels. Direction: Chang Yan. Screenplay: Chang Yan, Li Yuquan. Cinematography: Chang Yan. Art Direction: Zhang Yan. Music: Yang Yilun. Sound: Zhang Wen. Cast: Gao Fa as Feng Jiangchu, Li Zhonghua as Guangeng, Zhang Guowen as Liu Yahan

In the early 1930s, the Japanese impound for their headquarters a building in the Northeast China city of Haerbin. Chinese working in the building soon report ghost sightings, but police officer Feng Jiangchu is prevented from investigating by a Japanese refusal to cooperate and by local police officials. He continues to look into the situation privately, and at last finds the case revolves around a cache of weapons hidden in the building which had to be left behind by the anti–Japanese Volunteer Army when it withdrew from Haerbin. Feng at last solves the secret of the "ghosts" while he helps the Volunteers recover the weapons.

738. *The Ghost in the Palace (Sheng Dian You Ling)*

1989. Xiaoxiang Film Studio. Color. Wide screen. 9 Reels. Direction: Xue Yicang. Screenplay: Chen Baiqin, Qiu Ren. Cinematography: Zhao Peng. Art Direction: Na Shufeng. Music: Zhang Naicheng. Sound: Liu Feng. Cast: Wang Huichun as An Rushan, An Kejian as Ouyang Long

In the 19th century, in a small town in South China, a man starts a campaign to combat the area's growing opium problem. He receives anonymous threats to stop his efforts, but ignores them. His daughter is abducted, and the dragon flag symbolic of a secret society is left behind. The girl's fiance An Rushan angrily wants to attack the society, but is stopped by his father Ouyang Long, who discloses that he is the head of the secret society, and someone else has framed them because of their anti-opium activities. The father promises to help find the girl, and the members of the society follow clues to a church run by a foreign missionary called Little James. They rescue the girl, but in the battle Ouyang Long is killed, and An Rushan kills Little James.

739. *Ghost of a Policeman (Fei Hun Xing Jing)*

1992. Emei Film Studio. Color. Letterboxed. 9 Reels. Direction: Mi Jiashan. Screenplay: Xu Guangshun. Cinematography: Li Sheng. Art Direction: Wei Feng. Music: Lin Youping. Sound: Tu Liuqing. Costume: Lu Yankun. Makeup: Hu Chaohong. Cast: Kou Zhanwen as Xu Tianao, Lu Yao as Zhang Jiaping, Mo Qi as Mu Hongkun, Ai Junmai as Shao Guangmin, Wu Wenhua as Lang Dawen

Police detective Xu Tianao is working on a particularly frustrating case: he is certain that the chief accountant of a certain corporation was murdered by another employee, but he has been unable to find the evidence which will break the case. But during the course of the investigation, the detective is himself run over by a train. When he arrives in heaven, he pleads for a little more time to solve the case. God grants him five more days, but since his own body is now unusable, his soul is attached to the bodies of several other people at various times, and he continues his investigation through these surrogates. At last, Xu brings the criminals to justice and dies content.

740. *Ghost Shadow Under the Cross (Shi Zi Jia Mo Ying)*

1994. Xiaoxiang Film Studio. Color. Letterboxed. Letterboxed. 9 Reels. Direction: Wang Xuexin. Screenplay: Ding Mu. Cinematography: Ning Changcheng, Liu Weiwei. Art Direction: Guo Dexiang. Music: Guo Xiaotian. Sound: Liu Feng. Costume: Jiang Jianping, Li Huimin. Makeup: Yang Huiming. Cast: Lu Xiaohe as Long Yixiong, Zhang Jibo as Jia Zhenkui, Xiao Yang as Qin Guozhen, Yi Cuilan as Ye Qiuhong, Zhang Yuan as A Ying, Liu Yongji as Gu Shiwen, Cui Dai as Liao Dazhong

In 1949, when the PLA occupies a city near the Bingjiang River, an undercover Nationalist spy ring decides to implement its "midnight ghost" plan aimed at assassinating PLA and Communist Party leaders. One night, a PLA regimental commander and a Party worker are killed in the local hospital by injections of poison. The PLA intelligence chief takes charge of the investigation, and at last pinpoints the hospital's chief of security as the killer. Through this spy, the chief and his men expose the plot and round up the spy ring.

741. *The Giant Panda's Story (Xiong Mao De Gu Shi)*

1988. Emei Film Studio, Japan Denchu Company and China Film Company Co-Production. Color. Letterboxed. 11 Reels. Direction: Xin Chengzuo (Japan). Screenplay: Shuidaozhong (Japan). Qian Daoyuan. Cinematography: Fanchina (Japan). Art Direction: Luo Zhicheng, Qitengjianan (Japan). Music: Xiyeqingcheng (Japan). Sound: Wu Jing (Japan). Cast: Fang Chao as Longlong, Bamuxiaozhi as Miss Jiadai

The famous giant panda of China faces extinction as the global demand for bamboo steadily wipes out its main food supply. A woman researcher from the Tokyo Zoo undertakes a study of the animal's food-gathering habits, and during her work finds an orphaned panda cub struggling to stay alive. She and a young Tibetan boy take the cub to the research center and save its life. On one occasion the cub escapes from the center, and the researcher is injured saving it once more. The researchers name the panda "Huahua." A year later, Huahua returns to the wilds to live independently and the researcher completes her studies and returns to Japan. Longlong, the Tibetan boy, misses his friends.

742. *The Girl Being Followed (Bei Gen Zong De Shao Nu)*

1986. Youth Film Studio. Color. 9 Reels. Direction: Ma Jingwu. Screenplay: Li Baolin. Cinematography: Shen Xingao. Art Direction: Li Gengcheng. Music: Ma Ding. Sound: Lai Qijian. Cast: Zhao Yanhua as A Ting, Zhang Weike as A Hai, Gao Changli as Long Wa, Cai Hongxiang as Old Gui, Wang Zhicheng as Huang Xiang

When their boat capsizes, a couple, their daughter and a passenger named Huang Xiang are tossed into the sea. When A Ting, the daughter, wakes up she is lying on the beach with only the passenger's suitcase nearby. She opens it and finds it stuffed with smuggled contraband. She starts looking for help, and finds she is being followed by Huang Xiang, also a survivor. She eludes him, but soon realizes he has been joined by an accomplice in their pursuit. At last they catch up with A Ting, but just at that time the PSB, which has been following her pursuers, move in and arrest the smugglers.

743. *The Girl Does Not Want to Be an Actress (Bu Xiang Dang Yan Yuan De Gu Niang)*

1983. Tianshan Film Studio. Color. 10 Reels. Direction: Guang Chunlan. Screenplay: Li Hun. Cinematography: Yu Shishan. Wang Hugang. Art Direction: Zhang Tiren. Music: Shao Guangsheng. Sound: Zhang Xicheng. Cast: Meili Guli as Mayila, Reyihan as Amina, Hamusi as Aimaiti, Yibulayin as Nuer

After the Cultural Revolution ends, famous dancer Amina is permitted to resume her career. She wants to pass on what she knows to young people, so she and composer Nuer travel to the South Tianshan Mountains to recruit new students. They find Mayila, a young girl of great promise there, but her father Aimaiti refuses to allow her to go with them. He and his wife had once adopted another little girl, Ayixiamu, who he turned over to a dancing troupe, and he believes she came to a bad end as a result. He fears the same thing will happen to Mayila. But later he finds out that Amina is that same little girl, and he hears of how she had lost her husband and been persecuted during the Cultural Revolution. It also turns out that Amina is Mayila's birth mother. Aimaiti relents, Mayila joins the dancing troupe, and mother and daughter perform together.

744. *Girl Fortune Teller (Tuo Lu Shen Gua Nu)*

1991. Xi'an Film Studio. Color. Letterboxed. 9 Reels. Direction: Zhang Jingrong. Screenplay: Wang Shouyi, Cinematography: Zhang Faliang, Zhao Yimin. Art Direction: Yan Pingxiao. Music: Chang Yuhong. Cast: Zhao Xiaorui as Tuolong, Dili Nuer as Jin Chizhi, Zhang Zhaozhao as Naixiong, Zhao Chunmin as Boss Liu, Wang Deli as Zhu Tietou

745. *Girl Friends of the Same Age (Tong Ling Nu You)*

1987. Guangxi Film Studio. Color. 10 Reels.

Direction: Dai Zongan, Deng Ruzhuo. Screenplay: Dai Zongan, Kang Rong. Cinematography: Zhang Jiwu. Art Direction: Jin Bohao. Music: Wang Liping. Sound: Li Zhuwen. Cast: Zhen Zhenyao as Liu Qing, Wu Haiyan as Qian Yeyun, Guo Qi as Cai Shuhua, Dai Zongan as Wei Lingling

Four good friends since childhood, Liu Qing, Qian Yeyun, Wei Lingling and Cai Suhua get together again at Qian's home after a 20-year separation. Cai Suhua is a female deputy cadre, and while she works very hard at helping other families work out their problems, her own husband and children do not understand her. Qian Yeyun is very beautiful, three times married and twice divorced, but she always persists in being what she considers a real woman. Wei Lingling perhaps has the most reason to be happy, being married to a famous singer and having no lack of the material things in life. But she abandoned her medical career to be a full-time housewife, and while her loving husband is grateful for her support, she feels a bit sad deep down inside. Liu Qing is a strong and independent woman who never married. She has been a rural teacher for 15 years, and has the obvious affection and respect of the village people and her students.

746. *Girl from Hangzhou (Xi Zhi Gu Niang)*

1983. Changchun Film Studio. Color. 10 Reels. Direction: Lu Jianhua. Screenplay: Fang Zhi, Wen Xin, Lu Jianhua, Mi He. Cinematography: Xu Souzen. Art Direction: Ye Jiren. Music: Wang Ming. Sound: Wu Bike. Cast: Zhang Xiaolei as Pan Jiemei, Lin Qiang as Chang Lei, Zhang Xiaoming as Liu Wan, Yang Yaqing as Huang Ying, Zhang Fei as Professor Du

Pan Jiemei's gardener father died during the Cultural Revolution, and she herself was disabled helping a classmate who was attacked. Now she is permitted to return to her native city of Hangzhou, but is unable to find work. The people on the street where she grew up give her enough support to open her own small floral shop. With the notebook in which her father recorded all his work experience, she also sets up experimental flower beds in the suburbs where she develops new varieties, including the legendary "Ju" plant which had disappeared many years before. At a flower show, the "Ju" draws high praise from both Chinese and foreign observers.

747. *Girl from Huangshan Mountain (Huang Shan Lai De Gu Niang)*

1984. Changchun Film Studio. Color. Letter-boxed. 10 Reels. Direction: Zhang Yuan, Yu Yanfu. Screenplay: Peng Minyan, Bi Jiancang. Cinematography: Wang Jishun. Art Direction: Wu Qiwen, Du Wencheng. Music: Wu Damin. Sound: Chen Wenyuan, Fu Lingge. Cast: Li Ling as Gong Lingling, Ding Yi as the farm woman, Zhang Junyin as Wang Weiping, Hu Huiling as Qi Xiaojuan, Zhao Yamin as Liu Hongrong, Tian Chengren as Grandpa Zhou, Mi Lan as Zhou Xingxing

When young country girl Gong Lingling arrives in Beijing from her Anhui home seeking work, she is first employed by the Qi family as a housekeeper. Mrs. Qi's strictness and constant criticism soon drive her away, and she is employed by Liu Hongrong, a single mother abandoned by her husband. The two young women become good friends, but soon Liu is unable to afford her, and Gong must again find another job. At last she is employed by the Zhou family. She becomes like one of the family to them, and when granddaughter Zhou Xingxing starts a restaurant, she hires Gong Lingling as a buyer, traveling the countryside purchasing foodstuffs for the restaurant.

Best Actress Li Ling, 1985 Golden Rooster Awards.

Best Supporting Actress Ding Yi, 1985 Golden Rooster Awards.

748. *Girl from Hunan aka: Married to a Child (Xiang Nu Xiao Xiao)*

1986. Youth Film Studio. Color. 9 Reels. Direction: Xie Fei, Wu Lan. Screenplay: Zhang Xian. Cinematography: Dong Yaping. Art Direction: Xing Zhen. Music: Ye Xiaogang. Sound: Ju Min. Cast: Na Renhua as Xiaoxiao (as a child), Deng Xiaoguang as Hua Gou, Liu Qing as Xiaoxiao (as a teenager), Jiang Hong as Qiaoxiu's mother

In an isolated village in west Hunan province shortly after the founding of the Republic of China (c1913), a 12-year-old girl named Xiaoxiao is married to a 2-year-old boy, Chunyuan. Six years later, Xiaoxiao is a mature young woman in love with a co-worker, Hua Gou, by whom she is pregnant. Since the traditions of the time mean such behavior will be punished severely by other villagers, the frightened Xiaoxiao flees and gives birth to her son elsewhere. Ten more years pass, and Chunyuan, now a student with progressive ideas, renounces his feudal arranged marriage. By this time, Xiaoxiao has lost her enthusiasm for pursuing a new life of her own. Following the traditional practice, she arranges an adult bride for her now 10-year-old son.

749. *Girl in Red (Hong Yi Shao Nu)*

1984. Emei Film Studio. Color. 10 Reels. Direction: Lu Xiaoya. Screenplay: Lu Xiaoya. Cinematography: Xie Erxiang. Art Direction: Chen Ruogang, Zhou Jinglun. Music: Wang Ming. Sound: Wen Guang. Cast: Zhou Yitian as An Ran, Luo Yan as An Jing, Zhu Xu as Father, Wang Ping as Mother, Li Lan as Wei Wan, Gu Qun as Zhu Wenjuan

A coming-of-age story focusing on An Ran, a 16-year-old girl. An Ran is very close to her sister An Jing, a magazine editor. An Jing encourages the younger girl to achieve the "three excellencies" school award; students who achieve this award three years in a row are virtually assured admission to a good university. At this time, China is starting to become more open in many ways, including dress. When her sister gives An Ran a red skirt, it draws much commentary from her classmates, most of it negative. An Ran also gets on the wrong side of her teacher Wei Wan when she corrects the teacher's incorrect pronunciation in class. But when Wei Wan writes a very inferior poem that her sister's magazine publishes anyway, the teacher gives An Ran the desired "excellence" award. An Ran finds growing up very confusing.

Best Picture, 1985 Golden Rooster Awards.

Best Picture, 1985 Hundred Flowers Awards.

750. *The Girl Is 28 Years Old (Gu Niang Jin Nian Er Shi Ba)*

1984. Shanghai Film Studio. Color. 10 Reels. Direction: Tang Huada, Yu Jie. Screenplay: Li Tianji. Cinematography: Yu Shishan. Art Direction: Wang Xingcang, Ning Futing. Music: Xiao Yan. Sound: Huang Dongping. Cast: Li Lan as Fang Xiuying, He Ling as Zeng Qiang, Zhan Pingping as Liu Shan, Mao Yongming as Ding Baopei

Textile worker Fang Xiuying is repeatedly going out of her way to help others, whether friends, co-workers, or even total strangers. Once some frozen pork falls from a passing truck and Fang devotes considerable time and effort to tracking down the driver to return it. Her fiance Zeng Qiang urges her to stop paying so much attention to the affairs of others. She says she will try, but soon there is a fire in a mill workshop and she is the first on the scene to help. Unfortunately, the circumstances are such that her swift response makes her an arson suspect. At last, the real cause of the fire is detected, and she is exonerated. Fang and Zeng finally get married.

751. *The Girl Ming (Ming Gu Niang)*

1984. Beijing Film Studio. Color. Wide Screen. 10 Reels. Direction: Dong Kena. Screenplay: Hang Ying. Cinematography: Zhang Shiwei. Art Direction: Tu Juhua. Music: Hu Weili. Sound: Wang Dawen. Cast: Zhang Yu as Ye Mingming, Zhang Guomin as Zhao Chan, Zhang Lin as the Workshop Director

Zhao Chan, an outstanding student in the Beijing University Physics Department, is suddenly and unexpectedly struck blind, shattering his confidence and will to go on living. By chance he meets a girl named Mingming, whose understanding and gentle persuasion help to restore his confidence somewhat. Although he does not know it at first, Mingming is herself blind. Later, he visits the factory where Mingming works, a facility that employs only the visually impaired. Her encouragement brings Zhao Chan back, and he decides to be a person in control of his own fate. Later, Mingming accompanies Zhao Chan to see a specialist who holds out hope for the young man, although Mingming realizes her own blindness is irreversible. Zhan Chan regains his sight, and excitedly proposes marriage to Mingming. Mingming rejects him, for she feels that what he believes is love is really gratitude and sympathy. She urges him to resume his college studies. He finally accepts her advice and leaves.

752. *Girl Students' Dormitory (Nu Da Xue Sheng Su She)*

1983. Shanghai Film Studio. Color. 9 Reels. Direction: Shi Shujun. Screenplay: Yu Shan, Liang Yanjin. Cinematography: Zhao Junhong. Art Direction: Xue Jianna. Music: Liu Yanxi. Sound: Zhou Yunling. Cast: Luo Yan as Kuang Yalan, Xu Ya as Xin Gan, Chong Hongmei as Song Ge, Li Xia as Luo Xuemei, Jiang Yiping as Xia Yu

In the early 1980s, five freshmen women with very different backgrounds and experiences arrive at Southeast University. They are: Kuang Yalan, with an unhappy past; Xin Gan, spoiled and willful; Song Ge, who tends to be a bit extreme in her views; Luo Xuemei, an open-hearted and generous country girl; and shy Xia Yu. Thrown in together, the five at first have a series of misunderstandings and conflicts, but in time pull together to help out Kuang Yalan. Kuang, whose parents separated during a time of political upheaval, is having financial problems and looks for a weekend job so she can remain in school. It turns out her mother later remarried and has another daughter who gets all her support. The five girls pull together and solidify their friendship.

753. *Girl Swineherd (Yang Zhu Gu Niang)*

Direction and Screenplay collectively by the faculty of the Shanghai Film School. Cast: Yan Yongxuan, Zhong Jingwen

Wang Xiuhong, a girl swineherd in a commune, responds to the Party's call for development of swine husbandry by studying hard, accelerating her production speed and gaining advanced experience.

754. *The Girl, the Fugitive, and the Dog (Shao Nu Tao Fan Gou)*

1987. Tianshan Film Studio. Color. 9 Reels. Direction: Da Qi. Screenplay: Jin Xing. Cinematography: He Qin. Art Direction: Gao Feng. Music: Chen Yuanlin. Sound: Li Bing. Cast: Bolisha as the girl, Adijia as the fugitive, Rexiti as Mansumu, Wei Jianfang as Jiang Ao

A criminal escapes a labor reform farm, pursued by PSB officers. He meets a Weiwuer nationality girl who offers to share her precious water with him, but the fugitive flees with all of her food and water. The girl continues on her way, accompanied by her big yellow dog. At night, while she is sleeping, the fugitive steals her camel, food and water. When she awakens, she chases after him. When the fugitive is cornered by a bear, the girl kills the bear, but her dog is killed also. The girl leaves for her destination and the fugitive thoughtfully watches her go.

755. *Girl Using Drugs (Bai Feng Mei)*

1995. Pearl River Film Company, Wang's Film & Television Screenplay Corp. Ltd. Co-production. Color. Letterboxed. Direction: Zhang Liang. Screenplay: Wang Jingzhu, Zhang Liang. Cinematography: Wu Benli. Cast: Liu Wei as Zeng Xiaodan, Zhu Manfang as Xie Jiexin, Chen Zhijian as Zhou Jian, Zhang Tianxi as Xiong Jian

In Guangzhou, Zen Xiaodan was once a model teenage girl, a good student and very pretty. However, her parents suddenly break up, leaving Xiaodan without financial resources. Xiaodan and a boy named Zhou Jian, who also has family problems, begin hanging out at a dance hall. The woman manager there introduces the teenagers to marijuana, and both become drug users. Xiaodan meets a crime boss, who seduces her and she becomes his mistress for a time, until he dumps her. Drugs become her sole support in life. Zhou Jian is arrested by public security officers, but with the help of a woman reporter he starts to give up drugs. But it turns out to be too late for Xiaodan.

756. *Girls Against Drugs (Ji Du Shao Nu)*

1992. Yunnan Minority Film Studio & China Film Release Company Co-Production. Color. Letterboxed. 9 Reels. Direction: Shi Xi. Screenplay: Shi Xi, Xu Zhiqiang. Cinematography: Feng Bingyong. Art Direction: Wang Guizhi, Zhao Zhengxue. Music: Wang Xian. Cast: Pang Yan as Bai Wanchun, Wang Lisha as Bai Wanxia, Wang Sheng as Bai Wanqiu, Yan Dake as Meng Shaoxiong, Shi Xi as Bai Yifeng

At the end of the 1930s in the Southwest China border area, police chief Bai Yifeng leads his men in attacks on bandits smuggling opium. One night, the bandits retaliate when a dozen of them attack the home where Bai lives with his wife and three teenage daughters Wanchun, Wanxia and Wanqiu. In the attack, Bai Yifeng and his wife are killed. The daughters escape and start their own drug war against the smugglers, and at last kill the chief bandit and the real kingpin behind the smuggling. In the final battle, Wanchun's fiance Meng Shaoxiong and her sister Wanxia are killed. Surviving sisters Wanchun and Wanqiu sadly leave home after the battle.

757. *Girls and Boys at the Best Age (Gu Niang Xiao Huo Zheng Dang Nian)*

1984. Xiaoxiang Film Studio. Color. Wide

Screen. 10 Reels. Direction: Hua Yongzuang, Luo Zhen. Screenplay: Liang Jianhua, Song Zhenguo. Cinematography: Feng Guiting, Chen Yan. Art Direction: Jin Bohao. Music: Lu Yuana. Cast: Wang Yajun as Luo Xiaoling, Li Qiang as Xiang Zhiqiang, Wun Xiying as Master Worker Xiang, Liu Jinglin as Factory Director Luo, Xuo Pingguo as Xiao Lizhi, Wang Xiaoyan as Chen Yu

Female college graduate Luo Xiaoling is assigned to a steel mill as a technician. Soon after she arrives, she seriously criticizes safety violations by fellow worker Xiao Lizhi. Her action angers many of the other workers, including workshop head Xiang Zhiqiang. She draws support, however, from Xiang Zhiqiang's father, Master Worker Xiang, who insists that Luo be put in charge of her work group. Over time, Luo and young Xiang develop a grudging respect, then admiration which turns to love and marriage.

758. *Girls in the SEZ (Te Qu Gu Niang)*

1985. Xiaoxiang Film Studio. Color. 9 Reels. Direction: Hu Shue, Liu Guanxiong. Screenplay: Qi Jianren. Cinematography: Zhao Zelin, Yan Yunzhao. Art Direction: Yang Li. Music: Wei Jingshu. Sound: Liu Yishen. Cast: Wu Haiyan, Cui Chaomin, Chen Shaoze, Wu Jing, Cai Fang, Zhang Yunli

A group of educated young people work hard and make a duck farm profitable, despite such obstacles as parents who want them to apply their learning to less physical pursuits.

759. *Girls Should Get Married When They Grow Up (Nu Da Dang Hun)*

1982. Shanghai Film Studio. Color. 6 Reels. Direction: Yang Lanru. Screenplay: Zhang Gang, Lu Yulei. Cinematography: Zhen Xuan. Art Direction: Li Runzhi. Music: Xiao Yan. Sound: Yang Liangkun. Cast: Song Yining as Luo Ermei, Zhang Zhihua as Luo Xuemei, Hu Dagang as Miao Sheng, Zhou Guobing as Xiao Tie, Shi Yuan as Second Uncle, Wang Wei as Ermei's mother, Gong Yulan as Aunt Labahua

In a mountain village, sisters Luo Ermei and Luo Xuemei have reached marriageable age. They decide to let their future husbands Miao Sheng and Xiao Tie marry into their family, which is contrary to conventional practice. Ermei's aunt Labahua, wife of production unit director Luo Youfu, earlier forced Ermei's mother to adopt her 8-year-old son, planning

for him to someday obtain the Luo family home. Seeing the girls' intentions as a threat to her scheme, she sets out to thwart them. After Xuemei and Miao Sheng are married, she spreads rumors the couple are having extramarital affairs. Finally Miao Sheng cannot bear this and leaves. Ermei is determined to go ahead with the plan, and still wants Xiao Tie to marry into her family. But he is too frightened by Miao Sheng's experience to go along with it. Encouraged by other young people, Ermei posts signs throughout the village advertising for someone willing to marry into her family. Xiao Tie actually loves Ermei, so her boldness moves him to answer the ads. Finally, Labahua corrects her attitude and goes to invite Miao Sheng to come back home. The story ends happily.

760. *Girls to Be Married (Chu Jia Nu)*

1990. Pearl River Film Studio and the Hong Kong Sil-Metropole Organization Co-Production. Color. Wide Screen. 10 Reels. Direction: Wang Jing. Screenplay: He Mengfan. Cinematography: Zhao Xiaoshi. Art Direction: He Qun. Music: Wang Shi. Sound: Deng Qinhua. Cast: Shen Rong as Mingtao, Tao Huiming as Aiyue, Ju Xue as Hexiang, Gu Xuemei as Guijuan, Chi Huaqiong as Jin Mei

In pre-liberation China, in a remote mountain village, there is a "visiting garden," popular among young local girls as a place where they can go to indulge their hopes and dreams together. The story tells of five teenage girls who are in despair over the hopeless outlook for girls such as they, with little to look forward to but arranged marriages and hard lives. They have heard that those who die with their virginity intact go to a "visiting garden" in heaven, where they are happy forever. The five girls commit mass suicide by hanging themselves.

761. *A Girl's Tomb (Gu Niang Feng)*

1982. Tianshan Film Studio. Color. 9 Reels. Direction: Tang Guangtao, Tuohutasheng. Screenplay: Ali Mujiang. Cinematography: Wang Hugang. Art Direction: Zhang Tiren. Music: Ma Shizen, Yu Tianfu. Sound: Zhang Xicheng. Cast: Kabila as Xiaer Bati, Mohe Taer as Hali, Baya Ahong as Mayi Basi, Tuohe Tasheng as Dakai

On the West China prairie, beautiful Xiaer

Girls to Be Married. **One of the ill-fated girls in the story gazes longingly at a boat leaving the village where she faces so unpromising a future. 1990. Pearl River Film Studio.**

Bati is a hunter's daughter, the sweetheart since childhood of Ha Li. Mayi Basi, the largest landowner in the area, wants the girl for himself. For personal gain, he instigates a fight among the different tribes of prairie herdsmen, but his plot fails. Ha Li, meanwhile, has been busy organizing the tribes for a prairie rebellion. At the wedding of Xiaer and Ha, the couple is arrested by local police in the pay of Mayi. The girl escapes in the night, and Ha's friends make plans to rescue him. One of their number infiltrates police headquarters and his escape is successful. Xiaer Bati and Ha Li lead a successful rebellion, and vow to carry on the revolution together.

762. *Girls' Village (Gu Niang Zai)*

1987. Yunnan Film Studio. Color. 9 Reels. Direction: Xu Jihong. Screenplay: Cheng Zhi, Lang Zhen. Cinematographer: Huang Zhuxing, Ning Jiakun. Art Direction: Jia Xianjie. Art Direction: Xu Kaicheng. Music: Jin Fuzhai. Sound: Jia Xianjie. Cast: Huang Zhiling as Jin Feng, Lu Qin as Ang Xintai, Zhang Zhiqiang as the old village director, Zang Qian as Gao Meiying

In the hills of eastern Yunnan province, there are villages inhabited largely by people of the Shani nationality. One is called Girl's Village, and one is called Jinniu Village. The population of the latter includes a large number of single men. After the 3rd Plenary Session of the 11th Party Congress, Jinniu Village grows prosperous, and the village director's wife wants to help these young bachelors win over the girls in Girls' Village. The film tells how several young men and women get paired off.

763. *A Girl's Wish (Gu Niang De Xin Yuan)*

1981. Emei Film Studio. Color. 11 Reels. Direction: Mao Yuqing, Teng Jingxian. Screenplay: Xu Jihong, He Tianbao. Cinematography: Xie Erxiang. Art Direction: Liu Nanyang. Music: Chang Sumin, Tao Jiazhou. Sound: Shen Guli. Cast: Jiang Lili as Wei Zhihua, Du Xiongwen as Ma Gu, Li Qide as Lu Huaibing, Li Xinmei as Yang Ru, Lu Fei as the hospital director

When she is discharged from the army, young medical worker Wei Zhihua goes to work at a hospital in South China where her lover Lu Huaibing is a doctor. She asks for and receives an assignment in tumor research, because her family's medical history leads Wei Zhihua to suspect that she herself carries a terrible disease. She works hard but often examines herself. Her fears are realized when she learns she has incurable liver cancer. She keeps her secret and carries on with her research work. She faints on the job once, causing a laboratory accident in which Ma Gu, the tumor research division head, suffers a burnt cornea and loses his sight. His fiancee Yang Ru, part of a border area medical team, is shocked at the news and greatly concerned about their future life together. Wei Zhihua dedicates herself to helping Ma Gu get through this most difficult time, comforting him and raising his spirit and will to go on. She does this despite the fact that it makes Lu Huaibing jealous. She suppresses her feelings and refuses Lu Huaibing's love while working to keep Ma Gu and Yang Ru to stay together. She finally succumbs to the cancer, but just before she dies she donates her cornea to Ma Gu to help him regain his vision.

764. *Go Ahead, Don't Look Back (Chao Qian Zou, Mo Hui Tou)*

1994. Xiaoxiang Film Studio. Color. Letterboxed. 9 Reels. Direction: Zhang Xin. Screenplay: Zhang Xiaoling. Cinematography: Yang Weidong, Zhang Yuefu. Art Direction: Yang Li. Music: Yang Xiwu. Sound: Huang Siye. Costume: Li Huimin, Jiang Jianping. Makeup: Liu Xiaonan. Cast: Feng Guoqing as Long Bo, Xu Lei as Chu Huilan, Chao Li as Wu Limin, Wang Ban as Du Kejian, Jia Zhijie as Jin Mengqiao, Wu Mian as Ye Yuan, Li Yunjie as Yang Ming, Ma Jie as Zuo Wentao, Wang Haiyan as Wang Li, Liang Danni as Dua Yu, Zhang Zhen as Tongtong, Xing Jizhou as Du Tianlei

The Xingzhou Glass Factory's new director Long Bo concludes that the plant's repeated shortage of coal would be best handled by converting to oil instead. People vary in their reactions to his plan, and most try to stop it. But Long Bo's determination and devotion to reform finally changes the opponents' attitude and he succeeds.

765. *God of Hunters Leaves the Mountain Valley (Lie Shen Zhou Chu Shan Gu)*

1986. Emei Film Studio. Color. 10 Reels. Direction: Zhang Yi. Screenplay: Huang Fang. Cinematography: Sun Guoliang. Art Direction: Zhang Xuezhong. Music: Song Daneng. Sound: Shen Guli. Cast: Li Xiangang as Meng Yuan, Du Yuan as Tie Lida, Song Tao as one arm Zhang, Zhang Qi as Chunliu

Meng Yuan, called the "God of Hunters" by people in his mountain village, now decides to take up the leather business. This shocks the village people, and puts Meng in direct conflict with the father of his lover Chunliu. In anger, the father withdraws his permission for Meng Yuan and Chunliu to marry, and pressures her to marry another strong and capable young man, Tie Lida. When Chunliu swears she will have no other than Meng Yuan, Tie Lida begins to regard Meng as a rival. He issues a challenge to Meng Yuan to see which can outdo the other in a contest of their hunting skills. Meng does not take the competition too seriously, as his ego is not the type to be damaged if he is outdone, and Tie Lida takes an early lead in the competition. However, Tie gets into trouble and when his life is in danger, Meng Yuan saves his life. Tie Lida leaves the area so that Meng Yuan will have no rival for Chunliu. As he leaves, he wishes them well.

766. *God of Mountains (Shan Shen)*

1992. Beijing Film Studio, China Film Co-Production Corp. and Hong Kong Aolisi Film Company. Color. Wide Screen. 11 Reels. Direction: Huang Jianzhong. Screenplay: Zhang Jiping. Cinematography: Yu Xiaoqun, Zhang Jiang. Art Direction: Liu Shi. Music: Zou Ye. Sound: Gu Changning. Costume: Fan Gang. Makeup: Xia Juan. Cast: Shen Junyi as Shi Zhu, Ge Lili as Yingzi, Wang Fuli as Cuihuan, Deli Geer as Wu Dajian, Niu Ben as Yingzi's father, Ji Jun as Cui Batou, Xu Ming as Er Laizi

Shi Zhu and Yinzi are lovers, and Yinzi is pregnant. The sole product of their mountain village is ginseng, and when the harvest season comes, Shi Zhu practices hard to climb the mountain and obtain a near-legendary root called the "big one," an effort which has claimed eight lives in the past. At last, Shi Zhu climbs the treacherous cliff and gets the "big one," but this turns all the village people against the couple, for the people believe this particular ginseng root is the God of the Mountain. The couple are punished, and put in jail. The widow Cuihuan, who has secretly loved Shi Zhu for a long time, secretly comes and releases them. The young couple leave the village to move elsewhere.

767. *God of the Road (Lu Shen)*

1992. Changchun Film Studio. Color. Letterboxed. 9 Reels. Direction: Ma Huiwu. Screenplay: Gui Yuqin. Cinematography: An Zhiguo, Dong Yinde. Art Direction: Song Honghua. Music: Si Wanchun, Wang Yuemin. Costume: Hu Lianzhong. Makeup: Zhang Xiaoming, Lu Huamin. Cast: Guo Bichuan as Xia Long, Zhu Decheng as Tong Wu, Ma Shuchao as Jiang Baohai, Kelao Diya as Tilun, Liu Yan as Yang Debiao, Li Hu as Guan Degui

With World Bank investment, construction is under way on China's first freeway. Part of the road is deemed unacceptable and must be rebuilt within 15 days so as not to disrupt the overall schedule for completion. The construction team, headed by Xia Long, is badly in need of a break, but continue to drive themselves and accomplish the task on the 14th day.

768. *Going East to the Native Land (Dong Gui Ying Xiong Zhuan)*

1993. Inner Mongolia Film Studio. Color. Letterboxed. 9 Reels. Direction: Saifu, Mailisi. Screenplay: Zhao Yuheng, Xin Jiapo, Sai Fu, Yu Chenghui. Cinematography: Geritu. Art Direction: Mo Nayintai. Music: Cao Daoerji. Sound: Buren Bayaer. Costume: Ru Meiqi. Makeup: Ren Qinhua, Chao Ying. Cast: Ba Sang as Qian Huzhang, Ye Hui as Sanggeer, Wang Lu as Ninina, Ererdeng Mutu as Menglike, Zhang Shen as Tu Maer

In 1771, oppression and racial discrimination by the Czarist regime leads the Tueryte tribe to move back east to their Chinese homeland from Russia, where they have resided for the past 200 years. Tribal chief Alatasang leads his people east, but along the way they are harassed by a rival tribe which covets the map which will guide them. Alatsang guards the map zealously, but realizes he is dying. Before he dies, he confides to his daughter that the only genuine copy of the map is tattooed on his back, and to lead their people home, she must take some post-mortem steps she will probably find distasteful. She is very upset, but fulfills her father's dying wish.

Best Cinematography Geritu, 1994 Golden Rooster Awards.

Best Music Cao Daoerji, 1994 Golden Rooster Awards.

769. *Going Into Business (Xiao Sa Yi Hui)*

1993. Beijing Film Studio. Color. Letterboxed. 9 Reels. Direction: Xu Tongjun. Screenplay: Gao Mantang. Cinematography: Li Jianxin. Art Direction: Zhou Dengfu. Music: Gao Erdi. Sound: Wang Dawen. Costume: Zhang Xiaojing. Makeup: Dong Zhiqin. Cast: Chang Lantian as Mei Guo, Ma Ling as Wu Xiao, Kong Ling as Xiao Lili, Ma Enran as Chen Jiayi, Niu Zhenhua as Lu Tianyu

The director of a financially strapped opera company gets an infusion of cash from a businessman opera fan. This inspires the opera director to try his own hand at various types of business, but nothing seems to work for him. In addition, his happy family life is disrupted by his wife's misunderstanding of his relationship with one of the female performers. The couple at last reconcile, and while he has not been a business success, his wife tells him they will be parents soon.

770. *Going to That Side of the Mountain (Dao Qing Shan Na Bian Qu)*

1987. Beijing Film Studio. Color. 10 Reels. Direction: Xie Yucheng. Screenplay: Xie Yucheng, Li Zhiwei. Cinematography: Xing Peixiu. Art Direction: Chen Jiyun, Yao Wen. Music: Jin Zhengping. Sound: Zhang Jiake. Cast: Ju Chunhua as Mr. Ma, Zhang Qide as Professor Liu, Cui Xinqing as Mrs. Shi, Zhu Xiaoming as He Feng, Wang Hui as Wun Fei, Han Song as Luo Chonggao

In the early 1940s, the Japanese army occupying Beijing orders a roundup of left-wing Chinese students. The CPC underground arranges for Professor Liu and several of his students to escape to a Communist-held area before they can be arrested, led by a CPC agent known only as Mr. Ma. They finally make it to safety, but Ma is killed protecting them.

771. *Going Toward Brightness (Po Wu)*

1984. August First Film Studio. Color. Letterboxed. 9 Reels. Direction: Yan Jizhou. Screenplay: Wang Xiancai, Li Jing, Chun Chao, Sun Mu. Cinematography: Wang Mengyuan. Art Direction: Jiang Zhenkui. Sound: Shi Pingyi. Cast: Xu Min as Ding Zhaoyu, Zhang Yan as Duanmu Liting, Xia Hui as Meina, Han Zaisheng as Huang Jingjiang, Zhao Xiaomin as officer Tian, Sun Xianyuan as commander Han, Peng Qiyu as Ding's father, Lin Muyu as Ding's mother

Shortly after World War II, Chiang

Kaishek breaks the ceasefire with the Communists and attacks the areas they control. Air Force pilot Ding Zhaoyu, recently returned from advanced training in America, is assigned to bomb Communist positions. But he is greatly troubled when he finds out that the target zones were actually civilian areas, and many civilians were killed, including women and children. The last straw for Ding is the suicide of Duanmu Liting, a patriotic woman entrepreneur who was falsely accused and put out of business by the Nationalist government. Ding decides that only Communism can save China, and he defects.

772. *Going West to Baizhang Gorge (Xi Qu Bai Zhang Xia)*

1984. Liaoning Science Film Studio. Color. 9 Reels. Direction: Cheng Rui, Lu Ninan. Screenplay: Ouyang Jiyuan, Cheng Rui. Cinematography: Li Qinyu. Art Direction: Chen Bing. Music: Qian Yuan, Yao Di. Sound: Wang Chunbao. Cast: He Ling as Chen Fang, Wang Deshun as Zhong Fuhai, Jia Yongzhi as Han Gengbao, Hui Juanyan as Tonghua, Cui Muyan as Liu Yuqin, Li Hong as County Director Ma

When County Director Ma's request for wood products for a factory is rejected by forester Zhong Fuhai on environmental grounds, the angry director asks County Forest Bureau Supervisor Chen Fang to look into the matter. Chen goes to visit Zhong Fuhai, and finds the veteran forester is sincere in his concern for preserving timber resources. Chen recalls the days of the Great Leap Forward, when many people sought to cut down vast areas of timber for use in local steel mills, and how Zhong had resisted the excessive demands even though it led to his demotion. Chen Fang returns and reports County Director Ma's excessive demand to provincial authorities.

773. *Gold and Silver Beaches (Jin Yin Tan)*

1953. Shanghai Film Studio. B & W. 12 Reels. Direction: Lin Zhifeng. Screenplay: Lin Yi. Cinematography: Li Shengwei and Miao Zhenhua. Set Design: Ge Shichen. Music: Xu Huicai and Wang Haitian. Sound: Ding Bohe and Song Liangcheng. Cast: Enhesheng as Duobuling, Zhulan Qiqike as Zuoma, Sun Xi as Suonanjia, Xi Liang as Dalijie, Zhang Yan as the PLA Commander and County Director, Wun Xiyin as County Director Gaiba

In Tibet, two clan groups, the Taxiu and the Alicang, live at Gold Beach and Silver Beach respectively. The army of Nationalist warlord Ma Bufang attempts to exploit clan rivalries in order to divide and conquer. When the Nationalist commanders sense their days are numbered, they begin expropriating horses for their retreat, and incite the two clans to armed conflict with each other. Two secret lovers, a young man from Gold Beach named Duobuling, and a Silver Beach girl named Zuoma, see through the conspiracy, and persuade their families that the clans are being used. Zuoma's father Caiku calls for a ceasefire, but is accidentally wounded. This arouses the clans' several thousand households to turn their fury on the Nationalists. The PLA liberates Gold and Silver Beach. The CPC's new policy on ethnic minorities unites the two clans.

774. *The Gold Mandarin Duck (Jin Yuan Yang)*

1988. Emei Film Studio. Color. Letterboxed. 9 Reels. Direction: Ren Ren, Zhang Yiheng. Screenplay: Fang Yihua. Cinematography: Zhang Jiwu. Art Direction: Wang Tao, Li Xianglin. Music: Gao Weijie. Sound: Hua Yuezu. Cast: Ge Lili as Shen Weiniang, Li Lianyuan as Mister Wei, Hua Xiaoqin as Suer

Wealthy businessman Mister Wei returns to his hometown to find Hengniang, the wife he left 18 years before, and the child he has never seen. Wei fails to find any of his relatives. To pass the time, he has one of the hotel staff find him a girl to keep him company for the evening. He does not know the call girl sent over, Shen Weiniang, is really his daughter; her mother Hengniang had fallen ill and died after Wei left town, and she has always hoped her father would someday return for her and take her to a better life. Mister Wei decides he wants to spend the night with Weiniang, but she declines, claiming she doesn't feel well. She sends her girl friend Suer over to his hotel in her place. When Suer and Wei are together, he finds she is wearing the gold mandarin duck, a keepsake piece of jewelry he had given his wife 18 years before. Thinking that the girl is aware of his past, Wei murders her to keep her silent about his secret. Shen Weiniang becomes worried about Suer and goes to the hotel. When she arrives and finds her friend dead, she kills Wei and recovers the gold mandarin duck she had loaned to her friend.

775. *Gold Shoe (Jin Xie)*

1988. Beijing Film Studio. Color. 9 Reels. Direction: Wang Binglin. Screenplay: Wang Binglin. Cinematography: Guan Qinwu. Art Direction: Hao Jingyuan. Music: Wun Zhongtian. Sound: Li Bojiang. Cast: Chen Yude as Liu Liushun, Li Lina as Song Jinzhi, Liu Peiqi as Zhao Tuzhi

Liu Liushun and his wife Song Jinzhi operate a small restaurant in a town in north China. They argue constantly. One night, tomb robber Zhao Tuzhi comes into the restaurant, bringing with him a gold shoe he has stolen. The sight of the gold shoe inspires Liu with dreams of wealth. The couple and their son go to the tomb the same night and dig up the other gold shoe in the pair. They sell their business to his sister, as they plan to make huge money from the shoe. However, Zhao and other thugs chase them, and at one point Liu is almost killed. At last, Liu Liushun realizes that his pursuit of a fortune has brought them nothing but trouble. He goes to Zhao Tuzhi and the other thieves and gives them the shoe.

776. *Gold Smuggler (Huang Jin Da dao)*

1989. Changchun Film Studio. Color. 10 Reels. Letterboxed. Direction: Li Geng, Bei Yucheng. Screenplay: Wang Shouyi. Cinematography: Ning Changcheng. Art Direction: Mu Er. Music: Fan Weiqiang. Sound: Zhen Yunbao. Cast: Chen Xinli as Xue Lianhua, Xu Wenguang as Yang Kai, Zhu Shibin as Ma Jinhu

After a failed romance, goldsmith's daughter Xue Xiaofeng quits her job and moves back to her hometown to start over again. After she meets a man named Ma Jinhu, she changes her name to Xue Lianhua, and with his help opens a grocery store. Ma is engaged in illegal gold transactions, among other things. He bribes officials, and by sleeping with Xue Lianhua gets her to involve her brother in selling gold for him. He then hires Xue Lianhua's father to make gold statues of Buddha which Ma smuggles out of the country. The goldsmith is murdered, and detective Yang Kai collects sufficient evidence to prove to Xue Lianhua that Ma Jinhu is the killer. Xue Lianhua vows to avenge her father, and goes after Ma herself…

777. *Gold Smuggling Enforcement Team (Huang Jin Ji Si Dui)*

1989. Tianshan Film Studio. Color. Letter-boxed. 9 Reels. Direction: Tuohe Tasheng. Screenplay: Zhang Jianfu. Cinematographer: Gao Huanggang. Art Direction: Ma Zhili, Maimaiti. Music: Zhu Hengqian, Jiang Yimin. Sound: Wun Gang, Ba Hati. Cast: Zhang Yongxiang as Brother Li, A Dong as Director Sha, Bayan as Zhahan, Ye Erjiang as Little Bazi, Ye Erken as Wang Jingsheng, Gulaizai as Guli

A timid man called simply Li is hired to work in a mine just at the time China's gold fields have a continuing problem with gold being illegally taken from the mines and smuggled out of the country. Government anti-smuggling forces are frustrated in their efforts to stop it. It turns out that Li is an undercover police officer. He at last gathers enough information for the public security forces to move in, but sacrifices his life to protect the operation.

778. *Golden Dream (Jin Se De Meng)*

1985. Pearl River Film Studio. Color. Letter-boxed. 10 Reels. Direction: Lin Li. Screenplay: Zhao Qin, Lin Li, Ai Ling. Cinematography: Liu Huizhong. Art Direction: Mei Leiping. Music: Ye Xiaogang. Sound: Li Xun. Cast: Zhao Qing as Lu Dan, Li Ruping as Hua Da, Wang Lei as Xiaofeng, Wuyun Siqing as Meiling, Wang Zhenrong as the art director

The decade-long Cultural Revolution brought a premature end to dancer Lu Dan's performing career, and now she works as an accountant at an agricultural bank. Her husband Hua Da is a successful composer, they have a small child, and the three people are a very happy family. But Lu Dan still longs to make a career of the dancing she loves, and hopes to someday return to the stage. Her husband uses various excuses to oppose her comeback plans, based on his belief that a wife should sacrifice for her husband's career. After much hard work, she again becomes a professional dancer, but the couple separate. In addition to this distraction, Lu Dan also suffers abuse from woman dancer Meiling, whose jealousy leads her to blame Lu for everything that goes wrong. Lu Dan endures all this for her dancing career. One day she happens to meet her husband in a coffee shop, and he tells her he understands at last.

779. *Golden Fingernails (Jin Se De Zhi Jia)*

1989. Shanghai Film Studio. Color. 10 Reels.

Direction: Bao Zhifang. Screenplay: Zhang Chongguang, Lan Zhiguang. Cinematography: Shan Lianguo. Art Direction: Qu Ranxin. Music: Liu Yanxi. Sound: Lu Xuehan, Jin Fugeng. Cast: Fu Yiwei as Cao Mei, Wang Hui as Su Yafeng, Zhang Min as Shen Xiuwen, Guo Guan as Yu Xiaoyun

The colorful and sometimes tragic stories of five young women living in a large modern city. Cao Mei falls in love, and when she discovers the man is already married, decides to fight for him. So her story becomes that of two women and a man. Su Yafen is deserted by her husband, which turns out to be the best thing that could have happened to her, for it frees her to find true love at last. When we meet Shen Xiuwen, she is already divorced. She finds love again but concludes that the third party in divorce cases should never be condemned. Yu Xiaoyun, single and unattractive to men, devotes herself to her studies. She also searches for true love, if only to prove that she can overcome any problem. Ye Rui, the fifth woman, is a sophisticated woman who must resolve a family crisis when her husband announces he has fallen for another woman.

780. *A Golden Late Fall (Jin Se De Wan Qiu)*

1983. Shanghai Film Studio. Color. 10 Reels. Direction: Fu Chaowu, Xu Weijie. Screenplay: Wang Di, Duan Chengbing. Cinematography: Cha Xiangkang. Art Direction: Li Huazhong, Ning Funing. Music: Xiao Yan. Sound: Huang Dongping. Cast: Lu Yulei as Du Jian, Zhang Xian as Chen Zhuang, Shi Weijian as Su Haipeng, Gao Cui as Qin Yulan

When the Hainan Steel Corporation's mill director Chen Zhuang learns that company's CEO Du Jian is suffering the recurrence of an old illness, he is worried about his old colleague. While Du recuperates he gives considerable thought to the company, and by the time he returns to work he has decided that the current management team members like himself are too old and out of date. He begins a program to force them into early retirement and let younger and more vigorous people take over. His first target is Chen Zhuang, a conservative man with little education. Du Jian's reform measures run into a stone wall of opposition, mostly from his older colleagues' refusal to cooperate. Du is very upset with their attitude, but he is at last able to get Chen Zhuang removed from his post, and replaces him with

Su Haiping, a young engineer. Su Haiping's new ideas about management quickly turns around the mill's production downturn, and convinces everyone of the wisdom of reform, even Chen Zhuang. Tired and feeling his health is failing again, Du Jian retires and leaves for a resort.

781. *Gongbake Is Not Quiet (Bu Ping Jing De Gong Ba Ke)*

1986. Tianshan Film Studio. Color. Letterboxed. 9 Reels. Direction: Tang Guangtao. Screenplay: Hasimu, Zhang Shengtang. Cinematography: Hali Kejiang. Art Direction: Sun Changxi. Music: Nusi Laiti. Sound: Gong Zhengmin, Wun Gang. Cast: Polida as Sailimai, Sun Ai as Li Li, Boha Erding as Alimu, Mulati as Pulati, Abajiang as Suoshengcai, Wupuer Haili as Rejiepu

782. *A Good Child (Hao Hai Zi)*

1959. Haiyan Film Studio. Color. 8 Reels. Direction: Yang Xiaozong. Screenplay: Wang Sujiang, Sun Zhen, Bujiali, Liao Long, Zhang Qingfeng, Mochou and Bailu. Cinematography: Cao Weiye. Art Direction: Zhong Yongqing. Music: Xiang Yi. Sound: Wu Yin. Cast: Chen Chaoyin as Mingkui, Tong Yaming as Baomei, Wu Limin as Ahu, Geng Xinyu as Xiaoqing, Hu Xiaodong as Bean, Jin Xiaojing as Honghong, He Liji as Cai Fa, Xiang Mei as Teacher Tian, Li Baoluo as Grandpa, Zhang Yinjie as Commune Director Chen, Mao Lu as Secretary Qian, Liang Ming as Xiaoqing's grandmother

In rural Southeast China, commune director Chen is known as the "Number One Scholar of Wheat Planting." Chen's son Mingkui, supported by his fifth grade elementary school classmates, wants to plant some experimental cotton. But his father believes students should concentrate on studying, so he denies them a piece of land. They covertly find a plot of fallow land, plant their experimental cotton, and ask the grandfather of one of them to be their technical advisor. Their secret is eventually discovered by Director Chen and Secretary Qian, who are deeply moved by the children's love of work. So they formally grant this plot of land to the children. Inspired and taught by Teacher Tian, they set up a "Young Pioneer team," work and study together, and obtain a large harvest from their cotton field.

783. *A Good Guy Must Be a Soldier (Hao Nan Yao Dang Bing)*

1992. August First Film Studio. Color. Letterboxed. 9 Reels. Direction: Huo Deji. Screenplay: Li Pingfeng. Cinematography: Gao Jiuling. Art Direction: Chen Dong. Music: Yang Xiwu. Sound: Zhen Mingzhe. Costume: Nie Shuli. Makeup: Chen Jiaping. Cast: Zhao Liang as Wang Leshan, Shen Fa as Minister Sun, Chen Ping as Liu Quanding

A comedy about a farm boy's attempts to enlist in the army. With his father's approval, Wang Leshan tries to join up but is turned down. So he and his father travel to the city where an uncle lives, hoping the relative can get Wang in "through the back door," i.e., by pulling strings to get around the regulations. After a series of comic incidents, the young man's dedication and desire to serve at last moves a recruiter who approves his application.

784. *Good Luck (Zhu Ni Hao Yun) (orig: A Good Dream Comes True/Hao Meng Cheng Zhen)*

1992. Inner Mongolia Film Studio & Shanxi Film Studio Co-Production. Color. Letterboxed. 9 Reels. Direction: Lei Xianhe, Yang Shiguang. Screenplay: Jiang Yi. Cinematography: Jin Yixun, Zhang Weimin. Art Direction: Cui Junde. Music: Wu Ye. Cast: Niu Ben as the assistant director, Liu Xiaolingtong as director Zhang, Jia Ni as Liangliang, Liu Jiang as Director Gong, Qi Tao as Wang Feng, Zhan Qingbo as Da Shan, Niu Yingjiang as Xinxin, Jiang Xiaomu as Xin Ying

After his latest film bombs at the box office, an international award-winning director decides his usual type of film is passe, and starts work on a radical and risky departure for him, an action film titled "Good Luck." A sub-plot concerns the assistant director, who becomes a stunt man in order to earn the extra money he needs to buy a piano for his daughter.

785. *Good Luck (Yi Lu Shun Feng)*

1984. Nanjing Film Studio. Color. 9 Reels. Direction: Jin Jiwu. Screenplay: Peng Yongshui. Cinematography: Can Xingliang. Art Direction: Xiao Feng. Music: Ma Youdao. Sound: Han Weijun, Hong Di. Cast: Chen Baoguo as An Dele, Ren Yexiang as Huaihua, Gao Baocheng as Uncle, Xia Keqing as Auntie

Young truck driver An Dele contracts to transport a shipment of honey to South China. The shippers, an older couple called Uncle and Auntie, along with their niece Huaihua, accompany An Dele on his trip. An Dele keeps stopping to make money along the way, for example by letting hitchhikers ride part way for a small fee. This bothers the others, but there is nothing they can do. When the truck blows a tire, Huaihua sells some of the honey to buy a replacement; when Dele falls ill, the others take good care of him. He is so moved by their generosity that he promises to return next year.

786. *Good Morning, Beijing (Bei Jing, Ni Zao)*

1990. Youth Film Studio. Color. 10 Reels. Wide Screen. Direction: Zhang Nuanxin. Screenplay: Tang Danian. Cinematography: Zhang Xigui, Hua Qing. Art Direction: Li Yongxin. Music: Guo Wenjing. Sound: Hu Linping. Cast: Ma Xiaoqing as Ai Hong, Wang Quan'an as Zou Yongqiang, Jia Hongsheng as Keke, Jin Tiefeng as Wang Lang

The story of three ordinary young working people trying to cope with the rapid changes taking place in contemporary China. Ai Hong, her boyfriend Zou Yongqiang and their friend Wang Lang all work together on a Beijing bus. The rapid pace of economic reform soon disrupts the routine existence of the three. Wang Lang leaves his job without authorization in order to make money in the embryonic private sector, while Ai Hong tries to transfer to a Sino-foreign joint venture company. Zou Yongqiang is hard-working and simple, and wants things the way they have always been. He and Ai Hong break up. Ai Hong then meets Keke, an unemployed young man posing as a "student from Singapore." She falls under his spell, he seduces her and leaves her alone and pregnant.

787. *A Good Woman (Liang Jia Fu Nu)*

1985. Beijing Film Studio. Color. 10 Reels. Director: Huang Jianzhong. Screenplay: Li Kuanding. Cinematographer: Yun Wenyue. Art Direction: Shao Ruigang. Music: Si Wanchun. Sound: Zhen Chunyu. Cast: Chong Shan as Xingxian, Zhang Weixin as Wuniang, Wang Jiayi as Yi Shaowei, Zhang Jian as Brother Kaibing, Liang Yan as Third Sister-in-Law

In an isolated mountain village in Guizhou

province, on the eve of liberation, traditional feudal marriage customs are still the norm. Xingxian, an 18-year-old village girl, finds herself engaged to marry an 8-year-old boy; her prospective mother-in-law Wuniang is just 26. When Kaibing, a man about Xingxian's age, comes to the village as a temporary farm laborer, Xingxian falls for him, but local customs demand this sort of thing be punished severely. At this time, a land reform work team enters the village and from them Xingxian learns that the law now guarantees freedom of choice in marriage. So Xingxian goes public about her relationship with Kaibing, touching off a fierce emotional struggle among the villagers. After this, Xingxian and Kaibing elope, making her the first girl in her village's history to break free of this feudal tradition.

Grand Prix, International Critics Award, 25th Karlovy Vary International Film Festival.

Best Picture Award, Andalusian Critics Award, Film Club Award, 18th Atlantic International Film Festival.

788. *Goodbye to Death's Head Island (Gao Bie Ku Lou Dao)*

1989. August First Film Studio. Color. Letterboxed. 8 Reels. Direction: Gong Yiqun. Screenplay: Li Baolin. Cinematographer: Cai Shunan, Wang Weidong. Art Direction: Niu Xiaolin, Zhang Guozhen. Music: Wang Xiaoyong. Sound: Shen Guorui. Cast: Zhang Mo as Yangyang, Cao Dingding as Yanzhi

Two boys find a book called "Death's Head Island," a blood-and-thunder pirate story. They become so obsessed with the book that they begin to emulate the behavior of the pirates in the story, which soon lands them in trouble at school. With the guidance of an understanding teacher, they come to realize the book's bad influence, and turn it in to a government censor.

789. *The Gourmet (Mei Shi Jia)*

1985. Shanghai Film Studio. Color. 10 Reels. Direction: Xu Cangling. Screenplay: Xu Cangling. Cinematography: Can Lianguo. Art Direction: Qiu Yuan. Music: Huang Zhun. Sound: Zhou Yunling, Jin Fugeng. Cast: Xia Tian as Zhu Zhizhi, Wang Sihuai as Gao Xiaoting, Zhan Pingping as Kong Bixia, Lu Qin as Bao Kunnian

After the 11th Party Conference, Suzhou restaurant manager Gao Xiaoting wants to resume preparing the famous traditional dishes of Suzhou, a traditional skill discarded during

the Cultural Revolution. Bao Kunnian, one of his workers, suggests inviting Zhu Zizhi to give cooking lessons. Zhu is a man totally obsessed with food: before liberation, he had eaten three meals each day in restaurants, and this practice has continued for 40 years. Although Gao dislikes this "greedy man," Zhu's cooking lesson is so popular invitations pour in from everywhere asking him to give lessons. He enthusiastically starts a cooking association. Zhu wants to be elected president of the new association, so he has his wife Kong Bixia prepare a banquet to impress the rest of the members. After sampling Kong's marvelous food, Gao decides that since he cannot understand or agree with Zhu's popularity, he might just as well offer Kong Bixia the job of supervising the restaurant's kitchen.

790. *Grade Five, Section Two (Wu Er Ban)*

1984. Hubei Film Studio. Color. Letterboxed. 9 Reels. Direction: Xu Boran. Screenplay: Shen Hongguang. Cinematography: Yang Zhixue, Liao Shusheng. Art Direction: Cao Liangjun. Music: Wang Yuanping. Sound: Tang Rongchun, Zhang Minkui. Cast: Wu Wenhua as Teacher Le, Kang Ling as Nina, Qu Pu as Jidong, Zhang Yu as Wu Yong, Jin Xing as Lang Jun, Hu Jing as Tong Minmin

The students in Teacher Le's Grade 5, Section 2 elementary class come from a wide variety of family backgrounds. Over the course of a year, we see them develop and grow under the teacher's dedicated and loving guidance.

791. *Grain (Liangshi)*

1959. Beijing Film Studio. B & W. 10 Reels. Direction: Wei Rong. Screenplay: Pan Wenzhan, based on the novel of the same name. Cinematography: Li Wenhua. Music: Lu Ming. Sound: Cai Jun, Wang Zeming, Liu Shida. Cast: Zhang Ping as Kang Luotai, Qing Han as Xin You, Wang Yunxia as Xiulan, Ge Chunzuang as Qingshui, An Zhengjiang as the fourth Buddhist monk, Fang Hui as Li Desheng

In 1943, the Japanese and the Chinese collaborationist army often confiscated grain from the villages in a remote mountain area to prevent its being supplied to the Communist Eighth Route Army. Because the Communists cannot ship the grain out for at least three days, village chief Kang Luotai has the villagers hide their supplies. Kang Luotai also exploits the frequent disputes between the Japanese soldiers and the collaborationists, often instigating these. When the shipment must be further delayed, he devises another ruse which buys more time. His strategies make it possible for the villagers to pass through the enemy lines and deliver the grain safely to the revolutionary base.

792. *Grandson and Grandpa (Long Ye Hu Sun)*

1993. Emei Film Studio. Color. Letterboxed. 9 Reels. Direction: Miao Yue, Sun Ming. Screenplay: Miao Yue. Cinematography: Luo Xun, Xiao Guizhong. Art Direction: Chen Desheng. Music: Lin Ping. Sound: Luo Guohua. Costume: Yu Dezhao. Makeup: Wang Zezhen. Cast: Yang Chiyu as Grandpa, Hu Bing as Hu Tou, Deng Yulin as Boss, Luo Shiping as Little Bear, Zhou Jinquan as the man, Pan Yong as Hu Laoliu

Little Hu Tou's parents are divorcing, so they send him to Chengdu to stay with his grandfather. At the airport, a man is abducted by two gangsters, but before being taken away he slips a game card box to Hu Tou. The man is later killed, and in the box the little boy finds a map and the address of the man's father, a bank president in Chengdu before liberation. Hu Tou helps his grandfather, a retired police officer, solve the mystery, which involved hidden gold and gangsters.

793. *Grass Grows on the Kunlun Mountains (Kun Lun Shan Shang Yi Ke Cao)*

1962. Beijing Film Studio. B & W. 6 Reels. Direction: Dong Kena. Screenplay: Hua Ming and Dong Kena, based on the novel "Hui's wife" by Wang Zongyuan. Cinematography: Gao Hongtao. Art Direction: Zhang Xiande. Music: Liu Zhuang. Sound: Liu Shida. Cast: Liu Yanjing as Hui's wife, Li Mengrao as Mr. Hui, Wang Zhelan as Li Wanli, Zhao Wande as Xiao Liu, Yang Zongjing as Xiao Chen, Song Ge as Xiao Jiang

In the Kunlun Mountains by the rugged Qinghai-Tibetan Plateau, a woman called Hui's wife establishes a dormitory to house the drivers who crisscross the plateau by day and night. She becomes acquainted with other newcomers assigned by the government to build the plateau's economy. One of these is Li Wanli, a young Shanghai woman just graduated from a geological university, but fearful of the harsh life on the plateau. Hui's wife tells Li Wanli of her own experiences, after which Li goes happily to her new job.

794. *Grasslands (Cao Di)*

1986. August First Film Studio. Color. 9 Reels. Direction: Si Wei. Screenplay: Wang Yuanjian. Cinematography: Wu Fei. Art Direction: Ma Yibiao. Music: Du Xingcheng. Sound: Li Qinheng. Cast: Han Zhenhua as Chang Zhi, Li Yufeng as Xiao Guocheng, Huang Tao as Xiao Qin, Ji Ping as Huang Su, Sun Haiyin as Zeng Libiao

A war story, following the personal interactions and life-and-death struggles of a group of Red Army soldiers crossing a seemingly endless prairie.

795. *Gravel (Sha Li)*

1984. Beijing Film Studio. Color. Wide Screen. 10 Reels. Direction: Li Wei. Screenplay: Xia Zhixin, Xu Tesheng. Cinematography: Wang Liansheng, Liu Jirui. Art Direction: Li Zhongzhi. Music: Jin Xiang. Sound: Sun Yumin. Cast: Wang Yongge as Su Wang, Zhang Liwei as Li Man, Ahe Maiti as Hadeer, Qi Kejian as Fang Yushu, Song Jingsheng as Guda

When Su Wang is discharged from the army he volunteers for road maintenance work in the isolated Talimu Desert. When she hears this, his fiancee breaks off their relationship. Life in the desert is terribly difficult and depressing, and Su Wang himself almost goes mad. He survives and overcomes the difficulties, however, and helps his colleague Hadeer get back together with his girl friend. In time Su Wang himself meets Li Man, a girl who delivers water to the road crews. They find they have the same goals in life, and eventually marry.

796. *Gravity and Hostility in Heaven (Tian Guo Chou Heng)*

1985. Xiaoxiang Film Studio. Color. 10 Reels. Direction: Zhou Kangyu. Screenplay: Wang Zixing, Wang Jinbao. Cinematography: Zhou Shengtong. Art Direction: Jin Bohao, Guo Dexiang. Music: Shi Fu, Yi Xuezhi. Sound: Liu Yishen. Cast: An Yaping as Gao Yulong, Chen Kang as Bai Wenbing, Fang Jian as Luo Dafeng, Pang Lintai as Gao Dekun, He Fusheng as Luo Sizhu, Sha Xiaokui as Gao Delin, Yan Hua as Gao Yulong (as a child)

In 1864, the Taiping Rebellion is in its final days. The remnants of the Taiping army are surrounded by imperial forces, and Taiping

Grass Grows on the Kunlun Mountains. **1962. Beijing Film Studio.**

leader Hong Xiuquan falls ill and dies. Led by one of Hong's generals, Gao Dekun, a Taiping force protecting Hong's small son breaks out of the encirclement. General Gao is later killed in battle by imperial officer Bai Wenbing, but his son Gao Yulong escapes and takes refuge with his uncle Gao Delin. Years pass, and as Yulong grows to manhood he acquires outstanding martial arts skills. When his uncle dies, Gao Yulong prepares for a new rebellion. Eventually, the rebellion starts under his leadership, and in battle Gao Yulong kills Bai Wenbing, avenging his father's death.

797. *The Great Carpenter (Da Mu Jiang)*

1957. (Unreleased.) Beijing Motion Picture Academy Film Studio. B & W. 3 Reels. Direction: Wu Gongyi, et al. Screenplay: Wu Gongyi. Cinematography: Yang Qiming, Cao Zuobing and Zhen Guoen. Art Direction: Li Yongxin and Xu Jiacang. Sound: Zhang Ruikun, Li Ruinan and Hu Zhaohua. No Cast Credits

During the Great Leap Forward Campaign, a good carpenter is trying to make a rice transplanter at his rural home. His wife asks

him to put it aside and go into town to purchase a welcome gift, as today will be the first visit from their future son-in-law. On his way into town, the carpenter meets a young man on his way to visit relatives. He and the younger man get into a serious discussion of the rice transplanter and he totally forgets about the gift. The two go to his workshop and began working on the project together. Just as they get it finished, the carpenter's wife comes in and is angry when she finds her husband did not get the gift. Her anger is short-lived, however, when the young man reveals that he is their future son-in-law. Both parents love the capable young fellow.

798. *The Great Conqueror's Concubine (Xi Chu Ba Wang)*

1994. Sil-Metropole Organization Ltd. Color. Wide Screen. 17 Reels. Direction: Xian Qiran (Stephen Shin). Screenplay: Liu Heng, Xiaohe, Xian Qiran, Si Yangping. Cinematography: Zhen Zhaoqiang. Art Direction: Ma Guangrong. Music: Huang Zhan, Dai Lemin. Costume: Mo Junjie. Makeup: Pan Minghua, Qiu Ruixian, Chen Xiuxian, Huang Shunhui, Shi Haijun, Ke

Qian, Li Yanping. Cast: Lu Liangwei (Ray Lui) as Xiang Yu, Zhang Fengyi as Liu Bang, Guan Zhilin (Rosamund Kwan) as Lady Yu, Gong Li, Liu Xun, Wu Xingguo, Xu Jinjiang, Chen Songyong, Du Shaojin, Ye Quanzhen, Xu Xiangdong, Zhu Mu, Xu Zhan, Zhang Shi

An epic historical drama. Generals Xiang Yu and Liu Bang join forces to bring down the cruel Qin Dynasty (221–207 B.C.). After the victory, however, the two revert to the more familiar roles of rivals. Military genius Xiang Yu lacks the diplomatic skills to outmaneuver his rival Liu Bang, a peasant warrior with a politically clever wife. After many battles and negotiations, Liu Bang eventually emerges the victor and founds the Han Dynasty (206 B.C.–220 A.D.), the first great dynasty in Chinese history.

799. *A Great Cotton Harvest (Xue Hai Yin Shan)*

1959. Xi'an Film Studio. B & W. 6 Reels. Direction: Sun Jing. Screenplay: Zong Jiming. Cinematography: Cao Jinshan. Art Direction: Zhang Jingnan. Music: Wei Ruixiang. Sound: Hong Jiahui. Cast: Liu Yanping as Li Chunlan, Wang Lan as Zhang Xiufang, Zhao Zimin as Secretary Chen, Chen Xin as Tie Shuanpan, Zhao Guilan as Li Dasheng, Gao Zhijiu as the commune director

Li Chunlan, youth director at the "East Wind" farm commune, leads a dozen girls in a cotton-planting experiment designed to increase output, supervised by Party secretary Chen. She challenges the neighboring commune's famous cotton planter Zhang Xiufang to a contest. Due to the young women's lack of experience, their cotton has some problems. Chunlan goes to Zhang Xiufang for advice. Although she is his competitor, Zhang Xiufang is willing to help Chunlan resolve her problems with growing cotton, and saves her experimental field. Chunlan is deeply moved by Xiulan's style and attitude.

800. *The Great Dragon Penetrates the Mountain (Chuan Shan Ju Long)*

1957. (Unreleased.) Beijing Motion Picture Academy Film Studio. Color. 4 Reels. Direction: Graduates of the Class of 1956, Beijing Motion Picture Academy Directing Department. Screenplay: Zeng Xiandie, Lu Youhan. Cinematography: Gan Quan, Gu Wenka and Liao Jiaxiang. Art Direction: Li Yongxin. Music: Chen Yuping.

Sound: Zhang Ruikun. Cast: Zhang Debao as Secretary Hong, Zhou Shengguan as Grandfather Zhang, Wang Bingxu as Zhang Guoxiang, Ma Jingwu as Zhang Long, Li Erkang as the assistant driver, Wang Tianpeng as the stoker

Zhang Long, a young driver on the Longwei Railway section's "Great Dragon" Train, boldly seeks new methods. He proposes using the "Great Dragon" to conduct a test while fully loaded with transuranium, but runs into opposition from his father and supervisor Zhang Guoxiang, who is more conservative. Because the "Great Dragon" train is the pride of the railway section, and three generations of Zhang's family have been drivers of the train, Zhang Guoxiang fears that a failed test could ruin his family's honor. Zhang Long conducts the test without his father's knowledge, but fails, and is criticized as a result. As he prepares for another test, the news arrives that another train has had an accident on this newly created line, so some of his crew lose confidence. Party Secretary Hong helps them to analyze the cause of the failure, and supports them in conducting a second test. Aided by the party secretary and Grandfather Zhang, they succeed in the attempt this time. In the face of the facts, Zhang Guoxiang realizes his mistake.

801. *The Great Gorge (Da Xia Gu)*

1991. Yunnan Film Studio. Color. 9 Reels. Direction: Sun Sha. Screenplay: Tang Shijie. Cinematography: Gao Hongyu, Huang Zuxing and Wu Fei. Art Direction: Song Honghua. Music: Ma Ding. Sound: Liu Qun, Zhang Lifeng. Costume: Qi Chunzhi, Zhao Qiongxian. Makeup: Lei Longlong, Yang Meixin and Yin Hong. Cast: Zhen Zhaishi as Hong Hanxi, Pan Weixing as Qin Lanshi, Tong Ruixin as He Nanyang, Ni Xuehua as Shen Adi, Wang Changlin as Li Jian, Zhang Lin as Heizhi, Zhu Xuedong as Lin Shunzhi

As part of reform and opening, the Japanese Global Construction Company participates in the building of the Big Gorge Water Conservancy Project in Yunnan Province. The Japanese advanced technology and management combined with the hard work of the Chinese workers accomplish the massive task. At the same time, a deep friendship is built up between the Chinese and Japanese on the project.

The Great Leap's Sound Is Everywhere
see *A Thousand Miles a Day*

802. *The Great River Rushes Forward (Parts One and Two) (Dahe Benliu)*

1978. Beijing Film Studio. Color. (Wide & Narrow Screen). 21 Reels. Direction: Xie Tieli, Chen Huaiai. Screenplay: Li Zhun. Cinematography: Qian Jiang, Li Chengsheng, Zhou Jinxiang. Art Direction: Chen Yiyun, Hao Jingyuan. Music: Wang Yanqiao. Sound: Chen Yanxi, Gui Zhilin. Cast: Zhang Ruifang as Li Mai, Chen Qiang as Hai Qin, Zhang Jinling as Liang Qing, Zhao Lian as Hai Changsong, Liu Yanli as Tian Liang, Li Xiumin as Song Ming

In 1938, the Nationalist Army blows up the Huayuan Dam over the Yellow River in the attempt to cut off the Communist forces from participating fully in the anti–Japanese war. This causes much suffering among the people of the area, and many take to the streets to protest. One of these is Li Mai, female servant in the home of a landlord, and at the demonstration she meets and becomes friends with another woman, Communist Party cadre Song Ming, who is one of the protest demonstration organizers. Shortly after this, Li Mai joins the Communist Party to work for revolution. After the victory in World War Two, Li Mai returns to her hometown as district director, leading the people there in exploring and developing uncultivated land. She is introduced to Chairman Mao Zedong and Premier Zhou Enlai. Under Li Mai's leadership, the local people conquer the exceptionally great flood of 1958, and realize a huge harvest.

803. *Great Wall Decisive Battle (Chang Cheng Da Jue Zhan)*

1988. Guangxi Film Studio and Hong Kong Jinma Film Company Co-Production. Color. Letterboxed. 9 Reels. Direction: Lu Xiaolong, Zhang Ning. Screenplay: Wen Gui, Meng Haipeng. Cinematography: You Qi, Chen Shenkai. Art Direction: Wu Zhaohua. Music: Li Haihui. Sound (Dolby): Lin Lin. Cast: Lu Xiaolong as Hua Zhiqiang, Yang Weixin as Zhang Xiaoye, Luchun Taixiang as Xiaochilang

After the "September 18th Incident" at Marco Polo Bridge near Beijing, the Chinese Nationalist government's policy of non-resistance allows Japanese troops to rapidly occupy the three provinces of Northeast China. Hua Zhiqiang's mother is killed by Japanese invaders, and while he and his lover survive the massacre, they become separated during their flight. To damage the Chinese national pride, the invaders send martial artist Xiaochilang to challenge Director Yang of the Chinese Martial Arts Institute. However, Yang is poisoned before he ever gets the chance to accept the challenge. Yang's student Huang Zhiqiang asks for a contest with the Japanese representative, and beats him handily. The vanquished fighter returns to Japan and polishes his skills, after which he returns and challenges Huang, the contest to be held at the Great Wall. The fight is a vicious affair unlike any other kung fu match in memory. Huang finally defeats Xiaochilang for a second time, but is then shot to death by the Japanese.

804. *Great Wall of the South Sea (Nan Hai Chang Cheng)*

1976. August First Film Studio. Color. 10 Reels. Direction: Li Jun, Hao Guang. Screenplay: Liang Xing, Dong Xiaohua. Cinematography: Zhang Dongliang, Yin Qiaofang. Art Direction: Kou Honglie, Liu Jingsheng. Music: Fu Gengcheng. Sound: Wu Hanbiao. Cast: Wang Xingang as Qu Yingcai, Liu Xiaoqing as Tian Nu, Gao Dawei as Qu Yingcai (as a child), Shi Ren as Old Woman Zhong, Li Tingxiu as Uncle Chiwei, Zhao Ruping as Secretary Jiang, Chen Zhurong as A Luo, Zhou Qu as Wei Taili

In 1962, a militia company at the port city of Danan capture a man impersonating a Chinese soldier. Company Commander Qu Yingcai determines the prisoner is enemy spy "09," and from him Qu learns details of the enemy's "Shark Special Action" invasion plan. They devise a plan of defense, but naive young militiaman Jingzai leaks their plan to Wei Taili, another enemy agent who has gained the young soldier's trust. Qu Yingcai helps Jingzai to improve his class awareness, awakening him to the consequences of his carelessness. After obtaining Wei's intelligence, the enemy changes their original landing plan and land on Jinxing Island, but Qu Yingcai's militia company is ready for them, and wipe out the invaders.

805. *Great Waves Washing Ashore (Da Lang Tao Sha)*

1966. Pearl River Film Studio. B & W. 13 Reels. Direction: Yi Ling. Screenplay: Zhu Daonan, Yu Bingkun and Yi Ling. Cinematography: Liu Jingtang. Art Direction: Jiang Jin. Music: Che Ming. Sound: Li Liehong. Cast: Yu Yang as Jing Gongshou, Jian Ruichao as Gu Daming, Du Xiongwen as Yang Rukuan, Liu Guanxiong as Yu

Great Waves Washing Ashore. Jing Gongshou (Yu Yang, second left front) and fellow students enthusiastically join in the revolution. 1966. Pearl River Film Studio.

Hongkui, Shi Jing as Zhao Jingzhang, Wang Pei as Xie Hui

In 1925, young intellectuals Jing Gong-shou, Gu Daming and Yang Rukuan leave their hometown in search of greater opportunity. On the way they rescue Yu Hongkui, a young man fleeing a forced marriage. Swearing to become brothers, the four travel to the city of Jinan and enroll in Shandong No. 1 Normal University. They study with both Communist and Nationalist teachers, often stay up late discussing and reading revolutionary theory together. Caught up in the spirit of revolution sweeping China, they join the Northern Expeditionary Army to put down warlords. However, Yu Hongkui turns traitor and betrays the revolution, while Yang Rukuan leaves the army in depression and disappointment at the rigid military life. Gu Daming and Jing Gongshou bear up under the trials. They capture and execute their traitorous former friend Yu Hongkui. The continue their revolutionary work by joining the Qiushou rebellion led by Mao Zedong, maturing in the storms of revolution.

806. *A Great Young Man (Da Xiao Huo Zi)*

1983. Changchun Film Studio. Color. 10 Reels. Direction: Chen Zhanhe. Screenplay: Si Minshan, Zhou Yang, Wu Bengwu, Sun Xiongfei. Cinematography: Duan Zhenjiang. Art Direction: Gao Guoliang. Music: Gao Feng. Sound: Jue Jingxiu, Wang Lin. Cast: Hao Yiping as Da Wei, Zhang Yuhong as Jingjing, Chen Guojun as Da Liu, Zhang Chunfeng as Lili, Zhao Fan as Mr. Ji, Yang Xiaodan as Da Long, Xu Jinzen as Plant Director Gao

An unemployed young man named Da Wei becomes acquainted with Mr. Ji, the recently retired director of the Xinxin Electronics Company. Da Wei has outstanding mechanical skills, and has some innovative ideas about energy efficiency. Mr. Ji recommends the younger man to his old employer at the same time a smaller, struggling competitor is trying to recruit him. Da Wei chooses to go with the competitor, the Yong Fu Transport Parts Plant, because he feels they need him more. A fierce competition follows, with each company vying to bring out their energy efficient machine before the other. The larger Xinxin Company tries to use their larger size and production capacity to drive the Yong Fu Plant out of the race, but at last the smaller company wins out and gets a large contract with a transport company.

807. *Greatness Forever (Feng Liu Qian Gu)*

1981. Emei Film Studio. Color. 11 Reels. Direction: Kou Jiabi, Li Jiefeng. Screenplay: Kou Jiabi, Wang Peijiang. Cinematography: Gu Wunhou. Art Direction: Xia Zhengqiu. Music: Chang Sumin, Tao Jiazhou. Sound: Lin Bingcheng. Cast: Ji Zhenhua as Lu You, Wang Fuli as Tang Wan, Zhao Ge as Lu Zhai, Guo Fazen as Chen Daguan, Tu Zhongru as Li Chengzhao

Lu You (1125–1210) is a famous patriotic poet of the 11th Century. Although very talented, he fails the imperial exams because his patriotic papers do not match the ideas of the premier Qin Kui, who advocates China surrender to the Jin barbarians' invasion. Lu You marries his childhood sweetheart Tang Wan, and they are very happy together. One day, Lu You's good friend Chen Daguan writes to say that he is collecting funds to purchase arms for the resistance of the Jin invasion, and asks Lu You for a donation. Tang Wan donates some priceless gold jewelry left to her by her mother. However, when Chen Daguan puts this jewelry up for sale, it is recognized by store owner Li Chengzhao, an informer for Qin Kui. Li Chengzhao sends the jewelry back to Lu You's parents, and plants rumors which imply a plot involving Tang Wan and her parents. Lu You's parents order Lu You to divorce Tang Wan, and while Lu is very upset about this, under the feudal laws of the time he cannot refuse his parents' order. He loses all hope. Ten years later, Lu You has remarried a woman named Wang, and Tang Wan has remarried a man named Zhao Shicheng. In 1153, Lu You fails the imperial exams again, for reasons similar to the first time. He is very upset and angry. In 1155, Tang Wan and Zhao Shicheng happen to meet Lu You, and to express his feelings Lu You writes a poem "A Pair of Phoenicis." When Tang Wan reads his poem, so full of sorrow and suffering, she is so overcome with despair that she falls ill. She soon dies of sorrow. The poem becomes famous in Chinese literary history.

808. *Green Bamboo Mountain (Zhu Shan Qing Qing)*

1982. Xiaoxiang Film Studio. Color. 9 Reels. Direction: Hu Shuer, Pan Xianghe. Screenplay: Hu Shuer, Pan Xianger. Cinematography: Wang Kekuan, Yu Yejiang. Art Direction: Rao Weiquan, Zhou Yi. Music: Wei Jingshu, Ouyang Zhanwen. Sound: Liu Feng. Cast: Huang Ailing as Limei, Li Tan as Qin Gengwu, Zhu Sha as the Matchmaker, Huang Wansu as Li's mother, Shi Jing as Director Dao, Wang Ye as Li Shangyou

After losing his wife early in marriage, Qin Gengwu has raised their children alone. Now he is worried about getting his eldest son Chunsheng married, for he cannot seem to collect sufficient money to satisfy the demands of the bride-to-be's parents. The matchmaker suggests he first find a wealthy husband for his daughter Li Mei, demand a large sum from the groom, and then use this money to find a wife for his son. But Li Mei already has a lover, Li Shangyou. Although the couple tries very hard to collect the money her father needs so she will not have to marry someone else, they are unsuccessful. At last, Li Mei decides to take a stand, oppose her father and find her own marital happiness, and she finally wins out.

809. *Green Covered Land (Lu Ying)*

1984. August First Film Studio. Color. Letterboxed. 10 Reels. Direction: Chen Xinzhi. Screenplay: Kou Honglie, Wang Jia. Cinematography: Yang Guangyuan, Yang Xiuqin. Art Direction: Shi Pingyi, Sun Xuezhen. Music: Wang Ming. Sound: Zhao Changsheng. Cast: Sun Caihua as Shen Qiao, Li Qihou as Tang Tianxu, Ma Hongying as Gu Yushi, Zhu Cangmin as Luo Pu, Yang Fei as Xiao Luying

During the Cultural Revolution, a scientific institution engaged in military research is ordered to transfer its operations to the desert. The institution's director, Tang Tianxu, leads his entire staff on the long and arduous trek to its new facility. After a while, Tang marries the institution's archivist, who later dies giving birth to a son. Tang enlists one of his researchers, Shen Qiao, to help raise the child. When the Gang of Four falls, and intellectuals are permitted to return to the cities, Tang and Shen stay on to complete their research. Tang dies of overwork.

810. *Green Fields Again (Tian Ye You Shi Qin Sha Zhang)*

1986. Changchun Film Studio. Color. 11

Reels. Direction: Li Qiankuan, Xiao Guiyuan. Cinematography: Wang Jishun, Zhao Zhongtian. Art Direction: Wang Xingwen. Music: Si Wanchun, Zhu Lianjie. Sound: Yin Wenyu, Fang Yongming. Cast: Li Wei as Wang Changsheng, Huang Zongluo as Mr. Ding Hua, Hong Xuemin as Xiao Yingzi, Huang Zongluo as Mr. Ding Hua, Li Rentang as County Director Gong, Lu Xiaohe as He Da

After years of political and economic turmoil, prosperity returns to northeast China. But a new disturbance soon arrives when reform sweeps the country. This comedy shows the everyday lives and work of the residents of Elm Village, and the varying ways in which its citizens react to reform. Among the more than 40 characters we meet are Wang Changsheng, enamored of anything new; Mr. Ding Hua, superstitious and conservative; Xiao Yingzi, who goes with the flow no matter where it may lead, etc. The story is told with humor and considerable introduction to distinctive northeast China customs.

811. *The Green Jade Hair Clip (Bi Yu Zan)*

1962. (Unreleased). Haiyan Film Studio & Hong Kong Dapeng Film Studio Co-Production. Color. 13 Reels. Direction: Wu Yonggang. Screenplay: Wu Yonggang, based on the script for the Shanghai Yue Opera Troupe's production. Cinematography: Luo Chongzhou and Peng Enli. Art Direction: Zhang Xibai. Sound: Wu Jianghai and Zhou Hengliang. Cast: Jin Caifeng as Li Xiuying, Chen Shaochun as Wang Yulin, Zhou Baokui as Mrs. Lu, Qian Miaohua as Li Tingpu, Wei Fengjuan as Gu Wenyou, Zhen Zhongmei as Wang Yu

Li Xiuying, the intelligent and beautiful daughter of Minister of Justice Li Tingpu, marries Wang Yulin, the son of her father's good friend. Her jealous cousin Gu Wenyou attempts to destroy the marriage by leaving a forged love note and Xiuying's green jade hair clip in the bridal chamber where Yulin will find it. After finding this, Yulin angrily abandons his bride on their wedding night. Yulin shows the evidence to Li Tingpu, who investigates and determines the truth. Yulin is very regretful, but Xiuying, very hurt, rejects his apology. Yulin studies hard and attains the highest marks on the imperial examinations. In time, through his repeated pleadings and the urgings of their families, the young couple are reconciled.

812. *A Green Land's Victory Song (Lu Zhou Kai Ge)*

1959. Haiyan Film Studio and Xinjiang Film Studio Co-Production. Color. 11 Reels. Direction: Zhao Ming, Chen Gang. Screenplay: Wang Yuhu, Fan Yiping, Lin Songchun, Quan Kuanfu, You Suofu and Haojieyefu. Cinematography: Chen Zhenxiang, Liu Jingtang. Art Direction: Hu Zuoyun, Li Zongzhi. Music: Gao Tian, Kuerban. Sound: Zhou Hengliang, Zhang Xicheng. Cast: Shilajiding as Balati, Tuohudi Maolataji as Aximu, Nuer Maimaiti as Yulayin, Rena as Aixiamuhan, Ayixiamu as Ayimuhan, Tulankezi as Niyazihan , Maimaiti Yibulayin as Tuohuti

At the foot of Mount Tianshan in the Xinjiang Uighur Autonomous Region, woman team director Ayimuhan is an enthusiastic commune worker, while her husband engages in illegal but profitable grain sales. Because Ayimuhan refuses to go along with this, her whole family turns against her. Ayimuhan was once in love with the commune director Balati when they were young, and they still have considerable contact at work. Hidden reactionary Yulayin exploits the situation by arousing the jealousy of Ayimuhan's husband, and the latter beats her badly. This is part of a larger conspiracy to destroy the commune. Malaimuhan, another woman commune member, learns of the conspiracy and reports it to Ayimuhan. The conspiracy is defeated. In the end, Ayimuhan divorces her husband and is sent by the Party for advanced training.

813. *The Green Net (Lu Se De Wang)*

1986. Yunnan Minority Film Studio. Color. 9 Reels. Direction: Li Wenhua. Screenplay: Peng Xingfeng. Cinematography: He Qin. Art Direction: Hao Jingyuan, Xu Kaicheng. Music: Nie Lihua, Cao Xuean. Sound: Zhang Baojian, Fei Xianjie. Cast: Li Wa as Yuxiang, Cui Weining as Gao Han, Shen Guanchu as Yanbing

Along China's border with Vietnam, three women soldiers are ambushed by Vietnamese soldiers. Two of the women are killed, and the third, Yuxiang, escapes into the forest. In the forest she meets Gao Han, a man who claims to be a PLA soldier. Later, Yuxiang meets Yanbing, another man claiming to be a PLA soldier who lost his way while pursuing some Vietnamese who had crossed into Chinese territory. She has trouble determining which, if either, is telling the truth. As the story develops, it turns out that Gao Han is the genuine PLA soldier and Yanbing a Vietnamese spy.

814. *The Green Wallet (Lu Se Qian Bao)*

1981. Changchun Film Studio. Color. 10 Reels. Direction: Sun Yu, Wang Qimin. Screenplay: Liu Houmin, Xiao Yixian. Cinematography: Wang Qimin, Han Dongxia. Art Direction: Liu Jinnai, Gao Tinglun. Music: Wu Damin. Sound: Chen Wenyuan. Cast: Liang Bing as Han Xiaoyuan, Hu Ao as the school principal, Zhu Decheng as Teacher Wu, Wang Zhiqiang Hu Ao as the old principal, Wei Li as Wildcat, Zuang Wenyin as Xin Hong

On a crowded Beijing bus, Han Xiaoyuan, a boy of about 13, steals a green wallet from an old man while a young man known as "Wildcat" covers him. When Han Xiaoyuan makes a second attempt in a restaurant, he is caught by Xin Hong, a young woman working there. For this he is sent to reform school. He does not behave well in reform school either, stealing peaches from the next door production team's tree, etc. Later, "Wildcat" gets Han to escape from the school by claiming the boy's mother is seriously ill, then forces Han to steal again. When caught, Han is very close to being declared incorrigible and being charged as an adult, but the school's old principal will not give up on him and requests the boy be released. His caring deeply moves Han, and from then on the boy really straightens up, working hard and making good grades. Some time later, he happens upon "Wildcat" engaging in illegal activity, and helps catch him red-handed.

815. *Grieved Gunfighter (Bei Qing Qiang Shou)*

1994. Shanghai Film Studio. Color. Letterboxed. 10 Reels. Direction: Yu Benzheng, Wu Tianci. Screenplay: Zhang Zuoyan, Wu Tianci, Lan Zhiguang. Cinematography: Shen Miaorong. Art Direction: Chen Chunlin. Sound: Gong Dejun. Costume: Zhang Xuelin. Makeup: Zhu Peizhen. Cast: Zhou Lijing as Leng Yixiao, He Ling as Dong Aoran, Gao Ying as Xiao Lan, Pan Jie as Chen Lina, Huang Daliang as Xu Daxiong, Tan Pengfei as Xiao Jierong, Tan Zengwei as A Si, A Weiguo as A Dong

In pre-war Shanghai, Japanese agents prepare for the conflict to come. Their first priority is to eliminate the powerful triads which control the city and its commerce. They draw up a plan to stir up trouble between two rival lieutenants of the Tianlong triad, Leng Yixiao and Dong Aoran. Their machinations result in the triad's boss Xiao Xierong expelling Leng from the triad. Dong then marries the boss's daughter Xiao Lan, Leng's former lover. Leng is helped by woman reporter Chen Lina, who gets him a job as a bodyguard. When someone starts a battle between the Tianlongs and another triad, with many deaths on both sides, Leng is blamed for it. Beginning to suspect that someone is setting him up, Leng sets out to find who is really to blame. He fights with Dong Aoran, who he suspects. At last, Leng finds that the helpful reporter Chen Lina is really a Japanese agent, and the whole thing was planned. Everyone who survived the triad war, including Leng and Xiao Lan, are shot by the Japanese.

816. *Growing Up in Battle (Zhan Dou Li Cheng Zhang)*

1957. August First Film Studio. B & W. 10 Reels. Direction: Yan Jizhou, Sun Min. Screenplay: Hu Ke, based on his stage play of the same title. Cinematography: Jian Shi. Art Direction: Kou Honglie. Music: Gong Zhiwei. Sound: He Baoding. Cast: Tian Dan as Zhao Tiezhu/Zhao Gang, Li Jian as Tiezhu's wife, Jia Liu as Zhao Zhizhong, Zhang Shuming as Zhao Shitou, Wang Chengyou as the young Zhao Shitou, Wu Zhenjun as Yang Youde, Wang Xiaozhong as Yang Yaozu

In 1937, in Shanxi province, governed by the warlord Yan Xishan, farmer Zhao Zhizhong's land is forcibly expropriated by landlord Yang Youde and his son Yang Yaozu with the support of government officers. With no future, Zhao commits suicide. His son Zhao Tiezhu sets fire to the landlord's house, then leaves his home village. Fearing the landlord's revenge, his wife also flees the village with their son, changing the boy's name to Shitou, or "Little Rock." For years, they drift around China living as beggars. Ten years later, the son, now an adult, joins the Eighth Route Army and is assigned to battalion headquarters as a journalist. At first he does not recognize battalion commander Zhao Gang but eventually discovers the latter is his father Zhao Tiezhu. After the liberation of their native village, father and son recognize each other and the family is reunited.

817. *Gu Shangzhao's Story (Gu Shang Zhao Wai Zhuan)*

1989. Chinese Film Company and Hong Kong Dajie Company Co-Production. Color. Wide Screen. 9 Reels. Direction: Liang Zhiyong. Screenplay: Zhao Shunqi, Li Dongqun. Cinematography: Liang Zhiyong, Tian Jianmin. Art Direction: Xiao Chuan. Music: Shi Xin. Sound: Liang Zhiyong. Cast: Hou Yueqiu as Gu Shangzhao, Wang Hongtao as Sheng Tiefu, Shu Yaosuan as Gao Qiu

A story of rebellion during the late 11th century, centering on a thief who becomes a rebel leader.

818. *Guan Hanqing (Guan Han Qing)*

1960. Haiyan Film Studio And Pearl River Film Studio Co-production. Color. 14 Reels. Direction: Xu Tao. Screenplay: Guangdong Puren Yue Opera Company, based on the stage play of the same title by Tian Han. Cinematography: Chen Zhengxiang. Art Direction: Ding Cheng. Music: Guangdong Yue Opera Company Orchestra. Sound: Wu Ying. Cast: Ma Shizeng as Guan Hanqing, the "Red Thread Lady" as Zhu Lianxiu, Wen Juefei as Ye Hepu, Tan Yuzheng as Zhu Xiaolan's mother-in-law, Lin Xiaoqun as Sai Lianxiu, Shao Kunlun as Wang Zhu

In the Yuan (Mongol) Dynasty the regime is very oppressive and feudal, and the lives of the Chinese people are miserable. The great dramatist Guan Hanqing (c1210–c1298) witnesses the case of Zhu Xiaolan, a young woman executed after her conviction on trumped-up charges. Outraged, and feeling it his duty to expose the truth, he writes a drama called "Douer's False Case" based on her story, with the famous singing and dancing performer Zhu Lianxiu in the part of Douer. Although the play meets with warm public approval, its criticism of official corruption angers the emperor's aides. They demand the play's revision, but Guan Hanqing and Zhu Lanxiu both refuse. For refusing, they are sentenced to death and imprisoned. While in prison, Guan and Zhu fall in love. The massive public protest of their imprisonment results in the court commuting the couple's death sentence. Instead, the court orders Guan Hanqing exiled to South China, and Zhu Lanxiu ordered to be a singer and dancer at court. Her pleas to accompany Guan are denied, and the couple tearfully say farewell.

819. *The Guandong Hero (Guan Dong Da Xia)*

1987. Changchun Film Studio. Color. 10 Reels. Direction: Bai Dezhang, Xu Xunxing. Screenplay: Wang Zonghan, Bai Dezhang. Cinematography: Guo Lin, Zhang Zhongwei. Art Direction: Liu Huanxing. Music: Fan Weiqiang. Sound: Yi Wenyu, Fang Yongmin. Cast: Liu Wei as Guan Yuntian, Yu Lan as Er Lanzhi, Li Xiangang as Gao Yucheng, Pan Demin as Guo Jianglong, Yan Bide as Fu Diancheng

In northeast China in the 1930s, a village lies sleeping on a bitterly cold night. Among these is Guan Yuntian, a hunter. Suddenly, landlord Gao Shijia and Japanese soldiers attack the village, killing many of the people and burning their homes to the ground. Guan's family is among those killed. Seeking revenge for both himself and his country, Guan Yuntian organizes the village hunters into a group of forest bandits. His reputation earns him the title, the "Guandong Hero" (Guandong being another name for northeast China). His band wages guerrilla warfare against the Japanese and kill collaborators who help the invaders, which greatly harasses the enemy. Unfortunately Guan's struggle ends in tragedy.

820. *Guandong Heroine (Guan Dong Nu Xia)*

1989. Changchun Film Studio. Color. Letterboxed. 9 Reels. Direction: Bai Dezhang, Xu Xunxing. Screenplay: Zhang Xiaotian, Li Jie. Cinematography: Gao Hongbao. Art Direction: Wang Di. Music: Fan Weiqiang. Sound: Zhang Wen. Cast: Yu Lan as the Guandong heroine, Liu Wei as Lei Sihu

When the Japanese invade China in the early 1930s, a group of their soldiers rape a Chinese girl. After the attack, she is given sanctuary by some "greenwoods bandits." Several years pass, and the girl has become a superior kung fu artist, and now leader of the greenwoods bandits, which she has converted to an anti–Japanese guerrilla force. Local people call her the "Guandong heroine," for their frequent successful raids on the invaders. (Guandong being another name for northeast China.) Lei Sihu, one of the heroine's lieutenants, grows to love her and burns to avenge her. So he has his men kidnap and gang-rape a Japanese girl. The Guandong heroine decides that while Lei Sihu's action is a capital crime which cannot be pardoned, since he did it out of love for her she will marry him, then have him executed three days later. The couple are married and spend two days together. But on the third day, the Japanese attack the guerrilla base and kill most of the people there. The Guandong heroine and Lei Sihu are captured and executed by the Japanese.

821. *Guangzhou Story (Guang Zhou Gu Shi)*

1995. Pearl River Film Company. Color. Letterboxed. Direction: Meng Hongfeng. Screenplay: Kong Liang, Zeng Yingfeng. Cinematography: Zhang Yuan. Art Direction: Xu Xiaoli, Tan Xiaogang. Music: Li Fang. Cast: Tao Huiming as Xiao Lingmei, Guo Yong as A Qiang, Chen Xiaoyi as A Wen, Pan Yu as San Gupo, Pan Muzhen as Guifang

Xiao Lingmei is an actress in the Guangdong style of Chinese opera. One of her admirers is construction worker Awen, a childhood friend of hers. Lingmei marries and has a daughter. Later on, her husband abandons her. Several years pass, and Lingmei, no longer an actress, learns that the building she lives in will be razed for new construction. Worried about where she and her daughter will live, she goes to see the head of the construction crew, and it turns out to be Awen. He gives a lot of help to Lingmei and her daughter, for he has never stopped loving her, although he is now married to someone else. Life goes on.

822. *Guardians of Peace (He Ping Bao Wei Zhe)*

1950. Beijing Film Studio. B & W. 6 Reels. Direction: Shi Lan. Screenplay: Hu Ke, adapted from the novel "Six A.M.," by Liu Baiyu (1916–). Cinematography: Su Heqing and Liu Shide. Art Direction: Wang Yongjie. Music: Wang Hua, Kuo Xing and Yao Jingxin. Sound: Gao Min. Cast: Ge Zhenbang as Battalion Commander Sheng, Liu Jia as the Division Commander, Wang Shui as the Commissar, Yang Zhenqing as Zhao Zhuzhi, Luo Hui as the first soldier, Bai Ping as the second soldier, Xia Baocun as the third soldier, Zhu Xing as the fourth soldier, Zhang Shihua as the medical corpsman, Xie Guocheng as the radioman

On October 1, 1949, as a certain PLA division pursues remnants of the enemy fleeing south, Battalion Commander Sheng begins thinking seriously of leaving the army to enjoy the bright, post-liberation future. But with the aid of his division commander and some part-time education, he comes to realize that Chi-

ang Kaishek and his American allies are unlikely to accept defeat; therefore, the only way to consolidate victory and safeguard peace is through military power. Just then, the division commander learns that the enemy is preparing to blow up a key bridge after fleeing across it, so he orders Sheng to capture the bridge before 5 AM, to ensure that the PLA can continue pursuit. In the fierce battle which follows, Sheng's best fighter Zhao Zhuzhi is seriously wounded, but his battalion is eventually victorious, allowing the main PLA force to cross the bridge and wipe out the remaining enemy force.

823. *Guarding the Fruits of Victory (Bao Wei Sheng Li Guo Shi)*

1950. Northeast Film Studio. B & W. 10 Reels. Directors: Yi Ling, Li Enjie. Screenplay: Yu Shan, based on an original work by Gao Yuan. Cinematography: Li Guanghui. Set Design: Li Enjie. Music: Zhang Dicang. Sound: Zhang Jiake, Gao Dao, Sha Yuan. Costume: Wang Huaiguo. Makeup: Li Jingwen, Li Shouren. Cast: Liu Chunlin as Liang Yongqing, Che Yi as Chun Ni, Suli as Kou Yucheng, Li Huiying as Big Jun, Cheng Peicai as Zhang the Ox

In 1946, the Nationalist-Communist peace agreement falls apart, and civil war erupts. In one liberated rural area, Nationalist soldiers loot a village and take several pro–Communist farmers prisoners. They are saved by the PLA, and several of them, including Liang Yongqing and Kou Yucheng, decide to join the PLA to safeguard the freedoms they had struggled so hard to obtain. But on a reconnaissance mission, the inexperienced Liang fires his weapon too soon, alerting the enemy and causing the wounding of another soldier. With the help of Zhang the Ox, a veteran, Liang becomes a well-trained, good soldier, finally distinguishing himself in battle and capturing one of the enemy's commanders. After the liberation of the whole nation, the army sends Liang, Kou and Zhang for advanced military training.

824. *Guerrillas on the Plain (Ping Yuan You Ji Dui)*

1955. Changchun Film Studio. B & W. 10 Reels. Direction: Su Li and Wu Zhaodi. Screenplay: Xing Ye and Yu Shan. Cinematography: Li Guanghui. Set Design: Wang Guizhi. Music: Che Ming. Sound: Jue Jingxiu. Cast: Guo Zhenqing as Li Xiangyang, Wang Enqi as Guo Xiaobei, Zhang Ying as the District Branch

Guangzhou Story. **A Wen (Chen Xiaoyi) again meets Xiao Lingmei (Tao Huiming), the great love of his life, too late for them to have a happy ending. 1995. Pearl River Film Company.**

Commander, Du Defu as Hou Dazhang, Ma Shida as Sun Changqing, Jin Li as Dacheng, Fang Hua as the Japanese Commander, An Zhenjiang as Yang Laozong, Pan Demin as Lao Mei

In the fall of 1943, as the invading Japanese army prepares to carry out "mopping up" operations in North China, the base of anti-Japanese resistance, a guerrilla troop led by Li Xiangyang moves into a village in the flatlands behind Japanese lines. Their mission is to tie up the Japanese forces there. Tipped off by Yang Laozong, a collaborationist landlord, the Japanese search the village, but Li moves the guerrilla troop and local people into underground tunnels to protect the villagers and to carry out guerrilla operations. At a time when the guerrilla force is out of the town, Yang Laozong helps the Japanese find an entrance to the tunnel. They force the villagers out of it, kill some of them, and confiscate the food stored there. Li Xiangyang disguises himself and reenters the city, where he burns the enemy's grain and kills the Chinese traitor Yang Laozong. He then organizes the guerrilla troop in an attack on the Japanese troops in the village, and wipes them out.

825. *Guerrillas on the Plain (Ping Yuan You Ji Dui)*

1974. Changchun Film Studio. Color. 11 Reels. Direction: Wu Zhaodi, Chang Zhenhua. Screenplay: "Guerrillas On the Plain" Writing Team. Cinematography: Shu Xiaoyan, Wang Qimin. Art Direction: Liu Xuerao, Wu Qiwen. Music: Lei Zhengbang. Cast: Li Tiejun as Li Xiangyang, Song Xiaoying as Cui Ping, Gu Zhi as Meng Kao, Liu Yanjing as Mrs. Li, Li Fengping as the regimental commander, Yang Zhonglu as Guo Xiaobei, Nian Fan as Hou Dazhang

This is a remake of the same studio's 1955 black and white movie of the same title.

826. *Guerrillas on the Railway (Tie Dao You Ji Dui)*

1956. Shanghai Film Studio. B & W. 9 Reels. Direction: Zhao Ming. Screenplay: Liu Zhixia, based on the novel of the same title by Liu Zhixia. Cinematography: Feng Shizhi. Art Direction: Zhang Hancheng. Music: Lu Qiming. Sound: Lu Zhongbo. Cast: Cao Huiqu as Liu Hong, Qin Yi as Fanglin's wife, Feng Ji as Li Zheng, Feng Qi as Wang Qiang, Feng Xiao as Xiao Po, Deng Nan as Lu Han

Guerrillas on the Plain. Li Xiangyang (Guo Zhenqing) leads a guerrilla brigade into a flatlands village behind Japanese lines. 1955. Changchun Film Studio.

During World War II, a guerrilla troop operates along the south Shandong railway. Under the leadership of their commander Liu Hong and Political Commissar Li Zheng, they specialize in sabotaging Japanese rail transport, harassing enemy troops and coordinating the main anti-Japanese forces in battle. The Japanese, along with Nationalist collaborators, attempt to surround and annihilate the guerrillas. Liu Hong is wounded, and while he recuperates in the home of a widow called Fanglin's wife, they fall in love. Frustrated with their failure to wipe out the guerrillas, the Japanese burn several villages and take many civilians hostage, including Fanglin's widow. This infuriates Liu Hong, and he rashly decides to have it out with the enemy in a decisive battle. Li Zheng hurries to dissuade him from this, but is wounded on the way. In the battle, the outnumbered guerrillas are cut to pieces and only a strategic retreat saves them from total annihilation. They withdraw to the relative safety of Lake Weishan. There, they enlarge their forces and hold out against a subsequent attack. The Japanese commander commits all his forces, Japanese and Chinese,

to surrounding Lake Weishan, but Liu Hong leads a breakout of the guerrillas. Just before the final victory of World War II, Li Zheng rejoins the troop. The railway guerrillas defeat the collaborators, free Fanglin's widow and the other prisoners, and attack the fleeing Japanese invaders.

Remade in 1995 by the Emei Film Studio, with the title "Flying Tiger Brigade."

827. *The Guest from California (Jia Zhou Lai Ke)*

1986. Nanhai Film Company. Color. Wide Screen. 9 Reels. Direction: Liu Guanxiong. Screenplay: Qi Jianren. Cinematography: Liu Yuefei. Art Direction: Rao Weiquan. Music: Wang Ming. Sound: Lin Guang. Costume: Zhu Jingyi. Makeup: Ming Xiaomei, Yin Xiaoxiao. Cast: Wu Haiyan as Mei Xiuyun, Gan Zelan as Ann, Liu Guanxiong as Fang Ruishan, Wang Xiaoyan as Mei Yuzhen, Qi Mengshi as Teacher Chen, Dianne as Helen

Guerrillas on the Railway. **During World War II, the widow Fanglin's wife (Qin Yi) finds love with railway guerrilla troop leader Liu Hong (Cao Huiqu). 1956. Shanghai Film Studio.**

828. *Guest with a Sword (Wang Fu Dao Ke)*

1990. Changchun Film Studio. Color. Wide Screen. 9 Reels. Direction: Liu Zhongmin, Ji Shimin. Screenplay: Yi Ming, Wen Dong, Dong Lin. Cinematography: Li Juntun, Lin Boquan. Art Direction: Guo Yansheng. Music: Lei Lei. Sound: Zhang Fenglu. Cast: Jing Weimin as Qian Bingzhang, Zhao Yang as Hong Tao, Tao Qin as Tang Xiaomei

Towards the end of the Ming dynasty (c1640), a child is on the throne and the court is dominated by a crafty sycophant, powerful Qian Bingzhang. Qian and his network of spies are challenged by honest Prince Cheng, supported by a small force of folk heroes led by Hong Tao.

829. *The Guide (Xiang Dao)*

1979. Tianshan Film Studio. Color. 10 Reels. Direction: Wang Xinyu, Zhen Dongtian. Screenplay: Deng Pu. Cinematography: Meng Qingpeng, Ma Yanji. Art Direction: Li Jushan. Music: Chen Xin. Sound: Zhang Ruikun, Zhang Xicheng. Cast: Abulimiti as Yipulayin, Gesha as Tailai, Tuyigong as Biqikefu, Abuliahti as Bawudong

Towards the end of the 19th century, European explorer Tailai comes to the town of Kesheger in Xinjiang looking for a Chinese artifact more than 1,000 years old. He bribes the Manchu governor of Xinjiang to let him search an ancient desert town for the legendary article. An old man named Yipulayin is assigned to guide them. In order to protect the Chinese antique, Yipulayin deliberately misleads them, having them travel around the desert in circles, burning out their energies. When the ruse is discovered, the old man is left out in the sun without water to die. Tailai is successful in stealing a map of the ancient town where the artifact is supposed to be hidden, but the map is stolen from him by a Russian officer and sent to St. Petersburg. A decade later, a Russian army unit returns to Xinjiang and prepares to cross the Talimu River on the Sino-Soviet border. Yipulayin's grandson Bawudong destroys their boat for revenge. After liberation, Bawudong volunteers to be a guide for a PLA prospecting team moving toward the Talimu River. But a group of Russians ambush him. Outnumbered, Bawudong goes down fighting.

830. *Guitar Music (Ji Ta Hui Xuan Qu)*

1986. Guangxi Film Studio. Color. 10 Reels. Direction: Zhang Ning. Screenplay: Wang Lian. Cinematography: Liao Fan, Mo Shaoxiong. Art Direction: Li Qining, Xu Zhaozuang. Music: Su Yue. Sound: Han Weijun. Cast: Xu Zhongquan as Town Administrator Jia, Yu Fei as Wu Wenpei, Zhu Kexin as Qiu Ying

Wu Wenpei, a young man who loves to play guitar, is also a skilled photographer. He helps his village attain prosperity by making advertisements for the bamboo products the village makes. However, conservative village chief Jia thinks this is somehow an economic crime, and he forces Wu to leave the village. The sister of Wu's girlfriend is engaged to a man who writes television screenplays, and he invites Wu to play in a TV show which tells the guitar player's story. The film ends with village chief Jia inviting Wu Wenpei back to the village as manager of the bamboo products factory.

831. *Guixiangou Village (Gui Xian Gou)*

1988. Changchun Film Studio. Color. 9 Reels. Direction: Xiao Guiyun, Li Qiankuan. Screenplay: Li Jie. Cinematography: Sun Guangwen. Art Direction: Wang Xingwen. Music: Chen Shouqian. Sound: Yi Wenyu. Cast: Liu Tingrao as Tang Zhendong, Xu Zhongquan as Loudspeaker Cheng, Ruan Furen as County Director Liu, Wang Lihua as Yehuaxiang, Xia Hui as Hu Banxian, Yang Xiaojun as Chunshui, Liu Feng as Qitou

The lovely village of Guixiangou has grown prosperous from the excellent ginseng it produces. After village chief Tang Zhendong takes over management of the local ginseng company, he allocates funds to restore the local temple and invites all the village's former residents to come back and worship there. When his elderly mother falls ill, he calls upon the "spirits" to heal her, rather than a doctor. One of the people returning to the village to worship is a woman who had years before been the wife of the local elementary school teacher, a man persecuted to death during the Cultural Revolution. She is shocked to find her late husband's old school in a deplorable state of disrepair while the temple is so well-kept, and that a young man who greatly resembles her husband, probably her own lost son, is totally illiterate. She reports her findings to the county director. Soon after, Tang Zhendong's mother dies, and when the county director visits to investigate the woman's charges, he is aghast at the scale and grandeur of the funeral Tang holds for his mother. The county director criticizes Tang for his neglect of education, and the woman visitor donates all her considerable savings to the local school.

832. *Gun, Shooting from Behind (Qiang, Chong Bei Hou Da Lai)*

1987. Beijing Film Studio. Color. 8 Reels. Direction: Liu Qiuling. Screenplay: Lin Amian. Cinematography: Yan Junsheng. Art Direction: Ning Lanxin. Music: Li Baoshu. Sound: Wang Sheng. Cast: Yan Wunjun as Yanjian, Xiliwan as Yubo, Ma Shuchao as Shanbing, Hu Ran as Bohan, Zhao Zheng as Bai Lang, Wang Jie as the mute

During his summer break from school, Yanjian, a 12-year-old Dai nationality boy, goes to visit his grandfather in a village on China's southern border. One day, he and his grandfather go into the forest to rescue a wounded mother bear, and the two become separated. In the forest, Yanjian encounters a young woman called Sister Yubo struggling with a criminal. The boy intervenes to help, and later learns there is a drug-smuggling gang operating in the forest. He involves himself in the anti-smuggling effort and discovers the identities of the gang members. But when he goes to report what he has learned, a covert member of the gang called Shanbing shoots him in the back.

833. *Gunfire at the Secret Bureau (Bao Mi Ju De Qiang Sheng)*

1979. Changchun Film Studio. B & W. 12 Reels. Direction: Chang Yan. Screenplay: Zhen Quan and Jin Deshun, based on the novel "Battling the Enemy At His Headquarters" by Lu Zheng. Cinematography: Chang Yan, Gao Hongbao. Art Direction: Wang Guizhi. Music: Lou Zhanghou. Sound: Tong Zongde. Cast: Chen Shaoze as Liu Xiaochen, Xiang Mei as Shi Xiuyin, Ni Zhenghua as Zhang Zhongnian, Song Jingcang as Leng Tiexin, Wang Baohua as Yang Yulin, Li Qimin as Chang Liang

During the Chinese Civil War in the late 1940s, with Shanghai still under Nationalist government control, a Communist working under cover in the government's intelligence bureau is betrayed by a traitor and killed. The Communists then assign Liu Xiaochen to infiltrate the bureau, but when he tries to contact another Communist agent Shi Xiuyin, he is recognized by the traitor Huang Xiancai. Liu immediately shoots and kills Huang, then shoots and wounds himself to fool investigators. Various tricks are set up to test him, but all fail, and he eventually wins the trust of Zhang Zhongnian, the bureau's chief of intelligence. Liu gets Shi Xiuyin out of danger, and then exploits an internal bureau dispute to aid the Communist cause. Just before Shanghai is liberated, Liu Xiaochen finds Zhang Zhongnian's secret plans for the city's defense and makes a successful escape.

834. *The Gunman from Paris (Ba Li Lai De Qiang Shou)*

1989. Fujian Film Studio. Color. Wide Screen. 9 Reels. Director: Zhang Xing. Screenplay: Wang Subing. Cinematography: Wang Xili, Zhen Wencang. Art Direction: Han Qinguo, Gao Dalin. Sound: Liu Tonghe. Cast: Xu Yajun as Can Ke, Jiang Shan as Xia Zhu

When the Germans occupy Paris early in World War II, they intern a visiting Chinese professor and his son as enemy aliens, sending them to separate camps. The son, Can Ke, later escapes and tries to find his father. He meets one of his father's former students, who tells him the professor was murdered by a German prison camp commander named Neumann. Can Ke makes his way back to China alone. When he gets back, he rescues a group of local people led by a girl named Xia Zhu. He joins them in their anti–Japanese guerrilla actions. Later, he hears that a nearby Japanese military unit has a German liaison officer with them, a man named Neumann. After a complicated series of investigations, Can Ke learns the officer is indeed the same one who killed his father. He sets out for revenge, and at last encounters the German in a bloody fight to the finish. At the critical moment, Xia Zhu intervenes to help Can Ke kill his enemy. Can Ke and Xia Zhu leave the area together.

835. *Gun Shots from the Wasteland (Huang Dao Qiang Sheng)*

1986. Zhejiang Film Studio. Color. Wide Screen. 9 Reels. Direction: Jiang Haiyang. Screenplay: Zhao Fengkai. Cinematography: Zhang Yongjiang, Zhang Dongdong. Cast: Yuan Yuan as Jiang Jieming, Fu Lili as Yu Ping, Sun

Chun as Lu Jian, Chou Yongli as Liu Yulin, Hong Danqing as Guan Xiaohu

836. *Gunshots in the Suolun River Valley (Suo Lun He Gu De Qiang Sheng)*

1985. August First Film Studio. Color. 10 Reels. Direction: Jing Mukui. Screenplay: Li Yinjie. Cinematography: Gao Jiuling. Art Direction: Cui Qinsheng. Music: Zhen Qiufeng. Sound: Xiang Zhiliang. Cast: Zhang Guomin as Xian Wengong, Tao Zeru as Wang Ziwei, Zhao Jun as Liu Mintian, Zhao Ying as Li Luolan

When young military officer Xian Wengong joins his new unit, he immediately sees several areas where the company needs improvement. He suggests various changes to Company Commander Wang Ziwei, but Wang takes offense, misunderstanding Xian's motives. In time, Wang comes to realize his own lack of expertise in training troops is the cause of the company's shortcomings, and he puts Xian in charge of training. The company improves markedly.

837. *Gunshots on the Prairie (Chao Yuan Qiang Sheng)*

1980. Tianshan Film Studio. Color. 10 Reels. Direction: Meng Qingpeng, Song Jie. Screenplay: Shen Kai, Xia Zhixin. Cinematography: Liu Yongshi. Art Direction: Li Jushan. Music: Waliraola, Chen Xin, Zhu Hengqian. Sound: Zhang Xicheng. Cast: Azhati as Asilebaike, Fadiha as Kalipa, Mutelifu as Hali, Halunbaike as Suerdan

One dark night, a horse runs wildly toward the Sino-Soviet border, the sound of gunshots behind it. The horse's rider is Asilebaike, a man abducted and taken across the border by Soviet agents when he was prospecting on the prairie. He has tried many times without success to escape and return to China, why is he so successful this time? His original abduction was part of a plot by the Soviets to provide cover for Suertan, a Soviet spy operating among the prairie people. After Asilebaike was safely out of the way Suertan had used false pretenses to gain the trust of Asilebaike's father Hali and then marry Asilebaike's fiancee Kaliba. After Asilebaike returns, Suertan spreads many rumors about him among the people, but under the leadership of the county Party committee, they finally realize what is going on. When Suertan sees that he is about to be exposed, he plans to abduct some people and livestock back across the border. Asile-baike sees through the plot, but cannot persuade others, including his father, to believe him. With no other choice, he goes after Suertan himself and shoots and kills the spy on the border.

838. *Gunslinging Singer (Dai Qiang De Ge Nu)*

1993. Changchun Film Studio. Color. Letterboxed. 9 Reels. Direction: Xu Yunsheng. Screenplay: Cao Zhaohong. Cinematography: Su Weiping. Art Direction: Li Taiping. Music: Fan Weiqiang. Sound: Wang Baosheng. Costume: Yang Shu. Makeup: Pan Li. Cast: Tian Ming as Diao Yali, Yu Yunhe as Zhang Yeshe, Li Yongtian as Lin Guoxiong, Zhang Xuejie as Guo Shaotang, Li Yinqiu as Jin Yanmei, Zhang Jibo as Gao Da, Zhang Zihong as Zhenni

China's national police headquarters is informed by Interpol that a Hong Kong drug ring is moving into a South China city. Hong Kong officer Zhang Yese and mainland detective Gao Da are assigned to a joint operation, coordinated by Interpol officer Ling Li, a woman who goes under cover as a night club singer. They catch the head of the ring, and destroy his organization. Ling Li is wounded during the last shoot-out, but she and Zhang fall in love during the investigation.

839. *Hai Rui Reprimands the Emperor (Hai Rui Ma Huang Di)*

1985. Pearl River Film Studio. Color. Wide Screen. 10 Reels. Direction: Xu Qiang. Screenplay: Jin Yang Writing Group. Cinematography: Li Ping, Xie Yongyi. Art Direction: Qin Hongyi. Music: Zhang Hong. Sound: Li Bojian. Cast: Tao Jin as the Emperor, Du Xiongwen as Hai Rui, Li Juanjuan as Hua Feihua, Wang Xiaozhong as Wang Jin, Xu Dongfang as Shen Shien

During the reign of the Ming Emperor Jiajing (r1522–1567), the emperor is obsessed with longevity, which leads many to take advantage of him, including Taoist priest Wang Jin. The emperor's obsession leads him to construct a spirit platform at great expense and considerable disruption to the people's lives. Minister Hai Rui witnesses how the emperor's corruption is hurting the people, so he speaks out on their behalf. He writes and submits a memorial to the throne listing the consequences of the emperor's behavior. The people all admire this great minister for his brave action, but the emperor is outraged and wants to have Hai Rui put to death. But when the people collectively petition on Hai Rui's behalf, the sentence is commuted and Hai Rui imprisoned. In 1567, the Jiajing Emperor suddenly dies from eating a so-called spirit drug.

840. *Hai Xia (Hai Xia)*

1975. Beijing Film Studio. Color. 12 Reels. Direction: Qian Jiang, Chen Huaikai, Wang Haowei. Screenplay: Xie Tieli, based on the novel "Island Militia Woman" by Li Ruqin. Cinematography: Qian Jiang, Wang Zhaoling, Li Chengsheng. Art Direction: Chen Yiyun, Yang Zhanshuan. Music: Wang Ming. Sound: Liu Shida. Cast: Wu Haiyan as Hai Xia, Cai Min as Hai Xia as a child, Zhao Lian as Supervisor Fang, Tian Chong as De Shun, Chen Qiang as Wang Fa, Yan Zenhe as Shuang He, Li Lin as Chen Zhanao

Before liberation, a fishing couple on Tongxin Island abandon their newborn daughter at sea, but she is fortunately rescued by a fisherman called Uncle Liu, who names the baby Hai Xia. After liberation, with help and education from the Party, Hai Xia organizes the women of Tongxin Island into a militia brigade. Past resident of the island Chen Zhanao, who had fled to Taiwan just before the island's liberation, is now sent back as a spy. After secretly landing on the island, he does whatever he can to hamper construction of the island's defenses. Hai Xia calmly analyzes the complicated situation and launches an investigation. With close cooperation between her brigade and the PLA, she finally uncovers Chen's spy ring and in a gun battle kills Chen Zhanao. The smashing of the spy ring halts the enemy's conspiracy to invade the island.

841. *Hail the Judge (Jiu Pin Zhi Ma Guan) (alternate title: Bai Mian Bao Qing Tian)*

1994. Yunnan Nationalities Film Studio, Yongsheng Film Production Corporation Ltd., Shanghai Film Studio Co-Production. Color. Letterboxed. 10 Reels. Direction: Wang Jing. Cinematography: Zhong Zhiwen. Art Direction: Mo Shaoqi. Music: Hu Weili. Costume: Wen Runxiong, He Shaoying. Makeup: Wen Runling, Zhu Huifang. Cast: Zhou Xingchi as Bao Longxing, Zhang Ming as Qin Xiaolian, Wu Mengda as Bao Youwei, Zhong Liti, Xu Jingjiang, Cai Shaofeng, Ni Xing, Fan Qiongdan, Cheng Dong, Liang Rongzhong

Hai Xia. Hai Xia (Wu Haiyan, right) organizes the women of Tongxin Island into a militia brigade. 1975. Beijing Film Studio.

Bao Longxing was taught to be honest and to battle injustice wherever he finds it. When he grows up, his family buys a low-ranking title for him. He learns of a person being falsely accused, but standing up for the accused lands Bao himself in prison. He breaks out of jail and goes to Beijing to appeal the case. At last, orders clearing him arrive, and justice is served. Bao Longxing resigns his title, and leaves with his faithful wife Wu Haoti to start a new life.

842. *Half Flame, Half Brine (Yi Ban Huo Yan, Yi Ban Hai Shui)*

1989. Beijing Film Studio. Color. 9 Reels. Letterboxed. Direction: Xia Gang. Screenplay: Wang Shuo, Ye Daying, based on the novel by Wang Shuo (1958–). Cinematography: Li Tian. Art Direction: Huo Jianqi. Music: Li Lifu. Sound: Wu Ling. Cast: Luo Gang as Zhang Ming, Ji Ling as Wu Di, Gao Jie as Hu Yin

A young man named Zhang Ming, something of a charming ne'er-do-well, meets attractive female university student Wu Di. Enchanted by Zhang's cynicism and humor, the innocent girl falls hard for him. But to Zhang

Ming she is just another affair, one of a succession of women in his life. In despair and feeling betrayed, she seeks to get even with him by becoming a prostitute. Zhang Ming is deeply hurt by Wu's behavior. He regrets his past treatment of Wu Di, but it is too late, and she ends up a suicide. Zhang Ming lands in jail. Two years later, the prison authorities release him to a sanitarium, where he becomes acquainted with a girl who resembles Wu Di in every way.

843. *A Half Ink Stone (Jing Tan Hong Bai Hei)*

1992. Xi'an Film Studio. Color. Letterboxed. 9 Reels. Direction: Zhang Yumin. Screenplay: Ni Feng. Cinematography: Nie Tiemao. Art Direction: Liu Xinghou. Music: Tao Long. Cast: Liu Jie as Hong Yun, Wang Zhigang as Dongfang Ke, Yang Jing as Ouyang Yu, Bai Junjie as Zhong Jicang, Wang Guanghui as Hong Xiaobing, Chu Zhihong as Bai Dafa

Taiwan policewoman Hong Yun steals one half of an antique inkstone from a museum, then flees with it to the Chinese mainland, where she hopes to get the other half from her cousin Hong Xiaobing. Meanwhile, Taiwan special investigator Dongfang Ke, Hong Kong jeweler Zhong Jicang and Hong Kong triad boss Xia Jingjing all come to the mainland with the same idea in mind. Chinese PSB officer Ouyang Yu helps Dongfang defeat the others and recover both halves of the stone.

844. *Half of an Engagement Photo (Banzhang Dinghunzhao)*

1980. Shanghai Film Studio. Color. 4 Reels. Direction: Sha Jie. Screenplay: Collective, written by Tang Junhua. Cinematography: Jian Shuzhen, Wu Liekang. Art Direction: Pu Jingsun. Music: Zhang Linyi. Sound: Yang Liangkun, Jin Fugeng. Cast: Lu Qin as Qu Xinde, Chen Ye as Lanlan, Yu Zhenghuan as Qi Zhongqi, Yuan Lin as Young Pioneer member, Geng Shengzhi as the fat lady

Young Qu Xinde is going to see his girl friend Lanlan, a hospital nurse. They plan to see a play and then have their engagement photo taken. However, that day Qu Xinde follows a fat lady, a Young Pioneer member and a magician in order to cheat them out of theater tickets, an umbrella, etc. Later, when he is with Lanlan, these people all recognize him and publicly denounce his behavior. Although Qu Xinde and Lanlan have taken their engagement picture, it turns out to be only half a picture, because Lanlan realizes this man's true nature, angrily tears off her half and takes it away.

845. *Happiness (Xin Fu)*

1957. Tianma Film Studio. B & W. 10 Reels. Directors: Tian Ran and Fu Chaowu. Screenplay: Ai Mingzhi. Cinematography: Gu Wunhou. Art Direction: Xu Keji. Music: Zhang Linyi. Sound: Zhu Weigang. Makeup: Wang Kai. Cast: Han Fei as Wang Jiayou, Zhang Fa as Papa Hu, Feng Xiao as Liu Chuanhao, Wang Pei as Hu Shufeng, Shi Yuan as a gossip, Yang Hua as Party Secretary Qian

Wang Jiayou, a young machine shop worker, is influenced by capitalist thoughts. He lives a dissolute life, with no labor discipline, seeking only pleasure and the company of women, particularly that of Hu Shufeng, a young woman factory worker. But Hu is in love with Wang's good friend, a college secretary named Liu Chuanhao. At a party, Wang Jiayou's improper behavior causes a misunderstanding between Liu Chuanhao and Hu Shufeng and they break up. After that, Wang

Jiayou sends anonymous love letters to Hu Shufeng and makes a date to meet her at a club. Gossip that Wang Jiayou is after Hu Shufeng spreads quickly, and leads to an argument between Hu Shufeng and her father, because Hu Shufeng thinks the letters come from Liu Chuanhao. In front of the club, Wang Jiayou boldly declares his love to Hu Shufeng, but she ignores him, expecting Liu Chuanhao to arrive soon. In the end, the misunderstanding between Hu Shufeng and Liu Chuanhao is resolved, and they reconcile. Wang Jiayou is chastened a bit by the experience.

846. *Happiness Doesn't Come Automatically (Xin Fu Bu Shi Mao Mao Yu)*

1987. Shanghai Film Studio. Color. 10 Reels. Direction: Yu Jie. Screenplay: Zhang Li, Liang Xingmin. Cinematography: Kong Guoliang. Art Direction: Wu Weifei. Music: Cai Lu. Sound: Ni Zheng. Cast: Chen Rui as Liu Ming, Lin Xiaojie as Xu Minzhu, Yu Ya as Wang Youchun, Wang Zhongchao as the fat guy

In a south China Special Economic Zone, when a transport company lays off some of its workers, the newly unemployed gather together and decide to start their own business. They open a bar near the beach, and it becomes a popular tourist hangout. Later, they meet with a group laid off from another company, and jointly form a travel services center.

847. *Happiness Is Beside You (Xin Fu Zai Ni Shen Bian)*

1984. Hubei Film Studio. Color. Direction: Xiao Lang, Liu Shuan, Qiu Liping. Screenplay: Lu Xinger, Chen Kexiong. Cinematography: Wun Zhixian, Li Jichun. Art Direction: Chen Xiaoxia. Music: Li Wanli. Sound: Tang Rongchun, Hu Kaixiu. Cast: Wan Qiong as Rongrong, Lu Jun as Shu Cheng, Chen Butao as Zhao Guokai, Chen Xiaoyi as Xiao Diandian, Chen Maya as Qin Xin, Wu Suqing as Teacher Wu

Rongrong was sent to live in rural North China when she was 15, and 10 years later she marries Shu Cheng, a young man just accepted for college study. After graduation, Shu Cheng secures a job in the city as a journalist, and Rongrong travels to join him. She gets pregnant soon after she arrives, but also finds after a while that Shu Cheng's attitude toward her has grown colder. She has an abortion, moves out and enrolls in college to study English.

In college, Rongrong meets graduate student Zhao Guokai, who likes her very much. But when Zhao Guokai finds out she is married, and that she and her husband are separated, he urges her to reconcile with her husband. Meanwhile, Shu Cheng is not as happy as he expected, and although he tries to lose himself in his work, it does not help. One day, Zhao Guokai shows up at Shu Cheng's home. Zhao tells him how Rongrong misses him, and urges the husband to reconcile with her, to keep the happiness he already has. Rongrong and Shu Cheng get back together.

848. *Happiness Knocks at the Door (aka The In-Laws) (Xi Ying Men)*

1981. Shanghai Film Studio. Color. 11 Reels. Direction: Zhao Huanzhang. Screenplay: Xin Xianling. Cinematography: Peng Enli, Cheng Shiyu. Art Direction: Zhao Yixuan. Music: Yang Shaolu. Sound: Xie Guojie. Cast: Wang Shuqing as Wang Qiangyin, Wen Yujuan as Xue Shuilian, Wang Yumei as Mother, Zhang Liang as Chen Renwen, Hong Xueming as Chen Renfang, Ma Xiaowei as Chen Renwu

In a North China mountain village, Chen Renwu takes Xue Shuilian as his wife. She presents quite a contrast with his elder brother's wife Wang Qiangying, a selfish woman who tries to get all she can from her mother-in-law. With the arrival of the new bride, this extended family's situation grows more complex. Qianying wants the Chen brothers' younger sister out of the house, so she arranges a marriage for her although she already has a lover. When Qiangying embarrasses her husband by preparing good food for her husband, daughter and son, but gives poor food to her grandfather-in-law, he angrily slaps her. Qiangying leaves home and moves in with her mother, who supports her daughter, causing a big argument between the two families. The kind and unselfish Shulian provides some wise counsel to her sister-in-law, after which Qiangying apologizes to the grandfather. The family is happy again.

Best Picture, 1982 Hundred Flowers Awards.

Best Music Yang Shaolu, 1982 Golden Rooster Awards.

849. *Happiness Mansion (Suo Ming Xiao Yao Lou)*

1990. Beijing Film Studio. Color. Wide Screen. 10 Reels. Direction: Li Wenhua, Li Ni. Screenplay: Ke Zhangru, Wang Ruiyang. Cinematographer: Tu Jiakuan. Art Direction: Zhen Huiwen, Song Zhengshan. Music: Guo Wenjing. Sound (Dolby): Zhang Baojian. Cast: Wang Hongtao as Bai Xian, Wang Chi as Can Biao, Yang Fengyi as Can Er, Huang Guoqiang as Shen Long, Zhou Zhou as Bai Jifu, Wang Guier as Ling's

A complex tale of vengeance. During the reign of the Qing Tongzhi Emperor (1862–1875), high-ranking military official Bai Chong entertains lavishly at his mansion. His mansion compound is really an impregnable fortress, with very sophisticated security devices protecting it. Eighteen years earlier, Bai Chong had tricked a simple thief named Can Biao into killing another official, Wen Yuan. After the killing, Can took the murdered man's daughter and raised her as his own, calling her Can Er. Now he and the girl are dedicated to killing Bai Chong. Bai Chong himself took Wen Yuan's son and raised him as his own, calling him Bai Jifu. When the revenge-seekers finally are able to penetrate the compound's security, Bai Jifu captures and then rapes Can Er. When he finds out she is his own sister, his shame drives him to suicide. The grief-stricken Bai Chong lets down his guard and is killed by Can Er.

850. *Happiness of Farm Families (Nong Jia Le)*

1950. Shanghai Film Studio. B & W. 9 Reels. Direction: Zhang Ke. Screenplay: Sun Qian. Cinematography: Gu Wenhou. Music: Ge Yan. Cast: Zhang Fa as Zhang Laowu, Qing Yi as La Ying, Wei Yuping as Zhang Guobao, Bai Mu as Du Tiancheng, Wang Li as County Committee Member, Mo Chou as Zhang Laowu's wife, Zhong Xinghuo as the Village Head, Fu Huizhen as Du Tiancheng's wife

The liberated farmers of Dujia village receive their land allocations, and enthusiastically start farming for themselves. Among the villagers are Zhang Guobao, a recently demobilized war veteran, and his father Zhang Laowu, head of the village production team. The latter is very conservative in his thinking, trusting only the old ways of doing things. One of the new innovations he rejects is planting imported cotton varieties, which the government advocates. This puts him at odds with his son, who is enthusiastic about the imported varieties. Eventually the elder Zhang comes to see the superiority of this and other new things, and he helps convince other conservative farmers. The result is a bumper cotton harvest.

851. *Happiness on Top of Success (Jinshang Tian Hua)*

1962. Beijing Film Studio. B & W. 8 Reels. Direction: Xie Tie and Chen Fangqian. Screenplay: Xie Tie, Chen Fangqian, Chen Qicang and Luo Guoliang. Cinematography: Zhang Qinghua. Art Direction: Mo Renyi. Music: Tang Ke. Sound: Cai Jun. Cast: Han Fei as Duan Zhigao, Zhao Zhiyue as "Old Trouble-shooter," Tian Lie as "Old Pocket Watch," Chen Zhijian as "Broadcast" Qing, Ling Yuan as "Chubby," Chang He as Tieying. Wang Bing as Tieying's father, Huang Suying as Tieying's mother, Cao Changhuan as "Little Discoverer," Xiong Saisheng as "Broadcast"'s wife, Huang Zongluo as the traveller

The director of a small railway station who carries the nickname of "Old Trouble-shooter" falls for the director of a nearby people's commune, a woman called "Chubby." She also finds him attractive, but both are too shy to make their feelings known, so many opportunities are lost. When a new power generator project is begun in the area, "Old Trouble-shooter" joins in to help with the construction. When the project is almost finished, he begins talking in his sleep about his feelings for the woman, and is overheard by "Broadcast," his neighbor. The neighbor had always though the two would make a good match, so he goes at once to "Chubby's" home to talk to her. At the dedication ceremony for the new power project, the two shy people are married.

852. *Happy, Angry, Sad, Cheerful (Xi Nu Ai Le)*

1986. Changchun Film Studio. Color. 9 Reels. Direction: Qin Bosheng, Qiao Keji. Screenplay: Jiao Shiyu. Cinematography: Xing Eryou. Art Direction: Wang Jiru. Music: Zhang Qianyi. Sound: Wang Fei, Gu Xiaolian. Cast: Chen Zhifeng as Chen Ao, Tang Jing as Miao Xiang, Li Xuliang as Miao Jiangong, Sui Jingying as Yang Cagu, Shu Yaoxuan as Yan Min, Xu Jinzen as Zhou Yinzhi

Everyone at the Beigang City medical equipment plant is shocked at the mysterious disappearance of one of its workers, Chen Ao.

Chen is a bright and ambitious young man who in a period of reform was making frequent suggestions and proposals for improving the plant's poor sales. Some people suspect plant manager Miao Jiangong: Miao never supported the young man's ideas, and in addition strongly disapproved of Chen dating the manager's daughter. But then word comes that Chen Ao is safe in a hospital, rescued by a boat after he jumped into the river to rescue a child. Chen Ao's courageous act draws considerable attention, and the city's deputy mayor comes to the plant for a visit. The official notes the many problems that exist there, and declares his support for Chen's suggested reforms. The plant manager begins to change his attitude, and at last he and his wife approve of their daughter's relationship with Chen.

853. *Happy Bachelors (Kuai Le De Dan Shen Han)*

1983. Shanghai Film Studio. Color. 11 Reels. Direction: Song Chong. Screenplay: Liang Xingmin, Yang Shiwen. Cinematography: Zhang Yuanmin. Art Direction: Zhang Chongxiang. Music: Lu Qimin. Sound: Liu Guangjie. Cast: Liu Xingyi as Shi Qilong, Gong Xue as Ding Yujue, Ma Xiaowei as Liu Tie, Zhan Che as Master Worker Qin, He Ling as Sun Zhimin

The young men working in the Zhonghua Shipyard are honest and hard-working, but they lack formal education. When the shipyard sets up an evening school for its workers, a young woman named Ding Yujue is assigned to be its first teacher. At first, the young workers are unhappy at being ordered to give up some of their evenings for classes, and they do not like to study. But in time, with Ding's patient teaching, they begin to appreciate the importance of an education. One of the men, Shi Qilong, falls for the teacher, but when he confides in his co-worker Liu Tie he finds that Liu has similar feelings for the woman but has a problem: Liu's mother was once the Ding family housekeeper, and while Liu and Ding are attracted to each other he is troubled by the social and economic gap in their backgrounds. Shi goes to Ding to tell her of his feelings, but when she tells him she already loves Liu Tie, Shi Qilong convinces the two to break with tradition and get together.

Best Supporting Actor Liu Xingyi, 1984 Hundred Flowers Awards.

854. *Happy Meeting (Xi Xiang Feng)*

1988. Shanghai Film Studio. Color. Letterboxed. 11 Reels. Direction: Zhao Huanzhang. Screenplay: Yu Li, Yin Dunhuang. Cinematography: Can Lianguo. Art Direction: Jin Qifeng, Chen Chunlin. Music: Xiao Yan, Lu Qimin. Sound: Tu Minde. Cast: Lin Qiang as Niu Shuanghu, Zhao Yanhong as Lan Ni, Qiang Yin as Cai Lian, Chen Yude as Shang Gou, Zhang Yuan as "Big Shrimp," Zhou Guobing as Zhang Qing

In exchange for the opportunity to gain some practical business experience she can use in writing her thesis, college student Lan Ni agrees to also act as personal tutor of the son of transportation company general manager Niu Shuanghu. Niu Shuanghu appoints Lan Ni to the position of company secretary. She does not receive a warm welcome: Cai Lian, who had been caring for the child, feels threatened by Lan Ni's arrival, for she is in love with Niu Shuanghu; some other employees of the company also want to get rid of Lan Ni, for various reasons. The business later falls apart, and by then Shuanghu has fallen in love with Lan Ni, but she rejects him. Shuanghu then hopes to get together with Cai Lian, but in her earlier sorrow Cai Lian has now turned to Zhang Qing, a man who truly loves her. These setbacks in love and business cause Shuanghu to leave; he goes to the mountains to become a shepherd. Cai Lian and Lan Ni persuade Shuanghu to return to the company and lead it back to prosperity, and at this point Lan Ni decides to leave.

855. *Happy Xiaoliang River (Huan Teng De Xiao Liang He)*

1976. Shanghai Film Studio. Color. Wide Screen. 11 Reels. Direction: Liu Qiong, Shen Yaoting. Screenplay: Wang Lixing and Gao Xing, based on the novel of the same title. Cinematography: Shen Xilin, Ju Jiazheng. Art Direction: Xue Jianna, Zhong Yongqin. Music: Liu Yanxi. Cast: Ma Cangyu as Zhou Canglin, Wang Qun as Li Yuhua, Gu Yuqing as Yu Zhifang, Lu Qin as Zhang Erquan, Gao Cui as Yao's mother, Pan Hong as Jiang Chunmei, Wen Xiying as Deputy Director Xia

In a commune in the Xiaoliang River area, Second Unit director Zhou Canling is considered a rebel when he suggests exploiting the river would help develop the collective economy. Ninth Unit director Xu Zhenghua likes the idea of "being more prosperous," but is op-posed to treating the river. In the ensuing struggle, the county committee, led by its deputy director Xia, puts pressure on Zhou, while secret capitalist Bai Hancheng tries to sabotage Zhou's efforts. In the struggle, Zhou Canglin is victorious, and Xia is criticized for being "an absolutely unreconstructed capitalist roader."

856. *Happy Zoo (Kuai Le De Dong Wu Yuan)*

1983. Beijing Film Studio. Color. Wide Screen. 3-D. 6 Reels. Direction: Yang Qitian, Zhang Zhucheng. Cinematography: Zhang Zhucheng. Art Direction: Yu Fengming. Music: Lu Zhulong. Sound: Dong Qiuxiang. Cast: Sun Jingxiu, Jiang Kun, Li Wenhua, Lu Xingqi, Lu Sai

A comedy film in which the main characters are the animal residents of a zoo. Some of these are Yingzhi the Gorilla, the zoo's performing star, who is obsessed with keeping the zoo clean; Panda, Cockatoo, and others. The highlight is an animal basketball game organized by Little Monkey and Big Bear. All the human characters in the film play themselves, such as famous Chinese cross-talk comedians Jiang Kun and Li Wenhua, who appear as referees at the game.

857. *Harbin Massacre (Ha Er Bin Da Tu Sha)*

1985. Changchun Film Studio. Color. 10 Reels. Direction: Lin Ke. Screenplay: Li Zhen, Xu Luyin. Cinematography: Sun Hui. Art Direction: Wang Jiru. Music: Gao Feng, Chen Shouqian. Sound: Liu Wenzhang. Cast: Wang Hui as Li Zhaoling, Zhu Yidan as Yu Guoxiong, Kasimu Bolida as Ge Ling, Li Jiabing as He Qiu, Ren Yi as Guan Weimin, Zhang Yanzhu as Hu Ji, Tang Na as Jin Shuwen

In October of 1945, the Nationalists and Communists sign a pact intended to avert a civil war. In accordance with the agreement, the Communists withdraw their forces from the northeast Chinese city of Harbin. CPC General Li Zhaoling resigns his position as Deputy Governor and takes a position as Associate Director of the Sino-Soviet Friendship Association in Harbin. He looks forward to a new era of cooperation between the two Chinese political parties. One night, Nationalist agent He Qiu tries to assassinate Li; the attempt misfires, and a reporter is killed instead.

Li conscientiously does his job, publicizing widely the CPC's policies and principles. The opposition steps up its efforts to eliminate Li, and at last succeed. This results in most of Harbin's people turning on the Nationalists.

858. *The Harmful Yiguan Way (Yi Guan Hai Ren Dao)*

1952. Beijing Film Studio. B & W. 12 Reels. Direction: Li Enjie and Wang Guangyan. Screenplay: Yan Yiyan and Xia Youhong. Cinematography: Gao Hongtao and Qian Yu. Set Design: Li Enjie and Zhang Zhenzong. Music: Li Ning. Sound: Chen Yanxi and Cai Jun. Makeup: Zhang Jing. Cast: Yao Xiangli as Xu Fengsheng, Yang Jing as Liu Wenhui, Bai Ming as Guo Shufang, Han Dan as Xu Zhonghou, Zhang Qingjian as Xu Shuyun, Lin Yangyang as Zhang Jianhua (as a boy), Li Keng as Zhang Jianhua (as a man), Li Jingbo as Wang Jishan, Zhou Daio as Li Xianjun

In pre-liberation China, Xu Fengsheng and her father Xu Zhonghou run a grocery store in Beijing. In the year that Fengsheng is 16, they are swindled by Wang Jishan, head of the Yiguan (persistent) Way, a gang. The daughter despairs of ever escaping the Way's dominance and intimidation, and decides the only way to survive is to go along. Fengsheng's aunt, the widow Xu Shuyun, is raped after she refuses to join the Way, but she dares not speak out against them. The Way also takes all the property her husband had left her. Xu Shuyun's son Zhang Jianhua is a progressive youth, and is engaged in revolutionary work in a liberated area. Later, Xu Zhonghou is again swindled, and this time loses his business, forcing him to earn his living by cleaning a temple. Xu Zhonghou and Xu Shuyun learn the methods by which the Way swindles people, so are killed by Li Xianjun, a gunman secretly employed by the Nationalist government. Li and Wang deceive Fengsheng into thinking that her father and aunt were killed by the CPC. After liberation, Xu Shuyun's son Zhang Jianhua enters the city with a PLA cultural troupe and finds his cousin Fengsheng. Li and Wang fear that she will tell what she knows about them, so they plan to kill her, but she is saved by PLA public security workers. Li Xianjun and Wang Jishan are arrested, and during the trial, Fengsheng learns the truth, that the Yiguan Way committed the murders. Regretting her past acceptance of the Way, she testifies against them in court. Correcting her own past errors, she begins a new life.

859. *Harmony Love (Qing Tou Yi He)*

1986. Ministry of Machinery Audio-Video Technology Center. Color. Wide Screen. 3-D. 6 Reels. Direction: Liu Huizhong, Screenplay: Fang Feng, Wan Mei. Cinematography: Li Tingzheng. Art Direction: Chang Yanlong. Music: Hu Weili. Sound: Li Jingcheng, Wang Dawen. Cast: Pao Haihong as Lan Ying, Zhu Yali as Zijuan, Ge You as Ke Nian, Zhou Zhou as Cheng Wang, Wang Lixiang as Hua Jia, Liu Zhao as Engineer Qin, Yang Xueming as Shuxian

860. *Harvest (Fen Shou)*

1953. Northeast Film Studio. B & W. 10 Reels. Direction: Sha Meng. Screenplay: Sun Qian and Lin Shan. Cinematography: Bao Jie. Set Design: Lu Jin. Music: Zhang Dicang. Sound: Sha Yuan and Chen Wenyuan. Cast: Li Shutian as Chen Chuyuan, Zhao Zhiyue as Sun Fugui, Zhang Ping as County Commissioner Wang, Lin Nong as Little Dong, Wang Pei as Jin Hua, Xu Liankai as Yang Mingyuan, Fu Jie as Old Mr. Fu Shan

Chen Family Village's agricultural cooperative has had several consecutive years of good harvest, but Associate Director Sun Fugui worries that production may have reached its peak. A model worker named Chen Chuyuan returns from Beijing where he has attended a "Model Workers Conference," and declares that increased production must be their goal. Sun Fugui and By-products Director Yang Mingyuan believe the goal too hard to achieve. In order to assure increased production, Chen suggests digging a well as a precaution against drought. The more idealistic young people, including Sun's son and Chen's daughter, support his plan, but opposition from such authorities as Sun Fugui and Yuang Mingyuan result in the well digging plan failing to pass. But with the support and encouragement of the county commissioner, Chen Chuyuan convinces Sun and Yang that peak production still lies ahead. The well is dug, previously arid land is irrigated, and Chen Family Village's harvest far surpasses previous records.

861. *Hassan and Djamileh (Ha Sen Yu Jia Mi La)*

1955. Shanghai Film Studio. B & W. 11 Reels. Direction: Wu Yonggang. Screenplay: Wang Yuhu, Buhala. Cinematography: Xu Qi. Set Design: Wang Yuebai. Music: Xu Huicai. Sound:

Zhang Fubao. Cast: Abulai as Hassan, Falida as Djamileh, Tulaer as Djamileh's mother, Awubeike as Djamileh's father, Zegeng as Shelike, Kuliqiang as Kulan

Hassan and Djamileh are two young Kazakh nationality lovers in the Xinjiang Autonomous Region of Northwest China. The son of a major herd owner wants Djamileh and using his power and influence claims her for his own, forcing Hassan to leave the village. The lovers, aided by the herdsman Shelike, flee into the mountains and live a primitive life there in a cave, in time having a baby. Soon after, the Nationalist government attempts to consolidate its control of the Xingjiang area with the aid of the powerful herd owner. In return, they agree to have soldiers search for the couple, and Hassan and Djamileh are caught. Hassan escapes from jail and joins a minority army troop which liberates the village and rescues Djamileh. They look forward to a happy, free life together.

862. *Having Nothing (Yi Wu Suo You)*

1989. Shanghai Film Studio. Color. Letter-boxed. 10 Reels. Direction: Jiang Haiyang. Screenplay: Gu Bai. Cinematography: Zhang Er. Art Direction: Shen Lide. Music: Yang Mao. Sound: Lu Jiajing. Cast: Shen Junyi as Luo Lie, Zhuge Min as Jin Si, Yuan Yuan as Hei Bao, Zhang Hong as Xiao Juan

Prewar Shanghai is dominated by triad gang organizations, and Luo Lie and Hei Bao are heavily involved young men. They had once been close friends, Hei Bao at one time even saving Luo Lie's life; but Luo was forced to flee overseas for a time, and the two became enemies after that. During Luo's absence, Hei Bao got together with Luo's girlfriend Xiao Juan, but when Luo returned Xiao Juan went back to him. On their wedding day, Luo kills Hei Bao. When Xiao Juan learns that Hei Bao had intended to turn over his power base to Luo for Xiao Juan's sake, she realizes that it was Hei Bao she really loved. Xiao Juan lies down next to Hei Bao's body and kills herself with his pistol.

863. *He Chose Murder (Ta Xuan Ze Mou Sha)*

1988. Shenzhen Film Corporation. Color. 9 Reels. Direction: Guo Baochang. Screenplay: Guo Baochang, Hou Yong. Cinematography: Hou Yong. Art Direction: Li Hong. Sound: Lin Lin. Cast: Xia Zongxue as Professor Su Xia, Jiang Chen as Jiang Hu, Yu Shaokang as Liu Wen, Zhang Yanli as A Qiong

Professor Su Xia is at the peak of his scientific career, selected to receive the prestigious Darwin Prize. As he prepares to leave for England to accept the prize, he begins receiving a series of anonymous threatening letters and phone calls. In addition, his favorite student Jianghu starts behaving differently towards him. All this is connected to a tragedy that took place some 30 years earlier. At that time, Su Xia and his fellow research students Li Bolin and Liu Fei were part of a scientific expedition in a remote part of China. Li Bolin lost his life on the trip when Su Xia refused to help him out of a dangerous situation. Su later took over Li's scientific findings. It turns out that Jianghu is Li Bolin's son, and has just learned from Liu Fei the story of what happened on the ill-fated expedition. Jianghu is now determined to avenge his father's death, so much so that he is ready to cast aside his bright future and turn to murder.

864. *He Is in the Special Economic Zone (Ta Zai Te Qu)*

1984. Pearl River Film Studio. Color. Wide Screen. 10 Reels. Direction: Ding Yinnan. Screenplay: Lu Yanzhou. Cinematography: Zhen Yuyuan. Art Direction: Huang Derong, Qin Hongyi. Music: Wang Yiyong. Sound: Lin Guoqiang. Cast: Li Weixin as Zhen Jie, Zhang Xiaolei as Fang Lan, Li Xuehong as Wei Bing, Zhang Qiaoqiao as Xiaojiao, Zhang Tianxi as Xiaobo, Zhang Weila as Longzhai

Zhen Jie, Director, and Fang Lan a woman engineer, are pioneers at setting up the Hukou Special Economic Zone (SEZ). In just two short years, the SEZ develops to a high state of prosperity. Development is not easy, as many people accuse them of trying to reinstate capitalism. Zhen Jie pushes ahead despite the attacks, some of which comes from within his own family. Finally, Fang Lan is honored with a summons to Beijing to report their progress to the State Council.

865. *Heading for the New China (Zou Xiang Xin Zhong Guo)*

1951. Beijing Film Studio. B & W. 10 Reels. Direction: Wu Tian. Screenplay: Wu Tian. Cinematography: Lian Cheng. Set Design: Liu Rui. Music: Ma Ke, Ju Xixian, Liu Zhi and Zhang

Wengang. Sound: Chen Yanxi. Makeup: Zhang Jing. Cast: Lan Ma as Chang Weiliang, Sang Fu as Plant Director Ding, Zhang Qingjian as Chang's wife, Chen Fangqian as Xu Min, Wang Run as Chang's daughter, Zhang Yan as the Policeman, Xie Tian as the General Manager

Metallurgical engineer Chang Weiliang returns home from study in the U.S., but in old China under Nationalist rule, his dream that "industry will save the nation" is soon shattered. Even after the liberation of his home city, he remains depressed because of labor disputes in his plant: he fails to understand the workers, and they reject his modern ideas. Military representatives help resolve the situation, educating the workers on one hand, and improving his awareness of the workers as a force on the other. When they work together, they overcome technical problems and all become enthusiastic builders of the new China.

866. *Heading South (Nan Xing Ji)*

1990. Emei Film Studio. Color. 9 Reels. Wide Screen. Direction: Zhou Li. Screenplay: Ji Xing, Xian Ziliang. Cinematography: Qiang Jun. Art Direction: Zhou Qing. Music: He Xuntian. Sound: Luo Guohua. Cast: Lei Han as the drifter, Tan Xiaoyan as the street performer, Zheng Zhenyao as Big-footed Woman, Zhang Fengyi as the opium dealer, Sun Min as the young man, Tang Zuoqun as the fortune-teller, Wang Zhi as the owner, Ma Rui as the owner's wife

In the late 1920s a group of northerners are traveling through the open country of Southwest China's Yunnan Province — a drifter, an opium dealer, a young man, two street performers and an old fortune-teller. In the strange, vast, semi-tropical wilderness, this disparate group finds themselves unlikely traveling companions on a long and dangerous journey. They struggle with an unkind environment and are preyed upon by bandits. The hardships reveal the differing personalities and temperaments of each. Cowardice, betrayal, companionship and degeneracy are brought out as they proceed with their journey, a metaphor for life.

867. *Heading Toward Zhongyuan (Ting Jin Zhong Yuan)*

979. Emei Film Studio. Color. 10 Reels. Direction: Zhang Yi. Screenplay: Li Linmu, Wang Zhunxi. Cinematography: Li Erkang. Art Direction: Li Fan. Music: Fu Gengcheng. Sound:

Zhang Jianping. Cast: Wang Zhigang as Zhou Damin, Wang Danhua as Fang Jun, Zhou Chu as Bai Jianye, Yu Li as Laidi

In 1947, Liu Bocheng and Deng Xiaoping lead an army of 100,000 across the Yellow River against the Nationalists. As the army advances, soldiers find and adopt a young girl called Laidi. When the Liu/Deng army arrives at Mount Dabie, it links up with local guerrillas and sets up a people's government. Laidi becomes the district chairman. In the spring of 1948, the PLA launches a major counterattack. Laidi volunteers to scout the enemy's situation, but she is killed on her way back to report what she has found. In the ensuing battle, the outnumbered Communists completely rout the Nationalist forces.

868. *Headless Arrow (Wu Tou Jian)*

1988. Yunnan Minority Film Studio. Color. Letterboxed. 9 Reels. Direction: Huang Ling, Huang Yanen. Screenplay: Shi Yong. Cinematography: Si Yongmin, Yang Changsheng. Art Direction: Sun Changfang, Qi Deyu. Music: Nie Lihua. Sound: Chen Baolin. Cast: Liu Xiaomin as Gebu, Li Xuesong as Sai Xiaomeng, Wang Xinjian as Kaluo

A PLA unit in western Yunnan province receives an urgent message, delivered by headless arrow, that some illegal activities are going on in an Aini nationality village near the border. Army scout Gebu is sent to the village, but when he arrives he finds his designated contact has been murdered. He is helped by an Aini girl called Sai Xiaomeng, and she sacrifices her own life to protect the scout. At last, with the help of the local militia, Gebu succeeds in capturing the bandits' chieftain and smashing his plot to smuggle weapons in across the border.

869. *Heartaches (Ku Nan De Xin)*

1979. Changchun Film Studio. Color. 11 Reels. Direction: Chang Zhenhua. Screenplay: Zhang Xian. Cinematography: An Zhiguo. Art Direction: Gao Guoliang, Ming Zongshi. Music: Wu Damin. Sound: Li Zhengfeng. Cast: Kang Tai as Luo Bingzhen, Song Xiaoyin as Yuwei, Shi Kefu as Tian Gang, Wang Baohua as Yang Fan, Li Junhai as Xu Jiamao

In the fall of 1975, famed cardiologist Luo Bingzhen is recalled from the rural practice he had been consigned to during the Cultural Revolution. With the help and support of the hospital's Party deputy secretary, he begins laboratory research on a new heart surgery procedure. But when the "Gang of Four" launches the political movement called "anti-restoration," they label Luo's heart operation "laboratory research restoration" and brand him a counterrevolutionary. When a seriously ill patient is brought to him for emergency care, Luo Bingzhen performs the necessary operation, and although the patient is saved Luo himself collapses from political and physical stress. With his life in danger, one of the Gang's followers Xu Jiamao takes him to a place of safety. After the Gang is defeated, Luo Bingzhen is invited as a guest of honor at the National Science Conference, but the good doctor dies before he can attend.

870. *Heartline Dam (Lian Xin Ba)*

1977. Shanghai Film Studio. Color. 10 Reels. Direction: Xu Weijie, Huang Shuqin. Screenplay: Collective, recorded by Zhang Fengsheng and Yang Shiwen. Cinematography: Luo Zhensheng, Sun Yeling. Art Direction: Mei Kunping. Music: Yang Shaolu. Sound: Feng Deyao. Cast: Ma Guanyin as Zhang Miaoyu, Zhao Guobing as Chun Hou, Pan Xiping as Ma Fengcheng, Zhao Jiayan as Chen Mao, Sun Yufeng as Long Quan, Hong Rong as Cha Hua

On the banks of the Qinlong River live people of the Tujia minority people, the Miao minority and the majority Han Chinese. Before liberation, Chinese domination of the river's waters often led to violence among different ethnic groups. When their fathers are killed by a tyrant, three boys — Zhang Miaoyu, a Han Chinese, Ma Fengcheng, a Miao, and Chun Hou, a Tujia — bond together and grow up as close as brothers. After liberation, Zhang Miaoyu, now a discharged soldier, returns to their hometown and suggests that building a dam will alter the area's chronic water shortage. Deputy Secretary Quan Zhanshan, in league with Ma Zhongnian of the Miao minority, stirs up a series of ethnic disputes to disrupt the project. The relationship of the three old friends is also harmed. However, by relying on the Party organization and the people, Zhang Miaoyu is able to overcome class enemies Quan Zhanshan and Ma Zhongnian. The dam is built, a monument to ethnic unification.

Hearts for the Motherland **see** *Loyal Overseas Chinese Family*

871. *Hearts Link with Hearts (Xin Lian Xin)*

1958. Changchun Film Studio. B & W. 10 Reels. Direction: Wu Tian. Screenplay: Collective, recorded by Wu Tian and based on the novel, "People Whose Hearts Link With Hearts" by Yang Runshen. Cinematography: Su Xiaoyan. Art Direction: Xu Wei, Music: Chen Zi, Du Yu. Sound: Sui Xizhong. Cast: Huang Zong as Tian Ernu, Shi Kefu as Liu Dong, Lu Xun as Li Daoxuan, Yang Wei as Yang Laozheng, Han Shaojun as Fuchou, Cao Shangao as Liangzi

On the eve of World War II, poor farmer Tian Ernu borrows a sum of money from landlord Yang Laocheng to dig a well on his land, but his earnings are so small he cannot even pay the interest on the loan. His other attempts to make money are just as unsuccessful, and he has to give up his small plot of land to the landlord. One night, Yang Laocheng captures Liu Dong, a Communist Party member, and sentences him to be publicly executed. At the risk of his own life, Tian Ernu rescues Liu Dong. The Communist educates him, and Tian joins in the work of organizing the poor farmers of the area to oppose the landlord. When the war begins, Tian becomes an organizer of anti–Japanese resistance in his native village. He later joins the Eighth Route Army to fight for the liberation of all China.

872. *Heaven and Hell (Di Yu Tian Tang)*

1989. Shanghai Film Studio. Color. Letterboxed. 10 Reels. Direction: Yang Yanjing. Screenplay: Zhang Xian, Qin Peichun. Cinematography: Sun Guoliang. Art Direction: Huang Qiagui. Music: Xu Jingxin. Sound: Ni Zheng. Cast: Fang Wenjie as Huaer, Wu Wenlun as Ma Long, Da Wuchang as Dr. Wen Qing, Yu Hui as Jing Ling, Ren Wei as Nai Quan

The story takes place among the Chinese community overseas. After her mother dies from spousal abuse, a young girl named Huaer is raped by her stepfather Ma Long. He is sent to prison for this, and Dr. Wen Qing adopts the girl, taking her with him to the city and changing her name to Jing Ling. Ten years later, she is an adult, devoted to her adoptive father. She gains the love of fashion photographer Nai Quan, but when Ma Long is released from prison he tells Nai Quan that he had raped Jing Ling years before, which causes a blowup between the young couple. Later, Ma Long abducts Jing Ling and rapes her again.

Ma Long kills himself out of self-loathing, and just as Wen Qing and Nai Quan show up, Jing Ling takes her own life.

873. *Heaven's Banquet (Tian Tang Yan Hui)*

1987. Shanghai Film Studio. Color. 10 Reels. Direction: Zhong Shuhuang. Screenplay: Zen Zhaohong, Zhang Ronghua. Cinematography: Sun Guodong. Art Direction: Qin Bosong. Music: Xu Jingxin. Sound: Xu Xiushan. Cast: Zhang Xiaoli as Cai Ling, Lu Ying as Liu Yao, Zhou Jinzhen as Zhou Ting, Ye Hui as Luo Dan, Ma Tianfang as Pang Dali, Zhou Guobing as Zhu Gui

Woman college student Cai Ling really loves to cook, so she naturally loves her business school major of restaurant management. Her boyfriend, art education major Luo Dan and his mother both deplore Cai Ling's choice of career and urge her to change to something else. Cai Ling refuses, and breaks off the relationship with Luo Dan. Later, her wonderful cooking gains the approval of people from all over, including Luo's mother. Cai Ling and her boyfriend come to a new understanding, but first she and two other girl students are selected to attend and participate in an international food fair.

874. *Heaven's Pride (Tian Jiao)*

1983. Liaoning Science Film Studio. Color. 10 Reels. Direction: Wu Guojiang. Screenplay: Wang Chitao, Liu Jianmin. Cinematography: Wu Guojiang, Xing Eryou. Art Direction: Huang Jianfeng. Music: Qin Yongcheng. Sound: Wang Chunbao. Cast: Qiao Qi as Wu Min, Du Xiongwen as Yang Qi, Wang Zhihua as Zhou Shaoyan, Wu Lilin as Yuelan, Song Dewang as Peng Bo

After 10 years of intensive research, elderly scientist Wu Min completes a major project of solar analysis. At this time, he also looks forward to the return of his best student, Yang Qi, labeled a counterrevolutionary and sent away during the Cultural Revolution. When Yang returns to the research institute, however, he points out several critical errors in Wu's work. This at first hurts the two men's relationship, but after thinking it over Yang Qi wisely invites Wu Min to help him revise the paper and refute his own theory. Wu accepts the offer, and the new research results completely overturn Yang Qi's original findings.

875. *Hello, Bikini (Ha Luo, Bi Ji Ni)*

1989. Inner Mongolia Film Studio. Color. Letterboxed. 9 Reels. Direction: Mailisi, Guangbudaoerji. Screenplay: Xiao Yixian, Zhen Jingang. Cinematography: Narisu. Art Direction: Du Changshun. Music: Yang Yilun. Sound: Zhen Yunbao. Cast: Liu Diancheng as Tan Dun, Sun Song as Wei Jian, Xu Rihua as Fang Xiaoxu, Jia Ruixin as Su Meihua

When athletic authorities decide to hold China's first beauty contest, they set off a major controversy by declaring that all entrants must perform in bikinis. The film takes a humorous look at various people's reactions. Art Institute director Wei Jian has a huge argument with girlfriend Fang Xiaoxu over her decision to participate and provincial sports director Tan Dun forbids his own daughter from competing. But young worker Su Meihua and newlywed couple Li Hongli and Zhang Yaping are enthusiastic. In the end, China's first such contest is a big success.

876. *Hello! Pacific (Ni Hao, Tai Ping Yang)*

1990. Shenzhen Film Corporation. Color. 9 Reels. Wide Screen. Direction: Chen Jialin. Screenplay: Liu Xing, Liu Xueqiang. Cinematography: Liu Jiankui, Su Li. Art Direction: Han Gang. Music: Jin Fuzai. Sound: Li Bojiang. Cast: Cao Can as Deng Xiaoping, Zhao Youliang as Jiang Han, Liu Wenzi as Hao Guochang, Chen Baoguo as Wang Haipeng, Wu Haiyan as Feng Jieyi

A semi-documentary look at the Shenzhen Special Economic Zone and its achievements after a decade of economic reforms.

877. *Hello, Sisters! (He! Jie Men)*

1988. Changchun Film Studio. Color. 10 Reels. Direction: Jiang Shusheng, Ji Shimin. Screenplay: Peng Mingyan. Cinematography: An Zhiguo. Art Direction: Yuan Dianmin. Music: Guo Feng. Sound: Kang Ruixin. Cast: Gao Junxia as Dongdong, Xu Min as Zhao Hanzhi

Self-employed Dongdong takes the money she makes operating a street food stall and buys her own taxi. She is married for a time to Shunzi, a film studio makeup artist, but the two fight constantly and at last break up. The film studio hires Dongdong to drive actors to a location filming site each day, and she in doing so she soon becomes obsessed with actor Zhao

Hanzhi. At first Zhao ignores her, but when he learns how much money she has earned over the years in business, he responds to Dongdong's advances and soon gets her pregnant. Zhao asks her to have an abortion, and she does. But when he learns that she actually has little money left he breaks off their love affair. Her naivete and his selfishness have left both feeling like losers in real life.

878. *Helpful Young Man (Zhang Yi Xiao Huo Er)*

1987. Beijing Film Studio. Color. 3-D. Direction: Huo Zuang. Screenplay: Xu Xiaoxing, Huo Zuang. Cinematography: Li Tingzhen. Art Direction: Yang Yuhe, Yang Xiaowen. Music: Wang Ming. Sound: Li Jingju, Zhang Zhian. Cast: Lu Liang as Fang Fan, Zhao Dafu as Zhao Dajie, Yuan Mei as Xiao Xue, Huang Suying as Fei's mother, Mo Qi as Huang Douyaer

Construction worker Fang Fan has a reputation for meddling in the affairs of others. While his frequent attempts to help are always done from a sense of justice or kindness, they are not always appreciated. He finally finds romance with Xiao Xue, a young woman who has the same trait.

879. *Her Smile Through the Candlelight (Zhuo Guang Li De Wei Xiao)*

1991. Shanghai Film Studio. Color. 10 Reels. Letterboxed. Direction: Wu Tianren. Screenplay: Wu Tianren. Cinematography: Yu Shishan. Art Direction: Zheng Changfu, Ye Jingming. Music: Xu Jingxin. Sound: Tu Minde. Cast: Song Xiaoying as Wang Shuangling, Ding Jiayuan as Daliiu, Yang Jin as Zhou Liping, zhang Hongwei as Li Xiaopeng, Tang Li as Lu Ming

Wang Shuangling is a middle-aged fourth grade teacher. Experienced and patient, she quickly wins the support of her pupils. She decides to call on the parents of three students who concern her. Lu Ming is a clever student who seems a bit more mature than other children his age. Li Xiaopeng, on the other hand, has developed some bad habits because of his parents' lack of culture. The third problem student, Zhou Liping, is a new kid in town and is discriminated against by other children. Zhou seems depressed, and Wang Shuangling finds that the girl's mother is cold and weird. Wang is so concerned for these children that

she neglects her health and ends up hospitalized for a heart attack.

Best Actress Song Xiaoying, 1992 Golden Rooster Awards.

880. *Herding Song of North Shaanxi (Shan Bei Mu Ge)*

1951. Beijing Film Studio. B & W. 8 Reels. Direction: Lin Zhifeng. Screenplay: Sun Qian. Cinematography: Wang Qiming. Set Design: Qing Wei. Music: Liu Zhi. Sound: Wang Shaozhen. Costume: Zhang Caiping. Makeup: Li Ende. Cast: Liu Bing as Cheng Baowa, Zhang Jiquan as Bai Xiulan, Zhang Yun as Bai Haiwang, Pei Ran as Mr. Li, Guo Yangting as Ma Sanbao, Wang Xuewen as Fu Gui, Bai Long as Zhang Ruitang, Cheng Yi as Commander Qiu

In 1935, farmers in the town on Woniu, North Shaanxi province, can no longer bear the oppression of their landlords and the Nationalist government, and secretly organize a Red Guard team to assist the Red Army when it attacks villages in the area. White Army regimental Commander Qiu and landlord Zhang Ruitang are ordered to search out those working for the Red Army. One of those pursued is Mr. Li, a guerrilla leader, but he is hidden by young shepherd Cheng Baowa and his girlfriend Bai Xiulan. One day, White Army soldiers confiscate two of the sheep tended by Cheng Baowa, and landlord Zhang Ruitang wants the youth executed for losing them. But Bai Xiulan's father Bai Haiwang gives his daughter's favorite bracelet to the landlord as compensation for the sheep. His life spared, the shepherd runs away and joins the guerrilla forces. The landlord wants to send Bai Xiulan to Commander Qiu as a concubine, but Mr. Li leads the Red force in rescuing her. Shortly afterwards, the North Shaanxi Red Army links up with the guerrilla forces, and they attack Woniu town. The town soon falls, and the Nationalist Army is defeated there. Cheng Baowa executes despotic landlord Zhang Ruitang. Farmers in Woniu receive the land, Cheng Baowa and Bai Xiulan get married and join the Red Army together.

881. *Herdsman (Mu Ma Ren)*

1982. Shanghai Film Studio. Color. 10 Reels. 106 min. Direction: Xie Jin. Screenplay: Li Zhun. Cinematography: Zhu Yongde, Zhang Yongzheng. Art Direction: Chen Shaomian. Music: Huang Zhun. Sound: Zhu Weigang. Cast: Zhu Shimao as Xu Linjun, Chong Shan as

Li Xiuzhi, Liu Qiong as Xu Jingyou, Niu Ben as Guo Pianzhi, Lei Zhongqian as Old Man Dong

In the fall of 1980, overseas Chinese entrepreneur Xu Jingyou returns from America, and in the Northwest China grasslands finds his son Xu Lingjun, who he has not seen since leaving for the U.S. 30 years before. Xu Jinggou feels guilty for not taking care of his son, and now that he is back he plans to bring his son to America. However, Xu Lingjun feels uncomfortable with his father, and the two have difficulty communicating, with seemingly nothing in common. One night, Xu Lingjun tells his father of his unfortunate past experiences. In 1957, he was falsely accused of being a "rightist" and sent to work in the northwest China grasslands. The natural beauty of the land purified his thinking, and the warm-hearted sincerity of the local people softened his heart. Their kindness and caring restored Xu Lingjun's courage and will to live. During the Cultural Revolution, a girl named Li Xiuzhi came to the grasslands from her home in rural Sichuan to avoid starvation. Although there was 15 years age difference between them, Li and Xu Lingjun got married, had a son Qinqin, and built up a warm and loving family life. In 1979, Xu Lingjun's "rightist" label was corrected and he became a teacher of grasslands children. Xiu Lingjun thinks of his beloved wife and son, and informs his father that could never leave the country that had given him such a fulfilling life and so much love, despite the hard times. Xu Jingyou no longer tries to persuade his son. The older man feels that although he is a billionaire, he is poor in affection. He tells his son that he plans to be buried in his motherland after he dies. Xu Lingjun returns to his wife and son.

Best Picture, 1983 Hundred Flowers Awards.

Best Supporting Actor Niu Ben, 1983 Golden Rooster Awards.

Best Supporting Actor Niu Ben, 1983 Hundred Flowers Awards.

882. *Here Comes a Man (Lai Le Yi Ge Nan Zi Han)*

1984. Henan Film Studio. Color. 9 Reels. Direction: Han Xiaolei. Screenplay: Zhang Shiqi, Li Zenheng. Cinematography: Liu Yongshi. Art Direction: Zhao Yixuan, Ning Futing. Music: Wang Liping. Sound: Cui Weimin. Cast: Ju Naishe as Li Qiusheng, Li Xiaoyan as Chen Li, Xu Zhongquan as Wang Yungui, Li Guozhong as Chen Gui, Sha Weiqiao as Zhao Geng, Song Chunli as the woman factory director

Army officer Li Qiusheng retires from the PLA to a city in South China, taking a job in an industrial plant. He has several problems: he really wants a job which would better use his military experience, such as police work; he knows nothing about business; and finally, his leadership experience doesn't help him in supervising his all-female staff. Li decides that China's future lies in its industry, and he begins a steady process of self-education. During the nationwide call for reform, his plant's reform plan is rejected at first, but Li does not give up, and leads his staff in drawing up a plan that is finally accepted.

883. *Hermit of the Bamboo Forest (Zhu Lin Yin Shi)*

1985. Fujian Film Studio. Color. Letterboxed. 10 Reels. Direction: Wang Xiuwen. Screenplay: Li Dong, Ni Feng, Wang Xiuwen. Cinematography: Cai Naide. Art Direction: Liu Nanyang. Music: Chen Yongtie. Sound: Wu Hua. Cast: Lin Jianrong as Zhen Yan, He Ling as Liu Zilin, Feng Qi as Art Institute Director Zhen, Tu Zhaohui as Fangmei, Geng Junqi as Mr. Wang, Gu Yang as Fu Zhaoshou

Female art school student Zhen Yan meets Liu Zilin, an outstanding talent from a nearby art institute. Liu encourages Zhen to go into the wilderness to observe and paint her favorite subject, the giant panda. Zhen does this, and the two fall in love.

884. *A Hero as Brave as a Tiger (Ying Xiong Hu Dan)*

1958. August First Film Studio. B & W. 9 Reels. Direction: Yan Jizhou, Hao Guang. Screenplay: Ding Yishan. Cinematography: Jiang Shi. Art Direction: Kou Honglie. Music: Gao Ruxing. Sound: Li Bojian. Cast: Yu Yang as Zeng Tai, Zhang Yongshou as Geng Ao, Li Po as Political Commissar Ma, Liu Bingzhang as Regimental Commander Lin, Zhu Qi as the company commander, Li Li as the old hunter, Fang Hui as Li Hanguang, Hu Minying as Li Yuegui

In the days just after liberation, the people living in Guangxi province's Shiwan Mountain region are still harassed by a holdout force of Nationalists operating as bandits and led by Li Hanguang and his wife Li Yuegui. PLA reconnaissance section chief Zeng Tai pretends to be a former Nationalist deputy commander just returned from overseas with intelligence obtained from the PLA. In this guise he infiltrates the enemy headquarters. Zeng Tai is subjected to four very tough and risky tests, but through his cunning and the support of the PLA, he finally wins their trust. He eventually rises to an influential position in the gang and uses an old hunter living in the mountains as a courier to provide the PLA with the intelligence needed to round up the bandits.

885. *Hero Beggar Su (Ying Xiong Hao Jie Su Qi Er)*

1993. Pearl River Film Studio, Hong Kong Yihai Film Company Co-Production. Color. Letterboxed. 9 Reels. Direction: Yuan Jingtian, Jiang Yecheng. Screenplay: Chen Qiansong, Liu Damu, Huang Yonghui, Xu Dachu. Cinematography: Ma Guanhua, Pan Deye. Art Direction: Li Pingye. Music: Hu Weili. Costume: Zhou Jianying, Li Yuer, Liu Jian. Makeup: Wu Zhixin, Lai Fang, Feng Zude. Cast: Wang Yu as Huang Feihong, Zhen Zidan as Su Qier, Chen Shulan as Xiao Yazhen, Wu Mengda as Su Ren, Yuan Jieying (Fenny Yuen) as Dai Yide, Pao Fang as Lin Zexu

On the eve of the Opium War (1840–1842), Huang Feihong (Cantonese: Wong Fei Hung) helps Commissioner Lin Zexu stamp out the opium trade in Guangzhou. This earns him the hatred of the British. When martial artist Su Qier and Huang have a quarrel over some relatively minor matter, British administrator Bailey exploits this to drive a wedge between the two. At last, Huang and Su settle their differences and join forces against the British opium traders.

886. *A Hero of the Bush (Cao Mang Ying Xiong)*

1986. Emei Film Studio. Color. 10 Reels. Direction: Liu Zhinong. Screenplay: Zhao Erhuan, Xie Hong, Li Tianxiong. Cinematography: Xie Erxiang. Art Direction: Xie Huibing. Music: Tao Jiazhou, Yu Yu. Sound: Peng Wenguang. Cast: Xia Zongyou as Luo Xuanqin, Zhang Guoli as Tang Bingxian, Wang Ji as Chen Shanmei, Guo Jiaqin as Wang Yunlu, Wun Xianqiao as Li Chenghua, Zhao Xiaorui as Luo Xiaohao

In the fall of 1911, on the eve of the Qing Dynasty's overthrow, Sichuan province is swept by a wave of patriotic opposition to selling railway rights to foreigners. A railway protection commission is established in the province's six southern counties, with strong-

man Luo Xuanqin elected its head. The commission soon finds itself at loggerheads with the imperial government, which follows a policy of appeasing the foreigners. The movie relates the struggle of these anti-foreign, anti-Qing patriots, as they struggle to the bitter and bloody end.

887. *Hero of the Dragon Group (Long Hu Qun Ying)*

1993 Xiaoxiang Film Studio. Color. 9 Reels. Direction: Liu Xiaoning. Screenplay: Hu Zongyuan, Zhang Dongpan. Cinematography: Sun Xiaoguang, Ma Ning. Art Direction: Jia Feng. Music: Zou Ye. Sound: Liang Jiadong. Costume: Wei Rao. Makeup: Hong Quanli. Cast: Liu Xiaoning as Wu Long, Ge You as Li Hawang, You Yong as Chang Shaolong, Li Haibing, Bayin, Li Shiming, Pan Jie, Zhou Bo, Bo Shaozhen, Hao Hanfeng, Fan Jianguo, Wei Rao

At a laboratory in North America, work is under way on development of a new weapon of mass destruction. Two of the key scientists working on the project are Chinese, one from the PRC and one from Taiwan. A secret organization out for world domination kidnaps the two scientists and takes them to an island. The counterintelligence organizations of the PRC and Taiwan work together to rescue them.

888. *Hero on the Wrong Way (Qi Lu Ying Xiong)*

1994. Yunnan Nationalities Film Studio. Color. Letterboxed. 9 Reels. Direction: Wang Rui. Screenplay: Xu Jianhai. Cinematography: Ning Jiakun, Li Erjing. Art Direction: Xu Shaojun. Music: Chen Xingguang. Costume: Fu Ping. Makeup: Yang Meixin. Cast: Chang Rong as Luo Wei, Yan Bingyan as Xiao Jun, Li Changyuan as Xie Ming, Yang Dekun as Qin Laoda, Liu Yongming as "White Face," Liu Fan as the director, Zhong Changde as the assistant director

Luo Wei's girlfriend Xiaojun is gang-raped one night on her way home from work. Although she wants to report this to the police, the furious Luo Wei stops her, insisting he will personally avenge her. He takes leave from work to devote full time to this. Luo eventually learns the identities of the gang members responsible, and kills them. After he returns to work, however, other members of the same gang abduct Xiaojun, seeking their own revenge. Luo and an old army buddy go after the gang themselves, and this time Xiaojun is shot and killed in the fight. Luo Wei realizes that by going it alone he has accomplished nothing.

889. *A Hero Standing by Justice (Zhang Yi Ying Xiong)*

1992. Guangxi Film Studio. Color. Letterboxed. 9 Reels. Direction: Qiu Lili. Screenplay: Ni Feng. Cinematography: Ning Jiakun. Art Direction: Chen Xiaoxia. Music: Li Wanli. Costume: Yang Yuling, Zhang Dezhong. Makeup: Guan Jun, Yang Wenxuan. Cast: Guo Weihua as Zhou Dachuan, Li Yunjuan as Fenggu, Xu Xiaojian as Yan Shaojie, Li Hui as Shanhu, Huang Zizhi as Xingzhi, Zhou Xiaoling as Bian Lingzhi

When a large sum of money donated by overseas Chinese to the anti–Japanese cause disappears on the way, a Chinese guerrilla troop led by Communist liaison Zhou Dachuan sets out to look for it. In their search, they encounter a defeated Nationalist Army unit led by Yan Shaojie, retreating from Japanese attack. Zhou also meets again his former lover Fenggu, now the leader of group of greenwoods bandits. After overcoming considerable difficulties, Zhou reconciles with Fenggu and unites her bandits and Yan's soldiers with his own. Their added strength enables them to defeat the Japanese and continue with their search for the money.

890. *Hero Without Tears (Ying Xiong Wu Lei)*

1991. Inner Mongolia Film Studio. Color. 9 Reels. Direction and Screenplay: Jiang Hao. Cinematography: Yi Huhewula. Art Direction: Wang Xiaohong. Music: Sun Gang. Sound: Hu He. Cast: Liu Xiaoning as Li Qiang, Luo Lan as Wei Ling, Cao Li as Ha Lei

Chief of detectives Li Qiang carries out a new attack on the underworld, an all-out attack on gang activities in his city. Knowing Li is the principal obstacle to their continued success, gang boss Halei sets up and frames Li Qiang, resulting in the latter's dismissal from the force. But the ex-detective does not give up, and continues to battle organized crime on his own.

891. *Heroes' Calamities (Ying Xiong Jie)*

1993. Beijing Film Studio. Color. Letterboxed. 9 Reels. Direction: Du Min. Screenplay: Gu Bai. Cinematography: Yan Junsheng. Art Direction: Yang Wan, Zhang Wenqi. Music: Bian

Liunian. Sound: Wu Ling. Makeup: Liu Dan. Cast: Jiang Wu as Zhao Daman, Liu Yunlong as Qian Erbao, Zhang Yue as Sun Sanqiang, He Bing as Li Biao, Yuan Yin as Ouyang Jiedan, Zhou Qi as Mai Qi

The story takes place in North China during World War II. Four young men fight for justice against a local despot.

892. *Heroes for Justice (Qi Xia Wu Yi)*

1994. Fujian Film Studio, Taiwan Liufu Film Industry Corp. Co-Production. Color. Letterboxed. Direction: Chen Muchuan. Screenplay: Xi Si. Cinematography: Peng Dawei, Yu Xiaojun. Art Direction: Han Guoqing. Cast: Lin Wei, Li Zhixi, Shi Zhongtian, Zhen Aonan, Fang Zhongxing, Yang Liqing, Ren Shiguan

A historical sword epic. In the 11th Century, at a time of major political instability for China, seven heroes emerge. They make a vow to uphold the "five morals" and fight for justice.

893. *Heroes in a Time of Chaos (Luan Shi Ying Hao)*

1988. Fujian Film Studio and Hong Kong Zhengye Film Company Co-Production. Color. Wide Screen. 10 Reels. Direction: Xie Yucheng. Screenplay: Yao Wentai. Cinematographer: Cai Naide, Yu Xiaojun. Art Direction: Tang Peijun. Music: Ma Ding. Sound: Chen Binglian. Cast: Li Yunjuan as Chang Er, Huang Guoqiang as Chengsheng, Chen Jianjun as Guishan Xiaochiliang

The story begins more than 70 years ago in Shanghai, when a triad boss learns a treasure is hidden in Chang Family Village in the countryside. His gang stages a bloody raid on the village, but are unsuccessful in getting the treasure. Many years later, the triad boss tries again, and while he kills the villager protecting the treasure, it remains hidden. The hunt for the treasure is soon joined by a Japanese killer and a Western adventurer. At last, there is a fierce battle for the treasure, successfully protected for the nation by some village heroes.

894. *Heroes of Luliang (Lu Liang Ying Xiong)*

1950. Beijing Film Studio. B & W. 10 Reels. Directors: Lu Ban, Yi Ling. Screenplay: Lin Shan, based on the novel of the same title by Ma Feng (1922–) and Xi Rong. Cinematography:

Gao Hongtao. Set Design: Yu Yiru. Music: Li Jida. Sound: Cai Jun, Niu Lanrui. Costume: Wei Bangjun. Makeup: Wang Xizhong, Sun Hongkui. Cast: Li Baiwan as Zhu Zhi, Guo Yuntai as Erwa, Fu Ke as Old Zhang, Li Jingbo as Kang Xixue, Xue Tao as Xiuyin, Zhou Diao as Mr. Ma

In the spring of 1942, villagers in a remote area of the Luliang Mountains suffer frequent harassment by the Japanese invaders. One of the villagers, Zhu Zhi, is nominated to lead a civil guard, but his inexperience makes the initial effort unsuccessful. Under the tutelage of an upper level Communist Party organization, Zhu gradually becomes a mature leader. In the fall, when the wheat crop matures, Zhu leads his civil guard in protecting the harvest from enemy grain looters. However, village traitor Kang Xixue betrays the guardsmen, resulting in serious Chinese losses. Zhu and several others are taken prisoner and tortured. Party District Director Mr. Ma regroups the remaining civil guard, and in a counterattack they free Zhu and the other captives, kill the Japanese commanding officer and the traitor Kang, and liberate a nearby town occupied by the Japanese. After the eventual Japanese surrender, Zhu Zhi joins the PLA.

895. *Heroes on Snowy Mountain (Xue Shan Yi Xia)*

1991. Tianshan Film Studio. Color. Letterboxed. 9 Reels. Direction: Dong Ling, Ha Lun. Screenplay: Zhang Pufu, Pu Zhaoyu. Cinematography: Gao Huanggang. Art Direction: Sha Deke. Music: Mu Hong. Sound: Lu Zhengyi. Costume: Liu Lihong. Makeup: Wang Mana. Cast: Wang Quanan as Sangmu, Zhao Qian as Zhang Xueping, Bayan as Habai, Ye Erjiang as Hasai, Hu Xiaoguang as Jin Shangjian, Lu Yaoxing as Zong Sheng, Yang Xiaomao as Wang Hubiao, Xie Xinzhi as Huo Jixian

After the collapse of Boxer Rebellion, three heroes swear to be brothers and sisters. They continue resisting the foreign invasion, but give their lives in the effort.

896. *The Heroic Driver (Ying Xiong Si Ji)*

1954. Northeast Film Studio. B & W. 11 Reels. Direction: Lu Ban. Screenplay: Yue Ye. Cinematography: Gao Hongtao. Set Design: Zhang Hancheng. Music: Zhang Guocang. Sound: Sui Xizhong. Makeup: Bi Zepu. Cast: Guo Zhenqing as Guo Dapeng, Wang Qiuyin as Meng Fanju, Yan Meiyi as Jin Yanchi, Xu Liankai

as Liu Ziqiang, Shang Fu as Director Tang, Zhao Zhiyue as Old Man Xu, Huang Ruomin as Deputy Minister Lu

In the summer of 1950, Anping Station in Northeast China is laboriously loading goods for shipment. Guo Dapeng, driver of Train No. "999," suggests a new loading method which could resolve their delivery problems, but is opposed by conservative section director Meng Faju. With the aid and support of Party Branch Secretary Liu Ziqiang, Director Tang Likai and a Soviet expert, Guo's advanced experience gains the attention of the Railway Ministry, and at the National Work Conference on Trains, Railway Deputy Minister Lu encourages Guo to not only ship more but run faster. That winter, Guo requests that "999" be reassigned to a new line, but is opposed by Meng Fanju, who is worried because of a recent accident caused by a train. He is criticized by Deputy Minister Lu for his conservative thinking. At a celebration, the entire crew of "999" is awarded "heroic driver" flags.

897. *A Heroic Epic (Ying Xiong Shi Pian)*

1960. Pearl River Film Studio. B & W. 9 Reels. Direction: Lu Yu, Si Meng, Wang Weiyi and Xu Yan. Based on the "Makou Incident." Cinematography: Jian Shi, Li Shengwei, Shen Minghui, Long Qingyun and Wang Yunhui. Principal Cast: Zhang Zhen, Li Changhua and Hong Bing

A fire breaks out in a paper plant in the Makou area of Guangdong's Yingde County, injuring many people. A military police unit located at Makou goes to do rescue work, during which many people are injured, including the military police chief and another policeman, both of whom later die from their burns. The story describes the rescue efforts of the county, the railway system and the air force.

898. *Heroic Island (Ying Xiong Dao)*

1959. August First Film Studio. Color. 9 Reels. Direction: Feng Yifu, Shi Wenzhi. Screenplay: Lu Zhuguo. Cinematography: Cao Jingyun. Art Direction: Tong Yuting. Music: Li Weicai. Sound: Guo Dazheng. Cast: Yang Jing as Hong Xiuhai, Tao Yuling as Hong Xiujiang, Liang Zhipeng as Hong Yashi, Zhang Huaizhi as Hong Yasha, Jia Liu as Hong Jiushu, Huang Suying as Hong Jiu's wife, Li Xuehong as Xueqin, Zou Darong as Hong Xiaosha

On an island of strategic importance to

China's coastal defenses, the commune's female director Hong Xiuhai leads the island's residents in combating the attempts of the U.S.-backed Nationalists to take over the island. At the same time, they continue to carry out production. One after another, they repulse invasions of their island, but in one battle, Xiuhai is wounded protecting a cannon. Her younger sister — elementary school teacher Xiujiang — and her younger brothers Yashi and Yasha devise an island communications net using such simple tools as kites and bamboo rafts. They capture all of the enemy invaders. Xiuhai's brother, forcibly conscripted by the Nationalist Army nine years earlier, escapes and returns to the island for a reunion with the family.

899. *Heroic Land, Heroic Tears (Ying Xiong Di, Ying Xiong Lei)*

1992. Shanghai Film Studio & the Hong Kong Jinli Film Company Ltd. Co-Production. Color. Letterboxed. 10 Reels. Direction: Li Jiansheng. Screenplay: Nan Yan, Han Kun, Qiu Ting. Cinematography: Shen Miaorong. Art Direction: Shen Lide. Music: Mai Zhenhong. Sound: Xie Guojie. Costume: Jin Jitai, Lin Rongqing. Makeup: Zhu Peizhen, Luo Yuchou. Cast: Yi Minyang as Luo Zhixing, Zhang Yaoyang as Huang Dagang, Chen Qiuling as Yuyu, Yu Li as Nan Qian, Liu Songren (Damian Lau) as Boss Wei, Peng Jiali as Xiao Pei

The death of usurper and would-be emperor Yuan Shikai in 1916 sets off a scramble among various warlords seeking to fill the power vacuum, plunging China into chaos and civil strife. Shanghai triad chief Huang Dagang is exploited by Boss Wei, a Japanese collaborator, to help the Japanese ship weapons illegally into China. Wei's main opposition comes from a patriotic underground group called the "Little Knives." Huang Dagang realizes he is being used when his girlfriend commits suicide after being raped by a Japanese agent. He joins forces with the Little Knives against Boss Wei to intercept a trainload of military supplies headed for the Japanese.

900. *Heroic Minority Women Fighting with Japanese Invaders (Mang Nu Zui Hun)*

1990. Yunnan Film Studio. Color. 9 Reels. Direction: Miao Yiqi. Screenplay: Ni Feng, Wang Wenzhi. Cinematography: Ning Jiakun, Wang Jiangdong. Art Direction: Li Zhixin, Wang Zhichao. Music: Nie Lihua. Sound: Chen Baolin. Cast: Li Yunjuan as Malu, Gao Baobao as Ayi, Li Baodheng as Amang

Preparatory to their invasion of Yunnan province during World War II, the Japanese military sends a special unit into the province to foment antagonisms among the several minority peoples there. As a result, three nationality groups are on the verge of civil war. But they discover the conspiracy before it is too late and unite to oppose the Japanese.

901. *Heroic Sons and Daughters (Ying Xiong Er Nu)*

1964. Changchun Film Studio. B & W. 12 Reels. Direction: Wu Zhaodi. Screenplay: Mao Feng and Wu Zhaodi, based on the novel "Reuniting" by Ba Jin (1905–). Cinematography: Shu Xiaoyan. Art Direction: Xu Wei, Wang Chong. Music: Liu Zhi. Sound: Huang Lijia. Cast: Tian Fang as Wang Wenqing, Zhou Wenbing as Wang Fubiao, Liu Shangxian as Wang Fang, Liu Shilong as Wang Cheng, Zhe Dazhang as Zhao Guorui, Guo Zhengqin as Zhang Zhenhua

Wang Wenqing and Wang Fubiao were old military comrades. Although unrelated, they shared the same surname and felt like brothers. Years later, during the Korean War, Wang Wenqing, now the political commissar of a PLA division, has a chance encounter with the son of his old friend, a young soldier named Wang Cheng. The young soldier mentions that his younger sister, Wang Fang, is also in the army. When Wang Cheng dies heroically in action, Wang Wenqing seeks out the sister to pay his respects. When they meet, he recognizes that she is his own daughter from whom he had become separated 18 years earlier. But he chooses not to tell her this; rather, he encourages her to be a good soldier and emulate her brother's example. Wang Fang is injured, and is sent back to China to recover. At last, Wang Wenqing, Wang Fubiao and Wang Fang reunite again, and Wang Fubiao decides it is time to tell the girl the truth about her parentage. Wang Wenqing encourages his daughter to carry on as a new revolutionary generation.

902. *Heroic Spirit (Xiong Hun)*

1990. Xiaoxiang Film Studio. Color. 9 Reels. Wide Screen. Direction: Zhang Jinbiao. Screenplay: Meng Lie, Liang Xiaosheng. Cinematography: Ding Xiaodong. Art Direction: Li Runzhang. Music: Yang Qing. Sound: Liu Yishen.

Cast: Lu Yi as Da Peng, Cao Peichang as Guo Wei, Gao Junxia as Xu Wenjuan, Wang Yuzhang as Xiao Zhenwu, Shu Yaoxuan as He Bin

On September 18, 1931, Japanese troops occupy Shenyang in Northeast China. This invasion, referred to as the "September 18th Incident," shocks the whole world. Every Chinese is faced with a choice of either resisting Japan or surrendering. Guo Wei, Commander of the 305th Regiment of the Northeast Army, and Da Peng, former leader of a group of greenwoods bandits, become bold and courageous resistance fighters. Long-time personal enemies because of a historic family feud, the two are now forced by circumstances to become military allies. But Chinese traitors sow discord between them.

903. *Heroic Tank Crew (Ying Xiong Tan Ke Shou)*

1962. August First Film Studio. B & W. 9 Reels. Direction: Li Ang. Screenplay: Zhou Jianhua. Cinematography: Xue Boqing. Art Direction: Zhen Tuo. Music: Fu Gengcheng. Sound: Kou Shenkang. Cast: Wang Ren as Zhang Yong, Gao Baocheng as Yang Dehou, Zhao Ruping as Wang Dagang, Zhang Lianfu as Sheng Libiao, Zhang Kefang as Liu Ping, Li Po as the infantry division commander

In 1952, PLA Volunteer Army tank platoon leader Zhang Yong and his tank crew lose contact with the rest of their tank group on route to battle. They pass through many dangers before reaching the front lines. In the battle they fulfill their mission, destroying an enemy tank.

904. *The Heroine of Lake Tianhu (Tian Hu Nu Xia)*

1988. Changchun Film Studio. 9 Reels. Direction: Qiao Keji, Zhao Weiheng. Screenplay: Ni Feng, Shen Qing. Cinematography: Chen Chang'an, Wang Jian. Art Direction: Guo Yansheng. Music: Bi Xiaoxing. Sound: Li Zhenduo. Cast: He Yan as the female "Water Bandit," Wang Jianjun as Yun Zhongyan

Near the end of the Qing Dynasty, a treasure, the "Qiling Five-Colored Ball" is found buried beneath the waters of Great Tianhu Lake. The treasure is coveted by both French and Japanese, and a struggle begins to prevent the foreigners from stealing a national treasure. Their efforts are thwarted by the "Water Bandit," a Lake Tianhu heroine, along with her kung fu instructor and others. She kills a Chinese traitor Yun Zhongyan and counters vari-

ous opposition tricks to save the treasure for China.

905. *Hero's Blood Bank (Ying Xiong Xue An) (alternate title: Cue An Qing Chou)*

1993. Xiaoxiang Film Studio. Color. Letterboxed. 10 Reels. Direction: Wang Xuexin. Screenplay: Jiang Qinmin, Liu Yong. Cinematography: Ning Changxin, Lu Beiyu, Wu Pei. Art Direction: Sui Zuangji, Li Shu. Music: Guo Hongjun. Sound: Yuan Xuefeng. Costume: Li Huiming, Li Shuyan. Makeup: Wang Xiaoling, Xu Yunjie. Cast: Huang Guoqiang as Gong An, Han Yongqin as Liu Pingping, Wang Andong as Zhao Zhongquan, Shi Lei as Liu Zhuli, Zhang Jibo as Zhao Nantian, Wang Xianwei as Wu Chenglong

Around 1920, a man named Liu brings his family to a small town in Southeast China, where they begin farming a small plot of land. Local tyrant Zhao Dingjin redivides the land, giving part to another family named Gao, which makes it very difficult for the two tenant families to survive. Twenty-six years pass, and the Liu, Gong and Zhao family children are all grown. When the Gong family's eldest son and his mother return from overseas, they want to use their savings to build a river port, but once again the Zhaos bully and persecute the others and destroy their plan. The inter-familial conflicts lead to a tragic outcome.

906. *Hibiscus Town (Parts 1 & 2) (Fu Rong Zhen)*

1986. Shanghai Film Studio. Color. Wide Screen. 17 Reels. Direction: Xie Jin. Screenplay: A Cheng and Xie Jin, adapted from the original novel by Gu Hua (1942–). Cinematography: Lu Junfu. Art Direction: Jin Qifeng. Music: Ge Yan. Sound: Zhu Weigang. Cast: Liu Xiaoqing as Hu Yuyin, Jiang Wen as Qing Shutian, Zhen Zaishi as Gu Yanshan, Zhu Shibin as Wang Qiushe, Xu Songzi as Li Guoxiang, Zhang Guangbei as Li Mangeng

Hibiscus Town is a simple Chinese town in a beautiful scenic setting. It draws its name from the hibiscus blossoms which fill the town with their fragrance every autumn. In the town, kind-hearted and pretty Hu Yuyin and her husband Guigui earn their living by selling a local variety of beancurd they make from rice. Through hard work and frugality they finally put aside enough money to build a home of their own. Unfortunately, this brings them nothing but trouble. During the "Four Clean-ups" political campaign of 1964, they are branded as "newly rich peasants," resulting in confiscation of their house and Guigui's suicide. Party Secretary Li Mangeng, once in love with Hu Yuyin, and Gu Yanshan, manager of the local grain supply center, are both implicated in the campaign and discharged from their posts, while local ne'er-do-well Wang Qiushe becomes a key political figure. When the "Cultural Revolution" begins, he is made Party Secretary, and once-lovely Hibiscus Town becomes a place of darkness and terror. Several local citizens, including Hu Yuyin, are placed on trial as "Rightists." She is sentenced to sweep the streets every day with Qing Shutian, a local known as "Madman," whose crime consisted of having received a Western education. Through helping each other survive the ordeal, they gradually fall in love and eventually marry. But their political troubles continue: the jealous Wang Qiushe has Qin sentenced to 10 years in prison and during the first winter after he leaves, Hu Yuyin goes into a difficult labor. She is saved by Gu Yanshan, who has an army vehicle take her to a military hospital, where she gives birth to a son. In the end, Qin Shutian is released from prison and returns home. Private enterprise is now encouraged and the couple take up the profitable beancurd business Hu Yuyin had pursued once before. Everyone is still haunted by memories of the bitter past, however.

Best Actress Liu Xiaoqing, 1987 Golden Rooster Awards.

Best Supporting Actress Xu Songzi, 1987 Golden Rooster Awards.

Best Art Direction Jin Qifeng, 1987 Golden Rooster Awards.

Best Picture, 1987 Hundred Flowers Awards.

Best Actor Jiang Wen, 1987 Hundred Flowers Awards.

Best Actress Liu Xiaoqing, 1987 Hundred Flowers Awards.

Best Supporting Actor Zhu Shibin, 1987 Hundred Flowers Awards.

Grand Prix, Crystal Ball, Jury Award of Czechoslovakian Dramatist Association (Xu Songzi), 26th Karlovy Vary International Film Festival.

Special Jury Award, Audience Award, 33rd Valladolid International Film Festival

Critique Award of Best Foreign Features, German Film Association.

Golden Panda Award, 5th Montpelier Film Festival.

Honorary Award, 40th Working People's Film Festival (Czechoslovakia).

907. *Hidden Rock (An Jiao)*

1977. Changchun Film Studio. B & W. 9 Reels. Direction: Guang Dao, Lin Ke. Screenplay: Xue Shouxian. Cinematography: Tang Yunsheng. Art Direction: Cui Yongquan. Music: Lei Zhengbang, Lin Xuesong. Sound: Huang Lijia, Wang Wenlei. Cast: Li Ge as the PSB Director, Ding Xiaoyi as the Chief Inspector, Chi Zhiqiang as Chen Ming, Wang Guofeng as Guo Ling, Jin Yi as Gao Yin, Ran Jie as Fang Mingxin

In the summer of 1964, in order to damage China's relations with the Third World, Nationalist officials on Taiwan hatch a plot to blow up the Chinese transport ship "Friendship" as it carries a large group of technical experts, students and materials to China from Africa. The plotters dispatch covert agents to the Chinese port city of Binghai, where they make contact with members of an organization called "the lizards," under cover since 1949. A suitcase containing the bomb is loaded on the ship when it stops at Binghai, but the Chinese security forces detect and smash the plot.

908. *Hidden Shadows (Qian Ying)*

1981. Guangxi Film Studio. Color. 10 Reels. Direction: Guo Baocang, Huang Ling. Screenplay: Ji Hongxu, Ji Shanmeng. Cinematography: Yang Yuming, Jiang Weimin. Art Direction: Zhang Yafang. Music: Li Yanlin. Sound: Lin Lin. Cast: Yuan Yuan as Xiao Ling, Chi Zhiqiang as Luo Jie, Han Yueqiao as Lu Yihua, Li Ping as Luo Ming

One night during a thunderstorm, in the Ningwang Palace Museum, curator Lu Yihua is frightened to see the sudden appearance of strange shadows on a wall. One is the image of a Qing Dynasty emperor's concubine, the other a modern person in a raincoat. She reports the apparition to local Public Security Bureau investigator Luo Jie. Luo Jie finds out that Lu Yihua's boyfriend Xiao Ling happens to be studying means of projecting images on surfaces, but what about the dark shadow of the man in a raincoat? Things turn serious when Xiao Ling's coworker Chang Wenhu is murdered. After some very complicated developments, prime suspect Xiao Ling is proven to be innocent and the real killer is caught.

909. *High Expectations for a Son (Wang Zhi Cheng Long)*

1986. August First Film Studio. Color. 9 Reels. Direction: Jia Shihong. Screenplay: You Fengwei. Cinematography: Dong Liang. Art Direction: Fei Lansheng. Music: Li Weicai. Sound: Wang Lewen, Zhang Lei. Cast: Jia Liu as Wang Mi, An Qi as "Lady Half Spirit," Zhu Xiaoming as Wang Chenglong, Wu Lanhui as Li Ruoyu

In a small town, porcelain maker Wang Mi operates a profitable small business making fine china from secret techniques given him by his father years ago. Wang believes that such secrets should only be transmitted from fathers to sons, and decides the time has arrived to share his secrets with his son Chenglong. However, the young man tells him he has no interest whatever in making china. As an alternative, Wang Mi feels the next best recipient of the secret would be a son-in-law. He is actually very fond of his capable apprentice Li Ruoyu, but Wang's daughter already has a lover and flatly refuses to even consider an arranged marriage. In time, Wang Mi begins to alter his traditional thinking. He comes to the conclusion that with reform in China, the young will choose their own careers and arrange their own lives, just as the old must arrange theirs. He decides to go see his lady friend, a local shopkeeper, and propose they start arranging their lives together.

910. *Highrise Pagoda (Tong Tian Ta)*

1986. August First Film Studio. Color. 10 Reels. Direction: Cai Jiwei, Lu Zhuguo. Cinematography: Wang Jiaxi. Art Direction: Ren Huixing. Music: Gong Zhiwei. Sound: Shi Pingyi. Cast: Cun Li as Zhou Tao, Tian Hua as Zhen Ying, Huang Ailing as Zhou Bing, Chen Jianfei as Zhou Sha, Zhou Hongshan as Zhou Shan

Zhou Tao is the chief of telecommunications at a military satellite launching base. His devotion to his work leaves his family feeling neglected, and alienates his daughter Zhou Bing and son Zhou Shan. But as the launch date draws closer, Zhou Tao's family gradually begins to understand and sympathize with the father's enthusiasm for the mission. By the time the satellite is launched successfully, the entire family shares his zeal.

911. *High-Speed Ball Bearing Trains (Gang Zhu Fei Che)*

1959. Changchun Film Studio. B & W. 8 Reels. Direction: Zeng Weizhi. Screenplay: Wang Gengzhu. Cinematography: Yang Cong. Art Direction: Ji Zhiqiang. Music: Wang Bo. Sound: Li Zhenduo. Cast: Shen Yin as Dahu, Ren Weimin as "Slicker than a Ghost," Tian Hongchao as Erren, Yang Huang as Erniu, Ren Wenxiu as Yuling, Liu Ru as the secretary

During the Great Leap Forward campaign, an agricultural commune at an isolated mountain village in Heman province conducts a contest in order to resolve their transport problem. One team of women, led by Erniu, remodeled wood bearings to ball bearings, but her brother Dahu, head of the train team, distrusts ball bearings and rejects them. At the next day's contest, the team competing with wood bearings loses to another using ball bearings. This causes Dahu to realize his mistake, and with new confidence in the technological revolution, he accomplishes the transport mission ahead of schedule.

912. *Hills Bathed in Sunset (Qing Shan Xi Zhao)*

1984. Youth Film Studio. Color. Wide Screen. 9 Reels. Direction: Zhao Min, Situ Zhaodun. Screenplay: Yang Tao, Kong Du. Cinematography: Pao Xiaoran. Art Direction: Xing Zheng, Han Gang. Music: Hu Weili. Sound: Wang Junzhi, Ma Yaowen. Cast: Cao Huiqu as Liu Hong, Qin Yi as Wang Xiu, Zhong Xinghuo as Peng Liang, Feng Qi as Wang Qiang, Feng Xiao as Xiao Po, Liu Fei as Yan Fuyou

In the twilight of his career, Ministry of Railways official Liu Hong and his wife Wang Xiu travel to the Weisanghu area where they had both served when young. Liu Hong recalls their railway work during the war, and then in the early years of the People's Republic, as China was upgrading its railways.

913. *His Little World (Ai You, Ge Ge!)*

1987. Shanghai Film Studio. Color. 8 Reels. Direction: Jin Shuqi. Screenplay: Wang Yanzhen. Cinematography: Cheng Shiyu. Art Direction: Guo Dongcang. Music: Liu Yanxi. Sound: Liu Guangjie, Gong Dejun. Cast: Guan Peipei as Little Bean, Chun Xiao as Da Gan, Ma Dalong as Father, Xu Zhiyi as Xiao Tu

Doudou is a young boy who has an

insatiable thirst for knowledge but tends to live in fantasy. He worships his older brother Dagan and sets him up as a role model. Like a typical teenager, sometimes Dagan is rude to his little brother and doesn't want to play with him. Dagan lives in his own world, but of course, Doudou is very interested in what Dagan is doing. When Dagan doesn't take an interest in him, Doudou feels lonely and depressed, but he never stops admiring his brother. In a composition entitled "His Little World," Doudou unveils his innermost thoughts in the hope Dagan will understand him.

914. *Hit Woman (Nu Jie Sha)*

1993. Guangxi Film Studio. Color. Letterboxed. 9 Reels. Direction: Wang Wenzhi. Screenplay: Zhao Xuebin. Cinematography: Cai Xiaopeng. Art Direction: Qiu Hongjun. Music: Niu Shisheng. Costume; Chen Weixing. Makeup: Zhao Zhiming. Cast: He Wei as Ren Yulan, Zhao Liping as Bai Xue, Xu Jianing as Jin Yongle, Wang Xiaozhong as Guitian, Sun Wei as the woman bandits chief, Kuang Kuang as Zhen Yuanji, Tang Zhongting as Hou Tai, Bai Yun as Ren Yuzhu

On the eve of the founding of the PRC in the late 1940s, Professor Ren Yan, a scientist renowned for his weapons research, secretly leaves the U.S. to return to China. Nationalist Chinese intelligence on Taiwan assigns woman agent Bai Xue to intercept the scientist and abduct him to Taiwan, with orders to kill him if necessary to keep him away from the Communists. Meanwhile, Ren's nieces, sisters Yulan and Yuzhu, travel to meet him and escort him back to China. The two sisters fight a running battle with the agent, foiling each of the latter's attempts to get close to the scientist. At last, Bai Xue reaches her quarry, only to discover the man she has been pursuing is a decoy, and the real Ren Yan has arrived safely in Beijing. Unable to face returning to Taiwan a failure, the Nationalist agent takes her own life.

915. *Holy Fire at a Border Guard Station (Tian Bian You Yi Chu Sheng Huo)*

1990. August First Film Studio. Color. Wide Screen. 10 Reels. Direction: Song Zhao. Screenplay: Zhen Zhenghuan. Cinematography: Zhang Chi, Ye Naijun. Art Direction: Sun Guoqing.

Music: Wang Xiaoyong. Sound: Li Qingheng, Shi Pingyi. Cast: Wei Jian as Lan Heer, Wang Liyun as Qiaoqiao, Zhang Guangbei as Liu Qinjian

At a lonely outpost in the Chinese desert, a small group of PLA soldiers serve their country in isolation, and we learn some of their stories. Platoon leader Lan Heer has called the desolate station home for over 10 years; his wife Qiaoqiao hopes that some day she will be approved to live with him as a military spouse. In order to help the station out of some difficulty, however, Lan Heer volunteers to take early retirement from the army. Another soldier, deputy platoon leader Liu Qinjian, gives up his chance to teach at a military school and returns to the outpost instead. The soldiers all put their duty ahead of their personal desires.

Homemade Cement **see** *Abandon Superstitions*

916. *Homesick (Xiang Si)*

1985. Jiangxi Film Studio. Color. 10 Reels. Direction: Qi Shilong, Wu Anping. Screenplay: Wang Yimin. Cinematography: Zhen Xuan. Art Direction: Li Youren. Music: Ma Ding. Sound: Yu Meiqiang, Li Jianyun. Cast: Ying Tingru as Zhou Lianggu, Zhang Guoli as Chen Zhuan, Wei Jian as Zhou Daoshan, Che Li as Teacher Mei

In rural northern Jiangxi province, Li Ming abandons his young wife Zhou Lianggu when he gets the opportunity to work and live in the city. His abandoned wife tries to overcome her pain through hard work. A former classmate of Li Ming's, a nice young teacher named Chen Zhuan, is sympathetic to her plight, and in time she falls in love with Chen, only to find that he is having an affair with another teacher named Mei. Zhou Lianggu survives this second lost love, and hides her feelings. She later receives an award for her contributions to agricultural production.

917. *Hometown (Lao Xiang)*

1986. August Film Studio. Color. 9 Reels. Direction: Wang Xiaotang. Screenplay: Wang Xiaotang, Huang Xiaohua. Cinematography: Cai Shunan, Jiang Jingde. Art Direction: Zhang Zheng. Music: Zhang Peiji. Sound: Song Tianpei. Cast: Zhang Fengyi as Yu Mang, Tong Li as Du Shuangbao, Dong Yugang as Zhao Huadong, Qiu Li and Grandma Wang

High-ranking army officer Yu Mang makes

a nostalgic visit to the town which was his old wartime base, where he is surprised and dismayed to find the poor living conditions of some of the veterans and their families. Yu Mang feels very guilty about the neglect and lack of care of these people, so he finds a capable developer he knows, Du Shuangbao, and convinces him to develop the town. The old village begins to prosper, and Du Shuangbao grows to like the place so much he decides to make it his home.

918. *Hometown Accent (Xiang Yin)*

1983. Pearl River Film Studio. Color. 9 Reels. Direction: Hu Bingliu. Screenplay: Wang Yimin. Cinematography: Liang Xiongwei. Art Direction: Li Xin. Music: Jin Youzhong, Situ Kang, Ding Jialin. Sound: Wu Chengxin. Cast: Zhang Weixin as Tao Chun, Liu Yan as Yu Musheng, Zhao Yue as Xingzhi, Chen Rui as Minhan

Yu Musheng and his wife Tao Chun are a happily married farm couple with two children. When a new railway station opens in the nearest town, some 10 miles distant, Tao Chun expresses a desire to go see it. Her husband expresses considerable surprise at her request, as she has practically never left home in her life. He tells her to stay where she is, and she obeys him as she always has. When Tao Chun tells him she is experiencing abdominal pains, Yu shows little concern, and just gets her some pain killer. When a new clothing store opens in their village, and Tao Chun tells her husband how pretty the dresses are, he tells her a farm woman like her should only wear plain clothing, and again she obeys him. When she has a recurrence of the abdominal pains, he again tells her to just take something for it. But this time her sister intervenes and insists Tao Chun go to the hospital, where she is diagnosed as having liver cancer. This shocks Yu, and he deeply regrets having for so long delayed her getting a diagnosis and treatment. He tells her he will now accede to whatever she wants. Tao Chun tells him she just wants to see the new railway station.

Best Picture, 1984 Golden Rooster Awards.

919. *Hometown at the Foot of the Mountain (Shan Xia Shi Gu Xiang)*

1983. Pearl River Film Studio. Color. 10 Reels. Direction: Liu Hongming. Screenplay: He Mengfan, Wang Hong. Cinematography: Wang

Yunhui, Zhu Junheng. Art Direction: Li Wenguang. Music: Cheng Dazhao. Sound: Lin Guang. Cast: Pao Guoan as Chang Mao, Liang Yuejun as Yushao, Ju Wancheng as Huaijin, Guo Qihai as Heiwa

One day in early spring, Chang Mao returns to his hometown after being away for some time working in the city as a carpenter. When he arrives, he learns that former production team director Huai Yu has just been killed in an accident. This saddens Chang Mao, for the two had been childhood playmates. No one else is grieving, however, for Huai Yu's silly policies had brought hardship to everyone in the village, including Chang Mao, whose wife died having a miscarriage directly attributable to Huai Yu's incompetence. At this time, Huai Yu's widow Yushao comes to Chang Mao begging him to help her and her 11-year-old son Heiwa: not only is she now without any means of support, she cannot bear the mockery and abuse of the villagers who hated her husband. Kindly and forgiving Chang Mao decides to help them, although the boy Heiwa is strongly opposed to his mother's getting together with Chang Mao. Chang Mao determines to break through the villagers' hostility to Yushao, and in time he wins the boy over as well.

920. *Hometown of Overseas Chinese (Qiao Xiang Qing)*

1989. Nanhai Film Company and Aofeng Film Company Co-Production. Color. Letterboxed. 9 Reels. Direction: Liu Xin. Screenplay: Ruo Gu, Liu Xing. Cinematography: Han Xingyuan. Art Direction: Zhu Jinhe. Music: Zhang Jielin. Sound: Lu Minwen. Cast: Situerde as John, Sangqita as Helen, Xie Fang as Liang's wife

John and Helen Liang are a Chinese-American brother and sister who arrive in China seeking their family's ancestral native village, Rongshu Village. By following clues left them by their late father, they succeed in locating Rongshu. Their mother then joins them, bringing along her late husband's ashes for burial in his native soil. The family then finds that a woman living in Rongshu is known as "Liang's wife," and it turns out she was the late Mr. Liang's wife before he left China. Although the first wife had not heard from him for many years, she always remained faithful, and is now very upset to hear of his death. She and the second Mrs. Liang build a close relationship based on mutual understanding and sympathy, and the two children acknowledge they have two mothers.

921. *Hometown Rhythm (Gu Xiang De Xuan Lu)*

1984. Tianshan Film Studio. Color. 9 Reels. Direction: Ma Jingwu. Screenplay: Liu Cheng, Xia Lan. Cinematography: Liu Yongsi. Art Direction: Kang Lin. Music: Zhou Ji, Aibai Dula. Sound: Lai Qijian. Cast: Pahaerding as Dilixiate, Gulizhaer as Shaniya, Aersiye as Sailimu, Dalilihan as Haimiti, Mulati as Aihamaiti, Palida as Fadima, Reshalati as Paxia

A Uighur student who has been studying music in Beijing returns to Xinjiang to collect folk songs. He searches for a legendary old folk singer, and romances a local girl. He successfully gets the songs he wants, but the girl tells him she loves another.

922. *Hometown Romantic Tune (Jia Xiang Lang Man Qu)*

1989. Youth Film Studio. Color. Letterboxed. 9 Reels. Direction: Duan Jishun. Screenplay: Dong Shengtao. Cinematography; Gao Lixian. Art Direction: Liu Changbao. Music: Yang Nailin. Sound: Zhang Yaling. Cast: Zhao Liang as Ding Shitou, Liu Jing as Qiaoyun, Yang Shihua as Xiulan, Shan Zenghong as Wang Xinhua, Zhao Xiaochuan as Ding Mingli

Years ago, a young man named Ding Shitou left his rural village to work in the city. Now he returns, bringing along a group of young people like himself. They plan to open a stone-cutting team. They fail, but later find a spring, which leads them to open a soft drink plant. This is more successful, and meanwhile several romances blossom among the young entrepreneurs.

923. *Honeymoon Conspiracy (Mi Yue De Yin Mou)*

1985. Xi'an Film Studio. Color. 9 Reels. Direction: Li Yucai. Screenplay: Li Rui. Cinematography: Zhang Faliang, Ma Shusheng. Art Direction: Zhang Qi, Ge Yue. Music: Li Xudong. Sound: Chen Li. Cast: Li Xida, Hao Yiping, Xu Zhiwei, Wen Qian, Tian Ying

In the fall of 1970, a newlywed couple is returning to their home in the city after their honeymoon. However, the bride Qiao Li is abducted and driven off in a jeep, along with one of their suitcases. When the husband Ding

Jiayi returns home he finds their home has been broken into and everything in it stolen. It also develops that the woman he married is not who she claimed to be, an ordinary factory worker named Qiao Li. PSB Chief Investigator Yang Lin takes the case. He learns that the whole business was a conspiracy led by a city government clerk named Chen. Chen had blackmailed a woman named Liu Ping into taking the name Qiao Li and getting involved with Ding Jiayi to get him out of the way. While Ding was away, Chen's gang searched Ding's house for a fortune in gold they believed hidden there. After the criminals are caught, Ding Jiayi sees Liu Ping again. He considers her as much a victim as himself, and still loves her anyway.

924. *The Honeymoon Returns (Mi Yue Zai Lai)*

1992. Shanghai Film Studio. Color. Letterboxed. 10 Reels. Direction: Bao Qicheng. Screenplay: Li Yunliang. Cinematography: Peng Enli. Art Direction: Wang Xingcang. Music: Su Junjie. Sound: Tu Mingde. Costume: Ding Shulan. Makeup: Wang Jingxian. Cast: Ru Ping as Xia Yu, Ning Li as Lin Mu, Lu Yinzhi as Fang Xiaoqi, Liu Cangwei as Fang Xiaoqi, Zhong Canghuo as Fang Hongbo, Cao Kefan as Lu Yi

A photographer's jealous wife always suspects her husband of having affairs with the many women he comes into contact with at work, although her husband is very obedient to her. At the same time, a computer expert's psychologist wife is very dominant in their relationship, but also suspects him of being unfaithful. After a series of misunderstandings, the two couples are able to work out their difficulties and put love back in their relationships.

925. *Hong Yu (Hong Yu)*

1975. Beijing Film Studio. Color. 12 Reels. Direction: Cui Wei. Screenplay: Yang Xiao and Cui Wei, based on the novel of the same title by Yang Xiao. Cinematography: Nie Jing, Zhou Jixun. Art Direction: Yu Yiru. Music: Su Min, Wang Jixiao. Sound: Zhang Jiake. Casting: Zen Xiushan as Hong Yu, Wun Gang as Xiao Shun, Chen Guoxi as Qin Lin, Tian Chengren as the stonesmith, Shao Wanlin as Er Huai, Fang Hui as Sun Tianfu

In a mountain village, a young boy named Hong Yu dreams of becoming a rural doctor serving the farmers. One day he sees that Sun

Fu, a pharmacist in the old society, is still selling counterfeit drugs. In order to have total control of the village's medical care, Sun Fu petitions to become the local physician, and the village chief approves this. This sets off a controversy over who should become the local physician, with the final decision being to send Hong Yu to a training unit for rural doctors. Sun plants many vicious rumors about Hong Yu, and upon his return Hong Yu has many run-ins with Sun. But Hong Yu's medical skills improve steadily, and he becomes increasingly trusted by people.

926. *Honggu Village Love and Hostility (Hong Gu Zai En Chou Ji)*

1988. Beijing Film Studio. Color. 9 Reels. Direction: Duan Jishun. Screenplay: Liang Xing. Cinematography: Wang Zhaolin. Art Direction: Cheng Rongyuan, Wang Xinguo. Sound: Zhao Jiping. Music: Li Bojiang. Cast: Zhang Mingming as Honggu, Xiong Dahua as Huo Gongzhi, Li Jian as Old Honggu, Zhu Xiaomei as Hongmei, Chong Lin as Wang Jinhu

Toward the end of the Ming dynasty (c1625), governmental corruption makes the people's lives almost unbearable. A woman named Honggu is a performer with a traveling family acrobatic troupe. But no matter where they perform, they are persecuted by Huo, a senior court official who has a high military position. Once, when their situation seems desperate, they are rescued by Huo's son, a young man who is honest and sympathetic. Honggu realizes that as a result of the official's persecution, more than 50 people from the acrobatic company have lost their lives in just one generation. She decides to avenge this by killing Huo. But just at this time, the official dies suddenly, and according to Chinese custom his son should become the target of her revenge. The story ends with Huo's son at last deciding to go with Honggu's people in joining a peasant rebellion under Li Zicheng.

927. *Honorable Family (Guang Rong Ren Jia)*

1950. Northeast Film Studio. B&W. 9 Reels. Direction: Ling Zifeng. Screenplay: Sun Qian. Cinematography: Qian Jiang, Yan Dekui. Set Design: Zhu Ge. Music: Gao Tian. Sound: Lu Xiancang. Costume: Liu Jingying. Cast: Chen Ke as Tian Yongtai, Huang Ling as Elder Daughter-in-Law, Li Xiaogong as Second Daughter-in-Law, Lu Fei as Elder Brother, Sun Yuezhi as Second Son

In the winter of 1948, the final battle begins for the liberation of northeast China. Millions of farmers in the northeast liberated areas volunteer to join civilian work teams helping in the front lines. Although older than 50, Tian Yongtai enthusiastically volunteers and is accepted as a stretcher bearer at the front lines. There he meets his second son, and then rescues and cares for his wounded eldest son. He encourages his sons to kill the enemy and render outstanding service. Later, both of the sons are decorated for meritorious service. Tian Yongtai himself captures an American-made gun. His first and second daughters-in-law remain home, but become worker-heroes. Tian Yongtai's family is given the title of "Honorable Family."

928. *Hoofbeats (Ma Ti Sheng Sui)*

1987. Xiaoxiang Film Studio. Color. 9 Reels. Direction: Liu Miaomiao. Screenplay: Jiang Qitao. Cinematography: Zhang Li, Yan Yuanzhao. Art Direction: Yang Li. Music: Wun Zhongjia. Sound: Huang Shiye. Cast: Bianba Danzi as Chen Zhikun, Yang Qiong as Feng Guizhen

In 1935, inept political interference results in the Red Fourth Army being forced back to the north in retreat. Regimental Commander Chen Zhikun is given the mission of blowing up a bridge, and on his way back he meets five extremely fatigued women soldiers. He tells them he is returning to the main Red Army force, and they travel together. But then Chen accidentally breaks both legs and, knowing he cannot go on, takes his own life. The five women press on. On the road they see the bodies of many Red Army soldiers, most of them starved to death. Even the grass has been eaten by the desperate troops. At one point the women feed themselves by cooking and eating their leather jackets. They doggedly advance through many hardships, and after many days they at last catch up with the main force of the Red Army.

929. *Hope (Liu An Hua Ming)*

1979. Beijing Film Studio. Color. 13 Reels. Direction: Guo Wei. Screenplay: Chen Dengke, Lu Yanzhou, Xiao Ma, Jiang Sheng. Cinematography: Ge Weiqing. Art Direction: Chen Xiaoxia. Music: Shi Lemeng, Lu Zhulong. Sound: Zhang Jiake, Dong Qiuxin. Cast: Chen Dazhu as Mrs.

Tian, Tian Jingshan as Geng Changgui, Zhang Ping as the old county director, Li Yaling as Wu Chunzheng

After her husband is persecuted to death during the "Cultural Revolution," Mrs. Tian and her six-year-old daughter Xiao Lan are declared "relatives of counterrevolutionaries" and driven from their Liugang production unit. The two travel to the production unit at Huaxi. The director at Huaxi, Geng Changgui, is sympathetic to her plight and allows Tian to join their unit. Tian applies to her work the things she had learned from her late husband, and the Huaxi unit soon flourishes. In time, Geng Changgui and Mrs. Tian fall in love. But a faction of "Gang of Four" followers represented by the provincial secretary destroys Huaxi's excellent production situation. In addition, her past catches up with her, and the Gang of Four persecutes Mrs. Tian and the former county director. At last Mrs. Tian is imprisoned, but after the Gang is smashed, she regains her freedom.

930. *Hope Over the Ocean (Hai Wang)*

1981. Pearl River Film Studio. Color. 10 Reels. Direction: Liu Hongming. Screenplay: Chen Jian, He Jun, Tao Baili. Cinematography: Liu Hongming, Ye Weimin. Art Direction: Li Wenguang. Music: Zhen Qiufeng. Sound: Lu Minwen. Cast: Chen Xiguang as Bai Yunfei, Wang Xiyan as Minister He, Zhang Fa as Zen Zhiyuan, Qi Mengshi as Bai Yongqin, Liu Guanxiong as Zhang Bing, Sun Yan as Zen Qiuping

Nationalist pilot Bai Yunlong loves China, but his entire background and training have led him to believe that only the Nationalist Party can preserve and protect China's people and culture. After the mainland falls to the Communists in 1949, he and his wife Qiuping are separated by the Taiwan Strait. Bai Yunlong hears that his wife has been executed by the Communists. In 1955, he participates in aerial bombing of the mainland. When he is sent on a second bombing run, he is shot down and bails out into the sea. He is picked up, taken to the mainland and hospitalized. In the hospital he sees how many innocent civilians have been hurt by the bombing he took part in. At last, he unexpectedly meets his wife Qiuping who he has not seen for 13 years. Bai Yunlong undergoes a conversion, and joins the mainland Chinese Air Force.

931. *Horrible Ghost Forest (Kong Bu De Gui Sheng Lin)*

1987. Xi'an Film Studio. Color. 3-D. 8 Reels. Direction: An Qinyun. Screenplay: An Qinyun, Yuan Xianan, Zhang Eryang. Cinematography: Zhao Zhiyu. Art Direction: Liu Xinghou, Li Zhengshen. Music: Zhang Yangao, Li Jimin. Sound: Chen Li. Cast: Si Fengyong as Ge Long, Han Bingjie as Gu Ming, Ma Huiyin as Pu Liruo, Zhao Chunmin as Mang Lege, Li Jinbang as Geng Bu

Shortly after the founding of the People's Republic, a PLA company is sent to China's southern border to round up a bandit gang operating in that region. The film tells how they pursue and at last round up all the bandits.

932. *The Horror Boxer (Kong Bu Quan Wang)*

1993. Changchun Film Studio. Color. Letterboxed. 9 Reels. Direction: Bei Zhaocheng, Li Geng. Screenplay: Huang Yazhou. Cinematography: Li Geng. Art Direction: Zhong Quan, Mu Er. Music: Fan Weiqiang. Sound: Zhen Yunbao. Costume: Chen Xiaoling. Makeup: Wang Xiaoling, Wang Xiaoqiong. Cast: Li Hu as Tao Sixiong, Xin Ying as Fei Li, Wan Zhihua as Lou Yi, Xu Wenguang as Liang Haihai

Tao Sixiong is a well-known and successful boxer, but lacks a legal sense. His wife Fei Li had been a popular singer, but gave up her career when they married. When someone rapes his wife, Tao vows revenge, although he has no idea who did it. He often suspects strangers and beats them up, for which he is repeatedly arrested. Fei Li later discovers that her attacker was her husband's friend Lou Yi, but fearful of her husband doing something stupid again, she keeps silent about it. Tao finds out the truth anyway, and attacks Lou Yi, beating him until the police arrive to intervene. Fei Li leaves, and resumes her singing career. Tao feels very lost, coming home every night to an empty apartment. Then he receives another notice from the police, ordering him to turn himself in.

933. *Horse (Ma)*

1956. Changchun Film Studio. B & W. 5 Reels. Direction: Yuan Nancheng. Screenplay: Lei Jian, based on the novel by Wang Di. Cinematography: Ge Weiqin. Art Direction: Wang Chong. Music: Li Ning. Sound: Zhang Jianping. Cast: Fang Hua as Old Chang, Xiong Shaisheng as Chang's wife, Xi Yuming as Chang Xiulan, Pan

Deming as Wang Che, Ren Weimin as Bao Hua, Ma Shida as the tall guy

During a meeting to upgrade a junior commune to senior status, farmer Old Chang sneaks out of the meeting hall, for he worries the commune will undervalue his horse. After the meeting, his daughter Xiulan wants to take the horse herself and join the commune, but Chang tries to stop her. Father and daughter argue over this, and Chang's wife sides with the girl. Commune director Wang Che mediates the disagreement, patiently persuading and educating Old Chang as well as advising Xiulan to be less pushy in getting her father to join the commune. When Old Chang later sees his horse evaluated fairly and reasonably, he brings the horse with him and joins. The members elect him director of the commune horse ranch. Xiulan marries commune director Wang Che, and the family lives happily.

934. *Horse Running at the Screen (Beng Xiang Ying Mu De Ma)*

1985. Changchun Film Studio. Color. 10 Reels. Direction: Wang Xuexin. Screenplay: Wang Xingdong, Wang Zhebing. Cinematography: Meng Xiandi. Art Direction: Ju Lutian. Music: Wan Weiqiang. Cast: Su Yala as Zhen Daqun, Wang Chunli as Chen Xiaoqiu, Xie Yuan as Liu Ruozen, Wang Shu as Huang Mu

To obtain a horse for an upcoming movie, assistant film director Chen Xiaoqiu goes to an army cavalry company for help. The assignment is given to soldier Zhen Daqun, who finds an excellent white horse for the filmmakers. But while the horse is beautiful, it is also very spirited. Zhen works very hard to train the horse, and is chosen to stand in for actor Hao Wei in the riding scenes. The film is a big success.

935. *Horse Spirit (Long Ma Jing Shen)*

1965. Beijing Film Studio. B & W. 11 Reels. Direction: Shi Yifu, Chang Gengmin. Screenplay: Li Zhun. Cinematography: Zhu Jinming. Art Direction: Mo Renji. Music: Lu Yi. Sound: Sun Yumin. Cast: Pang Jianmin as Han Mangzhong, Lu Jingqi as Changshui, Jia Linqing as Li Shishan, Su Zhen as Cai Xiuzheng, Wang Shanbao as Liang Dou, Guo Yi as Liu Cuixiang

In rural Henan, the Shishugou production unit is very poor, lacking water and large livestock. Commune member Han Mangzhong

buys a cheap, skinny horse for the commune at a goods fair. The commune's stockman Liang Dou is a selfish upper-middle class farmer, who had wanted to buy this thin horse himself, then fatten it up for resale at a profit. So he rejects the horse and refuses to feed it for the commune. Mangzhong brings the horse to his own home and cares for it out of his own pocket. Liang Dou tries to foster disputes between Mangzhong and his wife Cai Xiuzheng, and does succeed in getting the couple to argue about the horse. However, Mangzhong does not give up, and continues to work very hard at feeding and caring for the horse until it is at last very strong and healthy. The couple also reconcile. Later, the production unit finds that Liang Dou has been illegally stealing and selling feed intended for the commune's horses, and assigns Mangzhong to take over Liang Dou's work.

936. *Horse Thief (Dao Ma Zei)*

1986. Xi'an Film Studio. Color. Wide-screen. 9 Reels. Direction: Tian Zhuangzhuang. Screenplay: Zhang Rui. Cinematography: Hou Yong, Zhao Fei. Art Direction: Huo Jianqi. Music: Ju Xiaosong. Sound: Hui Dongzi. Cast: Cexiang Rigzin as Rorbu, Dan Zhiji as Djoma, Daiba as Grandma, Gaoba as Nowre, Jayang Jamco as Drashi, Drashi as Grandpa

A leisured exploration of the way of life of the Tibetan people, and a demonstration of the key role their religion plays in the people's lives. The simple plot follows Rorbu, who supports his family by stealing horses. When his son dies, Rorbu expresses his repentance for his way of life in the "Ghost Dance," and tries to go straight. However, poverty drives him back to theft again after his second son is born, this time with tragic consequences.

Grand Prix of Fribourg Municipality, 4th Film Festival of the Third World.

937. *The Horse Thief's Wife (Ma Zei De Qi Zi)*

1988. August First Film Studio. Color. 9 Reels. Direction: Yang Zhaoren. Screenplay: Wang Chonghan. Cinematography: Cai Shunan. Art Direction: Sun Guoqing. Music: Du Xingcheng. Sound: Zhang Lei. Cast: Wu Gang as Qu Wenhan, Wu Lijie as Qin Yuzhu

In rural Northeast China in the 1930s, Beifeng Town school teacher Qin Yuzhu is raped by town administrator Cao Shilin. She begs her fiance Qu Wenhan to avenge her. Qu, an anti–Japanese Volunteer Army branch director in the nearby town of Changbai, immediately leads his force in an attack on Cao's mansion, but Cao Shilin suddenly announces he is establishing an anti–Japanese Volunteer Army Beifeng branch. Qu has to control his anger and join forces with the Beifeng branch in the anti-Japanese effort. Qin Yuzhu leaves him and marries another "greenwoods bandit," Chao Shangfei. To avenge his new wife, Chao Shangfei surrounds the Beifeng branch when the Changbai branch is off with other troops preparing to attack a railway station. Qu later kills Cao Shilin after learning Cao is really a Japanese collaborator, but Qu himself is then killed by the enemy. Qin Yuzhu grieves for him.

938. *Hot Youth (Gun Tang De Qing Chun)*

1993. Tianshan Film Studio. Color. Letterboxed. 9 Reels. Direction: Guang Chunlan. Screenplay: Wei Rongsu, Guang Chunlan. Cinematography: Li Yuebin, Yu Shishan. Art Direction: Zhang Xiaochun. Music: Nusilaiti. Sound: Liang Jiadong, Yan Ming. Costume: Yang Shixin. Makeup: Bai Nisha. Cast: Bierxun Nayi as Bai Mei, Mulading as Shabier, Muketaisi as Gulina, Abu Lizi as Nijiati, Maimaiti Aili as Abudula, Apurili as Nishahan

Two young people from Xinjiang, Uighur singer Shabier and young girl Bai Mei, both work in a folk culture village in a prosperous Chinese city. They are good friends and spend much of their spare time together. They are given the choice of staying with urban life or returning to Xinjiang to help develop its southern region. Shabier decides to return to his hometown, where he has a girlfriend Gulina waiting for him. Bai Mei then realizes their friendship can never develop into love, but she decides to make a trip to Xinjiang since her father once lived there. It turns out that Bai Mei is really a Uighur, and she decides to stay. Shabier marries Gulina, and Bai Mei becomes engaged to a young man named Nijiati. Everybody is happy.

939. *Housekeeper (Jia Wu Qing Guan)*

1982. Changchun Film Studio. Color. 11 Reels. Direction: Guangbudao Erji. Screenplay: Zhang Xiaotian. Cinematography: Dansheng Nima. Art Direction: Liu Sheng. Music: Gao

Feng. Sound: Wang Wenfu. Cast: Ma Qun as Liang Yu, Wang Suya as Yang Qinwei, Pu Ke as Xiao Peng, Li Junhai as Chi Junfang, Geng Xiaolu as Saibei

The 3rd Plenary Session of the 11th Party Congress leads aging and ailing city Party Secretary Liang Yu to think about retirement. He thinks he should step aside and give some younger, more energetic person a chance. Liang Yu's wife Yang Qinwei strongly opposes her husband's retirement decision, for fear of losing political influence. The whole family argues about it. Societal pressures mix in with the family dispute. All of this stress causes a reoccurrence of Liang Yu's heart trouble. Yang Qinwei then realizes she has been behaving improperly, and with the help of friends and relatives, Yang Qinwei corrects her attitude, and Liang Yu's family unites in support of his retirement decision.

940. *How Many Levels Has Hell? (Di Yu Jiu Jing You Ji Ceng)*

1994. Guangxi Film Studio, Hong Kong Lu Xiaolong Film Company Co-Production. Color. Letterboxed. 9 Reels. Direction: Lu Xiaolong, Zhang Ning, Jiang Yang. Screenplay: Xiao Ma, Li Zhipu. Cinematography: Cai Xiaopeng. Art Direction: Li Qining. Sound: Lin Lin. Cast: Li Lili as Qiushan Hemei, Lu Xiaolong as Zhongchun Qianyi, Yuanwen as Xinjing Qingzhi, Tang Jun as Cui Lianyu, Yang Dichang as Gongben, Tian Ye as Chuanqi, Zhang Ning as Qiushan Hong

During World War II, Qiushan Hemei, a half–Chinese, half–Japanese woman reporter, interviews some "comfort women" (sex slaves for the Japanese army). Shocked at the inhumane lives these women are forced to lead, she determines to tell the world about it. But before she can write the story she is arrested. A Japanese officer rapes the reporter and forces her to become a comfort woman herself. Qiushan organizes the other women for a mass escape, but it fails. Qiushan wants to kill herself, but a Japanese comfort woman encourages her to write out the story. Qiushan starts to write "How Many Levels Has Hell," but her captors find the manuscript and burn it. The attempted cover-up eventually fails, as some comfort women survive to tell the truth.

941. *Hua Tuo and Cao Chao (Hua Tuo Yu Cao Chao)*

1983. Shanghai Film Studio. Color. 11 Reels.

Direction: Huang Zhumo. Screenplay: Tao Yuan, Yu Fang. Cinematography: Shen Miaorong. Art Direction: Chen Shaomian. Music: Xiao Yan. Sound: Wu Honghai, Wang Shu. Cast: Zhen Qianlong as Hua Tuo, Wang Hongsheng as Cao Chao, Gong Xue as Yunqin, Ding Jiayuan as Xun Yu, Zhang Yiran as Xu Zhe, Dong Wengang as Cao Chong, Yang Xinzhou as Cao Pei

In 200 A.D., General Cao Chao has a sudden recurrence of severe headache just before his troops are to engage the enemy at the decisive battle of Guan Du. Hua Tuo, known as the "miracle doctor," is brought to the general and quickly relieves his pain. Cao Chao is so impressed he demands the doctor stay and serve him, but Hua Tuo is devoted to treating the illnesses of common people, so he declines the offer. Besides, he wants to develop a new anesthetic, and feels he cannot do that in the general's service. Hua Tuo tries to leave but Cao Chao forces him to stay against his will. Hua Tuo grows increasingly unhappy at being the general's personal physician, and at last finds an excuse to leave for a while. He travels about treating common people again, and in time develops his anesthetic, called "ma-fushan." When he at last has to go back, Cao Chao is so unhappy at his late return he decides to lock up the doctor for a time to teach him a lesson. The guards, thinking Hua Tuo is just another prisoner, brutalize and then kill him. Soon, when Cao Chao has a recurrence of his severe headache, he calls for Hua Tuo to be brought again to treat him, but it is too late. Cao Chao dies as well.

942. *Huaishu Village (Huai Shu Zhuang)*

1962. August First Film Studio. Color. 11 Reels. Direction: Wang Ping. Screenplay: Hu Ke, adapted from his stage play of the same title. Cinematography: Cai Jiwei. Art Direction: Kou Honglie. Music: Cheng Geng. Sound: Wu Hanbiao. Cast: Hu Peng as Mrs. Guo, Kong Rui as Liu Laocheng, Ge Zhenbang as Liu Gengzhu, Che Yi as Laocheng's wife, Jiang Zeshan as Mr. Tian, Feng Xiangru as Jinmei

In 1947, farmers in the North China village of Huaishu initiate land reform under the leadership of Communist Party members Mrs. Guo and Liu Laocheng. State administrative cadre Cui Zhiguo is a malcontent, opposed to the movement for reasons having to do with his family's landlord background. Guo leads the people in struggling with Cui, and the land reform is finally accomplished. Six years later, Mrs. Guo and Liu Laocheng, the latter now a CPC veteran, set up a farm co-op. In 1957's anti-rightist campaign, Cui Zhiguo foments discontent in Huaishu Village. Guo struggles with Cui under the leadership of upper division Party leaders, and makes sure that production goes as it should. In 1958, when Huaishu Village sets up a people's commune, Guo is elected commune director and goes to Beijing for a worker heroes' reception.

Best Director Wang Ping, 1963 Hundred Flowers Awards.

943. *Huang Tianba (Jin Biao Huang Tian Ba)*

1987. Beijing Film Studio. Color. 9 Reels. Direction: Li Wenhua. Screenplay: Zhang Xian. Cinematography: Guan Qinwu. Art Direction: Hao Jingyuan. Music: Wun Zhongyou. Sound: Zhang Baojian. Cast: Wang Qun as Huang Tianba, Chen Yongxia as Zhang Guilan, Liu Gui as Zhang Qi, Renxiang as Si Shilun, Song Wenhua as Wu Tianqu, Zhang Xucheng as Pu Tiandiao

During the reign of the Emperor Kangxi (1662–1723), four bandits dominate South China: Pu Tiandiao, Wu Tianqu, Huang Tianba and He Tianbao. Government forces enter the region on an extermination campaign, and He Tianbao is the first to be captured. At last they corner Huang Tianba, who kills his two remaining "brothers" to prove his loyalty to the throne, saving his own neck by sacrificing the other two.

944. *Huang Yinggu (Huang Ying Gu)*

1980. Changchun Film Studio. Color. 11 Reels. Direction: Xing Jie, Shu Xiaoyan. Screenplay: Chen Lide. Cinematography: Shu Xiaoyan. Art Direction: Gong Minhui. Music: Qiao Yu. Sound: Zhang Fenglu. Cast: Zhang Jinling as Huang Yinggu, Wu Lusheng as Geng Tieshuo, Li Chengbing as Liu Qinlin, Lin Qiang as Shuangxi, Miao Zhuang as Yingsheng, Zhu Decheng as Zhou Xiaolong

During the Chinese Civil War, Huang Yinggu, female leader of a band of "greenwoods heroes," is very powerful in her locality. Red Army political supervisor Liu Qinlin contacts her and proposes that she affiliate her band with the Red Army, joining them in their anti-government struggle. The local landlords, all with ties to the Nationalist government, hate Huang and have tried for years to wipe out her band. The next time the landlords' mercenaries attack, the bandits are saved by the intercession of Liu Qinlin's force. Huang Yinggu proposes to her deputy commanders that the band merge into the Red Army, but her chief deputy and former protégé Geng Tieshuo opposes her and tries to take control of the band. He does this by spreading rumors about Liu Qinlin, fomenting trouble between Huang Yinggu and the local Communist Party representative, and cooperating with Yingsheng, a traitor. When Liu finds that Geng is working against the amalgamation, he moves to stop him, but is murdered by Yingsheng. Just before he dies, Liu Qinlin tells Huang Yinggu that she has the makings of an excellent Party member. Huang then leads Liu's Red Army troops against a Nationalist regiment and routs it. She then leads her band into the Red Army and develops into an excellent commander.

945. *Huanghua Mountain Ridge (Huang Hua Ling)*

1956. Central Newsreel and Documentary Film Studio. B & W. 7 Reels. Direction: Jin Shan. Screenplay: Jin Shan, based on the novel of the same title by Shu Hui. Cinematography: Gao Hongtao. Art Direction: Qin Wei. Music: Ge Guangrui, He Fang, Sound: Xue Shengxing. Cast: Cui Wei as Li Hongkui, Zhang Yunfang as Songer's wife, Wang Ban as Li Chuntang, Shao Hua as Song Fushan, Zhang Silian as Song Fushan's wife

Widowed when very young, a poor woman known only as Songer's widow lives alone and supports herself by raising peaches. When times become especially difficult, she seeks help from her late husband's brother Song Fushan, but he belittles her for her poverty and unmarried status. Later, he decides to take over her peach garden and blocks her from joining the local agricultural cooperative. Songer's widow at last breaks through the feudal code of ethics and obtains the help she needs by joining the cooperative union.

946. *Huangpu River Story (Huang Pu Jiang De Gu Shi)*

1959. Haiyan Film Studio. Color. 11 Reels. Direction: Zuo Lin. Screenplay: Ai Mingzhi, Chen Xihe. Cinematography: Xu Qi. Art Direction: Ding Cheng. Music: Wang Yunjie. Sound: Chen Jingrong. Cast: Wei Heling as Chang Xinggeng, Zhang Fa as Chang Guishan, Zhou Liangliang as Yang Zhaodi, Ji Qiming as Fang Zhenhai, Tan Yun as Xinggeng's wife, Chen Xu as Zhu Acai

During the last years of the Qing Dynasty (c1910), fisherman Chang Xinggeng is put out of business when his fishing boat is sunk by a British gunboat in the Huangpu River near Shanghai. To support his family, Chang finds work at the British-owned Shenjiang Boat Plant, where he and the other Chinese workers are badly abused by the British managers. Twenty years later, his son Chang Guishan becomes a worker at the same plant. Chang Guishan joins the CPC, and marries another CPC member, young worker Yang Zhaodi. During WWII, the plant is taken over by the Japanese, but Chang Guishan continues working at the plant in preparation for destroying it. After the war, the father returns to work at the plant, but now he is bullied by the Americans and Chinese Nationalists who run the plant. After liberation, vast changes occur at the plant, and with the workers now in charge, they build a 10,000-ton class ship.

947. *Huangwa (Huang Wa)*

1989. Changchun Film Studio and Tianjin Film Studio Co-Production. Color. Letterboxed. 9 Reels. Direction: Xing Shumin. Screenplay: Xia Lan. Cinematography: Xing Shumin. Art Direction: Wang Fengshu, Meng Zhonghua. Music: Yao Min. Sound: Yao Guoqiang. Cast: Guo Zhenqin as the County Director, Wang Wei as Dongdong

A former county director returns to his old hometown when he retires. There, he decides to start a school to improve the people's situation. At first, no one shows up to register, but he keeps trying to attract the village children, and at last succeeds.

948. *Huanhuan, Xiaoxiao (Huan Huan Xiao Xiao)*

1981. Beijing Film Studio. Color. Three dimension. 6 Reels. Direction: Liu Qiulin, Qin Zhiyu. Screenplay: Lin Ji, Liu Qiulin. Cinematography: Zhang Zhucheng. Art Direction: Cheng Rongyuan. Music: Li Wanli, Wang Xiling. Sound: Wei Xueyi. Cast: Dai Zhaoan as Yang Huanhuan, Han Yueqiao as Liu Xiaoxiao, Chen Meijuan as Lili, Qin Wen as Auntie, Yuan Yuan as the Tough Guy, Liang Danni as Little Sister

Yang Huanhuan, a sincere and honest young worker in a roast duck restaurant, is dumped by his girlfriend Lili, causing him to lose interest in his job. One day, on his way to meet a girl someone wants to introduce to him, he sees a girl being assaulted by a young tough. Huanhuan intercedes to help, and it turns out the girl happens to be the one he was going to meet, Liu Xiaoxiao. The two like each other right from the start, but Huanhuan covers what he does for a living, claiming he works at a "food import and export company." When Xiaoxiao later finds out the truth she feels very hurt that Huanhuan lied to her. She decides to hurt him back a bit. Xiaoxiao's father, an upper-level official in the city's food service oversight agency, is familiar with Huanhuan. When he learns of his daughter's relationship with the young man, he gives her sound advice on how to handle the matter. Xiaoxiao begins sincerely helping Huanhuan, and he soon adjusts his attitude towards his work. Their romantic future looks bright.

949. *Huge Disturbance (Ju Lan)*

1978. Beijing Film studio. Color. 12 Reels. Direction: Dong Kena, Jue Wen. Screenplay: Lu Yanzhou, Xiao Ma, Jiang Sheng. Cinematography: Xu Xiaoxian, Zhang Zucheng. Art Direction: Hao Guoxin, Wang Dawen. Music: Tian Feng. Cast: Zhang Lianwen as Zhong Yuan, Du Peng as Zhang Ruochuan, Li Xiumin as Fengni, Yu Ping as Li Xiang, Chen Ying as Manager Du, Yang Wei as Master Long

In the fall of 1950, a series of storms batters the Huai River area, endangering the lives and property of many. Volunteer Army Divisional Commander Zhong Yuan, originally planning to go to Korea, instead takes on the assignment of leading the Huai River dam project. Former commander Zhang Ruochuan has already contracted the project to Shanghai capitalist Manager Du. Du is anxious to implement his original design, while a covert imperialist spy named Gu Leisi plans to use his important ministerial position to destroy any Huai River project. After making an onsite investigation, Zhong Yuan throws out the original plan and consults with many local people in drawing up a new plan. Although his enemies use every possible means to frighten Zhong off the project, including an attempt on his life, the commander stays on the project and carries the project through to a successful conclusion.

950. *The Hui People's Detachment (Hui Min Zhi Dui)*

1959. August First Film Studio. Color. 12 Reels. Direction: Feng Yifu, Li Jun. Screenplay: Li Jun, Ma Rong, Feng Yifu. Cinematography: Cao Jingyun. Art Direction: Xu Run. Music: Gao Ruxing, Li Weicai. Sound: Guo Dazheng. Cast: Li Po as Ma Bengzai, Jia Liu as Political Commissar Guo, Hu Peng as Ma's mother, Liu Jiyun as Old Mr. Li, Wang Runsheng as Han Fushun, Li Huijian as Li Maocai, Wang Xiaozhong as Bai Shouren

In Hebei province in 1938, Ma Bengzai of the Hui nationality organizes an anti–Japanese volunteer army. In one battle, they are almost decimated, but fortunately the Eighth Route Army joins in the battle and saves the Hui volunteers from extinction. Ma Bengzai allies his remaining forces with the Eighth Route Army. At one point he finds that his second-in-command Bai Shouren is scheming to betray them to the enemy, and Ma Bengzai is force to execute Bai. Another time, Ma Bengzai's mother is captured by the enemy and dies in captivity. Ma Bengzai's application to join the CPC is approved, and his volunteer force of Huis develops into a true revolutionary army.

951. *The Hunting (Da Wei Bu)*

1991. Guangxi Film Studio. Color. Letterboxed. 9 Reels. Direction: Luo Yuzhong. Screenplay: Zhu Zhongping, Li Xian. Cinematography: Ye Ruiwei. Art Direction: Huang Shu. Music: Li Yanlin. Sound: Han Weijun. Cast: Wang Runshen as Leng Chongwu, Bi Fu as Tang Jingui, Hu Yunqi as Lei Shaoyun, Chi Zhiqiang as Zhong Chao, Geng Ying as Yu Zhongkui, Wang Yue as Xuan Xiaofei, Ma Junqin as Sufeng, Zhang Fengxiang as Liu Juncheng, Zhou Xuqi as Pao Ao

Two convicts escape from a labor camp and make their way to a secret government plant, where they kill the Party Secretary and steal many classified documents which they hope will help them flee the country. Public security forces move in and start their action of surrounding and blockading the area, and at last recapture the killers.

952. *Huo Wa (Huo Wa)*

1978. Beijing Film Studio & Beijing Film Academy Co-Production. B & W. 9 Reels. Direction: Xie Fei, Zhen Dongtian. Screenplay: Ye Xin and Xie Fei, based on the novel "High Miao Mountain Range." Cinematography: Ge Weiqin, Zhou Kun. Art Direction: Li Jushan. Music: Tian

Liantao. Sound: Lu Xiancang, Zhang Ruikun. Cast: Baima Zhaxi as Huo Wa, Ji Ping as Brother Sun, Ma Jingwu as Rongcang, Qi Guirong as A Ma, Feng Enhe as Father, Liu Jiang as Shan Mowang

In 1950, some villages in the mountainous area peopled largely by the Miao minority are still controlled by remnants of the defeated Nationalist Army and the reactionary local Miao governor. One day, PLA scout Xiao Sun comes to the area in pursuit of a bandit chieftain, but is attacked by Shan Mowang, an associate of the bandit. Xiao receives a leg wound, but is helped by Huo Wa, a boy tending oxen nearby. Shortly after, the PLA surrounds the village, but Shan Mowang digs in for a last stand. Huo Wa goes to the bandit headquarters to obtain information, but is detected and put into jail, where he finds his mother. She and other prisoners help him escape to deliver the information to the PLA. With the information he provides them, the PLA is able to overrun the bandits' headquarters, and their chief and Shan Mowang receive the fate they deserve.

953. *Hurricane Action (Ju Feng Xing Dong)*

1986. Shenzhen Film Studio. Color. 9 Reels. Direction: Teng Wenji. Screenplay: A Cheng, Dong Wen. Cinematography: Zhu Dingyu, Zhi Lei. Art Direction: Yao Qin. Music: Guo Feng. Sound: Gu Changning. Cast: Zhang Yi as Luo Ao, Shen Ming as Ouyang Hua

An earthquake turns up a rare mineral previously unknown to exist in China. When it disappears, and an international conspiracy is suspected, Chief Inspector Luo Ao investigates, assisted by his girlfriend, TV reporter Ouyang Hua.

954. *Hurricane Over the Sea (Da Hai Feng)*

1993. Fujian Film Studio. Color. Letterboxed. 10 Reels. Direction: Yu Xiaoyang. Screenplay: Gao Mantang, Sun Jianye, Han Yu. Cinematography: Li Sheng. Art Direction: Chen Bing. Music: Chen Shouqian. Sound: Lai Qizhen. Cast: Zhou Lihua as Huo Yunhua, Jin Xing as Liang Laosan, Yu Yang as Factory Director Qi, Yu Shaokang as Lao Wutou, Xing Minghua as Glass Ball

The Huanghai Shipyard pushes its workers around the clock in order to fulfill a contract with a foreign company before a typhoon hits the Fujian coast. When Huo Yunhua, director of an electric welding team, faints from overwork, her team, which includes a veteran worker past retirement age, a brash youngster and several other varying types of people, commits themselves to work even harder. They work until no one can go on any more. The factory puts office workers and Party cadres into the workforce to help, and at last the project is completed a bit ahead of schedule. Everyone celebrates.

955. *A Husband's Secret (Zhang Fu De Mi Mi)*

1985. Pearl River Film Studio. Color. 10 Reels. Direction: Zhang Gang. Screenplay: Zhang Gang. Cinematography: Hu Zhaohong. Art Direction: Wang Rencheng. Music: Wang Ming. Sound: Jiang Shaoqi. Cast: Mao Yongming as Huang Aman, Gao Ying as Xu Yunzhen, Yang Liyi as Du Juan, Cheng Pang as Zhong Xuejian, Huang Minsheng as Tielong, Xue Guoping as Zhang Yibing

Worker Huang Aman joins a cooperative security team, but hides the fact from his wife, for fear she will worry about his volunteering for such potentially dangerous work. His frequent excuses for leaving the family arouse her suspicions, however, and the truth comes out. He decides to resign from the team for family considerations and family life is tranquil again. But when he sees many young children getting mixed up in criminal activity, and especially when he witnesses the death of a poor boy Xiao Dujuan, his sense of social responsibility prods him to join in the search for the killer.

956. *Husbands' Secret Savings Accounts (Da Zhang Fu De Si Fang Qian)*

1989. Shanghai Film Studio, Shanghai Shansi Film Company Co-Production. Color. Letterboxed. 10 Reels. Direction: Yu Jie. Screenplay: Huang Jingjie. Cinematography: Zhou Zaiyuan. Art Direction: Zhang Wanhong. Music: Cai Lu. Sound: Xie Guojie. Cast: Mao Yongmin as Li Yuwen, Zhang Wenrong as Doctor Mei, Huang Yijuan as Zhou Yun, Huijuan as Sister Qin, Niu Beng as Teacher Lu

The stories of three men who have savings accounts they keep secret from their wives. Senior engineer Li Yuwen saves his bonuses and part-time income in order to help with his sister's medical expenses. Liu Xinghua uses his to buy expensive gifts for another woman. Li Yuwen's neighbor, Teacher Lu, saves his extra money to help his brother. In each of these stories, their wives find out about the secret accounts, and in two cases misunderstand their husbands' intentions. All is resolved happily in the end.

957. *I Am Not a Hunter (Wo Bu Shi Lie Ren)*

1984. Changchun Film Studio. Color. Letterboxed. 8 Reels. Direction: Xu Chuanzhen. Screenplay: Huo Da. Cinematography: Gao Jun. Art Direction: Wang Jiru. Music: Zhang Fuquan. Sound: Zhang Fenglu. Cast: Yang Tong as Chang Le, Shi Jun as Lin Wa, Li Xuesong as Xiao Qing

Each summer vacation, elementary school student Chang Le goes to visit his uncle, an animal keeper in a nearby city zoo. The boy loves animals, and when he later gets the chance to go with his friend Lin Wa to a forested mountain area to observe some in their native habitat, he quickly accepts. The youngsters become lost in the forest, and in trying to find their way out they come upon a man hunting in a wildlife sanctuary. When the children are reported missing, the zoo sends out a search team to look for them. Led by Lin Wa's grandfather, the search team finds Chang Le and Lin Wa, who help the searchers catch the illegal hunter.

958. *I Am Very Ugly, But I Am Very Sweet (Wo Hen Chou, Ke Shi Wo Hen Wun Rou)*

1991. Shanghai Film Studio. Color. Letterboxed. 10 Reels. Direction: Zhuang Hongsheng. Screenplay: Zhang Xian, Zhuang Hongsheng. Cinematography: Shen Miaorong. Art Direction: Xue Jianna. Music: Liu Yanxi. Sound: Ren Daming. Cast: Wei Zongwan as Li Laifu, Ning Jing as Liu Tingting, Ying Jilun as Chouchou, Fang Qinzuo as the meat lady, Wang Weiping as Chouchou's father, Cui Jie as Xiao Wang, Ni Yilin as Sister Ma

Homely and simple, but kind and hardworking umbrella repairman Li Laifu looks forward to his impending marriage to Rou Shao. On the eve of their wedding, however, a baby boy turns up on his doorstep. His fiancee misunderstands, and cancels the wedding. Li Laifu takes care of the baby while searching diligently for its parents. He eventually finds out that the boy's father had abandoned the mother, Tingting, and they both refused to take responsibility for the child, the father because a child would hamper his Bohemian lifestyle, and Tingting because she is determined to marry someone who will take her overseas. But at last Laifu's obvious devotion to the child moves Tingting, and she returns to her child, giving up her chance to go abroad. At last, the child brings the glamorous young woman and the good-hearted older man together as parents in reality.

959. *I Am with Them (Wo Zai Ta Men Zhong Jian)*

1982. Emei Film Studio. Color. 10 Reels. Direction: Chong Lianwen, Lu Xiaoya. Screenplay: Yu Hongjun. Cinematography: Li Baoqi, Lu Rongqi, Lu Rongqin. Art Direction: Wu Xujin. Music: Shu Zechi. Sound: Shen Guli. Cast: An Qi as Director Li, Liu Guoxiang as Director Luo, Si Jieqiang as Wu Fang, Zhao Yaming as Tao Yiping

When Director Li comes to her new position at a stocking mill, she finds that her main problem is that her young female employees are obsessed with boys and dating. She decides that production will increase if she can better control their various affairs, so she adopts a series of regulations the women consider unrealistic. She really cares about her employees, but her efforts don't come across that way. Her former colleague, repair shop director Luo, confines himself to economic reform and ideological guidance for his employees. Director Li changes her approach when she sees Luo's results, and her new methods get the young people to realize their shortcomings while improving their morale.

960. *I Have a Daughter (Wu Jia You Nu)*

1994. Children's Film Studio. Color. Letterboxed. 9 Reels. Direction: Ma Chongjie. Screenplay: Liang Xiaosheng. Cinematography: Yang Ying. Art Direction: Yang Qingsheng. Music: Liu Weiguang. Sound: Zhang Ruikun. Cast: Qiu Yue as Xiaowen, Wang Kuirong as father

A newspaper columnist frequently writes columns which are based on the doings of his teenage daughter Xiaowen, a practice she really dislikes. They quarrel about it, but still love each other. The mother works overseas, and often writes to urge that Xiaowen join her. The worried father at last admits to Xiaowen he is not her real father. Xiaowen's father was killed in an auto accident, after which the girl's mother left Xiaowen with the newspaperman, a close friend of the parents. The revelation upsets Xiaowen greatly, but she says she still loves her bogus father.

961. *I Only Cried Three Times (Wo Zhi Liu San Ci Lei)*

1987. Children's Film Studio. Color. 10 Reels. Direction: Qiqin Gaowa. Screenplay: Wang Xingdong, Wang Zhebing. Cinematography: He Guojun. Art Direction: Duan Zhenzhong. Music: Liu Changyuan. Sound: Chen Yixi. Cast: Fang Chao as Ma Yue, Zhu Shimao as Father, Ding Yi as Auntie, Zhang Weixin as Teacher Song, Liu Zhao as Uncle

Ma Yue, 10, throws himself into his father's arms when he finds out his father is leaving to go fight at the front. After the truck takes his father away, Ma Yue goes alone to live with his aunt, but he has a quarrel with his cousin and a fight with a classmate who insults his father. Ma feels all alone and misses his father very much. The little boy does make one close friend in Xiaoxiao, his teacher's daughter, a little girl whose father is also in the army. When word comes that their fathers have been wounded and hospitalized, Ma Yue goes to visit his father, taking with him Xiaoxiao's greetings to her father. Unfortunately, when he gets there he learns his father has already recovered and been sent back to the front, while Xiaoxiao's father has died of his wounds. Ma Yue bursts into tears and wonders how he will ever be able to tell Xiaoxiao the terrible news.

962. *I Still Love You (Wo Xin Yi Jiu)*

1991. Beijing Film Studio. Color. Letterboxed. 9 Reels. Direction: Xia Gang. Screenplay: Meng Zhu. Cinematography: Ma Xiaoming. Art Direction: Gai Wa. Music: Fu Lin. Sound: Zhang Zhian and Guan Jian. Cast: Li Ting as Ye Xiaozhen, Shao Feng as Luo Jie, Xie Lei as Minmin, Lu Zhong as Mother, Tan Feng as Xiao Guang, Shi Weijian as Father, Zhang Fan as Grandma, Lei Zheng as A Huang

Ye Xiaozhen, who works in an editorial office, meets her former high school classmate Luo Jie, sent to reform school several years before and now a temporary laborer in a printing plant. During their school days, Luo had secretly loved Ye, and had once intervened when he came upon another boy assaulting her. The attacker had fallen in the struggle and was dis-

abled. But when he accused Luo Jie of attacking him, Ye had not spoken up in Luo's defense, something she has always regretted. The two now begin a romance, but her parents object so strongly that her father arranges for Ye Xiaozhen to go abroad for study. She determines to marry Luo Jie anyway, but when she catches him with another woman, she angrily decides to take the opportunity to go abroad. As she is about to leave, however, Ye learns that Luo's apparent cheating was false, that he staged the whole thing after learning he had terminal brain cancer. Ye decides she will never leave Luo Jie again. She gets a marriage license and goes to the hospital, but arrives to find only an empty bed: Luo has died.

963. *I Want to Have a Home (Wo Xiang You Ge Jia)*

1992. Changchun Film Studio. Color. Letterboxed. 10 Reels. Direction: Wang Fengkui. Screenplay: Fei Min, Wang Fengkui. Cinematography: Li Li. Art Direction: Ju Lutian. Music: Yang Yilun. Sound: Zhang Wen, Meng Gang. Costume: Liang Xuejie. Makeup: Ji Weihua. Cast: Huang Meiying as Meng Bai, Ma Xiaoqing as Jiuzhi, Wang Sihuai as Su Yi, Hou Yaohua as Bao He, Jia Hongsheng as Xiao Bang

In Beijing, high school music teacher Meng Bai wants to study overseas. She meets Jiuzhi, a young girl just arrived from the countryside, and lets her stay at the teacher's place while Meng Bai is out of the country. Jiuzhi later becomes a singer in a music hall, and makes quite a bit of money. So Meng borrows the money she needs to go abroad from the newly prosperous Jiuzhi, using her house as collateral. After Meng leaves, Jiuzhi is cheated out of most of her money by her boyfriend. At this time, Meng Bai unexpectedly returns from overseas, which was not as satisfactory as she expected.

964. *I Want to Live (Wo Yao Huo Xia Chu)*

1995. Beijing Film Studio, Hong Kong Dongfang Film & Television Co. Ltd. Co-Production. Color. Letterboxed. Direction: Li Huimin (Raymond Lee). Screenplay: Liang Fengyi, based on her novel. Cinematography: Ma Chucheng. Art Direction: Zhuang Zhiliang. Music: Chen Jiande, Wu Guoen. Cast: Zhang Aijia (Sylvia Chang) as Bei Xing, Yuan Yongyi (Anita Yuen) as Ye Fan, Zhou Huajian as Wen Zhiyang, Zhao Wenxuan as Gao Jun

So that her grandmother may go abroad for medical treatment, Bei Xing sacrifices her love for Wen Zhiyang and marries another man by whom she has a daughter Ye Fan. Bei Xing becomes a successful businesswoman and enters a marriage of convenience to lawyer Gao Jun, giving him half of her business in exchange for legal protection for the business. At this time, Wen Zhiyang comes into her life again, and her daughter Ye Fan falls for her mother's old love. Bei Xing's past relationship with Wen drives the mother and daughter apart, but at last Ye Fan and Wen Zhigang are married.

965. *I Want to Marry You (Jiu Yao Jia Gei Ni)*

1991. Xiaoxiang Film Studio and Liaoning Film Studio Co-Production. Color. Letterboxed. 9 Reels. Direction: Xu Xiaoxing and Huo Zuang. Screenplay: Xu Xiang, Shou Shan. Cinematography: Qiu Yihong, Zhang Jinning. Art Direction: Wang Guizhi, Zhao Zhenxue. Music: Xu Jingqing. Sound: Wang Chunbao. Costume: Zhang Wei, Pang Yan. Makeup: Li Rui, Cheng Hong. Cast: Xie Yuan as Wang Shichuan, Ye Ping as Miao Fengxia, Dong Yunling as Liang Chunli, Wen Pudong as Miao Wancheng, Zhang Hongxing as Wang Jingyuan, Zhang Xiaodong as Tian Zuyi, Tong Daqiang as Lanfang

In 1930s Shanghai, a triad chief's daughter rejects the marriage he wants to arrange for her. She seeks her own lover by scanning the city streets with a telescope, and watches some interesting stories develop.

966. *I, You, Him … (Wo, Ni, Ta …)*

1982. Liaoning Science Education Film Studio. Color. 10 Reels. Direction: Ma Jingwu, Liu Sibing. Screenplay: Li Ranran, Ma Jingwu. Cinematography: Han Jianwen. Art Direction: Wang Jianjin. Music: Mu Hong. Sound: Zhu Qizhen. Cast: Ma Jingwu as Mai Wenhui, Li Ranran as Meng Yu, Cui Xinqing as Meng Nan, Wang Chenglian as Xiao Yiren, Cheng Xiaoying as Song Fengling

Mai Wenhui returned to China from study abroad in 1950. But his life since then has not been as happy as he anticipated. Years later, he has a wife and a son, but his wife is obsessed with material possessions and has little interest in her banking job. Mai works very hard with little thought of return. One day by chance he meets his old girl friend Meng Nan. They had been forced to separate during the Cultural Revolution, and now at the age of 40 and still single, her life is very depressing. Mai Wenhui tries to instill in her his deep affection for China and its people. She is very surprised to find that others who suffered during the Cultural Revolution can still contribute so much toward building the nation. Later, Mai's sister suggests he go back overseas, a prospect which greatly excites his wife. But Mai decides to stick with his own life's goals and remain in China.

967. *Ice Mountain Snow Lotus (Bing Shan Xue Lian)*

1978. Emei Film Studio. Color. B & W. 10 Reels. Direction: Xiang Ling. Screenplay: Gu Gong. Cinematography: Li Erkang. Art Direction: Lin Qi. Music: Xu Qinhua, He Min. Sound: Zhang Jianping. Cast: Qiongpei Luosang as Yue Fengyun (Zhaxi), Ouyang Fengqiang as Zhaxi (as a child), Deqin Zuoma as Yang Jin, Dawangdui as Rebu, He Xiaoshu as Ming Yumei, Yang Jiancheng as Yue Tianyu, Zhong Wei as Jinzhu (as a child), Zhao Zheng as Jinzhu (as a young woman)

In 1935, as the Red Army on the Long March passes through Tibet, they rescue poor stonemason Rebu and his son Zhaxi from persecution by local Buddhist priests. Regimental Commander Yue Tianyu and his doctor wife have just had a baby, a girl they name Jinzhu. They leave the girl with Rebu and his wife and take Zhaxi with them. After the Red Army leaves, the priests want to hurt the baby. Rebu saves her, but is himself killed. Rebu's wife then raises Jinzhu. In 1951, a Red Army road building crew comes to that area of Tibet, led by Zhaxi, now a battalion commander. He meets Jinzhu but they of course do not recognize each other. Later, during a battle with Tibetan reactionaries, Jinzhu is critically wounded, but fortunately her real parents have also come to Tibet and her mother saves Jinzhu's life. The family is reunited, and Zhaxi is reunited with his mother.

968. *The Icy River Line of Death (Bing He Shi Wang Xian)*

1986. Shanghai Film Studio. Color. 10 Reels. Direction: Zhang Jianya. Screenplay: Zhen Yi. Cinematography: Qiu Yiren, Huang Renzhong, Shen Xingao. Art Direction: Qiu Yuan. Music: Yang Mao. Sound: Zhan Xin. Cast: Zhuge Min as the old boatman, Ping Lanting as Niu Changtai, Lu Yilan as Gong Xiaojie, Nai She as Shi Wei, Zhang Jing as Hei Man's father

At a small Yellow River crossing station one day in early spring, 40 passengers board for the crossing. But when the boat reaches the middle of the river, it is struck by two huge chunks of ice. The boat takes on some water, and while it stays afloat, it cannot be controlled, marooning the passengers in mid-stream. As it gets dark and the temperature drops, the passengers grow cold and hungry. County Party Secretary Niu arrives with a rescue party, but none of their several attempts at a rescue are successful. Finally, Niu requests helicopter support from the PLA, and the grateful passengers are rescued.

969. *Ideological Problems (Si Xiang Wen Ti)*

1950. Wenhua Film Company. B & W. 11 Reels. Directors: Zuo Lin and Ding Li. Screenplay: Lan Guang and Liu Canglang. Cinematography: Xu Qi. Set Design: Wang Yuebai. Sound: Shen Yimin. Costume: Ma Shuqiu, Cai Jian. Makeup: Ni Yifei. Cast: Ji Qiming as Li Zhenwei, Chen Qi as Gao Jie, Hu Delong as Liu Jing, Jiang Jun as Zhou Zhenghua, Pan Rui as Hu Biao, Nong Zhongnan as Yu Zhirang, Cheng Cheng as Wang Changsheng, Yuan Zhiyuan as He Xiangrui, Zhang Manping as Yuan Meixia, Ding Wen as Director Zhao, Fang Xing as Assistant Director Chen

Shortly after Shanghai's liberation, a group of intellectuals from a variety of backgrounds are enrolled in the Northeast People's Revolutionary College. Group leader Li Zhenwei works enthusiastically but has the problem of trying to do too much too fast, wishing to change his own group into a model group immediately. His group of students is particularly complex in background and thinking: college student Zhou Zhenghua received an American style education and looks down upon everything; Hu Biao comes from a reactionary Nationalist military family; special agent He Xiangrui loves to spread rumors; Yu Zhirang is a clerk who enrolled simply because the students receive meals; Yuan Meixia is a city woman interested only in dining, drinking and having a good time; Wang Changsheng is a landlord's son. At first, Li Zhenwei has difficulty in reforming these people's thinking, but with Director Zhao's help and criticism, Zhou makes headway. After three months' study, each person has made considerable progress, and each is ready and eager to participate in revolutionary work. Li Zhenwei himself overcomes his problem of trying to rush everything.

970. *If There Is Love in Heaven (aka Motherliness) (Tian Ruo You Qing)*

1992. Beijing Film Studio. Color. Letterboxed. 9 Reels. Direction: Shi Xi. Screenplay: Wang Tianyun, He Guopu, Shi Meijun. Cinematography: Li Jianxin. Art Direction: Zhang Wenqi, Liu Changbao. Music: Li Haihui. Sound: Wei Xueyi, Liang Jiadong. Costume: Wang Rong. Makeup: Liu Ying. Cast: Zhao Kuier as Zhou Guiyin, Wang Limin as Chen Gengbao, Xu Jun as Yangyang, Nin Yuanyuan as Tiantian, Wei Nan as Shi Feng, Yi Tian as Tiedan

In the summer of 1991 Central China is struck by massive floods, killing many people and destroying the farms and homes of many others. The story focuses on one ordinary family suffering from the disaster. The wife, Zhou Guiyin, is a cleaning woman, and her husband Chen Gengbao a truck driver. They adopt three children whose parents were killed in the flood. Later, Chen Gengbao sacrifices himself in helping other flood victims.

971. *I'll Answer You Tomorrow (Ming Tian Hui Da Ni)*

1981. Changchun Film Studio. Color. 9 Reels. Direction: Wang Yabiao. Screenplay: Wang Xingdong, Wang Zhebing. Cinematography: Zhui Yanting, Xing Eryou. Art Direction: Gao Guoliang. Music: Lei Zhenbang, Cao Shuzuang. Sound: Hong Di, Wang Wenfu. Cast: Yang Rong as Lu Xi, Wei Wei as Manye, Sun Yanjun as Feng Shaoheng, Li Xiaoli as Yi Wenxiu, Wang Runsheng as Feng Decang, Liu Junsheng as Yang Shiyan

Woman engineer Lu Xi, who lost her husband during the Cultural Revolution, and young engineer Feng Shaoheng work together on a machine automation project. His father, their supervisor Feng Decang, is suspicious of what his son and Lu Xi are doing in their workshop because they often work late. Yang Shiyan, who works with them, makes advances to Lu Xi and when he is rejected spreads rumors about Lu and Feng's relationship. Lu Xi cannot bear the gossip and whispers, and wants to change to some other work. Feng Shaoheng criticizes her for this and encourages her to continue the project. Feng Shaoheng's girl friend Yi Wenxiu believes the rumors and breaks up with Feng. Confused and hurt by his father and others misunderstanding him, Feng Shaoheng leaves home. Feng Shaoheng sincerely proposes marriage to Lu Xi but she angrily refuses him. Their hard work at last pays off, and the computerized machine operation is successful. His father Feng Decang is convinced by the evidence of success. As everyone is celebrating the project's successful conclusion, Lu Xi quietly leaves the plant and moves to a new job. She leaves a letter to Feng Shaoheng as her response to him.

972. *Illegal Gunman (Fei Fa Chi Qiang Zhe)*

1989. Emei Film Studio. Color. Letterboxed. 9 Reels. Direction: Zhang Xihe. Screenplay: Xiong Yu, Luo Xing. Cinematography: Wang Xiaolie. Art Direction: Xia Zhengqiu. Music: Wang Hong. Sound: Tu Liuqing. Cast: Wun Haitao as Hao Wei, Xia Zongyou as the teacher, Bai Ling as the woman taxi driver

In a certain city, a man is killed by a single bullet in the eyebrow, and passerby Hao Wei recognizes the bullet used as coming from a rare type of handgun made during the Cultural Revolution. During that time, Hao Wei had been a technician assigned to make this type of gun, designed by one of his teachers. He also recalls that his teacher always aimed for the eyebrow. Hao Wei later becomes a suspect in the case, and sets out to prove his innocence. He has a final confrontation with his old teacher, in which they are both killed.

973. *Illegal Migrant (Mang Liu)*

1987. Xi'an Film Studio. Color. 9 Reels. Direction: Xu Huanshan. Screenplay: Zhen Dingyu, Huang Xin. Cinematography: Luo Yongjian, Wen Shibing. Art Direction: Zhang Gong. Music: Zhu Shirui. Sound: Xiong Huajuan. Cast: Zhang Chao as Shi Dainian, Jiang Hong as Qu Doumei, Wang Yuanbang as Cui Liandeng, Wang Borui as Old Tietou, Cai Hongxiang as He Huanxi

Shi Dainian escapes from prison and boards a freight train headed for northwest China. Also boarding the train is Qu Doumei, a girl trying to find her father. They are detained as illegal migratory workers and separated. At the migrant labor camp, Shi Dainian becomes acquainted with an old man named Cui Liandeng, who is very ill. Before he dies, Cui tells Shi that he has a daughter called Qu Doumei. Qu Doumei shows up at the camp, looking for Shi Dainian, and tells him she wants to marry him. Later, Shi is cleared of the charges which originally sent him to prison, and he and Qu Doumei look forward to a new life together.

974. *Illusive Girl (Huan Nu)*

1993. Xi'an Film Studio. Color. 9 Reels. Direction: Shao Qi, Huangpu Yichuan. Screenplay: Zhao Heqi. Cinematography: Zhao Yimin. Art Direction: Cheng Mingzhang. Music: Zhang Dalong. Sound: Ji Changhua. Costume: Su Jianjun. Makeup: Ai Hui. Cast: Lan Lan as Lu Xiaoya, Qu Guoqiang as Ren Tiangao, Ling Zongying as Zhao Ping, Li Guiqing as Hu Xiuxiu, Huang Siwei as A B, Haire Guli as Lan Lini

A fantasy mystery set in a modern Chinese city. Zhao Ping, a middle-aged overseas woman, comes to China to invest and do research, as stipulated in her father's will. Ren Tiangao, a famous kung fu master, is blackmailed by a mysterious figure known as "Black K" to kill Zhao Ping. Xiao Ya, a young girl who dreams of someday meeting the mother she has never seen, is painting a picture in an isolated spot. Suddenly, a man starts to attack her, and when she resists, Xiao Ya finds she has an almost superhuman strength she was unaware of, allowing her to cast her attacker aside like a rag doll. When the girl happens to see Zhao Ping for the first time, she has a feeling this may be her mother, her dream. Meanwhile, the killer is planning to do away with Zhao Ping, but Xiao Ya has a premonition, and becomes the older woman's protector. From then on, the two always stay together, as if mother and daughter. Finally, with the help of police, Xiao Ya defeats the conspiracy.

Imperial Eunuch Li Lianying see *Li Lianying*

975. *Imperial Nun (Huang Jia Ni Gu)*

1990. Changchun Film Studio. Color. Wide Screen. 8 Reels. Direction: Yu Xiaoyang. Screenplay: Zhen Yanying. Cinematography: Li Sheng. Art Direction: Wei Hongbao. Music: Chen Shouqian. Sound: Fu Yong, Liu Wenzhang. Cast: Jin Lili as Princess Guo, Wang Jianjun as Qi Xiaopeng, Hou Tianlai as the new emperor

When the old emperor dies, his favorite concubine Princess Guo is sent to the royal temple as a nun. But years of court intrigue have given her too great a desire for power to accept this; she wins the love of chief monk Qi Xiaopeng, then uses him to gain access to the new emperor as a means of returning to court. The empress sees what Guo is up to, and tries to have the deposed concubine assassinated.

Court officials also want to stop Guo by having her killed, but the monk protects her each time. With his help Guo at last regains the pinnacle of power at court, then casts him aside when he is no longer of use.

976. The Impulse of Youth (Qing Chun Chong Dong)

1992. Beijing Film Studio. Color. Letterboxed. 9 Reels. Direction: Zhou Xiaowen. Screenplay: Zhou Xiaowen. Cinematography: He Qin. Art Direction: Zhang Daqian. Music: Shi Song. Sound: Zhen Chunyu. Costume: Ren Zhiwen. Makeup: Li Dongtian, Liu Xiaoyang. Cast: Shi Lan as Ai Fei, Chang Rong as Gao Dalong, Jing Gangshan as Wu Ji, Liu Xiaoning as Han Shaoyi

Beijing taxi driver Gao Dalong and his girl friend A Fei rely heavily on each other, as neither has any relatives in the city. A Fei's singing talent is at last discovered by a night club boss, and she soon becomes popular among club patrons. Gao picks her up every night after her show, and one night he arrives just as some toughs are assaulting A Fei. He intervenes, but accidentally causes the death of an innocent bystander. Gao Dalong is sent to a prison farm. A Fei stays on in Beijing, and soon acquires two successful businessmen as suitors. But realizing something is missing from her life, A Fei gives up her career and moves to a small town near the prison farm to work at a restaurant. Five years later, Gao Dalong is released to find A Fei waiting for him.

977. In a Distant Land (Zai Na Yao Yuan De Di Fang)

1993. Hong Kong Jianian Film Studio & Xi'an Film Studio Co-Production. Color. Letterboxed. 10 Reels. Direction: Teng Wenji. Screenplay: Wang Shi, Li Hua, Liang Zongzhu, Yu Zhongwei. Cinematography: Zhi Lei. Art Direction: Yang Gang. Music: Luo Dayou. Sound (Dolby): Gu Changning. Costume: Zhang Yaodong, Liu Yanping. Makeup: Zhao Heping, Liu Jishu. Cast: Zhang Hongliang as Huang Zhong, Chen Hong as Jiang Xue, Hu Jing as Wu Duomei, Dawa Yangzong as Zuo Ma

978. In a Minefield Thinking of Trees (Lei Chang Xiang Si Shu)

1986. August First Film Studio. Color. 11 Reels. Direction: Wei Lian. Screenplay: Jiang Qitao, Cinematography: Xu Lianqin, Xu Jian-

sheng. Cast: Wu Gang as Mu Tao, Hu Yajie as Qiu Yuan, Zhang Jianmin as Ji Gang, Zhao Jun as Cai Nong, Shen Xiaoqian as Zhong Yi

When the Sino-Vietnamese border war starts, five college students from varying backgrounds decide to leave school and enlist in the army together. They are assigned to a combat unit, and in one battle, one of their number is killed and another is crippled for life. When the war ends, one of the young men returns to civilian life. Back in the crowded and bustling city streets, he cannot rid himself of his emotions and memories of war and his sacrificed comrades-in-arms.

979. In an Elevator (Dian Ti Shang)

1984. Xi'an Film Studio. Color. Letterboxed. 9 Reels. Direction: Yu Lianqi. Screenplay: Xie Fengsong, A Sheng. Cinematography: Zhu Dingyu. Art Direction: Cheng Minzhang. Music: Xiang Yin. Sound: Hong Jiahui, Li Ping. Cast: Xiao Xiong as Qin Shuang, Yang Hailian as Shi Yaqin, Zhao Youliang as Zhen Zhuang, Han Ying as Xiao Lingxia, Shi Yu as the old professor

The many residents of a Beijing apartment building often see each other only in the elevator. One day, portrait artist Zhen Zhuang recognizes the new elevator dispatcher as Qin Shuang, a former ballet dancer he had painted several years before. Now she lives simply with her two children, having been abandoned by her husband when he went overseas. Zhen Zhuang is very sympathetic to her, and in time the two fall in love. Their relationship causes other residents to start being more neighborly with each other.

980. In and Out of Court (Fa Ting Nei Wai)

1980. Emei Film Studio. Color. 9 Reels. Direction: Cong Lianwen, Lu Xiaoya. Screenplay: Song Yuexun, Chen Dunde. Cinematography: Feng Shilin. Art Direction: Wu Xujin. Music: Wang Ming. Sound: Zhang Jianping. Cast: Tian Hua as Shang Qing, Zhou Chu as Director Xia, Lin Muyu as Liu Rulian, Chen Peisi as Xia Huan, Huang Yuemei as Tang Xiaosu, Liu Xuling as Jiang Yanyan

In the city of Wunquan, a district court hears a traffic case: Xu Dahuai, the driver for the city's revolutionary committee Director Xia, is charged with killing female gymnast Jiang Yanyuan while he was driving drunk. The court rules it an accident, and because he turned himself in, clears of Xu of any criminal liability. Public outrage over the judgment results in the case being taken to the city's intermediate court. Court justice Sang Qing learns that although Xu turned himself in, he could not have been the driver that day. But who should be the defendant? Sang's attempts to get at the truth run into all sorts of evasions and political pressures. At last she learns that Director Xia's son Xia Huan is the real criminal: he had raped the young woman, then ran her down with the car to cover up his crime. Sang Qing at first finds herself over her head, as there are some powerful political figures involved. But support comes from an unexpected source: when Director Xia sees the irrefutable evidence of his son's crime, he comes down firmly on the side of Sang Qing and justice. Xia Huan is tried and convicted of rape and murder, and is sentenced to death.

981. *In Expectation (Wu Shan Yun Yu)*

1995. Beijing Film Studio, Beijing East-Earth Cultural Development Co. Co-Production. Color. 100 minutes. Direction: Zhang Ming. Screenplay: Zhu Wen, from an idea by Wang Xingyu, Liu Yongzhou and Jiang Yuanlun. Cinematography: Yao Xiaofeng, Zhou Ming and Ding Jiancheng. Art Direction: Zhang Hongwen. Sound: (Dolby), Wang Weiyan. Costume: Feng Jianrong. Cast: Zhang Xianmin as Mai Qiang, Zhong Ping as Chen Qing, Wang Wenqiang as Wu Gang, Yang Liu as Lily, Li Bing as Lao Mo, Wang Shengguo as Wang Jie, Jiang Xin as Liang Er

In the industrial city of Wuhan, introverted Mai Qiang passes his days at the boring job of changing traffic signals for the boats that traffic the Yangtse River. The only thing of interest that happens is when his buddy Wu Bang pays a visit to Mai, bringing along his bored girlfriend Lily. Wu encourages the two to get together, and Mai and Lily wind up in bed. Meanwhile, Chen Qing, a widow who works as a desk clerk at a small, nondescript hotel, attempts to raise her young son while fending off the unwelcome advances of the hotel's manager, Lao Mo. Lao knows a young policeman named Wu Gang, and tells him that he suspects Mai of raping Chen, which starts an investigation that throws the lives of all concerned into upheaval.

982. *In Pursuit of the Sun (Zui Gan Tai Yang De Ren)*

1991. Changchun Film Studio. Color. 9 Reels. Letterboxed. Direction: Pang Hao. Screenplay: Zhang Xiaotian, Wu Qitai, Pang Hao. Cinematography: Wu Benli. Art Direction: Ye Jiren. Music: Yang Yilun. Sound: Jiang Yan. Cast: Kou Zhenhai as Li Azai, Pang Xueqin as Zhang Nanjian, Liu Xuling as Su Lin, Lu Jilan as Fang Guanrong, Tao Hong as Ou Mei, Liang Yin as Lu Peng

Through a focus on one company, this film traces the development of the Hainan Special Economic Zone in Hainan Island, south of the Chinese mainland. Li Azai, the new President of the South Mainland Group Company, discards his original organizational construction program and promotes Su Lin, an M.A. student returned from the United States, and Lu Peng, a brilliant middle-aged engineer. Su Lin and Lu Peng discover that the company has purchased obsolete equipment. So Li Azhai dismisses the employees who purchased the equipment, which shocks the whole company. Company ex-president Fang Guanrong and his men try to frame Li Azai. Li's case is at last cleared up and he is reinstated and ready to resume his work.

983. *In the Heat of the Sun (Yang Guang Can Lan De Ri Zi)*

1993. Hong Kong Dragon Film Intl. in association with China Film Co-Production Corp. Color. 139 minutes. Color. Direction and Screenplay: Jiang Wen, based on the novel "Dongwu Xiongmeng" ("Vicious Animals") by Wang Shuo (1958–). Cinematography: Gu Changwei. Art Direction: Chen Haozhong. Music: Guo Wenjing. Sound (Dolby): Gu Changning. Costume: Liu Huiping. Cast: Xia Yu as Ma Xiaojun (Monkey), Ning Jing as Liu Yiku, Geng Le as Liu Yiku, Shang Nan as Liu Sitian, Tao Hong as Yu Beipei; also: Dai Xiaopo, Wang Hai, Siqin Gaowa, Wang Xueqin, Fang Xiaogang, Wang Shuo

Some teenage boys in Beijing during one hot summer in the 1970s, with events described years later by one of the boys as he remembers them happening, not necessarily as they really occurred. The boys, "army brats," spend their time idly around the compound where the military houses their families, roughhousing, getting into minor trouble and hanging out with girls of varying degrees of virtue. The boys' leader is Liu Yiku, whose girlfriend Yu Beibei is not above flirting with a younger boy called Ma the Monkey, in his own turn infatuated with an older woman.

Best Actor (Xia Yu), 50th Venice International Film Festival.

984. *In Their Teens (Dou Kou Nian Hua)*

1989. Children's Film Studio and Nanjing Film Studio Co-Production. Color. 10 Reels. Wide Screen. Direction: Qiu Zhongyi, Xu Geng. Screenplay: Xu Geng, Cheng Wei. Cinematography: Shan Xingliang, Wu Yun. Art Direction: Xiao Feng, Chen Zhaoyuan. Music: Wang Xiaoyong. Sound: Zhou Xiaomin. Cast: Zhang Xi as Cao Mimi, Miao Miao as Yao Xiaohe, Cai Xiangliang as Xia Yu, Zhou Zhengbo as Ge Ping

A coming-of-age movie focusing on a group of 16 and 17-year-old girl students, facing normal teenage problems in addition to fierce academic pressures at Longcheng Middle School. In addition, we meet Xia Yu, a young teacher displaying his talent for the first time, and graduating senior Ge Ping, who fails to pass the university examination.

985. *An Incomplete Moon (Can Yue)*

1984. Pearl River Film Studio. Color. Letterboxed. 9 Reels. Direction: Cao Zheng. Screenplay: He Jiesheng. Cinematography: Wei Duo. Art Direction: Tan Ancang. Music: Du Jiangang, Wang Liping. Sound: Jiang Shaoqi. Cast: Zhen Zhenyao as Mother, Zhao Erkang as A Fu, Hong Rong as Xiufang, Luo Xueying as Xiuzhen, Huo Xiu as Xiulan, Zhang Jie as He Tao, Xu Songyuan as Ma Jie

A young widow raises her five daughters by herself, assisted only by a kindly neighbor named A Fu. With his help, she gets through the tough years. In time, a true affection grows between the two, but distant relatives of her late husband spread malicious gossip about them which causes A Fu to go away. After liberation, with her daughters grown, Mother and A Fu meet again, and want to marry. But now her five adult daughters protest, and Mother abandons her last chance at romance. Not long after, the eldest daughter's husband dies, and the daughter's grief brings her to realize the pain and loneliness her mother has suffered over the years. The daughters decide to give their mother their blessing, but she dies.

986. *Incredible Kids from Shaolin (Shao Lin Tong Zi Gong)*

1986. Henan Province Performing Company & Hong Kong Jinma Film Company Co-Production. Color. Wide Screen. 9 Reels. Direction: Xue Hou. Screenplay: Hou Houxian. Cinematography: Wun Gui. Art Direction: Li Min, Li Zhi. Music: Wang Jixiao. Cast: Wang Lisha as Cuicui, Zhang Long as Tong Deng, Wang Qingyu as Guang Ci, Shao Zhaoming as Tong Ling

Kung fu film set at the end of the Ming Dynasty (ca1644).

987. *Independent Troop (Du Li Da Dui)*

1964. Changchun Film Studio. B & W. 12 Reels. Direction: Wang Yan. Screenplay: Lu Zhuguo and Wang Yan. Cinematography: Wang Qiming. Art Direction: Wang Tao, Wang Jixian. Music: Zhang Dicang. Sound: Chen Wenyuan. Cast: Zhong Shuhuang as Ye Yongmao, Guo Zhengqing as Ma Long, Pang Xueqing as Diao Feihu, Sun Xiaofei as Li Denggao, Da Qi as Niu Gu, Wang Jieren as Wang Ziqi

In 1946, guerrilla headquarters in North Guangdong sends Ye Yongmao as a liaison to a "greenwood" band which had broken away from the Nationalist Army. Bandit chief Ma Long, influenced by his sworn brothers Diao Feihu and Li Denggao, is suspicious of Ye Yongmao. Diao Feihu in particular exploits his special relationship with Ma Long to commit various outrages. When new recruit Niu Gu exposes Diao's crimes, the other soldiers all demand Diao be executed but Ma Long pardons him. Later, after Ye Yongmao is successful in persuading Ma to reorganize his troops, Diao and Li conspire to set Ma up for ambush. Ma is wounded, but Ye Yongmao brings some troops to intercede at a critical moment and save Ma Long. After this bloody experience, Ma Long voluntarily converts his independent troop into Troop No. 4 of the North Guangdong guerrillas.

988. *The Indian Ocean Sinking of the H.M.S. Leibeili (Lei Bei Li Hao Chen Mo Zhai Yin Du Yang)*

1985. Changchun Film Studio. Color. 10 Reels. Direction: Jin Tao. Screenplay: Zhang Xiaotian. Cinematography: Wang Lianping. Art Direction: Hao Bing, Jiao Zhenmin. Music: Tan

Dun. Cast: Lei Luosheng as Zhuang Haiquan, Ling Hui as Tang Mei, Xu Caihua as Shi Hua, Wang Jiancheng as Zhuang Sangeng, Wang Wensheng as Li Yingmin, Wei Zongwan as Zhang Shuihou

During World War II, a British freighter with a mostly Chinese crew steams across the Indian Ocean with a cargo of arms intended to supply the anti–Nazi resistance in Europe. The ship is torpedoed and sunk. The captain and some crewmen go down with the ship, but Machinist's Mate Zhuang Haiquan leads the survivors to a deserted island. The movie tells of their struggle for survival until they are rescued.

989. *Indulge in Fantasy (Xiang Ru Fei Fei)*

1990. Youth Film Studio. Color. Wide Screen. 9 Reels. Direction: Zhang Gang. Screenplay: Zhang Gang. Cinematography: Shen Xilin, Zhang Jian. Art Direction: Liu Bo, Wang Renling. Music: Wang Ming. Sound: Zhu Yong. Cast: Yao Erga as Ding Aman, Chang Lantian as Mr. Zhong

In a certain city, the bureau of light industry's chief Mr. Zhong discovers that ordinary worker Ding Aman has an extraordinarily large capacity for alcohol. He begins using Ding to entertain prospective clients, and this leads to the young man's hiring by a joint venture company for the same purpose, a "designated drinker." He meets and falls for a girl named Meimei, but she breaks off with Ding when she learns what he does for a living. Depression over the failed love affair brings a decline in Ding's ability to hold liquor, and puts him in disfavor with his employers and the bureau. Meimei later finds she is pregnant by another man, and comes back to Ding, figuring an alcoholic husband with a job is better than none at all. She convinces him the child is his, but just as they prepare to marry, Zhong tells Ding Aman his services are no longer needed because the Party now advocates healthful practices in work and lifestyles.

990. *Indulge in the Wildest Fantasy (Yi Xiang Kai Tian)*

1986. Pearl River Film Studio & Hongkong Tianhu Film Company Jointly. Color. 10 Reels. Direction: Wang Weiyi. Screenplay: Zhang Xianliang. Cinematography: Chen Xianghe. Art Direction: Huang Zhaohui. Music: Ding Jialing, Jin Youzhong, Si Tukang. Art Direction: Huang

Zhaohui. Cast: Yao Peide as Xu Peizuo, Xu Weiming as Zhang Xiaoyu

Xu Peizuo is a young employee of a Shanghai company who escapes from his humdrum daily existence through daydreams. Once, he finds himself gifted with extraordinary physical capabilities, which he puts at the service of the nation. When an aircraft is hijacked, he intervenes to stop it, and from this goes on to other super and heroic adventures. Suddenly he awakens to realize it was just a dream after all.

991. *The Inextinguishable Flame (Pu Bu Mie De Huo Yan)*

1955. Changchun Film Studio. B & W. 10 Reels. Direction: Yi Ling. Screenplay: Xi Rong, Ma Feng. Cinematography: Wang Qiming. Art Direction: Tong Jinwen. Sound: Shen Guli. Cast: Ge Zhenbang as Jiang San, Du Zheng as Jiang Er, Ding Weiming as Jiang's mother, Wang Zhifang as Liu Yumei, Han Yan as Wang Liqing, Wang Jingfang as Political Commissar Wang

In 1942, CPC member Jiang San returns to his hometown in Shaanxi province to mobilize the people there for struggle against the Japanese. His elder brother Jiang Er is a collaborationist officer in a Japanese occupied area. Backed by Japanese power, he rules the people there with a cruel iron fist, but Jiang San still believes in his brother's basic good nature, and hopes he can win him over. But when Jiang Er tricks Jiang San into exposing his guerrilla troop's base location and then uses this information to wipe out most of them, the two brothers split and become sworn enemies. They wage a fierce struggle. Later, after Jiang San has executed a village chief who was a notorious criminal, the Japanese commander in the area orders Jiang Er to capture Jiang San within a certain number of days. Jiang Er arrests and interrogates their mother and Jiang San's wife Liu Yumei, forcing them to confess Jiang San's whereabouts. Jiang San rescues the two women, then leads his reconstituted guerrilla band in at last wiping out Jiang Er and his troops.

992. *Infiltrator (Wo Di)*

1992. Shanghai Film Studio. Color. Letterboxed. 9 Reels. Direction: Shen Yaoting. Screenplay: Gu Bai. Cinematography: Si Junping. Art Direction: Zhang Wanhong. Music: Yang Shaolu. Sound: Xu Xiushan. Costume: Zhang Fucai. Makeup: Zhang Anlin, Hong Meijuan. Cast: Wang Sihuai as Zen Shufan, Wang Weiping as

Chou Keruo, Zhou Xiaoli as Jia Xuefang, Zhang Xiaoqin as Liu Xianglin

In 1914, Yuan Shikai's spymaster Chou Keruo secretly comes to Shanghai to set a trap for Sun Yatsen and his chief of staff. He plants an infiltrator inside Sun's revolutionary team. One of Sun's advisors, theater manager Zen Shufan, suspects that one of their number is a spy, and pretends to betray the revolution in order to flush out the infiltrator. His apparent treachery estranges him from his wife Jia Xuefang, but he sticks to his mission. At last, his wife is killed by the enemy, but Zen succeeds in killing both Chou Keruo and the spy.

993. *The Injustice to Dou Er (Dou Er Yuan)*

1959. Changchun Film Studio. Color. 13 Reels. Direction: Zhang Xinshi. Screenplay: Shanxi Jinnan Drama Society, Shanxi Jinnan Pu Opera Troupe, based on an original work by Guan Hanqing. Cinematography: Bao Jie. Art Direction: Liu Xuerao. Music: Shanxi Jinnan Pu Opera Troupe Music Team. Sound: Huang Lijia. Cast: Wang Xiulan as Dou Er, Yan Fengchun as Dou Tianzhang, Yang Hushan as Tao Wu, Zhu Yuelai as Zhang's father, Zhang Qingkui as Huang Qi, Zhu Yuanna as Mrs. Cai

Douer lost her mother at a very early age, and shortly after her own marriage her husband dies. Dou Er moves in with her mother-in-law, Mrs. Cai, the two widows supporting each other.

A man named Zhang Luer falsely accuses Mrs. Cai of murdering his father, and bribes the county administrator to torture the old woman. Fearing that her mother-in-law cannot bear the ordeal, Dou Er confesses to the murder. She is sentenced to death, and at her execution she predicts that in return for the injustice to her, strange phenomena will occur: it will suddenly snow in summer, a usually rainy region will suffer three years of drought, etc. All these things happen just as she predicts.

Six years later, Douer's father Dou Tianzhang passes the imperial examinations and is appointed to a very high position. One night, while reading some cases, he suddenly sees his daughter Dou Er begging him to right the injustice. The next day, Dou Tianzhang re-opens the case and discovers the truth. Zhang Luer and a confederate are sentenced to the death penalty.

The In-Laws **see** *Happiness Knocks at the Door*

994. *An Innocent Babbler (Za Zui Zi)*

1992. Children's Film Studio. Color. Letter-boxed. 9 Reels. Direction: Liu Miaomiao. Screenplay: Yang Zhengguang, Liu Miaomiao. Cinematography: Wang Juwen. Art Direction: Liu Jian, Liao Yongjun. Music: Wun Zhongjia. Sound: Huang Siye, Wang Zhihong. Cast: Li Lei as Minsheng ("Babbler"), Cao Cuifeng as Shuyin, Yuan Jing as Qunsheng, Lu Xiaoan as Yan Mai, Guo Shaoxiong as teacher Wang, Ma Zongzhi as Diandian

Jixiang Village boy Minsheng so loves to talk that he is called "Babbler." In addition to liking to talk, he also has a penchant for being outspoken, which sometimes gets him in trouble. At last, the boy decides to hold his tongue and becomes silent. Unfortunately this leads to disaster for Minsheng and his family.

995. *Inside an Old Grave (Gu Mu Huang Zhai)*

1991. Beijing Film Studio. Color. 3-D. 10 Reels. Direction: Xie Tieli. Screenplay: Xie Fengsong and Xie Tieli. Cinematography: Zheng Yuyuan. Art Direction: Yang Yuhe and Wei Feng. Music: Wang Ming. Sound: Liu Shida. Cast: Xing Minshan as Yang Yuwei, Fu Yiwei as Lianshuo, Zhou Xun as Jiaona, Wu Tiange as Nie Xiaoqian

This film is based on eight stories from the Ming Dynasty collection "Liao Zhai Zhi Yi" (Strange Stories from a Chinese Studio) by Pu Songling (1640–1715).

Scholar Yang Yuwei secludes himself in a tomb-like desolate house in order to study in private for the imperial examinations, the entry to an official career. There he meets Lian Suo, a strange girl who is really a ghost, and the two fall in love. With the help of friends, Yang battles predatory ghost Bai Wuchang, enabling Lian Suo to return to life. But Lian Suo's parents look down on Yang, and force the couple to separate. Lian Suo stands up against them. On his way to the imperial examinations, Yang falls ill. Witnessing the tragedy, Qiao Na, a fox spirit, saves Yang. With help from the flower spirit Nie Xiaoqian, Yang passes the examination and becomes a high official. But on returning to Lian Suo's mansion, he finds her dead.

996. *Insight and Loyalty (Huiyan Danxin)*

1960. Pearl River Film Studio. B & W. 10

Reels. Direction: Yin Ling. Screenplay: Zhang Moqing, Lian Yubing and Chen Ke. Cinematography: Jiang Shi. Art Direction: Ge Xinger. Music: Yang Ye. Sound: Chen Bang and Li Ming. Cast: Zhang Anfu as Feng Zhiqing, Wang Xin as Li Sufang, Zhang Anfu as Party Secretary Liu, Tong Linxi as Xiao Zhou, Song Lanbo as Li Hua, Gao Cui as Jin Feng

In 1950, during an all-out effort to prepare materials for Chinese forces in Korea, young machine plant worker Feng Zhiqing is blinded in an explosion while saving another young worker Xiao Zhou. With the Party's care and comrades' encouragement, he overcomes his handicap through strong will, and returns to his work station. He is also lucky in love, and happily marries Li Sufang. He later upgrades the plant's technology by designing a new type of screw for use in military vehicles, and after repeated experiments, is ultimately successful.

997. *Intelligence Station on the Isolated Island (Gu Dao Qing Bao Zhan)*

1990. Changchun Film Studio. Color. 9 Reels. Direction: Guo Lin. Screenplay: Zhen Qin. Cinematography: Zhang Zhongwei. Qian Weizhe. Art Direction: Liu Hong. Music: Fan Weiqiang. Sound: Cao Feng. Cast: Wanlijia (American) as Johnson, Li Youbing as Liu Jianfeng, Liu Weihua as Shen Chongmin

Before U.S. entry into World War II, Japanese soldiers in Shanghai stage a surprise raid on the offices of the "Far East Weekly," an English language newspaper. Their objective is a confidential document obtained by the paper, showing that Chiang Kaishek is engaged in secret negotiations with the Japanese. Johnson, an American employee of the paper, flees with the document and seeks help from the Chinese Nationalist government. Chinese officials pretend to offer him aid while actually making it easier for the Japanese to capture him. Nationalist agent Liu Jianfeng is unaware of the government's duplicity, and gives Johnson all the help he can. Also trying to help him is the Communist underground, in the person of agent Shen Chongmin. Johnson eventually comes to realize who his friends are, and decides to trust the Communists. Nationalist agent Liu and Communist agent Shen join forces to help the American escape from Shanghai.

998. *An Intelligent Person (Cong Ming De Ren)*

1958. Haiyan Film Studio. B & W. 10 Reels. Direction: Xu Tao, Pan Wenzhan. Screenplay: Xu Tao, based on the stage play, "The Indigenous Specialist" by Li Zhun and Wang Yanfei. Cinematography: Wu Weiyun. Art Direction: Qiu Yiren, Wang Zhichu. Music: Wang Yunjie. Sound: Zhou Hengliang. Makeup: Yao Yongfu. Cast: Wun Xiying as He Guangming, Zhang Yunxiang as He Shigan, Fan Lai as Secretary Wang, Di Fan as Mu Xiuyin, Pang Jianbing as He Laogang, Lu Jingqi as Kong Jingxi

He Guangming, deputy director of a farm commune, invents a new, upgraded farm implement. However, he is opposed by his father, the commune director He Shigan, who does everything by the book. But with the support and encouragement of Party Secretary Wang, he is eventually successful in getting the new tool adopted.

999. *The Intercepted Order (Mi Ling Jie Ji)*

1986. Changchun Film Studio. Color. 10 Reels. Direction: Hua Ke. Screenplay: Bi Bicheng. Cinematography: Liu Fengli. Art Direction: Guo Yansheng, Liang Xianchuan. Music: Zhang Peiji. Sound: Liu Xingfu, Fu Yong. Cast: Zhao Runfeng as Luo Beiyue, Gan Yuzhou as General Shirakawa, Cao Peicang as Shanxia, Xu Yuejie as the "Comfort Woman," Jiang Defu as Liu Degui, Liu Tongyan as Qiu Hancheng

Towards the end of World War Two, as they face impending defeat, the Japanese military government sends a secret order to Japanese Army Headquarters in Shanxi, China, ordering General Shirakawa to return at once to Japan. Shirakawa is a favorite of the Japanese High Command, and they believe he will be safer as a prisoner of the Americans than of the Chinese. Eighth Route Army Headquarters at Taihang learn of the General's secret orders. To the Chinese, flight to Japan by a man they consider a butcher responsible for the deaths of countless innocent Chinese is unthinkable. So they order a group of commandos headed by Luo Beiyue into the enemy-occupied city of Taiyuan to kidnap Shirakawa before he can get away. Through clever tactics and some bloody fighting, the commandos succeed in their mission of taking him prisoner.

1000. *Interesting and Happy Lovers (Xi Xiao Yuan Yang)*

1995. Beijing Film Studio, Shandong Jinan Xingyou Industrial Development Co. Ltd. Co-Production. Color. Letterboxed. Direction: Tang Yanlin. Screenplay: Nai Xun. Cinematography: Li Xiong. Art Direction: Chen Yiyun. Music: Liu Weiguang. Cast: Tian Shaojun as Qin Yihe, Liu Tao as Ding Shouzhong, Pan Hong as Wei Zhen, Gao Yuan as Bai Miaoxiang, Liu Haonan as Wei Qiulan

In the early 17th century, towards the end of the Ming Dynasty, the lives of ordinary people are miserable. The governor of Hexi, who already has seven wives, wants more women and chooses two girls already engaged to marry. They and their lovers at last have a happy ending.

Interim Father **see** *Temporary Dad*

1001. *International Rescue (Guo Ji Da Ying Jiu)*

1990. Emei Film Studio. Color. Wide Screen. 10 Reels. Direction: Xie Hong. Screenplay: Qian Daoyuan. Cinematography: Zhang Jiwu. Art Direction: Xia Xinqiu. Music: Xie Jun. Sound: Wang Guangzhong. Cast: Xiaoen Bona as Anderson, Steven Zhang Mindao as Shanbuluo

A World War II story of Chinese minority people in Yunnan Province helping U.S. intelligence agents rescue an American pilot shot down and captured by the Japanese. The rescue effort succeeds, but all the Chinese are killed.

1002. *Intimate Friends (Zhi Yin)*

1981. Beijing Film Studio. Color. 11 Reels. Direction: Xie Tieli, Chen Huaiai, Ba Hong. Screenplay: Hua Ershi. Cinematography: Nie Jing, Ru Shuiren. Art Direction: Qin Wei, Chen Zhaomin. Music: Wang Ming. Sound: Chen Yansi. Cast: Wang Xingang as Cai Er, Zhang Yu as Xiao Fengxian, Yin Ruocheng as Yuan Shikai, Zhang Yisheng as Jiang Chaozong, Wang Pei as Yuan Keding

After General Yuan Shikai takes control of the Chinese government from Sun Yatsen in the early period after the Republic Revolution in 1911, a subordinate general of Yuan's named Cai Er is transferred to Beijing. Cai is very unhappy with Yuan Shikai's policies, and is particularly unhappy with the relocation. Yuan realizes this, and wants Cai Er nearby to keep an eye on him. Yuan has Cai Er introduced to the famous courtesan Xiao Fengxian, hoping to distract Cai Er from political activity. The Japanese force Yuan to sign the "21 Articles," a treaty which sold out China in exchange for Japanese support of Yuan's attempt to install himself as emperor. Recognizing Yuan's true nature from this, Cai Er begins organizing military forces throughout China to rebel against Yuan. Xiao Fengxian is very impressed with Cai Er's reputation and behavior, but his suspicions of her and some misunderstandings on her part keep the couple from becoming really close although they stay together. One day, Xiao Fengxian tells Cai Er of her tragic background and her desire for revenge on Yuan for killing her father. Cai Er is excited and moved to learn that she is a woman who has made elimination of Yuan Shikai her life's goal, and the two then become intimates for the first time. Just before Yuan plans to declare himself emperor, Cai Er secretly leaves Beijing for Yunnan, where he launches the anti–Yuan rebellion. Every province in China responds to his call. Less than a year later Yuan dies, his dream of empire at an end. Weary and sick from so many hard years as a soldier, Cai Er decides to go to Japan for medical treatment to restore his health. He dies there, leaving behind a grieving Xiao Fengxian.

Best Actor Wang Xingang, 1982 Hundred Flowers Awards.

1003. *Intruders (Chuang Ru Zhe)*

1993. Beijing Film Studio, Shijiazhuang Huajun Real Estate Corp. Ltd. Co-Production. Color. Letterboxed. 9 Reels. Direction: Zhang Guoli. Screenplay: Ke Zhanghe, Zhang Guoli. Cinematography: Wang Song. Art Direction: Zi Heng. Music: Li Lifu. Sound: Zhang Baojian. Costume: Wang Rong. Makeup: Xue Yuanyuan. Cast: Yuan Yuan as Zhao Chuan, Wang Zhixia as Lu Li, Zhao Jun as Ding Weiguo, Fang Zige as Pixiong, Hou Yaohua as Hou Sanhu, Bi Yanjun as Tiecheng, Wu Xiaodong as Ji Yun, Tian Ming as Huang Meigui, Zhang Xiao as Nana

Neglected by her work-obsessed husband Tie Cheng, pretty young Lu Li is having an affair with Ji Yun. The two have their trysts while her husband is at work. One day, she answers a knock at the door, and two drug dealers on the run from police burst into the house. They take Lu Li and her lover hostage at gunpoint. Later that day, when Tie Cheng comes home with their daughter, he and the child are also taken hostage. It does not take long for Tie to realize the relationship of his wife with Ji Yun, but he knows they must first of all work together to thwart their captors. When they at last make their move, Lu Li is killed in the fight, taking a bullet intended for her husband. The police take the drug dealers into custody, and Tie Cheng and Ji Yun are both left to mourn the woman they loved.

1004. *The Invisible Front Line (Wu Xing De Zhan Xian)*

1949. Northeast Film Studio. B&W. 10 Reels. Direction: Yi Ming. Screenplay: Yi Ming. Cinematography: Fu Hong, Chen Minhun. Sound: Chen Wenyuan. Cast: Zhang Ping as Zhang Yong, Lu Ban as Zhou Shaomei, Yao Xiangli as Cui Guofang, Liu Xilin as the old watch repairman, Liang Yin as the young engraver

After the liberation of Northeast China, several Nationalist agents remain behind as potential saboteurs. Their leader Zhou Shaomei orders one of the agents, Cui Guofang, to get a job in a certain factory so that he might steal production information. In making contact with another agent, Cui is arrested by security police and converted by re-education. Armed with information he supplies them, the police smash the spy ring, and Cui is given the chance for a new start in life.

1005. *The Invisible Net (Qian Wang)*

1981. Beijing Film Studio. Color. 10 Reels. Direction: Wang Haowei. Screenplay: Yao Yun, Wun Zhennian. Cinematography: Li Chengsheng. Art Direction: Hao Jingyuan. Music: Wang Liping. Sound: Gui Zhilin. Cast: Liu Xiaoqing as Luo Xuan, Zhang Guomin as Chen Zhiping, Chen Shaoze as He Kan, Zhang Ping as He Fangde, Xiang Lei as Luo Zhongwen, Lin Bing as Luo's wife

Professor's daughter Luo Xuan falls in love with soccer player Chen Zhiping. However, Luo's parents object, as they like neither the young man's poor family background nor his career. Instead, the parents want Luo Xuan to marry their old friend, college president He Fangde's son He Kai. He Kai and Luo Xuan grew up together, and he is now a mate on an oceangoing ship. Although she is very fond of Luo Xuan, she does not love him. Meanwhile, Chen Zhiping's parents also disapprove of their son's relationship with Luo Xuan, for they do

not want him entering a family with higher social status than theirs. Unable to get together, the two marry other people: Chen marries A Hui, a worker, and Luo Xuan later marries shipyard worker Guo Feng. Neither marriage goes well. Guo Feng is killed in an industrial accident, leaving Luo Xuan with a little girl. He Kai still loves Luo Xuan, and has waited for her for years, but now it is his parents who disagree with the choice, for they do not want their son involved with a widow with a child. He Kai courageously stands up to this feudalistic thinking and goes to Luo Xuan hopefully. But she turns him down again, for she has decided that she has gone through so much she deserves to devote some time to building a career.

1006. *The Invisible Ph.D. (Yin Shen Bo Shi)*

1991. Xi'an Film Studio. Color. Letterboxed. 9 Reels. Direction: Zhang Yuen. Screenplay: Xiao Mao. Cinematography: He Qin. Art Direction: Wang Yanlin. Music: Zhao Jiping, Bian Liunian. Sound: Hui Dongzhi. Cast: Chang Lantian as the Ph.D., Bai Lanmei as Xiao Yan, Jiang Jingyu as Xiulan, Wang Quanan as Erguo, Shi Guoqing as deputy director

After dreaming about human invisibility, a Ph.D. who is an amateur inventor creates a drug which accomplishes just that. His girl friend's brother steals the drug and uses it to rob a bank. This starts a succession of troubles for the Ph.D., but it ends that the whole affair was just a dream.

1007. *Irony of Fate (Ji Du Feng Hua Ji Du Chou)*

1991. Shanghai Film Studio & Taiwan Wanli Film Company Ltd. Co-Production. Color. Letterboxed. 9 Reels. Direction: Xie Dengbiao. Screenplay: Fei Xuejiao. Cinematography: Zhang Er. Art Direction: Zhang Wanhong. Music: Liu Yanxi. Sound: Zhou Hengliang. Cast: Wu Yujuan as Bai Mei, Tao Jin as Xin Jia, Yu Hui as Xu Youyou, Zhang Hong as Li Shaozhu, Liang Boluo as Tong Ping, Zhang Wenrong as Bai's mother, Zhu Manfang as the regimental commander

Young, beautiful and pregnant dancer Bai Mei returns to her home town, where she delivers a baby girl. The dancer had left with high hopes for a dancing career, but she was seduced then abandoned by the troupe's dancing coach Tong Ping. Bai Mei buries her sadness deep in her heart. A few years pass, and she meets and falls in love with Xin Jia, a Beijing choreographer. They marry, but a few years later he abandons her as well. Bai Mei has matured, and vows to carry on despite her broken heart.

1008. *It's a Wonderful Life (Da Fu Zhi Jia)*

1994. Shenzhen Film Company. Color. Letterboxed. 9 Reels. Direction: Gao Zhisen (Clifton Ko). Screenplay: Du Guowei. Cinematography: Li Jiagao. Art Direction: Wan Ying. Music: Huang Shichang. Costume: Wang Hong. Makeup: Wu Jing, Zhao Wenqiang. Cast: Guan Dexing as Grandfather Ren, Cao Dahua as Ren Dakuan, Li Xiangqin as Ren's wife, Huang Baiming as Ren Qiufu, Liang Jiahui (Tony Leung) as Ren Qiugui, Zhang Guorong (Leslie Cheung) as Robert, Yuan Yongyi (Anita Yuen) as He Shoujie, Zheng Yuling (Carol "Dodo" Cheng) as He Shouzhen, Feng Baobao as Yue Rong, Mao Shunyun (Teresa Mo) as Ren Qiuan

A complex saga of a Hong Kong family, four close-knit and interacting generations. The family has no money concerns, but the relationships among family members are very complex. The film follows the separate lives of the family's three sons and one daughter and their own families.

1009. *Its Fragrance Spreads for Thousands of Miles (Xiang Piao Wan Li)*

1959. Tianma Film Studio. B & W. 11 Reels. Direction: Fu Chaowu. Screenplay: Chen Jubing, Zhou Wenju, Pang Suyang, Fu Chaowu. Cinematography: Zhang Xiling. Set Design: Liu Pan. Music: Huang Zhun, Xiao Peiyan. Sound: Yuan Qingyu. Cast: Wei Yuping as Lu Huaming, Mu Hong as Liu Nianbeng, Shangguan Yunzhu as Gao Lan, Han Fei as Meng Shaode, Bai Mu as Director Zhou, Feng Xiao as the political instructor, Shi Jiufeng as the company commander, Su Yin as Wuwa, Yu Fei as Engineer Yang, Feng Huang as the technician, Yu Chong as Mr. Qian, Jiang Shan as the old hunter, Jiang Mianfang as the ticker seller, Xuan Jinglin as the girl

In 1958, Lu Huaming, a buyer for a Shanghai chemical products raw materials station, leads a small group to look for "mother of essence"—a sweet grass rumored to grow along the Southwest China border area. Yang, engineer at the regional botanical institute, believes that no such plant grows in the Southwest; among his own team, scent expert Liu Nian-

beng suggests importing the desired grasses. Armed with clues provided by the botanical institute, Lu Huaming leads his team deep into the Fenghuang Mountains. They encounter many difficulties and have several humorous incidents, but with the help of local peasants they finally discover the sweet grass high in the mountains.

1010. *It's Not Easy Being a Man (Nan Ren Ye Nan)*

1994. Beijing Film Studio. Color. Letterboxed. 9 Reels. Direction: Ru Shuiren, Wang Chi. Screenplay: Zhao Haicheng, Wang Chi. Cinematography: Ru Shuiren, Song Yazhou. Art Direction: Wang Xinguo. Music: Gao Erdi. Sound: Guan Jian. Costume: Zhang Yongyi. Makeup: Guo Jingxia. Cast: Wang Chi as Tong Shun, Yang Qing as Wang Yuzhi, Huang Zongluo as Uncle An, Ma Ling as Pan Mengting, Wang Xiaofei as Sun Qian, Zhou Zhou as Qian Xiaoyi, Zang Jinsheng as the taxi driver, Zhang Jing as the woman ticket seller, Zhang Shan as the truck driver, Yi Wei as Director Ding

Shopping mall employee Tong Shun is very concerned about his future, as his store is about to close. At the same time, he writes letters to an old man named An, whose daughter is dead. Tong comforts the old man by pretending she is still alive. Learning of Tong Shun's close relationship with An, a real estate development company approaches Tong about helping them take possession of the old man's house. His pregnant wife also wants the house, which they could then convert into a restaurant. Tong Shun has a difficult time withstanding all this pressure, but he stands by his principles, and does nothing to cost An his home.

1011. *Jackals and Wolves Enter the Room (Chai Lang Ru Shi)*

1991. Xi'an Film Studio. Color. Letterboxed. 9 Reels. Direction: Qiang Xiaolu. Screenplay: Qiang Xiaolu. Cinematography: Song Chao. Art Direction: Cheng Mingzhang, Li Zhengshen. Music: Zhang Dalong. Sound: Wei Jia. Costume: Liu Jianzhong. Makeup: Zhu Jian. Cast: Liang Danni as the woman, Feng Yuanzheng as the big guy, Weiqin as the child, Xu Jingyi as the fat man, Niu Yinghong as the college student, Gao Ming as the executive, Wang Yingquan as Big Liu

A man wanted for murder looks for a way to get money and false identification in order to flee the country. In a bar, he targets a young, single mother, a designer with a decorating firm, and with a good income. He follows the woman to her office, but she realizes what he is up to and runs home. He pursues her there and takes over her home, holding the woman and her little boy against their will. Their lives are constantly in danger, but when the child's tutor arrives, he grows suspicious and at last gets a message to the police. The fugitive is at last apprehended.

1012. *Jade Brings Down the Royal Palace (Yu Sui Gong Qing)*

1981. Changchun Film Studio. Color. 9 Reels. Direction: Gao Tianhong. Screenplay: Tian Ye. Cinematography: Liu Fengdi. Art Direction: Gong Minhui. Music: Liang Kexiang. Sound: Zhang Fenglu, Dong Baosheng. Cast: Lin Fangbing as Princess Tana, Ge Chunzhuang as King Ganzhuer, Li Xiangang as Hong Guer, Yu Xiaoping as Chisang Gebuzhaer, Jin Weimin as Tuo Rihan

The beautiful Princess Tana, beloved daughter of the Mongolian King Zhuer, meets young hunter Hong Guoer one day, and they fall in love. A nobleman, Sanggeerzhabu, has planned to marry Tana himself in order to gain the throne. When he learns of the princess's love for Hong Guer, he plots to kill the hunter. Meanwhile, King Zhuer objects to the princess's marrying Hong, and puts her under house arrest. Princess Tana has an insane elder sister who tells Tana that 10 years before, the elder sister had secretly married a man with low ranking at court. Their father the king, wanting to marry the elder daughter to a rival emperor, had his daughter's husband and child murdered. This was what drove her insane and why she has been locked in the palace for years. Tana continues to resist her father, and with her sister's help escapes from the palace to find Hong Guer. She finds him dead. At this point Sanggeerzhabu arrives and persuades Tana to return to the palace. She goes along, but now, recognizing her father's true nature, she kills her father and then herself.

1013. *The Jade Colored Butterfly (Yu She Hu Die)*

1980. Emei Film Studio. Color. 10 Reels. Direction: Zhang Fengxiang. Screenplay: Zhao Danian, Fan Jihua. Cinematography: Zhang Shiwei, Gao Lixian. Art Direction: Chen Desheng. Music: Lu Yuan. Sound: Lin Bingcheng. Cast:

Wang Danfeng as Zhunei Jundai, Xiang Lei as Qiutong, Zhang Fengxiang as Lingmu, Huang Daliang as Wangdong, Yu Yana as Changnian Zhongzi

In Japan in the 1930s, a Chinese student named Mu Rongqiu meets and falls in love with Jundai, a Japanese girl. They marry and have a son. When the child is five, Japan invades China and Mu Rongqiu is forced to leave Japan and Jundai, taking the boy back with him to China. The couple loses all contact, but Jundai remains faithful to her husband and devotes herself to becoming an expert entomologist. During the Cultural Revolution, Mu Rongqiu (now called Qiutong) is labeled a traitor and loses his right to hold a job. After the Gang of Four is defeated, Jundai is at last able to travel to China to search for her husband, bringing with her a daughter and a granddaughter. They find Qiutong in Beijing, restored to his old job. The couple, separated for 40 years, is together again at last. But Qiutong believes his wife must have remarried, for she now has a daughter. The situation is clarified, and three generations of the family are together at last.

1014. *The Japanese Warrior (Dong Ying You Xia)*

1991. Fujian Film Studio and Hong Kong Sil-Metropole Organization Ltd. Co-Production. Color. Letterboxed. 9 Reels. Direction: Zhang Xingyan. Screenplay: Lin Xiangpei, Zhang Xingyan. Cinematography: Zhou Bailing, Li Ming. Art Direction: Han Qingguo. Music: Zhang Shaotong, Chen Yongtie. Costume: Lu Yueying, Li Yanwen. Makeup: Li Yuping. Cast: Yu Rongguang as Ueichi, Yang Liqing as Cui Gu, Xu Jie as Xiao Maotou, Jin Demao as Hong Tianpeng, Yu Hai as Lin Tongshan, Ge Chunyan as Chen Yazhen, Ji Chunhua as Kawashima, Chang Rong as Xu San, Li Zhizhou as Yamura

Through a depiction of the adventures of the Japanese samurai warrior Ueichi, who came to China's Fujian Province in the Ming Dynasty (1368–1644) to look for the sources of the Japanese martial tradition, the film reveals the origins of karate. Reflecting the changing political trends, the film also plays up traditional Chinese-Japanese friendship.

1015. *Ji Hong (Ji Hong)*

1979. Changchun Film Studio. Color. 12 Reels. Direction: Zhang Xinshi. Screenplay: Er Hua. Cinematography: Dan Sengnima. Art

Direction: Wu Qiwen, Sun Shixiang. Music: Lou Zhanghou. Sound: Wun Liangyu. Cast: Pu Ke as Cheng Ruisheng, Gong Xue as Zhou Yingtong and Cheng Yingtong, Lin Qiang as Xu Hongyu, Guan Changzhu as Zhou Dan, Song Jingcang as Feng Jiabao

Ji Hong is a well-known and precious type of porcelain. In 1929, porcelain maker Cheng Ruisheng, a specialist in making Ji Hong, his daughter Ying Tong and his son-in-law Xu Hongyu live a poor life as a porcelain-making family. Then Feng Jiabao arrives in their town under Nationalist government orders to find the precious porcelain and get as much of it as possible. The plan is to give the porcelain to foreigners in exchange for weapons to be used by Chiang Kaishek's anti-revolutionary army. Cheng Ruisheng refuses to work for Feng Jiabao. Later Xu Hongyu joins a guerrilla troop and with the troop's director Zhou Yu organizes a porcelain workers' strike. Feng Jiabao kills Xu Hongyu and jails his pregnant wife, who delivers a baby girl in jail. The baby is later rescued by a guerrilla troop headed by Zhao Dan, who adopts her. After 1949, the daughter grows up a porcelain worker, and one day, in front of her parents' tomb, Zhao Dan and the girl meet Cheng Ruisheng. When Cheng Ruisheng successfully creates a truly beautiful Ji Hong vase for the tomb, his daughter suddenly appears. It turns out that she had escaped during a transfer of prisoners to Shanghai, joined a guerrilla brigade and after 1949 was sent to work overseas. Now, father, daughter and granddaughter are united.

1016. *Ji Hongcang (Parts 1 & 2)* (*Ji Hong Cang*)

1979. Changchun Film Studio. Color. 18 Reels. Direction: Li Guanghui. Screenplay: Chen Lide. Cinematography: Li Guanghui, Wang Jishun. Art Direction: Li Wenguang, Cui Yongli. Music: Lei Zhengbang. Sound: Huang Lijia. Cast: Da Qi as Ji Hongcang, Bai Dezhang as Huo Jinlong, Zuo Fu as Zhou Guangyuan, Zhao Hengduo as Chiang Kaishek, Zhang Xiqi as Zhen Guilin, Liu Han as Tang Gui

In 1931, Nationalist commander Ji Hongcang finds his army defeated time and again by the Communists. He sees that one reason for the Communists' success is that they have so much support from the common people. To find the reasons for this support, Ji Hongcang goes incognito to the Communist-controlled area and sees how the people live there. After

this, he decides to fight the Red Army no more. When Chiang Kaishek orders him to fight again, he refuses and moves abroad. After the "December 8th" incident, Ji returns to China and joins the Communist Party. In 1933, Ji Hongcang organizes the Volunteer Army in Tianjin to resist the Japanese invasion, directly contrary to the Nationalist government's appeasement policy of the time. Chiang tries to force Ji to disband his army, but he refuses. Chiang then has spies arrest and abduct Ji, but Ji continues his resistance, despite being tortured in jail. Finally Chiang has Ji Hongcang executed.

Best Picture, 1980 Hundred Flowers Awards.

Best Screenplay Chen Lide, 1980 Hundred Flowers Awards.

1017. *Jiang City's Strange Story* (*Jiang Cheng Qi Shi*)

1990. Shanghai Film Studio. Color. Wide Screen. 10 Reels. Direction: Pao Zhifang. Screenplay: Zhao Zhiqiang, Hu Huiying. Cinematography: Qiu Yiren, Zhang Hongjun. Art Direction: Shen Lide. Music: Liu Yanxi. Sound (Dolby): Feng Deyao. Cast: Lin Jifeng as Meng Tao, Wang Zhihua as Gao Feng, Tong Ruixin as He Yiming

In Jiangling City, newly assigned Mayor Gao Feng finds that his former schoolmate Meng Tao is head of the city's theatrical troupe. The two discuss a recent incident at the local jade sculpting plant, a typical example of what unhealthy social customs can bring about. Gao Feng suggests Meng Tao write and perform a play about it, to make more people aware of the problem. Meng agrees, and takes the show on the road. The film follows the experiences of the drama group as they tell audiences some things they often don't want to hear about unhealthy and unethical practices.

1018. *Jiao Yulu* (*Jiao Yu Lu*)

1990. Emei Film Studio. Color. 10 Reels. Wide Screen. Direction: Wang Jixing. Screenplay: Fang Yihua. Cinematography: Qiang Jun. Art Direction: Lu Qiming. Sound: Wang Guangzhong. Cast: Li Xuejian as Jiao Yulu, Li Rentang as Agent Zhao, Zhou Zongyin as Pan Jian, Tian Yuan as Wu Rongguang, Zhang Ying as Wu Junya

The biography of a Communist Party hero. Lankao County in Henan Province has long been plagued by sandstorms, floods and saline-alkali soil. In 1962, the county suffers another natural calamity, but at this critical juncture, Party Secretary Jiao Yulu, assisted by the prefectural agent, the county magistrate and the local people, determines to save the county from its poverty and backwardness. He is devoted to carrying out his public duty. Although he dies prematurely of liver cancer on May 14, 1964, the people of Lankao will remember him forever.

Best Picture, 1991 Golden Rooster Awards.

Best Picture, 1991 Hundred Flowers Awards.

Best Actor Li Xuejian, 1991 Golden Rooster Awards.

Best Actor Li Xuejian, 1991 Hundred Flowers Awards.

1019. *Jin Luer (Jin Lu Er)*

1982. Beijing Film Studio. Color. 5 Reels. Direction: Dong Kena. Screenplay: Hang Ying, Dong Kena, Zhang Shiwei. Cinematography: Zhang Shiwei. Art Direction: Hao Guoxin. Music: Hu Weili. Sound: Wang Dawen. Cast: Leng Mei as Jin Minglu, Si Jianlan as Wang Shuxian, Zhang Guomin as Shi Yongli, Lei Min as Mr. Guo

A retail store's customers select a woman named Jin Luer as the store's best salesperson. However, controversy soon follows the vote. Rumors spread saying the only part of the job Jin Luer likes is dressing up and wearing fancy clothes to work, that she really dislikes the actual work of selling. This leads the company's Youth League Secretary Wang Shuxian to conduct an investigation of her. Wang Shuxian finds out that Jin Luer truly loves her work, that she has excellent skills and service techniques, and that her customer service manner is warmly welcoming and sincere. At the same time, Jin Luer likes having an attractive appearance too. Wang Shuxian gains an understanding of Jin Luer through probing conversations with her, and is soon able to dispel all the misunderstandings and biases.

Ji Hongcang (Parts 1 & 2). **Volunteer Army commander Ji Hongchang (Da Qi) inspects his troops. 1979. Changchun Film Studio.**

1020. *Jin Suo (Jin Suo)*

1976. Shanghai Film Studio. Color. 6 Reels. Direction: Da Shibiao. Screenplay: Collective, recorded by Da Shibiao, and based on the novel of the same title. Cinematography: Zhang Yuanmin. Art Direction: Zhu Jiancang. Music: Yang Shaolu. Cast: Huan Rong as Jin Suo, Dong Qinwei as Xiao Niu, Fu Hengzhi as Jin Suo's father, Xu Caigeng as Zhong Chun, Shi Ling as Shi Degui

During World War Two, the Japanese search for the Communist New Fourth Army's secret munitions plant in rural China. After a succession of failures, they attempt to cut off the plant's sources of material by rounding up all scrap metal from the villages. Children's brigade member Jin Suo bravely and cleverly struggles with the Japanese, and collects a large quantity of scrap metal in support of the New Fourth Army.

1021. *Jin Yuji (Jin Yu Ji)*

1959. Changchun Film Studio. Color. 11 Reels. Direction: Wang Jiayi. Screenplay: Wang Jiayi, Ji Ye. Cinematography: Wang Chunquan. Art Direction: Shi Weijun. Music: Pu You, Gao Zhixing, Lei Zhenbang. Sound: Lin Bingcheng. Cast: Bai Yang as Jin Yuji, Shi Yan as the political commissar, Shi Kefu as Director Cui, Xu Dongzhi as a veteran soldier, Dong Runquan as leader of the third division team, Bao Xuegang as leader of the second division team, Guo Wenlin as Jin Zhaoming

During the anti–Japanese War, Korean nationality woman soldier Jin Yuji leads a unit of the Volunteer Army in a successful attack on Japanese forces in the Changbai Mountains. She is later assigned with staff officer Jin Zhaoming to locate grain supplies in the mountains. But Jin Zhaoming has turned traitor, and betrays her to the Japanese. Jin Yuji is captured, tortured and finally executed. But some local people find her still breathing and save her life. After her recovery, Jin Yuji leads mine workers to fight against the Japanese. The traitor is captured and punished. After the war, she returns to her hometown, and vows to continue the revolutionary struggle.

1022. *Jinggang Mountains (Jing Gang Shan)*

1993. Beijing Film Studio and Jiangxi Film Studio Co-Production. Color. Wide Screen. 11 Reels. Direction: Li Xin. Screenplay: Cao Shuolong, Liu Rende. Cinematography: Yun Wenyue, Gao Jie, Liu Xiaoling. Art Direction: Zu Shaoxian, Wang Xinguo. Music: Zhang Qianyi. Sound: Wu Ling. Costume: Zhang Dezhong. Makeup: Liu Changzheng. Cast: Wang Zheng as Mao Zedong, Wang Zhixia as He Zizhen, Zhang Xinyuan as Wang Zuo, Hong Tao as Yuan Wencai, Xu Jianguo as He Changgong, Liang Li as Shuisheng, Zhao Dengfeng as Zhu De, Guo Jiangxi as Chen Yi, Zhang Ping as Wan Xixian, Shi Lei as Zhang Ziqing

On September 22, 1927, Mao Zidong leads the survivors of the failed Qiushou farmers' rebellion to the Jinggang Mountains to recover from their severe losses. In the mountains, Mao develops and expands his band of workers and farmers. At the same time, he struggles with Communist Party leadership over what he perceives as their incorrect political line. On April 28, 1928, Mao and General Zhu De merge their troops to form a new force in the Chinese Communist Party and start a new chapter in China's revolutionary history.

1023. *Jingpo Girl (Jing Po Gu Niang)*

1965. Changchun Film Studio. Color. 10 Reels. Direction: Wang Jiayi. Screenplay: Yang Su, Li Jianrao and Wang Jiayi. Cinematography: Wang Chunquan. Art Direction: Liu Xuerao. Music: Lei Zhengbang. Sound: Lin Bingcheng. Cast: Meilu Malu as Dainuo, Muding Madu as Leding, Daqi as Wenshuai, Zhang Yuan as Doctor Li, Su Mai as Dong Muna, Shi Mabo as Mu Lan

In Dulong Village on a mountain in Yunnan province, a Jingpo nationality girl named Dainuo is a household serf of mountain owner Zhaokun. Unable to bear the mistreatment she suffers at the hands of his family, Dainuo runs away to find the PLA. Soon afterwards, a PLA work team comes to Dulong village to help the Jingpo people carry out democratic reforms. To turn the Jingpo people against the PLA, Zhaokun spreads the rumor that Dainuo's disappearance is due to her having been abducted by the soldiers. The girl's lover Leding particularly hates the PLA work team. But the work team's Doctor Li converts their thinking by providing the Jingpo people with excellent medical care. He also makes suggestions on how they can reform their traditional forms of farming. Shortly after, Dainuo returns, and explains that she has been working with another PLA team to successfully resolve disputes among different villages. When they learn the truth, the Dulong village people rise up and overthrow Zhaokun. Then they establish a village people's government, electing Dainuo village head.

1024. *Jiu Xiang (Jiu Xiang)*

1995. Changchun Film Studio. Color. Letterboxed. Direction: Sun Sha. Screenplay: Du Lijuan. Cinematography: Zhang Songping, Zhang Luming. Art Direction: Qi Ming. Music: Yang Yilun. Cast: Song Chunli as Jiu Xiang, Zhang Guisheng as Guan Zhenliang, Zhang Hongjie as You Tuhu, Qiang Yin as Yue Gui

In a small mountain village in Northeast China, young and beautiful Jiu Xiang becomes a widow with five children when her house collapses, killing her husband. Her husband's co-worker Mr. Guan devotes considerable time and effort to helping the family, and in time he and Jiu Xiang fall in love. However, her children will not accept him, so Jiu Xiang defers to them and lets love pass her by. Unable to bear being so close yet apart, Mr. Guan moves to the city. Many years later, her children having grown up and left, old and lonely Jiu Xiang goes to the city to look up Mr. Guan, only to find he died nine years before. Jiu Xiang suddenly grows very feeble and sick. Her children bring her back to the home where they were raised, and they all feel very guilty about their old mother.

1025. *Joint Investigation (Lian Shou Jing Tan)*

1990. Shenzhen Film Corporation and Hong Kong Sil-Metropole Organisation Ltd. Jointly. Color. 9 Reels. Wide Screen. Direction: Guo Baochang. Screenplay: Wu Qitai, Guo Baochang. Cinematography: Hou Yong. Art Direction: Li Hong. Music: Li Lifu. Sound: Huang Minguang. Cast: Yu Rongguang as Huang Tao, Guo Xiuyun as Shao Xiafei, Jiang Han as Chen Qingyun, Ji Chunhua as Pan Jiu, Zhang Yanli as A Qi

In the forests along the Shenzhen–Hong Kong border, a corpse and some counterfeit HK bank notes are discovered. Huang Tao, a policeman from Shenzhen, crosses the border and infiltrates the Hong Kong underworld to investigate the case. Huang gains a partner in Hong Kong policewoman Shao Xiafei as he takes on the Hong Kong underworld.

1026. *Journeying West to Kill the Demon (Xi Xing Ping Yao)*

1991. Xiaoxiang Film Studio and Hong Kong Changhe Film Company Co-Production. Color. Letterboxed. 9 Reels. Direction: Zhang Che. Screenplay: Zhang Che and Chen Baoxun, from the novel by Wu Cheng'en (ca1500–ca1582). Cinematography: Zhao Peng, Liu Weiwei. Art Direction: Yang Li. Sound: Deng Shaolin. Costume: Liu Xuequn, Li Huiming. Makeup: Wu Yan, Liu Ying and Liu Jianping. Cast: Jia Yongquan, Chen Jiming, Du Yumin, Mu Lixin, Dong Zhihua, Yu Jia

A dramatization of a story in the classic Chinese novel *Xi You Ji* ("Journey to the West"), in which a Tang dynasty monk and his apprentices travel to the far Western regions to bring the classic Buddhist scriptures back to China.

1027. *Joy at Moon Bay (Yue Liang Wan De Xiao Sheng)*

1981. Shanghai Film Studio. Color. 9 Reels. Direction: Xu Sulin. Screenplay: Jin Haitao, Fang Yihua. Cinematography: Zhang Er. Art Direction: Wang Xingcang. Music: Xu Jingxin. Sound: Ren Xinliang. Cast: Zhang Yan as Jiang Maofu, Zhong Xinghuo as Qing Liang, Gu Yuqing as Lanhua, Kou Zhenhai as Guigeng, Tan Pengfei as Deshan, Ouyang Ruqiu as Lanhua's mother

Jiang Maofu is an ordinary peasant in Moon Bay Village. Because of his skill raising fruit, he is more prosperous than others, and is labeled "typical of those traveling the capitalist road." The father's political status prevents his son Guigeng finding a wife. Guigeng falls in love with peasant girl Lanhua, but her father objects. Later, with a change in the political atmosphere, Jiang Maofu overnight becomes a model of the new prosperity, and now Lanhua's father Qing Liang regrets his earlier decision. He decides to get his daughter married into Jiang Maofu's family, and after initial rejection by Jiang, the marriage is approved. But when the Gang of Four begins criticizing the "rightist conversion wind," Jiang Maofu is branded a "capitalist" once more. Qing Liang interrupts the wedding and drags his daughter away. After the downfall of the Gang of Four, Jiang Maofu is again restored to political respectability, and Guigeng and Lan Hua are still unfulfilled lovers. Lanhua's mother takes matters in hand and forces her husband Qing Liang to see Jiang Maofu and ask for the marriage. In spite of his anger with Qing Liang, Jiang faces reality and again approves of the match.

Best Actor Zhang Yan, 1982 Golden Rooster Awards.

1028. *Ju Dou (Ju Dou)*

1990. Tokuma Shoten Publishing, Tokuma Communications, China Film Co-Production Corp., China Film Export & Import Corp. Co-Production. Color. 10 Reels. Direction: Zhang Yimou, in collaboration with Yang Fengliang. Screenplay: Liu Heng (1954–), based on his novel "The Obsessed." Cinematography: Gu Changwei, Yang Lun. Editor: Du Yuan. Music: Zhao Jiping. Sound: Li Lanhua. Costume: Zhang Zhian. Makeup: Sun Wei. Cast: Gong Li as Ju Dou, Li Baotian as Yang Tianqing, Li Wei as Yang Jinshan, Zhang Yi as Yang Tianbai (as a child), Zhen Jian as Yang Tianbai (as a young boy)

In the 1920s, the middle-aged owner of a small town dyeing mill, Yang Jinshan, keeps buying young women as his wives in fruitless attempts to produce a male heir. The latest of these brides is a pretty young girl named Ju Dou. Outraged and frustrated at his own impotence, Yang beats the young woman nightly. Aware of her nightly suffering but powerless to help is Wang's young nephew Tianqing, the operator of the mill. Ju Dou begins to flirt with the nephew during the day, and soon entices him into an affair. She becomes pregnant, and the delighted Yang Jinshan is easily convinced he is the father. The birth of a son takes things out of their hands: the nephew naturally wants his son to love and respect him, but the opposite is the case, as the boy increasingly comes to resent the presence of "Uncle," actually his father. Ju Dou wishes the old man dead, especially after a stroke leaves him a demanding and abusive paraplegic. The old man dies at last. After that, her son's resentment of Tianqing turns to hatred, especially as the boy (who turns out to have the same brutish nature as the old man) spitefully observes the sexual relationship of his mother and her lover, his real father. In the end, the boy kills Tianqing, and Ju Dou burns down the dyeing mill.

Luis Bunuel Award, 43rd Cannes Intl. Film Festival.

Golden Hugo Award, 26th Chicago Intl. Film Festival.

Golden Wheatsheaf Award, Best Picture, 35th Semana Intl. de Cine de Valladolid.

Eastman Kodak Award for Excellence in Photography (Gu Changwei), the 10th Hawaii Intl. Film Festival.

1029. *July (Qi Yue Liu Huo)*

1981. Shanghai Film Studio. Color. Letterboxed. 10 Reels. Direction: Ye Ming. Screenplay: Lin Gu. Cinematography: Cha Xiangkang, Wun Shijie. Art Direction: Zhong Yongqin, Xie Muqian. Music: Wang Yunjie. Sound: Tu Minde. Cast: Chen Dazhu as Hua Suyin, Li Zhiyu as Wen Yuanqiao, Wang Suya as Jin Guangcai, Gong Xue as Ni Youyun, Shi Shugui as Guan Tong, Zhang Wenrong as Wu Zhen

In 1939 Shanghai, Hua Suying, a covert member of the Communist Party, organizes her fellow professional women into a club. The club holds various charity fund-raising sales, but the funds are actually for the anti-Japanese New Fourth Route Army. These activities arouse the suspicions of "No.76," a Chinese collaborationist organization. It assigns woman lawyer Du Jinguang to join the women's club in order to gather information and disrupt its activities. Her efforts set back the club's fundraising. On top of her other problems, Hua Suying's mother dies. Since her work will not allow her to leave, Hua asks her fiance Wen Yuanqiao to make the funeral arrangements, but he accuses her of not having fulfilled her duties as a daughter, and breaks off their engagement. Hua is at last able to get the volunteers' work going again, so the collaborators decide the only way to stop her is to kill her. They decide her mother's funeral will present the ideal opportunity. Tipped off by a spy at government headquarters, the Party organization warns her to stay away from the funeral, and makes arrangements to relocate her to work at a Communist liberation base. Before leaving, Hua goes to see Wen, and asks him to think about joining her. As her friends are seeing her off, a hired gunman shoots and critically wounds Hua, and she is rushed to the hospital. Wen Yuanqiao visits her there, and Hua Suying apologizes for having made him wait so long. After having sacrificed her love for her mother and her lover for the revolution, she breathes her last.

1030. *The July 7th Incident (Parts 1 & 2) (Qi Qi Shi Bian)*

1995. Changchun Film Studio. Color. Letterboxed. Dolby Sound. Direction: Li Qiankuan, Xiao Guiyun. Screenplay: Long Jianhua. Cinematography: Li Li. Cast: Wu Guiling as Song Zheyuan, Li Fazeng as Tong Lingge, Wu Jingan as Zhao Dengyu, Zhen Bangyu as Zhang Zhizhong, Du Zhiguo as He Jiyang, Li Zhixin as Feng Zhian, Shi Xianfu as Jin Zhenzhong, Zhou Shouchao as Yimu Qingzhi, Su Lin as Zhou Enlai, Gu Yue as Mao Zedong, Xu Daolin as Chiang Kaishek

Following their occupation of Northeast China in 1937, the Japanese push into North China. Wanping County stands between the invaders and the cities of Beijing and Tianjin, so Chinese 29th Army commander Song Zheyuan decides to make his defense there. The Japanese first offer the Chinese the opportunity to withdraw, but when this is refused the invaders move closer to the town of Wanping. In docudramatic style, the film relates the defense of North China by such commanders as Song, Tong Lingge, Zhao Dengyu and He Jifeng. At last, the Chinese are forced to withdraw from the Marco Polo Bridge (Luk-ouqiao), permitting Japanese forces to cross the bridge into Beijing. This was the start of full-scale hostilities between the two armies.

1031. *Juvenile Delinquents (Shao Nian Fan)*

1985. Shenzhen Film Studio. Color. 10 Reels. Direction: Zhang Liang. Screenplay: Wang Jingzhu, Zhang Liang. Cinematography: Yan Xuzhong. Art Direction: Wang Meifang. Music: Yang Shaolu. Sound: Hou Shenkang. Cast: Lu Bing as Fang Gang, Jiang Jian as Xiao Fu, Zhu Manfang as Xie Jiexin, Shen Guangwei as Feng Guangwei, Zhao Zhichang as Director Zhao, Wang Jue as Shen Jinmin

Veteran woman reporter Xie Jiexin is assigned to look into her city's juvenile crime problem. She investigates the cases of three delinquents, then writes a series of articles which call for society to be more understanding of youth such as these. She urges that they not be abandoned, but offered a second chance at school and jobs. Her series ignites strong reactions and much commentary, but just at this time her own son is arrested on sex-related charges. Xie finds herself questioning whether she has also neglected her son's upbringing for her career.

Best Picture, 1986 Hundred Flowers Awards.

Best Actors Award of Youth Film Competition, 7th Fajr International Film Festival.

1032. *Kangxi Upsets Wutai Mountain (Kang Xi Da Nao Wu Tai Shan)*

1989. Pearl River Film Studio. Color. 10 Reels. Direction: Yu Deshui. Screenplay: Song Da'en. Cinematography: Wu Benli. Art Direction: Huang Zhaohui. Music: Cheng Dazhao. Sound: Li Xun. Cast: Wang Jue as Kangxi, Yang Dezhi as the Monk, Zhang Dongsheng as Ma Mingyang, Xu Weirong as Zheng Ke

In the latter part of the 17th Century the Emperor Kangxi travels to Mount Wutai disguised as a knight-errant. He hopes to find his father the Emperor Shunzhi, who abdicated and became a monk many years before. Kangxi and his men meet up with Ma Mingyang, a rebel who aims to kidnap Shunzhi as a hostage to blackmail Kangxi into giving up some of his territory in southeast China. In the course of unraveling Ma's conspiracy, Kangxi is shattered to learn that he cannot prevent his own father's death.

1033. *Kawashima Yoshiko (Chuan Dao Fang Zi)*

1989. Xi'an Film Studio. Color. 10 Reels. Wide Screen. Direction: He Ping. Screenplay: Zhu Zi. Cinematography: Nie Tiemao, Ma Delin. Art Direction: Cheng Mingchang. Music: Tao Long. Sound: Dang Chunzhu. Cast: Zhang Xiaomin as Kawashima Yoshiko, Gao Fa as Iwahara Kazuo, Yuan Yan as Tanaka Ryukichi, Gao Ming as Captain Koomoto

Kawashima Yoshiko, a descendant of the Qing court, is the step-daughter of a Japanese rojin. She becomes a renowned Japanese spy in the 1920s and 1930s. This film depicts only part of her career. In April 1928, the Japanese army in Northeast China decided to eliminate Zhang Zuolin, the warlord there. Kawashima approaches Zhang's aide-de-camp Chen Jin, and steals secrets concerning Zhang's travel schedule. This action results in Zhang's death when the Japanese blow up his personal train. After that, she receives orders to go to Tianjin disguised as a man and kidnap Empress Wan Rong of the Qing court, which was in exile there. Another mission takes her to Shanghai, the largest city in China and a center of intrigue at that time... To realize her dream of restoring the Qing dynasty, she goes to any length, often even surprising her Japanese masters. But when the Japanese feel that she is too difficult to control, they send her former lover to secretly get rid of her...

1034. *Kidnapping Karajan (Bang Jia Ka La Yang)*

1988. Shanghai Film Studio. Color. 10 Reels. Direction: Zhang Jianya. Screenplay: Du Xiaojuan. Cinematography: Jiang Shuzhen. Art Direction: Qiu Yuan. Music: Ju Xiaosong. Sound: Zhan Xin. Cast: Zhen Dasheng as Da Long, Chen Yi as Fangfang, Yao Erga as Xiao Huan, Sang Wei as A Liang

Four youngsters are desperate to attend a concert conducted by the renowned conductor Von Karajan. However hard they try, they fail to get the tickets for the performance. So finally they devise a scheme for kidnapping the artist.

1035. *Kids Inviting Treasure (Zhao Cai Tong Zhi)*

1987. Children's Film Studio. Color. 9 Reels. Direction: Liu Guoquan. Screenplay: Wang Binglin, Zhang Liang. Cinematography: Wang Jiuwen. Art Direction: Zhang Yafang. Music: Wang Ming. Sound: Wu Ling. Cast: Wang Huili as Xiangni, Zhang Li as Shiye, Cao Xuewen as Tianbao, Chen Yude as Tian Shan

In Hongshi Village, 15-year-old Shiye assumes a heavy work load after her mother's death. Her father Tian Shan likes money but never seems to make any. A new boy named Tianbao comes to Shiye's school, following his mother when she remarries. The movie follows the young people's struggle to get an education. They are helped greatly when the Chinese government makes nine years of education compulsory.

1036. *Kids' Restaurant (Wa Wa Can Ting)*

1986. Shanghai Film Studio. Color. 9 Reels. Direction: Shi Xiaohua. Screenplay: He Guopu, Shi Meijun. Cinematography: Yin Fukang. Art Direction: Zhen Changfu. Music: Liu Yanxi. Sound: Xie Guojie. Cast: Pan Feng as Luo Jia, Lin Jian as Ma Haisheng, Yin Qinlan as Gu Yan, Li Ding as Fat Grandpa, Zhou Liangliang as the old director

During summer vacation from school, a childrens' activity center organizes a Young Pioneers' Restaurant. Because the entire staff from management to kitchen help to servers consists of children about the age of 10, it becomes known as the "Kids' Restaurant." A man named Luo Jia volunteers to be the general manager, and a superior chef called Fat Grandpa is invited to be head chef. The problem is he does not take the children seriously, although they are very serious about the project. The story tells how the various children work together to make up for their individual shortcomings. Finally, Fat Grandpa goes to Beijing for a gourmet food exhibition, and the children keep the restaurant open during his absence. When he returns, he finds the business not only is running well, but the children have invented several new dishes they invite him to try.

1037. *Kill the Northeast King (Mou Ci Guan Dong Wang)*

1993. Changchun Film Studio. Color. Letter-boxed. 9 Reels. Direction: Liu Zhongming, Liu Erwei. Screenplay: Ma Junxiang, Liu Ying. Cinematography: Yu Zhenhai. Art Direction: Liu Sheng. Music: Chen Chunguang. Sound: Zhang Qingjiang. Costume: Yang Shu, Zhao Xiaohua. Makeup: Li Yang, Sheng Libo. Cast: Shen Junyi as Song Tianfeng, Wang Gang as Qige Qiao, Su Tingshi as Zhang Zuolin, Chi Zhiqiang as "Glasses," Lu Xiaohe as Li Cheng, Jia Ni as Suyu

Early in the 20th century, warlord general Zhang Zuolin's ambiguity regarding the Japanese leads a group of progressive generals led by Guo Songling into a movement to force Zhang Zuolin out of power. The result is that Guo is killed. After his death, several of his followers secretly organize a hit squad to assassinate Zhang, who is protected by the Japanese. The plotters come to a tragic ending, with their leaders blowing themselves up with Zhang's Japanese bodyguards.

1038. *The Killer and the Coward (Xiong Shou Yu Nuo Fu)*

1987. Shanghai Film Studio. Color. 10 Reels. Direction: Da Shibiao. Screenplay: Yang Shiwen, Liang Xingmin. Cinematography: Zhang Er. Art Direction: Wang Xingcang, Shen Lide. Music: Xiao Yan. Sound: Yin Zhiping. Cast: Tian Shaojun as Song Yang, Xiao Yan as Li Zhen, Yu Feihong as Lu Xiaofeng, Li Weitian as Liu Jiaye, Guo Lianwen as Zhang Fengling, Zhang Weigang as Lin Abao

PSB investigator Li Zhen's preparations for her forthcoming wedding to athlete Liu Jiaye are interrupted when she is called out to look into a particularly violent case: a girl, Chen Xiaofeng, has been raped and murdered and a badly beaten young man was found at the scene. The beating victim, Zhang Fengling, tells Li and her partner Ma Long that his injuries are the result of attempting to rescue the murdered girl. The detectives find out Chen Xiaofeng had a boyfriend named Song Yang, who has disappeared. They suspect he was somehow involved, and when they at last find Song Yang, he leads them to the startling truth: on the fatal night, Song Yang and Chen Xiaofeng were out on a date, when Zhang Fengling and some other hoods attacked them. They raped Chen Xiaofeng, but the cowardly Song only kneeled to beg the criminals to spare him. After the attack, Song's reaction swung to the opposite extreme and he savagely beat Zhang Fengling, then ran off. Most surprising for Li Zhen, however, is the revelation that another person was at the scene: when Chen Xiaofeng was being raped, the detective's fiancee Liu Jiaye happened to pass by; he wanted to rescue her, but backed off when Zhang Fengling threatened him with acid. The case is cleared up and all criminals are caught. Li Zhen breaks off her engagement with Liu Jiaye.

1039. *The Killers' Passion (Sha Shou Qing)*

1988. Xi'an Film Studio. Color. 11 Reels. Direction: Yan Xueru. Screenplay: Yan Xueru. Cinematography: Mi Jiaqing, Feng Wei. Art Direction: Li Xingzheng. Music: Cheng Baohua. Sound: Li Lanhua. Cast: Shen Junyi as Song Guang, Shi Ke as Han Meiyun, Wang Chi as Gao Dahu, Zhang Chunzhong as Sun Li, Li Yan as Han Yunshan

In 1914, Yuan Shikai sends agents throughout China to suppress all opposition to his seizure of power. Two of his hired killers are sent to assassinate an anti–Yuan movement leader and locate his hidden arms cache. One of the assassins is Su Lu, who allies himself with powerful local despot Gao Dahu. The other, Han Yunshan, employs his adopted daughter Han Meiyun to ingratiate herself with Sun Li, their target. But a third killer complicates their plans: Song Guang, whose brother Song Liang was killed two years earlier by Gao Dahu while passing through the area on a business trip. Song Guang has come for revenge. In the course of avenging his brother he encounters three very different women, and they all fall in love with him. Intrigues and passions lead to a series of bloody murders.

1040. *Kindly People Have No Enemies (Ren Zhe Wu Di)*

1995. Inner Mongolia Film Studio. Color. Letterboxed. Direction: Chen Xunqi. Screenplay: Zhou Zhenying, Li Bingguang. Cinematography: Wu Rongjie. Cast: Di Long as Fu Hongxue, Chen Xunqi as Ye Kai, Yuan Yongyi (Anita Yuen) as Ding Lingling, Cen Yulian as Shen Sanniang, Ju Ying as Ding Baiyun

An action film.

1041. *King Lanling (Lan Ling Wang)*

1994. Shanghai Film Studio. Color. Direction: Hu Xuehua. Screenplay: Hu Xuehua, Wang Peigong. Cinematography: Hu Xuehua. Art Di-

rection: Han Sheng. Music: He Xuntian. Cast: Ruo Lanzuo, Yang Liping, Ning Jing, Wang Xueqi, Ning Qi

In ancient Chinese legend, there was once a Southwest China tribe which worshipped the peacock. The head of the tribe was a beautiful woman, who had a son she named Lanling. When Lanling grew up, he accepted his duty of defending the tribal honor, but because of his handsome face, almost as lovely as that of a girl, no one would take him seriously as a warrior.

1042. *King of Heaven Conquers the Earthly Tiger (Tian Wang Gai Di Hu)*

1990. Shanghai Film Studio. Color. Wide Screen. 10 Reels. Direction: Wu Tianren. Screenplay: Lan Zhiguang, Ling Shu. Cinematography: Yu Shishan. Art Direction: Guo Dongmao. Music: Xu Jingxin. Sound: Zhao Jianzhong. Cast: Ju Naishe as Li Zheng, Feierdaweisi as Da Wei, Jiang Boping as Gu Lan, Wang Weiping as Xia Changhou

The wreckage of a Chinese Nationalist airplane is found in the desert, where it had apparently crashed 38 years earlier. However, investigation shows that some things were missing from the plane, notably some weapons and a priceless copy of the Koran. As detective Li Zheng and policeman Da Wei investigate, a Hong Kong triad learns that a mainland smuggling ring has the Koran, and sends professional killer Xia Changhou to get it from them. Xia kills the smugglers and takes the Koran, but the police officers intercept him before he can return to Hong Kong. In the final shoot-out, Xia kills Da Wei and Li Zheng kills Xia.

1043. *The King of Masks (Bian Lian)*

1995. Youth Film Studio, Shaw Bros. (Hong Kong) Co-Production. Color. Letterboxed. 97 minutes. Direction: Wu Tianming. Screenplay: Wei Minglun, based on Chen Wengui's original story. Cinematography: Mu Deyuan. Art Direction: Wu Xujing. Music: Zhao Jiping. Cast: Zhu Xu as Wang, Zhou Renying as Gouwa ("Doggie"), Zhang Ruiyang as Tian Ti, Zhao Zhigang as Liang, Jia Zhaoji as the dealer in humans, Chen Li as Miss Wen, Dong Jiannan as the wet nurse

In Sichuan in the 1920s, an old folk artist

The King of Masks. Old Wang (Zhu Xu) learns to truly love his adopted "grandson" Gouwa (Zhou Renying). 1995. Youth Film Studio, Shaw Bros. Co-Production.

known as the King of Changing Faces follows the tradition of passing on his art to sons only, and not to daughters. The "King" finds a market in humans, and adopts a grandson from it. He greatly enjoys his grandson, who he names Gouwa. But one day he discovers that Gouwa is actually a girl, and this makes the old man very unhappy. To please her adoptive grandfather, little Gouwa one day lets an apparently homeless three-year-old boy come into their home to stay. This makes the King very happy, until the police arrive to get the boy, who turns out to be the lost child of the city's wealthiest man. The King is jailed for kidnapping the boy. But Gouwa and a woman actress called the "Living Kuanyin" save the old man. From then on, he treats Gouwa as his own grandson.

1044. *The King of Panners (Tao Jin Wang)*

1985. Shanghai Film Studio. Color. Wide Screen. Direction: Shen Yaoting. Screenplay: Wang Shouyi. Cinematography: Ju Jiazheng. Art Direction: Huang Qiagui. Music: Xiao Yan. Sound: Li Bingkui. Cast: Zhang Jinsheng as Xu

Tianxiong, Song Jia as Xiao Luzhu, Niu Beng as Wang Baozi, Zhou Zhiyu as Guan Shan, Dong Ling as Ba Zhangui, Liao Xueqiu as Jincao

In the early years of the 20th century, a group of fortune hunters travels to Xinjiang in search of gold. One of these is Xu Tianxiong, a tough but good guy with a past, wanted by the government for having killed some agents in a gold mining incident. He rescues a man called the "King of Panners" from persecution by a mine boss. Xu wins the trust of all the miners, and in time becomes the new "King." He leads them in the search for a gold cave which could make them all rich. The miners find the gold, but it does not bring them happiness, as disaster strikes.

1045. *King of Shooters (Yi Dai Qiang Wang)*

1989. Changchun Film Studio. Color. Letterboxed. 9 Reels. Direction: Yu Mei, Yang Jing. Screenplay: Zhong Yuan. Cinematography: Gao Hongbao. Art Direction: Wang Chong. Music: Wang Liping. Sound: Luo Huailun. Cast: Wang Qun as Cheng Zhiqin, Zong Qiaozhen as Lianhua, Xiang Mei as Lin Luomi, Aer Silang as Clinton

During the Boxer Rebellion in 1900, armies of eight foreign nations occupy Beijing. Although the Boxer movement is a patriotic one, the corrupt and decadent Qing court withholds its support so as not to offend the foreigners. Cheng Zhiqin, one of the rebel leaders, argues that government support is key to their success, and that it is worth trying to win the government over to their side. But his argument is interpreted by some as weakness and betrayal of the rebel cause. As a result, orders are issued for Cheng to be killed. In the bloody fighting that ensues between the Boxers on one side and the joint foreign military force and the Qing army on the other, the hopelessly outgunned Boxers are destroyed, realizing too late that Cheng Zhiqing was not a traitor, and ignoring his advice was a fatal error.

1046. *The King of Sulu and the Emperor of China (Parts 1 & 2) (Su Lu Guo Wang Yu Zhong Guo Huang Di)*

1987. Beijing Film Studio & Philippines Cultural Center Co-Production. Color. 17 Reels. Direction: Xiao Lang, Eddie Romero, Qiu Lili. Screenplay: Su Shuyang, Zhai Jianping, Mao

Rong, Liu Qingyuan, Eddie Romero. Cinematography: Ru Shuiren, Manolo Abaya. Art Direction: Chen Xiaoxia, Zushaoxianfeier Tuobate. Music: Wang Liping, Lei Shi. Sound: Wang Yunhua. Cast: Wang Xinggang as Emperor Zhudi, Vic Vargas as the King of Sulu, Tang Aerwaluo as Ayoubu, Liu Qiong as Zhang Qian, Zhang Jie as Zhen He, Liu Jiafu as Ji Gang

In 1417, the enlightened domestic and foreign policies of the Emperor Zhudi have made China stable and prosperous. The King of Sulu's great admiration for China and the Emperor prompts the King to make an official visit. After overcoming many challenges on the long, hard journey, he successfully arrives in China.

But his difficulties are far from over, as schemers at both the Sulu and the Chinese courts are bent on destroying the mission. Only after prolonged and dangerous investigation is their plot smashed. The Emperor of China and the King of Sulu cement the relationship between their countries. Tragically, just as he is about to return home, the King of Sulu dies in China.

1047. *King of the Children (Hai Zi Wang)*

1987. Xi'an Film Studio. Color. 10 Reels. Direction: Chen Kaige. Screenplay: Chen Kaige and Wan Zhi, based on the novel of the same name by A Cheng (1949–). Cinematography: Gu Changwei. Art Direction: Chen Shaohua. Music: Xiao Song. Sound: Tao Jing, Gu Changning. Cast: Xie Yuan as King of the Children, Yang Xuewen as Wang Fu, Chen Shaohua as the Principal

In a poor mountainous region during the Cultural Revolution, a young farmer named Lao Cha is honored by being named "King of the Children," and assigned to be a teacher. He is first assigned to teach junior high school students, but fails miserably, a failing the school principal attributes to the fact Lao Cha himself has only a primary school education. He is reassigned to teach an elementary class. Since there are no textbooks, the students have to copy them, and without a good textbook Lao Cha's dictionary becomes the children's "Bible." The prescribed teaching content calls for the students to read theoretical texts, which means they are unable to understand and write compositions. So Lao Cha teaches them the fundamentals of composition. As the children become more armed with knowledge, they be-

come more puzzled and curious about the world. The bureaucracy dismisses Lao Cha for deviating from prescribed content and methods, and he returns to the farm.

Best Cinematographer Gu Changwei, 1988 Golden Rooster Awards.

Best Art Direction Chen Shaohua, 1988 Golden Rooster Awards.

Future Director Award (Chen Kaige), 17th Rotterdam International Film Festival.

Educational Contribution Award, 4th Cannes International International Film Festival, France.

Exploratory Film Award, Film Exploration Critics Activities in '88, Belgium.

1048. *Kisses for Russian Lovers (Kuang Wen E Luo Si)*

1994. Beijing Film Studio. Color. Letterboxed. 10 Reels. Direction: Xu Qingdong. Screenplay: Ma Junxiang. Cinematography: Xie Ping, Sun Xiaoguang. Art Direction: Song Jun. Music: Gao Erdi. Sound: Liu Xiaodong. Costume: Chen Yulian. Makeup: Chen Aihua. Cast: Feng Gong as Da Jiang, Yeliena Boershekewa as Kajia, Niu Zhenhua as Shuangcheng, Lijiya Kuziniezuowa as Natasha, Ma Jingwu as grandpa, Longli Xieerbining as A Liaosha, Liu Yingtao as Yu, Wang Xi as Xiao Li

Based on the novel "In the Far East" by Deng Gang. After his divorce, middle school music teacher Dajiang wants a career change. He travels with his friend, businessman Shuangcheng, to Russia to learn to do business. Shuangcheng's Russian partner is a woman, who introduces Dajiang to her sister, pretty Katya. Dajiang and Katya fall in love. Their romance develops around a series of humorous incidents which befall the two Chinese businessmen learning to conduct trade in an unfamiliar culture and language.

1049. *Kitchen Symphony (Guo Wan Piao Peng Jiao Xiang Qu)*

1983. Xi'an Film Studio. Color. 9 Reels. Direction: Teng Wenji. Screenplay: Teng Wenji. Cinematography: Zhao Haifu. Art Direction: Zhang Zhien. Music: Li Yuedong. Sound: Dang Chunzhu. Cast: Sun Chun as Niu Hong, Yin Tingru as Liu Junying, Chen Ye as Niu Hua, Liu Xiaochun as Man Feng, Qiu Yuzhen as Sun Lianxiang, Sun Ming as Qiu Erbao, Li Wei as Shi Xinju, Wang Dawei as Zhao Yongli

Early one summer, Beijing food service company office worker Niu Hong is re-assigned to manage a restaurant which has been losing money for years. Impressed with Niu's new status, his former girl friend Man Feng wants to get back together, but he refuses. Under Niu's management, the restaurant improves every day, and business grows. Niu Hong is very attracted to Liu Junying, one of his employees, but she already has a boy friend, and soon marries. In spite of the restaurant's success, Niu Hong is accused of raking off some of the profits, and suspended from his post pending investigation. This depresses him terribly. Finally, the investigation is completed, he is cleared of any crimes and restored to his position. He decides to express his love for Shi Xinju, another girl he meets there, but he finds out she is already engaged.

1050. *The Kite (Fengzheng)*

1958. Beijing Film Studio & French Jialangshi Film Studio Co-Production. Color. 10 Reels. Direction: Wang Jiayi and Luoxie Billkuo. Screenplay: Wang Jiayi and Luoxie Billkuo. Chief Cinematography: Henry Elkang. Cinematographers: Wu Shenghan and Aimiller Weilaieribo. Music: Duan Shijun. Sound: Chen Yanxi, Cast: Paitelike Te Baerdina as Biailuo, Xierweiyena Luoshengbaoa as Nigaoer, Qianli Qimanshiji as Beibeier, Xie Tian as the antique shop owner, Zhang Chunhua as the Monkey King, Yuan Diwang as Linlin

A kite bearing the Monkey King's image is borne by the wind to Paris. Three Parisian children, Biailuo, his sister Nigaoer and their playmate Beibeier, find the beautiful kite with a letter written in Chinese attached to it. Biailuo goes to a Chinese antique shop owner to have it translated, and learns that it was sent by Song Xiaoqing, a child in Beijing. The letter requests that whoever finds the kite write back to him and become his penpal. Beailuo is eager to do this, but naughty Beibeier is jealous, and takes the return address. That night, Beailuo dreams that the Monkey King helps him, and that he and his sister go to Beijing and finally find Song Xiaoqing, the kite's owner. When he awakens, Beibeier comes to apologize and return the address. So the two jointly write an answering letter to Song Xiaoqing. They also write another letter which they tie to the kite, hoping it will help them find another friend.

1051. *KMT Special Action Team (Jun Tong Te Qian Dui)*

1990. Changchun Film Studio. Color. Letterboxed. 9 Reels. Direction: Qiao Keji. Screenplay: Pan Jianqing. Cinematography: Han Dongxia, Qian Damin. Art Direction: Gao Tinglun. Music: Yang Yilun. Sound: Yu Kaizhang. Costume: Ouyang Yongkuan, Liu Tao. Makeup: Yan Zhenying. Cast: Li Dingbao as Dai Li, Zhang Zhonghua as Du Yuesheng, Wun Guojun as Zhou Fohai, Chen Yi as 5th wife, Wang Xinjian as Cheng Kexiang, Zhang Xingya as Yang Er, Tian Ming as Luo Man, Chen Jianxin as Bai Yunsheng

When World War II ends, the people of Shanghai demand that China's wartime traitors be executed. Zhou Fuohai, one of the worst of the traitors, appeals to Chiang Kaishek for protection by threatening to blackmail the Generalissimo with a secret letter Chiang sent Zhou before the war. Chiang sends a team of spies headed by his intelligence chief Dai Li to Shanghai to retrieve the letter. Meanwhile, Shanghai Triad head Du Yuesheng also wants the letter, hoping to use it to strengthen his own power in the city. A fierce and bloody three-way struggle ensues for control of the letter. At last, Dai Li gets the letter and leaves Shanghai. Public pressure forces Zhou's arrest, and he is sent to prison. He falls ill and dies behind bars.

1052. *Knew That Three Years Ago (Sannian Zao Zhidao)*

1958. Changchun Film Studio. B & W. 9 Reels. Direction: Wang Yan. Screenplay: Wang Yan, based on the novel of the same title by Ma Feng (1922–). Cinematography: Yin Zhi. Art Direction: Wang Xingwen. Music: Gao Ruxing. Sound: Chen Yudan. Casting: Chen Qiang as Zhao Mantun, Ma Shida as Dalong, Wang Chunyin as Hu Zhi, Ma Yu as Old Man Hu, Xia Peijie as Hu Fengyin, Liu Xilin as Zhang Mingshan

Farmer Zhao Mantun is nicknamed "Knew That Three Years Ago" because no matter what the topic, he evaluates everything by what is in it for him personally. During the agricultural commune campaign, he avoids joining for fear of personal financial loss. His younger brother, a soldier, writes that he plans to join the commune, and if Mantun does not it will split the family. So Mantun joins, reluctantly, and is assigned to care for the commune's livestock. However, he continues to do everything from the angle of his own self-benefit. But with the help and education of the commune director and other people, he finally realizes his mistakes, becomes an enthusiastic member, and is ultimately appointed head of the commune's water conservation project.

1053. *Knight's Honor (Qi Shi De Rong Yu)*

1984. Beijing Film Studio. Color. Wide Screen. 10 Reels. Direction: Yu Yang, Dele Geerma. Screenplay: Yinde Sier, Cao Shuolong. Cinematography: Shao Yueqing, Wusi Riqingtu. Art Direction: Yang Zhanjia. Music: Yiner Jimin. Sound: Wang Zemin. Cast: Cui Dai as Yideer, Zhao Erkang as Chen Yong, Suyala Dalai as Saiyin, Enhe as Hu Riqing, Jiang Gengcheng as Tao Gao, Da Lintai as Bao Yintu

In 1945, a cavalry unit made up of Mongolian nationality soldiers rebels against its collaborationist Chinese commanders and sets out on its own to fight the Japanese. The CPC assigns one of its best political officers in the region to be the Political Commissar of the Mongolian troops. The unit's new commander Yideer is receptive to the new arrival, but his sworn brother Tao Gao is more interested in the rank and possible monetary rewards that could result from allying their troops with anti–Japanese Chinese troops. He lobbies with Yideer to reject the CPC's advice, which brings him into conflict with Chen Yong. A series of bloody incidents, including the death of Yideer's actual brother Saiyin, expose Tao Gao's treachery. The simple and honest Yideer realizes that the only future for his people lies in following the CPC along the revolutionary road.

1054. *The Kong Family's Unknown Story (Parts 1 & 2) (Kong Fu Mi Shi)*

1987. Beijing Science Film Studio. Color. 17 Reels. Direction: Lin Nong. Screenplay: Kong Defan, Ke Lan. Cinematography: Yang Haigeng. Art Direction: Ning Lanxin, Hu Weiye. Music: Zang Dongsheng, Zhang Jiye. Sound: Shu Shuiping. Cast: Xu Guiyin as Madam Tao, Guan Jian as Kong Lingyi, Li Jing as Baocui, Zhang Yan as Qi Shun

Kong Dafan, a descendant of Kongzi (Confucius) recalls her mother Wang Baocui, concubine to Kong Lingyi, 76th generation grandson of Kongzi. Kong Lingyi's wife Tao abuses

Baocui. Later, Kong Lingyi dies in his 50s without leaving a male heir, but fortunately before his death he learns his concubine Baocui is pregnant. Baocui does give birth to a son, the 77th grandson of Kongzi, but Tao murders the concubine in order to maintain her own status in the Kong family.

1055. *Korean Woman Hero (Bing Xue Jin Da Lai)*

1963. Changchun Film Studio. B & W. 10 Reels. Direction: Zhu Wenshun. Screenplay: Guan Monan. Cinematography: Bao Jie. Set design: Liu Jinnai. Music: Lou Zhanghaou. Sound: Tong Zongde. Cast: Li Songzhu as Kim Su-jia, Pu Ke as Father-in-Law, Shi Kefu as Wang Chengan, Xia Peijie as Mother-in-Law, Bai Yingkuan as Cui Chenglong, Li Ying as Zhao Ming

Kim Su-jia, a Korean woman, migrates to Northeast China from her Japanese-ruled homeland in search of a better life. She meets and marries a Chinese man, Cui Chenglong, but when the Japanese invade China, he leaves to join an anti–Japanese guerrilla troop. At first, Kim Su-jia had been content to be a simple housewife, looking forward to motherhood, but her husband's joining the guerrillas leads to her own arrest. Tortured in prison, she goes into premature labor and miscarries. Tutored by a woman guerrilla troop member, Zhao Ming, Kim Su-jia learns revolutionary ideas. After Zhao is killed by the Japanese, Kim is released. She joins the guerrillas, fighting the Japanese at her husband's side.

1056. *Kuan Yin Is 12 Years Old (Guan Yin Jin Nian Shi Er Sui)*

1988. Pearl River Film Studio. Color. Letterboxed. 9 Reels. Direction: Yu Shibing. Screenplay: Huang Yazhou. Cinematography: Liu Xinmin. Art Direction: Li Wenguang. Music: Du Jiangang. Sound: Lu Minwen. Cast: Xue Bai as Teacher Bai, Zhou Mi as Hai Ling, Zhao Xiaopeng as Chang Xiaotu

In a shabby temple in a remote mountain village, a few rooms are set aside as classrooms for the local elementary school. However, worshippers frequently disturb the classes. Teacher Bai has on several occasions asked the village chief to do something to alter the situation, but the chief just goes to the temple and prays for the village's prosperity. Girl student Hai Ling is very upset about the situation, so she and classmate Chang Xiaotu figure out a means of coping. One morning, Hai Ling sits beneath a big tree in the village, claiming that she is now possessed by Guan Yin, the Buddhist Goddess of Mercy. Hai Ling asks every worshiper to carry 49 bricks to the temple to repair the school. Hai Ling exposes the corrupt activities going on at the temple, and makes devout worshippers understand.

1057. *Kung Fu Girl (Jiang Hu Mei Zi)*

1989. Changchun Film Studio. Color. Letterboxed. 10 Reels. Direction: Lu Jianhua, Yu Zhongxiao. Screenplay: Xie Wenli, Han Qipeng. Cinematography: Zhang Songping. Art Direction: Sui Zuangji. Music: Wang Ming. Sound: Huang Lijia, Shi Lin. Cast: Zhen Shang as the Kung Fu Girl, Chen Yude as the Inspector

Near the end of the Qing Dynasty (c.1910), a young woman renowned for her kongfu skills lives in a village on the southeast China coast. In addition to helping people who are oppressed or unfairly treated, she is also a healer who cures many sick and injured people. She runs into trouble when the new magistrate begins to lust for her, and she foils his advances through a practical joke. He orders her arrest. In fighting with the magistrate's men, the kongfu girl is wounded. Local people who she helped in the past now rally to her aid and get her to safety. However, she has to leave her home and move elsewhere.

1058. *A Kung Fu Hero's Unusual Adventure (Shao Xia Qi Yuan)*

1988. Pearl River Film Studio. Color. Wide Screen. 9 Reels. Direction: Wang Yi. Screenplay: Huangpu Keren, Zhang Xiaojing. Cinematography: Wang Hengli. Art Direction: Guan Yu. Music: Ding Jialing, Situ Kang. Sound: Jiang Shaoqi. Cast: Xiang Minhua as Zhi Ren, Dong Honglin as Yu Jingwu, Yang Xiaojun as Qianying

At the end of the Qing Dynasty, the revolutionary Tongmeng League decides to send a treasure chest overseas to Dr. Sun Yatsen with which to buy arms. Kung fu heroes Zhi Ren and Yu Jingwu are entrusted with getting the treasure safely to its destination. The Qing government knows what is going on, and sends agents to follow the heroes. A series of life and death struggles ensue, but Zhi Ren and Yu Jingwu continue on to their destination with the help of a girl called Qianying.

1059. *Kung Fu Master (Xian E Jiang Hu Xiao Yao Jian)*

1989. Pearl River Film Studio. Color. Letterboxed. 10 Reels. Direction: Deng Yuan. Screenplay: Deng Yuan. Cinematography: Gang Yi. Art Direction: Zhang Song. Music: Zhang Hong. Sound: Deng Qinhua. Cast: Sun Chenxi as Ye Nianci

A guard from the Jinshi Security Agency is delivering an extremely valuable pearl, when he is killed and the pearl stolen. The agency asks one of its former guards to come out of retirement and find it. He does, but is also killed. His son, kung fu master Ye Nianci, determines to avenge his father. He tracks down the pearl, going through many battles on the way. None know till the end that his reckless disregard for his own safety is because he suffers from an incurable illness.

1060. *The Kunlun Column (Parts 1 & 2) (Wei Wei Kun Lun)*

1988. August First Film Studio. Color. 18 Reels. Wide Screen. Chief Direction: Hao Guang. Direction: Jing Mukui. Director of Cinematography: Wei Duo. Cinematography: Wang Jiaxi, Zhu Junheng. Art Direction: Cui Denggao, Niu Xiaolin. Music: Xiao Yan. Sound: Shi Pingyi. Cast: Zhang Keyao as Mao Zedong, Su Lin as Zhou Enlai, Guo Fazeng as Liu Shaoqi, Liu Huaizheng as Zhu De, Liu Xi as Ren Bishi, Lei Fei as Peng Dehuai, Fu Xuecheng as Liu Bocheng, Qiang Meidi as Deng Xiaoping, Liu Xitian as Chen Yi, Wang Tianpeng as He Long, Sun Feipeing as Chen Geng, Sun Feihu as Chiang Kaishek

World War II has no sooner concluded than Chiang Kaishek, head of the Nationalist government, undertakes military action against the Communists. China is once again plunged into civil war. After failing in a general offensive against the Communists, he begins an attack against key sectors in March, 1947. Yan'an, headquarters of the Central Committee of the Communist Party, is one of the key objectives of the offensive, and Mao Zedong evacuates all departments of the Central Committee from Yan'an. Chiang orders Hu Zongnan to lead an army of 200,000 against the city. The Communist high command meets and decides that Mao Zedong, Zhou Enlai and Ren Bishi should stay with the defenders of northern Shaanxi province, code named "The Kunlun Column," and commanded by Ren; Liu Shaoqi and Zhu De will then take the rest of the Central Committee leadership to the east side of the Yellow River. The Kunlun Column succeeds in halting the Nationalist advance, and the Communists' Northwest Field Army launches a massive counterattack. Then Liu Bocheng and Deng Xiaoping lead their army to the Dabieshan Mountains, starting a massive counter-offensive.

Best Picture, 1990 Hundred Flowers Awards.

1061. *Labor's Flowers Bloom (Lao Dong Hua Kai)*

1952. Changjiang/Kunlun Associated Film Studios. B & W. 11 Reels. Direction: Chen Liting. Screenplay: Ke Lan. Cinematography; Yao Shiquan. Set Design: Ding Chen. Music: Chen Gexin. Sound: Li Liehong and Wu Hua. Costume: Jin Ke. Makeup: Yao Yongfu. Cast: Wei Helin as Party Secretary Wang, Lan Ma as Engineer Zhang, Zhong Shuhuang as Representative Zhao, Zhang Yi as Liu Jianyun, Shangguan Yunzhu as Zhang's wife, Jiang Tianliu as Liu's wife

Soon after liberation, Western economic sanctions against China lead to a shortage of gasoline by the Shanghai public transportation company, and many buses may have to be removed from service. The company's party secretary and workers are creative in finding other fuels, relying especially on Engineer Zhang's experience and expertise. Zhang at first is not confident that government leaders and the masses of the people will throw their support behind alternative fuels, but with the encouragement and support of Party Secretary Wang and the company's military representative Mr. Zhao, he soon designs a bus that runs on white coal. First testing is unsuccessful, but the enthusiasm of Zhang's wife helps him overcome his keen disappointment. After much further testing and revision, the white coal bus finally succeeds, resolving the fuel supply problem and reversing the company's losses.

1062. *Ladies (Da Xiao Fu Ren)*

1988. Changchun Film Studio. Color. 10 Reels. Direction: Li Geng, Bei Yucheng. Screenplay: Tan Li, Zhang Yinghui, Shan Shan. Cinematography: Zhang Shaoge. Art Direction: Yuan Dianmin. Music: Fan Weiqiang. Sound: Zhen Yunbao. Cast: Li Ding as Chief Zhen, Liu Jun as Jiang Minfeng, Bai Hai as Sun Yuping, Wu Jinhua as Liu Xiaorong

In ancient China "lady" (*furen*) was an honorific title for the wife of a duke or a prince, but by the 17th century the wives of the highest ranking officials were also addressed as "lady." By the 20th century people who wanted to show off their status would call their wives "lady." The ladies in this film symbolize power. The story takes place in a spare-time art school. The "ladies" include the wives of a bureau chief, of a school president, of the newly promoted vice minister... The film comically depicts these power-crazed wives and their social milieu.

1063. *Ladies' Choice (Nu Ren De Xuan Ze)*

1994. Xiaoxiang Film Studio. Color. Letterboxed. 9 Reels. Direction: Chen Lu. Screenplay: Wu Jiaxin. Cinematography: Wang Kekuan, Liu Weiwei. Art Direction: Tan Shengshan. Music: Ji Xiping. Sound: Liu Yishen, Jiang Ping. Costume: Liu Nian. Makeup: Zhang Yinghua, Cheng Hong. Cast: Kong Ling as Xia Lan, Hu Qiang as Da Gou, Li Mingzhu as Mu the village head, Jiang Hualing as Uncle Laogeng, Fu Yiping as Chunlan, Wang Duan as Xie Xiaoyu, Tao Ye as Qiulan

Daju comes home from military service, wanting to do something about the poverty in his hometown. He goes to another village, prosperous Baohe Village, and takes a job there with pig farmer Mu, intending to master pig-raising skills to take back with him. But Mu only lets Daju work, and doesn't teach him anything. In time, Daju falls for Mu's daughter Xialan, but while she also loves him, so do her sisters Chunlan and Qiulan. Their father wants Daju to marry Qiulan. Daju's devotion to making his hometown prosperous finally changes Mu's attitude. Chunlan and Qiulan hide their feelings and wish Daju and Xialan well.

1064. *The Lady in the Painting (Hua Zhong Ren)*

1958. Changchun Film Studio. Color. 11 Reels. Direction: Wang Bing. Screenplay: Liang Yan and Yin Su, based on Liang Yan and Xiong Shaisheng's dramatization of a classic Chinese fairy tale. Cinematography: Fang Weiche. Art Direction: Lu Gan. Music: Ma Ke. Sound: Shen Guli. Makeup: Bi Zepu. Cast: Li Yilan as Sister Qiao, Bai Dezhang as Brother Zhuang, Chen Qiang as the Emperor, Li Jie as the evil administrator, Pu Ke as the old stonesmith, Xu Lan as the female immortal

When a young woman is chosen to be the

unwilling concubine of the emperor, a female immortal changes her into the image on a painting, which she later leaves in order to marry her lover. But they are both arrested and taken to the palace. With the help of the immortal, they are able to overcome the emperor's forces and are reunited.

1065. *A Lady Left Behind (Liu Shou Nu Shi)*

1991. Shanghai Film Studio. Color. 10 Reels. Letterboxed. Direction: Hu Xueyang. Screenplay: Zhang Xian, Yu Yun. Cinematography: Gao Ziyi. Art Direction: Guo Dongchang. Music: Su Junjie. Sound: Zhan Xin. Cast: Xiu Jingshuang as Nai Qing, Sun Chun as Jia Dong, Zhao Ying as Qiqi, Jin Meng as A Xiu

The Chinese fervor for going abroad creates a large number of temporary widows and bachelors. This film focuses on one such, Nai Qing, a woman whose husband is abroad. One day she meets a taxi driver whose wife has also gone overseas. The two become acquainted and eventually fall in love, but they remain lonely, confused and lost. To solve her emotional problems, Nai Qing decides to go abroad and find her own worth.

1066. *A Lady of Good Family (Liang Jia Fu Nu)*

1985. Beijing Film Studio. Color. 10 Reels. Direction: Huang Jianzhong. Screenplay: Li Kuanding. Cinematography: Yun Wenyue. Art Direction: Shao Ruigang. Music: Si Wanchun. Sound: Zhen Chunyu. Cast: Chong Shan as Xingxian, Zhang Weixin as Wuniang, Wang Jiayi as Yi Shaowei, Zhang Jian as Brother Kaibing, Liang Yan as Third Sister-in-Law

In an isolated mountain village in Guizhou province, on the eve of liberation, traditional feudal marriage customs are still the norm. Xingxian, an 18-year-old village girl, finds herself engaged to marry an 8-year-old boy; her prospective mother-in-law Wuniang is just 26. When Kaibing, a man about Xingxian's age, comes to the village as a temporary farm laborer, Xingxian falls for him, but local customs demand this sort of thing be punished severely. At this time, a land reform work team enters the village and from them Xingxian learns that the law now guarantees freedom of choice in marriage. So Xingxian goes public about her relationship with Kaibing, touching off a fierce emotional struggle among the vil-

lagers. After this, Xingxian and Kaibing elope, making her the first girl in her village's history to break free of this feudal tradition.

1067. *The Lamp of Baolian (Bao Lian Deng)*

1959. Tianma Film Studio. Color. 8 Reels. Direction: Ye Ming. Cinematography: Feng Shizhi, Lu Junfu. Set Design: Lu Jingguang. Music: Zhang Xiaohu. Sound: Zhou Yunling. Cast: Zhao Qing as Lady Shansheng, Fu Zhaoxian as Liu Yancang, Chen Yunfu as Chengxiang, Sun Tianlu as the spirit Erlang, Fang Bonian as Daxian, Chen Hua as the spirit dog

On his way to the capital to take the imperial examinations, scholar Liu Yancang stops to rest at a temple. There he sees a statue of the temple spirit, Lady Shansheng. He so admires her beauty that he writes a poem expressing his admiration on her scarf, then falls asleep. Lady Shansheng has grown tired of the life of a spirit, and is so impressed with the young man's poetry she falls in love with him. When he awakens she appears before him. She worries about how the spirit world will react to such a match. But with Liu's appeals and encouragement, she finally breaks through the restriction of feudal thinking and gives her love to him. Protected by Shansheng's powerful magic weapon, the Lamp of Baolian, they live together, and a year later have a daughter Chenxiang. Shansheng's brother spirit Erlang steals the magic lamp and entombs Shansheng underneath Hua Mountain. Fifteen years later, Chenxiang has grown up determined to rescue her mother. She defeats Erlang, recovers the Lamp of Baolian and frees Shansheng. The couple and their daughter are finally reunited.

1068. *Land (Tu Di)*

1954. Northeast Film Studio. B & W. 11 Reels. Direction: Shui Hua. Screenplay: Mei Bai, Shui Hua, Yu Lin, Li Bing and Guo Xiaochuan. Cinematography: Bao Jie. Set Design: Liu Xuerao. Music: Zhang Dicang. Sound: Chen Wenyuan. Cast: Li Po as Xie Chenggang, Pei Ran as Wang Zhengliang, Wang Yizhi as Xiu Laoshou, Li Binglin as Shi Daquan, Hu Peng as Xie Chenggang's mother, Huang Lin as Mr. Shou's wife, Ye Xiangyun as Xie Zizhai

In 1930, far from the Communist Party's base area, the town of Zhulin is carrying out land reform under the leadership of Xie Yousheng, a local CPC member. The effort is soon suppressed by counterrevolutionaries led by landlord Xie Zizhai and his brother, nick-named "Devil." Xie Yousheng is burned to death. Twenty years later, the country is liberated, and Xie Yousheng's son Xie Chenggang takes over leadership of the land reform movement. In addition to the two landlord brothers, he has to battle long-standing enmity between the Xie clan and the Shi clan, which is incited by the counterrevolutionaries.

1069. *The Land Mine War (Di Lei Zhan)*

1962. August First Film Studio. B & W. 8 Reels. Direction: Tang Yingqi, Xu Da, Wu Jianhai. Screenplay: Liu Qihui, Qu Hongchao, Chao Guangsheng. Cinematography: Zhen Zhiguo, Cai Sheng. Art Direction: Mai Yi. Music: Li Tongshu, Li Yansheng. Sound: Hou Shenkang. Casting: Bai Dajun as Zhao Hu, Zhang Changrui as Director Lei, Wu Jianhai as Grandpa Shi, Zhang Dajie as Third Uncle, Zhang Hanying as Dayong, Lu Zaiyun as Yulan

During the anti–Japanese war, Zhaojia Village and a few other villages in eastern Shandong suffer from raids and "sweeping" of the crops from their fields by the troops from a nearby Japanese base, making it impossible for them to earn their livelihood. Under the leadership of Party District Director Lei, civil militia from Zhaojia and the other villages form a guerrilla defense team to carry out armed resistance. They create various kinds of homemade land mines which seriously disrupts the enemy. They invent a homemade chemical land mine, and thwart the enemy's plans to dig up their land minds. At last the guerrillas coordinate with the Eighth Route Army in an attack on the enemy base, and win a total victory.

1070. *Lanlan and Dongdong (Lan Lan He Dong Dong)*

1958. Tianma Film Studio. B & W. 6 Reels. Direction: Yang Xiaozong. Screenplay: Du Xuan. Cinematography: Shi Fengqi. Art Direction: Wei Tiezhen. Music: Huang Zun, Lu Qiming. Sound: Wu Hua. Makeup: Chen Yan. Cast: Chen Yiyin as Lanlan, He Haixi as Dongdong, Ding Ran as Father, Shu Yi as Mother, Shi Jiufeng as Zhen Daguang, Zhang Hongmei as Xiao Tao

Lanlan and Dongdong are a sister and brother living in a Shanghai kindergarten after their physician parents are assigned to work in Beijing. The concerned parents arrange for the children's transfer to a Beijing school, but since they cannot get time off to bring the kids themselves they entrust the Shanghai Railway Bureau to escort them. Vacationing train attendant Zhen Daguang and his radio announcer wife Xiao Tao are put in charge of the children en route. The impish children involve the grownups in various humorous incidents during the trip. When the train finally arrives in Beijing, the father cannot meet them due to an emergency, and when the mother arrives at the station she finds that another passenger's child is ill, so she accompanies that child to the hospital. Zhen Daguang and Xiao Tao give up their plans for going to the theater that evening and take the two kids home with them.

1071. *The Last Aristocrats (Zui Hou De Gui Zu)*

1989. Shanghai Film Studio and Sil-Metropole Organisation Ltd. (Hong Kong) Co-Production. Color. Wide Screen. 12 Reels. Direction: Xie Jin. Screenplay: Bai Hua, based on the novel by Taiwanese author Bai Xianyong. Cinematography: Lu Junfu. Art Direction: Chen Shaomian. Music: Jin Fuzai. Sound: Zhu Weigang. Cast: Pan Hong as Li Tong, Pu Cunxin as Chen Yin, Li Kechun as Huang Huifen, Xiao Xiong as Lei Zhiling, Lu Ling as Zhang Jiaxing

In the late spring of 1948, life seems to hold it all for Li Tong. At her family's Shanghai mansion, her diplomat father is holding a lavish celebration of her birthday on the eve of Li Tong's departure for college in the U.S. Young, gifted and beautiful, Li Tong gives little thought to the imminent downfall of her father's government and Shanghai's aristocracy. She and her girlfriends Huang Huifen, Lei Zhiling and Zhang Jiaxing leave for America and soon settle happily into their studies and campus life. But suddenly word comes that Li Tong's parents have been killed when their ship sinks en route to Taiwan. Although her boyfriend and three girlfriends try to console her, there is little they can do: Li Tong is adrift without support in an alien land. She disappears unexpectedly, and her life goes steadily downhill after that. Her friends hear something of her from time to time, none of it good: she becomes an aimless drifter, working for a time as a model, then becoming a wealthy businessman's mistress. She hits the depths when she is arrested in a police roundup of prostitutes. Her friends are devastated by the change. She eventually drifts to Venice, where she was born, and we last see her sadly staring down at the waters… Filmed mostly on location in New York City.

1072. *The Last Eight People (Zhi Hou Ba Ge Ren)*

1980. Changchun Film Studio. Color. 11 Reels. Direction: Yu Yanfu. Screenplay: Xu Zhiheng, Wan Jie. Cinematography: Xu Shouzeng. Art Direction: Huang Zhaohui. Music: Wu Damin. Sound: Kang Ruixin. Cast: Luo Guoliang as Bai Yunlong, Hou Guanqun as Ma Changhe, Ju Xuanhe as Wang Yuguang, Zhao Yamin as Bai Hua, Liu Hanpu as Jiang Chunjiang, Xu Cangxi as Grandpa Jin

In the snow-covered forests of Northeast China, a regiment of the anti–Japanese Volunteer Army is betrayed by a spy in their midst and surrounded. Commander Bai Yunlong selects seven of his troops to help him find a way the regiment can break out from the encirclement. Ma Changhe, their chief scout, is sent to contact the local Party organization but he is later found unconscious by another of the group, Wang Yuguang. After Ma comes to, he privately tells Bai Yunlong that Wang is the traitor. Bai angrily orders Wang's execution, but the other members of the group are very suspicious of Ma's information and protect Wang. Bai rescinds the execution order and the eight resume their search for an escape route. Tempers become frayed, and Wang accuses Ma of framing him because they both love Bai Yunlong's daughter Bai Hua. The group experiences many difficulties, while Bai Yunlong continues looking for the spy. He finally determines that Wang Yuguang is indeed the spy, but he must first contend with the regiment being surrounded. In the end, Bai Yunlong accompanies Wang Yuguang to the enemy camp to negotiate a surrender, but during the negotiations Bai pulls out a gun and kills Wang and the enemy commanders before he himself is cut down.

1073. *The Last Empress (Mo Dai Huang Hou)*

1986. Changchun Film Studio. Color. 10 Reels. Direction: Chen Jialin, Sun Qinguo. Screenplay: Zhang Xiaotian. Cinematography: An Zhiguo. Art Direction: Jin Xiwu, Lu Qi. Music: Jin Fuzhai. Sound: Zhang Fenglu, Wang Baosheng. Cast: Pan Hong as Wan Rong, Fu Yiwei as Tan Yuling, Jiang Wen as Pu Yi, Zhang Hua as Li Chang'an, Liu Wei as Li Yueting, Zhu Yin as Wen Xiu

In December, 1922, the deposed last Manchu emperor Pu Yi and his bride Wan Rong preside over a huge wedding celebration. Although politically irrelevant, they still enjoy wealth and a luxurious lifestyle. Nine years pass, and things are quite different: the imperial household has been driven from the Forbidden City; Imperial Concubine Wen Xiu has divorced Pu Yi, creating a national scandal; and the neglected and unhappy Empress Wan Rong increasingly takes solace in alcohol and drugs. In 1932, Pu Yi goes to Northeast China with the Japanese invaders and becomes a collaborator, accepting the title Emperor Kangde of the Japanese puppet state of Manchukuo. Lonely, and disgusted with their life, Wan Rong has an affair with a one of Pu Yi's court officers, Li Yueting. She has a baby by him, but Pu Yi has the baby killed and its father executed. Wan Rong loses her mind and abandons herself totally to drugs. In order to tighten their control over Pu Yi, the Japanese select Beijing high school student Tan Yuling to be his new wife, but kill her in 1942 when they find her uncontrollable. The Japanese then choose another 15-year-old to be Pu Yi's last concubine.

1074. *The Last Imperial Concubine (Zui Hou Yi Ge Huang Fei)*

1988. Changchun Film Studio. Color. 11 Reels. Direction: Sun Sha. Screenplay: Zhang Xiaotian. Cinematography: Zhong Wenming. Art Direction: Yang Baocheng. Music: Xu Zhijun. Sound: Yi Wenyu. Cast: Li Ling as Li Yuqin, Hou Tianlai as Pu Yi, Li Xiaoli as Wan Rong

After the Empress Wan Rong becomes mentally deranged, Imperial Concubine Wen Xiu is granted a divorce, and his second concubine Tan Yuling dies, China's last emperor — Aisin Gioro Pu Yi — is a lonely man, deprived of the women in his life. He selects a new bride by shuffling through a stack of photographs of girl students presented as likely candidates. From the candidates, he selects 15-year-old Li Yuqin. Summoned to Pu Yi's palace, Li is destined to live no longer as a commoner but to become the last imperial concubine of China's last emperor. By this time Pu Yi is Emperor of China only in name, the puppet emperor of Japanese-controlled Manchukuo. As the puppets of a puppet, the imperial concubines have even less sovereignty over their own lives. After the Japanese surrender, Pu Yi is tried as a war criminal. Li Yuqin divorces Pu Yi and regains her freedom.

1075. *The Last Military Salute (Zui Hou Yi Ge Jun Li)*

1982. August First Film Studio. Color. 9 Reels. Direction: Ren Pengyuan. Screenplay: Fang Nanjiang. Cinematography: Ding Shanfa. Art Direction: Cui Denggao. Music: Peng Xiuwen. Sound: Zhen Minzhe. Cast: Ma Cangyu as Geng Zhi, Chen Dazhu as Geng's wife, Xing Minhua as Wei Cheng, Du Yuan as Lu Erkun

Geng Zhi, political supervisor in a military company, has been in the army for 13 years. After two more years of service, his wife and child will be eligible to live with him in military housing, and the whole family looks forward to it. Then his commander informs Geng that he is being sent into mandatory early retirement due to a PLA reduction in force. This is a major disappointment to the family, but Geng Zhi accepts the decision and persuades his family to make their home in the place where he grew up, knowing his background will get him a good job there with the county. On their way, they come across a car stuck in an iced-over river; Geng organizes others to get the car out. When they arrive at their destination, Geng Zhi gives up his chance to work for the county, and instead volunteers to work at the local commune. He is answering the call of duty one more time.

1076. *Last Sunshine (Zui Hou De Tai Yang)*

1986. Shanghai Film Studio. Color. 10 Reels. Direction: Jiang Haiyang. Screenplay: Fu Xiaomin, Jiang Haiyang. Cinematography: Cai Zhengchang. Art Direction: Chen Shaomian. Music: Yang Mao. Art Direction: Lu Jiajing. Cast: Liu Qiong as Wang Wenhui, Zhang Yan as Jin Ageng, Jiang Jun as Yan Fei, Lin Bing as Li Shufeng, Zhang Fa as Yuan Shengli, Yang Baohe as Old Drummer

Four retired men happen to meet on the street one day and become acquainted. Wang Wenhui was a symphony conductor who misses his music and hates the pop music of today; former Bureau of Culture Director Yan Fei has no idea what to do with his time; retired worker Jin Ageng has so much excess energy he gets out in the street and directs traffic; and the fourth, "Old Drummer," is nearly 70 and very lonely. The four talk, and decide to form a senior citizens' chorus. They work hard at organizing the group and holding rehearsals. The chorus gives performances in theaters, fac-tories and on campuses. Life is once again interesting and fun.

1077. *The Last Tragedy (Yu Ba Tian Xia)*

1994. Emei Film Studio. Color. Letterboxed. 9 Reels. Direction: Jing Gang. Screenplay: Luo Xing, Du Bohang. Cinematography: Tu Dongxiang, Cheng Xinghuai. Art Direction: Xie Huibing. Music: Ao Ying. Sound: Zhang Mingyi, Tu Liuqing. Costume: Liu Changxiu, Luo Ping. Makeup: Yang Jie, Wang Yi. Cast: Zhang Weijian as Qiu Zihong, Jiang Qinqin as He Yao, Luo Changan as He Yong, Tong Tong as Yao Xiaojun, Zhen Zeshi as Yao Dachuan, Yu Daijun as Kang Zhenzong, Wun Hong as Yu Lizhen, Di Wei as Jiang Dongping, Zhang Jianli as Yuan Wu, He Jiaju as Jin Jiuhua

Shanghai in the 1940s is dominated by triads, and the three largest of these gangs maneuver for overall control of the city. Opposing them is Chief of Police Kang Zhenzong, but he has his own agenda: Kang's strategy is to play each triad off against the others in the expectation they will wipe themselves out. If this happens, Kang will be certain to become Shanghai Police Commissioner. After ambitious and capable young Qiu Zhihong comes to Shanghai from the countryside, the chief has an opportunity to observe the newcomer's courage and skills. He recruits Qiu as an unofficial hit man for the police. Qiu undertakes a mission of assassinating triad chieftains, and since the gangs suspect each other, the gang competition erupts into all-out warfare. At last, Kang accomplishes his goal and is appointed commissioner. But instead of rewarding Qiu, he kills him. Just before he dies, Qiu Zhihong realizes how he has been used to satisfy the ambitions of another.

1078. *A Late Spring (Chi Dao De Chun Tian)*

1980. Emei Film Studio. Color. 9 Reels. Direction: Ma Shaohui, Tai Gang. Screenplay: Rao Qu, Tan Su. Cinematography: Mai Shuhuan. Art Direction: Lin Qi. Music: Xiong Jihua, Zhao Yulong. Sound: Zhang Jianping. Cast: Zhang Jiatian as Zhao Cheng, Xiang Hong as Zeng Xiaopei, Chen Ming as Wang Mingyao, Chen Qiguo as Li Chong

Everyone who knows them is shocked when Zhao Cheng and his wife Zeng Xiaopei separate, for they had seemed a very loving and devoted couple. Party Secretary Wang

Mingyao investigates. It turns out that Zhao Cheng had been listed as one the "five types of bad people" because his father had been labeled a "rightist" during the Cultural Revolution, giving him much in common with Xiaopei, labeled the daughter of a capitalist. Their mutual support led to love and the couple later married. After the Gang of Four was deposed, Zhao wanted to take the college entrance exams, although Xiaopei warned that his political background would still bar him from admission. He wants it so badly, however, that she supports him in moving from the countryside to the city. Zhao believes that if he does well enough on the exams he can break the pattern of discrimination and bias. While his exam scores are outstanding, he is still rejected as the son of a "rightist." To Xiaopei, this affirms her views, and she expects they will return to the countryside. But her husband is determined to stay and retake the exams the following year. This had led to the argument which drove the couple apart. Wang Mingyao points out how their love had given them strength during the worst of times, and this matter was relatively unimportant. They reconcile. Not long after, Zhao Cheng is notified that a policy change has led to a review of some people previously excluded, and he will be admitted on that basis.

1079. *Laughing Is Better Than Crying (Xiao Bi Ku Hao)*

1981. Ministry of Machinery. Color. 10 Reels. Direction: Ma Jingwu, Qian Xuege, Zhang Shouguang. Screenplay: Zhang Shouguang. Cinematography: Yang Shijiang, Yu Desheng. Art Direction: Pu Zhi. Music: Ma Ding. Sound: Liu Jingui. Cast: Cao Peng as Cheng Liang, Guo Jing as Liang Yan, Wei Ke as Fu Fangqi, Mei Yanping Cheng Hui

Young worker Cheng Liang is the careless cause of many work-related accidents, but does nothing to correct his problem until the day his carelessness seriously injures his girl friend Liang Yan. Meanwhile, Cheng Liang's older sister Cheng Hui, a teacher in the factory's off-duty education program, is very fond of Cheng Liang's workshop instructor Fang Qi. But Fang Qi loves the factory manager's only daughter Lu Xiaofeng. When Fang Qi is blinded in an explosion in the plant, Lu Xiaofeng cannot accept this and abandons him. Cheng Hui quietly provides Fang Qi with the support he needs to go on, and finally the two

together complete the design for a new type of safety equipment.

1080. *Lawyer on Probation (Jian Xi Lu Shi)*

1982. Youth Film Studio. Color. 10 Reels. Direction: Han Xiaolei. Screenplay: Han Xiaolei. Cinematography: Pao Youran. Art Direction: Wang Jianjin. Music: Wang Liping. Sound: Shui Xizhong, Zhang Yaling. Cast: Sun Chun as Yan Wengang, Wang Yongge as Wei Zekuan, Wang Anli as Li Mang, Liu Dong as Lu Xiaoqiao, Yuan Yuan as Zhao Dawei, Li Shourong as Judge Wang

Yan Wengang is a law student at Yanbei University. He is often confused about life and his role in society, sometimes resolute and sometimes indecisive. Like all young people who went through the Cultural Revolution, he was caught up in the insanity of the era and did some things he now regrets. The one thing he is now sure of is that he wants to do something good for his fellow Chinese. He often discusses the future with his girlfriend Lu Xiaoqiao but she sometimes finds it difficult to understand him. During his internship, Yan is assigned to defend a man accused of robbery and murder, and although the young lawyer is convinced of the man's innocence, his defense fails. After graduation, Yan doggedly continues trying to prove his client's innocence. Lu Xiaoqiao begins to understand him better.

1081. *The Leading Criminal Is Beside You (Zhu Fan Zai Ni Shen Bian)*

1985. August First Film Studio. Color. Letterboxed. 10 Reels. Direction: Wang Mengyuan. Screenplay: Shi Chao, Liang Xing. Cinematography: Chen Zhenzhong. Art Direction: Fang Xuzhi. Music: Tan Dun. Sound: Guo Yisheng. Cast: Shang Lijuan as Yu Qian, Xiao Lin as the judge, Shi Xilai as Shen Jiwen, Yu Chunmian as Deputy Secretary Kong

At one time, woman public defender Yu Qian was a PSB investigator in a coastal city. More than a decade before, when the Gang of Four was in power, she was involved in a complex case which resulted in a great deal of personal suffering for her. At that time, the city's PSB Director obtained evidence that someone in the city was forging documents designed to falsely incriminate Premier Zhou Enlai in a conspiracy. The director was murdered on his way to the provincial capital to report the matter. His successor, Deputy Secretary Kong, assigned this case to their most experienced investigator, Yu Qian's fiance Shen Jiwen. Shen seems to be making progress, but on their wedding night Shen is called out to investigate something else, and disappears. Now, Yu Qian picks up the investigation her husband had started years before, and finds evidence that the main criminal is Kong, now the city's Deputy Party Secretary. She takes the supporting documents and leaves to report everything to the central government authorities.

1082. *Leftover Snow (Can Xue)*

1980. Changchun Film Studio. Color. 10 Reels. Direction: Jiang Shusehng. Screenplay: Huo Zuang, Xu Xiaoxing, Huang Jianzhong. Cinematography: Chen Chang'an. Art Direction: Song Honghua, Liu Huanxing. Music: Wu Damin. Sound: Li Zhenduo. Cast: Li Yan as Zhou Feng, Siqin Gaowa as Zhang Xiuyun, Xu Zhan as Zhou Weiguang, Yao Xiangli as Du Yuanzheng, Li Qimin as Hu Pei, Chen Rubing as the court justice

After the Gang of Four is smashed, Xinjiang forest technician Zhou Weiguang is thrilled at the news that his father Zhou Feng, previously exiled to the countryside, has been restored to his official post. Zhou Weiguang is unhappy with his own life, however, and decides to divorce his loyal wife Zhang Xiuyun. After divorcing her, Zhou Weiguang returns to Beijing and finds a job by using his father's influence. He hides the fact of his divorce from his father Zhou Feng and his mother Du Yuanzheng. The following summer, Zhou Feng receives an anonymous letter from Xinjiang which is harshly critical of his son's divorce, claiming it was obtained through improper means and had a disruptive influence on the local people there. Shocked to hear the truth, Zhou Feng and his wife leave immediately for Xinjiang to visit their former daughter-in-law, but she at first refuses to see them. When she finally receives them, the older couple make a heartfelt expression of their pain and regret for what their son has done. Zhang Xiuyun and her family are impressed by the couple's sincerity. After he returns to Beijing, Zhou Feng learns that his son is preparing to marry again. He brings Zhou Weiguang back into his home and patiently explains things to him. Zhou Weiguang begins to wake up to the realities of life, and not long after happily boards a train to Xinjiang.

1083. *The Legend of Daliang Mountain (Da Liang Shan Chuan Qi)*

1988. Emei Film Studio. Color. Letterboxed. 10 Reels. Direction: Zhang Xihe. Screenplay: Huang Yuexun, Wang Caiying, Qi Hai. Cinematography: Song Jianwen. Art Direction: Cheng Jinyong. Music: Tang Qinshi. Sound: Tu Liuqin, Zhang Minyi. Cast: Hu Zhiqi as Shama Mujia, Han Haihua as Tiebo, Li Dianfang as Meng Ge

In 1863, Taiping General Shi Dakai is defeated by the Qing army in the battle of Daduhe River. Ten years later, Shi Dakai's followers persuade Yi nationality chieftain Shama Mujia to lead his people once more in rebellion, and send him a bag containing a map of the region where a huge cache of weapons is stored. Their enemies get the bag, however. The movie tells how the rebels attack government troops and from them seize many weapons which compensate for loss of the bag. Mujia wages a struggle to the death with Menggan, an enemy of the Taipings years before, and at last Menggan is killed.

The Legend of Fong Sai-yuk **see** *Fang Shiyu*

1084. *Legend of Girls (Rong Zhou Chuan Qi)*

1990. Emei Film Studio & Hong Kong Hezhong Film Company Co-Production. Color. Wide Screen. 9 Reels. Direction: Li Junjie. Screenplay: Luo Xing, Li Junjie. Cinematography: Du Xiaosi. Art Direction: Lin Qi. Cast: Deng Cuiwen as Xiao Lan, Huang Yanmeng as Jin Sheng

In North Sichuan legend, there was in ancient times an evil Taoist named Babila who blocked water resources, resulting in a drought. The people were saved by 18 capable girls who dug out the huge rocks blocking the river. They succeeded but were turned into 18 white stones. Babila has gone through many reincarnations, and still makes trouble for the people, but one of the girls, Xiao Lan, counterbalances his evil.

1085. *Legend of Lu Ban (Lu Ban De Chuanshuo)*

1958. Jiangnan Film Studio. B & W. 9 Reels. Direction: Sun Yu. Screenplay: Zhu Xin. Cinematography: Yao Shiquan. Art Direction: Ge Shicheng. Music: Ji Ming. Sound: Gong

Zhengming. Cast: Wei Heling as Lu Ban, Li Baoluo as Master Zhao, Ji Hong as the first stonemason, Li Wei as the second stonemason, Xu Mu as Wei Fangshi, Zhang Wan as the old woman

Lu Ban was the legendary "ancestor of carpenters" in the Spring and Autumn Period of Chinese history (770–476 B.C.). One day, Lu passes a place in Sichuan province where a large stone bridge is being built. Arrogant master worker Zhao has made a design error, so the two main sections of the bridge cannot be linked. Lu Ban digs up a great stone which he sends to a poor girl who wants to marry but lacks the money for a dowry. At the critical moment when the bridge sections must be linked, the poor girl donates the stone, which completes the bridge. For this she is rewarded with money. In Southeast China, Lu Ban comes upon some people building a temple. He devises two unique methods which enabled the project's completion. Another time, the emperor wants a building which must have many very special features. Although many workers have tried and failed at such a design, Lu Ban completes the design after just a few days thought.

1086. *The Legend of Sculptor Chang (Ni Ren Chang Chuan Qi)*

1983. Beijing Film Studio. Color. 10 Reels. Direction: Li Wenhua, Du Yu. Screenplay: Chen Aimin, Li Wenhua. Cinematography: Zhen Yiyuan. Art Direction: Mo Kezhan. Music: Fan Zhuyin. Sound: Zhang Baojian. Cast: Zhang Yi as Chang Jiabi and Chang Qinshan, Shao Wanlin as Mr. Liu, Xin Jing as Zhao Canghai, Xiang Hong as Chang Jiayu, Huang Xiaolei as Yang Jingbao, Zhang Ju as the Living Zhuge

In old China, people like Chang Jiabi and his sister were vulnerable and living at the bottom of society. They are sculptors who support themselves by selling their artworks for whatever they can get. Their skills have been handed down over four generations. An antiques dealer named Zhao Canghai is so impressed with Chang's skill that he lets them make artworks for his shop, which Zhao sells at a huge profit. When Chang discovers the dealer has been falsely marketing Chang's sculptures as antiques, he quits Zhao and opens his own shop. Zhao does not want to lose this moneymaker, so he does all he can to drive Chang out of business, persecuting Chang and his family as well. Chang loses his

shop and his wife leaves him. He and the rest of his family have to leave their hometown, but Chang Jiabi is determined to keep his family's traditional skill pure, for it belongs to the Chinese people.

1087. *Legend of the Cixi Tomb Treasure (Ci Xi Mu Zhen Bao Chuan Qi), Part 1— The Dongling Robbery (Dongling Dadao), Part 2—Fighting for Treasure at Pingjin (Pingjin Duo Bao)*

1986. Xi'an Film Studio. Color. Wide. Color. 19 Reels. Direction: Li Yundong. Screenplay: Su Jinxing. Cinematography: Yang Baoshi. Art Direction: Cheng Xiangzhang. Music: Guo Shuyin. Sound: Hong Jiahui, Li Ping. Cast: Hu Qinshi as Sun Dianying, Hao Zhibeng as Na Xinting, Peng Jun as Zhang Houqi, Jiang Hua as Tan Wunjiang, Sun Feihu as Jiang Jieshi (Chiang Kaishek), Fu Xuecheng as Zhu Shou

Part 1: After his victories in the Northern Expeditionary Campaign of the 1920s, Chiang Kaishek begins an expansion and reorganization of his military forces. This includes weeding out those forces he considers insufficiently loyal to him. Among these forces is the army of warlord Sun Dianying. Sun wants to build up his own strength as a counter-balance to Chiang, but lacks the funds to do so. So he breaks into the tomb of Dowager Empress Cixi, and loots it of the massive treasures buried there. When his action becomes known, the Chinese media demands the crime be punished and these Chinese national treasures recovered.

Part 2: Sun Dianying sends his regimental commander Zhang Houqi to Japan to sell the treasures. But another warlord also wants the treasure, and fighting over the riches breaks out between the two warlord armies. Meanwhile, his emissary strikes a deal with some Americans to turn the treasure over to them in exchange for enough arms and equipment to outfit five army divisions. But just when the treasure is about to be delivered, it is all stolen by two mysterious masked people.

1088. *Legend of the Cixi Tomb Treasure (Ci Xi Mu Zhen Bao Chuan Qi) Parts 3 & 4 — The Dongling Robbery (Dong Ling Da Dao)*

1987. Xi'an Film Studio. Color. Wide Screen. 17 Reels. Direction: Li Yundong. Screenplay: Su

Jinxing, Dou Bing. Cinematography: Yang Baoshi. Art Direction: Cheng Minzhang. Music: Guo Shuyin. Sound: Hong Jiahui, Li Ping. Cast: Hao Zhibeng as Na Xinting, Hu Qingshi as Sun Dianying, Fu Xuecheng as Zhu Shouguang, Bo Guanjun as Xu Yuanquan, Wang Xiaozhong as Shen Jiu, Ding Lan as Zuo Hong, Sun Feihu as Jiang Jieshi (Chiang Kai-shek), Jiang Hualin as Yu Yuexian, Dou Bing as Yan Xishan, Hao Zhiben as Na Xinting, Zhao Minjie as Shen Hui, Cheng Mingzhang as Shen Puxiu, An Ruiyun as Guo Song, Ren Quanhua as Hua Caishi

Part 3: After the Dongling treasures are stolen, Chiang Kaishek assigns one of his officers Zhu Shouguang to investigate. Zhu learns the details of Sun Dianying and Xu Yuanquan conspiring to exchange the treasures for armaments, and reports this to Chiang. Meanwhile, another investigator, General Na Xinting, tracks the masked robbers to a Taoist temple. One of them tries to kill Na, but he is protected and given sanctuary by Shen Jiu, master of a Taoist temple. Shen Jiu agrees with Na that the national treasures should be preserved in one location and not spread out throughout China or the world, but he believes the temple is the best location for this. Another Taoist priest, Shen Hui, wants to get rid of Na, so he spreads a rumor that the general has violated the rules of their mountain temple and should be arrested. Na bravely prepares for the worst.

Part 4: Shen Hui's plot against Na Xinting is detected by temple master Shen Jiu, and the officer is saved. But Na continues to insist that the temple should turn the treasures over to the government, angering the priest. Meanwhile, Sun Dianying's men are looking for Na with the intent of bribing him to give up the treasure. After a series of complicated adventures, Na proposes to Chiang Kaishek three conditions under which the temple will agree to relinquish the treasures: that a date be set for the public display of the treasures; Sun Dianying be arrested and put on trial; and a national museum be built to house the treasures. Chiang accepts all three conditions.

1089. *The Legend of the Eight Immortals (Ba Xian De Chuan Shuo)*

1985. Shanghai Film Studio. Color. 11 Reels. Direction: Zhao Huanzhang. Screenplay: Xiao Wun. Cinematography: Peng Enli, Zhang Yong-

zheng. Art Direction: Ding Cheng, Li Jinggui. Music: Xiao Yan. Sound: Wang Huimin. Cast: Wang Futang as Cao Guoju, Shi Weijian as Lu Dongbing, Zhao Qiansun as Tie Guaili, Tie Niu as Han Zhongli, Yuan Zhiyuan as Zhang Guolao, Sun Jian as Han Xiangzhi

A folk legend. Seven immortals once lived at Penglai. One of them, Tie Guaili, calls the others together for a banquet, at which he suggests they make a good man named Cao Guoju an immortal as well. That way, they will be eight in number, a perfect situation since eight is the most auspicious number in Chinese folk belief. The movie tells how they go about persuading the initially reluctant Cao Guoju to become one of them.

1090. *Legend of the Emperor Yan (Yan Di Zhuan Ji)*

1994. Xiaoxiang Film Studio, Hong Kong Jiahui Film Corp. Ltd. Color. Letterboxed. 16 Reels. Direction: Li Jingsong. Screenplay: Li Shuxing, Sheng Heyu, Mao Xiecheng, Chi Feng. Cinematography: Liu Yuefei, Cao Peng. Art Direction: Liu Shibiao, Long Wei. Music: Zhang Qianyi, Luo Xiaojian. Sound: Lai Qizhen, Wang Xueyi. Costume: Long Xiaoping. Makeup: Yang Huiming, Cao Shizhen. Cast: Tian Shaojun as Emperor Yan, Li Ming as Emperor Huang, Gao Xian as Chi You, Shao Bing as Rong, Yan Qing as the witch, Xie Lan as Haven, Liu Shuling as Fu Ba

A story set in remote antiquity, and concerned with shifting tribal relationships. Yan, the hero, unites his people with those of a rival named Huang to defeat another tribe and unite the country. Yan then hands over leadership to Huang, and returns to a his previous simple life.

1091. *Legend of the Royal Horses (Yu Ma Wai Zhuan)*

1981. Shanghai Film Studio. Color. 6 Reels. Direction: Li Xiepu. Screenplay: Zhao Zhiqiang, Li Xiepu. Cinematography: Dai Qimin. Art Direction: Li Wenkang. Music: Yang Shaolu. Sound: Xu Junlin. Cast: Cheng Zhi as Pu Tianguo, Gu Langhui as Pu Naiqing, Zhu Yuwen as Ding Lili, Ma Guanyin as Pu Naijian, Sun Yan as Zhao Guifeng

Antique collector Pu Tianguo acquires a pair of bronze royal horses. At the first Spring Festival after the defeat of the Gang of Four, Tianguo happily returns home to see his two sons and the daughters-in-law he has never met. He gives the horses to the two couples as wedding gifts. The elder son Pu Naiqing had been given a bronze horse earlier, but had sold it to buy a TV set and other luxury items. He and his wife Ding Lili now want another horse, because the buyer will give 30,000 yuan for a second horse to make a pair. Pu Tianguo's youngest son and daughter-in-law treat him very lovingly, but the elder couple are only interested in getting the horse. This so upsets Pu Tianguo that he falls ill and enters the hospital. Pu Naiqing and his wife finally learn the horse's location from the old man's talking in his sleep. They sell the horse. But much to their chagrin, the couple is nabbed in an anti-smuggling campaign and are arrested for selling a national treasure, the royal horse.

1092. *The Legend of Tianyun Mountain (Tian Yun Shan Chuan Qi)*

1980. Shanghai Film Studio. Wide Screen. Color. 12 Reels. Direction: Xie Jin. Screenplay: Lu Yanzhou. Cinematography: Xu Qi. Art Direction: Ding Cheng, Chen Shaomian. Music: Ge Yan. Sound: Zhu Weigang. Cast: Shi Weijian as Luo Qun, Wang Fuli as Song Wei, Si Jianlan as Feng Qinglan, Zhong Xinghuo as Wu Yao, Hong Xueming as Zhou Yuzhen

In the early 1950s, two young women, recent college graduates Song Wei and Feng Qinglan, join the Tianyun Mountain prospecting team. At the same time, young and capable Lun Qun is named to replace Wu Yao as the team's political commissar. Luo Qun is a charismatic leader who fires the team members' enthusiasm for their work. Song Wei and Luo Qun fall in love. In 1957, when the anti-rightist campaign begins, Wu Yao is assigned to head up the movement in the Tianyun Mountain area, and he falsely labels Luo Qun a rightist. Young, and a new Party member, Song Wei is confused by this political movement; she finally gives in to the Party organization's persuasion, separates from Luo Qun and marries Wu Yao. Although Luo Qun suffers greatly from the attacks on him, he still loves and is loyal to the revolution. At this time, Feng Qinglan enters his personal life, offering her support and affection. Despite having very little money and facing a bleak future, the two get married. During the Cultural Revolution, the couple pass a hellish 10 years. At one time, Feng Qinglan almost loses her life protecting some documents that could send Luo Qun to prison. Fortunes change, and Wu Yao finds himself labeled a "capitalist authority," and persecuted. After the defeat of the Gang of Four, Wu Yao becomes prefectural Party Deputy Secretary and a department director, but he selfishly refuses his wife's urgings to intervene on the side of justice for Luo Qun. Song Wei insists on disclosing the whole truth to upper level leadership, and finally Luo's case is heard and he is pardoned. But the good news arrives too late for Feng Qinglan, whose pure heart finally gives out after having borne so much hardship for so long.

Best Picture, 1981 Golden Rooster Awards.

Best Picture, 1981 Hundred Flowers Awards.

Best Director Xie Jin, 1981 Golden Rooster Awards.

Best Cinematographer Xu Qi, 1981 Golden Rooster Awards.

Best Art Direction Ding Cheng and Chen Shaomian, 1981 Golden Rooster Awards.

1093. *Legendary Romance in the Forbidden City (Zi Jin Cheng Qi Lian)*

1994. Beijing Film Studio. Color. Letterboxed. 9 Reels. Direction: Duan Jishun. Screenplay: Lao Jun, Duan Jishun, Fang Yuan, Xiao Lu. Cinematography: Gao Lixian. Art Direction: Liu Changbao. Music: Ai Liqun. Sound: Zhang Zizhong. Costume: Li Fengju. Makeup: Liu Jianping, Liu Li. Cast: Xiulan Limei as Wen Rui, Kong Zhewen as Charles, Lingna as Anna, Li Shijiang as Wangye

At the end of the 19th century, the Russian ambassador in Beijing becomes enamored of Chinese art and antiques. While he indulges himself in his avocation, his beautiful wife Anna has an affair with Charles, a British translator. A few days before the couple's scheduled return to Russia, Anna is found murdered. Clues at first point to Charles, believed to be a jealous, spurned lover. Charles sets out to prove his innocence, aided by Wen Rui, a young noblewoman at the Qing court. The solution to the mystery turns out to be that the art-obsessed ambassador murdered his wife, not because of her infidelity, but in order to obtain a painting he coveted. During the course of getting to the truth, Charles and Wen Rui fall in love and at last leave together for England.

1094. *Lei Feng (Lei Feng)*

1964. August First Film Studio. B & W. 10 Reels. Direction: Dong Zhaoqi. Screenplay: Ding Hong, Lu Zhuguo, Cui Jiajun and Feng Yifu. Cinematography: Li Erkang. Art Direction: Liu Qian, Music: Fu Gengcheng. Sound: Wu Hanbiao. Cast: Dong Jintang as Lei Feng, Yang Guifa as Wang Dali, Dang Tongyi as Wu Kui, Yang Qinhua as the big careless guy, Yu Chunmian as the supervisor, You Ling as Director Liang

Lei Feng was a PLA soldier, and an almost mythical figure in modern Chinese history. This is his story. It begins with Lei Feng telling a group of Young Pioneers of his miserable childhood. We see him working to improve himself, studying the works of Chairman Mao and performing a variety of good deeds: stopping on his way to receive medical attention to help deliver bricks to a construction site; accompanying an old lady returning to her rural home during a storm; anonymously sending money for medical treatment to a co-worker's ailing mother; donating his labor and money to a disaster stricken area, etc. After Lei Feng is killed in a work-related accident, his memory receives a variety of honors, including publication of a famous essay by Mao Zedong, "Learn From Lei Feng." Today, Lei Feng's image and the exhortation to emulate his example can be seen on billboards throughout China.

1095. *Lei Feng's Song (Lei Feng Zhi Ge)*

1979. August First Film Studio. Color. 10 Reels. Direction: Wang Shaoyan. Screenplay: Wang Deyin, Jing Hong, Bai Lao. Cinematography: Yin Qiaofang. Art Direction: Kou Honglei, Li Jian. Music: Lu Yuan. Sound: Liu Qi. Cast: Li Shixi as Lei Feng, Huo Ke as Old Mrs. Zhang, Lin Huachun as Li Houliang, Xie Wuyuan as Jin Dali

Orphaned before liberation, Lei Feng's childhood is very hard. He grows up to become a military driver. His hard work and study make him outstanding at his work. He helps those who are traditionalist in their thinking, those in need of money, and others who need assistance in making progress. One cold winter, he travels to the town of Hongshi, far from his base, to buy Mao Zedong's writings, and on the way back stops to help strangers pull a truck stuck in an icy river. When fellow soldier Li Houliang's hometown is struck by floods, Lei Feng goes to visit Li's parents and mails 200 yuan of his own money to help with disaster relief. When he is killed in a trucking accident, Chinese soldiers and civilians all mourn, everyone calling his name and recalling the many good things he had done for others. His name becomes a symbol of revolutionary spirit and of helping others.

1096. *Let the Smile Come Back (Hui Lai Ba! Wei Xiao)*

1987. Shanghai Film Studio. Color. 9 Reels. Direction: Shen Yaoting. Screenplay: Zhang Xiaoling. Cinematography: Can Lianguo. Art Direction: Mei Kunping. Music: Liu Yanxi. Sound: Li Bingkui. Cast: Ning Haiqiang as Zhang Letian, Lu Qin as Wang Yixiao, Chang Baoting as Guan Ren, Wu Jing as Chen Huan, Sun Ming as Jiang Mi

Department store salesman Zhang Letian attends a personality improvement training session designed to give him a better, more winning smile. The trainer applies all sorts of advanced equipment and technology in his attempt to help his trainees get their smiles back. At last, he comes to realize that sincere smiles can only come from within, and Zhang Letian learns that only by treating others sincerely and giving them happiness can he himself be happy.

1097. *The Letter with Feathers (Ji Mao Xin)*

1954. Shanghai Film Studio. B & W. 8 Reels. Direction: Shi Hui. Screenplay: Zhang Junxiang, based on the novel of the same title by Hua Shan. Cinematography: Luo Congzhou. Set Design: Wei Tiezhen. Music: Huang Yijun. Sound: Huang Lijia. Makeup: Yao Yongfu. Cast: Cai Yuanyuan as Hai Wa, Ma Li as Gui Niu, Cai An'an as Gou Wa, Shu Shi as Papa, Li Baoluo as Farmer Committee Cadre, Cao Duo as Head of the Civil Militia

During the anti–Japanese war, at a North China resistance base, Longmeng Village's childrens group head Hai Wa accepts an assignment to deliver to the Eighth Route Army a "letter with feathers" (an urgent priority message) from the militia. On the way he runs into some Japanese troops and is taken prisoner. Through cunning and courage, he not only protects the letter but also lures the enemy into the mountains where they are wiped out by the Eighth Route Army. The Communist forces then act on information contained in the letter and launch a successful

The Letter with Feathers. Hai Wa (Cai Yuanyuan, left) accepts the mission of delivering an urgent letter from the head of the civil militia (Cao Duo, right). 1954. Shanghai Film Studio.

attack on the Japanese base, capturing the enemy commander.

1098. *Letters from the Front (Qian Fang Lai Xin)*

1958. Tianma Film Studio. B & W. 7 Reels. Direction: Fu Chaowu. Screenplay: Fu Chaowu, based on the novel by Li Zhun. Cinematography: Yao Meisheng. Art Direction: He Ruiji. Music: Huang Zhun. Sound: Huang Dongping. Makeup: Chen Yan. Cast: Jiang Tianliu as Shen Zhilan, Fan Xuepeng as the mother, Qi Heng as Secretary Zhang, Zhang Fa as Wang Hui, Su Yi as Liu Guiyin, Jin Naihua and Ma Xiao as Volunteer Army representatives, Jiang Shan as Old Zhao, Yu Chong as Uncle Zhou, Zeng Ji as Xiao Hu, Yu Mingde as the postman

When Shen Zhilan learns of her soldier husband's death at the front in Korea, her Party training enables her to bear up under the grief. Fearful that her aged mother-in-law will not be able to bear the sorrow, she keeps the news to herself for the time being, and composes letters purportedly from him, which she reads to the old woman. Through these letters, she educates her mother-in-law in international politics, and raises the older woman's

ideological awareness. So when the soldier's mother finally learns of her son's death, she is able to turn her grief into power, joins a support group going to Korea, and makes a contribution to the Campaign to Resist America and Aid Korea.

1099. *Li Bing (Parts 1 & 2) (Li Bing)*

1983. Changchun Film Studio. Color. 16 Reels. Direction: Wang Yabiao. Screenplay: Chen Zeyuan. Cinematography: An Zhiguo. Art Direction: Wang Xingwen. Music: Lei Yusheng. Sound: Kang Ruixin. Makeup: Wang Fengrui, Ji Weihua. Cast: Hu Qinshi as Li Bing, Mao Yanhua as Hua Yang, You Jiangxiong as Wang Zhui, Li Yuanyuan as Du Juan, Li Jie as Sun Ruo, Li Liansheng as Huayang Lielong

In the late 3rd century B.C., the prefecture of Shu suffers an annual series of floods which nearly destroys the people's livelihood. Li Bing is assigned to the governor of Shu, with orders to handle the disaster. The story focuses on how he carries out the project while coping with opposition from senior official Hua Yang. Li Bing also makes use of prisoner Wang Zhui, convicted after he advocated a new flood control method. Li's flood control plan alarms Hua Yang who with his son plots to defame Li Bing. Li does not give up, even when his own son is killed in a construction accident. One year later, Shu is again struck by a flood of unprecedented size, but Li Bing's method is successful, and the people all worship him. The imperial court decides to promote him to a high-ranking position in the capital. Just at that time, word comes that Li Bing's wife has died. In his grief, he decides to remain in Shu and serve the people there.

Best Art Direction Wang Xingwen, 1984 Golden Rooster Awards.

1100. *Li Lianying (aka Imperial Eunuch Li Lianying) (Li Lian Ying)*

1990. Beijing Film Studio and Hong Kong Shijia Film Company with the cooperation of China Film Co-Production Corporation. Color. 10 Reels. Wide Screen. Direction: Tian Zhuangzhuang. Screenplay: Guo Tianxiang. Cinematography: Zhao Fei. Art Direction: Yang Yuhe, Yao Qing. Music: Mo Fan. Sound: Wu Ling. Cast: Jiang Wen as Li Liangying, Liu Xiaoqing as Cixi, Zhu Xu as Prince Chun, Xu Fan as Imperial Concubine Zhen

Li Liangying (1844–1910), is the favorite eunuch of the Empress Dowager Cixi, who he has served for 52 years. After her death, he leaves the Forbidden City and moves to the imperial tombs where he tends her grave until his death. The film highlights Li Lianying's role in the momentous political events that take place in his lifetime and examines his private life.

1101. *Li Shanzi (Li Shan Zi)*

1964. Unreleased. Haiyan Film Studio. Color. 11 Reels. Direction: Zhen Junli. Screenplay: Wang Lian, based on the North Korean stage play "Red Propagandist." Cinematography: Luo Chongzhou, Feng Shizhi, Wang Zhichu. Art Direction: Hu Dengren. Music: Ge Yan. Sound: Zhou Hengliang. Cast: Zhang Ruifang as Li Shanzhi, Zhang Yan as Cui Zhenwu, Lin Bing as Fushan's wife, Kang Tai as Cui Guanbi, Wun Xiying as Pu Zhixu, Wang Qi as An Bingxun

Li Shanzi is a woman propagandist in an agricultural co-op, influencing backward people to participate in collective work. Her painstaking ideological work results in the co-op realizing a big harvest.

1102. *Li Shizhen (Li Shi Zhen)*

1956. Shanghai Film Studio. B & W. 12 Reels. Direction: Shen Fu. Screenplay: Zhang Huijian, based on the life of Li Shizhen (1518–1593). Cinematography: Luo Chongzhou. Art Direction: Hu Zuoyun. Music: Ji Ming. Sound: Ding Bohe. Cast: Zhao Dan as Li Shizhen, Shu Shi as Li Yueci, Zhong Xinghuo as Tian Heng, Gu Yelu as Shenbao, Gao Xiaoou as Mr. Zhang, Deng Nan as Little Lu's father

Distinguished Ming Dynasty pharmacologist Li Shizhen learned medicine from his father. In order to create an "Herbal Catalog" for Chinese medicine, he scours the mountains and rivers collecting herbal samples. For 30 years he suffers every sort of hardship, including mockery from lowlifes and gentlemen alike. He perseveres in his work with no thought of winning rank or money, and finally completes the 52 volume "Herbal Catalog" which serves Chinese physicians for many generations.

1103. *Li Shuangshuang (Li Shuang Shuang)*

1962. Haiyan Film Studio. B & W. 11 Reels. 110 min. Direction: Lu Ren. Screenplay: Li Zhun, based on his novel "The Story of Li Shuangshuang." Cinematography: Zhu Jing. Art Direction: Zhong Yongqing. Music: Xiang Yi. Sound: Chen Jingrong. Cast: Zhang Ruifang as Li Shuangshuang, Zhong Xinghuo as Sun Xiwang, Zhang Wenrong as Sun Guiying, Li Kanger as Erchun, Zhao Shuyin as Dafeng, Liu Fei as Jin Qiao, Zhi Shiming as Sun Youpo, Cui Wenshun as Sun You, Ma Ji as Yan Fang's wife, Cao Duo as Yan Fang, Li Baoluo as Old Uncle Jin, Shao Li as Secretary Liu, Shi Yuan as Xiao Wang, Mao Lu as Old Uncle Geng

In her commune, Li Shuangshuang is known as a straightforward, bold and energetic woman who refuses to put up with selfishness and traditional behavior. Her husband Sun Xiwang is basically good and honest, but timid and easily persuaded by others. After Xiwang is named the commune's accountant, his family convinces him to exploit his new position for his and their gain. When Li Shuangshuang is elected director of the women's team, she promptly exposes the corruption of several commune officials, including her husband. Xiwang is unhappy and leaves home, taking a transportation job with backward deputy director Jin Qiao. At harvest time, when Xiwang sees how the production team has realized a

Li Shizhen. Li Shizhen (Zhao Dan, right) devotes his whole life to finishing his "Herbal Catalog." 1956. Shanghai Film Studio.

bumper harvest under Shuangshuang's leadership, he approaches her about a reconciliation. While they talk it over, he reveals that he has been working on turning Jin Qiao and others away from their corrupt actions. After he leaves, she follows him, and finds out he was telling the truth about helping the others to realize their mistakes. Li Shuangshuang and Sun Xiwang reconcile.

Best Picture, 1963 Hundred Flowers Awards.

Best Screenplay Li Zhun, 1963 Hundred Flowers Awards.

Best Actress Zhang Ruifang, 1963 Hundred Flowers Awards.

Best Supporting Actor Zhong Xinghuo, 1963 Hundred Flowers Awards.

1104. *Li Siguang (Li Si Guang)*

1979. Beijing Film Studio. Color. 12 Reels. Direction: Ling Zhifeng. Screenplay: Zhang Nuanqing, Yao Shuping, Li Tuo. Cinematography: Yu Zhengyu. Art Direction: Zhang Jinbiao, Song Hongrong. Music: Du Mingxin. Sound: Wang Zeming. Cast: Sun Daolin as Li Siguang, Wang Tiecheng as Zhou Enlai, Yu Ping as Xu Shubing, Wen Pudong as Song Xuetao, Shi Xian as Zhen Sheng, Tu Zhongru as Wu Huanmin

Film biography of a famous Chinese geologist. After obtaining his Master's degree in England, Li Siguang returns to China as a Professor at Beijing University and marries music teacher Xu Shubing. The various warlord battles going on around China have plunged the nation into chaos. Li's unconventional geological theories soon draw criticism both in China and abroad. During World War Two, Li and his geological institution colleagues move to the wartime capital of Chongqing to carry on their work. Li is visited by Communist Premier Zhou Enlai, who gives Li encouragement to go on, and suggests he go abroad to work for a while. Later, when the PRC is founded, Li Siguang returns to China, and with the support of the Party he makes great contributions to the development of geological science in China.

1105. *Liao Zhongkai: A Close Friend of Sun Yatsen (Liao Zhong Kai)*

1983. Pearl River Film Studio. Color. 11 Reels. Direction: Tang Xiaodan. Screenplay: Lu Yanzhou. Cinematography: Shen Xilin, Liu Jingrong. Art Direction: Ge Sicheng, Wang Huixun, Wang Xingcang. Music: Chen Qixiong. Sound:

Li Shuangshuang. **Outspoken, bold and energetic Li Shuangshuang (Zhang Ruifang) is frustrated with how her timid husband Sun Xiwang (Zhong Xinghuo) is so easily manipulated by others. 1962. Haiyan Film Studio.**

Li Bojian. Cast: Dong Xingji as Liao Zhongkai, Liang Yuejun as He Xiangning, Zhang Jie as Sun Yat-sen, Zhang Yan as Song Qingling, Yu Zijian as Li Dazhao, Liu Guanxiong as Hu Hanmin

In 1922, Liao Zhongkai is Doctor Sun Yansen's trusted assistant as well as director of Guangdong's financial bureau. After the Chen Jiongming rebellion starts, Liao Zhongkai meets with Li Dazhao of China's fledgling Communist Party and tells him of Sun's new policy of making common cause with the Communists. In 1923, after Chen Jiongming is defeated, Liao becomes Governor of Guangdong as well as its chief financial officer. He makes great contributions to Doctor Sun's efforts to combat the Nationalist Party's right wing, particularly in fund-raising. Liao's assistance to Sun in formulating the "Three Principles of the People" makes him a target for the rightists, especially warlord Chen Lianbo, commander of the Shangtuan Army in Guangzhou (Canton). In 1925, during the Sheng-Gang general workers' strike, Liao Zhongkai stands with the workers, making Chen Lianbo and others hate him even more. On August 20th, 1925, Liao Zhongkai is assassinated.

Best Director Tang Xiaodan, 1984 Golden Rooster Awards.

Best Actor Dong Xingji, 1984 Golden Rooster Awards.

1106. *Liberating Shijiazhuang (Jie Fang Shi Jia Zhuang)*

1981. August First Film Studio. Color. 10 Reels. Direction: Wei Jia, Su Fan. Screenplay: Jiao Yanting, Li Fengzhu. Cinematography: Bai Fujin. Art Direction: Song Tianpei. Music: Li Weicai, Zhao Qiong. Sound: Liu Yushu. Cast: Wang Yuxiao as Zhong Tianmin, Zhao Juanjuan as Qu Yun

In July, 1947, the PLA launches an overall offensive against the Nationalist forces, aimed at capturing the key city of Shijiazhuang. The story relates the long-range struggle between the PLA commander and his opposite number commanding the Nationalist Third Army. The PLA strategy hinges on luring their enemy out of the city and then attacking it, but the Nationalist commander doesn't fall for it. The PLA then adjusts its strategy to fool Chiang Kaishek into overruling his commanders and ordering them out of the city. When this succeeds, the PLA springs the trap and quickly takes Shijiazhuang.

1107. *Liberation (Jie Fang)*

1987. Changchun Film Studio. Color. 11 Reels. Direction: Qi Xingjia. Screenplay: Wang Xingdong, Wang Zhebing. Cinematographer: Gao Hongbao. Art Direction: Liu Huanxing. Music: Huang Duo. Sound: Zhang Qinjiang. Cast: Zhao Youliang as Peng Han, Li Jiabing as Su Zong, Zhang Jinling as Han Kefeng, Liu Zhibing as Li Bengzhi

A North China factory with a staff of thousands faces a production crisis. The "Liberation" brand trucks the factory manufactures aren't selling. Company president Peng Han in desperation decides to develop a totally new model. The factory's workers reluctantly bid farewell to the old-style "Liberation" trucks and start figuring out ways to make money to produce new ones. Finally, the new "Liberation" brand truck is entered in an international truck race and also gets the seal of approval from Beijing. By totally restructuring production, the "Liberation" truck factory beats the crisis, but competition for the factory is not over because the reforms must still continue.

This film received an award from the Ministry of Radio, Film and TV in 1987.

Best Makeup Wang Fengrui and Ji Weihua, 1984 Golden Rooster Awards.

1108. *Lie Detector (Ce Huang Qi)*

1993. Xi'an Film Studio. Color. Letterboxed. 9 Reels. Direction: Zhou Xiaowen. Screenplay: Wang Yugang. Cinematography: Lu Gengxin. Art Direction: Zhang Daqian. Music: Wei Yang. Sound: Zhen Chunli. Costume: Ren Zhiwen. Makeup: Lu Yingchun. Cast: Sun Cun as Tang Kai, Fu Lili as Zhou Yi, Xiao Xue as Yu Xiaoying, Zhao Chunmin as Li Qiang, Liu Yali, Zhang Daqian, Han Zecheng, Cao Jianye, Zhao Qingxin, Li Chunming

Successful businesswoman Zhou Yi meets handsome Tang Kai, and after a whirlwind courtship they marry. Actually, Tang only wants her money, and his amorous pursuit is just part of a scheme by the man and his lover Yu Xiaoying to kill Zhou and inherit her wealth. After several failed or missed opportunities, Tang at last secretly sabotages Zhou Yi's boat, and the two murderous lovers happily listen to her fading radio signals for help. They begin enjoying Zhou's house and money, but soon strange things begin to occur. Small indications of Zhou Yi's presence show up, even her footprints across the floor. One unexplained incident follows another, and soon Yu begins to believe the house is haunted with the murdered woman's ghost. She starts to lose her mind, and then Tang's grip on reality goes as well. The two are committed to an insane asylum, and Zhou Yi, still alive, comes out of the hiding place from which she had driven them mad.

1109. *Lies (Gui Hua)*

1951. Northeast Film Studio. B & W. 3 Reels. Direction: Wang Jiayi. Screenplay: Wang Jiayi, based on an original story by Zhao Shuli (1905–). Cinematography: Fu Hong. Art Direction: Liu Xuerao. Music: Zhang Guochang. Sound: Sha Yuan. Cast: Zhao Zhiming as Zhou Cheng, Huang Ling as Zhou's wife, An Qi as Little Rong, Gao Ping as You Fu, Yang Wei as Little Feng, Zhao Guozhang as the militia commander

During the Korean War, a reactionary group called the Eternal Way attempts to destroy the Chinese campaign to "resist America and aid Korea." One of their methods is to make themselves up as ghosts, greatly feared by the peasants, and spread rumors. Gullible farmer Zhou Cheng was often fooled by Eternal Way in the past, and this time is no exception — he believes the rumors. Zhou Cheng's younger sister Xiao Rong, a member of the Young Pioneer youth organization, mistrusts the Eternal Way, and tries without success to convince her brother of the group's deception. At last, the Eternal Way assigns a distant relative of Zhou Cheng, a special agent named You Fu, to play ghost and frighten Zhou's family. Word of this incident reaches the district militia, who search for and apprehend You Fu. Zhou Cheng then comes to realize he has been deceived all along.

1110. *Liezi No.99 (Liezi Jiu Shi Jiu Hao)*

1978. August First Film Studio. Color. 12 Reels. Direction: Yan Jizhou. Screenplay: Zhou Zhentian, Li Yang. Cinematography: Xue Boqin, Bai Fujin. Art Direction: Liu Jingsheng, Tang Shiyun. Music: Li Weicai. Sound: Zhen Minzhe. Cast: Chen Huiliang as the Chief Inspector, Zhang Liwei as the female detective, Fu Qinzen as the male detective, Tian Hua as the Party Committee Secretary, Li Po Director of the Public Security Bureau, Sun Xianyuan as the Chief Administrator, Yang Yi as Doctor Wu

In the city of Haizhou, Plan No. 817 has developed an important product code-named "Liezi No.99." The Public Security Bureau learns that security has been compromised by someone secretly taking a picture of the product. An intercepted telegram discloses that a spy called "AC" has been in contact with a foreign intelligence agency, and the clues seem to point to Doctor Wu Shiqiu of the plant's medical station. It was the spies' plan to cast suspicion on the doctor, but since he has information which can expose them, they plan to kill him. He is saved by security officers, who capture the assassin. The assassin leads the officers to arrest Plant 817's administrative department director Sun Yugeng, the "AC" who had been under cover in the plant for many years.

1111. *Life (Parts 1 & 2) (Ren Sheng)*

1984. Xi'an Film Studio. Color. Wide Screen. 9 Reels. Direction: Wu Tianmin. Screenplay: Lu Yao. Cinematography: Chen Naicai, Yang Baoshi. Art Direction: Lu Guangcai. Music: Xu Youfu. Sound: Chen Yudan. Cast: Zhou Lijin as Gao Jialin, Wu Yufang as Liu Qiaozhen, Gao Baocheng as Grandpa Deshun, Jia Liu as Gao Yude, Li Xiaoli as Huang Yaping, Qiao Jianhua as Zhang Kenan

Gao Jialin is dismissed from his teaching position and replaced by the son of the production unit Party Secretary. Gao has to return to his village. Pure and simple country girl Liu Qiaozhen has loved Gao Jialin for years, but has feared to tell him because he is a teacher and she is illiterate. Her warmth and innocence at last attract Gao Jialin, and he returns her love. An uncle in the prefectural labor bureau helps Gao Jialin obtain a journalist's job in the county seat. He works hard and shows his talent, although he has no formal journalism training. A local radio announcer named Huang Yaping falls in love with him, and Gao decides to leave Qiaozhen. Qiaozhen is devastated, and decides to marry another man to prove an illiterate country girl can live a good life. Meanwhile, Gao's irregular means of obtaining his job comes to the attention of higher authorities, and he is dismissed and returned to the countryside. Huang Yaping cannot return with him, so he seems to have lost everything. Gao realizes he must give some serious thought to his future.

Best Picture, 1985 Hundred Flowers Awards.

Best Actress Wu Yufang, 1985 Hundred Flowers Awards.

Best Music Xu Youfu, 1985 Golden Rooster Awards.

1112. *The Life and Death Card (Sheng Shi Pai)*

1959. Haiyan Film Studio and Hunan Film Studio. B & W. 12 Reels. Direction: Zhang Tianxi. Screenplay: Xiao Xiang. Cinematography: Gu Wunhou. Art Direction: Wu Qiwen. Music: Li Yongming. Sound: Lu Zongbo. Cast: Wang Xiaozhi as He Shanlang, Dong Shaohua as Jialang, Zhang Fumei as Mrs. Zhang, Zuang Lijun as Wang Yuhuan, Liu Chunquan as Huang Boxian, Dong Wuyan as Chief Military Officer He

When Wang Yuhuan goes to visit her dead mother's tomb she is set upon by He Shanlang, who attempts to rape her. She runs away from him, but in chasing her the man falls into a river and drowns. He Shanlang's father, a high-ranking military officer, accuses Yuhuan of murdering his son and orders county magistrate Huang Boxian to execute the young woman, otherwise he will kill Huang. Huang, an honest official, learns the truth from Yuhuan, and also discovers that her father was a man who had once saved his life. So he determines to let Yuhuan escape. Huang's daughter Xiulan and his adopted daughter Qiuping both offer to die in Yuhuan's place, but she refuses their offer, and the three argue about it. Finally, they decide to draw cards in a dark room, with whoever draws the death card being the one to die. Huang's own daughter Xiulan draws the death card. At the execution site, a strange figure in the crowd turns out to be the disguised Hai Rui (a famous figure among the Chinese, representative of justice) on an inspection trip. He quickly determines the truth, frees the young woman and others wrongly accused, and charges Chief Military Officer He with crimes.

1113. *Life and Death Critical Moment (Sheng Si Guan Tou)*

1994. Changchun Film Studio. Color. Letterboxed. 9 Reels. Direction: Yang Jing. Screenplay: Zhu Xiaocai. Cinematography: Su Li. Art Direction: Sui Zuangji. Music: Guo Xiaotian. Sound: Wang Xinchao. Costume: Zhang Shufang, Li Xiuzhi. Makeup: Zhao Li, Dan Xiangshuo. Cast: Ren Mei as Shi Ying, Li Yunjuan as Fang Hong, Liu Zhibing as Yang Shouzhi, Li Yongtian as Qi Zhanchi, Zhang Yufei as Liu Sha

In the North China city of Geshan, when policewoman Shi Ying and her partner Gao Tian finally corner drug dealer Huang Mingsheng, Gao is killed. As Huang attempts to drive away, Shi Ying riddles the criminal's car with bullets, only to find afterwards that Huang's small son had been in the car and died with his father. The distraught policewoman is placed on leave to pull herself together, little knowing that Huang's widow Feng Hong is plotting to revenge her husband and child. She exchanges drugs for guns, then hires some thugs to help her. They invade Shi Ying's home and kidnap the policewoman's daughter Liu Sha. Shi Ying goes after them to save her daughter, and a series of gun battles follows. At last, at the critical moment, little Liu Sha shoots Feng Hong and is saved.

1114. *Life and Death Tree (Sheng Si Shu)*

1984. Shenzhen Film Studio Corporation Ltd. Color. Direction: Zhen Huili. Screenplay: Guo Wenli. Cinematography: Zhang Huijun. Art Direction: Lu Zhicang, Han Gang. Music: Wang Ming. Sound: Han Weijun. Cast: Liu Qianyi as Zhang Xiujiao, Sha Jingcang as Chen Fengyuan, Pan Yu as Third Aunt, Lin Naizhong as Ninth Uncle

In rural Guangdong Province some years before liberation, farmer Chen Fengyuan and village girl Zhang Xiujiao fall in love. At first, the feudal customs of the times require them to keep their love secret, but when Xiujiao becomes pregnant they marry. Two days later, however, Fengyuan leaves to go abroad and claim some money promised him as a wedding gift by overseas relatives. Zhang Xiujiao waits patiently for his return, and bears a baby girl. Four years later, word comes that her husband has been seriously injured overseas. Xiujiao wants to go to him, and travels as far as the border, where she is turned back. Unable to leave the country, she returns home to find her daughter has been sold. Xiujiao falls ill and dies. Twenty years later, Fengyuan returns from abroad and finds his daughter.

1115. *Life During Wartime (Zhan Dou Nian Hua)*

1982. Xi'an Film Studio. Color. 9 Reels. Direction: Zhang Qicang. Screenplay: Xie Fengsong, Liang Xing. Cinematography: Zhangfa Liang, Zhu Kongyang. Art Direction: Wang Fei. Music: Xie Tiyin. Sound: Chen Zhiyuan. Cast: Gao Changli as He Long, Xu Yuanqi as Li Kuan, Jin Di as Mo Mang, Wang Xiaoyan as Zen Xiu, Guo Gang as Gui Juanguo, Yang Yazhou as Gui Xianguo, Zhou Xiaoren as Huan Youren

In Northwest China during the period of Communist-Nationalist wartime collaboration against the Japanese, General He Long's division of the Eighth Route Army comes upon a group of young people who want to help somehow in the revolution. He Long decides that they can for the present help best by forming a basketball team; this would suit their physical characteristics and provide some badly needed entertainment for his troops. After a time, the team is matched up against a team of Nationalist soldiers, and the competition on the court brings both sides to realize the importance of allying against the Japanese. One of the Nationalist soldiers, Huan Youren, even defects to the more revolutionary Communist side.

1116. *Life Gets Easy Even Among Those Who Hate Each Other (Yuan Jia Lu Kuan)*

1981. Changchun Film Studio. Color. 9 Reels. Direction: Lin Ke, Chen Zhenan. Cinematography: Jia Shouxing. Art Direction: Sun Shixiang, Dong Ping. Music: Shi Fu. Sound: Liu Xingfu. Cast: Chun Li as Gao Guangle, Li Zhan Wen as Gao Zhengyuan, Ma Ling as Gao's wife, Yang Xiaofan as Lu Canghua, Pan Demin as Jiang Tai

Gao-Jiang Village's two clans, the Gao and the Jiang, have been feuding for many years. When Gao Guangle is elected head of the village, he determines to handle all matters brought before him impartially. When there is a dispute between Gao Ershen and Jiang Tai, he decides that Gao Ershen should pay Jiang Tai's medical expenses, but Gao Ershen refuses to pay. To set an example, Gao Guangle pays the amount required out of his own pocket. Gao Zheng, Gao Ershen's son, falls in love with Jiang Tai's daughter but is rejected by her family. Gao Erhshen solves many nagging disputes through his patience and impartiality, which improves the relationship between the Gao and Jiang clans. The children marry, and Jiang Tai and Gao Ershen put aside their feud to become relatives.

1117. *Life Has No One Way (Ren Sheng Mei You Dan Xing Dao)*

1984. Xi'an Film Studio. Color. Wide Screen. 9 Reels. Direction: Jin Yin. Screenplay: Shi Chao, Li Pingfeng, Lu Wei. Cinematography: Zhao Haifu, Nie Tiemao. Art Direction: Liu

Xinghou, Sun Baoxi. Music: Wang Liping. Sound: Che Ziyuan. Cast: Wang Gang as Pu Yumin, Liu Xuling as Ding Lei, Lin Xiaojie as Ye Juan, Ruan Ruxin as the boyfriend

Mill director Pu Yumin's desires for reform in the mill do not extend to his personal life. He demands that his wife Ye Juan, a professional woman, sacrifice her career to stay home and be a traditional housewife. She refuses, they argue, and she files for divorce. Pu's friends and colleagues all side with Ye Juan, and criticize Pu Yumin for his old-fashioned stance. At the same time, his cherished reform plan is disapproved by higher authorities. When the couple get to court, civilian court worker Ding Lei is able to get them reconciled. Finally, Pu's reform plan is approved.

1118. *Life in a Song (Sheng Huo Zai Ge Chang)*

1989. Emei Film Studio. Color. Letterboxed. 9 Reels. Direction: Yang Gaisen. Screenplay: Yang Yingzhang. Cinematography: Li Baoqi. Art Direction: Cheng Jinyong. Music: Yang Shuzheng. Sound: Zhang Jianping. Cast: Chou Yongli as Zhou Yuangang, Li Xiaojia as A Fang, Chen Lu as Xiao Lin, Han Fang as Xiao Ma

Zhou Yuangang and his wife A Fang are employees of a coastal city hotel. Zhou's apprentice Xiao Ma has a girlfriend Xiao Lin who also works at the hotel. The hotel manager criticizes Xiao Lin because she so often sings while she works. When a talent contest is held, Zhou Yuangang encourages his wife to enter one of her songs, and they ask Xiao Lin to perform it. The story ends with the contest judge, a famous music professor, praising A Fang's song highly and inviting Xiao Lin to attend his school.

1119. *Life Is Good (Sheng Huo Shi Mei Hao De)*

1982. Liaoning Science Education Film Studio. Color. 10 Reels. Direction: Lu Jianhua, Yu Zhongxiao. Screenplay: Lu Jianhua, Dong Jingsheng, Yu Zhongxiao, Xu Shutian. Cinematography: Yi Zhi. Art Direction: He Ruiji. Music: Gao Fei. Sound: Yuan Minda. Cast: Huang Daliang Ding Yaxin, Hao Yiping as Xu Weiping, Zhao Fengxia as Jiang Xiaoli, Wang Fuyou as Zhen Yunpeng, Jin Yi as Qin Suzhen, Yang Xiaofan as Guo Ling, Shi Lihua as Song Juan, Wang Baosheng as Xiao Chen

Ding Yaxin is the Youth Secretary at the Limin Shipyard. When he learns that so many of the young men in the yard are frustrated by their inability to find girlfriends, he decides to set up a dating service to help young people get together. Director Song opposes this, believing it has no place in the organization. But Ding's service is a success: through helping people with the social relationships, it fires their enthusiasm to work hard, and production goes up steadily. Director Song now realizes the important role romance plays in young people's lives, and the responsibility the older generation has to help the young.

1120. *The Life of Wu Xun (Parts 1 & 2) (Wu Xun Zhuan)*

1950. Kunlun Film Company. B & W. 24 Reels. Direction and Screenplay: Sun Yu, based on the life of Wu Xun (1839–1896). Cinematography: Han Zongliang. Set Design: Ding Sheng. Music: Huang Yijun. Sound: Yuan Qinyu. Costume: Jiang Zhengqin. Makeup: Wang Tiebin, Yao Yongfu. Cast: Zhao Dan as Wu Xun, Huang Zongyin as the woman teacher, Sun Donguang as Wu Xun (age 7), Zhen Dawei as Jiu Ren, Jiang Tianliu as Fourth Wife

December 5th, 1949 is the 110th anniversary of the birth of Wu Xun. In front of the Wu Xun Memorial in the east China town of Liulin, Tanyi County, Shandong Province, a woman teacher relates Wu's story to a group of children.

Wu Xun is born into a poor farmer's family. His father dies when the boy is five, after which his mother supports them for two years by begging for food. One day, with 200 yuan he has worked very hard to earn, Wu Xun goes to a private school and pleads with the teacher to accept him as a student. However, he is rejected by the other students, all sons of wealthy men. Upon his return home, he learns that his mother has died. He is raised by an aunt for seven years, then he works as a common laborer and is a homeless wanderer. At the age of 17, he becomes a laborer for a big landlord named Zhang and is often mistreated. In Zhang's home, he grows to realize the suffering illiteracy brings to the poor, and vows to devote his life to building a public school for poor children.

Wu Xun begins a new life as a clown, making people laugh although he is inwardly unhappy. Ten years pass, and Wu Xun has saved a tidy sum of money, which he deposits with Gao Chunshan, an outwardly upstanding citizen. Unfortunately, Gao embezzles all of it.

Wu does not give up, but starts over again, building up savings from his clown work. After another 20 years, he finally succeeds in founding his school for the poor, but to his disappointment, he finds the students who enroll in his school have no interest in working after graduation, but rather hope their attendance will lead to cushy official appointments. Later, to appease the peasants who love Wu Xun and deter them from rebelling, the imperial court honors Wu by naming a highway after him and bestowing five honorific titles. But Wu Xun finds the reality very painful. He often admonishes poor children, "when you grow up, never forget you are the children of peasants!" He leaves his hometown and spends his last days as a wanderer.

The woman teacher finishes the story in front of Wu Xun's tomb. They all seem to see Wu Xun in his old age walking slowly and firmly across North China's fields.

1121. *Life on a String (Bian Zhou Bian Chang)*

1991. Beijing Film Studio, China Film Corporation, Pandora Film (Germany) in association with Herald Ace (Japan), Film Four International, Berlin Film Fordereung (Germany), Diva Film (Italy), Cinecompany (Netherlands). Color. 120 minutes. Executive Producer: Cai Rubin, Karl Baumgartner. Producer: Don Ranvaud. Direction: Chen Kaige. Screenplay: Chen Kaige, based on a short story by Shi Tiesheng (1951–). Cinematography: Gu Changwei. Art Direction: Shao Ruigang. Music: Qu Xiaosong. Sound: Tao Jing, Martin Steyer. Costume: Liu Jizong, Chen Jidong. Makeup: Wang Liqiu, Hu Chaohong. Cast: Liu Zhongyuan as the old master, Huang Lei as Shitou, Xu Qing as Lanxiu, Zhang Zhengyuan as the noodle stall owner, Ma Ling as the noodle stall owner's wife, Zhang Jinzhan as Lanxiu's father, Zhong Ling as the pharmacist, Yao Erga as the retarded man at the noodle stall

On his deathbed, a master of the three-stringed guitar called the *sanxian* tells his blind apprentice the boy's blindness can be cured by a prescription inside his guitar; but it will only be effective after the boy has broken 1,000 strings while playing his instrument. Now, many years later, the apprentice is the master, wandering the wastelands of Northwest China. He has broken 995, but he does not have that much time left to attain his lifelong dream, the vision he never had. The old man has his own apprentice now, a blind teenager called Shitou. When the two arrive at a desert valley village

inhabited by two feuding clans, the feud is put on hold out of deference to the master, revered by the people as a saint. During their stay, Shitou becomes involved with Lanxiu, a village girl, and begins to neglect his playing and singing. The old man is unhappy with this, for it recalls his own lifelong repressed desires. The old man falls ill, but when a fight breaks out between the two clans, he gets out of his sickbed to stop it. Later, while playing his guitar in the sun, the 1000th string breaks, but not from his playing, as he thinks. The old man leaves at once for a town where he can at last have his prescription filled.

With the old man away, Lanxiu's clan members beat up Shitou out of anger at the blind youth's romancing a village girl. Lanxiu, realizing their love is hopeless, gives Shitou a letter she has written, then throws herself from a cliff. Meanwhile, the old man has learned that his carefully preserved prescription is merely a blank sheet of paper. He furiously smashes his own master's gravestone, then makes his way back to the desert village, bringing a butterfly kite as a gift for Shitou and Lanxiu. When Shitou tells him what developed in his absence, the old man tells Shitou to always keep Lanxiu's letter. The old man gives one more musical performance for the peasants, then dies during the night. After his master's funeral, Shitou hides Lanxiu's letter in his guitar, rejects the villagers' desire to make him the new saint, and goes off on his own. The villagers watch him disappear over the horizon, then see the butterfly kite flying in the distance.

1122. *Life Starts from Here (Sheng Huo Cong Zhe Li Kai Shi)*

1983. Changchun Film Studio. Color. 11 Reels. Direction: Li Geng, Bei Zhaocheng. Screenplay: Li Yanguo, Zhang Fagui, Li Genghong. Cinematography: Meng Qingpeng. Art Direction: Yuan Yimin. Music: Lu Yuan. Sound: Xing Guocang. Cast: Xu Zhan as Xiao Jinhe, Zhang Qing as Long Bing, Ren Weimin as Tian Zhijing, Wang Xinghua as Feng Daquan, Li Yufeng as Zhong Ding, Xing Minhua as Guan Yingsheng, Dong Hui as Long Yuxiu

Xiao Jinhe, director of the workshop at the Huanghe Chemical Products Plant, is the lead singer for the plant's off-duty chorus. His singing attracts the attention of the provincial singing and dancing troupe, and they recruit him to join their troupe full-time. His girlfriend Long Yuxiu is especially enthusiastic about his prospective career change. Just before Xiao Jinhe leaves his old job, however, a fire rips through the chemical plant, burning it to the ground and injuring many employees. Xiao Jinhe decides he must stay and help rebuild the plant. His girlfriend thinks his decision foolish, and breaks off their relationship. The plant employees are so inspired by Xiao's dedication and loyalty to them that they elect him the new director. He promises everyone he will resume full production and implement a new management system within one year, and although they meet many difficulties they at last reopen their plant with new workshops and a state-of-the-art fire detection and alarm system.

1123. *Life's Marathon (Sheng Huo De Ma La Song)*

1987. Emei Film Studio. Color. 9 Reels. Direction: Ma Shaohui. Screenplay: Luo Xing, Xiong Yu. Cinematography: Mai Shuhuan, Du Xiaoshi. Art Direction: Yan Dingfu. Music: Ao Cangqun. Sound: Wang Guangzhong. Cast: Gao Weiqi as Liu Shiting, Yan Cheng as Han Bing, Wang Runsheng as Xin Zhongyuan, Mao Yanhua as Ye Tongmin

The film tells the story of four retirees: famous radio announcer Liu Shiting, Red Army veteran Xin Zhongyuan, spinster Han Bing and She Xiling, a recent widower. Their lives take a positive turn when they begin taking adult education classes in a college. Each of them acquires a new, refreshed outlook on life, and romance blossoms between Liu and Han.

1124. *Life's Spray (Sheng Huo De Lang Hua)*

1958. Beijing Film Studio. B & W. 11 Reels. Direction: Chen Huaiai. Screenplay: Sun Wei. Cinematography: Qian Jiang, Yu Suzhao. Set Design: Yu Yiru. Music: Su Ming, Li Jida. Sound: Wang Zeming. Makeup: Wang Xizhong. Cast: Yu Yang as Jin Zhang, Yang Jing as Ye Suping, Wei Heling as the School Director, Yin Zhimin as Bo Kang, Ye Xiaozhu as Xiao Qi, Liu Chunlin as Team Director Tang

At a hospital-affiliated medical school, young doctors Jin Zhang, Bo Kang and Xiao Qi are good friends. While they are all very fond of a girl named Ye Suping, she only has eyes for Jin Zhang, a very good doctor but conceited and arrogant. His overconfidence leads him to seriously mishandle an operation on Tang, director of a prospecting team, and Jin is seriously criticized for this. Out of jealousy over Ye Suping, Bo Kang seizes the opportunity to attack Jin Zhang. After the incident, Ye goes to Jin to help him realize his mistakes, but he accuses her of turning on him as well, and she leaves angrily. In time, with the help of his professors and fellow doctors, Jin Zhang comes to realize his errors. He is later assigned to serve on the prospecting team, directed by Tang, his former patient. Tang again is in need of surgery, and this time Jin Zhang's actions save him. Meanwhile, Ye Suping learns the true selfish nature of Bao Kang, and she goes to the prospecting site to start a new life with Jin Zhang.

1125. *Life-Taking and Soul-Catching Guns (Zhui Ming Duo Hun Qiang)*

1992. Changchun Film Studio. Color. Letterboxed. 9 Reels. Direction: Sun Guoqin, Teng Guoyin. Screenplay: Hu Shanxiang, Pei Xi. Cinematography: Sun Guangwen. Art Direction: Guo Yansheng, Zhang Hui. Music: Guo Xiaotian. Sound: Jiang Yan. Costume: Zhang Shufang, Liu Tao. Makeup: Liu Jiao. Cast: Yu Jian as Feng Tianlong, Zhu Decheng as Jin Zishou, Zhao Yan as Zhu Juxian, Hou Yueqiu as Wai Lian, Li Li as Jingxin, Zhao Naixun as Sun Weitian

In 1915, Feng Tianlong, an agent of Sun Yatsen, goes to the city of Longcheng to discuss a plan to overthrow Yuan Shikai. Feng carries a pistol he calls the "soul-catching" gun. Also going to Longcheng is Yuan's follower Jin Zishou, who eight years before killed Feng's father and took his weapon, the "life-taking" gun. Jin plans to get the "soul-catching" gun from Feng and present it to Yuan Shikai as a gift when Yuan is installed as emperor. The two at last shoot it out, Feng kills Jin and recovers his late father's "life-taking" gun.

1126. *Light (Deng)*

1978. Changchun Film Studio. Color. 10 Reels. Direction: Yi Yiqin. Screenplay: Yan Yi. Cinematography: Wang Lei. Art Direction: Wang Chong. Music: Wu Damin. Sound: Li Zhenduo. Cast: Zhang Zhan as Chu Ge, Pu Ke as Du Yuan, Qin Wen as Jin Xiu, Jiang Changhua as Shen Ning, Ren Yi as Ge Hua, Fu Xuecheng as Huang Xuan, Luo Wenrui as Zhuang Ping

In 1974, just as the "Gang of Four" makes its move to seize power in China, Jiangcheng

Shipping Plant engineer Chu Ge is busy at
work on a remote controlled navigation light.
Supporters of the "Gang of Four," led by plant
Party Deputy Secretary Huang Xuan and
Deputy Director Zhuang Ping, label scientific
researchers such as Chu Ge "black models"
who "only care about production," in the attempt to stop their design work. Chu Ge resists their pressure with the support of bureau
Party Secretary Du Yuan. Just at that time,
Chu Ge is discovered to have an incurable illness and given only seven months to live. But
he carries on bravely, exposing the machinations of Huang and the rest. With the best of
health care in his final days, he finally completes the remote control navigating system.

1127. The Light in the Mines (Kuang Deng)

1959. Beijing Film Studio. B & W. 10 Reels.
Direction: Li Enjie. Screenplay: Lin Yi, Cui
Guoyin, Tian Runlin. Cinematography: Li Wen-
hua. Art Direction: Yang Yuhe. Music: Zhang
Lu. Sound: Fu Yinjie. Cast: Zhao Lian as Stone,
Hong Niuniu as Stone as a child, Wang Huaiwen
as Road, Yu Qiding as Road as a child, Wang
Yuanlu as Second Bean, Hong Shenshen as Sec-
ond Bean as a child, Huang Fei as Shunzi, Wang
Wuyi as Shunzi as a child, Yang Jing as Big Ju,
Ma Haixing as Big Ju as a child, Yu Yang as Fu
Shandong, Zhao Ziyue as Li Jingchun, Huang
Zongjang as Wang Fuhou

In a mining region of North China under
British control, the mine workers and their
families lead a miserable existence. This is especially so for child laborers such as Road,
forced to work in the mines when orphaned at
13. Road and his friends Stone, Shunzi, Second
Bean and Big Ju are taken in by elderly miner
Wang Fuhou, who gives the children a home
to return to from the mines. When World War
II comes along, the Japanese military adds
brutality to their lives. When his age makes
Wang Fuhou too weak to work any longer, the
mine overseer has the kindly old man fed alive
to dogs. The children plot to revenge him by
killing the overseer, but they botch the attempt and Stone is killed. In the end, the miners are inspired and led by undercover Communist agent Fu Shandong in organizing a
successful strike and achieving liberation.

1128. Light Spreads Everywhere (Guang Mang Wan Zhang)

1949. Northeast Film Studio. B&W. 10 reels.
Direction: Xu Ke. Screenplay: Chen Boer. Cine-
matography: Fu Hong. Set Design: Xu Wei.
Music: He Shide, Su Min. Sound: Sui Xizhong.
Costume: Xue Yan. Makeup: Li Ying. Cast:
Zhang Ping as Zhou Mingying, Wang Weiwei as
Zhou Xiaozi, Ouyang Ruqiu as Mrs. Zhou,
Zhang Qi as Li Hai, Yu Yanfu as Wang Jing-
sheng, Zhang Ying as Mr. Song

During the Civil War, Nationalist forces
retreating from Northeast China blow up a
power plant, costing a loss of jobs for the
workers there. After liberation, attempts to restore the plant to operation are initially
thwarted by the cautious approach of the
plant's chief technicians, and their reluctance
to take responsibility. However, Zhou Mingying, an older worker, unites masses of people
and fires their enthusiasm for the project. Even
an act of sabotage by Wang Jingshen, a secret
agent for the enemy, does not deter Zhou
Mingying's confidence and resolve. Ultimately,
the plant is rebuilt, and the city again supplied
with power.

1129. Lightning (Shan Dian Xing Dong)

1987. August First Film Studio and Hong
Kong Sil-Metropole Organisation Co-Produc-
tion. Color. 9 Reels. Direction: Zhu Yan, Liang
Zhiqiang. Screenplay: Liu Qihui. Cinematogra-
phy: Chen Yuanliang. Art Direction: Zhang
Zheng. Music: Yang Xiwu. Sound: Li Lin. Cast:
Du Zhenqin as Liu Kaihua, Chu Zhibo as Liang
Guozhu, Zhao Xiaorui as Ruan Xiong, Zhang
Ling as Yuemei, Zhu Xinyun as Lin Xiaoliang,
Sun Haiyin as Jiang Yuan

During the Sino-Vietnamese border war,
an elite Vietnamese unit known as the Magic
Guns occupies some Chinese territory, and are
counterattacked by the Chinese own special
unit — Lightning, led by their commander Liu
Kaihua. The fighting is fierce, and while the
Lightning troop finally succeeds in wiping out
the Magic Guns, not many of the victors survive either.

1130. Lightning Action (Pi Li Xing Dong)

1988. Beijing Film Studio. Color. 9 Reels.
Direction: Teng Wenji. Screenplay: Teng Wenji,
Han Yu, Wang Qinchuan. Cinematography: Zhi

Lei. Art Direction: He Zhiming. Music: Gao Dalin. Sound: Hua Juan. Cast: Jin Hong as Luo Ao, Duan You as Shen Dandan, Li Zhiming as Liu Weilong, Zhang Qingzu as Lin Sheng, Du Xiongwen as Zhang Yifu, Xu Lin as Zhao Liping

Late one night, the Huasheng Company's safe is broken open, and the intruder flees through a window. But investigation shows that nothing was taken. A few days later, Lin Sheng, a key figure in the company, finds that someone is following him. Lin is involved in an auto accident, after which he disappears, and an important contract he was carrying has disappeared as well. It turns out that Lin's company had signed the contract with another businessman named Liu Weilong. When Liu learned he had been cheated in the contract, he arranged the accident, abducted Lin and took the contract. Liu Weilong is caught. A concurrent plot line depicts the unusual involvement of Lin Sheng's lover Zhao Liping and company CEO Zhang Yifu. The safecracking incident is related to their relationship, and the two make plans to abscond. They are caught before they can get away.

1131. *Lightning-Irrawaddy (Shan Dian-Yi Luo Wa Di)*

1995. Yunnan Film Studio, Shanghai Yongle Film Production Company Co-Production. Color. Letterboxed. Direction: Zuang Hongsheng. Screenplay: Guang Sheng, Tu Yue. Cinematography: Dan Lianguo. Art Direction: Wang Xingchang. Cast: Xiao Rongsheng as Huang Guoxiong, Zhang Yonggang as Cai Mingquan, Wang Peng as Guo Qinglong, Li Guixi as Ma Laihua, A Li as Yin Yalong, Zhou Guobing as Zhong Huashan, Yu Guichun as Wang Hu, Song Ningning as Cha Erdun

World War II in the Pacific starts with a string of victories by the Japanese, as they quickly conquer Hong Kong, Singapore and the Philippines. British General Alexander asks the Chinese Army for help. In Kunming, Chinese battalion commander Huang Guoxing is ordered to escort a convoy delivering supplies and equipment to the Burmese border, then reconnoiter the Irrawaddy River area along the border for the main Chinese force. The film relates the bloody struggle of Huang's battalion in accomplishing its mission. Three days later, armed with the intelligence supplied to it by Huang, the Chinese Army launches its "Lightning-Irrawaddy" attack, relieving General Alexander and 7,000 British troops. Ten days after that, the Chinese pour 100,000 troops into Burma to fight the Japanese.

1132. *Lily Flower (Bai He Hua)*

1981. Youth Film Studio. Color. 6 Reels. Direction: Qian Xuege, Zhang Xin. Screenplay: Zhang Xin. Cinematography: Meng Haifeng, Gu Wenkai. Music: Ma Ding. Sound: Zhang Ruikun. Cast: Cui Xinqing as Lu Lan, Ge Jianjun as the young soldier, Shen Danping as Hehua (Lily), Li Huiying as the neighbor

In the fall of 1946, Lu Lan, an entertainer in a PLA performance troupe, is assigned to help in the work of a frontline medical aid station. On route, she meets a young soldier traveling to the same destination. After they arrive, Lu Lan asks the young soldier to accompany her in borrowing comforters from the village people for use in the aid station. When they come to the home of Hehua, a newlywed bride, they borrow a comforter from her. But after the young soldier learns this was the only wedding possession the young bride has, and something she had worked hard to save for, he wants to return it. However, Hehua refuses to take it back. When the battle starts, the young soldier leaves for the front, while Lu Lan and Hehua continue preparing the aid station. As the wounded are brought in, they bring news of the battle's progress, and how the Communist forces are winning. When the fighting nears its end, a mortally wounded soldier is brought in, who turns out to be the shy young soldier they knew. There is nothing that can be done for him and he dies. Tearfully, Hehua covers his body with her new comforter she saved for her wedding.

1133. *Lin Chong (Lin Chong)*

1958. Jiangnan Film Studio. B & W. 9 Reels. Directors: Shu Shi and Wu Yonggang. Screenplay: Huang Shang, based on the story of Lin Chong in the classic Ming Dynasty novel, *Shui Hu Zhuan* ("Outlaws of the Marsh," also known as "All Men Are Brothers.") Cinematography: Yao Shiquan. Art Direction: Hu Zuoyun, Sun Zhang. Music: Xiang Yi. Sound: Ding Bohe. Costume: Hu Xuguang. Makeup: Da Xu. Cast: Su Shi as Lin Chong, Zhang Yi as Lu Zhisheng, Lin Bing as Zhang Zhenniang, Jin Chuan as Officer Gao, Feng Qia as Lu Qian, Gao Xiaoou as Fuan, Wei Shi as Jiner

Lin Chong, a military instructor of 800,000 troops, accompanies his wife Zhan Zhenniang to worship in their local temple.

When he is called away temporarily, an officer named Gao, son of a high-ranking official, rapes Zhenniang. Although humiliated and powerless to do anything about it, Lin Chong takes her back. Later, the Gaos set Lin Chong up on an attempted murder charge. Lin is reduced to the rank of common soldier and banished to a remote area. There, the Gaos have arranged for Lin's murder. But he is saved by Lu Zhisheng, a farmer turned greenwoods bandit. Lu's band tries to persuade Lin Chong to join them, but he is determined to return home and clear his name. Upon his return, he finds that his wife, after suffering further harassment and humiliation, has committed suicide. He is assigned as caretaker at a granary, but when another attempt to kill him goes awry, burning down the granary, he is falsely accused of arson. This time, with no options left, Lin Chong leaves to join the bandits.

1134. *The Lin Family Shop (Lin Jia Pu Zhi)*

1959. Beijing Film Studio. Color. 9 Reels. Direction: Shui Hua. Screenplay: Xia Yan, based on the novel of the same title by Mao Dun (1896–) Cinematography: Qian Jiang. Art Direction: Chi Ning. Music: He Shide. Sound: Cai Jun. Cast: Xie Tian as Boss Lin, Ma Wei as Lin Mingxiu, Han Tao as Chairman Yu, Liang Xin as the store helper, Cai Yuanyuan as A Si, Guo Bing as Boss Chen, An Ran as Mr. Wu

Following the 1931 Japanese invasion of China, there is a nationwide boycott of Japanese goods, but some seize this as an opportunity for personal gain. In one Southeast China town, a merchant named Lin uses bribery, extortion and intimidation to get around the boycott and obtain Japanese goods to market. He also uses these means to force other businesses with less assets out of business. However, he himself is exploited by the bank's high interest rates and is blackmailed by government officials. All of this backstabbing and infighting finally results in Lin declaring bankruptcy, closing the store and leaving town with his daughter. It turns out that the biggest losers are the town's citizens, many of them poor and weak, who had deposited money at Lin's store: he embezzles all of their deposits when he leaves.

1135. *Lin Zexu (aka The Opium War) (Lin Ze Xu)*

1959. Haiyan Film Studio. Color. 11 Reels. Direction: Zheng Junli, Cen Fan. Screenplay: Ye Yuan, based on events in the life of Lin Zexu (1785–1850). Cinematography: Huang Shaofeng, Cao Weiye. Art Direction: Han Shangyi, Hu Dengren. Music: Wang Yunjie. Sound: Wu Jianghai. Cast: Gao Zheng as Wen Ning, Xia Tian as Mu Zhanga, Zhao Dan as Lin Zexu, Han Fei as Qi Shan, Yang Hua as Yu Lei, Liang Shan as Wu Shaorong, Gerald Tannebaum as the British Consul, Li Yong as Den Tingzhen, Deng Nan as Guan Tianpei, Jiang Rui as Han Zhaoqing

In the late 18th Century, the British East India Company began exporting opium into China from India, and by the 1830s, thousands of Chinese had become addicted. Chinese efforts to stop the drug traffic are futile and half-hearted. But in 1836 the Qing Dynasty Emperor Daoguang appoints as Imperial Commissioner Lin Zexu, a radical advocate of banning the drug completely. Lin arrives in the South China city of Guangzhou (Canton) to find he is opposed by military governor Mu Zhanga and the governor of Zhili Qi Shan, both of whom are sharing in the profits of the drug trade. Lin is able to enlist the aid of several honest officials, including Deng Tingzhen, governor of Guangdong and Guangxi provinces, and Guan Tianpei, Guangzhou's naval governor. They adopt a strategy of rebuilding China's deteriorated coastal defenses in preparation for the anticipated British invasion while detaining British ships and confiscating the opium. Lin at one point burns over 20,000 chests of the drug. While he makes considerable headway in controlling the Chinese side of the drug traffic, the foreign side is largely beyond his control. In May of 1840, British forces invade China, beginning the Opium War. Out of fear of the British army, the emperor loses his nerve, removes Lin Zexu from his position as imperial commissioner and reassigns him to remote Xinjiang as punishment.

1136. *Lingjiao General (Ling Jiao Jiang Jun)*

1987. Children's Film Studio. Color. 9 Reels. Direction: Qiu Zhongyi. Screenplay: Song Zhenguo. Cinematography: Can Xingliang. Art Direction: Xiao Feng. Music: He Zhanhao. Sound: Zhou Xiaomin. Cast: Zhan Haixiang as Tian

The Lin Family Shop. 1959. Beijing Film Studio.

Xiaoman, Gao Cang as Erniu, Xu Hui as Little Stone, Qiu Shuang as Zhu Wenhua, Bian Tao as Tian Guyu, Chi Peng as Pan Yufeng

Tian Xiaoman is a natural leader among the children in prosperous and beautiful Lingjiaowan Village, but has a tendency to get into mischief. Young teacher Pan Yufeng recognizes Tian's ambition and organizational ability, so he appoints the boy to a position of leadership in the village school, in charge of maintaining discipline. Tian Xiaoman surprises everyone by doing very well with this responsibility. He organizes the children to help some of the village adults conquer their addiction to gambling, which helps the village chief recognize his own bad social habits.

1137. *Lion Dancer's Legend (Wu Shi Ren Chuan Qi)*

1985. Pearl River Film Studio. Color. 10 Reels. Direction: Xing Jitian. Screenplay: Zhou Yiru. Cinematography: Xie Yongyi. Art Direction: Du Xiufeng. Music: Zhen Qiufeng. Sound: Li Bojian. Cast: Wang Runshen as Chen Jianhong, Wang Yu as Huo Shilong, Shen Guangwei as Xing Yapu, Wang Liping as Wang Haitao, Zhou Peihong as Tong Kun

Chen Jianhong, a performer of traditional lion dancing, kills landlord Qi Menglong for revenge. The landlord had killed Chen's wife, abducted their daughter and stolen the family heirloom, a jade sculpture of a lion. Chen finds a home for their small son Huzai with a fellow performer, then leaves to roam the country under a different name. Twenty years pass, and the now-elderly Chen Jianhong runs a famous martial arts training hall in Guangdong, only now he calls himself Jiang Bonan. Huzai is now an adult, known as Huo Shilong. Opium smuggler Xing Yapu, pretending to be a philanthropist, hires Huo Shilong as a guard for his opium shipments. In time, Huo and his father meet, recognize each other, and decide to join together in the nation's interest to combat Xing Yapu and other opium smugglers. Xing Yapu discovers that Jiang Bonan is the man who killed his father 20 years ago, and has him captured. At the critical moment, Xing's wife Chen Shuixian releases Jiang Bonan when she learns that he is the father from whom she was separated 20 years before. The Chen family is at last reunited, but Chen Shuixian dies.

Lin Zexu. Imperial Commissioner Lin Zexu (Zhao Dan, right) learns that his effective opposition to the British drug trade has gained him banishment to the frontier for his efforts. 1959. Haiyan Film Studio.

1138. *Lion in the Desert (Huang Mo Zhong De Si Zhi)*

1987. Inner Mongolia Film Studio. Color. 9 Reels. Direction: Zuo Gehe. Screenplay: Zuo Gehe. Cinematography: Yi Hu, Hewula. Art Direction: Aori Lige. Music: Du Zhaozhi. Sound: Aosi. Cast: Hasi Gaowa as Kangkelai, Ning Cai as Xiage Daer, Er Changlin as Zhaoke Labutan, Jiang Bula as Hari Bandi

In a desert area of Inner Mongolia, a ruthless landlord evicts herdsmen from the prairie where their people have earned their living for generations. Xiage Daer leads a people's revolt. The rebel leader is wounded in a battle, but is rescued by young and beautiful widow Kangkelai and her father-in-law. Kangkelai falls in love with him. But when her father-in-law Zhaoke Labutan learns that Xiage is the man who killed his son Gamola, he opposes the romance and begins plotting to kill Xiage. But at last he gives up his dreams of personal revenge when he sees how the people need Xiage's leadership. Kangkelai has to struggle with her own emotions, but at last she decides her love for Xiage is too strong and she goes to him. However, Xiage Daer is betrayed and killed by his friend Hari Bandi, who is in turn killed by Kangkelai.

1139. *Lion Trainer Sanlang (Xun Shi San Lang)*

1985. Shanghai Film Studio. Color. 3-D. 8 Reels. Direction: Yu Jie. Screenplay: Lu Yuzhong, Liu Yonglai, Rui Baoluo. Cinematography: Wun Sijie. Art Direction: Shen Lide. Music: Cai Lu. Sound: Huang Dongping. Cast: Mao Yongming as Liu Sanlan, Jing Lanying as Meimei, Li Zhengbing as Luo Yi, Yang Hongwu as Guan Tao, Yang Kaixuan as Liu Jianguo, Huang Longzhu as the pretty girl

Although noted for his timidity, acrobat Liu Sanlang volunteers to replace his circus troupe's lion trainer when the trainer suffers an injury during a performance. Sanlang decides the first step is to train himself to be brave. He loves Meimei, an actress, but when he learns she already has a boyfriend Guan Tao, he selflessly sets out to make them happy. Meanwhile, Sanlang devotes himself to learning lion training, and a girl in the troupe falls in love with him. Liu Sanlang has succeeded in both love and work.

1140. *Little Bell (Xiao Ling Dang)*

1964. Beijing Film Studio. Color. 7 Reels. Direction: Xie Tian, Chen Fangqian. Screenplay:

Xie Tian, Chen Fangqian, Cinematography: Zhang Qinghua. Art Direction: Yang Yuhe. Music: Qiao Gu. Sound: Fu Yinjie. Cast: Shi Xiaoman as Xiaoman, Ma Jia as Xiaojia, Guan Weiji as Little Bell's puppeteer

Two children, sister and brother, find a puppet lost by a puppet troupe, an audience favorite called "Little Bell." The girl, Xiaojia, urges they return the puppet immediately, but her brother Xiaoman disagrees and runs away with the puppet. He falls asleep on a boat in a park and dreams that a huge man looking exactly like himself comes and takes Little Bell away, making the little boy very angry and upset. After he wakes up, Xiaoman realizes his sister was right, so he returns Little Bell to the troupe.

1141. *Little Bell (Sequel) (Xiao Ling Dang)*

1986. Children's Film Studio. Color. Letterboxed. 8 Reels. Direction: Xie Tian. Screenplay: Xie Tie, Chen Hongguang. Cinematography: Sun Yongtian. Art Direction: Jia Youke. Music: Huang Xiaofei. Sound: Fu Jinjie. Cast: Liang Jinqi as Little Fatty, Ma Jia as Ma Jia, Shi Xiaoman as Xiao Man

After they have seen the movie "Little Bell," Little Fatty and his playmates talk about finding someone really like the title character to put on a show for them. They find a man who has been asleep in a cellar for 23 years. Since he has missed so much during that time, he is naturally curious and does not recognize many things. For example, he does not know about robots, and has no idea what is a "Special Economic Zone." So when he gives his performance he just makes up humorous stories about what these might be. Little Fatty suddenly awakens to realize it was all a dream.

1142. *The Little Black Box (Hei Xia Die Xue Ji)*

1986. Shanghai Film Studio. Color. 10 Reels. Direction: Zhong Shuhuang. Screenplay: Xie Wenli. Cinematography: Zhang Er. Art Direction: Qin Bosong. Music: Xu Jingxin. Sound: Tu Mingde. Cast: Wen Xitai as Jin Biao, Li Xiaoyan as Nan Guiying, Zhang Anji as Wang Jianxiong, Tang Junliang as Liu Shan, Han Zhikai as Policeman Hu

On the eve of the 1911 Revolution, kung fu master Jin Biao is sent to South China by revolutionary leaders. His mission: get a secret document from the revolutionaries in Wuchang city. He finds his contact, Nan Renjie, and obtains from him the black box holding the document, but their meeting is interrupted by government troops searching for the two. Nan Renjie sacrifices his own life so that Jin Biao can escape. In addition to the government troops, Nan's daughter Guiying and Nan's nephew Wang Jianxiong set off in pursuit of Jin Biao, each for his or her own reasons. Jin Biao concludes that Wang Jianxiong is the traitor who betrayed the revolutionaries, and when they reach the banks of the Yangtse River, Jin Biao kills him. In the struggle to protect the little black box, Jin Biao and his fellow kung fu fighters battle to the last man.

1143. *Little Cavalry Boy's Adventure (Xiao Qi Bing Li Xian Ji)*

1988. Children's Film Studio. Color. 8 Reels. Direction: Lu Gang. Screenplay: Ding Renyan. Cinematography: Sun Yongtian. Art Direction: Guo Juhai, Sun Guojun. Music: Fu Gengcheng. Sound: Zhen Chunyu. Cast: Fu Dalong as Lian Fu, Xu Rihua as Section Chief Wang

In 1947, 12-year-old cavalry stableboy Lian Fu falls from his beloved red pony. When he regains consciousness, he sees an enemy cavalryman bearing down on him. He is saved when a woman shoots the enemy soldier. After he rejoins his unit, the boy learns his rescuer is Reconnaissance Section Chief Wang. Lian Fu is later captured, and again sees Wang at the enemy's headquarters, where she has been badly tortured. The PLA attacks the enemy headquarters town, and in the battle Wang protects Lian Fu a second time. This time the woman is killed. Lian Fu brings his red pony to stand by her flag-draped body. He thanks her and calls her "Mom."

1144. *Little Cowherd (Er Xiao Fang Niu Lang)*

1992. Anhui Film Studio & Beijing Film Studio Co-Production. Color. Letterboxed. 8 Reels. Direction: Zhang Chi. Screenplay: Xiong Yu, Xiao Yixian. Cinematography: Liu Ping. Art Direction: Chen Xiaoxia. Music: Liu Kexin. Costume: Zhang Yongyi, Chen Songlin. Makeup: Guo Jinxia, Liu Chun. Cast: Ding Yan as Wang Erxiao, Shen Danping as Lanyin, Liu Guanjun as Da Niu, Li Jiaxi as Niuniu, Zhao Xiaofei as Qiaoqiao

During World War II, young cowherd Wang Erxiao loses both his parents. The little boy bravely does what he can to resist the invaders, protecting Chinese soldiers and guiding local people to safety. At last he successfully lures some Japanese soldiers into an encirclement by Eighth Route Army troops, but he sacrifices his own life to do this, a war casualty at the age of nine.

1145. *The Little Deyuelou Restaurant (Xiao Xiao De Yue Lou)*

1983. Shanghai Film Studio. Color. 9 Reels. Direction: Lu Ping. Screenplay: Ye Min, Xu Cangling. Cinematography: Zhang Guifu. Art Direction: Zhang Wanhong, Yang Shaolu. Sound: Xie Guojie. Cast: Mao Yongmin as Yang Maotou, Lu Chengsheng as Yang's father, Gu Xiang as Qiao Mei, Zhang Weijing as Hanhan, Zhen Jingsheng as Duoduo, Ye Xiaozhen as Bai Niangniang

In the East China city of Suzhou, a hot spot for tourism, the shortage of acceptable restaurants has become a real problem. Seeing an opportunity, Yang Maotou, a young waiter in Suzhou's famous Deyuelou Restaurant, proposes to his friends Qiao Mei, Hanhan and Duoduo that they start a branch operation to be called the "Little Deyuelou." They make a presentation of their idea to Yang Maotou's father, the Deyuelou's manager, but he turns them down because he does not trust the young people's competence. The young people keep trying, and finally get their restaurant up and running, despite Manager Yang's objections. At last even he is convinced.

1146. *Little Eighth Route Heroes (Ying Xiong Xiao Ba Lu)*

1961. Tianma Film Studio. B & W. 10 Reels. Direction: Gao Heng. Screenplay: Zhou Yuhui, based on the stage play of the same title by Chen Yun. Cinematography: Shi Fengqi. Art Direction: Zhen Jieke, Zhou Qingling. Music: Ji Ming. Sound: Gong Zhenming. Casting: Hong Zhosheng as Guojian, Lu Ning as Lin Yan, Wu Limin as Tieniu, He Liji as Xiaoming, Li Yixing as Xiao Hua, Wang Qi as Party Secretary Zhao

In a village of Fujian province, directly across the Taiwan Straits, Young Pioneers Guojian, Lin Yan, Tie Niu, Xiao Ming and Xiao Hua carry on the revolutionary tradition of their forebears by engaging in various activities which support the work of the PLA. Once, they capture a man they suspect of being a spy, but find he is a PLA regimental commander on an undercover inspection tour. They win praise for their diligence. Later, a real spy sent from Taiwan arrives pretending to be Xiao Ming's uncle. But the clever boy is suspicious and captures the spy. Finally, the five Young Pioneers render valuable service to the Red Army during a counterattack on Jinmen Island (Quemoy).

1147. *Little Flower (Xiao Hua)*

1979. Beijing Film Studio. Color, B & W, 10 Reels. Direction: Zhang Zheng. Screenplay: Qian She. Cinematography: Chen Guoliang, Yun Wenyao. Art Direction: Liu Xuan. Music: Wang Ming. Sound: Wang Yunhua. Cast: Tang Guoqiang as Zhao Yongsheng, Chen Chong as Zhao Xiaohua, Liu Xiaoqing as He Cuigu, Ge Chunzhuang as Ding Shuheng, Wang Biao as Ding Shi, Fu Zhucheng as Dong Xiangkun

In 1930, the impoverished Zhao family is forced to sell their newborn baby daughter Xiaohua ("Little Flower"). But later that same night, revolutionary Dong Xiangkun and her husband Doctor Zhou ask their friends the Zhaos to care for their daughter Dong Hongguo while the parents are on the run from government troops. For her protection, Hongguo is renamed Zhao Xiaohua, after the baby girl the Zhaos had just sold. A few years later, after Xiaohua's adoptive parents are both killed by the army, she and her foster brother Zhao Yongsheng raise each other. Later, the brother has to flee to avoid being drafted into the Nationalist Army. In 1947, the PLA comes to the area, and Zhao Xiaohua. now 18, meets PLA regimental Doctor Zhou, but father and daughter do not recognize each other. Zhao Yongsheng's real sister who was sold as a baby is now called He Cuigu, and has become an outstanding guerrilla fighter. By chance, Zhao Xiaohua, Zhao Yongsheng and He Cuigu meet and all notice Cuigu's striking resemblance to Zhao Yongsheng's mother. Following this clue, the three young people seek to find out which is the sister and which is the real Xiaohua. The story ends with He Cuigu and her brother Zhao Yongsheng reunited, and Xiaohua reunited with her parents Dong Xiangkun and Doctor Zhou.

Best Picture, 1980 Hundred Flowers Awards.

Best Actress Chen Chong, 1980 Hundred Flowers Awards.

Best Cinematographer, Chen Guoliang and Yun Wenyao, 1980 Hundred Flowers Awards.

Best Music Wang Ming, 1980 Hundred Flowers Awards.

Little Flower. **Zhao Xiaohua (Chen Chong/Joan Chen, left) and He Cuigu (Liu Xiaoqing) chatting happily on a river bank. 1979. Beijing Film Studio.**

1148. *Little Flying Hero (Xiao Fei Xia)*

1995. Changchun Film Studio in cooperation with Hainan Nanyang Film Company. Color. Letterboxed. Dolby Sound. Direction: Lin Weilun, Meng Li. Screenplay: Liang Weiting, Situ Huizhuo, Zuo Bing. Cinematography: Zhen Zhaoqiang. Art Direction: Guo Shaoqiang, Yang Guomin. Cast: Xie Miao, Wu Mengda, Lu Huiguang, Zhen Bolin, Ni Xing, Luo Huijuan

On a visit to Hong Kong, Xie Fei and his father are mistaken by police for two suspects in a murder case. Father and son become separated while running from the police, and Xie Fei meets a noodle seller called Big Shanyuan and his son Chumian. They help the little boy, and he has a series of adventures. Xie Fei's father rescues his son, and kills a policeman who was the actual murderer. Xie Fei and his father bid a fond farewell to their new friends.

1149. *Little Goldfish (Xiao Jin Yu)*

1982. Shanghai Film Studio. Color. 10 Reels. Direction: Zhang Junxiang, Li Xiepu, Wang Ji. Screenplay: Ai Minzhi. Cinematography: Yin Fukang. Art Direction: Huang Qiagui, Zhu Jiancang. Music: Huang Zhun. Sound: Feng Deyao. Cast: Lu Qin as Hu Sheng, Zhang Yu as Xie Xiaoyin, Zhong Xinghuo as Teacher Zhong, Zhen Shuzhi as Xie's mother

Unable to bear the discipline at reform school, Hu Sheng runs away. His father and former classmates no longer accept him, so he becomes a homeless person. Meanwhile, Teacher Zhong from the reform school searches for the boy, wanting to help him. Hu Sheng happens to meet some boys playing soccer. He joins in the game, and impresses them with his skill. One of the boys, Xie Yonghong, invites him to stay at his home. Xie Yonghong's older sister Xie Xiaoying is a vivacious and sincere girl who works as the youth association secretary at a street-run factory. She helps Hu Sheng, encourage him to do volunteer work at her factory, and the person in charge there also takes to Hu Sheng. Hu Sheng thrives in the new environment. Teacher Zhong also visits Hu Sheng's family to help him out, and everyone pitches in to help Hu Sheng. Hu Sheng is now being cared for and educated by those from the reform school and from society at large, and now is determined to get on with his new life.

1150. *Little Guest (Xiao Ke Ren)*

1987. Tianshan Film Studio. Color. 9 Reels. Direction: Li Shifa. Screenplay: Li Pengcheng. Cinematography: Gao Huanggang. Art Direction: Xiang Shaowei. Music: Zhou Ji. Sound: Liu Honggang. Cast: Du Jian as Nannan, Mayila as Manlizhou, Silayin as Kadeer, Asi Haer as Sailike, Mulati as Uncle Aili, Rehaman as Grandfather

Little Nannan, growing up on the banks of the Jialing River, thinks of his grandfather in Xinjiang, who he has never met. One day he leaves his parents and follows his Uncle Aili on a business trip to Chongqing and then to Xinjiang. The story tells how Nannan eventually meets his grandfather.

1151. *Little Hedgehog Sonata (Xiao Ci Wei Zou Min Qu)*

1983. Children's Film Studio. Color. 8 Reels. Direction: Qiqing Gaowa. Screenplay: Yao Yun. Cinematography: Wang Zhaoling. Art Direction: Duan Zhengzhong. Music: Jin Zhengping. Sound: Wang Zemin. Cast: Liu Di as Doudou, Chelaixi as Lumengtuo, Maide as Tingka, Jin Feng as Grandpa, Ali Telaaolei as Lumengtuo's mother

A six-year-old boy named Doudou lives with his grandfather near a rural resort. The boy loves small animals, and one day finds and picks up a small hedgehog which he keeps as a pet. One day, the hedgehog disappears. When Doudou goes to look for his pet he finds that two foreign boys staying at the resort now have it. He argues with the two boys, Lumengtuo and Tingka, and finally gets the hedgehog back. When he tells his grandfather about this, the old man encourages him to go back and make friends with the foreign boys. He does so, and the three become pals, often playing with the hedgehog together. When it comes time for the foreign boys to return to their own country, the three exchange gifts. They decide to give the little hedgehog a gift as well, and release him back into the wilds where he belongs.

1152. *Little Herdsman Joins the Army (Mu Tong Tou Jun)*

1957. Haiyan Film Studio. B & W. 9 Reels.

Direction: You Long. Screenplay: Wu Qiang, based on the story "He Raises a Shining Gun." Cinematography: Cha Xiangkang and Lu Junfu. Art Direction: Huang Jianfeng and Wu Qiwen. Music: Liang Hanguang. Sound: Ren Xinliang. Cast: Yang Sengcang as Li Xiaohu, Gao Zheng as the Company Commander, Cao Duo as the Political Instructor, Wang Qi as Platoon Leader Hong, Sun Yongping as Yu Guocai, Yang Gongming as Yuan Chunsheng, Liang Shan as Hu Si, Gao Xiaoou as Zhou Shigui

During the Chinese Civil War, 14-year-old herdsman Li Xiaohu flees from the Huda Village landlord who beats him, and seeks sanctuary with a unit of the Eighth Route Army which is in the area. He finds a home with the army, doing odd jobs for them, but when the unit moves out, the company commander feels he is too young to go with them, so temporarily places the boy in the home of local administrator Zhou Shigui. In time, however, Zhou decides to curry favor with the landlord by inviting him to a banquet. Li Xiaohu is discovered by the landlord and turned over to the Nationalist Army, which tries to get the boy to tell what he knows about the PLA. The boy escapes but is recaptured. He escapes a second time and this time reaches the PLA. In a battle at Yang Village, Li Xiaohu helps the PLA wipe out the enemy force and capture their chief of staff. After the battle ends, the PLA pretends to be the Nationalist Army and traps the landlord Hu Si. Huda village is liberated. Finally, Xiaohu officially joins the PLA.

1153. *The Little House Under the Moon (Yue Guang Xia De Xiao Wu)*

1985. Inner Mongolia Film Studio. Color. 9 Reels. Direction: Zhang Yuqiang. Screenplay: Xiao Zengjian, Ji Weihua. Cinematography: Guan Qingwu. Art Direction: Kou Honglie. Music: Jin Xiang. Sound: Lan Fan. Cast: Zhang Xianheng as Wang Eryao, Yao Jiwen as Hei Gou, Zen Bingbing as Ma Gou, Gao Chang as Hui Gou, Wu Yunfang as Director Li

Convicted robber Wang Ermo is released from prison ahead of time for good behavior, and returns to his hometown on the south China coast. He finds his wife has died during his absence, and the lack of parental supervision has brought his three sons under bad influences. The boys are also hostile towards their father. By his own behavior, Wang slowly builds up a relationship of trust with his boys, and eventually they accept him and begin a new life.

Outstanding Foreign Film — Family Entertainment, 8th Los Angeles International Children's Film Festival.

1154. *Little Island (Xiao Dao)*

1985. August First Film Studio. Color. 10 Reels. Direction: Zhang Lun. Screenplay: Wang Haiou, Zhang Lun. Cinematography: Zhang Lun. Art Direction: Fang Xuzhi. Music: Zhen Qiufeng. Sound: Song Tianpei. Cast: Lin Muyu as Sister Su, Yue Hong as Han Ling, Qin Ling as Cai Xiaojie, Xiao Yan as Yuan Hui, Wang Yuzhang as Wang Fuxing

Three young women medical professionals had joined the army together eight years before, but now their lives have taken different paths. Doctor Yuan Hui has earned her medical degree and is now preparing to marry a man she loves; pharmacist Cai Xiaojie has twice failed to gain admission to graduate school, and has lost the confidence to try again; nurse Han Ling is lonely, taking solace in her love of reading and writing poetry. Hospital Director Su patiently counsels the three on handling their lives and careers. In the end, Cai gets her confidence back and Han finds love with construction battalion chief Wang Fuxing. All three look forward to bright futures.

1155. *A Little Night Music in the Castle (Gu Bao Xiao Ye Qu)*

1987. Changchun film Studio. Color. 10 Reels. Direction: Zhou Wei. Screenplay: Fu Xing. Cinematography: Chen Chang'an. Art Direction: Li Junjie. Music: Liu Xijing. Sound: Liu Jingui, Wang Wenfu. Cast: Wu Yufang as Sheng Qing, Lu Jun as Ouyang Cheng

Sheng Qing has passed 26 uneventful years in an old, depressing, castle-like house with her parents, uncle and aunt, four very strange old people. The boring pattern of her life changes when a friend introduces her to Ouyang Cheng, a young, handsome and energetic manager of an electrical power plant. But her father cannot stand Ouyang Cheng's free and open manner, so he angrily drives Sheng Qing and Ouyang Cheng from the "castle." The young couple move to the suburbs, but after a while Sheng Qing starts to miss her family. At the same time, she cannot understand the bold reforms Ouyang Cheng is insti-

tuting at his plant. The young man loves Sheng Qing very much, but her lack of support combined with the criticisms he received from others cause him considerable pain and loneliness. Sheng Qing returns home, and is surprised to find the old people so influenced by Ouyang Cheng that they are starting their lives anew. Sheng Qing thinks of Ouyang Cheng and returns to their suburban home.

1156. *Little Playmates (Xiao Huo Ban)*

1956. Shanghai Film Studio. B & W. 8 Reels. Direction: Ge Xin. Screenplay: Hai Mu, based on the novel of the same title by Liu Zhen. Cinematography: Shi Fengqi. Art Direction: Zhong Yongqin. Music: Guan Yingcheng. Sound: Wu Hua. Cast: Cai Yuanyuan as Xiao Wang, Zhao Yurong as Xiao Rong, Guo Yuntai as Chief Zhao, Qi Heng as Old Mr. Sun, Wu Yin as Old Mrs. Zhang, Mochou as Xiao Rong's mother

A little boy named Xiao Wang is a messenger for the Eighth Route Army. His playmate, a little girl named Xiao Rong, greatly admires him and wants to be a little Eighth Route Army soldier. When Xiao Rong's messenger mother is arrested, the little girl completes her mother's mission. Xiao Wang brings the homeless Xiao Rong to the army, which collectively adopts her. She grows up rapidly in her new "family," and becomes a bright and brave messenger. She and Xiao Wang carry out many important assignments together, and help in the apprehension of the traitor who betrayed her mother. Her mother is later released and reunited with Xiao Rong. Near the end of World War II, the two young people are selected to receive further education which will prepare them for greater responsibility in the coming revolution.

1157. *The Little Shell Trumpet (Xiao Luohao)*

1975. Pearl River Film Studio. Color. 7 Reels. Direction: Liu Xin. Screenplay: Liu Xin. Cinematography: Liang Xiongwei. Art Direction: Mo Renji. Music: Tan Zhibing. Sound: Jiang Shaoqi. Casting: Wu Dongsheng as Hai Long, Can Hong as Xiao Min, Yi Xiawen as Hai Mei, Xing Jitian as Party Secretary Chen, Jian Ruichao as Rong Aliu, Jin Tao as Shi Yongbo

After oil workers come to a small island in the South Sea, Young Pioneers often help the workers by bringing food gifts, etc. While playing near the work site, the children note some suspicious activity by local resident Rong Aliu. They follow him and finally observe him sending covert radio messages. Their alertness leads to the exposure of a conspiracy to sabotage the oil project.

1158. *Little Soccer Team (Xiao Zu Qiu Dui)*

1965. Haiyan Film Studio. B & W. 9 Reels. Direction: Yan Bili. Screenplay: Ren Deyao, Shi Fangyu and Lin Puhua, based on the stage play of the same title. Cinematography: Gu Wunhou. Art Direction: Fu Shuzhen. Music: Wang Yunjie. Sound: Wu Yin. Cast: Wang Jiner as Jiang Li, Si Rong as Li Ming, Zhang Guoping as Lu Yang, Liang Boluo as Wu An, Li Baoluo as Uncle Zhao, Xie Yibing as Grandma

High school student Lu Yang is the key player on his soccer team, but he always looks for ways he can stand out from the rest of the team, ignoring the collective good. He rejects criticism from teacher and classmates, and leaves the collective, organizing a "nameless team" outside of school with a few other students. Under the influence of Wu An, his coach outside of school, Lu Yang gradually becomes more individualistic, and his grades begin to fall as well. School principal Jiang Li strengthens his education of Lu Yang and the other boys, while continuing to oppose Wu An's individualistic thinking. Lu Yang at last comes to realize his mistakes and returns to his school soccer team.

1159. *Little Soldier Zhang Ge (Xiao Bing Zhang Ge)*

1963. Beijing Film Studio. B & W. 11 Reels. Direction: Cui Wei, Ouyang Hongying. Screenplay: Xu Guangyao. Cinematography: Nie Jing. Art Direction: Qin Wei, Cheng Rongyuan. Music: Liu Zuang. Sound: Wang Yunhua. Cast: An Jisi as Zhang Ge, Wu Keqing as Fatty, Li Xiaoyan as Yuying, Zhang Ping as Zhong Liang, Zhang Ying as Luo Jinbao, Yu Shaokang as the District Director

During World War II, in central Hebei Province, a little boy named Zhang Ge witnesses his grandmother's execution by the Japanese for having given shelter to soldiers of the Eighth Route Army. Soon after, the Japanese capture his uncle Zhong Liang, an Eighth Route Army reconnaissance company commander. To save his uncle and revenge his grandmother, the boy goes to live with the guerrilla army. In one battle, Zhang Ge finds an enemy pistol, but he violates discipline by keeping the gun for himself instead of turning it in. While scouting the enemy's defense of a town, he is himself detained for interrogation, but he is able to get away and with the information he has gained, coordinates the guerrilla's successful attack on the enemy base. His Uncle Zhong is rescued. After the battle, Zhang Ge turns in the pistol he had hidden to the army. His actions lead the district director to officially announce Zhang Ge's acceptance as an Eight Route Army scout, and issues the pistol back to him.

1160. *Little Treasure (Bao Bei)*

1981. Jiangsu Film Studio. Color. 8 Reels. Direction: Guang Chunlan. Screenplay: Chen Tongyi, Tang Junhua. Cinematography: Dan Xingliang, Zhang Pingqiang. Art Direction: Liu Mintai. Music: Chen Pengnian. Sound: Feng Kaitan. Cast: Liu Dong as Pang Jun, Cheng Jun as Chen Meijuan, Ma Junqing as Teacher He

Chen Meijuan adores her only child, her son Pang Jun. However, she mothers him so much that he is often teased at school about being tied to her apron strings. At summer camp, Pang Jun starts swimming lessons, but when the mother hears about it she becomes frightened and comes to the camp to bring him home. She falls into the lake and is saved from drowning by the children. From this rescue, Pang Jun really learns to swim. Chen Meijun thinks about Teacher He's words, that children must learn some things away from books and classroom, and she begins to understand.

Little Weather Station see *Young Masters of the Great Leap Forward*

1161. *The Little White Flag Dispute (Xiao Bai Qi De Feng Bo)*

1956. Shanghai Film Studio. B & W. 6 Reels. Direction: Gao Heng. Screenplay: Bao Shi, based on the novel by Ji Xuexu. Cinematography: Shen Xilin, Dian Guohao. Art Direction: Huang Jianfeng, Wu Qiwen. Music: Liang Hanguang. Sound: Ren Xingliang. Cast: Jiang Tianliu as Ye Junyin, Li Wei as Li Liangyu, Wu Yin as Liangyu's mother, Jiang Shan as Uncle Zhengde, Wang Ti as Xiao Lin, Cao Duo as Dalong

In their cooperative association, Li Liangyu

is head of production and his wife Ye Junyin is the co-op's deputy head. When the co-op holds a work competition, Li Liangyu's crew concentrates on doing the fastest job of hoeing weeds, and consequently they leave quite a few. Uncle Zheng of the judging committee does not want to damage his friendship with Li, so he awards their effort a red flag anyway. When Junyin hears others' negative comments about this, she goes to see the land herself, and replaces the red flag with a little white flag which means her husband's crew should do it over. Yuliang completely loses his temper over this, for he thinks she is doing it just to irritate him. But he later is moved by his wife's impartiality and her desire for him to excel. He comes to realize his error, so he and his crew redo the land, and this time everyone is agreed they should be the winners. This time, Junyin awards them a red flag, and after this little dispute, the couple loves and respects each other more than ever.

1162. *A Little Witness (Ti Xin Diao Dan)*

1992. Shanghai Film Studio & Nanchang Film & Television Creation Institute Co-Production. Color. Letterboxed. 9 Reels. Direction and Screenplay: Zhang Gang. Cinematography: Zhang Jian. Art Direction: Wang Renchen. Music: Xu Jingxin. Sound: Liu Guangjie. Costume: Dai Yili, Wang Huiling. Makeup: Fang Fang, Zhou Liangeng. Cast: Wen Kai as A Man, Hu Zongqi as Guo Tie, Ni Yuanyuan as Weiwei, Wu Mian as Chen Yu

A little girl named Weiwei happens to see a man killing another man. When the killer Guo Tie realizes there is a witness to his crime, he chases after the girl. She runs to the house of a man named A Man, who takes her in not knowing she is in danger. Guo Tie also shows up, but faints from the exertion of his previous struggle with his victim. With the help of police officer Chen Yu, A Man sets out to find Weiwei's parents. They also take Guo Tie into custody. It turns out that Guo Tie is not really a villain, but a man pushed to his limit: the man he was trying to kill was his boss Qian, who had raped Guo's wife. Fortunately, Qian survives. Guo is sent to prison for a year, and after his release he and A Man become good friends with Weiwei.

1163. *Liu Fei's Will (Liu Fei De Yi Shu)*

1988. August First Film Studio. Color. Wide Screen. 10 Reels. Direction: Yan Jizhou. Screenplay: Li Jing. Cinematography: Zhu Lutong. Art Direction: Jiang Zhenkui. Music: Li Weicai. Sound: Shen Guorui. Cast: Ying Xin as Liu Fei, Zhao Hongna as Leng Hui, Zhang Xiaoli as Qu Lili, Tian Hua as Mama

Liu Fei is a bright and pretty Chinese student in Japan. Among her classmates are Taiwanese student Leng Hui and her boyfriend, and others. But these people she thinks of as friends are actually international spies. Liu Fei's father is an important person in China's national defense industry, so their objective is to gain vital intelligence through Liu Fei. They eventually recruit Liu Fei into helping the spy agency that employs them. Liu Fei in turn tries to recruit another girl Qu Lili into the agency, but Qu is a patriotic girl. She refuses to join the organization and urges Liu Fei to confess her errors. Female chief investigator Lin Xiao arrives to save Qu's life, and discovers Liu's involvement. Leng Hui is arrested at the airport. Liu Fei in despair commits suicide. She leaves behind a will in which she expresses her regrets.

1164. *Liu Haishu (Liu Hai Shu)*

1993. Pearl River Film Studio. Color. Letterboxed. Direction: Yao Shoukang, Zhang Xin. Screenplay: Zhang Xin, Xu Shehua. Cast: Ma Xiaowei

In 1921, Shanghai Art Institute director Liu Haishu and young teacher Ding Xiao advocate the school add a course in painting the nude female form. A courageous girl named Li Xiaoer becomes China's first nude model. Li is subjected to massive personal stress for going against tradition in this way. Liu and Ding also suffer personal attack and public ridicule. More than a half-century later, Ding Xiao is now the institute director, and with the aged Liu Haishu's support she advocates the school try it again. Ding's granddaughter brings them A Kui, a girl from the countryside, who makes a perfect figure model. A Kui is also subjected to attack from all directions, but she says her grandmother understands and supports her, which gives her the strength to withstand the criticism. Ding and Liu later find that her grandmother is their first model, Li Xiaoer.

Little Soldier Zhang Ge. Little Zhang Ge (An Jisi) joins the anti–Japanese resistance after witnessing his grandmother's execution by the invaders. 1963. Beijing Film Studio.

1165. *Liu Hulan (Liu Hu Lan)*

1950. Northeast Film Studio. B & W. 9 Reels. Direction: Feng Bailu. Screenplay: Lin Shan. Cinematography: Yan Dekui. Art Direction: Liu Xuerao. Music: Chang Sumin, Liu Wenjin. Sound: Zhao Hongjun. Costume: Liu Jingying. Makeup: Bi Zepu. Cast: Hu Zongwun as Liu Hulan, Lu Xiaoya as the child Liu Hulan, Pan Demin as Liu's father, Zhang Qi as Liu's grandfather, Zhuang Yan as Liu's mother, Sun Yuezhi as Guihua's mother, Yuan Shida as the landlord, Huang Lin as the landlord's wife, Ma Lu as Comrade Sun, Gao Jun as Xiao Qing

As Liu Hulan grows up in rural Shanxi province, she hears many stories of revolution from Red Army soldier Comrade Sun, which inspires her to become a revolutionary. In the course of her work, she meets and falls in love with a young man named Xiao Qing. When the Japanese occupy their county, Xiao Qing joins the Red Army and Liu Hulan joins the resistance. Her hard work and success win her a position of leadership and CPC membership. After the Japanese surrender, Xiao Qing returns and the two lovers are reunited, but only briefly, for the Communist-Nationalist civil war starts. Xiao Qing returns to the army, and

Liu Hulan joins other civilians in supply work. However, she is captured by the Nationalists and is executed. Mao Zedong writes that she "was born to greatness and died honorably."

1166. *Liu Mingzhu (Liu Ming Zhu)*

1964. Pearl River Film Studio & Hong Kong Hongtu Film Studio Co-Production. Color. 12 Reels. Direction: Tan Youliu. Screenplay: Zhen Wenfeng, based on a popular legend. Cinematography: Shen Minghui. Art Direction: Huang Zhiming. Music: Ma Hui. Sound: Lin Guang. Cast: Fan Zehua as Liu Mingzhu, Zhang Changcheng as Hai Rui, Hong Biao as the empress, Chen Wanxi as Zhu Houpan, Zhu Chuzhen as Hai Rui's wife, Wun Miaohui as Yingfeng

In the 1620s, General Liu Guangcheng is murdered by evil official Zhu Houpan. Seeking justice, Liu's daughter Liu Mingzhu travels to Beijing with some evidential documents her father had left. When she arrives, she happens to meet Hai Rui, an official famed in Chinese history for his honesty and devotion to justice, and he gives her temporary lodging in his home. Hai Rui obtains an audience with the empress for Liu Mingzhu, at which Liu presents the evidence which proves Zhu Houpan's crimes. But the empress only dismisses Zhu Houpan from his official position. Liu Mingzhu, unable to control her hatred for Zhu, attacks and murders him on the spot. The furious empress wants to charge Liu Mingzhu, but Hai Rui and other officials all protect her. The empress then dismisses the case and has the girl ejected from court. Hai Rui resigns his position, and proudly leaves with Mingzhu.

1167. *Liu Shaoqi's 44 Days (Liu Shao Qi De Si Shi Si Tian)*

1992. Xiaoxiang Film Studio. Color. Wide Screen. 10 Reels. Direction: Zhang Jinbiao. Screenplay: Liu Xingliang, Luo Zhijun, Peng Lunhu and Tan Dongmei, based on events in the life of CPC leader Liu Shaoqi (1898–1974). Cinematography: Xu Hongliang. Art Direction: Tan Shengshan. Music: Liu Zhengqiu. Sound: Liu Yishen, Yu Wei. Costume: Lei Xiaoxiang, Jiang Jianping. Makeup: Zhang Yinghua. Cast: Guo Fazen as Liu Shaoqi, Liu Xiujie as Wang Guangmei, Shao Xiaowei as Yu Manzhen, Li Wei as Deng Desheng, Meng Chunjiang as Zhao Xing, Wang Ren as Mao Zedong

From April 1st to May 15th, 1961, Liu Shaoqi, Vice Chairman of the CPC and President of the PRC, makes an inspection tour of rural Hunan a province he had left 40 years ago. He is accompanied by his wife Wang Guangmei, who serves as his secretary. During his 44 days' stay there, Liu Shaoqi visits the farmhouses and fields, listens to what the ordinary people say and shows concern for their well-being. During his investigation, he uncovers problems like falsified production statistics and finds ways to improve the lot of the peasants.

1168. *Liupan Mountain (Liu Pan Shan)*

1978. Xi'an Film Studio. Color. 11 Reels. Direction: Guo Yangting, Liu Bing. Screenplay: Yao Yizhuang. Cinematography: Chen Wancai. Art Direction: Zhang Xiaohui, Lu Guangcai. Music: Wei Ruixiang, Li Zhonghan. Sound: Che Zhiyuan. Cast: Zhang Ping as Hai Laoning, Chen Xuegang as Hong Zhen, Gao Fang as Guihui, Ding Weiming as Hada Ma, Wang Suhong as Xi Jicao, Li Chaoyang as Haqi Zhi, Duan Yuanhe as Nashi

In October 1935, China's worker and farmer Red Army crosses through Liupan Mountain on its way North to resist the Japanese invasion. Despotic local landlord Nashi is hostile to the Red Army, and spreads rumors about it as it passes through the area. Old hunter Hai Laoning and his adopted daughter Xi Jicao welcome the Red Army, and under the tutelage of the Red Army commander they oppose the landlord. When the Red Army arrives at Nashi's mansion they release all the people he has jailed in the compound. In a small back room in his mansion they find a sick and elderly woman working. It turns out she is Xi Jicao's biological mother, confined by Nashi 14 years earlier when she had refused to become his concubine. After the Red Army defeats warlord Ma Bufang's army, mother and daughter are reunited.

1169. *Live for Life (Mou Sheng Qi Yu)*

1992. Changchun Film Studio. Color. Letterboxed. 9 Reels. Direction: Lu Shaolian, Yang Xiaodan. Screenplay: You Xuezhong. Cinematography: Li Junyan. Music: Wang Meng. Sound: Wang Baosheng. Costume: Yang Shu, Chen Xiaoling. Makeup: Liang Ling, Zhao Liying. Cast: Chang Rong as Qian Weiyi, Liu Bing as Ouyang, Geng Ge as Guo Qianyu, Dai Xiaoxu as Pan Heping

Four graduate students, three men and a woman, decide to spend their summer break in the city. They hope to earn some money while gaining experience in the real world. Each has an adventure, sometimes comic, sometimes serious: in a foreign joint-venture company, as a nightclub waiter, as part of an ambulance crew and as an assistant soccer coach. When they meet again at the train station to return to campus, they have all grown by experience, and feel the world has been their classroom.

1170. *Living a Vagabond Life (Chuang Jiang Hu)*

1984. Tianjin Film Studio & Tianjin People's Art Troupe. Color. Letterboxed. 10 Reels. Direction: Chen Fan, Fang Rong. Screenplay: Wu Zhuguang. Cinematography: Yang Chong, Yang Delin. Art Direction: Dong Jingwen. Music: Gao Wei. Sound: Zhou Yunling. Cast: Li Baotian as Zhang Letian, Zhang Anli as Yang Caixia, Zhen Dan as Zhang Yiting, Li Fengping as Commander Li, Han Yuanyuan as Ying Lingzi

During World War II, Zhang Yiting is patriarch of an opera troupe in Tianjin. His daughter Ying Linzi, the troupe's leading lady, announces she will marry Nationalist Army Commander Li and retire from performing. This infuriates her father. Meanwhile, Zhang Yiting's godson Zhang Letian is in love with another young woman in the troupe, Yang Caixia. They marry and soon have a baby. Ying Linzi's dreams of happiness are shattered when she learns that her lover already has a wife, and in addition has a reputation within the army as being a cold-blooded killer, a battlefield butcher. The troupe is bullied by the authorities to the point they must leave Tianjin. They move to Qingdao, but things go even worse there, so bad that Zhang Letian sells his blood to support them. His wife Yang Caixia also decides she must sacrifice to help out, and sells herself to a corrupt government official as his mistress. Zhang Yitian's health declines. After the war, things begin to change. The troupe returns to Tianjin, where Lingzi's false lover Commander Li is arrested and executed by the Eighth Route Army for war crimes and collaborating with the Japanese. Caixia leaves the man to whom she had sold herself, and runs to rejoin the troupe.

1171. *The Living and Dead Fa Wang (aka My Flying Wife) (Yin Yang Fa Wang)*

1992. Beijing Film Studio & Hong Kong Xin Baoda Film Company Ltd. Co-Production. Color. Wide Screen. 9 Reels. Direction: Hu Jinquan. Screenplay: Hu Jinquan and Zhong Acheng. Cinematography: Pan Deye. Art Direction: Wang Jixian, Liang Huasheng. Music: Mo Fan. Cast: Zhen Shaoqiu as Wang Shunsheng, Wang Zuxian (Joey Wang) as You Feng, Hong Jinbao (Samo Hung) as Taiyi Shangren, Liu Xun as Yuqin the Taoist Priest, Lin Zhengyin as Lin Zhengren, Jia Qingfang as Wang's wife; also: Zhang Yaoyang (Roy Cheung), Yuan Jieying (Fennie Yuen), Huang Guangliang (Tommy Wong)

A scholar named Wang Shunsheng saves a woman You Feng from suicide by drowning and takes her home, but soon finds she is a ghost. In a previous life she had been an actress, persecuted to death by a man with magic powers. Now she is seeking vengeance on the man who persecuted her, as well as Scholar Wang for intervening to save her, as her own suicide would have permitted her son's reincarnation. Wang asks Yuqin the Taoist priest to help her, after which she returns to the world

of the dead. Shortly thereafter, Wang's wife presents him with a baby boy, who may be the reincarnation of the actress's son.

1172. *Living Dream (Qian Niu Hua)*

1995. Shanghai Film Studio in association with China Network Group. Color. Letterboxed. 104 minutes. Direction: Hu Xueyang. Screenplay: Hu Xueyang. Cinematography: Ju Jiazhen. Art Direction: Xue Jianna. Music: Su Junjie. Sound: Feng Deyao. Cast: Jindao Xingxing as Xiao Tu (Rabbit), Zhang Mengxin as aunt Lianzi, Chang Rong as Shuichuan, Chen Duo as Great-uncle, Zhou Tao as Shui Zhuzi, Zhang Jing as Weigu, Fu Lihua as "My" mother

A story of his childhood told in the first person by a young man, "I." Twenty years ago, the then nine-year-old narrator is sent to live temporarily in his parents' home town. He is assigned to the care of Lianzi, a girl just graduated from high school. He also meets an aggressive young man, Shuichuan, who secretly steals and hides Lianzi's underwear. The little boy's fondness for Lianzhi prompts him to tell Shuichuan to stop this practice, in exchange for which Shuichuan whips him. Later, while she is taking an ox to the veterinarian, Shuichuan attacks Lianzhi and rapes her, then notices she has stopped breathing during the ordeal. He buries her, leaving the ox as the only witness. The ox leads the little boy to the spot, and he digs her up in time for her to recover. In the spring, the boy leaves for school, and he and Lianzhi part as close friends.

1173. *Living Forever in Burning Flames (Lie Huo Zhong Yong Sheng)*

1965. Beijing Film Studio. B & W. 15 Reels. Direction: Shui Hua. Screenplay: Zhou Jiao, based on the novel "Red Rock" by Luo Guangbing and Yang Yiyan. Cinematography: Zhu Jinming. Art Direction: Qin Wei. Music: Zhu Jianer. Sound: Cai Jun, Zhang Jiake. Cast: Zhao Dan as Xu Yunfeng, Yu Lan as Sister Jiang, Li Jian as Xu's mother, Zhang Ping as Li Jingyuan, Cai Anan as Hua Wei, Lin Ying as Sun Mingxia, Cai Songling as Hua's wife

In 1948, on the eve of the liberation of Chongqing, the husband of Communist Party member Sister Jiang is killed by government agents. Although grieving deeply, she goes to the Huaying Mountain area to participate in the armed struggle in the countryside there. Later, Sister Jiang and the Chongqing undercover Party organization leader Xu Yunfeng are betrayed by a traitor and arrested. Government intelligence agents try unsuccessfully to intimidate or turn Xu Yunfeng. They torture Sister Jiang, but she refuses to divulge any information about the Communist underground. At the beginning of 1949, the PLA crosses the Yangtse River, meaning Chongqing will soon be liberated. Xu Yunfeng and Sister Jiang lead the other prisoners in planning a mass prison break. Their liaison with the outside is the regional Party Secretary Hua Zhiliang, who has worked at the prison as a cook and for 15 years has pretended to be crazy. But just before the break is to take place, Xu Yunfeng and Sister Jiang are executed. Hua Zhiliang leads the prison break and links up with the Huaying Mountain guerrilla troop. Hua Zhiliang is also reunited with his wife, the legendary "double handgun old lady," commander of the Huaying Mountain guerrilla troop.

1174. Local Residents (Xiang Min)

1986. Pearl River Film Studio. Color. 9 Reels. Direction: Hu Bingliu. Screenplay: Zhang Zhiliang. Cinematography: Han Xingyuan. Art Direction: Zhang Zhichu. Music: Cheng Dazhao. Sound: Lu Minwen. Cast: Wei Beiyuan as Han Xuanzhi, Zhao Zhili as Wang Cai, Lin Xiaojie as Bai Ying, Chen Rui as Erbei, Guo Jianguo as Gousheng, Huang Yating as Huazhi

Two older men, retired teacher Han Xuanzhi and businessman Wang Cai, engage in a competition for respect and influence among their fellow residents of the town of Jiaode in the Qingling Mountains.

1175. Lonely Sword (Du Gu Jiu Jian)

1994. Xi'an Film Studio, Hong Kong Xianda Film Company Co-Production. Color. Letterboxed. Direction: Yu Mingsheng. Screenplay: Li Mingcai, Liang Jianhao. Cinematography: Zhen Zhaoqiang, Shang Zhaolin, Huang Baowen. Art Direction: Liu Mingxiong. Music: Zeng Yefa. Sound: Zeng Jingxiang. Cast: Li Jiaxin as the Jin Princess, Liu Ximing as the Xia Prince; also: Yang Lijing, Li Zixiong, Liu Xun

At an ancient time when China is wracked by frequent wars among various small kingdoms, the princess of the Kingdom of Jin is in flight from the enemy. She carries an extremely valuable jade flute which could help her king-

dom's recovery. She is saved by the prince of the Xia Kingdom, who has a sword emblematic of his country's power. They join to fight the enemy Yang kingdom. Xia is ordered to kill the princess, but realizes this is not the sort of life he wants. The prince and princess make their own peace, throw the sword and flute into a deep canyon, and leave to start a new life together.

1176. Lonely Traveler (Tian Ya Gu Lu)

1986. Shanxi Film Studio. Color. Letterboxed. 10 Reels. Direction: Guangbu Daoerji. Screenplay: Huang Shiyin, Sai Fu. Cinematography: Liu Xing, Yan Zhubing. Music: Wu Daming. Sound: Hong Di. Cast: Sun Fengyin as Lan Hua, Zong Ping as Yuan Ye, Hou Hua as Liangzi, Liu Runcheng as Old Jia, Zhao Yuqi as Mr. Qin

1177. The Loner (Gu Du De Mou Sha Zhe)

1986. Guangxi Film Studio. Color. Color. 10 Reels. Direction: Zhang Junchao. Screenplay: Ci Minghe. Cinematography: Qin Jinghong, Xiao Feng. Art Direction: Zhang Yafang. Music: Chen Yuanlin. Sound: Lin Lin. Cast: Sun Genga as the Loner, Dong Xiaodong as Canna, Liu Qixin as Elder Brother, Zhou Chuanshi as Huang Zhang

In Guangxi province in 1884, 20 years after the failure of the Taiping Rebellion, former Taiping general Huang Zhang is now serving in the army of the Qing (Manchu) emperor. He returns to Guangxi to celebrate his mother's birthday, but to forestall any possible attempts on his life, he orders the arrest of all descendants of Taiping leaders, resulting in the deaths of many innocent people. To avenge the massacre, a kung fu hero and Taiping descendant known only as the Loner takes on the job of killing Huang Zhang. After many plot twists, the Loner fulfills his mission during the old lady's birthday party.

1178. Long Live Women (Nu Ren Wan Sui)

1994. Tianshan Film Studio. Color. Letterboxed. 10 Reels. Direction: Zhang Gang. Screenplay: Zhang Gang. Cinematography: Shen Xilin, Zhang Jian. Art Direction: Mei Kunping. Music: Dong Weijie. Sound: Liu Guangjie. Costume: Zhou Wenzhe. Makeup: Yuan Guimin, Yan Huiming. Cast: Hou Changrong as Aman,

Living Forever in Burning Flames. Communist organizers Xu Yunfeng (Zhao Dan, left) and Sister Jiang (Yu Lan) bravely face their upcoming execution. 1965. Beijing Film Studio.

Zhong Ping as Huo Lanlan, Niu Ben as Zhong Yuanzhang, Li Ding as Huo Qingquan, Hui Juanyan as An Chunlan, Zhou Liangliang as Tao Xiuzhi, Fang Qingzuo as Chen Sanyi, Dong Huaiyi as Governor Liu, Ma Xiaoning as Feng Haonian

Ignorance combined with a traditional desire for sons has left some parts of China with a serious gender imbalance. A job-seeking man named Gao Aman disguises himself as a woman in order to get a job in a daycare center, while a woman name An Chunlan goes about dressed as a man to avoid excessive male suitors. A series of funny incidents occur which teach people some lessons about their own anti-female prejudices.

1179. *The Long March (Jin Sha Shui Pai)*

1994. Yunnan Nationalities Film Studio. Color. Wide Screen. 11 Reels. Direction: Zhai Junjie. Screenplay: Gan Zhaopei. Cinematography: Guo Jingliang, Huang Zuxing. Art Direction: Ren Huixing, Liu Wei. Music: Xiao Geng, Cao Pengju. Sound: Zhang Lifang. Costume: Zhang Heru, Jiang Xiaoyun. Makeup: Yang

Meixin. Cast: Li Kejian as Mao Zedong, Qi Rong as Wang Fei, Wang Limin as Fu Lianzhang, Wang Hui as He Zizhen, Yang Gang as Hou Zhen, Zhang Hui as Qian Xijun, Li Yunliang as He Mingren

In February of 1935, the Chinese Communist forces are beaten back, and the revolution is at its lowest point. Mao Zedong leads his forces to the southwest. Mao and his wife He Zhizhen have difficulties in their personal lives as well, and are forced to give up their newborn baby daughter while they are on the march. Then He Zhizhen's brother is executed for violating strict rules of conduct laid down by Mao. He Zhizhen is later badly injured, and for a time is near death. Years later, after the People's Republic is founded, Mao searches for his abandoned daughter, but never finds her.

1180. *The Long March (Lu Man Man)*

1981. August First Film Studio. Color. 10 Reels. Direction: Cai Jiwei, Gu Dexian. Screenplay: Li Maolin, Du Zhimian, Tang Wei. Cinematography: Cai Jie, Xu Lianqin. Art Direction:

Ren Huixing, Fei Lansheng. Music: Lu Yuan. Sound: Wu Hanbiao. Cast: Jin Xing as Zhu Hua, Tang Guoqiang as Cheng Kang, Zhao Xiuli as Sister Xi, Huang Meiying as Hu Xiangyu, Bai Zhidi as Hu Yuan

In the early 1920s, young farmer Zhu Hua fights back when bullied by a landlord and for this is driven from his hometown. He joins a warlord army and later gets the chance to study at a military school. There he meets progressive, revolutionary soldier Cheng Kang. With Cheng Kang's help, Zhu Hua is introduced to progressive thinking and gains in political awareness. After he graduates, Zhu Hua is assigned to be a part of Chiang Kaishek's Northern Expeditionary Army. When the army arrives at the city of Wuchang, Zhu Hua is surprised to find Cheng Kang one of the leaders attacking it. Cheng is a member of the Communist Party, at that time still the Nationalist Party's left wing, and he teaches Zhu Hua some of his party's political theory. After Chiang Kaishek turns on the Communists in 1927, and many party members and their sympathizers are killed, Zhu Hua breaks with the Nationalists, goes over to the Communists and leads his regiment in rebellion.

1181. *Long Time Friendship (You You Gu Ren Qing)*

1984. Beijing Film Studio. Color. Wide Screen. 11 Reels. Direction: Wang Yan. Screenplay: Wang Yan, Ding Rongyan. Cinematography: Ru Shuiren. Art Direction: Hao Jingyuan. Music: Du Mingxin, Zhang Peiji. Sound: Wang Yunhua. Cast: Ding Xiaoyi as Peng Dehuai, Ma Changyu as Jiang Zhigu, Shen Dezhen as Zhu Yuzhi, Fang Shu as Gutian, Zhang Baoru as Grandpa Ding, Niu Shengwen as "Little Dog," Yang Jiabao as Commander Xun, Wang Yan as Zhou Xingyu

After his pardon from false charges, old cadre Jiang Zhigu takes his wife Zhu Yuzhi and their daughter Gutian to revisit the CPC's old revolutionary base in northern Shanxi province. They first encounter an old man who had been a cook in the army of General Peng Dehuai, then they meet "Little Dog," the general's onetime bodyguard, now a commander. At Yan'an, the family meets an old man Zhou Xingyu, once a Nationalist division commander who was captured, then became an admirer and follower of Peng Dehuai for the second half of his life. After finishing his visit to the former base, Jiang Zhigu deeply

misses Peng Dehuai, and is inspired by Peng's memory.

1182. *Long Yun and Chiang Kaishek (Long Yun He Jiang Jie Shi)*

1989. August First Film Studio. Color. 10 Reels. Letterboxed. Direction: Ren Pengyuan. Screenplay: Wang Chaozhu, Wang Zunxi. Cinematography: Shen Jie. Art Direction: Liu Yushu. Music: Lu Zulong. Sound: Zhen Minze. Cast: Qi Mengshi as Long Yun, Sun Feihu as Chiang Kaishek

After the Japanese defeat in World War II, Chiang Kaishek resumes his pre-war campaign to eradicate the Chinese Communists. One of his highest-ranking generals is Long Yun, a warlord known as the "King of Yunnan" because he has governed it for so many years. But Long has grown increasingly sympathetic to the ideas of the Communist Party and has become increasingly liberal and democratic in his administration. Chiang views the Yunnan warlord as a threat, one he wants to be rid of, so he reassigns the bulk of Long's Yunnan Army to Vietnam, then has his loyal crony Du Yuming take this opportunity to foment a rebellion in Yunnan against Long's administration. Chiang then sends the remainder of the Yunnan Army to fight the Communists in Northeast China, and forces Long Yun to transfer to Taiwan. With the help of an American friend, Long Yun is able to escape and flees to Hong Kong instead. Chiang refuses to give up, and sends agents to Hong Kong to kill Long Yun. Long Yun escapes the assassination attempt, then holds a press conference at which he exposes the corruption of the Nationalist government and calls for an uprising in Yunnan.

1183. *Long Zhong (Long Zhong)*

1982. Ningxia Film Studio. Color. 10 Reels. Direction: Luo Tai. Screenplay: Zhang Xianliang, Luo Tai. Cinematography: Wun Zhixian. Art Direction: Ma Gaiwi. Music: Yang Shuzheng. Sound: Jin Wenjiang. Cast: Guo Yuntai as Long Zhong, Yu Ping as Mu Yushan, Li Yan as Jiang Lu, Ren Xiaying as Zhen Fulin, Xie Wanhe as Director Sun, Yang Shulin as Si Guang

When Long Zhong assumes his new post as Party Secretary on a Northwest China collective farm, he finds a depressing situation: morale is very low, and the unit has suffered massive economic losses. His investigation attributes the problems to two things: leftover bad feelings from the 10 years of Cultural Revolution and shortcomings of the economic management system. Long Zhong adopts some firm countermeasures, including downsizing his management staff and implementing a contract responsibility system. This bring Zhen Fulin and some others into conflict with Long, and subjects him to personal attacks as well. When provincial Party Secretary Jiang throws his support behind Long, he renews his resolve to continue his reforms.

1184. *The Longest Rainbow (Zui Chang De Cai Hong)*

1994. Fujian Film Studio. Color. Letterboxed. 9 Reels. Direction: Ge Xiaoying. Screenplay: Du Xiaoou. Cinematography: Zhang Guoqing, Wang Shen. Art Direction: Zhao Shaoping. Music: Zhang Shaotong. Sound: Guan Jian, Chen Binglian. Costume: Lu Yueying. Makeup: Hu Baojia. Cast: Man Xuchun as Shang Jing, Xu Fei as Xu Fei, Cao Chun as Geda, Zeng Guohua as Teacher Mo, Cui Yong as Xu Fei's father, Luo Tuo as Grandpa Gao, Xu Zhicheng as Party Secretary Lu, Li Yapeng as Xiao Hou

Shang Jing is a child with musical talent. Particularly good at the guitar, he dreams of becoming another Elvis Presley. He quits school to work on this, but one day a dedicated teacher in a mobile school convinces the boy that musicians can benefit by studying other subjects than just music. Shang Jing returns to school and joins the school's chorus. Later, the chorus director selects Shang Jing to represent the school in a Beijing singing competition.

1185. *Longing for Home (Xiang Qing)*

1981. Pearl River Film Studio. Color. 10 Reels. Direction: Hu Bingliu, Wang Jing. Screenplay: Wang Yimin. Cinematography: Liang Xiongwei. Art Direction: Li Xin. Music: Yang Shuzheng. Sound: Jiang Shaoqi. Cast: Huang Xiaolei as Tian Gui, Ren Yexiang as Cuicui, Wu Wenhua as Tian Qiuye, Huang Jingtang as Liao Yiping, Wang Jing as Kuang Hua

When they leave to participate in the revolution, Kuang Hua and his wife Liao Yiping leave their son with a neighbor woman, a kindly and honest peasant woman named Tian Qiuye. She lovingly raises him as her own son, called Tian Gui, and also adopts a daughter called Cuicui. The children grow up together and eventually fall in love. As the village prepares for their wedding, word arrives that Tian Gui's birth parents are alive and looking for their son. Tian Qiuye postpones the wedding and sends Tian Gui to the city to meet his parents. It turns out that Kuang Hua and Liao Yiping now have important positions in the city, and Liao Yiping intends to use her excellent political and economic situation to change her son and build a bright future for him. However, Tian Gui can think only for his adoptive mother and his fiancee, both of whom he misses terribly. Kuang Hua, who had been busy at work, realizes his wife's plans have made Tian Gui unhappy, so he gives the boy permission to bring Tian Qiuye and Cuicui to the city. But Liao Yiping sends a letter which gives only Cuicui permission to come. Tian Qiuye keeps her pain to herself, wanting Tian Gui to unite with his parents. She comes to the city later and by chance finds that Liao Liping is a woman she had risked her own life to save during the war. Even then, she does not speak out. Kuang Hua criticizes his wife, and he and others point out the realities to her. She begins to change her attitude, and at last everyone goes together to find Tian Qiuye before she leaves the city.

Best Picture, 1982 Hundred Flowers Awards.

1186. *Look at Me, Miss (Gu Niang, Wang Zhe Wo)*

1985. Beijing Film Studio. Color. 10 Reels. Direction: Xing Rong. Screenplay: Da Li. Cinematography: Yu Zhenyu. Art Direction: Yang Yuhe. Music: Wang Ming. Sound: Wang Yunhua. Cast: Guo Xuxin as Xu Yanfu, Chen Yongjian as Lu Jiaqi, Niu Na as Cai Lanzhi, Ma Jing as Cui Jie, Shan Yun as Ding Ruoyi, Zhu Decheng as Xiao Yixiong

Doctor Xu Yanfu is justly renowned for the excellent quality of the eye care he gives his patients. But he has a secret guilt: while out boating eight years before, he had struck a small fishing boat. The fisherman had been fatally injured, but his small daughter survived. The doctor had fled in a panic, and has lived with his guilt ever since. One day, a young female patient is brought in for treatment of an injury to her eyes; the doctor recognizes the girl, Cai Lanzhi, as the little girl on the other boat. Although he can restore her sight surgically, Doctor Xu knows that when she recovers she might recognize him as the man who caused the fatal accident. Xu struggles with himself, and at last decides to do what he can for the girl. When he is certain she will recover her vision, he discusses the matter with his wife, and with her support the doctor goes to turn himself in.

1187. *Looking for a Real Man (Xun Zhao Nan Zhi Han)*

1987. Guangxi Film Studio. Color. 9 Reels. Direction: Zeng Xueqiang. Screenplay: Sha Yexin, Sha Yinnong. Cinematography: Meng Xiongqiang, Cai Xiaopeng. Art Direction: Tan Zhong. Music: Jin Fuzhai. Sound: Li Yunping. Cast: Wu Mian as Shu Huan, Liu Wenzhi as Jiang Yi, Lu Xiaohe as Zhou Qiang, Li Zongqiang as Situ Wa

Sculptress Su Huan, a single woman, is looking for a real man in her life. The "Global Marriage Introduction Institute" introduces her to a man called Situ Wa, but Su Huan disappointedly drops him. She then meets Zhou Qiang, division head at a research organization, but Su Huan eventually breaks with this man because he toadies to those in power. More men are introduced to her, but for various reasons none of these relationships turn out. One day, Su Huan meets company executive Jiang Yi. Jiang Yi's ambition, self-confidence and understanding of others makes Su Huan feel that he is the one she has been seeking. However, it turns out that Jiang Yi has come to the matchmaking service seeking a girlfriend for one of his colleagues.

1188. *Looking for Shelter (Bi Nan)*

1988. Emei Film Studio. Color. Letterboxed. 10 Reels. Direction: Han Shanping, Zhou Li. Screenplay: Li Kewei, Li Gui, Yan Geling. Cinematography: Rao Ren, Luo Xun. Art Direction: Wang Longsheng. Music: Tang Qinshi. Sound: Li Jian. Cast: Feilande (American) as Father Warden, Fu Lili as Yang Liufeng, Liao Xueqiu as Hu Zuihua

In the early spring of 1938, after the atrocities at Nanjing, invading Japanese soldiers occupy a small town in south China, and begin a massacre there. In the midst of the slaughter, Father Warden takes into his church a few women seeking sanctuary. The women, unknown to the priest, are hookers Yang Liufeng and Hu Zuihua, and opera actress Xiao Caiyue. The women's rudeness and coarse behavior is definitely out of place in church, but the priest tolerates them anyway. Later, a few wounded Chinese soldiers also come to the church seeking sanctuary, and they are taken in as well. But Japanese soldiers invade the church and brutally kill the Chinese soldiers. The Japanese tell the women they will be spared if they consent to provide sexual services for the Japanese troops. Late at night, the three women walk out of the church, and while the Japanese are celebrating their victory, the three low-class women show their heroism by blowing up the Japanese soldiers and themselves.

1189. *Lord Guan (Parts 1 & 2) (Guan Gong)*

1989. Beijing Film Studio. Color. Letterboxed. 19 Reels. Direction: Yang Jiyou. Screenplay: Yang Jiyou. Cinematography: Li Yunguang, Yu Bo. Art Direction: Bian Qiyi. Music: Wang Ming. Sound: Li Guangtian. Cast: Zhao Yanmin as Kong Min, Hou Shaokui as Guan Yu, Wang Wenyou as Liu Bei, Tian Chunhu as Zhang Fei, Li Yusheng as Cao Cao, Chen Daomin as Zhou Yu

Part 1: Early in the 3rd Century A.D., the Eastern Han Dynasty was on the verge of collapse from excessive corruption. In the Kingdom of Zuo, three men, Liu Bei, Guan Yu and Zhang Fei, meet in a peach garden, take an oath as blood brothers and decide to raise an army to restore the Han regime. Part 1 tells the story of how Guan Yu loyally contributes to the expansion of Liu Bei's power and influence as he combats enemy generals Cao Cao and Yuan Shao.

Part 2: The three blood brothers make three visits to the home of General Kong Min before they at last prevail on him to join in helping Liu Bei. Cao Cao occupies the city of Jingzhou, and meets Liu Bei in battle. The result is total defeat for Cao Cao, and his army of 830,000 men is completely destroyed. Guan Yu is very kind to the defeated general, and lets him escape into exile. But Cao Cao uses this opportunity to raise a new army, and now Zhou Yu, Cao Cao and Liu Bei are once again engaged in a struggle for the country. In 213 A.D., Liu Bei establishes the Kingdom of Su, and from that point, the country is divided into three kingdoms, the Wei, the Su and the Wu.

1190. *Losing Track of "Xuebao" (Xue Bao Xia Luo Bu Ming)*

1990. Guangxi Film Studio. Color. Wide

Screen. 9 Reels. Direction: Zhao Wendeng. Screenplay: Zhou Weixian, Wang Chenggang, Fang Hongyou. Cinematography: Zhu Dingyuan, Xie Zhijun. Art Direction: Zhang Yafang. Music: Ma Ding. Sound: Lin Lin. Cast: Zhang Ning as "Polo," Hu Xiaoguang as Ertou, Liang Baoxiang as Heima, Jia Ruixin as "Hollywood," Huang Ailing as Mingming

In order to be upgraded in status by the local bureau of industry, a toy company offers a prestigious "Xuebao" brand motorcycle to a bureaucrat as a bribe. However, the employee assigned to deliver the gift loses it. Unable to go to the police, he hires "Polo," a part-time investigator, to recover the motorcycle. Polo at last finds the lost cycle and attempts to return it to the company, but to cover their bribe attempt they deny any knowledge of the matter, refuse to pay Polo and kick him out. He angrily goes to the police and offers his cooperation in the case.

1191. *The Lost Dream (Shi Qu De Meng)*

1990. Xiaoxiang Film Studio. Color. 9 Reels. Wide Screen. Direction: Dong Kena. Screenplay: Shao Hongda, Gao Junshan. Cinematography: Tu Jiakuan. Art Direction: Tan Shengshan. Music: Wang Liping, Wang Shi. Sound: Wang Yunhua. Cast: Li Kechun as Li Mengqiu, Liu Jiuhu as Chen Xiaofei

Hard-working and kind-hearted Li Mengqiu is an illiterate peasant woman. She places all her hopes for the future on her son Chen Xiaofei, planning and dreaming that the boy receive the good education which will guarantee him a bright future. Giving up a good job and leaving her husband, she moves with her son to a large city in northern China, where she finds employment as a temporary worker and soon saves 3,000 yuan to pay her son's college expenses. She is strict with her son, forcing him to study hard. But the pressure she puts on him actually retards his progress in the classroom. He fails an exam, and in her frustrated anger and worry she beats the boy, accidentally killing him. The last shot is of the woman walking across snowy fields, a red scarf across her shoulders, walking toward a vision of her son — her lost dream.

1192. *The Lost Hero (Mi Tu Ying Xiong)*

1992. Guangxi Film Studio. Color. Letterboxed. 9 Reels. Direction: Chen Jialin, Liu

Jiankui, Guo Shaoxiong. Screenplay: Hu Yuewei. Cinematography: Liu Jiankui. Art Direction: Lu Qi. Music: Gao Feng. Sound: Wang Baosheng. Costume: Zhao Li. Makeup: Ji Weihua, Yang Shudong. Cast: Chen Peisi as Chen Bide and Long Tailiang, Gao Baobao as Feifei, Zang Qian as Fang Xiaoyuan

A comedy set in 1933. At a show commemorating the Mukden Incident, which the Japanese used as an excuse to invade Northeast China, Japanese agent Long Tailiang notes that one of the actors, Chen Bide, is almost his identical twin. By exploiting the actor's patriotism, the spy gets the simple and honest Chen to kill a Chinese general by deluding him into thinking his target is really the Japanese spy. When he discovers the truth, Chen battles the spies with the help of his wife and co-performers.

1193. *The Lost Kerchief (Piao Shi De Hua Tou Jin)*

1985. Changchun Film Studio. Color. 9 Reels. Direction: Song Jiangbo. Screenplay: Xiao Yixian, Liu Jie. Cinematography: Yu Bing. Art Direction: Wei Hongyu. Music: Liu Xijin. Sound: Wun Liangyu, Luo Huailun. Cast: Yang Xiaodan as Qin Jiang, Hui Juanyan as Shen Ping

Merchant seaman Qin Jiang drifts aimlessly through life until one day he chances to meet Shen Ping, a girl on her way to start college in Beijing. Her ideals and life goals make a great impression of Qin Jiang, and when he learns she had prepared for college through self-study he vows to achieve the same goal and some day be worthy of her. Two years later, he is admitted to the same university. When he again sees Shen Ping, he is shocked at the dramatic change in her: having abandoned her previous idealistic goals, she now devotes herself to having a good time. When Qin tells her of his love for her, Shen laughs at him; she wants to date lots of men, not settle down with one. Later, when the two meet again, she now feels only pain and guilt over what she has done with her life. But Qin Jiang still offers her hope and encouragement.

1194. *Lost My Love (Yong Shi Wo Ai)*

1994. Hainan Nanyang Film Studio and Beijing Film Studio Co-Production. Color. Letterboxed. 10 Reels. Direction: Feng Xiaogang. Screenplay: Wang Shuo, Feng Xiaogang, based on the original novel of same title by Wang Shuo

(1958–). Cinematography: Wu Di. Art Direction: Feng Xiaogang. Sound: Li Bojiang. Costume: Hou Jingli. Makeup: Shen Sheng. Cast: Guo Tao as Su Kai, Xu Fan as Lin Gege, Ju Xue as Yang Yan

Taxi driver Su Kai meets flight attendants Lin Gege and Yang Yan. Su and Lin immediately fall in love, Su Kai builds a house for them and they happily make marriage plans. Then Su Kai learns he has an incurable disease, so he initiates a plan to make Gege think he is dumping her for her friend Yang Yan. Unaware of the truth, Gege is of course heart-broken. Meanwhile, Yang Yan unselfishly begins caring for Su Kai, and gives him her love. He accepts her love, and responds to her care with a renewed will to live his remaining days to the fullest. A few years later, Su Kai's ghost appears before the two women, thanking them for the love they both gave him, and wishing them happiness.

1195. *Lost Partner (Yi Shi De Ban Lu)*

1988. Changchun Film Studio. Color. 10 Reels. Director; Lu Shaolian. Screenplay: Liang Yan, Liang Xiaosheng. Cinematography: Zhong Wenmin. Art Direction: Liang Shukui. Music: Fan Weiqiang. Sound: Zhang Fengxing. Cast: Chen Ying as Xu Tianfang

Commerce Bureau Director Xu Tianfang retires, but his life is now very lonely. None of his children still live with him, and he misses his wife who died many years before. Kindly neighbor Tang Xiuyun is very sympathetic with Xu's situation, and offers him a great deal of help with household matters, but Xu still cannot shake off his loneliness. A seniors' organization eases his pain for a time by finding him some worthwhile volunteer work, but then he suffers some new blows: his son is cheated out of the money he has set aside to study abroad, and Xu Tianfang's home is burglarized. The old man sinks into depression once more.

1196. *Lost Song (Shi Qu De Ge Sheng)*

1984. Tianjin Film Studio. Color. 8 Reels. Direction: Si Wei. Screenplay: Lin Hongtong, Luo Qisheng, Sun Zonglu. Cinematography: Zuang Yongxing. Art Direction: Wang Zhongyu, Wang Tianshi. Music: Tian Feng. Sound: Feng Ling, Zhao Jun. Cast: Liu Fang as Liang Lili, Xia Mu as Tiezhu, Chang Ruyan as Mother, Liu

Wenzhi as Father, Wu Jing as Qiu Ping, Qu Yun as Grandma

Liang Lili is a talented little girl with a lovely singing voice. But she becomes depressed and stops singing after her parents divorce and her mother moves to another city. One day she returns home to find her father has taken a new wife, a woman named Qiu Ping. In addition, Qiu Ping has brought her own son into the household, a little boy named Tiezhu. At first the two children detest each other, but after a time they find mutual comfort in the fact that each misses a parent: Lili misses her mother, and Tiezhu his father. They become friends. When Tiezhu tells her that his fondest wish is to visit his father, she decides to help, and gives him all the money she has saved so he can buy a train ticket. After this, Lili decides to start saving again so she can go visit her mother.

1197. *Love Affairs at the Gingkgo Tree (Ying Xing Shu Zhi Lian)*

1988. Guangxi Film Studio. Color. Letterboxed. 10 Reels. Direction: Qin Zhiyu. Screenplay: Zhang Xuan. Cinematography: Li Duyan. Art Direction: Ma Jiesheng. Music: Jin Xiang. Sound: Li Zuwen. Cast: Wang Wei as Chang Yan, Su Ling as Meng Lianlian, Ma Chongle as Yao Mingsheng, Zhu Zhaorong as Fang Xiang

On her way to conduct an interview, "Woman's Life" magazine reporter Chang Yan gets together with her old friend, village elementary school teacher Meng Lianlian. She learns that the teacher's lover Yao Mingsheng has dumped her now that he has been promoted to work at the county Party committee. Chang Yan is disgusted with Yao's treatment of his lover, but meanwhile Chang Yan's own love life is not going so well: her lover Fang Xiang is a construction engineer, in the midst of applying for study abroad. Chang hopes very much that they will marry before he leaves, but Fang does not want to be tied down before leaving. In order to get a promotion, Yao Mingsheng marries Meng Lianlian, and when Chang meets her again, Meng is already pregnant, and although she knows Yao does not really love her, she is content. Now Fang Xiang brings his passport and proof of marriage eligibility to Chang, and proposes marriage to her. But Chang Yan suddenly decides to choose another road in life, and the two start arguing again.

1198. *Love and Death in a Place of Evil (Mo Ku Sheng Si Lian)*

1992. Beijing Film Studio. Color. Letterboxed. 10 Reels. Direction: Song Chong. Screenplay: Zhang Zhuoyan. Cinematography: Sun Yongtian. Art Direction: Wang Xingcang. Music: Xu Jingxin. Sound: Wu Guoqiang. Cast: He Zhenjun as Yang Zhengren, Xin Ying as Zhu Lirong, Qi Mengshi as Zhu Manqing, Zhao Jing as Zhu Manlin, Zhen Jiasheng as Cao Jinsheng, Ren Shen as Liu Wensi

Shanghai in 1947 is booming yet sinister, a place where money takes priority over everything and official corruption is the order of the day. Bank president and city councilman Zhu Manqin is also head of the city's largest drug ring. Initially elated when his sister Zhu Manlin's husband Liu Wensi is named head of the Shanghai anti-smuggling department, he is disappointed when Liu refuses to cooperate. So the drug dealer has his brother-in-law killed, and frames his daughter's narcotics agent boyfriend for the crime. The daughter shoots and kills her boyfriend for murdering her father, then kills herself when she learns of his innocence. The drug dealer's sister Zhu Manlin, insane with grief at having lost her entire family, turns on her evil brother and shoots him to death.

1199. *Love and Hate (Ai Yu Hen)*

1985. Beijing Film Studio. Color. 10 Reels. Direction: Li Wenhua. Screenplay: Liang Xiaosheng. Cinematography: Ru Shuiren. Art Direction: Hao Jingyuan. Music: Mu Hong. Sound: Fu Yinjie, Li Bojiang. Cast: Yu Li as Xu Jingjing, Wang Bozhao as Yulong, Zhang Ju as Ge Quande, Li Wei as Ge Xiujuan, Hou Guanqun as Dai Xun, Shao Wanlin as Xu Weicang

The film revolves around the complex relationships of four families: that of retired construction worker Ge Quande, local PSB Director Gao, local Commerce Bureau Director Xu, and Mayor Dai. Ge's son Ge Yulong had once loved Xu's daughter Xu Jingjing, but she was forced to marry the mayor's younger son Dai Zheng after the latter raped her. The mayor has a good elder son, Dai Xun, who falls in love with Ge Quande's daughter Ge Xinjuan. Xu Jingjing and Dai Zheng eventually divorce, and her father hopes she can put her painful past behind her and get back together again with Ge Yulong. Dai Zheng, meanwhile, is in league with Gao's second son Gao Zhenwu in criminal activity. When evidence of this and earlier such actions comes to their attention, the Mayor and the PSB Director decide that as good cadres they must order the arrest of their two criminal sons.

1200. *Love and Hate in Fire (Lie Huo En Yuan)*

1992. Youth Film Studio & Nanhai Film Company Co-Production. Color. Letterboxed. 9 Reels. Direction: Xie Yucheng. Screenplay: Xie Yucheng. Cinematography: Zhao Xiaoding and Yu Xiaojun. Art Direction: Zhang Zhili. Music: Hao Jian. Sound: Ju Ming, Yang Shunli. Costume: Zhao Hui. Makeup: Zhang Li, Wu Guihua. Cast: Tao Zeru as Cai Zude, Xiao Lei as Ajiao, Hu Jun as Cai Xiuming, Ma Ling as Xiao Cui, Yang Qing as Xiuyuan

In Taiwan in the 1960s, a young woman named Ajiao comes to a remote, heavily forested area to care for her paralyzed sister Xiuyuan and the latter's eight-year-old son Xiuming. One day, a massive forest fire starts, and while Ajiao is able to rescue the child, her sister perishes in the fire. A rumor spreads among local people that Ajiao and her sister's husband Cai Zude started the fire intentionally, and they are driven from the area. Twenty years pass, and Xiuming is now a prominent Taipei attorney. One day on the street he unexpectedly meets Ajiao, who has lived alone since the fire. He tells her of his suspicions about the fire, which upsets her greatly. To prove her innocence, Ajiao commits suicide right in front of him, in public. The fire of 20 years before has claimed another life.

1201. *Love and Hate in Snow Country (Xue Guo Qing Chou)*

1993. Xiaoxiang Film Studio. Color. Letterboxed. 9 Reels. Direction: Zhao Weiheng. Screenplay: Ni Feng. Cinematography: Yu Bing, Su Zaidong. Art Direction: Ju Lutian, Li Taiping. Music: Guo Xiaotian. Sound: Sheng Hongtao. Costume: Chen Hua, Hu Liya. Makeup: Liu Jiao, Tan Shumei. Cast: Ni Xuehua as Xue Gu, Lu Xiaohe as Dechang, Zhang Yechuan as Deguo, Guo Yong as Degang

Early in the 17th century, landlords and despots throughout China contend for a special seal issued by the government which conveys special privileges and powers to the person who possesses it. Decang, the warlord ruler of Ahasi, orders his servant girls Juyun and Juyue to use their exceptional kung fu skills to obtain the seal for him. Another girl, Xuegu, attempts to stop them. At last, Juyun and Juyue realize the evil of their master, and join forces with Xuegu against him.

1202. *Love and Hostility in the World (Ren Jian En Yuan)*

1987. Xiaoxiang Film Studio. Color. Letterboxed. 9 Reels. Direction: Xue Yicang, Xing Dan. Screenplay: Wang Binglin. Cinematographer: Liu Yuefei, Meng Fanjun, Li Xiaoping. Art Direction: Yang Yuhe, Zhao Zhenxue. Music: Liu Soula. Sound: Huang Yinxia, Wang Yunhua. Cast: Zhang Yan as Yang Laowu, Liu Bin as Yang Xiaohu, Sun Weiliang as Shao Qiang, Ling Yuan as Mrs. Yang, Tian Zuang as Yang Xiaorong, Han Ying as Mrs. He, Liu He as He Jinfeng

Yang Laowu is a well-known tofu maker in his community, loved and respected for his honesty and kindness to others. His son Yang Xiaohu is something quite different, selfish and spoiled by his family. When Xiaohu begins to date He Jinfeng, he passes himself off as the son of a "senior government administrator" in order to impress her. When she learns the truth, however, the girl angrily breaks off their relationship. Yang Laowu believes that his downhearted son can get her back by securing a regular job. After a series of comic incidents, Xiaohu at last finds a job at a hotel, and he and Jinfeng are reconciled. She soon gets pregnant, and the family must arrange a rush wedding for the young couple. The parents even relinquish their own room for the newlyweds. Although the parents continue to sacrifice, they still smile contentedly at seeing their son so happy.

1203. *Love and Legacy (Ai Qing Yu Yi Chan)*

1980. Xi'an Film Studio. Color. 10 Reels. Direction: Yan Xueshu. Screenplay: Li Yunliang. Cinematography: Zhang Faliang. Art Direction: Zhang Xiaohui. Music: Xie Tiyin. Sound: Chen Yudan. Cast: Zhang Yuyu as Wei Wei, Yuan Zongfu as Zhong Hai, Zhou Jingtang as Wei Jia, Han Yueqiao as Han Shasha, Bao Yanhua as Wei Cangzhou

Wei Wei, a young woman eye doctor, is in love with sailor Zhong Hai. Wei Wei's younger brother, newspaper reporter Wei Jia, only appreciates physical beauty. He has fallen for Han Shasha, a ballerina. When Zhong Hai is blinded in a training mishap, he is sent to a naval hospital in Qingdao. Wei Wei and her eye specialist father Wei Cangzhou are invited to come from Nanjing to assist in his treatment. When Wei Wei arrives she learns the patient is her lover. Zhong Hai has asked his nurse to destroy all of Wei Wei's love letters to him, for he thinks that as a blind man he will only bring her pain. But Wei Wei tells him that if his blindness should be permanent, she will always be his eyes. She informs her father of the patient's relationship to her, so her father performs the operation instead of her. Meanwhile, Han Shasha, whose life centers around money, overhears Wei Cangzhou mention that his "greatest treasure" is kept somewhere in a strongbox. She and Wei Jia begin dreaming of how they will spend all that money after inheriting it. When Wei Cangzhou learns how his son and future daughter-in-law are thinking, it so upsets him that he has a recurrence of a heart problem and dies. After his death, Wei Wei finds the unfinished manuscript of a book he had been working on, one that would have been a major contribution to vision research. Wei Wei decides to devote herself to completing her father's work. Wei Jia and Shasha finally find the strongbox, but to their shock and dismay find instead of cash a receipt for having "paid a 50,000 yuan membership fee" to the Communist Party. The dream of wealth shattered, Han Shasha leaves the Wei home. Only then does Wei Jia realize what a fool he has been.

1204. *Love and the Hero (Qi Qing Xia Lu)*

1988. Yunnan Minority Film Studio. Color. Letterboxed. 10 Reels. Direction: Wang Wenzi. Screenplay: Ni Feng, Wang Wenzi. Cinematography: Xu Shouzhen, Huang Zuxing, Ning Jiakun. Art Direction: Ju Lingtian, Xu Kaicheng. Music: Lei Lei. Sound: Liao Yongliang. Cast: Kou Zhanwen as Bai Jianqin, Li Lingyu as Ningning, Hu Yingjie as Jin Ruyi, Hou Yongsheng as Wu Shangu

Bai Jianqin, a sword-for-hire during the 17th Century reign of the Emperor Kangxi, is ordered by the emperor to kill a political rival named Wu Shangu. On route to fulfill his mission, Bai meets a female martial artist named Ningning who accompanies him for a time. It turns out that Ningning is the daughter of his target as well as her father's bodyguard. She has learned of the emperor's order, and has been alert for the killer's arrival. While she has admired and grown to love Bai Jianqin, when she learns his identity she tells him she is willing to die for her father, and he must make a choice. Bai is torn between love and duty, but at last he chooses love.

1205. *Love at Three Gorges (San Xia Qing Si)*

1983. Hubei Film Studio. Color. 9 Reels. Direction: Xu Jihong, Zhang Wenjia. Screenplay: Liu Zhendong, Wang Peigong. Cinematography: Zhao Junhong, Pan Dingshi. Art Direction: Cao Gengjun. Music: Ma Ding, Wang Yuanping. Sound: Tang Rongchun, Hu Kaixiu. Cast: Li Wenbo as Ouyang Minguang, Guo Jing as Li Lan

Cinematographer Ouyang Minguang is devoted to his art and his profession. After he marries Li Lan, a young teacher in an art institute, they begin to argue over their differing views: he strongly believes art should be founded in real life, and she does not. Li Lan decides to get away for a while, and travels to the Three Gorges site. All along the way she hears people's compliments about Ouyang's documentary film about Three Gorges, and she comes to realize his contribution. Now she brings this same understanding to her career and their life together.

1206. *Love for Amoy (Qing Gui Ludao)*

1991. Fujian Film Studio. Color. Letterboxed. 9 Reels. Direction: Hu Gai and Liu Baolin. Screenplay: Xia Feng. Cinematography: Zhen Wangong and Yang Minghua. Art Direction: Cai Dongdong. Music: Chen Danbu. Sound: Zhu Wenzhong. Cast: Zhou Lijing as Zhang Lie, Du Peng as Yang Fengwu, He Xiaoshu as Luo Wanfeng

In the booming coastal city of Xiamen (Amoy), Taiwan businessman Yang Fengwu comes seeking investment opportunities. Yang, who left the mainland in 1949, also wants to find Xiao Bao, the son he has not seen in 40 years. Yang becomes president of an electronics enterprise, and hires as his vice-president a man named Zhang Lei. Actually, Zhang Lei is Yang's son Xiao Bao, whose name was changed by the family which adopted him years before. A misunderstanding ensues when Zhang Lei believes Yang to be the man who killed his adoptive mother's husband during the Civil War. But at last father and son work it out and reconcile.

1207. *Love Hurts (Ku Cang De Lian Qing)*

1986. Fujian Film Studio. Color. 9 Reels. Direction: Wu Jianxin, Nie Xinru. Screenplay: Wu Jianxin. Cinematography: Li Shen, Li Ming. Art Direction: Tang Peijun. Music: Zhang Shaotong. Sound: Liu Guohe. Cast: Gu Yan as Yuefang, Niu Shijun as Da Han, Wang Qi as Old Grandma Chen, Zhen Zhongan as Wu Shuang, He Lin as Chen Danggui

Although her fisherman husband disappeared at sea some 12 years earlier, Yuefang is now pregnant, initiating considerable gossip among her fellow villagers and rampant speculation about who might be the father. They finally conclude it is Da Han, a bachelor stonemason. Da Han bears the accusations for Yuefang's sake, and quietly offers to marry her to solve the problem. Much to his surprise, however, Yuefang rejects his proposal. She keeps her secrets to herself, doggedly pursuing her solitary existence as she has for years. Only the ever-growing pressure of her thoughts disturbs the regular pattern of her life. Baffled and a bit hurt, Da Han is now determined to find out who impregnated Yuefang. He turns into an amateur sleuth, shadowing her and watching her home around the clock. He eventually catches the guilty party, but it turns out to be someone totally unsuspected by all. Da Han is faced with the dilemma of what to do with knowledge he now wishes he did not have.

Best Music Award, Nantes Film Festival, France, November 1988.

1208. *Love in a World of Upheaval (Gun Gun Hong Cheng) (aka Red Dust)*

1990. Changchun Film Studio & Hong Kong Dongxi Film Company, Ltd. Co-Production. Color. 9 Reels. Director: Yan Ao. Screenplay: Shan Mao. Cinematographer: Pan Hengsheng. Art Direction: Gong Minghui. Cast: Lin Qingxia (Brigitte Lin) as Shen Shaohua, Qin Han as Zhang Nengcai, Zhang Manyu (Maggie Cheung) as Yue Feng, Gu Meihua (Josephine Koo) as Su Yin, Wu Yaohan as Boss Yu, Yan Ao as Xiao Yong, Li Xiaoli as the young wife, Zhang Yuan as Yu Lan, Zhang Guowen as the young husband

During World War II, independent-minded girl student Shen Shaohua believes in freedom of marriage, so she repeatedly opposes her traditional father's attempts to find her a husband. She becomes a writer, and meets middle-aged Zhang Nengcai, who works as a cultural officer for the Japanese. They fall in love, but he disappoints her, shattering her dreams for the future. Zhang realizes his mistakes, but the upheaval going on in the world soon separates them before he can seek a reconciliation. When the People's Republic is founded, Shen becomes a reformed, liberated, new woman, and writes a popular novel which tells of her love, her hatreds and hopes. Twenty years later, Zhang Nengcai returns from overseas to seek a reunion with Shen, but fate separates them forever.

1209. *Love in Calligraphy (Bi Zhong Qin)*

1982. Shanghai Film Studio. Color. 10 Reels. Direction: Yan Bili. Screenplay: Jiang Xun. Cinematography: Shen Xilin, Chen Yongjun. Art Direction: Jin Qifeng. Music: Ge Yan. Sound: Xie Guojie. Cast: Wang Bozhao as Zhao Xuzhi, Zhao Jing as Wenjuan, Ding Jiayuan as Xu Anmin, Cheng Zhi as Qi Shen, Chi Zhongrui as Heng Xu, Zhang Wei as Yu Juan

Young calligrapher Zhao Xuzhi is talented and handsome, which attracts the attention of Administrator Qi Shen's eldest daughter Wenjuan. She falls in love with him, and when her father arranges a house party to pick a future son-in-law for Wenjuan, Zhao Yuzhi is one of the young men invited. But Zhao is also somewhat egotistic, and assuming he will be the natural choice, he runs away from the party before Wenjuan is introduced. When Zhao Xuzhi later gets the chance to see Wenjuan, he is immediately impressed by her beauty and talent, and regrets having rejected his earlier chance. When he goes to ask for her hand in marriage, however, General Heng Xu, another suitor, is already there presenting his suit. So he has missed another opportunity. Zhao Xuzhi leaves home and goes on a long trip to visit many famous scenic sites and improve his calligraphy. At last, he realizes that his shortcomings have been his devotion to calligraphy to the point of neglecting others, and his arrogance. The story ends with Wenjuan and Zhao Xuzhi at last getting together and having a perfect marriage.

1210. *Love in Crisis (Ai Qing Wei Ji)*

1992. Changchun Film Studio. Color. Letterboxed. 9 Reels. Direction: Guo Lin, Le Yinjie. Screenplay: Zhang Guanglie, Guo Lin. Cinematography: Zhao Bo. Art Direction: Min Jianguo, Li Taiping. Music: Xu Zhijun. Sound: Liu Qun, Zhao Xudong. Costume: Liang Xuejie.

Makeup: Guo Zhen, Pan Li. Cast: Liu Zifeng as Qin Qing, Bai Han as Ai Yuan, Guo Xiao as Li Liye, Lu Liang as Zhang Shixin, Huang Xia as Li Li, Zhang Huizhong as Doctor Liu

After 20 years of marriage, renowned archeologist Qin Qing and his wife Aiyuan believe their life is as close to perfect as it could be. But one day they take a quiz designed to assess a couple's marital relationship, and find that they grade very low. The couple then undertake a series of activities designed to improve the quality of their marriage, which leads to a succession of funny incidents.

1211. *Love in Crisis (Bai Sha Hen)*

1992. Xiaoxiang Film Studio. Color. Wide Screen. 14 Reels. Direction: Zhou Kangyu. Screenplay: Wang Yuefeng, Lin Yuan, Zhou Kangyu. Cinematography: Zhang Jianzhong. Art Direction: Guo Dexiang. Music: Xu Jingxin. Sound: Liu Feng. Costume: Sheng Lingzhen. Makeup: Zhang Jing. Cast: Lu Xiaohe as Wang Guoxing, An Yaping as Po Jingyong, Chen Kang as Li Shaoqiu, Ruan Baoliang as Wang Yujing, Shu Yaoxuan as Jiang Bidong

When the Japanese invade Hainan Island, the Nationalist Army offers no resistance, but instead withdraws to Baisha County, home to Li and Miao nationality people. There, the soldiers live off the fat of the land, raiding people's homes for what they need, forcing the young men into the army, and in general making nuisances of themselves. Wang Guoxing, respected head of the local people, eventually rebels, but his men suffer heavy casualties. At last, Wang Guoxing leads his people to join the Communist military forces.

1212. *Love in Dance (Wu Lian)*

1981. Emei Film Studio. Color. 10 Reels. Direction: Jiang Shixiong, Wen Lun. Screenplay: Jia Mu. Cinematography: Cao Zhuobing, Zhang Wenyin. Art Direction: He Baotong, Xing Zheng. Music: Tian Feng. Sound: Zhang Jiake. Cast: Cheng Xiaoyin as Qumu Azhi, Zhang Jizhong as Xiang Feng

Twenty years earlier, calligrapher Xiang Feng met talented Yi nationality girl Qumu Azhi. They fell in love and married, and she created a special dance expressing their love. However, during the Cultural Revolution Xiang Feng collapsed under political pressure and betrayed her. Today, viewing a presentation of minority people's dances, he unexpectedly meets Qumu Azhi. She coldly rejects him because of how shamefully he had betrayed their love during the Cultural Revolution. However, when Qumu Azhi sees Xiang Feng is very regretful and has been guilt-ridden for 20 years about his actions, and how he has raised their child Huahua all by himself, she begins to forgive him. They finally get together, and the start a new life together, working to develop the nation's minority dancing.

1213. *Love Is Forever (Bu Neng Mei You Ai)*

1992. Beijing Film Studio. Color. 9 Reels. Direction: Li Zhiyu. Screenplay: Xiao Mao. Cinematography: Li Sheng. Art Direction: Yu Maiduo. Music: Gao Erdi. Sound: Chao Jun. Costume: Hou Xiaojie. Makeup: Yu Xiaoting. Cast: Wang Ban as Zhao Shengtian, Kong Ling as Li Xiaolan, Li Haiyan as Cui Xiaoguang, Lu Hanbiao as He Dalu, Qu Yan as Hong Lili

On the rebound from being dumped by his girlfriend Hong Lili, driver Zhao Shengtian meets another girl Li Xiaolan. When she unexpectedly gets pregnant, they decide to marry. They begin having troubles soon after the child is born, however. His mother has steadily refused to accept Li, and the young wife herself begins to feel she gave up too much by marrying and having a child so soon. They quarrel often. But when Zhao is arrested in connection with a traffic case, Li shows her love by taking care of his mother. Her kindness moves the mother to accept her at last. When Zhao is released and returns home, the young couple recognize their love again and start life anew.

1214. *Love Is Not Far Away (Ai Bing Bu Yao Yuan)*

1983. Longjiang Film Studio. Color. 10 Reels. Direction: Jiang Shusheng. Screenplay: Wang Ronghui. Cinematography: Wu Benli. Art Direction: Gong Minghui, Li Deyu. Music: Liu Xijin. Sound: Dong Baosheng, Zhang Jun. Cast: Wang Fuyou as Zhen Xin, Han Guangping as Sun Wei, Du Yuan as Liu Meng, Tu Ruyin as Jin Mei, Chen Limin as Zhang Lanlan, Jiang Ruilin as Hao Hong, Li Dan as Pang Zhang

When Zhen Xin receives a prestige assignment to head up an oil drilling team in an undeveloped area, he happily goes to tell his fiancee Zhang Lanlan. To his surprise, she reacts negatively and delivers an ultimatum: get a city job and marry her, or else their relationship is finished. He chooses his career, and

travels to the oil field exploration site near Moon Lake. He builds up a strong friendship with the project's woman director Sun Wei. At the same site, drilling technician Liu Meng and nurse Jin Mei fall in love but then break up. They meet again when Jin Mei comes back to Moon Lake on a medical emergency, and after talking it over they reconcile. A third story involves Hao Hong, a young worker dumped by his city girl friend, who wins the love of woman driver Pang Zhang.

1215. *Love Me or Love My Cow (Chi Nan, Yuan Nu He Niu)*

1994. Changchun Film Studio. Color. Letterboxed. 9 Reels. Direction: Yu Xiangyuan. Screenplay: Yu Xiangyuan, based on the novel "Fu Niu" by Zhou Daxin. Cinematography: Zhang Songping, Ma Weiye. Art Direction: Zhang Yan. Music: Fan Weiqiang. Sound: Meng Gang. Costume: Wu Boqiao. Makeup: Qiu Hong. Cast: Liu Guanjun as Zhou Zhaojing, Ge Nan as Xilan, Zhu Na as Qiaoqiao, Wang Jichun as Liu Guanshan, Lin Ke as Erxing, Qian Ling as Zhaojing's father, Tian Jiefu as grandpa Qishun, Jin Liang as Sanleng, Ju Jiajia as little fatty

In the rural village of Fu Niu, two young men, Zhaojing and Erxing, are both in love with the same girl, Xilan. The village's domineering and selfish chief coerces Zhaojing into marrying his daughter Qiaoqiao, a mute. Their marriage is an unhappy one, as Zhaojing is bitter and resentful and Qiaoqiao neglected and unloved. Erxing, after leaving the village for a time to work in the city, now returns with money he has saved for a business. He and Xilan start a leather goods factory together, and in time she accepts his proposal of marriage. Meanwhile, Zhaojing has also become successful by immersing himself in his work to compensate for his anger at his fate. When his life is in peril, Qiaoqiao sacrifices herself to save him, leaving Zhaojing regretful that he for so long neglected his wife and refused her love, and saddened at the thought of what he might have had if he had tried.

1216. *Love of Silk in Water Town (Shui Zhen Si Qing)*

1983. Xi'an Film Studio. Color. 9 Reels. Direction: Li Yundong. Screenplay: Huang Yazhou. Cinematography: Chen Wancai, Yang Baoshi. Art Direction: Zhang Zhien. Music: Xu Youfu. Sound: Che Zhiyuan. Cast: Wu Haiyan as Xu Meizhi, Guo Xuxin as Zhang Xiaobai, Gao

Baocheng as Deputy Factory Director Ji, Wang
Aibing as Cui Yan, Zhao Youliang as Wang Jialie,
Sun Ai as Bafeng, Chen Rishun as Little Bobo

In the spring of 1981, Xu Meizhi is ill with
terminal cancer. Now out of the hospital and
back at her job as director of a silk mill, she
wants to devote her final days to produce a
type of high quality silk called 6A. After many
long days and nights of effort, the first samples
sent to the provincial capital for testing do not
meet the 6A standard. Xu analyzes the reasons
for the failure, and prepares to try again, but
her deteriorating condition prevents her from
carrying on. The mill's entire staff pulls together and succeeds. Xu Meizhi receives the
news in her hospital bed, as the nurses prepare
her for transfer to a hospital in Shanghai.

1217. *Love of the Forest (Lin Hai Qing)*

1984. Liaoning Science Film Studio. Color.
10 Reels. Direction: Ding Ni. Screenplay: Yan
Wenjing, Shi Lishu, Li Qidong, Jiang Zhao-
cheng. Cinematography: Yang Shijiang. Art Di-
rection: Wang Jihou, Deng Yong. Music: Lei
Yusheng, Yang Guang. Sound: Wang Wenfu.
Cast: Li Muran as Ye Sucheng, Chen Ying as Lin
Ao, Zhang Hanjun as Liu Shaoqi, Wang Damin
as Deputy Bureau Director Shi, Zhou Hong as
Xiaoman, Wang Guiqing as Shanfeng

When Forest Bureau Director Ye Sucheng
is released in 1979 from 13 years unjust imprisonment, he returns to his old position. He is
upset to find that unregulated cutting of trees
has now become the norm, and reinstates the
regulations controlling this. One of the worst
offenders has been Lin Ao, director of a machine tool plant, and he and Ye Sucheng clash
over the new regulations. When a flash flood
hits the area, killing many of the residents and
destroying the homes of many others, Lin Ao
sees the value of maintaining an environmental
balance.

1218. *Love on a Camel's Hump (Tuo Feng Shang De Ai)*

1985. Beijing Film Studio. Color. 9 Reels.
Direction: Yang Jing, Yu Yang. Screenplay: Feng
Lingzhi. Cinematography: Yang Wenqin. Art Di-
rection: Zhen Huiwen. Music: Moer Jihu.
Sound: Zhang Zhian. Cast: Fang Chao as Ji Ya,
Siqin Gaowa as Yilina, Cui Dai as Sunite, Yin Na
as Tana, Shu Mei as Mother, Hasi Gaowa as
Badama

Mongolian farmer Sunite's three-person

family was very happy at first. But when his
active wife Yilina joins a spare-time song and
dance troupe for recreation and finds she has
considerable talent, Sunite becomes very jealous and takes to drinking. When he drinks he
gets very abusive, so at last Yilina can bear it
no longer and leaves their home, their poor little son Ji Ya remaining behind with his dad.
Over time, the pure and innocent nature of
the little boy brings the estranged couple to
face the realities of their life. They grow
ashamed over their behavior and reconcile.

1219. *Love on a Far-Off Mountain (Yuan Shan Qing)*

1992. Guangxi Film Studio. Color. Letterboxed. 10 Reels. Direction: Zen Xueqiang. Cinematography: Cai Xiaopeng. Art Direction: Chen
Yaogong. Music: Du Jiangang. Sound: Li Yunping. Costume: Huang Liqin. Makeup: Gan Jun,
Liu Keyong. Cast: Chen Hong as A Liu, Liu
Yanjun as Jin Zai, Tao Zeru as Jiang Shun, Li Xiaohong as A Huo, Meng Weimin as Hua Ge

In a small town in Guangdong Province,
20-year-old A Liu's parents arrange a marriage
for her with Jiang Shun, a wealthy man 30
years her senior. She falls in love with Jin Zai,
a young laborer. Later, she and Jiang Shun are
divorced, and the money she receives in the
settlement allows her to open a flower shop.
She gets together with Jin Zai, who makes and
sells furniture, and they have a comfortable
life. But A Liu is ambitious, more so than Jin
Zai, who is content with things as they are.
The couple quarrels over this, and A Liu leaves
Jin Zai, who loves his wife although he does
not understand her. He thinks long and hard
about it, comes to the conclusion his wife is
right, and goes to find her.

1220. *Love on Green Mountain (Qing Shan Lian)*

1964. Haiyan Film Studio. B & W. 10 Reels.
Direction: Zhao Dan, Xu Tao, Qian Qianli.
Screenplay: Ai Mingzhi, Zhao Dan, Xu Tao,
Qian Qianli. Cinematography: Qiu Yiren, Fan
Houqing. Art Direction: Huang Jianfeng. Music:
Wang Yunjie. Sound: Lin Bingsheng. Cast: Zhao
Dan as Lu Chun, Gao Bo as Zhan Guocai, Zhu
Xijuan as Shanque, Wu Wenhua as Xu Ying,
Huang Daliang as Ji Wang, Zhou Kangyu as
Wang Dehua

In the spring of 1959, Red Army veteran
Lu Chun retires from the army to his hometown, where he begins tree farming. He is soon

joined by a group of young intellectuals from Shanghai. Although they are energetic, the young people's motivations and dreams vary greatly. Some are practical and down-to-earth; some care only for their own personal interests. One of the latter, recent graduate Ji Wang, wants to do technical work rather than manual labor, so he pays slight attention to his work, which leads to an accident. Unfortunately, he learns little from this episode. In time, however, with Lu Chun's help and guidance, he improves his awareness, corrects his shortcomings, and devotes himself to the work of raising trees.

1221. *Love on Ice (Bing Shang Qing Huo)*

1990. Pearl River Film Studio. Color. 9 Reels. Direction: Deng Yuan. Screenplay: Deng Yuan, Gang Yi. Cinematography: Gang Yi. Art Direction: Liang Hong. Music: Fang Xiaoming. Sound: Li Yan, Lu Hong. Cast: Sun Zhou as Lin Jiajun, Yu Li as Zhao Yayi, Zhang Yongling as Wang Kai, Li Qiang as Lang Ren

Skater Lin Jiajun kills a Hong Kong businessman in an automobile accident. During the investigation, the PSB discovers the businessman was also a member of a Hong Kong triad, and apparently was in mainland China to pick up a cache of drugs he had hidden there earlier. The PSB launches a search for the drugs, but they are not alone: the triad sends a killer called "Wolfman" to find it first. As both sides search for the drugs, the skater finds himself being pursued by the killer, as the triad believes the car crash was no accident. Not trusting the police at first, Lin Jianjun at last decides to cooperate with them to find the drugs. "Wolfman" is killed in a final shootout.

1222. *Love on the Changing Stage (Cang Sang Li Yuan Qing)*

1993. Children's Film Studio. Color. Letterboxed. 9 Reels. Direction: Sun Yongtian, Ma Rongjie. Screenplay: Li Weiyi. Cinematography: Sun Yongtian, Yang Ying. Art Direction: Chen Aosi. Music: Liu Weiguang. Sound: Lan Fan. Cast: Diao Yunling as Shi Xiaolong, Zhao Hongfei as Yu Youchun, Zhang Yunxi as Yu Chunling, Zhen Rong as Yu Chunpeng

A boy named Shi Xiaolong, whose grandfather has instilled in him a love of Beijing opera, is introduced to famous performer Yu Youchun, and asks to become his student. Yu rejects the youngster because of lingering bad feelings stemming from a disagreement the old artist had many years before with Xiaolong's grandfather. The boy is upset but does not give up. He practices hard to hone what skills he has, but again is rejected by Yu Youchun. At last, the older performer is moved by the boy's dedication to the art, and he accepts Shi Xiaolong as his student.

1223. *The Love Song on a Lu (Lu Sheng Lian Ge)*

1957. Changchun Film Studio. B & W. 10 Reels. Direction: Yu Yanfu. Screenplay: Peng Jingfeng and Chen Xiping. Cinematography: Wang Qiming. Art Design: Wang Tao. Music: Lei Zhenbang. Sound: Hong Jiahui. Cast: Wang Jie as Zhatuo, Song Xuejuan as Nawa, Li Jingbo as Aqi, Chen Guangting as Shuangbao, Sun Yu as Zhamu, Xia Peijie as Nawa's mother

In the valley of the Lancang River in China's Yunnan province live the Lagu nationality people, among them Zhatuo, a young Lagu huntsman, and his lover, the beautiful Nawa. But the Lagu people suffer terribly under Nationalist rule. The brutal oppression and mistreatment they receive at the hands of Nationalist soldiers pushes the Lagu to armed rebellion. Nawa, along with the other women, the children and the elderly, evacuate the village, while the Lagu young men fight. However, their homemade weapons are no match for the U.S.-equipped government forces, and they are soon forced into a nearby forest, where all except Zhatuo are killed. To gain revenge, Zhatuo stays at large, living a primitive life in the forest. After liberation, a geological prospecting party goes there looking for mineral resources and sight a mysterious, unidentified savage. They follow him deep into the forest, and find a "lu," a traditional Lagu reedpipe wind instrument, and a mineral stone they were looking for. Their guide, a village elder, is certain that this is Zhatuo, who had been missing for two years. But Zhatuo cannot imagine these are friendly people, so he repeatedly shoots arrows at anyone who comes near. He wakes up to reality when Nawa uses the wind instrument to play the love song that had been their favorite. Zhatuo tearfully comes to his pursuers, and the two lovers are at last reunited happily.

1224. *Love Spray (Qing Hai Lang Hua)*

1991. Shanghai Film Studio. Color. Wide Screen. 10 Reels. Direction: Pao Zhifang. Screenplay: Hu Huian and Zhao Zhiqiang, based on the novel "Spray" by Qiong Yao (1938–). Cinematography: Ju Jiazheng. Art Direction: Ju Ransheng, Sun Weide. Music: Liu Yanxi. Sound (Dolby): Feng Deyao. Cast: Yu Lan as Qin Yuqiu, Tong Ruiming as He Junzhi, Wu Jing as Wanling, Tong Ruixin as He Zijian, Kong Ling as Dai Xiaoyan, He Yongfang as He Peirou, Guo Dongwen as Jiang Wei, Gao Qiang as Du Zhonghao

A common devotion to art brings together painter Qin Yuqiu and gallery curator He Junshi, the latter a man with a boring and loveless family existence. Although He Junshi's children are avid in their own pursuits of romance, they cannot understand similar longings in their parents. When Qin Yuqiu learns that by winning the man she loves she will destroy a family, she firmly determines to leave him.

1225. *Love Story in Tong Minority Mountain Village (Gu Lou Qing Hua)*

1987. Guangxi Film Studio. Color. 10 Reels. Direction: Li Xiaolong. Screenplay: Mao Zhengshan. Cinematography: Yang Yuming, Liu Baogui. Art Direction: Li Qining. Music: Chen Yuanxing. Sound: Lin Lin. Cast: Li Zhi as Long Beng, Wang Juan as Su Na, Kuang Hongyan as Liang Yin

Minority college student Su Na comes to a mountain village populated by people of the Tong nationality. She wants to learn the spiritual strength of a nationality which has existed for more than a thousand years but does not have its own language. Through a series of events, Su Na realizes the Tong nationality's undying resolve for self-development.

1226. *Love That Cannot Be Chased Back (Zhui Bu Hui Lai De Ai Qing)*

1990. Emei Film Studio. Color. Wide Screen. 9 Reels. Direction: Li Shaoxu. Screenplay: Li Shaoxu, Xu Haibing. Cinematographer: Shen Xianao. Art Direction: Zhou Jinglun. Music: Tang Qinshi. Sound: Zhan Xin. Cast: Chen Rui as Xu Haiping, Wu Ying as Xiao Wan

Xu Haiping and Xiao Wan are lovers, but after Xiao Wan gets pregnant, circumstances force her to opt for an abortion. After the operation she sinks into deep depression, and leaves Xu. Three years later, Xu Haiping has become quite successful, but Xiao Wan has sunk into a dissolute life. Xu at last finds Xiao Wan, and wants to resume their past relationship. She gives it a try, but the past always crops up to spoil things. At last, she leaves him again. Xu is shocked at first, but finally comes to understand her feelings. On Chinese New Year's Eve, he goes to look for Xiao Wan to tell her of his love, but arrives just as she is being taken away by police.

1227. *A Love That Surpasses Life (Chao Yue Sheng Ming De Ai)*

1992. Inner Mongolia Film Studio. Color. Letterboxed. Direction: Sun Tianxiang, Bao Nayintai. Screenplay: Wang Zhengping, Hasi Chaolu, Sun Tianxiang. Cinematography: Na Risu. Art Direction: Mo Nayintai, Ali Musi. Music: Yong Rubu. Cast: Hasi Gaowa as Qimuge, Cheng Xiangying as Hude, Du Juan as Xiao Wen, Guan Qige as Secretary Ba, Wu Rigeng as Gongbu, Li Ying as Teacher Xiao

In the early 1960s, Mongolian couple Gongbu and Qimuge adopt four Chinese children orphaned by a natural disaster. Later, they adopt another girl. During the Cultural Revolution, Gongbu is persecuted and Qimuge loses her unborn baby, as well as her ability to have her own child. After Gongbu dies, Qimuge's adopted children provide her with the strength to carry on. She raises them by herself, and at last passes away with her grateful and grieving children around her.

1228. *Love to Shanxi (Qin Chuan Qing)*

1985. Shanghai Film Studio. Color. Wide Screen. 10 Reels. Direction: Huang Zhumo. Screenplay: Zhen Yanyin. Cinematography: Shen Miaorong. Art Direction: Zhu Jiancang. Music: Lu Qimin. Sound: Wang Shu. Cast: Lu Xiaohe as Zhuangzhuang, Yu Ya as Yu Qianer, Dawa Pingcuo as Da Xi, Zhang Wenrong as the widow, Zhan Che as the production team leader

In 1976, 14-year-old Yu Qianer and her father leave their famine-stricken village and move to another village. Soon after, the father dies, and Zhuangzhuang, a bachelor about her father's age, helps Qianer bury her father. With encouragement from local people, the two get together and agree to marry when

Love on the Changing Stage. **1993. Children's Film Studio.**

Qianer grows up. Five years pass, and Qianer is now a grownup young woman. She meets and falls in love with Da Xi, a successful young farmer. But Qianer feels guilty about Zhuangzhuang, who has given her so much support through the years. Zhuangzhuang knows how she feels, so he attempts suicide in order to get out of the young couple's way. Yu Qianer and Da Xi intervene to save his life, and they rush him to the hospital, caring for Zhuangzhuang as Qianer did for her father. As they leave, a village widow insists on going along. As Qianer notes the way in which the widow looks at and cares for Zhuangzhuang, Qianer sees an obvious resolution to their problem.

1229. *Love Trip (Ai Qing De Lu Cheng)*

1985. Youth Film Studio. Color. 9 Reels. Direction: Liu Cheng, Feng Ji. Screenplay: Xiao Zenjianj, Guo Lingling. Cinematography: Zhu Junhuan. Art Direction: Hu Rongfa, Song Meizhen. Music: Ma Ding. Sound: Sun Xin. Cast: Zhang Tianxi as Lu Wei, Zhou Yue as Xiao Qian, Zhang Ling as Xi Mei, Geng Xiaolu as Ai Mei

In a small city in south China, young taxi driver Lu Wei has two regular female passengers with whom he frequently converses. He falls in love with one of them, a young woman called Xiao Qian. He keeps his feelings to himself. One day he learns that she had a boyfriend who abandoned her when she became pregnant. At first, she had wanted to kill her lover, but now she learns he has been sent to prison. He had turned to crime in order to raise money to meet her excessive material demands, so now she feels very regretful. She at last goes to visit him in prison, and they reconcile. At this time, Lu Wei's other regular female passenger, Xi Mei, tells him she loves him. The taxi driver, who has loved Xiao Qian for so long, now has an important decision to make.

1230. *Love, What's Your Last Name? (Ai Qing A, Ni Xing She Me?)*

1980. Shanghai Film Studio. Color. 10 Reels. Direction: Yan Bili. Screenplay: Li Tianji. Cinematography: Ma Linfa. Art Direction: Jin Jifeng, Qiu Yuan. Music: Huang Zhun. Sound: Li Bingkui. Cast: Wang Weiping as Li Zhenggang, Yan Zhengan as Lin Rongrong, Lu Yulei as Ying

Xianzhang, Wu Yunfang as Xie Xuefang, Qiao Qi as Guan Ming, Sun Jinglu as Xiao Cui, Wang Dinghua as Qin Tian, Kou Zhenhai as Zhong Qiang, Hong Xuemin as Ye Hongying

In the spring of 1980, a group of tourists visit Suzhou and Lake Tai. Two of these, Lin Rongrong and Li Zhenggang, are lovers. While Li is a nice young man, Lin's mother opposes the relationship because Li's parents' lack high social status. Ying Xianzhang and Xie Xuefang, forced to divorce during the Cultural Revolution, are now being pushed to reconcile by their daughter Ying Wei and son Ying Jun. An older couple, Guan Ming and his wife Xiao Cui, are not getting along because he does not like spending his retirement idly and wants to find a job, while she just wants them to have an easy, comfortable life. Another young couple, Zhong Qiang and Ye Hongying, meet on the tour bus and fall in love. After one day's travel, everybody's problems are resolved during their visit to these scenic spots. All learn the lesson that love is not money or power, but trust, hope and strength.

1231. Love with a Spirit (Chi Nan Kuang Nu Liang Shi Qing)

1993. Beijing Film Studio. Color. Letterboxed. 9 Reels. Direction: Huo Zuang, Xu Xiaoxing. Screenplay: Li Dong, Huo Zuang, based on the story "Lu Gong's Daughter" by Pu Songling (1640–1715). Cinematography: Liu Xiaomei. Art Direction: Hao Jingyuan. Music: Zhang Fuquan. Sound: Wang Yunhua, Xu Huiju. Costume: Zhang Dezhong, Lu Baozhong. Makeup: Liu Ying, Li Xia. Cast: Huang Guoqiang as Zhang Yudan, Zhao Xueqin as Lu Feifei, Miss Lu, Wang Shuo as Wang Sheng, Xia Zongxue as Lu Hubu

Scholar Zhang Yudan meets and falls in love with a beautiful girl, Lu Feifei. He goes to her family's home to call on her, and is informed she has just died. The film then follows their attempts to fulfill their love while in two worlds, trying to get her back to the world of the living.

1232. The Loved One (Qin Ren)

1985. Tianshan Film Studio. Color. 9 Reels. Direction: Yu Deshui. Screenplay: Sha Ying. Cinematography: Liu Jingtang, Baihaiti. Art Direction: Ma Shaoxian. Music: Ma Shizeng. Sound: Li Bing. Cast: Waersi as Bolati, Song Dewang as Li Weixuan, Liu Yan as Li Xiaoqing, Wu Wenhua as Wang Mei, Mutai Lifu as Uncle Hashan

Riding back from visiting a patient, Xinjiang veterinarian Li Xiaoqing collapses from overwork and falls from her horse. A local high school teacher finds her unconscious and helps her. She is the daughter of Li Weixuan, chief engineer at the city's chemical industrial plant. Her father had volunteered for work in Xinjiang many years earlier, but his wife Wang Mei was forced to remain in Guangdong because of the demands of her scientific research. Wang Mei writes him to say her project is finished, and she can transfer to Xinjiang to join him. But before she arrives, Li Weixuan is killed in an chemical explosion at the plant. Wang Mei and the daughter both decide to remain in Xinjiang because their loved one is buried there.

1233. Loveless Lover (Wu Qing De Qing Ren)

1986. Pearl River Film Studio. Color. 11 Reels. Direction: Chen Guojun. Screenplay: Chen Guojun. Cinematography: Li Zhibing. Art Direction: Zhen Huiwen. Music: Lu Yuan. Sound: Li Xun. Cast: Liu Xiaoqing as Namei Qingchuo, Zhang Kanger as Duojisang, Li Wei as Lang Zha, Wu Xiqian as Quelu Danzhu

On the Tibetan plateau, a beautiful girl named Namei Qingchuo nurses thoughts of revenge in her heart. Her parents were murdered when she was very small, and she lives for the day she will be able to avenge them. She meets a brave and handsome young man named Duojisang, and they fall in love. Later, however, she discovers that Duojisang's father is the man she has been searching for all her life — Quelu Danzhu, the man who murdered her parents. In a climactic shootout, Namei accidentally kills her lover Duojisang instead. In her sorrow over what has happened, she lets down her guard and is shot to death by Quelu.

1234. A Lover's Blood Is Especially Red (Qing Ren De Xue Te Bie Hong)

1994. Yunnan Nationalities Film Studio. Color. Letterboxed. 9 Reels. Direction: Zhan Junke. Screenplay: He Lan. Cinematography: Qiu Yiren, Yang Changsheng. Art Direction: Li Zhengxin. Music: Xu Jingxin. Sound: Ou Lifeng. Costume: Wang Guangqun. Makeup: He Yaling. Cast: Shen Lizi as Li Yun, Qu Yan as Hua Qing, He Zhenjun as Doctor Tang, Liu Wenzhi as the father, Zhang Yan as the mother, Wang Zhi as the butler

Li Yun has been raised by her father in the South Pacific, and after his death in the 1920s she inherits the old family home in South China. She returns to find the house she recalls as a stately mansion is now in a terrible state of disrepair. In addition, her stepsister Huaqin acts strangely, not at all as Li Yun remembers. Also in the home is sinister Doctor Tang. These circumstances, combined with her recollection of how her stepmother had died suddenly and strangely years before, prompts Li Yun to investigate. It turns out that when Li Yun's stepmother married her father, the woman brought her grown daughter Huaqin to live with them. Li's father subsequently had an affair with his stepdaughter, which drove the stepmother to suicide. Li Yun's father then took his own daughter Li Yun and left for the South Pacific, which broke Huaqin's heart. Doctor Tang moved in on Huaqin, killing her when she resisted his advances. The evil doctor later found a woman who resembled Huaqin and occupied the Li family home with her. Doctor Tang and the bogus Huaqin are brought to justice. Although she has the family home now, the saddened and disappointed Li Yun leaves to seek a new life elsewhere.

1235. *Lover's Last Kill (Qing Ren De Zui Hou Yi Chi Mou Sha)*

1989. Changchun Film Studio. Color. Letterboxed. 9 Reels. Direction: He Misheng, Cheng Ke. Screenplay: Yu Ji, He Zhizuang. Cinematography: Lei Xianhe. Art Direction: Gao Tinglun, Zhang Yan. Music: Yang Yilun. Sound: Cao Feng. Cast: Zi Yitong as He Chengzu, Li Xiangang as Lin Dawei

He Chengzu, San Francisco's Chinese-American district attorney, completes a plan to raid and smash the headquarters of a Chinatown gang called the "Black Hands." But one suspicious incident after another prevents him from implementing it. Then his supervisor orders He Chengzu to take a vacation. He decides to spend his vacation in China, and travels there, not knowing he is being followed by Lin Dawei, a hit man known as "Lover" who has been hired by the Black Hands. Shortly after arriving in China, He Chengzu takes a tour boat down the Yangtse River, where a series of murders occur. At last, He Chengzu outwits "Lover" and kills him. He Chengzu boards a Japanese airliner to return to the U.S.,

but high above the Pacific a group of armed men hijack the plane.

1236. *Lovers Who Are Personal Enemies (Chou Lu)*

1982. Changchun Film Studio. Color. 11 Reels. Direction: Chang Zhenhua. Screenplay: Yang Peijing. Cinematography: An Zhiguo. Art Direction: Song Honghua, Liu Huanxing. Cast: Lou Zhanghou. Sound: Li Zhenduo. Cast: Ma Guanyin as Zhao Quansheng, Huang Ailing as Fengmei, Wang Baohua as Li, Wu Xiqian as Zhang Wanan, Zhang Jiatian as Zhao Wangchun, Zhu Jianping as Donggua

In Jiangxi province, a place called Shunta is divided into east and west towns, which have been hostile to each other for longer than anyone there can remember. Twelve years before, a west town young man named Dongguan accidentally kills an east town man named Zhao. The victim's son Zhao Quansheng leaves home to study martial arts in order to avenge his father. But Zhao Quansheng's life takes a different course and he becomes a practitioner of Chinese medicine, then joins the revolution. Now he has been sent back home by the CPC to organize armed rebellion, but he is worried that his return will call up old hatreds which could interfere with his mission. But when Zhao Quansheng meets Fengmei, the sister of Dongguan, he puts the old bitterness aside forever, and works with west town people in his organizational effort. The hostilities between the two towns do hamper his work quite a bit, but he is eventually successful in leading the people against counterrevolutionary forces. Zhao Quansheng and Fengmei marry and devote their lives to the revolution.

1237. *Loving Heart (Cun Cao Xin)*

1983. Guangxi Film Studio. Color. 9 Reels. Direction: Wu Tianren. Screenplay: Zhang Xiaoling. Cinematography: Liao Fan. Art Direction: Wu Zhaohua. Music: Yang Shaoyi. Sound: Li Zhuwen. Cast: Bo Han as Chen Ying, Xi Lei as Li Yang, Jin Ya as Ren Guangyuan, Pu Chaoyin as Lin Huan, Zhang Miaoling as the Head Nurse, Jiang Xinai as Liu Min

Nurse Chen Ying marries painter Li Yang. All goes well until Li Yang wins an award at an art exhibit and becomes a celebrity. He gets involved with another woman, which hurts his pregnant wife very much when she learns of his affair. Chen Ying leaves him and after the baby is born devotes herself to her career and child. When his flattering temporary friends drift away from him, Li Yang comes back to earth. He looks up his old teacher Liu Min, and after a long talk with Liu, Li realizes what he has lost. He sees his wife and daughter again at an art exhibit, and everyone knows they will get back together.

1238. *Loyal Hearts on the Green Sea (Bi Hai Dan Xin)*

1962. August First Film Studio. B & W. 11 Reels. Direction: Wang Bing. Screenplay: Liang Xing. Cinematography: Chen Jun. Art Direction: Jiang Zhenkui. Music: Leng Bing. Sound: Li Lin. Cast: Li Changhua as Xiao Ding, Tian Hua as Jin Xiaomei, Feng Yifu as Commander Ding, Shi Chunyu as Jin Dayi, Li Tingxiu as the second squad leader, Li Baiwan as Su Cheng

In 1949, Company One of a PLA Fourth Field Army Division pursues a retreating Nationalist force to the tip of the Leizhou Peninsula in South China, but a lack of boats prevents their crossing the Qiongzhou Strait to liberate Hainan Island on the other bank. They then wait and carry out training in invasion by sea. They invade and take Hainan the following year.

1239. *Loyal Hero (Xia Gu Feng Liu)*

1992. Beijing Film Studio. Color. Wide Screen. 10 Reels. Direction: Li Hongsheng. Screenplay: Xie Fengsong and Gu Naihua. Cinematography: Ru Shuiren and Hou Yuzhi. Art Direction: Li Bojiang. Music: Wang Ming. Makeup: Liu Changzheng, Xu Qiuwen. Cast: Dong Hongling as Wei Chigong, Yang Fengyi as Bai Suhua, Zhao Jian as Li Jiancheng, Sun Desheng as Li Yuanji

At the beginning of the 7th century, China is wracked by wars as the Sui Dynasty is about to give way to the Tang. The common people suffer greatly. Wei Chigong, an honest blacksmith and kung fu master, leaves home to join the army. He finds his talents and yearnings for a strong country stymied by corrupt officials, so he returns home to resume his trade of blacksmith. One day, honest officials come in a delegation to request he return to service and lead them. From then on, Wei Chigong becomes marshall of the Tang Dynasty and leaves an outstanding historical record.

1240. *Loyal Overseas Chinese Family (aka Hearts for the Motherland) (Hai Wai Chi Zi)*

1979. Pearl River Film Studio. Color. 12 Reels. Direction: Ou Fan, Xing Jitian, Wan Yunji. Screenplay: Hu Bing. Cinematography: Huang Yonghu. Art Direction: Huang Tongrong. Music: Zhen Qiufeng. Sound: Lin Guang. Cast: Qin Yi as Lin Biyun, Deng Xing as Lin Biyun (as a youth), Shi Jing as Huang Deshen, Lang Yongmin as Huang Desheng (as a youth), Chen Chong as Huang Sihua, Xing Jitian as Sima Wei, Du Xiongwen as Huang Siguo, Liu Zhiwei as Han Shan, Gang Qingguang as Tang Qingyu

Young girl Huang Sihua is gifted with a beautiful voice, but when she applies to join a PLA musical troupe she is turned down because she has overseas Chinese connections. The troupe's director Sima Wei disagrees with this decision, and sends Han Shan to investigate the girl's family background. It turns out that Huang Sihua's father Huang Desheng lived overseas as a child, coming to China with his wife after the PRC was founded to become director of a large, beautiful and prospering farm. But later, when Lin Biao and the Gang of Four began to interfere with farm production, he was labeled a capitalist roader and a spy. Huang's wife tells Han Shan about the injustice suffered by her husband, and how they have struggled with Gang follower Tang Qingyu. After the Gang is smashed, Huang Sihua gets the chance to resume her career as a musical performer.

1241. *Loyal Partners (Qing Chang Yi Shen)*

1957. Tianma Film Studio. B & W. 11 Reels. Direction: Xu Canglin. Screenplay: Xu Canglin. Cinematography: Yao Shiquan. Art Direction: Zhang Hanchen. Music: Chen Gexin. Sound: Huang Dongping. Makeup: Xu Ken. Cast: Shu Shi as Hong Leiguang, Shangguan Yunzhu as Shao Qiong, Zhang Zhiliang as Jin Kang, Xiang Lei as Huang Weiwen, Li Ming as Peifang, Cui Chaoming as the doctor, Zhang Liang as the messenger, Shi Hui as Old Zhou, Zeng Chang as Deng Wei, Wang Wei as Young Zhou

Microbiology research institute director Hong Leiguang and his sister's husband, bacteriologist Huang Weiwen, have been good friends for many years, but now argue over the development of a new antibiotic for treating the "302" disease. The chief problem is Huang's conservative approach to research.

The two men patch up their differences, but when Hong later delivers a speech at a conference criticizing conservative thinking, Huang knows he is the target and angrily applies for transfer to another institute. When Hong contracts the "302" disease, Huang stays on and, using Hong's methods, develops the new antibiotic and saves his old friend's life. Their friendship is once again secure.

1242. *Lu Ping, the Gentleman Thief (Xia Dao Lu Ping)*

1989. Shanghai Film Studio. Color. Letterboxed. 10 Reels. Direction: Shen Yaoting. Screenplay: Gu Zemin, Meng Shenghui. Cinematography: Ju Jiazhen. Art Direction: Xue Jianna. Music: Liu Yanxi. Sound: Qian Ping. Cast: Zhou Mei, Wang Zhihua as Guo Jing, Dong Ling as Zhuang Chengyi, Lin Jifan as Chen Miaogeng, He Ling as Lu Ping

When World War II ends, "gentleman thief" Lu Ping returns to Shanghai. Passing himself off as famous detective Guo Jing, Lu gains entrance to the home of wealthy Japanese collaborator Zhuang Chengyi, who Lu knows is in possession of stolen diamonds. Lu steals the diamonds, and returns them to the rightful owner. Chen Miaogeng, an officer in the government property registration office, blackmails former Japanese collaborators by using Lu Ping's name. When Lu finds this out, he sets up Chen to be arrested as Lu Ping. Chen is murdered soon after his release from jail. Lu Ping and Guo Jing work together to solve the murder, and at last conclude the killer is Japanese spy "Blue Snake." They catch the killer spy, but when Lu and Guo meet again, they have a final confrontation.

1243. *Lu Siniang (Shen Long Jian Xia Lu Si Niang)*

1989. Changchun Film Studio. Color. Letterboxed. 10 Reels. Direction: Gao Tianhong. Screenplay: Han Rubing, Xu Yali. Cinematography: Ning Changcheng, Wang Erjiang. Art Direction: Gao Guoliang. Music: Lei Yusheng. Sound: Dong Baosheng, Luo Huailun. Cast: Zhang Bing as Ma Long, Yi Tieguang as Nalan Wende, Zhang Dehui as Wang Xian, Chen Yongxia as Lu Siniang, Wang Zhicheng as Chou Ying, Gao Hongping as Sister Wen

When Manchu Emperor Qin Long learns that Ma Long, one of his generals, has thrown his support behind rebellious Prince A Kui, the emperor sends official Nalan Wende to investi-

gate. On the way, Nalan is attacked and chased by rebels led by Wang Xian. He is rescued by the intervention of Lu Siniang, who happens to be passing through that area. Chou Ying and Sister Wen, allied with Lu Siniang, later come into possession of Prince A Kui's secret orders calling the rebels into action, and Lu orders them to turn these over to Nalan Wende in the interests of national unity. This puts Lu in direct conflict with Ma Long and Wang Xian. In a final showdown, Lu kills both of the rebels.

1244. *Lucky Man (Xin Yun De Ren)*

1986. Beijing Film Studio. Color. 10 Reels. Direction: Dong Kena. Screenplay: Chong Shen. Cinematography: Zhang Shiwei. Art Direction: Zhang Xiande. Music: Liu Zuang. Sound: Wang Dawen, Ning Menghua. Cast: Tao Yuling as Ye Runfang, Xu Huanshan as Huang Yanfu, Li Rentang as Liang Zhengben, Xie Fang as Qu Wenjing, Xu Zhiqun as Zhenzhen, Du Yulu as Shi Yupu

In a major city in north China, the city's electronics appliance plant Party Secretary Ye Runfang hires an intellectual named Huang Yanfu to help him turn around the plant's money-losing situation. This is a controversial move, as Huang is not a Party member, and is considered to be a "political problem." Huang quickly makes the plant profitable. But further reforms bring new pressures on Ye and Huang, and new controversies. Ye Runfang resists the pressures and even nominates Huang Yanfu as a candidate for the provincial Party Committee. This shocks officials such as Liang Zhengben, director of the city's bureau of light industry.

1245. *Lucky Search (Xin Yun Sou Suo)*

1992. Children's Film Studio. Color. Letterboxed. 9 Reels. Direction: Luo Xiaoling. Screenplay: Li Haihang. Cinematography: Liu Yongsi. Art Direction: Xiao Gan. Music: Lu Shilin. Costume: Du Jingmei. Makeup: Yuan Lin. Cast: Cao Chun as Gao Cheng, Ma Enran as Gao Erfu, Yang Lili as Jiang Mengru, Zhang Ying as Wei Yin, Liu Shuming as Yan Huaihua, Wang Shu as Grandpa

Eleven-year-old Gao Cheng's mother died when he was very small, and now it is just him and his father Gao Erfu, a very busy scientist. Father and son agree that a wife and mother in their home would greatly improve their lives.

When Gao Cheng notices that his father seems to like the boy's teacher Jiang Mengru, he determines to make a match. He goes to considerable effort to set up situations which might lead to romance, but they all prove in vain when it turns out his teacher already has a serious boyfriend. But then Gao Erfu introduces his son to Yan Huaihua, a woman the father has found on his own. Young Gao Cheng sees hope for the future once more.

1246. *Lucky Star (Xing Yun De Xing)*

1989. Beijing Film Studio. Color. Wide Screen. 10 Reels. Direction: Xu Qingdong. Screenplay: Du Xiaoou. Cinematography: Li Yuebing. Art Direction: Shi Jiandu. Music: Wun Zhongjia, Shi Zhiyou. Sound: Liu Xiaodong. Cast: Liu Xuling as Bingma and Duma, Gao Du as Da Ying

Bingma and Duma are twin sisters. Bingma is an actress with the Beijing Central Minority Song and Dance Company, and when the troupe returns from an overseas tour, she tells her boyfriend Da Ying she is leaving for her hometown to visit her sister, and experience some of Duma's life there in a chemical factory. Later, Duma visits Beijing, where everyone mistakes her for her twin sister Bingma and try to drag her back to the chemical factory, since she wanted to experience life there. A series of humorous incidents ensue from everyone's mistaking Duma for her sister. At last Bingma shows up to straighten things out.

1247. *Luo Cheng the Handsome Guy (Qiao Luo Cheng)*

1992. Liaoning Film Studio & Xiaoxiang Film Studio Co-Production. Color. Wide Screen. 10 Reels. Direction: Yao Shougang. Screenplay: Xie Fengsong, Gu Naihua. Cinematography: Song Chao, Zhang Jinglin. Art Direction: Zhang Lin, Zhao Zhengxue. Music: Xiang Yin. Sound: Zhang Baojian, Xu Ziping. Costume: Pang Yan, Liang Ting, Liu Nian. Makeup: Liu Xiaonan, Cheng Hong. Cast: Sun Chengxi as Luo Cheng, Dong Ping as Zi Yan, Ma Shengjun as silly auntie, Yang Shu as Xian Niang, Guo Yuling as Wu Kui, Run Huaili as Yang Li

The story of the early 7th century general Luo Cheng and three women in his life, all of whom he must eventually avenge.

1248. *Luo Xiaolin's Resolution (Luo Xiao Lin De Jue Xin)*

1955. Changchun Film Studio. B & W. 5 Reels. Direction: Yan Gong. Screenplay: Wang Jiayi, based on novel "The Story of Luo Xiaolin" by Zhang Tianyi. Cinematography: Lian Cheng. Set Design: Lu Gan. Music: Quan Rufeng. Sound: Hong Di. Cast: Chen Jialin as Luo Xiaolin, Zhang Junying as Wang Xiuqin, Lu Dayu as Liu Hui, Li Xixiang as Wei Jiaming, Chen Keran as the tall student, Shi Yuan as Luo Xiaoyuan, Shi Lin as Mama Luo, Xie Tian as the old goldfish seller, Zhang Yukun as Uncle Liu, Liu Zhenzhong as Uncle Guo

Sixth grade student Luo Xiaolin has trouble with his schedule because of his curiosity and fondness for playing. With the encouragement of Uncle Liu Wengui, a worker, Luo Xiaolin determines to correct this shortcoming of liking play too much. However, many interesting things still distract him and for a time cause his resolution to waver. But Luo Xiaolin's strong character, combined with the supervision and help of workers, his classmates and his mother, result in his finally becoming a good student who can keep to a schedule.

1249. *Ma Jia and Ling Fei (Ma Jia He Ling Fei)*

1982. Children's Film Studio. Color. 4 Reels. Direction: Wang Yiwan, Lu Gang. Screenplay: Wang Luyao. Cinematography: Wei Tong. Art Direction: Chen Zhuo. Music: Liu Weiguang. Sound: Zhang Zhian. Cast: Wang Jianing as Ma Jia, Lei Ting as Ling Fei

Good friends Ma Jia and Ling Fei are student leaders in their fifth grade class at Xinhun Elementary School. One afternoon, Teacher Xu tells the two to notify everyone in the class that there will be an exhibition of the children's artworks the next morning, and stresses that everyone should be there on time. Three students in the class are late nearly every day; how to get them there on time? Ma Jia suggests telling everyone the meeting time is 30 minutes earlier, and that way everyone will be on time even if someone is a half hour late. Ling Fei insists on getting everyone there at the time specified by the teacher, so she works hard to make it happen. The next day, all the students arrive on time, but Ma Jia is almost late. At the exhibition, Ling Fei's painting is awarded a first class prize, which carries the opportunity of a visit to Beidaihe beach resort, but Ma Jia only receives a second class award. Ma Jia looks at the seascape he painted, and thinking of his father who was lost at sea, starts to cry. Ling Fei realizes that Ma Jia needs to see the ocean more than she does, so she volunteers to let Ma Jia take the trip. Children's Palace teacher Zhao is moved by the children's friendship and decides to let both of them go to Beidaihe. In their happiness, Ma Jia has learned something.

1250. Ma Lan's Success (Ma Lan Hua Kai)

1956. Changchun Film Studio. B & W. 12 Reels. Direction: Li Enjie. Screenplay: Lin Yi. Cinematography: Han Zongliang. Set Design: Wang Xingwen. Music: Lei Zhenbang. Sound: Hong Jiahui. Cast: Qing Yi as Ma Lan, Gao Bo as Wang Fuxing, Pu Ke as political instructor Xu, Mu Hong as Hu Ageng, Huang Fei as Jin Tong, Wang Cunyin as Lihai

Homemaker Ma Lan wants to learn tractor driving so she can participate in building New China. She gets no support from her family and friends, but with the encouragement of the Party, her husband and mother change their mind, and Ma Lan finally gets the chance to learn. After she gains some experience she is assigned to learn operation of earth moving equipment, and is teamed for training with veteran worker Hu Ageng. Hu Ageng is very traditional in his thinking, especially about women in the workplace. Each time Ma Lan makes a mistake, he loses his temper and criticizes her harshly. She begins losing her confidence, but political instructor Xu encourages her to keep going. Her determination finally changes Hu Ageng, and he teaches her all he knows. She finally succeeds in making the transition from full-time homemaker to skilled equipment operator.

1251. Ma Suzhen's Revenge (Ma Su Zhen Fu Chou)

1988. Shanghai Film Studio. Color. Letterboxed. 9 Reels. Direction: Shen Yaoting. Screenplay: Shen Yaoting, Shen Yaohua. Cinematography: Zhou Zhaiyuan. Art Direction: Zhang Wanhng, Ye Jingmin. Music: Xu Jingxin. Sound: Qian Ping. Cast: Li Yunjuan as Ma Suzhen, Guo Weiping as Ma Yongzhen, Lin Jifan as Bai Laili, Li Xiangchun as Cai Jiuyun

At the end of the Qing Dynasty (c1910), Shandong martial arts hero Ma Yongzhen is invited to Shanghai by Cai Jiuyun. At that time, a British bank has taken over some Chinese property to build a racetrack, and have arranged for Chinese gangster Bai Laili to keep any protesting Chinese in line. Ma Yongzhen beats all the foreigners and their collaborators, and at last Bai Laili conspires with some local thugs to murder him. When Yongzhen's sister Ma Suzhen learns of her brother's death, she comes to Shanghai looking for Bai Laili and seeking vengeance. At last Ma Suzhen chases Bai Laili over a cliff, killing him and avenging her brother.

1252. Madam Shexiang (She Xiang Fu Ren)

1985. Zhejiang Film Studio. Color. Wide Screen. 9 Reels. Direction: Chen Xianyu. Screenplay: Zhu Yunpeng, Chen Xianyu. Cinematography: Zhou Ping. Art Direction: Wang Hanjun. Music: Si Wanchun. Sound: Cui Weimin. Cast: Huer Xide as Madam Shexiang, Li Shaoxiong as Ma Ye, Wang Chunli as Shezhu, Yu Ming as Cao Kelong, Gege as Liu Shuzhu, Da Qi as Zhu Yuanzhang

In the late 14th century, Guizhou Province is beset with natural disasters, as well as heavily taxed. Madam Shexiang, a leader of the Guizhou people, petitions for a reduction in the tax burden. For doing so, she is beaten by local Commander Ma Ye. The movie relates Madam Shexiang's tireless efforts to have her petition heard. At last, the imperial court hears and approves her petition. The court also orders that Ma Ye be executed for the way he treated her. But Madam Shexiang sympathizes with Ma Ye, and writes another petition asking his sentence be commuted.

1253. The Magic Beggar (Shen Gai)

1987. Changchun Film Studio. Color. 10 Reels. Direction: Gao Tianhong. Screenplay: Gao Tianhong, Chen Aimin. Cinematography: Wang Lianping. Art Direction: Lu Qi. Music: Huang Weiqiang. Sound: Zhang Fenglu. Cast: Wang Qun as Yang Luchan, Xu Yuanguo as Chen Changxing, Chen Yongxia as Chen Shimei, Hu Yinjie as Zong Shengsun

In the early years of the 19th century, farmer Yang Lucan follows his teacher Liu Ligong's advice and goes to Chengjiagou Village to ask Taiqi master Chen Changxing be his teacher. Unfortunately, the master rejects Yang Luchan as a student. After that, Yang Luchan passes three years wandering the country as a beggar. He at last returns to ask Chen

Changxing to take him as a student, and this time his plea moves the master, who is surprised to find this is the same person he rejected before. So Yang Luchan is accepted as Chen's last student. Yang Luchan in time becomes a kung fu practitioner with super skill.

1254. *The Magic Emeralds (Shen Qi De Lu Bao Shi)*

1983. Emei Film Studio. Color. 10 Reels. Direction: Ma Shaohui. Screenplay: Liang Shangquan, Song Qingtao. Cinematography: Wang Wenxiang, Shang Defu. Art Direction: Xie Huiyue. Music: Si Guangnan. Sound: Luo Guohua. Cast: Chiren Ouzhu as Dage, Gaixi Lamu as Shemu, Yang Chiyu as King Longshan, Chen Xiaoyi as Princess Xuebao

In a legendary place called Jiuzaigou, famed in China for its scenic beauty, the many ponds are made of emeralds. A cruel and avaricious king named Longshan steals the emeralds, turning Jiuzaigou into a barren desert. Dage, a young peasant boy, obtains a magic horse, and after many adventures and hardships he arrives at King Longshan's palace. With the help of the king's daughter he is able to recover the emeralds and return them to their rightful place. From then on, Jinzaigou's mountains and waters become lovelier than ever.

1255. *Magic Legs (Wu Di Yuan Yang Tui)*

1988. Beijing Film Studio. Color. 9 Reels. Direction: Li Wenhua. Screenplay: Hai Peng, Zhou Zhencang, Cai Rongchuan. Cinematography: Guan Qinwu. Art Direction: Hao Jingyuan. Music: Wun Zhongjia. Sound: Ning Menghua, Li Bojiang. Cast: Wang Qun as Wu Jiatai, Wang Chi as Hei Shazhuang, Zong Qiaozhen as Zhu Fengni, Li Guang as Fengni's father, Tao Qiufu as Wu Laodong

To defend a young lady's honor, Wu Laodong and his son Wu Jiatai fight a local tyrant, but Wu Laodong is killed. Before he dies, Wu makes his son promise he will master the "magic legs" martial arts technique. In a fury, Wu Jiatai ignores his father's last request and decides to fight the tyrant single-handed. He is beaten badly and injured. Later, he meets Zhu Fengni, a young woman performer in a traveling troupe, who also has a score to settle with the same tyrant. Wu Jiatai saves Zhu's life and she promises to marry him. Zhu's father becomes Wu Jiatai's teacher and

helps him master the "magic legs" skills. One day during their workout the tyrant breaks into Zhu's home, kills Zhu's father and leaves Wu and Zhu unconscious. When the couple come to they swear to avenge Zhu's father's death, undertake an arduous training program, and wait for their chance to catch the tyrant off guard.

1256. *The Magic Needle (Mo Zhen)*

1986. Tianshan Film Studio. Color. 9 Reels. Direction: Zhou Shaofeng, Zhao Jiajie. Screenplay: Lan Tianmin. Cinematography: Zhang Xijun, Wang Shiji. Art Direction: Chen Shuwen. Music: Du Jiangang. Sound: Li Lehua. Cast: Yi Xuezhi as Huang Shiping, Bao Ming as Qiuyun, Wang Guisheng as Luo Zi

In the early years of the Republic of China (c1914), Huang Shiping is an expert at the ancient healing art of qigong. He is able to cure the severe and recurring headaches of dictator Yuan Shikai where German physician Luo Zi failed. Doctor Luo gradually builds up a close friendship with Huang, but the German hospital president hates him. Huang Shiping and Luo Zi learn from each other, and gain an appreciation of each other's medical science. But at last Yuan Shikai orders Huang Shiping arrested because Yuan's foreign supporters are unhappy with the Chinese physician. Luo Zi is ordered back to Germany. He and Huang have a sad farewell.

1257. *Magic Powers (Mo Li)*

1988. Beijing Film Studio. Color. 9 Reels. Direction: Xiao Lang, Qiu Lili. Screenplay: Huang Shiyin. Cinematography: Ru Shuiren. Art Direction: Chen Xiaoxia. Music: Li Wanli. Sound: Wang Yunhua. Cast: Zhang Jing as Fang Jiajia, Guan Shisen as Fang Mimi, Guan Zongxiang as Daddy Fang, Wang Biao as Principal Guan, Song Ge as Chief Editor Hu, Lu Jie as Qian Feifei, Gao Jianhua as Mi Lan, Sun Lijuan as Huang Mao, Cheng Xueqin as Man Tianfei, Guo Weihua as Scarface

Fang Jiajia and his sister Fang Mimi have special magic powers. One day while shopping for food, the two display their powers, shocking the entire city. The Fangs' home and school are swamped with reporters and others such as scientists wanting to conduct tests on them. In addition, gangster Man Tianfei wants to get control of them to exploit their talents to commit crimes. The brother and sister have quite a tussle with the criminals, but win out with the help of the police. Jiajia and Mimi are sent to Beijing to attend a conference on human physiology.

1258. *Magic Sword (Shen Jian)*

1994. Xi'an Film Studio, Taiwan Film Culture Company Co-Production. Color. Letterboxed. 10 Reels. Direction: Ding Shanxi. Screenplay: Zhang Dachun, Xia Yan. Cinematography: Ma Delin, He Yongzheng. Art Direction: Xiao Rong. Music: Zhao Jiping. Cast: Tuo Zonghua as Gan Jiang, Jin Sumei as Mo Xia, Wang Dao as He Lu, Kuang Mingjie as Mei Nu, Tai Shan as Qing Ji, Liao Jun as Yao Li

Similar in theme to the 1995 film "Swordmaking" (q.v.). This historical drama relates the story of master swordsmiths Ouyang Zhi and Gan Jiang, and their struggles with an evil king.

1259. *The Magic Thief (Bai Bian Shen Tou)*

1989. Shanghai Film Studio and Sil-Metropole Organization (Hong Kong) Ltd. Co-Production. Color. Letterboxed. 10 Reels. Direction: Liang Zhiqiang. Screenplay: Liang Zhiqiang. Cinematography: Ju Jiazhen. Art Direction: Zhong Yongqin. Music: Cai Lu, Xiao Yan. Sound: Liu Guangjie. Cast: Chun Yushan as Bao De, Zhou Lijing as Xia Bingyun

In the 1930s, master thief Bao De is one of Shanghai's most wanted criminals, although ordinary people love him for the fact he robs from the rich and gives to the poor. When many are made homeless by flooding in north China, the Shanghai Disaster Relief Committee raises over 2 million yuan to help. Xia Bingyun, a crooked lawyer chairing the committee, embezzles the money. When Bao De tries to steal it back, he is caught. Bao later escapes, and with the help of some street kids learns that Xia used the money to buy diamonds, and where he has probably hidden them. Bao steals them back and exposes Xia's crime, then turns the diamonds over to the relief committee.

1260. *The Magic Watch (Mo Biao)*

1990. Children's Film Studio. Color. Wide Screen. 9 Reels. Direction: Xu Geng. Screenplay: Zhang Zhilu. Cinematography: Wang Jouwen. Art Direction: Chen Zhaoyuan. Music: Wang Xiaoyong. Sound: Du Xiaohua. Cast: Jin Jia as Kang Bosi (as a child), Zhang Xiaotong as Kang Bosi (as an adult), Yu Dexian as Manager Ma

Kang Bosi is a small and thin boy who wishes he were big. One day, he finds a magic watch which instantly turns him into an adult. However, nobody recognizes him, and he soon finds he would rather remain a child. A department store manager steals the watch and uses it to make himself into a child. At last, caught in a rainstorm, both return to their original status.

1261. *The Mahjong Set (Fei Cui Ma Jiang)*

1987. Beijing Film Studio. Color. 9 Reels. Direction: Yu Xiaoyang. Screenplay: Zhong Yuan. Cinematography: Yan Junsheng. Art Direction: Yang Wan, Zhang Guojun. Music: Su Yue. Sound: Lai Qizhen. Cast: Cai Hongxiang as Chen Ting, Zhou Wenqiong as Lan Yun, Wang Hui as He Jian, Yuan Yuan as Tang Xiaoliang

One foggy, snowy morning, two girls in helmets ride a motorcycle onto an overpass and continue for some time along the same road. One of the girls is Lan Yun, the other He Chen. Suddenly the motorcycle speeds up, breaks through the railing and falls from the overpass... Days later, woman singer Song Yuan is murdered, and there are clues connecting her to the two girls killed in the motorcycle accident. Lan Yun and He Chen used to be good friends, their fathers worked in the same office. They were both in love with the same badminton player, Pei Ning. Investigators have many unanswered questions: Why did they both apparently commit suicide? Why was Song Yuan murdered? Could these incidents all be related to a mahjong set?

Maidens of Heavenly Mountain see *Dragon Chronicles, Part 1*

1262. *The Main Lesson (Zhu Ke)*

1976. Guangxi Zhuang Minority Autonomous Region Film Study Class. Color. 9 Reels. Direction: Guangbu Daoerji. Screenplay: Collective. Cinematography: Dansheng Nima, Meng Xiongqiang. Art Direction: Yun Chuan. Music: Zhu Songfeng, Yang Shaoyi. Sound: Li Zhuwen. Casting: Yu Haipeng as Feng Chunsong, Chen Limin as Li Kai, He Jinling as Li Ming, Yang Lingyan as Boniang, Zhao Wenqin as Ya Tao, Li Dingfeng as Tan Agong

A live-action version of a puppet show film "The Main Lesson," made by the Shanghai Cartoon Film Studio in 1975.

1263. *Mai's Love (Mai Mai Ti Wai Zhuan)*

1987. Tianshan Film Studio. Color. Direction: Guang Chunlan. Screenplay: Guang Chunlan, Duan Baoshan. Cinematography: Qi Xing, Nijiate. Art Direction: Xie Ri, Zha Ti. Music: Yikenmu. Sound: Li Bing. Cast: Tuerxunayi as Dilinar, Mulading as Maimaidi, Feierda Weisi as Xilipu, Ahzi Guli as Bainisha

Xilipu, a driver for a local travel agency, and Bainisha, a singer, are planning their wedding. One of their biggest worries is choosing the attendants for the event. The bridesmaid is Dilinar, a graduate of the Beijing Dance Academy, so Bainisha wants to be sure the best man is a match in appearance and social status. The groom asks his best friend Maimaidi, a restaurant owner, to be his best man, but at the wedding Maimaidi passes himself off as an interpreter named Alimu. "Alimu" plays his role successfully and of course Dilinar falls in love with him. Unfortunately, "Alimu" has to keep his distance because he's afraid Dilinar will find out the truth. Seeing a resemblance between "Alimu" and a restaurant owner named Maimaidi, Dilinar suggests they meet, but "Alimu" refuses. Finally Maimaidi tells Dilinar the whole story, to which she replies she loves him.

This film won an "Outstanding Feature Film" award from the Ministry of Radio, Film and Television in 1987.

1264. *The Makeup Artist and the Cartoonist (Hua Zuang Si Yu Man Hua Jia)*

1987. Guangxi Film Studio. Color. Letterboxed. 9 Reels. Direction: Zhao Wen. Screenplay: Ding Chanbang. Cinematography: Liao Fan. Art Direction: Lao Guanneng, Lei Xiaolan. Music: Su Tie. Sound: Han Weijun. Cast: Sun Song as Hao Erdan, Mai Xiaoqing as Zhen Fengya, Zhao Lijuan as Su Shanshan, Xie Zhou as Du Ke, Gao Qun as the director, Zhang Xiaoling as Xiao Rong, Li Jinfei as Da Long

Beauty salon makeup specialist Hao Erdan meets high school art teacher Zhen Fengya. They have a strong mutual attraction, but the relationship starts to founder over his lack of respect for her work. They get together for good when he comes to understand that proper makeup can also enrich people's lives.

1265. *Making a Living in Beijing (Hun Zai Bei Jing)*

1995. Fujian Film Studio, Hainan Nanyang Culture Group Corporation Co-Production. Color. Direction: He Qun. Screenplay: Suo Fei, based on Hei Ma's novel of the same title. Cinematography: Hou Yong, Shang Yong. Art Direction: Li Bing. Music: Zhang Shaotong. Cast: E Yang as Men Xiaogang, Fang Zige as Zhe Yili, Lu Xiaoyan as Zhang Xiaoyan, Feng Yuanzheng as Mao Shoucai, Mao Haitong as Huihui, Bi Yanjun as Hu Yi, Zhang Guoli as Sha Xin, Jin Shunzi as Xiao Qin, Xi Meijuan as Teng Baiju, Ju Xue as Ji Zi, Xiu Zongdi as Lao Sigui, Luo Xiaohua as Huang Yehong

The housing provided by the Xiangdo Publishing House for its employees consists of one-room apartments in a nondescript building. Through the lives of these people, the film examines the lives of intellectuals in China today, particularly how reform is affecting their lives. Sha Xin holds a master's degree in literary criticism, and has high standards concerning the company's output. He is also the most outspoken about the staff's shabby living conditions. Beautiful art editor Jizhi dreams of going overseas. Zhe Yili, a self-styled poet, becomes the most financially successful person in the building by writing lyrics to pop songs. He is having an affair with pop singer Huang Yehong. Mao Shancai is a naive young man from the countryside, attracted to Zheng Xiaoyan, a young woman just out of college but having trouble finding a permanent job. Reform has made Yu Huihai and his wife Teng Boju ambitious, and they now dream of converting the old publishing house into a source of popular best sellers. So they at last implement a company reorganization which eliminates Sha Xin's job, and results in Jizhi leaving for a new life in Hainan. Zhe Yili is dumped by his pop star girl friend, leaving him distraught but with new ideas for ballads. Mao and Zheng get married, figuring they can make it on their combined meager incomes. The reforms have affected everyone.

1266. *Making Langhong (Shao Lang Hong)*

1992. Xi'an Film Studio, Taiwan Taizi Film Co. Ltd. Co-Production. Color. Letterboxed. 10 Reels. Direction: Li Jia. Screenplay: Chen Wengui. Cinematography: Lin Zhanting. Art Direction: Yan Pingxiao, Dou Guoxiang. Music: Zhao Jiping. Sound: Hua Juan. Costume: Hai Qin,

Chang Rongfang. Makeup: Zhu Jian, Cheng Yin. Cast: Zhang Shi as Han Dong, Zhang Peifeng as Chunmei, Wang Yuwen as Gu Ping, Huang Daliang as Gu Zhi, Hong Rong as Han's mother

In eastern Jiangxi Province lies Jingde Town, renowned for centuries for producing the fine porcelain ware known in the West as "china." One particular type of china made there is called "Langhong," exceptionally difficult to make, so naturally very precious. The film relates the story of how in 1911 the government organized the production of Langhong. The master Quan is the natural choice for the job, but his apprentice Han Dong challenges him. Han's talent and devotion to the task finally makes Quan turn the job over to the apprentice.

1267. *Making Up Each Other's Deficiency (Qu Chang Bu Duan)*

1985. Shanghai Film Studio. Color. 9 Reels. Direction: Zhang Huijun. Screenplay: Huang Jingjie. Cinematography: Zhou Zhaiyuan. Art Direction: Yao Wei. Art Direction: Yao Wei. Music: Xiao Yan. Sound: Dong Jujing. Cast: Li Xiaqin as Yang Hua, Ji Ping as Niu Zhicheng, Tie Niu as Assistant Director Niu, Xie Yan as Sun Jinmu, Yang Shihua as Gu Yaonan, Jin Rong as Zhang Wei

Chunjiang County's Assistant Director of Transportation Niu happily welcomes the delivery of three new buses with three woman drivers just graduated from driving school. He assigns them to three veteran male drivers for training. Petite Yang Hua is assigned to big and crude Li Tielin; sweet Li Yuping to Zhou Xiaosong, a man greatly concerned with his personal appearance; and beautiful Gu Yaonan is assigned to Sun Jinmu. The comedy tells how these young people fall in love in pairs, but not with their assigned training partners.

1268. *Making Up Missing Classes (Bu Ke)*

1977. Shanghai Film Studio. Color. B & W. 5 Reels. Direction: Huang Zhumo, Liao Ruiquan. Screenplay: Collective effort of the Shanghai No. 3 Steel Mill's "No.57" High School and the Shanghai Dramatic Troupe, based on the stage play of the same title. Cinematography: Chen Ling. Art Direction: Lin Qi. Music: Yang Shaolu. Sound: Wu Jianghai, Yang Liangkun. Cast: Si Xilai as Teacher Jin, Li Junxi as Master Worker Li, Chen Ning as Teacher Zhang, Wang Zhijun as Li Gang, Wang Jian as Zhou Ming, Bi Zhijun as Gao Xiang

While teachers Jin and Zhang are both zealous about their students making up missed classes, the two disagree in their thinking about supervising these makeups: Zhang cares not at all about ideology, while Jin feels that ideological concerns should be paramount. Helped by Jin, visiting schoolmaster Zhao and some Red Guards, Zhang comes to realize he must alter his own thinking in order to change the thinking of his students. His method of having his students do makeup work was changed from then on.

1269. *The Malan Flower (Ma Lan Hua)*

1960. Haiyan Film Studio. B & W. 9 Reels. Direction: Pan Wenzhan, Meng Yuan. Screenplay: Ren Deyao, based on the children's stage play of the same name. Cinematography: Zhu Jing. Art Direction: Ding Cheng. Music: Yan Jinxuan, Zhang Hongxiang. Sound: Wu Ying. Cast: Wang Pei as Big Lan and Little Lan, Liu Angu as Ma Lang, Dong Ming as Old Cat, Lian Dezhi as Little Monkey, Li Baoluo as Old Wang, Ma Ji as Mother

In legend, a spirit named Ma Lang lived at the top of Mount Malan, where he planted a beautiful Malan flower, supposed to have magic powers. At the foot of the mountain lived two sisters: Big Lan was lazy while Little Lan was diligent. Presenting the Malan flower to the girls' father, Ma Lang petitioned for marriage to one of the sisters. Big Lan was reluctant to marry Ma Lang because she thought that life on the mountain would be too hard, so Little Lan married him. Not long after the wedding, Little Lan came to visit her parents bearing many gifts. Her obvious happiness and prosperity aroused her elder sister's jealousy. She temporarily lost her mind and, using the flower to change her into a wolf, attacked her sister. Later, being moved by the kindness and patience of Ma Lang, she confessed and repented for what she had done. Ma Lang and Little Lan then lived together happily again.

Best Art Direction Ding Cheng, 1962 Hundred Flowers Awards.

1270. *Male Citizens (Nan Xing Gong Min)*

1986. Shenzhen Television Station. Color. 10 Reels. Direction: Guo Baochang, Li Xiaolong. Screenplay: Guo Baochang, Lu Kejian.

Cinematography: Huang Renzhong. Art Direction: Sun Lin, Ji Qiao. Music: Liu Yanxi. Sound: Lin Bingsheng, Yu Xiaoming. Cast: Kong Xiangyu as yang Lei, Wang Runsheng as Su Zhen, Lu Ming as Lu Tianjie

During development of the Shenzhen Special Economic Zone, Yang Lei, CEO of a road construction corporation, overcomes all kinds of difficulties to initiate a large-scale project. However, just before the project is completed, Yang Lei makes an error which incurs heavy economic losses. He does not let this setback defeat him, however, and does his best to recover his losses. In the process, he also raises his personal standards, through the many internal and external conflicts within the company.

1271. *Mama, Where Are You? (Ma Ma, Ni Zai Na Li?)*

1982. Changchun Film Studio. Color. 9 Reels. Direction: Li Hua. Screenplay: Li Shaoyan, Qian Daoyuan, Yang Yinzhang. Cinematography: Duan Zhengjiang. Art Direction: Liang Shukui. Music: Quan Rufeng. Sound: Liu Xingfu. Cast: Song Chunli as Ming Wen, Yang Tong as Xiao Liang, Ni Changbo as Cao Jian, Zhao Wenyu as A Zhen, Huang Ailing as Waner, Kang Baomin as Gu Ageng

In 1927, CPC member Jian Hua is executed by the Nationalists on the same day his son is born. His wife Ming Wen is wanted as well, so she takes the baby and flees to a Communist controlled area. She gives the baby to worker Gu Ageng's family to raise. The Gu's are very poor, and in time the boy, named Xiao Liang, loses contact with the family. When Xiao Liang is 10 years old, he returns to Shanghai to look for his birth mother. Ming Wen is in Shanghai working for the Party, but they do not meet each other. Xiao Liang later goes to Wuhan and becomes a young revolutionary. Ming Wen is also there, and learns of his presence, but cannot contact him for fear of blowing her cover as a teacher in the home of a Japanese collaborator. In the end, mother and son are reunited at Yan'an.

1272. *Mama's Hand (Ma Ma De Shou)*

1992. Guangxi Film Studio. Color. Letterboxed. Direction: Zhang Junzhao. Screenplay: Ci Minhe, Zhang Junzhao. Cinematography: Cai Xiaopeng. Art Direction: Li Qining. Music: Wang Xiaoyong. Cast: Zhu Ling as Anna, Li

Qiang as Doctor Lin, Zhen Xiao as Teacher Wang, Jiang Lu as Xiao Zhen

Anna is a nurse in a Taipei hospital. Her husband takes a new lover and deserts Anna and their crippled daughter Xiaozhen. Anna works very hard to raise sufficient money for Xiaozhen's medical treatment, and begins to suffer the effects of overwork. Doctor Lin gives her an injection he says will counter this, but it actually makes her an addict. To obtain the drugs she needs, Anna becomes Doctor Lin's mistress. Anna is caught stealing drugs from the hospital and is fired, since nobody believes her story of how she got into her present situation. In despair, Anna kills herself. A few years later, Xiaozhen's former teacher sees her and she says she now lives with her father.

1273. *A Man and a Woman (Mo Nan He Mo Nu)*

1988. Pearl River Film Studio. Color. 10 Reels. Direction: Wang Di. Screenplay: Wang Lian, Li Yunliang. Cinematography: Luo Yan, Gang Yi. Art Direction: Li Wenguang, Liang Xiongguo. Music: Yang Shuzheng. Sound: Deng Qinhua. Cast: Zhang Kaili as Han Peipei, Zhang Guomin as Kang Kai, Wang Ping as Gu Yan, Ling Hui as Shen Bali

A new version of the theme presented in "The Shop Around the Corner" and its musical remake "In the Good Old Summertime." Two lonely people living on separate floors of a high-rise apartment building in South China come into conflict whenever they meet, unaware that each is the other's anonymous pen-pal.

1274. *Man Married into the Court (Jia Dao Gong Li De Nan Ren)*

1990. Chinese Film Company & Taiwan Zuofan Company Co-Production. Color. 9 Reels. Direction: Bai Jingrui. Screenplay: Wang Shuyuan. Cinematography: He Qin. Art Direction: Yu Maiduo. Music: Su Chong. Cast: Zhang Liji as Yongfu, Wang Yuling as Manzhu, Siqin Gaowa as Cixi, Zhang Zhenhua as Tongzhi, Gu Feng as Sun's father, Gui Yalei as Man's mother, Huang Yanmeng as Yongshou, Chen Honglie as Li Lianying

In the 1860s, in a suburb of Beijing, a young man named Yongfu falls in love with neighbor girl Manzhu. But Manzhu is selected to serve the Emperor Tongzhi at court. Yongfu travels to Beijing to find his beloved, but there he is tricked and turned into a eunuch. He later becomes an intimate confidant of the emperor. In 1875, after Tongzhi dies of syphilis, the Dowager Empress Ci Xi orders the death of everyone who knows the truth about Tongzhi's illness. Manzhu and Yongfu flee the Forbidden City for their old home in the suburbs, but there they find that all their relatives have been killed. In the end the lovers also fall victim to Ci Xi's terror.

1275. *A Man of Love (Ren Fei Cao Mu)*

1992. Shanghai Film Studio. Color. Letterboxed. 10 Reels. Direction: Zhang Gang. Screenplay: Zhang Gang. Cinematography: Shen Xilin, Zhang Jian. Art Direction: Sun Weide, Wang Renchen. Music: Wang Ming. Sound: Liu Guangjie. Costume: Dai Yili, Yuan Manfeng. Makeup: Zhou Liangeng. Cast: Liu Jinshan as Ye Aman, Zhang Kaili as Du Lan, Han Tongsheng as Director Zhong, Jin Meng as Wang Lili, Ni Yuanyuan as Lanlan, Zhuge Min as Wang Zhiyi

Deliveryman Ye Aman so loves his job that he often works for others. He meets Wang Lili, whose lover stole all her money and left her pregnant. Ye sells his own possessions to pay off her debts, and befriends her. In time, Wang falls in love with him. Ye also helps Du Lan, a librarian who has an unfaithful husband.

1276. *A Man or a Monkey (Ren Hou Da Lie Bian)*

1992. Xi'an Film Studio. Color. Letterboxed. 9 Reels. Direction and Screenplay: Pan Peicheng, Lin Yu, Zhang Rui, based on Zhou Daxin's original story. Cinematography: Shang Yong, Li Xiaoping. Art Direction: Wang Caibing. Music: Zhang Dalong. Sound: Li Tie, Xu Qian. Costume; Liu Qingang. Makeup: Shao Zhen. Cast: Xu Fan as Xun'er, Zhang Qiuge as Sha Gao, Zhang Xiaotong as Zhen Ping, Cao Jingyang as Shao Laokuan

Farmer Sha Gao hires Zhen Ping to catch a monkey he can put on display. Zhen catches several monkeys, but in doing so injures his leg. While he is recuperating, Sha Gao's family assumes Zhen's debts. During this time, Zhen convinces Sha Gao that it would be more profitable if they worked up a circus act with the monkeys. The act they decide on is called "Man and Monkey Fight." It proves popular with rural peasants, but is really degrading. At last, Sha Gao's wife Xun'er convinces Zhen to give this up and do something worthwhile and meaningful. Xun'er then frees all the monkeys into the mountains.

1277. *Man Who Deals with Devils (Yu Mo Gui Da Jiao Dao De Ren)*

1980. Pearl River Film Studio. Color. 11 Reels. Direction: Lin Lan. Screenplay: Liu Shizheng. Cinematography: Liu Jingtang. Art Direction: Zhou Chengren. Music: Ding Jialing. Sound: Deng Qinhua. Cast: Guo Yuntai as Yu Haitao, Chu Ming as Du Kangfu, Zhu Manfang as Wang Huiru, Fang Hua as Yan Kefei, Lu Shuren as Zhao Yibiao, Wang Zhigang as Yu Haibao

In Shanghai in 1947, Chiang Kaishek issues secret order "A," intended to take the fullest advantage of his government's support in economic circles. CPC undercover operative Yu Haitao infiltrates the Nationalists by posing as Zhang Gongpu, CEO of the Rongcang Company. To accomplish his mission, Zhang Gongpu often has to put his personal feelings aside. One time, he is visited by his brother Yu Haibao, a Red Army logistics officer he has not seen in 10 years. Yu Haibao appeals to his brother to help the Communist cause by getting military materials to their forces. When his brother turns him down to protect his cover as Zhang Gongpu, the officer leaves in anger. Zhang Gongpu's son Zhang Wu is enthusiastic about the anti–Chiang activity, but he misunderstands his father's actions and cuts off all ties with the family. Later, the Party makes contact with Zhang Gongpu through a young woman liaison named Ai Di. When Zhang and his wife Wang Huiru realize that Ai Di is their own daughter, they keep their emotions to themselves and do not tell her. Wen Ai Di is arrested, they control themselves and refrain from helping her so as not to arouse Nationalist suspicions. When Ai Di dies in captivity, the couple grieve, but are proud of their daughter. Zhang Gongpu exploits the Nationalists' internal conflicts and finally succeeds in thwarting the secret order "A" conspiracy.

1278. *The Man Who Stopped the Hearse (Lan Ling Che De Ren)*

1986. Shanghai Film Studio. Color. 10 Reels. Direction: Li Xiepu. Screenplay: Jin Damo, Yan Jifeng. Cinematography: Cao Weiye. Art Direction: Xue Jianna. Music: Xu Jingxin. Sound: Ren

Daming, Xu Xilin. Cast: Wang Zhihua as Jiang Wenjing, Wu Jing as Yuyin, Yang Kaixuan as Tang Hui, Liao Xueqiu as Liu Na, Zhou Yuyuan as Mei Yugui

As a funeral procession makes its way through the streets, it is suddenly stopped by Doctor Jiang Wenjing, who demands there first be an autopsy. The autopsy discloses that the deceased, son-in-law of the county Party Secretary, has not died of natural causes but has been murdered. The prime suspect is his wife Luo Na, the Party Secretary's daughter. She is detained for questioning, but absolutely refuses to cooperate with investigators. She is released for lack of evidence, and the political nature of the case puts heavy pressure on the PSB to solve it soon. At last their investigation leads back to the original suspect Luo Na, and she is brought to trial.

1279. *The Man Will Take a Long Trip (Nan Er Yao Yuan Xing)*

1987. Changchun Film Studio. Color. 9 Reels. Direction: Guangbu Daoerji. Screenplay: Huang Shiyin. Cinematography: Sun Hui, Zhang Shaoge. Art Direction: Wei Hongyu. Music: Wu Damin, Yang Yilun. Sound: Zhen Yunbao. Cast: Ma Cangyu as Liang Zheng, Lin Qiang as Fu Ping, Liang Tongyu as Long Dahai

The lives and loves of some oil workers and their families. Geological engineer Yuan Fang and his wife An Jing are a devoted couple, and she is very supportive of his work. Director Liang Zheng's wife asks for a divorce because her husband's work takes him away for long periods of time. Yuan Fang is killed in an accident. The oil exploration work at the bottom of the South China Sea ends, and the team prepares to move on to the East China Sea. Their families sadly see them off, but they understand.

1280. *Managing the Weather (Geng Yun Bo Yu)*

1960. Beijing Film Studio. B & W. 8 Reels. Direction: Wei Rong. Screenplay: Li Zhun. Cinematography: Li Wenhua. Art Direction: Zhang Xiande. Music: Shi Lemeng. Sound: Lu Xiancang, Liu Shida. Cast: Yu Ping as Xiao Xiaoying, Lu Fei as Secretary Guan, Yu Zhongyi as Bronze Hammer, Wang Zhifang as Commune Director Zhang, Guo Shutian as Xu Xiangchao, Wang Yunxia as Sister-in-Law, Chen Qiang as Xiao Kuan, Zhang Ping as the County Secretary, Zhao Lian as Li Chun, Huang Suying as Aunt Xiao

Xiao Suying, a young woman in the Dan River people's commune, establishes a rural meteorological observatory. Her first, amateurish efforts are mocked by the commune's agricultural department director Xu Xiangchao and by her own brother "Bronze Hammer." She is encouraged to keep trying by commune secretary Guan, however, and as she gains more knowledge of scientific forecasting, combined with the experience of local farmers, her accuracy improves steadily. After the wheat harvest there is a major drought. The county meteorological observatory forecasts a storm, so the country Water Conservancy Bureau orders the water released from the commune's reservoir for the safety of those living in the lowlands near the Dan River. But Suying forecasts it will not rain, and argues against the release. After much debate, her judgment is accepted, and her forecast proves accurate. Since the reservoir is not drained, the commune is guaranteed sufficient water for irrigation.

1281. *Manchurian Traveling Performers (Jiang Hu Guai Lang)*

1990. Changchun Film Studio. Color. Letterboxed. 9 Reels. Direction: Qiao Keji. Screenplay: Ouyang Chongxian, Liu Zhicheng. Cinematography: Liu Fengdi. Art Direction: Guo Yansheng, Meng Xiangchun. Music: Liu Xijing. Sound: Yang Yuedong, Zhen Yunbao. Cast: Mao Yanhua as Boss Jin, Luo Jiujiang as dragon, Li Chiyou as Xizi, Shi Lei as Tie Tou, Liu Jihong as Jin Cui, Yan Shirong as Wang Ping, Lu Qiwen as Little Bean

In the 1940s, Jin's Acrobatic Troupe roams from town to town in Northeast China, often having to bear the bullying of Japanese soldiers in the audience. At this time, the Japanese Army is running seriously low on medical supplies, and constant allied bombardment prevents new supplies from coming in. After discovering that the acrobatic troupe has a very effective homemade medication they use for treating injuries, the Japanese demand the formula. Out of patriotic motives, the acrobats refuse to share the formula, which results in severe enemy persecution. At last, the acrobats are able to escape.

1282. *Man's World (Nan Ren De Shi Jie)*

1987. Guangxi Film Studio. Color. 10 Reels.

Direction: Wang Weiyi. Screenplay: Wang Hui-quan, Wang Weiyi. Cinematography: Shen Xilin. Art Direction: Han Shangyi. Music: Jin Fuzhai. Sound: Zhou Minzong, Lin Lin. Cast: Hou Wei-wen as "A," Wang Fuli as the woman director

A futuristic tale. In order to ensure their having male babies, thousands of women undergo an operation designed to separate the XY DNA. The operation has a 99 percent success rate. A man referred to simply as "A" and his wife want a boy very badly, but are in the one percent that produces a girl. More than a decade later, the first male generation is growing up, and society is starting to experience the consequences of their not finding wives. So "A" is very popular because he has a daughter. This is one of a series of stories pointing out the problems of a society which has only boys.

1283. *Mansions and Humble Homes (Da Sha Xiao Wu)*

1986. August First Film Studio. Color. Color. 9 Reels. Direction: Ren Pengyuan. Screenplay: Huang Yazhou. Cinematography: Zhang Chi. Art Direction: Li Cuihua. Music: Liu Tingyu. Sound: Duan Huilai. Cast: Hasi Bageng as Ye Jin, Liang Yujing as Luo Yue, Wang Qingxiang as Wang Zhilong, Xu Zhan as Station Director Song

At a key construction project in the city of Kunshan, trouble erupts when a resident of the construction area makes some outrageous demands before agreeing to relinquish his property. Local TV reporter Ye Jin suspects there is something else behind the resident's irrational behavior, and with strong support from the station director, launches an investigation. Ye Jin's probe at last turns up evidence that the true owner of the house is Wang Zhilong, head of the business department at the city's Bureau of Industry, who stands to make a considerable amount of money if he handles it right. Ye Jin uses the evidence he gathers to make a video tape exposing the bureaucrat's conflict of interest and corruption, but Wang uses every means at his command to stop the tape's being put on the air. At last the tape is broadcast, shocking the population of Kunshan, but the station staff knows the battle against official corruption is far from over.

1284. *Mao Zedong and His Son (Mao Ze Dong He Ta De Er Zi)*

1991. Xiaoxiang Film Studio. Color. 10 Reels. Wide Screen. Direction: Zhang Jinbiao. Screen-play: Fang Taochu, Luo Ju. Cinematography: Yang Wei. Art Direction: Li Renzhang, Cao Bin. Music: Yang Qing. Sound: Liu Yishen. Cast: Wang Ren as Mao Zedong, Wu Gang as Young Mao Zedong, Yao Gang as Mao Anying, Ming Zi as Mao Anying (as a boy), Xu Yang as Liu Siqi

In the summer of 1950, the Korean War begins, and by fall China begins to feel threatened. Mao Zedong decides to organize the Chinese People's Volunteers to aid North Korea. Mao's eldest son Mao Anying goes to the front under Peng Dehuai, commander-in-chief of the Volunteer Army. Not long afterwards, Mao Anying dies in battle. Though grieving deeply over the loss of his son, Mao arranges that the widow is not informed. Unaware of her husband's death, Mao Anying's wife Liu Siqi waits for his return. Mao Zedong overcomes his grief and puts all his energy into his work, but his daughter-in-law's weekly visits often plunge him into deep sorrow. Encouraged by Premier Zhou Enlai, Mao is finally able to tell Liu Siqi about his son's death. Liu leaves in tears, and Mao reminisces about all those close to him who have already died.

1285. *Mao Zedong's Story (Mao Zedong De Gushi)*

1992. Emei Film Studio. Color. Wide Screen. 15 Reels. Direction: Han Sanping, Mao Mao, Luo Xing. Screenplay: Han Sanping. Cinematography: Luo Xun. Art Direction: Wu Xujing, Chen Desheng. Music: Guo Wenjing. Sound: Tu Liuqing. Costume: Shuai Furong, Wang Nailong, Chen Jiying. Makeup: Wang Qingping, Zeng Xiaozhen, Wang Yi. Cast: Gu Yue as Mao Zedong, Sun Ming as Zhong Erniu, Sidifeng Chakadi as David Eisenhower, Luosaila Badeluqi as Julie Nixon, Ma Shuangqing as the village head, Yang Chunming as the teacher, Wei Tiantang as Zhang Ershun, Yu Lan as Ershun's mother

One evening in 1975, former President Nixon's daughter Julie and her husband David pay a call on Mao Zedong, bringing him a personal letter from her father. As they while away the evening in pleasant conversation, Mao looks back over his 80 years, recalling the anti–Japanese resistance, his organizational work among the peasants in Shaanxi Province, the post–World War II conflict with the Nationalists, the American-brokered peace negotiations, the establishment of the PRC, the Korean War (which cost Mao his son), the Great Leap Forward, the Cultural Revolution years and many other events along the way. Back in the present, Mao tells the American couple that he still hopes to someday see and swim in the Mississippi River.

1286. *Map-Tattooed Bodies (Duan Ming Wen Shen)*

1991. Changchun Film Studio. Color. Letterboxed. 9 Reels. Direction: Zhao Weiheng. Screenplay: Zen Xiaohui. Cinematography: Yu Bing. Art Direction: Liu Zhonghong, Ming Jianguo. Music: Guo Dingli. Sound: Wun Liangyu and Chen Fan. Cast: Ma Chongdong as Si Daocheng, Xia Jing as Qing Ye, Zhou Zhou as Wang Ping, Ge Chunzuang as Cui Wenxi

In 1915, martial arts instructor and revolutionary Cui Wenxi raids a Japanese weapons storehouse. He escapes, but is forced to bury the weapons. He tattoos a map of the hiding place on the bodies of his five apprentices and his daughter. The film follows the efforts of the Japanese and their Chinese collaborators to get the maps.

1287. *Maple (Feng)*

1980. Emei Film Studio. Color. 10 Reels. Direction: Zhang Yi. Screenplay: Zhen Yi. Cinematography: Li Erkang, Wang Wenxiang. Art Direction: Xie Huibing. Music: Fu Gengcheng. Sound: Zhang Jianping. Cast: Xu Feng as Lu Danfeng, Wang Erli as Li Honggang

In 1966, millions of young Chinese are caught up in the fervor of the Cultural Revolution, among them a girl named Lu Danfeng and a boy named Li Honggang, two young students who are also lovers. However, the political atmosphere changes rapidly, and the two find themselves following rival political lines, presenting them with the painful choice between love and revolution. One day, an armed fight begins between the two factions, and each tries to persuade the other to defect, without success. Finally, in despair, she jumps from a building and is killed, leaving Li Honggang grieving. He finds he cannot go on without her and leaves the organization. But he finds no peace: two years later, the faction Lu belongs to gains power, and Li Honggang is executed as a counterrevolutionary for having driven Lu Dangeng to her death.

1288. *Maple Bay (Fengshu Wan)*

1976. Pearl River Film Studio. Color. 13 Reels. Direction: Lu Yu, Liu Xin, Lin Lan.

Screenplay: Collective, recorded by Chen Jianqiu, and based on the Hunan Provincial Dramatic Company's stage play of the same title. Cinematography: Huang Yonghu, Li Shengwei, Wei Duo. Art Direction: Mo Renji, Huang Chong. Music: Bai Chengren, Tan Zhibing. Cast: Liao Bingyan as Zhao Haishan, He Ningkang as Cheng San, Lu Xiangzhang as Miao Wangchun, Li Bo as Zhao's mother, Ye Junwu as Niu Yazhi, Di Xiaohui as Lian Meizhi, Sun Qichang as Tang Hanchi, Liu Yungji as Tang Jiaju.

In the fall of 1926, as the Communist Party's influence grows rapidly among workers and farmers, Party cadre Zhao Haishan is assigned back to his hometown of Maple Bay which he had been forced to leave years before. He organizes a farmers' association and sets up a farmers' self-protection group to struggle with their main enemy, tyrannical local landlord Tang Hanci and his son. The Tangs conspire to wipe out the farmers' movement. Zhao also has to contend with rightist line carried out by county agricultural department head Hu Siu. The farmers execute Tang Hanchi, and in what becomes known as the Fall Harvest Rebellion, they defeat a private army raised and led by Tang Jiaju.

1289. *Maple Leaves Cover the Small Road (Hong Ye Pu Man Xiao Lu)*

1983. Emei Film Studio. Color. 10 Reels. Direction: Zhang Yi. Screenplay: Wang Yuejun, Long Tailing, Cui Hongcang. Cinematography: Li Dagui. Art Direction: Wang Tao. Music: Yu Linqin. Sound: Shen Guli. Cast: Li Kechun as Tian Chuanmei, Zhu Yanping as Director Chu, Fu Lili as Lanzhi, Zhuo Lei as Shui Xiang, Tang Xiaobing as a young soldier

Just at the time that warlord General Liu Xiang amasses a force of 120,000 to launch a fall offensive against a Communist-held area, Red Army political instructor Tian Chuanmei sets out to contact the local county Party Committee. She is accompanied by two other women: Lanzhi, a medic, and Shui Xiang, a soldier. On the way, they meet Chu, a Red Army intelligence officer. Chu places Tian Chuanmei under arrest because her husband Li Baogui has "rebelled," thereby making her suspect as well. On the way to Intelligence Bureau headquarters, however, Chu is injured. The women still take care of him and make no attempt to either abandon him or escape. Tian Chuanmei's strong will and obvious loyalty impresses Chu and he later sacrifices his own life to cover the women. They still proceed to bureau headquarters to clear Tian's name.

1290. *Marching South, Fighting North (Nan Zheng Bei Zhan)*

1974. Beijing Film Studio. Color. (Wide and Narrow Screen), 13 Reels. Direction: Cheng Yin, Wang Yan. Screenplay: Shen Ximeng, et al. Cinematography: Nie Jing, Chen Guoliang. Art Direction: Yang Yuhe. Music: Yan Ke. Sound: Lu Xiancang. Cast: Wang Sangxing as the Division Commander, Zhang Lianfu as the Political Commissar, Lu Fei as Regimental Commander Liu, Zhang Yongshou as Battalion Commander Gao, Tian Baofu as the Advisor, Bai Zhidi as Company Commander Zhang

This is a remake of the Shanghai Film Studio's 1952 black and white film of the same title.

1291. *Marksman Without a Gun (Wu Qiang Qiang Shou)*

1988. August First Film Studio. Color. 10 Reels. Direction: Hu Mei. Screenplay: Wang Zequn. Cinematography: Wu Feifei. Art Direction: Cai Weidong, Hu Shumin. Music: Guo Feng. Sound: Xiang Zhiliang. Cast: Zhang Yi as Situ Minjie, Wang Xian as Chang Guchuan

Situ Minjie had been a noted chief of detectives, but was removed from his position for violating regulations during an investigation. His good friend Zhang Cheng, Chief Justice of the Maritime Court, asks him to look into a salvage case involving a sunken ship. Through his former lover Yan Hong's will, Situ Minjie finds some evidence in the salvage dispute, a roll of film which records the damage down to the ship by a Japanese ship the "St. Mary." Situ comprehensively analyzes the whole situation, and at last the court issues an order detaining the "St. Mary" and ordering it to pay compensation.

1292. *Marriage (Jie Hun)*

1983. Youth Film Studio. Color. 5 Reels. Direction: Jin Tao, Zhou Wei, Wang Zhiyin. Screenplay: Jin Tao, Zhou Wei, Wang Zhiyin. Cinematography: He Qing, Sun Cheng, Gu Changwei, Wu Fei. Art Direction: Zhen Wei. Music: Ai Liqun. Sound: Kong Lingyan, Huang Yinxia, Sun Xin. Cast: Lei Gesheng as Old Liang, Hou Kemin as Young Liang, Cao Pengju as Xiao Chen

In the countryside outside of Beijing live two bachelor brothers, both orphaned in early childhood. Old Liang is now in his 40s and resigned to being a bachelor all his life although he hopes his brother Young Liang will be able to find a wife. Old Liang saves all he can to send Young Liang to technical school in the city and also for his brother to someday have a fine wedding. After graduation, Young Liang gets a factory job where he meets a girl named Xiao Chen. They get engaged, and Young Liang asks his brother for the wedding money, which is gladly handed over. On the day of the wedding, Old Liang travels to Beijing to attend, but at the celebration his younger brother refuses to introduce him to anyone because the older man's appearance is so shabby. Hurt and angry, Old Liang leaves and goes home. Young Liang feels so guilty that he collapses. When he recovers, Young Liang and his bride travel to the countryside to visit and apologize to his older brother.

1293. *Marriage in a Trap (Xian Jing Li De Hun Yin)*

1993. Shanghai Film Studio & Beijing Jidi Film Technology Development Company Co-Production. Color (70mm). 10 Reels. Direction: Song Chong. Screenplay: Song Chong. Cinematography: Liu Lihua. Art Direction: Xue Jianna, Zhu Jiancang. Music: Xu Jingxin. Sound: Feng Deyao. Costume: Dong Zhongmin, Zhao Yingwu. Makeup: Wang Jingjuan, Zhu Liping. Cast: He Zhenjun as Ji Jiaqi, Chen Wei as Mei Xiushan, Xia Jun as Tao Zhengde, Cui Jie as Li Jinkui, Yan Xiang as Ji Guojun, Yu Fei as Ya Erxun

In order to develop the insurance industry in China, Ji Jiaqi and his father Ji Guojun start the Jiaxing Insurance Company in Shanghai in 1932. This does not set well with the United Asian Insurance Company, a foreign firm headed by Ya Erxun, and which had dominated the Chinese market. A triad abducts campus beauty Mei Xiushan and orders her to marry Ji Jiaqi; otherwise, her boyfriend Tao Zhengde will be killed. She consents in order to protect Tao, but on her wedding night attempts to kill Ji. When she finds that he is wholly innocent of the plot, she tells him that the marriage was a trap set for him. It develops that her boyfriend Tao set up the plot, as part of a scheme to destroy the Jiaxing Company. Tao also arranges for a ship to have an accident, prompting thousands of victims to file insurance claims with Ji's company. Mei and Ji lead the struggle against his company's unethical competitor and its allies in organized crime, and they really fall in love in the process.

1294. *Marriage of the Borrowed Bride (Jie Qing Pei)*

1959. Changchun Film Studio. B & W. 10 Reels. Direction: Fang Ying. Screenplay: Yang Ming, based on the Yunnan opera of the same name. Cinematography: Liu Yongzhen. Art Direction: Wang Yongkang. Music: Jin Hui, Chen Qifang. Sound: Kang Ruixin, Cast: Qiu Yunsun as Wang Zhengkui, Zhou Huinong as Grandma, Cai Xiangzhen as Zhang Guiyin, Peng Guozhen as Li Chunlin, Zhao Yintao as Father-in-Law, Hui Yaoping as Mother-in-Law

To give her dead father a proper funeral, Zhang Guiying indentures herself as a servant in the household of Wang Zhengkui. After a few days, he tries to force her to become his concubine, but she refuses. Wang's younger cousin Li Chunlin visits Wang, seeking his help in "borrowing" a wife. It seems that after Li's wife died, he had difficulty raising the money to travel to Beijing for the Imperial examinations to become a scholar-official. Meeting his former father-in-law on the street one day, the older man assumed that Li had taken a new wife, and said that if Li brought his bride to see him the father-in-law would give him the money he needed for the trip. Wang lends Zhang Guiying to Li, and she accompanies him to the in-laws home. The older couple are charmed by the young woman, and Zhang Guiying really falls for Li, giving him many hints as to her background. Their attempts to marry hit a snag when Wang Zhengkui makes some accusations in court, but finally their marriage is approved.

1295. *A Married Couple (Er Nu Qing Shi)*

1950. Beijing Film Studio. B & W. 8 Reels. Direction: Du Shenghua. Screenplay: Du Shenghua. Cinematography: Han Gangzhi. Set Design: Qin Wei. Music: Zhang Linyi. Sound: Gao Min. Costume: Liu Dongmu. Makeup: Sun Hongkui. Cast: Shi Wei as Li Xiulan, Huang Fei as Wang Guichun, Li Jingbo as Li Laocuan, Di Li as Old Lady Li, Fang Hua as Zhao Laoman, Su Wei as Director of the Women's Committee, Wang Weiguang as the Village Head, Sang Fu as the District Director, Yan Zengho as Zhao Dakui

After the issuance of China's first marriage law, in the village of Dongzhao, Hebei Province, two village young people named Wang Guicun and Li Xiulan fall in love and want to marry. However, Xiulan's conservative father Li Laocuan is bitterly opposed to the match, as he wants his daughter to marry Zhao Da, a well-to-do farmer in a nearby village. Xiulan stands up to her father, and enlists the support of the local Women's Committee director. The director convinces Xiulan's mother of the harm caused by arranged marriages, and the mother drops her opposition to the daughter choosing her own mate. But when the young couple go to the village government to register their marriage, they encounter Xiulan's father Li Laocun, who produces a marriage certificate for his daughter and Zhao Da, obtained with the aid of a rather muddled village head. Again the Women's Committee director intervenes, criticizing the village head's error and accompanying the young couple to register with the district government. After explanations, Li Laocun agrees to cancel his daughter's engagement with Zhao Dakui, but he reaffirms his opposition to her chosen marriage and breaks off relations with the couple. But after the marriage, when he sees how happy they are together, Li Laocun is reconciled with his daughter.

Married to a Child **see** *Girl from Hunan*

1296. *The Marshall and the Soldier (Yuan Shuai He Shi Bing)*

1981. Changchun Film Studio. Color. 9 Reels. Direction: Zhang Hui. Screenplay: Yan Yi, Guo Shaogui, Chen Zhonggan, Su Shaoquan. Cinematography: Liu Yongzhen. Art Direction: Hu Pei. Music: Qin Yongcheng, Li Yanzhong. Sound: Jue Jingxiu, Fu Linge. Cast: Wang Tianpeng as Marshall He Long, Liang Tongyu as Yang Guoguang, Wang Zhifang as Mother, Bao Ming as Li Jimo

The story of Marshall He Long's interest in pingpong in China, and how he cared for and trained an athlete, Yang Guoguang. Yang Guoguang is a Hong Kong athlete. When he fell ill and had to be hospitalized, the marshall goes to visit him and organizes a medical team for his care. Marshall He's enthusiasm for the Chinese Pingpong team greatly encourages the young man, so when he recovers he practices very hard, finally becoming the first Chinese world champion in international competition.

After that, the marshall arranges for Yang to become coach of the Chinese women's ping-pong team. This leads to romance and marriage for Yang and woman player Li Jimo. Yang lifts the Chinese women's team to world class, and they also win a world championship. This so excites and pleases the marshall that he approves Yang Guochang's taking the women's team to visit some friendly countries.

1297. *The Marshall Is Missing (Yuan Shuai De Si Nian)*

1990. Youth Film Studio & Shanxi Film Studio Co-Production. Color. Wide Screen. 10 Reels. Direction: Wei Linyu, Qika Kuerban. Screenplay: Shi Qinshuo. Cinematography: Wei Linyu. Art Direction: Fang Xuzhi. Music: Jin Fuzhai. Sound: Ni Zheng, Xie Ao. Cast: Dong Shize as Xu Xiangqian, Yuan Zhishun as the young Xu Xiangqian, Lu Xi as Liang Peihuang

Red Army Marshall Xu Xiangqian looks back over his career during the civil war of the late 1940s. In March, 1948, Xu was commander of Communist forces in Shanxi, Shandong and Henan provinces. In the drive toward Lingfen, he pushes back Nationalist commander Liang Peihuang, despite the latter's overwhelming numerical superiority. On April 10th, Xu's army takes Xiacheng, the last objective before Lingfen, and on May 7th they destroy the defenders of Lingfen, taking Liang Peihuang prisoner in the process.

1298. *The Martial Angel (Shen Wei Tian Shi)*

1993. Inner Mongolia Film Studio. Color. Letterboxed. 9 Reels. Direction and Screenplay: A Buer. Cinematography: Ge Lisheng. Art Direction: Bu Ren. Art Direction: Wang Xiaohong. Music; Wei Jianian. Sound; Buren. Costume: Tang Baoli. Makeup: Su Bude. Cast: Gong Youchun as Ya Hong, Ren Naichang as Gao Shiyin, Wei Daming as Little Fatty, Zhang Fuzhi as Fu Zhu, Jia Ruixin as Lina

Middle-aged bachelor farmer Fu Zhu pays 7,000 yuan to buy a bride, college student Li Na. The girl was abducted by a crime ring headed by Gao Shiyin which specializes in abducting girls and selling them to farmers as wives. Police officers investigating the girl's disappearance follow the trail to the countryside, and are able to rescue Li, who has been raped and held against her will by Fu Zhu. In a final confrontation, the officers kill the criminally insane and vicious Gao Shiyin.

1299. *Martial Woman 13th Sister (Xia Nu Shi San Mei)*

1986. Beijing Film Studio, Japan Shi Optical Research Institute Co-Production. Color. 3-D. Wide Screen. 10 Reels. Direction: Yang Qitian, Chunchuantou. Screenplay: Meng Lie, Yang Qitian, Zhang Zhucheng. Cinematography: Zhang Zhucheng, Jingshangwan. Art Direction: Luo Yurong. Music: Wang Ming. Sound: Lan Fan. Cast: Ding Lan as He Yufeng, Wang Bozhao as Sir An, Qiu Jianguo as Han Yong, Wang Qun as Hua Biao, Ge Chunzuang as Ji Xiantang, Li Junfeng as Tie Luohan

During the reign of the Emperor Yongzheng (c1730), famous and powerful General Ji Xiantang becomes increasingly abusive of his power. One of his subordinates, He Qi, is an honest officer with a beautiful daughter, He Yufeng. General Ji wants Yufeng to be his daughter-in-law, but when her parents refuse, Ji Xiantang has the entire family killed, with only Yufeng escaping. The girl devotes herself to the study of kongfu, and takes the kongfu name "13th Sister." With help from older fellow students, 13th Sister finally kills General Ji and avenges her parents.

1300. *Mary from Beijing (Meng Xing Shi Fen)*

1993. Beijing Film Studio and Hong Kong Shaw Brothers Film Company Co-Production. Color. Letterboxed. 10 Reels. Direction and Screenplay: Zhang Aijia (Sylvia Chang). Cinematography: Du Kefeng. Art Direction: Zhang Shuping. Costume: Lu Xiafang. Makeup: Lu Ruilian. Cast: Gong Li as Mali (Mary), Zhong Zhentao (Kenny Bee) as Wang Guowei, Lin Junxian (Wilson Lam) as Peter, Lin Haifeng (Jan Lam) as Ming Zai, Bai Hua as Mary's father, He Hongwan as Peter's mother, Zhu Mu as Peter's father

After graduation from college, Mali goes to Hong Kong, hoping to relocate. After 10 months there, she still has been unable to obtain a permanent residence card, so cannot find work. Peter, son of a wealthy jeweler, falls for her and sets her up in an apartment as his mistress. They often talk about marriage, but Peter avoids mentioning the subject to his parents, and only comes to visit Mali occasionally. A new neighbor in Mali's apartment building is Wang Guowei, a Chinese who grew up in Britain but has now returned to build up his business with China. However, Guowei's wife has refused to accompany him, and they are in the process of getting a divorce. He and Mali meet by chance, and become good friends. When Wang goes to the mainland on business, he visits her parents, and he and Mali grow closer. Mali finally tires of her pointless relationship with Peter, and she moves out on her own. She finally gets her residence card and finds work as a tour guide. One day, she and Guowei run into each other and are delighted to get together again.

Masters of the Skies **see** *Vast Oceans and Skies*

1301. *A Matter of Life and Death (Xing Ming Jiao Guan)*

1986. Shanghai Film Studio. Color. 9 Reels. Direction: Shi Xiaohua. Screenplay: Miao Yikang, Xu Weixin. Cinematography: Qiu Yiren, Li Chongjun. Art Direction: Zhen Changfu. Music: Xu Jingxin. Sound: Xie Guojie. Cast: Xie Yuan as Yao Rao, Ye Zhikang as Fei Yimin, Shi Ling as Su Zongtang, Sun Min as A Lu, Ding Jiayuan as Chang Chunlai, Wang Jingguo as Lu Daniu

In a South China hospital during the Cultural Revolution, the new liaison from central Party headquarters changes the hospital's name to "Oppose Deviationism Hospital" and orders the institution's revolutionary committee to fire all "intellectuals" on the staff. She instructs them to use youthful Red Guards or promote ordinary workers to professional positions. Worker propaganda team director A Lu appoints hospital cook Yao Rao a surgeon. The hapless Yao cannot turn down this honor, and starts to perform an operation although he is terrified. After the first operation, Yao Rao is publicly hailed as a "model doctor." The film tells how Yao Rao finally comes to realize he is being used as a tool in a political conspiracy.

1302. *Mayor Chen Yi (Chen Yi Shi Zhang)*

1981. Shanghai Film Studio. Color. Letterboxed. 10 Reels. Direction: Huang Zuolin, Luo Yizhi, Fu Jinggong. Screenplay: Sha Yexin. Cinematography: Qiu Yiren, Zhou Zhaiyuan. Art Direction: Xu Run, Mo Shaojiang. Music: Shen Liqun. Sound: Liu Guangjie, Lu Xuehan. Cast: Wei Qimin as Chen Yi, Zhang Fei as Fu Yile, Xu Chengxian as Qi Yangzhi, Wang Xiyan as Tong Dawei, Su Shucai as Peng Yihu

On May 27, 1949, Shanghai is liberated, and Chen Yi becomes mayor of China's largest city. When he takes office, the city is in chaos: businesses of every sort are bankrupt, there are shortages of food and fuel, and unemployment is rising steadily. Chen Yi implements the Communist Party policy of relying on the working class, revolutionary cadres and intellectuals, and uniting Chinese capitalists behind the revolution. To accomplish the last point, Chen Yi and Bureau of Industry Director Gu Chong hold a conference at the home of textile manufacturer Fu Yile to explain the Party's economic policy toward Chinese capitalists. This bolsters the manufacturers confidence in the city's future. In the fall of 1949, the Shanghai Number One Department Store opens for business, a milestone in the city's economic recovery. Chen Yi visits the famous chemical industrialist Qi Yangzhi to discuss ways of alleviating the city's severe shortage of medicines. Over time, Chen Yi displays his leadership qualities, bringing labor and management together to relieve capitalist-worker conflicts. His enthusiasm is even successful in persuading his father-in-law to move back to Shanghai. In less than a year, he accomplishes an economic rebirth for Shanghai.

1303. *Me and My Classmates (Wo He Wo De Tong Xue Men)*

1986. Shanghai Film Studio. Color. 9 Reels. Direction: Peng Xiaolian. Screenplay: Xie Youchun. Cinematography: Liu Lihua. Art Direction: Zhou Xinren. Music: Liu Yanxi. Sound: Dong Jujing. Cast: Bu Lan, Zhou Jingzhou, Yang Chunlei, Yong Jingxing, Yu Lei

In Guangming High School in Shanghai, Senior student Zhou Jingzhou is a member of the city basketball team as well as the star of his class team at Guangming. He is also his class athletic representative on the Athletic Council, so when he announces that he will soon be moving to the city of Dalian with his parents, the class must elect a new representative. Bu Lan, who everyone calls "Dancer," is elected to the post. The story tells how Bu Lan, Zhou Jingzhou and their classmates work together to make up for each other's shortcomings and at last win the school's basketball championship.

1304. *Medicine (Yao)*

1981. Changchun Film Studio. B & W. 9 Reels. Direction: Lu Shaolian. Screenplay: Xiao

Yixian and Lu Shaolian, based on the story of the same title by Lu Xun (1881–1936). Cinematography: Han Hanxia. Art Direction: Lu Xin. Music: Si Wanchun, Li Xian. Sound: Ting Zongde. Cast: Liang Yin as Huang Laoshuang, Chen Qi as Xia's wife, Qu Yun as Hua's wife, Bai Mu as Master Xia, Yue Minqiang as Hua Xiaoshuang, Lu Zhongtang as the revolutionary, Chen Guojun as Xia Yu

Toward the end of the Qing (Manchu) Dynasty, the corrupt and decadent government is wildly killing all revolutionaries in a desperate attempt to remain in power. When a young teacher named Xia assassinates a government officer, his own uncle secretly informs on him. The young man is arrested and executed, but goes to his death bravely. His mother Lady Xia still believes her son was a good man, and often dreams he is with her again. Meanwhile, a man named Hua Laoshuang and his wife Lady Hua earn their living by operating a small teahouse. They are both over 50 and have only one son, Hua Xiaoshuang, who is seriously ill with consumption. The couple has heard that the disease can be cured by eating bread dipped in human blood, so they spend most of their money to obtain some human blood, the blood of Teacher Xia. But the little boy's illness quickly worsens, the bread failing to save his life. He soon dies. The Huangs go to mourn their son at his grave, and there Xia's mother is mourning her son as well. Lady Xia finds a flower laying on her son's grave. She does not know who put it there.

1305. *Meeting (Xiang Hui)*

1984. Changchun Film Studio. Color. Letterboxed. 9 Reels. Direction: Huang Yanen. Screenplay: Qiao Man, Wang Jie. Cinematography: Shu Xiaoyan. Art Direction: Liu Huanxing. Music: Quan Rufeng. Sound: Tong Zongde. Cast: Tian Jihai as Fang Kehan, Liang Tongyu as Feng Zhicai, Li Hong as Ma Xing, Zhao Yaming as Zhao Mengjun, Guo Yong as Zhao Mengqi, Song Lijie as Wang Xiaoxing, Li Ying as Wang Jieyin

Fang Kehan, a senior official in the Lanzhou city government, worries about the long-term pattern of economic losses by Lanzhou's publicly owned industries. He concludes the core problem is the low caliber of managerial and technical personnel they have, so he sends the city's Personnel Director, his wife Wang Jieyin, to the provincial capital to recruit more talented people to work for the city. Meanwhile, he starts a national campaign to recruit scientific and technical people, and

many respond. Opposition to his plan soon develops among people in his own organization. One experienced telecommunications engineer he recruits, Feng Zhicai, is so good that Fang soon appoints him plant director. This infuriates Fang's old friend Ma Xing, who feels he should be in line for that appointment. Fang patiently convinces Ma to get over it and cooperate with the new director. Gradually, the situation in Lanzhou improves, and Fang Kehan is assigned new, more responsible duties by the province.

1306. *Meeting in the Dark (Ren Ye Huang Hun)*

1995. Hong Kong Siyuan Film Company with the cooperation of Shanghai Film Studio. Color. Letterboxed. Dolby. Direction: Chen Yifei. Screenplay: Wang Zhongru. Cinematography: Xiao Feng. Art Direction: Chen Shaomian. Music: Ye Xiaogang. Cast: Liang Jiahui (Tony Leung) as "I," Zhang Jingqiu as "Ghost"

In Shanghai one late fall night in 1937, the narrator, identified only as "I," meets a woman who calls herself "Ghost." The two agree to meet again, and after a few dates they seem to be falling in love. But then she disappears. When "I" goes to the address she had given him, he is told the woman he seeks has been dead for several years. Moreover, at the time of her death she had been the prime suspect in the murder of her husband. "I" sets out to investigate the old murder case, and at last finds who actually killed her husband. After the case is closed, "I" walks out into the rain, and sees "ghost" standing there; she smiles at him, then disappears into the mist. "I" stands crying in the rain.

1307. *The Melons Are Ripe (Gua Shu Di Luo)*

1983. Xi'an Film Studio. Color. 9 Reels. Direction: Li Yucai. Screenplay: Xin Xianling. Cinematography: Zhang Faliang. Art Direction: Zhang Xiaohui. Music: Wang Yan. Sound: Xiong Huajuan. Cast: Yang Fengliang as Jin Dashan, Yang Hailian as Xiang Qiu, Wang Runshen as Old Watermelon, Fu Chengxun as Manager Cui, Wang Shuqing as Su the Gossip

When Jin Dashan is discharged from the army, he returns to his native village with plans to settle down there. His father ("Old Watermelon") and his fiancee Xiang Qiu, however, want him to take advantage of his outstanding service record and find a good job in the city. Dashan sticks to his resolve to stay in the village, which so upsets Xiang Qiu she leaves for the booming port city of Qingdao. There she finds a job as a contract employee and meets a smooth young man named Cui who tells her he is a company director. Actually, he is a smuggler. He further ingratiates himself with Xiang Qiu by nurturing her dreams of becoming an actress. So she feels very foolish when he is arrested. When the watermelons grow ripe, her native village has a big harvest, and Dashan writes asking her to return. Xiang Qiu realizes how much she now misses the old place, and happily starts back home.

1308. *Men and Women (Nan Ren Men He Nu Ren Men)*

1985. Pearl River Film Studio. Color. 10 Reels. Direction: Yu Shibing. Screenplay: Liu Shugang. Cinematography: Han Xingyuan. Art Direction: Tan Ancang. Sound: Lin Guoqiang. Cast: Zhang Ling as Lu Yeping, Liang Jingsheng as Luo Nan, Wan Qiong as Pan Qiu, Tao Baili as Bai Rujun, Pu Chaoying as Li Xiaodian

As a graduation project, young woman college student Lu Yeping proposes a study of the urban marriage situation, particularly the issue of divorce. Her project is accepted by the city's marriage and family studies association and the local women's association. Courthouse employee Luo Nan, a former boyfriend, is designated to assist her on the project, and they conduct interviews together. When Lu meets with Luo Nan, she learns he is now married and his wife is in the countryside, but the two former lovers rekindle their romance anyway. When Luo Nan's wife Pan Qiu learns of their affair, she agonizes over the development but at last agrees that Lu and Luo are more suitably matched. Luo Nan is certain he loves Lu Yeping, but when his wife files for divorce he is very confused. He has mixed feelings about the whole thing, and is uncertain what to do.

1309. *Men and Women Are Different (Nan Nu You Bie)*

1988. Xiaojiang Film Studio and Jiangxi Film Studio Jointly. Color. Letterboxed. 9 Reels. Direction: Zhang Gang. Screenplay: Zhang Gang. Cinematography: Wang Kekuan, Tang Yulin. Art Direction: Li Youren. Music: Wang Ming. Sound: Yu Meiqiang, Wang Zhihong. Cast: Li

Changqing as Yang Aman, Zhang Baishuang as Shi Xiaoliu, Huang Jingtang as Xu Wei

Middle-aged painter Yang Aman and his wife Shi Xiaoliu travel to their provincial capital to attend an art exhibition. But because the couple neglected to bring their marriage certificate with them, they are forced to stay in separate rooms. Meanwhile in the same hotel, Aman's painting "Pure Girl" is viewed by hotel manager Xu Wei as being pornographic, and he reports the matter to the police. Aman is put under surveillance. Aman decides to withdraw from the exhibition, but Cultural Bureau worker Zhong Shijian apologizes to Aman, and lets him submit his painting for judging although Zhong himself has not seen it. After seeing the painting, however, Zhong Shijian bars Aman from participating in or even attending the exhibition. But this time the director of the Cultural Bureau approves the painting. Then the woman who modeled for the painting demands Aman withdraw it because of the social pressures it has brought her. Cultural Bureau director Wu's daughter now volunteers to be the model, and lets Aman paint another version. At last, "Pure Girl" is shown, and after all his problems, Yang Aman leaves the provincial capital.

1310. *Men Are Puzzled, So Are Women (Nan Ren Kun Huo, Nu Ren Ye Kun Huo)*

1989. Changchun Film Studio. Color. Letterboxed. 10 Reels. Direction: Chang Yan. Screenplay: Li Lingxiu. Cinematography: Zhou Kun. Art Direction: Ye Jiren. Music: Mo Fan. Sound: Zhang Wen. Cast: Liu Yancheng as Qian Shenglin, Sha Jinyan as Tao Qian, Ma Dalong as Zhen Jian, Liang Tongyu as Zhang Yongqin, Guo Bichuan as Siqiang

Police investigate the murder of Tao Qian, wife of Qian Shenglin, director of the city's household electronics appliance factory. In addition to the dead woman's husband, Inspector Zhen Jian has two other suspects: Zhang Yongqin, husband of the city Economic Committee director, and Si Qing, reporter on a legal newspaper. It turns out that Qian Shenglin was in league with Hong Kong businessman Huo Xiaoning to use his authority for personal gain, and when his wife tumbled to their crime Qian killed her to keep her from informing on them.

Meeting in the Dark. "Ghost" (Zhang Jingqiu) only appears at night. 1995. Hong Kong Siyuan Film Company, Shanghai Film Studio Co-Production.

1311. *Meng Genhua (Meng Gen Hua)*

1979. August First Film Studio. Color. 11 Reels. Direction: Li Shutian. Screenplay: Yun Zhaoguang, Aodesier, Zhang Changgong, Jia Man. Cinematography: Huang Fuxiang. Art Direction: Jiang Zhengkui. Music: Tang Ke, Ererdun, Zhao Lu. Sound: Li Yan. Cast: Yang Yaqing as Meng Genhua, Xiang Lei as Gongbu, Song Yemin as Ding Shan, Luo Hui as Eryoucai, Lan Faqin as Bashi, Liu Long as Pi Zhanbiao

In the winter of 1924, on the Huhe Prairie, young Mongol couple Su He and Meng Genhua and young Han Chinese couple Ding Qinyun and Zhao Mei hold a joint third birthday celebration for their two 3-year-old sons Mulun and Ding Shan. Local governor Gongbu is childless, so the Nationalist warlord Eryoucai gives Gongbu's wife permission to take the hearts of the two little boys and use them to prepare a potion that will give her a son. So Mu Lan and Ding Shan are kidnapped and taken to the governor's mansion. Their parents rescue the children, but Ding Shan's father Zhao Mei is killed in the effort. The other mother, Meng Genhua, gives her son Mulun to old Mrs. Liu for safekeeping and

flees the prairie taking Ding Shan with her. Twelve years later, Meng Genhua and Ding Shan find Ding Shan's mother, now an Eighth Route Army captain, and Meng learns that her husband Su He has been killed fighting the Japanese. She decides to carry on for her husband, and changing her name to Yinghua, returns to her hometown with her guerrilla troop. Er Youcai, Gongbu and Japanese spy Hutian are in alliance to fight Yinghua. They also encourage Batu to murder Yinghua. Yinghua captures Batu and when interrogating him realizes he is her son Mulun. Meng Genhua uses his information to learn the location of Gongbu's troops, lures them into ambush, and defeats them. Mulun and Ding Shan now join together to fight the common enemy.

1312. *Menglong Desert (Meng Long Sha)*

1960. August First Film Studio. Color. 10 Reels. Direction: Wang Ping and Yuan Xian. Screenplay: Luo Shui, based on the stage play "Remote Menglong Desert." Cinematography: Xue Boqing. Art Direction: Wang Wei. Music: Yang Fei. Sound: Guo Dazheng. Cast: Wang

Xingang as Jiang Hong, He Meiping as Meien, Li Jiayang as Shuaien, Guan Yixing as Leheng, Wu Nanshan as Poman, Zhao Yan as Mitao, Cao Ying as Dao Ailing

In the days shortly after liberation, PLA border defense forces political instructor Jiang Hong leads a work team into the Yunnan province Dai nationality area called Menglong Desert. Woman spy Dao Ailing, working for the Americans, instigates the local head to forbid the local people having any contact with the work team, making it hard for the team to do its work. Jiang Hong has his soldiers do all sorts of good things for the local people, as well as setting an example himself. This slowly wins over the local people and the work spreads that the Communists are helping the people. Half a year later, Dao Ailing arranges a plot to blow up the Menglong Bridge. Jiang Hong sees through the plot and leads the local militia in arresting Dao.

1313. *Meridian of War (Zhan Zheng Zhi Wu Xian)*

1990. Youth Film Studio. Color. 9 Reels. Wide Screen. Direction and Screenplay: Feng Xiaoning. Cinematography: Chen Jun, Zhang Guoqing. Art Direction: Han Yunfeng. Music: Guan Xia. Sound: Zhao Jun, Li Wei. Cast: Fu Dalong as the Old Soldier, Shen Danping as the Nurse

An old woman walking west in the mountains along the Great Wall outside Beijing reminisces about events half a century ago. In 1942, in the same mountains, she is one of 13 young people, children really, walking in the morning mist. They come upon a badly wounded Chinese soldier who gives them a document he had been taking to Chinese headquarters. The children take over the soldier's mission, passing the document from one to another as the Japanese close in. The last person to receive the document is a little girl. There is a huge explosion, and all the children but one are killed. We find ourselves back in the present on the same part of the Great Wall. The old woman, the sole survivor, seems to see her childhood friends again, passing in front of her along the Great Wall toward the west.

1314. *Merry World (Kuai Le Shi Jie)*

1989. Tianshan Film Studio. Color. 10 Reels. Letterboxed. Direction: Guang Chunlan. Screenplay: Duan Baoshan, Guang Chunlan. Cine-

matography: Qi Xing. Art Direction: Adixia. Music: Nuslaiti. Sound: Aierkeng. Cast: Mulading as Asihar, Gulizhar as Ayixiamu, Mahemuti as Abudula

A group of youngsters headed by dancer Asihar decides to leave the exciting and comfortable life of the city and organize a dance troupe to perform for peasants. They are warmly received wherever they travel. By chance, they come upon secluded and backward Yangle Village, where they get involved in the intricate relationships of the people there: the melancholy director of the village's hat factory, Ayimuxia, the conservative diehard village leader, Abudula, and the ill-fated Aihetair... Everything is mysterious. The youngsters bring a new viewpoint which challenges backwardness and obstinacy, but the conservative forces are a powerful enemy.

1315. *Metropolis in 1990 (Yi Jiu Jiu Ling Da Cheng Shi)*

1990. Changchun Film Studio. Color. 9 Reels. Wide Screen. Direction: Sun Sha. Screenplay: Xiao Yixian. Cinematography: Gao Hongbao, Huang Yinde. Art Direction: Yang Baocheng. Music: Yi Wenyu, Liu Qun. Sound: Yi Wenyu, Lou Qun. Cast: Kong Xiangyu as Yan Honghuan, Zhao Fan as Gao Bonian, Fan Zhiqi as Yang Jianhua, Liu Yubin as Kang Kejian

In mid-life, Yan Honghuan becomes the mayor a of a northern Chinese city. He is determined to modernize the old city, beginning with the city's transport and housing problems. Supported by the Municipal Party Committee led by Party Secretary Gao Bonian, Yan organizes the demolition of old, sub-standard housing. He takes strong measures against the bureaucracy and replaces the city's incompetent cadres. He adopts other tough measures to eliminate the corruption, which results in children of privileged cadres forcibly occupying apartments intended for working class people. Yan encounters great opposition. He is the victim of rumors and frame-ups. But he never retreats.

1316. *Metropolitan Romance (Du Shi Qing Hua)*

1993. Shanghai Film Studio. Color. Letterboxed. 10 Reels. Direction: Xu Jihong. Screenplay: He Guopu. Cinematography: Zhao Junhong. Art Direction: Mei Kunping. Cast: Bai Han as Luo Naiqian, Shang Rongsheng as Li Yiming, Ding Jiayuan as Song Yi, Wu Jing as

Zhao Peihong, Zhang Hong as Zhang Jinxiang, Wang Dong as Lin Zhi, Wang Ling as Zhou Xi, Xiang Yongcheng as A Kuan

Luo Naiqian, woman director of a Shanghai silk factory, insists that reform be implemented throughout her plant, even firing her close friend Zhao Peihong when the latter resists the reforms. Zhao then uses her husband's connections to land a job as Shanghai representative for an Italian company. But when Luo's reforms are admired and advocated by her new employers, Zhao again balks. Meanwhile, Luo and her husband Li Yimin are having problems in their relationship: he has an invitation to Japan which could lead to long-term residence there, but she is too busy to accompany him. They separate for a while, but Li Yimin finally understands her feelings and helps her import some new equipment. At last, he decides to remain in China.

1317. *Metropolitan Saxophone (Du Shi Sha Ke Si Feng)*

1994. Shanghai Film Studio. Color. Letterboxed. 9 Reels. Direction: Shi Xiaohua, Bao Qicheng. Screenplay: He Guopu, Zhao Huanan. Cinematography: Liu Lihua. Art Direction: Guo Dongchang. Music: Jin Fuzai, Dong Weijie. Sound: Tu Mingde. Costume: Zhang Chunzhong, Le Guofeng. Makeup: Yin Shangshan. Cast: Tong Fan as Luo Yi, Xia Lixin as Huizi, Ye Mang as Lingbu, Liu Qing as Tian Zhongxiong, Jin Ange as Luo Ning, Ning Li as Xiao Bo, Cao Kunqi as Li Hui, Gao Meiqing as Yang Li

Accompanied by Lingbu, her chief designer, Japanese clothing manufacturer Huizi comes to China to invest. Lingbu is also romantically interested in his boss. In China she hires Luo Yi, a very talented young Chinese who had studied clothing design and management in Japan. She likes Luo Yi, which makes Lingbu very unhappy. Luo Yi understands Chinese workers, and his cooperation with them helps the company win out in the market. Huizi and Luo Yi grow closer.

1318. *Miao Tan the Sleuth (Miao Tan)*

1991. Beijing Film Studio. Color. Letterboxed. 9 Reels. Direction: Li Wei. Screenplay: Li Yunliang, Lin Xiping. Cinematography: Yang Wenqin, Li Xiong. Art Direction: Chen Xiaoxia. Music: Ma Ding. Sound: Zhang Zhizhong. Cast: Che Yue as Miao Tan, Fang Qinzuo as Miao Lan, Ma Xiaoqing as Xiao Shilian, Zhou Zhou as Tong Xin, Mu Ning as Bo Yun, Fang Zhige as Xia Tian

Naval Intelligence specialist Miao Tan retires to his home town, where he finds his sister Miao Lan suspects her husband Tong Xin of having an affair with his assistant Bo Yun. She asks her brother to investigate the matter. Miao Tan follows Tong Xin and the woman, and soon determines their relationship is quite innocent. But his sister refuses to believe the evidence, and decides to make trouble for the others through their company. Miao Tan tries to stop her, and a series of comic incidents happen when the two women meet. The truth finally comes out, and all ends well.

1319. *Miaomiao (Miao Miao)*

1980. Beijing Film Studio. Color. 9 Reels. Direction: Wang Junzheng. Screenplay: Yan Tingting, Kang Liwen. Cinematography: Zhen Yiyuan, Zhou Jinxiang. Art Direction: Liu Yi. Music: Liu Zhuang. Sound: Sun Yumin. Cast: Li Ling as Han Miaomiao, Wang Jianing as Yang Xiaoliang, Guan Qiang as Xu Peipei, Cao Cuifeng as Gao Ying, Zhu Yurong as Fang Yu, Jiang Yunhui as Principal Chen

Young girl Han Miaomiao had wanted to be an athlete, but is instead assigned to teach in an elementary school, a job she accepts with reluctance. But when she arrives at the school and finds the children in her class to be very ill-behaved, Miaomiao becomes interested in guiding these children in the right direction. By making herself into a good example for them, she gradually improves the image of the class, with even the worst behaved making progress. However, dealing with children of such different backgrounds is no easy task. For example, Bao Rui, the grandson of a high-ranking military officer, is very proud of his political privilege, and when Miaomiao wants to talk with the grandfather, she cannot get by his secretary. The mother of student Peipei makes false accusations against the teacher. Miaomiao is on the verge of quitting, but all the students in the class beg her to stay. When Miaomiao's efforts are acknowledged by the parents, she is inspired to stay and devote herself anew to her job.

1320. *Midnight (Zi Ye)*

1981. Shanghai Film Studio. Color. Wide Screen. 14 Reels. Direction: Sang Hu, Fu Jinggong. Screenplay: Sang Hu, based on the novel of the same title by Mao Dun (1896–).

Cinematography: Qiu Yiren. Art Direction: Han Shangyi, Ju Ransheng, Li Huazhong. Music: Lu Qiming. Sound: Miao Zhenyu, Feng Deyao. Cast: Li Rentang as Wu Sunpu, Qiao Qi as Zhao Botao, Cheng Xiaoyin as Lin Peiyao, Gu Yelu as Du Zhuzhai, Zhang Fa as Master Wu, Ling Yun as Sun Jiren, Shi Jioufeng as Wang Hepu

The setting is Shanghai in 1930. Wu Sunpu, chief executive of the Shanghai Yuhua Silk Company, wages many struggles: with plant workers, with strikers, others in his industry, and most of all with bourgeois comprador Zhao Botao. Capitalists and other figures in Shanghai's industrial and commercial community come and go. They out-maneuver and cheat one another, first this one gaining the upper hand, then that one. The strategy finally comes down to a head-to-head confrontation between Wu and Zhao Botao, but the latter has support from America and plans to take over Wu Sunpu's plant. Wu faces a choice of surrender to Zhao or declaration of bankruptcy. His situation is so bad that he considers suicide, but decides to go on vacation with his wife Lin Peiyao on Mount Lushan. As they leave Shanghai at midnight, Wu paces the deck of the ship, reviewing and pondering his life and his fate.

Best Art Direction Han Shangyi, Ju Ransheng and Li Huazhong, 1982 Golden Rooster Awards.

1321. *Midnight Song (Ye Ban Ge Sheng)*

1985. Shanghai Film Studio. Color. Wide Screen. 10 Reels. Direction: Yang Yanjing. Screenplay: Xu Yinghua, Shen Ji. Cinematography: Sun Guoliang. Art Direction: Wang Xingcang. Music: Xu Jingxin. Sound: Ren Daming. Cast: Ju Naishe as Song Danping, Li Yun as Li Xiaoxia, Wang Weiping as Sun Xiaoou, Wei Guochun as Tang Jun, Li Tianji as the doorkeeper, Zhang Qi as Ludie, Li Zhiyu as Li Xianchen, Wang Jingan as the mother

A Chinese version of "Phantom of the Opera." In the late 1930s, actor Song Danping's anti–Japanese play "Love to Yellow River" is very popular wherever he appears. In one town, a local girl named Li Xiaoxia falls for the handsome and famous actor. Her father, local despot Li Xiaocheng, cannot bear his daughter being involved with an actor, so he has someone throw acid in Song's face, permanently disfiguring him. He disappears from public view, but finds a hiding place in a secret

area of the theater. When Li Xiaoxia learns her lover is still alive, she blinds herself because she knows Song wants to keep his disfigured image from her. She finds him, but the couple is prevented from finding happiness together when enemies burn down the theater and Song and Li perish in the fire.

1322. *Midnight Taxi (Wu Ye Chu Zu Che)*

1992. Changchun Film Studio. Color. Letterboxed. 9 Reels. Direction: Yang Jing. Screenplay: Zhong Yuan, Wang Yao. Cinematography: Wang Changning. Art Direction: Wang Di. Music: Shu Zechi. Sound: Wang Qinchao. Costume: Zhao Huijie. Makeup: Sun Xueguang. Cast: Xu Xiaojian as Ban Hai and Ban Long, Bai Zhidi as Chen Ting, Ma Chongle as Feng Kebing, Wang Xiaofang as Zhen Anqi

A gang specializing in hijacking taxis mistakes policeman Ban Hai for his twin brother, taxi driver Ban Long. The PSB decides to take advantage of this opportunity by letting Ban Hai continue pretending to be his brother. The major conflict erupts when gang boss Feng Kebing discovers the ruse, and orders Ban Hai be killed. In the final battle, Ban Hai succeeds in capturing the entire gang.

1323. *Military Depot No, 51 (Wu Shi Yi Hao Bing Zhan)*

1961. Haiyan Film Studio. B & W. 10 Reels. Direction: Liu Qiong. Screenplay: Zhang Weiqing, Liang Xin, Liu Quan. Cinematography: Qiu Yiren. Art Direction: Ding Cheng, Zhang Wanhong. Music: Xiang Yi. Sound: Lu Zhongbo. Casting: Liang Boluo as Liang Hong, Zhang Yi as Mr. Yang, Gao Bo as Wu Peng, Gu Yelu as Mr. Song, Zhou Han as Master Worker Zhou, Sun Yongping as Xiao Sun

During World War II, Communist military cadre Liang Hong is assigned to a depot in Shanghai, working undercover as an apprentice. By cleverly playing off Japanese and Chinese collaborationist intelligence agents against each other, he is finally successful in getting a large quantity of military supplies shipped to the Red Army instead of to the enemy.

1324. *Military Life (Rong Ma Sheng Ya)*

1990. Emei Film Studio. Color. Wide Screen. 10 Reels. Direction: Zhang Yi. Screenplay: Hu Yuewei, based on events in the life of Guo Moruo

(1892–1978), scholar and literary figure. Cinematography: Li Baoqi. Art Direction: Xie Huibing. Music: Yu Linqin. Sound: Shen Guli. Cast: Liu Jihong as Guo Moruo, Guo Weihua as Zhou Enlai, Xu Daolin as Chiang Kaishek

When the May 4th Movement sweeps through Chinese intellectual circles after 1919, student Guo Moruo returns from abroad to enter the Whampoa Military Academy. There he meets Zhou Enlai, director of the school's political department, and is nominated by school director Chiang Kaishek for promotion to captain and department headship. When Chiang later turns on the Communists, the Nationalist Party's left wing, Guo writes an essay attacking Chiang. Guo finds his own ideas increasingly matching those of the Communists. He participates in the August 1st Nanchang Rebellion, and later gains CPC membership.

1325. *Military Post in the White Birch Forest (Bai Hua Lin Zhong De Shao Suo)*

1982. Xi'an Film Studio. Color. 9 Reels. Direction: Yao Shougang. Screenplay: Wang Xingdong, Liu Minsheng, Wang Zhebing. Cinematography: Wang Hui. Art Direction: Liu Xinghou. Music: Xu Youfu. Sound: Hua Juan. Cast: Lu Jun as Lu Xing, Han Yueqiao as Bai Ruhua, Wang Bingyan as the supervisor, Wang Yingquan as the company commander, Wang Dawei as Guo Zhenhai, Zhao Guang as Liu Changjiang, Bai Lin as Hu Jiacai

During the time the Gang of Four is in power, educated youth Lu Xing and Bai Ruhua, who are also lovers, are sent from Beijing to work in Heilongjiang Province in Northeast China. The first winter after the Gang of Four's downfall, Lu Xing enlists in the army and is assigned to the canine corps as a dog keeper. Meanwhile, Bai Ruhua becomes an actress and returns to Beijing, where she becomes interested in a TV director. When Lu Xing visits Beijing three years later, he is very upset at the change in Bai Ruhua and returns to the army in disgust. The TV director, a man who has gone through considerable suffering himself, soon comes to realize Bai's true nature and leaves her as well.

The Miners' Song **see** *Tin City Story*

1326. *Miracle Cat and Steel Spider (Shen Mao Yu Tie Zhi Zhu)*

1989. Inner Mongolia Film Studio. Color. Wide screen. 10 Reels. Direction: Zhongshu Huang, Dong Tao. Screenplay: Ye Zuxun, Zhang Lequn. Cinematography: Geritu. Art Direction: Tong Yonggang. Music: Wang Xiling. Sound: Hu Linping. Cast: Li Xiaoyan as Steel Spider, Du Zhenqing as Miracle Cat, Zhong Xinghuo as Wen Zhonghan

In the early years of the Republic of China (ca1914), Congressman Lu Zhiling is murdered at his Nanjing home, and a valuable diamond necklace taken. Several detectives are killed or disappear while investigating the case. Two famous detectives called "Steel Spider" and "Miracle Cat" are brought in from another part of China to take up the case. It turns out that on one of the diamonds in the necklace is engraved a name list of military officers who oppose Yuan Shikai's efforts to seize power, and that Yuan has hired a gunman to steal the necklace and the list. After a battle with Yuan's agents, the two detectives recover the necklace.

1327. *Miracle Doctor Bian Que (Shen Yi Bian Que)*

1985. Changchun Film Studio. Color. 9 Reels. Direction: Cui Ying. Screenplay: Xie Wenli. Cinematography: Sun Hui, Jin Hengyi. Art Direction: Wang Xingwen. Music: Lou Zhanghou. Sound: Hong Bo. Cast: Ge Dianyu as Bian Que, Liang Yin as Old Duke Shi, Ji Hengpu as Qi Henghou, Xu Jingzhi as Yu Jie

In the 5th Century B.C., highly skilled physician Bian Que is famed as China's legendary "Miracle Doctor." In addition to serving the people through treating their ailments, he also teaches them that only medicine can cure illness. This makes him a threat to China's many shamans. So when Bian Que cures the emperor's son, the court physician, himself a shamanist, has Bian Que murdered and all his medical research records burned.

1328. *Miracle Land (Shen Qi De Tu Di)*

1984. Changchun Film Studio. Color. Wide Screen. 10 Reels. Direction: Gao Tianhong. Screenplay: Gao Tianhong. Cinematography: Wang Lianping, Yu Bing, Liu Xing. Art Direction: Hao Bing. Music: Qin Yongcheng, Huang Weiqiang. Sound: Kang Ruixin. Cast: Hu Jinjin as Li Xiaoyan, Yang Xiaodan as Chen Si, Zhang Fengyi as Wang Zigang, Fu Yiwei as Shanshan

In the early years of the People's Republic, a military construction team is sent to Heilongjiang to explore some virgin territory for possible development. They encounter many difficulties and hardships and two of their key figures perish: woman Political Commissar Li Xiaoyan of illness, and a brave soldier named Wang Zigang in fighting a wolf. The rest of the team carries on. Today this region is a developed and prospering agricultural area.

1329. *Miracle Sword Pagoda (Shen Qi De Jian Ta)*

1984. Shanghai Film Studio. Color. Letterboxed. 9 Reels. Direction: Liang Tingduo. Screenplay: Cheng Zhi, Liang Zhen. Cinematography: Luo Zhengsheng. Art Direction: Zhang Chongxiang. Music: Liu Yanxi. Sound: Jin Fugeng. Cast: Yang Tong as Ahu, Dong Wengang as Hailong, Mao Yongming as Brother, Huang Daliang as the reporter

In a Bai nationality fishing village, junior high school students Ahu and Hailong are saving their money to attend a historical camp at Xi'an during their summer break from school. When summer nears and their funds are still insufficient, they seek ways of making some. One day, they by chance find a gold sculpture of a local tower, but disregard it. When they find out the sculpture is a precious and very valuable antique which had been stolen, they return for it but find it gone. The film follows the two boys' efforts to find the stolen antique and solve the mystery of its theft. Working in cooperation with the PSB, they find out that Hailong's older cousin is the thief. The relevant authorities give Ahu and Hailong a reward which pays their expenses to camp.

1330. *Miraculous Flying Mouse (Fei Tian Sheng Shu)*

1990. Pearl River Film Studio. Color. Wide Screen. 10 Reels. Direction: Wang Wei. Screenplay: He Houchu. Cinematography: Zhen Kangzheng. Art Direction: Du Xiufeng. Music: Zhang Hong. Sound: Lu Minwen. Cast: Huang Guoqiang as Zhao Gou, Sun Chengxi as Li Ma, Lu Ying as Da Shan, Wang Yan as Xiao Shan

In the early 5th Century, a group from the Kingdom of Jin abducts Zhao Gou, king of the rival Song people. Li Ma, a loyalist hero called the "Miraculous Flying Mouse," leads a group of fighters to rescue him. On the way, they help a man being persecuted by some villains, and he asks Li Ma to protect his daughters Da Shan and Xiao Shan. Li Ma and his band fight their way through terrible hardship to rescue their king, and along the way he and Xiao Shan fall in love. However, Zhao Gou rewards Li Ma's unswerving loyalty by having him put to death. Xiao Shan leads an army of thousands of volunteers to the border to resist the Jin invasion.

1331. *The Miraculous Policemen and the Magical Thief (Shen Jing Qi Tou)*

1992. Shanghai Film Studio & Shanghai Film and Television Literature Institute Co-Production. Color. Letterboxed. 9 Reels. Direction: Shi Xiaohua. Screenplay: Lu Shoujun, Guo Bingyi. Cinematography: Lu Junfu. Art Direction: Ye Jingmin. Music: Pan Guoxing. Sound: Dong Yan. Costume: Zhang Xing. Makeup: Shen Keqiang. Cast: Wang Yan as Lu Fang, Jin Lili as the Magical Thief of a Thousand Faces, Tong Ruixin as Xiao Zhao

A series of robberies leads larceny detectives to conclude the almost legendary "Magical Thief of a Thousand Faces" has come to their city. It turns out the thief is a woman, and when her own daughter becomes shamefully aware of her mother's occupation, the thief turns herself in to the authorities.

1332. *Miraculous Sword in the Temple (Shen Zhai Qi Jian)*

1990. Xi'an Film Studio. Color. Wide Screen. 9 Reels. Direction: Zhang Yumin. Screenplay: Li Yanxi, Tian Pei. Cinematography: Nie Tiemao. Art Direction: Yan Pingxiao. Music: Tao Long. Sound: Dang Chunzhu. Cast: Dong Xiaoxia as Han Dazhu, Zhao Kemin as Liu Shanpu, Zhao Jian as Zhao Tonghai

During World War II, jeweler Han Tiankui and his daughter Han Dazhu entrust another store owner, Liu Shanpu, with a suitcase full of jewelry donated to raise money for the anti–Japanese effort. They take with them only a short, jewel-encrusted sword to serve as identification for the person who later claims the case. On their way home, the Hans are attacked by a masked person, and the jeweler, mortally wounded, hurls the sword into a lake before he dies. Han Dazhu escapes, and dedicates herself to getting the sword back. After many struggles, her search finally leads her to Liu Shanpu as the one who killed her father. She also exposes Liu as a Japanese spy. The treasure is recovered and delivered to the anti-Japanese front.

1333. *The Miraculous Whip (Shen Bian)*

1986. Xi'an Film Studio. Color. 10 Reels. Direction: Zhang Zhien. Screenplay: Zhang Zhien. Cinematography: Gu Changwei. Art Direction: Zhang Hong, Li Xingzheng. Music: Li Yaodong. Sound: Gu Changning. Cast: Wang Yawei as the Man, Chen Baoguo as Boli Hua, Xu Shouli as Juhua

In Tianjin during the last years of the Qing (Manchu) Dynasty, a stupid-looking man called Shaer is famed for the whip he always carries, a whip with seemingly miraculous powers. He marries Juhua, a neighbor girl, and they have a good life together. Later, the Boxer anti-foreign movement reaches Tianjin, and Shaer is asked to join. He does, but in an ensuing battle, a foreigner's bullet strikes and breaks his whip. The anti-foreign forces regroup, and a few years later Shaer and Juhua return to their home with handguns. His whip is gone, but he still carries its spirit.

1334. *Miss An Li (An Li Xiao Jie)*

1989. Beijing Film Studio. Color. 10 Reels. Letterboxed. Direction: Qin Zhiyu. Screenplay: Zhang Xian, Qin Zhiyu. Cinematography: Yun Wenyao. Art Direction: Huo Jianqi. Music: Wang Ming. Sound: Wang Dawen. Cast: Zhang Yanli as An Li, Tang Guoqiang as Lin Yiping, Liang Guoqing as Feng Guojiang, Xia Zongxue as Ou Luyi

In a special economic zone in South China, police investigate an alleged case of profiteering in color TV sets. Miss An Li, the Chinese manager of a Sino-Hong Kong joint venture, is a suspect in the case. She meets again two men who had previously played a big role in her life: her lifelong enemy is aligned with her boss against her, while her former lover is the investigator. At first, as the prime suspect, she is the focus of the case, but as the investigation progresses she is able to clear herself and help the police solve it.

1335. *Miss Jiaojiao (Jiao Jiao Xiao Jie)*

1986. Children's Film Studio. Color. Letter-boxed. 8 Reels. Direction: Chen Jingshu. Screenplay: Wang Feng, Chen Yuezhi. Cinematography: Wang Jiuwen, Zhang Shunqi. Art Direction: Ju Ransheng, Sun Weide. Music: Li Haihui. Sound: Wang Zhongli, Gu Quanxi. Cast: Gong Xundong as Jin Xiaolong, Cheng Haiguang as Da Lishi, Zhu Yuwen as Mother, Hua Xue as Xiang Yuling, Zhang Xundao as Gu Erkang

Jin Xiaolong is a talented but mischievous child who loves animals. He is recruited by a circus troupe to train a giant panda called "Jiao-jiao." He works hard with the panda, and in time trains it to eat Western-style food, kick a ball and ride a motorcycle. Miss Jiaojiao becomes the hit of the show and Xiaolong grows up to be an excellent actor. Even his previously reluctant mother now believes his time has not been wasted.

1336. *Mr. Qiao Rides a Sedan Chair (Qiao Lao Ye Shang Jiao)*

1959. Haiyan Film Studio. B & W. 8 Reels. Direction: Liu Qiong. Screenplay: Tian Nianxuan, Liu Qiong. Cinematography: Qiu Yiren, Li Chongjun. Art Direction: Hu Zuoyun. Music: Xiang Yi. Sound: Liu Guangjie. Cast: Han Fei as Qiao Xi, Li Baoluo as boatman, Sun Jinglu as Lan Xiuyin, Wu Yunfang as Qiuju, Yang Hua as Lan Musi, Chen Xu as Lan Xinhui

In old China, scholar Qiao Xi meets Lan Xiuyin, daughter of an official, and there is an instant mutual attraction between the two. That evening, the scholar goes to her home to get a glimpse of her, but is mistakenly abducted by Xiuyin's brother, who in the dark thinks Qiao is a girl he wants to marry. The abductors put Qiao into a sedan chair, and take him to the Lan family home. He keeps silent in order to protect the girl who was the intended abductee. When Xiuyin finds what her brother has done, she is angry with him, and tells the servants to put the "girl" in her room, while she goes to talk to her mother about releasing her. But the mother takes her son's side, and orders Xiuyin to persuade the "girl" to marry her son. Xiuyin goes to persuade the "girl" but discovers the family's prisoner is the scholar she met that day. Xiuyin is at first upset with Qiao's ruse, but when he explains what happened, she is impressed by his sacrificing himself to rescue another, and falls for him. At this time, the guests invited to the brother's wedding begin to arrive, so to save the family from embarrassment, Xiuyin convinces the mother to turn her brother's wedding into hers and Mr. Qiao's.

1337. *Mr. Wang's Burning Desires (Wang Xian Sheng Zhi Yu Huo Feng Sheng)*

1993. Shanghai Film Studio. Color. Letterboxed. 10 Reels. Direction: Zhang Jianya. Screenplay: Xu Xiaofan and Zhang Jianya, adapted from a cartoon story by Ye Qianyu. Cinematography: Huang Baohua. Art Direction: Zhou Xinren. Costume: Dong Zhongmin, Zhao Yingwu. Makeup: Shen Dongsheng, Yin Lihua. Producer: Yang Guang. Cast: Lin Dongpu as Mr. Wang, Zhang Yu as Yi Wen, Zong Xiaojun as Xiao Chen, Wang Wenli as Mrs. Wang

Mr. Wang complains his wife is interested in only two things: asking him for money and playing mah-jongg. Now he unhappily notes that his daughter Ayuan is turning out the same. Wang's friend Xiao Chen is poorly treated by his wife, so he often visits Zhaofang Park hoping to find romance there. The two men go to a night club together, and there they meet singer Yi Wen. The young woman is in danger from triad figures, and since she needs a place to hide Wang takes her home with him. Mrs. Wang lets her stay with Aman. That night Mr. Wang and Xiao Chen both dream of having affairs with Yi Wen. She already has a boy friend Yu Desheng who she has corresponded with for years, unaware that he has changed his name and become a Japanese collaborator. When she discovers the truth, Yi Wen dumps him. She says goodbye to the Wangs and leaves, hoping that someday she can find a clean place in the world.

1338. *Mixed Feelings (Bei Xi Rensheng)*

1991. Inner Mongolia Film Studio. Color. Letterboxed. 9 Reels. Direction: Mailisi and Sai Fu. Screenplay: Kang Liwen. Cinematography: Lin Jian. Art Direction: Han Jinfeng. Music: San Bao. Sound: Hu Linping. Cast: Ma Jingwu as Zhu Feng, Hou Yaowen as Lin Shan, Huang Meiying as Jiang Nan, Ma Ye as son, Wang Hong as Liu Jia

Famous comedian Zhou Feng is in a deep state of depression. His wife is unhappy over his devotion to his career and neglect of his family, and he has just been informed he has a disease of the vocal cords which will soon cost him his voice. However, Zhou figures out a new way to perform: pantomime. His new act is a huge success. One day, his audience expectantly awaits as usual, but Zhou Feng does not show up. It turns out he has collapsed and died of heart failure on the way to the theater. The great performer, deprived of the chance to say goodbye to his loyal fans, will always be remembered by them.

1339. *A Model Husband (Mo Fan Zhang Fu)*

1981. Xiaoxiang Film Studio. Color. 9 Reels. Direction: Zhou Kangyu. Screenplay: Zhao Danian. Cinematography: Ding Xiaodong. Art Direction: Li Runzhang. Music: Liu Nianxun. Sound: Yan Ji. Cast: Li Jiayao as Yu Papa, Zhu Xijuan as Liu Li, Xiao Yuan as Wang Qiang, Zhang Miaozhen as Wu Yu, Fu Hengzhi as Yan Ren, Cao Xilin as Liu Ju

Every morning at six, while it is still dark, electronics institute director Yu Papa quietly rises and goes to the kitchen to prepare breakfast for his family, his wife, son and daughter. When breakfast is ready, he then wakes up his wife Liu Li, a judge at the People's Court. Liu Li is currently handling the divorce case of engineer Wan Qiang (an employee at the electronics institute) and his wife Wu Yu. Liu Li's investigation has determined that the cause of the couple's breakup is that Wan Qiang is a very macho man: while he devotes his time to his career, he insists his wife, a working woman, also handle every housekeeping detail including taking care of him. He is rude to his wife when he is dissatisfied with the care he receives. Through the divorce process, Liu Li shows the couple that men and women should both have careers they are fond of, and this brings the couple to begin to understand each other. In order to show Wan Qiang a man's role in family life, Liu Li arranges a special Sunday show for the couple: she has her husband Yu Papa display what he does everyday. Yu Papa prepares food skillfully and does the laundry quickly. Wan Qiang, who has always looked down upon housework, is shocked when he sees his respected director doing these thing so naturally and skillfully. The two couples now both appreciate their husband or wife's work more.

1340. *The Modern Generation (Dang Dai Ren)*

1981. Xiaoxiang Film Studio. Color. 10 Reels. Direction: Huang Shuqing. Screenplay: Zhao Danian, Bian Zhengxia. Cinematography: Wang Kekuan. Art Direction: Xia Rujin. Music: Si Guangnan. Sound: Liu Yishen, Huang Shiye.

Cast: Zhang Jiatian as Cai Min, Bian Ju as Xu Yan, Zhang Xiaolei as Wang Weizhou, Wang Shuqing as Liu Yufang, Zhong Xinghuo as Wang Kaiji, Liu Houen as Zhang Jie

In a South China city, the Forward Tractor Plant is in a state of economic and productive crisis: its product inventory is growing due to a high rate of return for poor quality. Newly assigned deputy plant director Cai Min, an engineer, on one hand pushes improving product quality and on the other hand stresses post-sales technical service. However, Cai Min's reform methods are resisted by conservative forces: department heads Chen and Wu and by cadre department head Liu Yufang and workshop director Li Baoben. At last, Cai Min's sincere attitude and hard work, combined with the achievements of his work, educates the people in the plant. Old plant director Wang Kaiji becomes convinced that Cai Min is a person to trust, so he abolishes the old restrictive and conventional practices and turns over the plant managerial authority to Cai Min.

1341. *Modern Wrestler (Xian Dai Jiao Dou Shi)*

1985. Changchun Film Studio. 10 Reels. Direction: Bai Dezhang, Xu Xunxing. Screenplay: Li Hun, Xu Xunxing. Cinematography: Liu Fengdi. Art Direction: Gao Guoliang. Music: Wu Damin, Yang Yilun. Sound: Kang Ruixin. Cast: Yang Liqin as Xilin, Bai Dezhang as Ming Shan, Zhang Xuzhong as Jin Dongao, Bao Zhenhua as He Hui, Liu Jing as Yin Dengmei

The story of a wrestler, a young man of the Xibo nationality, and his struggles to rise from champion of his autonomous region through national competition and to eventual success in European competition. Against this background, the film focuses on the wrestler's relationship with his coach and romance with a figure skater.

1342. *Moment (Shun Jian)*

1979. Changchun Film Studio. Color. 11 Reels. Direction: Zhao Xinshui. Screenplay: Peng Ning, He Kongzhou, Song Ge. Cinematography: Wu Beingli. Art Direction: Li Junjie. Music: Si Wanchun, Wang Jianzhong. Sound: Wang Fei. Cast: Liang Yuru as Wu Ao, Liang Boluo as Shi Feng, Huang Meiying as He Yansheng, Sheng Guangwei as Fu Xiohu, Zhu Decheng as Song Xiaolu, Shen Liang as Yu Fuli

Air Force aeronautical engineer Shi Feng is assigned to the Lushan Air Base to design a new type of fighter plane. Shortly after his arrival, he sees again old cadre Wei Tiegong, who had saved Shi Feng's life during the war. He learns that Wei, a worker at the site, has been falsely accused. When Lin Biao's conspiracy to assassinate Mao Zedong is smashed, agents of Lin arrive at the site and try to hijack a plane to flee the country. Wei Tiegong is killed stopping their hijacking attempt. Shi Feng is deceived into piloting the plane on which the conspirators mean to escape. But once in the air, when he learns of their plan to flee to a foreign country, he intentionally crashes the plane, sacrificing himself to kill the conspirators.

1343. *The Money Dream (Jin Qian Meng)*

1981. Shanghai Film Studio. Color. 5 Reels. Direction: Feng Xiao. Screenplay: Feng Xiao, Jiang Liangsheng. Cinematography: Zhen Xuan. Art Direction: Pu Jingsun. Music: Liu Yanxi. Sound: Ni Zheng. Cast: Han Fei as Father, Zhao Xiuli as Yinyin, Zhang Ying as Auntie, Zhou Guobing as Dawei

Yingying and Dawei are lovers, and today Dawei is to meet Yingying's father. While Yingying bustles in the kitchen, Yingying's father learns the young man works in a small factory making only 90 cents salary a day, and lives in a tiny single room. He immediately objects to the match. The humiliated Dawei leaves, but forgets to take along his bookbag. Later, the father looks into the bag and finds a bundle of foreign cash in it. He immediately changes his mind and wants the couple back together. When Dawei returns to pick up the bag, Yingying's father wants to hang on to this windfall, and rushes the couple out the door, insisting they get married right away. When Yingying and Dawei are away on their honeymoon, Yingying's father learns the "foreign currency" is superceded currency, and almost worthless.

1344. *Money Stuff (Qian Zhe Dong Xi)*

1985. Tianshan Film Studio. Color. 10 Reels. Direction: Jin Shuqi. Screenplay: Tuerxun Younisi. Cinematography: Yu Zhenyu. Art Direction: Gao Feng. Music: Chen Sanquan, Nusi Laiti. Sound: Du Shouyin. Cast: Tuyigong as Kezimu, Ati Kemu as Tai Laihan, Julaiti as Aili, Aini Waer as Dili Xiati, Azi Guli as Ruxian Guli

Kezimu the shoemaker is a greedy old man with no sense of business ethics. His son is much like him, but his daughter deplores her father's actions. She believes the only proper way to prosperity is through hard work. In the same village, a woman called Tai Laihan the carpet maker and her daughter are much like Kezimu and his son, but her son is honest. The two families become involved when the children get together, and all ends happily for the honest young couple.

1345. *The Mongolian Captive (Bei Fang Qiu Tu)*

1987. Inner Mongolia Film Studio. Color. 9 Reels. Direction: Abuer, Chen Hongguang. Screenplay: Jiang Ao. Cinematography: Hu Linping. Art Direction: Han Jingfeng. Music: Mori Jifu. Sound: Hu Linping. Cast: Qina Ritu as Chagan, Byin Errile as Yideng, Bao Hailong as the deputy

This action movie follows the shifting relationship between captive and warder. Chagan, a famous horse thief from the Mongolian steppes in the 1930s, is arrested and put under the guard of Yideng. One of Yideng's prison horses is stolen by a gang. The gang members belong to a family bent on revenge for Yideng having earlier arrested one of their members. Yideng refuses to be beaten. He orders Chagan to get the horse back, and the latter, afraid for his pregnant wife, dares not refuse. At first, Chagan's sympathies lie with the gang members, and he works hard to protect them from Yideng at the same time he tries to recover the horse. But the more he learns about Yideng's suffering at their hands and the crimes they have committed, the more he comes to understand the officer. With a plot full of double-crosses and stabs in the back, the movie builds rapidly to a bloody and tragic climax. When a third man intervenes, neither of the two heroes survive.

1346. *Monk "Tieluohan" (Tong Tou Tie Luo Han)*

1989. Shanghai Film Studio. Color. Letterboxed. 10 Reels. Direction: Bao Qicheng. Screenplay: Liu Tielong. Cinematography: Luo Zhengsheng. Art Direction: Wu Tianci. Music: Lu Qimin. Sound: Tu Minde. Cast: Fang Hu as Bujie, Xu Xueli as the merchant, Li Haoling as Wuji, Xie Yan as Han Dilei, Gao Hongping as Hua Mianhu

Adventurers and fortune-hunters from throughout China battle for possession of a precious and extremely valuable book, "Original Interpretations of Buddhism." The hero is a young monk named Bujie, representing the White Horse Temple.

1347. *The Monks from Shaolin (Zhi Yong He Shang)*

1991. Emei Film Studio and Taiwan Golden Tripod Film Co. Ltd. Co-Production. Color. Letterboxed. 9 Reels. Direction and Screenplay: Zhang Pengyi. Cinematography: Peng Dawei. Art Direction: Zhang Linwan. Music: Zhang Liao. Sound: Xinyi Recording Studio. Cast: Chen Guanhong as Gu Xiaoyun, Xu Chengyi as Zhi Shan, Lin Wei as Wei Zhongxian, Zhen Yanfeng as Miaomiao, Wu Ma as the unknown person, Xu Zhongxing as the silly monk, Kong Fanmian as Master Xinmin

In the Ming Dynasty, eunuch Wei Zhongxian persecutes and causes the murders of three court officials who block his path to power. The young daughter of one of the murdered men flees the court and takes sanctuary in the Shaolin Temple. There, she finds the child of another loyal official. The story tells how the Shaolin kung fu masters oppose the evil eunuch and protect the children.

1348. *Moon at the Moon Festival (Yue Dao Zhong Qiu)*

1983. Nanjing Film Studio. Color. 10 Reels. Direction: Yan Gong. Screenplay: Zhou Anhe. Cinematography: Wang Yizhi. Art Direction: Jin Bohao. Music: Wang Yunjie. Sound: Shen Guli. Cast: Xia Zongxue as Ling Mengqin, Yuan Mei as Fang Shu, Tan Mindi as Juanjuan, Liu Ming as Peng Sheng

Now in their 40s and having gone through the difficult Cultural Revolution years, museum antiques expert Ling Mengqin and dance troupe costume designer Fang Shu marry and look forward to peaceful and happy family life. But when he moves into Fang Shu's home, her children from her first marriage make him feel very unwelcome. He firmly believes that his warm expressions of affection for them will overcome their hostility, and at last the children come to respect and like their new stepfather. When the Moon Festival begins, the whole family celebrates together in the moonlight.

1349. *Moonlight in Spring (Er Quan Ying Yue)*

1979. August First Film Studio. Color. 11 Reels. Direction: Yan Jizhou. Screenplay: Guo Yunwen, Liu Baoyi, Rong Lei. Cinematography: Xue Boqin, Bai Fujin. Art Direction: Liu Jingsheng, Tang Shiyun. Music: Zhang Rui, Gong Zhiwei. Sound: Xue Boqin, Bai Fujin. Cast: Zhen Songmao as A Bing, Shao Hua as Mr. Zhong, Yuan Mengya as Sister Qing, Ning Hualu as Hua Xuemei, Dong Yugang as Tiger Li

Folk musician A Bing loses his mother at an early age and becomes a Taoist priest with his father. He loves music, and by his teen years has become famous as a musician at the Taoist temple in Wuxi. When his father dies he is left with just two classical Chinese instruments. Befriended by folk artist Mr. Zhong, A Bing continues learning from him. Then Zhong becomes seriously ill, leaving his daughter Sister Qing with no means of livelihood. A Bing leaves the temple to marry Qing, and they eke out a living as street performers. The two lead a very hard life in the old society, suffering considerable mistreatment and humiliation. Police chief Tiger Li lets the couple play for him, but takes offense at a satirical song A Bing performs. In anger, Li has the musician beaten, blinding him in one eye, and also takes Sister Qing away. After liberation, A Bing gains a new life and very happily gives stage performances which celebrate China's liberation. Then he learns that Sister Qing killed herself to escape Tiger Li's sexual demands. A Bing sits in front of Qing's tomb, and plays for her "Moonlight in Spring" which he has composed.

1350. *Morning Song (Chen Qu)*

1982. Shanghai Film Studio. Color. 5 Reels. Direction: Zhao Mao. Screenplay: Shi Yong, Zhao Qinrui, Jin Damo, Ding Yuling. Cinematography: Zhang Hongjun. Art Direction: He Zhaojie. Music: Xu Jingxin. Sound: Lu Jinsong. Cast: Na Renhua as Fang Lei, He Ling as Xiao Jinzhou, Wang Weiping as Sun Mu, Ling Jiayun as Xiao Xiong

Fang Lei is assigned a job in a kindergarten, but since her dream is to be an actress, working with small children holds no interest for her. Fang Lei's boyfriend Sun Mu, a hospital worker, also wants Fang Lei to change jobs. But through her work, Fang Lei comes to realize the importance of child care in helping parents who are busy making contributions to the nation. She becomes very serious about her work, but Sun Mu cannot believe it. He fakes a diagnosis of a contagious disease for Fang in order to get her transferred out of the kindergarten. The two finally break up over this. Fang Lei is now devoted to the small children she works with, and decides to devote herself to preschool education.

1351. *Morning Star at Green Field (Lu Ye Cheng Xing)*

1983. Inner Mongolia Film Studio. Color. 9 Reels. Direction: Gegeng Tana. Screenplay: Sai Fu. Cinematography: Xia Lixing, Bao Qin. Art Direction: Monayintai, Shen Minquan. Music: Da Renqin. Sound: Chen Hongen, Nashun. Cast: Qina Ritu as Chaoluomeng, Li Kechun as Wurihan, Aori Gele as Bateer, Shu Hai as Sangbu

Young Mongolian girl Wurihan returns to her home town to a new job teaching in a commune elementary school. There she meets a young man named Chaoluomeng, who for some reason is very cool toward her. She is also puzzled why he does not get along with commune director Sangbu, an old friend of her family. She soon learns that Chaoluomeng and the other young people in the commune work very hard to make their home town prosperous and beautiful, but the director's attitude and policies get in their way. Wurihan and the others build up mutual respect and understanding over time, and in the end she and Chaoluomeng are married.

1352. *Mother (Mu Qin)*

1956. Shanghai Film Studio. B & W. 12 Reels. Direction: Ling Zhifeng. Screenplay: Hai Mu. Cinematography: Zhu Jing. Art Direction: Lu Jingguang. Music: Wang Yunjie. Sound: Zhu Weigang. Cast: Zhang Ruifang as Mother, Jin Yan as Mr. Deng, Zhang Yi as Wang Laode, Zhang Zhiliang as Liang Chengwen, Qin Wen as Yan Jia, Yang Gongming as Liang Chengwu, Shi Wei as Xi Que, Li Nong as Liang Yuhou, Chen Shu as Shi Mopo, Zheng Min as Shi Huide

In 1922, when massive flooding devastates eastern Hebei province, a woman everyone calls "Mother" moves her family out of the flooded area to avoid starvation. On the road, they take in Xique, a homeless girl. The refugees are helped in resettling by two underground CPC workers, Mr. Deng and Wang Laode. After Mother's husband Liang Yuhou dies, she comes increasingly under the political influence of Mr. Deng, and she too joins the

Mother. Mother (Zhang Ruifang, left) is a Communist devoted to revolution and national liberation during World War II and the Chinese civil war. 1956. Shanghai Film Studio.

CPC. Later, Mr. Deng and Mother's son Liang Chengwen are betrayed by a government agent in the Party and arrested. Mr. Deng is executed. After the son is released, he goes into the countryside to do organizational work. The Party organization sends Yan Jia to contact Mother, and they join Wang Laode in organizing an armed rebellion. After the rebellion succeeds, Wang Laode and Mother's second son Liang Chengwu lead a general strike of workers in the city. In providing a cover for Yan Jia, Mother is arrested, then tortured in jail. Her adopted daughter Xi Que is abducted by secret police chief Shi Mopo to be his mistress. Mother is kept in jail until the end of World War II, and upon her release sets up an underground communications network for the Communists during the ensuing Civil War. Xi Que assists her by supplying information about the secret police's operations. When the Red Army nears the city, Shi Mopo orders that all the city's factories be blown up. Xi Que hurries to inform the Party underground of this, and Mother again gets herself arrested covering her. After liberation, Mother and her children are at last reunited.

1353. *Mother (Ma Ma)*

1990. Xi'an Film Studio. Color. 9 Reels. Wide Screen. Direction: Zhang Yuan. Screenplay: Qin Yan. Cinematography: Zhang Jian. Art Direction: Su Gang. Music: Wang Shi. Sound: Zhang Lei. Cast: Qin Yan as Liang Dan, Huang Haibo as Dongdong, Pan Shaquan as Chi Li, Ma Zheng as Xiao Zhang, Yu Shaokang as the old man

The film tells the story of Liang Dan, a single mother with a retarded child, Dongdong. Liang is a librarian who courageously faces up to the challenges of her life and tenaciously takes on the burden of trying to give her son a normal life.

1354. *Mother and Daughter Teachers (Mu Nu Jiaoshi)*

1957. Changchun Film Studio. B & W. 9 Reels. Direction: Feng Bailu. Screenplay: Ji Yie. Cinematography: Wang Yuru. Art Direction: Zhang Jingnan. Music: Li Xi. Sound: Hong Di. Cast: Lin Muyu as Shen Shuyan, Zi Qian as Lin Yueying, Zhang Hui as Chen Wei, Li Yalin as Zhang Zhigao, Liu Baoshu as Wang Damao, Zhang Juguang as Director Wu

Shen Shuyan and her daughter Lin Yueying

are both rural elementary school teachers. The mother has devoted all of the last 30 years to rural education, while the daughter is just enthusiastically beginning her new career. The two differ on their philosophies of education: the mother (who is also the school principal) advocates discipline with students, believing that "students will not become talented people if they are not disciplined." But the daughter advocates earnest instruction and enthusiastic help. The two have a falling out over this. Later, the mother attempts to resign over her guilt for dismissing student Wang Damao by mistake. With the trust and encouragement of the Party and government, and her coworkers' sincere request that she stay, Principal Shen realizes her mistake, and mother and daughter reach an understanding.

1355. *Mother Lake (Mu Qin Hu)*

1982. Inner Mongolia Film Studio. Color. Letterboxed. 10 Reels. Direction: Sun Tianxiang. Screenplay: Yun Zhaoguang. Cinematography: Wulan Mulin. Art Direction: Mo Nayintai. Music: Ala Tengaole. Sound: Li Juncheng. Cast: Suyaer Dalai as Chagan, Ha Da as Nayin Tai, Qiao Lu as Ning Bu, Li Youzhong as Huang Yading

In the late 1940s, on the shores of Inner Mongolia's "Mother Lake," Communist Party underground prefectural secretary Nayin Tai holds a wedding ceremony for his daughter and a young Party member named Cha Gan. However, the ceremony is disrupted by Nationalist soldiers still in the area. The furious Chagan vows he will never marry until all reactionaries are defeated. He joins the private military force of local warlord Ning Bu, hoping by that means to infiltrate the Nationalists. Chagan eventually works himself into the position of Ning Bu's bodyguard, a position from which he can closely monitor the actions of Nationalist commander Huang Yading and his intelligence chief. That winter, the underground prefectural committee receives a telegram from Chagan giving them the information they need for a decisive attack. The PLA and the prairie guerrillas jointly attack Huang Yading and wipe out his forces at icy Mother Lake. After the area is secured, Chagan is at last able to marry.

1356. *Mother Wants Me to Marry (Ma Ma Yao Wo Chu Jia)*

1956. Changchun Film Studio. B & W. 8

Reels. Direction: Huang Shu. Screenplay: Ji Ye, based on the novel "Sister Chun" by Liu Zhen. Cinematography: Chen Guohun. Art Direction: Dong Ping. Music: Li Ning, Wang Bo. Sound: Hong Di. Cast: Bo Ruitong as Li Yuchun, Jiangyan as Yuchun's mother, Liu Shilong as Liu Minghua, Ren Weiming as Tie Dan, Huang Shuying as Minghua's Mother, Liu Bo as Jiuxi

In a place called North Village, a girl named Li Yuchun falls in love with Liu Minghua, a young man from the South Village agricultural co-op. However, Yuchun's mother disapproves, because she thinks that co-op members will always be poor. Matchmaker old Woman Wang works on Yuchun's mother, persuading her to marry her daughter to Jiuxi, a local businessman. But Yuchun's best friends Xiufang and Ermei enthusiastically work to get Yuchun and Minghua together. After Yuchun and Minghua obtain a marriage license, the girl's mother kicks her out of the house. Later on, Yuchun's mother realizes the advantages of cooperatives, and finally recognizes Liu Minghua as her son-in-law. Mother and daughter are reconciled.

1357. *Motive for Murder (Sha Ji Bei Hou)*

1989. Inner Mongolia Film Studio. Color. Letterboxed. 9 Reels. Direction: Dong Tao. Screenplay: Tuo Ya. Cinematography: Geng Guangyuan, Lin Jian. Art Direction: Wang Xiaohong, Hou Yan. Music: Alatengaoqing. Sound: Zhao Aosi. Cast: Zhang Zhaobei as the killer, Zhang Dawan as Zhen Fuxiang, Hasibageng as Asier, Chen Qi as Fangfang

A convicted murderer breaks out of prison and flees to Inner Mongolia, where he finds employment with Hong Kong businessman Zhen Fuxiang, who hires him to find a map of prairie mine locations. The fugitive, who always wears black, kills one person after another in his search for the map. Chief investigator Asier tracks down the killer, and in the course of his investigation also learns that some supposedly upstanding local businessmen are involved in illegal tobacco dealings with Zhen. At last, the gunman in black is killed in a gun battle with police.

1358. *Mountain Flower (Shan Hua)*

1976. Beijing Film Studio. Color. Wide Screen. 13 Reels. Directors: Cui Kui and Sang Fu. Screenplay: Sun Qian, Ma Feng and Guo Ende. Cinematographers: Gao Hongtao and Yu

Zhenyu. Art Direction: Liu Yi and Yang Zhanjia. Music: Gong Zhiwei. Sound: Wang Yunhua. Cast: Xie Fang as Gao Sanhua, Zhang Ping as Hu Gengmao, Wang Xianghong as Gao Sanhua (as a child), Yang Wei as Shi Rushan, Lei Min as Ma Qijia, Fu Zhucheng as Feng Tianbao

Sun Guangzong, from a capitalist background, allies himself with a corrupt Party secretary to hinder farm production at the Huang Tupo production unit. Party Secretary Gao Sanhua detects their plot and exposes it, in spite of opposition from her stepfather Hu Gengmao, who believes she is being unnecessarily suspicious.

1359. *Mountain People (Shan Li De Ren)*

1958. Beijing Film Studio. Color. 9 Reels. Direction: Chen Huaiai. Screenplay: Liang Xiucheng. Cinematography: Nie Jing. Art Direction: Qing Wei. Music: Su Ming. Sound: Chen Yanxi. Cast: Gao Shiyin as Huang Liying, Yu Zhongyi as Zhang Dahong, Gao Changde as Lin Apang, Zhang Yan as Steel Hammer Huang, Shi Meifeng as Pan Zhu, Tian Feng as Village Chief Fang

When a railway construction team comes to build a railway in a remote mountain area, veteran blacksmith "Steel Hammer" Huang insists on helping, although he is well over the age limits. His daughter Huang Liyin also wants to help, but he forbids her from doing so, so she only helps when he is absent from the site. Unfortunately, Steel Hammer's conservative insistence on quality above quantity in everything seriously impedes the progress of construction. Criticism from his work team about this only makes him more set in his ways. His daughter's team successfully upgrades their technology and greatly improves their work efficiency. Eventually, Steel Hammer Huang becomes more progressive through inspirational talks with the construction team director and his daughter's experience.

1360. *Mountain Village Accountant (Shan Chun Kuai Ji)*

1965. Changchun Film Studio. B & W. 8 Reels. Direction: Yi Yiqing. Screenplay; Yang Runsheng. Cinematography: Zhang Yun. Art Direction: Tong Jingwen. Music: Chen Ming. Sound: Jue Jingxiu, Hong Bo. Cast: Guo Jun as Jiang Xixi, Ai Hongli as Tian Laoda, Du Defu as Zhou Laoshi, Pan Shulan as Junqing, Huang Ling as Liu Yingduo, Li Keming as Guigui

The Zhaiyinggou production group's accountant Zhao Youcai, whose family had been rich farmers, is dismissed from his position for poor performance. He is replaced by his cousin Jiang Xixi, formerly a cook in the Eighth Route Army. At first, Zhao does not take Jiang seriously, thinking that the latter's low education level will prevent him from discovering that Zhao had been embezzling. However, Jiang Xixi devotes himself to serving the commune's members, studies and works hard, and gradually finds some clues that point to the former accountant's crimes. When Zhao realizes he may soon be in danger, he tries and fails to win over Jiang by taking advantage of the fact they are relations. Zhao then tries to foment dissent among less-progressive commune members, but Jiang Xixi is able to show a key potential witness who is the real criminal, turning the witness against Zhao in court.

1361. *Mountain Village Sisters (Shan Cun Jie Mei)*

1965. Beijing Film Studio. B & W. 10 Reels. Direction: Zhang Zhen. Screenplay: Liu Houmin. Cinematography: Xu Xiaoxian. Art Direction: Yang Yuhe. Music: Su min. Sound: Zhang Jiake. Cast: Gao Aisheng as Jin Yan, Qiu Lili as Jin Ling, Chen Lizhong as Qi's mother, Guo Shutian as Old Geng, Huang Zhong as Old Qingcheng, Huang Fei as Zhao Mingli

In 1963, two young sisters live in a village in the far suburbs of Beijing. Jin Yan, the elder of the two, has voluntarily relinquished her teaching job in the city to return to her hometown and work as a farmer. The younger sister Jin Ling, spoiled by their parents, has been influenced by capitalist ideas. She only wants to pursue pleasure. She is introduced to Zhao Mingli, a young man from a more prosperous area seeking a wife, and to avoid the hard life of their mountain area, she marries him. But Jin Ling soon discovers that even those in prosperous villages do not live as she imagined they did, and that her husband has actually gone heavily into debt in order to marry her. She is very regretful. Her older sister Jin Yan works with the village's young people in learning to plant Chinese flowering crabapple trees. She is finally successful at this. Jin Ling also decides to work with her sister in building a new mountain village.

1362. *A Mountain Village's Struggle (Zhan Dou De Shan Cun)*

1958. Haiyan Film Studio. B & W. 9 Reels. Direction: Su Shi. Screenplay: Wang Yun, Suo Yunping. Cinematography: Zhu Jing. Art Direction: Zong Yongqing. Music: Jiang Yulin. Sound: Lu Zongbo, Feng Deyao. Makeup: Tian Zhigao. Cast: Ling Zhiao as Ding Deming, Shao Li as Secretary Wang, Deng Nan as Chen Yingtang, Sha Li as Chen Xiumei, Zhao Guoxiang as Liu Haiwang, Cha Mannuo as Liu Yuzhen

During the agricultural commune campaign, discharged soldier Ding Deming returns to his hometown in the Yimeng Mountains. He donates his mustering out bonus to help his neighbors dig a well that will resolve their long-standing problem with water resources. He also suggests building a water tunnel to bring the waters of the Qing River to the mountain area, but this is opposed by conservative thinkers in the commune, led by director Chen Yingtang. With the support of County Secretary Wang, Ding Deming leads commune members in changing the way they look at the mountains. Ding's fiancee Chen Xiumei, who had planned to leave the mountain area to study in the city, now sees the wonderful future of the mountains, so she determines to stay and help in building the area.

1363. *Mountains and Rivers (Shan Chong Shui Fu)*

1980. Beijing Film Studio. Color. 12 Reels. Direction: Wu Zhaodi. Screenplay: Ding Yishan, Wu Zhaodi. Cinematography: Wang Zhaoling. Art Direction: Mo Kezhan, Shao Ruigang. Music: Lou Zhanghou. Sound: Wang Yunhua. Cast: Feng Chunchao as Chen Yi, Bai Zhidi as Han Shanhe, Nie Yaliang as Feng Zhihuan

In 1937, the Chinese Communist Party proposes "stopping the Civil War and uniting against the Japanese." Chen Yi carries the Party's orders to the Wohu Mountains, where he meets guerrilla brigade commander Han Shanhe, and conveys to Han the Party's orders about establishing an anti–Japanese united front. He asks Han to immediately reorganize his guerrillas into an anti–Japanese brigade. Han Shanhe cannot understand this: to him, cooperating with the Chinese Nationalist Party is tantamount to surrender. He mistakenly suspects Chen Yi of being a traitor, and orders his arrest. Chen understands Han's feelings, and works patiently to persuade Han, but with no success. Meanwhile, a Nationalist spy, Feng Zhihuan, creates an incident designed to cast further suspicion on Chen Yi's loyalties. Han decides to kill Chen Yi. However, he begins in time to see the light, and comes to understand both Chen Yi and the Party's orders.

1364. *The Mountain's Final Song (Shan Ye Jue Chang)*

1992. Changchun Film Studio & Anhui Film Studio Co-Production. Color. Letterboxed. 9 Reels. Direction: Zhang Zhongwei. Screenplay: Fang Yihau. Cinematography: Huang Qiao. Art Direction: Zhu Jiaxin. Music: Fan Weiqiang. Sound: Zhang Wen, Gu Kejian. Costume: Wu Xiufeng, Wang Zixiang. Makeup: Liao Yonghua. Cast: Lu Xiaohe as Yue Pengcheng, Zhang Jing as Qiuling, Li Ping as Yingguan, Li Lan as Shuzhen, Liu Xuefang as wife Xiaoyun, Fang Qingzi as Xiao Yu

Yue Pengcheng starts a wood products plant in his village, hiring many of his fellow villagers. He makes a lot of money, but in time becomes a very corrupt local despot, even taking his secretary as his mistress. His son Yingguan starts his own business, and in time beats out his father in market competition. No matter what the father tries to beat him, the son always wins. With inevitable failure staring him in the face, Yue Pengcheng feels tired, weak and defeated for the first time in his life.

1365. *Mountains of the Sun (Tai Yang Shan)*

1991. Fujian Film Studio. Color. 9 Reels. Direction: Wu Ziniu. Screenplay: Sima Xiaojia. Cinematography: He Qing. Art Direction: Zhao Shaoping. Music: Zhang Shaotong. Sound: Liu Tonghe. Cast: Zhang Liwei as A Ning, Tao Zeru as A Xiang, Liu Zhongyuan as Li Daxi, Dong Jie as A Ming

In a northern Fujian mountain village in the 1950s a deranged woman hangs herself, leaving her six-year-old crippled son to fend for himself. The child is adopted by A Ning, a woman teacher at the mountain school. A Xiang, a young man from the mountains, extends a helping hand and is interested in A Ning, but she still misses her husband who had been evacuated to Taiwan when the Nationalist army and government fled the Chinese mainland. One day, while A Xiang is out gathering medicinal herbs for the woman and the child, he falls from a cliff and disappears. When a search party finds him, badly injured but still alive, A Ning embraces him tightly

Mountains of the Sun. **A Ning (Zhang Liwei, right) adopts and raises a handicapped boy (Dong Jie, left). 1991. Fujian Film Studio.**

and swears she will never let him get away from her again. The couple pass 30 peaceful and harmonious years together. But their lives are disrupted by the unexpected arrival of A Ning's former husband from Taiwan. The three now elderly people now confront a shock to their sentiments and souls…

1366. *Moving Forward Shoulder to Shoulder (Bing Jian Qian Jin)*

1958. Changchun Film Studio. B & W. 8 Reels. Direction: Yan Gong. Screenplay: Wu Zhaodi, Yin Yiqing and Ji Ye, based on the novel, "Snow and Ice Melt" by Li Zhun. Cinematography: Liu Yongzheng. Art Direction: Tong Jingwen. Music: Li Xi. Sound: Jue Jingxiu. Cast: Li Mengrao as Zhen Deming, Guo Shutian as Wei Hutou, He Xiaoshu as Zhen Xiuzhi, Wang Feng as Liu Mainao, Liu Shilong as Wei Xiaosong, Ren Weimin as Li Sheng

During the agricultural commune movement of 1955, Liu Mainao, deputy director of the Red Flag agricultural commune, is arrogant and conceited about the commune's achievements. Director Wei Hutou of the Sunlight commune, heavily influenced by his deputy

Liu Erxing, pays more attention to the shipping business than he does to agricultural production. Liu Mainao, instead of offering constructive criticism of Wei's mistakes, satirizes and attacks him, which leads to a split in the two communes' unity. Red Flag director Zhen Deming's daughter Zhen Xiuzhi and her lover Wei Xiaosong, Wei Hutu's son, argue with their fathers, and get them to see the error of their ways. Their leaders' shortcomings having been overcome, the two communes unite for mutual progress.

1367. *Moyadai (Mo Ya Dai)*

1960. Haiyan Film Studio. Color. 12 Reels. Direction: Xu Tao. Screenplay: Ji Kang, Gong Pu. Cinematography: Luo Chongzhou. Art Direction: Hu Dengren. Music: Ge Yan. Sound: Miao Zhengyu. Cast: Qing Yi as Mihan and Yilaihan, Wei Heling as Boyihan, Kang Tai as Yanwun, Chang Tai as Mr. Cao, Xia Tian as Laoba, Deng Nan as Zhaogui Bosha

In Yunnan province before liberation, Mihan, a beautiful woman of the Dai nationality, resists the advances of a man named Laoba. In retaliation, he accuses her of being a witch who spreads diseases, and she is burned to death. Eighteen years later, just after liberation, Mihan's daughter Yilaihan is grown up and in love with Yanwun, a young farmer. Laoba frames Yilaihan for witchcraft as well, and she and her ailing father are driven from their village to seek refuge elsewhere, and the father dies on the way. Orphaned, and mistakenly thinking Yanwun has changed his mind and rejected her, the young woman jumps into a river to commit suicide, but is rescued by some PLA soldiers. Two years later, Yilaihan has became a doctor trained by the Party, and is assigned to her native village. She cures so many patients that she smashes Laoba's lies about "witches" spreading disease. She also meets again with Yunwun, and after clearing up their misunderstanding, the young couple are married. Laoba is tried and punished for his crimes. Land reform is successful, and the people's lives are much better.

1368. *Mumian Patchwork Clothing (Mu Mian Jia Sha)*

1984. Fujian Film Studio & Hong Kong Jiamin Film Corporation. Color. 9 Reels. Direction: Xu Xiaomin. Screenplay: Zhang Hua, Ye Nan, Xu Xiaomin. Cinematography: Li Wanjie. Art Direction: Liu Nanmei. Cast: Xu Xiangdong as Huineng, Lin Qiuping as Lin Ying, Yu Dalu as Wang Cheng, Yang Yongcai as Yuanhui, Yu Rongguang as Qi Tianyuan, Ding Jinyou as Quanji Zhenren

The title refers to the patchwork robes worn by monks. Near the end of the Ming Dynasty (ca1640), all of the groups rebelling against the Ming battled under the flag of Shaolin. Imperial forces commander Wang Cheng decides the Shaolin Temple must be brought to heel, so he names his underling Qi Tianyuan the next Master of Shaolin. His army surrounds the Temple, but the monks refuse to give in to Wang Cheng's demand they accept Qi Tianyuan as Master. Led by a hero named Huineng, they fight bravely and repel the attacks. After the battle is over, Huineng is named the 28th Master of the Shaolin Temple.

1369. *Murder at the Wedding (Hun Li Shang De Chi Ke)*

1989. Inner Mongolia Film Studio. Color. Wide screen. 9 Reels. Direction: Li Yucai, Baona Yintai. Screenplay: Li Rui, Li Yue. Cinematography: Chen Wancai, Du Rong. Art Direction: Mo Nayintai. Music: Moer Jihu. Sound: Buren Bayaer. Cast: Ge Batuqingele as Master Bayantala, Wurijiletu as Zhaoritu, Bashengzhabu as Jirigereng, Hasigaowa as Tana

At the end of the 1930s, Master Bayantala governs the beautiful and prosperous Bayantala Prairie of Inner Mongolia. As the patriotic Master Bayantala is considering throwing his support behind the growing anti–Japanese movement in China, the Japanese government sends a hit man to eliminate the Master and ease their path to an eventual invasion. The killer chooses Master Bayantala's wedding as the best time to make his move. But throughout the wedding and the gala reception that follows, a singer named Zhaoritu follows Bayantala at every moment and thwarts the attempted assassination.

1370. *Murder in an Island Nation (Dao Guo Mo Sha)*

1989. Changchun Film Studio. Color. Letter Box. 9 Reels. Direction: Wang Yabiao. Screenplay: Deng Chengxi. Cinematography: Lei Xianhe. Art Direction: Guo Yansheng, Zhang Yan. Music: Fan Weiqiang. Sound: Cao Feng. Casting: Su Ying as Crocodile, Qian Dongli as Aina

An international terrorist organization hires an expensive hit man called "Crocodile" to assassinate the Chinese Prime Minister while he is attending an international conference in an island nation. When Crocodile arrives on the island, he is able to take advantage of the local police chief's girl friend Aina to help him carry out his assignment. At the same time, a similar plan is being hatched by the U.S. CIA's local organization, a group headed by the police chief's wife. The story ends with Crocodile being shot to death by police, and the chief's wife committing suicide when her espionage activities are exposed.

1371. *Murder in an Isolated Village (Huang Yuan Sha Shou)*

1988. Beijing Film Studio. Color. 9 Reels. Direction: Huangpu Keren. Screenplay: Jiang Ao. Cinematography: Wang Lianping. Art Direction: Huangpu Keren, Wang Lianping. Music: Guao Xiaodi. Sound: Zhang Yu. Cast: Li Baotian as Zhao Feng. Also: Chen Shensheng, Zhang Peiyu, Ding Lan

In an isolated village near the border, Inspector Zhao Feng and his assistant investigate a murder case. Six years earlier, the district director had been murdered in the same village, and Zhao Feng had been in charge of that investigation as well. By following and analyzing the clues, Zhao Feng at last identifies the killer. But the clever criminal has covered his tracks so well that Zhao knows he lacks sufficient evidence to convict. He decides to take the criminal into custody anyway…

1372. *Murder Mystery (Xia Jiang Yi Ying)*

1985. Changchun Film Studio. Color. 10 Reels. Direction: Li Qimin. Screenplay: Xie Wenli. Cinematography: Gao Hongbao. Art Direction: Guo Yangsheng, Hu Pei. Music: Zhang Hong. Sound: Liu Wenzhang. Cast: Sun Jianmin as Lin Jie, Zhang Xiling as Mei Xia, Cui Yi as Da Hei

Towards the end of the Qing (Manchu) Dynasty, a secret democratic movement called the Tongmeng Association springs up throughout China, attracting many martial arts fighters to its membership. The Qing government reacts by dispatching hired killers to root out these revolutionaries. Mei Xia, daughter of an anti–Qing martial artist, comes to the city of Xiajiang seeking to join the revolutionary cause. She finds work as a servant in the home of a mysterious man named Hong Sheng, a martial arts expert and a covert leader of the Tongmeng Association. Another man who joins Hong's household is Lin Jie, secretly a Qing government spy. Lin Jie becomes very close with Hong Sheng's daughter Xiao Chui, and after much intrigue Lin Jie learns that Hong Sheng is a Tongmeng leader. He is successful in killing Hong, but Meixia saves Xiao Chui, however, and the two young women join the anti–Qing movement.

1373. *Murder of a Visitor from Hong Kong (Gang Ke Mou Sha An)*

1987. Pearl River Film Studio. Color. 9 Reels. Direction: Cao Zheng. Screenplay: Bai Yunsheng, Zhen Yifu. Cinematography: Wang Lianping. Art Direction: Wang Meifang. Music: Du Jiangang. Sound: Liu Haiyan. Cast: Wang Jiancheng as Liang Bing, Liu Gege as Li Li, Du Xiongwen as Bao Kezhi, Yu Haiyang as Ma Wen, Chen Xiaoming as Guo Youxiang, Wen Juefei as Liu Shoude

Several tourists come to a scenic spot near the city of Guangzhou. Among these are Liu Shoude, CEO of a large Hong Kong corporation, his mistress Li Li, his personal physician and his manservant. Following them is Li Li's old boyfriend Ma Wen. One morning, the tour group finds Liu lying dead in the woods. PSB investigator Liang Bing and his assistant Yang Guang are assigned to the case. They are given only three days to solve the crime, as the tour group is supposed to return to Hong Kong then. On the last day, as the group is preparing to depart, Liang Bing calls together the four people connected to the murdered man and announces that one of them will not be going back…

1374. *Muslim Funeral (Parts 1 & 2) (Mu Si Lin De Zhang Li)*

1993. Beijing Film Studio & Kangda Film Company Ltd. Co-Production. Color. Direction: Xie Tieli, Zhao Yuan. Screenplay: Huo Da, based on the novel of the same title. Cinematography: Zhen Yuyuan. Art Direction: Tu Juhua. Music: Zhang Qianyi. Cast: Wang Sihuai as Han Ziqi, Xue Shujie as Liang Zhijun, Gai Lili as Liang Bingyu, Shi Lanya as Xinyue

In the early summer of 1919, Yipulaxin, a young Muslim, arrives in Beijing where he meets the famous jade craftsman Liang Yiqiu. Liang takes him into his home and makes the young man his apprentice. Three years later, Yipulaxin is himself famous for his jade work, and he adopts the Chinese name Han Ziqi. After Liang dies, Han marries his mentor's eldest daughter Junbi, and they soon have a son Tianxing. Han's business grows and prospers through the 1920s. When the Japanese invade China, Han decides to leave China for London and get away from the war. But his wife Junbi refuses to leave her family. So Han Ziqi leaves for London, accompanied only by his wife's younger sister Bingyu. In London, they hear that the entire family has been killed in the war. Han and Bingyu get married, and have a daughter Xinyue. Years later, they return to Beijing, but find that Junbi and Tianxing are still alive. Although she loves Han and their daughter, Bingyu feels she must leave, painful though it is for her. Through the years, Xinyue grows up in a strange household, always aware of her stepmother/aunt's coldness towards her. In addition, the girl suffers from a severe heart ailment. The only hope in her life is her love for her college teacher Chu Yanchao. In 1979, Bingyu finally returns to China to visit her relatives. But she finds only Tianxing, who tells her she arrived too late. Everyone else has died.

1375. *The Mute Girl (Ya Gu)*

1983. Beijing Film Studio. Color. 10 Reels. Direction: Xiao Lang. Screenplay: Ding Zhengquan. Cinematography: Li Yuebing. Art Direction: Yang Zhanjia. Music: Li Wanli. Sound: Wang Yunhua. Cast: Wan Qiong as the Girl, Shen Guanchu as Chunge, Wang Baoshan as Uncle "Government," Wu Suqing as Old Mrs. Man, Ling Yuan as Grandma Lu Fu, Chen Yude as the Stranger

A young girl makes her way unsteadily along a rugged and muddy mountain road. She meets Chunge, a young man who raises ducks. That night, Chunge discovers the girl is so hungry she steals the ducks' food to eat. The girl stays temporarily in the village, and since she never speaks, everyone considers her a mute. In the short time she stays there, the village people see she is hard-working and diligent, and gradually come to like her. She helps Chunge and his son raise their ducks, and she and the widowed Chunge start growing fond of each other. Just when it appears she will settle down there, an old woman shows up and says she is the girl's mother. It turns out that the girl is from a very poor village, and her mother married her off to an old smuggler in order to pay off the family's debts. On the way to the wedding, the girl had fled and was wandering from place to place pretending to be a mute so no one would ask about her background. The next morning, the girl bids farewell to the village as she leaves with her mother. Chunge and his little boy stand watching silently until she is out of sight.

1376. *Mutiny (Hua Bian)*

1989. Guangxi Film Studio. Color. Letterboxed. 9 Reels. Direction: He Qun. Screenplay: Li Baolin. Cinematography: Liu Baogui, Fang Miao. Art Direction: Zhang Ruo. Music: Zhao Jiping. Sound: Lin Lin. Cast: Zhu Yidan as Zhongye, Chen Jianfei as Yue Tai, Zhang Guangbei as Cheng Huan

In 1943, the Japanese military high command orders the formation of Chinese units of the Imperial Army, offering a bonus to Japanese commanders for each Chinese they recruit. A corrupt Japanese division commander exploits this by regularly having a certain number of the Chinese killed off to make room in the ranks for more, thereby assuring himself a steady income of recruitment bonuses. The film relates how anti–Japanese emotions grow among the Chinese troops until they at last rebel against the real Japanese troops in a violent and bloody final confrontation.

1377. *My Country, My Mother! (Zuguo A, Muqin!)*

1976. Shanghai Film Studio. Color. 15 Reels. Direction: Tang Xiaodan, Zhang Huijun. Screenplay: Mala Qinfu. Cinematography: Shen Miaorong, Chen Yongjun. Art Direction: Ge Sicheng, Zhen Changfu. Music: Xin Huguang, Meili Qige. Sound: Tu Minde. Cast: Nige Mutu as Bateer, Zhou Zhiyu as Zhao Zhimin, Ta Na as Hong Geer, Ha Da as Re Xi, Yi Ruohu as Nabuqi, Zhu Yanqin as Shandan, Chen Da as Shamuteng

In Inner Mongolia soon after World War II, prairie governor Shamuteng, in league with the Nationalist Chinese government, attempts to destroy the Chinese people's growing sympathy for liberation by fostering a Mongolian people's "independence movement." The Communist Party sends Bateer from Yan'an to organize a counter-movement. He sets up a "Herdsmens' Association," wins the cooperation of local armed volunteers led by Hong Geer and defeats Shamuteng's conspiracy of holding Inner Mongolia for the government under the guise of seeking independence.

My Flying Wife **see** *Living and Dead Fa Wang*

1378. *My Memories of Old Beijing (Cheng Nan Jiu Shi)*

1982. Shanghai Film Studio. Color. Wide Screen. 10 Reels. 96 min. Direction: Wu Yigong. Screenplay: Yi Min, based on the novel by Lin Haiyin. Cinematography: Cao Weiye. Art Direction: Zhong Yongqin. Music: Lu Qiming. Sound: Xie Guojie. Cast: Shen Jie as Yinzhi, Zhen Zhenyao as Mrs. Song, Zhang Ming as the crazy woman, Zhang Fengyi as "that person," Yan Xiang as Father, Yuan Jiayin as Niuer

In old Beijing, Lin Yinzhi's family lives at the south end of the city. As a child, Yinzhi observes the world through the eyes of innocence, including many things she cannot understand. Yinzhi makes friends with a young neighbor woman named Xiuzhen who everyone says is crazy. Xiuzhen's former lover, a Beijing University student, was arrested. After the young woman gave birth, the baby was taken away from her. Yinzhi's playmate Niuer was abandoned and then adopted, but her adoptive parents abuse her. Yinzhi imagines Niuer is the crazy woman's daughter who was taken away from her at birth, so she brings Niuer to the crazy woman, figuring both need love. However, the two are soon killed in a train wreck. Yinzhi's family moves away and she makes a new friend. Having no other choice, he becomes a thief, but he too is soon taken away. Mrs. Song is the wet nurse for Yingzhi's younger brother, but Yingzhi cannot understand why the woman does not care for her own son, about the same age as Yingzhi's little brother. Yingzhi is soon in sorrow again because Mrs. Song's son drowns. Mrs. Song is taken away by her husband. Yingzhi's father is a kindly man and a good teacher. One day word comes that he has died in Taiwan, far from home. Yinzhi's childhood has ended.

Best Director Wu Yigong, 1983 Golden Rooster Awards.

Best Supporting Actress Zhen Zhenyao, 1983 Golden Rooster Awards.

Best Music Lu Qiming, 1983 Golden Rooster Awards.

The Equator Award, 10th Quito International Film Festival.

1379. *My Native People (Xiang Qin Men)*

1993. Emei Film Studio and Tianjin Film Studio. Color. Letterboxed. 9 Reels. Direction: Wang Jixing Cinematography: Qiang Jun. Art Direction: Chen Jinyong. Sound: Wang Guangzhong. Costume: Feng Guilan. Makeup: Xiao Guiyuan. Cast: Huang Wenke as Ba Dakuan, Cao Dingding as Miaoxiu, Ding Yan as Zhouzi, Bai Zhidi as Uncle Lulu, Qu Yun as Old Lady Ji, Liu Zhongyuan as the rural gentleman, Liu Wei as Huo Chonglei, Zhao Jun as Brother Gouti

When the Japanese launch a sweep through central Hebei, three young Eighth Route Army soldiers, 12 and 13 years old, lose contact with their unit. They are hidden and given protection by village people. They continue harassing the invaders by night, and at last make contact with the local Communist Party committee, which helps them make their way back to their unit. But many villagers are killed during the effort, and at last the three young soldiers perish as well.

1380. *My September (Wo De Jiu Yue)*

1990. Children's Film Studio. Color. 9 Reels. Wide Screen. Direction: Yin Li. Screenplay: Du Xiao'ou, Luo Chensheng. Cinematography: Li Jianguo. Art Direction: Shu Gang, Meng Jiyuan. Music: Liu Weiguang. Sound: Zhen Chunyu. Cast: Zhang Meng as An Jianjun, Zhang Chen as Liu Qinglai, Fan Dongsheng as Lei Zhenshan, Zhang Guoli as the Teacher

An Jianjun, nicknamed Big Fool, is a shy but friendly 4th grade schoolboy. His stuck up classmate Liu Qinglai and many others think that An is so weak that he is an easy target. During a school fund drive to raise money to support the Asian Games, Liu frames An Jianjun so that An is blamed for something he never did, allowing Liu to take credit for An's contribution to the fund drive. An becomes a laughing-stock. Realizing the boy's torment, a teacher encourages him to be brave and confident and convinces him he is as good as the others. Finally, An Jianjun crosses the first hurdle in gaining self-confidence. In that unforgettable September of his new self-confident life, An determines to excel in martial arts.

1381. *My Ten Classmates (Wode Shige Tongxue)*

1979. Emei Film Studio. Color. 10 Reels. Direction: Ye Min. Screenplay: Yang Yinzhang. Cinematography: Feng Shilin. Art Direction: Wang Tao. Sound: Hua Yaozhu. Cast: Yang Yaqing as Fang Ming, Lu Guilan as Shen Yujie, Zhao Youliang as Li Dazhi, Lu Xiaohe as Zhou Mengjia, He Xiaoshu as Qin Youlan

In 1977, universities intensively discuss the "Two Evaluations" theory. In order to let "facts" prove the theory, Southwest College woman teacher Fang Ming decides to investigate some graduates' behavior after graduation. She investigates many graduates and realizes the "Two Evaluations" theory is wrong. Happily, on the train on her way to see the final graduate, she hears that the People's Daily is criticizing the "Two Evaluations," and that a mountain of evidence has proven the "Two Evaluations" a false theory.

1382. *The Mysterious Buddha (Shen Mi De Da Fo)*

1980. Beijing Film Studio. Color. 10 Reels. Direction: Zhang Huaxun. Screenplay: Xie Hong, Zhang Huaxun, Zhu Hongsheng, Lu Shoujun. Cinematography: Chen Guoliang,

Liang Zhiyong. Art Direction: Wang Yi. Music: Xiong Yihua, Xie Jun. Sound: Wang Dawen. Cast: Zhang Shunsheng as Si Tujun, Liu Xiaoqing as Meng Jie, Jiang Gengcheng as Wun Jianming, Guan Zongxiang as Haineng, Wang Biao as Zhen Han, Ge Chunzhuang as Shatuo, Li Liansheng as Little Monk

In the days before the Chinese revolution, a legend holds that a fortune in treasure is hidden in a secret tomb somewhere around the huge statue of Buddha on Mount Le in South China. Many had gone to the mountain in search of the treasure, but all were killed at the foot of the Buddha by a man with a strange face. Si Tujun, an overseas Chinese from Southeast Asia, comes to the town at the foot of the mountain on what he says is important business with his uncle. He refers to his relative as An Kang, a name no one in town recognizes. His arrival creates a considerable stir among the local people: policemen keep an eye on his movements, local despot Master Shatuo has him followed, and Shatuo's family tutor Meng Jie is his frequent guide around town. Si Tujun finally contacts his uncle, who turns out to be Haineng, a Buddhist master. Si Tujun realizes his life is in danger. On the night he and his uncle finally meet to hold their talks, the strange-faced man attacks, wanting Haineng to tell the secret of the treasure. Meng Jie, who had been hiding in the shadows to protect Si Tuju, helps them overpower the attacker. Finally, Haineng guides Si and Meng to the treasure—a gold Buddha.

1383. *The Mysterious Camel Team (Shen Mi Tuo Dui)*

1985. Tianshan Film Studio. Color. 10 Reels. Direction: Guang Chunlan. Screenplay: Ma Yan, Duan Baoshan. Cinematography: Zhou Cuiyuan. Art Direction: Zhang Tiren, Gao Feng. Music: Nusi Jinti. Sound: Liu Honggang. Cast: Peier Daweisi as Sha Dike, Xiati Guli as Ayi Nuer, Tuer Xunjiang as Yusupu, Apureli as Guli

Lalai, a beautiful Uighur woman, is raped by foreign merchant Yusufu, resulting in her giving birth to twin girls. He drives out the mother and one girl, Ayi Nuer, and keeps the other baby girl, Mayi Nuer. Twenty years pass, and Xinjiang is about to be liberated, so Yusufu prepares to flee across the border. He finds he is being pursued by a mysterious camel team. It turns out to be PLA platoon leader Sha Dike and soldier Baibilu. They capture Yusupu and reunite the twin sisters.

1384. *Mysterious Couple (Shen Mi Fu Qi)*

1991. Beijing Film Studio. Color. Letterboxed. 9 Reels. Direction: Li Zhiyu. Screenplay: Xiao Mao, Wang Suo, Li Zhiyu. Cinematography: Li Tian. Art Direction: Huo Jianqi. Music: Wu Xia. Sound: Zhang Baojian. Cast: Jiang Wenli as Bai Li, Jia Hongsheng as Liu Zhibing, Zhao Chengshun as Dan Liren, Wang Yanping as Yao Jing

Advertising executive Liu Zhibing marries a woman for her money. He arranges for another man to rape his wife while the couple is on their honeymoon, planning to use the incident as part of an elaborate scheme to divorce her and obtain a sizable settlement. By chance, policeman Dan Liren is staying at the same hotel as the couple. He conducts his own investigation and at last exposes the plot and brings the scheming husband to justice.

1385. *Mysterious Dancing Hall Queen (Shen Mi De Wu Ting Huang Hou)*

1991. Changchun Film Studio. Color. Letterboxed. 9 Reels. Direction: Yu Zhongxiao. Screenplay: Li Mengxue. Cinematography: Chen Chang'an and Wang Jian. Art Direction: Feng Shukui and Liu Wenjing. Music: Gao Feng. Sound: Yi Wenyu and Liu Qun. Cast: Han Yueqiao as Xu Yafang, Guo Bichuan as Gao Li, Zhang Duofu as Yi Liquan, Guan Xinwei as Meng Xianbing, Lu Xiaohe as Director Liu, Yan Xiang as Wang Bohai

Xu Yafang, once a professional dancer but now a dance hall girl, has a chance encounter with her ex-husband. They spend some time together, but after leaving her he is killed. Xu then finds herself being pursued by thugs. At last she finds that her ex-husband had planted a secret formula in her clothing when she was unaware. When she finds she has the formula, she helps the public security forces protect the formula and thwart those trying to obtain it.

1386. *Mysterious Tourist Party (Shen Mi De Lu You Tuan)*

1992. Shenzhen Film Company & China Film Release Import And Export Company Co-Production. Color. Letterboxed. 9 Reels. Direction: Yu Shibing. Screenplay: Zhou Shi, Zhang Ming. Cinematography: Yu Xiaoqun, He Yongjian. Art Direction: Huang Chaohui. Music: Cao Guangping. Sound: Lin Guang. Costume:

Cai Peiqiong, Xie Huizhen. Cast: Xu Yongge as Liu Changfeng, Xu Lili as Fu Xiao, Miao Wanxia as Yang Tingyu, Zhou Renjie as Little Fatty, Zhang Ling as Tang Lijuan, Wang Weibo as Wang Yusheng, Chen Jianjun as Cao Laoshan

Tour guide Yang Tingyu begins to notice strange things about some of the passengers on the tour she is leading. The only person she knows she can count on is her boyfriend, martial artist Liu Changfeng. It develops that most of the passengers are drug dealers from Hong Kong, using the tour as a cover. But another passenger is policewoman Fu Xiao, and with Liu's help she succeeds in foiling the plot and capturing the criminals.

1387. *Mysterious Traveling Companions (Shen Mi De Lu Ban)*

1955. Changchun Film Studio. B & W. 10 Reels. Direction: Lin Nong and Zhu Wenshun. Screenplay: Lin Nong, based on the novel, "The Bell-less Pack Train" by Bai Hua (1930–). Cinematography: Nie Ping. Set Design: Liu Xueyao. Music: Zhang Dichang. Sound: Chen Wenyuan. Cast: Yin Zhiming as Feng Tinggui, Liu Zengqing as Zhu Linsheng, Li Jie as Wei Fu, Tian Lie as Xiao Wu, Wang Xiaotang as Little Li Ying, Xu Liankai as the Captain

Wei Fu and Xiao Wu, two secret agents in the employ of the U.S. and the Nationalists, are under cover as operators of a pack train in a border area. Among the goods on one trip, they hide weapons and communications equipment for delivery to Catholic priest Fan Kaixiu, another secret agent whose religious activity is a cover for his espionage work. They successfully avoid a border inspection station, but their behavior attracts the notice of a Yao nationality woman, who immediately notifies the captain of the border patrol. The captain assigns Platoon Leader Feng Tinggui and Yi nationality civil guardsman Zhu Linsheng to join the pack train and observe its movements. As they follow along, and covertly observe, Feng Tinggui becomes suspicious about the goods being shipped, and Zhu Linsheng falls for Little Li Ying, an Yi nationality girl employed by the smugglers to tend their horses. The secret agents try to lose their unplanned traveling companions, but Little Li Ying thwarts the effort. When the secret agents find she has fooled them, they intend to kill her to cover up their crimes, but Feng and Zhu show up before they can do so. When Feng realizes the agents are starting to suspect him, he pre-

tends to be very stupid to divert their suspicions. Finally, when the agents deliver the weapons and equipment to their destination, the border patrol soldiers are waiting for them.

1388. *Mysterious Woman (Shen Mi De Nu Ren)*

1988. Xiaoxiang Film Studio. Color. Wide Screen. 12 Reels. Direction: Zhai Junjie. Screenplay: Tian Junli, Ju Junjie. Cinematography: Shen Jie, Lei Jiaming. Art Direction: Wu Zhaohua. Music: Ai Liqun. Sound: Han Weijun, Ma Ting. Cast: Tao Zeru as I, Ren Meng as woman, Zhao Xiaorui as man

Over thirty years ago, the narrator, "I," goes deep into the mountains on a geological exploration for the military, and requests overnight lodging with a local family. The woman of the house, carrying a small child, reluctantly agrees. At midnight, an old man enters, utters some strange words and leaves, after which the woman hangs herself. "I" cuts her down and saves her. At that time, her husband returns home. The next day, "I" leaves the household, but feels very suspicious, so stops on the road not far from the house. Shortly after, the man leaves the house carrying the baby. He stops the man and tells him of the previous night's happenings, but the man knows nothing about it. The two return to the house, where the woman despairingly relates her background. Of mixed parentage, half–Chinese, half–Japanese, she had been a Tokyo University student during the war. In 1944, she was told her father was killed by the Chinese. To avenge him, she joined the Japanese secret service and was sent to China. But when she arrived she learned the truth, that her father had been executed by the Japanese for opposing germ warfare experiments on humans. She refused to serve as a spy any more, ran away and hid in the mountains, later marrying and having a child. Her enraged husband almost wants to kill her when he learns she had been a Japanese spy, but she bids him and their child goodbye and leaves to confess to the authorities. Thirty years later, "I" visits the place again and learns the woman has passed away, her husband living as if the dead woman's spirit is always with him.

1389. *Mystery at Lake Center Island (Hu Xin Dao Zhi Mi)*

1987. Changchun Film Studio. Color. 3-D.

Direction: Wu Guojiang. Screenplay: Tang Huanxin. Cinematography: Xu Shouzen, Dong Zhensheng. Art Direction: Wang Jiru, Ji Jingchun. Music: Chen Shouqian. Sound: Yu Kaizhang. Cast: Ji Chengmu as Wan Ke, Zhang Yinxin as Little Fatty, Shi Lei as Chen Xiaomin

Lin Si, key figure in a bank robbery, is poisoned by Lu Xiang, a woman gangster. Before dying, Lin telephones his partner to tell him where he hid the money and where Lu Xiang is hiding. However, the dying man misdials and calls the home of Wan Ke, a 14-year-old boy. Wan Ke doesn't understand the message, so he records it and then has his friend Little Fatty over to listen to the tape. The boys decide to call in two more friends to investigate with them, based on the information supplied on the phone. They first go to Lu Xiang's home, where she curses them and drives them away. Eventually, Wan Ke and Little Fatty track down the hidden suitcase full of money. Their lives are endangered, but PSB officers arrive to save them in the nick of time.

1390. *Mystery of Goddess Peak (Sheng Nu Feng De Mi Wu)*

1980. Guangxi Film Studio. Color. 10 Reels. Direction: Guo Baocang. Screenplay: Hu Bing. Cinematography: Yang Yuming. Art Direction: Lao Guanneng. Music: Li Yanlin. Sound: Li Zhuwen. Cast: Zhang Guomin as Jiang Jian, Zhao Shoukai as Tan Nan, He Ling as Zhao Xin, Hou Kemin as Wu Xinzhu, Yuan Wan as Tao Rongrong, Geng Ying as Bald Eagle

As a young woman named Zhao Xin is painting a landscape at Goddess Peak near Lijiang, she sees two men fighting near a cliff, and one goes over it. She immediately reports the incident to the police, but when she returns to the site with an officer nothing is found so no one believes her. But that night, a male corpse is found in the river at Lijiang. It is believed to be the body of the missing Tao Rongrong, son of Pan Fei, Deputy Director of the city's Bureau of Light Industry, but Pan refuses to identify the body as that of her son. It develops that Tao Rongrong was murdered by members of a gang of robbers he belonged to, and the mother refused to identify him for fear disclosure of the son's criminal activities would hurt her and her husband's careers. To find the killer, investigators Jiang Jian and Tan Na repeatedly question the witness Zhao Xin, and after going over the story many times she finally gives them some vital clues. They find

out that the fight involved some valuable ancient books hidden in a cave at Goddess Peak, books stumbled upon by young teacher Wu Xinzhu and his fiancee. They had brought the books back to read, but Tao had stolen them. Tracing the set of books leads the investigators to a museum receipt and then to Tu Ying, head of the gang and the actual murderer. Tu Ying attempts to escape, but the officers overpower and arrest him. The antique books are returned to the museum. Meanwhile, Jiang Jian and Zhao Xin have fallen in love.

1391. *Mystery of the Double Eagle (Shuang Tou Ying Zhi Mi)*

1987. Emei Film Studio. Color. 8 Reels. Direction: Zhang Xihe. Screenplay: Xiao Jian, Ni Feng, Xiao Yan. Cinematography: Wang Xiaolie. Art Direction: Cheng Jinyong. Music: Yang Fei, Tang Qinshi. Sound: Lin Bingcheng. Cast: Xu Xing as the drunk, Zhang Xiling as A Da, Mei Xiaozheng as Qing Gang, Yu Rongkang as the old man, He Jun as A Song, Cui Xiaoping as the fat man

Police track a smuggler code-named "Double Eagle" to the vicinity of a large burial ground in southwest China, and shortly after this the local chief of police is murdered. The police believe the murder is not the act of the smuggler, but rather has something to do with "Black Butterfly," a bandit operating in the area.

1392. *The Mystery of the Heavenly Kingdom's Treasure (Tian Chao Guo Ku Zhi Mi)*

1990. Shanghai Film Studio. Color. Wide Screen. 9 Reels. Direction: Xu Jihong. Screenplay; Zhao Ruiyong. Cinematography: Sun Guoliang. Art Direction: Ju Ransheng, Sun Weide. Music: Lu Qimin. Sound: Ge Weijia. Cast: Lu Liang as Ma Liang, Gai Lili as Yang Ling

In the 1920s, archaeologist Ma Liang stumbles onto clues which point to the location of the secret treasure warehouse of the Taiping rebels, the "Heavenly Kingdom" of the mid-19th Century. This attracts the attention of the Chinese government, the Japanese and triads. To protect this national treasure, Ma determines to find it first. Accompanied by girl student Yang Ling, he sets out for where he believes the treasure is hidden. On the way, they find themselves targets for the others. They finally arrive at the site, but so do the others, and a gunfight ensues. The man guarding the treasure is shot by Yang Ling, but when he cries out the building collapses, killing Yang Ling as well.

1393. *Naked Lives (Chi Luo Ren Xing)*

1993. Shanghai Film Studio. Color. Letterboxed. Direction: Xu Weijie. Cinematography: Ju Jiazhen. Art Direction: Yao Wei. Music: Liu Yanxi. Cast: Tang Zhenzong as Mu Yan, Xia Jing as Li Lin, Zhen Shuang as Du Wen, Qi Mengshi as Cai Yuanji

Although company president Cai Yuanji is seriously ill, he lets his son Cai Yiliang take his bride Du Wen to Suzhou on their honeymoon anyway. He also tells his son that while he is there he should look up a man named Mu Yan, as he should find it interesting. They find and contact Mu Yan, but before they meet Cai Yiliang is killed in an accident. When Mu Yan shows up for the meeting, Du Wen finds he is her husband's exact double. She hires Mu to substitute for her husband, so she can fulfill her dream of inheriting the family fortune. Mu consents, and replaces the dead man quite well, particularly in the business. However, he and his secretary Li Lin fall in love. But a blackmailer named Jiang discerns Mu is an impostor and threatens him with exposure. Further complications arise when Cai Yuanji suddenly discloses that Li Lin is his daughter, which infuriates Du Wen, for now she has a rival for the inheritance. In an argument with the persistent Jiang, Mu Yan kills the blackmailer, setting off a further round of intrigue and murder.

1394. *Nameless Heroes (Wu Ming Ying Xiong)*

1958. Jiangnan Film Studio. B & W. 11 Reels. Direction: Gao Heng, Screenplay: Du Xuan, based on his stage play of the same title. Cinematography: Ma Linfa. Art Direction: Shen Weishan, Fu Shuzhen. Music: Ji Ming. Sound: Ding Bohe. Cast: Mu Hong as Lin Weishi, Ji Ming as Liu Chuming, Li Wei as Chen Zhihang, Feng Qi as Li Buping, Qiao Zhi as Xu Hua, Feng Huang as Xiao Feng, Fu Huizhen as Li Buping's wife, Li Baoluo as Wang Huaizhong

Late in the Chinese Civil War, undercover Communist agents are assigned to incite rebellion among Nationalist naval forces, to make it easier for the PLA to cross the Yellow River and occupy Shanghai. Two CPC agents, Lin Weishi and Chen Zhihang, are under cover as enemy sailors. With the help of naval commander Wang's servant Xiao Feng they obtain the Nationalists' plans for defense of the Yellow River, and based on this they decide that the ship "Changhong" is the most likely enemy ship to rebel and defect to the Communist side. Lin and Chen join undercover CPC agent Fu Liang, already on board the "Changhong," to incite the rest of the men on the ship. But their actions arouse suspicion, and while Lin is able to escape in disguise, Chen and Fu are arrested and confined to the brig. But their plans succeed, for just when the "Changhong" is ordered to attack the PLA troops crossing the river, the "Changhong" crew rebels and brings the ship over to the Communists.

1395. *Nameless Island (Wu Ming Dao)*

1959. Beijing Film Studio. Color. 9 Reels. Direction: Xie Tieli. Screenplay: Zhao Zhong, Du Bingru, Guan Shinan, Wang Kai. Cinematography: Zhang Qinghua. Art Direction: Zhang Xiande. Music: Li Ning. Sound: Chen Xiyan, Liu Shida, Li Zhenduo. Cast: Li Baiwan as Wang Yongzhi, Zhao Wande as Lin Maocai, Li Lin as Wu Yehan, Fang Hui as Feng Zhankui, Li Mengrao as Sun Gui, Yan Zenhe as Jiao Liansheng

In the fall of 1958, a Nationalist landing ship is torpedoed and sunk by a Communist torpedo boat. Nationalist Captain Wu Yehan and four of his men swim to the north side of an unnamed island to await rescue. Communist naval political instructor Wang Yongzhi and torpedoman Lin Maocai land on the south side of the island, still very close to their enemy. In a situation where they are outnumbered, Wang Yongzhi plays a cat-and-mouse game with their enemy, finally killing them. Then, when the Nationalist rescue force arrives, he lures them into a trap which wipes them out.

1396. *The Nanchang Uprising (Nan Chang Qi Yi)*

1981. Shanghai Film Studio. Wide. Color. 11 Reels. Direction: Tang Xiaodan. Screenplay: Li Hongxin, Wu Anping, Xu Haiqiu, Zhou Dagong. Cinematography: Shen Xilin. Art

Direction: Han Shangyi, Yan Cangming, Ning Futing. Music: Lu Qimin. Sound: Zhou Hengliang. Costume: Cao Yingping. Cast: Kong Xiangyu as Zhou Enlai, Gao Changli as He Long, Liu Huaizheng as Zhu De, Li Xiangang as Shuangxi, Zhang Xiaolei as Heigu

In 1927, Wang Jingwei, head of the Chinese government, accelerates the movement to stamp out the Communist Party. The Communists' first try at rebellion fails, putting the future of their movement in serious doubt. At this critical juncture, some of their leaders such as Zhou Enlai, Yun Daiying and Li Lisan propose a "Nanchang Rebellion" to Party Central, which is approved. Zhou Enlai is named the rebellion committee secretary, and travels to Nanchang where he meets Zhu De to draw up the rebellion plans. When the Party central representative Zhang Guotao arrives in Nanchang from the city of Jiujiang, he tries to stop the plans from going forward. After a fierce debate, Zhang Guotao has to obey the majority decision. When everything is in place, Zhou Enlai learns that some traitors have leaked information concerning the rebellion, so he orders the rebellion to start ahead of schedule. The rebellion starts on August 1st, 1927. With Ye Ting in command, and Zhu De and He Long participating, the "Nanchang Rebellion" ends in victory, the first Communist military victory in the revolution that puts them in power over 20 years later.

Best Costume Cao Yingping, 1982 Golden Rooster Awards.

1397. *Nanjing in Political Storm (Parts 1 & 2) (Feng Yu Xia Zhong Shan)*

1982. August First Film Studio. Color. 16 Reels. Direction: Yuan Xian, Wei Linyu, Li Po. Screenplay: Ai Xuan, Liang Xing. Cinematography: Wei Linyu. Art Direction: Liu Jingsheng. Music: Fu Gengcheng. Sound: Li Lin. Makeup: Yan Bijun, Xu Jianxin, Li Zunxun and Zhang Jiafan. Cast: Zhang Keyao as Mao Zedong, Wang Tiecheng as Zhou Enlai, Sun Feihu as Chiang Kaishek, Yang Chiyu as Li Zongren, Zhi Yitong as Zhang Zhizhong

By 1948, the tide of civil war has swung to the side of the Communists after their three key victories in the battles of Liaoshen, Pingjing and Huaihai. Chiang Kaishek is forced to resign in an attempt to salvage the Nationalist cause, on the brink of collapse. The U.S. is able to get both sides to agree to

negotiate. The U.S. envoy suggests creating a North and a South China by dividing the country at the Changjiang (Yangtse) River. Li Zongren, succeeding to the presidency of the Nationalist government after Chiang's resignation, uses this idea of "division" as his side's negotiating position. Conversely, the Communist leader, Party Chairman Mao Zedong, takes the concept of "unification" as his side's basic position. On April 1, 1949, Communist Vice-President Zhou Enlai leads his delegation to the negotiations with the Nationalist delegation led by Zhang Zhizhong. The talks break down on April 20th, and fighting resumes. The PLA crosses the Changjiang, and quickly overruns the Nationalist Army, taking the capital city of Nanjing on the 23rd. By fall, all of China will be under Communist control.

Best Makeup Yan Bijun, Xu Jianxin, Li Zunxun and Zhang Jiafan, 1983 Golden Rooster Awards.

1398. *Nanjing Massacre (Nan Jing Da Tu Sha)*

1995. China Co-Production Corp., Taiwan Longxiang Company Co-Production. Color. Direction: Wu Ziniu. Screenplay: Xu Tiansheng, Zhang Jiping, Liang Xiaosheng, Hong Weijian. Cinematography: Hou Yong. Art Direction: Zhang Xiaobin, Lu Qi, Zhu Gang. Music: Tan Dun. Cast: Qin Han as Cheng Xian, Qiujijiu Meizi as Lihuizi, Ye Quanzhen as Liu Shuqin, Chen Yuda as Deng Tianyuan, Tao Zeru as Li Gengfa

In 1937, the Japanese encroachments into China become an all-out attack. The city of Nanjing, then the capital of the Republic of China, is surrounded by Japanese troops. The Chinese troops defending the city have pulled out, leaving behind only civilians, wounded soldiers too ill to travel and civil guards. Just before this, Chinese doctor Cheng Xian moves his pregnant Japanese wife, her daughter and his son Xiao Ling back to his home town of Nanjing from Shanghai. They arrive to find his family's home destroyed by bombs. When the Japanese troops enter Nanjing, the doctor and his wife become separated, and she takes the children to a shelter maintained by international relief agencies. They are still bullied and harassed by Japanese soldiers, however. Meanwhile, the Japanese troops launch an orgy of rape and murder in the city, sparing no one, regardless of status, gender or age. The slaughter is horrific. His clinic invaded and destroyed, Cheng Xian joins his family in the shelter just as the Japanese start to invade it. Most of the women are raped, including Xiao Ling's teacher, who had courageously protected all her students. The doctor's wife goes into early labor while trying to protect her daughter. In all, 300,000 Chinese were slaughtered in Nanjing, yet even today the official Japanese government position is one of denial.

1399. *The Nanjing Massacre Evidence (Tu Cheng Xue Zheng)*

1987. Fujian Film Studio. Color. 10 Reels. Direction: Luo Guanqun. Screenplay: Xie Guangning. Cinematography: Chen Minwei, Qiao Qicang. Art Direction: Liu Jiajing, Han Qinguo. Music: Liu Yanxi. Sound: Liu Tonghe, Xu Gang. Cast: Ju Naishe as Zhan Tao, Chen Daomin as Li Yuan, Wu Lijie as Liu Jingjing, Lei Luosheng as Fan Changle, Shen Danping as Bai Yan, Liu Jiang as Qiao Beng

On December 13, 1937, the Japanese Army enters the city of Nanjing and begins an orgy of rape and slaughter that lasts for six hellish weeks. Zhan Tao is the student of a foreign professor at Jinling University. Katie, the professor's daughter, loves the young man deeply and persuades him to go abroad with her family when they leave China. But as the casualties mount, Zhan Tao decides to stay on and use his medical skill to help Nanjing's people. A roll of pictures of Japanese soldiers systematically killing civilians falls into the hands of photo shop proprietor Fan Changle. Fan flees to the professor's home, and explains how this is evidence of the Japanese Army's war crimes. Various people sacrifice their lives to protect the photos, and at last Zhan Tao gives his life to get the precious roll of film to Katie. She leaves for abroad to tell the world what has gone on in Nanjing.

1400. *Nanjing Nights (Jin Ling Zhi Ye)*

1985. Beijing Film Studio. Color. 10 Reels. Direction: Qian Jiang. Screenplay: Cao Shuolong, Qian Jiang. Cinematography: Fu Ruisheng. Art Direction: Chen Xiaoxia, Guo Juhai. Music: Jin Xiang. Sound: Dong Qiuxin. Cast: Kong Xiangyu as Qian Zhuangfei, Zhu Decheng as Gu Shunzhang, Ai Junmai as Xu Enzeng, Liu Jian as Chen Lifu, Sun Feihu as Chiang Kaishek, Hu Ao as He Chengjun, Wang Tiecheng as Zhou Enlai

In 1927, Chiang Kaishek turns on the Communist left wing of the Nationalist Party and begins a series of executions of Party members. Covert CPC member Qiao Zhuangfei assumes the identify of a Doctor Zhang, and travels to Shanghai from his home in Beijing. Upon his arrival, he loses contact with his Party organizational contact for a time. After it is restored, the central Party organization grants his request to infiltrate Nationalist headquarters through a man named Xu Enzeng, brother-in-law of the Nationalist Party Chief Secretary Chen Lifu. The movie tells how Qiao is able to exploit Xu to gain information for the Communists, eventually helping the Shanghai Communist Party organization transfer to a place of safety before Chiang is able to put into effect his plan to arrest the entire CPC organization in Shanghai.

1401. *Nanpu Bridge (Qing Sha Pu Jiang)*

1991. Shanghai Film Studio. Color. 10 Reels. Letterboxed. Direction: Shi Xiaohua. Screenplay: He Guopu, Yang Shiwen. Cinematography: Ying Fukang. Art Direction: Huang Qiagui, Zhu Jianchang. Music: Yang Mao. Sound: Ni Zheng. Cast: Zhu Yanping as Luo Dawei, Zhang Xiaolin as Chen Hui, Zhao Erkang as Master Zhongfa, Zhang Mingyi as Chief Engineer Cheng, Yu Hui as Song Li

The story of the men who built the Nanpu Bridge and of their families. Luo Dawei, leader of the construction brigade, is so busy working on the construction site that his wife starts feeling neglected. Young worker Chen Hui is in love with Song Li, but doesn't know she has a terminal illness. But their family problems and their work difficulties do not discourage them. They work hard and complete the bridge on time.

1402. *Narrow Lane Celebrity (Xiao Xiang Ming Liu)*

1985. Emei Film Studio. Color. 9 Reels. Direction: Chong Lianwen. Screenplay: Liang Husheng, Luo Huajun. Cinematography: Li Erkang. Art Direction: Chen Desheng. Music: Tao Jiazhou. Sound: Shen Guli. Cast: Zhu Xu as Ma Shouxian, Ge Jianjun as Han Niushan, Sun Caihua as the Widow Zuo, Ren Weimin as He Laizhi, Liu Hai as Gao Feng, Zhang Xuemei as Dingxiang

In an old alley in a western Sichuan township live three families: that of Sima Shouxian, who sells funeral supplies; the widow Zuo who lives by selling used clothes; and Han Niushan, who earns his living killing dogs. All suffer during the Cultural Revolution. Zuo and her daughter are frequently bullied by Red Guards, but Niushan stands up in the women's defense. Widow Zuo is very sympathetic to Niu's having been orphaned at an early age, and this and gratitude lead her to decide that her daughter Dingxiang will someday marry Niushan, an idea supported by Sima Shouxian. Dingxiang's beauty and talent get her accepted into an opera company, but on her first day on the job she is raped by the Revolutionary Committee director and his son. Widow Zuo loses her mind over this, and is sent to an asylum. Ten years pass, and the small town has a brand new look, masking the pain its inhabitants still feel.

1403. *A Necklace (Yi Chuan Xiang Lian)*

1966. Xi'an Film Studio. B & W. 4 Reels. Direction: Wu Chun. Screenplay: Gansu Province Gannan Tibetan Nationality Autonomous Prefecture Dance and Singing Troupe. Cinematography: Yu Shuzhao. Art Direction: Zhang Xiaohui. Sound: Dang Chunzhu. Casting: Ji Jian as Sangba, Wen Maoji as Zhaxiji, Zhu Dongyan as Danmuduo

For Danmuduo's upcoming marriage, her mother Zhaxiji wants to buy her daughter a necklace by selling ox hair she has saved. However, Zhaxiji's husband Sangba wanted to take the hair to the village before the cold weather arrives, to keep the livestock warm. But Zhaxiji refused to give it to him. While the couple argues over this, their daughter quietly takes the hair to the village. When she returns, Danmuduo patiently explains the situation and helps her mother recall the bitter past life and compare it with the happiness of their present life. This awakens Zhaxiji, and she happily agrees to use ox hairs to make rope.

1404. *Neighbors (Lin Ju)*

1981. Youth Film Studio. Color. 11 Reels. Direction: Zhen Dongtian, Xu Gumin. Screenplay: Ma Lin, Zhu Mei, Da Jiangfu. Cinematography: Zhou Kun, Gu Wenkai. Art Direction: Yi Li, Wang Honghai, Liu Guangen. Sound: Zhang Ruikun. Cast: Feng Hanyuan as Liu Lixing, Zhen Zhenyao as Doctor Min, Wang Pei as Yuan Yifang, Wang Chong as Zhang Binghua, Xu Zhongquan as Xi Fengnian, Li Zhanwen as Feng Weidong

Living in an apartment building for engineering college employees are the school's head Yuan Yifang, school consultant Liu Lixing, plumber Xi Fengnian, Doctor Min from the school's infirmary, Assistant Professor Feng Weidong and Instructor Zhang Binghua. Their housing is substandard, but the families share life's joys and get along well. However, when an extra new apartment becomes available for one of these families, some unpleasant things happen. When an old friend of Liu Lixing, an American journalist named Agnes comes to visit him, Yuan Yifang's arranges for them to meet in a home all pretend is Liu Lixing's. These ordinary neighbors still have hope and a sense of justice. Another spring arrives, and the neighbors hold a party to celebrate their upcoming move into new housing. The one exception is Liu Lixing who has been hospitalized with cancer. But he has Yuan Yifang bring two roast ducks for the others, along with a letter in which he mentions every family but not himself. However, everybody feels he is right among them.

Best Picture, 1982 Golden Rooster Awards.

1405. *Neither Laughter Nor Tears (Ku Xiao Bu De)*

1987. Fujian Film Studio. Color. 10 Reels. Direction: Zhang Gang. Screenplay: Zhang Gang. Cinematography: Zhen Wangong. Art Direction: Liu Nanyang. Music: Chen Yongtie. Sound: Liu Weijie. Cast: Dao Zhaoan as Fang Aman, Shen Fa as Zhong Yijian, Tu Ruyin as A Ju, Kang Baomin as Song Wen, Li Aijie as Chen Lifang

On a trip to Guzhou City on the coast of southern Fujian Province, freelance writer Fang Aman stops at a hotel, but accidentally enters the wrong room and walks in on a couple making love. He is particularly embarrassed, for although the man is a stranger, he recognizes the woman as Chen Lifang, wife of famous writer Zhong Yijian. Zhong Yijian's success has largely been gained by hiring Fang Aman as a ghostwriter, and in fact Fang's business to Guzhou is in answer to a summons from Zhong, to write a screenplay for him. The two men go to a beach resort to get away and discuss the project, and there Fang finds romance with A Ju, a woman abandoned by her husband. He also meets Chen Lifang again, and learns that her husband Zhong Yijian's bad character is the reason she has sought out another man. At last, A Ju and Fang Aman decide to go away together, and Zhong Yijian is forced to at last reveal publicly that Fang has really written all the works attributed to Zhong.

1406. *The Net of Justice (aka The Law) (Tian Wang)*

1994. Beijing Film Studio, Nanjing Film Studio Co-Production. Color. Letterboxed. 9 Reels. Direction: Xie Tieli, Qiu Zhongyi. Screenplay: Xie Tieli, Gao Zhenhe, based on Zhang Ping's original novel. Cinematography: Zhen Yuyuan. Art Direction: Yang Zhanji, Liu Mingtai. Music: Wang Ming. Sound: Wang Dawen. Costume: Dong Xiuqin, Tang Li. Makeup; Sun Hong. Cast: Sun Feipeng as Qin Yumin, Dong Ji as Li Rongcai, Yong Heping as Jia Rengui, Wang Futang as Gu Jiacheng, Shi Xian as Shi Wude, Sun Qipeng as Xu Kejian, Xing Jigui as Zhang Guanghai, Li Zongquan as Yi Yuan, He Jiancai as Zhao Liang, Yang Jun as Wei Xiaoming, Chen Weifeng as Guo Mei, Song Ruijun as Wang Qing, Han Fuli as Han Fu

In a remote mountainous area in the early 1980s, newly arrived county director Qin Yumin finds an old man, Li Rongcai, sitting in front of the county administrative building. Li explains he was once the county's accountant, but when he found discrepancies in the accounts, a network of political cronies, relatives, etc., pulled together to frame Li for embezzlement. Jailed for a time and ousted from his position, the falsely accused accountant begins the long, perhaps hopeless, process of trying to clear his name. More than 20 years have gone by this way, during which Li's wife has lost her mind, his son left home, and the family lost everything they had. Qin Yumin starts to investigate the case, and layer by layer strips away the network that protected the guilty and framed Li Rongcai. At last, the old man receives the justice he sought for so long.

1407. *Never Forget (Qian Wan Buy Yao Wang Ji)*

1964. Beijing Film Studio. Color. 10 Reels. Direction: Xie Tieli. Screenplay: Xie Tieli and Cong Shen, based on the latter's stage play of the same title. Cinematography: Li Wenhua. Art Direction: Xiao Bing. Music: Li Ning. Sound: Liu Shida. Cast: Luo Yupu as Ding Shaochun, Peng Yu as Yao's mother, Qin Wen as Yao Yujuan, Zhang Ping as Ding Haikuan, Zhang Lun as Grandpa Ding, Bi Jiancang as Ji Youliang

Young worker Ding Shaochun, from a working class background, is at first enthusiastic about his job in an electrical machinery plant. But after he marries Yao Yujuan, from a bourgeois background, he falls increasingly under the influence of his mother-in-law, and becomes less serious about his work. Repeated warnings by his father Ding Haikuan and good friend Ji Youliang are of no effect. Encouraged by his mother-in-law, he even absents himself from work to go hunting, nearly causing a worksite disaster. This experience and the help and education of his father and co-workers wake Shaochun up. Yao Yujuan also learns from this, and makes an ideological break with her mother.

1408. *New and Old Hatreds (Xin Chou Jiu Hen)*

1992. Youth Film Studio. Color. Letterboxed. 10 Reels. Direction: Guo Lin. Screenplay: Ge Ritai. Cinematography: Dansheng Nima, Shu Shu. Art Direction: Zhang Yan. Music: Fan Weiqiang. Sound: Cao Feng, Zhang Xiaonan. Costume: Li Shuyan, Jiang Fenger. Makeup: Yan Zhenrong. Cast: Chen Xiaoyi as Wang Hong, Chen Xiaoyi as Zhao Meiyu, Xu Xiaojian as Li Ming, Shu Yaoxuan as Guan Huitang

Li Ming finds out his sister has been assaulted by her employer Guan Huitang, a powerful executive. He confronts Guan about this, they struggle, and the executive is injured. Li Ming is sent to prison. After his release, he chances upon information that Guan is involved in illegal business dealings, and determines to get to the bottom of it. Li Ming enlists the aid of a childhood friend, policewoman Wang Hong. Together they investigate Guan's dealings, and at last bring him to justice.

1409. *New Dragon Gate Inn (Xin Long Men Ke Jin)*

1992. Xiaoxiang Film Studio and Hong Kong Siyuan Film Corporation Co-Production. Color. Letterboxed. 11 Reels. Direction: Xu Ke (Tsui Hark) and Li Huimin (Raymond Lee). Screenplay: Su Shuyang and Zhang Tan. Cinematography: Liu Mantang, Huang Yuetai and Liu Weiwei. Art Direction: Liang Zhixing and Guo Dexiang. Music: Chen Feilei. Cast: Zhang Manyu (Maggie Cheung) as Jin Xiangyu, Lin Qingxia (Brigitte Lin) as Qiu Moyan, Liang Jiahui (Tony Leung) as Zhou Huaian, Zhen Zhidan (Donny Yen) as Cao Shuqin. Also: Liu Xun (Lau Shun), Wu Qihua (Lawrence Ng)

During the reign of the Ming emperor Jingtai (1450–1458), evil eunuch Cao Shuqin gains control of the emperor and ruthlessly kills everyone who gets in his way, including a patriotic court official. To protect the official's two children, woman warrior Qiu Moyan and her warrior lover Zhou Huaian attempt to smuggle them out of the country. They get as far as the New Dragon Inn near the border, where they are overtaken by Cao's men. The inn is a stopover point for the scum of the earth, every sort of rogue and cutthroat imaginable. Its sexy proprietress Jin Xiangyu keeps things under control, while supplementing her income by killing and robbing some of the inn's more deserving guests. A war of wits between the two sides erupts into a life and death battle when the eunuch arrives to take personal charge of his forces. Jin Xiangyu falls for Zhou Huaian, although she realizes he only loves Qiu Moyan. Someone must get the children to safety, and Qiu sacrifices herself so that Zhou can get them away. Jin Xiangyu and the hotel cook fight a delaying action against the eunuch, and at last kill him. She burns down her hotel, and leaves to follow Zhou Huaian.

1410. *New Fang Shi Yu (Xin Fang Shi Yu)*

1984. Hong Kong Liancheng Film Corporation & Guangzhou Culture Service Corporation Co-Production, assisted by China Film Producing Corporation. Color. Wide Screen. 9 Reels. Direction: Yang Fan, Wei Haifeng. Screenplay: Associated Writing Team. Cinematography: You Qi. Art Direction: Wu Zhendong. Music: Liu Changan. Costume: Shen Aojian, Yang Juanjuan. Makeup: He Xiaoying, Zhang Jiangjiang. Cast: Shi Baohua as Fang Shiyu, Guo Liang as Lei Hong, Chen Yongxia as Miao Cuihua, Du Xiongwen as Fang's father, Wu Meiling as Li Xiaohuan, Song Baosheng as Juehui

Fang Shiyu (Fang Sai-yuk in Cantonese dialect) was a legendary Chinese martial artist. When Fang was a year old, his martial artist mother Miao Cuihua fought and defeated a villain named Lei Hong and an evil Taoist priest. When the two return 10 years later to resume their feud with Fang Shiyu's family, Miao Cuihua convinces her husband they should send the boy to the Shaolin Temple to study martial arts. There, Fang Shiyu hones his talents, becomes China's top martial arts fighter, and at last kills Lei Hong and his cronies.

1411. *New Fang Shiyu (Part 2) (Xin Fang Shi Yu)*

1986. Hong Kong Lianxing Film Company, China Film Co-Production Corp. and Guangzhou Culture Service Company Co-Production. Color. Wide Screen. 9 Reels. Direction: Wei Haifeng. Screenplay: Collective. Cinematography: He Kewei. Art Direction: Ruo Zhi. Music: Liu Chao. Cast: Shi Baohua as Fan Shiyu, Li Zhizhou as Hu Huiqian, Zhou Gongjing as Zhi Shan, Xiao Qin as Da Hong, He Weiming as Niu Hualong, Cai Mingyuan as Da Fu, Lu Shuren as Uncle Hu, Zhang Hongmei as Hu Qiaozhen, Lin Quan as Niu Huajiao

Sequel to the 1984 film from the same studio, chronicling the further exploits of the 19th Century South China hero.

1412. *New Heroes and Heroines (Xin Er Nu Ying Xiong Zhuan)*

1951. Beijing Film Studio. B & W. 14 Reels. Directors: Shi Dongshan and Lu Ban. Screenplay: Shi Dongshan, based on the novel by Yuan Jing (1914–) and Kong Jue. Cinematography: Gao Hongtao. Set Design: Yu Yiru. Music: Huang Zhun. Sound: Cai Jun. Art Direction: Li Zhongyun. Costume: Wei Bangjun. Makeup: Wang Xizhong. Cast: Jin Xin as Niu Dashui, Yao Xiangli as Yang Xiaomei, Yan Zhenhe as Grandpa Niu, Xu Lan as Sister Biao, Zhao Yin as Mother Yang, Guo Yuntai as Gao Tu'ner, Xie Tian as Zhang Jinlong, Shi Kuan as He Shixiong

After the July 7th Incident of 1937, the first armed confrontation between Chinese and Japanese troops, farmers in Hebei province were constantly harassed by defeated soldiers and bandits. After the Eighth Route Army arrives in the area, many farmers join up to fight back. Farmer Niu Dashui is an enthusiastic volunteer, and fights bravely. He is soon joined by another volunteer, a distant relative named Yang Xiaomei, who has left her abusive husband, Zhang Jinlong. She later agrees to take her husband back, and helps him enlist in the anti–Japanese cause. Later, however, Zhang surrenders to He Shixiong, a Chinese collaborator, leading Yang Xiaomei to terminate their relationship once and for all. Yang Xiaomei is wounded in an enemy attack, and Niu Dashui is captured by Zhang Jinlong, now fighting for the Japanese. Niu is returned to the Chinese side in a prisoner exchange. Niu Dashui and Yang Xiaomei are sent to the same place to recuperate, and soon fall in love. After their recovery, they return to the war, and in a

New Heroes and Heroines. **Peasant militia set an ambush for the Japanese. 1951. Beijing Film Studio.**

subsequent engagement with the enemy, Niu Dashui leads the militia in capturing both He Shixiong and Zhang Jinlong.

1413. *The New Legend of Shaolin (Xin Shao Lin Wu Zu)*

1994. Beijing Film Studio, Taiwan Xinfeng Film Corp. Ltd. Color. Letterboxed. 9 Reels. Direction: Wang Jing. Screenplay: Wang Jing. Cinematography: Liu Mantang. Art Direction: Fu Delin, Li Jingwen. Costume: Chen Gufang. Makeup: Liu Dan, Liu Jianping. Cast: Li Lianjie (Jet Li), Qiu Shuzhen (Chingmy Yao), Ji Chunhua, Sun Jiankui, Ye Dexian, Chen Songyong, Xie Miao, Yang Wei, Sun Guannan, Fu Yu, Guan Peng, Wang Zifei

In the late 17th century, the Shaolin Temple allies with the Heaven and Earth Society to oppose the Qing government. The film tells how Shaolin hero Hong Xiguan, his son Ma Ninger and five temple masters combat the forces of evil.

1414. *A New Lesson (Xin De Yi Ke)*

1958. Changchun Film Studio. B & W. 7 Reels. Direction: Wang Yi. Screenplay: Changchun Film Studio No. Six Writing collective, recorded by a guest. Cinematography: Zhang Yi. Art Direction: Li Junjie. Music: Lin Xuesong. Sound: Zhang Fenglu. Cast: Wun Lingwei as Xiao Liu, Xu Yan as Chen Xiang, Bao Xueguang as Mr. Gao, Sun Ao as Wang Liang, Wang Dali as Xiao Dong, Jiang Changhua as Secretary Cao, Ma Loufu as Master Worker Zhang

In the 1957 campaign to adjust work methods, Ji Guifang, a female third-year student in a college chemistry program, suggests a new process for carbon black which would be more in line with the Party's principle that education should serve politics. She has the support of the department's Party branch, but is opposed by department conservatives like Zhou Shoufang and Professor Sun. However, the students dare to go forward with her plan, and with the help of old master worker Zhang, they are successful.

1415. *The New Member (Xin Dui Yuan)*

1960. Pearl River Film Studio. B & W. 8 Reels. Direction: Zhou Wei. Screenplay: the Guangdong Dongshan District Collective Writing team, recorded by Wang Rongyan. Cinematography: Long Qingyun. Art Direction: Lu

Shengfan. Music: Liang Lizhu. Sound: Lin Guang. Cast: Wang Gang as Huang Youdong, Liu Chunzhen as Zhang Yaoxing, Tan Jianzhang as Yang Ming, Jia Jianhe as Huang Youjun, Wang Zhijun as Hu Xiaoniu, Wang Li as Zhao Lingling, Huo Yinzhen as Teacher Feng

Elementary school student Huang Youdong is a new member of the Young Pioneers. A willful, undisciplined student at first, he begins to overcome his shortcomings with the help of Teacher Feng and his classmates. Once, on his way back to school after the Young Pioneers had made a field trip to a commune, he finds a package of seeds which had to be mailed to Beijing immediately; he makes every effort to get the package to the railway station, then arrives at school on time despite being very tired.

1416. *New Soldier Ma Qiang (Xin Bing Ma Qiang)*

1981. Beijing Film Studio. Color. 9 Reels. Direction: Yu Qin. Screenplay: Xu Guangyao. Cinematography: Wun Zhixian, Yang Haigeng. Art Direction: Yang Zhanjia, Luo Yurong. Music: Zhang Naicheng, Li Xian. Sound: Dong Qiuxin. Cast: Liu Yanli as Ma Qiang, Shen Guanchu as Gong Dafang, Xu Yuanqi as Jin Sihu, Li Lan as Xiao Luo, Dong Wenwu as the company commander

Ma Qiang is a new PLA recruit from the countryside. Although totally inexperienced at first, he becomes a sharp, battle-hardened veteran during the Sino-Vietnamese border war. He is wounded rescuing a Vietnamese child, and is hospitalized. Recovered, he returns to the frontlines and continues to serve valiantly, although he sees the deaths of two close friends, Gong Dafang and squad leader Jin Sihu.

1417. *New Song for the Great Wall (Chang Cheng Xin Qu)*

1975. Changchun Film Studio. Color. 9 Reels. Direction: Zhao Xinshui. Cinematography: Chang Yan. Art Direction: Shi Weijun. Music: Li Yuqiu. Cast: Lu Wulin as Bai Yufeng, Jiang Ruilin as Zhang Tiedun, Lu Junhai as the company commander, Yan Wenpan as the political supervisor, Liu Yanli as Cheng Siping, Zhang Kezhong as the regimental commander

PLA swineherd Bai Yufeng is implementing revolutionary feeding methods both inside and outside of the army. When he introduces his new methods to the peasants of Ying Village,

the landlord there poisons two pigs and plants evidence which makes it appear that Bai is trying to destroy the local pig business. To protect the PLA's relationship with the peasants, the commander changes Bai Yufeng's job. But he continues to encourage his fellow soldiers to continue the feeding revolution. It steadily becomes apparent to all that Bai's ideas are sound. When the military and the local people are carrying out a joint training exercise, the landlord poisons all the pigs. Bai Yufeng works with the local people to analyze the reasons for the pigs' death, and finds that all clues point to the landlord. After this class struggle exercise, the entire company successfully accomplishes its training mission and receives honors.

1418. *New Story of A Hun (A Hun Xin Zhuan)*

1984. Pearl River Film Studio. Color. Letterboxed. 9 Reels. Direction: Wang Weiyi. Screenplay: Xiao Cui, Wu Ren. Cinematography: Yan Xuzhong. Art Direction: Tu Benyang. Music: Shen Liqun. Sound: Le Dehua. Cast: Yan Shunkai as Du Xiaoxi, Ye Paobei as Xiao Meiyin, Wu Meimei as Grandma, Zhu Huiqing as Da Nan, Li Qin as Du Mengxiong, Wang Guilin as Zhou Minhui

The main character in this comedy is Du Xiaoxi, a young man nicknamed "A Hun" (Shanghai slang for someone who wants to get everything without doing anything in return). A Hun is an ordinary worker in a plant that makes animal feed. His brother-in-law Zhou Minhui invents a new material, and A Hun tries to horn in on the glory. He meets a girl, and to impress her gives the impression he has a technical job in the plant. But when her father asks him to show how it was done, his charade quickly becomes evident and he is shown the door. The girl impresses on him the importance of honesty, and he decides to start over.

1419. *New Story of a Killer (Ci Ke Xin Zhuan)*

1995. Yunnan Nationalities Film Studio, Beijing Film Studio and Hong Kong Changsheng Film Production Corporation Ltd. Co-Production. Color. Direction: Zhong Shaoxiong. Screenplay: Zhang Tan, Situ Huizhuo. Cinematography: Zhao Fei. Art Direction: Chen Xiaoxia. Music: Huang Bangxian. Cast: Zhang Fengyi as Tang Zhan, Guan Zhiling as Le Yao, Ni Dahong as Wei Zhongxian, Mo Shaochong as

Wang Kou, Zhang Guangbei as Song Zhong, Song Ge as Mi Gonggong

In the early 17th century, the Ming Dynasty court is controlled by eunuchs. To eliminate any potential rivals, chief eunuch Wei Zhongxian recruits condemned prisoners to be his killers. One of these is Tang Zhan, who had been condemned for attempting to elope with his lover Le Yao, a girl at court. Although not a killer to begin with, Tang Zhan becomes one of Wei's most reliable, dispatching one of the eunuch's rivals after another. One day Tang Zhan meets Le Yao, who urges him to stop the killing. Tang realizes she is right, but his attempt to resign makes him a target. The eunuch sends two other killers after Tang, and while he succeeds in killing them, Tang himself dies.

1420. New Story of an Old Soldier (Lao Bing Xin Zhuan)

1959. Haiyan Film Studio. Color. Wide Screen. 11 Reels. Direction: Shen Fu. Screenplay: Li Zhun. Cinematography: Luo Chongzhou. Art Direction: Hu Zuoyun. Music: Ge Yan. Sound: Miao Zhenyu. Cast: Cui Wei as Director Zhan, Sun Yongping as Xiao Dongzhi, Gao Bo as Director Li, Chen Xu as Old Wang, Gu Yelu as Zhou Qinghe, Cao Duo as Liu Chengguang

Shortly after the liberation of Northeast China, retired military cadre Zhan becomes director of a newly established farming community there. He clashes with Deputy Director Zhao Songjun, an agronomist who always goes by the book. Zhao believes that newly cultivated former wastelands should only be planted in alternate years, but Zhan feels that China's needs are so great they should plant annually. Director Zhan is supported by his young students, and when fall comes they have a bumper wheat crop. Many of the young people marry and decide to settle down where they have been farming. Director Zhan accepts a new assignment to explore wastelands in other places.

1421. New Story of Liang Shanbo and Zhu Yingtai (Liang Shan Bo Zhu Ying Tai Xin Zhuan)

1994. Nanhai Film Company. Color. 9 Reels. Direction: Liu Guoquan. Screenplay: Lang Wenyao, Liu Guoquan, based on a Chinese traditional opera. Cinematography: Li Dawei. Art Direction: Zhang Yafang. Music: Wu Jiaji. Sound: Zhang Baojian, Liang Jiadong. Costume: Yi Shenglin, Dai Lingling. Makeup: Zhao Zhiming, Huang Yueying. Cast: Hu Huizhong as Zhu Yingtai, Pu Chunxi as Liang Shanbo, Cheng Qian as Ma Wencai, Chen Xiaoyi as Yingxin, Xie Liasi as Siniang, Wang Jieshi as Zugong, Jing Gangshan as Sijiu

A legend of ancient China. Scholar Liang Shanbo meets Zhu Yingtai, a young woman disguised as a man so she may attend school, and they fall in love. Meanwhile, a man named Ma Wencai persuades his father to arrange a marriage for him with Zhu Yingtai. Her father agrees to the match, and calls her home under some pretense. Before she leaves, she and Liang Shanbo exchange betrothal vows. When word later reaches Liang that Zhu will be married to Ma Wencai, he dies of a broken heart. On her wedding night, Zhu Yingtai escapes, aided by her servant Sijiu. Zhu goes to Liang's tomb to grieve, but suddenly the tomb bursts open, and two butterflies fly out. Zhu sees Liang come to her, and the two lovers fly away together to a happier place.

1422. New Year's Sacrifice (Zhu Fu)

1956. Beijing Film Studio. Color. Direction: Sang Hu. Cinematography: Xia Yan. Screenplay: Qian Jiang, based on the novel by Lu Xun (1881–1936). Art Direction: Chi Ning. Music: Liu Ruzeng. Sound: Chen Yanxi. Cast: Bai Yang as Xianglin's wife, Wei Heling as Old Sixth He, Li Jingbo as Grandpa Fourth Lu, Shi Lin as Mrs. Fourth Lu, Di Li as Sister Liu, Li Jian as the Mother-in-Law, Guan Zongxiang as Old Second Wei

About the time of the fall of the Qing (Manchu) Dynasty in 1912, in a poor and remote village in East China's Zhejiang Province, a young widow known only as Xianglin's wife learns that her mother-in-law and a distant relative plan to sell her as a wife to a peasant living in the mountains. She flees and becomes a maid in the home of a local landlord, but she is soon caught, brought back and sold to the peasant. Their marriage still turns out to be a happy one, and a year later they have a son. As their many debts pile up, her husband works himself to death trying to pay them off. In addition, her cherished little boy is carried off by a wolf, and her brother-in-law seizes her home as part of the debt repayment. Xianglin's wife is forced to return to the landlord's home as a maid. Her ill fortune leads her employer to regard the widow as a jinx, and whenever sacrifices are performed during worship, she is

Top: New Story of an Old Soldier. 1959. Haiyan Film Studio. *Bottom: New Year's Sacrifice.* The servant called Widow Xianglin (Bai Yang, second right) happily makes arrangements for the New Year's celebration. 1956. Beijing Film Studio.

not permitted to touch the dishes, chopsticks or anything else used in the service. Later, she hears that she may be able to cleanse herself of bad luck by donating to the temple a threshold for everyone entering to walk on. She does this, and at the next sacrifice night, she happily takes out the sacrificial utensils for the family's worship service. However, the landlord's family angrily accuses her of trying to bring them bad luck, and drives her from the house. From then on, she lives the life of a homeless beggar, until finally, on a sacrifice night, she dies in a snowstorm, on the temple threshold that had been her donation.

1423. *Newsboys (Bao Tong)*

1979. Beijing Film Studio. Color. 12 Reels. Direction: Qian Jiang and Zhao Yuan. Screenplay: Qian Jiang, based on the novel of the same title. Cinematography: Sun Changyi. Art Direction: Yang Yuhe and Shen Xiaoding. Music: Du Mingxin and Yu Dacheng. Sound: Sun Yuming. Cast: Wang Tiecheng as Zhou Enlai, Li Ruojun as Shi Lei, Tan Kun as Chao Mang, Fang Jufeng as Ququ, Lu Guilan as Sister Li, Xu Tianxia as Zhao Xiu

In 1941, Nationalist government incompetence leads to the "Wannan Incident" in which more than 7,000 anti–Japanese officers and men are killed. Among those killed are the parents of Shi Lei, a Chongqing newsboy who sells the "New China Daily," a pro–Communist newspaper. Shi Lei and other employees of the newspaper work even harder to publicize Chiang Kaishek's responsibility for the tragedy. Chiang orders the paper closed down. Led by Communist Vice Chairman Zhou Enlai, the newspaper workers and vendors break through the army blockade and get their paper out to the street where everyone can read about the "Wannan Incident" and learn the truth. Some of the newsboys, including Shi Lei, grow up to become members of the New Fourth Route Army, struggling with the enemy.

1424. *Nie Er (Nie Er)*

1959. Haiyan Film Studio. Color. 13 Reels. Direction: Zhen Junli. Screenplay: Yu Ling, Meng Bo and Zhen Junli, based on events in the life of the composer Nie Er (1912–1935). Cinematography: Huang Shaofeng, Luo Chongzhou. Art Direction: Han Shangyi, Music: Ge Yan, Li Yinhai, Liu Fuan, Sound: Wu Jianghai. Cast: Zhao Dan as Nie Er, Wang Pei as Wan Qian-

hong, Deng Nan as Mr. Jiang, Zhao Shuyin as wife Jiang, Jiang Jun as Su Ping, Sun Yongping as Xiao Long, Zhang Ruifang as Zheng Leidian, Xia Tian as Zhao Meinong, Gao Zheng as Li Tianyin, Han Tao as Boss of the song and dance troupe, Huang Zongying as Fengfeng

In the summer of 1930, for having participated in a student demonstration, music student Nie Er is expelled from college and driven from his home in Yunnan by the government. He goes to Shanghai, where he at first works in a store, then becomes a musician for a burlesque song and dance troupe. He meets and has an affair with Zheng Leidian, a politically active young woman, and under her influence joins the Communist-led "Anti-Imperialist League." Nie soon joins the Communist Party of China, and leaves burlesque for a CPC musical group called the "Friends of the Soviet Union." During this period Nie writes many revolutionary songs. In the spring of 1935, when the government steps up its persecution of revolutionary artists, the CPC decides to send Nie Er to safety in the Soviet Union. However, he dies en route in Japan. Just before he leaves China, Nie Er composes the "March of the Volunteers," which eventually becomes the national anthem of the People's Republic of China.

1425. *Night Delivery Truck (Ye Xing Huo Che)*

1985. Film Association, Beijing Film Studio, Hebai Company, and Hong Kong Zhenye Film Company Ltd. Co-Production. Color. 10 Reels. Direction: Xie Yucheng. Screenplay: Wang Haitao, Xie Yucheng. Cinematography: Shen Xilin. Art Direction: Fu Delin. Music: Hou Dejian. Sound: Wang Zemin. Cast: Yu Shaokang as company door keeper Zhang, Zhang Fengyi as Zhan Yihong, Lin Fangbing as Liu Xiaoling, Han Yueqiao as Ai Lisi, Kou Zhenhai as Lin Rongping

Zhan Yihong is an employee of an American electronics company in Taipei. His abilities are appreciated and promotions come quickly. In addition, he and beautiful company secretary Liu Xiaoling are deeply in love. However, they become aware that there is a pattern of sexual harassment and racial discrimination within the company. The movie traces the couple's efforts to resist these inequities. At last, Zhan resigns in protest, and Liu Xiaoling abandons her idea of going to America to study. They have given up good jobs, but they have their principles and each other.

Nie Er. Soon after composing "The March of the Volunteers," later to become the PRC's national anthem, Nie Er (Zhao Dan, left) prepares to leave China for political safety. 1959. Haiyan Film Studio.

1426. *Night of Fear (Kong Bu Ye)*

1988. Emei Film Studio. Color. Letterboxed. 9 Reels. Direction: Mao Yuqing. Screenplay: Wang Chenggang. Cinematography: Zhang Huaming. Art Direction: Wu Xujin. Music: Jin Daiyuan. Sound: Peng Wenguang. Cast: Tu Zhongru as Qi Yuanjing, Wang Lingqian as Zhou Luo

Shortly after the establishment of the PRC in 1949, an outlaw band digs in for a last stand in the rugged mountains of western Sichuan province. Detectives Qi Yuanjing and Zhou Luo disguise themselves as businessmen to investigate a Taoist temple believed to be the bandit headquarters. Qi Yuanjing has been told the temple's Master Kong is a man of respect and honor, so he wants to contact Kong for help. Qi and Zhou also find an underground passage into the temple. They make contact with Master Kong, but soon find out he is a bogus priest who had killed the real Master Kong. Qi and Zhou have a violent battle with the bandits inside the temple, during which Kong is killed by Qi Yuanjing. The temple is peaceful once more.

1427. *A Night of Horror (Yi Ye Jing Xian)*

1993. Changchun Film Studio. Color. Letterboxed. 9 Reels. Direction: He Misheng. Screenplay: Mao Jie, Mao Xiaofeng. Cinematography: Shu Shu, Liu Tong. Art Direction: Liu Huanxing. Music: Guo Xiaotian. Sound: Cheng Xianbo. Costume: Li Xiuzhi, Li Fengwen, Zhang Jun. Makeup: Wang Fengbin. Cast: Yu Meng as Dengdeng, Zhang Ning as Juju, Wu Yu as Madam, Li Daqiang as the Professor, Liu Yan as Monkey Head

While her parents are visiting relatives in Los Angeles and her elder brother is away on business, little Lin Dengdeng stays by herself in a newly completed 26-story high rise apartment building. She and her playmate Juju spend much of their time playing with model airplanes. Meanwhile, one of the second floor units is rented to two men called "Professor" and "Houston," who with two other men are actually running a counterfeit money operation out of their apartment. One day while searching for a lost plane, the two girls accidentally enter the second floor apartment and witness the criminal activities going on there. The counterfeiters find out the children are on to them, which sets off a chase around the building, the criminals pursuing the girls, and the clever girls eluding them. At last, the police round up the counterfeiters and the little girls are heroines.

1428. *Night Pearl (Ye Min Zhu)*

1983. Zhejiang Film Studio. Color. 9 Reels. Direction: Liang Tingduo, Zuo Feng. Screenplay: Wang Yuan, Wei Er, Tao Qian, Jin Zhong. Cinematography: Zhang Yongjiang, Zhang Dongdong. Art Direction: Luo Depo. Music: Lu Enlai. Sound: Zhang Chenghua. Cast: Zhu Limin as Taotao, Wang Ying as Xiao Li, Lin Muyu as grandma Chen, Cai Xiang as Afa, Li Di as Niuniu, Wu Rui as Pingping, You Jia as Taotao's mother, Li Shouzhen as Afa's mother

During school vacation one summer, a group of children learn that Grandma Chen, a kindly woman who had once been their daycare provider, is losing her eyesight and is nearly blind. Their desire to help her leads them into several adventures, including trying to catch a large snake whose meat they hear will cure blindness. One day they see a newspaper article about a doctor in the provincial capital reported to have cured the blindness of more than 100 patients. They travel to see him. The doctor is very moved by the children and travels back with them to their hometown, where he restores Grandma Chen's sight.

1429. *Night Rain at Bashan (Ba Shan Ye Yu)*

1980. Shanghai Film Studio. Color. 9 Reels. Direction: Wu Yonggang, Wu Yigong. Screenplay: Ye Nan. Cinematography: Cao Weiye. Art Direction: Xue Jianna. Music: Gao Tian. Sound: Jin Fugeng, Yang Liangkun. Cast: Li Zhiyu as Qiushi, Zhang Yu as Liu Wenyin, Qiang Min as Li Yan, Ouyang Ruqiu as the old lady, Lin Bing as the woman teacher, Lu Qin as Song Mingsheng

Poet Qiu Shi, imprisoned for six years by the Gang of Four, is being returned by ship to his home city of Wuhan, escorted by two police officers, Li Yan and Liu Wenyin, the latter a woman officer. Qiu Shi is depressed and unhappy over the bitter turn his life has taken: his beloved wife died while he was in prison, and he has a young daughter he has never seen. There are nine passengers in all, eight adults and an ill-mannered little girl. On the trip, Qiu Shi's thoughts and behavior begin to shake Liu Wenyin's confidence in herself and

her political views. She starts to change from self-confident and unshakable to puzzled, confused and suspicious. She finally awakens to the fact that her political views have been wrong all along. When she learns that the little girl is Qiu Shi's daughter, she decides to help them. The captain, other passengers and the police officers help to get father and daughter acquainted. By the time the ship docks, the two are united and looking forward to a new life in freedom.

Best Picture, 1981 Golden Rooster Awards.
Best Screenplay Ye Nan, 1981 Golden Rooster Awards.
Best Actress Zhang Yu, 1981 Golden Rooster Awards.
Best Music Gao Tian, 1981 Golden Rooster Awards.

1430. *Nightless City (Bu Ye Cheng)*

1957. Jiangnan Film Studio. Color. 12 Reels. Direction: Tang Xiaodan. Screenplay: Ke Lin. Cinematography: Zhou Daming, Ma Linfa. Art Direction: Ge Shicheng. Music: Wang Yunjie. Sound: Liu Guangjie. Makeup: Xu Ken. Cast: Li Lingjun as Shen Yindi, Liu Fei as Ju Haisheng, Mao Lu as Ju Yonggeng, Li Jingkang as Qian Xiuzhu, Cui Chaoming as Zhang Yaotang, Sun Daolin as Zhang Bohan

During World War II, entrepreneur Zhang Bohan returns to Shanghai from studies in England to find his father Zhang Yaotang's textile plant forced into near-bankruptcy by Zong Yichun, a comprador for a Japanese textile plant which wants to buy out the Zhang family business. Zhang Bohan. believing that a booming industry is the way to save China, merges his father's plant with that of his father-in-law, which staves off the takeover attempt. He then produces a new type of blue cloth which, at a time when the Chinese people are boycotting Japanese goods, makes them rich. Just prior to liberation, with the Nationalist government close to losing power, Zhang's plant is also in danger, so Zhang makes a deal with Zong Yichu, now a comprador for the Americans, to obtain some American cotton business and rely on American banks for support. He almost goes bankrupt as a result. After liberation, Zhang's plant secures a large order from the new government, and his business flourishes again. However, Zhang Bohan has become obsessed with seeking huge profits and illegal money, and he becomes an illegal capitalist. He clashes with his daughter over this, causing her to leave home. Eventually Zhang comes to realize his mistakes, and makes a full confession of his illegal activities, for which he receives only a light penalty. He dedicates himself to finding ways for privately owned and publicly owned enterprises to cooperate.

1431. *Nine Dragon Beach (Jiu Long Tan)*

1978. Xi'an Film Studio. Color. 10 Reels. Direction: Lin Feng. Screenplay: Li Su, Feng Guangyu. Cinematography: Xu Deyuan. Art Direction: Liu Xinghou. Music: Wang Jinao, Zhang Zhengping. Sound: Dang Cunzhu. Cast: Zhen Danian as Zhao Zhijiang, Wang Zhi as Wang Baocheng, Gao Yang as Shi Changqin, Song Aiwu as Wang Jiyin, Bian Yongyuan as Tao Chunsheng, Bi Fusheng as Gu Huzhi

Wang Baocheng, a Red Army soldier since 1935, leaves in 1949 to become the director of a prefectural transport team, managing some shipping routes. In the economic crisis of 1961, some hidden class enemies seize the opportunity to throw the Nine Dragon Beach shipping route into chaos. At this time, an old army buddy of Wang's, Zhao Zhijiang, is assigned as Party secretary of the Bureau of Transport. The two work to formulate a plan for handling the route, but counterrevolutionary Wei Sheng plots to disrupt the route by planting explosives. Just as the plotters are about to set off the explosives, they are caught red-handed by militia troops who had been tipped off to the plot.

1432. *19 Years Old (Shi Jiu Nian Hua)*

1986. Xiaoxiang Film Studio. Color. 9 Reels. Direction: Luo Yin, Hua Yongqin. Screenplay: Deng Chengxi. Cinematography: Yu Liping, Li Xiaoping. Art Direction: Tan Shengshan. Music: Wei Jingshu. Sound: Ning Yuqin. Cast: Wang Yan as Li Qian, Zhang Jian as Lin Yishan, Zhu Xiaoming as Zhang Xiaoguang, Liu Di as Lin Lanlan

In 1934, at a Red Army school in north Fujian province, student Lin Yishan and his 19-year-old teacher Li Qian fall in love. After Lin Yishan graduates, he rises quickly to become a company commander. Li Qian is reassigned to work in a grain bureau, and volunteers for a mission to obtain grain sources from behind enemy lines. However, Li Qian is killed in the operation. Now, in the present,

Shanghai girl Lin Lanlan hears this story from a young man named Zhang Xiaoguang. She realizes that the Lin Yishan in the story is her own father.

1433. *Niujiaoshi (Niu Jiao Shi)*

1976. Beijing Film Studio. Color. 10 Reels. Direction: Shi Yifu. Screenplay: Cao Shuolong, Li Baoyuan. Cinematography: Zhu Jinmin, Wun Zhixian. Art Direction: Chen Rongyuan, Tu Juhua. Music: Liang Kexiang. Sound: Sun Yumin, Wang Jinxiang. Cast: Hu Jing as Qi Lanzhi, Yu Zhongyi as Wang Weizhong, Li Baiwan as Zhang Li, Guo Shutian as Niu Laomin, Mei Zhao Hua as Hai Liang, Cao Cuifeng as Xiu Zhen

In 1962, a corrupt prefectural-level official in league with some relatively well-off farmers tries to force the people of the Niujiaoshi Commune to implement a new policy which will make it easier to engage in speculation and other profiteering activities. The Party branch secretary leads the people in resisting this, and after a bitter political struggle the county Party Secretary intervenes on the anti-corruption side, and the corrupt official is dismissed from his position.

1434. *Niulang Seeks Zhinu (Niu Lang Xun Zhi Nu)*

1988. Beijing Film Studio. Color. 5 Reels. Direction: Jin Yanxi. Screenplay: Long Chuanren. Cinematography: Zhang Qinhua. Art Direction: Zhu Cao. Music: Gu De. Sound: Zhang Ye. Cast: Wang Yuejing as Niulang, Zhou Wenqiong as the guide, Xing Hong as Zhinu

July 7th is the date that two spirits called Niulang and Zhinu have agreed to meet at a bridge in the heavens. Suddenly, a UFO shatters the bridge, casting female spirit Zhinu from the heavens and into the human world. An alien from the UFO finds Zhinu and absorbs her into the UFO, which then lands in a forest near the Great Wall. After Zhinu awakens, she flees, but is now stranded in the world of humans. The rest of the film relates Niulang's search for Zhinu and her experiences in the human world. At last Niulang and Zhinu are reunited in the clouds and return to the spirit world together.

1435. *No Alternative (Bie Wu Xuan Ze)*

1991. Changchun Film Studio. Color. Letterboxed. 9 Reels. Direction: Mu Deyuan. Screenplay: Mu Deyuan, Chen Yanmin. Cinematography: Zhang Haimin. Art Direction: Gan Jun, Wang Di. Music: Gao Erdi. Sound: Zhang Haimin. Cast: Shi Zhaoqi as Xing Dong, Zhu Ling as Li Jing, Shen Junyi as Qu Xianguo, Zhao Xiaorui as Tutou, Zhang Fengyi in an unnamed supporting role

A training accident which also takes away his sexual ability forces Xing Dong into premature retirement from China's military special forces. His understanding wife, beautiful doctor Li Jing, tries to help him adjust to civilian life and regain his ability. At a loss for something to do, he happens to run into his old friend Qu Xianguo, now the CEO of a company threatened by mobsters trying to take it over. Xing Dong helps his old friend, but soon finds himself attracted to and increasingly involved with the mob activities. But Qu Xianguo is in fact an undercover public security bureau officer, and he at last corners Xing Dong and the other mobsters. Seeing no way out, Xing Dong commits suicide. Unfortunately, not all of the criminals are caught, and one who escapes is a mad dog killer called Tutou, a former cop gone bad. Tutou kills Xing's wife Li Jing, and abducts Xing Dong's son. In the final confrontation, the son turns the tables and kills Tutou.

1436. *No Compromise (Si Bu Liang Li)*

1993. Changchun Film Studio. Color. Letterboxed. 9 Reels. Direction: Gu Jing. Screenplay: Huang Dan, Tang Louyi. Cinematography: Shu Li, Liu Bing. Art Direction: Li Baoshu. Music: Zou Ye. Sound: Cao Feng, Zhang Xiaonan. Costume: Li Lei. Makeup: Wang Daiwu, Han Yi. Cast: Shi Zhaoqi as Zhao Jiannan, Xu Yang as Yunqin, Chen Mu as Tan Mengquan, Zhang Huizhong as Biao Shan, Jia Yongzhi as Bureau Chief Liu, Li Yunjuan as Yu Cai

Young policeman Zhao Jiannan is determined to bring down major drug dealer Tan Mengquan. His reasons are as much personal as professional, for he believes the gangster killed Zhao's father. During the course of his investigation, Zhao meets and falls in love with a girl named Yunqin. Zhao's boss, Chief Liu, strongly backs Zhao's efforts to gain his revenge, even at times hinting it would be better to bring the gangster in dead rather than alive for trial. Zhao finally corners Tan and is about to kill him when the gangster tells Zhao

his father had actually been killed by Liu, and that Yunqin is Liu's daughter. Liu and his men surround the site where Zhao and Tan waged their final struggle, and orders that Zhao be killed. Zhao turns on Liu and the two kill each other. The grieving Yunqin leaves the city for a remote area.

1437. *No Fur, But Precious (Wa, Mei Mao De Gou)*

1992. Xiaoxiang Film Studio. Color. Letterboxed. 9 Reels. Direction: Hu Zhongqiu. Screenplay: Zhao Junhai. Cinematography: Li Ping. Art Direction: Liao Jianheng. Music: Yang Xiwu. Sound: Huang Siye. Costume: Sheng Lingzhen. Makeup: Zhang Jing. Cast: Pao Zhanyuan as Cheng Jiu, Li Yonggui as Yong Ba, Zhang Li as Dezhu, Niu Yinghong as Zhen Xiu

In a small town in South China, two restive farmers who want to get rich quick hit on a scheme which focuses on exhibiting a supposedly special dog. They have some surprising initial success in rural villages, but as the money starts to come in they spend more time arguing and trying to cheat each other. They have a falling out, but are reconciled by their children.

1438. *No One Cheers (Wu Ren He Cai)*

1993. Beijing Film Studio and Yanming International Corp. Color. Letterboxed. 9 Reels. Direction: Xia Gang. Screenplay: Wang Shuo, Meng Zhu, from the novel of the same title by Wang Shuo (1958–). Cast: Ge Ke as Xiao Keping, Xie Yuan as Li Mianning, Ding Jiali as Han Liting, Fang Zige as Qian Kang

Attractive and talented musician Xiao Keping finds that her husband Li Mianning is unhappy and restive despite their comfortable life in Beijing. Years before, he had been a respected aeronautical engineer in Northwest China, but in order to be with her Li had relinquished his professional job and moved to Beijing, where he now works as a warehouse doorkeeper. His unhappiness gives rise to conflicts, and eventually the couple divorce. However, the shortage of housing forces them to continue sharing their quarters. Successful businessman Qian Kang begins a serious courtship of Xiao Keping, while Li has his own admirer in a young woman named Han Liting. Actually, Han's goal in marrying is to get Li's house. Eventually, Xiao and Li look at their

No One Cheers. Xiao Keping (Ge Ke) and her husband Li Mianning (Xie Yuan) face a crisis in their marriage. 1993. Beijing Film Studio.

situation differently and decide to get back together, while Han and Qian begin their own relationship.

Best Supporting Actor Fang Zige, 1994 Golden Rooster Awards.

Best Supporting Actress Ding Jiali, 1994 Hundred Flowers Awards.

1439. *No Regrets About Youth (Qing Chun Wu Hui)*

1991. Xi'an Film Studio. Color. 10 Reels. Direction: Zhou Xiaowen. Screenplay: Wang Shuo, Wei Ren. Cinematography: Zhou Xiaowen, Lu Gengxin. Art Direction: Qian Yunxuan. Music: Qian Yuanxuan. Sound: Hong Jiahui. Cast: Shi Lan as Mai Qun, Zhang Fengyi as Zhen Jianong, Liu Yunlong as Hu Songli, Lu Liping as Liu Jie, Liu Shu as Duoduo, Zhang Wankun as Zhang Haiming, Yang Lixin as Wu Jiang, Jin Yaqin as Hu's mother, Wei Qinghuai as Hu's father

A man and a woman who had once known each other in the army are again thrown together by fate. He was once an important figure in a frontier army battalion, but now he is a truck driver at a construction site. She used to be a nurse in an army hospital, but now works as a doctor at a local clinic. At one time, each saved the life of the other. They meet again in a hospital where he is terminally ill with cancer. She is his doctor. Neither has any regrets about their lost youth.

Best Supporting Actress Lu Liping, 1992 Hundred Flowers Awards.

1440. *No Shadow Scouting Team (Wu Ying Zhen Cha Dui)*

1989. August First Film Studio. Color. Letterboxed. 9 Reels. Direction: Hu Zhongqiu. Screenplay: Lu Wen. Cinematography: Cai Shunan. Art Direction: Ni Shaohua. Music: Yang Xiwu. Sound: Wang Lewen. Cast: Wang Huichun as Wei Hua, Wang Jing as Hu Shibei, Nei Jian as A Meng, Zhe Jiashe, Tan Weiming as Captain Li, Mu Liyyan as Xiao Fang, Zhu Shan as Kong Zhan, Shi Feng as Yan Jun

1441. *North China Red Beans (Bei Guo Hong Dou)*

1984. Beijing Film Studio. Color. Wide Screen. 10 Reels. Direction: Wang Haowei. Screenplay: Qiao Xuezhu. Cinematography: Li Chengsheng. Art Direction: Chen Yiyun, Lin Chaoxiang. Music: Zhang Peiji. Sound: Fu Yinjie. Cast: Liu Xiaoqin as Lu Xuezhi, Zhang Guomin as Jiang Youlin, Jin Xing as Fang Gengzhu, Yu Shaokang as Lu Minzi, Han Guiju as Sister

In 1971, Hebei peasant girl Lu Xuezhi settles down at her sister's home in the Daxinganling area, and finds work there as a forest worker. At work, she meets and falls in love with a co-worker, simple and honest Fang Gengzhu. Their relationship meets with the strong disapproval of her brother-in-law Lu Minzi, a cadre with some local power. He wants to advance himself politically by marrying her off to a powerful cadre of higher rank. Lu Xuezhi angers him by refusing. She then moves out of her sister's home. Fang Gengzhu's family, fearful of Lu Minzhi, sends him gifts as peace offerings. Fang's weakness so disappoints Lu Xuezhi that she loses hope and confidence in the future. She now feels distant from Fang, but does not want to give up completely on the nice young fellow. Fang also feels the change between them, and decides to prove himself by volunteering to fight a forest fire.

1442. *Not at All Without Feelings (Dao Shi Wu Qing Sheng You Qing)*

1983. August Film Studio. Color. 10 Reels. Direction: Wei Lian. Screenplay: Lu Zhuguo. Cinematography: Zhu Lutong. Art Direction: Zhang Zheng. Music: Gong Zhiwei. Sound: Wu Hanbiao, Liang Zuochun. Cast: Zhu Shimao as Yuan Han, Niu Qian as the regimental commander, Zhu Cuiming as Yuan's wife, Yang Tongshun as Luo Huaimu, Guo Gang as the platoon leader

A new regimental commander finds that while his 3rd Company is poorly trained, 1st Company Commander Yuan Han's troops are outstanding. Therefore, he puts Yuan in charge of the 3rd Company, with orders to bring them up to par. When Yuan takes over his new assignment he finds more problems than he had expected, including an almost total lack of discipline among the troops. Yuan straightens out the small problems first, then focuses on military training. His devotion to the task is such that he does not return home when his newborn twin girls are very sick, one dying. Under Yuan's leadership, the company comes up to the level of the rest of the regiment just as the Sino-Vietnamese border war starts. Yuan Han is promoted to battalion commander and leads his troops to the front.

1443. *Not for Love (Bu Shi Wei Le Ai Qing)*

1980. Emei Film Studio. Color. 10 Reels. Direction: Yin Xianglin. Screenplay: Yang Tao, Curi Changwu. Cinematography: Li Dagui. Art Direction: Xia Zhengqiu. Music: Huang Anlun. Sound: Lin Bingcheng. Cast: Li Shixi as Han Yu, Peilan Nikelaida as Wei Na, Liu Dong as Hong Mei, Yan Shikui as Pu Dahai, Cao Peng as Han Xin, Lu Fei as Secretary Li

Dancer Wei Na is an international orphan. When her fiance Pu Dahai is arrested for taking part in a public demonstration of grief over the death of Premier Zhou Enlai, she finds herself alone and under a political attack which causes her to lose her job. In despair and without the will to go on, Wei Na jumps into a lake to commit suicide. She is rescued by a young couple passing by, railway worker Han Yu and his girlfriend Hong Mei. Out of sympathy for Wei Na, Han Yu takes her in and gives her encouragement and material support. Hong Mei thinks Han Yu is going too far: she tries to get him to stop the involvement, and

threatens Wei Na if she doesn't get out of China. Finally, Hong Mei falsely accuses Han Yu of being a counterrevolutionary. When the Gang of Four's political persecution reaches Han Yu, he confronts it bravely, so impressing Wei Na that she falls in love with him. He returns her affection, and after the downfall of the Gang of Four, many people come to help Han and Wei with their wedding arrangements. But also showing up is her former fiance Pu Dahai, thought to have died in prison. Han Yu, saying that "love is linked to one's beliefs," controls his emotions and takes leave of Wei Na. He believes that the couple which had already suffered so much in life will be happier together.

1444. *Not Just One Person's Story (Bing Fei Yige Rende Gushi)*

1978. Emei Film Studio. Color. 11 Reels. Direction: Zhang Fengxiang. Screenplay: Zhao Danian. Cinematography: Gu Wunhou. Art Direction: Chen Desheng. Music: Tao Jiazhou. Sound: Shen Guli. Cast: Shi Weijian as Zhang Heng, Leng Mei as Li Nong, Gong Yiqun as Xu Qiang, Zhang Feng Xiang as Liu Yicheng, Xu Liankai as Bureau Director Sun, Yu Liwen as Yu Xueqin

At the time the "Gang of Four" is persecuting intellectuals, farm machinery engineer Zhang Heng secretly persists in his research. But co-worker Yu Xueqin and others at their institution who are in sympathy with the Gang persecute Zhang Heng and their supervisor Director Liu Yicheng. Zhang and Liu are forced to go to Ludipo Village for reform through labor, but the local people and village Party deputy secretary Miss Li Nong all show their support, especially after Zhang renovates their farm machinery. Later, with the support of the county Farm Machinery Bureau Director Sun, Zhang again starts doing research. Some Gang supporters in the area move to further persecute Director Liu, but their conspiracy is smashed by Li Nong and local people. After the Gang of Four is defeated, Zhang Heng's renovation of machinery succeeds; meanwhile he and Li Nong have fallen in love through their class struggle and scientific experience.

1445. *Nuer Nisha (Nu Er Ni Sha)*

1984. Tianshan Film Studio. Color. 10 Reels. Direction: Abu Dula. Screenplay: Maimu Tiyiming. Cinematography: Ai Lijiang. Art Direction:

Gao Feng. Music: Zhu Hongqian. Sound: Li Dehua, Li Bing. Cast: Reyihan as Nuer Nisha, Aili as Nijiate, Ahsi Kaer as Shabier, Aitanmu as Bake, Guzi Linuer as Polida

The romance of Nijiate and his girl friend Polida is disrupted when someone tells Polida her lover was born illegitimately, after which he was adopted by the people he believes are his parents. When she tells this to Nijiate, he is upset, and determines to find out the truth. His inquiries lead him to a woman named Nuer Nisha, who turns out to be his real mother. After he learns the true story of his background, and that he has nothing to be ashamed of, Nijiate returns and he and Polida are together again.

1446. *Number One Adventure Action (Yi Hao Tan Xian Xing Dong)*

1990. Changchun Film Studio. Color. Wide Screen. 9 Reels. Direction: Jin Tao, Sun Yan. Screenplay: Zhou Xinde. Cinematography: Gao Hongbao. Art Direction: Li Deyu. Music: Yang Yilun, Liu Kexin. Sound: Zhang Jun, Gu Xiao-lian. Cast: Peng Song as Haizhu, Li Songmao as Daping

Haizhu, Daping, and some of their elementary school classmates plan an adventure exploring a cave for their summer break from school. When they arrive at their destination, they find a suitcase loaded with pornographic video tapes. They use their carrier pigeon to send a message reporting the situation. Then a man arrives to pick up that suitcase, and he turns out to be Haizhu's father. Haizhu is so upset, he helps his classmates fight his father and turn him in to the police for smuggling.

1447. *Number One Killer in the East (Dong Fang Di Yi Chi Ke)*

1993. Guangxi Film Studio. Color. Letter-boxed. 9 Reels. Direction: Zhao Wenqin. Screenplay: Zhao Xuebin, based on Lu Tieren's novel "Number One Killer In Shanghai." Cinematography: Cai Xiaopeng. Art Direction: Li Qining. Music: Xian Hua, Xian Zhenzhong. Sound: Lin Lin. Costume: Chen Yixing. Makeup: Li Zun-xun. Cast: Shen Junyi as Wang Yaqiao, Xia Jing as Cuiqiao, Wang Zhifei as Wu Huaiyuan, Li Shusheng as Gong Chunpu, Guo Feng as Yu Likui, Zhou Zhihua as Sun Fengming, Li Ze-quan as Zhang Xiaolin, Guo Hong as Huang Shanshan as Tong Xue, Zang Qian as Wanjun, Ai Junmai as Zhao Tieqiao, Huer Xide as Meilier

Shanghai in the late 1920s is a battleground for triads. Chiang Kaishek's massacre of large numbers of Communists in April of 1927 infuriates Wang Yaqiao, head of the Futao triad and a revolutionary sympathizer. Wang orders one of his gunmen, Zhao Tieqiao, to assassinate Chiang. But Zhao betrays Wang and goes over to Chiang's side instead. Wang vows revenge, and winds up fighting Japanese, other triads and Nationalist government intelligence agents as well. He at last comes to realize that the Communists are the only force in China which shares his political views, but he is killed by government agents before he can escape Shanghai.

1448. *A Nurse's Diary (Hu Shi Ri Ji)*

1957. Jiangnan Film Studio. B & W. 11 Reels. Direction: Tao Jin. Screenplay: Ai Mingzhi. Cinematography: Chen Zhenxiang. Art Direction: Lu Jingguang. Music: Wang Yunjie. Sound: Lin Bingsheng. Makeup: Jiang Youan. Cast: Wang Danfeng as Jian Shuhua, Tang Huada as Gao Cangping, Li Wei as Shen Aoru, Jian Tianliu as Gu Huiying, Fu Botang as Mo Jiabing, Huang Wansu as Tang Xiaofang

After graduating from a Shanghai school of nursing, Jian Shuhua decides to work at a construction workers' clinic in a remote area of China, in spite of the objections of her fiancee Shen Aoru. When she arrives at her new work station, she finds that one of the clinic directors, Mo Jiabing, pays more attention to his love affair with nurse Gu Huiying than he does to his work. In addition, the arrival of a new nurse arouses Gu Huiying's jealousy. Jian Shuhua's hard work and personality soon overcome this, and she is also able to help Mo Jiabing correct his shortcomings. Her fiance Shen Aoru arrives, but he fears the hard life there, and tries everything he can to persuade her to return with him to Shanghai. She firmly refuses to leave, so Shen returns alone, and marries another woman. Jian Shuhua sticks to her hard work, eventually finding romance with Gao Cangping, another clinic director. Her enthusiastic and selfless work win her the affection and support of all the construction workers served by the clinic.

1449. *Obsession (Feng Kuang De Dai Jia)*

1988. Xi'an Film Studio. Color. 10 Reels. Direction: Zhou Xiaowen. Screenplay: Zhou Xiaowen, Lu Wei. Cinematography: Wang Xinsheng. Art Direction: Dou Guoxiang, Lu Wei.

Music: Zhu Shirui. Sound: Gu Changning. Cast: Wu Yujuan as Qingqing, Li Jing as Lanlan, Xie Yuan as Li Changwei, Chang Rong as Sun Dacheng

When their parents divorce, sisters Qingqing and Lanlan are abandoned, leaving the elder Qingqing to raise her younger sister. The experience teaches Qingqing to be tough and independent, while Lanlan is free to grow up as normally as possible. All this changes one night when Lanlan is raped while returning home from classes. The incident leaves Qingqing distraught and plunges Lanlan into expressionless silence. To avenge Lanlan, Qingqing begins a desperate search for the rapist. She borrows a camera from her boyfriend Li Changwei and starts taking photos of suspicious strangers for Lanlan to identify. Her photographic skills improve, but the criminal remains at large. During her summer vacation, Lanlan is minding Li Changwei's bookstore when she recognizes one of the customers as the man who raped her. Qingqing goes off in pursuit of the criminal, whom the police by now are also looking for. The rapist, Sun Dasheng, forces Qingqing at gunpoint to the top of a high building. The police arrive on the scene, but while they eventually capture the criminal, Qingqing kills the rapist by kicking him off the building. Qingqing must now face criminal charges of her own.

1450. *The Ocean Is Calling (Da Hai Zai Hu Huan)*

1982. Beijing Film Studio. Color. 10 Reels. Direction: Yu Yang, Yang Jing. Screenplay: Lu Junchao. Cinematography: Zhang Qinghua. Art Direction: Tu Juhua. Music: Wang Liping. Sound: Zhang Zhian. Cast: Yu Yang as Chen Hongzhi and Chen Haiwei, Qiu Yi as Wu Minyue, Fang Baoluo as Ma Bashuo, Aibi as Ba Boluo, Zhao Lian as Jin Ying, Cheng Qiang as Chen Hongye

After the Cultural Revolution, veteran sea captain Chen Haiwei resumes his command of the transport ship "Shanghai," hauling cargo and passengers throughout Southeast Asia. Its first trip out the ship runs into a storm in the Bay of Bengal, and the captain and crew need all their skills and experience to save it. When the ship is passing an lighthouse island, the lighthouse signals an emergency. The ship stops at the island, and Chen finds that the lighthouse keeper is ill and in need of immediate surgery. The keeper is also his old friend Ba

Boluo, a comrade from the days of maritime labor struggles more than 30 years before. Chen donates his own blood to Ba for the operation, and Ba's life is saved. In the keeper's illness, the navigation light has failed, but repairing it in the storm is very dangerous. Young crew member Wu Minyue volunteers to repair the light. He is successful, but gives his life in the effort. Chen Haiwei, his crew and passengers all deeply mourn the young man who had selflessly given his life, to be laid from rest so far from his home.

1451. *Ocean Ship Story (Yuan Yang Yi Shi)*

1986. Fujian Film Studio. Color. 9 Reels. Direction: Liu Miaomiao. Screenplay: Wu Jianxin. Cinematography: Zhen Wangong, Yang Ming. Cast: Liu Jiaoxin as Li Bing, Li Xiaoyan as Yu Yixing, Yang Zhichun as the old father-in-law, Liu Guodian as Zhang Jiu, Ye Hui as Zhen Wendu, Li Ping as Lin Yabing

1452. *Ocean Storm (Hai Shang Feng Bao)*

1951. Shanghai Film Studio. B & W. 9 Reels. Direction: Xu Xinzhi. Screenplay: Yu Shan, Huang Zongjiang and Zhou Xing, based on a novel by Jiao Fuchun. Cinematography: Miao Zhenhua, Shen Weikang and Wang Mingsheng. Art Direction: Wang Cangcheng and Yang Lingde. Music: Zhu Jianer. Sound: Ling Shengqing. Costume: Zhang Yongshan. Cast: Chang Qian as Commissar Gao, Le Yuhou as Commissar Liu, Wang Li as Regimental Commander Wang, Li Keling as another Regimental Commander Wang, Chen Hehua as Battalion Commander Sun, Shen Mujun as Company Commander Guo

A company of 42 PLA soldiers led by Commander Guo is sent to practice beachhead raids, but a storm washes them ashore on an isolated island. They are soon under attack from Nationalist troops dug in on another island nearby. The embattled PLA company holds out for a week against the enemy's greater numbers, in large part by deceiving the Nationalists into thinking the PLA troops are a much larger force. On the seventh night, Commander Guo sends two men back to the mainland to contact the division, and dispatches a platoon to stage a raid on the enemy island. The mission goes well, but leads to the enemy discovering the true size of Guo's unit, and attacking the island in force. Just as Guo's company is about to run out of food and am-munition, a PLA relief force arrives from the mainland, and the invaders are driven off.

1453. *The Ocean Through Glasses (Yan Jing Li De Hai)*

1989. Pearl River Film Studio. Color. Letter-boxed. 10 Reels. Direction: Chen Erlin. Screen-play: Li Chunli. Cinematography: Liu Xinmin. Art Direction: Du Xiufeng. Music: Miao Neng. Sound: Lin Guoqiang. Cast: Zhang Li as Xinxin, Xia Mu as Wang Le, Li Liwei as Su Fei

The joys and sorrows of a group of high school students. Xinxin loves painting, a talent unsupported by her parents. Bright Wang Le's independent thinking is often misunderstood by his teachers. Su Fei, raised by his divorced mother, faces a dilemma: his father wants him to join him overseas and eventually take over his father's business, or stay with his mother, who wants him always by her side. The class-room is like a small community, in which each of the citizens has his or her own problems and solutions.

1454. *Office Girls (Ao Fei Si Xiao Jie)*

1994. Shanghai Film Studio. Color. Letter-boxed. 10 Reels. Direction: Pao Zhifang. Screen-play: Yang Xingji, Shen Ningyue, Pao Zhifang. Cinematography: Zhao Junhong, Zang Hongjun. Art Direction: Zhou Qinren. Music: Liu Yanxi. Sound: Lu Jiajing. Costume: Zhang Huijuan. Makeup: Zhou Meihua. Cast: Ning Jing as A Meng, Zhou Xiaoli as Mimi, Li Hong as Yanyan, Xiao Rongsheng as Jiang Xiang, Tong Ruixin as Lin Geng, Gao Shuguang as Wang Ming, Wu Wenlun as Qiu Fanggui, Zhang Kanger as Qiaozhi, Tang Zhenzong as Wensheng

Ameng, Mimi and Yanyan are three young women of disparate characters. They all go to work for Shanghai joint venture companies. Mimi is only interested in earning sufficient money to go to bars and discos. Her husband is working in Tokyo, so when her company's CEO expresses a romantic interest in her she initially turns him down. When she learns that her husband has betrayed her in Tokyo, she gives in to the boss's advances. Yanyan turns to a foreign co-worker. Ameng is interested mainly in business achievement, but her career seems headed downwards when she rejects a contract with a company she believes makes poor quality products. However, she presents evidence at a board meeting which justifies her

actions and impresses the brass. A Taiwan cor-poration appoints her their Shanghai representa-tive. In addition, she finds romance with Jiang Xiang, a music school professor.

1455. *Oh! Sweet Snow (O! Xiang Xue)*

1989. Children's Film Studio. Color. 9 Reels. Letterboxed. Direction: Wang Haowei. Screen-play: Tie Ning, Wang Liu, Xie Xiaojin, based on an original story by Tie Ning (1957–). Cine-matography: Li Chengsheng. Art Direction: Lin Chaoxiang. Music: Zhang Qingyi. Sound: Tao Jing. Cast: Xue Bai as Xiangxue (Sweet Snow), Zhuang Li as Feng Jiao, Tang Ye as Duo'er

A train filled with passengers from the big city begins daily service to the small mountain village of Tai'ergou. The train shatters the vil-lage's tranquility but brings new hope to the people who live there. Xiangxue comes daily with her friends to see the train, and they learn much about the outside world. Xiangxue has long dreamed of owning a plastic pencil box. One day, she plucks up her courage to board the train, where she manages to trade some eggs for a colorful pencil box. But she forgets to get off the train in time, and has an unex-pected adventure.

1456. *OK! Big-belly Arhat (OK! Da Du Luo Han)*

1988. Beijing Film Studio. Color. 9 Reels. Direction: Zhang Huaxun. Screenplay: Zhao Bing. Cinematography: Tu Jiakuan. Art Direc-tion: Ma Gaiwa. Music: Xu Jingqin. Sound: Guan Shuxin. Cast: Gao Yinpei as Bao Lin, Wang Housheng as Yue Yi, Guo Qi as Hong Xiangqin

When a Sichuan opera troupe in a small town is invited to perform a famous classical Chinese opera abroad, many local people hav-ing little or no connection to the troupe see the opportunity for a possible junket. They comically resort to every possible means and pull every string to be part of the delegation. The delegation winds up teeming with officials and others with political connections but very few singers.

1457. *An Old and Well-known Steel-working Family (Gang Tie Shi Jia)*

1959. Tianma Film Studio. Color. 10 Reels.

Direction: Tang Xiaodan. Screenplay: Hu Wanchun. Cinematography: Shen Xilin. Art Direction: Zhang Hancheng. Music: Lu Qiming. Sound: Gong Zhenming. Cast: Qi Heng as Meng Cangtai and Meng Guangfa, Fan Xuepeng as Mrs. Meng, Wang Qi as Meng Daniu, Er Lin as Meng Xiaocui, Shi Jiufeng as Little Afang, Zhang Yan as Liu Guishan, Shi Shugui as Liu Guilan, Jin Naihua as Ma Zhenmin, Yu Fei as Engineer Tang

In pre-liberation Shanghai, three generations of Meng Guangfa's family are steelworkers in the same mill. Shortly after liberation, grandfather Meng Cangtai is murdered by an old enemy. Later, his grandson Meng Daniu has an accident when testing a new method for making steel rapidly because his lack of experience causes him to ignore the opinions of his fiancée, technician Liu Guilan. Her father Liu Guishan, who had been opposed to the new procedure from the start, demands Meng Daniu be punished and the testing discontinued. But with the encouragement of Party Committee Secretary Ma, Meng Guangfa continues to support his son's experiments. Soon after, Meng Guangfa is promoted to deputy director of the mill, and Daniu and Guilan are married. During the Great Leap Forward campaign, Meng Guangfa helps his son's in-laws to overcome their conservative thinking by using advanced production technology successfully and accomplishing the mill's production target ahead of schedule. Inspired by her father, Meng Guangfa's daughter Xiao Cui also becomes an outstanding woman steelworker.

1458. *Old Ge (Ge Lao Ye Zi)*

1993. Changchun Film Studio. Color. Letterboxed. Dolby Sound. Direction: Han Gang. Screenplay: Jiang Yi. Cinematography: Jin Zhi, Zhang Weimin. Art Direction: Li Yongxin. Music: Mo Fan. Cast: Li Baotian as Old Ge, Jiang Wu as Ge Jun, Ma Xiaoqing as Li Xia, Fang Shu as Su Jing, Liu Jian as Wang Xiang

In an industrial city in North China lives a man named Old Ge and his adult grandson Ge Jun. The younger man's parents had died years before, and he had been raised by his grandfather. When Old Ge retires, he still goes to the steel mill every day to pick up scrap metal to sell, and in this way supplement his pension. The grandson, manager of a fashionable cafe, dislikes his grandfather's life style and offers to support Old Ge in a more dignified manner. Old Ge cannot accept this; his life has always been lived a certain way, and he sees no reason

to change. The two often quarrel over the matter, and at last Old Ge packs his meager belongings and leaves, leaving his grandson very confused.

1459. *The Old Man and His Dog (Lao Ren He Gou)*

1993. Xiejin-Hengtong Film Company Ltd. Color. Wide Screen. 9 Reels. Direction: Xie Jin. Screenplay: Li Zhun, based on Zhang Xianliang's novel of the same title. Cinematography: Lu Junfu. Art Direction: Fei Lansheng. Music: Jin Fuzai. Sound: Guan Shuxin. Costume: He Juandi. Makeup: Gao Juan. Cast: Xie Tian as Xing Laohan, Siqin Gaowa as Nunu, Gao Baocheng as Wei Laohan, Feng Enhe as Director Wei, Meng Jing as Ma Shanpo

In the Northwest China countryside in the late 1970s, an old bachelor named Xing lives alone, with only his loyal dog for company. One day, a woman in her 30s comes to his door begging for food. The area she comes from has been devastated by a natural disaster, and the people there are starving. He gives her food and lets her stay. For the only time in his life, Xing has a wife. However, Nunu is worried because she left home without permission. One day, she gets word that her family has suffered further, and she is particularly worried about her 14-year-old child. So, after their short period of happiness, she leaves him. At that time, the village receives an order that all dogs must be killed to conserve food supplies, so the old man loses his faithful dog as well. Winter comes, and one cold morning when snow covers everything, his neighbors find the old man will never rise again.

1460. *Old Restaurant (aka Peking Duck Restaurant) (Lao Dian)*

1990. Shanghai Tianma Film Corporation and China Film Distribution and Exhibition Corporation Co-Production. Color. 14 Reels. Wide Screen. Direction: Gu Rong. Screenplay: Gu Rong. Cinematography: Shen Xilin, Qian Tao. Art Direction: Liu Fan, Shi Jianquan. Music: Ma Ding. Sound: Lu Jiajing, Zhang Ji. Cast: Chen Baoguo as Yang Mingquan, Xu Songzi as Yuhuan and the film director

A young woman, an overseas Chinese film director, pays a visit to the Great Wall. In a small village near the wall, she visits the grave of her grandmother, and there she meets Tian Shun, a centenarian who lives nearby. He relates to her the history of Beijing's famous

Old Restaurant (aka Peking Duck Restaurant). **Restaurant owner Yang Mingquan (Chen Baoguo, left) and his employee Tian Shun (Zhao Liang, second left) buying supplies for the soon-to-be-famous restaurant. 1990. Shanghai Tianma Film Corporation and China Film Distribution and Exhibition Corporation Co-Production.**

Quanjude Restaurant, world renowned for its roast duck. The old man had once been an employee of the restaurant, owned by a bright and ambitious man named Yang Mingquan. When Yang takes over, his first act is to hire the most skilled chef he could find, and this combined with Yang's excellent management makes the business prosper. But Yang's personal life is not so smooth. He loves Mrs. Yuhuan, a woman who must support a disabled husband. For a time he has a fling with Miss Jiaxiu, an upper-class woman who soon tires of him. Miss Yuhuan becomes pregnant, and soon afterwards her husband dies. Yang marries her, although he knows the child is not his. Violence erupts at their wedding celebration, and Yuhuan is killed. For half a century, Tian Shun tends their graves.

Best Sound Lu Jiajing and Zhang Ji, 1991 Golden Rooster Awards.

1461. *The Old Temple Bell Rings (Gu Sha Zhong Sheng)*

1958. Changchun Film Studio. B & W. 9

Reels. Direction: Zhu Wenshun. Screenplay: Liu Baode. Cinematography: Chen Minhun. Art Direction: Wang Tao. Music: Lou Zhanghou. Sound: Hong Jiahui. Cast: Pang Xueqing as Division Head Wang, Tian Lie as the old monk, Li Xida as Huzhi, Chen Keran as the little monk, Pu Ke as Minister Zhou, Kou Jianfu as the gangster chief

During World War II, a group of Japanese collaborator special agents hide out in an old temple to carry out sabotage activities. Chinese reconnaissance division head Wang and a soldier Huzhi enter the old temple in disguise, pretending to be pilgrims seeking restored health. There they find only an old monk and a mute little monk. From the little monk, they learn that gangsters had killed all the real monks in the temple five years before, then made the temple their sabotage base. The chief of the gang is a collaborationist brigade commander disguised as the old monk, and he has fed the little monk a potion which makes him mute. Wang finally discovers the enemy gang's hideout in the temple basement, then he leaves Huzhi to keep an eye on them while he goes back to headquarters to report. The old monk arranges to kill Wang on route, but he is saved by a local huntsman. Wang reports the situation at the temple, and Chinese soldiers round up all the Japanese collaborators there.

1462. *Old Well (Lao Jing)*

1987. Xi'an Film Studio. Color. Wide-screen. 14 Reels. Direction: Wu Tianming. Screenplay: Zheng Yi (1947–), based on his novel of the same title. Cinematography: Chen Wancai, Zhang Yimou. Art Direction: Yang Gang. Music: Xu Youfu. Sound: Li Lanhua. Cast: Zhang Yimou as Sun Wangquan, Liang Yujin as Zhao Qiaoying, Lu Liping as Duan Xifeng, Jie Yan as Sun Wangcai, Niu Xingli as Wan Shui, Zhao Shiji as Crazy Grandpa

Old Well is a village located deep in the Taihang Mountains. There are endless rock-covered mountains, but no water. Over the generations, the people here have dug 127 wells, the deepest more than 50 meters deep, but they have all been dry wells. The inhabitants fondest dream is that one day they will find water on their own land. Sun Wangquan, a native of the village, returns after finishing college determined to use his knowledge to dig a well and find water. His own family is very poor, consisting of five men, all of them bachelors. To reach his goal and to help his brothers get married, Wangquan himself marries Duan Xifeng, a young widow, and sacrifices his real love for Zhao Qiaoying. Led by Sun Wangquan, the villagers overcome many difficulties and finally succeed in digging a first well. Now, they have water.

Best Picture, 1988 Golden Rooster Awards.
Best Picture, 1988 Hundred Flowers Awards.
Best Director Wu Tianming, 1988 Golden Rooster Awards.
Best Actor Zhang Yimou, 1988 Golden Rooster Awards.
Best Actor Zhang Yimou, 1988 Hundred Flowers Awards.
Best Supporting Actress Lu Liping, 1988 Golden Rooster Awards.
Best Supporting Actress Lu Liping, 1988 Hundred Flowers Awards.
Best Picture, 2nd Tokyo International Film Festival.
Best Actor Zhang Yimou, 2nd Tokyo International Film Festival.
First Prize, 11th Salso International Film & TV Festival, Italy.

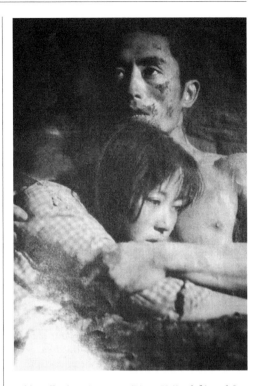

Old Well. Zhao Qiaoying (Liang Yujin, left) and Sun Wangquan (Zhang Yimou) cling to each other after a construction cave-in traps them underground. 1987. Xi'an Film Studio.

1463. *On a Small Street (Xiao Jie)*

1981. Shanghai Film Studio. Color. Letter-boxed. 11 Reels. Direction: Yang Yanjin. Screenplay: Xu Yinghua. Cinematography: Yin Fukang, Zhen Hong. Art Direction: Liu Pan. Music: Xu Jingxin. Sound: Lin Bingsheng. Cast: Zhang Yu as Yu, Guo Kaiming as Xia

A blind young man named Xia relates a tale to a film director. During the Cultural Revolution, Xia was an auto mechanic. He became acquainted with a handsome young person named Yu, a girl who disguised herself as a boy in order to hide her identity as the daughter of a woman labeled as "bad people," cutting her hair short and wearing male clothing to avoid attacks. Xia helps her, is beaten up for it, and loses his sight. After Xia gets out of the hospital, the girl has disappeared. Xia and the director now speculate about what might have become of her and three possible fates are presented: Yu may have ended tragically, ending her life of hardship; Xia hopes that her fate was a happy one, she is now the violinist she dreamed of becoming, and one day they will meet again, this time to stay together. In reality, Yu's fate was actually more ordinary: after fruitlessly searching for Xia, she has become a worker in a textile plant. One day they just happen to meet on a train, and will build a new life together.

1464. *On Misty Mountain (Yun Wu Shan Zhong)*

1959. Changchun Film Studio. B & W. 9 Reels. Direction: Huang Ye. Screenplay: Shi Chao, Wang Derong. Cinematography: Meng Xiandi. Art Direction: Li Junjie, Wang Jixian. Music: Chen Ming. Sound: Zhang Jianping. Cast: Bai Yinkuan as Tian Dongsheng, Xue Yandong as Zhu Dagang, Zhang Jianyou as Song Xiaochun, Ma Xiyu as the strong man, Ma Shida as the regimental commander, Wang Feng as the company commander, Liu Zengqing as Fang Youzhi, Li Zonglin as Wu Ba

After the liberation of Southwest China, bandit chieftain Wu Ba holes up for a last ditch stand in a naturally dangerous area known as Misty Mountain. To wipe out bandits and Nationalist agents still in the area, PLA platoon leader Tian Dongsheng leads his platoon to reconnoiter Wu Family Village on the mountain. During the operation, Tian attempts to free Fang Youzhi, a farmer held by the agents. Tian and Fang are able to escape, then Tian infiltrates the bandits' headquarters by pretending to be a liaison to them from the Nationalist agents. With the help of a gang member who wants to go straight, he finally coordinates the PLA's main force in wiping out the bandits and enemy agents.

1465. *On the Assassination List (Zai An Sha Min Dan Shang)*

1988. Fujian Film Studio. Color. 10 Reels. Direction: Wu Jianxin. Screenplay: Lu Ye, Cinematography: Xing Shumin. Art Direction: Luo Yurong, Zhao Shaoping. Music: Zhang Shaotong. Sound: Zhu Wenzhong, Chu Rongchun. Cast: Zhen Qianlong as Tao Jingguang, Hao Wenhai as Mao Zhaixing, Li Yongyong as Dong Shishi

In 1948, shortly before the fall of the mainland to the Communists, Nationalist intelligence chief Mao Renfeng arranges for the assassinations of several government officials believed to be Communist sympathizers. He also orders one of his intelligence officers to take some highly valuable treasures and rare books to Taiwan. The officer, Tao Jingguang, recognizes the Nationalists' corruption, so in order to have a future for himself, he takes the treasures to Hong Kong instead. The film tells how the CPC rescues Tao from assassination and help him return the treasures to the mainland and the Chinese people.

1466. *On the Banks of the Yellow River (Huang He Zhi Bing)*

1984. Changchun Film Studio. Color. Letterboxed. 10 Reels. Direction: Li Qiankuan, Xiao Guiyun. Screenplay: Zhang Xiaotian. Cinematography: Han Dongxia. Art Direction: Zhong Quan. Music: Si Wanchun. Sound: Yi Wenyu. Cast: Huang Kai as Wei Xingbang, Wang Yingshen as Geng Changfa, Zhu Decheng as Xin Zhaohai, Hong Xueming as Xiangni, Chen Huiliang as Liu Hui, Xie Fang as Su Hui

The struggles of an honest Party official through some difficult years. During the Great Leap Forward, Prefectural Secretary Wei Xingbang receives a letter from two old friends, Geng Changfa and his sister Xiangni, informing him that official production statistics he is receiving are grossly inflated. Wei investigates and confirms what they say. But when he relays his findings to higher authority he is disciplined and demoted to County Secretary. When the Soviet Union withdraws its financial aid and China enters three years of depression, Xiangni is unable to bear it any longer and commits suicide. Geng Changfa breaks off his relationship with Wei out of hatred for all officials. Later, after the 3rd Plenary Session of the 11th Party Congress, Wei works himself to death carrying out the reforms.

1467. *On the Banks of Yanming Lake (Yan Ming Hu Pan)*

1976. Changchun Film Studio. Color. 11 Reels. Direction: Gao Tianhong. Screenplay: Zhang Xiaotian and Wang Weicheng, based on the novel of the same title. Cinematography: Tang Yunsheng. Art Direction: Guo Yansheng. Music: Wu Damin. Cast: Zhang Liwei as Lan Haiying, Shi Kefu as Zhang Houde, Ye Zhikang as Song Changyou, Wang Haomin as Lan Haitao, Lu Yalin as Miao Chunlan, Da Lintai as Zhen Chengshan, Ge Cunzhuang as Lin Daquan, Zhang Zhanghua as Chen Tu

In 1971, to use it for illegal activities, Lin Daquan gains control of the medical aid station in a farm community. His various schemes include selling medicine at inflated prices and selling expired drugs, etc. Lan Haiying, a young woman from the city and recently graduated from college, detects and exposes Lin's crimes. But with the support of local cadres who have a weak sense of the class struggle, Lin is able to retain control of the station. When Haiying suggests that digging a new well would prevent disease by improving water quality, Lin Daquan attempts to destroy this project in order to keep up his drug sales. Lan Haiying is at last successful in exposing Lin's scheme.

1468. *On the Beat (Min Jing Gu Shi)*

1995. Eurasia Communications, Euskal Media and Beijing Film Studio Co-Production. Color. 102 minutes. Direction and Screenplay: Ning Ying. Cinematography: Zhi Lei, Wu Hongwei. Art Direction: Cheng Guangming. Music: Su Cong. Sound: (Dolby), Chao Jun. Cast: Li Zhanhe as Yang Guoli, Wang Lianggui as Wang Liangui, Li Jian as Li Jian, Shen Zhen'ou as Liu Jianjun, Wan Jianjun as Wan Jun, Li Chen'gang as the Precinct Chief, Li Wensheng as the Political Commissar, Pan Yongzhen as the Divisional Chief, Li Li as Yang's Wife, Zhao Zhiming as Wang Xiao'er, Liu Yingshu as Liu, the Vagrant

The daily life of a cop on the beat, portrayed as far from the usual movie or television image of the profession. Immediately after an inspirational speech to new officers, a cynical, world-weary veteran introduces one of the newcomers, Yang Guoli, to the realities of his beat, including what he terms the "granny cops," local women who maintain well-indexed and cross-referenced files on the entire neighborhood. Yang soon finds that daily police life holds little glamour, being taken up with such tasks as tracking down wild dogs, routine arrests, but always with the possibility of sudden and unexpected violence. He derives little respite from his life at home, where a nagging wife holds sway. At the same time, petty bureaucracy and an official preoccupation with the trivial appear to be the norm.

1469. *On the Enemy's Trail (Gen Zong Zhui Ji)*

1963. Pearl River Film Studio. B & W. 10 Reels. Direction: Lu Yu. Screenplay: Zhu Xiangqun, An Zhongmin. Cinematography: Shen Minghui. Art Direction: Huang Zhiming. Music: Wang Zhengdong. Sound: Lin Guang. Cast: Lin Lan as Li Minggang, Lin Shujing as Xiao Huang, Shi Jing as Qian Jiaren, Hong Bing as Xu Ying, Chen Tianzhong as Teacher He, Jian Ruichao as Lin Dexiang, Gu Langhui as Lin Yonggui

In 1961, Qian Jiaren and Lin Yonggui, agents in the employ of the U.S. and Taiwan, smuggle explosives into Guangzhou in preparation for subversive activities. Acting on the clue of an old lady's handbag being switched with another bag holding suspicious contents, Chinese public security officers Li Minggang and Xiao Huang learn that Lin Yonggui had made the exchange. They apprehend Lin and successfully turn him into a double agent, in hopes he will lead them to the rest of the agents. However, their counterespionage plan is detected by Qian Jiaren, who abandons Lin and the original plan. Qian plants the bomb in another location in the power station, wiring it to a timer. Li Minggang learns the new location and rushes to the power station in time to disarm the bomb. When Qian Jiaren and other agents attempt to flee, they are captured by the public security officers.

1470. *On the Hunting Ground (La Chang Zha Sha)*

1985. Inner Mongolia Film Studio. Color. 8 Reels. Direction: Tian Zhuangzhuang. Screenplay: Jiang Ao. Cinematography: Lu Le, Hou Yong. Art Direction: Zhang Xiaoan, Li Geng. Music: Ju Xiaosong. Sound: Wu Ling. Cast: Bayaertu as Wangsheng Zhabu, Laxi as Rigalang, Aotegeng Bayaer as Bayasi Guleng, Shewang Daoerji as Tao Getao

When Mongolian hunter Wangsheng Zhabu violates the traditional rules of the hunting ground, local administrator Bayasi Guleng sentences him to the traditional punishment of being beaten by his elderly mother. This so infuriates his brother Tao Getao that he decides to take revenge on Bayasi Guleng by leading a wolf to the administrator's sheep ranch. The movie tells how the brothers finally awaken to their own shortcomings and reconcile themselves to hunting ground rules.

1471. *On the Progressive Road (Zai Qian Jin De Lu Shang)*

1950. Northeast Film Studio. B & W. 10 Reels. Direction: Cheng Ying. Screenplay: Yue Ye. Cinematography: Wang Chunquan. Set Design: Xu Wei. Music: Gao Tian. Sound: Lin Bingcheng. Costume: Xiang Yuhuan. Makeup: Wang Shiru, Yang Shiya. Cast: Lu Fei as Luo Zhen, Gao Ping as Liu Si, Chen Ge as He Zhongguang, Zhang Wei as Jiang Hui, Bi Lianlu as Jin Kang, Lu Min as Luo Cunyu

In the winter of 1949, two former army

buddies are assigned the task of resolving the frequent traffic jams which plague rail transport in a certain Northeast China city. One of these, He Zhongguang, is somewhat over-confident because of his past successes, and decides on his own to resolve the problem by building a new railway yard. However, his friend Luo Zhen advocates the adoption of an advanced train allocation system used in the Soviet Union. The Railway Administrative Bureau backs Luo's plan, and the traffic jam problem is worked out successfully. Finally, upper level leaders decide to remove He from his position as Director of the railway branch, and he is sent for study.

1472. *On the 30th Floor (San Shi Chen Lou Shang)*

1986. Changchun Film Studio. Color. 10 Reels. Direction: Bei Zhaocheng, Li Geng. Screenplay: Mu Er, Ju Xiangqi, Zhang Yongming. Cinematography: Jia Shouxing. Art Direction: Gao Tinglun, Yang Baocheng. Music: Liu Yanxi. Sound: Huang Lijia, Fang Yongming. Cast: Yin Yanping as Jin Jingjing, Du Jieqi as Ma Feijin, Ling Yunyi as Yan Fangfang, Lu Chengsheng as Wang Boyong, Yin Yuguan as Huang Zhilang

A 30-story building is planned for a scenic site at Suzhou. Huang Zhilang returns to China from abroad to recruit people to landscape the building's grounds. A woman named Yan Fangfang contracts for the project but then must persuade her manager husband to cooperate with Huang.

1473. *On the 38th Parallel (San Ba Xian Shang)*

1960. August First Film Studio. B & W. 8 Reels. Direction: Shi Wenzhi. Screenplay: Ma Jixing, based on the PLA Frontline Cultural Troupe's stage play of the same title. Cinematography: Cao Jingyun. Art Direction: Fang Xuzi, Kou Honglie. Music: Wang Zhengya. Sound: Wu Hanbiao. Cast: Wang Boling as the old woman, Zhang Liang as Little Thing, Xing Jitian as the PLA senior general, Yang Zhenghuai as the company commander, Jia Xuewu as the squad leader, Yao Yongyue as Niu Dahai, Gao Junqin as Liu Xuezhi, Feng Zhenkun as Li Yulan

In 1953, after the Korean Cease Fire, an American general sends two agents across the border into North Korea to locate a Japanese war criminal. The agents are veteran Qiao Shan and a young Korean man named Cui

Chunsheng. The Japanese has been hiding in Korea for years, and has valuable military intelligence for the U.S. On their return, Qiao and Cui are discovered. In their flight, Cui suffers a leg wound and hides in the home of an old woman. Suspicious of the two, she tries to report them to the Chinese Volunteer Army, but Cui stabs the old woman and then flees. When the spies are caught by North Korean and Chinese soldiers, they at first refuse to talk. But then Cui discovers that the old woman he stabbed had been his own mother, whom he had not seen for many years. He had been deceived into believing the Communists had killed both his parents. Confronted by the facts, he awakens to reality and exposes the U.S.-South Korean conspiracy.

On the Train **see** *A Thousand Miles a Day*

1474. *On This Piece of Land (Zai Zhe Pian Tu Di Shang)*

1982. Pearl River Film Studio. Color. 10 Reels. Direction: Xu Dan, Wang Yi. Screenplay: Shi Yong, Meng Shenghui, Si Minshan. Cinematography: Lu Dongqin. Art Direction: Tan Ancang. Music: Tie Yuan Qin Yongcheng. Sound: Wu Chengxin. Cast: Zhang Jie as Tang Yuda, Wu Jiao as Yan Shougeng, Bai Li as Wan Tianhong, Liang Xueqiu as Mi Sihua

On the eve of the 3rd Plenary Session of the 11th Party Congress, Wan Tianhong arrives at a new construction site as deputy director of the technical department. There he meets Tang Yuda, an old colleague from 30 years before. Tang has been removed from his managerial post for urging technical renovation at the site. But Wan is also committed to renovation, and enlists Tang's support. Their main opposition comes from bureaucrat Yan Shougeng, who begins even further persecution of Tang. Tang collapses from pressure and overwork, and is hospitalized. The entire situation changes dramatically when the 3rd Plenary Session is held.

1475. *Once He Learned He Was Japanese (Hun Dang Dong Yang)*

1987. Pearl River Film Studio. Color. 9 Reels. director: Sun Yu. Screenplay: Meng Fan. Cinematography: Wu Libeng. Art Direction: Huang Chaohui. Music: Zhang Hong. Sound: Lin

Guoqiang. Cast: Chang Lantian as Hou Gennan, Yang Hongwen as Cheng Mancui, Guo Zhenqin as the Troupe Director, Li Wanfen as Mother-in-Law

Hou Gennan wants to be an opera performer, but his skills are so minimal the local troupe cannot even offer him supporting roles. In order to at least be on the periphery of the art, Hou contracts to do cleaning work outside the theater. His life takes a sudden and dramatic turn when his mother tells him he is not Chinese, but a Japanese orphan she adopted from a "Mrs. Kong" some 40 years before. Learning he has Japanese blood excites Hou, and he finds that others change their attitude toward him as well. Even the opera troupe changes its evaluation of his talent, and assigns him a leading role in a major production. His nagging wife and mother-in-law change their treatment of Hou from hostility to respect and admiration. He undertakes to find his birth mother and learn more details of his background. However, when he finds Mrs. Kong, she is too old and feeble to provide any details of his background, or even confirm that he really is Japanese. Hou Gennan's Japanese dream is shattered.

1476. *Once Upon a Time in China III (Shi Wang Zheng Ba)*

1993. Beijing Film Studio & Hong Kong Film Workshop Company Ltd. Co-Production. Color. Wide Screen. 12 Reels. Direction: Xu Ke (Tsui Hark). Screenplay: Xu Ke, Zhang Tan, Chen Tianxuan. Cinematography: Liu Weiqiang. Art Direction: Yuan Bing. Cast: Li Lianjie (Jet Li) as Huang Feihong (Cantonese: Wong Fei Hung), Guan Zhilin (Rosamund Kwan) as 13th Aunt, Mo Shaochong, Liu Xun, Xiong Xinxin, Zhao Jian, Ge Chunzuang, Meng Jing, Huang Deren

During a troubled time in China in the late 1800s, the corrupt Empress Dowager and her favorite senior official Li Hongzhang decide to hold a Lion Dance Competition. But the Lion Dance (martial arts) schools see the competition as an opportunity to boost their strength, causing much chaos and fighting. Huang Feihong, the best martial artist in China, travels to Beijing to visit his father, a lion-head manufacturer, and is forced to defend his father's school against an aggressive rival. Huang manages this, but 13th Aunt, his fiancee, runs into an old Russian boyfriend who gives her a motion picture camera as a gift. The camera captures a plot by the Russian officer to assassinate Li Hongzhang during the Lion Dance Competition. Huang enters the Competition to stop the attempted assassination.

Best Co-Production picture, 1994 Hundred Flowers Awards.

1477. *Once Upon a Time in China IV (Wang Zhe Zhi Feng)*

1993. Beijing Film Studio & Hong Kong Film Workshop Company Ltd. Co-Production. Color. Wide Screen. 10 Reels. Direction: Yuan Bing. Screenplay: Xu Ke (Tsui Hark), Deng Biyan, Cheng Tianxuan. Art Direction: Li Jingwen, Fu Delin. Music: Hu Weili. Sound: Zhou Shaolong, Zhou Jingrong. Costume: Huang Baorong. Makeup: Guan Lina, Yu Baozhong, Li Lihua. Cast: Zhao Wenzhuo as Huang Feihong (Cantonese: Wong Fei Hung), Wang Jingying as 14th Aunt, Mo Shaocong as Liang Kuan, Liu Xun as Huang Linying, Xiong Xinxin as Gui Jiaoqi, Wang Jinghua as Miao Sanniang

In 1900, when the eight allied foreign armies invade North China to help suppress the Boxer Rebellion, they are opposed by a group called the Red Lanterns. Folk hero Huang Feihong, about to return to his home in Guangzhou, decides to stay and help the resistance. Many Chinese fighters are killed by the foreigners' superior weaponry but at last Huang gains some vengeance in a fight. As the foreign armies mass for a push on Beijing, Huang realizes that one man alone cannot change the course of history or the fate of an entire nation. He leaves for Fushan temporarily to await further opportunities to fight for China in the future.

1478. *One and Eight (Yi Ge He Ba Ge)*

1984. Guangxi Film Studio. Color. Letterboxed. 9 Reels. Direction: Zhang Junzhao. Screenplay: Zhang Ziliang, Wang Jicheng. Cinematography: Zhang Yimou, Xiao Feng. Art Direction: He Qun. Sound: Zhang Yu. Costume: Chen Bona. Makeup: He Hong, Zhu Xiaoling. Cast: Tao Zeru as Wang Jin, Chen Daomin as Xu Zhi, Zhao Xiaorui as Da Tuzi, Zhao Jianwen as Cu Meimao, Lu Xiaoyan as Yang Qiner, Wei Zongwan as Lao Wantou, Ju Chunhua as Shou Yangui, Xin Min as Da Gezi, Liu Honggang as Little Dog, Xie Yuan as spy

On the Jinzhong Plain of North China during World War II, Eighth Route Army political instructor Wang Jin is accused of spying for the Japanese. While there is no evidence of this, and the man making the accusation is himself believed to be a traitor, Wang is arrested pending further investigation. Wang, very upset and demanding a full review by higher authority, is put in a cell with eight prisoners being transported for trial or military court martial. The eight, who had been planning an escape, are at first suspicious the newcomer may be an informer planted among them. In these hostile surroundings, Wang maintains his dignity and conducts himself as an officer should. The other prisoners acquire a growing respect for Wang, and at last conclude he is innocent. At this time, the Japanese cut off all contact the troops have with the outside, and during a firefight, the only person who can prove Wang's innocence is killed. Company Commander Xu Zhi realizes they must get out of their situation, and leads a breakout, taking the shackled prisoners along. The company suffers severe casualties as they travel and fight, and when Commander Xu is wounded, he orders the prisoners released to fight as well. Most of them go down fighting bravely while Wang's accuser reveals he really is a traitor and is killed. At last, Wang Jin, Xu Zhi and escaped convict Chu Meimao reach safety. Just before they arrive at the army base, Chu Meimao says goodbye: he promises never to oppose the Communists, fight the Eighth Route Army or harm common people. He leaves, and Wang and Xu continue on to their base.

1479. *One Family, Two Systems (Yi Jia, Liang Zhi)*

1994. Shenzhen Film Company. Color. 10 Reels. Direction: Chen Guoxing. Screenplay: Liu Xueqiang, Ju Sheng. Cinematography: Zhao Xiaoding. Art Direction: Yang Hong. Music: Chen Xiangyu. Sound: Guan Jian. Costume: Liu Huiping. Makeup: Cui Jie. Cast: Tang Zhenzong as A Wen, Yan Xiaoping as Xiao Jia, Zhang Zhen as Uncle, Wen Bo as Kun Shu, Li Li as Xixi, Wu Weidong as Engineer Zhang

A Wen is the CEO of the Lanyu Electronics Company, of which his uncle is president. A Wen has a dispute over a technical design matter with Xiaojia, a woman engineer. A Wen's uncle is pressuring the younger man to get married, something A Wen is not anxious to do. To appease his uncle, and assure he will inherit control of the company in the future, A

Wen asks Xiaojia to pretend to be his wife; although they don't get along, she is about the only single woman he knows. She agrees, and it turns out the uncle thinks she is marvelous, the best decision his nephew ever made. When the company is in a competitive struggle, A Wen and Xiaojia work closely together, and in the process really fall in love. At last, in spite of their differing backgrounds and personalities, they start a real family together — one family with two systems.

1480. *One Man's Family (Xiao Da Lao Zhuan)*

1987. Yunnan Film Studio. Color. 10 Reels. Direction: Zhang Gang. Screenplay: Zhang Gang. Cinematography: Zhen Wangong. Art Direction: Wang Renchen. Music: Jin Fuzhai. Sound: Zhu Yong. Cast: Zhong Xinghuo as Luo Laoman, Dai Zhaoan as Daman, Sun Yanan as Luo Xiuzhi, Liu Junxiang as Xiaoman

Kindly and honest old worker Luo Laoman becomes a volunteer reserve policeman assigned as a traffic cop. While his son Daman is an honest and conscientious worker at a plush restaurant, Laoman's daughter Luo Xiuzhi is so anxious to go abroad that she stoops to doing some rather disgraceful things. At last, Xiuzhi is exploited by a confidence man claiming to be an overseas Chinese. Although Laoman's life is basically happy, things such as this sometimes make him want to cry.

1481. *One Night Is a Hundred Years (Yi Xi Shi Bai Nian)*

1991. Pearl River Film Studio. Color. Letterboxed. 9 Reels. Direction: Chen Ying, Shao Xuehai. Screenplay: Yang Jifu. Cinematography: Wu Yukun. Art Direction: Gu Jiadong. Music: Yu Linqin. Sound: Liu Haiyan. Cast: Hu Yajie as Li Tao, Ju Xue as Xiuzhi, Tang Lu as Liying, Hou Jilin as Yulan, Song Dewang as Uncle, Fu Yunxian as Mother, Liu Tongwei as Sha Jizu

The lives and romantic pursuits of some young intellectuals in the 1940s. The story focuses on a college student and his relationships with three young women.

1482. *One Night Pop Star (Yi Ye Ge Xing)*

1988. Shanghai Film Studio. Color. Wide Screen. 15 Reels. Direction: Zuang Hongsheng. Screenplay: Han Jingting. Cinematography: Shen Miaorong. Art Direction: Wang Xingcang.

Music: Xu Xinjing. Sound (Dolby): Ren Daming. Cast: Liu Xiaomin as Da Bao, Liu Xiaochun as Bao Zhu, Jin Meng as Xiao Xue, Tong Jiaqi as Da Kang

An arts company is on route to give a performance in a certain city, when its star singer Jiang Fei is delayed for personal reasons. Troupe manager Da Kang finds a man named Da Bao who is amazingly like Jiang Fei in both voice and appearance, so he has the man replace Jiang Fei for one evening's show. Da Bao is an enormous success, so when the real Jiang Fei is further delayed, the manager keeps Da Bao on. But the instant success and acclaim go to Da Bao's head; he becomes very greedy, demanding such things as residence in a hotel presidential suite, and before long he even abandons his fiancee Xia Xue. Later, Dao Bao develops a throat ailment which ends his career, and Da Kang and his wife flee when they see the hoax will be discovered. Jiang Fei finally goes to meet Da Bao and encourages him to be a true person and not live a fantasy.

1483. *The One Who Helped Me Get on My War Horse (Fu Wo Shang Zhan Ma De Ren)*

1983. Children's Film Studio. Color. 8 Reels. Direction: Zhao Yuan, Zhen Jianmin. Screenplay: Zhang Yingwen. Cinematography: Yu Zhengyu. Art Direction: Cheng Rongyuan. Music: Yan Fei. Sound: Ren Shanpu. Cast: Lei Fei as Peng Dehuai, Zhang Weimin as Gouwa, Zhou Haibin as Qiangqiang, Xue Junjie as Xiao Yang, Cui Tong as Da Yang, Zhang Dayong as Huzi, Zhang Yansong as Xiao Liu, Tan Xin as the big guy

A group of boys who call themselves the "Eight Tough Guys" live in a riverside village in northern Shanxi Province. Their leader is a boy named Gouwa. One day PLA Deputy Commander Peng Dehuai comes into their village on a white horse. The kids love the horse, and dream of someday riding it. Peng's army is encamped nearby, and he is in the village to establish an anti–Japanese village school. When he learns the boys' desire to ride the horse, he tells them that if the "tough guys" will set an example for the rest of the village children and study hard, the best student will get to ride his white horse. The eight boys do exactly that, and finally Gouwa gets the ride. He feels as if he is a soldier riding his horse on the battlefield.

1484. *One Who Lights the Morning Sunlight (Dian Ran Zhao Xia De Ren)*

1984. Changchun Film Studio. Color. Letterboxed. 10 Reels. Direction: Su Li. Screenplay: Wang Dongman. Cinematography: Liu Yongzhen. Art Direction: Wang Guizhi, Liang Guangchuan. Music: Gao Feng. Sound: Tong Zongde. Cast: Yi Fuwen as Ruan Jinbiao, Zhao Fengxia as He Dafeng, Song Ge as Wan Jingui, Liu Qun as Xinghua, Yi Ga as Li Ergui

After the 3rd Plenary Session of the 11th Party Congress, one brick-making plant decides to sub-contract some of its work to individual entrepreneurs. A group of young people led by Ruan Jinbiao gets the contract, but run into opposition from veteran brickyard worker Wan Jingui. Ruan's group expands its team, purchases new facilities and is successful.

1485. *The Open Window (Chang Kai De Chuang Hu)*

1982. Children's Film Studio. Color. 4 Reels. Direction: Shi Lin. Screenplay: Yang Fuqin, Shi Lin, Shi Heng. Cinematography: Wei Tong. Art Direction: Chen Zhuo. Music: Li Wanli. Sound: Zhang Zhian. Cast: Li Yintao as Niu Qiang, Liu Qin as Lin Xiaojuan, Wu Wei as Teacher Jin

Elementary school student Niu Qiang is honest, brave and considerate of others. He is also a star on his class soccer team. He courageously criticizes Teacher Jin by telling him that the teacher assigns too much homework every day, putting excessive pressure on the students. When Zhang Dajun, a bad student who often bullies other students, tries to bully Niu Qiang and his friend Lin Xiaojuan, Niu fights him. Teacher Jin, still smarting from being criticized by a student, punishes Niu Qiang without investigating the incident at all. But Lin Xiaojuan and class leader Xu Jianmei go to Teacher Jin's home to tell the facts about the fight. Teacher Jin is moved, feels guilty, and concludes the problem lies in his teaching. One night, Teacher Jin goes to Niu Qiang's home, acknowledges his mistake and gives the boy a pair of sports shoes. With the barriers between teacher and students now gone, they are finally communicating.

1486. *The Opera House Legend (Li Yuan Chuan Qi)*

1982. Emei Film Studio. Color. 10 Reels. Direction: Yang Gaisheng, Zhang Lukun.

Screenplay: Wei Minlun, Nan Guo. Cinematography: Cheng Zhaoxun, You Zongshi. Art Direction: Chen Desheng. Music: Tian Feng, Chen Zhimei. Sound: Zhang Jianping. Cast: Zhang Xianheng as Yi Danda, Zhu Ling as Hua Xiangrong, Liu Jian as Jiu Lingtong, Guan Zongxiang as Le Shanren, Yan Pide as Ma Wuye, Zhao Shulan as Yi's wife, Guo Qi as Ma's wife

Toward the end of the Manchu Dynasty (c1910), the Sanhe Opera Troupe arrives in a small town to perform, but are stopped from doing so by Le and Ma, two local thugs. The head of the troupe, Yi Danda, struggles with the two, and at last the troupe is able to perform. The harassment goes on, though, as both Le and Ma desire the actress Hua Xiangrong. The troupe continually outwits the two men, however, and at last leaves town. They realize, sadly, that no matter where they go in that society there will be no place for them.

1487. *Opera Teacher and Students (Ying Yan Tao Li)*

1984. Shanghai Film Studio. Color. Letterboxed. 9 Reels. Direction: Wu Wenpu. Screenplay: Zen Shaohong, Zhang Ronghua. Cinematography: Can Lianguo. Art Direction: Li Runzhi, Lin Guoliang. Music: Yang Shaolu. Sound: Feng Deyao. Cast: Gu Yongfei as Liu Ying, He Qing as Bai Tao, Chen Shujun as Xia Yan, Dong Peifen as Bai Li

Liu Ying, a famous opera singer, accepts music student Bai Tao as her apprentice. The girl progresses rapidly under Liu Ying's tutelage, and receives a performing award. Rapid success soon goes to Bai Tao's head. She begins missing rehearsals, and even skips a performance to attend to personal business. In her absence, the troupe replaces her with another young singer, and when Bai Tao returns she finds she is no longer being cast in lead roles. She creates a lot of unpleasantness about this, but at last she faces reality and realizes her mistakes. She vows to start over again, work hard, and win back her stardom.

1488. *Opium Enforcement Gunman (Jing Yan Qiang Shou)*

1990. Shanghai Film Studio. Color. Wide Screen. 10 Reels. Direction: Da Shibiao. Screenplay: Gu Bai. Cinematography: Cheng Shiyu. Art Direction: Zhang Chongxiang. Music: Liu Yanxi. Sound: Gong Dejun. Cast: He Ling as Lin Zemin, Jin Lili as Qin Ya, Shen Ming as Wen Kejun, Yu Luosheng as Zhen Zhongyi

In the 1930s, Shanghai is awash in illegal drugs. An innocent bystander, a teacher, is killed during one of the gang wars. One of the teacher's former students, drug enforcement agent Lin Zemin, vows to kill all drug dealers in revenge. Song Jiliang, the biggest drug dealer of them all kidnaps Lin's former girl friend Qin Ya, who is helping the agent. Pursued by the drug kingpin's men, Lin escapes to the home of film make-up artist Wen Kejun, who agrees to help him because both of her parents had died of opium addiction. It turns out that Qin Ya is really a member of the drug ring, and that her abduction was really a ruse designed to trap Lin. Lin Zemin kills both Song and Qin, and Wen Kejun sacrifices her own life to protect Lin.

1489. *Opium Murderer (Xue Bo Di Xiao)*

1994. Emei Film Studio. Color. Letterboxed. 9 Reels. Direction: Zhang Xihe, Hu Tu. Screenplay: Deng Jiahui, Mao Mao. Cinematography: Li Dagui, Zhang Keyi. Art Direction: Cheng Jinyong. Music: Lin Youping. Sound: Tu Liuqing. Costume: Feng Guilan, Zhou Ailing. Makeup: Cao Songlin, Zeng Xiaozhen. Cast: Wen Haitao as Fei Wende, Wu Jian as Xutian Chilang, Xu Xing as Wu Jili, Gao Yuchang as Tang Ruifu, Cheng Xi as Xiangyue Zhizi, Li Li as Luo Li, Li Jing as Leng Xing

After instigating the clash between Japanese and Chinese troops that becomes known as the "September 18th Incident," the Japanese step up their invasion plans. About this time, young Chinese doctor Fei Wende opens a drug rehabilitation clinic in Beijing. A Japanese business which is really a front for drug dealing plans to eliminate this new threat to their business, so they plant an agent in the clinic as an employee. Soon, some of Fei's patients die, and the doctor is blamed. He is beaten up and his clinic destroyed. Fei Wende learns the truth and sets out for revenge. At last, he locates the place where the Japanese process the drugs they sell, and attacks it. His girl friend Luo Li is killed in the fight. The Chinese police arrive in time to rescue Fei Wende. A few days later, the Japanese invade Beijing.

The Opium War **see** *Lin Zexu*

1490. *Orange Garden (Ju Yuan Qing)*

1984. Liaoning Science Film Studio. Color. 10 Reels. Direction: Gao Zheng. Screenplay: Li Daoji, Li Huiming. Cinematography: Xie Erxiang. Art Direction: Si Qiping. Music: Wang Qiang. Sound: Chang Bosheng. Music: Li Li as Chen Chunming, Huang Daliang as Du Xinhe, Wen Xiying as Father, Zhou Liangliang as Grandma

When an unexpected crisis occurs, the families of two lovers, Chunming and Xinhe, pull together for mutual support.

1491. *Orange Harvest Along the Min River (Min Jiang Juzi Hong)*

1955. Shanghai Film Studio. B & W. 9 Reels. Direction: Zhang Ke. Screenplay: Fujian Province Cultural Association Creative Group. Cinematography: Yao Shiquan, Art Direction: Ge Shicheng. Music: Li Yinghai. Sound: Chen Jingrong. Cast: Li Lingjun as Li Yinhua, Zhang Fa as Yang Caifa, Dai Yu as Aunt Yang, Shi Jiufeng as Yang Xiaolong, Zhang Yan as Uncle Wang Hu, Bai Mu as Hu Fuxiang, Xie Yibing as Fuxiang's servant girl, Shi Yuan as An An

Near the Ming River, Li Yinghua, the orange growers' mutual aid association head, and a young man named Yang Xiaolong fall in love while working together. Yang Xiaolong's father, Yang Caifa, confident in his individual skills at orange-growing, chooses to seek his own prosperity rather than join the association, a view his son opposes. At first, the association's inexperience causes some inequities in distribution, prompting some members to threaten to resign. Later, Li Yinghua and her uncle Wang Hu devise and implement a distribution method based on individuals' contribution of labor, which sparks the farmers' enthusiasm. The orange trees suffer a serious insect attack, and veteran farmer Yang Caifa's family secret recipe for insect treatment is ineffective. At this time, the government steps in and lends a hand, and the association overcomes the disaster under Li Yinghua's leadership. It also helps Yang Caifa and other non-member households. Yang Caifa learns from the incident, and he and the other non-member households decide to join the association after all. Li Yinghua and Yang Xiaolong find their love has grown stronger through this.

1492. *An Ordinary Career (Ping Fan De Shi Ye)*

1958. Haiyan Film Studio. B & W. 8 Reels. Direction: Lin Yang. Screenplay: Huang Zongyin. Cinematography: Chen Zhengxiang. Art Direction: Sun Zhang. Music: Ji Min. Sound: Ren Xinliang. Cast: Wang Pei as Lin Peimin, Lu Min as Principal Lu, Huang Wansu as Li Juan, Li Lingjun as Fang Fang, Huang Xiaoqing as Honghong, Zhi Shimin as Mrs. Pan

High school graduate Lin Peimin is assigned to be a caregiver at a kindergarten. At first, she looks down upon nursery work, and pays little attention to it. In addition, co-worker Li Juan teases her, and at one time she almost resigns in anger. But with the help and teaching of Principal Lu she improves her understanding and becomes fond of the children under her care, gradually coming to realize the importance of child care. She finally comes to love her work, and helps Li Juan, who has also been inattentive to her work, realize her errors.

1493. *An Ordinary Household (Pu Tong Ren Jia)*

1984. Beijing Film Studio. Color. Letterboxed. 9 Reels. Direction: Duan Jishun. Screenplay: Ma Lin, Jiang Dafu, Zhu Mei. Cinematography: Li Yuebing. Art Direction: Chen Zhaomin. Music: Wang Ming. Sound: Fu Yinjie. Cast: Zhang Lianwen as Yang Dagan, Wang Shuqing as the wife, Zhang Ping as Master Worker Liu, Li Jian as Grandma, Chang Rong as Li Chi, Tan Tianqian as Engineer Jiang

Life is good for Yang Dagan. Placed in charge of a construction company's carpentry workshop while still very young, he is happily married and has a bright son. Life changes when his neighbor Doctor Ling receives a color TV set as a gift from an overseas relative. It becomes important to Yang to earn more money so he can buy a TV for his family, so he begins moonlighting to earn more, and in time even begins phoning in sick to gain more time for his extra employment. The change in his father begins to affect Yang's son Xiaobao, and Yang also becomes involved in some improper financial dealings. Yang Dagan now regrets that he ever got into this, as he now sees the pursuit of money as dangerous to family life. He decides to return to being the man he used to be.

1494. *Oriental Beauty (Dong Fang Mei Nu)*

1989. Xiaoxiang Film Studio. Color. Letter-boxed. 9 Reels. Direction: Li Jingmin. Screenplay: Lin Yuan. Cinematography: Yan Yunzhao. Art Direction: Li Runzhang. Music: Lu Qimin, Chen Xinguang. Sound: Liu Feng. Cast: Zhang Yiran as Gongteng, Can Xingmei as Yi Jianmei, Si Dasheng as Huang Deshan, Jiang Niao as Zhou Shixiong

When the Japanese occupy Hainan Island, their commander Koteng receives from Chinese traitor Huang Deshan a map detailing where the island's natural resources are located. In addition, the commander claims a beautiful local girl, Yi Jianmei. But Yi is a kung fu master, and uses her skill to put the Japanese commander to sleep. She then runs off with the map. The pursuing enemy kills her father, but with the help of her friend Zhou Shixiong, she at last executes the traitor and the enemy commander.

1495. *The Orient's Greatest Magician (Dong Fang Da Mo Wang)*

1985. Changchun Film Studio. Color. 9 Reels. Direction: Zhu Wenshun, Chen Zhanhe. Screenplay: Xu Jinyan, Zhang Daguang. Cinematography: Dansheng Nima. Art Direction: Gao Guoliang, Du Wencheng. Music: Lei Zhenbang. Sound: Wang Lin. Cast: Han Fei as Zhang Ruosong, Chang Guiju as Du Fangbing, Pang Wanling as the foreigner

In the earliest years of the Republic of China (c1915), Zhang Ruosong, billed as "The Orient's Greatest Magician," is forced to leave his home when his act is interpreted as critical of General Yuan Shikai, China's self-proclaimed new emperor. He changes his name to Chen and travels to Hangzhou in south China where he joins a troupe led by woman magician Du Fangbing. Zhang is excited when the news arrives that Yuan's power grab has been smashed. When he and Du learn that some foreign magicians touring China are giving some performances humiliating to Chinese people, Zhang challenges them. When the foreigners plot to murder him, Zhang is tipped off so he and the troupe can flee Hangzhou to safety.

An Orphan on the Streets **see** *The Watch*

1496. *Ou Mei (Ou Mei)*

1984. Xiaoxiang Film Studio. Color. Letter-boxed. 10 Reels. Direction: Peng Ning. Screenplay: Peng Ning. Cinematography: Zhang Li, Chen Yan. Art Direction: Zhao Jianxi. Music: Si Wanchun. Sound: Lu Xichun. Cast: Shen Hong as Ou Mei, Ma Huiwu as Jin Dou, Wu Qi as Grandma, Wang Yumei as Su Sheng, Yan Bide as Master Worker Dong, Zhao Fan as Lu Shi, Huang Suqi as Liang Boming

Orphaned while just a little girl, Ou Mei is raised by her wet nurse, and grows up with the latter's little boy Liang Boming. Ou Mei loves Boming, and when she grows up determines to save enough money to help him go abroad to study. One day, Ou Mei sees an advertisement recruiting factory workers, she applies and is hired. Her hard work pays off, and Liang Boming goes abroad to attend college. Back at the factory, Ou Mei rises to become factory director, then in time moves up to chief executive of the company which owns the plant. Her methods are not always popular, but they are successful, and the company moves into international trade. Finally, Liang Boming returns, and Ou Mei happily goes to see him. He tells her that he now has another girl friend he met overseas. The disappointed Ou Mei returns to again dedicate herself to her work.

1497. *Our Discharged Soldier (Za Men De Tui Wu Bing)*

1985. Shanghai Film Studio. Color. 10 Reels. Direction: Zhao Huanzhang. Screenplay: Ma Feng, Sun Qian. Cinematography: Peng Enli. Art Direction: Zhu Jiancang. Music: Xiao Yan. Sound: Wang Huimin, Xie Yuao. Cast: Wang Baosheng as Erhu, Fu Yiwei as Shui Xian, Xue Shujie as Yu Ya'nan, Chen Yude as Tiedan, Ding Yi as Xiushao, Wen Yujuan as Yanu, Cao Duo as Lao Da

When his six years of military service are up, Erhu returns to his hometown. His older brother Dahu is doing very well in his transport business, and he invites Erhu to join him. But when Erhu finds that most of the village people are not as prosperous as his brother, he decides to unite these people in seeking prosperity together. He proposes they start a factory, which greatly upsets his brother and Erhu's girl friend Shui Xian, who leaves him. Erhu perseveres, and the lives of the village's poor are greatly improved. In addition, he finds true love with one of his co-workers, Yu Ya'nan.

Best Picture, 1986 Hundred Flowers Awards.

Best Supporting Actor Chen Yude, 1986 Hundred Flowers Awards.

1498. *Our Fields (Wo Men De Tian Ye)*

1983. Youth Film Studio. Color. 10 Reels. Direction: Xie Fei. Screenplay: Pan Yuanliang, Xie Fei, Xiaojian. Cinematography: Meng Qinpeng, Gan Quan. Art Direction: He Baotong. Music: Ma Ding. Sound: Kong Lingyan, Zhao Jun, Ma Yuewen. Cast: Zhou Lijing as Xi Nan, Zhang Jing as "July," Lei Han as Little Brother, Lu Xiaogang as Qu Lin, Lin Fangbing as Ning Yu

One beautiful fall day, five young people arrive in the primitive and undeveloped Beidahuang area of Northeast China, sent by the government to develop this virgin land. But though their spirits are high, the life there is hard, and before too long Ning Yu returns to the city to marry, never coming back. Qu Lin also finds a reason to go back. The girl nicknamed "July" dies helping others in a forest fire. A few years later, Xi Nan leaves to finish college, and when he returns on a visit everyone hopes he will stay as his younger brother has decided to do. As Xi Nan thinks about his brother and their lives at Beidahuang, he concludes that although their generation has been treated very unfairly by history and politics, he decides he will return and help finish the job into which he and the others have put so much blood and sweat.

1499. *Our Little Cat (Women De Xiao Hua Mao)*

1980. Shanghai Film Studio. Color. 4 Reels. Direction: Wu Yigong, Zhang Yuqiang. Screenplay: Wang Tianyun, Zhang Yuqiang, Wang Runsheng, Wu Yigong. Cinematography: Wen Sijie, Sun Guoliang. Art Direction: Yao Wei. Music: Chen Dawei. Sound: Zuang Yongnan, Xu Xilin. Cast: Bai Mu as the old professor, Zhao Shuyin as Grandma, Chen Wenjie as Kangkang

An old professor who has been in prison for political reasons is released and allowed to return home. However, he is only allowed to stay in the storeroom of his house. Young boy Kangkang who lives underneath the professor's room has a lovely cat. Curious Kangkang discovers the professor is doing research on fish in the storeroom, and the two become good friends, the professor teaching the boy quite a lot about fish. One day, when Kangkang comes to visit the professor, he finds the fish tank smashed and his little cat eating the fish. Kangkang, thinking his little cat had caused the accident, sends the cat to a fisherman. But the professor tells him that the tank was smashed by his political enemies, and not the cat. A few years later, the old professor is restored to his job in oceanic exploration. He finds the little cat with the fisherman and gets it back. Kangkang, waiting in port for the old professor, is overjoyed to have his cat back.

1500. *Our Niu Baisui (Za Men De Niu Bai Sui)*

1983. Shanghai Film Studio. 10 Reels. Direction: Zhao Huanzhang. Screenplay: Yuan Xueqiang. Cinematography: Zhu Yongde. Art Direction: Li Jinggui. Music: Xiao Yan. Sound: Huang Dongping. Cast: Liang Qingang as Niu Baisui, Wang Fuli as Ju Hua, Qian Yongfu as Niu Tiansheng, Ding Yi as Qiu Shuang, Chen Yude as Tian Fu, Dawa as Niu Qi

When a rural commune divides its members into work teams, none of the teams are willing to accept the more lazy and backward members such as Niu Qi, Xin Liang, the widow Ju Hua, Tian Fu and Niu Tiansheng. Party member Niu Baisui decides to organize this group of misfits into a separate team, and takes on the responsibility of leading them. He stipulates that his group will work under the contract responsibility system and encourages them to think of themselves as new people with a fresh start. They of course encounter many difficulties, and some of the group want to quit. Even Niu Baisui becomes discouraged and thinks the task may be impossible to achieve. Then the widow Ju Hua comes to him and tells him how much she likes the changes that have taken place since he assembled the team, and encourages him not to give up. Niu Baisui gains new confidence from this, and keeps his team together. They have an excellent fall harvest, and the several former misfits have a new self-image. The other commune members now respect them as productive contributors to the collective effort.

Best Picture, 1984 Hundred Flowers Awards.

Best Supporting Actress Wang Fuli, 1984 Hundred Flowers Awards.

1501. *Out of Life and Death (Chu Sheng Ru Si)*

1990. Beijing Film Studio. Color. Wide

Screen. 9 Reels. Direction: Xu Qingdong. Screenplay: Fu Xuwen. Cinematography: Li Xiong. Art Direction: Huo Jianqi. Music: Li Lifu. Sound (Dolby): Liu Xiaodong. Cast: Wang Xu as Bao Gaiding, Lu Jianmin as Cheng Li, Hu Mei as Xie Hongshi, Jia Hongsheng as Ha Jie, Meng Chunhong as Yu Luoxi, Wang Handong as Da Fan, Zhang Jianli as Xiao Xia, Xue Chao as Hezi Pao, Liu Yi as Liu Lianzi

A sequel to the 1989 film "Woman Detective Bao Gaiding" from the same studio. Chief Investigator Ning Xiaoyu returns, this time to investigate the "Red Dragonfly" case, and once again she is personally involved with the principals. Her childhood friend Xie Hongshi, now the top woman executive at the Tailong Group, is suspected of having mob connections. Further investigation shows that another old friend, Ha Jie, is part of a counterfeiting ring. Bao once more overcomes her personal feelings and rounds up all the criminals, including her old friends.

1502. *Out of My Control (Shen Bu You Ji)*

1993. Shanghai Film Studio. Color. 9 Reels. Direction: Fu Dongyu. Screenplay: Dongfang Abai, Dong Yu, based on Qiu Weiming's novel "High Tide, Low Tide." Cinematography: Ju Jiazhen. Art Direction: Zhu Jianchang. Music: Zhen Fang. Sound: Gong Dejun. Costume: Xiao Yingjuan, Lin Rongjing. Makeup: Tao Meichun. Cast: Liu Xiaoning as Xue Biao, Tian Ge as Danni, Li Ping as Sister Bao, Qiu Shide as Liu Guosong, Huang Daliang as Chi Jingzhou, Lu Ye as Pan Mazi, Shao Zhiyu as A Chang

A young stockbroker on a streak of bad luck, including losing his girl to a successful businessman, meets another girl who plays the market using techniques taught her by her father. The two young people join forces to play the market and fulfill her father's dream of making a million before he passes away. Along the way the couple fall in love, but the relationship is complicated by his memories of his old girl friend and the out-of-wedlock baby they had together.

Overjoyed **see** *Vast Oceans and Skies*

1503. *The Ozone Layer Vanishes (Da Qi Chen Xiao Shi)*

1990. Children's Film Studio. Color. 10 Reels. Wide Screen. Direction: Feng Xiaoning. Screenplay: Feng Xiaoning. Cinematography: Zhang Guoqing. Art Direction: Jin Tonglin. Music: Guan Xia. Sound: Zhen Chunyu. Cast: Lu Liping as the woman, Wu Jiangan as the driver, Wang Yongge as the professor, Zhang Ning as the boy

A train is hijacked and a highly toxic poison begins leaking from three of the boxcars. As the poison gas covers the countryside, all living creatures in the area fall ill and are close to death. Pollution experts called in fail to find the source of the toxic gas leak. A young boy who can communicate with animals sets out with a cat and a dog to look for the toxic source together. He soon acquires two unusual human companions on route—a woman who has been involved in a bank robbery and a timber thief. But they all find themselves stranded when a cloud of toxic gas surrounds the car they are traveling in. The thief and the woman die, but the boy, the cat and the dog struggle on and at last arrive at the boxcars. The boy is about to enter one with a torch, but the dog rushes into the smoking car before him, setting off a massive explosion. Soon all is again quiet. TV broadcasts relay scientists' prediction that the world's ozone layer is threatened by this environmental pollution.

1504. *The Pack Horse Teams' Bells Ring in the Mountains (Shan Jian Ling Xiang Ma Bang Lai)*

1954. Shanghai Film Studio. B & W. 10 reels. Direction: Wang Weiyi. Screenplay: Bai Hua. Cinematography: Luo Chongzhou, Set Design: Han Shangyi and Wang Tao. Music: Lu Yun. Sound: Lin Bingyi. Cast: Feng Qi as the District Party Secretary, Wu Yang as Company Commander Zhang, Yu Yang as Dai Yu, Sun Jinglu as Lan Pang, Liu Qiong as La Ruoai, Fan Xuepeng as Daiwu's mother

Shortly after liberation, the Party and government send a large number of pack horses to ship necessities of living and production supplies to China's southern border for the minority peoples who live in that region. Miao village home guard director Dai Yu and the local PLA company commander jointly lead guide a guard unit to meet the pack horse teams. Before meeting the teams, however, they have to fight off and eventually wipe out a local gang which tries to steal the supplies.

1505. *A Pair of False Products (Yi Dui Mao Pai Huo)*

1986. Guangxi Film Studio. Color. Letterboxed. 10 Reels. Direction: Lu Dongqin, Mao Jian. Screenplay: Gu Gong, Hu Huiling. Cinematography: Lu Dongqin, Fang Miao. Art Direction: Tang Xinghua. Music: Jin Fuzhai. Sound: Zhang Qinjiang, Zhou Minzong. Cast: Tu Ruyin as Sun Mulan, Shen Guanchu as Xin Qi, Lin Xibiao as Qiao Jin, You Lihua as Fang Yan

Electronic appliance saleswoman Sun Mulan wants to introduce the products of her company to Hushi City. Qiao Jin and Fang Yan, two salesmen from a rival plant already entrenched in Hushi, try every trick they can think of to block her getting into the Hushi market. Sun Mulan is confident of her sales ability, and at last exposes Qiao and Fang's anti-competitive deceptions. When Sun Mulan gets her company's products into Hushi, their superiority wipes out the competition.

1506. *A Pair of Safety Belts (Yi Fu Bao Xian Dai)*

1974. Shanghai Film Studio. Color. 5 Reels. Direction: Song Ningqi, Zhao Huanzhang. Screenplay: Shanghai People's Huai Opera Troupe, based on the stage play of the same title by the Shanghai Jiading County Recreational Artistic Team and the Taopu Commune's Recreational Opera Team. Cinematography: Sheng Xilin. Art Direction: Zhao Jiwen. Music: Xu Jingxin. Cast: Wang Zheng as Hongyin, Qian Hongjuan as Xiao Yang, Zhan Che as Uncle Li, Zhong Xinghuo as Uncle Wang, Feng Qi as Qiu Jincai

Capitalist thoughts influence Xiao Yang, a young electrician in a Shanghai suburban people's commune. Unhappy that her regular safety belt is unattractive, and encouraged by Qiu Jincai, an accountant dismissed from his position, she orders a pair of leather safety belts on her own. Young woman accountant Hongyin refuses to put this on the commune's accounts, basing her stand on the principles of thrift and hard work. Hongyin realizes that underneath this affair of the safety belts lies a class struggle issue. While educating Xiao Yang, Hongyin also investigates Qiu Jincai, and discovers he has been engaged in illegal business. Further investigation reveals he is the head of a robbery ring. Xiao Yang realizes everyone must adhere to the traditional revolutionary style of thrift and hard work to develop a socialist nation.

1507. *Panda the Sun*

1995. Chi (HK) Film Production Co. Ltd. production in association with My Way Co. Ltd., the Children's Film Studio and the China Co-Production Corp. Color. 98 minutes. Direction: Yang Likuo. Screenplay: Xie Ting, Xiao Yang. Cinematography: Li Tingzheng. Art Direction: Hsu Hailin. Music: Liu Weiguang. Sound: Lan Fan. Cast: Jin Ming as Wen Chuan, Ku Xiaotu, Hsu Lemei, Tsao Jian

Nine-year-old Wen Chuan's dreams of Olympic gymnastic glory are put on indefinite hold by an auto mishap. While recovering, she visits her mother, a zoologist at a sanctuary for endangered species. After a while, she goes to visit her grandfather in the mountain village where he lives, where she quickly becomes friends with the village children. The new playmates find a wounded panda hiding in her grandfather's barn, and they nurse it back to health. When the animal recovers, and the children take it back to the mountains, they encounter the poachers responsible for wounding the panda. The children show they have fighting skills, capturing the villains and turning them in to the police.

1508. *Paratrooper (San Hua)*

1983. Tianshan Film Studio. Color. 9 Reels. Direction: Jing Mengling, Zhang Zhuoyin, Zhu Yingzhi. Screenplay: Li Hun, Shen Kai. Cinematography: Yu Zhenyu, Jiang Yanzhou, Qi Xing. Art Direction: Sun Changxi. Music: Chen Zhiquan. Sound: Yan Min. Cast: Dani Yaer as Aerkeng, Ali Muhazi as Sailike, Tuoerhong as Tuerxun, Aiergen as Rejiepu

Paratroop training company commander Aerkeng takes a very serious approach to his work, and is very strict about the training of his men. One of his new recruits, Tuerxun, lost his parents very early and had grown up very undisciplined as a result. He often violates military discipline, but company cadres show him the importance of regulations as a part of training. Sailike, a recruit from the prairie, has difficulties in training exercises because he is so bowlegged, but through hard work he attains the required standard. Rejeipu comes from an intellectual family background and is arrogant, but with the help of others he also at last measures up.

1509. *Partners (Sheng Si Pai Dang)*

1994. Beijing Film Studio. Color. Letterboxed. 9 Reels. Direction: Jiang Cheng, Cheng

Jie. Screenplay: Jiang Cheng. Cinematography: Fu Jingsheng. Art Direction: Yang Wan. Music: Guo Wenjing. Sound: Lai Qizhen, Gu Yu. Costume: Li Jiqing. Makeup: Liu Qiuxiang, Ma Shuangying. Cast: Li Xuejian as the chief of detectives, Jiang Cheng as Gao Xiong, Qu Yan as Ye Jun, Zhang Chenghao as Shou Zhou, Guo Tao as Qiangge

Policeman Gao Xiong and his supervisor Director Li crack a counterfeiting ring with the assistance of Ye Jun, a woman at first exploited by the counterfeiters.

1510. *Party Branch Team Head (Dang Xiao Zu Zhang)*

1986. Beijing Film Studio. Color. Letterboxed. 10 Reels. Direction: Yang Zhaibao. Screenplay: Ma Lin. Cinematography: Gao Lixian. Art Direction: Wang Xinguo. Music: Jin Fuzhai. Sound: Lu Xianchang. Cast: Chen Xiaolei as Yang Yang, Li Po as Bureau Director Liu, Zhang Jiasheng as the office director, Wen Xiying as Commander Ding, Liu Xiaohua as Mrs. Mei

After his army discharge, 22-year-old Yang Yang gets a job as driver for his city's water bureau. His adherence to principle, going strictly "by the book" in everything he does, so impresses Bureau Director Liu that he recommends the young man be named Party Team Leader. In his own work, Director Liu is the complete antithesis of Yang, often postponing payment of the Party membership fee, using public buildings for private endeavors, taking family trips in bureau vehicles, etc. Till now, everyone has been too timid to say anything, but Yang Yang becomes Liu's constant critic. Before long, the young man is demoted from car driver to truck driver, but he still retains his confidence.

1511. *Passage to the Black Mountain (Hei Shan Lu)*

1992. Xi'an Film Studio. Color. Letterboxed. 10 Reels. Direction: Zhou Xiaowen. Screenplay: Zhu Jinxin. Cinematography: Zhou Xiaowen. Art Direction: Dou Guoxiang. Music: Zhao Jiping. Sound: Hui Dongzhi. Costume: Ren Zhiwen. Makeup: Zhao Gang. Cast: Ai Liya as the woman, Zhao Xiaorui as Brother Gong, Xie Yuan as Xiao Liuzi

In the late 1930s, Brother Gong, a strong but rough peasant, heads a transport team in the mountains of Northwest China. He is injured at work, and lodged in a small inn to recover. A local woman is assigned to care for

him. Gong desires the woman, but she rejects him. When he discovers her with Xiao Liuzi, one of his men, he jealously beats up her lover. But he also cares about the other man. When the Japanese arrive, Gong starts to organize his men and the local people to resist, but he is captured instead. The Japanese force Xiao Liuzi to act as their guide in the area. The woman persuades Xiao to rescue Gong, and although the rescue is successful, the woman and many of Gong's men are killed in the effort. When freed, Gong at first confronts Xiao angrily, but the two men decide to fight the Japanese together.

1512. *Passing Death (Chao Yue Si Wang)*

1992. Tianshan Film Studio in association with the Beijing Aohua International Culture Entertainment Company Ltd. Color. Letterboxed. 9 Reels. Direction: Zhang Huaxun. Screenplay: Zhao Suya, Xia Luohui. Cinematography: Zhao Peng, Liu Weihua, Ma Rongsong. Art Direction: Shi Jiandu. Music: Xue Ruiguang. Costume: Li Changzhao. Makeup: Wang Lingzhi. Cast: Ji Yuan as Hua Han, Ying Xiu as Ye Lanshan, Gao Fa as "the Destroyer"

In a coastal city, scientist Qi Boru and his assistant and lover Ye Lanshan have just completed their work on a new, experimental energy source when two gunmen from overseas invade the laboratory, kill all the personnel there and steal the computer disks containing all the research findings. Chief of detectives Hua Han is baffled to find that Qi and Ye are not among the bodies; they seem to have just disappeared. It turns out that Ye has taken it on herself to get the stolen materials back, but her plan is to take the disks to America, where she and her lover can get rich by selling their findings to the highest bidder. Qi angrily dissents, as he wants to keep the discovery in China. At last, Ye dies fighting the overseas gunmen, after which the police rescue Qi Boru and kill the criminals.

1513. *Passing the Ghost Town at Night (Ye Zhou Gui Cheng)*

1989. Xi'an Film Studio and Hong Kong Hanshan Film Company jointly. Color. Wide screen. 9 Reels. Direction: Hu Gang. Screenplay: Hu Gang. Cinematography: Wang Yongrong. Art Direction: Lu Guangcai. Music: Deng Shaolin. Sound: Wang Zuopan. Cast: Wang Wensheng as General Hu, Guo Jianyong as Tao Yu, Li

Passage to the Black Mountain. **Pack mule team leader Brother Gong (Zhao Xiaorui, right) and his crew face the prospect of opposing the Japanese invaders. 1992. Xi'an Film Studio.**

Jiancheng as Fatty, Hao Min as the old woman's ghost

Shortly after the fall of the Qing Dynasty in 1911, warlord General Hu plans to use his army for opium smuggling. Two adventurers, Tao Yu and his sidekick Fatty, discover the general's plot. When Hu learns his plot has been discovered, he orders the deaths of Tao, Fatty, and two others who had been duped into making the opium delivery. When they learn of this, the four get together and make plans to kill Hu first.

1514. *Passing Time (Shui Yue Chong Chong)*

1986. Pearl River Film Studio. Color. Letterboxed. 10 Reels. Direction: Cao Zheng. Screenplay: Xu Yan. Cinematography: Wu Yukun. Art Direction: Zhu Jinhe. Music: Zhang Hong. Sound: Li Bojian, Liu Haiyan. Cast: Wang Fuli as Gu Ying, Xu Zhan as Xia Xinhua, Li Jingli as Wang Yaqin, Qi Jianqiu as Da Biao

Gu Ying was once the prima donna of many an operatic production, but in middle age she finds herself relegated to supporting roles only. She vows to regain her status as a lead, despite a lack of support from her husband Du Biao. Gu Ying calls in every IOU, every connection she has from her past triumphs to get auditions, but finds her age prevents her from competing with younger actresses. She gets an offer to make a movie, a kung fu epic, but finds she is just wanted as a stand-in for the younger woman playing the lead. At last Gu Ying gains a new understanding of life and her need to find another outlet for her creativity. She becomes an instructor at an opera training school.

1515. *The Passion, the Sense and the Law (Qing-Li-Fa)*

1994. Tianshan Film Studio, Hong Kong Mingshi Film Company Co-Production. Color. Letterboxed. 9 Reels. Direction: Chen Dongchun, Li Pengcheng. Screenplay: Li Tongcai, Li Pengcheng. Cinematography: Luo Dacheng. Art Direction: Wu Chaoliang, Ma Shaoxian. Sound: Liu Honggang. Costume: Mo Yinglong. Makeup: Shao Jianan, Wang Wanbin, Yi Yilin. Cast: Lu Liangwei (Ray Lui) as Dan Huaming, Ye Yuqing (Veronica Yip) as Lan Qiuping, Xu Jingjiang as

Baitou Lao, Li Weiming as Dan Huahui, Lin Wei as Wu Bingzheng, Li Yin as Ailing, Wen Aihong as Meiling

Young Hong Kong art student Dan Huahui travels to Beijing to continue his studies. One day, he intervenes to help a girl being assaulted by thugs, and accidentally kills one of them. He flees in panic, and becomes a fugitive. His brother Huamin, a Hong Kong lawyer, assisted by a Beijing woman named Tie Ping, investigate the case. At last, young Huahui is exonerated and justice is served.

1516. *The Passionate Detective (Ji Qing Jing Tan)*

1993. Shanghai Film Studio. Color. 10 Reels. Direction: Wu Tiange, Huang Hai. Screenplay: Wu Tiange, Huang Hai. Cinematography: Gao Ziyi. Art Direction: Sun Weide. Music: Su Junjie. Sound: Qian Ping. Costume: Zhang Lifang. Makeup: Zuang Yazhen. Cast: Xie Yuan as Li Zhusheng, Zhang Xiaolin as Qian Hui, Ma Ling as Yi Teng, Li Ying as A Fang, Qiu Shide as Zuoteng, Zhang Yuan as Li Gengfa, Qu Jingyun as Ren Zhong

Shanghai detectives Li Zhusheng and Qian Hui have been good friends since police academy. When offered a chance to go to Japan and enter private business, Qian Hui resigns from the force and leaves his girl friend Yi Teng. A few years pass, during which time Li Zhusheng rises through the detective ranks, at the same time developing a close relationship with Yi Teng. When Qian returns, obviously prosperous and successful, Yi Teng excitedly gets back together with him. Qian asks Yi Teng, who works for a Japanese company, to introduce him to her boss. While this is going on, Li Zhusheng is investigating a case of counterfeiting, with all the clues pointing to Yi Teng's employer. The woman tells Li that her relationship with Qian is going so well, she is sure that she and the successful cop-turned-businessman will marry soon. Li meanwhile, is worried about the involvement of his old friend with the suspected counterfeiters. As it develops, Qian is really an undercover agent for Interpol, and his reconciliation with Yi Teng just a way of infiltrating the counterfeit ring. It is also found that Yi Teng is involved in the criminal operations, and the two detectives sadly watch together as a police car takes her away.

1517. *Passionate Hats (Duo Qing De Mao Zi)*

1986. Guangxi Film Studio. Color. Letterboxed. 10 Reels. Direction: Zhang Gang. Screenplay: Zhang Gang. Cinematography: Sun Lixian, Chen Shenkai. Art Direction: Zhang Yafang. Music: Yang Shaoyi. Sound: Zhou Minchong, Lin Lin. Cast: Mao Yongming as Chen Aman, Gao Ying as Tian Jing, Shen Fa as Zhong Kejian

Chen Aman struggles along as a band musician. He is very honest, but unlucky in love. One day he and his old school friend Zhong Kejian eat at a restaurant, and get to talking with the proprietor about the lack of real progress in their careers. He suggests the two men start a hat factory together. Chen is initially reluctant because of their inexperience, but Zhong Kejian sees dollar signs and persuades Chen to try it. They produce many new style hats, but there is no market for them. Chen pours more money into the business, selling all his possessions to do so, and before long spending all his savings to pay their debts. He meets a girl named Tian Jing, who offers her help. She advises Chen on how to pay off his debts, and shows him how to sell his hats without losing money. In the process of getting the business going, Chen Aman and Tian Jing fall in love.

1518. *The Path Takes Me Home (Cun Lu Dai Wo Hui Jia)*

1988. Beijing Film Studio. Color. Letterboxed. 10 Reels. Direction: Wang Haowei. Screenplay: Tie Ning. Cinematography: Li Chengsheng. Art Direction: Shao Ruigang, Hi Hongyuan. Music: Zhang Peiji. Sound: Zhang Baojian. Cast: Li Ling as Qiao Yeye, Wang Yongge as Jin Zhao, Chen Qin as Ou Duanyang, Chong Lin as Song Kai, Liang Guanhua as Pan Yu

After graduating from middle school, a sweet girl named Qiao Yeye goes to live and work in the countryside. Also there are her childhood sweetheart Song Kan, honest young peasant Pan Yu who cares for her deeply, and Jin Zhao, a demobilized soldier who also finds her attractive. Through a matchmaker, Yeye marries Pan Yu, but he soon dies, leaving her alone and pregnant. Song Kan is admitted to a college in the city, but before leaving he promises to return and bring Yeye back to the city with him after graduation. Yeye's life as a single mother is hard but she waits patiently for Song Kan to return. Meanwhile, economic reforms and the responsibility system are introduced in the countryside, and Jin Zhao becomes the richest man in the village. He still cares for Yeye. After graduating from college, Song Kan comes to take Yeye back to the city but his feelings about her are now somewhat mixed. During the night after her return to the city, Yeye carefully considers her situation, and the next morning she takes the bus back to the village. As the bus travels the familiar country road back, Jin Zhao follows the bus on his motorbike, back to their common destiny.

Best Art Direction Hu Hongyuan, 1989 Golden Rooster Awards.

1519. *Peace Hotel (Lao Ban De Gu Shi)*

1995. Shanghai Film Studio. Color. Shanghai Film Studio, Hong Kong Jin Gongzhu Film Production Corporation Ltd. Co-Production. Direction: Wei Jiaxiang. Screenplay: Wei Jiaxiang. Cinematography: Wei Jiaxiang. Cinematography: Huang Yongheng. Art Direction: Xi Zhongwen. Music: Huang Jiaqian. Cast: Zhou Runfa (Chow Yun Fat) as Wang Aping, Ye Tong (Cecilia Yip) as A Man, Liu Xun (Lau Shun) as Ding Man

In Shanghai in 1921, the triads all agree that the Peace Hotel is off limits for violence; anyone who flees to the hotel will be safe from attack there, but vulnerable after leaving. Wang Aping, the boss of the hotel, was once a professional killer who had no equal in a gun battle. Now he has retired to run the hotel as a respite from gang warfare. One day, a woman singer named Aman comes to the hotel seeking sanctuary. She and Wang Aping fall in love, and Wang decides to extend protection to her after she leaves. The whole thing was set up by triads in order to induce Wang to break his own rule. Therefore, the triads start to attack the hotel. Wang is so driven to anger that he starts to kill again. Just as before, none can match his superior gunfighting. Aman realizes what she has done, but her appeals have no effect now on Wang, who has reverted to the cold, killing machine he was before. He now believes there is no love in the world. He leaves the hotel, leaving Aman in tears, surrounded by dead bodies.

1520. *A Peaceful Spring (Tai Ping Chun)*

1950. Wenhua Film Company. B & W. 11 Reels. Direction: Sang Hu. Screenplay: Sang Hu.

Cinematography: Huang Shaofeng. Cast: Shi Hui as Liu Jinfa, Shangguan Yunzhu as Liu Fengying, Shen Yang as Zhang Genbao, Cui Chaoming as Master Zhao, Cheng Zhi as Regimental Commander Wang, Lin Zhen as Mrs. Zhao, Wang Min as Jin Fa's wife, Yu Zongyin as Li Gui, Zhou Min as Mother Zhang, Tian Zhendong as Wang Damao

Before liberation, in a small town in eastern China, tailor Liu Jinfa's daughter Fengying and his apprentice Zhang Genbao fall in love and are engaged to marry. But Master Zhao, a despotic landlord, forces Fengying to be his concubine. Her father objects, so Zhao contacts the area regimental commander and has him conscript Zhang Genbao as a laborer. Not knowing that Zhao arranged this, the tailor goes to the landlord and asks his help in freeing the young man. Zhao agrees to intercede if Fengying will marry him, and she agrees in order to save her lover. After Genbao returns and learns what happened, he asks Fengying to flee with him. She at first refuses, as she fears doing so will make trouble for her father. On the day of the wedding, however, they do run away with the aid of some village people. In a rage, Master Zhao demands that Commander Wang arrest her father and others who had helped the couple get away. But just then word comes that the PLA has crossed the Changjiang River, and Zhao prepares to make his own escape. Since he cannot take all his possessions, he exploits Liu's honesty by getting him to take care of the property left behind, and gives him some money as a retainer. After liberation, Fengying and Genbao return to their hometown and prepare for their wedding. Her father wants to spend the landlord's money on a wedding gift, but the young couple persuade him to turn in the property and the retainer to the new people's government. He does so, and is praised and rewarded for it.

1521. *Peach Blossom Party (Jing Hun Tao Hua Dang)*

1994. Xiaoxiang Film Studio. Color. Letterboxed. 9 Reels. Direction: Zeng Jianfeng. Screenplay: Yuan Ye, based on the novel by Liu Zongdai. Cinematography: Wang Xili, Ye Nanqiu. Art Direction: Guo Dexiang. Music: Xu Jingxin. Sound: Wang Zhihong. Costume: Lin Heming, Liu Xuequn. Makeup: Yang Huiming. Cast: Wang Luyao as Mei Ya'nan, Wen Haitao as Hua Xin, Yang Chiyu as Jiye, Liu Libin as Jimei Liangzi, Wen Hao as Songtian, Zhang Tao as Wu Chuanyu, Gao Dehua as Zuomu Ling, Nian Fan as Sun Zhuguang, Tong Jiaqi as Gao Runshan, Ning Guoyu as Zhao Ruowen

In Japanese-occupied Tianjin, prominent private investigator Hua Xin is asked by occupation authorities to look into a series of murders of prominent Chinese citizens. Hua Xin detects a pattern to the methods used in the killings, which appear to be imitations of those used by the Peach Blossom Triad which dominated pre-war Tianjin. This clue at last leads him to an old girl friend, reporter Mei Ya'nan. When Hua confronts her with his findings, the woman freely and proudly admits to being the murderer: all the victims were Japanese collaborators, and since China is at war she considers herself a soldier fighting for her homeland. She presents the detective with a choice: let her continue her work as she plans to do, or turn her in, thereby becoming a collaborator himself. Hua Xin tries to travel an intermediate path: report he has been unable to solve the killings, and dissuade her from committing any more, as he fears she will soon be tripped up and caught anyway. But all his persuasion is ineffective: Mei Ya'nan continues killing Chinese traitors, until at last her luck runs out and she and Hua Xin are both killed.

1522. *Peach Flower Fan (Tao Hua Shan)*

1963. Xi'an Film Studio. B & W. 12 Reels. Direction: Sun Jing. Screenplay: Mei Qian and Sun Jing, based on Kong Shangren's Qing Dynasty play "Peach Flower Legend" and Ouyang Yuqian's modern play "Peach Flower Fan." Cinematography: Wang Zhixiong. Art Direction: Dong Ping, Hu Qiangsheng. Music: Fan Buyi, Wei Ruixiang. Sound: Hong Jiahui, Meng Fuyin. Cast: Wang Danfeng as Li Xiangjun, Feng Ji as Kou Chaozong, Yu Junfang as Zhen Tuoniang, Han Tao as Ruan Dacheng, Zhen Danian as Yang Youlong, Li Qianying as Li Zhenli

In 1627, scholar Kou Chaozong, a leader in the "Ming Dynasty Restoration League," boldly criticizes powerful official Ruan Dacheng. For this, he gains the admiration of famous Nanjing courtesan Li Xiangjun. Kou sends Xiangjun a fan as an engagement gift. Ruan Dacheng later wants to marry Li Xiangjun, but she rejects his petition. The next year, the Ming emperor dies, and Ruan Dacheng orders the arrest of all scholars in the Restoration League. Kou Chaozong has to leave Nanjing and bids Xiangjun farewell. When Xiangjun and others are forced to perform as singers and

dancers for Ruan Dacheng, Xiangjun makes up her own lyrics to criticize Ruan Dacheng. The furious official orders her arrest but she escapes. At this time, Kou returns to Nanjing to see Xiangjun and is arrested. Xiangjun makes her way to a nunnery in the mountains and finds sanctuary there. Eight years later, Kou Chaozong comes to the nunnery looking for Xiangjun. At first she is delighted to see him again, but when Xiangjun learns that he has changed his mind and gone over to the Manchu side, she harshly criticizes him and tears up the peach flower fan. She refuses to have anything more to do with Kou, and spends the rest of her days in the nunnery.

1523. *The Peacock Flies to Awa Mountain (Kong Que Fei Lai A Wa Shan)*

1978. Emei Film Studio. Color. 10 Reels. Direction: Zhang Qi. Screenplay: Lin Yu. Cinematography: Feng Shilin. Art Direction: Wang Tao. Music: Yang Fei. Sound: Lin Bingcheng, Hua Yaozhu. Cast: Li Yalin as Bai Wenjing, Lu Xiaohe as Ai Huolong, Yan Xiaowen as Ye Mei, Wang Zhe as Wo Langkang, Tian Yuan as Headman Aiga, Yan Zenhe as Ai Chu

In the spring of 1950, a PLA minority work team led by Captain Bai Wenjing and his deputy Zhang Hui arrives in Yunnan province to work among the Awa tribe in the mountains. They make four attempts to enter the mountains but are turned back each time by the local people. But the work team does not give up. Captain Bai is able to make friends with Ai Huolong, a young archer who was first hostile to the work team, but now with some understanding of the team's purpose he and Bai become blood brothers. When local headman Wo Langkang is deluded by Nationalist agent Li Shikui into reaching an agreement on the area's governance, Ai Huolong brings Bai Wenjing to the meeting place and the two together expose the Nationalist conspiracy. Later, with the help of some minority people, the PLA wins over Wo Langkang, kills Li Shikui, and wipes out the remnants of the Nationalist Army still in Tibet.

1524. *The Peacock Princess (Kong Que Gong Zhu)*

1982. Beijing Film Studio. Color. Letterboxed. 12 Reels. Direction: Zhu Jinming, Su Fei, Xing Rong. Screenplay: Bai Hua. Cinematography:

Du Yizuang. Art Direction: Wang Jixian. Music: Tian Liantao. Sound: Fu Yinjie, Ren Shanpu. Cast: Li Xiumin as Namunuona, Tang Guoqiang as Zhaoshutun, Chen Qiang as Zhao Zuangxiang

In an ancient Dai nationality legend, there lives a young man called Zhaoshutun, the son of the King of the Menbanzh court. Zhaoshutun is handsome, brave and intelligent, fond of freedom and nature. He and the beautiful peacock princess Nanmunuona fall in love and marry. However, when the happy newlyweds return to the Menbanzh, the court is closed to them and the king refuses to receive them. It turns out that a wizard who hates Zhaoshutun has cast a spell on the king. On the couple's wedding night, the wizard casts another spell which causes a war. Zhaoshutun has to leave and fight the enemy, and in his absence the wizard makes the king even more corrupt and ignorant. When the wizard tells the king that Nanmunuona is an evil spirit the king sentences her to death. On the date of execution, Nanmunuona takes peacock form and flies away. When the husband returns and finds his wife is not there, he sets out on a long and arduous quest to find her. The story ends happily with the reunited lovers killing the wizard which breaks the spells. They forgive the king and queen, and everyone lives happily ever after.

Peintre, La **see** *Soul of a Painter*

Peking Duck Restaurant **see** *Old Restaurant*

1525. *People Cutting Into Mountains (Kai Shan De Ren)*

1976. Xi'an Film Studio. Color. 12 Reels. Direction: Wei Rong. Screenplay: Collective, recorded by Yan Yi. Cinematography: Chen Guoliang, Meng Qinpeng. Art Direction: Lu Xin, Zhang Xiaohui. Music: Xu Youfu, Xie Tiyin. Sound: Chen Yudan. Cast: Xia Zongyou as Lu Hai, Zhe Danian as Political Commissar Zhou, Zhang Keyao as Liang Zhixiang, Li Guiping as Zhang Hua, Wang Tongle as Liu Tie, Chun Li as Zhen Gugong, Cheng Senlin as Chen Ke

In 1964, "Backbone Project Team" Director Lu Hai leads his team to the work site of the Ziyunshan tunnel project, abandoned two years before because of an incorrect political line. The team encounters many difficulties. Project department director Liang Zhixiang can think only of the poor natural conditions,

so refuses to build; hidden counterrevolutionary engineer Chen Ke also blocks construction. But Lu Hai resolves every problem. Finally, Chen Ke sets up a construction collapse, but Lu Hai catches him red-handed. This awakens Liang Zhixiang to the realities. With the team united, the successfully finish the Ziyunshan tunnel.

People Daring to Create **see** *Abandon Superstitions*

1526. *People Leaving Home to Make Money (Chu Men Zheng Qian De Ren)*

1983. Beijing Film Studio. Color. Letterboxed. 10 Reels. Direction: Zhang Yuqiang. Screenplay: Chen Shilian. Cinematography: Huang Xinyi, Kang Kai. Art Direction: Ning Lanxin, Yu Fengming. Music: Jin Xiang. Sound: Zhang Zhizhong. Cast: Liu Cangwei as Duo Shun, Wang Xian as Liu Chengye, Zhang Yan as Old Mr. Ma, Chen Peisi as Dabao, Lamaoxian as Sairichuo, Bai Mu as Director Wang

Four farmers leave their homes to make money elsewhere. They happen upon a herd of sheep with no apparent owner. The story centers around their efforts to deal with the sheep. At first they argue, with two wanting to sell the sheep and split the money, and two wanting to find the owner and collect a reward. At last they find the owner, return the sheep, and get no money for it. They agree the best way they can make money is by working hard.

1527. *People Living Along the Huai River (Huai Shang Ren Jia)*

1954. Shanghai Film Studio. B & W. 13 Reels. Direction: Zhang Junxiang. Screenplay: Yuan Jing. Cinematography: Yao Shiquan. Set Design: Wei Tiezheng. Music: Huang Zhun. Sound: Zhu Weigang. Cast: Feng Ji as Gao Heizi, Wang Pei as Kui Hua, Wei Helin as Kui Hua's grandfather, Dai Yun as Gao Heizi's mother, Zhang Yan as Gao Heizi's father, Shi Yuan as Ding Xier, Ding Ran as Xiong Taibo

In 1938, Chiang Kaishek orders the destruction of the Yellow River dam at Huayuan, a disaster for the people living along the banks of its Huai River tributary. Between their oppressive landlord Xiong Taibo and recurring floods, young farmers Gao Heizi and Kui Hua find it almost impossible to make a living. After liberation, they join in the Huai treatment project. But their former landlord, although having lost much of his power, continued to work underground to sabotage the Huai treatment work, and Kui Hua is injured as a result. This incident awakens the political awareness of Ding Xier, a backward laborer. Before the dam is finished, Xiong Taibao and other covert anti–Communist agents try to kill Gao Heizi and stop completion of the dam. Ding Xier reports this conspiracy to the PSB in time for them to round up Xiong Taibo and the other saboteurs. The big dam project is completed successfully and the Huai River's wild flooding is finally brought under control, promising a bright future for the people along both banks of the river.

1528. *People Moving Up (Ren Wang Gao Chu Zou)*

1954. Northeast Film Studio. B & W. 7 Reels. Direction: Xu Sulin. Screenplay: Lan Fengtong, Li Xinbing and Li Yongzhi. Cinematography: Wang Qimin. Set Design: Du Rongmao. Music: Chen Ming. Sound: Sheng Guli. Cast: Liu Maoqing as Old Sun, Huo Yingzhen as Yu Meizi, Li Qingyou as Diao Liu, Wang Huian as Director Wang, Jin Daiying as Old Sun's wife, Li Qichang as Xin Liang

In a Northeast China village, Old Sun, a newly middle-class farmer, is concerned only with his own family's prosperity. On the advice of stockbroker Diao Liu, he opts out of joining the agricultural association's union. When a natural disaster occurs, he cannot cope with it alone, and faces ruin. But the union helps him, and disaster is averted. This event brings him to realize that cooperative action is the way to go. Finally, he joins the agricultural cooperative union.

1529. *People of the Grasslands (Cao Yuan Shang De Ren Men)*

1953. Northeast Film Studio. B & W. 10 Reels. Direction: Xu Tao. Screenplay: Hai Mu, Mala Qinfu and Da Mulin, from Mala Qinfu's novel of the same title. Cinematography: Wang Chunquan, Fu Hong and Li Guanghui. Set Design: Wang Tao. Music: Xiang Yi and Tong Fu. Sound: Wu Jianghai. Makeup: Bi Zepu. Cast: Wu Rina as Sharen Gewa, Enhesheng as Shangbu, Zhao Lu as Bai Yire, Shu Hai as Bao Lu, An Qi as Wuer Shana, Ye He as Amu Gulang

Shala Gefu and hunter Shang Bu are lovers. They work hard building their beautiful grasslands. Undercover agent Bao Lu attempts unsuccessfully to sabotage the local mutual assistance group, first by stampeding their horses during a storm, then by poisoning a well which infects Sharen Gefu with a sheep's disease, and finally by starting a fire during the annual festival. Sharen Gewa and Shangbu uncover the conspiracy, and all the saboteurs are rounded up.

1530. *People of the Great Northern Wilderness (Bei Da Huang Ren)*

1961. Beijing Film Studio. Color. 11 Reels. Direction: Cui Wei, Chen Huaiai. Screenplay: Collective work by the Mudan River Agricultural Development Bureau's Cultural Work Brigade, recorded by Xiao Fan, and based on a stage play of the same title. Cinematography: Nie Jing. Art Direction: Qing Wei. Music: Ju Xixian, Zhang Wengang, Luo Zhongrong. Sound: Chen Yanxi. Casting: Zhang Ping as Gao Jianxin, Cui Kui as Huang Laoqing, Yu Shaokang as Ji Qingshan, Wang Binghuo as Che Xiangyang, Liu Shulin as Jiang Zhihong, Yuan Mei as Huang Yanzhi

In 1958, retired soldier Gao Jianxin brings a group of military retirees to develop the wild area in the Great Northern Wilderness near Yanwo Island. There, Gao meets Huang Laoqing, father of his best army buddy Huang Yonghe who had been killed 18 years earlier, and a little girl named Yanzhi once saved by Gao. In cultivating the lands, Gao Jianxin depends on the people, resists conservative opposition, and is ultimately successful in upgrading the people's technology to where they can cultivate the wasteland, receiving a big harvest.

1531. *People Who Spread Joy (Bo Zhong Xin Fu De Ren)*

1981. Shanghai Film Studio. Color. 6 Reels. Direction: Yao Shoukang. Screenplay: Song Chong, Zhao Fujian, Si Xilai. Cinematography: Yin Guohao, Shen Miaorong. Art Direction: Shen Wanchun. Music: Xu Jingxin. Sound: Xie Guojie. Cast: Cui Xinqing as Zhang Yin, Zhen Jiasheng as Hu Jin, Gao Cui as Mother, Tu Ruyin as Hu Ping, Ye Zhikang as Song Lide

Zhang Ying, a physically challenged young woman, is a secretary at the young people's college in the Guangmin Silk Plant. She is named the Worker of the Year in the plant, but she is surprised that Hu Ping, the previous year's winner, was not named again. Zhang Ying decides to find out why, and learns that Hu Ping has had a serious falling out with her

People of the Grasslands. **1953. Northeast Film Studio.**

mother because of Hu Ping's love for street cleaner Song Lide, and this disagreement has caused a decline in Hu's output. Zhang Ying wants to help her out, and her sincere friendship moves Hu Ping. Zhang Ying talks to the mother, and presents her with the realities of the situation. The mother changes her attitude and accepts Song Lide. Zhang Ying's selfless assistance to the lovers greatly impresses Hu Jin, a local college teacher. He expresses his love to Zhang Ying.

1532. *The People's Huge Palm (Ren Min De Ju Zhang)*

1950. Kunlun Film Company. B & W. 10 Reels. Direction: Chen Liting. Screenplay: Xia Yan. Cinematography: Hu Zhenghua. Set Design: Ding Chen. Music: Chen Gexin. Sound: Li Liehong. Costume: Jiang Zhengqin. Makeup: Yao Yongfu. Casting: Wei Helin as Zhang Rong, Zhang Gan as Huang Zihe, Wang Pei as Zhang Xinghua, Fu Botang as Li Fusheng, Zhang Yi as Xiao Liang, Gao Zheng as Xue Jiaqi

On the eve of the liberation of Shanghai, government agent Zhang Rong is assigned to work under cover in a thread mill and infiltrate leftist workers by pretending to be a radical. Led by the chief agent Xiao Liang, he contin-

ues pretending to be progressive and instigates labor-management conflict through extremist speeches. He also mentors a young special agent named Li Fusheng in sabotaging equipment. But Li arouses the suspicions of plant labor union cadre Zhu Yuqing, and when confronted Li makes a full confession of his own guilt without implicating anyone else. PSB officers suspect Zhang Rong as well, and hope he will implicate himself. Zhang is caught when he tries to arrange the bombing of the plant. Eventually, all the enemy agents are rounded up.

1533. *People's Soldiers (Ren Min De Zhan Shi)*

1950. Northeast Film Studio. B & W. 10 Reels. Direction: Ju Qiang. Screenplay: Liu Baiyu. Cinematography: Fu Hong. Set Design: Wang Tao. Music: Yan Ke. Sound: Lu Xiancang. Makeup: Liu Yutian, Hu Honghua. Cast: Li Changhua as Liu Xing, Liu Xin as Wan Liangcai, Song Guanghan as the Deputy Commander, Miao Qing as the Division Commander

In 1946, Nationalist forces on three occasions cross the Songhua River to launch all-out attacks on the liberated areas of Northeast China, but each time they are driven back across the river. The farmers living south of the river are severely persecuted by the soldiers occupying their region. One of these farmers, Liu Xing, joins the PLA in search of revenge, and is assigned to the same unit as Wan Liangcai, from the same village. That winter, the PLA counterattacks, driving south of the river, and Wan Liangcai is seriously wounded covering Liu Xing. After Liu Xing recovers and returns to the army, he takes part in a criticism campaign which raises class awareness in the military. Finally, the two army buddies are reunited on the battlefield, and both are decorated for bravery.

1534. *The Person Playing the Monkey (Wan Hou De Ren)*

1984. Henan Film Studio. Color. Wide Screen. 10 Reels. Direction: Wang Fengkui, Ma Ling. Screenplay: Wang Fengkui, Chen Mengbai. Cinematography: Qiao Yanting. Art Direction: Wang Yunzuang. Music: Ma Jinggui. Sound: Sun Yan. Cast: Ran Furen as Luo Baiyuan, Chen Dazhu as Ma Yunhua, Zhang Shifa as Zhao Liangeng, Wang Shanlin as Gao Shouzheng

During the Cultural Revolution, Luo Baiyuan and his wife Ma Yunhua try to make a little extra money by raising and selling chickens. For this "capitalist" activity, they are forced to leave their home town, and for some years after support themselves and their small son by putting on street performances with a trained monkey. After the downfall of the Gang of Four, Luo Baiyuan hears that their old home town is now a great place to live. The homesick Luo decides to see if this is true, so he and the little boy return home for a visit. He finds everything as wonderful as he had heard, and he sends for Ma Yunhua. Their new neighbors help them find housing, and they start a new business using Yunhua's talent at making things from bamboo.

1535. *The Phoenix's Song (Feng Huang Zhi Ge)*

1957. Jiangnan Film Studio. B & W. 10 Reels. Direction: Zhao Ming. Screenplay: Lu Yanzhou. Cinematography: Feng Shizhi and Qian Yu. Art Direction: Ge Shicheng. Music: Ji Ming. Sound: Zhang Fubao. Makeup: Kong Lingqi. Cast: Zhang Ruifang as Jin Feng, Li Ming as Wang Qi, Kang Tai as Wu Guisheng, Wang Jingan as Wu Yulan, Zhou Ming as Mrs. Zhang, Cui Wenshun as Li Tianchen, Deng Nan as Li Yuanmin

On Jinquan Mountain there are two villages: Li and Wu. Years of drought and competition for water and other life necessities have led to a longstanding feud between the two. A Li Village woman named Jin Feng, purchased as a child as a future bride and then abandoned by her fiance, still works as a laborer for the family who bought her. After liberation, the Communist Party launches the "Cooperation Campaign," encouraging villages to work together; as a part of this, Jin Feng joins the local agricultural cooperative movement, and comes under the tutelage of woman political instructor Wang Qi. With the latter's guidance, the young laborer breaks through many feudal traditions and falls in love with Wu Guisheng, a Wu Village cadre. To stop the co-op's work and instigate violence between the two villages, rich farmer Li Yuanmin transplants a blight to Wu Village, and accuses the Wu people of having abducted Jin Feng. Jin Feng tries to prevent the villages from fighting, but gets caught between then and is almost beaten to death. In the nick of time, Wang Qi arrives with the police to stop the fight. Li Yuanmin's sabotage is exposed, and Jin Feng's courage wins the respect of the people of both villages, who name her the co-op director. She openly declares her love for Wu Guisheng, and begins a new, happy life.

1536. *Piano Longings (Qin Si)*

1982. Emei Film Studio. Color. 9 Reels. Direction: Xiang Lin. Screenplay: Xiang Liang. Cinematography: Li Erkang, Wang Wenxiang. Art Direction: Yan Dingfu. Music: Shu Zeci, Wang Liping. Sound: Lin Bingcheng. Cast: Wang Jiang as Zhang Bo, Jiang Yunhui as Zhu Zhilan, Wei Qixian as Fang Bing, Li Xiaoyan as Du Xiaoning, Wang Yuzhen as Zhang Bo's mother, Guo Qi as Auntie

When little Zhang Bo's father dies, he goes to live with his mother at the Zhu family home, where his mother is employed as a servant. The Zhu's daughter Yalan loves music and spends much of her time playing piano. When by chance she discovers Zhang Bo has musical aptitude she teaches him piano and he becomes her student. Zhu Yalan's boyfriend Xiao Xue is a violinist. Yalan is convinced the only way they can become great artists is by studying at a famous music institute overseas, but he is becoming more interested in politics. She goes abroad and he stays behind, eventually going to Yan'an join the Communist forces there. Zhang Bo later gets the chance to go to music school, and in time becomes a famous pianist. Forty years pass, and Zhu Yalan returns to China on a visit where she meets Zhang Bo, her old piano student. He is surprised to find that she has abandoned music as a career and now operates a large restaurant. Her old boyfriend Xiao Xue is now called Fang Bing, and is a famous conductor. Zhu Yalan has very complex feelings about the course her life has taken.

1537. *A Pigeon Fancier's Adventure (Ge Zi Mi De Qi Yu)*

1986. Children's Film Studio. Color. Letterboxed. 10 Reels. Direction: Yu Yanfu, Zhang Yuan. Screenplay: Wang Zhebing, Wang Xingdong. Cinematography: Li Tingzheng. Art Direction: Wu Qiwen. Music: Jin Xiang. Sound: Zhang Zhian. Cast: Zhang Fengyi as Du An, Su Ning and Li Shengpei as Tiantian, Zhang Xiong as Father, Wang Suya as Qin Ying

Young steelworker Du An is a pigeon fancier. One day, he finds an abandoned infant girl who he brings home and adopts, giving her the name Tiantian. His father really dislikes the idea and urges his son to put the baby up for adoption. Du An keeps the girl, but his father makes him move out; Du An also finds life as a single parent much busier than before. When Tiantian is two, Du An's parents relent and let him and the little girl move back with them. A steady stream of marriageable young women are introduced to Du An, but all break off the relationship when they find out about Tiantian. One day, a young woman named Qin Ying shows up claiming to be Tiantian's natural mother. The possibility of losing the little girl creates some deep conflicts with Du An. But after spending some time with the little girl and her adoptive father, the woman abruptly leaves them, without explanation. It turns out she is not Tiantian's mother, but someone who was familiar with their story and wanted the little girl as a replacement for the child she had lost. She later sends a telegram to Du An, telling him that his treatment of the child has won her heart, and offering to be his wife if he will have her. He and Tiantian happily go to meet their new wife and "Mama."

1538. *Pigeon Guard in the Blue Sky (Lan Tian Ge Shao)*

1983. Shanghai Film Studio. Color. 9 Reels. Direction: Da Shibiao. Screenplay: Zhao Baohua,

Luo Huajun. Cinematography: Ju Jiazhen. Art Direction: Li Runzhi. Music: Xiang Yi. Sound: Yin Zhiping. Cast: Jin Yi as Lin Xi, Yuan Yuan as Han Ming, Zhou Jian as Lin Xi (as a child), Su Xudong as Xiao Haizi, Wu Jiao as Grandpa Song, Zhu Yaying as Xiao Yu

A tragic love story about two people who meet when he is 13 and she is 12. They share their dreams and become close friends. When the Cultural Revolution tears them apart, they follow different paths in life. Years later they meet again and realize how much they love each other. They are torn apart forever when he meets with a fatal accident.

1539. *Pine Trees Can Never Grow Too Old (Bu Lao Song)*

1959. Jiangnan Film Studio. B & W. 8 Reels. Direction: Fang Huang. Screenplay: Zhang Ming, Fang Huang. Cinematography: Yao Shiquan. Art Direction: Zhang Xibai. Music: Gao Tian. Sound: Gong Zhenming. Cast: Zhang Fa as Old Zhou, Mu Hong as the plant director, Wang Yi as Zhou Qiaozhen, Qiu Deshun as Chen Deshan, Mo Chou as Mrs. Wu, Wang Yunzhen as the chairman of the workers' union, Jiang Guiying as the little girl

Veteran textile mill worker Zhou has retired, but he still has too much energy to just take it easy. When the Great Leap Forward campaign begins, he joins with some other retirees in demanding the mill director give them some work to do. To appease them, the director assigns them some light work to do, but they tackle it enthusiastically, competing with younger workers for high production output. Their attitude fires the enthusiasms of workers throughout the mill, and in the end the mill wins the "Red Flag" award for production.

1540. *A Place Far Beyond the Crowd (Yuan Li Ren Qun De Di Fang)*

1983. Changchun Film Studio. Color. Letterboxed. 11 Reels. Direction: Bai Dezhang, Xu Xunxing. Screenplay: Zhang Xiaotian, Zhang Tianmin. Cinematography: Meng Xiandi. Art Direction: Liu Huanxing. Music: Gao Feng. Sound: Liu Jingui. Cast: Huang Zhongqiu as Li Daping, Zhu Ling as Tan Hong, Ma Qun as Tan Huaiyuan, Yan Meiyi as Zhao Shihan, Shao Hua as Yang Zeshi, Wang Tao as Yi Juan

At a forestry research institute in a remote part of Southwest China, assistant researcher Li Daping discovers a tree which is a major archaeological finding. Academy of Science journalist Tan Hong writes an article about it, and Li Daping is invited to the Beijing Academic Conference. Surprisingly, he does not show up. In his place is a woman named Zhao Shihan, director of the research institute's office. To learn why, Tan Hong travels to the institute and finds that Zhao Shihan severely suppresses Li Daping, and fears that his scientific breakthrough might harm her chances of promotion. Tan decides to investigate further.

1541. *A Place Reborn (Zai Sheng Zhi Di)*

1983. August First Film Studio. Color. Wide Screen. 11 Reels. Direction: Yan Jizhou, Yang Guangyuan. Screenplay: Wang Yongzhi. Cinematography: Yang Guangyuan. Art Direction: Fei Lansheng. Music: Yang Xiwu. Sound: Shi Pingyi. Costume: Fei Lansheng, Zhu Fengtang, Li Qing. Cast: Xia Zongyou as Pan Yun, Hu Ao as Yiteng Hongyi, Zhan Yupin as Tong Jingyang, Siqin Gaowa as Daozhen Meizi

In the winter of 1950, the Soviet Union hands over to China a group of Japanese charged with serious war crimes. They are put in the Fushun War Criminals Prison. In accordance with Premier Zhou Enlai's orders, Prison Director Pan Yun and Reform Department Head Tong Jingyang undertake difficult and complex reform and reeducation work among the prisoners. At first, the prisoners are hostile and uncooperative, resisting all efforts to reform them. But gradually they start to realize how serious were the crimes they committed against the Chinese. In 1956, China's Highest People's Court puts the Japanese on trial, during which they all acknowledge their crimes. Two years later, they are all released by the Chinese government and permitted to return to their homes.

Best Cinematographer Yang Guangyuan, 1984 Golden Rooster Awards.

Best Sound Shi Pingyi, 1984 Golden Rooster Awards.

Best Costume Fei Lansheng, Zhu Fengtang and Li Qing, 1984 Golden Rooster Awards.

1542. *Placing Hope (Ji Tuo)*

1976. Emei Film Studio. Color. 11 Reels. Direction: Ye Min, Zhang Yi. Screenplay: Gao Ying, Yi Qi, Yang Yinzhang. Cinematography: Gu Wenhou, Feng Shilin. Art Direction: Wang Tao, Lin Qi. Music: Zhang Chun. Cast: Rong Xiaomi as Wang Xiaolei, Niu Qian as Chen

Chunrong, Liu Lianchi as Shen Jitao, Song Tao as Boyanban, Feng Xiaoyuan as Ai Jiang, Zen Haiyan as Li Ping, Tian Yuan as Du Shiyou

Du Shiyou, in charge of the Manfeizai farm, engages in speculation and profiteering. But when young Red Guard Wang Xiaolei is assigned to the farm, he soon puts a stop to these illegal activities. However, farm director Li Ping sides with Du, and blames Xiaolei, leading to Li being criticized by Party committee secretary Shen Jitao. Later, Xiaolie criticizes Li for providing material incentives to the workers, and as a result Li is criticized and Xiaolei assigned as the No. 2 person in the farm leadership. Du Shiyou causes serious flood damage to the farm by not releasing a weather bulletin, then tries to shift the blame for this to Wang Xiaolei. In the end, Du is arrested, and Director Li is removed from his position.

1543. *Platoon Commander Guan (Guan Lian Zhang)*

1951. Wenhua Film Company. B & W. 12 Reels. Direction: Shi Hui. Screenplay: Yang Liuqing, adapted from an original work by Zhu Ding. Cinematography: Ge Weiqing. Art Design: Wang Yuebai. Cast: Shi Hui as Platoon Commander Guan, Yu Zongyin as the instructor, Yu Ding as the political officer, Cheng Zhi as Mr. Dong, Zhang Hejun as the messenger, Jiang Shan as Mr. Pan

Just before the liberation of Shanghai, PLA Platoon Commander Guan and his troops are assigned for rest and rehabilitation. During this time they are given further training and are introduced to formal study. Since Guan and his men are all peasants with little or no education, they find study very difficult. But with the help of their instructor and the encouragement of their political officer, they make rapid progress. In the battle to liberate Shanghai, the platoon is held in reserve for later use. However, at the height of the conflict, unable to control themselves any longer, Guan's troops plead with the commander to let them go in. He at last accedes to their request, and moves his troops to the enemy's rear to attack their headquarters. As they near the objective and prepare to attack, Guan discovers that the building used as the enemy headquarters is an orphanage, with several hundred orphans still inside. In order to accomplish the mission without endangering the children, Guan decides to abandon his original plan to bombard the building with artillery fire, and orders his troops to use only bayonets in the attack. They overwhelm the enemy, but with severe losses among their own troops, among them Platoon Commander Guan, who dies heroically.

1544. *Playing the Flute in a Different Way (Dong Xiao Heng Chui)*

1957. Haiyan Film Studio. B & W. 10 Reels. Direction: Lu Ren. Screenplay: Hai Mu. Cinematography: Yao Meisheng. Art Direction: Zhong Yongqing and Tang Menwen. Music: Ge Yan. Sound: Zhou Hengliang. Makeup: Wang Hanyong. Cast: Zhang Zhiliang as Liu Jie, Wang Yunxia as Yang Yilan, Fan Lai as An Zhenbang, Zhong Xinghuo as Wang Jinkui, Cui Wenshun as Yang Wanfu, Li Yong as Wang Yongxiang

Demobilized soldier Liu Jie returns to his native village to farm and help build a cooperative union of the poor farmers in the village. However, their efforts to organize are thwarted by An Zhensheng, the bureaucratic county Party Secretary. Also, village chief Wang Jinkui is dedicated only to seeking individual prosperity, and tries unsuccessfully to get Liu Jie to join him. He then organizes the more prosperous farmers to oppose Lin Jie's poorer union. He also coerces his long-time farm hand Ma Deyi into not joining Liu Jie's union. With the support of veteran local secretary Yang Yilan and the poor farmers in the village, Liu Jie resists Secretary An. Liu writes letters to the central government and to Chairman Mao explaining the situation. Chairman Mao sends the deputy governor of the province to investigate the situation. As a result of his investigation, illegal grain brokering activities by village chief Wang Jinkui are exposed, Secretary An's bureaucratic methods are criticized, the obstacles to establishing the union are cleared.

1545. *Please Care About It (Qing Duo Duo Guan Zhao)*

1988. Xi'an Film Studio. Color. Letterboxed. 9 Reels. Direction: Chen Xingzhong. Screenplay: Wang Huiquan, Chen Xingzhong. Cinematography: Nie Tiemao. Art Direction: Wang Yanlin. Music: Wang Xiling. Sound: Hong Jiahui. Cast: Ren Guangzi as Dong Dahai, Wang Liansheng as Li Min, Xia Shasha as Ling Yan, Li Yude as Liu Lin, Wang Shuangqin as Zhang Gengbao, Qiao Qi as Kong Xiaohai, Guo Haibing as Wang Qi

A minor figure in the Xingrong Machine Factory, Kong Dahai, is elected the new factory director. The factory has been suffering losses for many years. Kong issues a series of regulations and rules to manage the enterprise, and even tries withholding bonuses, previously unheard of. But to no one's surprise, there is no improvement, and the problems continue to exist. At last, the troubled factory implements a new system called the "director for a day" system.

1546. *Please Leave the Letter (Qing Ba Xin Liu Xia)*

1984. Changchun Film Studio. Color. Letterboxed. 10 Reels. Direction: Qin Bosheng. Screenplay: Wang Xingdong, Wang Zhebing. Cinematography: Wang Qimin, Li Junyan. Art Direction: Ju Lutian. Music: Wu Damin. Sound: Yu Kaizhang. Cast: Hong Jiantao as Shu Xiaochun, Zhao Fuyu as Jie Chunan, Xiu Jian as Zuang Duan, Shen Danping as Yunzi

Pigeon fancier Su Xiaochun has won two awards for his carrier pigeons. At a pigeon show, he meets and begins a gentle relationship with elementary school teacher Yunzi. Xiaochun was orphaned when very young, and the lonely young man dreams of someday having a real family. Xiaochun joins the PLA and is assigned to raising and caring for carrier pigeons. When he leaves, Yunzi gives him her favorite pigeon. In the army, Xiaochun's pigeons are very successful at delivering messages, and he is encouraged to train more. In addition, the warmth and friendship of his comrades overcomes his psychological pain and loneliness for the first time, becoming the family he never had. When the Sino-Vietnamese border war erupts, Su is sent to the front, and later gives his life to save others.

1547. *The Plough (Part 1) (Bei Dou)*

1979. Changchun Film Studio. Color. 9 Reels. Director: Zhou Yu. Screenplay: Hu Su. Cinematographer: Yan Xuzhong, Duan Zhengjiang. Art Direction: Wang Xiangwen. Music: Huang Zhun. Sound: Yu Kaizhang. Cast: Huang Zhongqiu as Shen Changyuan, Li Yuanhua as Guilan, Du Defu as Xie Xiangfu, Wang Runsheng as Shen Duoyu, Tang Ke as Gan Wenrong

In 1933, when a major drought hits northern Shanxi province, young village singer Shen Changyuan and his girlfriend Guilan marry and leave their hometown to seek a life elsewhere. In a Shanxi border town, warlord Gan

Wenrong takes both into a performing troupe he operates. A year later, Guilan has become a skilled and beautiful performer, arousing the warlord's desire. When he tries to rape her, Guilan and Changyuan run away, but in their flight he falls from a cliff and she is captured. To avoid Gan's advances, she attempts suicide. Although Guilan survives, the attempt gains her some time to avoid the warlord. Shen recovers from his injuries and becomes a drifter. In 1935, he meets a Communist underground worker, and under his tutelage concludes that China will have no future unless they follow the Communist Party's revolutionary path.

1548. *The Plough (Part 2) (Bei Dou)*

1980. Changchun Film Studio. Color. 9 Reels. Direction: Zhou Yu. Screenplay: Hu Su. Cinematography: Yan Xuzhong, Duan Zhengjiang. Art Direction: Wang Xingwen. Music: Huang Zhun. Sound: Yu Kaizhang. Cast: Huang Zhongqiu as Shen Changyuan, Li Yuanhua as Xie Guilan, Wang Runsheng as An Zhaoxiang, Yuan Zhiguang as Liu Zhidan, Su Lin as Zhou Enlai

Xie Guilan and Shen Changyuan are together again, but their life is miserable. Shen Changyuan had joined the revolutionary struggle after the Red Army led by Liu Zhidan liberated his hometown. Later, Xie Guilan is rescued by Liu Zhidan, who introduces her into his revolutionary team. However, at that time, Xie and her husband did not actually join the Red Army. Shortly afterwards, leftist opportunists made their move for power, and Xie Guilan is jailed by the Red Army as an "enemy." Finally, even Liu Zhidan becomes a target of the leftism line, and he is jailed too. Shen Changyuan cannot understand this, so he goes north to look for the Central Red Army. After he reports the matter to the Party, Deputy Chairman Zhou Enlai orders the release of Liu Zhidan and all other revolutionary comrades. Shen Changyuan and Xie Guilan are finally reunited as part of the revolutionary team.

1549. *Plum Blossom Mansion (Mei Hua Gong Guan)*

1993. Changchun Film Studio. Color. Letterboxed. 9 Reels. Direction: Zhu Wenzhi. Screenplay: Xue Shouxian, Xue Cheng. Cinematography: Qian Damin. Art Direction: Ju Luhui. Music: Gao Xiaotian. Sound: Meng Gang, Jiang Yan. Costume: Chen Hua, Tao Ni. Makeup: Liu

Xiaona, Yan Zhenrong. Cast: Hajie as Sha Feng, Dudu as Qingzi, Ni Xuehua as Zhao Yaqiu, A Wei as Can Qicai, Ju Yong as Dong Hanwen, Zhang Shuangli as Qi Zhixiu, Bai Yun as Tian Guizhi, Guo Yong as Chen Guang

In 1925, the Communist Party Central Committee sends young Xiaoping to the Northeast China city of Jinan to deliver their orders to members there concerning economic work. While passing through the city of Jinling on route, Xiaoping and several others are abducted by spies and taken to Plum Blossom Mansion, used by the spies as a safe house. But when the time comes for serious interrogation of Xiaoping, his captors find they have two Xiaopings, and they have no idea which is the one they want. Both Xiaopings escape to safety, the beneficiaries of a deception set up by the Party and a Japanese woman working for an antiwar group.

1550. *Plum Blossoms Bloom Twice (Er Du Mei)*

1959. Wuhan Film Studio. B & W. 12 Reels. Direction: Tao Jin. Adapted from the traditional script for the opera of the same name. Cinematography: Yao Meisheng. Art Direction: Li Pingye. Music: Zhang Dinghe. Sound: Wang Zhongxuan, Tang Rongchun. Cast: Chen Bohua as Chen Xingyuan, Wang Xiaolou as Mei Liangyu, Hu Guilin as Chen Risheng, Tong Jinzhong as the wife, Zhu Qingyu as Chen Chunsheng, Lei Jinyu as Cui Huan, Zhang Chuntang as Lu Qi

In the late Tang Dynasty (9th century A.D.), the family of official Mei Bogao is attacked by Prime Minister Lu Qi. Bogao's son Mei Liangyu flees, changes his name to Xitong, and becomes a gardener in the home of Chen Risheng, who had earlier been removed from his official position. In time, Liangyu and Chen's daughter Xingyuan fall in love, although the young man's lower status requires they keep their relationship secret.

One day, plum blossoms bloom everywhere in Chen Risheng's garden, causing Chen to miss his good friend Mei Bogao. Suddenly a strong wind blows away all the plum blossoms. That night, Chen's daughter Xingyuan learns that Xitong was really Liangyu. With the two young people beseeching them fervently, the plum blossoms bloom once more. Observing this phenomenon, Chen Risheng gives his permission for Liangyu and Xingyuan to marry immediately. But at this moment, Lu Qi orders Xingyuan to go to Hefan (a remote western border area) for a diplomatic marriage. Xingyuan must go, or everyone in her family will be endangered. Liangyu vows to avenge her. On route to Hefan, Xingyuan jumps from a cliff, sacrificing herself out of devotion to Liangyu. At that moment, the female spirit Zhaojun appears, and lets Xingyuan reunite with Liangyu.

1551. *Plum-Flower Embroidery (Mei Hua Jing)*

1980. Pearl River Film Studio. Color. 11 Reels. Direction: Zhang Liang. Screenplay: Wang Jingzhu, Zhang Liang. Cinematography: Li Zhexian. Art Direction: Zhang Zhichu. Music: Fu Gengcheng. Sound: Li Bojian. Cast: Wang Qingbao as Hongmei and Baimei, Zhang Jie as Guo Yueting, Qi Mengshi as Xia Yueqin, Huang Wansu as Lady Feng, Du Xiongwen as Shi Lei, You Lihua as Meiyu

Guo Yueting, an elderly Chinese now living overseas, had been an actor some 40 years earlier, while his wife Meiyu was very skilled at embroidery. The couple and their twin daughters had a very hard life in old China. When a local despot named Qiu Long tried to take his wife from him, Yueting fought the man and injured him. For this Guo had to leave, taking with him just a corner of one of her embroideries, a scarf with a plum blossom pattern. Now, on a trip back to China, Guo Yueting goes to see a play with the curious title, "The Plum Blossom Scarf." As the play unfolds, it recounts precisely the events of his own life. His wife Meiyu died shortly after he fled, and the twin girls Baimei and Hongmei were separated. Baimei lived by embroidering, while Hongmei became an artist, neither knowing where the other was. After 1949, the twin sisters were reunited. Watching the performance, Guo Yueting can control his emotions no longer. He stands up in the audience and approaches the actress Hongmei, then shows her the precious corner of the plum blossom scarf. Baimei, also in the audience, and her twin sister also take out other corners of the scarf. The family which had been separated for 40 years is together again.

Golden Eagle Honorary Award, First Manila International Film Festival, 1982.

Golden Statue Honorary Award, 7th Cairo International Film Festival, 1983.

1552. *The Poachers (Peng Hai Ren)*

1984. Changchun Film Studio. Color. Letterboxed. 10 Reels. Direction: Wang Feng, Screenplay: Da Li, Deng Gang, Cinematography: Meng Xiandi, Art Direction: Li Junjie, Music: Wang Ming, Sound; Wen Liangyu, Cast: Zhang Fengyi as Hai Long, Ren Mei as Bai Ou, Ma Ming as Group Leader Zhang, Ge Jianjun as Hai Tuzhi, Zhao Lu as "Dog," Liu Xueting as Bai Shan, Zhan Qinbo as Old Fatty

In a certain coastal city illegal fishing becomes popular with some people, including Hai Long, a temporary worker in a small manufacturing plant, and his brother, railway electrician Hai Tuzhi. They meet and become acquainted with a girl named Bai Ou. Disgusted by their activities, she severely criticizes them and convinces them to stop. Hai Long is particularly impressed with the young woman's sincerity and personal conduct, and with her help he begins training very hard to be a diver.

1553. *Poet and Hero Xin Qiji (Xin Qi Ji Tie Xue Chuan Qi)*

1993. Emei Film Studio. Color. Letterboxed. 9 Reels. Direction: Li Lingmin. Screenplay: Wang Zixing. Cinematography: Xie Erxiang. Art Direction: Yan Dingfu. Music: Mu Hong. Sound: Qiu Shuchuan. Costume: Zhang Pei. Makeup: Tang Shuangju, Wang Wanxiong. Cast: Liu Yanjun as Xin Qiji, Hu Zhengzhong as Dang Huaiyin, Jiang Qingqing as Fan Ruyu, Yang Xinzhou as Zhan Deli

The story of the military exploits of Xin Qiji, a famous Chinese poet and martial artist of the 12th century. This particular film deals with Xin's early career, when as a young man he helped repel an invasion of China by the Kingdom of Jin.

1554. *Poetess Li Qingzhao (Li Qing Zhao)*

1981. Xi'an Film Studio. Color. 11 Reels. Direction: Zhang Jingrong. Screenplay: Wang Yinqi. Cinematography: Zhang Jiaqin, Kou Jie. Art Direction: Wang Fei. Music: Tu Zhijiu. Sound: Xiong Huajuan. Cast: Xie Fang as Li Qingzhao, Feng Fusheng as Zhao Mingcheng, Ding Jiayuan as Lu Dafu, Zhu Yurong as Lingxiang, Zhi Yitong as Li Gefei

Li Qingzhao (1081–ca.1141) is a famous woman poet in 11th century China. She and her husband, archeologist Zhao Mincheng, are intimate friends as well as lovers, living in harmony while each cultivates a career. Much of Zhao Mingcheng's time is devoted to visiting historical sites, and during his absences Li Qingzhao composes many poems expressing her longing for him. These poems have become classics loved by the Chinese throughout history. When the Jin barbarians' invade China, the couple is separated, and while looking for her husband Li Qingzhao witnesses the suffering the invasion causes for the people. Zhao Mingcheng is persecuted to death, after which Li Qingzhao lives alone, wandering from place to place but never ceasing to write. In her later years she accomplishes her late husband's dream, completing his anthology of many famous Chinese poets. The work is a great contribution to Chinese literature.

1555. *Poetry Wars Pavilion (Dou Shi Ting)*

1960. Tianma Film Studio. B & W. 11 Reels. Direction: Yin Yunwei. Screenplay: Hu Xiaohai, based on a script from the Zhejiang No. 2 Yue Opera Company. Cinematography: Ma Linfa, Ren Zhixin. Art Direction: Ge Shicheng. Music: Zhou Dafeng. Sound: Ding Bohe, Gong Zhengming. Cast: Wang Aiqing as He Qiaohong, Cao Rongfang as Tian Xianghong, Zhang Ronghua as Lin Xiaohong, Liang Yongzhang as Tian Sibao, Jiang Tao as Tian Shangqing, He Ya as Old Lady He

In 1958, a group of young girls led by He Qiaohong attempts to produce high output cotton. Their commune gives them a small wheat field near a place called "Third World Pavilion," and production team director Tian Sibao is assigned to be their technical advisor. However, Tian Sibao thinks the girls' ideas are nonsense. Although the girls work very hard, the cotton does not grow well. Soon, mocking poetry appears on the walls of "Third World Pavilion." After their little cotton field is rated third class by the inspection team, more such poems appear. To show their determination to succeed, each girl writes a poem on the pavilion refuting the poems of their critics. Finally, their hard work pays off with a good cotton harvest. The name of the pavilion is changed to "Poetry Wars Pavilion."

1556. *Poison Strawberries (Du Chao Mei)*

1991. Changchun Film Studio. Color. Letterboxed. 9 Reels. Direction: He Misheng. Screen-

play: Lu Chen. Cinematography: Shu Li, Su Weiping. Art Direction: Ye Jiren. Music: Ye Jiren. Sound: Zhen Yunbao, Jiang Yan. Cast: Zhao Hengxuan as Ding Lin, Zhang Jiatian as Ma Zhao, Xin Xin as Ahong, Zhao Yanhong as Bai Ting

The 14K Group, a Hong Kong triad, is involved in smuggling along the South China border. Chinese special police intercept them, and inflict major financial and personnel losses. The triad swears revenge on the Chinese police and sends a professional killer into China to carry out a campaign of assassination against Chinese officials.

1557. *The Poisonous Kiss (Du Wen)*

1992. Xi'an Film Studio. Color. 9 Reels. Direction: Chen Xingzhong. Screenplay: Zhe Fu. Cinematography: Yang Baoshi, Wang Dong. Art Direction: Zhang Qi. Music: Li Yaofei, Tao Long. Sound: Hong Yi. Costume: Ren Zhiwen. Makeup: Zhao Gang, Liu Xiaoqiao. Cast: Yan Qin as Lin Nuo, Gao Min as Lin Fei, Xu Lei as Zhang Lan, Wu Bo as Sansan (as a youth), Li Bing as Sansan (as a child), Yang Fan as Sansan (as an adult)

Science fiction with an environmental message. A boy named Sansan is born with the ability to kill people, the result of extreme environmental pollution. He kills many people, including his own parents. As an adult, he is sent to prison, but escapes and flees to the mountain area where the city's water source lies. Military forces and helicopters are sent to catch him before he poisons the water supply, but before they can do anything, a brilliant light strikes Sansan, and he disappears in cloud of smoke and fire.

1558. *Police and Detectives (Jing Guan Yu Zhen Tan)*

1988. Emei Film Studio. Color. Letterboxed. 9 Reels. Direction: Mao Yuqing. Screenplay: Xu Bentian, Jiang Yunbiao. Cinematographer: Zhang Huaming. Art Direction: Yan Dingfu. Music: Jin Daiyuan. Sound: Yang Benzhen. Cast: Chen Xu as Qiao Longchi, Li Ping as Di Lan

Hong Kong businessman Qiao Longchi returns to the Chinese mainland to attend a trade conference, but as soon as he arrives he walks into a frame-up arranged by gangsters. He finds himself a wanted man and the PSB in pursuit. The officer in charge of the case is young woman police officer Di Lan, a recent police academy graduate. Desperate to clear himself, Qiao Longchi begins his own investigation. At last, he and Di Lan work together to clear his name and smash a smuggling ring's conspiracy to smuggle antiques.

1559. Police Heroes (Jing Jie Ying Xiong)

1991. Beijing Film Studio. Color. Letterboxed. 9 Reels. Direction: Zhang Zeyu. Screenplay: Fu Xuwen. Cinematography: Zuo Xinhui. Art Direction: Zhang Guojun. Music: Zhang Qianyi. Sound: Guan Shuxin. Cast: You Yong as Luo Jianfeng, Xu Yajun as Hou Jie, Liang Danni as Ge Ping, Lin Jinglai as Wan Zilong, Yan Qing as Ge Shan, Wang Fuyou as Shen Yang, Xing Yinglian as Yue Juan, Li Shijiang as Gao Dazuang, Yang Nan as Huzi

Police detective Luo Jianfeng, investigating a series of robberies, finds that his own sister-in-law Ge Shan possesses loot from the thefts. Luo suspects that Ge's boyfriend, company manager Wan Zhilong, is really a criminal who has been exploiting Ge's job in a bank to commit the robberies. He assigns police officer Hou Jie to follow the woman, and she and Hou Jie become attracted to each other. When Wan Zhilong tells Ge Shan of his plans to rob a bank, she refuses to cooperate further. Wan realizes that police surveillance of Ge Shan is linked to him, and tries to flee. In doing so he takes Ge Shan hostage. In a final gun battle, Hou Jie is killed protecting Ge, and Wan is shot to death.

1560. Police in the Year of the Dragon (aka Dragon Year Cops) (Long Nian Jing Guan)

1990. Beijing Film Studio. Color. 10 Reels. Wide Screen. Direction: Huang Jianzhong, Li Ziyu. Screenplay: Wei Ren. Cinematography: Zuo Xinhui, Zhang Jiang. Art Direction: Ning Lanxin. Music: Ge De. Sound: Guan Shuxin. Cast: Zhang Fengyi as Fu Dong, Zhang Yanli as Yang Aling, Wu Yujuan as Zhong Xiaomei, Lu Liping as Sun Yan

In 1988, two violent criminals escape from Qinghai Prison. They head for Beijing to take revenge on Fu Dong, the police captain who captured them years before. The two fugitives turn it into a crime spree, committing several crimes on their way to Beijing. In the end, Fu captures them again. Against this background the film also follows Captain Fu's complex relationships with three women: his ex-wife Sun

Yan, who he still loves although he deserted her; model Yang Ailing, whom he finds fascinating; and his partner and friend Zhong Xiaomei.

Best Supporting Actress Wu Yujuan, 1991 Hundred Flowers Awards.

1561. Police Officer Tie Zhongying (Shen Bu Tie Zhong Ying)

1991. Pearl River Film Studio. Color. Letterboxed. 10 Reels. Direction: Wang Wei. Screenplay: Ya Ling. Cinematography: Zhen Kangzheng. Art Direction: Guan Yu. Music Zhang Hong. Sound: Lu Minwen. Cast: An Yaping as Tie Zhongyin, Zhao Xueqin as Han Caiyun, Zhang Qi as Changsha Wang, Sun Chengxi as Zhou Feng, Wei Beiyuan as Chen Liao, Xu Songyuan as Jingzhou Wang

When the emperor dies, a struggle for succession breaks out among his five princes, leading to the murder of one in what becomes known as the "Duanzhou Murder Case." Beijing Chief of Police Tie Zhongjie is killed by an arrow while protecting the emperor's will. His younger brother Tie Zhongying takes over the investigation. One of the surviving princes sends a masked assassin to kill two of the others, then place the blame on Han Caiyun, a lady-in-waiting at court. At last, Tie Zhongying cracks the case, after which he and Caiyun leave the city together to lead a secluded life in the mountains.

1562. Police Officer with Special Identification (Te Shu Sheng Feng De Jing Guan)

1982. Xiaoxiang Film Studio. Color. 10 Reels. Direction: Zhou Kangyu. Screenplay: Mao Yicang, Yao Zhihao, Zhou Kangyu, Hu Linling. Cinematography: Teng Xihui, Ding Xiaodong. Art Direction: Li Runzhang, Yang Li. Sound: Yan Ji. Cast: Zhao Erkang as Jiang Wanhe, Yang Dezhi as Luo Baiqian, Yang Baohe as Qin Bangye, Kang Tai as Li Yuanfeng, Liu Guanxiong as Zhang Qian, Li Lanfa as Commissioner Wang

On a spring evening in 1932, Jinfeng County Commissioner Wang Guoci is arrested. Under interrogation, he admits to being a Communist Party member and agrees to lead the police to the local Party's underground headquarters. One of the officers assigned to escort Wang there is Chief of Detectives Jiang Wanhe, a Communist underground in the police department. On the way, Jiang creates an incident which gives him the chance to kill Wang. The Jiangsu provincial police bureau sends their top operative Qin Bangye to lead the investigation and purge of Communists in the county. Jiang Wanhe walks a tightrope in the days to come: while coordinating delivery of arms to guerrillas in the countryside, he must also appear to be investigating Communist activity at the same time he avoids being caught himself. Qin Bangye becomes increasingly suspicious of Jiang, and at last there is a showdown when the arms are being delivered. In a furious gun battle, Jiang holds off police and government agents. He kills scores of them, including Qin Bangye, until at last Jiang Wanhe himself goes down.

1563. *Police Trainees (Yu Bei Jing Guan)*

1983. Pearl River Film Studio. Color. 9 Reels. Direction: Luo Shuqi, Jiang Rui. Screenplay: Chen Jian, Luo Shuqi. Cinematography: Lu Dongqin, Wang Shiji. Art Direction: Tan Ancang. Music: Yang Shuzheng. Sound: Jiang Shaoqi. Cast: Liu Jizhong as Hou Guang, Zhang Tianxi as Liu Dachuan, Xu Ruiping as Xiao Yan, Wu Yufang as Yao Lanlan, Chen Butao as Shen Youcai, Ma Ting as Li Hong, Wang Jing as Grandma

In 1980, a new group of cadets enters the police academy. They vary considerably in their backgrounds and motivations. Hou Guang and Liu Dachuan have the opportunity to conduct their own investigation outside of school, and with the help of the academy director and instructors, uncover a case of economic crime. Yao Lanlan has dreams of becoming the next Sherlock Holmes, but he has trouble adjusting to the strict regulations of the academy. Xiao Yan, Li Hong and He Yingdi have to battle and overcome anti-female prejudice. The film follows the class through to graduation.

1564. *Policeman's Honor (Xing Jing Rong Yu)*

1993. Youth Film Studio, Hong Kong Dihao Film Entertainment Corp. Ltd. Co-Production. Color. 9 Reels. Direction: Mu Deyuan. Screenplay: Li Yiming, Mu Deyuan. Cinematography: Xing Shumin. Art Direction: Zhang Zili. Music: Gao Erdi. Sound: Zhang Wen. Cast: Sun Chun as Tian Zheng, Zhao Xiaorui as Zhao Qingkai, Zhu Jie as sister Yue, An Chi as Quanzi, Wang Xinhai as Xing Dong

When undercover cop Tian Zheng makes his move on the gang he has infiltrated, he kills the wife and brother of gang chief Zhao Qingkai, but Zhao himself escapes Beijing and flees to the prairie province of Qinghai. Tian and other detectives pursue Zhao and arrest him, but when the car transporting the criminal back to Beijing crashes in the mountains, everyone is killed except Tian, who is injured, and Zhao, who escapes again, this time taking Tian's gun and identification. Tian checks in at a hotel, and sets up new headquarters there, this time pretending to be a visiting officer. When Tian recovers, he sets out again after the criminal, but has trouble getting people to believe he is a policeman. At last, he finds the criminal and kills him.

1565. *Policemen in Pursuit (Zui Sha Xing Jing)*

1988. Changchun Film Studio. Color. 10 Reels. Direction: Jin Tao. Screenplay: Qiu Dui. Cinematography: Jin Yixun. Art Direction: Ye Jiren. Music: Xu Suya. Sound: Zhang Wen. Cast: Liu Wei as Zhou Lanfeng, Ru Ping as Xia Ying, Zhang Zhaobei as Qian Zhengyi

Policeman Zhou Lanfeng uncovers evidence that Nanyang Trading Company CEO Cheng Zhaoxiang and his secretary Liu Ge are involved in smuggling activities. He reports what he has found to Chief of Police Qian Zhenyi. Cheng Zhaoxiang decides to kill Zhou Lanfeng before the investigation goes any further. Zhou escapes death when he is tipped off by detective Liu Ge, who has infiltrated Cheng's organization, but Zhou's girlfriend Xia Ying is abducted. Xia Ying is killed by the mob, but not before she is able to get critical information to Zhou concerning the criminals' hideout. Zhou Lanfeng leads a raid on the criminal organization, and at last all the smuggling ring members are captured.

1566. *Policemen's Children (Jing Men Hu Zi)*

1990. Beijing Film Studio. Color. Letterboxed. 9 Reels. Direction: Du Min, Luo Hangmin. Screenplay: Fu Xuwen. Cinematography: Yan Junsheng. Art Direction: Wang Jixian. Music: Lei Lei. Sound: Liu Shida. Cast: Yu Meng as Yuanyuan, Ji Chengmu as Xiaowen, He Ling as Peipei

Yuanyuan, Xiaowen, Peipei, Shuaike and Yanjing are classmates and good friends. Four of the youngsters are children of policemen, Peipei being the lone exception. When Yuanyuan's father is killed in the line of duty, Yuanyuan vows to catch the person responsible, and the others of course help him. However, their investigation soon turns up evidence that Peipei's mother may be implicated in the case Yuanyuan's father was investigating at the time of his death. At this time, to retain their control over his mother, the gang responsible for the killing kidnaps Peipei. The other children send for the police, then rescue their friend. The police arrive in time to round up the whole gang.

1567. *Policewoman's Duty (Nu Jing Tian Zhi)*

1993. Shenzhen Film Company and Hong Kong Jianeng Film Company. Color. Letterboxed. 9 Reels. Direction: Huo Jingwei. Screenplay: Liang Husheng. Cinematography: Cao Anchun, Chen Chuanli. Art Direction: Xie Huibing. Sound: Deng Ronggong. Costume: Zhang Pei. Makeup: Yao Yubao, Yao Xiaomiao. Cast: Xue Li as Cheng Huizhong, Xu Jingjiang as Cheng Huiren, Di Wei as Wan Tianbao, Gui Zhong as Shen Qi, Shen Wei as Shousi, Lin Chong as Shuyi

In Hong Kong, a gang led by Wan Tianbao robs a bank and then discusses how to distribute the money. A joint Hong Kong-PRC police investigation begins, including mainland policewoman Cheng Huizhong. As the investigation comes to a climax in a final confrontation, Huizhong is shocked to find that one of the gang members is her brother Huiren, who she has not seen for years. Huiren at last realizes the wrong course he has taken and kills Wan Tianbao. Huizhong tearfully puts the cuffs on her brother.

1568. *Pomegranate Blossom (Shi Liu Hua)*

1982. Shanghai Film Studio. Color. 11 Reels. Direction: Tang Huada, Wang Xiuwen. Screenplay: Gao Xing. Cinematography: Peng Enli. Art Direction: Zhen Changfu. Music: Liu Yanxi. Sound: Zhou Hengliang. Cast: Gong Xie as Shi Liuhua, Dai Zhaoan as Chen Xiang

Shi Liuhua, adopted from an orphanage when very young, has grown up to value love. When she meets a blind boy named Chen Xiang, she takes it upon herself to escort him to and from school. Chen Xiang devotes his life to playing piano, and overcomes massive difficulties to play it well enough to major in piano at college. Shi Liuhua likes Chen Xiang's strong character and determination to have a career. Later, Shi Liuhua is disabled by an automobile accident, and while she at first finds it difficult to cope with this, she soon accepts the reality and becomes an assembler in a plant employing the disabled. A new medical procedure restores Chen Xiang's vision, and after graduating from college, he proposes marriage to Shi Liuhua. Shi Liuhua loves Chen Xiang deeply, but she does not want be a burden to him. Wanting to pursue the sort of life she can live on her own, she leaves for a school in South China to be a teacher of blind children. Chen Xiang and Shi Liuhua get together at the blind children's school in the south, and vow they will never part again.

1569. *Pop Song (Jie Shi Liu Xing Qu)*

1986. Pearl River Film Studio. Color. 10 Reels. Direction: Yu Shibin. Screenplay: Huang Jinhong. Cinematography: Liu Xinmin, Pang Lei. Cast: Du Ming as Amei, Chen Rui as Ajian, Wang Weibo as Ajin, Yuan Xingze as Afang, Huang Jingshang as Mother

In an old, three-story building in a humble neighborhood of Guangzhou a young woman named Amei lives with her mother. Amei, called "Golden Voice," has been pampered since childhood. Although she is 20, she idles away her days and shows no interest in getting a job. With the help of neighbors, Amei joins the All-Stars Band and before long becomes their lead singer, boosting her ego even further. She deliberately snubs her neighbors and a young man named Ajian, her childhood sweetheart. However, the band fires her because of her complacency. Harsh reality shocks her into seeing the light, but the love she longs for has been lost forever. Through her rise and fall, the film introduces many of the urban customs of Guangzhou, south China's largest city, and its unique form of pop music.

1570. *Popular Will (Tian Di Ren Xin)*

1994. Changchun Film Studio. Color. Letterboxed. 10 Reels. Direction: Wang Xuexin. Screenplay: Hu Zhengyan, Yin Xinglin. Cinematography: Ning Changcheng. Art Direction: Ji Shulin. Music: Guo Xiaotian. Sound: Zhang Hongguang. Costume: Yang Shu. Makeup: Pan

Li. Cast: Gao Qiang as Yang Shouben, Yue Hong as Wang Bing, Lu Xiaohe as Bao Zhiguang, Du Zhenqing as Wu Linshan, Ouyang Ruqiu as Old Lady Li, Zhao Chunming as County Director Guo, Di Li as Grandma Luo, Ji Chengmu as Yang Xiaoguang

When Yang Shouben assumes the directorship of the county grain bureau, he quickly discovers many corrupt practices such as embezzlement going on at the agency. His attempts to clean up the bureau runs head-on into opposition from a faction around his deputy bureau director Bao Bao. They use every means including personal attacks and an attempt to seduce the widowed Yang with a woman. The director's son Xiaoguang is preparing for his own marriage, when he gets a tip that Bao's followers are selling poor quality fertilizer. Xiaoguang goes to investigate the rumor, but he is killed and his body burned to conceal the murder. The perpetrators are caught, but the grieving father almost gives up his crusade. However, many local people come to him to express their sympathy and appreciation for his work on their behalf. This outpouring of support gives him the strength to carry on.

1571. *The Port Is Not Calm (Gang Wan Bu Ping Zheng)*

1983. Guangxi Film Studio. Color. 9 Reels. Direction: Zen Xueqiang. Screenplay: Chen Duode. Cinematography: Meng Xiongqiang, Chen Shengkai. Art Direction: Zhang Jingnan. Music: Li Yanlin. Sound: Li Zhuwen. Cast: Gu Yongfei as Cao Fan, Wu Jiao as Yu Qianshan, Yan Xiang as Rong Jiecheng, Zhang Lifa as Guo Dazhu, Zhang Tieyin as Bian Yang, Wu Cihua as Meng Ke

At the South China port of Jinsha at the end of the 1970s, a conflict arises between construction speed and quality. The Commercial Examination Bureau receives a letter reminding them that only 20 days remain for them to demand compensation should there be quality problems with their last shipment of imported steel piping. Unfortunately the shipment was shipped directly to Jinsha when received, and was never inspected. The Bureau sends young woman inspector Cao Fan to Jinsha. She has suspicions about the quality of the pipes, and suggests the project be shut down temporarily. Construction site chief Yu Qianshan opposes her for personal reasons: he has misused his import rights to bring in inferior materials and get a kickback from foreign businessmen, a major economic crime. Cao Fan calls on the support of workers and leadership at all levels to verify the pipes' poor quality and request compensation before the deadline expires, thereby protecting the national interest.

1572. *Posted to the Front (Qian Shao)*

1959. Changchun Film Studio. B & W. 11 Reels. Direction: De Guangbudaoerji. Screenplay: Zhou Jiuhu, De Guangbudaoerji. Cinematography: Li Huailu. Art Direction: Liu Jinnai. Music: Lou Zhanghou, Lin Xuesong. Sound: Wang Fei. Cast: Li Yalin as Gu Dapeng, Xu Liankai as Geng Jian, Ma Loufu as Director Fang, Wang Chunyin as Linhai, Yao Yin as Mrs. Zhao, Mang Yiping as Cai Meimei, Jin Lin as Chen Jiachang, Li Wanfu as the company commander, Li Yingju as Xiao Ming, Hou Jianfu as 404 (Jiang Renjun), Liu Ru as 42 (Hu Guang), Shi Kefu as 43 (Lu Shiying), Zou Wenlin as Liu Dao

A U.S. spy agency sends a unit of Nationalist agents headed by "No. 404" to gather intelligence from a small town on China's southeast coast. PLA counterintelligence sends Gu Dapeng to the town in the guise of a restaurant waiter. Staff officer Geng Jian's housekeeper Cai Meimei is the mistress of Huang Qi, one of the spies. When she tries to steal Geng Jian's briefcase, she is caught and Huang Qi is killed. Gu Dapeng is also able to thwart 404's plan to steal military maps. To catch all the spies, Gu Dapeng assumes the identity of the already-dead Agent 41, infiltrates the spies' headquarters, and gains their trust. From there, Gu coordinates the police and the PLA special agents in wiping out the enemy agents.

1573. *Postman (You Chai)*

1995. United Frontline. Color. 102 min. Direction: He Jianjun. Cinematography: Wu Di. Screenplay: He Jianjun, You Ni. Art Direction: Li Mang. Music: Otomo Yoshihide. Sound: Gu Yu, Guan Jian. Costume: Dong Yingchun. Cast: Fang Yuanzheng as Xiao Dou, Liang Danni as Sister, Pu Quanxin as Sister's boyfriend, Huang Xing as Qing Yun, Liu Zhizi as the postal station manager, Chen Jue as Chen Jie, Ge Zhixing as Old Wu, Zheng Tianwei as Wan Juan

An introverted young man, detached and uninvolved with the world about him, is by chance offered a job as a letter carrier. A good worker at first, he soon becomes bored, and to pass the time begins opening and reading letters intended for people on his route. He soon is addicted to following the events in the lives of these people, and at last becomes obsessed with them. His obsession leads him to go beyond just reading, to actually intervene in the lives of the addressees. His obsessive intervention at lasts leads to tragedy, an outcome from which he remains detached.

1574. *The Postponed Trial (Yan Qi Shen Pan)*

1992. Inner Mongolia Film Studio. Color. Letterboxed. 9 Reels. Direction: Sun Zhiqiang. Cinematography: Lin Jian. Art Direction: Han Jingfeng. Music: Bing He. Sound: Bu Ren. Costume: Tang Baoli. Makeup: Dong Weidong. Cast: Pan Zhiqi as Pang Weili, Han Yueqiao as Bi Lan, Ding Xin as Deng Hua, Gu Zhi as Zhen Huanyu, Li Yuling as Gu Kai

A serious accident in a chemical plant production line leaves 7 people dead and 30 injured. The man directly responsible for the line is placed on trial for criminal negligence, but the proceedings are disrupted when his wife enters the court protesting that an injustice is being done: the real culprit is the company CEO Gu Kai, so the court decides to postpone the trial. Investigator Pang Weili encounters numerous blocks, threats and at last the murder of a witness before he gets the real criminal Gu Kai on trial.

1575. *Prairie Eagles (Cao Yuan Xiong Ying)*

1964. Beijing Film Studio. Color. 10 Reels. Direction: Ling Zhifeng, Dong Kena. Screenplay: Wu Yuxiao, based on the stage play "Youth in a Remote Place." Cinematography: Qian Jiang. Set Design: Yang Yuhe. Music: Shao Guangsheng. Sound: Fu Yinjie. Cast: Abudulaheman Awazi as Kadeer, Nuernisha Simayi as Amina, Shadeke as Ali, Lipo as Secretary Liu, Silajiding Silayin as the Yili Ranch director, Sha Hei as Hasheng

Veterinary graduates Ali and Amina receive work assignments at the Yili horse ranch in the Tianshan Mountains. There, Amina meets her former lover and classmate Kadeer, whose enthusiasm for public service and caring for horses is admired and praised by all the herdsmen. On the other hand, Ali seeks fame and is arrogant, while Amina concentrates on studying theory but disdains practice. Both of them look down on Kadeer. But Kadeer's actions in

such things as saving a sick horse by performing a difficult operation, and handling the difficult birth of a calf, gradually changes Amina's attitude toward her work and toward Kadeer. Her admiration soon turns to love. With the help of the Party organization and the people on the ranch, Ali in time also comes to realize his mistakes, and the three young people make progress together.

1576. *Prairie Morning Song (Cao Yuan Chen Qu)*

1959. Changchun Film Studio & Inner Mongolia Film Studio Co-Production. B & W. 11 Reels. Direction: Zhu Wenshun, Zhulanqiqike. Screenplay: Malaqinfu, Zhulanqiqike. Cinematography: Chen Minhun. Art Direction: Liu Jinnai. Music: Tong Fu. Sound: Huang Lijia. Cast: Enghesheng as Hu He, Zhao Lu as Liaxiningbu, Baoyinjiergalang as Jiamiyang, Zhang Juguang as Zhang Yuxi, Qiao Lu as Daoerji, Pan Ying as Zhang Xiuzhi

A group of young friends, Mongolian and Chinese, battle the Japanese invaders in the mining region of China's Inner Mongolia province. After the war, they work together through the Party to exploit the mines' resources for the betterment of the local people's livelihood.

1577. *Prairie Storm (Cao Yuan Feng Bao)*

1960. Xi'an Film Studio & Qinghai Film Studio Co-Production. B & W. 9 Reels. Direction: Lin Feng. Screenplay: Cheng Xiushan and Wang Wuzeng. Cinematography: Han Zhongliang and Lin Jing. Art Direction: Li Mingjiu. Music: Wei Ruixiang. Sound: Hong Jiahui. Cast: Sun Yonghe as Naibuzhang, Zhang Zuohan as Division Head Wang, Cui Shufeng as Cairencuo, Yi Donglin as Secretary Wanma, Bi Fusheng as Ranluo, Zhang Muqing as Xiuchiji

In 1958, the Tibetan people of Huangren County, Qinghai province, establish a stock-raising production cooperative. The high priest of the local temple, Deputy County Director Lamorong and other reactionary elements make common cause with undercover agent Ma Yinu. The group tries to exploit the people's religious superstitions to make the herdsmen suspicious of the co-op. Lamorong also arranges a conspiracy to destroy the co-op's work, and orders young lama Danzeng to carry out his orders. Stock-raising co-op director Naibuzhang wins over Danzeng by proving to him that Naibuzhang's wife and daughter have been abducted and the wife tortured on Lamorong's orders. The young lama investigates further and learns of the enemy's conspiratorial activities. When Lamorong realizes his conspiracy is exposed, he decides to launch his rebellion ahead of schedule. Coordinating his actions with the PLA, Naibuzhang leads the local militia in smashing the rebels' plot. Lamorong is captured and Nai's wife and daughter are rescued.

1578. *Praising Acupuncture in the Operating Room (Wu Ying Deng Xia Song Ying Zhen)*

1974. Shanghai Film Studio. Color. 5 Reels. Direction: Li Chongjun. Screenplay: Sang Hu, based on the stage play of the same title by the Shanghai Chest Hospital's Recreational Writing Team. Art Direction: Xue Jianna. Music: Xu Jingxin. Cast: Zhu Xijuan as Li Zhihua, Wang Zhigang as Master Worker Chen, Lou Jicheng as Master Worker Old Yang, Ding Jiayuan as Doctor Ding, Chen Xiuzhen as Xiao Feng, Qiu Shishui as Doctor Luo

Young Doctor Li Zhihua proposes treating old worker Yang's heart ailment through the use of acupunctural anesthesia, since the situation will not permit the use of regular anesthesia. Doctor Luo, Deputy Director of the Department of Surgery, has a perfect record with the acupunctural method, so he objects to using it on Yang. Doctor Li risks her life to test the method on herself and determine every type of complication possible. When Yang's situation begins to take a turn for the worse, Doctor Luo wants to evict Yang from the hospital, but Li insists he be allowed to remain. Finally, Doctor Li cures Yang's heart ailment, and Doctor Luo acknowledges his mistakes in light of the realities.

1579. *Precious as Gold (Jin Bu Huan)*

1984. Pearl River Film Studio. Color. Letterboxed. 10 Reels. Direction: Hong Ping, Yu Shibing. Screenplay: Gu Xiaoyan. Cinematography: Wang Henli, Han Xingyuan. Art Direction: Zhang Zhichu. Music: Lu Yuan. Sound: Li Xun. Cast: Wei Jian as Jin Yonghe, Chun Li as Xu Er, Qu Yun as Jin's wife, Liang Yujing as Yuxia

When County Deputy Director Jin Yonghe decides to leave political life and become an ordinary farmer, he settles down in a village where he had once served as director. He receives a mixed greeting: as director, he had been critical of those who sought "the capitalist road," seeking to become rich. Some of those now-prosperous farmers resent his return. When a flood hits, threatening some of the farmers with economic disaster, Jin Yonghe diverts the water to his own fields to protect the crops of others. For this, everyone comes to him and tells him that a true Communist is as precious as gold.

1580. *The Precipice (Xuan Ya)*

1958. Changchun Film Studio. B & W. 10 Reels. Direction: Yuan Naiceng. Screenplay: Nan Dan. Cinematography: Su Xiaoyan. Art Direction: Wang Cong. Music: Ge Guangrui. Sound: Zhang Jian. Cast: Qing Wen as Fang Qing, Zhou Zheng as Fan Jun, Zhou Zou as Professor Yuan Shisheng, Sun Jingjian as Zhang Xiaoyan, Zhang Fengxiang as Professor Chen, Duan Bing as Wang Duo

Fang Qing, a young woman about to graduate from medical school, is in love with classmate Fan Jun. When job assignments are made, Fan Jun requests work in Northwest China where working and living conditions are hard, but Fang Qing insists on working at the medical school, so the two break up. After Fang Qing stays at the school, she is seduced by her former lover's uncle Professor Yuan, who exploits her capitalist desires for fame and fortune. He lures her into helping him with the organization and lab tests for a book he is working on, and she becomes so involved with it that she neglects her own work, which further alienates her from Fan Jun. She falls completely under the unethical professor's power when he offers to put her name on the book as co-author. He proposes marriage, which she accepts. But at their wedding, Zhao Wen, an old colleague of Professor Yuan's, returns from abroad and exposes him as a fraud who was plagiarizing the work of her late husband. Through this painful lesson, Fang Qing begins to understand the criticism and help which the Party organization, her comrades and Fan Jun had offered before. She decides to move to another work assignment where she can rehabilitate herself.

1581. *The Pre-Dawn Cold (Wu Geng Han)*

1957. August First Film Studio. B & W. 11 Reels. Direction: Yan Jizhou. Screenplay: Shi Chao. Cinematography: Jiang Shi. Art Direction: Xu Run. Music: Gong Zhiwei. Sound: Li Bojian. Makeup: Li Hongquan. Cast: Yang Wei as Party Secretary Liu, Shi Kefu as Luo Wenchuan, Cao Ying as Qiao Feng, Li Xuehong as Mu Ying, Yang Xiuzhang as Nan Guoxiang, Liu Jiyun as Lao Liangcai, Li Li as Wang Tai, Qu Yun as Pan Mao, Zhu Zizheng as Mo Wenjie

In 1946, Chiang Kaishek commits 200,000 troops to an attack on the Communist-held China central plains. After the PLA main force in the area retreats, the Nationalists also capture the area around the Dabie Mountains. County Party Committee Secretary Liu and county organization department director Mo Wenjie lead a guerrilla troop which continues the fight. But Mo Wenjie soon defects to the enemy. Mu Ying, a CPC member and the wife of guerrilla fighter Nan Guoxiang, is captured by the enemy but released in the hope she will induce others to defect. Nan Guoxiang, always fond of ease and comfort, wavers at first; but Secretary Liu and the rest of the guerrillas always keep to the objective, waging constant attacks on the enemy under the most difficult of circumstances. Winter passes and with the arrival of spring the PLA launches a massive counterattack which wipes out the enemy in the Dabie Mountains.

1582. *Pre-Dawn Gunfire (Fu Xiao Qiang Sheng)*

1991. Emei Film Studio. Color. Letterboxed. 9 Reels. Direction: Zhang Xihe. Screenplay: Liu Jianan, Mao Mao. Cinematography: Song Jianwen. Art Direction: Xia Zhengqiu. Music: Tang Qingshi. Sound: Tu Liucheng. Costume: Yu Aiguo. Makeup: Cao Songlin and Liu Zhiyu. Cast: Shi Zhaoqi as Chu Ling, Tai Gang as Ji Fanyu, Li Guozhong as Zhang Hao, Wang Xueqing as Mother, Han Haihua as Wailong, Yuan Zhishun as Commander, Zhang Xihe as Hei Laodiao

In the days just after the Communist victory in 1949, the Nationalists refuse to give up and have spies on the mainland instigate bandit raids. The PLA's intelligence branch and local public security forces work together to smash the conspiracy.

1583. *Pretty Girl A Ping (Jing Nu A Ping)*

1985. Pearl River Film Studio. Color. 3-D. 6 Reels. Direction: Er Lin, Zhang Rongren. Screenplay: Er Lin. Cinematography: Zhou Jianhui. Art Direction: Man Qinhai. Music: Cheng Dazhao. Sound: Lin Guoqiang. Cast: Xu Ruiping as Fu Ping, Zhang Shen as Li Keming, Liu Yan as Fu Dong, Li Zhi as Huang Lu, Jian Ruichao as Li Keming's father

A girl named Fu Ping (nicknamed A Ping) is named general manager of Shunhai City's new farmers' amusement park, but before assuming her new post she first goes to visit her brother, Changjiang Amusement Park's general manager Fu Dong. There, A Ping meets a young man called Li Keming who is unhappy at the park. He is a Chinese from Australia visiting China for the first time with his family. Now his father has fallen ill and is hospitalized. A Ping understands Li's feelings, and keeps him company to cheer him up. Through her, Li develops very good feelings about China. His few days experience there gives him the idea of investing in China to support its modernization effort. His father is very supportive of this. In addition, father and son decide to invest in the farmers' amusement park.

1584. *Prison Car to the West (Xi Xing Qiu Che)*

1989. Pearl River Film Studio. Color. Letterboxed. 10 Reels. Direction: He Qun. Screenplay: He Jianmin, Jiang Ao. Cinematography: Zhao Xiaoshi, Gang Yi. Art Direction: Zhang Ruo. Music: Ma Ding. Sound: Huang Minguang. Cast: Du Zhiguo as Zhen Zhongli, Li Qiang as Du Ming, Liu Pei as Luo Ling, Zhang Xi as Wang Jichang, Zhang Dongsheng as Zhao Peng, Guo Jianguo as Luo Pan, Wang Zhenrong as Zhao Ri, Xu Dongfang as Da Li

A train transports some of China's most hardened criminals to a prison in an isolated part of west China. The mixed lot of felons includes Luo Pan, who had been one of the country's most wanted, and Du Ming, who arranged his own capture in order to help Luo escape. Meanwhile, Luo's former gang makes detailed arrangements to free him. The story traces the PSB's efforts to stop the breakout, and at last haul all of the convicts to prison.

1585. *Private Bodyguard (Si Ren Bao Biao)*

1992. Beijing Film Studio. Color. Letterboxed.

9 Reels. Direction: Wang Junzheng. Screenplay: He Zhizuang, Yang Jiang. Cinematography: Yan Junsheng. Art Direction: Yang Hong. Music: Hou Muren. Sound: Zhen Chunyu. Costume: Wang Jianqin. Makeup: Li Dongtian, Li Hui. Cast: Zhao Jun as Zhou Qiu, Wang Yanping as Kang Qian, Zhang Fengyi as Zuo Bingwei, Zhao Liping as Wei Li, Zhen Weili as Kang Lan.

Retired army veteran Zhou Qiu, a wartime hero, is hired by company director Wei Li as his personal bodyguard. When a girl named Kang Qian makes an attempt on the executive's life, Zhou intervenes to save him. The bodyguard then finds the girl was a victim of Wei Li's illegal business: recruiting young girls as models, then selling them into prostitution overseas. His sense of justice, and later his love for the girl, motivate Zhou to help Kang stop this illegal trafficking. In the final confrontation, Kang succeeds in killing Wei Li.

1586. *The Private Teaching Company (Pu Lai Wei Ti Che Gong Si)*

1989. Children's Film Studio. Color. Letterboxed. Direction: Qiqin Gaowa. Screenplay: Xia Youzhi. Cinematography: Sun Yongtian. Art Direction: Chen Zhuo. Music: Zhang Piji. Sound: Zhang Ruikun. Cast: Pu Ying as Qiaomaipi, Feng Lei as Siyan'er, Elia as Meilidou, Chen Gang as "Kentucky," Guo Jinglin as Logda

Logda, a precocious and independent high school student, plans to start a private teaching company of his own during the winter vacation. He hires four other high school boys to help him, Siyan'er, Qiaomaipi, Meilidou and Kentucky. The four figure this is a good way to earn some money while having fun. They become tutors, "private teachers," to four junior middle school students. After 10 days of this, they not only find they have earned no money, they are in an awkward situation. They quit the company, deciding they cannot stand it any longer. Logda tries to hire four more…

1587. *Probation Within the Village (Liu Cun Ca Kan)*

1994. Changchun Film Studio. Color. Letterboxed. 9 Reels. Direction: Lei Xianhe, Wang Xingdong. Screenplay: Wang Xingdong, Wang Zhebing. Cinematography: Hu Weidong, Su Zaili. Art Direction: Liu Huanxing. Music: Wu Daming. Sound: Cao Feng, Zhang Xiaonan. Costume: Zhang Shufang, Zhang Renchun. Makeup: Zhao Li, Liu Xiaohong. Cast: Wei Zi as Jian Zheng, Shen Danping as Luo Caiyun, Cui

Guojun as Zhao Xiang, Jia Fengsheng as village director, Xu Jianing as Mou Geng, Li Haoling as Mou Lan, Li Xiaolu as Fangfang, Wang Zhixia as Ning Meng

Before he has completed his one year probation, County Director Jian Zheng is dismissed from his post when his wife Ning Meng is found guilty of accepting a bribe and sentenced to seven years in prison. Jian Zheng decides to restart his career from scratch, and takes a position as director of "Mute Village," a place where all the residents are mute. Jian finds the source of this problem is the village's water source, and he proposes a water project to correct it. He approaches the provincial office for the funds, and after much petitioning and many meetings the project is funded. Two years after completion of the project, the village has rid itself of poverty and is on the road to prosperity. The county legislature reappoints Jian Zheng to his old post as county director, and all the village people come to see him off.

1588. *Probationary Army Officers (Lu Jun Jian Xi Guan)*

1987. Changchun Film Studio. Color. 11 Reels. Direction: Yu Yanfu, Zhang Yuan. Screenplay: Wang Xingdong, Wang Zhebing. Cinematography: Dansheng Nima. Art Direction: Shi Weijun. Music: Wu Damin. Sound: Kang Ruixin. Cast: Liu Jiaoxin as Ju Aosheng, Wu Ruopu as Kuang Yintao, Zhang Guangbei as Xiang Fan, Ji Ping as Kang Kai, Liu Xuhui as Di Lian

After four years of strict and arduous training, some PLA military academy students will soon graduate. The military district headquarters orders that 60 graduates be selected to serve internships with a battalion at the Yunnan front. They are given three days leave before shipping out. The film tells of their three days. Xiang Fan, handsome son of a general, meets and falls in love with Yamei, a girl with whom he spends one happy day. Di Lian is something of an outsider, and spends every day at school working out. Kuang Yingtao goes to a prison to visit his good friend Tiefu, who committed a crime for Kuang. Kang Kai goes to visit Fengxiu, the girl he dumped four years before, and she forgives him upon learning he will be going to the frontlines. Ju Aosheng visits his adoptive mother. Everybody is encouraged about leaving for the front lines.

1589. *Proposal (Yi Jian Tian)*

1954. Beijing Film Studio. B & W. 9 Reels. Direction: Li Enjie. Screenplay: Yan Yiyan and Gu Yu, based on the latter's novel of the same title. Cinematography: Nie Jing. Set Design: Yu Yiru. Music: Chen Di. Sound: Cai Jun. Costume: Wang Feng. Makeup: Zhang Jing. Cast: Li Jioufang as Jin Qing, Wu Bing as Jin Qing's mother, Chen Qiang as Si Laogang, Lin Yuan as Si's wife, Liu Yi as Gui Rong, Liu Liu as Pao Changlin

At a meeting of the Jinghe County People's Congress, District 3 Representative Jin Qing voluntarily withdraws his proposal that his district build a brick dam in support of attempts to get a railway through the area. Rather, he agrees that District 1's dam-building proposal be given a higher priority. His action does not sit well with District 3's other representative Si Laogang and some of his constituents. Jin Qing patiently explains that during the rainy season the water in Laolong Bay in District 3 could rise and flood District 1. When this does indeed happen, the people from District 1 are protected by their repaired dam, and gratefully offer their assistance to District 3. In the next year, a reservoir is constructed at an upper section of the river, so the county commission decides to repair a water gate for District 3. From all this, the people of District 3 come to realize the correct relationship between the general interest and self-interest, that it is wrong to seek only one's own immediate interest and not consider overall interest.

1590. *Prosecution (Qi Su)*

1986. Emei Film Studio. Color. 10 Reels. Direction: Jia Mu. Screenplay: Jia Mu, Yang Yinzhang. Cinematography: Cheng Zhaoxun, Zhang Huaming. Art Direction: Lin Qi. Music: Tang Qinshi. Sound: Luo Guohua. Cast: Wei Qimin as Ji Hongwei, Wu Yuhua as Bai Huiru, Wang Zhenjiang as Lu Yongquan, Du Xiongwen as Zhen Wanliang, Tu Zhongru as Liu Youzhi

A series of charges of economic crimes are brought by a city's prosecutorial office against officials of the Haiou Comprehensive Development Company. The cases are assigned for investigation and prosecution to Bai Huiru, a young woman just graduated from school. Her investigation proceeds smoothly until her office receives an order from higher up to release one of the principals in the case, a Hong Kong businessman. Seeing how justice and the law can be perverted, Bai Huiru determinedly sticks to her investigation and at last secures the convictions of the main conspirators in the case.

1591. *The Prosecutor (Jian Cha Guan)*

1981. Shanghai Film Studio. Color. Letterboxed. 9 Reels. Direction: Xu Weijie. Screenplay: Luo Huajun, Li Zhaizhong, Zhao Zhiqiang. Cinematography: Ju Jiazhen. Art Direction: Chen Fuxing. Music: Xiao Yan. Sound: Yin Zhiping. Cast: Li Muran as Xu Li, Wang Weiping as Zhang Hua, Hong Xueming as Tang Ming, Huang Daliang as Xu Wentao, Jia Deyin as Deputy Director Liang

In the summer of 1977, the police in the city of Lidao break up a criminal gang. Chief Prosecutor Xu Li learns that the previously unresolved Mu Xiaoli case was also the work of this gang, and that the head of the gang is Zhang Hua, a driver in a freezer plant. Xu Li issues an order for Zhang Hua's arrest but the accused has fled. When Xu Li learns that Zhang Hua is the man who had once saved Xu Li from some Red Guards during the Cultural Revolution, he cannot believe that Zhang has become a criminal. In time, the fugitive is apprehended and the two meet again. At the trial, Xu Li is shocked to come across evidence that the true criminal may be his own son Xu Wentao. He investigates this possibility, and confirms that Xu Wentao is indeed in with the gang while Zhang Hua is a victim. However, Xu Li's conclusion is opposed by Liang Jingyi, deputy director of the Public Security Bureau and his wife Liao Qi. Xu Li finally wins Zhang Hua's trust, and with the accused man's help he is able to clear up everything. Xu Wentao attempts to escape, but falls from a cliff and is killed. Xu Li demands the case be reopened, and based on what he has learned investigating his son, he arrests Liang Jingyi and Liao Qi.

1592. *The Prostitute and the Raftsman (Bei Lie Pai Bang)*

1992. Jiangxi Film Studio. Color. Letterboxed. 9 Reels. Direction: Huang Jun. Screenplay: Huang Jun, Li Zhichuan, Zhou Wen. Cinematography: Ning Changcheng. Art Direction: Zhang Yikuan, Gan Zongrong. Music: Liu Yuan. Sound: Feng Deyao. Costume: Chen Cheng. Makeup: Fu Zhenghua. Cast: Wang Gang as Shan Yu, Shi Ke as Lian Hua, Yuan Yuan as Shuisheng, Liu Zhongyuan as Drummer, Li Wenjun as Jiang Gou

In 1945, before withdrawing from the area, the Japanese heavily mine Lake Panyang in Jiangxi province. This makes it impossible for the people living around the lake to earn a living. The film introduces these varied individuals, and depicts their struggle to get rid of the mines and go back to a normal life. In the end, all are killed by a mine.

1593. *Protecting Home Through the Nation (Wei Guo Bao Jia)*

1950. Northeast Film Studio. B & W. 9 Reels. Direction: Yan Gong. Screenplay: Wang Zhengzhi. Cinematography: Nie Jing. Set Design: Liu Xuerao. Music: Xu Xu. Sound: Zhao Hongjun. Costume: Wang Xiuying. Cast: Yang Jing as Chen Guiying, Yu Yang as Yang Dezhi. Che Yi as Li Yutian, Zhang Yin as Chen Zhengyi, Xue Yan as Zhang Jingluan, An Qi as Zhao Xiaolan

After Chen Family Village is liberated, the inspiration and assistance of Li Yutian, an Eighth Route Army woman soldier, helps free Chen Guiying from a local landlord's attempts to force her into marriage. She organizes the local women into a spinning group and is elected Village Head. She later becomes engaged to Yang Dezhi, a young soldier awaiting call-up to active duty. But when the War of Liberation starts, her life has so improved that she tries to persuade her fiance to remain a civilian and settle down in the village. With the criticism and help of Li Yutian, Chen Guiying realizes that peace without final victory is still a dream, and she sends him off to the army. Five years later, he returns with the army, to build and protect China.

1594. *Protecting the Children of Jingwu Kung Fu Academy (Jing Wu Xia Yuan)*

1995. Long Wei Film Production Company, Shanghai Film Studio. Color. Letterboxed. Direction: Li Zhao, Cheng Jiaxiang. Screenplay: Huang Shoukang, Li Zhao. Cinematography: He Ming. Art Direction: Qin Baisong. Sound: Xu Hong. Cast: Qian Jiale as Huojian, Chen Mingzhen as Yueer, Lin Guobin as Bai Ying, Ye Fang as Xiao Ying

When Yuan Shikai's dreams of becoming emperor are thwarted in 1916, he orders his son Yuan Keqi to implement a crazed plan of revenge, to kill everyone at the Jingwu Kung Fu Academy. This action film tells how various heroes protect the academy's younger generations.

1595. *Prowess (Shen Tong)*

1993. Shenzhen Film Company & Hong Kong Changhe Film Company Co-Production. Color. Letterboxed. 9 Reels. Direction and Screenplay: Zhang Che. Cinematography: Liu Hongquan, Ma Delin. Art Direction: Cheng Lu. Music: Deng Shaolin. Sound: Deng Shaolin. Costume: Hai Xin. Makeup: Bao Sha. Cast: Chen Baigang as Yuji, Cheng Yaling as Mu Tong, Dong Zhihua as Sun Che, Mu Lixin as Jin Tong, Du Yumin as Tu Tong, Chen Dieyi as Da Qiao

During the Yellow Turbans Uprising at the end of the Eastern Han Dynasty (c200 A.D.), heroic Yuji and his five adopted children, all orphans of peasant soldiers, fight against tyranny and injustice.

The Puma Action **see** *Code Name: "Cougar"*

1596. *Pure Gold in a Raging Fire (Lie Huo Zhen Jin)*

1959. August First Film Studio. B & W. 8 Reels. Direction: Dong Zhaoqi. Screenplay: Shi Qingye. Cinematography: Kou Jiwen, Jin Ming. Art Direction: Mai Yi. Music: Chen Daying. Sound: Li Lin. Cast: Zhao Ruping as Wang Zhiqiang, Wang Ying as Jiang Ling, Bai Gang as army Doctor Yang, Li Jiufang as the political instructor, Shi Chunyu as the hospital director, Guan Suzhen as the chief nurse

The title is an idiom meaning that people of worth prove their quality when things are most difficult, i.e., when the going gets tough, the tough get going.

On the frontlines in Fujian province, PLA soldier Wang Zhiqiang is severely burned and wounded saving a cannon during a major fire. When he arrives at the hospital, people from all walks of life queue up wanting to donate blood for him. Many of the hospital staff, including Doctor Yang and nurse Jiang Ling, stay with him day and night. Wang Zhiqiang overcomes the unbearable pain by sheer force of will. Through all the combined efforts, he finally recovers and returns to the frontlines.

1597. *Purple Red Crown (Zi Hong Se De Huang Guan)*

1987. Shanghai Film Studio. Color. 10 Reels. Direction: Yu Bengzheng. Screenplay: Wu

Tianci, Dong Jingsheng, Gong Nan. Cinematographer: Zhu Yongde. Art Direction: Wu Tianci. Music: Liu Yanxi. Sound: Liu Guangjie. Cast: Yuan Yuan as Zhan Liangliang, Cui Dazhi as Wang Xiaobing, Zhen Qianlong as Chen Lei, Lan Zhiguang as Screenwriter Xin

After his parents divorce and his father moves to another city, a lonely young boy starts hanging out in the streets, and soon gets into trouble by defacing parked cars. But when the adults he has wronged learn the cause of the boy's actions, they forgive him and give him the warmth and fatherly guidance he lacks at home.

1598. *Purple Scar (Zi Heng)*

1991. Changchun Film Studio. Color. Letterboxed. 9 Reels. Direction: Cheng Ke. Screenplay: Du Lijuan. Cinematography: Duan Zhengjiang, Qian Damin. Art Direction: Ju Lutian, Zhu Jiaxin. Music: Yang Yilun. Sound: Dong Baosheng, Gu Kejian. Cast: Song Jia as Luo Bandi, Zhang Li as Zi Heng, Liu Jiaojiao as Zi Heng (as a child), Chi Zhiqiang as Jiang Hongxi, Li Zhiyu as Tu Yihao, Tian Chun as A Liang

In pre-liberation China, beautiful, cold and ruthless Luo Bandi plots with her lover Tu Yihao to kill her wealthy and elderly businessman husband. Luo then goes to an orphanage and buys a young girl called Zi Heng ("Purple Scar") to care for her insane son, A Liang. A Liang's cousin Jiang Hongxi is very sympathetic with the girl, and in time they fall in love. But Luo Bandi wants the handsome young cousin for herself, so she pressures Zi Heng to marry the mad A Liang, beating her when she refuses. Meanwhile, Luo's current lover Tu Yihao and his henchmen murder the family of a patriotic businessman. When Jiang Hongxi exposes their crime, he is also killed. Witness to the murder of her lover, Zi Heng stabs Luo to death. Zi Heng is sent to prison for murder.

1599. *The Pursuing Fish (Chui Yu)*

1959. Tianma Film Studio. Color. 10 Reels. Direction: Yin Yunwei. Screenplay: Collective. Cinematography: Ma Linfa. Art Direction: Ge Shicheng. Music: Gu Zhenxia, Du Chunyang. Sound: Ding Bohe. Makeup: Da Xu. Cast: Qian Miaohua as the bogus Judge Bao, Xu Huiqing as the real Judge Bao, Chen Lanfang as Guanyin, Xu Yulan as Zhang Zhen, Wang Wenjuan as the Carp Spirit and Phoenix, Zhen Zhongmei as Jin Chong, Zhou Yukui as the wife

Scholar Zhang Zhen and Prime Minister Jin's daughter Phoenix have been engaged since early childhood. But when Zhang's parents die, leaving him penniless, the Jins want to cancel the engagement. A carp spirit living in a nearby pond loves Zhang Zhen, so she turns herself into Miss Phoenix, and in that form meets Zhang Zhen every night. All goes well until one day Zhang and the spirit together run into the real Miss Phoenix, touching off a big argument over who is the real girl. The General of Heaven dispatches his soldiers to arrest the spirit for what she had done, but at this moment she decides to tell her story to Zhang Zhen, which makes the young man love her more than ever. Guanyin, the Goddess of Mercy, intercedes and orders all the soldiers of Heaven to withdraw. She offers to let the spirit join her in the South Seas. The spirit instead prefers that Guanyin take three of her scales, thereby relinquishing her spirit status and becoming an ordinary human being, living her life with Zhang Zhen.

1600. *Puzzling Case in the Forest (Lin Zhong Mi An)*

1984. Shanghai Film Studio. Color. 10 Reels. Director: Xu Weijie. Screenplay: You Xuezhong, Gu Zemin. Cinematography: Sun Guoliang. Art Direction: Chen Fuxing. Music: Liu Yanxi. Sound: Xu Xilin. Cast: Li Ding as Sun Honghui, Wang Weiping as Guo Jun, Yang Baohe as Liu the Cripple

While hunting in the mountains, retired criminal investigator Sun Honghui finds a dead body. The county PSB director Guo Jun and his assistant Xiao Wang investigate. A monkey provides the clue which leads to identification of the body. Their investigation eventually leads them to a restaurant which turns out to be the base for a smuggling ring. Further evidence at last points the PSB to the killer. A wild chase through the mountains ensues.

1601. *Qilian Mountain Echoes (Qi Lian Shan De Hui Sheng)*

1984. August First Film Studio. Color. Wide Screen. 10 Reels. Direction: Zhang Yongshou. Screenplay: Li Maolin, Zhang Yongshou, Zhang Fengchu. Cinematography: Ding Shanfa. Art Direction: Ni Shaohua. Music: Li Weicai, Yue Chun. Sound: Guo Yisheng. Cast: Ni Ping as Sister Wu, Wang BaoKun as Qiuju, Zhang Chao as Tian Lin, Zhou Sheng as Manniu, Zeren Lamu as Sangjicuo, Mu Yi as Miaogu, Liu Yi as Yangmei, Wang Ao as Little Thing

In the 1930s, the Red Army's first all-woman brigade volunteers to conduct a delaying action which allows the army's main force to withdraw. The withdrawal is successful, but the women are picked off one by one by warlord Ma Bufang's troops. At the end, the few survivors choose suicide over capture.

1602. *Qing Dynasty Artillery Battery (Da Qing Pao Dui)*

1987. Pearl River Film Studio. Color. 10 Reels. Direction: Chen Guojun. Screenplay: Yuan Fang, Yu Qi. Cinematography: Li Yuebing. Art Direction: Huang Tongrong. Music: Lu Yuan. Sound: Li Xun. Cast: Liu Xiaoqing as Feng Yushu, Xin Min as Yang Chengxiao, Ge Chunzuang as Ye Shouxing, Wu Guilin as Liang Baoshan, Chen Zheng as Li Youcai, Wang Gang as Wang Yansheng, Li Xiangang as Dogshead, Zhang Tao as Zhou Yunxi

During the Opium War (1840–1842), the Chinese government organizes the inhabitants of a small South China fishing village into a coastal artillery battery, promising them they will be paid. Included in the ranks of the volunteers is young woman Feng Yushu, who disguises herself as a man in order to earn some money. Although each of them fights bravely in defense of their country, this amateur force is no match for the well-trained and equipped British Navy, and at last they are all wiped out. Not even their names remain in China's military history.

1603. *Qingsong Mountain Range (Qing Song Ling)*

1965. Changchun Film Studio. B & W. 12 Reels. Direction: Liu Guoquan. Screenplay: Zhang Zhongpeng, based on his stage play of the same title. Cinematography: Shu Xiaoyan. Art Direction: Li Junjie, Li Fan. Music: Si Wanchun. Sound: Shen Guli. Cast: Liu Xiaomei as Xiumei, Ao Wenbing as Daren, Li Rentang as Zhang Wanyou, Qi Huimin as Mrs. Zhang, Yan Benan as Fang Jiyun, Zhang Baoru as Zhou Cheng, Li Shunan as Qian Guang

In the Qingsong Mountain range, a young girl named Xiumei is upset with her production team's wagon driver Qian Guang, for the man seems interested only in speculation and profiteering. Since there is no appropriate re-placement, she tries to learn carriage driving herself. Her first attempt is a disaster, with the horses rearing and dumping the wagon's cargo. But she has the support of newly assigned Party branch secretary Fang Jiyun, and with his help she starts a program to train wagon drivers. The resentful Qian Guang plans to spoil her efforts in a way that will make her look incompetent. Later, when Qian Guang refuses to work, it falls to Zhang Wanyou, aging and with a bad leg, to make the deliveries. He also has the horses rear up at the exact same location it had happened to Xiumei. It turns out that Qian Guang has deliberately trained the horses to rear in certain circumstances, so no one else can control them. Further investigation reveals that Qian Guang is really a rich farmer wanted by the authorities in another part of China. Vindicated, Xiumei carries on with training other young people to be drivers.

1604. *Qinsong Mountain Range (Qing Song Ling)*

1973. Changchun Film Studio. Color. 11 Reels. Direction: Liu Guoquan, Jiang Shusheng. Screenplay: Hebei Province Chengde Prefecture State Drama Troupe Collectively. Cinematography: Meng Xiandi. Art Direction: Tong Jingwen. Music: Si Wanchun. Sound: Kang Ruixin. Casting: Li Rentang as Zhang Wanshan, Zhu Longguang as Fang Jiyun, Liu Xiaomei as Xiumei, Zhang Baoru as Zhou Cheng, Feng Lianjie as Yang Laowu, Qi Huiming as Zhang's wife

This is a remake of the same studio's 1965 black and white film of the same title.

1605. *Qiu Jin—A Revolutionary (Qiu Jin)*

1983. Shanghai Film Studio. Color. 13 Reels. Direction: Xie Jin. Screenplay: Huang Zongjiang and Xie Jin, based on the life of Qiu Jin (1877–1907). Cinematography: Xu Qi, Zhang Yongzheng. Art Direction: Ding Cheng, Zhong Yongqin, Mei Kunping. Music: Ge Yan. Sound: Zhu Weigang. Cast: Li Xiuming as Qiu Jin, Li Zhiyu as Xu Xiling, Chen Xiguang as Chen Tianhua, Yu Shizhi as Gu Fu, Wang Fuli as Wu Zhiyin, Huang Meiying as Xu Jicheng

Toward the end of the Manchu Dynasty, Qiu Jin, whose progressive father had insisted she be educated, leaves her husband and two children and goes to Japan to study democratic principles. She has chosen to give up her role as housewife and mother and devote herself to the cause of reforming or overthrowing the corrupt Manchu government. In Japan she becomes acquainted with other Chinese revolutionaries like Xu Xiling, Chen Boping and Chen Tianhu. When Qiu Jin later returns to China, she meets Dr. Sun Yatsen, who assigns her important duties in the revolution. She returns to her hometown of Shaoxing to help organize rebellion in Zhejiang and Anhui provinces. But when Xu Xiling fails in his attempt to assassinate a Manchu official, she is arrested because of her association with him. Qiu Jin is executed, but goes to her death bravely and with no regrets.

Best Supporting Actor Yu Shizhi, 1984 Golden Rooster Awards.

Qiu Ju Goes to Court see *The Story of Qiu Ju*

1606. *The Queen of Hearts Under the Muzzle (Qiang Kou Xia De Hong Tao Huang Hou)*

1986. Guangxi Film Studio. Color. 10 Reels. Direction: Wu Tianren. Screenplay: Xiao Jian, Ni Feng. Cinematography: Yang Yuming. Art Direction: Li Qining. Music: Li Yanlin. Sound: Lin Lin. Cast: Fang Zhoubo as Mo Mu, Zhang Jiumei as Suo Xiaochan, Li Qing as Xiao Qing, Wu Baolin as Station Director Li, Song Yuhua as Lin Lifang

In the province of Yunnan, along China's southern border, Border Patrol inspection station director Li gets a tip that a smuggling ring is sending one of its key figures into the area, a mysterious person known only as the "Queen of Hearts." A crew filming a TV series arrives soon after that, among them three women: TV director Lin Lifang, young painter Mo Mu and Suo Xiaochan, whose exact business there is unclear. Director Li welcomes them warmly, but keeps alert. It turns out that Suo is an undercover investigator. She presents evidence that Lin Lifang is one of the smugglers. Lin confesses, but insists she is not the "Queen." At last, the real "Queen of Hearts" is identified.

1607. *Quiet Mountain (Ji Jing De Shan Lin)*

1957. Changchun Film Studio. B & W. 10 Reels. Direction: Zhu Wenshun. Screenplay: Zhao Ming. Cinematography: Bao Jie. Art Direction: Wang Guizhi. Music: Quan Rufeng.

Sound: Lin Bingcheng. Cast: Wang Xingang as Feng Guangfa, Bai Mei as Li Wenying, Pu Ke as Sun Weilian, Gao Ping as Guo Zhiquan, Che Quan as Pi Shili, Wang Jingfang as Director Zhang

Li Wenying, a female spy, is sent by U.S. intelligence into Northeast China from Hong Kong under cover of returning to visit her hometown. Through liberal use of her charms and money, she recruits agents to prepare for the airdrop of more U.S. spies. Chinese counter-intelligence learns of the plot, and assigns a Chinese agent in the guise of a businessman named Feng Guangfa to gain Li's confidence. He is successful in this, and through her infiltrates U.S. spy headquarters in Hong Kong. In time, Feng gains a position of leadership in the spy net, to the point of controlling several of their operations. Finally, the information Feng supplies the Chinese police enables them to round up all U.S. agents in Northeast China.

1608. *Quiet Orchids in a Small Alley (Xiao Xiang You Lan)*

1983. Liaoning Science Film Studio. 10 Reels. Direction: Kou Wei. Screenplay: Tao Zhonghua. Cinematography: Geng Xingyuan. Art Direction: He Ruiji. Music: Li Yanxue. Sound: Lin Zhi. Cast: Chen Maya as Fang Lan, Liu Suhong as Grandma, Tu Ruyin as Zhang Qi, Yu Yanping as Zhang Ming, Chen Yixin as Zhang Ying

A young woman falls in love with and marries a construction worker with five children. Her kindness and understanding helps her through the difficulties of being stepmother to so large a ready-made family.

1609. *Quiet Rain (Wu Sheng De Yu Si)*

1985. Shenzhen Film Studio. Color. 9 Reels. Direction: Wang Yabiao, Zhang Jianyou. Screenplay: Da Li. Cinematography: Jin Yixun, Lei Xianhe. Art Direction: Ye Jihong. Music: Du Mingxin, Li Bingyang. Sound: Zhang Biaojian. Cast: Na Renhua as Liu Liu, Du Zhenqin as Li Qian, Lu Jing as Dog, Li Ping as Qianqian, An Baiyin as the father, Qin Wen as the mother-in-law

A woman plumber named Liu Yin works at Beijing's Capital Airport, maintaining the public toilets. While her husband's family had earlier been only too eager to take advantage of her job status to get Beijing residents' permits for the rest of the family, now they all look down on her and the work she does. When Liu Yin has an idea for designing an automated water pump, and asks her husband to help her with it, he mockingly refuses. The family's discriminatory treatment of blue collar workers causes Liu Yin considerable emotional distress. Her life becomes even more unhappy when her daughter dies. The one escape for Liu Yin is working on her design, and when she at last succeeds and is honored by her employers for her innovation, the family starts to flatter her. Liu leaves a letter for the family telling them she must leave them.

1610. *Raftsmen (Fa Zi Ke)*

1991. Xi'an Film Studio. Color. Letterboxed. 9 Reels. Direction: Yao Shougang. Screenplay: Zhang Rui. Cinematography: Mi Jiaqing. Art Direction: Ge Yao. Music: Li Yaodong. Sound: Li Tie. Cast: Jin Xin as Stone, Hu Zhaofeng as Black Bull, Tao Hong as Xinhua, Xu Huanshan as Big Carter, Yang Ping as Fourth Master Ge

In the mid–1920s, in the upper reaches of the Yellow River, a girl called Xinghua is pursued by a local despot called Fourth Master Ge. She is seized and taken back to Ge's home as his 13th concubine. But just before entering the wedding chamber, she escapes from the house. Black Bull, a raftsman passing by on the river, rescues her and takes her to Majia Town. Fourth Master Ge has his minions searching everywhere for the girl, and when he finally discovers her escape was aided by raftsmen, he uses his power and influence to damage their livelihood. The raftsmen band together to oppose the despot and protect the girl. In the process, two of the raftsmen fall in love with her, setting up what they realize will be their own confrontation when the despot is defeated.

1611. *The Raid (Qi Xi)*

1960. August First Film Studio. B & W. 9 Reels. Direction: Direction: Xu Youxin. Screenplay: Li Yang and Zhen Hong. Cinematography: Cao Jingyun and Liu Ying. Art Direction: Mai Yi. Music: Li Weicai. Sound: Li Lin. Cast: Zhang Yongshou as Fang Yong, Xing Jitian as No. 1 Squad Leader, Huang Huanguang as Tang Hu, Qu Yun as the old lady, Zhang Zhongying as No. 5, Wang Lianhai as Li Jiang, Yuan Xia as Pak Kim-yi, Wan Diqing as an enemy colonel, Xie Wanhe as an enemy captain, Wang Xiaozhong as an enemy captain, Meng Qingfang as an enemy military police officer

In the Korean War, PLA Volunteer Army company commander Fang leads a patrol on a mission to blow up the Kangping Highway Bridge, in the hands of the enemy. However, in a highway they are spotted by a South Korean truck convoy, but are able to scare the Koreans off by disguising themselves in American uniforms. After that, in the guise of a South Korean patrol, they evade the Americans guarding the bridge and acquire information concerning the bridge's defense and structure. Finally, with the help of a Korean woman guerrilla soldier they succeed in blowing up the Kangping Bridge, cutting off the enemy's line of retreat. The Chinese main force then attacks and completely wipes out the enemy.

1612. *Raiding Athena (Jie Sha Ya Dian Na)*

1992. Pearl River Film Studio. Color. Letterboxed. 9 Reels. Direction: Zhang Zhongwei, Wang Qili. Screenplay: Yuan Fang. Cinematography: Wu Wen, Song Junsheng. Art Direction: Wang Di. Music: Xu Zhijun. Sound: Jiang Yan. Costume: Zhao Li. Makeup: Yan Zhenrong. Cast: Liu Weihua as Yuan Long, Liu Jiacheng as Liu Haimin, Lu Lin as Wang Qiangsheng, Hua Xianghong as Yang Dan, Pan Jie as Jiang Shan

Yuan Shuijiang, the head of a transnational software firm, makes two CDs: one is a virus he calls Athena, the other a satellite decoder. He plans to use them to destroy a nuclear power station. An international crime syndicate sends a gunman named Wang to get the CDs. He shoots Yuan and takes Athena. Before he dies, Yuan tells his adopted son Yuan Long to take the decoder CD and travel to the Chinese mainland; there he should find his stepsister Yang Yue. The matter comes to the attention of Chinese police, and when Yuan Long arrives in China, policeman Liu Haimin is assigned to follow him. At last, with Liu's help, Yuan Long finds and protects Yang Yue, then kills Wang.

1613. *Railroad Guards (Fu Hu Tie Ying)*

1993. Pearl River Film Studio. Color (70mm). 9 Reels. Direction: Yu Shibin. Screenplay: Wang Zhonggang. Cinematography: Zhang Jingwen, Yuan Hong. Music: Cao Guangping. Sound: Liu Haiyan, Dong Xiaozhi. Costume: Hu Hailiang. Makeup: Zhou Shaomei, Jin Lanming. Cast: Xu Dongfang as Yue Cheng, Sun Wangqun as Yanrong, Zhang Li as Tao Shixi, Huang Huiyi as

Linlin, Xu Yongge as Tie Wei, Zhang Yanping as Gouniu

An attempt to hijack a train goes awry. One of the gang is killed, but the others are able to escape. Detectives get a lead in their investigation when an attempt is made on the life of the dead man's daughter when she arrives to identify the body. The police are able to protect her from harm, and although she is unaware of what valuable information she possesses, she begins working with the police in their efforts to identify and locate the would-be train robbers.

1614. *Railway Guards (Tie Dao Wei Shi)*

1960. Changchun Film Studio. B & W. 11 Reels. Direction: Fang Ying. Screenplay: Shenyang Railroad Public Security Collective Writing Team. Cinematography: Yang Chong. Art Direction: Xu Wei. Music: Lou Zhanghou. Sound: Kang Ruixin, Hongdi. Cast: Yin Zhimin as Gao Jian, Song Xuejuan as He Lanying, Zhou Wenbing as Master Worker Zhao, Luo Tai as Ma Xiaofei, Ye Lingliang as Wang Manli, Fang Hua as Wu Jichun

During the Korean War, after a failed attempt to blow up the bridge over the Yalu River, the U.S. military sends special agent Ma Xiaofei into Northeast China. There, he links up with undercover agent Wu Jichun to blow up Chinese military trains. Chinese Public Security Bureau division head Gao Jian leads an anti-espionage struggle which after several setbacks is successful in removing a time bomb set by Ma. This allows the Chinese military to ship huge quantities of military materials to Korea in support of the North Korean war effort.

1615. *Rainbow (Hong)*

1982. Xiaoxiang Film Studio. Color. 10 Reels. Direction: Jia Mu. Screenplay: Jia Mu. Cinematography: Zhou Shengtong. Art Direction: Guo Dexiang, Tan Shengshan. Music: Zhen Qiufeng. Sound: Huang Shiye. Cast: Zhang Yuping as Jiang Xu, Zhou Liangliang as Teacher Ye, Li Shixi as Father, Ouyang Fengqiang as Jiang Hao, Wei Li as A Tang, Gao Hongliang as Minmin

Jiang Xu and her brother Jiang Hao are high school students. Their mother's embroidery is justly praised at the village factory where she works, while their father works in his unit's dining hall. Since he believes living in the city will help his two kids have a better chance of getting into college, the father finds a job in the city and moves them there. The two children contrast greatly: Jiang Xu studies hard, while taking care of the family housekeeping work and tutoring Jiang Hao, who does not like to study. The film tells of some of life's struggles, contrasting right and wrong, and new and old fashions. In the end, Jiang Xu works herself sick on the eve of college entrance exams, and loses her chance, while her brother and their friends are admitted.

1616. *Raise the Red Lantern (Da Hong Deng Long Gao Gao Gua)*

1991. ERA International (HK) Ltd., China Film Co-Production Corporation. Color. Letterboxed. 12 Reels. Executive Producer: Hou Hsiao-Hsien and Zhang Wenze. Producer: Chiu Fu-Sheng. Direction: Zhang Yimou. Screenplay: Ni Zhen, based on the novel "Wives and Concubines" by Su Tong (1963–). Cinematography: Zhao Fei. Editor: Du Yuan. Music: Zhao Jiping. Sound: Li Lanhua. Art Direction: Cao Jiuping, Don Huamiao. Costume: Huang Lihua. Makeup: Sun Wei. Cast: Gong Li as Songlian, Ma Jingwu as Chen Zuoqian, He Saifei as Meishan, Cao Cuifeng as Zhuoyun, Jin Shuyuan as Yuru, Kong Lin as Yan'er, Ding Weimin as Mother Song, Cui Zhigang as Doctor Gao, Chu Xiao as Feipu, Cao Zhengyin as the Old Servant, Zhao Qi as Chen Baishun (the Housekeeper)

After a father's death wipes out his family financially, his daughter Songlian is forced to leave college. Her stepmother contracts a marriage for the girl to Chen Zuoqian, wealthy scion of an old and powerful family. At her husband's house she soon learns the family's traditions, notably that of the red lantern: whichever wife is chosen to stay with the master overnight has the lantern in her courtyard lit. A wife's status in the household is largely dependent on the frequency of the master's visits, and the four of them compete vigorously for the honor. The first wife, Yuru, is now the elderly mother of an adult son, Feipu, called the young master. The second wife, Zhuoyun, has fallen into disfavor for producing a daughter. The third wife, Meishan, was a famous opera singer. Each of the wives has a personal maid, and Songlian finds that her own maid, Yan'er, had dreams of becoming the fourth wife herself, so she deeply resents Songlian's arrival. The old mansion also harbors dark secrets: Meishan is having an affair with the family physician, Doctor Gao; in a locked tower are found the remains of a wife who had been unfaithful in a previous generation of the master's family. To gain the master's favor, as well as additional privileges, Songlian fakes pregnancy; when second wife Zhuoyun tricks her into revealing the fraud, Songlian is cast into permanent disfavor with a black lantern hung in her courtyard. Angry and bitter at her fate and frustrated by her hopeless attraction to Feipu, the young master, Songlian takes it out on Yan'er, her ill-tempered maid. She searches the girl's room, and finds a secret cache of red lanterns and a doll which Yan'er has been using to put a curse on her mistress. In retaliation, Songlian exposes the girl's offense, for which Yan'er is made to kneel for hours in the snow until she apologizes. She stubbornly refuses, and at last collapses and dies. Guilty at having indirectly caused her maid's death, Songlian gets drunk, and in her ravings inadvertently tells conniving second wife Zhuoyun about Meishan's affair. Meishan and her lover are caught together at a hotel, and Meishan is taken to the tower and executed. The horror of this combined with her own cumulative guilt drives Songlian insane.

Silver Lion Award, 48th Venice International Film Festival.

1617. *Really Annoying (Zhen Shi Fan Shi Ren)*

1979. Guangxi Film Studio. B & W. 9 Reels. Direction: Wu Yingxun, Gao Bu. Screenplay: Zhou Minzheng, Wu Yingxun. Cinematography: Meng Xiongqiang, Liao Fan. Art Direction: Zhang Yafang. Music: Yang Shaoyi. Sound: Xu Zhenkui, Lin Lin. Cast: Wang Xiangpu as Zhu Zhifeng, Lu Shuren as Yang Cheng, Liu Guiqing as Yang's wife, Tang Xuefang as Wu Sulan, Tian Limin as reporter, Lan Zhenbo as Chen Fang

Farm implement plant director Yang Cheng pays the utmost attention to production and scientific research, but none at all to what is going on in his employees' lives. He assigns the design of a new model machine to the plant's chief technician Zhu Zhifeng, but the pressures of a deadline leave Zhu no time to do his laundry. When a woman reporter comes to interview him, Zhu has no clean clothes to wear, so although it is summer, he puts a winter coat on over his dirty clothes, which embarrasses everyone at the plant. Director Yang's wife urges him to resolve the problems in his workers' lives, and suggests he design a washing machine for them. Yang refuses. Unhappy

with Yang's attitude, she leaves home to teach him a lesson. One day, the woman reporter comes to interview him about the rumored washing machine. Yang, used to having his wife take care of all his needs, is the one without clean clothes this time. In a rush, he also pulls out and puts on a winter jacket, again embarrassing. Faced with the realities, Yang finally realizes that a good leader must also be able to take care of people's lives.

1618. *Really Unexpected (Zhen Mei You Xiang Dao)*

1982. Fujian Film Studio. Color. 4 Reels. Direction: Ma Minquan. Screenplay: Ma Minquan. Cinematography: Chen Minhui. Art Direction: Zhen Chunsong. Music: Chen Yongtie. Sound: Chen Binglian. Makeup: Zuang Xi. Cast: Wang Donghan as Li Yong, Zhang Fei as Zhou Ying, Zhang Peitian as Mr. Zhou, Yu Jingchang as Mrs. Zhou

As a young man named Li Yong hurries on his bicycle to meet his date, he runs a red light. He continues on, traffic officer Zhou in pursuit. Li knocks down a woman carrying groceries, and keeps going. He runs into a wedding procession and still keeps going, Officer Zhou still chasing him. He finally arrives to meet his girlfriend and finds the woman he knocked down is his future mother-in-law and Officer Zhou his future father-in-law. Li Yong is guilty and learns from his mistakes.

1619. *Rebel Cheng Yaojin (Hun Shi Mo Wang Cheng Yao Jin)*

1990. Xiaoxiang Film Studio & Liaoning Film Studio Co-Production. Color. Wide Screen. 10 Reels. Direction: Li Wenhua. Screenplay: Xie Fengsong, Gu Naihua. Cinematography: Tu Jiakuan, Zhao Peng. Art Direction: Wang Guizhi, Zhao Zhengxue. Music: Wen Zhongjia. Sound: Zhang Baojian, Wang Chunbao. Cast: Zhou Zhou as Emperor Sui Yang, Deligeer as Cheng Yaojin, Ge Batuqingele as You Junda, Wang Hongtao as Yang Lin, Wang Wensheng as Qin Qiong, Shao Wanlin as Xu Maogong

In the closing days of the Sui dynasty (589–618), Emperor Sui Yang becomes increasingly corrupt. A salt merchant named Cheng Yaojin is arrested and sentenced to death for publicly criticizing this. He escapes, however, and joins a rebel group. Later, he and his men rescue a father and daughter named Wang, who are being mistreated by some powerful people. After a series of adventures together, he and Miss Wang are married. Cheng is elected chief of the rebels, then he merges them with another rebel band to overthrow the corrupt regime.

1620. *Reborn Hero (Zai Sheng Yong Shi)*

1995. Shanghai Film Studio. Direction: Zhang Jianya, Li Guomin. Screenplay: Lai Yin, Mu Jiang. Cinematography: Shen Xingao. Art Direction: Hu Weiping. Cast: Zhen Aonan as Song Dawei, Wu Xuewen as Tang Rong, Zhang Zhijian as Yuanan, Mai Deluo as Siwen

Chief of Detectives Song Dawei is wounded in a gun battle with bank robber Yuan An, and lapses into a coma which lasts for seven years. Mu Xing, a Ph.D. candidate and son of famous geneticist Li Min, is experimenting with a drug he thinks may help the patient. He injects the drug into Song Dawei, who soon gains consciousness. Naturally, everything is very unfamiliar to the detective. Meanwhile, Yuan An is still pursuing his life of crime, and plans to abduct the scientist Li Min. To protect Li and his son, Song goes after Yuan and this time defeats him.

1621. *Recovering the Jade Dragon (Zhi Jie Yu Xiang Long)*

1981. Xiaoxiang Film Studio. Color. 9 Reels. Direction: Zhang Jinbiao, Pan Xianghe. Screenplay: Lu Wen, Gu Zemin, Lu Shoujun. Cinematography: Zhao Zelin. Art Direction: Wang Jixia. Music: Xu Jingxian. Sound: Liu Feng. Cast: Lin Daxing as Ouyang Mingyue, Zhao Lian as Zhen Guanchang, Ge Chunzhuang as Situ Yu, Lu Jun as Lin Maochun, Chen Xiaoyi as Shen Feifei, Wang Yiping as Situ Yan

In Haiwan City, a routine mail inspection turns up the Jade Dragon, a priceless antique which had disappeared many years before. Customs inspection chief Ouyang Mingyue finds that the name and address of the sender are false, indicating a case of antique smuggling. He follows the evidence, but all signs initially point to Professor Situ Yu and his daughter Situ Yan, Ouyang Mingyue's fiancee. Ouyang Mingyue pushes on with his detailed investigation, and after getting through many false clues set up to mislead them, he and the public security officers finally find the true criminal in the case.

1622. *Recovering the Sword (Jian Gui)*

1983. Anhui Film Studio. Color. 9 Reels. Direction: Hua Chun. Screenplay: Ding Yihong, Wang Jinsheng, Li Zhishui. Cinematography: Wang Wenxi, Chen Zhenghua. Art Direction: Lin Lichong, Zhang Lin. Music: Hu Shiping, Liu Yizhao. Sound: Chao Fuguo, Zhang Guangdi. Cast: Qi Mengshi, Liu Wei, Yu Fei, Ning Hualu

Near the end of World War II, in a rural county in northern Anhui province, elderly Chinese herbalist Lei Zhenhua and his daughter Lei Jianping keep hidden a national treasure—the sword of Taiping General Lai Weiguang. A Japanese captain discovers they have the sword and tries to take it by force, planning to sell it back in Japan. Lei and his daughter kill the captain and flee with the sword to the Southeast China home of their trusted friend Zhen Guoxiong. Lei Zhenhua is arrested by the Japanese for being in possession of a national treasure. The movie tells how Zhen and the Lei family protect the sword from the Japanese and the corrupt Nationalist government, at last turning it over to the new government in 1949.

1623. *Red and White (Hong Yu Bai)*

1987. Emei Film Studio. Color. 10 Reels. Direction: Lu Xiaoya. Screenplay: Lu Xiaoya, He Cihang. Cinematography: Qing Jun. Art Direction: Zhou Qin. Music: Guo Wenjing. Sound: Luo Guohua. Cast: Xu Huanshan as Pan Yiding, Xu Zhan as Pan Dacheng, Guo Yuntai as Gong Fan, Yu Ping as Ming Shufeng, Wen Xianqiao as Wang Ai

Medical school professor Pan Yiding is writing a book which analyzes cases of misdiagnosis he has encountered during his 40-year career. When his son Pan Dacheng, a hospital resident, tells him of an obvious case of malpractice which the hospital officials are trying to cover up, the father urges his son to reveal the truth and stop the conspiracy to whitewash the incident. The message is that finding the truth is paramount, even when it conflicts with one's personal interests.

1624. *Red Banners on Mount Cuigang (Cui Gang Hong Qi)*

1951. Shanghai Film Studio. B & W. 10 Reels. Direction: Zhang Junxiang. Screenplay: Du Tan. Cinematography: Feng Shizhi, Qiu Ge. Art Direction: Wang Cangcheng, Yang Lingde. Music:

Wang Yunjie. Sound: Lin Bingsheng, Wang Xingzhou. Costume: Lu Boqin. Makeup: Wang Kai, Wang Hanyong. Cast: Yu Lan as Xiang Wuer, Zhang Fa as Jiang Mengzhi, Pei Cong as Feng Laoshi, Chen Tianguo as Xiao Zhenkui, Bai Mu as Feng Zhigu, Mu Hong as Jiang Chunwang, Wang Zhu as Jiang Linzi

In 1933, their success against the Nationalists leads the Red Army to increase the size of their force through a recruiting drive in the Cuigang region of Jiangxi province. Jiang Mengzhi, a young farmer, encouraged by his bride Xiang Wuer, enlists and remains a soldier for many years. In 1934, he accompanies the Red Army on its Long March retreat to the north of China. The areas abandoned by the Communists are re-occupied by the Nationalists, who then launch a campaign to wipe out the families of Red Army troops. Among those hunted down and slaughtered are Jiang Mengzhi's father and sister. His wife changes her name and, taking their newborn baby, flees from their home village. She finds work as a wet nurse in the household of Feng Zhigu, a wealthy landlord supporting the government forces. There, she learns of plans by Nationalist commander Xiao Zhenkui to raid a nearby guerrilla camp. She gets word to them in time for the guerrillas to ambush the government forces, and inflict severe losses on the attackers. In 1949, the PLA advances to the south, and Xiao Zhenkuo retreats to Cui Gang Mountain to make a last stand. By this time, Jiang Mengzhi has risen to the rank of Division Commander. Acting on information furnished by the guerrilla commander aided by Xiang Wuer, Jiang's division wipes out the Nationalist troops. The fighting over, Jiang Mengzhi and Xiang Wuer are together at last.

1625. *The Red Basket (Hongse Bei Lou)*

1965. Beijing Film Studio. B & W. 10 Reels. Direction: Shi Daqian. Screenplay: Shi Daqian. Cinematography: Yu Zhenyu. Art Direction: Xiao Bing, Luo Yurong. Music: Wang Yanqiao. Sound: Cai Jun. Cast: Cheng Hankun as Wang Fushan, Huang Zhong as Li Jianmin, Li Yunong as Manager Ma, Han Yan as Accountant Sun, Du Defu as Yang Tian, Cheng Xueqin as Xiao Zhang

For the convenience of his customers in their North China village, retail store sales clerk Wang Fushan begins delivering goods to their door in a basket he carries. At first this is opposed by Accountant Sun, who is very traditional in his thinking, and by Manager Ma who has little interest in politics. But with the support of the County Party Secretary Li Jianmin, Wang continues to deliver his goods. Sun and Ma, caring only for profits, decide to deliver the goods which will bring more profit, but refuse to deliver urgently needed items of less profit. Wang Fushan studies the writings of Chairman Mao, and uses Mao's theories to change Sun and Ma's thinking.

1626. *Red Beads (Xuan Lian)*

1992. Produced with the support of the China Eastern Cultural Development Center. B & W. 88 minutes. Direction: He Yi. Screenplay: Liu Xiaojing, You Ni. Cinematography: Nie Tiejun, Yu Xiaoyang. Art Direction: Wang Wangwang. Music: Guo Xiaohong. Sound: Guan Jian. Cast: Liu Jiang as Jing Sheng, Shi Ke as Jiyun, Tian Gechen as Dr. Sha, Hu Zhi, Wang Yongsheng, Li Huo, Meng Yan, Han Jingru, Liu Zhiyi

Relationship between a young man and a neurotic girl who has strange dreams of "red beads."

1627. *Red Cherry (Hong Ying Tao)*

1995. Youth Film Studio, Beijing Economic Develop Investment Company Co-Production. Color. Direction: Ye Ying. Screenplay: Jiang Qitao. Cinematography: Zhang Li. Cast: Guo Keyu as Chuchu, Xu Xiaoli as Luo Xiaoman

During World War II, a group of teenagers, members of the Communist Young Pioneers, are sent to the Soviet Union for training at the International Children's Institute. Two of them, close friends Chuchu and Luo Xiaoman, become separated when the Germans bomb the school. Chuchu is captured and forced to be a servant to a German general, who tattoos a Nazi flag on her back. Later, when the German Army is forced into retreat, the general commits suicide. When the Soviet Red Cross frees the young people, Chuchu's gaudy fascist flag tattoo shocks everyone. Her identity is at last confirmed, and she returns to China. Doctors try various surgical and other means to remove the tattoo, but since the area covered is so large, nothing is effective. Chuchu never marries and lives alone for the rest of her life.

1628. *Red Children (Hong Hai Zi)*

1958. Changchun Film Studio. B & W. 11

Red Children. Two "red children" share a secret. 1958. Changchun Film Studio.

Reels. Direction: Su Li. Screenplay: Qiao Yu. Cinematography: Li Guanghui. Art Direction: Tong Jingwen. Music: Zhang Dicang. Sound: Jue Jinxiu. Cast: Chen Keran as Su Bao, Ning He as Sister Xi, Wang Heyong as Tiger Boy, Lu Zhenyi as Jin Geng, Guan Jinxi as little Dongya, Liu Chunshen as Shui Sheng

In 1934, after the Red Army moves north to resist the Japanese invasion, a Red Guard troop in the Communist-held area of Jiangxi province carries out guerrilla activities from a mountain base. Troop leader's son Su Bao and his young companions witness the violent actions of collaborators. The children vow to avenge their fellow villagers who are victims of this violence. Without telling their parents, they form a teenage guerrilla troop, kill many collaborators and capture many weapons. In one battle, Su Bao's father is captured, but the young people sneak at night into the compound where he is being held, rescue him, and kill the enemy regimental commander.

1629. *Red Coral (Hong Shan Hu)*

1961. August First Film Studio. Color. 11 Reels. Direction: Wang Shaoyan. Screenplay: Zhao Zhong, Chan Wen, Lin Yingwu, Zhong Yibing, based on a classic opera of the same title.

Cinematography: Zhang Dongliang. Art Direction: Zhang Zheng, Ren Huixing. Music: Hu Shiping, Wang Xiren. Sound: Li Lin. Cast: Xiao Jun as Sister Coral, Zhou Zutong as Wang Yonggang, Wang Yun as Xu Laoda, Cui Changchun as the night time teller, Ling Aiban as Haiwang's wife, Lin Donghua as Hai Wang, Dai Huaxue as Aqing, Chen Guangzhi as the first fisherman, Wu Boyuan as the second fisherman, Zhang Yanying as Seventh Grandma, Liu Ruilin as Sun Fugui

In 1950, the PLA is liberating some islands off the China coast. On Coral Island, a woman called Seventh Grandma exerts a tyrannical control over the fishing families. She attempts to force Sister Coral, an island girl, into prostitution. The girl escapes by jumping into the sea. She swims to another island and there encounters by chance her fiance Aqing and wounded PLA reconnaissance officer Wang Yonggang. After Wang recovers, he and Sister Coral return to Coral Island to organize the fishermen there in a struggle with Seventh Grandma, who has since allied her own organization with the Nationalists in a scheme to draft all the island's young men into the Nationalist Army. Wang alerts the PLA to this plot, and at a critical moment Sister Coral gives the signal which guides the PLA to Coral Island, despite being wounded in the effort.

The island is liberated and Sister Coral is united with Aqing.

1630. *The Red-Crested Crane (Fei Lai De Xian He)*

1982. Changchun Film Studio. Color. 10 Reels. Direction: Chen Jialin. Screenplay: Wang Xingdong, Wang Zhebing, Liu Zhicheng. Cinematography: Chen Chang'an, Zhang Baozhi. Art Direction: Jin Xiwu. Music: Jin Fuzhai. Sound: Han Weijun. Cast: Sun Caihua as He's mother, Zhang Weixin as Bai Lu, Wang Shangxing as He Fengyu, Yang Tong as Xiao Xiang, Li Tiejun as Ding Zhenpeng

During the Cultural Revolution, a kindly, hard-working, middle-aged couple living on the Nunjiang prairie adopt an infant boy they name Xiao Xiang. After the downfall of the Gang of Four, a ballet dancer named Bailu arrives in the area and discovers the boy is hers. She does not want to hurt the older couple after so many years of adoption of her son, but when they find out the truth they sacrifice their own feelings and let her take Xiao Xiang back with her to Beijing. However, Xiao Xiang does not fit in well with his new family. He particularly rejects his mother's arrangements for him, such as piano lessons and painting. Deciding he will always be a child of the prairie, Xiao Xiang returns to the Nunjiang prairie where he was raised.

1631. *Red Detachment of Women (Hong Se Niang Zi Jun)*

1961. Tianma Film Studio. Color. 12 Reels. Direction: Xie Jin. Screenplay: Liang Xin. Cinematography: Shen Xilin. Art Direction: Zhang Hancheng. Music: Huang Zhun. Sound: Gong Zhengming. Cast: Zhu Xijuan as Wu Qionghua, Wang Xingang as Hong Changqing, Xiang Mei as Fu Honglian, Jin Naihua as the Division Commander, Wang Li as the Company Commander, Tie Niu as Agui, Niu Ben as Xiao Pang, Zhang Meiming as Big Sister, Shi Shugui as Dan Zhu, Jiang Yifang as Big Ying, Weng Shuying as Grandpa, Chen Qiang as Nan Batian, Yang Mengchang as the old housekeeper, Feng Qi as Old Four, Liang Shan as Huang Zhenshan, Yu Fei as Old Goldtooth, Zhu Suo as Big Girl

During the Chinese Civil War in the late 1940s, on the island of Hainan, servant girl Qionghua keeps running away from the landlord household where she is subjected to repeated beatings and other abuse. She finally escapes when she is purchased by Hong Chang-

qing, ostensibly a wealthy Overseas Chinese businessman, but actually an organizer for the Communist Party. He takes her to the base of a Red Army women's detachment he heads, and she enlists. But on her first patrol, she sees the landlord and violates orders by shooting at him. Soon after this, Qionghua is wounded when the women's detachment liberates her old village. After she recovers, Qionghua is gradually educated by Hong Changqing to overcome her yearning for personal revenge and put the collective interest first. Hong Changqing sacrifices himself to save a mission, the last act in developing Qionghua from a revenge-obsessed former slave to steeled Communist revolutionary fighter.

Best Picture, 1962 Hundred Flowers Awards.

Best Director Xie Jin, 1962 Hundred Flowers Awards.

Best Actress Zu Xijuan, 1962 Hundred Flowers Awards.

Best Supporting Actor Chen Qiang, 1962 Hundred Flowers Awards.

1632. *Red Eagles Spread Their Wings (Hong Ying Zhan Chi)*

1960. August First Film Studio. B & W. 9 Reels. Direction: Shen Dan. Screenplay: Qun Zi. Cinematography: Li Erkang. Art Direction: Li Xinmao and Liu Qian. Music: Gong Zhiwei. Sound: Wu Hanbiao. Cast: Liu Lei as Huang Ping, Wang Ren as Liu Kai, Chen Yao as Zhao Hang, Zhang Zhang as Cai Jiefei, Zhao Ruping as Ma Yongkui, Sang Ping as Han Yushan

Shortly after liberation, a group of cadres from Yan'an begin preparation to build China's first military aviation school in Northeast China. Flying instructor Cai Jiefei, who had defected to the PLA from the Nationalist Air Force, is doubtful such a school can succeed, but Group Leader Liu Kai and Political Commissar Huang Ping are confident and determined. They guide the students in building China's first aviation school, and by setting a good example, succeed in getting all the students to solo successfully. They are also aggressive in using alcohol in place of gasoline, and succeed in training soldiers to be excellent pilots, the foundation of the modern People's Air Force.

1633. *Red Elephant (Hong Xiang)*

1982. Children's Film Studio. Color. 8 Reels.

Red Detachment of Women. **Red Army recruit Wu Qionghua (Zhu Xijuan, right) exposes her unit's position when she impetuously shoots the landlord who had abused her. 1961. Tianma Film Studio.**

Direction: Zhang Jianya, Xie Xiaoping, Tian Zhuangzhuang. Screenplay: Wang Duanyang. Cinematography: Zen Nianping. Art Direction: Ning Lanxin, Feng Xiaoning. Music: Xu Jingqin. Sound: Zhang Jiake. Cast: Yan Jiao as Yanluo, Zhai Ge as Yan Shuai, Xing as Yixiang

In Xishuangbanna, an area peopled by the Dai nationality minority, elementary students Yanluo and Yanshua are good friends. In school they hear a story about a miraculous red elephant living in the forest, so during summer break they decide to go look for it. As they enter the forest, they find they are followed by a little girl named Yixiang who also wants to solve the mystery. They let her join them, and eventually the children get a glimpse of the red elephant from a distance. Soon after, they happen upon a large trap in which is caught a young elephant. It is not easy, but the three children finally free the little elephant and make friends with it. The little elephant is the offspring of the red elephant. The red elephant comes to them and lets them climb up on its back for a ride. They happily ride back home on the red elephant, and are greeted by their teachers who have come looking for them.

1634. *Red Firecracker, Green Firecracker (Pao Da, Shuang Deng)*

1993. Xi'an Film Studio, Hong Kong Wen Partners Organization Co-Production. Color. Letterboxed. 12 Reels. Direction: He Ping. Screenplay: Da Ying, based on the novel by Feng Jicai (1942–). Cinematography: Yang Lun. Art Direction: Qian Yunxuan. Music: Zhao Jiping. Sound: Gu Changning, Zhang Wen. Costume: Ma Defan, Ma Jing, Zhao Yihong, Zhang Weijun. Makeup: Ma Shuang Ying. Cast: Ning Jing as Chunzhi, Wu Gang as Niu Bao, Zhao Xiaorui as Man Dihong, Gao Yang as the butler, Xu Zhengyun as Xu Laoda, Zhao Liang as Hei Liu

Young painter Niu Bao lives only for art, caring little for money and nothing for power. He is hired by a family with a large fireworks business to do some painting for them before Chinese New Year, their peak season. He is surprised to find that the head of the business is Chunzi, a woman who dresses as a man, and whom everyone treats as a man. Chunzhi is the last of her clan line, and is forbidden to marry. Niu Bao and Chunzi fall in love and have an affair, but the clan and local people (all of whom are dependent on the business for their

Red Firecracker, Green Firecracker. Niu Bao (Wu Gang) in the midst of the disastrous climactic firecracker contest. 1993. Xi'an Film Studio, Hong Kong Wen's Partner Organization Co-Production.

livelihood) exert massive pressures on them to stay apart. At last, the clan decides to permit Chunzi to marry, and decree that her husband will be either Niu Bao or the company business manager Man Dihong, the lucky man being the one who wins a firecracker contest. In the contest, something goes wrong and Nie Bao's genitals are blown off. Severely injured, the painter is taken away, but Chunzi is carrying his child.

Best Art Direction Qian Yunxuan, 1994 Golden Rooster Awards.

Best Director He Ping, 1994 Golden Rooster Awards.

Best Co-Production Picture, 1994 Golden Rooster Awards.

Grand Prize, 14th Hawaii International Film Festival.

1635. *Red Flower of Mount Tian (Tian Shan De Hong Hua)*

1964. Xi'an Film Studio & Beijing Film Studio Co-Production. Color. 12 Reels. Direction: Cui Wei, Chen Huaiai, Liu Baode. Screenplay: Ou Ling. Cinematography: Nie Jing and Lin Jing. Art Direction: Chi Ning, Zhang Jingnan. Music: Xu Youfu. Sound: Chen Yanxi, Hong Jiahui. Cast: Fadiha as Ayiguli, Mutelifu as Asihale, Alibieke as Wumaier, Shaheidan as Kayixia, Bieertehan as Hashimu, Bayahong as Shadike

In 1959, the members of a Hashake nationality co-op cattle ranch in Xinjiang elect as their director Ayiguli, a female Communist Party member. Hashimu, the reactionary son of the former ranch owner, is so frightened by this that he tries to get her out of her position by exploiting her husband Asihale's dream of becoming rich, thinking this will destroy the couple's relationship. Despite her husband's threats, Ayiguli leads the people in their production work. Finally, with the support of the local Party organization and the herdsmen, she is able to expose Hashimu's crimes, and get her husband to realize his errors. During the following year's election, Asihale sincerely supports his wife's re-election, and sends her a red flower.

1636. *Red Fox (Huo Hu)*

1993. Changchun Film Studio, Hong Kong Shengxing Entertainment Develop Corp. Ltd.

Co-Production. Color. Letterboxed. 10 Reels. Direction: Wu Ziniu. Screenplay: Wang Chunbo, Wu Ziniu. Cinematography: Yang Wei. Art Direction: Wu Yang. Sound: Zhang Lei. Makeup and Costume: Wang Xiaojie. Cast: Gong Hanlin as the skinny guy, Tu Men as Beard, Li Qin as the skinny guy's ex-wife, Sharen Gaowa as Beard's wife

A film operator, already depressed by a slumping film market, learns that the 69-year-old theater he works for is to be converted into a restaurant. He travels to a snow-covered forest region 1,000 miles distant to hunt for a legendary red fox believed to be there. When he arrives, he meets a strange hunter, a man who has been hunting the fox for six years. They have an initial mutual hostility, but have to rely on each other for survival during a snow storm, and come out of the experience good friends. Although the red fox never does appear, each finds he has regained his courage and confidence in life.

1637. *A Red Guard Troop in Honghu (Hong Hu Chi Wei Dui)*

1961. Beijing Film Studio & Wuhan Film Studio Co-Production. Color. 12 Reels. Direction: Xie Tian, Chen Fangqian, Xu Feng. Screenplay: Collective, recorded by Mei Shaoshan and Zhang Jingan, and based on the Hubei Opera Company's opera of the same name. Cinematography: Qian Jiang, Chen Guoliang. Art Direction: Yu Yiru, Xiaobing. Music: Zhang Jingan, Ouyang Qianshu. Sound: Lu Xiancang, Zhang Jiake. Cast: Wang Yuzhen as Han Ying, Xia Kuibing as Liu Chuang, Fu Ling as Qiu Jiu, Chen Renxuan as Haigu, Zhang Jichao as Kehu, Wang Zhengxiang as Chunsheng

In the summer of 1930, in the Honghu area of Hubei province, a tyrant named Peng allied with Nationalist army commander Feng raids the Red Army's Honghu base. Honghu Party Secretary Han Ying and Director Liu Chuang lead the local guards in an orderly withdrawal, but they later return to lead a raid on the enemy's weapons storehouse. In retaliation, Peng has some local people tortured to try to discover Han Ying's hideout. In order to protect his fellow villagers, Han Ying gives himself up. He escapes, although one of his deputies sacrifices himself in the effort. After Han escapes, she continues to lead the Red Guard troupe in their struggles with the enemy.

Best Music Zhang Jingan and Ouyang Qianshu, 1962 Hundred Flowers Awards.

The Red Medal **see** *Eternal Friendship*

1638. *Red Orange Yellow Green Blue Purple (Chi Cheng Huang Lu Qing Lan Zi)*

1982. Changchun Film Studio. Color. 11 Reels. Direction: Jiang Shusheng, Li Lingxiu, Cinematography: Tu Jiakuan. Set Design: Li Junjie. Music: Lei Zhenbang. Sound: Yu Kaizhang. Cast: Fang Shu as Jie Jing, Zhang Jiatian as Liu Sijia, Jiang Lili as Ye Fang, Zhu Decheng as He Shun, Chen Ying as Zhu Tongkang, Ren Weimin as Director Tian

Zhu Tongkang, Party Secretary at the No.5 Steel Mill, confers with Jie Jing, deputy director of the mill's delivery unit, and a woman in whom he has complete confidence. He wonders how to handle the case of Liu Sijia, an "unpredictable" young worker who has been doing strange things, most recently selling pancakes in a food market near the mill. Jie Jing disagrees with Zhu's system of worker discipline and punishment, and suggests it would be better to reform the mill's management style to allow for better communication with young workers like Liu. So she makes friendly contact with him, finds his strong points and shortcomings and points them out. Once, the mill's oil storage facility catches fire, and Liu risks his life to rescue Jie Jing and control the fire. As they get to know and understand each other better, Jie Jing even helps Liu and his girlfriend improve their relationship. Through her understanding of young people and her communication with them, she and the mill's young workers make progress together.

Best Supporting Actress Jiang Lili, 1983 Hundred Flowers Awards.

1639. *Red Peak Warship (Chi Feng Hao)*

1959. August First Film Studio. B & W. 8 Reels. Direction: Yan Jizhou. Screenplay: Yi Ding, Ke Lan, Tie Jianghai, Cao Fubing, Zhong An, Ye Xuyin, Ma Chongji. Cinematography: Cai Jiwei. Art Direction: Kou Honglie. Music: Gong Zhiwei. Sound: Li Bojian. Cast: Zhang Yongshou as Tie Haixiong, Zhang Lianfu as Political Commissar Gao, Xing Jetian as the commander, Wang Runsheng as Big Liang, Huo Deji as Little Liu, Zhu Qi as Big Zhen

In 1954, Dashan Island off Zhejiang province is harassed by warships from Taiwan which disrupt transport and fishing. Captain

A Red Guard Troop in Honghu. **Han Ying (Wang Yuzhen, foreground) appreciates that farming is an important part of her revolutionary work. 1961. Beijing Film Studio.**

Tie Haixiong of the Chinese warship "Red Peak" accepts the assignment of luring the Taiwan ships into an ambush. When the two sides make contact, the Red Peak finds itself outnumbered five to one. But the Red Peak is successful in luring the Nationalist ships to the ambush site, where the Nationalists' flagship is badly damaged. After that, the PLA and navy liberate Dashan island.

1640. *Red Peony (Hong Mu Dan)*

1980. Changchun Film Studio. Color. 10 Reels. Direction: Xue Yandong, Zhang Yuan. Screenplay; Yan Fengle. Cinematography: Meng Xiandi. Art Direction: Shi Weijun, Wen Jingmei. Music: Tang Ke, Lu Yuan. Sound: Liu Jingui. Cast: Jiang Lili as Wang Lian, Sun Shulin as Huang Puyi, Gao Baocheng as Old Zhao, Guo Bichuan as Wuling Tong, Zhao Fengxia as Jiu Yueju, Zhang Yisheng as Zhang Deren

Huang Puyi, a young man dissatisfied with his impoverished existence, leaves his wife and daughter in their hometown and finds work with a traveling circus troupe. A few years later, Huang Puyi is now the troupe's owner and has forgotten all about his family. In the meantime, his wife has died and the daughter

Wang Lian sold. By chance, Huang Puyi buys her. Ten years pass, and Wang Lian has become a star of the troupe, with the stage name Red Peony. She and fellow performers Wu Lingtong, Jiu Yueju and others work hard to line Huang Puyi's pockets. When Huang Puyi takes the troupe to Hong Kong to perform, he tries to force Red Peony to bestow sexual favors on Zhang Desheng, a powerful local gangster. She rebels against this, and this so angers the gangster that the troupe must rely on the help of local leftist forces in order to return to the Chinese mainland. In order to keep Red Peony working for him forever, Huang Puyi wants to make her his concubine. But by chance, he learns that she is actually the daughter he abandoned years before. Puyi then wants her to stay on as family, but Red Peony adamantly walks out on this beast she had long ago come to hate.

1641. *Red Plum Blossoms (Shan Li Hong Mei)*

1976. Pearl River Film Studio. Color. 10 Reels. Direction: Si Meng. Screenplay: Collective, recorded by Qiao Dianyun. Cinematography: Wang Yunhui, Liu Hongming. Art Direction: Li

Xing, Zhang Zhichu. Music: Liang Lizhu. Sound: Li Baijian. Casting: Zhen Youming as Shan Mei, Shi Jing as Shi Jian, Zhang Zhiliang as Chang Yun, Ye Jiangdong as Wei Ruxue, Xing Jitian as Grandpa Xishan, Jian Ruichao as Chen Damo

In 1971, after returning from an inspirational visit to Dazhai, Shanhe production unit Party Secretary Shan Mei revises the original water ditch plan for her unit. Her action is opposed by several corrupt local officials who are involved in profiteering by selling building materials meant for constructing the ditch. With the support of the Party Secretary, Shan Mei exposes the corruption, although she is subject to considerable pressure and even an attempt on her life. Shan Mei perseveres and is at last successful in ousting the corrupt officials.

1642. *Red Postal Route (Hong Se You Lu)*

1966. Beijing Film Studio. B & W. 10 Reels. Direction: Ma Erlu. Screenplay: Collective, recorded by Ma Erlu. Cinematography: Chen Guoliang. Art Direction: Cheng Rongyuan, Music: Zhen Lucheng. Sound: Fu Yingjie. Cast: Li Baiwan as Yu Changshui, Li Liansheng as Qin Liming, Zhen Baoming as Wang Lihe, Du Defu as Guo Lin, Huang Fei as Zhao Wenchang, Kou Guanqun as Sun Mingyi

Yu Changshui is director of a postal delivery team at a post office in the mountains west of Beijing. His service is excellent, and the mountain people look forward to reading the same paper every day. So when Yu Changshui suggests creating a new delivery route he gains the support of both leaders and people. Yu takes on this difficult route himself, and fulfills the wishes of the mountain people. He is awarded the highest class of model worker award, and the entire postal bureau begins a campaign of learning from Yu Changshui.

1643. *Red Room, White Room and Black Room (Hong Fang Jian, Bai Fang Jian, Hei Fang Jian)*

1988. Changchun Film Studio. Color. 10 Reels. Direction: Song Jiangbo. Screenplay: Qin Peichun. Cinematography: Guo Lin. Art Direction: Liu Zhongren. Music: Liu Xijing. Sound: Gu Xiaolian. Cast: Liu Wei as He Shuifu, Ni Ping as Ge Tengzhi, Wu Eryang as Old Mr. Ai

Old Mr. Ai and his two daughters live in a Western-style building in Shanghai, renting out their old garage on the lower level to a road construction crew headed by He Shuifu. A rural woman named Ge Tengzhi arrives seeking her fiance Li Hongxing, the father of her child, because Li Hongxing had rented from the Ai family two years earlier. In fact, her fiance is planning to marry another woman. But Ge Teng's kindness and sincerity so move He Shuifu and the others that they decide to help her by holding a wedding ceremony for her and Li Hongxing, although the latter is nowhere to be found. They hold the wedding with an absentee groom, and this unusual experience causes them all to think about life.

1644. *Red Rose, White Rose (Hong Mei Gui, Bai Mei Gui)*

1994. Tianshan Film Studio, Golden Flare Films Corp. Co-Production. Color. Letterboxed. 10 Reels. Direction: Stanley Kwan. Screenplay: Liu Heng, Edward Lam, based the novel by Zhang Ailing (Eileen Chang). Cinematography: Christopher Doyle. Art Direction: Pu Ruomu. Music: Xiao Chong. Sound: Zhan Xin. Costume: Feng Junmeng. Makeup: Nancy Tong. Cast: Zhao Wenxuan (Winston Chao) as Tung Zhenbao, Chen Chong (Joan Chen) as Wang Jiaorui, Ye Yuqing (Veronica Yip) as Meng Yenli, Zhao Chang as Tung Tubao, Sheng Tong Hua as Wang Zehong

The story relates the sexual odyssey of Tung Zhenbao, a young man of good family who returns from studies in Europe in the 1930s to embark upon a business career in his native Shanghai. His principal weakness is sex: in between liaisons with prostitutes and girls of lower social standing, he encounters the two women who, in the words of the narrator, "are found in the lives of most men — his 'Red Rose' and his 'White Rose'." The "Red Rose" is Wang Jiaorui, an old friend's mail-order bride from England, a headstrong, passionate, and unpredictable young woman of middle class origins. Dissatisfied with her life and her older husband, she readily begins an affair with Tung. They declare their love for each other, she impetuously tells her husband about the relationship. This destroys her marriage and sends her lover packing, for he knows his family would never accept her. Tung vows to be a better man in the future, and decides to marry, choosing as his bride (his "White Rose") Meng Yenli, a dull upper-class girl who makes him an even duller wife. His behavioral change is short-lived, however: he devotes his days to business, increasingly successful, and his nights to hookers, increasingly frequent. His neglected and lonely wife sinks into a form of madness, passing most of her days in her bath sitting on the toilet (she even has her meals there), venturing out only to be fitted for elegant dresses she never wears. Years later, Tung has a chance encounter on a streetcar with Wang, now remarried. After an exchange of pleasantries, she leaves. He sadly watches her go, and vows to be a better man in the future.

1994 31st Golden Horse Awards: Best Actress, Joan Chen.

1645. *Red Seeds (Hong Se De Zhong Zi)*

1958. Haiyan Film Studio and Jiangsu Film Studio Co-Production. B & W. 11 Reels. Direction: Lin Yang. Screenplay: Xia Yang. Cinematography: Xu Qi. Art Direction: Sun Zhang. Music: Ren Tao. Sound: Ren Xinliang. Cast: Qing Yi as Hua Xiaofeng, Sun Daolin as Leiming, Song Deyu as Wang Laower, Zi Shiming as Grandma Wang, Sheng Yufang as Zhang Suzhen, Gu Yelu as Qian Fucang

During the Chinese Civil War, a young woman Communist named Hua Xiaofeng is assigned to work in an area held by the Nationalists. Pretending to travel to visit a relative in the army, she boards a cargo ship owned by businessman Qian Fucang. On route, the cargo ship is stopped and seized by the Nationalist Army. Qian Fucang gets the commander to let him sell his goods ashore for a share of the profits, and while ashore he sells Hua Xiaofeng to farmer Wang Laoer as a wife. Xiaofeng reveals her true identity and mission to Wang Laoer and his mother, and gains their sympathy and promise of support. So, remaining in the village in the guise of Wang Laoer's wife, she organizes the farmers in Xiaowang Village, establishes a Party organization, implements a movement to assassinate Nationalist sympathizers and agents, and acts as matchmaker for Wang Laoer and local widow Zhang Suzhen. Later, Hua Xiaofeng's husband, county Party secretary Leiming, leads an armed force into Xiaowang Village, where they disarm the Nationalists and arm the local people.

1646. *A Red Skirt Is Fashionable on the Street (Jie Shang Liu Xing Hong Qun Zi)*

1984. Changchun Film Studio. Color. Letterboxed. 10 Reels. Direction: Qi Xingjia. Screenplay: Jia Hongyuan, Ma Zhongjun. Cinematographer: Zhang Songping. Art Direction: Shui Zuangji. Music: Zhang Peiji. Sound: Kang Ruixin. Cast: Zhao Jing as Tao Xinger, Jiang Lili as Ge Jia, Song Yining as A Xiang, He Xiaoshu as the Workshop Head, Wang Baosheng as Xiao Lingmu, Guo Bichuan as Dong Xiaoqing

A young woman named Tao Xinger is designated a model worker at the Dafeng Textile Plant. As usual with those so designated, Tao customarily dresses in the traditional worker's garb of white blouse and blue pants. Young colleagues make her more aware of the changing world outside the plant, however, and how most of her contemporaries are abandoning traditional outfits for more fashionable dress. She starts to dress a bit more modern, and starts to live as others do.

1647. *Red Sorghum (Hong Gao Liang)*

1987. Xi'an Film Studio. Color. Direction: Zhang Yimou. Cinematography: Gu Changwei. Music: Zhao Jiping. Art Direction: Yang Gang. Screenplay: Chen Jianyu, Zhu Wei and Mo Yan, based on the novel of the same title by Mo Yan (1956–). Sound: Gu Changning. Costume: Liu Jianzhong. Makeup: Sun Wei. Cast: Gong Li as "My Grandma," Jiang Wen as "My Grandpa," Ji Chunhua as Sanpao the Bandit, Teng Rujun as Uncle Luohan, Qian Ming as father of "My Grandma"

In the barren wilderness of North China in the 1930s, a young woman is being carried to the home of a leper who has purchased her as his wife. En route, bandits attempt to abduct the bride, but she is saved by one of the sedan carriers. He later claims her as his own, and she does not resist. After the leper is mysteriously murdered, perhaps by her rescuer, the two take over his winery business. The two lovers engage in a succession of trials of will, in which neither gains dominance. When they finally cooperate, they produce good sorghum wine, and in time a son. Their lives change forever when the Japanese arrive. The invaders first cut down the sorghum that is the heart of the area's economy, and then begin torturing and killing the locals. The couple lead a desperate attempt to gain their freedom through an act of sabotage, with tragic consequences.

Best Picture, 1988 Golden Rooster Awards.

Best Cinematographer Gu Changwei, 1988 Golden Rooster Awards.

Best Sound Gu Changning, 1988 Golden Rooster Awards.

Best Music Zhao Jiping, 1988 Golden Rooster Awards.

Best Picture, 1988 Hundred Flowers Awards.

Winner, Golden Bear Award for Best Film, 1988 Berlin International Film Festival.

Best Picture Award, Best Director (Zhang Yimou), and True and New Style Award, 15th Zimbabwe International Film Festival.

Sydney Film Critics Award, 35th Sydney International Film Festival.

Great Atlas, Gold Award for Director and Film Production, 1st Marrakesh International Film & TV Festival.

Best Picture of the Youth Jury of Belgian Radio and Television, 16th Brussels International Film Festival.

1648. *Red Spider (Hong Zhi Zhu)*

1988. Changchun Film Studio. Color. 10 Reels. Direction: Liu Wenyu. Screenplay: Xu Zhiqiang. Cinematography: Sun Hui, Yu Zhenhai. Art Direction: Gong Minhui. Music: Chen Shouqian. Cast: Liu Tingrao as Yan Fang, Tang Qun as Sheng Ying, Cao Shisheng as Lu Jiang, Yu Lan as Dai Ya

The foreign "M" Company develops a "331" computer, potentially of great value in both civil and military operations. The will of company CEO Mr. Milo stipulates that at his death all company property is to be transferred to his nephew Lu Jiang, a professor at a PRC university. When she learns of the will's contents, Milo's wife asks the "Shadow Headquarters," a spy agency, to stop this from taking place. The agency orders its mainland China operative "Red Spider" to abduct Lu Jiang and take him overseas. But investigator Yan Fang thwarts the Red Spider at every turn and at last catches the foreign agent.

1649. *Red Sun (Hong Ri)*

1963. Tianma Film Studio. B & W. 14 Reels. Direction: Tang Xiaodan. Screenplay: Ju Baiyin, based on the novel of the same title by Wu Qiang. Cinematography: Ma Linfa. Art Direction: Ge Shicheng. Music: Lu Qiming, Xiao Yan. Sound: Ding Bohe. Cast: Zhang Fa as Shen

Zhengxin, Gao Bo as Political Commissar Ding, Zhong Shuhuang as Chief of Staff Zhua, Li Nong as Division Commander Cao, Li Po as Liu Sheng, Kang Tai as Chen Jian

In the winter of 1946, Chiang Kaishek's army launches a massive attack on the Communist-held areas of Northeast China. PLA commander Shen Zhengxin's army successfully withdraws from Shandong after a fierce battle with Chiang's elite 74th Division, so enraging the 74th's commander Zhang Linpu that he attacks civilian, non-military areas. In the winter of 1947, Shen Zhengxin's army defeats the 74th division. In the battle, PLA company commander Shi Donggeng is deceived by the Nationalists' feigned surrender, causing serious losses to the PLA. After the battle, Shi becomes arrogant, but corrects his shortcomings with help from division commander Shen. In the final battle of Menglianggu, Shi Donggeng's company destroys the enemy's division command post, which leads to the 74th division's annihilation and Zhang Lingpu's death.

1650. *The Red Sun Over the Ke Mountains (Ke Shan Hong Ri)*

1960. August First Film Studio. Color. 12 Reels. Direction: Dong Zhaoqi. Screenplay: Chen Qitong, based on Chen Qitong's opera of the same title. Cinematography: Wei Linyue, Yang Zhaoren. Art Direction: Xu Run. Music: Zuang Yin, Lu Ming. Sound: He Baoding. Cast: Li Bing as Mai Lisheng, Jiang Honggang as Mia Song, Dong Zhiyuan as Kelu Yade, Can Di as Qingqing, Li Lulin as Bieta, Zhang Hailun as Kama

In 1950, a PLA unit enters the Ke Mountains in Tibet mountain. To increase the political awareness of the Tibetan people, they do not implement reforms immediately, but help the Tibetans do it themselves. A Tibetan anti–Chinese force called Gexia sends spy Luo Jia into the mountains, where he links up with undercover agent Yade in opposing the PLA. They carry out disruptive acts of sabotage and finally openly rebel. In these circumstances, the PLA is forced to take military action, bring the rebels under control and free slaves in the Ke Mountains area.

1651. *Red Swan (Hong Tian Er)*

1993. Guangxi Film Studio. Color. Direction: Gu Rong. Screenplay: Gu Rong. Cinematography: Shen Xilin, Qian Tao. Music: Ma Ding. Art Direction: Shi Jingquan, Chen Wei. Cast: Xu

Songzhi as Qiao Danying, Xing Mingshan as Zhong Xueyang, Xu Yajun as Zhu Tong, Dong Zizhi as Lin Hong

Shortly after the founding of the PRC in 1949, a group of ballet students, 16-year-old Zhong Xueyang, 14-year-old Qiao Danying, and 13-year-olds Lin Hong and Zhu Tong are sent to Moscow to study "Swan Lake." They return to China, and their performance of this classical ballet is a great success. Zhong proposes marriage to Qiao, but she refuses. Later, Qiao marries Zhu Tong, and Zhong marries Lin Hong. During the Cultural Revolution, Qiao is downgraded to the position of cleaning woman, and Zhu is also stripped of his right to perform. The couple divorce. Zhong becomes the leader of a group of rebels. In 1980, as reform sweeps China, "Swan Lake" is again cleared for public performance, but Zhu Tong does not show up as scheduled. Lin Hong decides to move to France. Before leaving, she divorces Zhong Xueyang, who is in prison.

1652. *Red Thread (Hong Xian)*

1982. August First Film. Color. 9 Reels. Direction: Wang Shaoyan. Screenplay: Luo Xuan. Cinematography: Chen Ruijun. Art Direction: Zhang Zheng. Music: Lu Yuan. Sound: Yan Birong. Cast: Yi Fuwen as He Shanhu, Chi Peng as Qi Zier, Liang Yuru as Qi Laobing, Liu Xitian as Chen Yi

1653. *Red Tide on Ba Mountains (Ba Shan Hong Lang)*

1961. Xi'an Film Studio. B & W. 10 Reels. Direction: Sang Fu. Screenplay: Huang Di and Sang Fu. Cinematography: Lian Cheng. Cinematography: Ling Yi. Art Direction: Tian Shizhen. Music: Ma Ke and Li Yaodong. Sound: Chen Yudan. Cast: Yang Huizhen as Qing Guilan, Qu Zhong as He Zhuang, Shen Shisheng as Xu Kang, Li Yue as Fan Qiguang, Mang Yiping as Gu Caifeng, Mu Weihan as Ding Dalu

In 1958, when his steel plant in the north range of the Ba Mountains has some notable production achievements, Director Fan Qiguang claims credit for himself and becomes arrogant. He is also very selfish, showing reluctance to support the south range plant managed by his brother. When the two plants are engaged in a competition, Fan Qiguang cares only for his personal accomplishments, and little for the south plant's needs. Qing Guitian, a woman newly designated as deputy director of the plant and concurrently the Party secretary, seriously criticizes his wrong behavior. She urges that the north range people lend grain to the south range, and the south range assist the north in resolving its ongoing problem of poor quality ores. Guilan's criticisms and analysis of the facts leads Director Fan to realize his mistakes. Finally, the south and north range plants expand and merge into a large-scale joint steel producing enterprise.

1654. *Red Waves on the Green Sea (Bi Hai Hong Bo)*

1975. Xi'an Film Studio. Color. 10 Reels. Direction: Direction: Liu Bing. Screenplay: Han Guang. Cinematography: Zhen Guoen, Lin Jing. Art Direction: Wang Fei. Music: Su Tie, Li Yaodong. Sound: Hong Jiahui. Cast: Bi Jiancang as Lei Bo, Chen Mingao as Huang Lihu, Huang Zhongqiu as Fang Cheng, Yang Fengliang as Yang Kai, Li Anqin as Zhen Dagang, Xu Xiaoxing as healthcare worker

During the Korean War, the U.S. Army plans to cut off Chinese supply lines through air power. The Chinese countermeasures to this plan, known as "Plan S," involve the use of radar. Their radar misleads American scout planes, then they plant mines to repel an attack of their radar stations. In the end, "Plan S" is defeated.

1655. *The Reexamination (Fu Shi)*

1957. Changchun Film Studio. B & W. 5 Reels. Direction: Ren Sun. Screenplay: Lin Shan, Ren Sun and Dong Jieshen, based on the novel of the same title by He Wei (1926–). Cinematography: Shu Xiaoyan. Art Direction: Wang Chong. Music: Lou Zhanghou. Sound: Yuan Mingda. Cast: Che Xuan as Professor Yan, He Xiaoshu as Lu Xiaomei, Zhang Fengxiao as the Old Friend, Bai Mei as the College Dean, Meng Shun as the Hospital Director

During entrance examinations, music professor Yan discovers that candidate Lu Xiaomei is a very talented vocalist. However, at the reexamination, Lu loses her voice and is rejected. Professor Yan conducts an investigation at the girl's home and work unit and finds that she had spent the entire night before the exam helping typhoon victims, which affected her voice. When the admissions panel learns this, they admit her to the college.

1656. *The Regimental Commander and His Wife (Tuan Zhang He Ta De Qi Zhi)*

1985. Changchun Film Studio. Color. 9 Reels. Direction: Liu Pei. Screenplay: Long Tailing. Cinematography: Duan Zhenjiang. Art Direction: Tian Feng. Music: Gao Feng. Sound: Liu Jingui. Cast: Xu Yuanqi as Jiang Bo, Zhang Yan as Li Yani

In the mountains of northeast China, PLA Regimental Commander Jiang Bo has gone for some time without a letter from his wife Li Yani. He recalls the days when he was a young soldier courting Yani at beautiful West Lake in Hangzhou. She had originally supported his career choice, but after a time asked him to leave the military so they could have a more stable life with a permanent home. He refused, and the two had bickered over the matter ever since. Now, he worries about the possible implications of her failure to write. Then a package arrives from Yani. In it, he finds a supply of his favorite tea, along with a letter saying Yani and their daughter will soon come to visit him. Jiang Bo relaxes.

1657. *Regret for the Past (Shang Shi)*

1981. Beijing Film Studio. Color. 10 Reels. Direction: Shui Hua. Screenplay: Zhang Yaojun, Zhang Lei. Cinematography: Zou Jixun. Art Direction: Chen Yiyun. Music: Du Mingxin. Sound: Lu Xiancnag, Lan Fuan. Cast: Wang Xingang as Junsheng, Lin Ying as Zijun, Li Liansheng as Little Thing, Liu Zhao as Old Thing, Li Changle as the low ranking official's wife, Liu Xiaohua as the woman servant

In pre-revolutionary China, Junsheng is a young man caught up in the progressive "May 4th Movement" of 1919, but while he is dissatisfied with traditional society he feels powerless to change it. Just at the time he is most lonely and restive, Zhijun comes into his life. Zhijun is a woman rebelling against the oppressions of the old society, seeking individual fulfillment and a break with the restrictions of her feudalistic family. Junsheng falls in love with her courage and spirit. They ignore society's criticisms and marry. Happy at first, they soon begin having conflicts. With no career of her own, Zhijun is unhappy with just keeping house, and this starts to affect their love life. They find they also have personality clashes and differences of opinion. There is the additional pressure of a society which does not tolerate their marriage. When Juansheng loses his job at the Bureau of Education, he at first naively believes he can support them by doing translating work and writing. This proves to be a fantasy, and Juansheng begins to feel that the marriage is ruining his chances of attaining his goals in life. The changes in Juansheng make Zhijun frightened and suspicious. Love dies and soon Zhijun dies too. After her death, Juansheng is filled with grief and regret. At first he wants to die so he can find her in the afterlife, but after a period of mourning he determines that he will instead take the first steps toward a new life.

Best Cinematographer Zou Jixun, 1982 Golden Rooster Awards.

1658. *Regret on Taiwan Island (Tai Dao Yi Hen)*

1982. Emei Film Studio. Color. Wide Screen. 11 Reels. Direction: Zhang Yi, Shen Mujun. Cinematography: Feng Shilin, Cui Yifeng. Art Direction: Lin Qi. Music: Ge Lidao. Sound: Shen Guli. Cast: Yang Hailian as Tiehu, Da Qi as Chen Wanji, Wang Fuli as Chen's wife, Fei Anqi as Dasi, Zhang Jizhong as Chen Qiu

After the Sino-Japanese War of 1894–95 ends in defeat for China, the Japanese invade Taiwan. General Chen Wanji, the Chinese commander on Taiwan, chooses a policy of non-resistance, but his younger brother Chen Qiu argues for fighting the invaders. Tie Hu, a young woman martial arts expert, goes to the general in the guise of a man to plead with him to resist, but when he discovers she is a woman, Chen Wanji tries to rape her. She kills him defending herself, and from then on Chen Qiu considers her his sworn enemy. Tie Hu organizes a Taiwanese volunteer army to resist the invaders. Chen Qiu takes command of the Chinese army, but soon finds his forces surrounded by the Japanese. Tie Hu offers her volunteers to fight alongside the Chinese, but Chen at first rejects this from his hatred of her. He comes to realize that the national interest must be put above the individual's, and they make common cause. When their joint forces finally engage the Japanese, the Chinese suffer severe losses. Chen Qiu and Tie Hu decide that she will remain in Taiwan to recruit a new army to wage guerrilla warfare against the Japanese, while Chen Qiu will return to the mainland to seek more support in the cities there.

1659. *The Reign Behind the Curtain (Chui Lian Ting Zhen)*

1983. China Film Cooperation Company and Hong Kong New Kunlun Company Co-Production. 10 Reels. Direction: Li Hanxiang. Screenplay: Yang Chunbing. Cinematography: Yang Guanling, Tang Musheng. Art Direction: Song Hongrong. Music: Ye Chunzhi. Cast: Liang Jiahui (Tony Leung) as Xian Feng, Liu Xiaoqing as the Concubine Yi, Xiang Lei as Shu Shun, Zhou Jie as the Concubine Li, Zhang Tielin as Yi Qing

Sequel to "The Burning of Yuan Ming Yuan."

The Manchu government signs a series of treaties with the British and French which in effect give away China's sovereignty. Emperor Xian Feng falls very ill and dies. The concubine Yi and her allies at court use British and French power to persecute and eliminate Shu Shun and seven other senior court officials she considers enemies. Those allied with Yi win the political struggle, and the eight officials are executed. From that time on, Yi rules China unchallenged for over 40 years as the Empress Cixi.

1660. *Remake Another Me (Zhai Su Yi Ge Wo)*

1984. Xi'an Film Studio. Color. Letterboxed. 9 Reels. Direction: Zhang Jingreng. Screenplay: Liu Shugang, Huang Jianzhong. Cinematography: Cao Jinshan. Art Direction: Liu Xinghou. Music: Li Zhonghan. Sound: Xiong Huajuan. Cast: Lei Ming as Su Yu, Wang Bingyan as Mo Lei, Fang Qinzhuo as Chi Bo, Gong Ren as Ning Lili, Tan Yuanyuan as Liang Hong

Screenwriter Su Yu's new play "The Ambitious One" gets mixed reviews, and he cannot understand why. He decides to investigate real life, so goes to a civil court to interview participants in a divorce case. He meets middle-aged sculptor Mo Lei, a man divorcing his wife of many years. The couple had met in college, and she has supported him until he achieved success. Now that he has it, Mo Lei has found a new, young lover, Ning Lili. In reality, none of these people are happy. Ning finally realizes her affair with Mo just will not do it for her, and she leaves him to find a new life. Su Yu sees that his life is paralleling that of Mo Lei, just to a different degree. With a new attitude towards life, Su Yu drops "The Ambitious One" and decides to write a new play, reflecting his new understanding of a writer's responsibility to society and a husband's responsibility to wife and children.

1661. *Remote Place (Yuan Fang)*

1984. Guangxi Film Studio. Color. 10 Reels. Direction: Wu Yingchun. Screenplay: Zhou Minzheng. Cinematography: Liao Fan. Art Direction: Wu Zhaohua. Music: Yang Shaoyi. Sound: Lu Zhuwen. Cast: Xiang Hong as Yang Chun, Guo Gang as Yu Shaomin, Ma Shuyun as Shi Hua, Ji Ping as Shi Ding, Xu Cangxi as Teacher Wei, Yang Jinlong as Ba Wei

Miao nationality college graduate Yang Chun and her lover Yu Shaomin pay a visit to her hometown, remote Gaoba Village. Realizing the backward situation there, Yang Chun decides to rebuild the village school. After the repairs are completed, they have trouble finding teachers. Her old high school classmate Shi Ding comes to teach, but is soon accepted by a college. Shi Ding decides to pass up the opportunity and stay on as a teacher. Yu Shaomin grows bored in the village, and argues with Yang Chun about their remaining. At last, Yang Chun decides to stay in her hometown and educate the children, while Yu Shaomin is undecided as to what he will do.

1662. *A Remote Village (Liao Yuan De Shan Cun)*

1950. Northeast Film Studio. B & W. 10 reels. Direction: Wu Yonggang. Screenplay: Yuan Wenshu. Cinematography: Bao Jie. Set Design: Zhu Ge. Music: Zhang Guocang. Sound: Chen Wenyuan. Costume: Li Rongwei. Makeup: Zhang Litang. Cast: Zhang Ping as Wang Hanlong, Huang Ruohai as Dong Batian, He Gaoying as Sun Xiumei, Wang Huimin as Li Jiatou, Su Fei as Zhang Juan, Chen Ge as the Provincial Chairman

Wang Hanlong is appointed the District Director of a newly liberated district in a remote area. A landlord named Dong Batian along with his daughter Sun Xiumei and Li Jiatou, a Nationalist secret agent, secretly plan how to subvert the work of the new director. They concentrate on fomenting discord between the district's east and north villages, with repair of a local dam being the main point of contention. The argument turns violent, resulting in injury to the west village's headman. Wang is able to bring about a change in the villagers' thinking through patient one-on-one discussions with village elders. His wife Zhang Juan does the same with village women. After the dam is built, Dong Batian and Li Jiantou try to blow up the dam, but their plot is thwarted by alert armed villagers. After that, the conspirators try to burn a public granary and are arrested.

1663. *Rena's Wedding (Re Na De Hun Shi)*

1982. Tianshan Film Studio. Color. 11 Reels. Direction: Guang Chunlan. Screenplay: Shishitiyimin Aeryemiti, Guang Chunlan. Cinematography: Hali Kejiang. Art Direction: Ma Shaoxian. Music: Yan Fei. Sound: Meili Guli as Rena, Feierda Weisi as Xiaohe Lati, Aishan as Yasheng, Kamili as Kadeer, Apu Reli as Botanmu, Azi Guli as Manlidan, Naman as Aili

Rena is a beautiful and hardworking hospital nurse, in love with Yasheng, a model teacher. Her mother opposes the relationship, however, as she wants her daughter to marry someone with better financial prospects. At the wedding of Rena's friend Kadeer, a slick young salesman named Xiaohe Lati sees Rena and wants her. He ingratiates himself to the mother, deceiving her into thinking his position is much higher than it really is. Rena's mother readily agrees to her daughter marrying Xiaohe Lati. Rena is very upset at this, and finally decides to oppose this traditional way of arranging marriages. With the help of her friends, she exposes Xiaohe Lati's deception and wins. The film ends with Rena and Yasheng's gala wedding.

1664. *Reoccurring Miracles (Qi Ji De Zai Xian)*

1985. Beijing Film Studio. Color. 10 Reels. Direction: Xiao Lang, Qiu Lili. Screenplay: Qiu Lili, Mei Qianfei, Chen Peizhan. Cinematography: Zhou Jixun. Art Direction: Tu Juhua. Music: Peng Xiancheng, Gong Guofu. Sound: Chen Yanxi, Hua Kaixiu. Cast: Zhou Jie as Xia Ying, Wei Guochun as Wang Chong, Dong Zhizhi as Li Ming, Xiang Lei as Mr. Xia

Xia Ying, a young woman dancer in a city's song and dance performance troupe, happens one day upon a set of ancient Chinese court instruments called Bianzhong. She gets the idea of putting together a program recreating the ancient Bianzhong style of music. When she tries to enlist the aid of her boyfriend Wang Chong, a composer with the music troupe, he has no interest. Later, Wang Chong is assigned to compose for the program, but his lack of enthusiasm causes him to fail. He and Xia Ying quarrel over this. Troupe Director Zhou gets them to discuss the matter, and

Wang Chong comes to understand. In the end, Xia and Wang's production of "Chu Palace Music" is a huge success. The two also find themselves in love.

1665. *The Republic Will Never Forget (Gong He Guo Bu Hui Wang Ji)*

1988. Guangxi Film Studio. Color. 12 Reels. Wide Screen. Direction: Zhai Junjie. Screenplay: Tian Junli, Zhai Junjie. Cinematography: Shen Jie, Lei Jiaming. Art Direction: Wu Zhaohua. Music: Ai Liqun. Sound: Han Weijun, Ma Ting. Cast: Zhai Junjie as Tian Geng, Zheng Zaishi as Shen Tianwen, Tang Guoqiang as Lan Yumen, Wang Ji as Feng Lu, Mu Ning as Jiang Jingwen

Tian Geng, who everyone calls Boss Tian, is the head of the Huajiang Steel Mill. His drive and determination to implement progressive policies have brought the mill from the verge of bankruptcy to prosperity. In his family life, however, Tian is a despot to both his wife and his daughter, who seeks marriage as a means of escape. His ruthlessness eventually loses the affections of his family and the friendship of his comrades. Tian is left alone, with his only consolation the bittersweet knowledge that while his steelmaking has been a great contribution to building China, in the end it is only the nation that will never forget him.

Best Picture, 1989 Hundred Flowers Awards.

1666. *Rescue Mission (Fei Yue Jue Jing)*

1991. Xi'an Film Studio. Color. Letterboxed. 9 Reels. Direction: Shi Zhanfeng. Screenplay: Sun Yian. Cinematography: Zhao Yaolin and Luo Yongjian. Art Direction: Wang Yingbing. Music: Cheng Baohua. Sound: Yan Jun, Dang Wang. Cast: Shi Xiaohong as Liu Jian, Wang Chao as Wang Longsheng, Yi Xinxin as Bai Xue, Ma Yinchun as Bai Yuhua

In 1964, the Chinese government decides to conduct its first nuclear test in a remote area of West China. Three days before the planned detonation, authorities discover that a group of people are moving into the test area. For humanitarian reasons, the government sends a rescue team into the area to evacuate the people, only to find they are a group of former Nationalist soldiers turned bandits. After many difficulties, the rescue team at last accomplishes its mission.

1667. *Rescuing Li Zicheng (Chou Zhong Chou)*

1990. Xiaoxiang Film Studio. Color. Wide Screen. 9 Reels. Direction: Zhou Kangyu, Screenplay: Zhang Ge. Cinematography: Zhang Jianzhong. Art Direction: Xia Rujin. Music: Xu Jingxin. Sound: Liu Feng. Cast: Wang Yuanlu as Ajige, Sun Xixi as Li Cuiwei, Jiang Biao as Ma Zhong, Chen Kang as Han Yimang

In 1644, Li Zicheng leads a farmers' rebellion attempting to defend the Ming dynasty against the Manchu invasion. Li and his fellow rebels fall into a trap set by Manchu general Ajige. Ajige then sends a martial arts expert to find Li and kill him. Li Zicheng's daughter Li Cuiwei and Ming general Ma Zhong try to find him first to protect him.

1668. *Reserve Team Member (Hou Bu Dui Yuan)*

1983. Xiaoxiang Film Studio. Color. 8 Reels. Direction: Wu Zhiniu, Chen Lu. Screenplay: Xie Wenli. Cinematography: Zhang Li, Wang Xiaoyue. Art Direction: Li Jingsong, Li Yongqi. Music: Tan Dun. Sound: Huang Yinxia. Cast: Jiang Shuo as Liu Kezhi, Liu Weihua as Coach Huang, Tian Ge as Song Ping, Li Wenling as Mother

Liu Kezhi is a fourth-grade student interested only in martial arts. Since his grades are so poor, he is ineligible for the school's martial arts team. One day, the team coach sees Kezhi practicing by himself, and recognizes his talents. He encourages Kezhi to study, and while Kezhi does make substantial progress his grades are still not high enough. The coach probes further, and finds out that Liu Kezhi's father works outside of the city, leaving the mother with heavy family responsibilities. As a result, she has little time to help Kezhi at home. At last, Kezhi gets the tutoring he requires to get him on the team.

1669. *The Retired Soldier and the Girl Electrician (Lao Ban Ge He Dian Mei Zhi)*

1984. August First Film Studio. Color. Letterboxed. 10 Reels. Direction: Yang Guangyuan, Zhao Jilie. Screenplay: Chen Dunde, Gu Hua. Cinematography: Yang Guangyuan, Yang Xiuqin. Art Direction: Zhao Changsheng. Sound: Shi Pingyi, Sun Juzhen. Cast: Jin Xing as Mo Fenglin, Song Jie as Zhao Yuzhi, Xu Zhiwei as Yang Yeye, Zhang Baoru as Yang Laosi, Jin Hua as

Mao Laoguan, Xin Min as Shu Gu, Zhang Fan as Fenglin's mother, Xing Jizhou as Director Cao

When Mo Fenglin is separated from the army after 14 years service, he returns to his old home town planning to use his retirement bonus to buy the contract to operate a grain mill. His parents strongly oppose this, as does Yang Yeye, the fiancee selected for Mo by his parents. He has many problems and setbacks at first, but gets considerable aid and support from Zhao Yuzhi, a young woman electrician. At last, his mill begins to turn a profit, and Mo shocks everyone locally by declaring his own choice for a wife is Zhao Yuzhi. Mo is supported by the government in his decision.

1670. *Return to Our Army (Hui Dao Zi Ji De Dui Wu)*

1949. Northeast Film Studio. B & W. 8 reels. Direction: Cheng Yin. Screenplay: Cheng Yin. Cinematography: Li Guanghui. Set Design: Zhu Ge. Music: Wu Yin, Gong Zhiwei, Zhang Dichang. Sound: Chen Wenyuan. Makeup: Luo Tai. Cast: Lin Ke as Wu Dagang, Guan Guixiang as Wu Gensheng, Wu Taodi as Papa Wu, Sai Sheng as Mama Wu, Sun Hui as the Political Instructor, Cao Rui as Chen Yong, Wang Bing as Wang Dahe, Li Siye as Zhang Long, Su Li as Enemy Company Commander, Li Meng and Li Weixin as Enemy Platoon Leaders

During the war of liberation, Nationalist troops raid a small town. One of the homes sacked is that of a Nationalist soldier, Wu Dagang, and his father is badly beaten. When the town is liberated by Communist forces, a PLA political instructor educates Papa Wu to the point where he goes to the battlefield to encourage his son and other Nationalist soldiers to defect. In the next battle, Wu Dagang and others take their hated company commander prisoner, and go over to the other side.

1671. *Return to the Hometown (Huan Xiang)*

1983. Shanghai Film Studio. Color. 6 Reels. Direction: Bao Qicheng, Ye Dan. Cinematography: Cheng Shiyu. Art Direction: Chen Fuxing. Music: Xiang Yi. Sound: Tu Minde. Cast: Wu Haiyan as Xiao Qin, Li Zhaiyang as Zhu Geng

On route to a visit to her old hometown, Xiao Qin runs into Zhu Geng. The two had been sent to work in Northwest China in the 1960s, and had become lovers during that time. But their different interests and ambitions had caused her to at last refuse him.

When Zhu Geng returned to his hometown making money became his primary interest, and now at this reunion he brags incessantly about his material wealth. This does not impress her as he had hoped, for Xiao Qin's life has taken a different turn: she has become devoted to building the northwest, and material things hold little interest for her.

1672. *Return to Xini River (Chong Gui Xi Ni He)*

1982. Inner Mongolia Film studio. Color. 10 Reels. Direction: Wu Lan, Chen Da. Screenplay: Feng Lingzhi. Cinematography: Xia Lixing, Bao Qin. Art Direction: Li Jinggui, Shen Minquan. Music: Mori Jihu. Sound: Bu Ren. Cast: Suya Ladalai as Harifu, Hasi Gaowa as Sharuna, Yirihu as Grandma, Zhao Lu as Jiang Bula, Enhesheng as Dun Debu

A young Mongolian man named Harifu lost his mother when he was very young and was raised on the prairie by his grandmother while his father worked in the city. His father at last persuades Harifu to come join him there, but when the father dies, Harifu's stepmother is so abusive the young man chooses to return to the prairie where he grew up. The local people welcome him warmly, but when word gets around that Harifu had been fired from his city job as a driver, they begin having less to do with him. The only person to continue supporting him is Sharuna, a local girl. Harifu is hurt by others shunning him, for the truth of the matter is that after his father's death the local Party organization assigned him to work as a driver. When his stepmother's own son was involved in an accident she arranged for the blame to be shifted to Harifu, who lost both his license and his job. When the true story comes out, everyone rallies to Harifu's support, and he and Sharuna look forward to a bright future together.

1673. *Return with the Moon (Yue Sui Ren Gui)*

1990. Shanghai Film Studio. Color. 10 Reels. Wide Screen. Direction: Wu Yigong. Screenplay: Wu Yigong. Cinematography: Xia Lixing. Art Direction: Xue Jianna. Music: Yang Mao. Sound: Liu Guangjie. Cast: Xia Zongyou as Zhang Hanyuan, Zhang Wenrong as Lin Mengyun, Xiang Mei as Ou Yufen

Zhang Hanyuan left mainland China nearly four decades ago because his pious Roman Catholic parents wouldn't allow him to marry Lin Mengyun, a non-Catholic. Now he is returning to Shanghai, accompanied by Ou Yufen, a woman pretending to be his wife in order to console his parents. But he has never forgotten Mengyun, the one great love of his life. He never expects that Lin Mengyun will be the first person he meets when he arrives at the Shanghai docks.

1674. *Returning from the Aged to the Young (Fan Lao Huan Tong)*

1958. August First Film Studio. B & W. 7 Reels. Direction: Wang Bing. Screenplay: Yu Zhaohan. Cinematography: Chen Jun, Chen Zhiqiang. Art Direction: Mai Yi. Music: Li Weicai. Sound: Kou Shenkang. Cast: Liu Yi as Li Yanfang, Guan Shuzhen as Yang Xiuer, Jin Xin as Political Commissar Sun, Xing Jitian as Deputy Director Fan, Chen Yao as the general, Wang Xinjian as Li Xuzhang

Li Yanfang, a young doctor in a military hospital, is blocked from testing a new method of curing neurasthenia by clinic director Qi and Professor Cui. With the support of the Party organization and Political Commissar Sun and the close cooperation of Deputy Director Fan, a patient, he finally achieves success after experiencing many failures. Later, Qi tries again to stop use of the new method when an accident occurs, but investigation shows it was a nurse's carelessness and not the new method that was the cause. Director Qi and Professor Cui are both criticized for wrong thinking.

1675. *Returning to the Hometown (Gui Xiang)*

1983. Changchun Film Studio. Color. 10 Reels. Direction: Chang Zhenhua. Screenplay: Li Junbing, Liu Yongji. Cinematography: Jia Shouxing. Art Direction: Wu Qiwen. Music: Zhu Guangqin. Sound: Liu Xingfu. Cast: Hao Zhibeng as Li Chunniu, Zhang Peiyu as Xia Gu, Li Yanlai as Mrs. Qiulin, Lu Xiaohe as Tie Bao, Ma Shaoxing as Uncle Baliang, Liu Fan as Yuanpo, Wang Jiaying as Ximei

After the Chinese civil wars have finally ended in a Communist victory, Red Army soldier Lin Chunniu returns to the hometown he left nearly 20 years before. He is shocked and angry to find his wife Xia Gu has married another man, Tie Bao, and they have a 10-year-old daughter Ximei. After much bitter arguing, Chunniu decides to leave town, but as he is leaving some local people stop him and relate the story of what happened in his absence. It turns out that Xia Gu and Tie Bao had assumed a false relationship as a married couple in order to protect themselves from the Japanese, who were conscripting and enslaving single people. In time their protecting and caring for each other turned to real affection. Later, when they heard that Li Chunniu had died in battle, they legalized the relationship. Although the townspeople beg him to stay, Chunniu decides he must go, and tearfully takes his leave of the town where he grew up. Tie Bao and Xia Gu ask his forgiveness, and Chunniu gives them an engagement gift — a jade bracelet he had kept for many years. He wishes them a lifetime of happiness.

1676. *Reunion After 20 Years (Er Shi Nian Hou Zai Xiang Hui)*

1984. Shanghai Film Studio. Color. Letterboxed. 10 Reels. Direction: Shi Xiaohua. Screenplay: Liang Xingmin and Yang Shiwen. Cinematography: Shen Miaorong. Art Direction: Ju Ransheng. Music: Huang Zhun. Sound: Xie Guojie. Cast: Qian Yongfu as Yuan Lang, Zhu Ling as Zhu Hui, Gao Fei as Feng Zhenyu, Liu Zifeng as Chen Qimin

Yuan Lang, Zhu Hui, Feng Zhenyu and Chen Qimin were college classmates in the 1960s. Zhu Hui and Feng Zhenyu had also been lovers, but broke up after graduation because Zhu did not want to accompany Feng when he had the chance to go abroad for graduate study. Now, 20 years later, Yuan Lang is director of a shipyard, assigned the task of manufacturing the export ship "Jiuhua," planned to be China's largest to date. By chance, Zhu Hui is assigned as the ship's inspector and Feng Zhenyu shows up as representative of the foreign company that is partner to the venture. At first, the rest are suspicious and resentful of Feng's obsession with quality control, but in time they come to understand that his attitude grows out of patriotism and a desire to see China build an outstanding shipping industry. By the time the "Jiuhua" is finished, the four old classmates have restored their close friendship of the past.

1677. *Reunited in Victory (Sheng Li Chong Feng)*

1951. Shanghai Film Studio. B & W. 10 Reels. Direction: Tang Xiaodan. Screenplay: Zhang

Junxiang, based on Li Yang's novel, "A Hero Returns Home." Cinematography: Fei Junyang and Jin Tiemin. Art Direction: Wang Cangcheng and Yang Lingde. Music: Liu Fuan and Xue Yan. Sound: Song Liangcheng. Costume: Zhi Guang. Cast: Feng Ji as Geng Hailin, Su Yi as Ji Yingxing, Ling Yun as Luo Zhiqing, Ding Ran as the Bandits' Company Commander, Zhang Yan as Potbellied Cai, Yang Mengxu as Old Ji, Fan Zhenggang as Old Geng, Jiang Yusheng as Cui Yuwan.

During World War II, in order to raise enough money for wedding expenses, young farmer Geng Hailing pawns his small farm to landlord Cai who immediately takes the land. Shortly after Geng Hailing is married, he is drafted into the Chinese army, where he is bullied by his Nationalist officers. After the Japanese surrender, the Nationalist forces launch attacks on the areas held by Communist forces, and Geng is sent to Northeast China to fight in the civil war. After he is liberated, he is put into the Northeast Democratic Associated Army, where he gradually comes to lose the bad habits he acquired in the Nationalist Army. He also distinguishes himself in combat. When the army moves south, he goes to his hometown and is reunited with his wife and son. In order to protect what has been gained in victory, Geng Hailing then goes further south with the Red Army to wipe out the enemy.

1678. *Reuniting After the Storms of Life (Feng Yu Gui Tu)*

1990. Shenzhen Film Studio. Color. Wide Screen. 9 Reels. Direction: Wen Lumin, Zhi Lei. Screenplay: Li Gongda. Cinematography: Zhang Xiaoguang. Art Direction: Yang Gang. Music: Chang Yuhong. Sound: Li Tie. Cast: Zhang Fengyi as Jin Fan, Chen Wei as Yayun

When some corrupt officials embezzle 500,000 yuan from Haijin City's machinery plant, they set up plant manager Jin Fan as the fall guy. He is convicted of the crime and sentenced to prison. His lovely wife Yayun still loves Jin Fan, but is left with no choice but to divorce him. After serving his sentence, Jin Fan is determined to clear his name through his own investigation. Meanwhile, a criminal gang is looking for the half million yuan, which was never found. Jin Fan is finally able to convince two police officers to assist him, and together they recover the money and clear Jin's name. He and his wife find their love has survived, and they get together again.

1679. *Revenge (Bao Chou)*

1993. Shanghai Yongle Joint Stock Company Ltd., Emei Film Studio & Taiwan Baoxiong Film Media Company Ltd. Co-Production. Color. Letterboxed. 9 Reels. Direction: Zhuang Yujian. Screenplay: Zhen Wenhua. Cinematography: Zuang Yinjian. Art Direction: Yan Dingfu. Music: Tang Qingshi. Sound: Pan Lizhong, Zhang Weimin. Costume: Liu Changxiu, Luo Ping. Makeup: Tang Shuangju, Zhu Meidi. Cast: Zhang Fengyi as Chou Feng, Liu Ximing as Di Qi, Luo Rui, Wu Shanshan, Zhang Jianli, Wang Xia, Xu Manhua, Ye Rongzu, Cai Hong

A gangster film set in 1930s Shanghai. An innocent young girl from the country travels to the city to seek her father and her lover and blunders into a triad war with tragic consequences.

1680. *Revenge in the Big World (Fu Chou Da Shi Jie)*

1989. Changchun Film Studio. Color. 10 Reels. Letterboxed. Direction: Wang Xuexin. Screenplay: Zhang Jiping. Cinematography: Jin Hengyi. Art Direction: Wang Chong. Music: Fan Weiqiang. Sound: Xing Guocang. Cast: Xu Xiaojian as Deng Tianye, Zheng Rong as Xu Fujian, Yang Chunrong as Ouyang Qiufeng, Liu Wenfeng as Li Xiumei, Dong Fang Wenyin as Li Xiuli

In 1930s Shanghai, the "adventurers' paradise," Deng Tianye returns from study at a German military academy to accept a captain's commission in the Chinese Northeast Army. The official government policy at the time is to collaborate with the Japanese occupying parts of China, so Deng's insistence on resistance lands him in jail. His wife Ouyang Qiufeng is abducted and sold to the Chunle Garden, famous Shanghai Brothel. When Deng goes to Shanghai to look for his wife after his release, he is beaten up by thugs employed by the brothel. With the help of a Miss Li, Deng finds his wife and helps her escape, only to be trapped again by crooks and policemen. In order to keep her honor, Ouyang commits suicide. Deng has to leave Shanghai and goes to the Northeast to fight against the Japanese.

1681. *Revenge of Three (Long Feng Jiao)*

1993. Beijing Film Studio. Color. Letterboxed. 9 Reels. Direction: Li Wenhua. Screenplay: Ke Zhanghe. Cinematography: Tu Jiakuan. Art Direction: Zhen Huiwen, Qin Duo. Music: Yao Ming. Costume: Zhu Yanyan. Makeup: Hao Xia. Cast: Zhao Jun as Hai Long, Liang Danni as Ning Tianfeng, Zhou Li as Jiao Mei, Zhou Zhou as Biao Shaoye, Li Zhenping as Ning Feihong, Bai Han as Aunt Cui

A tale of jealousy, lust and revenge, set during the early 1920s. Two friends love the same woman, and when she marries one, the rejected suitor rapes the woman and later kills her husband. The dead man's son grows up to avenge his parents.

1682. *Revenge on Mount Tai (Tai Shan En Chou)*

1991. Beijing Film Studio. Color. Letterboxed. 10 Reels. Direction: Li Wenhua. Screenplay: Liang Zhiyong, Ke Zhanghe. Cinematography: Tu Jiakuan. Art Direction: Song Zhengli. Music: Guo Wenjing. Sound (Dolby): Lai Qijian, Chen Binglian. Cast: Zhang Lianwen as Steel Hands Zhang, Zhang Hong as Xuelan, Huang Guoqiang as Gengsheng, Zhang Chao as Bai Lang, Xu Yuanqi as Songawa, Liu Peiqi as Yan Xibiao, Ji Yemu as the priest

Martial arts expert "Steel Hands" Zhang lives with his adopted son Bai Lang at the foot of Mount Tai. One day, he rescues a stranger in trouble, then has his son escort the man back to the city of Tianjin. Soon after, the Japanese army enters the area, and Zhang finds the man he rescued is Japanese commander Songawa. He deeply regrets his previous action. He undertakes his own guerrilla campaign against the invaders, and at last is forced to kill his son Bai Lang, who has become a Japanese collaborator. In a final struggle, Zhang and Songawa kill each other.

1683. *Reverberations of Life (Sheng Huo de Chan Yin)*

1979. Xi'an Film Studio. Color, W & B, 11 Reels. Direction: Teng Wenji, Wu Tianming. Screenplay: Teng Wenji. Cinematography: Liu Cangxun, Zhu Dingyu. Art Direction: Zhang Zien, Hu Qiangsheng. Music: Li Yaodong. Sound: Hong Jiahui. Cast: Shi Zhongqi as Zhen Changhe, Leng Mei as Xu Shanshan, Xiang Lei as Xu Yixiang, Fu Qinzhen as Li Lin

After the Gang of Four is defeated, young violinist Zhen Changde performs a number called "Wiping Away the Tears" at a Beijing concert. A young girl in the audience, Xu Shanshan, recalls the unforgettable events of 1976. At that time, stooges of the Gang of Four were chasing the young violinist, and at the critical moment, Xu Shanshan brought this stranger into her own home. The chief pursuer of Zhen was Wei Li, a deputy director in a department of the Ministry of Culture. After hearing Zhen perform "Mourn in January," a number mourning the death of Premier Zhou Enlai, she came to admire the young man greatly. For political reasons and personal jealousy, Wei Li wants to have Zhen Chengde killed, but the violinist is unafraid. To show his defiance, he holds a concert at Xu Shanshan's home to accuse the Gang of Four of high crimes, and to memorialize Premier Zhou.

1684. *Reverie in Old Shanghai (Shang Hai Wang Shi)*

1995. CCTV Film & Television Division, Wanbao Group Financial Corp., Guangdong New World Film Production Corp., Zhejiang Film Studio Co-Production. Color. Direction: Li Jun. Screenplay: Qiu Donghua, based on the original screenplay by Shen Ji, Shu Shi. Cinematography: Hua Qing, Xu Hongbing. Art Direction: Liu Weixin. Cast: Wang Jiancheng as Chang Tingshan, Hou Changrong as Fang Zhiqiu, Liu Lei as Yao Yuqin

In the 1930s, Yao Yuqin is the most popular actress at the Shanghai Lianhua Film Studio. She has a friend and protector in Shanghai triad head Chang Tingshan, a man who owes his life to Yao's brother, who sacrificed his own life to save that of the gangster's. Yao falls in love with Beijing opera star Fang Zhiqiu, but he leaves her to return to Beijing and marry his childhood fiancee. When the Japanese occupy Shanghai, Chang Tingshan refuses to collaborate with them, so he flees the city and moves to Chongqing, the wartime capital. After he leaves, playboy Wang Haishan gives Yao a big rush, and they are married. But after the marriage he shows his true colors, becoming a collaborator as well as abusing her. The desperate actress attempts suicide, and word of the situation reaches Chang Tingshan, who returns to Shanghai and kills Wang. All this makes Yao realize that his feeling for her is more than friendship. Since he still refuses to collaborate with them, the Japanese arrest Chang Tingshan under the excuse of cleaning up the triads. Yao is able to get him out of jail, but he has lost everything. At this point, her old lover Fang Zhiqiu turns up, seeking to reconcile with Yao, but she rejects him, choosing instead to make her life with the faithful Chang. They leave Shanghai together.

1685. *Revolutionaries in a Disturbed World (Luan Shi Piao Gai)*

1992. Xi'an Film Studio. Color. Letterboxed. 10 Reels. Direction: Zhu Dingyu. Screenplay: Shao Licheng, Xiang Jincheng. Zhu Dingyu. Cinematography: Liu Cangxu, Liu Xiaaojing. Art Direction: Cheng Minzhang. Music: Xu Youfu. Sound: Guo Chao, Feng Shihe. Costume: Liu Taigang. Makeup: An Hong. Cast: Wang Guanghui as Luozhi, Wang Yali as Huang's wife, Zhang Yuan as Jian Ji, Zhao Jian as Jian Chun, Chen Shuqin as the doctor, Li Jiancheng as Shan Gai

As the new Republic of China replaces the Qing Dynasty in 1912, revolutionary Huang Qingshan obtains the secret agreement between dictatorial President Yuan Shikai and the Japanese, an agreement which betrays the Chinese revolution. While taking it back to headquarters, Huang is killed by a father and son named Zhao, two local revolutionaries with personal grudges against him. Huang's wife sets out on course of revenge, and opens a restaurant as a cover while she awaits her chance. The revolutionary party's headquarters sends an agent named Luozhi out to find Huang Qingshan, and when he learns of Huang's death, joins with the dead man's wife against the Zhaos. They eventually kill the Zhaos as well as one of Yuan Shikai's spies they uncover in their midst. They also recover the secret document.

1686. *A Revolutionary Family (Ge Ming Jia Ying)*

1960. Beijing Film Studio. Color. 11 Reels. Direction: Shui Hua. Screenplay: Xia Yan and Shui Hua, based on Tao Cheng's autobiography "My Family." Cinematography: Qian Jiang. Art Direction: Chi Ning. Music: Ju Wei. Sound: Cai Jun. Cast: Yu Lan as Zhou Lian, Sun Daolin as Jiang Meiqing, Zhang Liang as Jiang Liqun, Liu Guiling as Xiao Lian, Shi Xiaoman as Xiaoqing, Luo Guoliang as Meng Tao

After her marriage to university student and political activist Jiang Meiqing, country girl Zhou Lian begins learning revolutionary theory. During the Northern Expedition, Meiqing serves in the coalition army. But in 1927, when Chiang Kaishek turns on the Communists, Meiqing is one of those killed. Zhou Lian takes up her husband's unfulfilled career, and becomes a revolutionary. In the early 1930s, she works in the CPC's Shanghai underground. Shortly after her elder son Liqun returns from training in the Soviet Union, the

A Revolutionary Family. After marrying student political activist Jiang Meiqing (Sun Daolin, seated), Zhou Lian (Yu Lan) begins studying revolutionary theory. 1960. Beijing Film Studio.

Party organization is destroyed, and Zhou Lian and Liqun are arrested. Her captors alternate threats and inducements in their attempt to get Zhou Lian to supply them with information about the relationship of the Shanghai CPC branch with the Communist-controlled areas, but she will not talk. Finally, she is offered Liqun's life in exchange for her own, and in the interest of revolution, she sacrifices her son. She is not released until the anti-Japanese war begins. The Party organization sends Zhou Lian, her daughter Xiao Lian and younger son Xiao Qing to the Party central headquarters in Yan'an.

Best Screenplay Xia Yan and Shui Hua, 1962 Hundred Flowers Awards.

1687. *Revolutionary Pioneer (Ge Ming Jun Zhong Ma Qian Zu)*

1981. Shanghai Film Studio. Color. Wide Screen. 11 Reels. Direction: Yi Min. Screenplay: Ye Yuan. Cinematography: Luo Chongzhou, Zhang Xiling. Art Direction: Ge Shicheng, Mei Kunping. Music: Liang Hanguang. Sound: Zhou Yunling. Cast: Zhang Yunian as Zhou Rong, Xi Yurong as Zhang Taiyan, Zhang Ming as Qin Fang

In 1901, 17-year-old Zhou Rong, second son of a wealthy Sichuan businessman, goes to Japan to study. He hopes to use his education to help save China and its people. In Tokyo, he participates in various patriotic movements, and writes the famous "Revolutionary Manifesto," which advocates the overthrow of the corrupt Qing (Manchu) regime and the establishment of a democratic government and a free China. His political activism gets Zhou Rong expelled from Japan. After arriving in Shanghai, Zhou Rong meets and becomes close friends with Zhang Taiyan, who helps him get the "Manifesto" published and widely disseminated in China. The Qing government has Zhou and Zhang arrested and put on trial in what becomes a historically famous case in China. Zhou Rong presents his arguments well in court, but is convicted and executed at the age of 21.

1688. *The Revolutionary Road (Zheng Tu)*

1976. Shanghai Film Studio. Color. 11 Reels. Directors: Yan Bili and Bao Qicheng. Screenplay: Collective, based on the novel of the same title by Guo Xianhong. Cinematographers: Luo

Chongzhou, Yin Fukang. Art Direction: Hu Dengren, Wang Xingcang. Music: Lu Qimin. Sound: Zhu Weigang, Yang Liangkun. Cast: Guo Kaiming as Zhong Weihua, Zhang Fa as Li Dejiang, Wang Suhong as Mei Yinzi, Zhao Xin as Tian Xiaobing, Qin Yi as Guan's wife, Zhang Yi as Grandpa Zhang, Feng Qi as Zhang Shan

When Zhong Weihua and other educated young people arrive at the Sino-Soviet border area to settle down and homestead, they determine to give equal time to guarding the border and building up the area. This frightens Zhang Shan, formerly a covert Japanese collaborator, who has secret ties with the Soviets. He first gains the trust of the production unit director, then stirs up conflicts between the director and the young newcomers. He is also successful at shaking the confidence of some of the young people about settling along the border. Under the leadership of the Party branch committee, Zhong Weihua leads his comrades in struggling with this class enemy. They catch Zhang Shan and some Soviet spies, and go on with their settlement of the area.

1689. *Revolutionary Sparks at Meiling (Mei Ling Xing Huo)*

1982. Pearl River Film Studio. Color. 12 Reels. Direction: Lu Yu. Screenplay: Shao Wu, Hui Lin. Cinematography: Li Shengwei. Art Direction: Zhang Zhichu. Music: Fu Gengcheng. Sound: Deng Qinhua. Cast: Liu Xitian as Chen Yi. Also featuring Zhang Jie, Zhu Jianmin, Huang Zhongqiu, Ni Ping, Ji Ping, Zhou Jingqun and Xu Jinzhi

In October, 1934, the main force of the Red Army is forced to retreat, and starts its famed "Long March" to the north. To keep the seeds of revolution alive in the south, Chen Yi remains behind as head of a small band of guerrillas, fewer than 100-strong. Inexperienced, and in many cases unused to hardship, the guerrillas make many mistakes, but the confident Chen Yi keeps them together. After the peaceful resolution of the "Xi'an Incident" in 1936, things go well for a time, but then Chiang Kaishek again turns on the Communists and the guerrillas find themselves surrounded. Chen Yi again leads them out of it. The Nationalist and Communists form a third alliance in the summer of 1937, and Chen Yi's forces grow rapidly. The are formed into the New Fourth Route Army, and move northward to battle the Japanese.

1690. *Rice (Mi)*

1995. Beijing Film Studio, Beijing Minquan New Technology Co., Yitong Investment Co. Co-Production. Color. Letterboxed. Direction: Huang Jianzhong. Screenplay: Shi Ling. Cinematography: Zhang Zhongping. Art Direction: Wu Xujing. Music: Zou Ye. Cast: Tao Zeru as Wu Long, Shi Lan as Zhiyun, Yang Kun as Yiyun, Zhu Decheng as A Bao, Xia Zongyao as Master Lu

In a small town in the 1920s, a man named Feng operates a rice shop. He has two daughters, Zhiyun and Yiyun. Zhiyun grows up man-crazy, and is quite happy to become the mistress of despotic local landlord Master Lu. She eventually gets pregnant, just at the time he tires of her and dumps her. Wu Long, a hungry peasant, comes to town looking for work, but practically all the townspeople bully and humiliate him. The only person who shows him any consideration is Feng, who gives the young man a job helping out in the store. Yiyun hates the newcomer and continues to humiliate him. Wu gradually toughens, and learns to hate everyone, which leads Master Lu to appreciate him and make the young man a protege. The lusty Zhiyun finds Wu especially attractive, and they have an affair, making Yiyun hate him all the more. She wishes him dead, especially when he attempts to rape her while his lover Zhiyun is in labor. When Mr. Feng dies, Wu Long takes over the store, and proceeds to now treat everyone as they treated him before. A triad war erupts, and many of the locals are killed. When Yiyun finds that Wu Long has survived, she vows to kill him someday.

1691. *The Rich Master from Hong Kong (Xiang Gang Shao Ye)*

1993. Tianshan Film Studio. Color. Letterboxed. 10 Reels. Direction: Zhang Gang. Screenplay: Zhang Gang. Cinematography: Shen Xilin, Zhang Jian. Art Direction: Tang Xinghua. Music: Dong Weijie. Sound: Liu Guangjie. Costume: Dai Yili. Makeup: Zhou Liangeng. Cast: Huang Aoyi as A Man, Wu Dan as Huang Caiyun, Shen Ge as Zhong Sijian, Xiong Wei as Lu Zheng

Aman, a wealthy young Hong Kong man, travels alone to the mainland on vacation. After checking in to a luxury hotel, he goes swimming but while in the water all his money and personal identification are stolen. Unfortunately, no one at the hotel recognizes him, and without any clothes or documents, they refuse him entry. Hungry and wandering the streets, he meets Huang Caiyu, a kind girl newly arrived from Sichuan. She helps him out, gives him a place to stay, and gets him a job at the construction site where she works. He tells her who he is, but she laughs at his story, believing he is joking. They fall in love. In time his father arrives from Hong Kong looking for his missing son. Aman tells Huang, who wants an ordinary working man for a husband, that he is not the person they are looking for.

Rickshaw Boy **see** *Xiangzi the Camel*

1692. *Ripples Across Stagnant Water (Kuang)*

1991. Hong Kong Shijia Film Productions Ltd. and Emei Film Studio Co-Production. Color. 10 Reels. Letterboxed. Direction: Ling Zifeng. Screenplay: Han Lanfang. Cinematography: Sun Yongtian. Art Direction: Yang Zhanjia. Music: Liu Zuang, Mo Fan. Sound: Lai Qijian. Cast: Xu Qing as Mrs. Cai, You Yong as Luo Desheng, Zhao Jun as Gu Tiancheng, Cheng Xi as Liu Zhijin, Yao Erga as Cai Xingshun, Liu Yajin as Lu Maolin

At the turn of the century, the Eight-Power Allied Forces invade China, and the Empress Dowager Cixi and Emperor Guangxu flee from Beijing. The 1911 Revolution and the Boxer Movement bring chaos to China. This film is about a group of men and women living in Sichuan Province during this period. Detesting village life, young and beautiful Deng Yaogu marries Cai Xingshun, the grocer of Tianhui Town. His cousin Luo Desheng is a bachelor who follows a free and unrestrained lifestyle. Mrs. Cai secretly has eyes for Luo, and Luo realizes what she wants. Knowing that the Eight-Power Allied Forces have wiped out the Boxers and entered Beijing, Gu Tiancheng, who has old grievances against Luo Desheng, tries to gain his revenge with the help of the foreigners. As a result, Cai Xingshun's grocery is smashed and sealed up, while Cai himself is imprisoned. Mrs. Cai lapses into a coma and Luo Desheng escapes without a trace. Taking advantage of her precarious position, Gu Tiancheng wants Mrs. Cai to marry him, and she unexpectedly agrees to marry an enemy who has tried to kill her husband and destroy her son's future.

1693. *River Without Navigation Signs (Mei You Hang Biao De He Liu)*

1983. Xi'an Film Studio. Color. 9 Reels. Direction: Wu Tianmin. Screenplay: Ye Weilin. Cinematography: Liu Cangxu, Zhu Kongyang. Art Direction: Lu Guangcai. Music: Xu Youfu. Sound: Chen Yudan. Cast: Li Wei as Pan Laowu, Tao Yuling as Wu Aihua, Hu Ronghua as Shi Gu, Tang Minqin as Zhao Liang, Li Shulan as Gaixiu, Yu Wenzhong as Xu Minghe

During the Cultural Revolution, life is hard for Pan Laowu, Shi Gu and Zhao Liang. Ordinary raftsmen, they roam up and down the river seeking work where they can. In between, they combat their depression by drinking and brawling. At one stop, they learn that Xu, the director of that district, has been dismissed from his position, jailed, and has almost been persecuted to death. This outrages the three men, as they know the director to be a decent and honest man. They decide to help him escape and take him by raft to a place of safety somewhere down the river. Even the very thrifty Zhao Liang takes the money he has saved for his daughter's wedding to buy medicine for the director. They are successful in freeing the prisoner and getting him to safety. But later, when a flood hits the area, Pan Laowu is killed protecting some others.

1694. *The Riverbank at Dawn (Li Ming De He Bian)*

1958. Changchun Film Studio. B & W. 9 Reels. Direction: Chen Ge. Screenplay: Jun Qing, based on his novel of the same title. Cinematography: Fu Jincheng. Art Direction: Wang Chong. Music: Li Yaodong. Sound: Zhang Jianping. Cast: Sun Yu as Xiao Chen, Zhang Yang as Chen Ketai, Wang Jianhua as Old Lady Chen, Wu Ning as Xiao Jia, Ai Hongli as the Chief of Staff, Zhang Fengxiang as Director Yao

In the fall of 1947, the Nationalist Army occupies the Cangwei plain. Due to a traitor's betrayal, a Communist armed construction brigade defending the east bank of the Shouwei River suffers major losses, and their commander is killed. Messenger Xiao Chen is sent to report the situation to the west bank headquarters. After learning the news, the headquarters sends Director Yao to assume command of the east bank brigade. As they help Director Yao cross the river, Xiao Chen's mother and sister are both killed by the enemy.

Rice. **Hungry peasant Wu Long (Tao Zeru), comes to town looking for work, but nearly everyone in town abuses and humiliates him, a decision they will come to regret. 1995. Beijing Film Studio.**

Xiao Chen's father takes over rowing the boat. An attempt by the traitor to kill Yao is thwarted by Xiao Chen, who is himself wounded. Shortly after, Director Yao leads the east bank armed construction brigade in a counterattack, and Xiao Chen and his father both take part in the battle.

1695. *Road (Lu)*

1983. Fujian Film Studio. Color. Letterbox. 10 Reels. Direction: Chen Lizhou. Screenplay: Chen Lizhou, based on Tian Fen's novel "Gold." Cinematography: Liang Min, Zhen Wangong. Art Direction: Lin Chaoxiang, Tang Peijun. Music: Ma Ding. Sound: Zhu Wenzhong. Cast: Wan Yan as Qiuhua, Zhang Fengyi as the older guy, Wang Xianghong as Shang Quan, Xie Yuan as Niuzhi, Chen Hongmei as Third Sister, Liu Jia as Huang Bing, Lin Fangbing as Xiao Han

Through the story of Qiu Hua, one young woman struggling to find a life after the Cultural Revolution, the film examines the problems of an entire "lost generation" of Chinese, unemployed and unskilled. Qiu Hua attempts to cope by starting her own company, a plant making young people's sweaters. She alters the traditional socialist allocation system, studies market demand and updates styles. Her products become so much in demand that her plant is a strong competitor with state-owned enterprises. She has created a road for herself and others, and established her status in society.

1696. *Road Test (Lu Kao)*

1965. Changchun Film Studio. B & W. 11 Reels. Direction: Zhou Yu. Screenplay: Zhang Tianmin and Zhou Yu. Cinematography: Wang Lei. Art Direction: Shi Weijun. Music: Jiang Wei. Sound: Hong Di. Cast: Shi Xian as Young Liang, Chen Qiang as Old Liang, Ren Yi as Director Wu, Chen Xuejie as Wen Ying, Liu Yushan as Mr. Ding, Liang Yin as Old Mr. Ma

Young Liang is a hero in his own mind, but his excessive driving speed accidentally kills a pig, bringing him criticism from his father Old Liang and the leaders of their transport team. Shortly after, on an emergency assignment, he almost causes an accident by trying to make his driving stand out from the rest. Director Wu patiently educates the boy, as does his father. Young Liang finally changes his attitude, when his girl classmate Wen Ying tells him what she has learned from studying the story of Lei Feng, that "there can be heroism in performing daily tasks." Later, to rescue a patient, he drives by night to the county hospital, and although he encounters a frightened horse on the way is able to control it and avoid hurting it. Although he himself is injured, Young Liang continues on his way, and his efforts are praised.

1697. *The Road to Heaven (Tian Tang Zhi Lu)*

1988. Inner Mongolia Film Studio. Color. 9 Reels. Direction: Yun Wenyao. Screenplay: Yun Wenyao, Ruan Meimei. Cinematographer: Yun Wenyao. Art Direction: Zhao Ke, Monayintai. Music: Wang Ming. Sound: Ning Menghua. Cast: Enlisheng as Sulede, Batuqingele as Garibu, Ailiya as Moergengtai

In the early 19th century, the people of the Mongolian prairie lead a miserable existence. Elderly Sulede, a kind and decent street performer, adopts two orphan children, a boy named Garibu and a girl named Moergengtai. The children bring some happiness into the old man's lonely life, and he takes good care of them until Garibu indentures himself to earn a living. Ten years later, he flees back to his hometown, but cannot find Sulede. He does find that Moergengtai is a household slave in the mansion of a local landlord and his son. Garibu opposes and at last kills them. In the same struggle, Moergengtai burns down the landlords' mansion, but she herself is killed. His dreams shattered, Garibu decides to turn to crime and becomes a "greenwoods bandit." In this new life he is unexpectedly reunited with old Sulede.

1698. *Roar, Yellow River! (Nu Hou Ba, Huang He)*

1979. August First Film Studio. Color. 11 Reels. Direction: Shen Dan, Jia Shihong. Screenplay: Wang Xingpu, Chen Ruijun, Gao Jiuling, Shi Pingyi, based on the stage play of the same title by Wang Xingpu. Art Direction: Zhang Zhen, Cui Denggao. Music: Wang Yanqiao. Sound: Shi Yiping. Cast: Zhang Ruifang as He Dan, Liang Yuru as Wang Zhengkui, Liu Shangxian as He Xiaoxi, Gao Min as Xiao Yuchi

In the fall of 1975, He Dan is ordered to return to Beijing from the Yellow River Cadre School she had been sent to several years earlier for "reform through labor." He Dan had

previously been in charge of a musical troupe. Upon her return, she learns the reason for her recall is that Liu Liangliang, current troupe leader, wants her to write an article for the "Gang of Four" criticizing a musical piece called "Yellow River Chorus." It turns out to be the 40th anniversary of the death of Nie Er, composer of the national anthem, and the 30th anniversary of the death of Xian Xinghai (1905–1945), another great Chinese composer. Premier Zhou Enlai has ordered a commemorative concert at which the "Chorus" will be performed, and the Gang wants to embarrass Zhou publicly as part of their power grab. But He Dan refuses to be used as a tool of the Gang, angering the Gang's representative in Ministry of Culture. He Dan continues her resistance, knowing the struggle with the Gang has just begun.

1699. *Robbing Princess Zhen's Tomb at Night (Parts 1 & 2) (Ye Dao Zhen Fei Mu)*

1989. Tianshan Film Studio and the Aomin Brothers' Film Company Jointly. Color. Letterboxed. 17 Reels. Direction: Cai Yuanyuan. Screenplay: Li Bingxin, Shi Yuxin. Cinematography: Han Dongxia. Art Direction: Jin Xiwu. Music: Guo Xiaodi, Li Haihui. Sound: Wang Yunhua. Cast: Gu Lan as Fuhai, Chen Baoguo as E Shicheng, Lei Luosheng as Li Yiguang

The body of Princess Zhen, an imperial concubine persecuted to death by Dowager Empress Ci Xi, is finally laid to rest in 1915 in one of the Qing tombs. Many treasures are buried with her. In 1938, an underworld figure named E Shicheng wants to organize a gang to avenge his father, killed in a gang war. To raise the funds he needs, Guo hits upon the idea of robbing the Princess's tomb. E and five henchmen go to the tombs, but are repeatedly thwarted by Fuhai, the loyal tombkeeper who lives only to fulfill his duty. Complicating matters is the arrival of the rival triad figures who killed E Shicheng's father and also want the treasures. While the two rival gangs try to outmaneuver each other, Fuhai secretly moves the treasures to another location. The movie ends with a gun battle in which all concerned are killed, leaving the treasures' location a secret to this day.

1700. *Rock Kids (Yao Gun Qing Nian)*

1988. Youth Film Studio, Beijing Film Academy. Color. 9 Reels. Direction: Tian Zhuangzhuang. Screenplay: Liu Yiran. Cinematography: Xiao Feng. Art Direction: Li Yan. Music: Xu Peidong. Sound: Zhao Jun. Cast: Tao Jin as Long Xiang, Ma Ling as Yuan Yuan, Shi Ke as Luo Dan, Zhu Xun as Xiao Xiao

Young dancer Long Xiang loses his job as a choreographer because of his highly individualistic approach to modern Chinese dance. Things do not go so well in his love life, either. The film traces his efforts to win freedom, love and career success.

1701. *Rocking Killer (Yao Gun Sha Shou)*

1993. Changchun Film Studio. Color. Letterboxed. 9 Reels. Direction: Cheng Ke. Screenplay: Jia Ruo. Cinematography: Meng Xiandi, Wen Hongzhou. Art Direction: Yang Guomin. Music: Liang Qing. Sound: Liu Hui, Zhao Xudong. Costume: An Lixin. Makeup: Zhou Yaping. Cast: Liang Qing as Li Sha, Wu Ruomu as Zhen Han, Zhang Yechuan as Zhu An, Li Yinqiu as Lin Qingniao, Zhang Yue as Luo Fei, Hou Tianlai as Lin Huan, Liu Shubing as Long Jingtang

In a Southeast Asian nation, shipping magnate Lin Zichong leaves three-fourths of his business empire to his daughter Qingniao. This infuriates his son Lin Hai, who blackmails a man named Zhou Tai into killing his sister. However, Qingniao is protected by her boyfriend Li Sha, a rock singer with superior kung fu skills. Li's obvious fighting skills come to the attention of a villain named Long Jingtang, who persuades Li to kill the head of a Southeast Asian weapons smuggling ring, Zhen Mo. So Li becomes a hired killer. However, after Li infiltrates Zhen's organization, the two become friends, and when at last cornered by police, they kill each other rather than be captured. Long Jingtang kills Qingniao. After she is dead, Lin Hai kills Zhou Tai.

1702. *Rolling Waves (Lang Tao Gun Gun)*

1965. Beijing Film Studio. B & W. 12 Reels. Direction: Cheng Ying. Screenplay: Cheng Ying, based on the novel of the same title by Shao Hua. Cinematography: Gao Hongtao. Art Direction: Yu Yiru. Music: Du Mingxin. Sound: Lu Xiancang, Wang Zemin. Cast: Qin Yi as Zhong Yeping, Chin Ge as Secretary Ni, Peng Qiyu as Feng Shukai, Zhen Danian as Chen Chaoren, Wei Rong as He Shougang, Gu Lan as Chief Engineer Zhang

In the spring of 1958, Zhong Yeping is assigned as Party Secretary of the Qinglong Reservoir construction zone. Shortly after her arrival, the Great Leap Forward begins. She and the reservoir workers propose completing construction of the dam one year ahead of schedule. Chen Chaoren, director of the provincial water conservance bureau, is adamantly opposed, but provincial Party Secretary Ni supports her plan. Chen insists his own plan be followed, and threatens to dismiss Zhong Yeping for opposing him. But Zhong, with the support of construction workers, continues her struggle with the supervisor, and reports the situation to Ni. The Party Secretary makes an inspection visit to the construction site, after which he supports Zhong and criticizes Chen Chaoren. But Chen carries on with his own plan, which causes a major accident. The big dam is finally built, after which Secretary Ni says that everyone must construct a big dam in their minds that can keep out old ways of thinking.

1703. *Romance at Sea (Hai Zhi Lian)*

1980. Shanghai Film Studio. B & W. 10 Reels. Direction: Zhao Huanzhang. Screenplay: Li Yunliang, Yang Shiwen, Wang Lian. Cinematography: Zhu Yongde, Cheng Shiyu. Art Direction: Ju Ransheng. Music: Wang Yunjie. Sound: Lu Jinsong. Cast: Mao Yongmin as Jie Fang, Ma Xiaowei as Nan Xia, Wang Guojin as Jian Guo, Meng Jun as Huan Qing, Hong Xueming as La Yue, Zhao Jing as Li Qiu

Jie Fang, Nan Xia, Jian Guo and Huan Qing are four young men of about the same age growing up together. They have a happy childhood, then in the early 1970s, Jie Fang joins the navy, Nan Xia and Huan Qing go to work in an oceanic research institution, and Jian Guo goes down to the countryside. Nan Xia falls in love with Li Qiu, a worker at a plant which makes ocean scientific instruments. However, Huan Qing becomes a follower of the Gang of Four and joins in the persecution of Nan Xia's father, an old cadre in the scientific institute. The old man dies, and Huan then falsely accuses Nan Xia of being a counterrevolutionary. This puts Liu Qiu's love for him to an extreme test. She is reluctant to

Roar, Yellow River! **Anti–Gang of Four musician He Dan (Zhang Ruifang) practicing the "Yellow River Chorus."**
1979. August First Film Studio.

make friends with Jian Guo, who has just returned from the countryside. Liu Qiu's younger sister La Yue, an outstanding athlete, meets and falls in love with Jie Fang. However, Huan Qing continues his political attacks, accusing Jie Fang and Nan Xia of being counter-revolutionary conspirators, but La Yue marries Jie Fang anyway. Although Nan Xia has already suffered a lot from Huan Qing's persecution, he insists on continuing his work; he also misses Liu Qiu. Later, Liu Qiu is faced with no other choice but to marry Jian Guo for political protection, although she still loves Nan Xia. But on the eve of the wedding, she learns that Nan Xia is on the verge of death from having been persecuted for so long. She immediately goes to the hospital, but Nan Xia has already passed away. Liu Qiu decides to break her engagement with Jian Guo.

1704. *Romance by the Jinsha River (Jin Sha Lian)*

1991. Guangxi Film Studio. Color. Letterboxed. 9 Reels. Direction: Tan Yijian and Wei Danqi. Screenplay: Wang Gongpu. Cinematography: Chen Shengkai and Zhao Xuxu. Art Di-

rection: Chen Yaogong. Music: Li Yanlin. Sound: Li Yunping. Cast: He Zhenjun as Luo Na, Mao Haitong as Matuwei, Yang Xiaoyan as Ma Nai-wei, Zhang Lei as A Long, Mi Xuedong as A Nuoba

Two Yi nationality sisters living on the banks of the Jinsha River, one a farmer and the other a singer and dancer, fall in love with the same boy, a college graduate who manages a township enterprise. The sisters are at last faced with a painful decision, and each tries to bow out in favor of the other. The story ends happily with true love for all.

1705. *Romance in Philately (You Yuan)*

1984. Shanghai Film Studio. Color. Letterboxed. 10 Reels. Direction: Sang Hu. Screenplay: Wang Lian, Sang Hu, Li Yizhong. Cinematography: Qiu Yiren. Art Direction: Pu Jingsun. Music: Lu Qimin. Sound: Lu Xuehan. Cast: Guo Kaiming as Ding Dasen, Chen Yanhua as Zhou Qin, Zhang Ming as Ding Huijuan, Wang Suya as Mother, He Ling as Gao Qiang

Although he is energetic and hard-working, young worker Ding Dasen has little formal education. In addition, his previous school experiences were so bad that he had little interest in gaining an education. One day he meets Zhou Qin, a young woman letter carrier who is also diligent, but who loves learning. They begin seeing each other regularly, and she gets Dasen interested in stamp collecting. As his interest in stamp collecting grows, so does the knowledge he gains from the subject. He begins to actually like studying and learning, and at last applies for and is admitted to night classes. Zhou Qin accompanies him to school, and they walk together through the bustling Shanghai night.

Youth Audience Award, Coulommiers International Entertainment Film Festival.

1706. *Romance in the Stock Market (Gu Shi Hun Lian)*

1993. Tianshan Film Studio and Nancang Film And TV Institution Co-Production. Color. Letterboxed. 10 Reels. Direction: Song Chong. Screenplay: Zhao Huanan. Cinematography: Qiu Yiren. Art Direction: Li Yongqiang. Music: Zhen Qian. Sound: Liu Guangjie. Costume: Xiong Huiqiong. Makeup: Li Ping. Cast: Ma Xiaowei as A Nai, Gong Xue as Chen Chun, Cui Jie as Wang Fa, Liu Wanling as Ding Zhiyin, Li Tianjia as Uncle Wang

In 1992, investment fever sweeps through the people of Shanghai. The five households residing at Courtyard No. 818 are no exceptions: Chen Chun, a divorced woman; unhappily married worker A Nai; retired worker Wang Fa; self-employed Da Bao; and professor Li Ying. Chen Chun is very sympathetic to A Nai when the latter is laid off from his job, and encourages him to assist her in stock market investing. They succeed and make a lot of money. The two were once lovers, but A Nai's mother forced him to marry his current wife. Chen Chun urges him to get a divorce. At last, she decides to move to a new home, and A Nai decides to divorce his wife.

1707. *The Romance of Porters (Hong Mao Zi Lang Man Qu)*

1994. Shanghai Film Studio. Color. Letterboxed. 9 Reels. Direction: Yu Jie. Screenplay: Wu Hongli, Shen Zhengdao. Cinematography: Yu Shishan. Art Direction: Wang Xingchang. Music: Yang Di. Sound: Xie Guojie. Costume: Zhang Huijuan. Makeup: Ma Guofang. Cast: Tong Ruixin as Da Long, Geng Ge as Xiao Qing, Ning Li as "Mickey Mouse," Mao Yongming as Director Niu, Wei Guochun as Yang Darong, Gao Ying as Xue Zhen, Dai Zhaoan as Ban Ma

At Shanghai's new railway station is the "Redcap Help Team," and this film relates some of their stories. Da Long loves his co-worker Xiao Qin, but she hopes to meet and marry a successful business executive. Another redcap is called "Mickey Mouse," and he always talks of getting a better-paying job. Employees come and go, including Mickey Mouse, but Da Long continues working hard, assisting travelers. Eventually he and Xiao Qin get together.

1708. *The Romance of Zhang the Blacksmith (Zhang Tie Jiang De Luo Man Shi)*

1982. Changchun Film Studio. Color. 11 Reels. Direction: Qi Xingjia. Screenplay: Qi Xingjia, Xu Shiyan. Cinematography: Zhang Songping. Art Direction: Hu Pei, Sui Zuangji. Music: Du Mingxin, Zhang Peiji. Sound: Kang Ruixin. Cast: Hou Guanqun as Zhang Yingshuo, Wang Fuli as Wang Layue, Shao Dan as Shuangwa, Liu Yu as Little Shuangwa, Ni Changbo as Xia Mo, Song Chunli as Li Dacui

In an isolated town in rural North China, blacksmith Zhang Yingshuo and Wang Layue are married. A few years later, Zhang is falsely accused of doing something illegal, and in a rage he beats up Xia Mou, deputy chair of the commune. He is sentenced to three years in prison for this. With no means of support, Wang Layue takes their three-year-old son with her into the mountains looking for a way to make a living. When she faints from lack of food she is rescued by a bachelor. The three make their living together. After Zhang is released from prison, he searches everywhere for his wife and son. On one occasion, he meets a beautiful widow named Li Dacui. She falls for him, but he honestly explains the situation to her and continues his search. He finally finds them and the family is reunited.

1709. *Romance on Lushan Mountain (Lu Shan Lian)*

1980. Shanghai Film Studio. Color. Wide Screen. 9 Reels. Direction: Huang Zhumo. Screenplay: Bi Bicheng. Cinematography: Chan Lianguo, Zhen Xuan. Art Direction: Zhu Jiancang. Music: Lu Qimin. Sound: Lu Xuehan. Cast: Zhang Yu as Zhou Jun, Guo Kaiming as Geng Hua, Wen Xiying as Geng Feng, Wu Jiao as Zhou Zhenwu, Zhi Shimin as Mother

The first autumn following the defeat of the Gang of Four, Zhou Jun, daughter of former Nationalist Army General Zhou Zhenwu, comes from her home in the U.S. to see Mount Lu again. Five years before, on her first visit to China, she had met a young man named Geng Hua at the mountain, and they had fallen in love. But at that time, China's political situation prevented their developing their relationship. Five years separation and longing have passed. Geng Hua, now a college student, also arrives for their meeting at the mountain. But this time they discover that Geng Feng's father Geng Hua and Zhou Zhenwu had once been military buddies, but had fallen out after the Nationalist-Communist split of 1927. They have spent more than half their lives opposing each other on the battlefield, how can they now become a family? The two young lovers use their father's mutual love of China to drive them to meet again on Mount Lu. Zhou Jun and Geng Hua also finally get together.

Best Picture, 1981 Hundred Flowers Awards.

Best Actress Zhang Yu, 1981 Golden Rooster Awards.

Best Actress Zhang Yu, 1981 Hundred Flowers Awards.

1710. *Romantic Affair in Provincial Capital (Sheng Cheng Li De Feng Liu Yun Shi)*

1993. Guangxi Film Studio. Color. Letterboxed. Direction: 10 Reels. Direction: Wu Yingxun. Screenplay: Ye Xin. Cinematography: Ye Ruiwei. Art Direction: Li Jushan, Fan Dongyang. Music: Ai Liqun. Sound: Han Weijun. Costume: Chen Weixing. Makeup: Mai Qingrong. Cast: Zhao Youliang as Xue Mu, Yuan Hua as Zhang Cuichun, Wang Luyao as Su Ning, Yang Guanghua as Li Guoxiang

Xue Mu, senior reporter on a provincial newspaper, is married to Su Ning, beautiful and capable, but so devoted to her career that she neglects her husband. He happens to meet Zhang Cuichun, winner of a provincial model worker award, but unhappily married to a coarse worker named Li Guoxiang, abusive out of jealousy over his wife's work success. Xue and Zhang fall in love. His wife Su Ning discovers the relationship, and goes to Xue Mu's supervisors hoping they will break up the affair and hush up the matter. But the story gets out and creates a public scandal, given the province-wide reputations of the two lovers. As a result, Xue Mu is punished by being re-moved from his position and Zhang Cuichun is demoted.

1711. *The Rose Should Not Have Withered (Bu Gai Diao Xie De Mei Gui)*

1981. Guangxi Film Studio. Color. 10 Reels. Direction: Zen Xueqiang. Screenplay: Li Yi. Cinematography: Meng Xiongqiang. Art Direction: Fang Xuzhi. Music: Si Yin. Sound: Lin Lin, Xu Zhenkui. Cast: Zhang Liwei as Ruan Zhen, Tong Ruiming as Wei Li, Shi Xian as Li Wenxiong, Zhang Yunli as Wei Chunshan, Shen Huaiqi as Yuan Dezhong, Zhen Songmao as Yuan Lu

Chinese soldier Wei Li and Vietnamese doctor Ruan Zhen grow up on each side of the Qili River on the Sino-Vietnamese border. The childhood playmates marry when they grow up and make their home in China. Ruan Zhen's father dies during the Sino-Vietnamese border war, and when she crosses the river to attend the funeral she is detained by an old enemy, Li Wenxiong. Li had wanted her years before, then made trouble for her after she turned him down. Back in China, Ruan and Wei's daughter Xiao Mei so misses her mother that she looks for her mother along the river and unfortunately steps on a land mine. When Ruan Zhen is at last released and tries to cross the river, she is shot by a Vietnamese soldier and falls into the water. Wei Li, witnessing this from the opposite bank, goes to help his wife, but Li Wenxiong shoots and kills them both.

1712. *Rose's Dream (Mei Gui De Meng)*

1992. Changchun Film Studio. Color. Letterboxed. 9 Reels. Direction: Li Geng, Bei Zhaocheng. Screenplay: An Boshun. Cinematography: Mu Er. Art Direction: Sui Zhuangji. Music: Fan Weiqiang. Sound: Zhen Yunbao, Zhao Xudong. Costume: Zhao Li, Tao Ni. Makeup: Wang Xiaoling, Sheng Libo. Cast: Su Ying as Fang Shi, Wang Huayin as Ge Ping, Pan Shaquan as Sha Na, Zhang Xin as Guo Jianglong

Poet Ge Ping publishes a successful novel, "Rose's Loves and Hates." Actually, he did not write it, but rather hired four other people to translate parts of a foreign best-seller which he then pieced together and passed off as his own. Playing the role of brilliant major novelist, he captivates young singer Sha Na, and lures her away from her boy friend Fang Shi. Later, Ge

Ping's deception is discovered and the book banned. In addition, various book dealers are after him for keeping too much of the sales income. Seeing his true nature, Sha Na gets over her delusions and reunites with Fang Shi to bring about the false intellectual's downfall.

1713. *Rosy Dawn (Zhao Xia)*

1959. Changchun Film Studio. Color. 8 Reels. Direction: Yan Gong. Screenplay: Liu Houmin. Cinematography: Li Guanghui. Art Direction: Tong Jingwen. Music: Quan Rufeng. Sound: Jue Jingxiu. Cast: Pang Xueqing as Lin Zheng, Ye Zhi as Teacher Jiang, Zhang Guilan as Meng Yin, Li Xida as Hong Dawei, Cheng Ling as Hua Xiaochuan, Liu Nailin as Fang Minzhu, Wang Minwei as Jin Dayu, Wang Yansheng as Secretary Liu

Lin Zheng, the new principal at the Xinhua Elementary School, sets up a small factory in the school to implement the city commission's directive that the school offer a work-study program. He does this over the strong objections of Teacher Jiang, and some of the students' parents, who believe the school should strengthen its classroom instruction. Several of the students make nails on their own in the factory, which upsets Teacher Jiang greatly, for she regards this activity as a distraction for the students. Later, with the help of Lin Zheng and Secretary Liu of the city commission, Jiang sees how the work-study involvement has improved the students' overall performance, and she changes her previous views.

1714. *Rosy Remote World (Mei Gui Tian Ya)*

1995. Beijing Film Studio. Color. Letter-boxed. Direction: Ma Bingyu, Wang Xingang, Zou Jixun. Screenplay: Wang Ying. Cinematography: Zou Xixun, Yang Wenqing. Art Direction: Zu Shaoxian. Music: Su Yue. Cast: Ning Jing as Xiao Ruxing, Ning Jing as Xiao Rumeng, Xing Mingshan as Cai Qiang

Xiao Rumeng and Xiao Ruxing are identical twin sisters. At the time the Japanese invade China, Rumeng attends a performance of an anti–Japanese acting company, where she meets and falls in love with progressive student Cai Qiang. When the play's run is over, he plans to leave Shanghai for Yan'an, and Rumeng agrees to meet him there. Her sister Ruxing arrives in Yan'an before Rumeng, and meets Cai Qiang. When word comes that Ru-

meng has died, the two draw together for comfort, and in time Ruxing falls in love with Cai. Later, when she learns her sister is still alive, Ruxing sacrifices her own love for her sister by marrying an American doctor. In August, 1945, the Japanese surrender, and Rumeng and Cai Qiang are reunited on the banks of the Yellow River. But their reunion is brief, for each has revolutionary work to do, and they must part again.

1715. *Royal Heart and Soul (Yi Dan Zhong Hun)*

1991. Shanghai Film Studio. Color. Letter-boxed. 10 Reels. Direction: Zhang Jianya. Screenplay: Lai Ying, Mu Jiang. Cinematography: Huang Baohua. Art Direction: Zhou Xinren. Music: Pan Guoxing. Sound (Dolby): Qian Ping. Cast: Zhang Kanger as A Li, Xiao Rongsheng as Bing Kun, Hu Tiange as Niangzhi

When a workers' uprising fails in Shanghai in the 1920s, Nationalist intelligence chief Yu Engsheng decides to handle opposition with an iron fist. Many revolutionaries are massacred, along with a number of innocent bystanders. To help with the bloodletting, Yu hires a Shanghai triad to carry out some of the killings. One of the survivors is young Communist Ali, who later finds his former colleague Bing Kun has also survived. The two continue seeking other surviving revolutionaries as well as carrying out sabotage activities against the Nationalist government. They are joined by a sympathetic woman named Niangzhi, and at last devise a plan for freeing some of their former colleagues from prison.

1716. *Royal Policemen (Yu Xue Wei Shi)*

1990. Pearl River Film Studio. Color. Wide Screen. 10 Reels. Direction: Wang Wei. Screenplay: He Houchu. Cinematography: Dai Dawei. Art Direction: Tan Ancang. Music: Lan Zai, Liang Jun. Sound: Jiang Shaoqi. Cast: Zhang Qi as Zhou Min, Li Ping as Ye Xian, Li Hu as Zhao Qi, Cao Yuwen as Zhang Zhengyi, Zhu Huiguo as Tianxin, Lin Ping as Zhang Dian, Xu Dongfang as Guo Xiaoting, Dai Dawei as Ma Lianyun, Pu Chaoying as Ma's wife, Wang Qing as Ma's wife, Wang Qing as Lili, Yu Weifu as the PSB chief

A hardened criminal breaks out of prison and goes on a cross-country crime spree. He repeatedly eludes police, until the final, violent confrontation.

1717. *The Ruan Family's Three Heroes (Ruan Shi San Xiong)*

1988. Henan Film Studio and Hong Kong Hailing Film Company Co-Production. Color. Wide Screen. 9 Reels. Direction: Jiang Yang. Screenplay: Liu Wenmiao, Nie Yanjun. Cinematography: Wang Yongrong. Art Direction: Ke Zhongqi, Zhao Guichun. Music: Wang Jixiao, An Zhiyu. Cast: Yu Rongguang as Ruan Xiaoer, Yu Huiguang as Ruan Xiaowu, Fan Dongyu as Ruan Xiaoqi, Diao Xiaoyun as Panqin

In the late 10th century, China is ruled by the very corrupt Emperor Xuanhe. Three fisherman brothers at last rebel and take to the Liangshan Mountains (famed in Chinese history as a gathering place for rebels).

1718. *Ruanshui River Story (Yan Chang He)*

1995. Hong Kong Jiahui Film Industry Company, Xiaoxiang Film Studio Co-Production. Color. Letterboxed. Direction: Li Jingsong. Screenplay: Ru Han. Cinematography: Liu Yuefei. Cast: Wang Lan as Meiniang, Luo Gang as Shi Shaoye, Ai Liya as woman bandit

Along the banks of the Ruanshui River at the beginning of the 20th century, it was traditional for young women to leave their villages for a few years to work as prostitutes serving the men who worked on the river. With the money they saved, they would then return home, marry and settle down to raise families. Against that background, this film tells the stories of several such women.

1719. *Ruined Dreams (Yuan Meng Jing Hun)*

1993. Changchun Film Studio. Color. Letterboxed. 9 Reels. Direction: Gao Tianhong, Teng Tu. Screenplay: Hao Suping. Cinematography: Xing Eryou. Art Direction: Lu Qi. Music: Guo Xiaotian. Sound: Zhang Fenglu, Gu Kejian. Costume: Bao Guiqin, Li Shuyan. Makeup: Yang Shiya, Yang Xueli. Cast: Lu Liang as Tong Nan, Yu Xiaohui as Li Sha, Zhou Zhou as You Lin, Wu Yu as Huang Huang, Xu Ming as Director Chang, Liu Tongyan as Juanmao

After five years of marriage, a young architect and his wife are still forced by their jobs to live in different cities, so he shares a two-person dormitory room with another man in a similar situation. When the roommate's wife arrives to visit him, they use the room, but suddenly the architect's wife shows up unexpectedly: she has received permission to leave for two years of training overseas and has just 20 hours before her plane departs. The couple has a series of misadventures searching for a place to spend their last hours together, but at last a hotel he designed offers them a free night.

1720. *Rumors Run Deep (Nu Ren Guo De Wu Ran Bao Gao)*

1987. Beijing Film Studio. Color. 11 Reels. Direction: Wang Yan, Yang Lanru. Screenplay: Qian Gongle, Ye Shisheng. Cinematography: Zhang Zhongping. Art Direction: Shi Jiandu. Music: Gu De. Sound: Zhang Ye. Cast: Shen Danping as Xiujuan, Ma Chongle as Zuhe, Tan Tianqian as Zusheng, Li Haoling as Xiamei, Cao Cuifeng as Zusheng's wife, Wu Yunfang as Qiu's wife, Zhang Hua as Zulian

In Wang Family Village, Zuhe's wife Xiujuan runs a store which does good business. Combined with the income her husband and his sister Xiamei earn ferrying people across the river on their boat, the family has a nice income. One day, following a visit by her brother-in-law Zusheng, Xiujuan finds all the cash in the store is missing. She goes to report this, but Zuhe withdraws the charge to avoids familial trouble. From that point on, Zusheng's wife begins spreading nasty rumors about a relationship between Zusheng and Xiujuan. The rumors become so widespread that Zuhe starts to believe his wife is having an affair with his brother. When her husband turns on her, Xiujuan in despair commits suicide. After her death, all of the relatives on her side descend en masse on Zuhe's home, totally destroying it and his boat, leaving Zuhe with nothing to support his little daughter, his sister and his aging mother.

1721. *Running from an Evil World (Tao Chu Zui E De Shi Jie)*

1986. Xiaoxiang Film Studio. Color. 9 Reels. Direction: Zhang Li. Screenplay: Gan Zhaopei, Liu Miomiao. Cinematography: Zhaou Xiaoping. Art Direction: Yang Li. Music: Li Lifu. Sound: Huang Yinxia. Cast: Wang Xueqin as Li Wenxin, Liu Zhongyuan as Guan Dehai, Xin Min as Da Paowang

More than 20 years earlier, the Nationalist Army on China's southwest border is ordered to Taiwan. Junior officer Li Wenxin, not wanting to leave China, flees to the base of another

Nationalist division to serve there. But when the Nationalist government cuts off all its support for the division, they are on their own, and life is very hard. Once, Li Wenxin stumbles onto a forbidden area and finds the stranded Nationalist troops supporting themselves by planting and harvesting drugs. He flees again, and after experiencing many hardships, he and a young soldier who accompanies him finally make it back to the Chinese side of the border.

1722. *Rush to Arrest (Jin Ji Zhui Bu)*

1990. Fujian Film Studio. Color. 9 Reels. Direction: Han Xiaolei. Screenplay: Chen Jianyu, Liu Niu, Wen Wenhua. Cinematography: Zhen Wencang, Ying Yan. Art Direction: Han Qingguo. Music: Zhang Tianlong. Sound: Chen Binglian, Xu Gang. Cast: Lin Zhiqian as Chen Liwei, Liu Di as Lin Xiaoying, Chen Yi as Zhen Yaling

When police descend on a South China luxury hotel to arrest a criminal charged with smuggling counterfeit currency, they find someone has gotten there first and murdered the suspect. Clues lead investigators to the city of Yunhai, where detective Chen Liwei goes in the guise of a drug store manager to infiltrate the counterfeiting ring's headquarters.

1723. *Ruthless Desires (Can Ku De Yu Wang)*

1988. Shanghai Film Studio. Color. 10 Reels. Direction: Xu Weijie. Screenplay: He Zhizuang, Li Rong, Zhu Yu, Zhao Yaomin. Cinematography: Ju Jiazhen. Art Direction: Zhu Jiancang. Music: Lu Qimin. Sound: Wang Huimin. Cast: Lin Fangbing as Ding Ni, Zhang Xiaolin as Liu Ke, Wang Zhengwei as Lei Ze, Zhen Jianhua as Shi Kangke, Yang Mingjian as Shi Xiaosong

Chinese-American Shi Shuoqin, a man who has made millions on the stock market, is found murdered in his hotel room. His wife Ding Ni was attending a concert at the time, and collapses when informed of her husband's death. Detective Lei Zi's investigation determines that the murdered man's true objective in visiting China was not business, but rather to find his illegitimate son Liu Ke, to recognize Liu as his son and arrange for the younger man to be his heir. The police detain Liu Ke at the airport just as he is leaving the country, to inform him of this. The detectives at last are cer-

tain that the widow Ding Ni and her concert pianist lover Zhang Ke had conspired to murder her husband to prevent his contacting his son. When the police go to arrest Ding Ni, they find her dead: a stock market fluctuation has wiped out the fortune, and when she heard this news the woman committed suicide.

1724. *Saber, Sword, Smile (aka Three Swordsmen) (Dao, Jian, Xiao)*

1994. Tianjin Film Studio, China Film Co-Production Corp. and Hong Kong Yongfa Film Corp. Ltd. Co-Production. Color. Letterboxed. 9 Reels. Direction: Huang Tailai. Screenplay: Li Shixiong. Cinematography: Zhou Jianming, Zhou Jichang. Art Direction: Zhao Mei, Liu Shiyun. Music: Guo Xiaolin. Sound: Dongfang Recording Studio. Costume: Zhang Jing, Lu Yunying, Huang Xiaoqiu, Li Shihua. Makeup: Zhang Huiling, Chen Zhenghui and Ke Meihua. Cast: Lin Qingxia (Brigitte Lin) as Ming Jian, Liu Dehua (Andy Lau) as Xiao Sanshao, Xu Jingjiang as Heng Dao, Yu Li as Gu Caiyi, Dong Weiwei as Gu Diewu, Siqin Gaowa as Mother

An action film in which three greenwoods heroes battle against evil and injustice.

1725. *Sacred Mission (Shen Sheng De Shi Ming)*

1979. Emei Film Studio. B & W. 10 Reels. Direction: Mao Yuqing, Teng Jingxian. Screenplay: Wang Yaping, Li Caiyong. Cinematography: Wang Wenxiang, Xie Erxiang. Art Direction: Liu Nanyang, Yan Dingfu. Sound: Shen Guli. Cast: Gao Bo as Wang Gongbo, Chen Shu as Yang Darong, Wang Ruoli as Lin Fang, Fu Hengzhi as Bai Shun, Jiang Lili as Yang Qiong, Ji Hengpu as Pei Fanian

In 1975, veteran public security cadre Wang Gongbo finds some suspicious things in an old case, so he decides to reopen the investigation. He goes to a prison farm to meet defendant Bai Shun, but finds he is followed and his work hampered by Pei Fanian and others connected with the Gang of Four. This makes him even more suspicious about the case. With the help of public security cadre Liu, Wang Gongbo finds the addresses of Bai Shun's wife Lin Fang and prosecutor Yang Qiong. However, the "counterattack the rightist revisionism" movement begins, and Wang finds himself under attack. He continues his investigation secretly, and persuades Yang Qiong to tell the truth. Yang Qiong finally agrees to speak out and tell the whole truth after eight years. Pei Fanian moves to kill Yang to shut him up, but Wang Gongbo sacrifices his own life to save Yang's.

1726. *Sacrifice of Youth (Qing Chun Ji)*

1985. Youth Film Studio. Color. 10 Reels. Direction: Zhang Nuanxin. Screenplay: Zhang Manling, Zhang Nuanxin. Cinematography: Mu Deyuan, Deng Wei. Art Direction: Wang Jianjing, Li Yongxin. Music: Ju Xiaosong, Liu Bozhu. Sound: Ma Yuewen. Cast: Li Fengxu as Li Chun, Guo Jianguo as the brother, Yu Dan as Yibo, Song Tao as the old landlord, Feng Yuanzheng as Ren Jia

Educated young girl Li Chun spends her youth among people of the Dai nationality. When she first arrives, she finds the adjustment difficult, but she eventually makes many friends. When she is permitted to return to the city some years later in order to attend college, she says goodbye to the local people, knowing she will never forget their kindness through the years.

1727. *Sacrificing for the Motherland (Xue Wo Zhong Hua)*

1980. Changchun Film Studio. Color. 11 Reels. Direction: Yi Yiqin. Screenplay: Fang Lan, Sun Bo, Zhou Yiru. Cinematography: Dan Shengnima, Sun Hui. Art Direction: Li Wenguang, Liu Sheng. Music: Xu Xinpu. Sound: Hong Di. Cast: Wei Xin as Fang Zhiming, Zhao Wenyu as Fang's wife, Chen Guojun as Zhang Huaizhi, Jin Weimin as Wu Yaozong, Xiao Xiang as Liu Yangzhai, Zhao Hengduo as Chiang Kai-shek

In the winter of 1935, Communist Fang Zhiming is betrayed, arrested and imprisoned. In prison, Fang Zhiming begins writing, summing up what he has learned from long experience as both a worker and a spare-time Communist activist. With his cell mates' help, Fang completes a large number of articles, in "Beloved China" and "Prison: the True Story." When his captors find out about his writings, they search in vain for them, and finally order him to hand them over under threat of death. They also make him watch his pregnant wife being tortured. But Fang is bravely unrelenting. Prison guard Zhang Huaizhi gradually becomes influenced by what Fang teaches him, and offers to protect Fang's papers. When Chiang Kaishek concludes that Fang Zhiming will

never change and come over to the Nationalist side, he orders Fang Zhiming executed. On the eve of his death, Fang entrusts Zhang to give his papers to the great Chinese writer Lu Xun. Late at night, Fang is executed. Zhang Huaizhi risks his life to deliver the papers to Lu Xun.

1728. *Saihu (Sai Hu)*

1982. Xiaoxiang Film Studio. Color. 9 Reels. Direction: Hua Yongzhuang, Luo Zhen. Screenplay: Bi Bicheng. Cinematography: Feng Guiting, Zhou Shengtong. Art Direction: Jin Bohao. Music: Zhang Ji. Sound: Wang Lin. Cast: Li Ao as Wangzai, Dai Qin as Xiaoqing, Zhao Yigong as Zhao Yutang, He Ningkang as Wangzai's father, Liu Yibing as the housekeeper

A boy named Wangzai lives in pre-liberation China with his woodsman father and his dog Saihu. The dog is very capable and intelligent, and when the son of local landlord Zhao Yutang sees how talented the dog is, he traps the dog and takes him to his own home. Wangzai frees the dog, however. A guerrilla band is operating in the area, and when Wangzai's father tries to take them some firewood he is caught by Zhao and put in jail. Wangzai helps his father escape, but the father is shot and killed by Zhao's men. Wangzai and his playmate Xiaoqing are caught by the gunmen, then tied up and left in the forest to die. Saihu comes and rescues his owner, and although the dog is later wounded by Zhao's men, Wangzai, Xiaoqing and Saihu find and join the revolutionary guerrillas.

1729. *Sailing (Yang Fan)*

1981. Pearl River Film Studio. 9 Reels. Direction: Zhan Xiangchi, Yu Shibing. Screenplay: Zhan Xiangchi. Cinematography: Wei Duo. Art Direction: Ye Jialiang. Music: Wang Ming. Sound: Li Bojian. Cast: Hu Weishan as Lu Yaqin, Ding Tiebao as Li Pingfan, Wei Ke as Hao Ping

Lu Yaqin has suffered a series of misfortunes. Her parents are both falsely accused and labeled counterrevolutionaries during the Cultural Revolution. A lost and lonely young woman, she becomes a Red Guard. One day when her group is harassing some older people, she strikes a female singer named Li Pingfan, causing the singer to lost her hearing and destroying her career. Later, Lu Yaqin meets and falls for a young man named Hao Ping, a pianist. When Hao Ping discovers that Lu Yaqin also has musical talent, he encourages her to apply for music school. After the Gang of Four is defeated, he takes her to meet his mother, who turns out to be Li Pingfan, the woman she had hurt so badly in the past. The two women are very uncomfortable with each other. Guilt-stricken, Lu Yaqin runs away. But after thinking it over, Li Pingfan finally overcomes her initial emotional response and decides not to let the past negatively impact the future. She decides to accept Lu Yaqin, but learns the young woman has gone to Inner Mongolia. Li Pingfan leaves to find Lu Yaqin and bring her back to school and her lover.

1730. *Sailing Girl (Fan Ban Gu Niang)*

1985. Changchun Film Studio. Color. 10 Reels. Direction: Wu Guojiang. Screenplay: Ding Chanbang. Cinematography: Li Chaoren. Art Direction: Wang Jiru. Music: Li Haihui. Sound: Yi Wenyu. Cast: Zhou Caizhen as Hao Ling, Du Xiongwen as Ouyang Chunshan, Zhang Mingyu as Luo Bingwu, Zhang Yuting as Xu Lili, Wu Lilin as Ju Yingjie

When Huanghai's city sailing club loses in national competition, their coach Ouyang Chunshan vows his team will finish in the top six next time. His chances improve greatly when he discovers Hao Ling, a girl with outstanding skills. Hao Ling has an unfortunate family background, and her family commitments prevent her getting sufficient practice time. The coach helps her resolve her difficulties, and she improves quickly. In the next national competition, she finishes in second place, and is chosen by the national sailing team to sail in Asia-wide competition.

1731. *Samsara (Lun Hui)*

1988. Xi'an Film Studio. Color. 14 Reels. Direction: Huang Jianxin. Screenplay: Wang Shuo (1958–), based on his novel "Emerging From the Sea." Cinematography: Zhao Fei. Art Direction: Yang Gang. Music: Qu Xiaosong. Sound: Tang Yuanping, Gu Changning. Cast: Lei Han as Shi Ba, Tan Xiaoyan as Yu Jing, Liu Lijun as Liu Hualing

Shi Ba, the son of a high-ranking official, lives alone in a large house after the death of his parents. He is self-employed, although some of his business activities are illegal. The carefree young man has a passion for everything and refuses to take life seriously. He is very attractive to women, including Yu Jing, an innocent and beautiful young dancer. But

when his businesses start to make real money, he finds himself being blackmailed. The blackmailers continue to squeeze him even when his businesses take a downturn. When he finally rejects their demands, he is beaten up. He had once been so successful, but now nothing is going right. One day, a woman engaged in some shady dealings of her own invites him to join her in blackmailing foreigners. He refuses, and decides now is the time to marry Yu Jing. But Yu Jing brings up some things which have been troubling her about their relationship. This leads to a quarrel and Shi Ba hurls himself from a balcony.

1732. *Satisfied or Not (Man Yi Bu Man Yi)*

1963. Changchun Film Studio. B & W. 9 Reels. Direction: Yan Gong. Screenplay: Fei Ke, Zhang Huan'er and Yan Gong, based on the Suzhou City Comic Opera Troupe's production of the same title. Cinematography: Fang Weiche. Art Direction: Lu Jin. Music: Jiang Wei. Sound: Shen Guli. Cast: Fang Xiaoxiao as Master Worker Shen, Zhang Huaner as Mr. Zhang, Gu Yueer as Xiao Gu, Little Yang Tianxiao as Yang Yousheng, Ding Fengying as Yang's mother, Yang Tianxiao as Mr. Ma

In Suzhou, restaurant worker Yang Yousheng looks down upon service occupations, and has a very negative attitude toward his job. Later, helped by Master Worker Shen, an outstanding service worker, he goes to the other extreme, showing an obviously false smile when serving customers. He is highly criticized for this, and tries unsuccessfully to change his job. Through carelessness, he breaks a leg. After he recovers and returns to work, he at last finds the roots of his dissatisfaction, and with a new attitude to service work improves his performance.

1733. *Savage Land (Yuan Ye)*

1988. Nanhai Film Company. Color. Wide Screen. 10 Reels. Direction: Ling Zi. Screenplay: Ling Zi, Ji Si, based on the novel by Cao Yu. Cinematography: Luo Dan. Art Direction: Zhan Jia. Music: Du Mingxin. Sound: Lai Qizhen. Costume: Chang Shuhua. Makeup: Wan Xiang. Cast: Yang Zaibao as Chou Hu, Liu Xiaoqing as Jinzi, Liu Jian as Jiao Daxing, Bu Yihan as Chang Wu, Sun Ming as Bai Shazi

Convict Chou Hu lusts for revenge, partly on his old enemies the Jiao family, and partly on his former fiancee Jinzi, who married into

Samsara. **Innocent and beautiful young Yu Jing (Tan Xiaoyan) finds herself increasingly attracted to carefree and Bohemian Shi Ba (Lei Han). 1988. Xi'an Film Studio.**

the Jiao family after he went to prison. So when the opportunity to escape appears, Chou Hu takes it. After returning to his hometown, he learns that the man he wanted most, the head of the Jiao family, has died. Then he is distracted from his thoughts of revenge when he meets Jinzi again, and hears how she has been abused by her mother-in-law. He and Jinzi resume their romantic relationship, but at last he remembers the reason for his coming there, and kills her husband Jiao Daxing. Jinzi's mother-in-law tries for some revenge of her own, but by mistake kills her grandson, Jinzi and Daxing's child. As the police move in, Chou Hu and Jinzi run into the forest, but their pursuers soon catch up with them. The last thing Chou Hu will accept is going back to prison, so he kills himself. In the savage land of the forest, the only sounds are Jinzi's screams.

Best Picture, 1988 Hundred Flowers Awards.

Best Actress Liu Xiaoqing, 1988 Hundred Flowers Awards.

1734. *Schoolmates (Si Jie)*

1992. Pearl River Film Studio. Color. Letter-boxed. Direction: Chen Ying, Shao Xuehai. Screenplay: Yang Jifu. Cinematography: Wu Yukun. Art Direction: Gu Jiadong. Music: Yu Linqin. Cast: Hu Yajie as Li Tao, Ju Xue as Xiu Zhi, Tang Lu as Li Yin

When the Japanese invade Shanghai, Dongji University relocates out of the city to a small town in the countryside. Physics student Li Tao falls in love with Xiu Zhi, a girl in a higher grade, but his dreams are shattered when she is raped and made pregnant by a local despot. When the war ends, Li Tao graduates and becomes a member of the college's faculty. When the school prepares to move back to Shanghai, his mother asks him to return to the family's ancestral hometown and marry Yulan, a girl there. On his way to meet Yulan, he passes through a small town where he finds Xiu Zhi living. The two are overjoyed to see each other and profess their mutual love. He travels on to meet Yulan, intending to tell her their relationship cannot be, but the village girl is so kind, innocent and eager to be his obedient wife that he is unable to refuse her. On the way back to Shanghai, he stops to see

Xiu Zhi but finds she has left China for Taiwan.

1735. *The Scientist Jiang Zhuying (Jiang Zhu Ying)*

1992. Changchun Film Studio. Color. Letterboxed. 10 Reels. Direction: Song Jiangbo. Screenplay: Wang Xingdong. Cinematography: Zhang Songping. Art Direction: Qi Min. Music: Wu Damin. Sound: Jiang Yan, Yi Zhe. Costume: Yang Jingyong, Liu Tao. Makeup: Wang Xiaoling, Wang Xiaoqiong. Cast: Wei Zhi as Jiang Zhuyin, Xi Meijuan as Lu Changqing, Bi Yanjun as Luo Keng, Tian Ming as Zhang Kun, Gu Lan as Jiang Shuming

A film biography of Jiang Zhuying, an outstanding researcher in the field of optics. Hard-working but overworked, Jiang died at middle-age, considered an example of many Chinese intellectuals who die at the peak of their careers.

Best Screenplay Wang Xingdong, 1993 Golden Rooster Awards.

1736. *Scout (Zhen Cha Bing)*

1974. Beijing Film Studio. B & W. 11 Reels. Direction: Li Wenhua. Screenplay: Li Wenhua. Cinematography: Sun Cangyi. Art Direction: Zhang Xiande. Music: Shi Lemeng, Lu Zhulong. Cast: Wang Xingang as Guo Rui, Jin Zhengyuan as Big Liu, Wang Dacheng as Platoon Leader Jiang, Zhen Zhong as the commander, Yu Yang as the political commissar, Cheng Xueqin as Little Hu

In 1948, Guo Rui leads a PLA scout team into the enemy-occupied Fengcheng area. On the way they rescue two local cadres from the enemy, and kill a criminal who had been preying on the local people. To obtain intelligence, Guo Rui pretends to be the enemy's incoming commander, and gains important information about the enemy's defense plans. Then, aided by local Party undercover agents, Guo's team captures some key enemy figures and coordinates the PLA's main force in wiping out the enemy in Fengcheng.

1737. *Scouting Across the Yangtze (Du Jiang Zhen Cha Ji)*

1954. Shanghai Film Studio. B & W. 11 Reels. Direction: Tang Xiaodan. Screenplay: Shen Mujun. Cinematography: Li Shengwei. Set Design: Ding Chen. Music: Ge Yan. Sound: Miao Zhenyu. Casting: Sun Daolin as Company Commander Li, Qi Heng as Wu Laogui, Sun Yongping as Xiao Ma, Kang Tai as Zhou Changxi, Zhong Shuhuang as Yang Wei, Mu Hong as the Chief of Staff

In 1949, millions of PLA troops prepare to cross the Yangtze River in the last all-out attack on the Nationalist Army. The Nationalists dig in at the river to make their last stand. Before crossing the river, a PLA company commander named Li leads a group of scouts across the river to reconnoiter the enemy's position and learn as much about their defense as possible. After crossing the river, Li disguises himself as an enemy soldier and infiltrates their headquarters. He obtains the Nationalists' defense plans, but is detected and has to shoot his way out. He returns to his scout unit, enemy troops in pursuit, and after much fighting and difficulty they get the plans back to the PLA command.

1738. *The Screen Adventure (Ying Ping Qi Yu)*

1991. Children's Film Studio. Color. 9 Reels. Director and Screenplay: Lu Gang. Cinematography: Wang Jiuwen. Art Direction: Hao Guoxin. Music: Wang Liping. Sound: Lan Fan. Costume: Guo Qi. Makeup: Yuan Lin. Cast: Man Xuchun as Qiqi, Jia Yonghong as Hongxing, Zhang Shaohua as Hongxing's father, Qi Jianqiu as Lu Kun, Zhou Ning as Ye Dan, Zhang Yin as Tiantian, Ling Yuan as Grandma Tian

A fantasy in which a magician's son watching a video tape gets caught up with the plight of Hongxing, the Ming Dynasty girl in the film. The boy, Qiqi, takes the handgun his father uses in his magic act, and shoots the bad guy persecuting the girl in the movie. To his surprise, the gun shatters the TV screen, and Hongxing escapes to Qiqi's side. They play together happily, but after a time Hongxing misses her father and returns to her movie world. The villain again catches her, and this time Qiqi takes his magic gun and enters the screen himself. He is caught and taken to the execution ground. But just then someone back in Qiqi's living room hits a button on the remote control, allowing the boy to jump back to the contemporary world.

1739. *Screws (Luosi Ding)*

Screenplay: Ye Ming, Qian Dingde. Direction: Yu Zhongying. Cast: Erlin as Wang Xiaojuan, Qiao Zhi as Yang Ling, Shi Jiufeng as Xiao Yu, Tu Zhengping as Zhang Bingshan, Jiangshan as Master Worker Jiang, Zhang Yan as Secretary Li

Inspired by the Great Leap Forward, young woman worker Wang Xiaojuan responds to her local Party committee's campaign that "one person work like one and a half people," by reducing the time for producing screws from 14 minutes to 3, greatly improving efficiency.

1740. *The Sea Hawk (Hai Ying)*

1959. August First Film Studio. Color. 10 Reels. Direction: Yan Jizhou. Screenplay: Lu Zhuguo, Zhang Yiming, Wang Jun, Wen Da. Cinematography: Cai Jiwei. Art Direction: Kou Honglie. Music: Gong Zhiwei. Sound: Li Bojian. Cast: Wang Xingang as Zhang Ming, Zhang Yongshou as Li Xiong, Wang Yi as Liu Tao, Huang Huanguang as Ma Ruhu, Jing Liming as the chief engineer, Zhang Lianfu as the assistant engineer, Wang Xiaotang as Wu Yufen, Xing Jitian as Uncle Wu

Zhang Ming, commander of the Chinese navy's speedboat "909" is assigned the mission of attacking a Nationalist transport ship at an island well away from the Chinese mainland. With the help of his wife Wu Yufen and her father, he hides his ship at the ambush site to lie in wait. Two years later, they attack the target transport, but the "909" is also hit and sunk. Zhang Ming and nine members of his crew float for two days and nights at sea, and have a battle with some of the enemy survivors on a reef. They kill all of the enemy, and return on a sampan they obtain from friendly islanders. On the way back, they are picked up and rescued by a boat from the mainland.

1741. *Sea Lion Dare-to-Die Corps (Hai Shi Gan Si Dui)*

1990. Guangxi Film Studio. Color. Wide Screen. 9 Reels. Direction: Lu Jianhua, Yu Zhongxiao. Cinematography: Xie Wenli. Cinematography: Zhong Wenmin. Art Direction: Zhang Songping. Music: Fan Weiqiang. Sound: Dong Baosheng. Cast: Zhang Duofu as A Qiang, Mu Qin as Zhang Fuyun, Fang Xinmin as Ma Tanshou

On the eve of Chinese Revolution of 1912 which overthrew the Qing dynasty, both sides know that a Shanghai rebellion in imminent. A suicide squad of revolutionaries called the "Dare-to-Die Corps" accepts the assignment of transporting a shipment of homemade bombs from Hangzhou to Shanghai within five days. The film tells how with the help of the Hang-

zhou governor's daughter, they accomplish this difficult mission despite some of the best imperial fighters' attempts to stop them.

1742. *Sea of Forests and Plains of Snow (Lin Hai Xue Yuan)*

1960. August First Film Studio. B & W. 12 Reels. Direction: Liu Peiran. Screenplay: Liu Peiran and Ma Jixing, based on the novel of the same title by Qu Bo. Cinematography: Chen Ruijun. Art Direction: Zhen Tuo. Music: Li Weicai. Sound: Kou Shenkang. Cast: Zhang Yongshou as Shao Jianbo, Wang Runsheng as Yang Zhirong, Liang Zhipeng as Liu Xuncang, Cui Rongjiu as Sun Dade, Zhang Liang as Gao Bo, Shi Wei as Bai Ru

In the winter of 1946, a small unit of the Northeast PLA led by staff officer Shao Jianbo enters a region called the Sea of Forests and Plains of Snow in pursuit of bandits. Scout platoon leader Yang Zhirong disguises himself as Hu Biao, lieutenant to a bandit chief, and infiltrates bandit headquarters in the Weihu Mountains. After passing many tests, he finally gains the trust of the Weihu Mountains' bandit chieftain, Big Eagle. On New Year's Eve, just as Yang Zhirong prepares to notify Shao Jianbo the time is ripe for a PLA attack on the bandits' base, an escaped bandit arrives at the base, one who could expose Yang. But Yang cleverly turns Big Eagle's suspicions toward the escaped bandit, and finally gets the latter executed. Yang then gets word to Shao Jianbo, who leads a PLA attack which totally wipes out the bandits.

1743. *Sea Prisoners (Parts 1 and 2) (Hai Qiu)*

1981. Beijing Film Studio. Color. 16 Reels. Direction: Li Wenhua. Screenplay: Hong Yonghong, Gao Zhenhe. Cinematography: Ma Linfa, Ren Zhixin. Art Direction: Mo Kezhan. Music: Li Yinhai. Sound: Zhang Baojian. Cast: Da Qi as Tang Jinlong, Zhang Lianwen as Zhang Tianyi, Xiang Lei as Pan Rufei, Ma Shuchao as Pan Huoshi, Shao Wanlin as Pan Yuankun, Wang Tunren as Pan Ruqing

After the Opium War ends in 1842, the British consul in the Chinese coastal city of Xiamen (Amoy), a man named Charles, receives a request to send 500 Chinese laborers to Australia to dig gold mines. Charles, in league with Chinese collaborator Pan Rufei, deceives a group of Chinese laborers into thinking they are signing up for work down

Scouting Across the Yangtze. **PLA Company Commander Li (Sun Daolin, center) leads a group of scouts on a reconnaissance mission near Nationalist lines. 1954. Shanghai Film Studio.**

the Chinese coast. He then hires two men to take the Chinese to Australia: Taylor, a trafficker in human beings, and Thompson, a ship captain. The Chinese suffer greatly on the ship, subjected to mistreatment and humiliation. Too late they realize they have been shipped to Australia. The Chinese, under the leadership of a worker named Tang Jinlong, rebel and kill Thompson and Pan Ruqing. They then try to sail the ship back to China, but Taylor escapes and informs the British navy, which pursues them. When the British attack, many of the Chinese are killed and Tang Jinlong is captured. A few Chinese, led by Pan Huosi, make it back to Xiamen and kill Pan Rufei, but are then arrested by the corrupt Qing (Manchu) government. The rebellion has failed, but Tan Jinlong and Pan Huosi go the execution ground honorably.

1744. *Searching the Ship Plant (Chuan Chang Zhui Zong)*

1959. Changchun Film Studio. Color. 7 Reels. Direction: Lin Nong. Screenplay: Fei Liwen (1929–), based on his novel of the same title. Cinematography: Wang Qimin. Art Direction: Sun Shixiang. Music: Gao Ruxing. Sound:

Chen Wenyuan. Cast: Ren Yi as Zhang Gengsheng, Zhang Yuan as Wang Xiuyin, Yan Xueqing as Director Zhao, Chen Qiang as Mr. Qing, Wu Bike as the technician, Zhang Jianyou as the kid

Zhang Gengsheng, a nationally famous model worker, comes to Dalian City to give an exhibition of high-speed metal cutting, and his speed amazes the entire city. Just as he is about to leave the city, he receives an anonymous letter simply signed "the kid" from the Dalian Ship Plant, and requesting a meeting with him at the plant. Zhang goes to the plant, and there he finds the letter writer, a man who as a child 15 years before had been tortured by the capitalists, but was saved by Zhang. Today "the kid" has grown to be the plant's maintenance director.

1745. *Searing Passion (Xue Lei Qing Chou)*

1989. Liaoning Film Studio and the Xiaoxiang Film Studio Co-Production. Color. 70mm. 10 Reels. Direction: Li Wenhua. Screenplay: Xue Cifu, Chen Kaiming. Cinematography: Zhao Peng. Art Direction: Zhao Zhenxue. Music: Wen Zhongjia. Sound: Zhang Baojian. Cast: Yu

Sea of Forests and Plains of Snow. **1960. August First Film Studio.**

Rongguang as Yue Feng and Donghu, Han Shanxu as Song Xiaoxian, Chen Xiaoyi as Song Liyuan, Bao Laifu as Huang Xuanfeng, Chen Kaiming as the Chief Bodyguard

In the late 19th century, Manchu official Song Xiaoxian kills Yue Sheng, a revolutionary. Yue's wife is able to escape with Yue Feng, one of their twin sons, but the other, Donghu, has to be left behind. Twenty years later, Yue Feng has grown up and become the second in command of the Tianlonghui — an association of "greenwoods bandits." Yue Feng makes several unsuccessful attempts to avenge his father by assassinating Song Xiaoxian. Meanwhile, Yue Feng's twin brother Donghua has become Song's bodyguard and fallen in love with the official's daughter. The twin brothers become enemies. When dictator Yuan Shikai attempts to have himself proclaimed emperor and start a new dynasty, Song Xiaoxian throws his support behind Yuan, which leads to a break between Song and Donghu. Donghu joins an anti-Yuan force called the National Salvation Army, which makes alliance with Yue Feng's band. At this time, Yue Feng and Donghua learn they are twin brothers. They make common cause against Song Xiaoxian, and avenge their father.

1746. *The Season for Love (Lian Ai Ji Jie)*

1986. Inner Mongolia Film Studio. Color. 9 Reels. Direction: Wu'er Shana. Screenplay: Wen Xiaoyu. Cinematography: Y. Huhewuna, Lin Jian. Art Direction: Han Jinfeng, Tong Yonggang. Music: Wei Jiawen. Sound: Ao Si, Hu Linping. Cast: Cong Shan as Zuo Li, G. Batuqingelei as Sulun Zhabu, Zhang Mingming as Liang Wei, Guan Huiming as Liu Zhanying, Jue Lijun as Lu Xun, Zhou Guobing as Zhang Yu

Philosophy graduate Zuo Li's intelligence and devotion to her career has tended to scare off prospective suitors, so she finds herself still single in her thirties. Beneath her self-assured manner, however, is a woman troubled by past regrets and the problems of her friends. During the Cultural Revolution she was uprooted from the city and assigned to hard labor as a shepherdess on the Mongolian steppes. There she fell in love with a Mongolian herdsman called Sulun Zhabu. She later gave him up, but now finds she cannot forget him. In addition, she finds that the friends she went through those hard times with either married badly through desperation, or else have become disillusioned cynics who care only for themselves.

Zuo Li decides she must find her own way out of her situation.

1747. *The Second Handshake (Di Er Ci Wo Shou)*

1980. Beijing Film Studio. Color. Wide Screen. 12 Reels. Direction: Dong Kena. Screenplay: Cao Shuolong, Dong Kena. Cinematography: Zhang Shiji. Art Direction: Yu Yiru. Music: Wang Ming. Sound: Wang Zemin. Cast: Xie Fang as Ding Jieqiong, Kang Tai as Su Guanlan, Yuan Mei as Ye Yuhan, Shi Yu as Su Fengling, Boerdun as Aomuhuosi

In the fall of 1956, medical school professor Su Guanlan has an unexpected visitor, a woman dressed like an overseas Chinese. The professor's wife Ye Yuhan warmly welcomes the unknown woman, but Professor Su himself is surprised and upset. The visitor looks at the couple and leaves in a hurry. The story is that in 1928, when Su Guanlan was a student on his summer break, he rescued a girl, Ding Jieqiong, who had fallen into a river. The two became acquainted and fell in love. But Su Guanlan's father Su Fengqi wanted his son to marry Ye Yuhan, the daughter of an old friend of the father. Su hoped to discourage Ye Yuhan by expressing a wish to put off the marriage for 20 years, but much to his surprise, Yue Yuhan accepts this. In order to get away from his father's restrictions, Su and Ding Jieqiong arrange to go the United States to study, but only she is able to get U.S. government clearance to go to the U.S. Ding received her doctoral degree in the U.S., but is later jailed there for demonstrating against use of the atomic bomb against Japan. Su Guanlan's father lies to his son, telling him that Ding has married an American scholar. Later, when Su Guanlan gets into a fight with an American spy, Ye Yuhan rescues him. Her devotion so moves Su that he marries her then. On the other side of the world, Ding Jieqiong has remained faithful to Su and their vows, rejects the true love offered her by the American scholar, and returns to China. When she arrives at Su's home and learns he has married Ye Yuhan, she is distraught and leaves. But with the help of Premier Zhou and her scientist colleagues, and with Su Guanlan and Ye Yuhan's sincere offers of friendship, Ding Jieqiong is able to put her unhappy past behind her, and facing the future with a new outlook, shakes hands again with Su Guanlan.

1748. *The Second Spring (Di Er Ge Chun Tian)*

1975. Shanghai Film Studio. Color. 11 Reels. Direction: Sang Hu, Wang Xiuwen. Screenplay: Liu Chuan and He Baoxian, based on the stage play of the same title. Cinematography: Xia Lixing, Shen Xilin, Shi Fengqi. Art Direction: Hu Dengren. Music: Gao Tian. Cast: Yu Yang as Feng Tao, Yang Yaqing as Liu Zhiyin, Jing Limin as Xia Changfa, Zhang Xian as Qi Datong, Gao Bo as Liu Zhiqiang, Kang Tai as Pan Wen, Mao Lu as Old Liang. Zhang Yu as Liu Zhihua

One spring in the 1960s, naval branch political commissar Feng Tao is assigned to be secretary to a ship manufacturer. His arrival coincides with the disastrous attempt to launch the first Chinese-designed and manufactured warship, the "Seagle." Shaken by this experience, Director Xia Changfa locks the "Seagle" in a warehouse, and puts his hopes on help from the Soviet Union. Feng Tao insists that the "Seagle" project be continued, for he realizes the Soviets want to control China. Shortly after, the Soviet Union breaks the "brother countries" relationship, abrogating all contracts and withdrawing their experts from China. Feng Tao leads the shipyard workers in making the "Seagle," and finally succeed in the second spring.

1749. *Secret Agent No. 5 (Wu Hao Ji Yao Yuan)*

1984. Changchun Film Studio. Color. Letterboxed. 9 Reels. Direction: Liu Wenyu. Screenplay: Mao Bingquan, Zhang Gang. Cinematography: Xu Shouzen. Art Direction: Gao Tinglun. Music: Jin Xiang. Sound: Li Zhenduo. Cast: Lin Qiang as Feng Ziqiang, Wu Yuhua as Lu Chan, Niu Na as Chen Lan, Ma Qun as Pan Guoliang, Wang Baohua as Wang Wenxuan, Hao Yiping as Yin Fei

In the early fall of 1931, the CPC Shanghai underground assigns their most reliable agent, a mysterious person known only as "No. 5" to carry some important documents to the city of Linhai in East China, to be relayed from there to the CPC base in Jiangxi. Feng Ziqiang is assigned to assist, although he has never seen No. 5. However, Police Chief Wang Wenxuan quickly learns who their contact is and orders her arrest. She is killed, and another woman, Chen Lan, replaces her. She also dies protecting Feng Ziqiang. In addition to the police, the underground is also seeking No. 5. At last, Feng makes contact with another agent called

"Red Bean" and they go together to meet No. 5.

1750. Secret Decree (Die Xue Hei Gu)

1984. Xiaoxiang Film Studio. Color. Wide Screen. Direction: Wu Ziniu, Li Jingmin. Screenplay: Cai Zhaisheng, Lin Qinsheng. Cinematography: Zhang Li. Art Direction: Xia Rujin. Music: Tan Dun. Sound: Huang Yinxia. Cast: Du Yulu as Wang Chaozong, Zhao Jianwen as Song Kesheng, Cui Minpu as Zhou Shihang, Pao Haiming as Xiong Guoxiang, Lin Hong as Ding Liyun

In 1939, the 1st Division of the Nationalist 84th Army is surrounded by the Japanese. The Japanese offer to negotiate with the 1st Division's commander Wang Chaozong. Chiang Kaishek sends Wang a private letter, instructing him to accept the negotiations, and request the encirclement be lifted. In return for this Wang will no longer fight the Japanese, but will instead turn his efforts to exterminating the Chinese Communists, anti–Japanese allies at the time. Wang Chaozong enters into the negotiations, but does not make the offer, since he does not want the Chinese people to later brand him a collaborator. When the Chinese media reports a rumor of Chiang's secret order, the Chinese Communists want to obtain the document as proof of Chiang's treachery. Chiang sends a secret agent to Wang to retrieve the order, but Wang refuses to give it up. Instead, Wang Chaozong turns the document over to the Communists.

1751. Secret Drawing (Mi Mi Tu Zhi)

1965. August First Film Studio. B & W. 8 Reels. Direction: Hao Guang. Screenplay: Shi Chao, Zhen Hong and Hao Guang. Cinematography: Chen Ruijun. Art Direction: Zhen Tuo. Music: Li Yiding. Sound: Kou Shenkang. Cast: Tian Hua as Shi Yun, Xing Jitian as Bureau Director Ding, Wang Xingang as Cheng Liang, Wang Yi as Xiao Cui, Qian Shurong as Lu Wenhui, Li Huijian as Zhou Ming, Li Li as Li Hua, Shi Wei as Fang Li, Liu Jiyun as Gu Zhongru

Scientist Li Hua's briefcase, containing a secret drawing, disappears at a railway station. Woman inspector Shi Yun is assigned to investigate. Shi Yun soon determines that the clues point to a hotel chef, and they arrest him the following day. But when Shi's husband, a security agent, tells her of his investigation of

musician Fang Li, the two conclude that there may be more to the railway theft than originally believed. The arrested man turns out to be a mere small fry sacrificed by a large criminal organization, headed by Gu Zhongru, who had originally tipped them off to the suspect. Gu tries to escape, but police pursue him to the border and arrest him with the evidence: microfilm of the secret drawings.

1752. Secret History of the "Blood Drop" (Xue Di Zhi Mi Shi)

1990. Shanghai Film Studio. Color. Wide Screen. 10 Reels. Direction: Yao Shoukang. Screenplay: He Zhizuang, Li Rong. Cinematography: Ying Fukang. Art Direction: Mei Kunping. Music: Jin Fuzhai. Sound: Ni Zheng, Dong Yan. Cast: Ye Zhikang as Yongzheng, Wang Hua as Zhong Qiuqi, Zhang Yiran as Nian Gengrao, Zhao Zhigang as Li Siting, Wang Meiling as Yinggu

After the Emperor Yongzheng ascends the throne in 1723, he orders the killing of all members of the "Blood Drop," a group of fighters who made great contributions to his struggle to become emperor. The only one to escape is super kung fu specialist Zhong Qiuqi. Yongzheng also turns on his most loyal and helpful general, Nian Gengrao, and demotes him in rank. To assist him, Yongzheng chooses Li Siting, known as "Number One Sword." Nian wants to capture Zhong Qiuqi and use him to make a political deal with Yongzheng, while also wants to find Zhong to learn from him the secret weapon the "Blood Drop" group had developed before their annihilation. Nian at last traps and kills Zhong Qiuqi, but is himself put to death by Yongzheng. In 1735, the Emperor Yongzheng is found in his garden, murdered. It is said that the killing style was that of the "Blood Drop" group.

1753. The Secret History of the Budala Palace (Parts 1 & 2) (Bu Da La Gong Mi Shi)

1989. Emei Film Studio and Tibetan Film Translation Company Co-Production. Color. 16 Reels. Direction: Zhang Yi. Screenplay: Huang Zhilong. Cinematography: Luo Xun. Art Direction: Lin Qi, Qiangba Gesang. Music: Luo Nianyi. Sound: Wang Guangzhong. Cast: Duobuji as the Fifth Dalai, Yaduoji as Gushihan, Zhaxi Dunzhu as Sangjiejiachuo, Qiongda as Danzenhan

In Tibet in the mid–17th century, the Fifth Dalai overthrows the Zhangbahan regime and establishes his own with the support of his advisor Gushihan. Fifth Dalai decides to expand the Budala Palace, and for the duration of the work turns Tibet's political and other matters over to another advisor Sangjiejiachuo. All goes well until Gushihan dies, to be replaced by his corrupt and incompetent son Danzenha, after which the government enters a state of steady decline. When Danzenha dies, Prince Lazhanglu seizes power, starting a violent and bloody period in Tibetan history. Sangjiejiachuo is killed on the battlefield.

1754. *The Secret of Axia River (A Xia He Se Mi Mi)*

1976. Shanghai Film Studio. Color. 10 Reels. Direction: Yan Bili, Shen Fu, Wu Zhennian. Screenplay: Collective, recorded by Cao Zhonggao. Cinematography: Qiu Yiren, Shen Miaorong. Art Direction: Huang Jianfeng, Jin Qifeng. Music: Huang Zhun. Cast: Liang Jingyang as Sun Daliang, Zhao Xixiong as Zhaxi, Yang Peiguo as Ma Jiajia, Wu Xiqian as Ma Qingshan, Chen Ye as Zuo Ma, Fan Xiao as a little Red Army soldier, Feng Chunzhao as Ma Hade

One summer, teenagers Sun Daliang, Zha Xi and Ma Jiajia, Chinese, Tibetan and Muslim respectively, are spending their summer break from school at a tree farm along the Axia River. There, they discover quite a bit of loose timber floating away down the river, so they get from the local Party committee permission to guard the river. Later, water shipping team director Ma Hade instigates an argument among the three youngsters and they split up. Grandpa Qingshan, a member of the tree farm's Party committee, teaches them that they must learn to distinguish bad people from good, and urges them to unify. Working together again, they discover that Ma Hade is working with a gang of river bandits that has been stealing loose timber and floating it down the river. With the help of the militia, they catch him and the rest of the gang.

1755. *The Secret of R₄ (R₄ Zhi Mi)*

1982. Xi'an Film Studio. Color. 9 Reels. Direction: Li Yundong, Li Andi. Screenplay: Huang Yazhou. Cinematography: Cao Jinshan. Art Direction: Zhang Xiaohui. Music: Lu Yuan, Tang Ke. Sound: Hong Jiahui. Cast: Zhang Liwei as Li An, Shao Huifang as Chen Xiaoxiao, Qiao Zhen

as Lu Sha, Chen Mu as the Director, Wang Bingyan as Department Head Feng, Shao Yueer as Kang Yiqiu

On a warm summer night in 1971, medical research assistant Chen Xiaoxiao is working late in the laboratory when she suddenly hears a piercing scream from the next room. She rushes in, and finds her boss Zhang Xiuxiu murdered. Investigation by female detective Li An builds a strong circumstantial case against Chen, believed to be a jilted woman seeking revenge. Chen Xiaoxiao is tried and convicted of the crime, then sentenced to 20 years imprisonment. Seven years after this incident, Li An meets and finds herself falling for a man named Lu Sha. She discovers that he had once been Chen Xiaoxiao's lover, and that he still carries a torch for the convicted woman. Li is unhappy to learn this, but in talking with Lu about Chen, the detective begins to see some strange points about the affair that had not come out earlier. She decides to reopen the case, and finally proves that Chen was innocent after all. The real killer was Lu Sha's uncle, another researcher named Kang Yiqiu: he killed Zhang because the supervisor was getting too close to discovering that Kang was secretly using the lab to develop R₄, a deadly poison, then he framed Chen for the crime. After Chen is freed, Li An gives up Lu Sha so the two original lovers can reunite.

1756. *The Secret of the Calabash (Bao Hu Lu De Mi Mi)*

1963. Tianma Film Studio. B & W. 8 Reels. Direction: Yang Xiaozhong. Screenplay: Yang Xiaozhong, Ying Zhi and Jiang Tianliu, based on Zhang Tianyi's fairy tale of the same title. Cinematography: Shi Fengqi. Art Direction: Wang Yuebai. Music: Wang Qiang. Sound: Gong Zhengming. Cast: Xu Fang as Wang Bao, Zhang Ning as Zhen Xiaodeng, Wen He as Su Mingfeng, Lu Wei as Yao Jun, Shao Yaoguo as Yang Dahai, Chen Ronghua as Xiao Mingsheng

Elementary school student Wang Bao dreams of having a calabash, which could allow him to have everything without doing any work. One day, his dreams come true, and whatever he wants appear before him immediately. But the calabash also brings him much trouble and embarrassment, giving him pain and trouble along with the pleasure. He gradually realizes that the calabash is evil, so he exposes its secret to his classmates and throws it away. It explodes with a huge noise. Wang Bao

Secret Drawing. Inspector Shi Yun (Tian Hua, left) on her way to investigate the case of a scientist's missing briefcase. 1965. August First Film Studio.

awakens to find it was all a dream. From the experience he vows to study hard and stop indulging in idle daydreams.

1757. *Secret Order on the Succession (Chuan Guo Mi Zhao)*

1988. Shanghai Film Studio. Color. Wide Screen. Stereo. 14 Reels. Direction: Yao Shoukang. Screenplay: Mu Sheng. Cinematography: Peng Enli. Art Direction: Ju Ransheng, Shen Lide. Music: Liu Yanxi. Sound: Feng Deyao. Cast: Xun Feng as Wang Ziming, He Wei as Zhu Ciniang, Wang Hui as the Queen Mother, Sun Gengfa as the scarfaced man

On the eve of the Ming Dynasty's downfall, the Emperor Chongzhen gives a secret order to his son Zhu Ciniang sending him to Nanjing, where the emperor hopes his loyal followers will support Zhu's succession as emperor. On the way to Nanjing, Zhu is pursued by many who want to get hold of the order. After many fights, Zhu arrives at Nanjing. But the invading Manchu army arrives and wipes out the Ming troops there. By this time, Zhu no longer wants to be emperor, and when his loyal follower Wang Ziming is killed in bat-

tling some Manchu soldiers, Zhu Ciniang in despair casts the secret order into a fire.

1758. *The Secret Service in Action (Te Gao Ke Zhai Xing Dong)*

1981. Xi'an Film Studio. B & W. 9 Reels. Direction: Li Yucai, Jin Yin. Screenplay: Xiao Yixian, Zhou Xinde. Cinematography: Niu Han. Art Direction: Yan Pingxiao. Music: Xie Tiyin. Sound: Chen Zhiyuan. Cast: Lei Ming as Zhou Yi, Ma Chongle as Xin Yuting, Li Jingli as Shen Hong, Yuan Chunhai as Qinmu, Guo Fazeng as Ding Yan, Sun Yuanxun as Mr. Fang

During World War II, in the Boai Hospital, Doctors Xin Yuting and Zhou Yi, nurse Shen Hong and gardener Mr. Fang all are very interested in a particular patient. Japanese spy master Qinmu receives a tip from an agent referred to as "No. 45," urging him to conduct an immediate search of the hospital. As the story develops, Zhou Yi is found to be working for the New Fourth Army, purchasing and delivering medical supplies to their troops, and Xin Yuting is Japanese agent "No. 45." Mrs. Wu, a Communist underground liaison, is able to warn Zhou Yi that the mysterious patient is another spy planted in the hospital by the Japanese, and the next delivery will spring a Japanese trap. But the Communists have their own person, Ding Yan, planted in the Japanese spy agency, and he is able to coordinate the delivery from there. In the end, the boat making the delivery leaves safely.

1759. *The Secret Treasure House (Mi Mi Jin Ku)*

1986. Xiaoxiang Film Studio. Color. 9 Reels. Direction: Jiang Weihe. Screenplay: Du Zhihai, Jiang Xun. Cinematography: Zhou Xiaoping. Art Direction: Yang Li, Tan Shengshan. Music: Su Yue. Sound: Huang Qizhi. Cast: Han Yuanyuan as Zhu Jieyun, Wang Guoqiang as Zhao Jingbo, Jin Ange as Fang Lede, Guo Ping as Yao Jiren

In the summer of 1948, as civil war rages throughout China, CPC agent Zhao Jingbo accepts the assignment of protecting the Communists' treasury hidden in a north China city occupied by the Nationalists. A traitor tips off the Nationalists that the treasure is somewhere in that city, and they undertake a massive search, forcing Zhao to find another hiding place. Zhao persuades Fang Lede to use his family's pharmacy as a front for the treasure. Then, when Zhao is killed leading the enemy astray, Fang and his wife Zhu Jieyun are left with responsibility for making the transfer. At last, the couple decide to transfer the treasure to a Communist-held zone themselves, although it means abandoning their business, more than 100 years old and which had been in their family for five generations.

1760. *The Secret War (Mi Mi Zhan)*

1989. Emei Film Studio. Color. Letterboxed. 10 Reels. Direction: Tai Gang. Screenplay: Mao Mao, Luo Gonghe. Cinematography: Zhang Huaming. Art Direction: Chen Desheng, Li Xianglin. Music: He Xuntian, Li Silin. Sound: Shen Guli, Qiu Shuchuan. Cast: Xi Taoqi as Lu Hanlin, Deng Qian as Xu Lingbing

During the anti–Japanese War, politician Wang Jingwei establishes a collaborationist puppet government in Shanghai as a counter to Chiang Kaishek's refugee government in Chongqing. The Chongqing government draws up the "blue collar plan" to destroy the puppet regime. Professional killer Lu Hanlin is sent to Shanghai to assassinate Pan Daxia, an important figure in the collaborationist government, and after succeeding at this Lu is ordered to kill Pan's son Pan Zhipei as well. His third target is Deputy Mayor Zong Shukai. As much as Lu looks forward to this hit, having a personal grudge against Zong, the target escapes and Lu Hanling finds himself the target of a citywide manhunt. Zong Shukai goes to the Shanghai docks to meet a new, formal representative from Chongqing.

1761. *Secret Watch in Canton (Yang Cheng An Shao)*

1957. Haiyan Film Studio. B & W. 10 Reels. Direction: Lu Yu. Screenplay: Chen Canyun. Cinematography: Zhu Jing. Art Direction: Huang Chong and Yao Mingzhong. Music: Shi Yongkang. Sound: Li Liehong. Makeup: Tian Zhigao. Cast: Yang Weiru as No. 209, Hong Xia as Liang Ying, Yu Fei as the Reconnaissance Chief, Feng Ji as Wang Lian, Ling Yun as "Little Spirit," Di Fan as Bagu, Xia Tian as Boss Ma, Liang Ming as Mrs. Liu (special agent Mei Yi), Li Huanqing as Li Xiuying, Han Tao as Doctor Chen

A spy called "Agent 209" is discovered inside Chinese intelligence headquarters and is killed trying to escape. Scout Wang Lian accepts the assignment of assuming the dead spy's identity and contacting the spy he was supposed to link up with, a woman called Ba Gu. Bagu has recruited a couple, Doctor Chen and his wife Li Xiuying by getting the doctor drunk and then having her assistant "Little Spirit" take pictures of Bagu and Doctor Chen in a staged compromising situation. She has used the photos and evidence of other things in Doctor Chen's past to blackmail the couple into joining the "Chinese People's Accusation Delegation" to slander New China at the United Nations. In despair at ever escaping the agents' clutches, the doctor attempts suicide but is saved by Wang Lian. Chinese public security officers help him realize how muddled his thinking has been, and he offers to help them solve the case. After Doctor Chen leaves the hospital, the enemy agents force him to board a ship bound for Hainan Island which they plan to hijack to Hong Kong. The officers know of the plot, and they arrange a trap for the spies. Wang Lian and Bagu board the ship together. Half way to Hainan, Bagu's housekeeper Mrs. Liu appears unexpectedly, and it turns out that she is Mei Yi, head of the spy ring. Mei Yi has ordered that a time bomb be planted in the ship's hold. She has also detected Wang Lian's true identity and orders him killed, but the public security agents spring their trap and arrest all the spies. After a frantic search, Wang Lian finds the bomb and hurls it into the ocean.

1762. *Secretly Recorded Video Tape (Tou Pai De Lu Xiang Dai)*

1992. Shanghai Film Studio. Color. Letterboxed. 10 Reels. Direction: Xu Weijie. Screenplay: Xu Haibing. Cinematography: Sun Guoliang. Art Direction: Zhao Xianrui. Music: Liu Yanxi. Sound: Wu Guoqiang. Costume: Zhao Baodi. Makeup: Tao Meichun. Cast: Ning Jing as Lai Yun, Zhang Xiaolin as Guan Dong, Zhou Guobing as Huang Shanyang, Xu Feng as Jin Shui, Zhang Hong as Gu Jianqin, Pan Liqun as Li Kaifang

Television news cameraman Guan Dong secretly loves his partner, anchorwoman Lai Yun. One evening, the two secretly videotape a drug deal taking place in a bar. Without knowing it, they also include in the tape a serial rapist, who worries he will be identified if the tape is broadcast. He goes to the station and threatens Lai Yun with violence if she does not give him the tape. At the same time, the drug dealers have learned of the tape and are after it as well. In the end, Guan Dong is killed protecting Lai Yun.

1763. *Sector No. 13 (Shi Shan Hao Di Qu)*

1984. Changchun Film Studio. Color. Letterboxed. 10 Reels. Direction: Chen Jialing. Screenplay: Zhang Xiaotian. Cinematography: Zhong Wenmin. Art Direction: Jin Xiwu. Music: Jin Fuzhai. Sound: Han Weijun. Cast: Jiang Lili as Shao Weiping, Hou Guanqun as Li Tianhou, Zhi Yitong as Yang Xuchu, Huang Xiaolei as Liu Dong, Li Yaohua as Zou Pin, Wang Zhihua as Tan Peihua, Li Jian as Grandma

In the fall of 1970, medical school graduate Shao Weiping is assigned to "Sector No. 13," an island leper colony. Her father is falsely accused by a man named Zou Pin, resulting in the father's exile to Qinghai in West China. For Weiping's fiance Tan Peihua, also a doctor, this is the last straw in a long list of criminal actions by Zou Pin, so Doctor Tan falsely diagnoses Zou as having leprosy. When Zou arrives on the island, however, Shao Weiping discovers he does not have the disease and asks her fiance to correct his diagnosis. Tan argues that Zou has caused so much pain and suffering to others that he deserves the prison-like isolation of the colony. Besides, correcting the diagnosis will damage his own professional reputation. Tan Peihua at last corrects the diagnosis, but he and Shao Weiping have argued so much about it that their own relationship is destroyed.

1764. *See You Later (Hou Hui You Qi)*

1990. Youth Film Studio & Hebei Film Studio Co-Production. Color. Wide Screen. 10 Reels. Direction: Song Chong. Screenplay: Jiang Cheng, Chen Ding. Cinematography: Liu Lihua. Art Direction: Zhu Jiancang. Music: Xu Jingxin. Sound: Gong Dejun. Cast: Wang Yuzhang as Wang Jian, Jiang Cheng as Hou Jun, Song Xiaoying as Xiao Fang, Sang Di as Miss Bai, Yang Lu as Man Na

In an international counter-terrorism competition held by Interpol, Chinese policeman Wang Jian loses out to Taipei policeman Hou Jun because of the latter's superior firearm. Hou Jun's father is really a covert Taiwan crime figure. After his father is killed by the mob, Hou Jun inherits his father's huge fortune, which he uses to kill all his father's old enemies. Hou then flees overseas, but he is now an Interpol target. In China, Wang Jian is named to head a special unit cooperating with Interpol, and eventually the two former rivals find themselves in a real competition. At last, Wang has Hou cornered, but the latter chooses suicide to apprehension.

1765. *Seeking the Devil (Xun Zhao Mo Gui)*

1988. Beijing Film Studio & Shanxi Film Studio Co-Production. Color. 10 Reels. Direction: Wang Haowei, Qika Kuerban. Screenplay: Liu Yazhou, Liu Weihong. Cinematography: Li Chengsheng. Art Direction: Wang Jixian. Music: Zhang Peiji. Art Direction: Wang Jixian. Cast: Zhang Guomin as Liu Qing, Feng Enhe as Lu Dadao, Tian Shaojun as Wang Hongshui, Mai Xiaoqing as Ayi Guli, Liu Peiqi as Zhang Liang

In the vast Northwest China desert is a town where a vast treasure is supposed to be hidden. In the early 1920s, many treasure-hunters come to the town seeking these riches, although an old saying holds that those who do so will only find the devil. The strongest teams are those headed by Liu Qing and Lu Dadao, but both are handicapped by their lack of a treasure map. Young physician Wang Hongshui accidentally stumbles upon the legendary map, touching off a series of machinations and bloody incidents connected to the treasure hunt. At last, all those who came to "seek the devil" are dead.

1766. *Seeking the Dream (Qian Li Xun Meng)*

1991. Shanghai Film Studio. Color. Letterboxed. 10 Reels. Direction: Yang Yanjing, Screenplay: Ai Minzhi, Xu Yinghua, Cinematography: Sun Guoliang, Art Direction: Zhong Yongqin, Chen Chunlin, Music: Xu Jingxin, Sound: Lu Xuehan, Cast: Qi Mengshi, Qin Yi, Shu Shi, Xiang Mei

Liu Zhenhua, formerly head coach of the Chinese national basketball team, was forced out of his position by ill health. Now fully recovered, he plans a run from Shanghai to Beijing to welcome the Asian Games to Beijing. The news brings Tian Jieqin, his lover of 40 years before, from Hong Kong in search of him. However, life changes and recovered love do not sway Liu's determination, and he continues to run.

1767. *Senji Dema (Sen Ji De Ma)*

1985. Inner Mongolia Film Studio. Color. 9 Reels. Direction: Chen Da. Screenplay: Lu Zirong. Cinematography: Guan Qingwu. Art Direction: Yi Qingbo. Music: Alapeng Aole. Sound: Bu Ren. Cast: Bulude Qiqige as Senji Dema, Wang Weiguo as Jieerge, Siqin Gaowa as Du Ma

Among the people of Inner Mongolia, a girl named Senji Dema is legendary for her purity, kindness and strength. She was born in the Qing Dynasty, and was married into the household of a local farmer, as the wife of his only son, who was in very poor health. The groom died on their wedding night, and under the customs of the time she was to remain a widow. A household slave, Jieerge, was very sympathetic to her, and eventually the two fall in love. But her mother-in-law sells her to a remote place, leaving the distraught Jieerge helpless to do anything.

1768. *Sentiment Confusion (Qing Huo)*

1991. Beijing Film Studio. Color. Letterboxed. 12 Reels. Direction and Screenplay: Chen Guoxing. Cinematography: Zhang Zhongping and Cai Huimin. Art Direction: Yuan Chao. Music: Gao Erli. Sound: Wei Xueyi and Li Lijing. Cast: Zhang Qiang as Mei Lin, Liu Bing as

Xiao He, Xie Yan as Tian Erhei, Cai Hongxiang as Di Ke

Young and beautiful psychoanalyst Mei Lin loves her work and is very caring of her patients, who in turn are grateful and admire her. An anonymous phone call related to a killing introduces her to Xiao He, a humorous cop. Mei Lin's involvement stems from the fact the sole witness to the killing is crane operator Tian Erhei, a secret admirer of hers. The effect on Tian of what he has witnessed is so strong that he gets "retrograde amnesia." The cop wants to solve the case, and the doctor wants to cure her patients. Their different occupations frequently bring Mei and Xiao into conflict, but a sense of responsibility to their professions makes them cooperate. At last her patient regains his memory, and Xiao nabs the killer.

1769. *Sentries Under Neon Lights (Ni Hong Deng Xia De Shao Bing)*

1964. Tianma Film Studio. Color. 13 Reels. Direction: Wang Ping, Ge Xing. Screenplay: Shen Ximeng, based on his stage play of the same title. Cinematography: Huang Shaofeng. Art Direction: Zhang Hancheng, Xu Keji. Music: Lu Qimin. Sound: Ding Bohe. Cast: Xu Linge as Lu Hua, Gong Zhipei as Lu Dacheng, Ma Xueshi as Chen Xi, Yuan Yue as Zhao Dada, Liao Youliang as Tong Anan, Liu Hongsheng as Hong Mantang

Shortly after the liberation of Shanghai, a PLA company enters the city and is billeted behind bustling Nanjing Road, in an area noted for its commerce, nightlife and vice. Some of the troops are influenced by their new surroundings in varying ways: platoon leader Chen Xi forgets the PLA's traditions of simple living and hard work; new recruit Tong Anan ignores the unit's strict class struggle exercises; squad leader Zhao Dada can not adapt to the metropolitan environment, and petitions for relocation to a combat zone. Company commander Lu Dacheng and Political Supervisor Lu Hua soon realize the seriousness of the problem and initiate class education. Finally, Chen Xi, Zhao Dada, Tong Anan and the rest improve their class awareness, and enthusiastically join in the work of eradicating capitalism. Shortly afterwards, when American imperialism starts the Korean War, Chen Xi and Tong Anan receive approval to transfer there.

1770. *September (Jiu Yue)*

1984. Kunming Film Studio. Color. 9 Reels. Direction: Tian Zhuangzhuang. Screenplay: Yan Tingting, Xiao Jian. Cinematography: Hou Yong. Art Direction: Huo Jianqi. Music: Xu Jingqin. Sound: Zhang Jiake. Cast: Jiang Yunhui as Gu Xiaoyu, Wu Tao as Liu Yuan, Wang Minzhi as Zhen Qitian, Zhen Xin as Tian Ling, Wang Tingyin as Xiao Min

Gu Xiaoyu, an elderly teacher at a Children's Palace, prepares her children's choir for an upcoming music festival, although she does not get the parental support she would prefer. One day, she receives a letter from someone named Zhen Qitian, who claims to have once been one of the children she taught, but is now a young man soon to be released from a reformatory. The letter says he would love to see her again and asks her to meet him. Although she doesn't remember him, she decides to go anyway. When she arrives at the meeting spot, Zhen Qitian is too embarrassed to identify himself to her, and after a while she leaves. After she leaves, Zhen Qitian thinks back over his life, and concludes that his days at the Children's Palace were truly the happiest of his life.

1771. *Serfs (Nong Nu)*

1963. August First Film Studio. B & W. 10 Reels. Direction: Li Jun. Screenplay: Huang Zongjiang. Cinematography: Wei Linyue. Art Direction: Kou Honglei. Music: Yan Ke, Luo Nianyi. Sound: Kou Shenkang. Cast: Wang Dui as Qiangba, Qiangba as Mama, Little Wang Dui as Qiangba as a child, Little Duojie as the blacksmith, Shicui Zuoma as Grandma, Baima Yangjie as Landuo, Qiongda as Resa Wangjie

All of Qiangba's Tibetan ancestors have been serfs. Shortly after his birth, his parents are tortured to death by serf owner Wangjie. In his teens, he becomes a household serf of Wangjie, and passes an inhuman existence. Qiangba from then on refuses to speak, showing his resistance through silence. After the PLA enters Tibet, Qiangba and female serf Landuo leave to find the PLA. Landuo is rescued by the PLA, changing her fate, but Qiangba is caught and taken back. The serf owner's son, with support from foreign imperialists, foments armed rebellion. After the rebellion is smashed, Qiangba is rescued by the PLA, and the serfs are liberated at last. Qiangba is reunited with Landuo, and begins to speak again after many years of silence.

Service see *Young Masters of the Great Leap Forward*

1772. *A Set of Pearl Jewelry (Shuang Zhu Feng)*

1963. Tianma Film Studio & Hong Kong Jinsheng Film Company Co-Production. Color. 12 Reels. Direction: Su Shi. Screenplay: Yu Jiejun. Cinematography: Cha Xiangkang. Art Direction: Ge Shicheng, Liu Pan. Music: Zhen Ye, etc., Cast: Yao Cheng as Wen Bizheng, Xu Hongfang as Huo Dingjin, Guo Dongnuan as Qiuhua, Wang Hanqing as Liu Jingan, Liu Hongru as Huo Tianrong, Wang Yuanyuan as Madam Huo

When Huo Dingjin, daughter of a high-ranking government official, accompanies her mother to the temple to worship, she loses one of her pearl jewels. It is found by Wen Bizheng, a young scholar. Smitten with Huo Dingjin's beauty and charm, he hides his true identity and enters the Huo household as a slave.

When Wen finally has the chance to speak to Miss Huo, he returns the jewel to her, reveals his true identity, and proposes marriage to her. Dingjin commits herself to him by giving him the pearls. But when Bizheng returns to his home to resume his studies, Dingjin's father Huo Tianrong betroths his daughter to the son of the emperor's brother-in-law. Dingjin tells her father of her relationship with Wen Bizheng, which enrages him. Dingjin flees from home. The furious Huo Tianrong then seeks to make trouble for Bizheng, but the young man also escapes. The following year, he becomes the number one scholar in the Imperial exams. He finds Dingjin, and they are married.

1773. *Set the Prairie Ablaze (Liao Yuan)*

1962. Tianma Film Studio. B & W. 13 Reels. Direction: Zhang Junxiang and Gu Eryi. Screenplay: Peng Yonghui and Li Hongxin. Cinematography: Zhou Daming. Art Direction: Zhang Hancheng. Music: Huang Zhun and Shen Tiekou. Sound: Yuan Qingyu. Cast: Wang Shangxing as Lei Huanjue, Wang Xiyan as Yi Mengzhi, Wei Heling as Old Yi, Zhu Xijuan as Qiuying, Qi Heng as Zhang Laogeng, Lu Shan as Shunzhi's wife

In 1905, coal miners in western Jiangxi province rebel against the harsh oppression

Sentries Under Neon Lights. **Two PLA soldiers patrolling Shanghai after their forces occupy the city. 1964. Tianma Film Studio.**

and exploitation imposed upon them, but the rebellion is suppressed. After the Communist Party is founded in 1921, the Party sends Lei Huanjie to run a night school where workers are taught Marxist theory. Lei Huanjie organizes the workers into a union which battles the capitalist legally and politically. In 1923, encouraged by the high number of workers' strikes across the country, Lei Huanjue organizes a large-scale walkout in western Jiangxi. Confronted by awakened and militant workers, their capitalist boss Wu was not only forced to call off his goons, he had to accept the workers' demands, a major victory for the strikers.

1774. *Setting Moon in the Gobi Desert (Ge Bi Can Yue)*

1985. Changchun Film Studio. Color. 10 Reels. Direction: Zhao Xinshui. Screenplay: Zhao Xinshui, Wang Zuo. Cinematography: Chen Chang'an. Art Direction: Li Junjie. Music: Lei Yusheng. Sound: Li Zhenduo. Cast: Feng Enhe as Nuerjiang, Djamila as Tiyahan, Mutalifu as Kumayi, Shi Rong as Bolida

As the PLA enters Xinjiang in 1949, Kumayi, a right-wing chief of the Hashake na-

tionality, leads an anti–Communist espionage effort under the banner of "Protect the Nationality and Religion." His plan is to establish an East Turkestan Republic. Against this background, there is a sub-plot concerning the reunion of a long lost brother and sister on each side of the struggle.

1775. *Seven Days and Nights (Qi Tian Qi Ye)*

1962. Changchun Film Studio & Xi'an Film Studio Co-Production. B & W. 9 Reels. Direction: Wu Zhaodi. Screenplay: Li Jing. Cinematography: Shu Xiaoyan. Art Direction: Wang Jixian. Music: Chen Ming. Sound: Shen Guli. Cast: Bai Dezhang as Su Qiang, Wang Yansheng as the brigade commander, Zhang Fengxiang as the political commissar, Zhang Yan as Uncle Guo, Song Baoyi as Wang Zhijian, Zhu Dazhang as Zhang Guohua

In March of 1947, Nationalist warlord Hu Zongnan sends his 15 brigades to attack Yan'an. A PLA company is ordered to hold Hill 92 and the Songshu range. Newly appointed political commissar Su Qiang helps the soldiers overcome their cockiness and

Serfs. **Downtrodden and oppressed serf Qiangba (Wang Dui), the latest in a long line of Tibetan serfs. 1963. August First Film Studio.**

overconfidence, better preparing them for the enemy attack. Their lone company is attacked by a brigade. They relinquish Hill 92 and fall back to the Songshu range. They hold out for seven days and nights against repeated attack, until the enemy attackers turn back.

1776. *The Seven-Star Jasper Sword (Qi Xing Bi Yu Dao)*

1991. Shanghai Film Studio. Color. Stereo. Letterboxed. 10 Reels. Direction: Yao Shoukang. Screenplay: Gu Zemin, Meng Shenghui. Cinematography: Can Lianguo. Art Direction: Chen Shaomian. Music: Jin Fuzhai. Sound: Lu Xuehan. Cast: Zhao Yang as Duan Yu, Li Siqi as Zhu Zhu, Can Xingmei as Hua Yelai, Han Zhikai as Tie Shui, Ma Shunyi as Qiao Laoshan, Han Tao as Zhu Erye

Duan Yu, son of a martial arts master, travels to Southeast China on his father's orders to ask for the hand in marriage of the daughter of martial arts master Zhu. He carries with him a gift of a special knife having seven jade stars in the handle. Along the way, however, he is frequently harassed by a woman bandit, part of a trap set by a gang angered at his father's refusal to join them.

Each time he is attacked, however, a strange girl calling herself Hua Huafeng shows up to intervene and help him. At last, it turns out his mysterious helper is Master Zhu's daughter. The young couple happily get together.

1777. *Seventy-Two Tenants (Qi Shi Er Jia Fang Ke)*

1963. Pearl River Film Studio & Hong Kong Hongtu Film Studio Co-Production. B & W. 9 Reels. Direction: Wang Weiyi. Screenplay: Huang Guliu and Wang Weiyi, based on the Shanghai Public Comedy Troupe's stage play of the same title. Cinematography: Liu Hongming, Wang Yunhui. Art Direction: Huang Chong. Music: Huang Jingpei. Sound: Lu Mingwen. Cast: Xie Guobi as Du Fulin, Shu Yi as Han, the Teacher's Wife, Pan Qian as Doctor Jin, Li Yanling as Axiang, Fang Wenxian as Fa Zhai, Yi Boquan as the Tailor, Zhong Guoren as Chang Ji, Wen Juefei as Bing Gen, Wang Zhong as "369"

In China before 1949, 72 poor tenants (all vendors, small craftsmen, art workers, etc.) live in an old and deteriorating building in Guangzhou. They are severely bullied by their tyran-

Seventy-Two Tenants. 1963. Pearl River Film Studio.

nical landlord Bing Gen and his wife. To increase their income from the property, the landlord couple plans to renovate the building and convert it into a "pleasure palace," offering food, liquor, gambling and prostitution. They try to cultivate policeman number "369," hoping he will evict the tenants. When their original plan fails, the landlords decide to give their beautiful adopted daughter Axiang to the chief of the local branch police station as a concubine, in order to obtain some political influence. However, Axiang rejects this arrangement and flees at the wedding banquet. The tenants are all sympathetic to Axiang, and hide her. The branch chief is angry with the landlords and puts them both in jail. Axiang is saved, and because of the failure of the "pleasure palace" plan, the 72 tenants look forward to staying in their homes instead of being turned into the street.

1778. *Sex Scandal (Tao Se Xin Wen)*

1993. Shanghai Film Studio. Color. Letter-boxed. 10 Reels. Direction: Da Shibiao. Screenplay: Li Jianguo. Cinematography: Cheng Shiyu. Art Direction: Zhang Chongxiang. Music: Liu

Yanxi. Sound: Gong Dejun. Costume: Ding Shulan, Zhang Fuzhen. Makeup: Yin Shangshan. Cast: Wang Zhenjun as Lu Shifeng, Zhang Aiping as Lu Qinqin, Zhang Tao as Feng Yuer, Zhou Xiaoli as Liu Jia

A certain city is shocked when the dead bodies of top model Feng Yuer and senior police detective Sun Xiaomin are found together nude in a hotel bed. It at first appears to be an illicit affair ending in a murder-suicide. But investigator Lu Shifeng is unconvinced. He finds that Lu Qinqin, the woman running Feng's model agency, had been providing Feng to the local trade bureau chief in exchange for certain favors such as economic information. When Sun Xiaomin's investigation was getting too close, Lu Qinqin killed the two and set up the scene. The overall plan was the work of Lu Qinqin's boss Zhao Bing and a shadowy figure called the "old man." Lu Qinqin is caught, but reporter Liu Jia is abducted by the "old man." Lu Shifeng rescues her after a fearsome battle with the tough and evil criminal.

1779. *Sha Ou (Sha Ou)*

1981. Youth Film Studio. Color. 9 Reels. Direction: Zhan Nuanqin. Screenplay: Zhang Nuanqin, Li Tuo. Cinematography: Pao Xiao-ran. Art Direction: Wang Jianjing. Music: Wang Ming. Sound: Zhang Ruikun. Cast: Chang Shanshan as Sha Ou, Guo Bichuan as Shen Dawei, Lu Jun as Doctor Han, Li Ping as Zhang Lii, Jiang Yunhui as Sha Ou's mother

After the defeat of the Gang of Four, China becomes more involved in contacts with the outside world. Woman volleyball player Sha Ou and her teammates practice hard for China's first international volleyball participation in years. When Sha Ou incurs a severe back injury, the team doctor recommends she drop the sport immediately to avoid possibly permanent damage. However, Sha Ou decides to go ahead and play, feeling her athletic career is drawing to a close anyway and this will probably be her last chance at a gold medal. She is supported in this by her boyfriend Shen Dawei, a member of the national mountain climbing team. When China fails to take the gold medal in women's volleyball, Sha Ou is very upset. After returning to Beijing, Sha Ou decides it is time to get married, and help Shen Dawei scale the heights in his career just as he helped her. Shen and his team do reach the mountain peak. Back home, Sha Ou happily prepares for their wedding. But then the news arrives that the team was caught in an avalanche, and Shen Dawei was killed. Sha Ou sinks into the depths of despair, bereft of love and career. But her spirit of honoring the nation finally returns, and she becomes a women's volleyball coach. The next generation of women volleyball players trained by Sha Ou finally defeat the Japanese and take the gold medal.

Best Sound Zhang Ruikun, 1982 Golden Rooster Awards.

1780. *Shadow in a Stormy Night (Yu Wu Mo Ying)*

1991. Changchun Film Studio. Color. Letterboxed. 10 Reels. Direction: Li Geng, Bei Zhaocheng. Screenplay: Wang Dacheng. Cinematography: Ning Changcheng. Art Direction: Yang Baocheng. Music: Fan Weiqiang. Sound: Zhen Yunbao. Cast: Zong Ping, Zhang Chao, Zhang Minquan, Wu Wenguang

A police procedural in which public security forces solve a murder and the theft of technical documents.

1781. *The Shadow in the Rose Building (Mei Gui Lou Mi Ying)*

1993. Beijing Film Studio. Color. Letterboxed. 9 Reels. Direction: Qin Zhiyu. Screenplay: Qin Zhiyu, Zhang Xuan. Cinematography: Gao Jie. Art Direction: Tu Juhua, Yang Tinghui. Music: Li Haihui. Sound: Guan Shuxin. Costume: Dong Xiuqin. Makeup: Shao Jie. Cast: Zhang Yong as Bai Xiaoer, Lu Fei as Wang Tianlong, Qin Zhiyu as Zhu Xiulan, Zhou Jie as Wu Jian, Liang Li as Zhang Lili, Zhang Jingsheng as Liu Biao, Huang Xiaolei as Cailiang, Xia Zongxue as Lawyer Chen, Chi Ming as Zhen Xiaoer, Chi Ming as Bai Suer, Guo Yuntai as Doctor Zhao

Wang Tianlong, CEO of a trading company, is terminally ill. His wife Zhang Lili does not love him, and she and her lover Liu Biao are already making plans for spending Wang's fortune. Wang's housekeeper Zhu Xiulan craves her own revenge, for Wang had her husband framed and sent to prison years ago. Meanwhile, Bai Xiaoer, Wang's daughter by a former lover, shows up to see him. Wang dies, but the investigation reveals someone could not wait: the man was poisoned. Bai Xiaoer falls in love with a man named Wu Jian, who turns out to be Wang's murderer, a professional killer hired by the housekeeper. But the killings do not stop there: the survivors prey upon each other, either for greed or hatred, until at last the only survivor is Wang's real daughter Bai Xiaoer.

1782. *Shajiadian Grain Station (Sha Jia Dian Liang Zhan)*

1954. Northeast Film Studio. B & W. 10 Reels. Direction: Gan Xuewei. Screenplay: Wu Zhaodi, based on the novel "A Wall Made of Bronze and Steel" by Liu Qing (1916–). Cinematography: Ge Weiqin. Set Design: Lu Gan. Music: Xu Xu. Sound: Lin Bingcheng. Cast: Zhang Ping as Shi Defu, Du Defu as Shi Yonggong, Zhang Ying as Shi Yongkai, Pu Ke as Assistant Director Ge, Li Qing as Secretary Jin, Zhou Diao as District Director Cao

In 1947, Nationalist forces attack the Shaanxi-Gansu-Ningxia boundary region in

West Central China. At that time, grain supplies had become the most important problem for the Red Army. To help the Communists, Shi Defu, Shi Yonggong and others working underground in the Shajiadian Grain Distribution Station take on the difficult mission of supplying grain to the Red Army. The mission and their lives are in constant danger: a landlord tries to burn down the station, but Shi Defu organizes the workers in transferring the grain elsewhere. When the Nationalist forces attack Shajiadian, some of the grain workers are killed and Shi Defu is wounded and taken prisoner, but Shi Yonggong is able to escape. Shi Defu is tortured, but refuses to divulge where the grain is, and later escapes with other prisoners. At the time the Red Army begins a major counterattack, Shi Defu meets Secretary Jin and Shi Yonggong on the Shajiadian battlefield. The grain is turned over to high-echelon CPC leaders, successfully accomplishing the mission.

1783. *Shaking Calabash (Hu Lu Huang You You)*

1986. Xiaoxiang Film Studio. Color. 9 Reels. Direction: Pan Xianghe. Screenplay: Guo Songyuan, Yang Jiyuan, Lin Meizhao. Cinematography: Yu Yejiang. Art Direction: Rao Weiquan. Music: Wei Jingshu. Sound: Huang Shiye. Cast: Zhang Jianjun as Gu Yongfa, Liu Songbing as Wen Tianbao, Li Fang as Chungu

In the major tea producing area of west Hunan province, Gu Yongfa's outstanding tea earns him the perennial title of "King of Tea" in each year's competition. Although many ask his secrets, Gu steadfastly refuses to share them, saying that when his daughter Chungu marries someday, he will turn the secrets over to Chungu and her husband. One year there is an upset in the competition when the winner is Wen Tianbao, a young technician at the county's tea-training school. This excites Gu Yongfa, for he interprets this as an omen of who his future son-in-law should be. But he changes his mind when he meets the young man and finds him to be a cripple. When Chungu meets Tianbao, however, she falls for him on her own, creating much confusion in her father's mind. After going back and forth on the matter, Gu finally happily accepts Wen Tianbao as his apprentice and future son-in-law.

1784. *Shali Make (Sha Li Ma Ke)*

1978. Beijing Film Studio. Color. 10 Reels. Direction: Yu Lan, Li Wei. Screenplay: Yao Yunhuan, Shen Yin. Cinematography: Luo Dean. Art Direction: Yang Zhanjia. Music: Yan Fei, Mei Jialin. Sound: Zhen Chunyu. Cast: Song Xiaoyin as Shali Make, Zhang Guomin as Kabu, Zhu Xinyun as Sha Te, En Hesheng as Kujiwang, Liu Jiafu as Shagele, Zhao Zhiyue as Grandpa Gongbu

In the foothills of the Qilian mountains, populated largely by minority people, the homes are so scattered that most children have no way of attending school. After Shali Make retires from the military and returns to his hometown, he operates a "school on horseback" with the support of the old Party secretary. This brings schooling to all the children in the area. Some of the "horseback school" children find horses rustled by rancher Tulu Hala, so to cover himself Tulu Hala tries to frame Shali Make by getting commune secretary Jiadeng to lie. At the commune membership meeting, poor and lower class horse raising farmers see through the frame-up and criticize Jiadeng. The commune Party secretary praises the "horseback school" and confesses his lies. Tulu Hala's crimes are completely exposed.

1785. *Shan Ding Dong (Shan Ding Dong)*

1984. Pearl River Film Studio. Color. Letterboxed. 10 Reels. Direction: Ou Fan, Er Lin. Screenplay: Yu Xiangyi, Yuan Bo. Cinematography: Wu Yukun. Art Direction: Shi Haiying. Music: Lu Yuan. Sound: Deng Qinhua. Cast: Li Huan as Aunt Yang, Xu Dianji as Changgeng, Liu Yanli as Zhong Yide, Liang Yuejun as Yi Daying, Wang Changhui as Ba Minji, Song Dewang as Professor Wu, Kang Lu as Liu Maoxun

A romance in which a recent music academy graduate and a folk singer are brought together by their mutual love of a type of folk music called "shan ding dong."

1786. *Shan Niang (Shan Niang) (original title: Chong Hui Yao Shan)*

1994. Youth Film Studio. Color. Letterboxed. 9 Reels. Direction: Xu Tongjun. Screenplay:

Zhao Tingguang, based on Zhao Tingguang's original epic poem. Cinematography: Zhang Guoqing. Art Direction: Zhou Dengfu, Jin Yaodong. Music: Fu Lin. Costume: Lei Jun, Wu Guihua. Cast: Zheng Zhenyao as A Ma, Xing Mingshan as Man Sai, Song Jing as Shan Niang, Lu Sikun as Hong Sai, Qi Xiyao as Ruan Gong, Wang Zhi as Zai Lao

As Qinshan Village holds its traditional ceremony honoring the passage of some of its children to adulthood, the despotic local landlord Master Yuan arrives to order those newly classed as adults to report for mandatory labor. Such forced labor usually results in either death or broken health. Bright village girl Shan Niang organizes the villagers to oppose this injustice and fight for their rights.

1787. *Shan Que'er (Shan Que Er)*

1987. Changchun Film Studio. Color. 10 Reels. Direction: Hua Ke. Screenplay: Li Kuanding. Cinematography: Li Junyan. Art Direction: Song Honghua. Music: Si Wanchun. Sound: Liu Xingfu, Fu Yong. Cast: Ru Ping as Shan Queer, Zhao Jun as Tietou, Yu Lingling as Feifei

Country girl Shan Que'er loves Tietou, blacksmith in her village, but her mother arranges her daughter's engagement to Qianger, son of a well-off family in the next village. Shan Que'er appeals to Qianger to cancel the engagement, and he, a relatively educated young man, understands and agrees. His father, however, demands the girl repay the 900 yuan he had given her mother. To earn the necessary money, Shan Que'er goes to the city and finds work as a housekeeper in the home of a professor. Shan Que'er not only improves her knowledge but undergoes a considerable change in her ideology and attitudes. Then Tietou comes to the city to take her back home. Economic reforms have made him quite prosperous, and he has already repaid Shan Que'er's debt. But Shan Que'er now realizes that Tietou is not just uneducated but actually somewhat dense. A series of incidents increases the gap between the two, and eventually she asks out of this engagement as well. But this time, the people in her native village do not support her, and Shan Que'er feels the oppression of ancient traditions weighing her down.

1788. *Shanghai Dancing Girl (Two Parts) (Shang Hai Wu Nu)*

1989. Shanghai Film Studio and Nanjing Film Studio Co-Production. Color. 18 Reels. Direction: Xu Weijie. Screenplay: Ye Dan. Cinematography: Luo Yong. Art Direction: Xiao Bing. Music: Lu Qimin. Sound: Wang Huimin, Qian Youshan. Cast: Zhang Xiaolin as Pao Wangchun, Zhen Shuang as Hua Hongyan, He Qing as Bai Dailin, Chen Shu as Jiang Diping, Huang Daliang as Gu Xiaotong

At the end of World War II, Shanghai's citizens find that their own corrupt government officials have replaced the Japanese as oppressors. Deputy police chief Jiang Diping targets businessman Hua Biting for extortion. Besides money, Jiang wants Hua's daughter Hua Hongyan, while her girlfriend, dancer Bai Dailin, is similarly harassed by government agent Gu Xiaotong. One of Gu's deputies, Pao Wangchun, obtains evidence that Bai Dailin's father Bai Libing, another police official, had been a Japanese collaborator. He wants to arrest Bai Libing, but is blocked by Gu Xiaotong, for unexplained reasons. In time, as it appears her father's life is in danger, Hua Hongyan becomes Jiang Diping's mistress in exchange for his assurances of protection, but Hua Biting is killed anyway. Pao Wangchun at last finds that Gu Xiaotong has been thwarting his investigation because he himself was a major Japanese collaborator during the war. He also learns that Bai Dailin is actually his own sister that he has sought for years. When Pao gets too close to the truth, he is killed. One night, as a big official celebration takes place at a hotel, Hua Hongyan shows up and guns down both Gu and Jiang.

1789. *Shanghai Fever (Gu Feng)*

1993. Xiaoxiang Film Studio, Hong Kong Yineng Film Corporation and China Film Import and Export Corporation Co-Production. Color. Letterboxed. 9 Reels. Direction: Li Guoli. Screenplay: Jia Hongyuan. Cinematography: Shen Miaorong. Art Direction: Li Lesi. Music: Hu Weili. Sound: Fu Ning. Producer: Gao Jiajun. Costume: Tao Jing. Makeup: Zhu Yi, Qiu Tingqi. Cast: Pan Hong as Fan Li, Liu Qinyun as A Lun, Wang Rugang as San Bao, Wang Huayin as Xu Ang

Shanghai ticket seller Fan Li meets A Lun, who has come from Shanghai to make money in the stock market. A Lun encourages her to get involved in the market, and later they join forces to make a lot of money. Fan's success draws considerable attention from neighbors and co-workers, and she becomes a local celebrity, investing others' money for them. But her preoccupation with the market brings her to neglect her husband Xu Ang and their daughter. Xu Ang's feelings of neglect creates problems for him at his work, and he starts feeling he must do something to match his wife's success. He uses 200,000 yuan of other people's money to take his own plunge into the market, and loses it all. Xu Ang goes to a tall building, planning to jump, but Fan Li shows up and talks him down, convincing him they can overcome the setback. The story ends with Fan Li's family happily moving to a new home in Shanghai's booming Pudong area.

Best Actress Pan Hong, 1994 Golden Rooster Awards.

Best Actress Pan Hong, 1994 Hundred Flowers Awards.

1790. *Shanghai Girl (Shang Hai Gu Niang)*

1958. Beijing Film Studio. Color. 10 Reels. Direction: Cheng Ying. Screenplay: Zhang Xuan. Cinematography: Zhu Jinming. Art Direction: Qin Wei, Music: Chen Zi, Du Yu. Sound: Cai Jun. Cast: An Ran as Xiao Li, Liu Zhao as Mr. Zhang, Li Keng as Xiao Zhao, Zhao Lian as Lu Ye, Qing Wen as Su Feng, Gao Shiying as Hui Juan, Ba Lihua as Manager Lin

Technician Lu Ye and construction site inspector Bai Mei, a Shanghai girl, are co-workers and lovers. Lu Ye impetuously adopts a new and untested construction method, and although she loves him, Bai Mei realizes it will affect construction quality, so she reports Lu's action to his supervisor, Manager Lin. But because of the bureaucratic system in effect, Bai Mei is the one criticized and reassigned to another job. Before leaving, she makes one final plea to Lu Ye to reconsider, but he is adamant in his decision. After the project is completed, Lu Ye finds it does not satisfy quality standards, bringing huge losses to the nation. Added to the guilt he already feels about Bai Mei, he falls ill. When he returns to work, he learns that Bai Mei is leaving that day for her new job assignment in Southwest China, that she had come to the construction site to say goodbye, but finding him absent, has left for the train station. He hurries to the station to see her, but arrives just in time to see her train moving away in the distance.

1791. *Shanghai in 1937 (Da Shang Hai Yi Jiu San Qi)*

1986. China Film Co-Production Corp. & Hong Kong Shanyang Film Company Co-Production. Color. 9 Reels. Direction: Sun Che. Screenplay: Ruan Yizheng. Cinematography: Huang Wenyun. Art Direction: Zhang Xibai. Music: Huang Zhan. Cast: Du Yumin as Du Yuesheng, Xu Xiaojian as Lin Huaibu, Sun Yiwen as Wang Yueying, Dong Zhihua as Yang Pan

In 1937, the Japanese invade China and occupy Shanghai that August. To that time, the life and business of Shanghai has been dominated largely by three triads, and the heads of these gangs react to the Japanese in different ways. Huang Jinlong closes his door and stays at home. Du Yuesheng flees to Hong Kong. Zhang Xiaolin becomes a collaborator, cutting the Japanese in on the action. The lieutenants of the three triad heads also react in varying ways, some becoming collaborators, some joining the anti–Japanese resistance. Lin Huaibu, one of Du's followers, kills Zhang Xiaolin with Du's indirect help, setting off a bloodbath.

1792. *Shanghai Triad (Yao A Yao Yao Dao Wai Po Qiao)*

1995. Shanghai Film Studio, Alpha Films, UGC Images, La Sept Cinema Co-Production. Color. Wide Screen. 108 minutes. Direction: Zhang Yimou. Screenplay: Bi Feiyu, based on the novel "Men Gum" (Gang Law) by Li Xiao. Cinematography: Lu Yue. Art Direction: Cao Jiuping. Music: Zhang Guangtian. Sound: (Dolby), Tao Jing. Costume: Tong Huamiao. Makeup: Yang Yu, Ma Zide. Cast: Gong Li as Xiao Jinbao, Li Baotian as Tang the Boss, Wang Xiaoxiao as Shuisheng, Sun Chun as Song (No. 2), Fu Biao as No. 3, Li Xuejian as 6th Uncle, Chen Shu as Shi Ye, Liu Jiang as Fat Yu, Jiang Baoying as Cuihua the widow, Yang Qianquan as A Jiao

In 1930, teenage Shuisheng is brought to Shanghai to start a career with the triad employing his uncle. Shuisheng is assigned as a servant to the triad master's mistress, Xiao Jinbao, a nightclub singer. Shuisheng at first dislikes Xiao Jinbao, a temperamental woman who abuses practically everyone around her. The boy soon learns as well that Song, the master's right-hand man, is sleeping with Xiao Jinbao. When a triad war erupts, Shuisheng's uncle is killed protecting his boss. Leaving his lieutenants to run things, the boss evacuates some of his organization, including Xiao Jinbao and Shuisheng, to an island on a lake inhabited only by a young widow and her 9-year-old daughter. On the island, Xiao Jinbao, Shuisheng and the two inhabitants become friends and enjoy each other's company. Xiao Jinbao's own background is rural, she empathizes with the simple peasants and the true warmth in her character emerges. But the boss has given strict orders that anyone approaching the island is to be killed without question, so when the widow's fiance visits her from another island he is promptly dispatched. This murder infuriates Xiao Jinbao. When Song arrives from Shanghai with a group of hit men to report on developments since the master left the city, the boss discloses that he is fully aware that Song started the triad war in order to kill the boss and take over his triad, and that the evacuation to the island was just a ploy to isolate Song out of the city. He also informs his discredited lieutenant and Xiao Jinbao that he has known about their affair all along. He has the lovers buried alive, but before that offers Xiao Jinbao the one last request of the condemned: she asks that the widow and her daughter be left alone. Unfortunately, he cannot fulfill the request, as he has already had the widow killed. The next day the boss returns to Shanghai with Shuisheng (bound and gagged for trying to intervene to help Xiao Jinbao) and the little girl A Jiao, who the boss sees as the eventual replacement for Xiao Jinbao as queen of the nightclubs.

1793. *Shanghai Vacation (Shang Hai Jia Qi)*

1992. Shanghai Film Studio & Taiwan Golden Tripod Film Company Ltd. Co-Production. Letterboxed. 9 Reels. Direction: Xu Anhua. Screenplay: Wu Nianzhen. Cinematography: Li Pingbing. Art Direction: Zhang Wanhong, Qin Baisong. Music: Chen Yang. Sound: Liu Guangjie. Costume: Zhang Zhenbao. Makeup: Li Ding. Cast: Wu Ma as Gu Dade, Huang Kunxuan as Gu Ming, Liu Jialing (Carina Lau) as Yao Li

Mr. Gu, a 61-year-old retiree, leads a comfortable and happy life in Shanghai. His tranquil solitude is disrupted when his grandson Gu Ming shows up unexpectedly to spend two months with Mr. Gu while the boy's parents are at a training session in Germany. Gu Ming was born in America, and as Mr. Gu puts it, he is "too American." Not only does he have a hard time adjusting to life with his grandfather in Shanghai, he is very ill-behaved in school.

After the boy has a big fight with a classmate, the angry Mr. Gu strikes his grandson, who runs away to the countryside. There, he is taken in by an anonymous farm couple, and he learns a lot from them about Chinese ways. He returns to Shanghai. The two months pass quickly, and grandfather and grandson are close now. As Gu Ming leaves, Mr. Gu tells him that no matter where he may go or live, to never forget he is a Chinese.

1794. *Shangrao Concentration Camp (Shang Rao Ji Zhong Ying)*

1951. Shanghai Film Studio. B & W. 11 Reels. Directors: Sha Meng and Zhang Ke. Screenplay: Feng Xuefeng. Cinematography: Zhu Jinming. Art Direction: Han Xin and Cheng Bosheng. Music: He Luding. Sound: Ding Bohe. Costume: Cao Ming. Makeup: Zhu Ruiyun. Cast: Tang Huada as Zhao Hong, Jiang Jun as Lu Gong, Lu Ming as Shi Zhen, Lin Nong as Li Hua, Sheng Yang as the old professor, Zhou Liangliang as Su Lin

In January 1941, the anti–Japanese coalition breaks down when units of the Nationalist army arrest over 700 officers and soldiers of the Communist-led New Fourth Army, in what becomes known as the "Wan Nan Incident." These troops, along with nearly 300 left-wing civilians, are interned in the infamous Shangrao Concentration Camp, where they are subjected to severe mental and physical abuse, the women prisoners in particular. One captured female soldier, Shi Zhen, is severely disabled from repeated rapes, but she continues to resist. Her strength helps and encourages the weaker women, such as Su Ling, a timid elementary school teacher. A psychological tactic used by the captors is to spread false rumors in the attempt to weaken the prisoners' will. One that almost works is that Zhao Hong, one of the New Fourth Army's commanders, has confessed past errors and defected to the Nationalists. In March, 1942, as the Japanese army approaches, the entire camp is moved south in a forced march. However, when they eventually reach an area where the Communist underground is strong, the prisoners are able to make contact with CPC agents and with their help successfully rebel against the captors.

1795. *Shaolin Heroes (Shao Lin Ying Xiong)*

1993. Shanghai Film Studio. Color. Letterboxed. 9 Reels. Direction: Li Zhao, Cheng Jiaji. Screenplay: Huang Zhaoji, Luo Qi, Li Jian. Cinematography: He Ming. Art Direction: Qin Baisong. Costume: Zhang Xuelin. Makeup: Wang Zhengrong. Cast: Qian Jiale as Fang Shiyu, Lin Zhengrong as Hong Xiguan, Siqin Gaowa as Miao Cuihua, Wu Ma as Kong Yiji, Sun Guomin as Gao Jingzhong, Zeng Dan as Yueming, Yao Fengsi as Li Xiaohuan, Guan Haishan as Fang De, Chen Shaopeng as Li Bashan, Li Peiyun as Zhang Hanxiang

During the mid–18th century, Shaolin hero Hong Xiguan is wanted by the government. A senior government official, Gao Jingzhong, is ordered to kill Hong. Hong flees with help from Shaolin heroes, and he rescues Fang Shiyu. Later, Fang goes to battle Gao, but is soundly beaten. His cockiness diminished by the defeat, Fang asks Hong for another chance, and this time seriously practices kung fu. He tries a second time, and kills Gao Jingzhong.

1796. *Shaolin Temple Monk Damo (Shao Lin Da Mo)*

1990. New Film Studio, Hong Kong Weiyi Film Company Co-Production. Color. 9 Reels. Direction: Yu Jilian. Screenplay: Zhou Linsheng, Wang Xiqian. Cinematography: Wu Rongjie. Art Direction: Zhao Guohua. Music: Mu Hong, Guangming Sound Room. Cast: Wang Aishun, Liang Zhenglong, Xu Xiangdong, Xia Lirong, Cai Liming, Wang Jianli, Guo Yaping, Zhou Linsheng, Yang Si

Indian monk Damo travels to China, bringing the 1,000 Buddhist canonical texts. Dazhao Temple sends Heipao and other Hongfu monks to obtain the texts, but Damo refuses, insisting the texts must go to the Shaolin Temple. Later, Heipao leaves his own temple and becomes a wanderer. He accidentally kills Tianyu, a general of the imperial court, so he helps to raise the general's son Xiaobao and helps his widow Qiu Qing. Qiu Qing sets out on a mission of vengeance against anyone who had ever wronged her late husband, and at last comes face to face with Heipao. They fight, and Heipao gets the upper hand. Rather than double what he considers his most remorseful act, Heipao spares the woman and kills himself.

1797. *Shattered Dream at Loulang (Meng Duan Lou Lang)*

1991. Joint Company. Color. Letterboxed. 10 Reels. Direction: Zhang Zien and He Qing. Screenplay: Xu Tiansheng. Cinematography: Feng Wei, He Qing. Art Direction: Yu Maiduo. Music: Zhao Jiping. Sound: Lai Qizhen. Costume: Zhang Ningxiu, Wu Zhiping. Makeup: Yin Yufeng, Tang Zhengjie. Cast: Jia Shitou as Peng Zhongxiong, Liu Pei as Lanlan, Muhe Taer as Wen Xiaohuan, Xu Huanshan as Ma Zhankui, Kou Zhanwen as Tian Yunpeng, Xu Yaqun as Cai Yun, Tang Yuanzhi as Zhang Hanbo, Na Jiadi as Dang Qi

An old scholar devoted to the study of Chinese culture is struck down and killed by a madman. A kung fu hero sets out to bring the perpetrator to justice.

1798. *She Came from the Fog (Ta Cong Wu Zhong Lai)*

1981. Longjiang Film Studio. Color. 9 Reels. Direction: Ke Ren. Screenplay: Zhang Xiaotian. Cinematography: Fu Jincheng. Cast: Zhou Lina as Chen Rong, Guo Yiwen as Mrs. Zhang, Yi Furen as Zhao Guang, Liu Guoxiang as the director, Zhang Yuhong as Can Meili

Chen Rong is released from a labor reform farm. She swears to be a new person and starts a new life. When she arrives home, she learns her father has passed away while she was gone, and now she has no place to stay. The street security office director Mrs. Zhang helps Chen Rong get a new start in life by letting the young woman stay with her family and helping her find a job. However, Chen Rong's criminal past is still fresh in the minds of some people, and she suffers discrimination because of this. While honest people shun Chen Rong, her former criminal partners are looking for her, hoping to get her into crime again. When Chen Rong refuses to rejoin the old gang, she is framed. After a series of bad experiences, struggling with others and her own personal demons, she finally gets free and starts on a new life.

1799. *She Knocked at My Door Last Night (Bang Wan Ta Qiao Kai Wo De Men)*

1994. Changchun Film Studio. Color. Letterboxed. 9 Reels. Direction: Wang Fengkui. Screenplay: Li Yawei. Cinematography: Qian Daming. Art Direction: Liu Huanxing. Music:

Yang Yilun. Sound: Jiang Yan, Yi Zhe. Makeup: Xu Fengrong. Cast: Hou Yaohua as Zhao Da, Dongfang Wenying as Ouyang Qiongma, Qiang Yin as Wu Nazhen, Zhou Li as Ning Li, Wang Fengkui as Boss Cao, Wang Ziyang as Shaer

In one of South China's newly opened cities, an executive of a privately owned company is kidnapped just after leaving a bank. The man, Zhao Da, escapes, after which he decides he must have a bodyguard's protection. The security company he hires sends a woman, Ouyang Qiongma, to protect him. This makes his wife very jealous and unhappy. Meanwhile, Zhao Da's old girl friend, now part of a criminal gang, is assigned by her boss to rekindle the relationship as a path to the executive's money. The gang makes their move, and Ouyang outwits them. Afterwards, the executive tells Ouyang that he has fallen for her, but she informs him that she is really an undercover police officer assigned to get the gang by working through him.

1800. *She Loves Her Hometown (Ta Ai Shang Le Gu Xiang)*

1958. Changchun Film Studio. B & W. 10 Reels. Direction: Huang Shu, Zhang Qi. Screenplay: Xie Liming, based on the novel "Plant in Spring, Harvest in Fall" by Kang Qu. Cinematography: Wang Chunquan. Art Direction: Shi Weijun. Music: Li Ning. Sound: Yuan Mingda. Cast: Lin Ruwei as Liu Yuchui, Sun Heting as Zhou Canglin, Meng Zhaobo as Wang Jian, Ma Loufu as Wang Cheng, Huang Zhanying as Shanniu, Liu Zenqing as Guisheng

After an unsuccessful job search in the city, high school graduate Liu Yucui returns to the countryside but is dissatisfied with farm work, feeling it beneath her talents. She accepts the land her father had set aside for her, but lack of interest makes her a poor farmer. Youth League cadre Zhou Canglin offers to help her, and recommends her for the post of village school teacher. This helps her realize the major role educated youth can play in the countryside. She changes her previous view and comes to love her hometown. Eventually she and Zhou Canglin are married.

1801. *Sheathed Sword (Qiao Zhong Zhi Jian)*

1986. Changchun Film Studio. Color. 10 Reels. Direction: Zhu Wenshun, Luo Heling. Screenplay: Huo Da, Bei Cheng. Cinematogra-

phy: Duan Zhengjiang. Art Direction: Ji Zhiqiang. Music: Lu Shouqian. Sound: Wang Lin. Cast: Liu Boyin as Xiao Jian, Wang Huayin as Doctor Ji, Yu Liping as Liu Longquan, Ma Zheng as Xiao Hanru, Wang Runshen as Sun Ao, Zhang Baoqiu as Pan Lu

In October, 1948, Chiang Kaishek assembles his commanders to plan a major offensive against the PLA. The movie tells how CPC agent Xiao Jian coordinates with the PLA forces to smash Chiang's plans and disrupt Nationalist supply lines. Xiao Jian is also successful in persuading a Nationalist general to defect to the CPC side with his army and protect Beijing in the final battle in the north.

1802. *Sheng Xia and Her Fiance (Sheng Xia He Ta De Wei Hun Fu)*

1985. Beijing Film Studio. Color. 10 Reels. Direction: Qin Zhiyu. Screenplay: Huo Zhuang, Xu Xiaoxing. Cinematography: Liang Zhiyong. Art Direction: Fu Delin. Music: Hu Weili. Sound: Wang Dawen, Ning Menghua. Cast: Xiao Xiong as Sheng Xia, Liang Tongyu as Ke Ping, Zhao Yue as Xiao Lajiao, Hong Ying as the fat girl, Xu Xiaoxing as Qin Yuan, Ge You as Wei Xuejing

In the 1980s, a mania for self-improvement through study sweeps Beijing. Among the many caught up in this is Sheng Xia, a young woman sales clerk in a grocery market's meat department. Sheng Xia recalls how her formal education had been interrupted by the Cultural Revolution, and that when she returned from the countryside six years before she had begun studying to take the national college entrance exams. On the eve of the exams that time, Sheng Xia discovered she was pregnant. Her boyfriend Ke Ping wanted to marry immediately to keep the child, but she refused because of the upcoming exams. Ke Ping could not understand this, and broke off the relationship. Between losing Ke Ping and getting an abortion, Sheng Xia was sufficiently distracted to fail the exams. Now, six years later, she begins studying again in her spare time, finding happiness in self-improvement.

1803. *Shenlong Special Performance Team (Shen Long Te Ji Dui)*

1988. Xi'an Film Studio. Color. Letterboxed. 9 Reels. Direction: Shi Chengfeng. Screenplay: Shi Chengyuan, Shi Chengfeng. Cinematography:

Feng Wei. Art Direction: Zhang Jianmin. Music: Bi Xiaosi. Sound: Hui Dongzi. Cast: Ma Yingchun as Song Zhao, Wang Chi as Wang Qin

A special team of stuntmen and women is hired to perform a series of risky stunts for a movie. The film shows how the team, under its leader Wang Qin, works with the director and his crew to do an excellent and successful job.

1804. *Sherlock Holmes in China (Fu Er Mo Si Yu Zhong Guo Nu Xia)*

1994. Beijing Film Studio. Color (70 mm). 9 Reels. Direction: Liu Yunzhou, Wang Chi. Screenplay: Ke Zhanghe, Li Changfu, Wang Fengkui. Cinematography: Cai Huimin. Art Direction: Lin Chaoxiang. Music: Gao Erdi. Sound: Guan Jian. Costume: Jiang Jingming, Cai Jun. Makeup: Liao Ruiqing, Mu Xin. Cast: Fan Aili as Sherlock Holmes, Xiulan Limei as Furong, Wang Chi as Jin Mazhang, Zhang Chunzhong as Tu Wu, Wang Hongtao as Du Wencai, Xu Zhongquan as Watson, Hanson as Henry

Early in the 20th century, Holmes and his faithful friend Dr. Watson travel on holiday to China. They stay at a hotel run by a young woman called Furong. One of the other guests is the outgoing British Ambassador, who is escorting some Chinese treasure back to England. During the night, the ambassador is murdered. A Qing government representative asks Holmes to look into the matter, although he makes it clear his government is certain the deed was done by the Boxers, the anti–Qing and violently anti-imperialist Chinese rebels. During Holmes's investigation, he discovers that Furong is a member of the Boxers, but he also finds himself increasingly in sympathy with their cause. Holmes at last pinpoints the murderous thief, and the Boxers led by Furong set the trap which proves that guilt.

1805. *Shining Arrow (Shan Guang De Jian)*

1980. Changchun Film Studio. B & W. 10 Reels. Direction: Wang Feng. Screenplay: Jiang Junfeng, Wang Zhewei. Cinematography: Tang Yunsheng. Art Direction: Gao Guoliang, Ju Lutian. Music: Wang Zhuo, Liu Feng. Sound: Wen Liangyu. Cast: Wang Tongle as Lei Zhenghu, Wang Feng as Fang Tie, Xu Haitian as Su Feng, Tang Ke as Deputy Commander Xu, Cai Yunqin as Zhou Enlai, Zhang Yi as Mr. Wu

At the end of the 1950s, China is hit by a succession of natural disasters which seriously hurt the economy. On Taiwan, Chiang Kaishek takes advantage of the situation to send numerous U-2 high altitude spy planes over the Chinese mainland on intelligence gathering missions. Since PLA aircraft could not fly high enough to intercept them, the U-2s could make these flights unimpeded. Things change when the Soviet Union fulfills its contract to supply China with ground-to-air missiles. Division Commander Fang Tie sets up the PLA's first missile unit. Fang and his men study and master missile technology, and succeed in finally bringing down a U-2 from Taiwan. But at this point, the Russians decide to abrogate their contract to supply the missiles, which puts Fang's unit out of operation. Premier Zhou Enlai, a strong advocate of a missile program for China, visits a military weapons factory and encourages the production of Chinese-made missiles. When the Nationalist military learns the Soviet Union has withdrawn its contract, they conclude the time is ripe to attack the mainland. Premier Zhou's analysis is that Chiang wants to attack the mainland before the PRC successfully makes its first atomic bomb. He calls together a top-level meeting of China's military leaders and gets them to approve giving a high priority to building a missile defense.

1806. *Shining Knife and Tiger (Dao Guang Hu Ying)*

1982. Changchun Film Studio. Color. 9 Reels. Direction: Zhu Wenshun. Screenplay: Xue Shouxian. Cinematography: Dan Shengnima. Art Direction: Wu Qiwen, Ji Zhiqiang. Music: Zhang Jingyuan. Sound: Tong Zongde. Cast: Chen Ye as Xiao Bing, Ge Yamin as Lu Laohu, Zen Jing as Jin Yongfu, Shao Chongfei as Jin Baiwan, Li Xida as Shen Zhongshun, Lin Wumei as Fengyin

In Shandong province during World War II, female guerrilla leader Xiao Bing and greenwood heroes leader Lu Laohu combine their forces to harass and attack the Japanese and their collaborators in Qinhe County. The guerrillas learn that Feng Qiuping, daughter of a senior official in the Shandong provincial government, will be passing through Qinhe County on a trip to Tianjin and that county director Jin Baiwan, a Japanese collaborator, has been asked to entertain her when she stops over in the county. So Xiao Bing's troop abducts Feng's daughter. Xiao Bing then disguises herself as Feng Qiuping and goes to the county government to deal with Jin Baiwan and his son Jin Yongfu. Xiao Bing's objective is to free three CPC leaders being held prisoner by the Jins. Xiao Bing sets up a plan which allows her guerrillas to capture Jin Baiwan, intending to exchange him for the CPC leaders. But the plan is interrupted when Lu Laohu arrives, demanding that Jin Baiwan be turned over to him, as Lu has a personal grudge against Jin. At last, Xiao Bing leads her troops in an assault on the Jin mansion, freeing CPC Secretary Yu. Documents recovered from the mansion disclose that Xiao Bing and Lu are brother and sister. Lu now decides to join her revolutionary band.

1807. *Shiny Colorful Ball (Shan Guang De Cai Qiu)*

1982. Shanghai Film Studio. Color. 10 Reels. Direction: Song Chong. Screenplay: Song Chong, Ju Xinhua, Wang Shengrong, Zhou Yang. Cinematography: Zhang Yuanmin. Art Direction: Zhang Chongxiang. Music: Lu Qimin. Sound: Huang Dongping. Cast: Zhao Jing as Fang Hua, Ding Jiayuan as Lin Yucai, Liang Boluo as Zhou Yumin, Chen Shimin as Li Xiaochun, Shen Lan as Wang Wei, Ruan Jie as Yang Jing, Gao Bo as Professor Lu

Elementary school students Li Xiaochun, Liu Ke and Jiang Jianping are very naughty children who consistently misbehave in class. Teacher Lin Yucai, in charge of the class, believes the way to handle ill-behaved students and those with bad grades is a special class, which unfortunately hurts these student's self-esteem. Teacher Fang Hua, on the other hand, thinks this method is too simple; she treats her students with patience, encouraging them to correct their shortcomings and work with her and each other. By organizing a spring break contest, the more backward students come to realize the importance of studying hard. Fang Hua also realize the importance of improving parents' awareness in educating their kids, so she often communicates with their parents. Fang Hua's efforts show good results, and at a school-wide test of intellectual level, Li Xiaochun receives top marks.

1808. *The Ship That Mysteriously Vanished (Shen Mi De Shi Zhong De Chuan)*

1990. Beijing Film Studio. Color. Wide Screen. 9 Reels. Direction: Li Hongsheng.

Screenplay; Qi Tianfa, Dai Weiruo, Wang Taorui, Li Hongsheng. Cinematography: Hou Yuzhi. Art Direction: Qin Duo. Music: Gao Feng. Sound: Li Bojiang. Cast: Wang Qingxiang as Fang Dayu, Ju Wancheng as Lu Ping, Jiang Gengcheng as Zhu Tianlong, Gao Baobao as Haiman, Jia Yulan as Wang Bamei

In 1947, Song Qingling (Madame Sun Yat-sen) arranges for a shipment of badly needed medical supplies from a foreign country to the Chinese Communist armed forces. The ship is intercepted and hijacked by mobsters headed by Fang Dayu. As Communist agents are dispatched to search for the precious cargo, Nationalist agents kidnap Fang's son to force him to hand over the ship. The gang boss is himself captured in attempting to rescue the boy, but the Communist agents free him, one of them sacrificing his own life in the effort. Fang Dayu decides to release the medical supplies to the Red Army, then he himself leaves to join their ranks.

1809. *Shocked (Da Jing Xiao Guai)*

1989. Shenzhen Film Studio. Color. Letterboxed. 9 Reels. Direction: Zhang Gang. Screenplay: Zhang Gang. Cinematography: Meng Weiqiang. Art Direction: Wang Renling. Music: Yang Shaoyi. Sound: Zhu Yong. Cast: Ma Jingwu as Mei Aman, Mo Qi as Zhong, Gao Ying as Xiang Chunmei

Elementary school teacher Mei Aman runs into a series of problems and comic incidents while on a business trip. When the trip is over, he finds that in spite of his troubles, nothing seems to have been accomplished.

1810. *Shocked Soul at Midnight (Ye Ban Jing Hun)*

1991. Shanghai Film Studio. Color. Letterboxed. 10 Reels. Direction: Xu Jihong. Screenplay: Zhao Zhiqiang, Hu Huiying. Cinematography: Sun Guoliang. Art Direction: Zhang Chongxiang. Music: Xu Jingxin. Sound: Lu Jiajing. Cast: Ling Zhiao as Qi Yanong, Wu Jing as Shu Qianyun, Yang Kun as Qi Rongrong, Zhou Yemang as Liao Muren, Huang Daliang as Yan Jiren

Professor Qi Yanong owns a precious stamp, the "Great Dragon," issued in 1878. His wife, daughter, son-in-law and friends all show considerable interest in it. The professor knows he has terminal cancer, so he intends to sell the stamp and use the money to provide for the future care of his retarded son by his first wife. He begins receiving anonymous calls attempting to blackmail him, his will disappears and then his retarded son is abducted. Detectives investigating the case at last determine that the villains are Professor Qi's wife Shu Qianyun and editor Yan Jiren. They knew that the stamp had actually belonged to the professor's teacher, who had intended for it to be turned over to the country. At last, Professor Qi turns in the stamp, and his retarded son happily enters a nursing home.

1811. *Silent Ice Mountain (Chen Mu De Bing Shan)*

1986. August First Film Studio. Color. 9 Reels. Direction: Zhang Yongshou. Screenplay: Tang Dong. Cinematography: Ding Shanfa. Art Direction: Zhao Changsheng. Music: Lu Yuan. Sound: Sun Juzhen. Cast: Zhang Chao as Yang Fu, Gu Yan as Gaigai, Han Xing as Ju Yin

When Yang Fu was a soldier, he never had time to care properly for his wife and child. When famine swept the harsh plateau where he was stationed, his family left home to look for food and never came back. After he is involuntarily retired from the army during a reduction in force, he finds work near his old base raising sheep for mutton which he sells to the army. One day he meets Gaigai, a young widow who similarly has nowhere else to go, and they get married. She helps him with his business, and before long the couple is expecting a baby. But while making a special meat delivery to the army base at Chinese New Year's, Gaigai is fatally buried in a snowslide. Yang Fu looks back at his unhappy life and decides he will stay on the plateau, although it is to blame for so much of his misery.

1812. *A Silent Place (Yu Wu Sheng Chu)*

1979. Shanghai Film Studio. 10 Reels. Direction: Lu Ren. Screenplay: Zong Fuxian. Cinematography: Zhang Yuanming, Ji Hongsheng. Art Direction: Zhong Yongqin. Music: Lu Qiming. Sound: Feng Deyao. Cast: Zhang Xiaozhong as Ouyang Ping, Yang Baoling as Mei Lin, Zhu Yuwen as He Yun, Feng Guangquan as He Wei, Pan Lijuan as Liu Xiuyin, Zhao Shusheng as He Shifei

In 1976, as veteran cadre Mei Lin and her son Ouyang Ping pass through Shanghai, they pay a call at the home of old military comrade He Shifei, whom they have not seen for nine years. He Shifei had some time before become a "Gang of Four" follower in order to further his political career, and had accused Mei Lin of treason. So He Shifei is not at all pleased about Mei Lin and her son's arrival. He's daughter He Yun is very attracted to Ouyang Ping, so when she learns that he is a nationally wanted fugitive for having participated in the January, 1976 demonstration at Tiananmen, she is very unhappy. He Shifei reports Ouyang Ping's whereabouts to the "Gang of Four." Mei Lin, who is suffering from terminal cancer, urges her son to continue to struggle with the enemy in court and in jail. He Shifei's wife Liu Xiuyin, who has suffered for years with the knowledge that her husband has falsely accused Mei Lin of treason, now steps forward to expose her husband, and He Yun also breaks with her father when the police come to arrest Ouyang Ping. In the end, the degenerate He Shifei is alone, when both his wife and his son He Wei leave him, vowing to smash the machinations of all Gang of Four followers.

1813. *Silent Xiaoli River (Mu Mu De Xiao Li He)*

1984. Xi'an Film Studio. Color. Letterboxed. 9 Reels. Direction: Zhang Zhien. Screenplay: Zhang Zhiliang. Cinematography: Zhu Dingyu. Art Direction: Zhang Zhien. Music: Xu Youfu. Sound: Gu Changning. Cast: Jia Liu as Grandpa, Chen Baoguo as Military Officer, Ding Weiming as Grandma, Yang Lili as the woman soldier, Shi Xiaolong as "Dog"

In the fall of 1947, along the Xiaoli River in North Shanxi, most of the people flee the village of Qinshimao as warlord General Hu Zongnan's army moves into the area. Only one family stays. One day, some of Hu's troops enter the village to set up a communications station. Grandpa, the patriarch of the family that remained, uses his son and grandson as liaisons to a guerrilla band in the area, and coordinates a successful guerrilla attack on the warlord troops.

1814. *A Silkworm-Raising Girl (Can Hua Guniang)*

1963. Tianma Film Studio. B & W. 11 Reels. Direction: Ye Ming. Screenplay: Gu Xidong. Cinematography: Lu Junfu. Art Direction: He Ruiji. Music: Huang Zhun. Sound: Gong Jianqing. Cast: You Jia as Tao Xiaoping, Zhu Manfang as Liu Qiaolian, Yu Guichun as Tao Jiulong,

Xie Yibing as Tao Liusheng, Jiang Shan as Grandpa, Cheng Zhi as Tao Laowu, Wu Yunfang as Xiaomei, Feng Ji as the director

In South China, young girl Tao Xiaoping has little interest in raising silkworms, the staple of her village's economy. Instead, she dreams of becoming an actress. Her sister-in-law Liu Qiaolian has learned to raise silkworms, and steadily improved her skills by diligent study. With Qiaolian's help, Xiaoping also begins to learn, changing people's view of her. But one night, she neglects her silkworms to watch a performance, and some of the silkworms die. When she is criticized for this, she angrily leaves the countryside and goes to the nearby town, where her classmate Xiaomei is now an actress in a performing troupe. She hopes Xiaomei will help her become an actress. But she witnesses an argument between Xiaomei and the troupe director over the size of a role in a play, and this awakens her some to the realities of life on the stage. Qiaolian arrives to visit her at this time, and moved by her sister-in-law's care for her, Xiaoping changes her mind, deciding to become a silkworm-raising country girl.

1815. *The Silly Boy and the Pretty Girl (Chi Nan Jing Nu)*

1992. Pearl River Film Studio. Color. Letterboxed. 9 Reels. Direction: Cao Zheng. Screenplay: Lin Xitian, Li Yunliang. Cinematography: Luo Yan. Art Direction: Tu Bengyang, Feng Zhili. Music: Fang Zhidan. Sound: Huang Mingguang, Pu Xiaonan. Costume: Li Changzhao. Makeup: Wang Lingzhi. Cast: Bai Chongxin, Tian Xiaohong

One day when shopping in Guangzhou's Duomeng Furniture Store, Wan Jialong falls for salesgirl Fang Ye. But on their first date, his clowning around and joking turns her off, not realizing this is the young man's way of masking his basic shyness. Later, Wan is cheated by another store, and sets out to expose counterfeit furniture activities in Guangzhou. His successful efforts are acknowledged by the Duomeng store, and wins him Fang Ye.

1816. *Silver Flowers in Blue Sky (Bi Kong Yin Hua)*

1960. Xi'an Film Studio. Color. 9 Reels. Direction: Sang Fu. Screenplay: Han Guang. Cinematography: Yu Shuzhao. Art Direction: Tian Shizhen. Music: Li Yaodong. Sound: Chen

Yudan. Cast: Lu Rongming as Bai Ying, Wang Fang as Lin Ping, Shen Rongping as Huang Xiaoyun, Zhen Danian as Director Liu, Li Sirong as Yu Shaofeng, Zhao Jianyin as Yan Cheng

For varying reasons, several young women including Bai Ying, a student at a normal university, and machine shop worker Lin Ping, sign up to learn parachute jumping in their spare time. Bai Ying wants instant success, so while she relishes the compliments of the other students, Lin Ping's well-intended constructive criticism makes her unhappy. She misunderstands, thinking Lin wants to outdo her. But later, when the group is involved in prairie fire rescue work, the two women's parachute cords become entangled in midair; to save Bai Ying's life, Lin Ping cuts her own cords and falls into the prairie fire. From this incident, Bai Ying realizes Lin Ping's nature, and in deep regret determines to build a sincere friendship with the other woman. Later, the two jointly set a new world's record for women parachutists.

1817. *The Silver Snake Murder Case (Yin She Mou Sha An)*

1988. Beijing Film Studio. Color. 9 Reels. Direction: Li Shaohong. Screenplay: Hu Bing. Cinematography: Zen Nianping. Art Direction: Shi Jiandu. Music: Gu De. Sound: Zhang Ye. Cast: Jia Hongsheng as Hao Feiyu, Li Qingqing as Qiao Meilun, Gao Baobao as Qiao Meihuan, Zang Jingsheng as Shi Hengshan, Wang Jiancheng as Zhong Dazhong, Zhang Jingsheng as Wen Yinghua, Zhu Xiaoming as Kong Xiangxiong

Motion picture theater worker Hao Feiyu is a homicidal maniac: he spies on young girls through a high-powered telescope, then lures them to remote places and kills them with poisonous snakes. While looking through his telescope one day, Hao Feiyu accidentally observes photographer Kong Xiangxiong taking repeated pictures of a bank's entire activities. When the bank is robbed a few days later, Hao Feiyu believes this is his chance to make a big score by blackmailing the photographer. He then learns that the bank president Shi Hengshan is having an affair with Qiao Meihuan, the girlfriend of the chief robber Zhong Dazhong. Hao Feiyu cannot pass up the opportunity to indulge his murderous passion, so he successfully lures Qiao Meihuan to a remote spot and kills her. Meihuan's sister Meilun decides to investigate the case on her own. The climax comes with the bank president killed by the robbers and Meilun driven mad. At last, all the criminals are rounded up by the PSB. Cornered, the insane Hao Feiyu takes his own life.

1818. *A Single Woman (Du Shen Nu Ren)*

1991. Beijing Film Studio. Color. 10 Reels. Direction: Qin Zhiyu. Screenplay: Zhang Xuan, Ni Zhen and Qin Zhiyu. Cinematography: Ru Shuiren. Art Direction: Hao Jingyuan and Qin Duo. Music: Guan Xia. Sound: Wang Dawen. Cast: Pan Hong as Ouyang Ruoyun, Chen Xiguang as Qi Fang, Jiang Shan as Shu Lei, Huang Xiaolei as Li Zhiliang, Yang Ren as Wei Li

Vice-president and chief designer for the Helena Fashion Company, a Sino-American joint venture, Ouyang Ruoyun is a beautiful, middle-aged divorcee with a five-year-old son. She has several suitors, including the chief editor of a newspaper, her assistant Li Zhiliang and the company's American chief executive. In the summer of 1989, the clothing market grows sluggish, and the firm's future is clouded. At this time, Ouyang happens to meet Qi Fang, a middle-aged economist whose wife is divorcing him. He is later instrumental in Ouyang's securing financing for her new clothing line, and the two eventually fall in love. Their relationship is complicated, however, by her past, her feelings about being single, and Qi Fang's ex-wife continuing to show up in his life. Ouyang's clothing line is a big success, the company's fortunes improve, and Ouyang and Qi Fang work out their problems. They plan to marry, but he is killed resisting some carjackers on the road. Ouyang will continue to be a single woman.

1819. *Sink or Swim (Gu Zhu Yi Zhi)*

1992. Changchun Film Studio. Color. Letterboxed. 9 Reels. Direction: Xu Shutian. Screenplay: Liang Guowei, Pu Shulin. Cinematography: Zhang Shaoge, Yue Yang. Art Direction: Wang Jiru, Meng Xiangchun. Music: Chen Shouqian. Sound: Sheng Hongtao, Gu Kejian. Costume: Zhou Xingguo. Makeup: Li Chunhai, Sheng Libo. Cast: Chou Xiaoguang as Chen Jianxiong, Zhang Jing as Su Shan, Chen Xuegang as Xie Fei, Wang Gang as Huangwei Yilang, Liu Weihua as the police chief

In the Northeast China city of Harbin, police officer Chen Jianxiong, a member of the Communist underground, runs into a woman he had once known as Su Shan. However, she refuses to acknowledge that identity. Later, Chen finds records which state Su Shan was executed some time before. He decides to investigate, and learns that Su Shan is the daughter of a Japanese general and his Chinese mistress; now, she is being used by Nationalist intelligence chief Xie Fei as go-between in a deal to exchange military supplies for the diary of a Chinese Volunteer Army general which Xie Fei possesses. Acting on orders from the Communist Party, Chen kills Su Shan, detains the military supplies and recovers the diary.

1820. *Sino-Russian Railway Robbery Case (Zhong E Lie Che Da Jie An)*

1995. Emei Film Studio. Color. Letterboxed. Direction: Mai Dangjie. Screenplay: Ai Anxue, Yang Haibo. Cinematography: Zhao Lei. Art Direction: Xia Nan. Music: Liu Zupei. Cast: Lu Liangwei as Xiang Chong, Lu Simai as Natasha, Zhou Hong as Lin Nan, Lu Fang as second sister

After 1989, many Chinese businessmen travel to the former Soviet Union to sell their goods, and the 9,500-kilometer Sino-Russian railway becomes very busy. Crime on the railway grows as well, with frequent incidents of robbery, rape and even murder. Chinese public security forces put officers on the trains to Moscow, fight crime on the train and trace the organized criminals to their source.

1821. *Sins in the Wutai Mountains (Wu Tai Shan Qi Qing)*

1989. Beijing Film Studio. Color. 10 Reels. Direction: Zhang Huaxun. Screenplay: Yang Maolin, Yang Shiwen. Cinematography: Zhang Zhongping. Art Direction: Wang Jixian. Music: Lei Lei. Sound: Zhang Baojian. Cast: Dong Honglin as Qu Fengwu, Wang Jianjun as Yuankong, Lu Li as Meizhen, Jiang Gengchen as Sima Zhen

On a tour of Mount Wutai — sacred to Buddhists — Qing Emperor Kangxi (r.1662–1723) fathers an illegitimate son by Meizhen, a peasant girl. In an outrage, Meizhen's lover Qu Fengwu mutilates the baby's testicles. The boy, named Long'er, becomes a monk and changes his name to Yuankong. Some 20 years later Kangxi grants him the title "Honored Monk," and he becomes a powerful figure among the Buddhists in the area around Wutai. After a time, the area is plagued by someone called the

"Black Dragon"; he always appears on wedding nights, violating the brides and castrating the grooms. By now Kangxi has died, and his successor the Emperor Yongzheng appoints Sima Zhen as imperial minister with authority to investigate the case. Sima Zhen recruits the assistance of Qu Fengwu, now a kung fu master, and after many dangerous encounters, Sima Zhen finally learns that the "Black Dragon" is none other than the crazed Yuankong. Pursued by government soldiers, Yuankong jumps from a cliff to his death. His mother, Meizhen, then commits suicide in despair. Meritorious minister Sima Zhen is rewarded for his diligence by being poisoned by Emperor Yongzheng. Qu Fengwu, who has never ceased to love Meizhen, leaves his home and becomes a monk.

1822. *Sins of Revival (Fu Huo De Zui E)*

1994. Changchun Film Studio. Color. Letterboxed. 9 Reels. Direction: Zhao Weiheng. Screenplay: Liang Guowei. Cinematography: Yu Bing, Su Zaidong, Sun Shengguang. Art Direction: Liu Hong. Music: Guo Xiaotian. Sound: Sheng Hongtao. Costume: Chen Hua. Makeup: Tan Shumei. Cast: Zhou Lijing as Tang Dalong, Cao Xi as Yanzi, Lin Zi as Zhang Lili, Gao Qiang as Zhang Baoshan, Yan Shuqin as Li Yuemei, Dong Guoguang as Yan Laoda, Fan Yanli as Liu Xiuyun, Song Xuejuan as Grandma, Wu Jiazhao as Liu Wenshu

Young and pretty Liu Xiuyun and her sister Yanzi are abducted by a gang led by Yan Laoda. Yanzi gets away and frantically searches for help. She meets Tang, a military officer changing trains in that city, and tells him the story. Before she had escaped, Yanzi received from her sister a message telling her where she was to be taken. The officer and the girl travel there, and on the bus meet Zhang Lili, an woman undercover police officer tracking traffickers in humans. Working with local police, they are able to smash the gang, and identify the head of the gang as a woman, Li Yuemei. They arrive too late to save Yanzi's sister Xiuyun, however.

1823. *Sister (Jie Jie)*

1984. Shanghai Film Studio. Color. Wide Screen. 10 Reels. Direction: Wu Yigong. Screenplay: Ye Nan. Cinematography: Cao Weiye. Art Direction: Huang Qiagui. Music: Yang Mao. Sound: Miao Zhenyu, Wang Huimin. Cast: Song Chunli as Sister, Chen Hong as the young sol-

dier, Wang Zhixia as the little girl, Shi Shugui as the old nun

On March 9 and 10, 1937, the Red Army in Gansu province is engaged in a major battle with the forces of Nationalist warlords Ma Bufang and Ma Buqing. Hopelessly outnumbered, the Communists are overwhelmed and nearly wiped out. One of the survivors, a girl soldier called Sister, flees on foot through the brush along Gansu's Xihe Corridor. She comes upon a young soldier lying in the brush, unconscious but still alive. She saves his life, and when he is able to travel the two travel north in search of the Communists' headquarters in North Shanxi. They meet a young girl of the Yugu nationality, and she joins them. The young soldier goes out looking for food and is killed. Sister had been slightly wounded in the battle, and the harsh journey has worsened her condition. Now, physically exhausted and unable to go any further, she lies down and dies. The young girl buries her, then continues northward in search of Communist headquarters.

1824. *Sister and Brother in the Remote Mountains (Yuan Shan Jie Di)*

1993. Hebei Film Studio & Changchun Film Studio Co-Production. Color. Letterboxed. 9 Reels. Direction: Chen Li, Ma Shuchao. Screenplay: Shen Xiaowen, Ma Shen. Cinematography: Cheng Shengsheng. Art Direction: Jiao Zhenqi, Hao Hongji. Music: Cong Ge. Sound: Liu Shida, Zhang Chaojia, Su Xiaorui. Costume: Jia Xiangju. Makeup: Cheng Rong. Cast: Zhou Mingming as Xiuxiu, Chen Si as Dandan, Li Yunjie as Xiuxiu's mother, Wu Ruopu as Teacher Chen, Yu Wenzhong as Grandpa Jiefang

In a small, backward mountain village, a widow struggles to raise her two children alone. Her husband had received a good education, but died young. Now the woman and her daughter Xiuxiu put everything they have into supporting her son Dandan at school. Unfortunately, Dandan has little interest in studies. Conversely, his sister Xiuxiu loves to study, but the mother ignores the little girl's frequent requests for an education. The little girl studies in secret. When the mother falls ill, news arrives that the provincial newspaper has published an article Xiuxiu has written.

1825. *Sister Enemies (Jie Mei Qing Chou)*

1990. Xi'an Film Studio. Color. 9 Reels. Direction: Zhu Jianxin. Screenplay: Liu Rong, Yu Qinquan. Cinematography: Wang Xiaomin. Art Direction: Dou Guoxiang. Music: Li Yaodong. Sound: Gu Changning. Cast: Chen Yi as Gu Yuzhi, He Qing as Gu Yuqian, Wang Zhengjun as Huang Zhinong

In 1941, at China's wartime capital of Chongqing, famous Chinese entrepreneur Gu Bingxun is murdered outside of the National Bank. After this incident, his daughters Gu Yuzhi and Gu Yuqian have a falling out and become enemies. Yuzhi joins the Communist Party and Yuqian becomes a Nationalist government spy. They contend for possession of telecommunications equipment. At last, Yuqian is killed by the Communists. Yuzhi buries her sister and allows herself a little time to grieve. Then she returns to her duties.

1826. *Sisters on Ice (Bing Shang Jie Mei)*

1959. Changchun Film Studio. Color. 11 Reels. Direction: Wu Zhaodi. Screenplay: Wu Zhaodi, Fang Youliang. Cinematography: Su Xiaoyan. Art Direction: Wang Chong. Music: Quan Rufeng. Sound: Sheng Guli. Cast: Lu Guilan as Ding Suping, Yu Zhongjing as Yu Liping, Yang Huang as Wang Dongyan, Li Yalin as Coach Chen, Bai Dezhang as Wang Dongzhou, Lin Ying as Li Xiaoling, Qin Han as Luo Lin, Wang Yansheng as the Mayor, Zhang Juguang as the workshop boss, Zhou Wenbin as the doctor, Zhang Wei as Ding's mother

One winter in a Northeast China city, Ding Suping, a new competitor in the women's figure skating provincial championships, wins a surprising victory over long-time champion Wang Dongyan. In her spare time, Ding Suping is an active and enthusiastic coach of younger girls, and one of her best students is high school student Yu Liping. However, her rapid success under Ding's instruction swells Yu's ego, and when the coach criticizes her one day, she quits the training class. In an accident during mountain climbing training, Ding Suping saves Wang Dongyan, but breaks her own leg in doing so. Yu Liping is deeply moved by this, and goes to the coastal resort where Ding is recuperating, to criticize herself before her former coach. At the resort, Ding Suping has met and fallen in love with a singer named Luo Lin who is appearing there, but when Luo

meets Yu Liping, he instantly falls for her. Seeing how he feels, Ding decides to get Luo and Yu together. But when she learns this, Yu Liping breaks off with Luo Lin and leaves. After Ding Suping returns from the resort, she brings about a reconciliation of Yu and Luo. Later, Ding Suping and Wang Dongyuan's brother fall in love. One year later, Ding Suping, Yu Liping and Wang Dongyan all participate in the national skating championships. Wang Dongyan sets a national record, but Ding and Yu both surpass her record and become national champions.

1827. *Sisters Stand Up (Jie Jie Mei Mei Zhan Qi Lai)*

1951. Wenhua Film Company. B & W. 10 Reels. Direction: Chen Xihe. Screenplay: Chen Xihe. Cinematography: Ge Weiqin. Set Design: Wang Yuebai. Music: Huang Yijun. Sound: Zhu Weigang. Costume: Qi Qiumin, Ma Hongxiang. Makeup: Ni Yifei. Cast: Li Meng as Da Xiang, Liang Ming as Tongli's wife, Li Wei as Shang Youlin, Shi Hui as Ma San, Li Linyun as Yanzhihu, Cui Chaoming as Cui Huzhi, Tian Taixuan as Aunt Sun

In the fall of 1947, in a suburb of Beijing, a woman known as Tongli's wife loses her livelihood when her husband is worked to death by his landlord. She and her daughter Daxiang go to live in the city with the mother's Aunt Sun, a laundress. In time, Daxiang falls in love with their neighbor Shang Youlin. But the aunt, abetting a gangster named Ma San, sells the girl to a house of prostitution, where she is treated cruelly. When a government inspector comes, she pleads that she is being held against her will, but the inspector accepts a bribe to not report it. In despair over her daughter's fate and the official corruption which keeps her there, the mother commits suicide. When Youlin attempts to buy Daxiang out, he is brutally beaten. After the liberation of Beijing, the new government closes all the whorehouses. Ma San and Aunt Sun are punished. Daxiang and the other prostitutes are freed, sent for vocational and political training, and are given productive work and new lives.

1828. *The Six Jin County Director (Liu Jin Xian Zhang)*

1983. Xi'an Film Studio. Color. 9 Reels. Direction: Guo Yangting. Screenplay: Chen Zhengqin, Tian Jingzhi. Cinematography: Zhang

Faliang. Art Direction: Zhang Xiaohui. Music: Li Yuedong. Sound: Dang Chunzhu. Cast: Cao Jingyang as Niu Lichun, Lei Fei as Director Xiong, Hui Songwang as Director Ji, Lu Yang as Nan Shanxiu, Si Yin as Nan's wife, Wang Jianjun as Gao Xiaomin, Wang Fang as Zhu Mudan

During the Cultural Revolution, the people living in the Shangluo Mountains of Shanxi have a very hard life. Their only subsistence is a monthly government handout of six jin (about three kilograms) of food per month. The people refer to county administrator Niu Lichun as the "Six Jin Administrator." Niu's dream is that to someday supply each person in his district with 60 jin of food a month. His hope is fulfilled after the 3rd Plenary Session of the 11th Party Congress, but he soon finds that while life is much better for the majority of the people, there are still a few farm families living in poverty. The story concentrates on how he helps improve the lot of the Nan family. At the end, the Nans have a prosperous chicken-raising business, a new home, a married daughter, and everyone happy.

1829. *The Slave's Daughter (Nu Li De Nu Er)*

1978. Emei Film Studio. Color. 10 Reels. Direction: Zeng Weizhi. Screenplay: Chun Ding, Yuan Shijin. Cinematography: Li Dagui. Art Direction: Li Fan. Music: Zhang Chun. Sound: Shen Guli. Cast: Pan Hong as Hailai Wujia, Tian Hua as Zeng Zhihua, Wu Yang as Grandpa Guer, Liu Yiman as Captain Tian, Ju Cunyuan as Hailai Waha, Ding Ni as Shama Muluo

Female slave Hailai Wujia is sold into the household of Luohong Dashi, the man who had killed her father 20 years before after a slave rebellion. Wujia in turn helps some other women slaves to escape, and for this is condemned to death and thrown into a holding cell to await execution. Before this takes place, however, she is rescued by a PLA "Democracy Reform" work team, and she leaves with them to join in their work. When the democracy reform movement expands, Wujia is put in charge of the reform in her village. She faces many obstacles, notably the low class awareness of village people who do not understand the reform, and the former slave owners who have lost power. Wujia finally overcomes all these obstacles and wins the support of the people.

1830. *The Slipped Girl (Tou Du De Nu Ren)*

1994. Youth Film Studio. Color. Letterboxed. 9 Reels. Direction: Xue Yandong. Screenplay: Wang Chen. Cinematography: Gao Hongbao. Art Direction: Yi Zhenzhou. Music: Yang Yilun. Sound: Sheng Hongtao. Costume: An Lixin. Makeup: Song Yingyuan. Cast: Shi Ke as Chen Fang, Ju Naishe as Ma Tou, Huang Xia as Liu Yiyi, Chen Yi as Rou Si, Liu Jun as Wu Fan, Wang Xinjian as brother Rong, Hou Tianlai as "Glasses," Wu Kejian as Baoluo

Acting on information that a ring smuggling people across the border may be operating out of a prison, policewoman Chen Fang goes under cover as a prisoner. Inside, she gets to know another prisoner Ding Hong, who indicates she is involved in the smuggling. To infiltrate the smugglers, Chen Fang helps the other woman break out of prison. They arrive at a boat filled with women trying to get out of the country. A former classmate, Ma Tou, is also on the boat and recognizes Chen Fang. A bitter fight ensues, and Chen Fang kills all the criminals, including her old classmate Ma Tou, who refuses to surrender.

1831. *The Slipway Struggle (Zhan Chuan Tai)*

1975. Shanghai Film Studio. Color. 10 Reels. Direction: Fu Chaowu. Screenplay: Du Zhiqiu, Liu Shizheng, Wang Gongxu and Ye Dan, based on the Shanghai Dramatic Company's stage play of the same title. Cinematography: Luo Chongzhou, Peng Enli. Art Direction: Han Shangyi. Music: Lu Qimin, Liu Yanxi. Cast: Wang Zhengjiang as Lei Zhengsheng, Guo Diancang as Wang Dachuan, Lou Jicheng as Zhao Ping, Ling Zhiao as Zhou Peixin, Zhang Yan as Shen Lingdi, Qiu Shide as Gao Weizhou

In the early 1970s, inspired by the spirit of the Ninth Party Congress, Lei Haisheng, a Dajiang Ship Manufacturing Company worker, proposes the company build a 10,000-ton ship. He has the support of the Party and all factory workers. However, the counterrevolutionary Dong Yiwen comes up with another plan, which although inferior to Lei's plan is accepted by Dong's exploitation of plant director Zhao Ping's conservatism. The Party committee ultimately overrules Zhao, and adopts Lei's proposal. When the ship is close to completion, Dong Yiwen tries to sabotage it, while spreading rumors which cast blame on technician Gao Weizhou, a strong ally of Lei

Haisheng. But Lei presents evidence of Dong's criminal actions. Zhao Ping also realizes his mistakes. From this struggle China's first 10,000-ton class ship is finally built on the plant's small slipway.

1832. *A Small Boat (Yi Ye Xiao Zhou)*

1983. Beijing Film Studio. Color. 9 Reels. Direction: Huang Jianzhong, Yu Zhongyi. Screenplay: Song Ci, Su Shuyang. Cinematography: Gao Lixian. Art Direction: Zhong Ling, Shao Ruigang. Music: Wang Xiling. Sound: Zhen Chunyu. Cast: Zhao Erkang as He Ming, Chen Zhurong as A Feng, Li Xiang as Zhou Datian, Xie Gang as Bingcang, Yu Zhongyi as Director Yu, Wang Biao as culture station director Wang

He Ming and his wife A Feng are a comfortably retired middle-age couple. He Ming had served three separate terms as Party Secretary of his production unit, and three times he had been brought down by political campaigns. He still carries the "rightist" label from one of these campaigns. Unexpectedly, he is called out of retirement by their commune's Party Committee, and appointed manager of the local theater. His previous label is erased, and he starts with a clean slate. All does not go well, however, and soon the old political charges resurface. A Feng's dreams of a peaceful retirement seem shattered, but she sticks with her husband in his efforts to ride out the political storms.

1833. *A Small Hotel in an Isolated Range (Gu Ling Ye Dian)*

1988. Emei Film Studio. Color. Letterboxed. 9 Reels. Direction: Xiang Lin. Screenplay: Liang Husheng. Cinematography: Mai Suhuan. Art Direction: Chen Desheng. Music: Tang Qinshi. Sound: Lin Bingcheng. Cast: Tian Zhonghe as the purchasing agent, Qinmei Duoji as Baqin, Wang Yue as the salesman, Ma Fang as Zhizi, Ao Lu as the prisoner, Xu Zhizhen as Xiao Du

In a remote mountainous area, young widow Zhizi runs the small "Guyanling Hotel." The lonely woman's best friend is Baqin, an old woodsman who had been a close friend of Zhizi's late husband. He helps her as much as he can and watches over her. One day, a group of tourists arrives at the hotel, and hidden among them is a desperate fugitive. When the fugitive is later exposed, the tourist group is endangered, but Baqin bravely rescues

them despite being wounded in the struggle. Village businessman Juexi, who had been in love with Zhizi loses her affection because of his cowardice when the fight began. In the end, the tourists leave the hotel, taking the fugitive back to justice and Baqin to the hospital.

1834. *Small Road (Xiao Lu)*

1981. Jiangsu Film Studio. Color. 10 Reels. Direction: Jin Jiwu, Feng Ji. Screenplay: Ge Xiaoyin, Jin Jiwu, Feng Ji. Cinematography: Luo Yong. Art Direction: Yue Rongfa, Xiao Feng. Music: Wang Ming, Guo Chengzhi. Sound: Qian Youshan. Cast: Zhang Hui as Teacher Yu, Zhang Qin as Teacher Zhou, Shen Zhimei as Teacher Lin, Yang Xiaodan as Ye Ao, Liang Baoqin as the teenaged Ye Ao

A young man named Ye Ao is helped in life by three teachers. In childhood, Teacher Lin gets him to open his heart and mind; during the Cultural Revolution, Ye Ao wandered through life like a rudderless boat, but Teacher Zhou provided him with guidance to find his life's direction; in his youth, a most painful and difficult time for him, it was Teacher Yu's friendship and support that get him through and enable him to move forward.

1835. *Smile of an Unhappy Man (Ku Nao Ren De Xiao)*

1979. Shanghai Film Studio. Color. 9 Reels. Direction: Yang Yanjing, Deng Yimin. Screenplay: Yang Yanjing, Xue Jing. Cinematography: Yin Fukang, Zhen Hong. Art Direction: Xu Jian, Mei Kunping. Music: Xu Jingxin. Sound: Lin Bingsheng. Cast: Li Zhiyu as Fu Bing, Pan Hong as his wife, Long Fei as his daughter, Shi Jiufeng as Reporter Li, Yuan Yue as Secretary Song, Cheng Zhi as the chief editor, Bai Mu as the old professor, Qiao Qi as old reporter, Qin Yi as the actress, Fu Hengzhi as the chief researcher, Qiu Shisui as the doctor

The winter of 1975 is a very difficult time for honest people with a sense of justice, with Premier Zhou dead and the "Gang of Four" in control. Newspaperman Fu Bing is one of these frustrated people: he cannot tell the whole truth, but neither does he want to lie. One day, his chief editor sends him to a medical school to interview a research professor who has been in opposition to the Gang's "counterattack revisionism" movement. When Fu sees how the old professor has suffered for his beliefs, he wants to write down the whole

Smile of an Unhappy Man. **Arrested for writing about the Gang of Four's crimes, journalist Fu Bing (Li Zhiyu) is seen off to jail by his wife (Pan Hong) and daughter (Long Fei). 1979. Shanghai Film Studio.**

story, but he worries about the hardship this could bring to his wife and family. His internal conflicts cause him so much agony that for the first time ever, he calls in sick, that he cannot write the article. However, the chief editor and Party Secretary Song perceive what is really going on. Finally, Fu Bing can bear no more, and he speaks out about the crimes of the Gang. Fu Bing is arrested but he believes that his suffering will not be long term, that there will a brighter future lies ahead.

1836. *The Snake Case (She An)*

1983. Emei Film Studio. Color. 9 Reels. Direction: Hao Weiguang, Wang Hongtao. Screenplay: Wang Jiaming. Cinematography: Hong Wenyuan. Art Direction: Wu Xujin. Music: Zhao Yulong. Sound: Peng Wenguang. Cast: Wu Xiqian as Hai Yang, Sun Bing as Lin Yingsheng, Li Ping as Jin Fengming, Zhang Bei as Lin Jinsheng, Tu Zhongru as Zhang Balian, Liu Boyin as Shi Xiulin

In Chunchen City, 68 precious antiques are stolen, including an extremely valuable pot in the form of an animal. Chief Investigator Hai Yang with his assistants Jin Fengming and Shi Xiulin go immediately into action to look into the matter. They find plenty of leads, but they either appear to be unconnected, or turn out to be false. Suspicion finally turns to Lin Yingsheng, seemingly a simple and honest driver for the Foreign Trade Bureau. When the investigation gets too close, Lin turns violent. After a battle the police recover the national treasures and capture Lin and his foreign accomplice.

1837. *Snow in a Mountain City (Shan Cheng Xue)*

1980. Emei Film Studio. Color. 9 Reels. Direction: Qian Qianli. Screenplay: Yan Yi. Cinematography: Hong Wenyuan. Art Direction: Chen Zhenghai. Music: Chang Sumin, Tao Jiazhou. Sound: Shen Guli. Cast: Wu Gang as Zhou Enlai, Xiang Lei as He Yinqin, Zhao Ge as Zhao Renhuan, Wu Dairao as Zhoye Erlang, Tu Zhongru as Zhong Zhi, Xiang Zhili as Captain Guan

In 1940, scientist Zhao Renhuan returns from abroad to help China resist Japanese aggression. Frustrated at the Nationalist government's corruption and collaboration with the invaders, he tries to commit suicide, but is rescued. Hearing the news, Communist Party Deputy Chairman Zhou Enlai decides this tragic incident might be used in the campaign to save China. He has the news published in the New China Daily, giving it wide dissemination, and he himself tries to help Western reporters understand the true nature of the anti–Japanese campaign by exposing the collaborationist nature of the Nationalist government. Zhao Renhuan begins to see hope for the nation. Chiang Kaishek creates the "Wannan Incident" in which New Fourth Army General Ye Ting is abducted and many of his troops are murdered. Zhou Enlai is outraged at this, and criticizes the Nationalist government publicly for it. The New China Daily publishes the truth about the incident. Japanese collaborator He Yinqin instructs a spy to assassinate Zhou, but a loyal soldier named Zhong Zhi sacrifices his own life to protect the Chinese leader.

1838. *Snowflake and Ball (Xue Hua He Li Zi Qiu)*

1980. Shanghai Film Studio. Color. 4 Reels. Direction: Yu Jie. Screenplay: Shao Hongda, Yu Jie. Cinematography: Tang Shibao, Wu Dewei. Art Direction: Chen Fuxing. Music: Wang Qiang. Sound: Tang Shibao, Wu Dewei. Cast: Gu Yelu as Director Wen, Gu Langhui as Committee Member Chen, Qi Yong as Yan Bao, Liu Tielei as Xiao Hong

In 1976, the Luocheng Animal Performance Troupe comes to Beizhou City to perform and is a great success. At the same time, the Beizhou City Dramatic Troupe's stage play "Song of Occupation," specially written to support the Gang of Four, is a horrible flop. Beizhou's Revolutionary Committee member Chen and its Bureau of Culture Director Wen are angry and jealous, and decide to destroy the animal troupe. One night, when Snowflake, a white dog, and Ball, a black bear, are performing, Chen abruptly has the theater's electric power cut off. Wen then announces the performance is illegal. The next night, as the "Song of Occupation" is about to begin, Ball runs into the theater and destroys the performance, embarrassing Wen in front of the audience. When Chen and Wen try to revenge on the animals, the people rise as one to protect the beloved creatures.

1839. *Snowman in the Sunshine (Tai Yang Xia De Xue Ren)*

1987. August First Film Studio. Color. 10 Reels. Direction: Zhao Jilie. Screenplay: Cui Qinsheng, He Xiaojiang. Cinematography: Ding Shanfa. Art Direction: Jiang Zhenkui. Music: Liu Qi. Sound: Sun Juzhen. Cast: Li Ping as Wen Qing, Ye Hui as Lin Kuang, Zhao Guang as Zhao Shishui, Cui Weining as Fei Ping

A high school girl named Wen Qing falls for a classmate, Lin Kuang. She disagrees with his decision to attend military academy after graduation, rather than a regular college. After he finishes his academy training and leaves for military service, she breaks off the relationship and later marries another young man named Fei Ping. Shortly after this, Lin Kuang is killed in the line of duty, and one of his military comrades visits Wen Qing. When he tells her about Lin Kuang in the army, and how respected and liked he was by his comrades, Wen Qing feels very remorseful for the way she treated him. Fei Ping loves Wen Qing very much, and tells her they will both learn and grow from this experience.

1840. *Snowy Wilderness (Huang Xue)*

1988. Shanghai Film Studio. Color. 10 Reels. Direction: Tang Xiaodan, Bao Zhifang. Screenplay: Xu Yali. Cinematography: Luo Zhensheng. Art Direction: Chen Fuxing. Music: Liu Yanxi. Sound: Lu Xuehan, Zhao Jianzhong. Cast: Lu Xiaohe as Xiong Kejian, Xu Songzi as Ma Dacui, Ruan Zhiqiang as Xiao Guocai

In the harsh and remote wilderness environment of North China, a man named Xiong Kejian takes to drinking heavily after his divorce. One day, Xiong gives the widow Ma Dacui a lift in his cart. Seeing how drunk he is, Ma Dacui tries to convince him that he cannot continue escaping from life as an alcoholic. He rewards her concern by unexpectedly raping her. When he has sobered up, Xiong is overcome with shame and quietly leaves the district, not knowing that Ma Dacui is now pregnant. After she gives birth, she and the child have a rough life. She buries the pain in her heart and tries to make the most of her situation. With the passage of time, Ma Dacui grows and becomes a strong woman. She also acquires a suitor, her childhood sweetheart Xiao Guocai. But then Xiong Kejian returns and wants to compete with Xiao for her hand in marriage. At first Ma Dacui is distressed by this turn of events, but finally settles for Xiong Kejian, believing that he is now a reformed man.

1841. *So Lovely a Landscape (Jiang Shan Duo Jiao)*

1959. August First Film Studio. B & W. 10 Reels. Direction: Wang Ping. Screenplay: Wang Yun, Huang Zongjiang. Cinematography: Xue Boqing. Art Direction: Li Xinmao. Music: Gao Ruxin. Sound: Li Yan. Cast: Tian Hua as Yue Xian, Ling Yuan as Grandma, Li Yan as Secretary Wen, Li Changhua as Gao Guolin, Tao Yuling as Fenger, Liu Lei as Yue Laoxing

An agricultural commune in Henan province organizes a youth "shock brigade" team to work specifically on developing their mountainous region. One of those who responds to the Party's call and joins the group is Yue Xian, an 18-year-old woman. During their time in the mountains, the young people encounter many difficulties, not the least of which is gossip about their activities among the very traditional local people, with even Yue Xian's fiancee suggesting she is behaving improperly. The situation is saved by the arrival of the county Party Secretary, who investigates and then names Yue Xian director of the brigade. With Secretary Wen's help and encouragement, she reorganizes the masses of the people, and expands the shock brigade's membership. After many days of hard work, they change the desolate mountains into a fruitful area.

1842. *Soaring (Xiang)*

1982. Emei Film Studio. Color. 10 Reels. Direction: Wang Xiaotang. Screenplay: Wang Xiaotang. Cinematography: Zhu Lutong. Art Direction: Wang Tao, Wang Zhengxian. Music: Zhang Peiji. Cast: Wang Xiaotang as Cai Pianpian, Wang Zhengtai as Yang Mindi, Liu Jia as Lu Bobo, Xie Dehui as Pei Na, Guo Ping as Professor Lin, Zhao Zhiyin as Mr. He

Horticulturist Cai Pianpian returns to China from abroad in the early 1960s, and concentrates on developing a yellow peony. But when the Cultural Revolution begins, she is separated from her colleague and boyfriend Yang Mindi and put in jail. Even in jail, Pianpian insists on writing a book, "Chinese Peonies." She is soon released and returns to the home of Mr. He, an old worker whose family she had lived with before. There she finds that the peonies she had planted are close to blooming, and that Mr. He has carefully

recorded for her every life stage of the flower's development. After the Gang of Four is smashed, she reunites with Yang Mindi and starts a new life.

1843. *Soccer Fans (Qiu Mi)*

1963. Tianma Film Studio. B & W. 9 Reels. Direction: Xu Cangling. Screenplay: Xu Cangling, based on the stage play "Outside the Soccer Field" by Jin Zhengjia. Cinematography: Shi Fengqi. Art Direction: Xu Keji. Music: Qi Wang. Sound: Zhou Yunling. Cast: Tie Niu as the driver soccer fan, Sun Jinglu as the driver's wife, Chen Xu as the doctor soccer fan, Zhang Ying as the doctor's wife, Wu Ying as the pregnant woman's mother, Ming Huiqing as the pregnant woman soccer fan

Soccer fans in a certain city are all excited about the championship game between two teams composed of transport workers and medical workers. This is the story of some of these fans, including a driver, his wife (who mixes their tickets into the food they bring), a small soccer fan, a doctor, a pregnant woman, etc. By the end of the day, none of these fans has had a good time due to various incidents. But they learn that due to a fluke a rematch of the championship is scheduled, giving them a second chance to enjoy the game and turning their disappointment into happiness.

1844. *A Soccer Fan's Obsession (Qiu Mi Xin Qiao)*

1992. Changchun Film Studio. Color. Letterboxed. 10 Reels. Direction: Cui Dongsheng. Screenplay: Wang Yucang, Zhao Yanhua. Cinematography: Zhang Shaoge. Art Direction: Meng Xiangchun. Music: Zhu Ganggang, Tang Yuanzhi. Sound: Yang Yuedong, Chen Peng. Costume: Bao Guiqin, Guo Xiuying. Makeup: Lei Longlong, Leng Xiaolan. Cast: He Wei as Zuo Qianfeng, Liu Lili as Chang Shufeng, Zhang Kao as Da Wei, Sun Haiyin as Bian Houwei

A salesman obsessed with soccer hooks up with a retired coach to start a training camp for teenage players. His wife, a busy restaurant manager, cannot understand the man and the boy's devotion to the game. The man and his son gradually win her over and convert her into a fan as well.

1845. *Sold Out by a Lover (Bei Fanmaide Qingren)*

1991. Emei Film Studio. Color. Letterboxed.

10 Reels. Direction: Li Deshu, Li Dagui. Screenplay: Chen Xinhao. Cinematography: Li Dagui, Cheng Xinghuai. Art Direction: Luo Zhicheng. Music: Guo Xiaodi. Sound: Luo Guohua. Costume: Lin Ailian. Makeup: Gong Ping. Cast: Sun Wentao as Zhong Rui, Li Yeping as Liu Manhua, Zhuang Li as Yao Lili, Wang Minggang as Li Qiming, Chen Changhai as Yang Mou, He Qian as Zhu Xiaoyan, Zhang Fengyi as A Xiang, Yu Lingda as Fatty

Businesswoman Liu Manhua realizes that young taxation officer Zhong Rui's investigation of her will soon expose her tax evasion. She has her good friend Yao Lili get close to Zhong and become his lover. On Liu's instructions, Yao puts a large sum of money in the tax official's safe deposit box to make it appear he has taken a bribe. Zhong is convicted and sent to prison. After his release, he begins his own investigation to clear his name, and learns the brains behind all this was another tax officer, Li Qimin. He is still unaware that his lover set him up until she guiltily confesses everything in court. His name is cleared, but what will he do about the lover that betrayed him?

1846. *Soldier Deng Zhigao (Liebing Deng Zhigao)*

1958. Changchun Film Studio. B & W. 8 Reels. Direction: Lei Qiang. Screenplay: Ma Yunpeng. Cinematography: Li Guanghui. Art Direction: Tong Jingwen. Music: Quan Rufeng. Sound: Jiang Junfeng. Cast: Zhang Jianyou as Deng Zhigao, Xu Liankai as the Deputy Company Commander, Ren Weimin as Yuan Yifeng, Song Baoyi as Zhang Dadao, Han Shaojun as the Squad Leader, Zhao Zimin as the Political Instructor

New army recruit Deng Zhigao is undisciplined and childish. His deputy commander, an old friend of his father's, tries to help young Deng but is unsuccessful due to his incorrect teaching methods. The unit's political instructor criticizes and corrects the teaching methods, and Deng soon corrects his mistakes and becomes an excellent soldier.

1847. *Solitaire (Du Xing Ke)*

1989. Super Star Film Company of the Shanghai Film Studio. Color. 10 Reels. Letterboxed. Direction: Xue Weijie. Screenplay: Li Xiao. Cinematography: Liu Lihua. Art Direction: Huang Baochang. Music: Lu Qiming. Sound: Wang Huimin, Wu Guoqiang. Cast: Yang Mingjian as Solitaire Yang, Zhao Xiaorui as Liu Heiqi,

Zhang Hui as Aunt Zhuo, Zhou Zhou as Wang Qi, Zhou Guobin as Li Tianchou

Towards the end of the Ming Dynasty (early 17th century), a martial arts expert called Solitaire Yang is blessed with unique skills but remains aloof and uninvolved with the evils and injustices of the society around him. When Li Le of the White Lotus Society, an anti–Ming Dynasty group, is betrayed by traitor Liu Heiqi, the rest of the society decide the only one who can avenge him is Solitaire Yang. To trick Yang into becoming involved, Li Le's brother Li Tianchou gets the Bamboo Hats, a gang allied with Liu Heiqi, to chase him to Yang's residence. There Li Tianchou appears to commit suicide. Yang angrily reacts by swearing to avenge Li Tianchou, and sets out after the Bamboo Hats. On the road, however, he finds himself surrounded by them. A bloody battle ensues, in which he is almost killed. As he gradually learns more about the traitor Liu, his outrage grows. He at last decides he can no longer remain uninvolved with the injustice around him, and sets out for a battle to the death with Liu.

1848. *Solving an Odd Case (Zi Po Qi An)*

1989. Shanghai Film Studio. Color. Letterboxed. 10 Reels. Direction: Xu Jihong. Screenplay: Fang Ai, Fang Hong. Cinematography: Xia Lixing. Art Direction: Zhao Xianrui. Music: Yang Mao. Sound: Ge Weijia. Cast: Qiao Qi as Gu Peng, Zhou Yemang as Xu Mengfei, Dai Zhaoan as Bao Lang, Ju Naishe as Huo Sang, Zhao Yanhong as Gu Wenjuan, Zhao Xueqin as Su Shuqing

In the fall of 1935, Shanghai literary circles are celebrating publication of "End of Urban Life," the latest novel by famous author Gu Peng. Everyone is shocked, however, when Gu's secretary Xu Mengfei announces that Gu's work is not original, but has been stolen from other people's works. The next morning, Xu is found murdered at his home, and Gu Peng is of course the prime suspect. Detective Huo Sang learns that Xu Mengfei had been dating Gu's daughter, and because Gu Peng opposed the relationship, was about to fire the younger man. Gu's daughter Gu Wenjuan comes to the detective and confesses that she killed Xu for disgracing her father, but the situation is further complicated when another woman named Su Shuqing shows up claiming she is the killer. To flush out the killer, Huo Sang plants stories in the paper saying that Gu Peng has evidence proving his innocence, but was hospitalized before the police could question him further. The killer walks into the trap but escapes from the hospital. Huo Sang follows to the railway station, and in their struggle the killer falls to the tracks and is killed. He turns out to be Xu Mengfei, who had faked his own death to frame Gu Peng.

1849. *Some Things Turn Out All Right After All (Hao Shi Duo Mo)*

1980. Shanghai Film Studio. Color. 10 Reels. Direction: Song Chong. Screenplay: Ye Dan, Huang Jingjie. Cinematography: Lu Junfu. Art Direction: Zhao Xianrui. Music: Liu Yanxi. Sound: Dong Juqing. Cast: Gong Xue as Liu Fang, Guo Kaiming as Shen Yuan, Gao Bo as Political Commissar Liu, Gao Cui as Wei Xia, Yuan Yue as Deputy Commander Xu, Li Zhaiyang as Zhao Yingwu

Naval Department Deputy Director Wei Xia likes to play matchmaker, and is determined to find a good husband for naval political commissar Liu's daughter Liu Fang. Wei Xia quickly identifies Shen Yuan, a naval worker, as a suitable match, and pushes him to commit to Liu Fang. But Wei Xia handles the situation in such a way that Shen has many misconceptions about Liu Fang, and although they marry, they are unhappy. Wei Xia forces Shen to relocate to the southern port city where Liu Fang lives, and not knowing the whole story, Shen takes his anger out on his wife. After Liu Fang's father sees how unhappy the young couple are, he has a heart attack and is hospitalized. Wei Xia's good intentions have now actually harmed three people, and her approach to the situation is seriously criticized by her own husband, Deputy Commander Xu. Later, Shen learns the truth of the story, which changes his attitude towards his wife. However, Liu Fang has already filed for divorce. Deputy Commander Xu intervenes to get the young couple to finally understand each other and reconcile.

1850. *Somebody Loves Me (You Ren Pian Pian Ai Shang Wo)*

1990. Beijing Film Studio. Color. Wide Screen. 9 Reels. Direction: Ning Ying. Screenplay: Xiao Mao. Cinematography: Li Tian. Art Direction: Shi Jiandu. Music: Gu De. Sound:

Zhang Hua. Cast: Chang Xiaoyang as Jita, Wang Ban as Diyin, Ma Xiaoqing as Mimi, Jiang Shan as Xiaoai

Jita and Diyin, newly hired musicians at the Black Cat Nightclub, accidentally discover the club owner is part of an antique smuggling ring. With the assistance of club singer Mimi, they collect enough evidence for the police to catch all the smugglers.

1851. *Someone Bold in Thought and Action (Gan Xiang Gan Zuo De Ren)*

1959. Shandong Film Studio. B & W. 10 Reels. Direction: Fang Huang. Screenplay: Wang Mingfu. Cinematography: Yao Shiquan. Set Design: Sun Zhang. Music: Yun Fan. Sound: Zuo Jie. Cast: Zhang Zhiliang as Zhang Yingjie, Su Yi as Zhang's mother, Wang Ti as Xiu Zhen, Lei Zhongqian as Wan Detang, Liu Zhiyun as Uncle Zhao, Liang Shan as Master Worker Yao

Zhang Yingjie, a young worker in a woodworking shop, suggests a plan for making an electronic jointer which he believes will improve production efficiency. Conservative shop director Wang Detang thinks this is impractical, and, spurred on by the villainous Song Xisan, halts Zhang Yingjie's tests. The shop's Party secretary Liu supports Zhang and criticizes Wang Detang. Zhang Yingjie works very hard day and night, and with his mother's encouragement and the Party organization's help, finally succeeds on his 28th try.

1852. *Son, Grandson and Seeds (Er Zi, Sun Zi He Zhong Zi)*

1978. Shanghai Film Studio. Color. B & W. 9 Reels. Direction: Liang Tingduo. Screenplay: Wu Zhongchuan, Hu Linsheng. Cinematography: Chen Ling, Cai Guangeng. Art Direction: He Ruiji, Zhang Zongxiang. Music: Yang Shaolu. Sound: Wu Hua, Ni Zheng. Cast: Wang Danfeng as Zhang Xiuyin, Yu Guichun as Ding Zhifu, Hong Rong as Xinmei, Ding Jiayuan as Ding Min, Xie Yibing as Mrs. Ding, Wang Qi as Mr. Tian, He Lin as A Long, Zhang Liwei as Lanzhen, Wei Fei as Ding Youli, Cheng Zhi as Uncle Gao, Mao Yongming as Chang Xi, Cao Kunqi as Jin Gen, Zhang Shazhen as Jin Gen's wife

After the "Gang of Four" is defeated, Dingwan Village in Southeast China is in a flourishing stage of development. Woman Director Xinmei sets an example for everyone in implementation of the One-Child Policy.

While she is supported by her husband Ding Min, her mother-in-law is obsessed with having a grandson, in spite of the fact the younger couple already has a daughter. Uncle Gao's son A Long loves science, and devotes himself to improving seeds. Local girl Ding Lanzhen loves A Long, but her parents oppose this relationship and try to arrange for her to marry someone else. Xinmei supports Lanzhen's freedom of choice and explains the situation to the partner arranged for Ding. Another woman, Zhang Xiuyin, had been a good worker, but having too many babies has ruined her health and she can no longer work. Xinmei patiently persuades Zhang's in-laws, and they finally support her desire to be sterilized. In the summer of 1980, Dingwan Village realizes a bumper harvest, and even Zhang Xiuyin is able to make contributions to China's "Four Modernizations."

1853. *The Son of Fishing Island (Yu Dao Zhi Zi)*

1959. Pearl River Film Studio. B & W. 7 Reels. Direction: Xu Yan. Screenplay: Sun Jingrui. Cinematography: Long Qingyun. Art Direction: Lai Shen, Luo Shengfan. Music: Liang Lizhu, Zhang Zhongchi. Sound: Lin Guang. Cast: Yuan Dongbao as Luo Haisheng, Zhang Ruxiao as Xiao Yu, Zou Peiying as Yamei, Chen Huailiu as Jin Fu, Chen Changjiang as Xiao Fa, Liu Mingjing as Fengying

On a South China Sea fishing island, Young Pioneer members Haisheng and Xiaoyu by chance happen upon a raft used by enemy agents for landing on their island. But when they bring some PLA soldiers to the spot, the raft has disappeared. The next day, the two youngsters find a radio transmitter at the mouth of a cave, but just as they are about to take it to the soldiers, one of the enemy agents comes out of the cave. They hide the transmitter in some tall grass, but are tricked and caught by one of the islanders secretly working for the enemy. Though tortured, they refuse to divulge where they hid the transmitter. The PLA arrives to rescue them and capture the spies and the traitor.

1854. *Son of Nature (Zi Ran Zhi Zi)*

1983. Xi'an Film Studio. Color. 9 Reels. Direction: Zhang Qicang. Screenplay: Xu Qinhua, Li Dong. Cinematography: Zhao Haifu. Art Direction: Yan Pingxiao. Music: Xie Tiyin. Sound: Chen Yudan, Chen Li. Cast: Tan Wenxi as Zhang Xiaoxi, Wang Ke as Father, Jiang Zhuling as Ji Laizhi, Wang Bingyan as Luo Wen, Pan Feng as Luo Xiaofei

A little boy named Zhang Xiaoxi was born in a mountain village. The combination of the scenic landscape, his mother's appreciation of art and the artworks of a neighbor instills in him an early love of painting. When he is just six years old, an old painter named Ji Laizhi discovers the boy's talent and brings him to the county seat for formal study. Luo Xiaofei, son of the county cultural station director Luo Wen, also has painting talent, but his father advises Xiaofei to develop his talent in the direction of political propaganda. Xiaoxi, on the other hand, focuses his talent on painting things of nature, such as animals and landscapes. Xiaofei criticizes and bullies Xiaoxi. In the end, Xiaoxi is the success, receiving a gold medal at the age of seven, and with great promise for a successful career.

1855. *Son of the Earth (Da Di Zhi Zhi)*

1982. Changchun Film Studio. Color. 11 Reels. Direction: Qi Xingjia. Screenplay: Qi Xingjia, Wang Boyang. Cinematography: Zhang Songping. Art Direction: Shui Zuangji, Hu Pei. Music: Du Mingxin, Zhang Peiji. Sound: Huang Lijia. Cast: Guo Yuntai as Zhang Shiyuan, Na Renhua as Haiyun, Lu Guilan as Qiuwen, Zhu Yuwen as Meilan, Zhuang Peiyuan as Dongdong, Wang Shanshu as Old Shuangfu

In 1949, young army officer Zhang Siyuan leads his troops in liberating a certain city, where he meets a young student named Haiyun. The two fall in love and marry, and soon have a son named Dongdong. As Zhang becomes more involved in his job as city Party Secretary, he becomes more neglectful and disrespectful of his wife, and the unhappy Haiyun leaves him. She is soon replaced by a woman named Meilan. When the Cultural Revolution starts, Zhang is dismissed from his position, and Meilan immediately divorces him. In 1971, Zhang Siyuan is released from prison and travels to a remote area to see his son. The young man is not pleased to see his father, but with the help of Qiuwen, a woman doctor and close friend of Dongdong, the two gradually rebuild their relationship. Back in Beijing, Zhang rededicates himself to his career and rises rapidly until he attains his present position of deputy minister. At this time, Meilan contacts him, wanting to remarry, but he rejects her. He travels back to the village where Dongdong lives, and asks his son to come with him to Beijing. When Dongdong refuses, Zhang Siyuan says that Qiuwen can come along. She explains to the father that they do not want to go to Beijing, as they feel they can never leave the simple rural people who helped them through the worst of times.

1856. *Son of the Herdsman (Mu Ren Zhi Zi)*

1957. Changchun Film Studio. B & W. 10 Reels. Directors: Zhu Wenshun and Guangbudaoerji. Screenplay: Guangbudaoerji and Te Damulin. Cinematography: Bao Jie. Art Direction: Wang Guizhi. Music: Tongfu and Li Yaodong. Sound: Lin Bingcheng. Cast: Wang Xingang as Deligeer, Gegeng Tana as Gegeng Taoya, Zhaolu as Amuga, Shuhai as Tegexi, Mazhanhua as Puren, Li Jie as Aershilang

Demobilized soldier Deligeer returns to his native village along the Yinhe River on the Inner Mongolian prairie as village chief, where he draws up a plan to develop the prairie pastureland. Some rich householders such as Aershilang, caring only for their own selfish interests and not for the long-term, collective interest, oppose this plan and attempt to sabotage his efforts. In addition, Deputy Director Amuga, desiring Deligeer's lover Gegeng Taoya, uses every bureaucratic means to stop Deligeer's plan from succeeding in order to discredit the village chief in her eyes. The bureaucratic District Director Puren is biased in his deputy's favor and removes Deligeer from his position as village chief. These setbacks in work and love throw Deligeer into a state of depression. Later, Gegeng Taoya, who had for a while misunderstood Deligeer, comes to him offering support and the two reconcile. With the help of the village Party Secretary Tegexi and the support of the Party committee, Deligeer fights back, leading the masses in building up the Yinhe and accomplishes his plan to develop the prairie pastureland.

1857. *Son of the Militia (Min Bing De Er Zi)*

1958. Changchun Film Studio. B & W. 8 Reels. Direction: Huang Can. Screenplay: Huang Can, based on the novel, "Changing Heaven" by Jun Qing. Cinematography: Wang Chunquan.

Set Design: Xu Zhenkun. Music: Li Ning. Sound: Sui Xizhong. Cast: Jia Naiguang as Laichun, Zhou Shengguan as Laichun's father, Huang Ling as Laichun's mother, Li Jie as Old Man Haowu, Liu Ru as District Director Wang, Liang Yin as the village chief, Ren Gu as Hao Hai, Jun Xuan as Hao Gen

In 1947, during the Chinese Civil War, deposed landlord Hao Hai and his son Hao Gen return to their home village in Shandong province with a private army linked to the Nationalists, preparing to massacre the entire village as revenge for their having been overthrown. Laichun, son of the village militia head, hears of this and rushes to tell his father, but learns that his father has been murdered by enemy agents. Though grief-stricken, the son then hurries to report the information to District Director Wang, commander of a Communist guerrilla troop operating in the area. Wang gives the young man the assignment of coordinating the guerrilla troop's movements. When Laichun returns to the village, he is captured by the enemy. Though tortured, he tells them nothing about the guerrillas' location. Just as the enemy is about to bury all the villagers alive, the guerrillas arrive, wipe out the invaders, and liberate the village once more.

1858. *A Song for the Qiangs' Whistle (Qiang Di Song)*

1960. Changchun Film Studio. B & W. 11 Reels. Direction: Zhang Xinshi. Screenplay: Lin Bing. Cinematography: Wang Lei. Art Direction: Liu Jinnai. Music: Che Ming. Sound: Tong Zongde. Cast: Zhang Yuan as Dong Yongzhen, Guo Zhenqing as Sha Gejia, Lin Na as Jin Tanmi, Sun Yu as Dong Yongming, Niu Qian as Cang Wangte, Mao Yinghai as the political commissar, Wang Zhenying as Zhang Huade, Li Yi as Chen Taibao

In 1935, as the Red Army passes through the Southwest Qiang nationality area while on the Long March, they liberate the Qiang people from government-backed warlord oppression. Red Army woman soldier Dong Yongzhen leads a working group into a Qiang village to teach revolutionary theory. During their time there she is injured while saving a small child from an accident. When the Red Army resumes its trek north, Dong stays on in the village to recuperate from her injury and to organize the villagers in tax resistance. Her efforts lead to her arrest by the chief government official in the area Zhang Huade and despotic landlord Chen Taibao. Although she is rescued by a Qiang guerrilla band led by Sha Gejia, she dies from the cumulative effect of her injuries. Qiang guerrilla chieftain Sha Gejia decides not to let the enemy know of her death, and puts up various posters over Dong's signature, continuing the struggle against the enemy. More than a decade later, the area is liberated again by the PLA. The Qiang people come to visit the local Tomb of the Martyrs, conveying their respect and grief for this heroic woman soldier.

1859. *Song Jingshi* (*Song Jing Shi*)

1955. Shanghai Film Studio. B & W. 13 Reels. Directors: Zheng Junli and Sun Yu. Screenplay: Chen Baicheng and Jia Qi. Cinematography: Zhou Daming. Art Direction: Lu Jingguang and Ge Shicheng. Music: He Luding. Sound: Ding Bohe. Makeup: Wang Tiebin. Cast: Cui Wei as Song Jingshi, Tao Jin as Yang Dianyi, Zhang Yi as Zhang Chongde, Wun Xiying as Liu Houde, Shu Yi as Xia Sangu, Zhang Liang as Xia Qi

In the mid–19th century, a time of frequent rebellion in China, farmer Song Jinshi leads a tax rebellion against the landlords in Tangyi County, Shandong province. His rebels are called the Black Flag Troop, and coordinate their fighting with members of the Bailian religion and the Nian army, another rebel group. The most powerful landlords in Tangyi County, Yang Mingqian and Wang Erxiang, send Wang Zhanbie, leader of their private army, to feign defection to the Black Flag side. When Qing government forces surround the Black Flag Troop, Wang Zhanbie coordinates their moves from the inside. In order to preserve his force from attack by superior numbers, Song Jingsi pretends to surrender to the Qing and go into exile in Shanxi. From that province he leads his troops in rebellion again. This time, they are successful in defeating the landlords' army, killing the landlords and the traitorous Wang Zhanbie in the process. After this, the Qing government moves to wipe out the Black Flag Troop once and for all, with the assistance of British forces in China. In the ruthless attack, many of Black Flag members' families are killed, including Song Jingsi's wife and mother. Song Jingsi persuades his surviving forces to follow him in crossing the Yellow River, where they join the Taiping rebel army, and continue their anti–Qing, anti–imperialist struggle from there.

1860. *Song of Happiness* (*Xin Fu Zhi Ge*)

1981. Tianshan Film Studio. Color. 10 Reels. Direction: Guang Chunlan. Screenplay: Guang Chunlan, Maimaiti Tajilike, Dong Zhenbo. Cinematography: Wu Puer. Art Direction: Lin Changxi. Music: Chen Xin, Siledeer. Sound: Jin Wenjiang. Cast: Tuyugong as Kelimu, Aibibai as Gulina Duolikun as Tuyihong

Kelimu, a young worker at a farm machinery plant, is assigned the task of repairing a water pump in an orchard. Through his own fault, he misses the bus and fails to get to the orchard, for which he blames a girl who works at the bus station. When his co-worker Tuyihong visits Kelimu's home after work to see why Kelimu did not go to the orchard, Kelimu pretends to be sick. So Tuyihong rides a bicycle to the orchard to finish the work for Kelimu. After the water pump is repaired, the manager of the orchard praises the job that "Kelimu" has done. A friend arranges a blind date for Kelimu with a girl named Gulina, who turns out to be the girl from the bus station. Gulina has heard so much from her father, the orchard manager, about what a great guy Kelimu is that she has really been looking forward to meeting him. But when everyone finds out who Kelimu really is, and what really happened that day, he is criticized by everyone. He vows to correct his mistakes and be more useful to society in the future.

1861. *Song of Mangguo* (*Mang Guo Zhi Ge*)

1976. Changchun Film Studio. Color. 9 Reels. Direction: Chang Yan, Zhang Puren. Screenplay: Collective, recorded by Zhen Quan, based on the short story "Overture" by Gu Yu. Cinematography: Chang Yan. Art Direction: Shi Weijun. Music: Li Yuqiu. Casting: Yu Ping as Xia Caiyun, Liu Wenzhi as Master Worker Tang, Zhou Lina as Zhou Dashuang and Zhou Xiaoshuang, Xu Zhan as Gao Shiwei, Mei Yuanqi as Zhao Dahai, Zuang Peiyuan as Liu Xiaozhou

In 1968, during the "Cultural Revolution," the Linxi City No.6 Textile Plant's "workers' propaganda team" led by Xia Caiyun arrives at the Eastern Textile Industrial College. College cadre Nie Jialiang largely controls the college organization. After the "worker's propaganda team" arrives, they arouse the young students in attacking the school organization's "revisionist educational line." They win over young teacher Yang Yangmin from this line and attack Nie Jialiang. The young students also achieve great unity and initiate the great "struggle, criticize and reform" campaign.

1862. *The Song of Mount Tianshan (Tian Shan Ge Sheng)*

1959. Xi'an Film Studio. B & W. 9 Reels. Direction: Wu Chun, Hua Yongzhuang. Screenplay: Hong Liu. Cinematography: Ling Xuan. Art Direction: Zhang Jingnan. Music: Xu Youfu. Sound: Hong Jiahui. Cast: Liu Ming as Secretary Rong, Wang Huayi as Director Wang, Shao Jinjian as Master Worker Xie, Deng Shutian as Secretary Sun, Geng Xia as Xiao Liu, Li Zhongyuan as Xiao Li

A railroad construction team is working in the Tianshan (Heaven Mountains) region of the Xinjiang Autonomous Region. Led by Secretary Rong they battle high winds and snow storms. In addition, Rong must deal with the backward, conservative thinking of Director Wang and Technician Kong. Rong is successful at motivating the mass of the people to upgrade their technology, work hard and wisely. With the Chinese and minority Uighur people cooperating, the railroad is finally built.

1863. *Song of New Customs (Xin Feng Ge)*

1976. Shanghai Film Studio. Color. 12 Reels. Direction: Zhao Huanzhang, Lu Ren. Screenplay: Zhang Youde, Duan Quanfa, Fan Junzhi. Cinematography: Zhu Yongde, Wu Lielian. Art Direction: Chen Fuxing. Casting: Zhao Jing as Song Wenying, Wang Shanpu as Chang Geng, Liu Minyi as Uncle Tiesan, Zhang Zhihua as Li Yinfeng, Ding Yi as Yimianluo, Da Shichang as Li Changshui

Soon after new bride Song Wenying comes to work at a brick factory, she is assigned the concurrent assignment of plant Party branch secretary. She learns that her brother-in-law, plant manager Li Changju, is engaged in illegal business dealings. She succeeds in stopping this activity, and criticizes Li Changju for following such capitalist customs as seeking special living arrangements, accepting bribes, etc. Li Changju rejects her criticism and gets his younger brother Li Changshui, Song's husband, to try to persuade Song Wenying to relocate. Li Changshui appeals to his wife to quit her job at the plant, but Song bravely refuses and continues to harshly criticize Li Changju's actions.

1864. *The Song of Shisanling Reservoir (Shi San Ling Shui Ku Chang Xiang Qu)*

1958. Beijing Film Studio. B & W. 9 Reels. Direction: Jin Shan. Screenplay: Jin Shan, based on the stage play of the same title by Tian Han. Cinematography: Chen Guoliang. Art Direction: Zhang Zhengyu. Cast: Deng Ziyi as the political commissar, Jiang Zhuling as Regimental Commander Guo, Wu Xue as Chen Peiyuan, Tian Long as Liu Shaoyi, Zhang Yisheng as Professor Feng, Mei Xi as Li Hao

A cultural delegation visits the Shisanling Reservoir construction site. Ten years later, several of them meet again at the reservoir, and by this time, the main obstacles have all been overcome.

1865. *Song of the Red Flag (Hong Qi Ge)*

1950. Northeast Film Studio. B & W. 10 Reels. Director and Screenplay: Wu Zuguang, adapted from the novel by Liu Canglang and Lu Mei. Cinematography: Fu Hong. Set Design: Wang Tao. Music: Li Xi. Sound: Lin Bingcheng. Cast: Lu En as Sister Ma Feng, Yue Shen as Jing Fang, Zhang Wei as Zhang Damei, Wang Lifu as Wan Guoying, Du Cuiyuan as Zhao Meigu, Ma Lu as Peng Gang

Before liberation, the workers in a textile mill are cruelly exploited and oppressed. An underground Communist Party cell tries to organize the workers in their anti-capitalist struggle, but their leaders are arrested. Assistant Manager Wan Guoying uses this as an excuse to fire one of his workers, Sister Ma Feng, for allegedly having leftist sympathies. Her father dies of shock when he hears of the incident. After liberation, Sister Ma Feng returns to the mill, but Wan Guoying, now a factory cadre, and his cohort Zhang Damei confuse her as to the true situation in the plant, making her politically regressive and backward. After the mill's labor union learns of the situation, it sends union activist Jing Fang to counsel Sister Ma Feng and to criticize Wan Guoying. The union's concern so moves Sister Ma Feng that she alters her attitude and devotes herself to the mill's Red Flag competition, which her work group wins.

1866. *Song of the Red Flag (Hong Qi Pu)*

1960. Beijing Film Studio & Tianjing Film

Studio Jointly. Color. 15 Reels. Direction: Ling Zhifeng. Screenplay: Hu Su, Ling Zhifeng, Hai Mu and Wu Jian, based on the novel of the same title by Liang Bing. Cinematography: Wu Yinxian. Art Direction: Yu Yiru. Music: Ju Xixian. Sound: Fu Yingjie. Cast: Cui Wei as Zhu Laogong and Zhu Laozhong, Chen Fan as Zhu Laozhong as a child, Cai Songling as Yan Laoxiang and Yan Zhihe, Wang Mianzhi as Zhihe as a child, Lu Fei as Jia Xiangnong, Zhao Lian as Yuntao, Ge Cunzhuang as Feng Lanchi, Yu Zhongyi as Dagui, Li Jianguo as Wu Laoba

In the early part of the 20th century, farmer Zhu Laogong and his son live by the Futuo River near the town of Shuojing, Hebei province. Financially and physically ruined by despotic landlord Feng Lanchi, the father dies, and his son Zhu Laozhong is forced to leave town. Twenty-five years later, Laozhong returns to his hometown, the desire for revenge burning in his heart. His own son Dagui is conscripted by Feng Lanchi to be a warlord soldier serving the Nationalist government. Zhu Laozhong becomes acquainted with undercover Communist Party member Wu Laoba, who introduces him to the area's CPC chief Jia Xiangnong. They instruct Laozhong in revolutionary theory, and he organizes the farmers in opposition to Feng Lanchi. After 1927, with the revolution at a low point, Feng once more exploits the farmers cruelly, levying a series of burdensome and unfair taxes on them. Zhu Laozhong joins the CPC, and he and his son Dagui (who has deserted the army) are active in a successful anti-taxation campaign led by Jia Xiangnong.

Best Actor Cui Wei, 1962 Hundred Flowers Awards.

Best Cinematographer Wu Yinxian, 1962 Hundred Flowers Awards.

1867. *Song of the Skies (Qing Yun Qu)*

1959. Changchun Film Studio. B & W. 9 Reels. Director: Huang Shu. Screenplay: Xie Xuechou. Cinematography: Wang Yizhi. Art Direction: Li Youren. Music: Che Ming. Sound: Yan Ji. Cast: Yang Qitian as Du Chunlin, Guo Wenlin as Zhao Sheng, Zhang Fengxiang as Political Commissar He, Zuang Yan as Du's mother, Dai Yongsu as Sulan, Wang Yansheng as Division Commander Gao

Young pilot Du Chunlin is assigned to fly wingman for veteran pilot Zhao Sheng. Although Zhao is a pilot with much combat experience, he is conceited, arrogant and conservative in his thinking. Zhao's errors cause them to lose their first two air battles. Following a huge argument about tactics, Zhao realizes his errors, and at the third battle the two coordinate closely and shoot down a significant number of enemy aircraft. During another battle, after Du has landed, Zhao Sheng's plane is crippled. Du takes off again to provide cover for Zhao to land, but Du's plane runs out of fuel before he can return. Ordered by the division commander to bail out, Du refuses and in order to protect the nation's property, bravely glides his plane back to base, and lands it safely.

1868. *Song of Youth (Qing Chun Zhi Ge)*

1959. Beijing Film Studio. Color. Directors: Cui Wei, Chen Huaiai. Cinematography: Nie Jin. Screenplay: Yang Mo. Art Direction: Qin Wei. Music: Qu Xixian. Sound: Cai Jun and Wang Zemin. Makeup: Sun Yuemei. Cast: Xie Fang as Lin Daojing, Kang Tai as Lu Jiachuan, Yu Yang as Jiang Hua, Yu Shizhi as Yu Yongzhe, Zhao Lian as Dai Yu, Qin Wen as Wang Xiaoyan, Zhang Yisheng as Hu Mengan, Ma Chenxi as Bai Liping, Zhao Yurong as Yu Shuxiu

In 1931, on the eve of the Japanese invasion, Lin Daojing, a young student, attempts to drown herself to oppose a marriage arranged by her family. She is saved by a Beijing University student, Yu Yongzhe, and the two fall in love and marry. But the marriage does not bring Ling Daojing the independent life and happiness she seeks. At this time, she meets Lu Jiachuan and other members of the Communist Party, and through their tutelage comes to realize that there will be a future for Chinese intellectuals only if they associate their personal futures with that of China and its people. Therefore, she determines to leave her materialistic husband, who does not share her political views. Lin Daojing matures into a staunch CCP member, and becomes one of the leaders of the "December 9th" student movement to oppose Japanese aggression.

1869. *Song Over the Reservoir (Shui Ku Shang De Ge Sheng)*

1958. Changchun Film Studio. B & W. 7 Reels. Direction: Yu Yanfu. Screenplay: Liu Dawei, based on his original story, "The Best News." Cinematography: Yin Zhi. Art Direction: Wang Xingwen. Music: Lei Zhenbang. Sound:

Chen Yudan. Cast: Pu Ke as Gu Jingchun, Zhang Guilan as Gao Lanxiang, Li Yalin as Gu Zhiqiang, Liu Bing as the political instructor, Zhao Zhiyue as the carriage operator, Zhang Yuan as Zhang Hong

In an agricultural commune in suburban Beijing, woman production director Gao Lanxiang plans to marry PLA platoon leader Gu Zhiqiang during the Spring Festival, but on the eve of the holiday Zhiqiang's unit is ordered to the Shishan Forest to build a reservoir, forcing postponement of their plans. By coincidence, the commune is also directed to participate in the construction, and Lanxiang, along with Zhiqiang's father Gu Jingchun, is sent to study the worksite. They meet Zhiqiang there, and on New Year's Eve, the couple is married at the building site in an unconventional ceremony. After the wedding, they devote themselves to hard work, and the reservoir is soon finished.

1870. *Songs in the Whirlpools (Xuan Wo Li De Ge)*

1981. Emei Film Studio. Color. 9 Reels. Direction: Liu Zhinong, Wu Lan. Screenplay: Liu Zhinong, Liang Yun, Mi Jiashan, Yu Yang. Cinematography: Li Zhenhuan. Art Direction: Wang Longsheng. Music: Chang Sumin, Tao Jiazhou. Sound: Shen Guli. Cast: Zhao Erkang as Jiang Lisheng, Yang Yaqing as Xin Yiwen, Pan Hong as Lin Juan, Wei Beiyuan as Jiang's father, Liu Zhinong as Song Qin, Lei Nan as Lin's mother

Although he comes from humble origins, Jiang Lisheng is blessed with singing talent, and through hard work and practice becomes famous. During the Cultural Revolution he is tried and convicted of some nonsensical crime, and his wife Xin Yiwen gives in to political pressure and divorces him. After his release from prison he returns to the Yangtze River village where he was born and grew up. He takes up his father's trade of boatman, and while he and his son Jiang Xiaomin have a difficult life, he still finds time to compose and sing songs for the local people. He meets a young woman doctor named Lin Juan, who is sympathetic with his unfortunate past. The two eventually fall in love. By chance he meets his ex-wife one day. She is married to a man named Song Qin, but their marriage is a rocky one, mostly due to her guilt about Jiang and her present husband's inability to understand her feelings. Meanwhile, Lin Juan's mother is adamantly opposed to her relationship with Jiang Lisheng, but Lin goes against her mother's wishes and at a party celebrating the defeat of the Gang of Four she professes her love to him. Reluctant to involve the doctor in his hard life, he rejects her. Xin Yiwen sees how selfish and weak she has been, and how true is Lin Juan's love for Jiang. At this time a foreign musician comes to China asking to meet with his old friend Jiang, and brings word that the government is preparing to reverse Jiang's earlier conviction and grant him a full pardon. Lin Juan hurries to tell Jiang the good news, and that she will wait for him forever.

1871. *Songzai Ganbu (Song Zai Gan Bu)*

1988. Tibetan Television Station. Color. Wide Screen. Direction: Yang Jizhi, Danzen. Screenplay: Li Yang, Minma Cairen. Cinematography: Li Zhiguang, Qiang Ba. Art Direction: Wang Guan, Pu Ba. Music: Bai Denglang, Ji Shenghua. Sound: Wei Xueyi, Li Tian. Cast: Dunzhuduoji as Dabo Shanger, Zhaxidunzhu as Songzai Ganbu

In the early part of the 7th century, Songzai Ganbu becomes the leader of the Tibetans. To consolidate his power he seeks to marry someone from the Chinese court. The story tells how he conveys this message to the Tang Dynasty court, and how he and the Princess Wencheng are at last married in the Tibetan Budala Palace.

1872. *Sons and Daughters (Bu Yi Le Hu)*

1992. Pearl River Film Studio. Color. Letterboxed. 9 Reels. Direction: Wang Weiyi, Lin Shujing. Screenplay: Tian Yuan. Cinematography: Wu Yukun. Art Direction: Du Xiufeng. Costume: Zhang Feiyan, Chen Xiaomei. Makeup: Liu Xiuming. Cast: Wu Yuanbiao as Song Hongyuan, Lu Niu as Ding Xing, Lin Xingyun as Ding Wang, Yuan Xingzhe as A Er, Jiang Zhiwen as Director Lin, Huang Huiyi as Yinghua, Zhou Minghong as Jin Dou

Director Lin comes to Song Village to help implement family planning work there. The film follows the grassroots work of the family planning committee in overcoming traditional thinking and carrying out official policies.

1873. *Sons and Daughters of the Miao Nationality (Miao Jia Er Nu)*

1958. Jiangnan Film Studio. B & W. 9 Reels.

Song of Youth. **In their prison cell, student activist Lin Daojing (Xie Fang, right) is comforted and encouraged by veteran revolutionary Lin Hong (Qin Yi). 1959. Beijing Film Studio.**

Direction: Tao Jin. Screenplay: Zhou Minzhen. Cinematography: Zhang Xiling. Art Direction: Lu Jingguang. Music: Huang Zhun. Sound: Chen Jingrong. Cast: Lin Zhiao as Kaliang, Jin Chuan as Lin Wenbo, Zhao Donghai as Guoliang, Zhu Sha as Maixiang, Liu Fei as Chunliang, Lu Ming as Kami, Lin Bin as Teacher Zhou, Shi Wei as Wu Lan, Cui Zhaoming as Xiangfu, Fu Potang as the commune secretary

This story takes place among the Miao nationality people of South and Southwestern China. When discharged soldier Kaliang returns to his home village, he is heartbroken to find that Maixiang, the girl he loves, has married commune director Chunliang. While Kaliang's mother Kami, the Party secretary, encourages her son to be strong and get on with his life, the disgruntled commune secretary tries to exploit Ka Liang's sorrow by inciting bad feelings between Kaliang and Chunliang. When Kaliang proposes exploring some uncultivated lands and forests, Chunliang listens to the commune secretary and misunderstands Kaliang, so he opposes the latter's suggestions. Kami, Maixiang and the rest of the commune members support Kaliang's ideas. Kaliang leads the commune's people in carrying out his proposals, and they achieve their plans for increas-

ing grain output. The government arrests the commune secretary for violating the law, and Chunliang realizes his errors.

1874. *Soong Family Dynasty (Song Jia Huang Chao)*

1995. "Soong Family Dynasty" Film Production Company. Color. Direction: Zhang Wanting. Screenplay: Luo Qirui, based on "Soong Dynasty" by Sterling Seagrave. Cinematography: Huang Yuetai. Art Direction: Ma Panchao, Liang Huasheng. Music: Xiduo Lang. Cast: Jiang Wen as Song Chali, Jin Yanling as Ni Guizhen, Yang Ziqiong (Michelle Yeoh) as Song Ailing, Zhang Manyu (Maggie Cheung) as Song Qingling, Wu Junmei (Vivian Wu) as Song Meiling, Niu Zhenhua as H.H. Kong, Zhao Wenxuan (Winston Chao) as Sun Zhongshan, Wu Xingguo as Chiang Kaishek

Song Yaoru, a man with progressive ideas, sends his daughters Ailing, Qingling and Meiling to study in the United States during the first part of this century. After their return, the three young women all become persons of considerable influence in China through marriage: Ailing to wealthy financier H.H. Kong; Qingling to Sun Yatsen, father of the Chinese Republic; and Meiling to Chiang Kaishek,

Soong Family Dynasty. **The three most famous daughters in China: from left, Soong Ailing (Michelle Yeoh), Soong Qingling (Maggie Cheung) and Soong Meiling (Vivian Wu). 1995. "Soong Family Dynasty" Film Production Company.**

Nationalist military commander and later president. The three sisters have differing personalities, politics and dreams for China, yet they still pull together in times of crisis, such as when the Japanese invade their homeland.

1875. *SOS Village (SOS Cun)*

1988. Beijing Film Studio. Color. 9 Reels. Direction: Wang Yiwan. Screenplay: An Xiaochuan, Wang Yiwan. Cinematography: Gao Lixian. Art Direction: Liu Changbao. Music: Ma Ding. Cast: Zhang Yuyu as Xia Yue, Ye Ling as Ganggang, Xia Yonghua as Mu Xiuhua, Zhu Yilu as Chunping, Gao Mingru as Haitao

A renowned Austrian physician founds the "SOS Village" in China, ushering in a new era in which orphans are cared for and raised in a family setting. Urban mothers are hired as the caregivers at SOS Village and prepare to welcome the first group of children. The film shows the development of relationships between orphans and mothers through the women's unselfish care. The children treat the women as if they were their real mothers.

1876. *Soul-Catching Woman (Gou Hun Nu Lang)*

1995. Beijing Film Studio. Color. Letterboxed. Direction: Yu Xiangyuan. Screenplay: Yu Xiangyuan. Cinematography: Song Dehua. Art Direction: Li Guo. Music: Guo Xiaotian. Cast: Chen Jiming as Sun Shaowu, Ma Jie as Tie Yanzi, Zhu Na as Liu Xiaoqiong, Ji Jun as Chief of Detectives Li, Shi Lan as Xiang Xue, Zhang Zhongxi as Shanben, Yang Yuanyi as Mr. Zhao

A mystery set during World War II, in which the victims in a series of murders are all linked to the theft of a device for decoding secret documents. Detective Sun Shaowu has the dual task of identifying the killer and recovering the device.

1877. *The Soul of a Brave Ancestor (Shen Zhou Jing Hun)*

1988. Pearl River Film Studio. Color. Letterboxed. 8 Reels. Direction: Lu Yu, Zhou Shaofeng. Screenplay: Gu Jiadong, Lu Yu, Zhou Shaofeng. Cinematography: Yan Xuzhong, Tang Bozhong. Art Direction: Ye Jialiang. Music: Zhen Qiufeng. Sound: Lin Guang. Cast: Du Zhengqin as Xi, Du Zhengqin as Dayu

In prehistoric times, when people survived through hunting and farming, a strange animal appears in the clouds one day, and brings all kinds of disasters to the humans. Xi, leader of the Xia tribe, takes on the mission of slaying the creature. Xi dies in the effort, but a young handsome man called Dayu is born from his body. In order to fulfill his father's unfinished task, Dayu finally conquers the evil creature.

1878. *Soul of a Painter (aka La Peintre) (Hua Hun)*

1994. Shanghai Film Studio & Taiwan Golden Tripod Film Company Co-Production. Color. Letterboxed. 14 Reels. Direction: Huang Shuqin. Screenplay: Liu Meng, Min Anqi, Huang Shuqin and Li Ziyu, adapted from the novel of the same title by Shi Nan. Cinematography: Lu Le, Xia Lixing. Art Direction: Zhen Changfu, Chen Chunlin. Music: Liu Yuan. Sound: Ge Weijia. Costume: Wang Youlong, Qian Qingqing. Makeup: Li Ding, Jin Ailan and Ding Wei. Cast: Gong Li as Pan Yuliang, Er Dongsheng (Derek Yee, Yee Tung-shing) as Pan Zanhua, Da Shichang as Wang Shouxing, Zhang Qiongzhi as Qian Shuihong, Shen Hairong as Fang, Xu Min as Xue Yuan, Gao Junxia as He Qiong

Pan Yuliang was a famous Chinese painter who began as a teenaged prostitute in a small town in southern Anhui province. Pan Zanhua, the chief local customs official, falls for her, buys her from the brothel and takes her to Shanghai, where they are married. When Yuliang shows a talent for painting, her husband encourages her to apply for the Shanghai Art Institute, and she is admitted. When Yuliang finds that she cannot bear children, she allows her husband's first wife to move to Shanghai, and soon the family has a son. Pan Yuliang goes to Paris for advanced study, and in time her painting "The Bathing Girl" is awarded a Grand Prize in competition. She returns to China to accept an appointment to a university art faculty, and she, her husband and the son settle down in Nanjing. But her paintings of women's bodies runs counter to traditional Chinese mores and her work is publicly criticized. In addition, jealous male colleagues at the university set out to destroy her reputation, using her early background in prostitution as the tool. The criticism and ridicule at last prove too much for her husband: he takes the son and returns to Anhui. Pan Yuliang returns alone to Paris, where she devotes the rest of her days to painting. She dies in Paris in 1977.

1879. *Soul of a Policeman (Jing Hun)*

1994. Pearl River Film Company. Color. Letterboxed. 9 Reels. Direction: Wang Wei. Screenplay: Li Yanxiong, Wang Dekang, Liao Zhikai. Cinematography: Wu Benli. Art Direction: Guan Yu, Feng Zhixun. Sound: Huang Mingguang, Wang Guang. Costume: Zhao Meizhi, Zhang Hui. Makeup: Wang Lingzhi. Cast: Feng Yuanzheng as Peng Baolin, Cai Hongxiang as director Lin, Liu Jiaoxin as Qu Yaohuang, Du Du as Ding Xiaoping, Guo Yong as Ye Jinshui, Si Dasheng as Long Guangyuan

A film biography based on the career of real-life police detective Peng Baolin. Peng, an outstanding crime fighter in the South China city of Huizhou, Guangdong Province, cracked several famous cases. Peng's life and career ended tragically when he was killed in the line of duty on the eve of his marriage.

1880. *Soul of Heroes (Hu Dan Ying Xiong)*

1993. Pearl River Film Company. Color. Letterboxed. 9 Reels. Direction: Chen Peise, Gui Qun. Screenplay: Xiao Yixian, based on the novel "White Channel Plan." Cinematography: Li Xiaoping, Zhu Xuejun. Art Direction: Dong Shijun, Xu Hailin. Music: Xiang Yin. Sound: Hua Juan. Costume: Liu Jicheng, Li Jin. Makeup: Zhao Liyang. Cast: Wu Xian as Sima Lei and Jiang Hailong, Aoli Qie as Sidifeng, Xue Bai as Xiang Nong, Huo Deji as the bureau director, Si Zhaoxin as Tang Ye, Guan Jingchun as Rongfa, Guan Chunhua as Kankun

Taiwan and mainland police team up with Interpol to destroy a drug processing base on the Yunnan Border.

1881. *The Soul of Monster Town (Mo Gui Cheng Zhi Hun)*

1986. Tianshan Film Studio. Color. 9 Reels. Direction: Zhang Fengxiang. Screenplay: Zhang Hongjun. Cinematography: Li Zhenghuan, Qi Xing. Art Direction: Ma Shaoxian. Music: Zhu Hengqian. Sound: Wang Huimin. Cast: Ruan Ruxin as Xing Keyi, Guo Yuantao as Wang Jianjiang

In a barren desert outpost called "Monster Town," an oil prospecting team becomes increasingly less efficient. Newly assigned director Xing Keyi learns that the problem is his workers' terribly low morale, as they all realize their lack of education will keep them doing the same repetitive, boring jobs forever. Xing Keyi believes he must explore and find a spiritual source among these people, so he contacts each young worker individually. He finds out about them and their families, and gradually gains their respect and trust. Morale improves, as does the workers' lives, and the oil prospecting succeeds.

1882. *Soul of the Pipa (Pi Pa Hun)*

1982. August First Film Studio. Color. 10 Reels. Direction: Yan Jizhou. Screenplay: Zhang Chongtian. Cinematography: Yang Guangyuan. Art Direction: Wang Wei. Music: Gong Zhiwei. Sound: Shi Pingyi. Cast: Xiang Hong as Su Xiaoqing, Lu Yukun as Father, Xu Guangmin as Fan Shaozhang, Yang Zhaoquan as Mr. Kun

In 1943, the Japanese succeed in severing the communication links between the New Fourth Route Army and the Communist underground in the city of Lianzhen in East China. Woman soldier Su Xiaoqing, a native of Lianzhen, volunteers to restore the flow of information. Su's parents had been famous performers of "pingtan," a form of entertainment featuring storytelling and ballad singing in the Suzhou dialect. Now, her mother was dead, a victim of a local despot's persecution, and her father was old and sick. Su Xiaoqing enters the city as part of a pingtan troupe, then contacts her father, reveals her identity to him and asks his assistance. Father and daughter perform as a team, Xiaoqing playing the pipa, a classical stringed instrument. Through their music, she sends coded messages to the underground organization, and restores the communications link. Once contact is made, the group is able to rescue the Communists' local chief from captivity. Unfortunately, Su Xiaoqing is shot and killed during the escape.

1883. *Soul of the Sea (Hai Hun)*

1957. Haiyan Film Studio. B & W. 10 Reels. Direction: Xu Tao. Screenplay: Shen Junmu and Huang Zongjiang. Cinematography: Xu Qi. Art Direction: Ding Chen and Ge Xinger. Music: Gao Tian. Sound: Wu Jianghai. Makeup: Yao Yongfu. Cast: Zhao Dan as Chen Chunguan, Cui Wei as Dou Erpeng, Liu Qiong as the Ship's Captain, Gao Bo as Old Leitou, Zhen Xu as the First Mate, Kang Tai as Managing Secretary Bai Wu, Wang Danfeng as Wen Mengyuan

Just before Shanghai falls to the Communists, the Nationalist warship "Gulang" flees to Taiwan. After they arrive, the crew find themselves despised and humiliated by American soldiers. The sailors grow increasingly resentful at the way the Americans treat them. One of the sailors, Chen Chunguan, becomes acquainted with a Taiwanese bar girl named Wen Mengyuan. On one occasion when he and his buddy Dou Erpeng stop by the bar where she works, they see Wen Mengyuan being abused by some American soldiers. They intercede and beat the Americans in a fight. However, Wen Mengyuan loses her job over the incident and commits suicide. This experience and the constant bullying they take at the hands of their officers and the Americans pushes Chen and the other sailors to the boiling point. When the "Gulang" is assigned to blockade the mouth of the Yangtze River, the seamen mutiny. They kill their officers, fight a running battle with enemy warships and airplanes pursuing them, and take the "Gulang" back to the mainland.

1884. *Soul of the Sword (Jian Hun)*

1981. Emei Film Studio. Color. 10 Reels. Zen Weizhi, Li You, Fuxing, Gong Jie. Cinematography: Zhang Jiwu. Art Direction: Wang Tao, Wang Yongkang. Music: Shi Fu. Sound: Zhang Jianping. Cast: Yuan Mei as Su Chunxiu, Shi Zhancheng as Qi Fang, Xin Guiping as Chen Tianfang as Fang Jiayuan, Xin Guiqiu as Nan Fang, Xin Guiping as Xiao Fang

College student Nan Fang is visiting a scenic area with her boyfriend Fang Jiayuan, a boxer. There, they meet Qi Fang and Su Chunxiu, a Chinese couple recently returned from abroad. Qi and Su have become accomplished fencers overseas, and have returned with the dream of training Chinese fencers and coaching China's first national fencing team. Fang Jiayuan and Nan Fang join the team and show rapid progress. But during the Cultural Revolution, Fang Jiayuan is arrested on false charges of spying for a foreign power. Qi Fang is persecuted to death. Su Chunxiu and their daughter Xiao Juan suffer as well, and Su Chunxiu is barred from practicing her profession. Nan Fang is sent to a reform through labor camp. When the Gang of Four is forced out of power, Fang Jiayuan becomes coach of his province's fencing team. Qi Fang's daughter Xiao Juan shows considerable potential at the sport, and is selected to the national team.

Soul of the Sea. Chen Chunguan (Zhao Dan, second left) and his fellow mutineers joyously see the Chinese mainland on the horizon. 1957. Haiyan Film Studio.

In the world's championships in Spain, she is wounded in one arm, but continues the contest through sheer will to overcome the pain. In the end she takes the Silver medal in the women's competition.

1885. *The Soul-Taking Knives (Xiao Hun Dao)*

1989. Shanghai Film Studio. Color. Letterboxed. 10 Reels. Direction: Li Xiepu. Screenplay: Li Xiao. Cinematography: Lu Junfu, Shen Xingao. Art Direction: Mei Kunping. Music: Liu Yanxi. Sound: Zhou Hengliang, Xu Xiushan. Cast: Wang Hua as Gao Tianxiao, Cui Dai as Yang Heng, Liu Xiaomin as Guo Leshui, Hong Zugeng as Er Xizhi, Zhen Yi as Lannu, Zhang Hongkui as You Guozhen, Wang Dunyao as Wu Wei

Near the end of the Ming Dynasty, a certain county is hit by a succession of murders. The victims are all local officials and merchants, and the persons claiming responsibility are self-styled the "soul-taking knives." It turns out that the murdered men had conspired to frame an honest official, and now five of his loyal soldiers are killing off the conspirators one by one.

1886. *A Sound Spring's Sleep (Chun Mian Bu Jue Xiao)*

1980. Changchun Film Studio. Color. 11 Reels. Direction: Su Li. Screenplay: Zhang Xiaotian. Cinematography: An Zhiguo. Art Direction: Guo Tingsheng. Music: Zhang Dicang, Gao Feng. Sound: Kang Ruixin. Cast: Pu Ke as Liu Zhengyan, Wang Runsheng as Liu Guanghou, Liu Long as Qu Wo, Liu Simin as Tang Zuoxin, Wang Lanyin as Liu Kangkang, Li Xiaofeng as Li Heping

The romances of some young couples are played out against the backdrop of a campaign to root out official corruption in a provincial bureau of agriculture.

1887. *Sour and Spicy Marriage (Suan La Yan Yuan)*

1985. Guangxi Film Studio. Color. 9 Reels. Direction: Song Jie, Zhang Ning. Screenplay: Dong Shengtao, Song Jie. Cinematography: Liao Fan, Chen Shengkai. Art Direction: Wu Zhaohua. Music: Su Tie. Sound: Li Zuwen. Cast: Xie Gang as Li Zhangkai, Zhao Yue as Lihua, Zhang Teng as Zhao Yong, Xu Yuejie as Chunman

In rural Shandong province, young farmer Zhao Yong loves a girl named Li Hua. However, while Li Hua's mother likes Zhao, she forces her daughter to break off the relationship because the mother plans to use her daughter in exchange for a wife for her son Zhangkai, a disabled army veteran. Seeing the pain this is causing his sister and her lover, Zhangkai refuses to be a part of the scheme. He devotes himself to raising rabbits, and in time meets a girl named Chunman who has similar interests. They fall in love, and now everyone is happy.

1888. South Boxing King (Nan Quan Wang)

1984. Nanhai Film Company, Hong Kong Lefeng Film Company. Color. Wide Screen. 9 Reels. Direction: Xiao Long. Screenplay: Zhang Jun. Cinematography: Hai Lie, Fan Dongni. Art Direction: He Ruiji, Zhu Jinhe. Music: Guan Shengyou. Cast: Qiu Jianguo as Lin Hainan, Song Qiaozhen as Yuqin, Li Yanlong as Shaojia, Sun Gengfa as Neihaerchi, Xu Li as Zhao Shixiong

In the mid–19th Century, martial artist Lin Hainan is entrusted by a group of overseas Chinese to carry money from them to help the Taiping Rebellion. On the way, however, Lin is attacked by agents of the imperial court. He is injured, and those traveling with him are killed. Lin comes to a red boat which is the headquarters of a performing troupe. The troupe leader and his son Shaojia offer him sanctuary. At the time, the troupe is being harassed by a local despot, Zhao Shixiong, who proclaims himself the "South Boxing King" for defeating all comers. Lin Hainan accepts the challenge and defeats Zhao, so all the local residents now call Lin "the King." Later, Lin fights and wipes out all those bullying the local people and the troupe. His friends want Lin to stay, but he bids them farewell, for he has chosen the path of revolution with the Taipings.

1889. The South China Coast (Nan Fang De An)

1984. Kunming Film Studio. Color. Direction: Cui Dongsheng, Yu Jiqiu. Screenplay: Kong Jiesheng, Cui Dongsheng. Cinematography: Si Yongmin, Ye Yongkang. Art Direction: Li Zhengxin. Music: Cao Xuean, Nie Lihua. Sound: Jia Xianjie. Cast: Li Zhanwen as Yi Jie, Liu Qianyi as Mu Zhen, Guo Jiangui, Jia Meiying as Xiao Ting, Cui Minli as the former company director

During the Cultural Revolution, two young men named Yi Jie and A Wei, and a young woman named Mu Zhen, were educated youth sent to work on Hainan Island off the south China coast. After they are permitted to return to the city, the three friends open a food stall. Although business prospers, Yi Jie is restless, for he cannot forget their former life on Hainan. One day they have a visitor, the director of the company they all worked for Hainan. During his visit they naturally discuss the old days, and after the director leaves, Yi Jie is more restless than ever. He decides to return to Hainan, and after discussing it with Mu Zhen, she agrees to go with him.

1890. South China in the North (Bei Guo Jiang Nan)

1963. Haiyan Film Studio. B & W. 13 Reels. Direction: Shen Fu. Screenplay: Yang Hansheng. Cinematography: Luo Chongzhou. Art Direction: Hu Zhuoyun. Music: Xiang Yi. Sound: Lu Zhongbo. Cast: Deng Nan as Dong Ziwang, Wei Heling as Dong Zizhang, Ma Ji as Zhizhang's wife, Wang Qi as Wu Dacheng, Qin Yi as Yinghua, Li Jing as Ding Xiaoshan, Li Baoluo as Qian Santai

In Huangtu Village in a remote area of North China, agricultural commune director Wu Dacheng and his wife Yinghua are enthusiastically planning a project to dig a well and plant a forest. Hidden counterrevolutionaries create a great deal of difficulties for the couple, so frustrating Yinghua that she loses her sight. In addition, a boy they raised since childhood becomes enamored of making money and leaves their home for the city. Finally, Wu Dacheng overcomes the difficulties and finishes the well. His wife's eyesight responds to treatment, and at last the once poor and backward village is on the road to prosperity.

1891. South China 1994 (Nan Zhong Guo 1994)

1994. Tianjin Film Studio, Shenzhen Film Company Co-Production. Color. Letterboxed. 9 Reels. Direction: Zhang Nuanxin. Screenplay: Huang Shiying, Cai Yibing. Cinematography: Pao Xiaoran. Art Direction: Wang Jie. Music: Chen Xiangyu. Sound: Lai Qizhen. Costume: Gong Yanru, Sheng Wei. Makeup: Zhang Huiling. Cast: Cheng Qian as Yuan Fang, Su Jing as Liang Yifan, Li Shixi as Xu Jingfeng, Tan Tianqian as Yu Jie, Duan Jianguo as Wang Chuanliang, Cao Chun as Liu Xiaofang, Tian Xue as Qiuying, Wang Bing as Xiao Hong

In an opened city in South China,

competition between joint venture companies is fierce, and competition between company employees no less so. Yuan Fang, an executive in one firm, suggests that treatment of workers should not be limited to punishments alone. He works with the company's party secretary to improve labor-management relations, and at last is recommended as the company's new CEO.

1892. *The South Pacific Tycoon (Nan Yang Fu Wen)*

1985. Guangxi Film Studio. Color. 10 Reels. Direction: Zhao Wenxin. Screenplay: Zhou Minzhen, Cai Liyang. Cinematography: Liao Fan, Xie Zhijun, Zhao Xuxu. Art Direction: Lao Guanneng. Music: Yang Shaoyi. Sound: Lin Lin. Cast: Ma Ji as Director Yuan, He Quanzhi as Huang Sandie, Ren Hongen as Xu Jiajin, Wan Baohong as Daxin, Zhao Yan as A Fu

Tobacco planting in the Shiwan Mountain area of Guangxi has made Huang Sandie prosperous to the point the locals call him "The Tobacco King." He takes his daughter Daxin on a visit to the city of Guilin, and a series of misunderstandings ensue: at first they are regarded as peasants, and then he is mistaken for a wealthy tycoon visiting from abroad. At last he meets the real overseas Chinese "Tobacco King," and the story traces the development of their friendship.

1893. *South Sea Storm (Nan Hai Feng Yun)*

1976. August First Film Studio. Color. 10 Reels. Direction: Jing Mukui, Zhang Yongshou. Screenplay: Lu Zhuguo. Cinematography: Cai Jiwei, Gao Jiuling. Art Direction: Ren Huixing, Zhang Zheng. Music: Lu Yuan. Sound: Zhen Minzhe. Cast: Tang Guoqiang as Yu Hualong, Zhang Yongshou as Liang Chonghai, Gao Baocheng as Father, Hong Xueming as Sister, Gan Hong as Sister (as a child), Bao Xun as the signalman

In the Xisha archipelago, Yu Hualong becomes separated from his family when their fishing boat is fired on and sunk by a Vietnamese warship. After being rescued by a PLA ship, he joins the navy. He works his way up to become captain of a warship. Years later, his ship is on patrol when they encounter a Chinese fishing boat being threatened by the same Vietnamese ship. Yu Hualong's ship intervenes and saves the fishing boat. It turns out the skipper of the fishing boat is Yu Hualong's father, and his sister is a member of the crew.

1894. *The Spacious Courtyard (Parts 1 & 2) (Ting Yuan Shen Shen)*

1989. Shanghai Film Studio. Color. 18 Reels. Letterboxed. Direction: Shi Shujun. Screenplay: Yan Mingbang and Shi Shujun, based on the novel by Taiwanese writer Qiong Yao. Cinematography: Zhao Junhong, Zang Hongjun. Art Direction: Dong Jingsheng. Music: Yang Mao. Sound: Feng Deyao. Cast: Song Jia as Zhang Hanyan and Fang Siying, You Yong as Bai Peiwen, Jin Meng as Ou Ailin, Jiao Huang as Jian Feifan, Bei Qingni as Tingting

Fang Siying, a recent education graduate, arrives at a small town in Taiwan from the U.S., looking for the once luxurious Hanyan Mansion. She finds it badly dilapidated and occupied by the current owner, blind Bai Peiwen, his wife and young daughter. Fang becomes a teacher at the local primary school, and takes special care of the daughter Tingting, bringing happiness to the life of this sad young girl. Bai is grateful and at his request, Fang moves to live in Bai's mansion. Fang restores life to the old place. Bai feels Fang is much like his beloved first wife Zhang Hanyan, who died some time ago. Bai's present wife Qu Ailin is a jealous woman who quarrels incessantly with him. At this juncture a mysterious man called Jian Feifan arrives in Taiwan from the U.S. to take revenge on Bai. A storm is gathering.

Best Music Yang Mao, 1990 Golden Rooster Awards.

Best Sound Feng Deyao, 1990 Golden Rooster Awards.

Best Actress Song Jia, 1990 Hundred Flowers Awards.

1895. *Sparetime Policeman (Ye Yu Jing Cha)*

1987. Xiaoxiang Film Studio. Color. 9 Reels. Direction: Yuan Ye. Screenplay: You Xuezhong, Yuan Ye. Cinematography: Wang Kekuan. Art Direction: Jin Bohao. Music: Fu Lin. Sound: Liu Feng. Cast: Feng Gong as He Dazuang, Ling Hui as Qiuping

In the city of Guangzhou, young worker He Dazuang is denied permission to take extension college entrance exams because his admission ticket is stolen by a thief. He Dazuang swears he will become a voluntary crime fighter in his spare time. There ensues a series of incidents in which he apprehends various kinds of thieves, usually in public settings, such as on buses, etc. Although he is sometimes outwitted by the thieves, and everyone including his girlfriend Qiuping questions his sanity, he eventually gains a reputation and respect through his unusual avocation. Eventually Qiuping realizes she loves him very much.

1896. *A Sparkling Red Star (Shan Shan De Hong Xing)*

1974. August First Film Studio. Color. 11 Reels. Direction: Li Jun, Li Ang. Screenplay: Collective, recorded by Wang Yuanjian and Lu Zhuguo, based on the novel of the same title by Li Xintian. Cinematography: Cai Jiwei, Cao Jingyun. Art Direction: Zhen Mingzhe. Music: Fu Gengcheng. Cast: Zhu Xinyun as Pan Dongzhi, Bo Guanjun as Wu Xiuzhu, Gao Baocheng as Old Song, Li Xuehong as Mother, Zhao Ruping as Pan Xingyi, Liu Jizhong as Chunyazhi, Liu Jiang as Hu Hansan

In 1931, when the Red Army liberates the town of Liuxi, Little Dongzhi is rescued from the clutches of local tyrant Hu Hansan. In the fall of 1934, the Red Army's main force has to move its central base, but before leaving Dongzhi's father gives him a red star. After the main force pulls out, the town is once again under Nationalist government control. Dongzhi's mother is put to death for covering some village people's flight to safety. The boy Dongzhi grows up with a deep longing for revolution, and is progressively educated by the local Party underground. As a young man, he smashes Hu Hansan's plan to root out guerrillas hiding in the hills, and even kills Hu himself. Dongzhi then coordinates a guerrilla attack of the town of Yaowan. Finally, in 1938, Dongzhi joins the Red Army, and meets his father at a military relocation base. He shows him the red star that he has kept for so many years.

1897. *Sparks from the Heart (Xin Ling De Huo Hua)*

1982. Zhejiang Film Studio. Color. 11 Reels. Direction: Shen Yaoting. Screenplay: Shen Yaoting, Chen Zhenjiang. Cinematography: Zhang Guifu, Zhou Ping. Art Direction: Lu Jun, Li Shuqi. Music: Lu Enlai. Sound: Zhou Yunling, Zhang Chenghua. Cast: Wang Suya as teacher Xu, Tu Ruying as Wang Chengjuan, Gao Cui as Wang's mother, Zhou Guobin as Wang Cheng-

lin, Ye Zhikang as Zhang Anping, Sun Dongguang as Director Lin, Zhang Xiaoqin as Xiao Li, Xue Shujie as Zhou Ying

Old worker Chen is understandably upset when his new bicycle is stolen. But two weeks later the thief quietly returns it along with 25 yuan in compensation. The film tells the tale of a young man named Wang Chenlin, a new worker in a machine shop, but part of a gang of delinquent bike thieves when young. Sent to reform school, he is been converted by a caring teacher. After his release, Wang determines to go straight, but his old pals on the street are not convinced and stole old Chen's bike for him as a "gift." Not wanting to mess up his new life, Wang has returned the bike to its owner.

1898. *Special Assignment (Te Shu Ren Wu)*

1978. Shanghai Film Studio. B & W. 10 Reels. Direction: Yu Bengzheng, Xu Jihong. Screenplay: Liang Xing. Cinematography: Xia Lixing, Cheng Shiyu. Art Direction: Guo Dongcang, Li Huazhong. Music: Huang Zhun. Sound: Huang Dongping. Cast: Ma Guanyin as Gao Heng, Lu Jing as Tian Li, Li Qinqin as A Jiao, Zhang Yunli as Ya Xiong, Liang Min as Old Woman Qi, Sun Yufeng as Political Commissar He, Qi Jianqiu as Special Agent Wu

In the closing days of World War Two, a Hainan Island guerrilla troop sends three of their number, Special Agents Wu, Gao Heng and Tian Li to nearby Japanese-held Bingland Island, to blow up an installation there. Wu is killed before they reach the island, but the other two hide in a cave. Tian Li risks his life to enter the enemy's air base, where he learns of Japanese plans to rebuild the air strip and bombard Hainan, information he successfully transmits to Gao Heng. Gao Heng then learns that the Japanese plan to kill all the workers after the airport is completed. They use this information to organize a successful rebellion of the local people. The rebellion is successful and the island is liberated from the Japanese.

1899. *Special Group (Te Jing Xiong Wei)*

1992. Shenzhen Film Studio and Hong Kong Jianeng Film Company. Color. Letterboxed. 9 Reels. Direction: Huang Weiye (Hong Kong). Screenplay: Rao Mu. Cinematography: Liu Hua. Art Direction: Yan Dingfu. Sound: Cao Guanghua. Costume: Yu Deli. Makeup: Zhu Meidi.

A Sparkling Red Star. Pan Dongzhi (Zhu Xinyun, left) shows his grandfather how he hid salt inside his clothes to pass through an enemy checkpoint. 1974. August First Film Studio.

Zeng Zhen. Cast: Hu Huizhong as Zhang Hong, Yang Fengfeng as Li Tong, Huang Jiada as Zhao Jie, Feng Fusheng as Director Yuan, Mai Deluo as Wei Nan, Lian Weijian as He Sheng, Yu Daijun as Hu Cang

Hong Kong police crack a drug smuggling case which is linked to an important Hong Kong businessman, He Sheng. Two officers, Wei Nan and his woman partner Li Tong, are sent to the mainland to deliver documents relevant to the case to public security forces there. They believe that He Sheng has been exploiting a certain mainland factory's exemption from customs inspection to hide drugs from the golden triangle in shipments from the factory, drugs which are then delivered to Hong Kong for transshipment overseas. Chinese and Hong Kong police work closely together to smash the drug ring, finally arresting He Sheng and two foreign drug dealers.

1900. *Special Naughty Team in Action (Te Hun Jian Dui Zhai Xing Dong)*

1989. Beijing Film Studio. Color. Letter-

boxed. 9 Reels. Direction: Ge Xiaoying. Screenplay: Li Yunliang. Cinematography: Ru Shuiren. Art Direction: Zhou Dengfu. Music: Jin Fuzhai. Sound: Wei Xueyi. Cast: Shan Dan as Dong Haixing, Li Gang as Xie Qian, Wang Dichun as Jin Baobei, Wang Qiang as Liang Chitao

Three fifth grade boys in a school for children of naval personnel misbehave constantly, bully girls in their school and never study. A new school supervisor, warship Captain Liang Chitao, gains the boys' respect and eventually gets them on the right course in life.

1901. *Special Policemen Go Into Action (Te Jing Chu Ji)*

1992. Xi'an Film Studio. Color. Letterboxed. 9 Reels. Direction: Zhu Jianxin. Cinematography: Wang Xiaomin. Art Direction: Dong Shijun. Music: Li Yaodong. Sound: Ji Changhua. Costume: Liu Qingli. Makeup: Zhu Jian. Cast: Gao Fa as Ouyang, Gu Liuyi as Wu Shaoheng, Liu Shuang as Xiao Dai, Zhou Yinhong as Wun She, Tang Zhenhua as Li Xiaoyun

Interpol notifies the Chinese Public Security Bureau that the number 2 man in a transnational criminal organization, a Chinese, has killed his boss and fled into China, taking with him the information necessary to tap into the organization's Swiss bank account. Special investigator Ouyang is put in charge of the case. Ouyang has a life and death struggle with the gangster and his henchmen, but at last defeats them and recovers the bank account information.

1902. *Special President (Fei Chang Da Zong Tong)*

1986. Shanghai Film Studio. Color. Wide Screen. 12 Reels. Direction: Sun Daolin. Screenplay: Sun Daolin, Ye Dan. Cinematography: Luo Chongzhou, Wu Liekang. Art Direction: Ge Sicheng, Wu Weifei. Music: Lu Qimin. Sound: Feng Deyao. Cast: Sun Daolin as Sun Zhongshan (Sun Yatsen), Zhang Xiaomin as Song Qingling (Madame Sun), Xie Weixiong as Deng Qiang, Ye Yizhe as Ye Ting, Wang Ganyi as Ye Ju, Yuan Xingzhe as Qi Meilan, Liu Ping as Ma Lin, Li Dingbao as Chen Jiongming.

In May of 1925 Sun Zhongshan (Sun Yatsen) is named "Special President" in Guangzhou, launching the "legal protection" movement. But conspiring against him is General Chen Jiongming, commander of the Republican Army, in secret alliance with anti–Sun officials in Nanjing. President Sun travels to Nanjing in the attempt to win Chen back to his side. Chen expresses sympathy for Sun's cause, but continues to work against him in private. Chen eventually rebels openly, and the betrayal sinks President Sun into deep depression. Sun realizes he must reform the Nationalist Party. He issues a new policy calling for cooperation with the Communist Party at home and alliance with the Soviet Union abroad.

Best Supporting Actress Zhang Xiaomin, 1987 Hundred Flowers Awards.

1903. *Special Prisoner (Te Shu Qiu Fan)*

1995. Inner Mongolia Film Studio. Color. Letterboxed. Direction: Zhao Guohua, Xie Tao. Screenplay: Lei Fu. Cinematography: Na Risu. Art Direction: Ana Musi. Cast: Basheng Zhabu.

During an investigation of a huge bank embezzlement case, detective Zhao Lu is murdered. His angry superior Batu vows to avenge his partner's death. He also adopts his dead partner's son Harifu. But Batu is set up and violates some departmental rules which get him

removed from the investigation. The detective goes outside the department to continue the probe on his own. He at lasts succeeds in tracking down and killing the man responsible for his partner's death, but goes so far outside the law in doing so that he winds up behind bars. His father brings Harifu to visit him, and they encourage him to do well in prison.

1904. *Speeding (Chao Su)*

1987. Beijing Film Studio. Color. 10 Reels. Direction: Qiqing Gaowa. Screenplay: Chen Yutong. Cinematography: Huang Xinyi. Art Direction: Cehn Xiaoxia. Music: Gu De. Sound: Zhang Ye. Cast: Zhu Shimao as Sheng Bainian, Fu Yiwei as Feng Yinan, Tang Jiezhong as the bureau director, Gu Lan as Professor Feng Yiju, Song Xiaoyin as Qiao Ming, Lao Li as Zhao Ruiguang, Qi Kejian as Yuan Xiliang.

When driver Sheng Bainian sees a girl on his route attempting to kill herself, he intervenes to save her. She is Feng Yinan, despondent because her boyfriend had dumped her. Because of what he thinks is unjust criticism from his boss, Sheng later resigns his job and contracts his services to a trading company. One of his friends there, Yuan Xiliang, will do just about anything for money, but this goes against Sheng Bainian's principles. He tells his friend that greed is like speeding: it may be initially exhilarating, but it is really dangerous. This is borne out when Xiliang gets in big trouble because of some of the people he contracts with. Meanwhile, Sheng Bainian and Feng Yinan fall in love.

1905. *Spirit of a Nation (Guo Hun)*

1991. Fujian Film Studio and Zhejiang Film Studio Co-Production. Color. Wide Screen. 10 Reels. Direction: Chen Xianyu. Screenplay: Tian Junli. Cinematography: Zhang Dongdong. Art Direction: Lu Jun. Music: Guan Xia and Lu Enlai. Sound: Guo Qiang. Cast: Li Lan as Li Lan, Gao Fa as Jiang Yonggui, Wang Jianjun as Zhang Man, Zhao Xiaochuan as Liu Yongqin, Jiang Hualing as Niu Mantun, Pu Chaoyin as Liu's wife.

In the 1980s, a serious dispute erupts among the membership of a county Party Committee over how to implement the central Party's new opening and reform policy in the countryside. One view holds that opening will result in farmers deserting the land and flooding the cities; the other believes that farmers who leave the land would have nothing, but they will stay on the land if given a diversity of operations there. The latter view eventually wins out, and they begin to show the farmers how to become prosperous together.

1906. *The Spirit of Heaven Is in Her Sword (Tian Shen Jian Nu)*

1992. Beijing Youth Film Studio & Yiying Film Company Co-Production. Color. Letterboxed. 9 Reels. Direction: Liang Yaoming. Screenplay: Liang Yaoming. Cinematography: Li Yingde, Liao Qingsong. Art Direction: Liang Yaoming. Music: Yang Qichang. Sound: Ah Qiang. Costume: Liu Jiyou. Makeup: Luo Lijuan, Wang Caiyun. Cast: Lin Junxian as Shizhong Yusheng, Zhou Huiming as Honghua, Wu Ma as Xiang Tian, Qin Pei as Danhuo Tianjun, Liu Xun as Xiao Jiuzhou

Orphaned when very young, Honghua devotes herself to mastering kung fu, and becomes an outstanding swordsmith as well. She makes one sword that is so good it frightens the wolf spirit, and he fights Honghua. This is all witnessed by a man named Shizhong Yusheng, who is really a spirit. He secretly aids Honghua, and they fall in love. This is disapproved of by Heaven, for it is forbidden for a spirit to love a mortal. The film relates how the couple fight for their love, and at last get together.

1907. *Spirits of the Sea (Hai Shen)*

1981. Changchun Film Studio. Color. 11 Reels. Direction: Zhao Xinshui. Screenplay: Zhao Xinshui, Ding Shan, Lu Wenao. Cinematography: Wu Bengli. Art Direction: Li Junjie. Music: Lei Yusheng. Sound: Wang Fei. Cast: Wang Tongle as Liang Yuhu, Li Junhai as Guo Jingyou, Jiang Zeling as Yang Chunjiao, Pang Ming as Ci Ping

In 1950, the PLA is rapidly moving south. Regimental Commander Liang Yuhu had been born into a poor fishing family, and 10 years before had fallen in love with a sweet girl named Yang Chunjiao, from another fishing family. They became engaged, but once when he was out at sea, his boat was sunk by a passing Japanese warship. He was rescued by the Communist Eighth Route Army, which he joined. Now, Liang Yuhu brings his army to liberate his hometown, and is anxious to see his lover. Unfortunately, Yang Chunjiao married another man and had a daughter. She had given up on Liang because everyone believed he had been drowned at sea. Her husband was later drafted into the Nationalist Chinese army and was killed. Liang Yuhu and Yang Chunjiao overcome their pain and misunderstandings, and start to get reacquainted. After the new China establishes its first naval forces, Liang Yuhu is given a command. There are holdout Nationalist forces on nearby Wanshan Island, and Liang decides to attack and liberate the island. Yang Chunjiao serves as their navigator. In the fierce fighting that ensues, Liang and Yang are both among those who give their lives. The people consider them the true spirits of the sea.

1908. *A Spoiled Young Wife Goes to Earn a Living (Xiao Jiao Qi Mo Sheng Ji)*

1995. Shanghai Film Studio. Color. Letterboxed. Direction: Shi Shujun, Gu Langhui. Screenplay: Xu Yinghua, Shu Shujun. Cinematography: Zhao Junhong. Art Direction: Zhou Xinren. Music: Xi Qiming. Cast: Zhou Xun as Yangyang, Cao Li as Fang Dazhong

Spoiled young wife Yangyang wants her husband Fang Dazhong to come home early from work, so she lies, telling him she is sick. Racing home to be with her, Dazhong loses control of his car and crashes into a store, injuring several people. He is sentenced to three years in prison. Yangyang is forced to go to work, since all the family's possessions have to sold to compensate the crash victims. She unsuccessfully tries a series of occupations, including raising ducks, working in a hotel, selling food, etc. At last, sadder and wiser, Yangyang is reunited with her husband on his release from prison.

1909. *Spray and Soft Sand (Lang Hua Xi Sha)*

1983. Shanghai Film Studio. Color. 10 Reels. Direction: Fu Jinggong, Shi Xiaohua, Li Xiepu. Screenplay: Qi Wenshao. Cinematography: Ying Fukang, Dai Qimin, Zhen Hong, Wun Sijie. Art Direction: Guo Dongcang, Pu Jingsun, Li Wenkang, Yao Wei. Music: Xu Jingxin. Sound: Jin Fugeng. Cast: Lu Shan as Old Grandma, Gong Xue as Chen Jing, Liu Xingyi as Xiao Qian, Li Jiayao as Director Chen, Zhong Xinghuo as Deputy Bureau Director Zhao

The film consists of several short stories. "Secret Information" criticizes some of the less healthy aspects of contemporary Chinese social relations. "Brother's Letter" praises the significant changes in the Chinese countryside since the 3rd Plenary Session of the 11th Party Congress. "Finding the Lost Materials" reflects on how the social atmosphere was destroyed by the Gang of Four, and how much better things are now. "Danger Is His Name" urges having the courage to admit one's mistakes and correct them. "Dental Office" shows how one's soul can be polluted by money. "Rainy Night" praises the new socialist custom of helping others.

1910. *Spring and Autumn in a Small Town (Xiao Cheng Chun Qiu)*

1981. Fujian Film Studio. Color. 9 Reels. Direction: Luo Tai. Screenplay: Jiang Yimu, Chen Geng, Luo Tai. Cinematography: Zhu Yongde. Art Direction: Wang Yuebai. Music: Zhang Shaotong. Sound: Wu Hua. Cast: Liang Boluo as Wu Jian, Zhao Zhilian as Zhao Xiong, Xu Jiayin as Shuyin, Zhang Zhiqiang as He Jianping, Liang Zhipeng as Wu Qi, Zeng Zhifang as Xiuwei

Just prior to the anti–Japanese War, during the "Resist Japan, Rescue the Nation" campaign, a traitor guides collaborationist government spies to a Communist cell. Their leader, Communist Party member Wu Jian, gets his comrades out in time, but he himself is arrested. After his arrest, every possible means of torture and interrogation is used to break him, but Wu Jian continues to resist. Aided by a Communist under cover inside enemy headquarters, Wu Jian and the other prisoners organize a prison break. The breakout begins at the time planned, and while his fellow prisoners get out successfully, the badly beaten Wu Jian falls behind. As the pursuing enemy closes in on him, he orders the others to run while he bravely holds off the enemy. When his ammunition runs out, he jumps off a cliff, dying honorably.

1911. *Spring Comes to the Marshes (Shui Xiang De Chun Tian)*

1955. Shanghai Film Studio. B & W. 11 Reels. Direction: Xie Jin. Screenplay: Pao Yu, Wang Puqing. Cinematography: Gu Wenhou. Set Design: Ling Lei. Music: Lu Qiming. Sound: Shao Zihe. Cast: Qi Mengshi as Ji Chunlin, Sun Jinlu as Cui Lian, Tan Yun as Ji's wife, Fan Lai as Tai Youcai, Zhou Min as Tai's mother, Tie Niu as Zhang Gen, Xia Tian as Kong Bingyuan

After the chief of Nanwan Village Ji Chunlin returns from helping with the Huai River treatment project, he proposes converting the village's ponds into rice paddies, an idea enthusiastically received by his wife, Cui Lian, and local civil guard chief Zhang Gen. But some local villains try to sabotage his plan for their own personal gain. Ji tries to carry out his plan alone, but his thinking this way is criticized by the local Party branch secretary. Under the leadership of the Party, Ji Chunlin relies on the masses of the people to begin his project. The government also gives them seeds and financial loans to help them get started. It is later discovered that the early difficulties were all part of a plot by Kong Bingyuan, a rich farmer, and the people, now politically aware, unite to repair the sabotaged dam. The ponds are finally converted into paddies, and Nanwan Village enjoys a bumper harvest in the fall.

1912. *Spring Comes to the Withered Tree (Kumu Feng Chun)*

1961. Haiyan Film Studio. Color. 10 Reels. Direction: Zhen Junli. Screenplay: Wang Lian and Zhen Junli, based on the stage play of the same title. Cinematography: Huang Shaofeng. Art Direction: Han Shangyi. Music: Ge Yan. Sound: Wu Jianghai, Casting: You Jia as Bitter Sister, Xu Zhihua as Fang Dong, Shanguan Yunzhu as Fang's mother, Qian Qianli as Fang's father, Liu Hongsheng as Luo Shunde, Jiang Tianliu as Li Gengxiang

The title is an idiom for "a new lease on life."

In pre-liberation China, an orphan girl called Bitter Sister is purchased by the Fang family as their son's future wife. She is treated very well by her fiance and future-in-laws, and looks forward to a happy life. All changes when an epidemic of schistosomiasis breaks out, forcing the family to migrate to safety. On the way, Bitter Sister becomes separated from her new family. With no way of making a living, she marries someone else. However, her husband soon dies of the disease, and she herself falls ill with it. After liberation, she meets again her former fiance Fang Dong, now a tractor driver. Their joy at reuniting is tempered by her sadness at still carrying the disease. With the care of the people's government, Bitter Sister's schistosomiasis is cured. She and Fang Dong are married and soon have a healthy set of twins. The family looks forward to a happy future.

Spring Comes to the Withered Tree. From left, Bitter Sister (You Jia), Fang Dong (Xu Zhihua) and Mama Fang (Shangguan Yunzhu) are happily reunited under the new people's government. 1961. Haiyan Film Studio.

1913. *Spring Drizzle (Chun Yu Xiao Xiao)*

1979. Pearl River Film Studio. Color. 9 Reels. Direction: Ding Yingnan, Hu Bingliu. Screenplay: Su Shuyang. Cinematography: Wei Duo. Art Direction: Li Xin. Music: Wang Yanqiao. Sound: Lin Guoqiang. Cast: Zhang Liwei as Gu Xiuming, Zhang Jie as Feng Chunhai, Lin Muyu as Xu Lang, Huang Wenkui as Chen Yang, Hu Lingling as Yu Jia

After the "Tiananmen Incident" of 1976, when a mass demonstration was held in opposition to the Gang of Four, nurse Gu Xiumin is on a train from Beijing to another city, caring for a wounded person. The train is stopped by Gu's husband Feng Chunhai, as he has an emergency order from the PSB, looking for a "counterrevolutionary" named Chen Yang, participant in the "Incident." After talking to her husband, Gu Xiumin realizes that Chen Yang is her patient, but out of love for Premier Zhou and hostility to the Gang of Four, she decides to try to protect Chen Yang. She does her utmost to persuade her husband, and when he finally sees her reasoning and rids himself of his feelings for the Gang, he lets Gu Xiumin

take Chen Yang from the train to a place of safety.

1914. *Spring Festival (Guo Nian)*

1991. Beijing Film Studio and Hong Kong Wanhe Film and TV Co. Ltd. Co-Production. Color. 10 Reels. Direction: Huang Jianzhong. Screenplay: Jiang Yi. Cinematography: Li Tian. Art Direction: Liu Shi. Music: Zou Ye. Sound: Li Bojiang, Guan Jian. Cast: Li Baotian as the father, Zhao Lirong as the mother, Liu Xiaolingtong as the first son, Ding Jiali as the first son's wife, Hu Yajie as the second son, Tan Xiaoyan as the second son's girlfriend, Liang Tian as the youngest son, Ma Xiaoqing as the youngest son's girlfriend, Wang Liyun as the first daughter, Ge You as the first daughter's husband, Shi Lanya as the second daughter, Shen Junyi as the second daughter's husband

Spring Festival is the traditional Chinese New Year, as important to Chinese as Christmas is to those in the West. When Spring Festival arrives, everyone has a feeling of rebirth, and a hope the year to come will bring happiness and prosperity and that any bad luck a person has will depart with the old year. This story takes place on New Year's eve in a snow-bound small town in China's far north. Amidst the revelry and family reunions all around them, old man Cheng and his wife are all alone. None of their children will visit, especially after what seems to have been a debacle of a reunion the year before. But on the next day, the first day of the lunar new year, sons and daughters start to return anyway, spouses, children and significant others in tow…

Best Supporting Actress Ding Jiali, 1992 Golden Rooster Awards.

Best Picture, 1992 Hundred Flowers Awards.

Best Actress Zhao Lirong, 1992 Hundred Flowers Awards.

Best Supporting Actor Ge You, 1992 Hundred Flowers Awards.

Jury's Special Award, Best Actress Award (Zhao Lirong), 4th Tokyo International Film Festival.

1915. *Spring Fills the World (Chun Man Ren Jian)*

1959. Tianma Film Studio. Color. 10 Reels. Direction: Sang Hu. Screenplay: Ke Lin, Xie Junfeng, Sang Hu. Cinematography: Zhou Daming. Art Direction: Wang Yuebai. Music: Ji Ming. Sound: Zhu Weigang. Cast: Bai Yang as Fang Qun, Bai Mu as Fan Jikang, Wei Yuwei as Ding Dagang, Wang Danfeng as Zhu Xiuyun, Zhong Shuhuang as Liang Shicang, Feng Xiao as the reporter, Zheng Min as Professor Bai

Steel worker Ding Dagang is hospitalized with severe burns incurred fighting a fire in his mill. Hospital surgical department director Fan Jikang asks several specialists in for consultation on the case. Professor Bai, who relies entirely on the medical literature of Western nations, thinks the patient's burns are so severe there is no way to save him. Hospital Party Secretary Fang Qun urges the medical personnel to overcome their slavish admiration of Western theories, and explore new ways of saving patients' lives. At one point, infection sets in and they consider amputating the patient's leg, but Secretary Fang supports a new method which is successful when tried. Finally, after being near death several times, the patient recovers and is able to return to his job.

1916. *Spring Hastens the Blossoms Blooming (Chun Cui Tao Li)*

1961. Haiyan Film Studio. B & W. 10 Reels. Direction: Lin Yang. Screenplay: Ru Zhijuan, Ai Mingzhi. Cinematography: Luo Chongzhou. Art Direction: Hu Zuoyun. Music: Gao Tian. Sound: Liu Guangjie. Casting: Sha Li as Gu Shanjuan, Sun Jinglu as Zhao Ling, Hong Xia as Xiuhua, Qi Heng as Director Tang, Tie Niu as Party Secretary Lu, Chen Shinan as Yao Ageng

In 1958, supported by the district Party committee, Shanghai housewife Gu Shanjuan sets up a privately run elementary school in spite of the mocking suspicions of others. Zhao Ling, one of the teachers she hires, uses the teaching methods she learned in old China, most notably disciplining students with physical punishment. Zhao and young teacher Xiuhua argue over how to deal with unruly student Yao Ageng, which ends with both resigning. Gu Shanjuan takes on their workload in addition to her own. Meanwhile, she continues to help and persuade Zhao Ling. The other two are moved by her dedication and hard work, and both return to the school. In time, with patience on the part of his teachers, Yao Ageng begins to make progress with his behavioral problem.

1917. *Spring in Autumn (Qiu Tian Li De Chun Tian)*

1985. Shanghai Film Studio. Color. Wide Screen. 12 Reels. Direction: Bai Chen. Screenplay: Zhang Xuan. Cinematography: Lu Junfu. Art Direction: Zhong Yongqin. Music: Liu Yanxi. Sound: Ge Weijia. Cast: Xu Lei as Zhou Lianghui, Tong Ruiming as Luo Liping, Lei Han as Yangyang, Wang Pei as the old military friend, Gao Weiqi as Brother

During the Cultural Revolution, the former Party Secretary of a South China city is persecuted to death, his wife Zhou Lianghui is dismissed from her job, and her young son Yangyang is bullied by others. Mail carrier Luo Liping, an honest young man with a sense of justice, is very sympathetic and helpful to the widow and her son. After the Gang of Four's downfall, Zhou is restored to her old job, and soon becomes director of the city's Women's Committee, Yangyang gets a good job, and their lives return to normal. Over the years, Zhou Lianghui has grown to love the man who gave them so much help, Luo Liping. The two start to date openly, but society (in the form of Yangyang and his future in-laws) opposes their relationship. For the sake of her son's happiness, she sacrifices her love. But

Spring Fills the World. Hospital Party Secretary Fang Qun (Bai Yang, right) and Zhu Xiuyun (Wang Danfeng) comfort each other in the face of reactionary criticism. 1959. Tianma Film Studio.

one day she and Luo meet unexpectedly on the street.

1918. *Spring Is Here (Chun Tian Lai Le)*

1956. Shanghai Film Studio. B & W. 11 Reels. Direction: Gu Eryi, Huang Zumo. Screenplay: Lu Yanzhou. Cinematography: Qian Yu. Art Direction: Wang Yebai, Music: Ji Ming, Sound: Wu Jianghai, Cast: Sun Daolin as Lu Huaisheng, Li Baoluo as Grandpa Mo, Jiang Shan as Erhei's father, Niu Beng as Little Parka, Bai Mu as Zhang Minglou, Tan Yun as Daxiang's wife, Zhang Yan as Fu Shun

Lu Huaisheng, Deputy Director of the Dong Village agricultural cooperative proposes a reform plan for developing village farm production, but is opposed by Director Zhang Minglou. The co-op's accountant Fu Shun exploits their disagreement to stir up bad feelings between the two directors for his own gain. Instead of looking into the dispute, the district political commissar just listens to Zhang Minglou and concludes Lu Huaisheng is just seeking individual glory and dismisses the deputy from his position. Lu is ordered to report to the county committee for self-examination,

but when he appears before the committee, Lu exposes Fu Shun's involvement in speculation, profiteering and other actions destructive to the co-op. Faced with the facts, Zhang Minglou finally wakes up and understands that Lu Huaisheng's plan is correct. Lu's ideas are implemented with the support of upper level leadership, and the following harvest is a record one for Dong Village.

1919. *Spring Orchid, Fall Chrysanthemum (aka Two Brands) (Chun Lan Qiu Ju)*

1982. Guangxi Film Studio. Color. 10 Reels. Direction: Guo Baocang. Screenplay: Ji Hongxu, Guo Baocang. Cinematography: Yang Yuming. Art Direction: Zhang Yafang. Music: Su Tie. Sound: Li Zhuwen. Cast: Zhang Jie as Xu Daming, He Ling as Qu Wendi, Chang Wenzhi as Liang Hua, Shi Weijian as An Xi, Huang Wanqiu as Hua Min

When Xu Daming graduates from college in the 1950s, he founds a wool sweater mill and is named its deputy director. He is labeled a "follower of the capitalist line" during the Cultural Revolution and sent down to the countryside. After the Gang of Four is brought down, he returns to the mill, this time as its director. He finds the quality of the mill's renowned "Spring Orchid" brand of sweater to be deteriorating and that this is directly related to the quality control measures of his wife, Deputy Director Qu Wendi. Xu Daming gives considerable attention to quality control, and introduces a new sweater line, the "Fall Chrysanthemum." His wife is bitterly opposed to this, and he finds it difficult to get the new equipment required. He finally succeeds, with the "Spring Orchid" line regaining its reputation and the "Fall Chrysanthemum" becoming successful enough to enter the international market.

1920. *Spring Returns to the Red Mansion (Chun Gui Hong Lou)*

1981. Changchun Film Studio. Color. 10 Reels. Direction: Xue Yandong. Screenplay: Yan Fengle. Cinematography: Meng Xiandi. Art Direction: Liu Xuerao, Xu Zhengkun. Music: Xiao Yan. Sound: Liu Jingui. Cast: Ni Zhenghua as Yang Jian, Pu Ke as Guan Handa, Guo Yiwen as Guan's wife, Guo Xuxin as Xiaosheng, Liu Kai as Guan Shufeng, Yu Yanping as Rong Guoqiang, Zhang Baishuang as Wang Yuhua

When the Cultural Revolution is over, Hubing County Director Yang Jian is restored to his post, and happily travels to the Yanjiantan Commune to attend his son's wedding. On the way, he runs into a group of bachelors. They complain about their commune's poverty, and about the lack of marriageable young women for them. They request his help. Yang Jian arrives at the site of his son's wedding where he sees many guests with many gifts, and his son's fancy new home, everything standing in sharp contrast to what he has just seen on his trip. The county director criticizes his son for taking the gifts, then asks his son to return the gifts and postpone the wedding. This makes everyone unhappy, his son and future daughter-in-law, her parents, and the county Party Secretary Guan Handa and his wife as well. To help alter the poor situation in the commune, Yang Jian visits the bachelors again to look into their situation more closely. However, his son Yang Xiaosheng has petitioned the commune leadership to have these people kicked out. Yang Jian gets the bachelors to engage in agricultural byproduct production to increase their income, and he arranges for some girls in another commune to meet the bachelors of Yanjiantan Commune. His son

Yang Xiaosheng changes his attitude and joins the bachelors' work team. The story ends with Yang's son and the many commune bachelors holding a collective wedding.

1921. *Spring Song (Chun Ge)*

1978. Pearl River Film Studio. Color. 10 Reels. Direction: Chen Gang. Screenplay: Li Keling, Zhang Shaoliang. Cinematography: Wei Duo. Art Direction: Li Xing. Music: Che Min. Sound: Li Baijian. Cast: Chun Li as Kang Laofang, Yu Xiuchuan as Tian Shuang, Liu Xiaoqing as Li Cuizhi, Zhang Dongsheng as Kang Eryue, Ma Ji as Cui Qinchang, Ma Xiu as Qinchang's wife, Zhou Huahua as Wang Xiaolan, Cai Jingyu as Li Mingshui

South and North Yangling are two competing production units, and farm machinery mechanic Liu Ruishan of the South unit marries into the North unit. South Yangling unit farm machinery plant director Kang Laofang argues about this with his wife Tian Shuang. Kang Laofang's only son Eryue works at his plant, and he is in love with Li Cuizhi, a key worker in the North unit. Cuizhi hopes Eryue will marry into her unit, making Kang Laofang very angry. But, once when South Yangling has trouble purchasing spare parts for their machinery, the North Yangling Party secretary sends people to deliver the urgently needed parts. From then on, the two units are united, and make progress together. Eryue, Cuizhi and other young couples also begin getting married according to their own wishes.

1922. *Spring Sunshine (Chun Hui)*

1982. Guangxi Film Studio. Color. 10 Reels. Direction: Wu Yinchun. Screenplay: Zhou Minzheng. Cinematography: Li Zhuwen. Art Direction: Wu Zhaohua. Music: Yang Shaoyi. Sound: Li Zhuwen. Cast: Tian Chengren as Teacher Ling, Chang Rong as Tan Jian, Wu Dan as Zhong Xiaoxing, Cheng Zhong as Ling Yan, Jiang Junnan as Li Min, Xia Jin as Lu Xia

On the eve of national university entrance exams, high school teacher Ling is busy preparing his students for the big day. Ling has a heavy burden to bear in addition to his work responsibility: his wife is paralyzed and his daughter Ling Yan, who failed the exams the previous year, decides to forego them this year to help her father care for the mother. Tan Jian, one of Ling's students, offers to help Ling Yan prepare, but in taking the time to do this he harms his own preparation, so Teacher Ling forbids him from helping. Another student, Zhong Xiaoxing, at first misunderstands Tan Jian's intentions but in time comes to help him with his studies. There is a happy and inspiring ending to the story.

1923. *Spring Thunder (Chun Lei)*

1958. Changchun Film Studio. B & W. 7 Reels. Direction: Huang Ye. Screenplay: Li Hongkui, Huang Fenglong, Cui Hengdong, Cui Xiansu. Cinematography: Feng Guiting. Art Direction: Wang Chong. Music: Pu You. Sound: Sheng Guli. Cast: Yin Zimin as Pu Rongji, Su Jianfeng as Li Mingsu, Jin Guangchu as the director of Shijian Mill, Wang Yansheng as the Party Secretary, Wang Yabiao as the Chief Engineer, Sun Xiaofei as Director Xu

Two paper mills hold a production competition. The Shijian Mill falls behind the Changbai Mill, so they study and learn from the latter's experience, which creates a new record. The competition between the two mills goes on.

1924. *Spring Tide Comes Rapidly (Chun Chao Ji)*

1977. Emei Film Studio. Color. 11 Reels. Direction: Zhang Fengxiang, Xiang Ling. Screenplay: Rao Qu, Ni Xiwen. Cinematography: Li Erkang, Li Dagui. Art Direction: Li Fan, Xia Zhengqiu. Music: Tao Jiazhou. Cast: Feng Chunyin as Li Ke, Wu Wenhua as Li Rang, Yuan Maochuan as Lin Fangcheng, Jiang Dexing as Jin Bengtian, He Meiping as Xu Yuanju, Meng Jude as Songlin

In Libeiyuan Village in the north of Sichuan province, Director Li Chunshan's involvement in illegal business is supported by deputy secretary Hu Xing and other local officials. But Party secretary Le Ke, a retired soldier, leads the area's poor and lower class farmers in opposition by setting up an agricultural cooperative. Li Chunshan refuses to accept this setback and allies himself with a rich farmer who wants to kill the newborn co-op. Li Ke relies on the poor farmers to expose the plot, and publicly criticizes Hu Xing and the other misguided officials.

1925. *Spring Waters Flow Long (Chun Shui Chang Liu)*

1958. Changchun Film Studio. B & W. 6 Reels. Direction: Chen Ge. Screenplay: Xu Jiaxian. Cinematography: Fu Jincheng. Art Direc-

tion: Wang Jixian. Music: Li Yaodong. Sound: Zhang Jianping. Cast: Ma Loufu as Master Worker Zhang Fu, Gu Qian as Du Laibao, Chong Lianwen as Du Xiaoyou, Zhen Wanyu as Du Erbao, Ma Ming as the woman community director, Hou Jianfu as Han Gui

In the spring of 1958, Flourishing Farm Commune adopts as its motto, "One year to cross the Yellow River, three years to cross Southeast China." The commune director leads the people in maximizing the output of their rice paddies. But the commune's deputy director Du Laibao is conservative in his thinking, and suggests less development of the paddies. With help from the automotive plant old master worker Zhang Fu who comes to help in agricultural construction and with encouragement from the commune members, Du Laibao changes his thinking and revises the motto from "three years to cross Southeast China" to "one year to cross Southeast China."

1926. *The Spring Wind Blows Over the Nuoming River (Chun Feng Cui Dao Nuoming He)*

1954. Northeast Film Studio. B & W. 11 Reels. Direction: Lin Zhifeng. Screenplay: An Bo, Hai Mu and Lin Zhifeng, based on the stage play of the same title by An Bo. Cinematography: Han Zongliang. Set Design: Liu Jinnai, Li Kefu. Music: Mu Sheng, Liu Shouyi and Yi Shengshan, Sound: Yuan Minda, Casting: Bi Xing as Gao Zhenlin, Jiang Li as Gao's wife, Zhang Xuecheng as Cui Cheng, Fu Yunhui as Cui Xiuyin, Ding Ni as Sun Shoushan, Zhao Changyin as Sun's wife

Director Cui Cheng of Zhaoyang Village, on the Nuoming River in Northeast China, has only a superficial understanding of the CPC's policies but expresses his views to anyone who will listen. In the agricultural co-op campaign, he is rude and intimidating to some farmers uncertain of joining the cooperative. Cui pushes through establishment of the co-op association too soon, which creates work chaos and unhappiness among the members. His relative Sun Shoushan demands he be allowed to withdraw, but Cui responds by criticizing Sun. Cui is then criticized by the Party Branch Secretary Gao Zhenlin, who adheres to the correct party principle, and agrees to let Sun withdraw. Later, the cooperative rectifies the earlier chaos, takes in a huge wheat harvest, and the members prosper. Sun now sees the advantages of the co-op and volunteers to join the association.

1927. *Springtime in Drum Township (Gu Xiang Chun Xiao)*

1983. Shanghai Film Studio. Color. 10 Reels. Direction: Ge Xin, Zhuang Hongsheng. Screenplay: Cao Yumo. Cinematography: Zhang Hongjun. Art Direction: Zhao Xianrui. Music: Gao Tian. Sound: Xu Xilin. Cast: Liu Falu as Ding Yingchuan, Niu Beng as Needle Nose, Jin Kangmin as Gao Fande, Chen Qi as Grandma Ou, Yan Shunkai as Zhu the Cripple, Fang Qinzhuo as Ou Yulian

In 1978, a natural disaster makes the lives of Anhui province's farmers harder than ever. Ding Yingchuan, prefectural Deputy Party Secretary, decides that agricultural reform is the best road to recovery, so he says nothing when the head of the production unit, a man called "Needle Nose," secretly starts the responsibility system. The new innovation quickly gives the unit a new, vigorous image, but when prefectural Party Secretary Gao Fande hears about it he is very upset, fearing it could lead to political errors. He orders the reforms halted, but at the critical moment the provincial Party Secretary arrives on an inspection visit and throws his support behind the reforms. Spring has come to Drum Township.

1928. *Springtime in the Desert (Sha Mo De Chun Tian)*

1975. Changchun Film Studio. Color. 11 Reels. Direction: Zhu Wenshun, Liu Zhongmin. Screenplay: Mala Qinfu. Cinematography: Li Huailu, Zhang Songping. Art Direction: Tong Jingwen, Ye Jiren. Music: Ala Tengaole. Cast: Tana as Na Renhua, Baosier as Buluogan, Er Changlin as Na Muhan, Da Lintai as Tala, Jin Yi as Lu Hua, Nige Mutu as Hatu

When natural disaster strikes Inner Mongolia's Buertala prairie, commune director Damulin plans to cope by selling off livestock and urging the people to go hunting. Commune deputy Party secretary Na Renhua disagrees and suggests reforming the desert instead. Damulin uses a ruse to gain the trust and support of Tala, the deputy Party secretary. Na Renhua does not give up, but leads the people in trying to convince Tala. At a critical juncture, the prefectural Party secretary Buluogan throws his support to Na, who presents evidence that Damulin has for many years been a covert class enemy. Na achieves victory in the class struggle and accomplishes her dream of reforming the desert.

1929. *Springtime in the Forest (Wan Mu Chun)*

1961. Changchun Film Studio. Color. 13 Reels. Direction: Yu Yanfu. Screenplay: Pan Qing, Hu Su. Cinematography: Meng Xiande. Art Direction: Wang Xingwen. Music: Lei Zhenbang. Sound: Wang Fei. Casting: Liang Yin as Qing Peide, Pu Ke as Jiang Dianwen, Guo Zhenqing as Luo Shoutang, Zhu Bing as old Rantou, Liu Zengqing as Wang Zhensheng, Fang Hua as Bu Qingyun, Sun Xiaofei as Gao Changsheng

Shortly after liberation, Qing Peide is named director of the forestry bureau in a forested area of Northeast China. Hidden counterrevolutionaries Bu Qingyun and Gou Changsheng deliberately taint the workers' food to create dissatisfaction. Qing Peide moves quickly, and after investigating, exposes the conspiracy. He unifies the workers, overcomes the deputy director's conservative thinking, and by initiating important new research, builds a new future for forest development.

1930. *Springtime on Mount Yao (Yaoshan Chun)*

1978. Changchun Film Studio. Color. 10 Reels. Direction: Wang Yabiao, He Keren. Screenplay: Zhou Minzheng, based on a Beijing opera of the same title. Cinematography: Xu Shouzen. Art Direction: Lu Xin, Guo Tingsheng. Music: Zhao Qin. Sound: Wun Liangyu. Cast: Li Junhai as Tan Shiqiang, Sun Xiaoyu as Mrs. Feng, Zhao Fan as Meng Jiugong, Chen Xiaomei as A Dan, Jiang Jin as Tao Jinbao, Xu Xiaoyuan as Jiang Zhuxuan

Just before the liberation of Guangxi province, Guangxi warlord Jiang Zhuxuan leads what is left of his defeated army onto Mount Yao, and continues his resistance from there. PLA commander Tan Shiqiang leads troops into the mountains to wipe out what is left of the resistance. Jiang Zhuxuan allies his force with those of Tao Jinbao, head of a ruling Yao group seeking to retain control of the Yao minority people. As part of their strategy, Tao Jinbao arranges for the release from prison of Mrs. Feng, a woman incarcerated 15 years before after an internal struggle between two Yao factions. Jiang and Tao seek to re-ignite the internal fighting among the Yao factions, so they spread a rumor that Mrs. Feng is planning to seize control. The people who had opposed Mrs. Feng in the past form a regiment to oppose her. Mrs. Feng wants to fight, but Tai Shiqiang is able to convince her that she and the other Yao people are being exploited by their common enemy. At a meeting to raise funds for the regiment, she speaks out and exposes the plot. Their awareness raised, both Yao factions unite and aid the PLA in wiping out the enemy and capturing Jiang Zhuxuan.

1931. *Spy (Jian Xi)*

1980. August First Film Studio. Color. 11 Reels. Direction: Hao Guang. Screenplay: Lin Yu, Chong Sheng, Liu Shuichang. Cinematography: Wei Linyu. Art Direction: Zhang Zheng, Cui Denggao. Music: Liu Tingyu. Sound: Shi Pingyi. Cast: Du Yulu as Gan Quan, Tang Tangmin as Ding Aozhang, Qiu Yinsan as Pan Dake, Zhou Lina as Lu Fengxian, Song Chunli as Du Zhiwen

With support and leadership from the Communist Party, a Northeast China Volunteer Army branch unit is beginning to become a real thorn in the side of the Japanese invaders. The Japanese commander asks a spy agency for assistance. The agency sends Pan Dake, one of their best operatives, to infiltrate the branch unit in the guise of CPC provincial committee representative Tian Xin. The Japanese know that Tian is dead, but this fact is still unknown to the Chinese. Pan Dake begins to foment trouble as soon as he arrives: he accuses branch director Ding Aozhang and his wife Doctor Du Zhiwen of treason, and puts the couple on trial. Pan's actions arouse the suspicions of Political Commissar Gan Quan, so he leaves for Harbin to ask the provincial Party committee to investigate Pan Dake. With Gan Quan absent, Pan Dake exploits Political Department Director Xiang Qun's extreme left-wing ideology to persecute Du Zhiwen to the point where she commits suicide. He also succeeds in obtaining a death sentence for Ding Aozhang. This so angers No. 5 branch team director Lu Fengxian that she gets some soldiers to spirit Ding Aozhang away to a place of safety. This leaves her with no choice but to leave the unit herself. When Gan Quan returns, he brings evidence from the provincial Party Committee exposing Pan Dake as a spy and traitor. Pan and his collaborators are themselves put on trial and punished. The branch unit's members are left to ponder the lessons of this experience.

1932. *Spy Shadows at Donggang (Dong Gang Die Ying)*

1978. Shanghai Film Studio. B & W. 10 Reels. Direction: Shen Yaoting. Screenplay: Meng Shenghui, Zhou Yunfa, Chen Zhenjiang. Cinematography: Chen Zhengxiang. Art Direction: Li Jinggi, Zhao Xianrui. Music: Xu Jingxin. Sound: Tu Minde. Cast: Da Shichang as Zhong Lei, Mao Yongmin as Tian Dayong, You Xi as Yu Fang, Wang Dinghua as Mr. Yang, Zhong Shuhuang as Zhao Fang, Wang Xiyan as Ding Yi, Zhu Manfang as Xia Yun, Da Shibiao as Shalin

In Donggang city, the Yaohua Shipyard is manufacturing a new model warship the "Donggang." A foreign intelligence agency sends a spy to steal the blueprints. Part of the "Donggang" prints are stolen from engineer Huang Zhenyi on his return to the yard from the design office. The PSB learns that the code name of one of those involved is "Yun," and that the behind-the-scenes spy master is an international spy. They follow clues which lead to the plant's technical librarian Xia Yun. It develops that the librarian has been duped into turning classified data over to the spy ring. Chinese security officers reeducate Xia Yun and with the information she gives them they arrest Shalin, a foreign sailor. This in turn leads them to the spy, a tourist named Hoffman who turns out to be a top foreign intelligence agent. The Chinese authorities round up the whole spy ring.

1933. *Spy Wars Are Unrelated to a Woman's Charms (Jian Die Zhan Yu Nu She Wu Guan)*

1989. Changchun Film Studio. Color. Letterboxed. 10 Reels. Direction: Wang Fengkui. Screenplay: Wang Weicheng, Li Jihe. Cinematography: Zhang Zhongwei. Art Direction: Xu Zhenkun. Music: Yang Yilun. Sound: Huang Yongqing. Cast: Luxiou Bading as Watling, Liu Dingcheng as Songgang Xiaolin, Meng Qingsheng as Sun Jiaju, Wang Fengkui as Shi Mo, Meng Qingsheng as Xiang Fei

In 1941, Nationalist Chinese intelligence employs a secret code-breaking system called the "RB" to learn in advance of Japanese plans for attacking Pearl Harbor. While the U.S. does not act on the information relayed to them by the Chinese, after the attack spies from several nations compete to obtain the RB system, including American, British and Japanese. In the end, the British spy kills the

Japanese and makes off with the system, but the one he obtains turns out to be bogus.

1934. *Stage Sisters (Wu Tai Jie Mei)*

1965. Tianma Film Studio. Color. 11 reels. Direction: Xie Jin. Screenplay: Ling Gu, Xu Jin, Xie Jin. Cinematography: Zhou Damin, Chen Zhenxiang. Art Direction: Ge Shicheng. Music: Huang Zhun. Sound: Zhu Weigang. Cast: Xie Fang as Zu Chunhua, Cao Yindi as Xing Yuehong, Feng Qi as Master Worker Xing, Gao Aisheng as Jiang Bo, Shen Fengjuan as Xiao Xiang, Xu Caigen as Jin Shui, Shangguan Yunzhu as Shang Shuihua, Ma Ji as Qian Dakui, Luo Jingyi as Yu Guiqing, Wu Baifang as Little Chunhua, Li Wei as Manager Tang, Deng Nan as the monk A Xing, Shen Gao as the Shen family housekeeper, Dong Lin as Third Master Ni, Ding Ran as Commissioner Pan

In the late 1930s, a traveling opera troupe rescues Zu Chunhua, a peasant girl fleeing an arranged marriage. She joins the company and becomes like a sister to Xing Yuehong, the owner's daughter. After the father's death, the troupe is disbanded and the girls join a Shanghai theater company, where they become star performers. They begin to grow apart, as Yuehong grows increasingly dissolute and materialistic and Chunhua develops a political consciousness. The latter forms her own theater company to exhibit leftist plays, which eventually gets her into trouble with the Nationalist authorities and their underworld supporters. The climax comes when Chunhua is framed and then placed on trial, and Yuehong is forced to appear as the chief witness against her. The story ends hopefully after 1949, with the two women reunited in a revolutionary opera troupe.

1935. *Stamp Trip (You Piao Lu Xing Ji)*

1988. Chinese Film Company and Canadian Film Entertainment Company Co-Production. Color. 10 Reels. Direction: Mike Luobu. Screenplay: Mike Luobu. Sound: Yi An. Cast: Liu Kasi Yiwensi as Laerfu, Andongni Luojiesi as Tom, Jier Sitanli as Nancy, Andelu Weitehaide as Aerbote, Baoluo Paoboweiqi as Kasi, Han Yun as Meiling, Chen Yuantao as Chen Tao, Kateling as Kalier

A young member of a Canadian elementary school stamp collecting club goes to Australia to look for a rare stamp album, but winds up in China instead, where he is warmly welcomed by some Chinese children who help him get to Australia.

1936. *Stand Straight, Don't Bend Over (Zhan Zhi Luo, Bie Pa Xia)*

1992. Xi'an Film Studio. Color. Letterboxed. 11 Reels. Direction: Huang Jianxin. Screenplay: Huang Xin. Cinematography: Zhang Xiaoguang. Art Direction: Zhang Zhili. Music: Zhang Dalong. Sound: Yan Jun, Dang Wang. Costume: Ding Ni. Makeup: Cheng Yin. Cast: Feng Gong as Gao Wen, Zhang Lu as Gao Taitai, Da Shichang as Cadre Liu, Liu Xiaohui as Liu's wife, Niu Zhenghua as Zhang Yongwu, Fu Lili as Zhang's wife, Ma Shuangqing as the old doorman

Soon after writer Gao Wen moves into his new home, he finds his next door neighbors the Zhangs are rather nasty people. The father, Zhang Yongwu, ignores the law, is discourteous and argumentative, and is a general nuisance to his neighbors. He particularly cannot get along with the family of Cadre Liu. However, when Zhang's fish-raising business improves, he needs help, and offers part-time jobs to all the neighbors. When he does that, everyone changes their attitude towards the Zhangs, and eagerly accepts his offer of employment. As Cadre Liu puts it, "Opening and reform changes people, and we should put aside our disagreements of the past."

Best Supporting Actor Feng Gong, 1993 Hundred Flowers Awards.

1937. *Star (Xing, Xing, Xing)*

1982. Xiaoxiang Film Studio. Color. 9 Reels. Direction: Luo Zhen. Screenplay: Lin Li. Cinematography: Zhao Zeli. Art Direction: Jin Baohao. Music: Lu Yuan. Sound: Liu Yisheng. Cast: Bai Mu as Mr. Ding, Kou Zhenhai as Ding Kai, Ye Lingliang as Ding's wife, Zhang Xiaomin as Shali, Zhong Ao as Erbao, Ran Zhijuan as Xiaofeng, Lu Jing as Xiaofei, Liu Zhongyuan as Deputy Bureau Director Yu

In the Qunxing Shoe Factory, Deputy Director Ding is confronted with a real problem: the factory's famous brand of shoe has suddenly gone out of fashion. His son Ding Kai is obsessed with studying shoe styles, and in the course of his research he meets a girl named Shali, who sells shoes. They do market research together, and Ding Kai excitedly tells his father their findings, emphasizing the economic efficiency of making new style shoes to

Stage Sisters. At one time close as sisters, opera stars Xing Yuehong (Cao Yindi, left) and Zu Chunhua (Xie Fang) find their differing lifestyles and values are pulling them apart. 1965. Tianma Film Studio.

meet consumer demand. Mr. Ding reluctantly accepts their ideas, and after a succession of false starts the product finally succeeds. Mr. Ding's family all wear the new style of shoes, and Mr. Ding is proud to learn his son is now dating Shali, daughter of Deputy Bureau Director Yu.

1938. *The Stars Are Bright Tonight (Jin Ye Xing Guang Chan Lan)*

1980. August First Film Studio. Color. 10 Reels. Direction: Xie Tieli. Screenplay: Bai Hua. Cinematography: Cai Jiwei, Xu Lianqin. Art Direction: Kou Honglei. Music: Jin Xiang. Sound: Li Yan. Cast: Li Xiumin as Yang Yuxiang, Tang Guoqiang as He Zhanyun, Huang Xiaolei as Xiao Yu, Liu Jizhong as Xiao Guo, Bao Xun as Xiao Sun

In the winter of 1948, despairing over the deaths of her father and brother at the hands of a local landlord, peasant girl Yang Yuxiang attempts to hang herself. She is saved by Xiao Yu, a PLA telecommunications specialist working in the area. Although she had not wanted to be rescued, Yang feels she must now show gratitude, so she commits herself to be Xiao

Yu's future wife. The startled young man does not know how to handle this offer, but he is able to get the homeless orphan girl accepted by his unit as a food service helper. When the PLA moves into position for a battle with the Nationalists, Xiao Yu is assigned to tap the telephone lines into enemy headquarters. He overcomes many difficulties to make the tap, but is killed in the effort. His death greatly saddens his comrades, but none know how to break the news to Yang Yuxiang, still daydreaming of someday marrying Xiao Yu. When she does learn the bad news, she cries bitterly, but gathers strength from the cause he died for. Yang joins a PLA medical team, and becomes a real soldier as the war progresses.

1939. *Steel Blood Gold Soul (Tie Xue Jin Hun)*

1990. Inner Mongolia Film Studio. Color. Wide Screen. 9 Reels. Direction: Zhuo Gehe, Chen Hongguang. Screenplay: Cao Jinmeng. Cinematography: Li Tingzheng. Art Direction: Du Changshun. Music: Moer Jihu. Sound: Sangsi Erfu. Cast: Ai Liya as Lanling, Gong Youchun as Lin Xi, Zhang Guangbei as Brother Fang

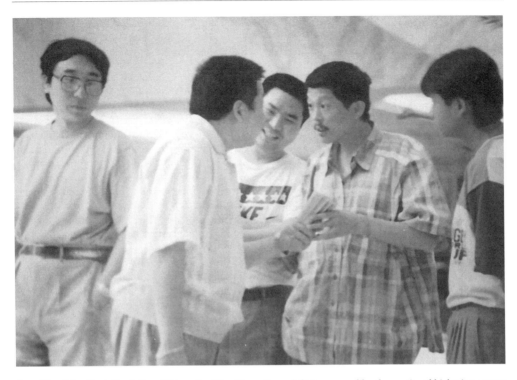

Stand Straight, Don't Bend Over. Writer Gao Wen (Feng Gong, left) is annoyed by the continual bickering among his new neighbors. 1992. Xi'an Film Studio.

Just after a bank holds a counter-robbery drill for its employees, a real holdup takes place, and a woman employee is killed. The killer, and organizer of the robbery, turns out to be another bank employee. The film climaxes in a massive gun battle at a construction site.

1940. *Steel Cavalry on Kunlun Mountain (Kun Lun Tie Qi)*

1960. Changchun & Xi'an Film Studios Co-Production. B & W. 10 Reels. Direction: Yuan Naicheng. Screenplay: Li Xilin. Cinematography: Wu Guojiang. Art Direction: Wang Chong. Music: Li Yaodong. Sound: Zhang Jianping. Cast: Bai Dezhang as Lei Jie, Guo Shutian as Mr. Zhou, Er Changlin as Mr. Zhang, Ma Loufu as the old doctor, Zhang Chongxiao as Wei Gang, Sheng Linzhong as the political instructor

In 1950, after the liberation of Northwest China, some of the defeated Nationalist army allied with local gangsters tries to escape to Northern Tibet to continue their resistance in the natural fortress of rugged Kunlun Mountain. A PLA cavalry company led by Lei Jie pursues them. Lei Jie sends platoon leader Wei Gang and staff officer Zhang to scout the enemy, but Zhang returns to report Wei has been captured. Wei is later rescued by some Tibetan hunters. When the battle comes, disagreements between the gangsters and the Nationalist commanders leads to their suffering major losses. Later, the PLA cavalry crosses Kunlun Mountain and wipes out the remaining Nationalist force.

1941. *The Steel File General (Gang Cuo Jiang Jun)*

1986. Emei Film Studio. Color. 12 Reels. Direction: Tai Gang. Screenplay: Bi Bicheng, Xiao Ma. Cinematography: Mai Shuhuan. Art Direction: Yan Dingfu. Music: Si Wanchun, Wang Haiping. Sound: Lin Bingcheng. Cast: Li Xuejian as General Li Li, Xiu Jingshuang as Lin Shuheng, Wang Ruoli as Zhou Qin, Cao Jingyang as Chen Tianshou, Wang Yingshen as Zhao Dashan, Tai Gang as Liang Jiuchun

In the late fall of 1978, former General Li Li recalls his past. In the fall of 1949, Li was Chief Secretary of a military administrative committee. He returns to Dongfang University, his alma mater, to visit his former English professor Zhou Qin, just returned from study in the U.S. Zhou introduces the young officer to a girl student named Lin Shuheng. Li and Lin are later married, and shortly after this Li meets a talented young college graduate named Liang Jiuchun and helps him find a job. This act of kindness comes back to haunt him later, when Liang is accused of spying. In his own job, Li intervenes when some officials persecute some intellectuals, such as engineer Chen Tiaoshou, a former Nationalist officer. When the Cultural Revolution comes, Li, by now a general, defends his old professor Zhou from charges that his U.S. experience has made him an enemy of the people. For helping his friends, Li himself is removed from his post. He suffers greatly during his years of inactivity. At last, back in 1978, he receives a letter from his former commander inviting him to return to his military work. As he leaves, his wife Liu Shuheng sees him off with very mixed feelings.

1942. *Steel Giant (Gang Tie Ju Ren)*

1974. Changchun Film Studio. B & W. 11 Reels. Direction: Yan Gong. Screenplay: "Steel Giant" Writing Group, collectively, based on the novel of the same title by Cheng Shuzheng. Cinematography: Meng Xiande. Art Direction: Liu Jinnai, Tong Jingwen. Music: Lei Zhengbang, Lin Xuesong. Cast: Li Yalin as Dai Jihong, Wang Wenlin as Wang Yonggang, Guo Zhenqin as Zhang Zhili, Jiang Changhua as Li Zhongcai, Liu Shilong as Yang Zhijian, Yan Fei as Tian Ming

In the winter of 1960, steel mill workshop director Dai Jihong assumes a leadership role in their assignment to produce China's first large-scale rolling mill. But plant director Li objects to this project on the grounds it is something totally new. There is a struggle between the working class represented by Dai and the diehard reactionaries represented by Li. Meanwhile, technician Liang Jun, who comes from a capitalist background, hates the socialist system and manifests his hostility by damaging machinery in the workshop. Dai Jihong, with the support of the Party committee, resolutely carries on the struggle and finally accomplishes the mission.

1943. *Steel Is Made This Way (Gang Tie Shi Zhe Yang Lian Cheng De)*

1995. Beijing Film Studio. Color. Letterboxed. Direction: Lu Xuechang. Screenplay: Lu Xuechang. Cinematography: Zhang Xiguo. Art Direction: Li Jixian. Cast: Zhu Hongmao as Zhou Qing, Yin Zongjie as young Zhou Qing, Li Qiang as Ji Wen, Zhu Jie as Fu Shaoying, Luo Jun as the girl, Li Xiaolong as Xiao Mo

In Beijing in the 1970s, a boy named Zhou Qing reads an inspirational Russian novel called "Steel Is Made This Way," concerned with how people form strong moral character. Later, when he gets a job at the Beijing railway station, he makes friends with a young man named Zhu Haolai, an educated youth returned from the countryside. Zhu tells young Zhou stories of his generation, further inspiring him. When Zhu leaves for South China to resume his education, he gives Zhou Qing a copy of "Steel," a precious item in China's anti-foreign environment of the time. When Zhou Qing finishes college himself, reforms are taking hold in China, and Beijing has changed greatly. A talented musician, Zhou signs a contract to play with a band at a club, but is upset by the drug use and loose morals of those who frequent the place. Zhou gets into a fight about this, and injures the other man so badly he winds up in prison for a time. Upon his release, he sees a new book has been published, also entitled "Steel Is Made This Way." Its author is his old friend Zhu Haolai, and he finds it as inspirational as its Russian namesake. His spirits restored, Zhou Qing calls his girlfriend, and they plan to go together to find Zhu Haolai.

1944. *Steel Leg Ma's Story (Ma Tie Tui Wai Zhuan)*

1986. Beijing Film Studio. Color. 10 Reels. Direction: Ling Zhifeng, Han Lanfang. Screenplay: Wei Xing, Han Lanfang, Luo Si. Cinematography: Zhou Jixun, Xing Peixiu. Art Direction: Wang Xinguo. Music: Liu Zuang. Sound: Fu Yinjie. Cast: Lei Gesheng as Steel Leg Ma, Gong Guyin as Ma's wife, Tong Jiaqi as Wang Dapao, Chen Huapu as Secretary Shuai, Zhong Yong as Xiao Bing, Zhu Yali as Xiao Yun

In a Chinese city in the early 1980s, an old worker called "Steel Leg" Ma and his wife have a pretty good life, except for the fact their son Xiao Bing is unable to return from the countryside. The son has a nice girlfriend, Xiao Yun, and the older couple hope the young people will marry soon. Unaware that a change in policy has made their son eligible to return already, Ma and his wife decide to seek his return by "going through the back door." A succession of humorous stories ensues, as the couple meet and attempt to curry favor with various bureaucrats. After all this, the son shows up at their door to announce he is returning to attend graduate school. A happy day for the whole family.

1945. *Steel Meets Fire (Parts 1 & 2) (Lie Huo Jin Gang)*

1991. Pearl River Film Studio and Nanyang Art and Culture Company of Hainan Co-Production. Color. 18 Reels. Letterboxed. Direction: He Qun, Jiang Hao. Screenplay: Jiang Hao, adapted from two novels by Liu Liu, *Brave Hero* and *Marvelous Hero*. Cinematography: Li Xiaolin. Art Direction: Zhang Ruo, Song Weidong. Music: Zhao Jiping. Sound: Liu Haiyan. Cast: Shen Junyi, Li Qiang, Zhao Xiaorui, Xu Dongfang, Song Chunli, Chen Wei

During World War II, an officer and two soldiers of the Eighth Route Army are cut off from their unit during mopping-up operations on the Hebei plains. They soon find themselves behind enemy lines. Meeting up with three Communist agents, they form a guerrilla unit to carry on the fight against the Japanese and Chinese collaborators.

1946. *Steeled Fighters (Gang Tie Zhan Shi)*

1950. Northeast Film Studio. B & W. 10 Reels. Director and Screenplay by Cheng Yin, based on an original story by Wu Zhaodi. Cinematography: Wang Chunquan. Set Design: Lu Gan. Music: Zhang Guocang. Sound: Chen Wenyuan. Costume: Xiang Yuhuan. Cast: Zhang Ping as Zhang Zhijian, Du Defu as Mr. Wang, Sun Yu as Xiao Liu, Zhang Xiqi as Qi Degui, Xu Liankai as Company Commander Zhao, Liu Ru as Wang Xiaoshuang

In the early summer of 1946, Chiang Kaishek concentrates a massive force in an attack on one PLA division. PLA Platoon Leader Zhang Zhijian leads his troops in a diversionary movement which allows the main PLA force to escape. They accomplish their mission, but Zhang and four of his men are captured when they run out of ammunition. The Nationalist division commander uses both rough and gentle interrogation methods in an attempt to get them to divulge where the PLA has buried some grain supplies. Finally, the Nationalist political officer brings in Zhang's mother and son, hoping that they will persuade him, but the mother does the exact opposite by urging her son to be strong and continue to resist. Later, a PLA counteroffensive overruns the Nationalist positions. Zhang Zhijian is rescued, and the Nationalist commander and his political officer are captured. When Zhang returns to his own unit, he is honored with a banner proclaiming him a "Soldier of Steel."

1947. *Stepmother (Jimu)*

1992. Shanghai Film Studio. Color. Letterboxed. 10 Reels. Direction: Sun Daolin. Screenplay: Xiao Fuxing. Cinematography: Ju Jiazheng. Art Direction: Mei Kunping. Music: Yang Mao. Sound: Ren Daming. Cast: Zhen Zhengyao as Stepmother, Jin Zhengwu as Father, Xing Mingshan as the adult Huazi, Jin Shuyuan as Aunt, Tang Jishen as Qiangzi's mother, Da Da as Qiangzi, Bai Lanmei as Yunyun, Wang Changer as Yuanyuan, Song Ruhui as Young Sister

In Beijing in the early spring of 1955, Huazi and his sister Yunzi are devastated by the loss of their mother. Their father soon brings home a shy girl to be their new stepmother. Huazi and Yunzi resent the newcomer and go out of their way to hurt her, while she is kind and does everything she can to please them. A decade goes by, the father has died, and the stepmother continues to work very hard to raise the children properly. She wants Huazi to go to college, and to accomplish this relinquishes her own chance to lead a comfortable life with her own, married daughter. Huazi is at last admitted to college, but the stepmother dies of overwork. Their aunt, their father's sister, visits Huazi and Yunzi and tells them that many years ago, the stepmother and their father had been lovers in their native village. The father's family had forced them to separate because the stepmother's family was so poor, and then forced the father to leave the village to earn a living elsewhere. The children at last realize their stepmother's feelings for their father and for them, but it is too late.

1948. *Stolen Love (Tou Lai De Ai)*

1987. Emei Film Studio. Color. 10 Reels. Direction: Wang Kanghua. Screenplay: You Fengwei. Cinematography: Xie Erxiang, Zhang Wenzhu. Art Direction: Xie Huibing. Music: Su Hanxing, He Xuntian. Sound: Hua Yaozhu. Cast: Lei Han as Yun Qi, Dong Zhizhi as the young girl, Zhu Xu as Uncle Changle, Niu Beng as Shunxing, Li Minzhu as Shunxing's wife, Chen Damin as Liansheng

The villages of Shangwan and Xiawan have little contact for fully a generation, due to a long-standing feud. Xiawan is as poor as Shangwan is prosperous, so a young Xiawan man named Yun Qi sneaks into Shangwan in order to learn the latest farming technology. He meets a young woman named Miaoling who enthusiastically shares with him her agricultural knowledge. They become lovers, and through them Xiawan starts to improve its economy and the two villages begin to reconcile.

1949. *Stories of Searching for Love (Xun Ai Ji)*

1957. Changchun Film Studio. B & W. 8 Reels. Direction: Wang Yan. Screenplay: Wang Yan. Cinematography: Fang Weiche. Art Direction: Shi Weijun. Music: Che Ming. Sound: Chen Yudan. Cast: Li Yunong as Li Yong, An Qi as Zhao Hui, Ren Weimin as Zhang Shilu, Su Jianfeng as Ma Meina, Gao Ping as Section Chief Zhang

Retail salesman Li Yong and department store cashier Zhao Hui have a traffic accident on their way to an advanced workers' conference. This unanticipated event causes the two to get acquainted, fall in love, and in time become a happily married couple. Zhao Hui's co-worker Ma Meina and Li Yong's co-worker Zhang Shilu are dissatisfied with commercial work, and regard sales as low, subservient work with no future. Ma Meina's idea of Mr. Right is someone who can help her change her occupation. At a dance party, she meets Zhang Shilu who passes himself off as a personnel division head, and the two are soon married. At the wedding, Ma Meina finally discovers that Zhang Shilu is not a personnel office head but a salesman, making her very regretful. After sincere advice and criticism from Li Yong and Zhao Hui, both Ma and Zhang come to realize the incorrectness of their thinking, and they happily look forward to life together.

1950. *Storm (Feng Bao)*

1959. Beijing Film Studio. Color. 12 Reels. Direction: Jin Shan. Screenplay: Jin Shan, based on the stage play "Red Storm." Cinematography: Zhu Jinming. Art Direction: Qing Wei. Music: Liu Zhi. Sound: Chen Yanxi. Cast: Li Xiang as Lin Xiangqian, Jin Shan as Shi Yang, Zhang Ping as Sun Yuliang, Wu Xue as Mr. He, Shi Yu as Bai Jianwu, Tian Hua as Chen Guizhen, Feng Yifu as Wu Peifu. Wang Ban as Wei Xueqin, Lu Fei as

Huang Defa, Yang Jing as Jiang's wife, Lin Dongsheng as Huang's wife, Meng Qinghe as Wu Bolin, Wang Pei as Wu Datou, Li Yaohua as Zhao Jixian

Based on historical events. In 1923, Beijing-Hankou Railway worker Lin Xiangqian and attorney Shi Yang establish a general workers union in the city of Zhenzhou under the supervision of undercover Communist Mr. He. Lin Xiangqian and other union leaders are expelled from the city by warlord Wu Peifu, and the union disbanded. After Lin and the others arrive in the city of Hankou, they arrange a strike. On February 4, 1923, the entire Beijing-Hankou Railway goes out on strike. On February 7, Wu Peifu puts down the strike in what becomes known as the "2–7 Massacre," shocking both China and international society. Shi Yang is arrested, but refuses to give in and cooperate with the authorities, who then turn to Lin Xiangqian to order the strikers back to work. Lin refuses and is subsequently killed.

1951. *Storm (Feng Lang)*

1979. Shanghai Film Studio. Color. 10 Reels. Direction: Zhao Huanzhang, Hu Chengyi. Screenplay: Gao Xing, Shi Yong. Cinematography: Zhu Yongde, Wu Liekang. Art Direction: Zhao Jiwen, Chen Fuxing. Music: Liang Hanguang. Sound: Zhou Yunling. Cast: Qin Yi as Xiao Yuhua, Sun Bing as Luo Fenggang, Kang Tai as Huangpu Weibang, Xu Zhan as Chang Hailin, Ding Jiayuan as Chang Haimin, Yao Minrong as Chang Hongxiang

A city's fishing boat plant secretary and a fishing company's Party secretary work together to smash a conspiracy of Gang of Four followers to convert the plant to the manufacture of armed ships, to be used in putting together a rogue naval force.

1952. *Storm in a Mountain Village (Shan Xiang Feng Yun)*

1979. Pearl River Film Studio. Color. 11 Reels. Direction: Fang Ying, Wu Ping. Screenplay: Wu Youheng and Fang Ying, based on the novel of the same title by Wu Youheng. Cinematography: Yao Meisheng, Li Zhexian. Art Direction: Zhang Zhichu. Music: Huang Jingpei. Sound: Jiang Shaoqi. Cast: Li Rong as Liu Qing, Yin Zhimin as Wan Xuanzhi, Hao Jialing as Chunhua, Jiang Rui as Liu Liren, Fang Ying as He Feng, Xie Weixiong as Heiniu

After victory in World War Two, the

Storm. 1959. Union leader Lin Xiangqian (Li Xiang, center) leads workers in an ill-fated 1923 railway strike. Beijing Film Studio.

Nationalists under Chiang Kaishek launch a major attack on the Communists' anti–Japanese bases. Liu Qing, the woman chief of a South China guerrilla troop, transfers her unit to the Naheng Mountains to establish a new base there. The mountain is controlled by landlord Pan Guiwang, an infamous despot allied with the Nationalist government. Liu Qing decides Pan must be driven from the mountains, so she makes plans to attack his base there. Pretending to be a teacher from Guangzhou province, Liu infiltrates Pan Guiwang's base and gains his daughter's trust. At the Moon Festival, when Pan Guiwang holds a "moon worship party" for his daughter, Liu Qing gives her troop the signal to attack the base, and they overwhelm Pan's private army. The victors then consolidate and expand their revolutionary base.

1953. *Storm in October (Shi Yue Feng Yun)*

1977. Emei Film Studio. B & W. 11 Reels. Direction: Zhang Yi. Screenplay: Yan Yi. Cinematographer: Li Erkang. Art Direction: Lin Qi. Music: Xiong Jihua. Sound: Zhang Jianping. Cast: Li Rentang as He Fan, Zhang Ping as Xu Jian, Zhu Yijing as Gao Shan, Ji Muxuan as Zhao Chun, He Xiaoshu as Wang Hua, Lin Wei as Sister Gu, Tang Guanghui as Xu Xuesong, Ye Linlang as Zhang Lin, Liu Zinong as Ma Chong

In a certain city, not long after the death of Chairman Mao, military plant Party secretary He Fan is hospitalized with an illness. Ma Chong, the city's Party secretary in charge of industry, orders the plant to produce obsolescent weapons. When He Fan is released from the hospital, he puts an immediate stop to this production. Ma Chong then accuses He Fan with having violated a "leader's" orders. Ma gets further support from reporter Zhang Lin, a special liaison to the plant from Wang Hongwen, one of the "Gang of Four." He Fan is forced out of his position because of his continued resistance to the scheme. Ma Chong arranges to have He Fan killed, but He Fan is saved when his driver Xu Xuesong sacrifices his own life. When Zhang Lin comes with an order from Wang Hongwen to take away the weapons, the Gang of Four's conspiracy is exposed, and Ma Chong and Zhang Lin are arrested.

1954. *Storm in Wuhan (Chu Tian Feng Yun)*

1981. Shanghai Film Studio. Color. Letterboxed. 10 Reels. Direction: Wu Yonggang, Li Changgong. Screenplay: Chen Binglei, Hua Zhongshi. Cinematography: Cao Weiye. Art Direction: Zhong Yongqin, Zhang Wanhong, Huangzhun. Sound: Wang Huimin. Cast: Zhen Rong as Dong Biwu, Xia Hanbi as Song Qingling (Madame Sun Yatsen), Gong Wue as Chumei, Feng Qi as Tang Yunjie, Xie Wuyuan as Zhen Hu, Zhang Yan as Kong Guinian

The story of Dong Biwu, an early Communist leader. Dong unites revolutionary forces in Wuhan to oppose Chiang Kaishek and Wang Jingwei's anti–Communist strategy. Dong wins over Tang Yunjie, a member of the Nationalists' Hubei Province Party standing committee, and teaches young woman student Chumei to improve her revolutionary skill and knowledge. He also clears a comrade who is framed and tried for the crime of another. His enemies decide Dong Biwu has to be killed, but Chumei gives her own life to save him. On July 15, 1927, Wang Jingwei publicly announces his collaboration with Chiang Kaishek in a joint anti–Communist stand. Song Qingling (Madame Sun Yatsen) announces her resignation from the Nationalist Party and Dong Biwu bids farewell to his old friends and leaves to join in the military struggle.

1955. *Storming the Darkness Before Dawn (Chong Puo Li Ming Qian De Hei An)*

1956. August First Film Studio. B & W. 10 Reels. Executive Director: Ding Li. Direction: Wang Ping, Liu Peiran. Screenplay: Fu Duo, based on a stage play of the same name. Cinematography: Cao Jinyun. Set Design: Wang Wei. Music: Li Weicai. Sound: Guo Dazheng. Cast: Jin Xin as Yan Zhigang, Li Qihuang as Yang Jinshui, Tian Yumin as Cui Zhenlei, Gao Baocheng as "Tiger," Xi Decang as Datun, Xing Zhixian as Qinglin

In 1942, Eighth Route Army platoon leader Yan Zhigang is seriously wounded but is rescued by old Mrs. Li and her daughter-in-law Fengxia. After Yan Zhigang recovers, he leads a guerrilla troop against the enemy, but a string of successive victories makes him careless. This results in unnecessary losses to his troops, for which he is criticized by superior officers. He applies himself to correcting his errors, and inflicts severe losses on the enemy through

such means as underground tunnels and land mines. After that, he also takes over the enemy base at Lijiaying, and rescues Fengxia, who had been taken prisoner.

1956. *Stormy Island (Feng Yun Dao)*

1977. Changchun Film Studio. Color. 9 Reels. Direction: Zhang Xinshi, Xue Yandong. Screenplay: Collective, recorded by Ming Guoku and Liu Xinzhi, based on a novel of the same title. Cinematography: Shu Xiaoyan. Art Direction: Liu Xuerao, Jin Bohao. Music: Quan Rufeng. Sound: Liu Jingui. Cast: Miao Zuang as Liang Lin and Liang Hongshan, Li Jiang as Liang Lin (as a child), Chen Guojun as Shen Chengjian, Pu Ke as Uncle Chunao, Li Hong as Jin Shuigeng, Jiang Ruilin as Zhang Hai, Fu Huiyuan as Liu Haishan, You Zhangke as Bi Jingui, Huang Ling as Lan Bajiao

In 1962, the Nationalist government on Taiwan makes plans to invade the Chinese mainland. Enemy commander Liu Haishan sends Bi Jingui to the island of Fengyun with orders for a spy known as "Agent 215" to steal PLA naval defense plans. After "215" obtains the plans, he hands them over to Liu Haishan's former mistress Lan Bajiao to give to Bi Jingui, but Bi is killed by the Chinese coast guard as he attempts to return to Taiwan, and the plans are recovered. Agent "215" then poisons Lan Bajiao to silence her. Naval commanders Liang Lin and Shen Chengjian analyze the situation and find a clue that points to their counterintelligence head Jin Shuigeng as "215." They draw up revised but false defense plans as a trap. When the advance contingent of the invasion arrives, Jin Shuicheng is caught red-handed setting signals for them, the advance force falls into the trap, and is wiped out.

1957. *Stormy Waves on the Shore (An Bian Ji Lang)*

1964. August First Film Studio. B & W. 8 Reels. Direction: Yuan Xian. Screenplay: Zhen Hong, Meng Jie and Yuan Xian. Cinematography: Cai Jiwei, Zhu Lutong. Art Direction: Ren Huixing. Music: Gong Zhiwei. Sound: Guo Dazheng. Cast: Zhao Ruping as A Bing, Kong Rui as Shan Shugong, Kong Xiuzhen as A Liang, Qu Yun as A Bing's mother, Liu Jiaoji as "Rubber Band," Li Jiufang as A Liang's father

In 1949, in a fishing village on the Southeast China coast, young farmer A Bing finds that a local tyrant is illegally shipping valuables out of the area before the PLA comes into the area. To silence him, the tyrant has A Bing abducted, but he is freed by the timely arrival of a guerrilla troop. After liberation, A Bing is named director of the local militia and shows his leadership in land reform and in countering the espionage activities of spies from Taiwan. At last the tyrant returns secretly with a small band of spies to engage in subversion. They take A Bing's son hostage, but with the help of the district public security forces, the militia wipes out all the enemy agents and free the little boy.

1958. The Story of a Eunuch (Tai Jian Mi Shi)

1990. Beijing Film Studio. Color. 9 Reels. Wide Screen. Direction: Li Wei. Screenplay: Shou Shan, Xu Xiang, An Ping. Cinematography: Zheng Yuyuan, Li Jianxiin. Art Direction: Yu Yiru, Zhang Xiande, Ma Zhaoren. Music: Wang Min. Sound: Lan Fan, Ke Hu. Cast: Hua Yajie as Yutai, Li Mengyao as Li Lianying, Meng Ying as Cixi

A young boy, Yutai, is forced by poverty to become a eunuch. He is duly castrated and sent to the imperial court, where he becomes one of the last generation of eunuchs serving the Qing dynasty. At court, he is humiliated and bullied by his master and other, older eunuchs. As an escape, he begins studying Peking Opera, and wins the favor of the Empress Dowager Cixi. To humiliate him, jealous chief eunuch Li Lianying forces him to dance with Wang Gege, who has just returned from abroad. The episode results in Yutai and Wang Gege being attracted to each other. Yutai learns to master the intrigue which is such a feature of court life, and at last succeeds in causing Li Lianying to fall from favor with Cixi. But he grows increasingly vicious and ruthless despite his wealth and high position.

1959. The Story of A Fu's Treasure Hunt (A Fu Xun Bao Ji)

1957. Jiangnan Film Studio. B & W. 8 Reels. Direction: Xu Sulin. Screenplay: Wang Ruowang. Cinematography: Shi Fengqi. Art Direction: Zhong Yongqing. Music: Zhang Linyi. Sound: Wu Hua. Makeup: Wang Hanyong. Cast: Qi Heng as Zhang Qixin (A Fu's father), Li Shoucheng as A Fu, Di Fan as Ruihua (A Fu's mother), Li Baoluo as Mr. Xu, Feng Qi as the Chief of Security, Zhang Qian as Xiao Xu

Zhang Qixin, a worker, brings home a sample Soviet-made drill bit used in petroleum drilling. His son A Fu, an elementary school student, sells the drill bit to buy a toy. When A Fu learns he has done something wrong, he is filled with regret and goes with his father and sister to look for the bit. Inquiries at the recycling store and a second hand shop are unsuccessful. When A Fu goes to search for the bit at the Shanghai No. 10 Steel Plant, he is arrested and questioned as a suspected spy by security officers. Finally, with the help of the plant's workers and chief of security, the steel bit is found in a sack of rubbish.

1960. Story of a Hairy Child Getting a Treasure (Xiao Mao Hai Duo Bao Qi Yuan)

1989. Nanhai Film Company & Hong Kong Hengxing Film Company Co-Production. Color. Wide screen. 9 Reels. Direction: Xiao Long. Screenplay: Collective. Cinematography: Yang Yongsong. Art Direction: Li Rongchun. Music: Guan Shengyou. Cast: Shao Zuorao as Liu Lang, Yu Zhenghuan as the small child, Xue Shujie as Wildcat

A man finds in the wilds a little boy with hair growing all over his body. He thinks the child is some sort of animal, and sells him to a pet shop owner. When the man learns the child is really a human and not an animal, he buys the boy back to spare him further humiliation. The hairy boy's picture gets in the papers, and the story is picked up by foreign wire services. Someone who sees the picture notes that the boy has a small metal plate on a chain around his neck, and connects that with an emerald hidden in a mountain cave. The boy is kidnapped and forced to lead the way to the treasure. When the child fails, his life is in danger. But the man who originally found him arrives in time to rescue the boy. The man and the boy find the jewel and make their escape.

1961. Story of a Knife (Da Dao Ji)

1977. Shanghai Film Studio. Color. 12 Reels. Direction: Tang Huada, Wang Xiuwen. Screenplay: Collectively, recorded by Qu Yankun and Qiu Xun, based on the novel of the same title by Guo Chengqing. Cinematography: Cao Weiye, Wun Sijie. Art Direction: Huang Qiagui, Zhong Yongqin. Music: Xiao Yan. Sound: Feng Deyao, Yin Zhiping. Cast: Yang Zaibao as Liang Baocheng and Liang Yongsheng, Pan Jun as Liang Yongshen (as a child) and Liang Zhiyong, Zhong Xinghuo as Meng Dahai, Shi Shugui as Cui Hua, Yang Yanxia as Cui Hua (as a child), Xu Bu as

Gao Shuqin, Li Wei as Jia Baoxuan and Jia Yugui, Chen Shu as Ma Tieda, Xu Zhao as Jia Yugui (as a child)

Landlord Jia Baoxuan has his henchman Ma Tiede beat tenant farmer Liang Baocheng to death. Liang Yongsheng tries to revenge his father but is unsuccessful, so he flees and goes into hiding, dedicating himself to mastering kung fu. Later, Liang Yongsheng leads the village people in their struggle with the landlord's bodyguards. Failing again, Liang Yongsheng travels to Yan'an, is educated by the Communist Party and becomes an Eighth Route Army commander. The Party sends him to his hometown, where he leads the people in battling the old landlord's son Jia Yugui. This time they achieve victory.

1962. *The Story of a Scar (Shang Ba De Gu Shi)*

1958. Changchun Film Studio. B & W. 8 Reels. Direction: Wang Jiayi. Screenplay: Sun Qian. Cinematography: Zhang Yi. Art Direction: Li Junjie. Music: Zhang Dicang. Sound: Lin Bingcheng. Cast: Wang Chengbing as Chen Youde, Pu Ke as Chen Xiude, Bai Ju as Liang Fengyin, Zhang Guilan as Liang Xiaofeng, Ai Hongli as Secretary Wei, Hao Guang as the Youth College Secretary

When discharged soldier Chen Youde returns to his hometown, he finds that his elder brother Chen Xiude has forgotten their hardscrabble existence of the past. Under the influence of his wife Liang Fengyin, Xiude wants to pursue individual rather than collective prosperity, loan money at high interest, and in general follow the road of seeking individual household prosperity. In addition, Fengyin is abusive to her younger sister Xiao Feng. Chen Youde is upset at this, for he loves the commune as if it were his home, and he wants his brother and sister-in-law to join the commune. But they mistrust his motives, the brothers argue and the household splits up. During the co-op campaign, Chen Youde becomes director of the co-op. He and Xiao Feng fall in love and marry. Finally, Youde finds that Xiude and Fengyin are selling grain for profit; the two brothers fight over this, and Xiude injures his arm, leaving a scar.

1963. *The Story of a Songstress (Nu Ge Xing De Gu Shi)*

1991. Changchun Film Studio. Color. Letter-boxed. 10 Reels. Direction: Song Jiangbo. Screenplay: Chang Qin, Chang Chunjie. Cinematography: Zhang Songping, Yan Songyan. Art Direction: Liu Huanxing. Music: Zhang Hongguang. Sound: Gu Xiaolian. Cast: Wei Wei as Chu Yun, Zhang Guoli as Yang Xiyang, Jiang Lili as Han Xue, Zhang Yonger as Xiaoxiao, Xu Ming as Xiao Guang

After winning a contest in Tokyo, Chinese singer Chu Yun becomes very popular. She has no shortage of suitors, and becomes involved with Yang Xiyang, a composer who also becomes her manager. Over time, his control over her increases, to the point where she is taken to court when Yang breaks a performance contract with a theater. When Yang meets an old girl friend who is now quite wealthy, he dumps Chu Yun and spreads rumors about her intended to destroy her career. Her world collapsing about her, Chu Yun loses the will to live. But with the help of a film star friend and another composer who has loved her secretly for some time, she regains her will and returns to the stage.

1964. *The Story of an Anti-Japanese Base (Feng Yun Chu Ji)*

1983. Changchun Film Studio. Color. 10 Reels. Direction: Luo Tai. Screenplay: Ren Yanfang, Yuan Naicheng. Cinematography: Chen Chang'an. Art Direction: Wang Chong, Guo Yansheng. Music: Lu Yuan, Tang Ke. Sound: Huang Lijia. Cast: Wu Dan as Chuner, Chang Rong as Mangzhong, Sun Shulin as Landlord Tian, Chen Shensheng as Tian Yaowu, Li Zequan as Gao Ba, Shui Yongqin as Shuer, Meng Shenqiu as Qiufen

When the Japanese invade China, the North China town of Zhiwu is thrown into chaos. In the midst of this, a man named Gao Chuner and his sister Qiufen return home to the town they had left 10 years earlier when a rebellion they joined had failed. Now they return as officers in the anti–Japanese Eighth Route Army. Also returning about this time is Tian Yaowu, son of the local landlord Tian Xiazhi. The older Tian advises his son to ally himself with senior officers in the Nationalist Army, which is collaborating with the Japanese invaders. The story follows the struggles between the Eighth Route officers on the one hand and the Japanese and their Nationalist collaborators on the other. It ends with the Gaos bringing their forces in to occupy the town and the Tians and their supporters fleeing.

1965. *Story of an Only Child (Yi Ge Du Sheng Nu De Gu Shi)*

1994. Changchun Film Studio. Color. Letterboxed. 9 Reels. Direction: Guo Lin. Screenplay: Zhao Junhai, Guo Lin. Cinematography: Zhao Bo, Wu Dongsheng. Art Direction: Li Guo. Music: Fan Weiqiang. Sound: Liu Qun, Zhao Xudong. Costume: Zhao Li. Makeup: Wang Keguang. Cast: Yang Suo as Zhang Mingming, Zhou Shuqin as Mother, Liu Baohua as Teacher Li, Zhao Xiuyun as Doctor Gao, Dong Ji as Grandpa Zhao, Zhang Yan as Father, Guo Ming as Aunt

After a girl named Zhang Mingming loses her father, she finds her mother's heart ailment grows worse from the stress of her husband's death. Mingming takes all the burden on her own shoulders, helping out economically, caring for her mother, doing all the household work and trying to get an education. But Mingming is very strong, and as she matures and becomes more in control of the situation things start to improve. Her mother regains her will to live, and both women face life bravely.

1966. *A Story of Being Born Again (Zai Sheng Ji)*

1960. Changchun Film Studio. B & W. 10 Reels. Direction: Liu Qun. Screenplay: The Third Collective Writing Team, recorded by Li Yuhua. Cinematography: Chang Yan. Art Direction: Yang Wei. Music: Chen Qifeng. Sound: Liu Xingfu. Cast: Li Chuncheng as Chen Shaohua, Qi Huatan as Huang Meiyin, Zhang Juguang as Zhou Daosheng, Meng Cuiyin as Jin Xiangcui, Tian Lie as An Ronggui, Zhao Baohua as He Weicai, Wu Bike as Ma Denglong

Before liberation, in a large city in North China, opera performers Chen Shaohua and Huang Meiyin are in love. In addition, their performance of Bangzhi (Hebei) opera is very popular with audiences. However, Ma Denglong, a special agent for the Nationalist government's Bureau of Investigations, desires Huang Meiyin and schemes to possess her. The actress's mother is aware of his plot and takes her daughter away to safety. Furious, Ma has Chen Shaohua beaten up and the opera company disbanded. In the meantime, Meiying has arrived in an area which is in Communist hands, but her mother loses contact with her and has to return to the city. One day, Chen Shaohua becomes acquainted with Zhou Daosheng, an undercover Communist agent, and with Zhou's help, Chen re-establishes the opera company. Their first performance is again disrupted by Ma Denglong. Meiying's mother dies, and Chen Shaohua suddenly goes blind while in a rage. After liberation, Shaohua and Meiying are reunited. They devote themselves to restoring and developing Hebei Bangzhi opera. During their performance of a classic play, Chen becomes so excited he regains his vision.

1967. *The Story of Liubao Village (Liu Bao De Gu Shi)*

1957. August First Film Studio. B & W. 9 Reels. Direction: Wang Ping. Screenplay: Shi Yan and Huang Zongjiang, based on the novel of the same title. Cinematography: Cao Jingyun. Art Direction: Kou Honglie. Music: Gao Ruxing. Sound: Li Yan. Cast: Liao Youliang as Li Jing, Xu Linge as the political instructor, Tao Yuling as Ermei, Kang Tianshen as Old Tian, Chen Donggang as Xiao Niu, Wang Jun as the No. 4 squad leader, Mo Yan as Liu Huzi

In the spring of 1944, a company of the New Fourth Route Army is on R&R at Liubao Village in Northern Jiangsu province. While recuperating from wounds at the home of a local family named Tian, No. 4 Squad's deputy squad leader Li Jing falls in love with the Tians' daughter Ermei. The political instructor talks with Li Jing and persuades him to break off the relationship, because PLA regulations forbid romantic relationships between military personnel and civilians during wartime. Although Li Jing agrees, he still loves Ermei deeply. After the troops leave the village, treacherous landlord Liu Huzi abducts Ermei to force her into marrying him. When word of this reaches Li Jing's company, they return to intercede, and Li Jing kills the landlord. After Ermei's rescue, she and Li Jing love each more than ever. With the army about to go on a long march, Li Jing finds himself in a painful dilemma. But with the help of the political instructor, he gives up his personal feelings and goes south with the army. Five years later, Li Jing has been promoted to the rank of company commander. When his company passes through Liubao Village, he finds Ermei, now a Party member and a cadre organizing farmers to supply frontline troops with food. She has been faithfully awaiting his return, and the two are finally reunited.

1968. *The Story of Qiu Ju (aka: Qiu Ju Goes to Court) (Qiu Ju Da Guan Si)*

1992. Hong Kong Sil-Metropole Organization Ltd., Beijing Youth Film Studio Co-Production. Color. Letterboxed. 11 Reels. Direction: Zhang Yimou. Screenplay: Liu Heng, based on Chen Yuanbin's novel "The Wan Family Lawsuit." Cinematography: Ci Xiaoning, Yu Xiaoqun and Lu Hongyi. Art Direction: Cao Jouping. Music: Zhao Jiping. Sound: Li Lanhua. Costume: Zhou Xiaoxing. Makeup: Sun Wei. Cast: Gong Li as Qiu Ju, Lei Luosheng as Wang Shantang, Liu Peiqi as Qinglai

In a small mountain village in Northwest China, a village man has an argument with village chief Wang Shantang, who at last angrily kicks the other man in the groin, injuring him. The injured man recuperates at home, ready to pass it off as just bad luck, but his six-months pregnant wife Qiu Ju is deeply offended. She feels that such an insult deserves an apology, which Wang Shantang flatly refuses to give. So she begins a long, arduous process of appeal, traveling by cart from town to county to city. At each level of bureaucracy, she receives a sympathetic ear, and even a ruling that her family receive monetary compensation, but who can force an apology? The only thing she can do is file a criminal charge. At last, Qiu Ju goes into a labor too difficult for the village midwives to handle. The village chief quickly organizes a team of volunteers to carry her to a distant hospital where she delivers a healthy son. Later, at a gala village celebration, word arrives that the village chief has been arrested and sent to jail for assaulting and injuring her husband. The case is over, and Qiu Ju has won, but not at all the victory she wanted.

Best Picture, 1993 Golden Rooster Awards.

Best Picture, 1993 Hundred Flowers Awards.

Best Actress Gong Li, 1993 Golden Rooster Awards.

Gold Lion Award, Best Actress (Gong Li), 49th Venice International Film Festival.

1969. *The Story of Qiuwen Encountering an Immortal (Qiu Wun Yu Xian Ji)*

1956. Shanghai Film Studio. B & W. 9 Reels. Direction: Wu Yonggang. Screenplay: Wu Yonggang. Cinematography: Zhou Shimu, Dai Sheng-chao. Art Direction: Hu Zhuoyun, Huang Chong. Music: Huang Zhun. Sound: Huang Dongping. Cast: Qi Heng as Qiuwen, Wang Xiaorong as the Peony Immortal, Guan Hongda as Judge Zhang, Wang Lan as Zhang Ba, He Jianfei as Yuwen, Chen Ke as Canwen

In Chinese myth, an old man named Qiuwen has a lifelong love of flowers, and spends all his time from morning to night caring for them and his beautiful flower garden. One day, Judge Zhang's housekeeper sells Qiuwen a dying peony bush which has not bloomed for three years. Under Qiuwen's care, the peony bush is saved and brings forth lovely blooms. When word of this reaches Judge Zhang he decides it is Qiuwen's garden that makes the difference, so he wants to buy the old man's land from him. When Qiuwen refuses, Zhang orders his thug Zhang Ba to destroy all the flowers. The peony immortal's magic touch restores all the flowers to life. When Judge Zhang hears of the flowers' survival, he has Qiuwen jailed for practicing witchcraft. But the peony immortal again uses magic powers to destroy the court house and frightens the officers into releasing Qiuwen. At last, Judge Zhang goes too far and is killed by the immortal's magic touch. From then on, hundreds of beautiful flowers bloom in Qiuwen's garden.

1970. *A Story of Scouting Across the River (Du Jiang Zhencha Ji)*

1974. Shanghai Film Studio. Color. 12 Reels. Direction: Tang Huada, Tang Xiaodan. Screenplay: Collective. Cinematography: Ma Linfa, Xu Qi. Art Direction: Ding Cheng. Music: Ge Yan. Cast: Wang Hui as Li Chunlin, Wu Xiqian as Wu Laogui, Li Chuanbing as Xiao Ma, Li Lanfa as Yang Wei, Zhang Xiaozhong as Zhou Changxi, Wun Xiying as the Chief of Staff

This is a remake of the same studio's 1954 black and white film, No. 1737.

1971. *Story of Suppressing Bandits in West Hunan (Parts 1 & 2) (Xiang Xi Jiao Fei Ji)*

1987. Xiaoxiang Film Studio. Color. 20 Reels. Direction: Zhou Kangyu. Screenplay: Zhou Kangyu, Xiao Qi, Shao Guomin. Cinematography: Ding Xiaodong. Art Direction: Guo Dexiang. Sound: Liu Yishen. Cast: Ding Rujun as Wu Bo, Xue Shujie as Ju Yuxiang, Chen Guodian as Xiao Bin, Ling Yun as Ju 24, Hu Xiangguang as Cai Jinhua, Wei Zongwan as Wei Biao,

Zhao Xiuli as Li Guifang, Wei Xiaohai as Cui Changjian, Zhou Yuyuan as Ouyang Jian, Yang Dezhi as He Wencai

Part 1: Just before liberation, as many as 70,000 bandits are hired by the Nationalists as mercenaries, becoming a major obstacle to the PLA's mission of liberating southwest China. In the fall of 1949, the PLA is ordered into west Hunan province to wipe out the bandits, and Battalion Commander Wu Bo brings his force into Fengshan County. Meanwhile, the bandits are welcoming a special train carrying Nationalist officer Jiu Xiangyu, sent to command the bandit force. The two forces do battle at a place called Niutoushan; it ends with a PLA victory, but Wu Bo's wife and son are taken captive by the bandits.

Part 2: After they are driven back at Niutoushan, Jiu Xiangyu leads the bandits deep into the mountains, pursued by the PLA. Wu Bo and some of his men disguise themselves and attend the wedding of bandit chieftain Si Yunze's nephew. At the wedding he meets Si Yunze and eventually wins him over. Si agrees to meet with the PLA for negotiations. Later, after learning that the bandits are in Pange village, the PLA launches a successful raid on the village, but some of the bandits escape, including Jiu Xiangyu. The PLA finally locates a large cave in which the last of the bandits are hiding. The trapped force refuses to surrender and decides to fight to the end.

The Story of "Three Hair" the Vagrant. Homeless orphan Three Hair (Wang Longji) struggles to exist on the streets of pre-liberation Shanghai. 1949. Kunlun Film Company.

1972. *Story of the Gold Bell (Jinling Zhuan)*

1958. August First Film Studio. B & W. 10 Reels. Direction: Liu Peiran. Screenplay: Zuo Lin. Cinematography: Chen Ruijun. Art Direction: Fang Xuzi, Kou Honglei. Music: Gong Zhiwei. Sound: Li Lin. Cast: Yang Wei as Director Liu, Yu Chunmian as Zhang Mancang, Xiao Chi as Li Lanyin, Yang Jing as Big Gold, Ling Yuan as Mancang's mother, Qu Yun as Lanyin's mother

High school graduate Li Lanyin and discharged soldier Zhang Mancang are model workers in their commune, and fall in love while working together. But Lanyin is influenced by "Big Gold," a girl in the commune who loves dressing well but does not like to work. Lanyin asks her brother, an army officer living in the city, to find her a husband there. Lanyin's brother criticizes her thinking, telling her she should stay at the commune with Mancang. Lanyin goes to the city by herself despite his advice. Criticized by Mancang at a cadre meeting, Lanyin feels very ashamed, and with the people's help, she gradually realizes her wrong thinking. Later, when Lanyin reads Mancang's progressive and advanced writings, the two are reconciled.

1973. *The Story of "Three Hair" the Vagrant (San Mao Liu Lang Ji)*

1949. Kunlun Film Company. B & W. 9 Reels. Direction: Zhao Ming, Yan Gong. Screenplay: Yang Hansheng, adapted from Zhang Leping's cartoon character. Cinematography: Han Zongliang, Qiu Ge. Set Design: Zhang Hanchen. Music: Wang Yunjie. Sound: Lin Bingsheng. Costume: Lu Boqin. Makeup: Yao Yongfu. Cast: Wang Longji as Three Hair, Guan Hongda as Uncle, Lin Zheng as the rich woman, Du Lei as the rich woman's husband. Cameo appearances by many leading contemporary Chinese actors and actresses

In pre-liberation Shanghai, a homeless vagrant child called "Three Hair" survives by selling newspapers, picking up discarded cigarettes and helping to push rickshaws. His efforts to lead an honest existence are repeatedly thwarted by misunderstandings, false accusations, and dishonest adults who take advantage of his youth and naivete. His luck appears to change when a wealthy woman adopts him, and he begins to receive an education. But he eventually comes to realize that he cannot accept the life of a rich family, so he returns to his beggar friends and his old, vagrant life. In an epilogue added later, after the Communist government had come to power throughout China, it is stated that he abandoned his vagrant lifestyle after liberation.

1974. *A Story of Visiting a Son (Tan Qin Ji)*

1958. Beijing Film Studio. B & W. 10 Reels. Direction: Xie Tian, Shang Fu. Screenplay: Yang Runsheng. Cinematography: Gao Hongtao, Chen Guoliang. Art Direction: Tian Shizhen, Zhang Xiande. Music: Shi Lemeng. Sound: Chen Yanxi, Fu Yinjie. Cast: Wei Heling as Tian Laogeng, Li Po as Captain Hu, Zhang Ping as the third son, Wang Renmei as Doctor Huang, Wu Yu as Director Su, Zhao Zhiyue as the cook, Zhang Yuan as Yushu

Stockman Tian Laogeng travels to Beijing from his rural home to visit his third son Tian Gang, whom he has not seen for more than 10 years. By coincidence, Tian Gang is away on a business trip, but his daughter-in-law Zhao Yushu lets the old man stay in their guest house. Tian Laogeng then happens to overhear Yushu mention to a friend that the old man's visit to Beijing was embarrassing; his feelings hurt, he decides to return home. But just at that time, Tian Gang returns home. To his surprise, Tian Laogeng finds that this Tian Gang is not his third son. It turns out that Tian Gang and Tian Laogeng's third son were close friends in the army, and the real third son had been killed in battle years before. For more than a decade, at his comrade's request, Tian Gang always wrote letters and sent money to the old man, treating him as if he were his own father. The old man was deeply moved by Tian Gang's friendship and loyalty to his son's memory. Tian Gang's wife Zhao Yushu also learns from this, and she respects the old man more after that.

1975. *The Story of Wei Baqun (Parts 1 & 2) (Ba Ge De Gu Shi)*

1978 (Part 1), 1979 (Part 2). Beijing Film Studio. Color. 21 Reels. Direction: Cheng Ying. Screenplay: Xie Fuming, Cheng Ying, Mao Zhengshan, Ma Yuanjie. Cinematography: Gao Hongtao, Xu Xiaoxian. Art Direction: Yu Yiru. Music: Li Yanlin. Sound: Liu Shida. Cast: Ma Cangyu as Wei Baqun, Xu Xiaoyuan as Wei Longpu, Lin Lan as Tan Feng, Feng Mingyi as Chen Tao, Xu Fuyin as Chen Da, Wu Xiongqin as Du Ba, Chen Zhijian as Pan Asi, Tan Weimin as Huang Bangwei

A true story from modern Chinese history. Part 1: After the revolution of 1911 which overthrew the Manchu Emperor, General Yuan Shikai attempts to have himself declared the emperor of a new dynasty. This causes an outbreak of civil wars in which various warlords fight among themselves, with resulting great hardship and suffering for the people of China. To find a better path for their country, such young men as Wei Baqun, Chen Da and Tie Min enlist in the army with more than 100 from their home town. Wei Baqun rises through the ranks to become a deputy company commander, but he loathes the corruption he sees everywhere in the army. When his frustration impels him to strike the company commander he is sent to prison. Upon his release he attends the Guozhou Military Academy, and after the "May Fourth" movement of 1919, is assigned to Chongqing as an army staff officer. Wei's liberal views in support of social revolution and military system reform land him in trouble again, so he leaves the army and returns to his hometown. There he leads a tax resistance movement and joins the local revolutionary association in attacking a local tyrant.

Part 2: In the early 1920s, after several

setbacks, Wei Baqun for a time loses sight of his goals. His spirit is restored after he reads Doctor Sun Yatsen's book "The Three Principles of the People." Wei enters the Guangzhou Farmers' Movement School in 1925, where he studies the writings of Mao Zedong and comes to understand the reasons for his earlier failures. He returns to his hometown and establishes a farmers self-defense troop. Shortly after this, Wei Baqun joins the Communist Party, and rejecting the blandishments of the warlord regime in Guangxi province, becomes a dedicated Communist. He defeats a warlord military attack and liberates Donglan County, establishing a Red regime there. In 1930, Deng Xiaoping and Zhang Yunyi lead the "Baise Rebellion," and found the "Chinese Workers' and Farmers' Seventh Army." Wei Baqun leads his farmers' self-defense troops to participate in this rebellion. From this point on, Wei Baqun's troop becomes a part of the Red Army.

1976. *The Story of Xiangyang Compound (Xiang Yang Yuan De Gu Shi)*

1974. Changchun Film Studio. B & W. 10 Reels. Direction: Yuan Naicheng. Screenplay: Collective, based on the novel of the same title by Xu Ying. Cinematography: Fang Weiche. Art Direction: Wang Xingwen. Music: Yan Zhuhua, Wu Daming. Cast: Pu Ke as Grandpa Shi, Zhang Shen as Tiezhu, Saihan as Heidan, Wu Yun as Xiuhua, Xu Tao as Shanhuzhi, Lin Jing as Hongxing

During the summer of 1964, retired worker Grandpa Shi houses at the Xiangyang Compound some school children on their summer break. The plan is for the youngsters to do some physical labor on a road construction site, learning from Lei Feng and exercising their minds. Hu Shouli, who also lives in the compound and still holds a reactionary position, hates this activity and uses various methods to try and corrupt the children. With the help of the local Party committee and some of the parents, Grandpa Shi and the children thwart his efforts. But Hu does not give up. He sets up a workplace accident in the attempt to injure some children and cast blame on Grandpa Shi. At the critical moment, Grandpa Shi risks his own safety to rescue the children. Hu Shouli is put on trial for his crimes.

1977. *The Story of Xiaofang (Xiao Fang De Gu Shi)*

1994. Shanghai Film Studio. Color. Letterboxed. 10 Reels. Direction: Jiang Haiyang. Screenplay: Wan Fang. Cinematography: Wang Tianling. Art Direction: Yi Xiaoming. Music: Su Junxie. Sound: Ge Weijia. Costume: Zhang Lifang. Makeup: Gui Shaolin. Cast: Hu Xin as Xiao Fang, Lu Liang as Chen Weidong, Ding Jiali as Qu Nannan, Wei Guochun as Qiao Anwen, Peng Bo as Qu Lang, Wu Haili as Jiang Xiaofei, Ding Huayu as Boss Hu

Chen Weidong is a songwriter, while his wife Qu Nannan is a the very capable manager of a music publishing company. But their marriage is unhappy. Chen writes a song "Xiao Fang," based on a romance he had with a village girl when he was sent down to the countryside. The song is a big hit. Chen returns to visit the village where it all took place, and finds that Xiao Fang is still there, a recent widow. Her life had been very hard after he left, but she at last married a wealthy overseas Chinese businessman, whose fortune she has just inherited. Chen returns to the city, asks his wife for a divorce, and she readily agrees. The divorce finalized, he returns once more to the village, only to find that Xiao Fang has just left with a new fiance. Chen knows she does not love the man, so he chases their car, and is injured. But he does succeed in stopping the ill-advised wedding. Xiao Fang nurses him back to health, and at last they get together.

1978. *The Story of "Yitian" and "Tulong" (Yi Tian Tu Long Ji)*

1995. China Film Co-Production Corporation, Hong Kong Yongsheng Film Production Co. Co-Production. Color. Letterboxed. Direction: Wang Jing, Hong Jinbao. Cast: Li Lianjie (Jet Li), Zhang Min, Qiu Shuzhen (Chingmy Yao)

An action film based on a kung fu novel of the same title by Jin Yong.

1979. *The Story That Should Not Have Happened (Bu Gai Fa Sheng De Gu Shi)*

1983. Changchun Film Studio. Color. 11 Reels. Direction: Zhang Hui. Screenplay: Wang Jie, Qiao Man. Cinematography: Liu Yongzheng. Art Direction: Xu Zhenkun. Music: Gao Feng. Sound: Hong Bo. Cast: Wang Runshen as Liang Cai, Lin Qiang as Han Xizhu, Li Junhai as Li Fachun, Xu Cangxi as an old farming committee member, Wang Shuyin as Leng's wife

In the winter of 1979, the 3rd Plenary Session of the 11th Party Congress issues a new rural economic policy, with a focus on the contract responsibility system for agricultural production. In commune elections in Minyue Village in Northeast China, the members vote Party member Li Fachun out of office as head of their production unit, replacing him with one of their own, Han Xizhu. When the commune reorganizes itself into work teams, no one wants to accept the Party members, classifying them with the weak and elderly. After a fierce ideological debate, the handful of Party members in the commune decide to set up their own "Party Member Team," headed by Liang Cai. All of them are out of shape after years of deskbound administrative work, but after a time they become more productive. A series of events helps both Party members and ordinary people come to understand each other better. A year later, the commune realizes a big harvest, and after that all the teams welcome Party members to join them.

Best Picture, 1984 Hundred Flowers Awards.

1980. *Strange Case at Meishan Mountain (Mei Shan Qi An)*

1985. Changchun Film Studio. Color. 10 Reels. Direction: Li Geng. Screenplay: Mu Er. Cinematography: Xu Shouzen. Art Direction: Gao Tinglun. Music: Fan Weiqiang. Sound: Tong Zongde. Cast: Wang Che as Han Zhong, Lin Qiang as Han Zhiwen, Fu Yiwei as Chen Lihua, Song Xuejuan as Wang Yaqin

The Meishan city PSB receives a call reporting a murder, and assigns Deputy Director Han Zhong to the case. When the investigators arrive at the crime scene, they find the body of Chen Lihua, a cashier at a local store. Han follows the clues, and at last the evidence points conclusively to the worst possible spot: to his own son Han Zhiwen. The son begs his father to forgive him and allow him to escape, and when Han Zhong refuses, Zhiwen tries to kill him. A chase ensues, at the end of which Han Zhong is forced to kill his own son.

1981. *Strange Case in the Year of the Tiger (Hu Nian Qi An)*

1987. August First Film Studio. Color. 10 Reels. Direction: Wang Mengyuan. Screenplay: Wang Mengyuan, Zhao Peng. Cinematography: He Qin, Wang Weidong. Art Direction: Ma Yib-iao. Music: Gong Yuehua. Sound: Zhu Junshan. Cast: Niu Piao as Wei Wei, Han Xing as Zhu Hong, Zhou Chu as Zhong Minda, Zhang Yunmin as Deputy Bureau Director Wang, Li Huan as Bei Meimei, Liu Boyin as Ji Tianli

One summer day in the city of Linjiang, a female zoo employee is found dead in front of the tiger's cage, and the tiger has disappeared. Investigation by PSB officers Wei Wei and Zhu Hong uncover a case of murder. The victim, Ping Ping, was the daughter of Du Kaiyuan, operator of a Chinese acrobatic troupe in a foreign country, and whom she had not seen in years. Du also had an adopted son, Ji Tianli. Just before Du Kaiyuan died, he told his old friend Zhong Minda that his will stipulated all his money should go to his daughter in China, from whom he had been separated for so long. The adopted son learned of this, and had gone to China and killed Ping Ping in order to be next in line for the money. Ji Tianli is arrested.

1982. *Strange Circle (Guan Quan)*

1986. Changchun Film Studio. Color. 10 Reels. Direction: Sun Sha. Screenplay: Fu Yanli. Cinematography: Zhang Songping, Sun Guangwen. Art Direction: Guo Yansheng. Music: Fan Weiqiang. Sound: Huang Shuiqin. Cast: Huang Meiying as Zhenni, Ge Yunping as Meizhen, Zhang Baishuang as A Man, Shen Ming as A Chun, Li Li as Xiao Ying, Wang Zhihua as Xiao Cheng, Wang Tang as A Long

A circle of close friends consists of four young women: Zhenni, Meizhen, A Man and A Chun. For individual reasons, they vow never to marry. But the death of an elderly woman she knows starts Zhenni thinking; she decides to leave the circle and find her own life. As the eldest of the four, Zhenni had considerable influence on the rest, and now with her gone they begin to drift away. A Man falls in love with a man named Xiao Cheng. Meizhen marries a painter. Eventually A Chun begins dating as well. Zhenni, meanwhile, has made a name for herself as a physician; she was the first to encourage the others to seek their own lives, and now she wonders what her future will be.

1983. *Strange City Romance (Du Shi Qi Yuan)*

1989. Youth Film Studio. Color. Wide Screen. 9 Reels. Jiang Weihe. Screenplay: Yu Yonghe, Liu Yiran. Cinematographer: Zhang Lubo, Li Dazhong. Art Direction: Kang Erjing.

Music: Li Lifu. Sound: Sun Xing. Cast: Tian Shaojun as Wang Laogan, Wu Yujuan as Liu Peipei

Wang Laogan, popular singer of folk songs in his native village, is on a visit to the city. Quite by chance, he finds himself impressed into service as a last-minute replacement for a girl singer named Liu Peipei, who does not show up that night. He is a success with the audience, but instead of being jealous, Liu Peipei helps him with his singing, and he improves quite a bit, so much so that he is signed to a contract by the provincial singing and dancing troupe. But Liu Peipei's boy friend comes to him and begs him to leave. After he finishes his final performance, as Liu Peipei is giving her performance, Wang Laogan quietly slips out of the theater and leaves.

1984. *Strange Friends (Mo Sheng De Peng You)*

1982. Beijing Film Studio. Color. 9 Reels. 90 min. Direction: Xu Lei. Screenplay: Li Baoyuan, Xu Lei, Xu Tianxia. Cinematography: Huang Xinyi. Art Direction: Duan Zhengzhong, Yi Hongyuan. Music: Zhang Peiji. Sound: Sun Yumin. Cast: Li Ling as the girl, Zhang Chao as Zhang Tongsheng, Zhan Jinbo as Du Qiu

On a train going from Beijing to Fuzhou, passengers notice the strange behavior of one young girl traveling alone. She never talks and never eats. They do not know her history: her parents were taken away during the Cultural Revolution; unhappy and on her own, the young girl had gotten into some trouble which landed her in reform school. After her release, she tried to find work and lead a useful life, but nobody ever made her feel welcome or trusted her. She was an outcast, and even framed for new crimes. In despair and without hope, she had boarded the train to leave. The girls unusual sadness and silence at last prompts her fellow passengers to show some caring and get her to talk about herself. One passenger in particular offers his help and protection: a young man named Tong Sheng who had once been a criminal but had since gone straight. The girl is moved and begins to have confidence in life again.

1985. *A Strange Guest from Far Away (Tian Ya Guai Ke)*

1989. Guangxi Film Studio and Haikou City Television Cultural Development Company Co-Production. Color. Letterboxed. 9 Reels. Direction: Zhao Wenqing. Screenplay: Xu Jinyan. Cinematography: Liao Fan, Zhu Dingyuan. Art Direction: Zhang Yafang. Music: Su Tie. Sound: Lin Lin. Cast: Li Lianyi as Lu Buping, Lu Ling as Yang Xuefang, Zhang Ning as Ding Tanzhu

A convention of Chinese magicians is held in Guangxi to choose one of their number to attend the World's Fair. Among the magicians who come from all over China is a strange man named Lu Buping. When the competition starts, Lu is clearly superior to all others, performing one baffling trick after another. Lu is the clear choice to attend the World's Fair, but suddenly disappears without a trace.

1986. *Strange Hero (Guai Xia)*

1989. Changchun Film Studio. Color. Letterboxed. 9 Reels. Direction: Chen Xuejie. Screenplay: Wang Tingjun. Cinematography: Sun Hui. Art Direction: Ye Jiren. Music: Wu Damin. Sound: Kang Ruixin. Cast: Hou Yuewen as Sun Nianzu, Huang Hong as Lin Cainiang, Zhang Lun as Xu Hanpeng, Liang Tongyu as Zhou Haifeng

A girl named Lin Cainiang is sent by county magistrate Sun Nianzu to serve as a mistress to governor Xu Hanpeng. But the morning after her first night there, the governor awakens to find Lin gone, half his hair missing, and a white lotus on the pillow next to him. This leads Sun Nianzu to conclude she is strange hero "White Lotus" the authorities have sought for some time, and he has her arrested. After the girl is jailed, a man calling himself Zhou Haifeng shows up and confesses that he is the true White Lotus and Lin Cainiang should be freed. Lin is released, and Zhou is sentenced to death. But on the way to execution ground, the real White Lotus shows up, rescues Zhou and takes his place in the execution cart. They finally arrive at the execution ground, but when the ax falls on White Lotus, it is the jailer's head that comes off instead.

1987. *Strange Incident of Returning a Sword (Huai Jian Qi Qing)*

1986. Pearl River Film Studio. Color. Wide Screen. 9 Reels. Direction: Hong Ping. Screenplay: Liao Zhikai. Cinematography: Wu Bengli. Art Direction: Li Xin. Music: Sun Yi. Sound: Lin Guoqiang. Cast: Tan Yuanyuan as Baozhu, Zhen Hui as Susu, Jiang Tao as Yun Wuyang, Jie Kejuan as Chen Qiujun, Tian Chunling as Mu Duyi, Wang Jue as Chen Xuanyi

Toward the end of the Yuan (Mongol) Dynasty (c.1360), a peasant rebellion breaks out. Rebel General Yun Wugang and his wife Chen Qiujun are cornered at a river by enemy troops. Yun treacherously pushes his pregnant wife into the river to kill her, then jumps in himself and swims to safety. Qiujun is rescued, however. She soon delivers her baby, a son she gives her own family name of Chen and the given name Xuanyi. Meanwhile, Yun Wugang remarries, to the daughter of kongfu master Mu Duyi, and they have a daughter Susu. Twenty years pass, and one day Yun Wugang has a chance encounter with his former wife Chen Qingyun. She tells her son the story of how Yun had pushed her into the river, and Xuanyi confronts his father for a battle to the death. Yun Wuyang commits suicide. Susu, overcome with grief at losing both her parents, jumps from a cliff.

1988. *Strange Love of a Ghost (You Hun Qi Lian)*

1992. Xiaoxiang Film Studio. Color. Wide Screen. 9 Reels. Direction: Qiu Lili. Screenplay: Zhang Jiaping. Cinematography: Zhao Peng, Ru Shuiren, Nie Zhanjun. Art Direction: Chen Xiaoxia, Liao Jianheng. Costume: Yang Yulin, Zhang Dezhong. Makeup: Guan Jun, Zhang Rong. Cast: Huang Guoqiang as Qi Tianyuan, Dong Xiaoyan as Mei Yin, Xu Xiaojian as Li Yin, Wang Qiong as Madam Huang

At a hotel in a remote mountain area, bandit Li Yuanfu commits a series of robberies and murders. The provincial government sends detective Qi Tianyuan to run down the criminal. He finds the situation more complex than originally believed, and at last concludes someone is committing the crimes in Li Yuanfu's name. Meanwhile the killings continue. With the help of Meiying, a girl ghost, Qi Tianyuan and Li Yuanfu join forces to find the real killer to be hotel owner Li Ying along with two accomplices. Li Yuanfu kills all three.

1989. *Strange Marriage (Qi Yi De Hun Pei)*

1981. Beijing Film Studio. Color. 8 Reels. Direction: Lin Nong. Screenplay: Xu Guangdong. Cinematography: Li Yuebing. Art Direction: Ye Jiren. Music: Huang Zhun, Lu Qimin. Sound: Ren Shanpu. Cast: Yan Shikui as Tiebo, Gao Lijuan as Xuelian, Li Renlin as Enzha Guha, Yan Pide as Su Ga, Qi Ping as the old woman

Enzhagua, a slaveholder of the Yi nationality, gives a Han Chinese woman named Xuelian to a slave named Tie Bo in order to secure the slave's loyalty. But the woman disappears on their wedding night, and Tie Bo is angered, thinking she had fled from him. Later, he hears that Xuelian had been abducted that night by a Han Chinese man called Qin Lin, and his attitude toward her changes to one of sympathy. He vows to someday avenge his loss. When one day the two do meet, Tie Bo shoots Qin Lin. At that time he learns that Qin Lin was actually Xuelian's husband, and had abducted his own wife to keep her from being given to another man. When he hears this, Tie Bo feels guilty and remorseful. Xue Lian convinces Tie Bo that this proves Enzhagua's evil nature, and asks him not to serve the slaveholder any more. Tie Bo finally rebels, and asks Xue Lian to run away with him. The two are pursued by the slaveholder's men. Xue Lian is shot and wounded. She falls into a deep valley but is saved by an old fisherman. The pursuers still search for her, and at last she is run down and shot to death. Tie Bo avenges her, shooting the gunmen with his bow. In his grief, he picks up Xuelian's body and carries her deep into the snowy mountains.

1990. *Strange Sound (Guai Yin)*

1989. Inner Mongolia Film Studio. Color. Letterboxed. 8 Reels. Direction: Wuer Shana. Screenplay: Zhan Daier, Zhang Zhengqin. Cinematography: Du Rong. Art Direction: Shen Minquan. Music: Wei Jianian. Sound: Huhe. Cast: Yi Gang as Yimin, Su Ya as Shaqier, Niu Ben as Grandpa Wang, Jiang Lieying as Tang Lei, Tian Ming as Fang Ling, Zhu Sha as Grandma Zhang, Zhang Chuanye as Yiming's mother

A boy accidentally records a scary sound emanating from a supposedly empty room. He and his friends decide to investigate the strange sound, which leads them to uncover a criminal conspiracy.

1991. *Strange Story at Laojun Village (Lao Jun Zai Qi Wen)*

1985. Changchun Film Studio. Color. 9 Reels. Direction: Jiang Yandong. Screenplay: Zhang Yigong. Cinematography: Li Chaoren. Art Direction: Liang Shukui. Music: Huang Weiqiang. Sound: Liu Jingui. Cast: Qian Yongfu as Guo Liang, Shen Dezhen as Cao Lan, Zhao Zhiying as Manager Hu, Wang Yinshen as Liu Zhong, Xu Quyu as Zhang Ming

In the isolated and backward mountain village of Laojun, high school graduate Guo Liang learns there is sulfur in the mountain. Tapping into the varying talents of the local commune members, he organizes them into a village business that turns Laojun around economically.

1992. *Strange Wedding (Ji Hun Guai Shi)*

1991. Youth Film Studio. Color. Letterboxed. 9 Reels. Direction: Jiang Shixiong. Screenplay: Bao Debin. Cinematography: Li Tingzhen. Art Direction: Liu Shi. Music: Yang Nailin. Sound: Sun Xin. Cast: Jin Jinglan as He Xian's mother, Zhang Shuangli as Huang Tianbang, Cai Wei as Li Fulai, Li Weijian as Tie Niu, Wang Fuer as Bai Juhua, Yun Yuchun as Fulai's mother, Liu Xingbang as Uncle Luoer

A farmer works very hard and saves his money, soon raising enough to buy a house and car. He becomes engaged to a nice girl, but before the wedding a series of bizarre and unhappy incidents take place, things they cannot control. It turns out a witch is casting spells which thoroughly disrupt the couple's lives and the lives of those around them. Their relationship is almost destroyed until they realize what is going on.

1993. *Stranger in Suzhou (Gu Su Yi Guai)*

1988. Changchun Film Studio. Color. 11 Reels. Direction: Sun Qinguo. Screenplay: Jin Botao. Cinematography: Gao Hongbao, Dong Yingde. Art Direction: Song Honghua. Music: Jin Junzai. Sound: Zhang Fenglu. Cast: You Bengcang as Ye Tianshi, Zhou Zhou as Liu Fengchun, Li Yuanyuan as Liang Meiniang, Yang Le as Zhang Yuchan

During the reign of Qing Emperor Yongzheng (1723–1736), Doctor Ye Tianshi lives in the city of Suzhou, and gains a reputation for helping people. When jeweler Liu Fengchun's home is robbed, his wife Liang Meiniang becomes very depressed, but Ye is able to cure her depression. The daughter of Wuzhong County Magistrate Zhang Yuchan becomes pregnant out of wedlock, and Ye helps her overcome the complications of her pregnancy, although the girl's father chooses not to thank the doctor for helping with something he considers shameful. Eventually Ye Tianshi wins the admiration and appreciation of the Emperor Yongzheng, who offers Ye a court position. But

Ye asks the emperor to allow him to return to Suzhou and continue serving the people there.

1994. *Street Guitar Players (Lu Bian Ji Ta Dui)*

1985. Changchun Film Studio. Color. 10 Reels. Direction: Chang Yan. Screenplay: Chang Yan, Wu Zenyan. Cinematography: Gao Hongbao. Art Direction: Wang Guizhi. Music: Wan Weiqiang, Zhen Fang. Sound: Kang Ruixin, Zhang Wen. Cast: Liang Qing as Xu Xiaoguang, Xu Lijuan as Shanshan, Ma Jun as Zhao Zhenggang, Hang Cheng as Luo Lanlan, Geng Tao as Gao Haiou, Zhu Feng as Huang Dongni, Zhu Jun as Xiaoguang's younger brother

Xu Xiaoguang and Zhao Zhenggang are young women workers who enjoy playing guitar in their spare time. They get up a band to give street performances. Disappointed that popular music is dominated by music from Hong Kong, Taiwan or abroad, they start composing their own. They are invited to perform at a music club which has till now only offered foreign music. One of their audience, the young woman owner of a coffee house, is so impressed that she joins the group. The one thing they lack is a singer, and Xiaoguang's sister Shanshan eagerly volunteers. Their father objects, but is converted when he hears Shanshan's beautiful singing voice.

1995. *Street Knight (Ma Lu Qi Shi)*

1990. Xi'an Film Studio and China Film Export and Import Corporation Co-Production. Color. 9 Reels. Wide Screen. Direction: Ge Xiaoying. Screenplay: Cui Jingsheng. Cinematography: Zhao Haifu. Art Direction: Liu Xinghou. Music: Xu Jingxin. Sound: Hui Dongzi. Cast: Xie Yuan as the Deliveryman, Ma Xiaoqing as the Girl, Yue Hong as the Deliveryman's wife, Jin Lili as the Doctor

A young girl with little experience of life gets pregnant, but because of her ignorance, fails to get an abortion. She longs for a "husband" to protect her, and chances to meet up with a deliveryman who cares for her out of a sense of guilt. His own wife is also pregnant. The deliveryman is caught between the girl, his wife and the hospital.

1996. *Struggle in an Ancient City with Wild Fire and Spring Wind (Yehuo Chunfeng Dou Gu Cheng)*

1963. August First Film Studio. B & W. 11

Struggle in an Ancient City with Wild Fire and Spring Wind. Yang Xiaodong (Wang Xingang, standing left) and Silver Ring (Wang Xiaotang, right) finally convince Guan Jingtao (Wang Runsheng) to defect from his collaborationist regiment. 1963. August First Film Studio.

Reels. Direction: Yan Jizhou. Screenplay: Li Yinru, Li Tian and Yan Jizhou, based on the novel of the same title by Li Yinru. Cinematography: Cao Jingyun, Zhang Dongliang. Art Direction: Zhang Zheng. Music: Gao Ruxing. Sound: He Baoding. Cast: Wang Xiaotang as Gold Ring and Silver Ring, Wang Xingang as Yang Xiaodong, Chen Lizhong as Yang's mother, Wang Runsheng as Guan Jingtao, Jin Qingyun as Xiao Tao, Zhao Ruping as Han Yanlai

In 1943, Yang Xiaodong, political commissar of a guerrilla troop, enters an old city in Northeast China in disguise to make contact with two undercover agents, twin sisters called "Gold Ring" and "Silver Ring." Their plan is to persuade Guan Jingtao, commander of a collaborationist regiment, to defect. At first, the agents meet with a series of disasters: Gold Ring bravely sacrifices herself to cover Guan Jingtao, who has fallen under the suspicion of his superiors; Yang's mother is betrayed by a traitor and arrested; Silver Ring inadvertently discloses she and Yang Xiaodong's rendezvous site, resulting in Yang's arrest. So that her son can concentrate on his work without worrying about her, Yang's mother commits suicide. The

tide turns when Silver Ring leads some armed members of the Party underground in rescuing Yang. The two are finally able to meet with Guan Jingtao and convince him to defect with his army. During their struggles, Yang Xiaodong and Silver Ring have fallen in love. His assignment fulfilled, he prepares to return to his own unit. As he says goodbye to Silver Ring, he gives her a red, heart-shaped ring his mother had been saving as a gift for her future daughter-in-law.

1997. *Struggle in Mind (Xin Ling De Bo Dou)*

1983. August Film Studio. Color. 9 Reels. Direction: Hao Guang. Screenplay: Mao Yan, Hao Guang. Cinematography: Zhang Dongliang. Art Direction: Zhao Changsheng. Music: Fu Gengcheng, Xu Xiyi. Sound: Zhen Minzhe. Cast: Zhen Songmao as Song Chunyang, Pan Xiping as Jiang Benzheng, Wang Baokun as Qu Suzhen, Zhen Baoguo as Ma Xiaobao, Zhang Mingliang as Wang Tianming, Wang Quan as Wang Tieshan

After Song Chunyang graduates from the

PLA school for political cadres, he is assigned to the 3rd Company of a certain division as political commissar. His bride Qu Suzhen accompanies him for a visit. As soon as Song arrives he is confronted with a major problem: the company is authorized to send one of their number for intensive advanced training, which usually assures rapid promotion. Some of the unit's officers, notably Song Chunyang's boss Regimental Commander Jiang Benzheng, want to send Wang Tianming, the son of Deputy Division Commander Wang Tieshan. The majority want to send Squad Leader Ma Xiaobao. The choice is given to Song. He compares the records of the two, and concludes that Wang Tianming is unqualified for selection. Jiang Benzheng is outraged, and threatens to have Song involuntarily retired from the army, a premature ending to his career with substantial loss of benefits. Song bravely sticks to his choice, and his name appears on the next list of retirees. Later, Deputy Commander Wang learns what has been going on, and highly praises Song Chunyang, removing his name from the list of retirees. Wang also calls in and chews out both his son Wang Tianming and Jiang Benzheng.

1998. *Struggles in the Big City (Du Shi Da Dou)*

1993. Guangxi Film Studio. Color. Letterboxed. 9 Reels. Direction: Lu Jiandai, Yu Zhongxiao. Screenplay: Huang Yazhou. Cinematography: Chen Chang'an. Art Direction: Long Xiaobo. Music: Fan Weiqiang. Sound: Dong Baosheng. Costume: Zhang Tianhong. Makeup: Gan Jun. Cast: He Wei as Li Ajing, Huang Meiying as Mai Lan, Wu Jianguang as Qiu Zhibing, Chen Yude as the Head of Contracting

Farmer Li Ajing comes to the city seeking work. He meets a woman store manager named Mai Lan, who takes a liking to him although she is already engaged to Qiu Zhibing, manager of a construction company. Ajing finds that Qiu has sub-contracted work to a low quality contractor in exchange for a bribe: a house which he needs for his marriage to Mai Lan. Not wanting to see Mai Lan involved in such dealings, Ajing sets out to gather evidence of Qiu's crime. But when he leaves Qiu's place, he falls into a trap Qiu set for someone else, and is badly beaten. This so angers Mai Lan she leaves Qiu. When Ajing recovers, he decides to return to the countryside. On the

boat, he finds Mai Lan on the shore smiling and waving to him.

1999. *Stubborn Man (Jiang Xiao Zi)*

1982. Shanghai Film Studio. Color. 7 Reels. Direction: Sun Yongping. Screenplay: Xiao Wun, Sun Yongping. Cinematography: Chan Lianguo. Art Direction: Ning Futing. Music: Gao Tian. Sound: Yin Zhiping. Cast: Liang Yanwen as Wu Ming, Cheng Zhi as Director Feng, Zhou Yazhou as Mother, Zhu Sha as Manager Song

A factory in the northeast China city of Songjiang is losing materials due to inept management. When 40 tons of coal are unaccounted for at the end of one month, Director Feng instructs warehouse worker Wu Ming how to cover up the loss, but the form she completes requires a stamp of approval from workshop director Pan Dakai. Pan realizes what is up, and refuses to go along. His stubbornness earns him considerable harassment from management and other workers. Even his family is affected, as his younger sister finds her job application rejected for no reason. Despite the unfair treatment, Pan refuses to give in, although his mother steals the seal and stamps the form. Pan Dakai's honesty moves Wu Ming, and she decides to cease cooperating with Director Feng. Wu Ming and Pan Dakai go to the Songjiang City Party Committee to report Feng, deciding they want justice even if it costs them their jobs.

2000. *The Stupid Heroes (Sha Xiao Zi Xing Xia Ji)*

1989. Pearl River Film Studio. Color. Letterboxed. 9 Reels. Direction: Wun Yanmei, Shao Xuehai. Screenplay: Wei Ning, Mei Yu. Cinematography: Wu Benli. Art Direction: Shi Haiying, Liang Guoxiong. Music: Wang Shi. Sound: Deng Qinhua. Cast: Liang Tian as Skinny, Ying Aiguo as Fatty, Liu Ling as Chunhua

Falsely accused and forced to flee the capital, the emperor's brother arrives in rural Tang Village, where he is given sanctuary in the home of the village chief. Because the common people know the charges against him are false, the chief's daughter Chunhua protects him, aided by her friends, Fatty the cook and Skinny the veterinarian. At last, when troops arrive to arrest the brother, Chunhua and her friends hold them off as long as they can while the quarry escapes, but are at last forced to flee their native village. Years later, when the brother succeeds to the throne as emperor, he finds Chunhua and rewards her by making her his empress. For Skinny and Fatty, however, life goes on as it always has.

2001. *Stupid Wang Laoda (Ben Ren Wang Lao Da)*

1987. Beijing Film Studio. Color. 12 Reels. Direction: Guo Wei. Screenplay: Guo Wei. Cinematography: Ge Weiqin. Art Direction: Zhang Xiande, Zhen Huiwen. Music: Liu Zhi. Sound: Wang Yunhua. Cast: Liang Qingang as Wang Laoda, Han Guiju as Dacui, Chen Guodian as Li Yongxu, Qi Guirong as the wife, Chang Wenzhi as Secretary Hu

Hard-working farmer Wang Laoda has difficulty speaking, so everyone calls him "Stupid Wang." Single and childless in his 30s, he adopts Xiao Goudan, a little boy abused by his natural parents, although Wang's one lady friend breaks off with him as a result. During the economically distressed early 1960s, he meets and marries a widow named Dacui, with whom he has three children. During the Cultural Revolution, Wang goes into the snow-covered mountains to find food for his family, slips off a cliff and is killed. In accordance with the hope expressed in his will, his adopted son marries his and Dacui's daughter.

2002. *Su Xiaosan (Su Xiao San)*

1981. Children's Film Studio. Color. 9 Reels. Direction: Pan Wenzhan, Yuan Yuehua. Screenplay: Hu Zhengyan. Cinematography: Guan Qinwu. Art Direction: Zhou Denggao. Music: Yan Fei. Sound: Zhang Jiake. Cast: Chen Xiaolei as Su Xiaosan, Zhang Ping as Zhao Xuchu, Wang Futang as Gao Wenlong, Ma Shuchao as Zhen Jian

In South China, after his parents are killed in a Japanese air raid, teenager Su Xiaosan is sold to an acrobatic troupe by Japanese collaborator Gao Wenlong. He at last is able to flee the troupe, but leads a homeless and miserable existence after that, thieves and beggars his only companions. One day he happens to meet Zhen Jian, director of a New Fourth Army guerrilla troop. Impressed with Zhen Jian's stories of fighting the Japanese, Su Xiaoshan begins looking for the New Fourth Army. Su's life finally changes one day when he enters the home of Zhao Xuchu, a well-known doctor but also an undercover agent for the Communist Party. Through Zhao, he finds the real

New Fourth Army, and becomes part of their support. He organizes the beggars into a network which delivers medicine from Doctor Zhao to the New Fourth. Su even saves the doctor's life by shooting a collaborator. Su Xiaoshan grows up as a young soldier of the revolutionary team.

2003. *Sub-Husband (Bian Wai Zhang Fu)*

1993. Fujian Film Studio. Color. Letterboxed. 9 Reels. Direction: Chen Minxing. Screenplay: Yang Xiaoxiong. Cinematography: Zhao Xiaoding. Art Direction: Yang Hong. Music: Shan Bao. Sound: Guan Jian. Costume: Tong Jingqin. Makeup: Cui Jie. Cast: Chen Peisi as Chen Yaozong, Ding Jiali as Dagui, Tian Ming as Ma Rui, Xie Yuan as Lu Qi, Da Shan as Ma Hongying, Ma Qi as Zhang Chao

A rumor spreads throughout a company that department head Chen Yaozong will be promoted to bureau chief when he returns from overseas, so on his arrival he is greeted and flattered by everyone. Instead of a promotion, however, Chen is fired. Jobless, and with little prospect of finding another position, Chen dares not tell his wife Dagui the truth. His behavior after the firing makes Dagui very suspicious. At last, Chen and his friend Ma Rui go into business together, starting a Sino-foreign racing club. Now a CEO, Chen has a new lease on life.

2004. *Such a Person (Zhe Yang De Ren)*

1984. Pearl River Film Studio. Color. Letterboxed. Direction: Wang Jing. Screenplay: Wang Peigong. Cinematography: Liang Xiongwei. Art Direction: Li Wenhua. Music: Cheng Dazhou. Sound: Lin Guang. Cast: Bai Zhidi as Liang Ziru, Wun Yujuan as Qin Lijuan, Jiang Guanjun as Deputy Division Commander Yan, Wang Shizhi as Han Feng, Guo Xuxin as Liu Zhizhong, Liu Ziuyun as Chunhua

When squadron leader Liang Ziru's ear disease forces him to discontinue flying, he is given a job as head of a PLA warehouse. Liang's criticism of his deputy head Han Feng for requisitioning wood to make furniture for Deputy Division Commander Yan leads to Liang's own demotion to ordinary warehouse worker. When Yan later summons Liang for criticism, Liang recalls a famous Chinese military campaign which embarrasses the commander about his own conduct. Han continues his single-minded persecution of Liang, and at last files false charges about him. But by now Yan has come to his senses and criticizes Han Feng, saying that Liang Ziru is a true Communist.

2005. *Such Affection (Ru Chi Duo Qing)*

1956. Changchun Film Studio. B & W. 7 Reels. Direction: Fang Ying. Screenplay: Luo Tai, based on the story "Love the Man, Not His Position" by Li Li. Cinematography: Ge Weiqin. Art Direction: Wang Tao. Music: Lou Zhanghou. Sound: Wang Lin. Cast: Ye Linlang as Fu Ping, Song Xuejuan as Xiao Zhang the nurse, Qin Han as Huang Shan, Zhou Ke as Bai Lang, Li Yalin as Manager Fei, Liu Zhenqing as Li Ming, Gao Ping as Wang the driver, An Zhenjiang as Zhao Xiangshi, Duan Wu as Department Head Li, Huang Wansu as Department Head Li's fiancee

Fu Ping falls for four men in succession. Today she dates this fellow, tomorrow she flirts with another. When she meets movie studio employee Bai Lang, she abandons college student Huang Shan; when she falls for Manager Fei, she then drops Bai Lang. Finally she meets Li Ming, an officer worker at the hydropower bureau. Mistaking him for a department head named Li, she dumps Fei, who truly loves her. She dreams of being the wife of an executive, and wants the money and position that would come with it. Although Li Ming keeps telling her that he is a clerk, she refuses to believe him and keeps repeating that "I love the man and not his position." She finally learns the address of Li the department head and goes to his home where she finds that the Li Ming she knows really is a clerk. When she learns the truth she is very embarrassed.

2006. *Such Parents (Ru Ci Die Niang)*

1963. Haiyan Film Studio. B & W. 9 Reels. Direction: Zhang Tianxi. Screenplay: Xiao Xixi, Lu Yang and Yie Yiqing, based on the Shanghai Public Comedy Troupe's stage play of the same title. Cinematography: Peng Enli. Art Direction: Zhang Wanhong. Music: Hu Dengliang. Sound: Ren Xinliang. Cast: Yang Huasheng as Sun Ping, Lu Yang as Zhu Juan, Xiao Xixi as Jiang Fugeng, Hong Liu as the Jiang family's grandmother, Zhang Qiaonong as Old Zhang, He Feng as Zhang Cuiying

Zhu Juan and Sun Ping both come from capitalist backgrounds, and after 1949 the cou-ple retain their previous bad habits, such as cheating on each other. It is no wonder that their 12-year-old son Xiaobao is lazy and greedy, often cutting school by feigning illness, and hanging out in the streets, which angers his parents. One Sunday, the parents go to a movie, locking Xiaobao in the house to force him to do some homework. On the way, the father loses his wallet, which is found and returned to them by a worker. But when it is discovered there is 10 yuan less in the wallet, Zhu Juan accuses the helpful worker of theft. At that moment, Xiaobao, steadily coming under the influence of one of his teachers, owns up that he had taken the money. His parents are very embarrassed.

2007. *A Sudden Tragedy (Huo Qi Xiao Qiang)*

1982. Shanghai Film Studio. Color. 10 Reels. Direction: Fu Jinggong. Screenplay: Ye Dan, Zhu Hongsheng. Cinematography: Li Chongjun. Art Direction: He Zhojie. Music: Yang Mao. Sound: Zhou Yunling. Cast: Wu Xiqian as Fu Lianshan, Yan Xiang as Liang Youhan, Zhao Jiayan as Secretary Guo, Li Dingbao as Big Wang, Wang Yiping as Dai Bing

After the 3rd Plenary Session of the 11th Party Congress, provincial Power Administration deputy head Fu Lianshan and his chief engineer Liang arrive at the Jiajing Power Bureau to reform the management system there, but the reforms are not welcomed by the Jiajing prefectural Party committee. After studying the situation, Fu Lianshan recommends downsizing the bureau's staff and merging the Jingou Power Station into the province's principal power network, thereby putting it under provincial administration. Since this would decrease the Jingou bureau's control, prefectural Party Secretary Guo breaks with Fu Liansha. Rumors and political pressures follow to plague Fu's efforts, and Chief Engineer Liang falls ill from stress. When a violent storm knocks out the power one night, Liang goes to the distribution station to deal with it himself, although he is very ill. Just as he gets the power restored, word comes that the Yingpeng station needs power, and Secretary Guo orders that some be sent from Jingou. Liang realizes this will overburden the system's capacity and cause an accident to the server. But he also knows that refusing Guo would be insubordination, so he decides to follows Guo's orders, hoping the inevitable accident will demonstrate the chaotic management of the bureau. The predicted disaster happens, and Liang is accused of incompetence. Fu Lianshan hopes that the ensuing hearing will show the real culpability of those responsible for the accident.

2008. *Summer Adventures (Xia Ri Li Xian)*

1991. Beijing Film Studio. Color. Letterboxed. 8 Reels. Direction: Du Min, Luo Hangmin. Screenplay: Zhou Qiying. Cinematography: Yan Junsheng. Art Direction: Wang Jixian. Music: Gao Erdi. Sound: Wu Ling. Cast: Gong Lifeng as Lao Wai, Fu Dalong as Lao Xia, Kang Xun as Da Kuan, Zhang Meng as Ku Desheng, Wang Chunzhi as Juanjuan, Liu Peiqi as the gang leader

During their summer break from school, four teenagers traveling to visit another city become good friends on the way and decide to stay together during their holiday. They accidentally stay at a warehouse being used by a gang of counterfeiters to store their product. The young people report their find to the public security forces, and have an exciting adventure helping the authorities round up the gang.

2009. *Summer Story (Xiatian De Gushi)*

1955. Changchun Film Studio. B & W. 10 Reels. Direction: Yu Yanfu. Screenplay: Sun Qian. Cinematography: Ge Weiqin. Set Design: Zhang Jingnan. Music: Li Xi. Sound: Huang Lijia. Cast: Zhao Lian as Tian Jinsheng, Li Songjun as Gao Ernu, Li Yin as Mu Yulan, An Qi as Tian Aizhen, Fu Ke as Liang Mancang, Wang Jianhua as Mrs. Tian, Bai Dezhang as Gao Baoming, Li Mengyao as Mi Sanduo, Zhou Senguan as Wang Dacheng, Zhang Ting as Wang Yongfu

Two recent junior high school graduates, a boy named Tian Jinsheng, and a girl named Mi Yulan return to Paomaobao Village to spend their summer vacation. They learn that the local agricultural cooperative cannot make any food allocations because the accounts were not cleared after the wheat harvest. It is rumored that the accounts were deliberately messed up by Wang Dacheng, an accountant of dubious reputation. When Tian Jinsheng sees the situation, he encourages and helps local girl Gao Erniu to learn accounting and oppose the villain. However, his classmate Mi Yulan is not interested in this at all. Shortly afterwards, senior high school admission

notifications arrive, granting admission to Tian Jinsheng but rejecting Mi Yulan. Tian Jinsheng tries to persuade Mi to remain in the village and do the badly needed accounting work, but Mi looks down upon all of the agricultural co-op's endeavors, as she is interested only in pursuing material wealth and pleasure. Her father then marries her off to a businessman in the city. In spite of his mother's objections, Tian Jinsheng decides not to return to school, but stay and help in building his hometown. In the end the co-op's accounts are cleared up, its members all receive their food allocations, and Tian Jinsheng and Gao Erniu fall in love.

2010. *The Summer Vacation Gift (Shu Jia De Li Wu)*

1961. Changchun Film Studio. B & W. 8 Reels. Direction: Cai Zhenya. Screenplay: the Anhui Huaiyuan County Film Screenplay Writing Team, recorded by Jiang Qingdi. Cinematography: Feng Guiting. Art Direction: Li Fan. Music: Lin Xuesong, Yan Zuhua. Sound: Zhang Jianping. Cast: Huang Qiming as Wang Xiaozhu, Zhang Jianwen as Zhang Shiyan, Cui Juanjuan as He Xiaoliu, Zhang Yali as He Shuangzhi, Yu Chunyan as Wei Lin, Jiang Ji as Jia Ping

During the Great Leap Forward, a troop of elementary school Young Pioneers near the Huaihe River collects scrap metal to raise funds over their summer vacation to purchase a tractor. With the help of Teacher Li and Commune Secretary Hong, they overcome many difficulties and salvage two large steel bells weighing 8,000 kg each. They are also successful in creating home-made fertilizers, and donate all these as a summer vacation gift to the commune.

2011. *Summer's Rain, Winter's Dream (Xia Zhi Yu, Dong Zhi Meng)*

1987. Changchun Film Studio. Color. 10 Reels. Direction: Chang Yan. Screenplay: Zhou Weixian, Wang Chenggang. Cinematography: Han Dongxia. Art Direction: Lu Qi. Music: Wu Damin. Sound: Zhang Wen. Cast: Ji Qimin as Wan Heming, Ye Meng as Shangguan Qiuyu, Shen Ming as A Fang, Zhang Xiaolin as Xiao Qiang, Tie Datong as Li Juhua

A Fang dislikes her job in a nursing home for the elderly. She is impatient with the people in her care, and cannot understand why they find certain things interesting, like going to the theater everyday to hear a story teller. The film tells the stories of some of these lonely older people and their personal tragedies such as neglect and abuse by their adult children. At last A Fang's own negligence results in one elderly woman dying of a heart attack. A Fang is very remorseful over the death. She gathers all the flower seeds the woman had bought before her death and spreads them on her tomb.

2012. *The Sun Has Ears (Tai Yang You Er)*

1995. Moonhill Intl. & China Starts U.S.A. Production in association with Changchun Film Studio. Color. Letterboxed. 108 minutes. Direction: Yim Ho. Screenplay: Yim Ho, Yi Ling. Cinematography: Zhao Fei. Art Direction: Gao Guoliang. Music: Otomo Yoshihide. Sound (Dolby): Gu Changning. Costume: Dong Chongmin. Cast: Zhang Yu as Youyou, You Yong as Pan Hao, Gao Qiang as Hu Tianyou, Jiang Yanqiang as the Widow Ma

In a remote part of North China during the early 1920s, warlords and bandits wield just as much power and control as the central government. When impoverished young bride Youyou collapses from hunger at the door of local bandit Pan Hao, he decides he wants her, in spite of his already having a lover, the Widow Ma. He makes a deal with Youyou's husband Tianyou, a man heavily in debt, to loan him the attractive young woman for 10 days. While Youyou complies reluctantly, she finds that Pan Hao's physical charms make for an enjoyable 10 days, at the end of which she returns to the impoverished Tianyou. When government troops on a bandit suppression campaign surround the village, Pan is wounded but manages to escape, taking Youyou with him. When he recovers, Pan returns to carry on the battle, with Youyou now carrying his child. After a complex succession of double-crosses in which everyone's life is changed, Youyou kills the bandit and starts life over again with her husband.

2013. *The Sun Just Came Over the Mountains (Tai Yang Gang Gang Chu Shan)*

1960. Changchun Film Studio. B & W. 8 Reels. Direction: Wang Yi. Screenplay: The Sixth Collective Writing Team of Changchun Film Studio, based on a novel by Ma Feng (1922–).

Cinematography: Wang Yizhi. Art Direction: Li Junjie. Music: Lin Xuesong. Sound: Yan Jin. Cast: Ren Yi as Director Gao, Liang Yin as Secretary Gao, Xia Peijie as the eldest son's wife, Zhang Qingjian as Dongmei, Guo Xiaoxi as Xiao Mei, Liu Zhenzhong as Secretary Guo

Director Gao of Liu Village's agricultural co-op worries that his co-op will not have sufficient machinery to draw the water it needs. He requests from his younger brother, the county Party secretary, permission to borrow more machinery. Secretary Gao finds that Liu Village has rich underground water resources, so he decides to concentrate on digging wells and building a canal, combining the well diggers of East and West Villages in Liu Village, aiming to set up a water station for the use of all three villages. But Director Gao is reluctant to cooperate, thinking his village can get a better deal by going it alone. With his younger brother's help he in time comes to realize his error. Soon after, the central government merges the three co-ops into a people's commune.

2014. *The Sun on the Roof of the World (Shi Jie Wu Ji De Tai Yang)*

1991. Guangxi Film Studio. Color. 10 Reels. Letterboxed. Direction: Xie Fei and Wang Ping. Screenplay: Huang Shiying. Cinematography: Liu Baogui. Art Direction: Zhong Guangling. Music: Shi Wanchun. Sound: Lin Lin, Ma Ting. Cast: Liang Guoqing as Fang Jingsheng, Jiao Huang as Fang Zheng, Shi Ke as Mi Lan, Wang Yumei as Leng Jing, Hu Peng as Granny, Feng Enhe as Feng Baolin, Ai Liya as Ni Ma, Bianba Renchi as Ge Sang

A young drilling engineer travels to Tibet to begin work on a geothermal development project. Soon after arriving, he receives a letter from his girlfriend Milan, a postgraduate student who urges him to rush back to Beijing and marry her. But his father Fang Zheng, supervisor-in-chief of the geothermal project, is firmly opposed to this. Ignoring his father, the young man returns to Beijing eagerly looking forward to married life. But Milan tells him her passport is ready and she plans to leave for the United States right after their marriage. Fang decides an absentee spouse is not what he had in mind, so he gives up the idea of marriage and returns to Tibet. Just when the geothermal project is in full swing, Milan arrives in Tibet to see Fang. The geological team members welcome her, and Fang and Milan spend a happy night together. Milan, now pregnant, finally goes to the States. She later writes Fang from the U.S. that she wants him with her and has arranged for him to join her in America. But Fang hesitates: he doesn't want to give up his career and the job he's now working on. On the night of a Tibetan festival, a rare blowout occurs at the project. In a desperate fight to shut the geothermal blowout down, Fang sacrifices his life.

2015. *The Sun Shines on Redstone Valley (Tai Yang Zhao Liang Liao Hong Shi Gou)*

1953. Wenhua Film Studio. B & W. 10 Reels. Direction: Lu Ren. Screenplay: Lu Ren. Cinematography: Xu Qi and Lin Fa. Set Design: Wang Yuebai. Music: Huang Yijun and Guan Keyan. Sound: Shen Yiming, Zhu Weigang, Guo Liang and Feng Deyao. Costume: Ma Hongxiang, Bai Jingzhong, Yao Gentao. Makeup: Cheng Zhi, Ni Yifei. Cast: Xi Feng as Ma Waibao, Yuan Baofeng as Mayipula, Cui Chaoming as Ma Xiren, Ding Jie as Comrade Li, Hua Cheng as Old Man Li, Wang Damin as Maahbudu, Cheng Zhi as Ma Yipu

Before liberation, in a village in the Redstone Valley of Northwest China, Hui nationality farmer Ma Waibao's elder son is killed by landlord Ma Xiren, who has links to Ma Bufang's warlord army. Seeking revenge, Ma Waibao trains his younger son Ma Yipu to become an expert hunter. When the PLA enters Northwest China, Ma Yipu is conscripted into the Nationalist army. Seeing that the locals welcome the Red Army, Ma Xiren spreads a rumor that the PLA intends to commit genocide of the Hui people. Comrade Li, the PLA work team director, widely publicizes the CPC's policy on minorities, which rapidly gains the people's trust and cooperation. Ma Yipu, learning that the PLA is the army of the poor, defects to the PLA and is reunited with his father. The PLA captures Ma Xiren.

2016. *The Sun Society (Guan Dong Tai Yang Hui)*

1993. Changchun Film Studio & Taiwan Muwei Film Company Co-Production. Color. Letterboxed. 9 Reels. Direction: Luo Qi. Cinematography: Luo Wen. Art Direction: Song Honghua, Wang Xouyuan. Music: Cheng Jingrong. Costume: Li Shuyan, An Lixin. Makeup:

Song Yingyuan, Song Xinying. Cast: Hu Huizhong (Sibelle Hu), Zhen Aonan , Mu Sicheng, Zhang Ruixi, Zhang Shenghe, Chang Shan

After the Japanese invasion and occupation of Northeast China, Li Jing, the woman manager of a dancing hall uses some of her employees to gain intelligence information from their Japanese clientele. Li then transfers the information to Chinese guerrillas through Meng Dezhao, operator of a local casino. The operation goes smoothly until the Japanese capture and kill Meng. His place is taken by Li Shangda, Meishun's former lover. Meishun is caught and killed when she tries to tell Li Jing of the Japanese plan to use human subjects in their secret germ warfare experiments. When Japanese soldiers block their path to escape, Li Shangda and Li Jing fight to the end and die bravely.

2017. *Sunrise (Parts 1&2) (Ri Chu)*

1985. Shanghai Film Studio. Color. Wide Screen. 16 Reels. Direction: Yu Bengzheng. Screenplay: Cao Yu and Wan Fang, based on the play by Cao Yu (1910–). Cinematography: Zhu Yongde. Art Direction: Ju Ransheng. Music: Xu Jingxin. Sound: Feng Deyao. Cast: Fang Shu as Chen Bailu, Wang Sihuai as Fang Dasheng, Wang Futang as Pan Yueting, Yan Xiang as Li Shiqin, Wang Fuli as Cuixi, Sha Wei as Huang Shenshan, Chen Dajun as Luo Heisan, Liu Qing as "Little Thing"

In the 1930s, a dissatisfied young woman named Chen Bailu leaves her poet husband and travels to Shanghai in search of a more exciting and glamorous life. She becomes quite prominent in the city's cafe society, a lavish party-giver and the mistress of prominent banker Pan Yueting. One night Chen returns home to find a frightened young girl hiding in her apartment. The girl, who everyone just calls "Little Thing," ran away when she was sold to a low-class brothel. Chen Bailu lets the girl stay with her, and makes protecting her a personal project. But at last the girl's whereabouts are discovered, and she commits suicide. Then, when Pan's bank goes under, he turns Chen's many debts over to a repulsive gangster who has long lusted for her. Chen Bailu realizes how vapid and miserable her life really is, and how powerless she is to change it. She decides that suicide is her only way out of this corrupt society.

Best Picture, 1986 Hundred Flowers Awards.

Best Actress Fang Shu, 1986 Hundred Flowers Awards.

Best Supporting Actress Wang Fuli, 1986 Golden Rooster Awards.

Best Supporting Actress Wang Fuli, 1986 Hundred Flowers Awards.

Best Screenplay Cao Yu and Wan Fang, 1986 Golden Rooster Awards.

2018. *Sunset (Can Zhao)*

1987. Emei Film Studio. Color. 10 Reels. Direction: Bai Hong. Screenplay: Li Kuanding. Cinematography: Song Jianwen. Art Direction: Chen Ruogang. Music: Tang Qinyun. Sound: Tu Liuqin. Cast: Yu Lan as Shan Yueer, Yang Zhichun as Shan Dacheng, He Wenyi as Pang Degui, Xu Xing as Pan Tianyan, Lei Han as Guo Wei

Shan Yueer is a nice girl in a mountain village, respectful to her elders and helpful to others. Her father Shan Dacheng is discriminated against because he is falsely labeled as being part of the rich farmer class. Shan Yueer's good friend Xueying loves young village elementary schoolteacher Guo Wei, but her mother Pang Erniang wants to improve the family's political status by marrying Xueying to commune director Cui Qinlian's nephew He Xianrong. Shan Yueer encourages Xueying to stand up to her mother. Hunter Pan Tianyan has a good relationship with Shan Yueer, and it looks promising for romance. However, Chi Qinlian begins to persecute Shan Yueer for trying to thwart his plans, so he has her labeled a counterrevolutionary and thrown into prison. Her father dies shortly after that, and her friend Xueying commits suicide rather than marry someone other than the boy she loves. When she kills herself, her mother Pang Erniang loses her mind. As the sun sets one winter day, a grieving Shan Yueer quietly weeps before her father's tomb, after which she and Pan Tianyan leave their hometown together.

2019. *Sunset Street (Xi Zhao Jie)*

1983. Beijing Film Studio. Color. 10 Reels. Direction: Wang Haowei. Screenplay: Su Shuyang. Cinematography: Li Chengsheng. Art Direction: Liu Yi. Music: Wang Liping. Sound: Gui Zhilin. Cast: Chi Zhiqiang as Shitou, Zhang Guomin as Wu Haibo, Song Xiaoyin as Zhou Yanyan, Yu Shaokang as Zhen Wanquan, Li Ding as Li Pengfei, Liu Yan as Xiao Na, Jiang Shui as Wang Pu, Lu Guilan as Liu Wen

The daily lives and personal struggles of several households on Beijing's Xizhao (Sunset) Street, an alley in a declining neighborhood. Among the residents are Shitou, an unemployed young man who has trouble finding work; Zhen Wanquan, a retired artwork framer who wants to start a snackfood business; model teacher Wang Pu and his wife Liu Wen, who want a good desk to work at; Doctor Zhou Yanyan, and others. The various residents achieve their dreams in their own ways. The story ends with the news that the neighborhood will be razed to make way for new housing construction. As they prepare to move, all look forward to a new, bright future.

2020. *Sunshine and Showers (Tai Yang Yu)*

1987. Pearl River Film Studio. Color. 9 Reels. Direction: Zhang Ming. Screenplay: Liu Xihong, Zhang Ming. Cinematography: Yao Li, Pang Lei. Art Direction: Peng Jun, Zhang Song. Music: Zhou Xiaoyuan. Sound: Lin Guang. Cast: Yan Xiaoping as Liu Yaxi, Sun Chun as Liu Yidong, Yi Xinxin as Kong Lingkai, Zhang Ling as He Nan, Zhang Yanli as A Yuan

This film depicts the new and different lifestyles of the young Chinese who live and work in the Shenzhen Special Economic Zone (SEZ). It focuses on the daily activities of a group of modern young women, and particularly the romantic relationship of one of them, Liu Yaxi. She and her boyfriend Liu Yidong seem perfectly compatible, but actually argue a great deal without understanding why. Things get worse when another woman enters their lives, turning conflict into crisis. The film's title refers to the alternating optimism and uncertainty characteristic of life in the economically booming SEZ, much like the South China weather.

2021. *Sunshine Through the Clouds (Tou Guo Yun Cheng De Xia Guang)*

1980. Xiaoxiang Film Studio. Color. 9 Reels. Direction: Ouyang Shanzhun. Screenplay: Liu Cheng. Cinematography: Shen Miaorong. Art Direction: Jin Bohao. Music: Du Mingxin. Sound: Yan Ji. Cast: Bi Jiancang as Zhen Yan, Pan Hong as Baimei, Liang Yuru as Hailao, Song Yining as Heimei

During China's dark historical period when the Gang of Four is in power, writer Zhen Yan goes into the hospital, where he falls in love with his doctor Baimei. While Baimei's sister Heimie approves of the relationship, her father Hailao disapproves because he does not trust writers. The two are forced to break off their romance. Later, Zhen Yan is assigned to cover an emergency rescue operation at sea, where he happens to meet Heimei and Hailao. On the ship, the two men become better acquainted, and Hailao sees Zhen Yan's honesty and sincerity. He approves of Zhen Yan's courtship of his daughter, and they notify Baimei to meet them when the ship docks. However, when she arrives, so do the police to arrest Zhen Yan for writing the truth about the Gang of Four. The young couple parts, and when will they meet again? When the sun shines through the clouds.

2022. *Suolong Lake (Suo Long Hu)*

1976. Changchun Film Studio. Color. 13 Reels. Direction: Zhou Yu. Screenplay: Yan Fengle, based on the novel, "The County Party Secretary." Cinematography: Wu Guojiang. Art Direction: Li Junjie. Music: Zhen Lucheng. Cast: Li Qi (Li Rentang) as Yang Kai, Song Xiaoyin as Gao Chunhua, Sun Feng as Gao Cangsong, Du Defu as Huang Mantun, Ci Zhiqiang as Wan Renxi, Liu Shilong as Guo Jun.

In 1963, newly assigned county Party secretary Yang Kai arrives in Xihu County, where he stays at the "advanced model" Huangjiawa production unit, set up by the deputy secretary Xiao Yifan. After investigation, he finds that serious problems exist: the unit Party secretary Huang Jinshan ignores agricultural production in order to stress production of by-products; Xiao Yifan and others thwart and attack cadre Gao Cangsong who has suggested a new means of flood prevention; Xiao has withdrawn accumulated public funds for his own use, etc. Yang Kai supports Gao Cangsong in his struggle with Huang Jinshan, and recommends to the county Party committee Huang's dismissal from his position. Xiao Yifan, although criticized for following the capitalist line, is still able to stay in his position by gaining the support of the prefectural secretary. At a mass Party conference, the two clash and Yang Kai's correct line is adopted by the prefectural Party committee.

2023. *The Super Reverent Monk (Tong Tian Zhang Lao)*

1990. Yunnan Nationalities Film Studio.

Color. Letterboxed. 9 Reels. Direction: Yao Shoukang. Screenplay: Song Gongquan, Luo Bangwu, Lu Shoujun. Cinematography: Liu Lihua, Yang Changsheng. Art Direction: Li Benzheng, Qi Deyu. Music: Jin Fuzai. Sound: Ni Zheng. Costume: Zhou Xingguo, Zhao Qiongxian. Makeup: Zhong Tiehui, Yang Meixin. Cast: Yu Hai as Tongtian, Li Dianfang as Gele Bao, Li Zhenping as Luo Siju.

During the reign of the Qing Emperor Jiaqing (1796–1821), armed conflict rages between Dragon Village and Tiger Village in southwest China. Dragon Village emerges the victor after fierce fighting, and Tiger Village Headman Xu is put to death. Xu's pregnant wife is captured as well. The chief abbot of the local Buddhist temple is distressed by these events and tries to save Mrs. Xu. To protect her, the monk routs the men of Dragon Village with his superb martial art skills, and forces Dragon Village Headman Luo to promise that the vendetta will be resolved by a duel between his son and Mrs. Xu's son when they reach maturity. Eighteen years later, as the date of the duel approaches, Dragon Village Headman Luo is overwhelmed by the fact that the boy he has brought up as his son turns out to be the son of his rival, because the monk had ingeniously arranged a swap when the two sons were still babies. Consequently, the duel is prevented, but the monk who has effected the truce finally sacrifices his own life.

2024. *Super Sleuth (Parts 1 & 2) (Da Zhen Tan)*

1988. Beijing Film Studio. Color. 10 Reels. Direction: Wang Junzheng. Screenplay: Guo Dayu. Cinematography: Sun Cheng. Art Direction: Wang Jixian. Music: Zhang Qianyi. Sound: Lai Qijian. Cast: Li Xuejian as Du Yipu, Qiao Qi as Wu Ciren, Yang Baohe as Associate Chairman Song, Wang Xin as Mr. Shen.

In the early 1920s, jeweler Shen Da dies unexpectedly. Private detective Du Yipu, nicknamed "Super Sleuth," is asked to look into the strange circumstances surrounding the death. His adopted daughter Shi Nan assists him in the investigation. Du learns that Shen Da had owned a rare pearl, which has been replaced by a fake since its owner's death. Du and his daughter later determine that the switch was made by Wu Ciren, a local politician with close ties to a foreign businessman who belongs to a dangerous cult. Du breaks into the foreign businessman's residence and recovers the pearl, but soon loses possession of it once more. A mysterious phone call leads him back to the pearl.

2025. *Super Thief (Xing Qie Da Shi)*

1988. Youth Film Studio. Color. 9 Reels. Letterboxed. Direction: Han Xiaolei. Screenplay: Qin Peichun. Cinematography: Zeng Nianping. Art Direction: Feng Fang, Zhong Guanglin. Music: Zhu Shirui. Sound: Zhang Ruikun. Cast: Ma Jingwu as Wang Shou, Liang Danni as Gao Xiaoli, Xu Yajun as Bai Jiesheng, Li Ning as the Japanese Merchant

Wang Shou, head of a circus troupe, is also a magician, well known throughout China for his sleight of hand. While performing in a small town, Wang's adopted daughter and assistant, Gao Xiaoli, learns by chance that a Japanese merchant residing there has in his possession a Chinese national treasure stolen during World War II. She asks her father to steal it back, but is disappointed when he refuses to do so. Father and daughter begin to drift apart and she becomes involved with Bai Jiesheng, a "gentleman" thief. At last, Wang decides to use his skills to recover the national treasure from the Japanese merchant. When the merchant discovers his prize is missing, he dispatches some of his thugs to find and kill Wang who is also being sought by the local police. The magician must now call on all his skills just to survive.

2026. *Superstar (Tian Huang Ju Xing)*

1990. Pearl River Film Studio. Color. Wide Screen. 9 Reels. Direction: Li Shu, Liao Zhikai. Cinematography: Xie Ping. Art Direction: Zhang Ruo. Music: Li Haiying. Sound: Lu Hong. Cast: Sun Ao as Ma Zhile, Shi Lanya as Tong Dan

Young Ma Zhile is a talented singer and dancer, but is repeatedly rejected in auditions because of her homely looks. One day, the younger brother of famous singer Tong Dan hears Ma sing, and persuades his sister to give the younger girl the break she needs. The film tells how Tong Dan helps Ma Zhile develop her style. At last, Ma appears on a nationally televised young singers' contest. She is a big hit, and a new star is born.

2027. *Surging River (Jiang Shui Tao Tao)*

1976. Shanghai Film Studio. Color. 10 Reels. Direction: Shu Shi, Zhao Hongbing. Screenplay: Collective, recorded by Shi Ming, and based on the novel of the same title. Cinematography: Peng Sili, Zuang Hongjun. Art Direction: Han Shangyi, Zhao Xianrui. Music: Wang Yunjie. Cast: Yang Zaibao as Lu Dacheng, Yuan Yue as Lu Ada, Wang Dinghua as Xu Jianhong, Zhang Fa as Ji Baoquan, Zhang Xuechun as Lin Yin, Qi Jianqiu as Tu Haigeng

Just before the liberation of the coastal city of Qinyang, young sailor Lu Dacheng and his fellow crew members foil a plot to hijack their ship to Taiwan. After 1949, Lu's ship, now named the "Liberation," is assigned a coastal defense mission. First Mate Bai Yunfei, an undercover Nationalist agent, sets out to disrupt this work, and tries to get himself named ship's captain. He is helped by the erroneous actions of project director Ren Yansheng. But the crew elects Lu Dacheng their captain, and after a fierce struggle with Bai Yunfei he finally succeeds in catching the spy attempting an act of sabotage. The "Liberation" successfully fulfills its assignment under Lu Dacheng's leadership.

2028. *Surly In-Laws (Jiang Gong Gong Jue Xi Fu)*

1985. Changchun Film Studio. Color. 10 Reels. Direction: Luo Qin. Screenplay: Li Dianchen and Niu Guanli. Cinematography: Zhong Wenmin. Art Direction: Ye Jiren. Music: Zhu Chaolun, Liang Sihui and An Zhiyu. Sound: Huang Lijia. Cast: Du Qitai as Liu Wanshun, Xie Huayuan as Gaigai, Wang Xiaofen as Jian Fang, Zhang Ping as Xiao Shan, Liu Xianpei as Uncle Jianguo, Liu Lanfang as Aunt Wangting

The revolutionary decisions of the 11th Party Congress inspire Henan province tofu maker Liu Wanshun to mobilize his entire extended family to get rich. But his dictatorial manner and the backward facilities quickly put a chill on the rest of the family's enthusiasm for the project. Meanwhile, another kind of "revolution" is taking place inside the family: their new daughter-in-law Gaigai challenges the old man, which angers him and leads to an ongoing argument. She eventually wins out, and at last the "Liu Wanshun Tofu Products Factory" is established. The family unites and all work hard together.

2029. *Surprise Move in Snake Valley (She Gu Qi Bing)*

1989. August First Film Studio. Color. 9 Reels. Wide Screenplay. Direction: Yu Yehua, Li Sanyi. Screenplay: Yu Yehua, Li Sanyi, Wang Xuewu. Cinematography: Wang Naicong, Zou Yongquan. Art Direction: Kuang Zeji. Music: Yang Xiwu. Sound: Wang Defan. Cast: Zheng Xiaoning as Xiao Jun, Li Yiqing as Hua Dong, Li Zhixiong as Sai Desheng, Gao Zhixiong as Shi Gang

A war movie set in the 1979 Sino-Vietnamese border war. The focus is on a Chinese tank battalion and their commander Xiao Jun. The battalion undertakes a mission to try to get behind the Vietnamese army. They eventually succeed and drive the enemy back, but only at a very high cost in casualties.

2030. *Suspect (Xian Yi Fan)*

1985. Youth Film Studio. Color. Letterboxed. 9 Reels. Direction: Han Xiaolei. Screenplay: Wang Peigong, Feng Gang. Cinematography: Zhang Huijun. Art Direction: Liu Guangen, Liu Ying. Music: Ju Xiaosong. Sound: Kong Lingyan. Cast: Wang Yongge as Ding Peng, Lu Yulei as Ma Shaolin, Zhen Shihe as Ouyang Zhi, Lin Muyu as Huang Qun, Zhang Guoli as Ma Bing

In the summer of 1983, Ding Peng is released from prison. Ding was imprisoned on suspicion of having murdered provincial Party Secretary Gao Changhe, for whom he was a bodyguard, during the Cultural Revolution. He goes to visit his ex-wife Liu Xiaodi, but she refuses to see him. Ding keeps trying because he wants to retrieve a diary he had stored at her home. When he finally gains entrance to the house he finds her dead. He goes to Ma Shaolin, director of the provincial disciplinary office, and demands the Gao Changhe case be reopened. Ding presents evidence that the real murderer is Ouyang Zhi, the current provincial committee chief, and that Ouyang killed Liu Xiaodi as well. However, the political currents are such that after exposing the real murderer, Ding Peng himself is jailed.

2031. *The Swallow Returns (Yan Gui Lai)*

1980. Shanghai Film Studio. Color. 10 Reels. Direction: Fu Jinggong. Screenplay: Shi Yong, Meng Shenghui, Si Minsan. Cinematography: Qiu Yiren, Zhou Zhaiyuan. Art Direction: Li Runzhi, Xie Hongru. Music: Ju Wei, Ji Min. Sound: Huang Dongping. Cast: Gao Yin as Lu Yan, Da Shichang as Lin Hanhua, Yang Rong as You Huimin, Yuan Yue as Xie Zhixin, Zhang Xiaolei as Wu Lan, Ma Xiaowei as Xie Feng

A boy named Xie Feng and a girl named Wu Lan are very much in love. One day, his father Xie Zhixin learns that Wu Lan's mother was a student named Lu Yan who the father 20 years before had labeled a "rightist," resulting in Lu Yan being sent to work in a remote, prairie region of China. To shield her boyfriend, Wu Lan's father, from the effects of this political attack, Lu Yan had broken off their relationship. When Xie Feng learns that his father had brought so much misfortune to Lu Yan, he is very ashamed and out of love for Wu Lan, tells her the truth. Unable to bear this, she announces their breakup. Wu Lan tells her mother about this. For the sake of her daughter's happiness, Lu Yan visits Xie Zhixin, who is at first too embarrassed and regretful about his past conduct to express an apology. Lu Yan tells him that the misfortunes of their generation should not be borne by their children, and that they should come to terms with the past on their own.

Best Actor Da Shichang, 1981 Hundred Flowers Awards.

2032. *The Swan Goose (Hong Yan)*

1960. Changchun Film Studio. B & W. 11 Reels. Direction: Zhao Xinshui, Chang Zhenhua. Screenplay: the Fourth Collective Writing Team, recorded by Zhang Tianmin. Cinematography: Liu Yongzhen. Art Direction: Wang Guizhi. Music: Lei Zhengbang. Sound: Sui Xizhong. Cast: Liu Shilong as Li Yunfei, Pan Demin as Mr. Zhen, En Hesheng as Jin Yingsong, Li Xida as Xiao Jin, He Xiaoshu as Fan Yulan, Zhao Wenyu as Pu Yunu

In the rural area around Northeast China's Mount Changbai, letter carrier Li Yunfei always delivers his newspapers, magazines and letters on time, as well as serving the people of the area as a "buyer" and a "selling agent." Farmer Pu Yunu does not concentrate on her pig raising, so Li patiently persuades and helps her when her pig falls ill. With Li's help, Yunu becomes a model worker. Li also takes on the assignment of creating a new postal service route in the mountainous area when another carrier Xiao Jin fails to climb Mount Changbai. Li overcomes extremely cold temperatures and a storm to successfully climb to the top of Mount Changbai on the eve of the 1959 Spring

Festival. He also finds the recipient of an un-addressed letter — WWII veteran Jin Yingsong, reuniting him with his daughter Yunu, from whom he had been separated for 19 years.

2033. *A Sweet Affair (Tian Mi De Shi Ye)*

1979. Beijing Film Studio. Color. 9 Reels. Direction: Xie Tian. Screenplay: Zhou Mingzheng. Cinematography: Huang Xinyi. Art Direction: Chen Zhaoming. Music: Lu Yuan, Tang Ke. Sound: Wei Xueyi, Zhang Zhian. Cast: Ma Ling as Aunt Tang, Liu Zhao as Uncle Tang, Lin Yuan as Mrs. Tian, Li Xiuming as Tang Zhaodi, Li Tang as Mr. Mo, Li Liansheng as Tian Wubao

Sugarcane grower Uncle Tang is devoted to sugarcane production, but he finds it increasingly hard to carry on alone. He and his wife Aunt Tang have five girls but want a son to help with the business. To change her mother's traditional thinking, their eldest daughter Zhaodi says she is willing to remain unmarried all her life in order to care for the parents when they grow old. This presents a problem for her boyfriend Tian Wubao, who hopes to marry Zhaodi. Tian Wubao decides to marry into Zhaodi's family, giving the parents the son they want, and the happy Aunt Tang makes plans for a sterilization operation. However, Tian Wubao's family is now unhappy, because the traditional way of doing things is for the girl to marry into her husband's family. The story ends with a happy marriage and both families content.

Best Director Xie Tian, 1980 Hundred Flowers Awards.

2034. *Sweet Glasses (Wen Rou De Yan Jing)*

1987. Guangxi Film Studio. Color. Direction: Zhang Gang, Screenplay: Zhang Gang. Cinematography: Chen Shenkai. Art Direction: Zhang Yafang. Music: Yang Shaoyi. Sound: Li Yunping. Cast: Fang Zhige as Zhou Aman, Wu Lijie as Wang Meijiao, Shen Fa as Zhong Bengjian, Wu Xiqian as Grandpa, Ye Lingliang as Wang Eryi, Tan Sijia as Lu Xiaolan

In the area around the town of Lujia, native place for many overseas Chinese, feudal thinking is still quite prevalent. Recent college graduate Zhou Aman is sent to Lujia to investigate what feudal practices might still be carried out there. The film tells how Aman learns the secret of Wang Eryi's "family inherited magic" — washing the head in a pot of boiling oil with her daughter's help. Zhou Aman falls in love with the daughter, Meijiao, and they become engaged. But Wang is angry at Zhou Aman for making her secret public, so she separates Meijuan and Aman, and breaks off their engagement. One month later, Aman returns to Lujia village, only to find that Meijiao has been married to a Hong Kong businessman. Aman leaves, very upset.

2035. *Sweet Matching in the Air Force (Tian Mi De Bian Dui)*

1987. August First Film Studio. Color. 10 Reels. Direction: Huang Fuxiang. Screenplay: You Fengwei, Liang Chunsheng. Cinematography: Cai Shunan, Yang Ke. Art Direction: Liu Yushu. Music: Yang Xiwu. Sound: Xiang Zhiliang. Cast: Li Changhua as He Yunpeng, Zhao Xiaomin as Sun Keqiang, Lan Fazuang as Zhao Yu, Lu Yujie as Zhang Changxi, Zhu Xiaoming as Xiao Gu, Yang Xiaojun as Xiao Yuling

After he retires from the Air Force, Division Commander He Yunpeng starts a second career as a matchmaker, finding suitable wives for young pilots. He arranges happy marriages for several young couples, although he himself is single, having been widowed for some years. His friend, retired Political Commissar Feng Guang, urges him to arrange a wife for himself, but this appears to be the one thing He Yunpeng does not do well. At last, he finds an ideal wife as well.

2036. *Sweetgrass (Huang Sha — Qing Cao — Hong Tai Yang)*

1994. Xi'an Film Studio. Color. Letterboxed. 9 Reels. Direction: Zhou Youchao. Screenplay: Yang Zhengguang. Cinematography: Zhao Fei, Li Xiaoping. Art Direction: Dou Guoxiang. Music: Zhao Jiping, Zhao Ling. Sound: Hong Ding, Yuan Xiaoyong. Cast: Zhen Tianwei as Gan Chao, Sun Haiying as Ba Dun, Wang Gang as Niu E, Liu Jishu, Xiao Xiao

Young widow Gan Chao and her small son live alone in their village. Local small businessman Niu Er is very kind to them, giving them considerable help to get by. Niu Er secretly loves Gan Chao, but realizes his cause is hopeless because of the widow's love for Badun, a man addicted to gambling. No matter how hard Gan Chao tries to persuade him, Badun cannot give it up, sometimes losing all the money he has. The one thing he never risks is his beloved red horse. But at last he risks the horse and loses it. Out of sympathy for him, Gan Chao steals the horse back. When the new owner of the horse comes to recover it, he ends up taking Badun a hostage. Badun's behavior leads Gan Chao to conclude the man she loves is a coward. Niu Er goes to help Badun, but in the fight that ensues, Badun is killed.

2037. *The Swindler (Zha Pian Fan)*

1993. Shanghai Film Studio. Color. Letterboxed. 9 Reels. Direction: Shen Yaoting. Screenplay: Shen Yaoting, Shen Yaohua. Cinematography: Zhang Er. Art Direction: Zhang Wanhong. Music: Yang Shaolu, Su Junjie. Sound: Xu Xiushan. Costume: Zhang Fucai. Makeup: Zuang Yazhen. Cast: Wang Sihuai as Qian Gengfa, Zhong Xinghuo as Gu Songlan, Zhou Xiaoli as Wenxiang, Huang Daliang as Huang Jiesheng, Xue Guoping as the detective, Chang Hongyan as A Si, Wu Kunlai as Xiao Xiang, Hong Rong as Li Zhiqing

In Shanghai in the 1940s, Gu Songlan tries desperately to support his family. He finally decides his only hope is his insurance policy, which will pay 100 million yuan if he is killed in an accident or murdered. He tries the first method, but his attempt to create an accident fails. Gu next sets about arranging his own murder: he finds out that hard-working and honest barber shop proprietor Qian Gengfa once struck and killed a girl while driving one rainy night. So he begins relentlessly blackmailing the poor man, hoping to force Qian to murder him. He at last makes Qian so desperate he does just that. Then the truth comes out: Gu leaves behind documents detailing his scheme and taking full responsibility for his own murder, so Qian just receives a year in jail. In addition, Gu leaves a letter to Qian telling the barber where the money is kept — all the money he paid the blackmailer. Qian bursts into tears when he reads this.

2038. *The Sword Stained with Royal Blood (Bi Xue Jian)*

1993. Pearl River Film Company, Hong Kong Shengyi Xi'an Film Corp. Ltd. Co-Production. Color. Letterboxed. 9 Reels. Direction: Zhang Haijing. Screenplay: Zhang Haijing, Wei Xin, based on Jin Yong's original novel. Cinematography: Liu Hongquan, Ma Jinxiang, Pan Deye. Art Direction: Shi Meiyi. Costume: Liang Yuzhen. Makeup: Chen Yingyi, Zhen Ruli, Huang Shunhui. Cast: Wu Ma as Sun Zhongshou, Huang Jingyan as Wun Laosan, Chen Long as Wen Laowu, Li Xiuxian as Xia Xueyi, Yuan Biao as Yuan Chengzhi, Zhang Min as the Ninth Princess, Wu Mengda as Gui Xinshu, Yuan Yongyi (Anita Yuen) as He Tieshou, Ye Quanzhen as Wen Qingqing, Li Meifeng as Lady Wen, Xu Jinjiang as Wen Baozhu, Shi Baohua as Niao Hake

An action film set in the latter half of the 16th century.

2039. *Swordsman and the General (Yi Jian Qi Xia)*

1992. Changchun Film Studio. Color. Letterboxed. 9 Reels. Direction: Yu Xiangyuan. Screenplay: Cheng Tianfa. Cinematography: Su Weiping. Art Direction: Liu Sheng. Music; Zhang Hou, Xue Feng. Sound: Zhang Hongguang, Liu Zhaoming. Costume: Wu Boqiao, Yu Hongming. Makeup: Feng Chunjie. Cast: Xu Xiaojian as Yu Liang, Li Yunjuan as Ge Chujuan, Huang Bangrui as Hongguang, Da Niya as Ge Lin, Song Linlin as Pulaishi, Li Wei as Zhang Guoshou, Li Xida as Bai Shulu

When the Opium War erupts in 1840, British troops invade an important port city and wipe out its Chinese defenders. The British commander orders that the head of Chinese general Ge Yunfei be exhibited above the city gate as a warning to possible dissidents among the citizenry. During the night, some patriotic Chinese led by Yu Liang, leader of an anti–British secret organization, are able to take the general's body away. For many years, there has been a feud between his family and the general's, but now Yu Liang joins forces with the late general's daughter Ge Chujuan to make common cause against the invaders. They succeed in getting the general's head and body to safety, and in the process find romance.

2040. *The Swordsman in Double Flag Town (Shuang Qi Zhen Dao Ke)*

1990. Xi'an Film Studio. Color. 9 Reels. Wide Screen. Direction: He Ping. Screenplay: Yang Zhengguang, He Ping. Cinematography: Ma Delin. Art Direction: Qian Yunxuan. Music: Tao Long. Sound: Wei Jia, Hong Yi. Cast: Gao Wei as Hai Gei, Zhao Mana as Good Sister, Chang Jiang as the Lame Man, Sun Haiying as Single Stroke Saint

Double Flag Town is an isolated castle in the West China desert terrorized by two brothers famed for their kung fu skills. The swordsman Hai Ge, carrying out his father's will, comes to the town to fetch his fiancee, Good Sister, promised to him by her father even

A Sweet Affair. Uncle Tang (Liu Zhao) finds that his wife's enthusiasm for having a big family makes it difficult for him to grow the sugar cane that is their livelihood. 1979. Beijing Film Studio.

before her birth. However, she and her innkeeper father give him a cold reception, and give him a menial job at the inn. One day, the younger of the two brothers comes and tries to rape Good Sister. Hai Ge kills him. The older brother, nicknamed Single Stroke Saint, comes to avenge his younger brother, but meets up with the same fate. At daybreak, Hai Ge leaves the haunted place on horseback together with his fiancee.

Best Art Direction Qian Yunxuan, 1991 Golden Rooster Awards.

2041. *Swordsman of the Yellow River (Huang He Da Xia)*

1987. Xi'an Film Studio and Zhongyuan Film Corp. Color. Letterboxed. 10 Reels. Direction: Zhang Xingyan, Zhang Zhien. Screenplay: Huang Maishuang. Cinematography: Zhou Boling. Art Direction: Dai Yuanzhong. Music: Xiang Yin. Sound: Huang Junshi, Zhang Wang. Cast: Yu Chenhui as Ma Yi, Chunyu Shanshan as Che Tian, Jin Demao as Duan Wang, Ji Chunhua as Liu Wang

During the Tang Dynasty, civil war breaks out in the northwestern lands around the headwaters of the Yellow River. The combatants are Princes Duan, Wang and Li. Each of them in turn tries to entice master swordsman Ma Yi into fighting for them, but he refuses to get involved. Outraged that Ma has refused him, Prince Li attempts to poison him. Prince Duan appears to be more benevolent, but he plans to kill Ma Yi once he has emerged triumphant over the others. When Ma Yi eventually learns of the plots against him, he unleashes his fury on the princes.

2042. *Swordsman Wang Wu (Da Dao Wang Wu)*

1985. Xi'an Film Studio. Color. 10 Reels. Direction: Yu Lianqi. Screenplay: Ma Xianda, Jia Qi, Wang Wuzen. Cinematography: Niu Han, Luo Yongjian. Art Direction: Lu Guangcai, Han Shihua. Music: Xiang Yin. Sound: Hong Jiahui, Li Ping. Cast: Wang Xiaozhong as Wang Wu, Zhao Changjun as Houxia, Ge Chunyan as Feifeng, Ji Qiling as Tan Citong, Wang Hua as Gou Fengtao, Niu Shengwen as the Emperor Guangxu

The end of the Qing Dynasty brings a struggle for power between supporters of the reactionary Dowager Empress Cixi and the reformist followers of the Emperor Guangxu. Foreign imperialist nations move to exploit the situation and grab control of Chinese territory. Beijing swordsman Wang Wu calls on all patriotic Chinese to join in defending China against the invaders. In the patriotic movement, he allies his followers with Tan Sitong, one of the Emperor Guangxu's chief advisors. After Cixi dismisses Guangxu, General Yuan Shikai's troops surround the Summer Palace and arrest Tan Sitong and other reformers. Tan Sitong decides his own martyrdom is the best way to arouse the Chinese people, so he rejects his friends' efforts to break him out of prison. Wang Wu hurries to intervene in the execution but arrives too late. In deep sorrow, Wang Wu bears Tan Sitong's body to his native place for burial.

2043. *Swordswoman in White (Bai Yi Xia Nu)*

1992. Liaoning Film Studio & Beijing Film Studio Co-Production. Color. Letterboxed. 9 Reels. Direction: Zhang Huaxun. Screenplay: Wang Zhanjun. Cinematography: Yang Wenqin. Art Direction: Qin Duo. Music: Yao Ming. Sound: Wang Dawen. Costume: Zhang Wei, Zhu Yan. Makeup: Hao Xia, Deng Jie. Cast: Wang Meiling as Wang Conger, Jia Ping as Daogu, Kou Zhanfu as Fan Renjie, Li Junfeng as Wang Qing, Jiang Gengcheng as Yang Guozhong, Li Yonggui as Liu Shanhuai

Near the end of the 18th century, 20-year-old Wang Conger becomes head of the White Lotus, a group of Chinese opposed to the Qing government. Wang, the bright and courageous daughter of a martial arts family, travels to meet with her father and his friend, a former military commander, to discuss raising forces to take military action. She is pursued by Qing soldiers, but eludes them. When she arrives at the meeting site, she finds her father has been murdered. It later turns out the killer is her father's old friend, actually a government spy. Things look bad for her rebels until a Qing general, his family betrayed by the government, brings his troops over to the White Lotus side. This starts the White Lotus Rebellion (1796–1804).

2044. *T Province in 1984 and 1985 (T Sheng De Ba Si, Ba Wu Nian)*

1986. Shanghai Film Studio. Color. 10 Reels. Direction: Yang Yanjing. Screenplay: Liu Guoqin. Cinematography: Zhang Yuanmin. Art Direction: Wang Xingcang. Music: Xu Jingxin. Sound: Ren Daming. Cast: Ye Zhikang as Guo Gang, Da Shichang as Cheng Ge, Guo Yuntai as Ma Yu, Lu Fei as Li Tao, Liu Zonghui as Dign Fei

In 1984 and 1985, a series of unusual events occur in China's "T Province." The focus of these is Cheng Ge, a man who contracts to direct a factory affiliated with the "T Province" Machinery Corporation. This factory has been running in the red, but after Cheng takes over, he implements a series of reforms which successfully get the factory back in the black. Surprisingly, despite Cheng's success, the Machine Corporation's Party committee decides to unilaterally cancel the contract and dismiss Cheng Ge from his post. Cheng angrily petitions the court for redress, and Guo Gang, judge of the local economic court and soon to be promoted to be the next head of the People's Court, agrees to hear the case. After a thorough investigation, Guo decides Cheng Ge has done nothing wrong and that the case should be heard by a jury, in strict accordance with the law. The jury decides Cheng's contract is valid and there is no reason for his dismissal. The case should have been closed at this point, but Guo Gang is unexpectedly transferred to a lower court in the suburbs, and the Party committee reaffirms the non-renewal of Cheng Ge's contract. Obviously, there is more to this than appears on the surface.

"Outstanding Film" award from the Ministry of Radio, Film and Television, 1986.

2045. *Tai Chi Master (Tai Ji Zhang San Feng)*

1993. China Film Co-Production Corp., Hong Kong Zhengdong Film Corp. Ltd. Co-Production. Color. Letterboxed. 9 Reels. Direction: Yuan Heping. Screenplay: Ye Guangjian. Cinematography: Liu Mantang. Art Direction: Fu Delin, Li Jingwen. Costume: Cai Huiying, Liu Weifeng, Tang Baoli, Wu Yongzhi, Cai Jun, Wang Junying, Zhang Qingxiang, Meng He. Makeup: Su Hong, Li Lihua, Zhao Fengling, Sun Bing, Zhang Teng, Xu Qiuwen, Guan Jun, Jiang Juanjuan, Wen Runling. Cast: Li Lianjie (Jet Li), Yang Ziqiong (Michelle Yeoh), Qian Xiaohao, Yuan Jieying (Fenny Yuen), Yu Hai

A fictional biography of the inventor of the Tai Chi martial arts style. Tianbao and Junbao, Shaolin Temple monks and friends since childhood, are expelled from the temple, and have to find new paths in life. The ambitious Tianbao joins the army and becomes right-hand man to the evil eunuch in power. Jun-bao, a man with a strong code of honor, allies himself with anti-government rebels. Tianbao betrays Junbao and kills many of the rebels, gaining himself a major promotion. Junbao dedicates himself to practicing his kung fu and finally the two former friends, now bitter ene-mies, meet in battle. Junbao kills Tianbao, then withdraws from this society to devote himself to Tai Chi.

2046. *Taibao: The Magically Fast Bike Rider (Shen Xing Tai Bao)*

1983. Shanxi Film Studio. 10 Reels. Direc-tion: Luo Guoliang, Shi Yushan. Screenplay: Guo Ende. Cinematography: Zhen Qinyu, Han Beiji, Wang Zhutian. Art Direction: Wang Zhenghua. Music: Zhang Pei. Cast: Liang Tongyu as Ma Ming, Wei Xin as Team Leader Qiao, Qi Ka as Ding Yiqun, Chen Limin as Wu Ruonan, Zhao Zhiyue as the Bicycle Shop Worker

A young bicycle rider is racing with two friends when he is spotted by the coach of a bicycle team. The coach gives him the chance to race in competition, and he eventually qualifies for China's national team, racing in international competition.

2047. *Taiji's Miraculous Power (Tai Ji Shen Gong)*

1985. Xi'an Film Studio, Hong Kong Han-shan Film Company And China Film Coopera-tive Company Co-Production. Color. 9 Reels. Direction: Qi Yixiong, Zhang Yumin. Screen-play: Qi Yixiong. Cinematography: You Qi. Art Direction: Zhang Xiaohui. Music: Li Xiaodong. Cast: Guo Liang as Zhu Haichou, Li Haiyan as Jinger, Chu Zhihong as Zhu Hanliang, Gao Lingxin as Kaier, Hong Tao as Sha Ying, Zhang Xianghua as Chen Jizong, Zhang Quanren as the Grand Master

During the reign of the Qing Yongzheng Emperor (1723–1736), villainous government official Sha Ying leads Qing soldiers in a sur-prise attack on a place called Zhu Family Vil-lage. The attack is related to the death 10 years earlier of General Nian Raogeng, executed on trumped-up charges. Before his death, Nian asked his old friend Zhu Wentian to raise his little son. Zhu raises the boy as his own son, with the name Zhu Haichou. Now Sha Ying has discovered Zhu Haichou's true identity and wants to kill him as well. Zhu Wentian

and his wife are both killed in the attack, but before dying he divulges to Zhu Haichou the young man's true identity as the son of Gen-eral Nian. Zhu Haichou escapes and later goes to a special martial arts school to study "mira-cle kongfu." After a few years' practice, Zhu Haichou finally kills Sha Ying with the help of many honest people, avenging both his family and the nation.

2048. *Taiwanese Lovers' Unusual Ex-perience (Tai Wan Qing Lu De Qi Yu)*

1988. Yunnan Minority Film Studio. Color. Wide Screen. 9 Reels. Direction: Luo Guanqun. Screenplay: Huang Enda. Cinematography: Qiao Jicang. Art Direction: Li Zhengxin. Music: Liu Yanxi. Sound: Jia Xianjie. Cast: Wang Baosheng as Chen Huai, Zhu Ying as Ma Li

In accordance with their parents' wishes, two lovers from Taiwan arrive in Yunnan province to have a Dai nationality wedding. Distracted by the beautiful scenery, the couple become separated from their tour group and enter a deep forest. There, they have a series of adventures. Meanwhile, the tourist bureau learns they are missing, and dispatches a heli-copter over the area to search for them. Al-though they are total strangers, the local peo-ple care for the young couple as if they were close relatives.

2049. *Taking His Name (Mao Ming Ding Ti)*

1987. Changchun Film Studio. Color. 10 Reels. Direction: Zhu Wenshun, Zhao Ruiqi. Screenplay: Xue Shouxian. Cinematography: Li Huailu. Art Direction: Liu Xuerao. Music: Chen Souqian. Sound: Liu Jingui. Cast: Shi Chongren as Qi Jianfu, Lin Qiang as Qi Haitao, Han Yue-qiao as Hai Yan, Li Ying as Geng Huiming

Gu Fei, mainland representative of a Tai-wan trading company, is actually a spy. He re-ceives orders to abduct and return to Taiwan a man named Qi Jianfu, who had defected to the mainland 30 years ago. Gu Fei forces Qi Jianfu's son Qi Haitao, an employee of the trading company, to persuade his father to vol-untarily go to Taiwan from the mainland. Other spies have already fooled Qi Haitao's mother Xia Menglan into going to Hong Kong, but when Qi Jianfu learns his son's true motivation for visiting him, he refuses. Haitao is moved by his father. At last, the spies' conspiracy is smashed, and Xia Menglan is returned to the Chinese mainland.

2050. *Taking Risks (Mao Mao Feng Xian)*

1988. Beijing Film Studio. Color. 9 Reels. Direction: Qiu Lili, Xiao Lang. Screenplay: Zhao Jun, Qiu Lili, Zhang Cuilan, Fu Qiang. Cinematography: Ru Shuiren. Art Direction: Wang Xinguo. Music: Li Wanli. Sound: Wang Yunhua. Cast: Wang Xueqin as Zhen Xingming, Shen Ming as Xiao Miao

Young inventor Zhen Xingming designs a car with a totally plastic body, but cannot find a manufacturer interested in producing it. He takes his new invention to the Shenzhen Special Economic Zone, and with the city's government's help, he receives a sufficient loan and establishes the "Chinese Automobile Company," which finally produces the first totally plastic car body. However, huge problems follow this success; for example, a group of investigators from Beijing accuse of him of taking bribes, and the company's bank organizes its own investigation and stops a loan to the company. The company does not even have the money to pay its employees at New Year. Zhen Xingming does not give up, and at last all the charges against him are dropped. Today, there are many plastic-bodied cars on the highways.

2051. *The Tall Center and the Short Coach (Gao Zhong Feng He Ai Jiao Lian)*

1985. Beijing Film Studio. Color. 10 Reels. Direction: Ji Wenyan. Screenplay: Li Yanguo, Li Yanan. Cinematography: Wang Zhaoling. Art Direction: Yu Yiru, Ning Lanxin. Music: Su Min. Sound: Wang Yunhua. Cast: Niu Beng as Coach Gao, Guan Jie as Wang Xiaoshan, Peng Yu as Gao's wife, Zhao Wenxin as Mr. Huang, Jin Qi as the old soldier, Sun Wanfan as Director Yu, Xu Yanqing as Master Du

A certain county athletic commission's basketball coach Gao, although himself a short man, is dedicated to the game and to recruiting young men to play it. This single-mindedness of purpose gets him into considerable trouble during the Cultural Revolution, but in 1974 he is back coaching again. One day, he meets a very tall but ungainly young man named Wang Xiaoshan, and determines he will make him into a player. Everyone ignores Coach Gao's recommendations about Wang, feeling he has no future in the game, so Gao must continue training the young man strictly by himself. Just when the coach starts to get discouraged, he meets an old soldier who had once worked for He Long, China's Commissioner of Sports. With the old soldier's help, Gao finally gets Wang Xiaoshan accepted by China's national team.

2052. *Tan Citong (Tan Ci Tong)*

1984. Changchun Film Studio. Color. Wide Screen. 14 Reels. Direction: Chen Jialin. Screenplay: Liu Genglu. Cinematography: An Zhiguo. Art Direction: Jin Xiwu. Music: Jin Fuzai. Sound: Zhang Fenglu, Wang Baosheng. Cast: Da Shichang as Tan Citong, Song Xiaoyin as wife, Wang Yumei as Cixi, Gu Lan as Wen Tonghe, Niu Xingli as Huai Tabu, Ma Lianji as Xiang Shengxiu, Jiang Yang as Lin Xu

In 1898, reformer Tan Citong is called by the Emperor Guangxu as an advisor on the reforms the emperor wishes to put in place. They have the support of the emperor's tutor Wen Tonghe, but the reactionary Dowager Empress Cixi dismisses Wen and sends him out of the capital. Tan Citong appeals for help to Yuan Shikai, commander of the Imperial Army, and while Yuan at first lends his support he at last betrays Tao and the emperor, throwing his support to Cixi. Tan Citong and other reformers are placed under house arrest. Although he is given the opportunity to escape, Tan chooses death as a martyr as a way of educating the people.

Best Supporting Actress Wang Yumei, 1985 Golden Rooster Awards.

2053. *Tank No. 008 (Tie Jia Ling Ling Ba)*

1980. August First Film Studio. Color. 9 Reels. Direction: Hua Chun, Ren Pengyuan. Screenplay: Jin Jingmai, Li Baolin, Sang ping. Cinematography: Wang Mengyuan, Ding Shanfa. Art Direction: Tang Shiyun. Music: Yan Ke. Sound: He Baoding. Cast: Li Shixi as Hunan, Li Lan as Tian Jing, Li Po as Nong Yige

When Tian Jing returns to her hometown upon graduation from medical school, her fiance Hu Nan gives up his opportunity to go to college, and enlists to go with the army to fight against the Vietnamese. He becomes the driver of tank No. 008. Tian Jing puts in a request to go to the frontlines as well. She and

Hu Nan meet there unexpectedly, and encourage each other to protect the motherland honorably. He and his crew are later ambushed at the entrance to a tunnel and Hu Nan sacrifices himself by driving the tank directly into the enemy gun emplacement and allowing the main Chinese force to move through the tunnel. Tian Jing takes strength from the sorrow and continues to fight on.

2054. *Task Force (Te Bie Gong Ji Dui)*

1992. Changchun Film Studio. Color. Letterboxed. 9 Reels. Direction: Xu Chuanzhen. Screenplay: Jiang Ao. Cinematography: Lei Xianhe, Yang Kai. Art Direction: Wang Di. Music: Wu Damin. Sound: Zhang Hongguang. Costume: Yang Jingyong, Li Lei. Makeup: Li Chunhai, Zhao Liying. Cast: Liu Weihua as Li Ao, Chen Yongxia as Feng Juan, Li Ming as Teng Qiuma, Yang Jing as Zhou Muyan, Luo Jiujiang as Zhou Fuxing, Jin Demao as Wang Yixing, Zhao Hui as Zhao Peng

In 1948, during the last phase of the Chinese Civil War, the desperate Nationalist command hopes to turn the tide through the use of poison gas. PLA intelligence learns of the plot, and the location of the warehouse where the gas is stored. A special army commando task force is formed to infiltrate behind Nationalist lines to the warehouse and blow it up.

2055. *The Tattooed Face (Du Long Wen Mian Nu)*

1993. Emei Film Studio. Color. Letterboxed. 10 Reels. Direction: Xie Hong. Screenplay: Xian Xiaowo, Xie Hong. Cinematography: Zhang Jiwu, Li Qin. Art Direction: Chen Ruogang. Music: He Xuntian. Sound: Wang Guangzhong. Costume: Wen Xiaoyan, Luo Ping. Makeup: Cao Songlin. Cast: Zhang Chunyan as A Nan, Li Jing as Dunzhu, Fan Chunxia as A Ni, Gao Qiang as Lei Muga, Cao Peicang as Mao Ding, Zhao Xiaorui as A Keng, Deng Yulin as A Luga

For several hundred years, people of the Dulong nationality have followed a custom whereby girls' faces are tattooed when they become adults, after which they are forbidden to marry outside of their own nationality group. A young girl named A Nan is one of those who oppose this barbaric practice and want freedom of choice in marriage. She flees from her people and goes to an area inhabited largely by Tibetan people. A young man named Mao Ding falls in love with her, but local custom pro-

hibits their getting together. The climax comes when the forces of a slaver named A Keng surrounds the Dulong village.

2056. *Tea Song of the Xique Mountains (Xi Que Ling Cha Ge)*

1982. Direction: Yu Shibing, Hong Ping, Screenplay: Jin Fan, Cao Chun, Xiao Jian. Cinematography: Wu Yukun, Zhao Jiajie. Art Direction: Ye Jialiang. Music: Fu Gengcheng. Sound: Lu Minwen. Cast: Wang Qingbao as Cahua, Zhao Chunchang as Liu Xinquan, Ren Yexiang as Xiaomei, Xing Mali as Xiaoliu, Xue Bai as Yujiao, Ping Weinian as Afa

In 1979, a self-educated young man named Liu Xinquan is unsuccessful at finding research work because he lacks formal academic credentials. Instead, the county science institute offers him temporary work as a cook. One day, the institute director gets an emergency call for technical assistance, but all of his technicians are off on other duties. He desperately searches the personnel files and finds that Liu the cook had once published a paper on prevention of tea disease. Having no other choice, he sends Liu into the mountains to help. When Liu arrives at the tea production unit, he joins a local girl named Cahua in her attempts to make the unit's methods more scientific. They encounter considerable difficulties, especially bureaucratic ones, In the end, they are able to convert everyone to their methods. Liu and Cahua also fall in love.

2057. *Teahouse (Cha Guan)*

1982. Beijing Film Studio. Color. Letterboxed. 12 Reels. Direction: Xie Tian. Screenplay: Uncredited, based on the stage play of the same title by Lao She (1899–1966). Cinematography: Zhen Yiyuan. Art Direction: Yang Yuhe. Music: Peng Xiuwen. Sound: Chen Yanxi. Cast: Yu Shizhi as Wang Lifa, Zhen Rong as Mr. Chang, Lan Tianye as Master Qin

Twentieth century Chinese history reflected in daily life at one Beijing teahouse. In 1898, with the corrupt and decadent Manchu Dynasty in its twilight, Yutai teahouse owner Wang Lifa does what he can to keep his business going. When the Manchu government falls, and the new Republic of China struggles to survive, imperialist nations and battling Chinese warlords inflict hardship and suffering on most of the Chinese people. Wang continues his struggle for economic survival, not knowing what the future holds. He is robbed, bullied and humiliated by corrupt officials and soldiers. Another 30 years passes and Wang Lifa is now an old man. He still tries his best to stay in business, and after the Japanese surrender, the U.S.-supported Nationalist government exploits the people even more. Anyone who opposes the authorities is dealt with harshly. One day in the late 1940s, two of Wang's old customers return to the teahouse: Master Chang Shi, an intellectual who was arrested and his career destroyed 40 years earlier when he was overheard voicing mild displeasure at official policy; and Qin Er, a merchant who had devoted his life to saving China through the development of industry, and failed. The three old men talk and from their own experiences criticize the evil society they have been a part of for so long. After spending this time with his old friends and speaking out after so many years of suffering in silence to keep his business going and support his family, Wang Lifa now feels relaxed. He decides to find a place to hang himself.

2058. *Team for Love (Qiu Ai Bie Dong Dui)*

1992. Tianshan Film Studio. Color. Letterboxed. 9 Reels. Direction: Guang Chunlan. Screenplay: Tu Erxun Younusi. Cinematography: Mu Lati. Art Direction: Xieer Zhati. Music: Yikemu. Costume: Amina, Dong Xiuhua. Cast: Reheman as Reheman, Dili Daer as Azhti Guli, Abu Lizi as Mulati, Meili Guli as Ala Muhan, Tuer Xunjiang as Zhayier

In Wulumiqi City in Xinjiang, three women employees of a rug factory are sent out to find a place that can produce a certain type of rug requested by a foreign tourist couple. After a succession of humorous incidents, they at last locate a family that can make such a rug. In the process, each of the three women finds love as well.

2059. *Tear Stains (Lei Hen)*

1979. Beijing Film Studio. Color. 12 Reels. Direction: Li Wenhua. Screenplay: Sun Qian, Ma Feng. Cinematography: Wu Shenghan, Chen Youqun. Art Direction: Mo Kezhan. Music: Shi Lemeng, Lu Zhulong. Sound: Zhen Chunyu. Cast: Li Rentang as Zhu Keshi, Xie Fang as Kong Nina, Yang Wei as Lu Mingyuan, Shao Fanglin as Zhang Wei, Fang Hui as Xu Guanxiong

When he arrives in Jin County to assume his post, the new County Secretary Zhu Keshi learns that the construction costs of a local

water conservancy project not only seem inordinately high, the project is opposed by the local people it is supposed to benefit. He is also suspicious of the circumstances surrounding the death of the former secretary Cao Yi, and the "mental illness" of Cao's wife, Kong Nina. When he sets out to investigate, he finds various obstacles thrown in his path by several officials, including his county office manager Zhang Wei. Zhu relies on the local people and continues his probing. He soon determines that Lu Mingyuan, the former director of the local Public Security Bureau, had been wrongly dismissed, and has Lu restored to his position. With the latter's help, he at last discovers the truth about Cao Yi's death, and that Kong is feigning insanity to protect herself. Zhu Keshi uncovers and smashes a wide-ranging conspiracy of fraud and murder.

Best Picture, 1980 Hundred Flower Awards.

Best Actor Li Rentang, 1980 Hundred Flowers Awards.

2060. *Tears Flowing on Red Candles (Liu Lei De Hong La Zhu)*

1983. Changchun Film Studio. Color. 11 Reels. Direction: Xue Yandong. Screenplay: Zhang Tingting, Liu Ling. Cinematography: Zhang Songping. Art Direction: Shui Zhuangji. Music: Zhang Peiji. Sound: Chen Wenyuan. Cast: Zhao Fuquan as Li Maishou, Ni Ping as Bai Xuehua, Lu Yuan as Old Mother, Shi Yan as Wang Dajiao, Liang Tongyu as Liu Xinchun, Fu Yiwei as Qiuju

In a remote mountain village, today is the wedding day of young Li Maishou and his fiancee Bai Xuehua. But just as the ceremony is about to begin, the bride rebels and refuses to go any further. It turns out that the marriage was arranged through a matchmaker, with a 1,000 yuan gift to the bride's parents. She already loves a boy named Liu Xinchun, and cannot bear to marry another just to make her parents rich. When the hurt and angry Li Maishou calms down, he starts to think back on his own experience. He had once loved a girl, but because he was poor then the girl's parents forced her to marry someone else. Li Maishou decides to step aside and let Bai Xuehua marry someone of her choice. His unselfish consideration for others is very impressive to Liu's younger sister Qiuju, and it is obvious Li Maishou's real romance is not far off.

2061. *Tears of Snow Mountain (Xue Shan Lei)*

1979. August First Film Studio. Color. 11 Reels. Direction: Hua Chun, Ren Pengyuan. Screenplay: Wang Ying. Cinematography: Zhang Lun. Art Direction: Zhang Guozheng. Music: Fu Gengcheng, Shi Feng. Sound: Li Lin. Cast: Dawangdui as Zhaxi, Zhaxilamu as Yang Jin, Cangmu as Suolangzhuma, Suonanraodeng as Langshe, Yangjinzuoga as Dawa, Zhaxilamu as Nima

Tibetan young people Zhaxi and Yangjin get married and soon have twin daughters. Tibetan monk Lang She wants the wife Yangjin for himself, so he has Zhaxi's left eye put out, on the excuse that their marriage violates the will of Buddha. Choosing to die rather than go with Lang She, Yangjin drowns herself in a river, leaving behind the couple's twins. The elder is called Dawa, the younger Nima. In 1957, when the girls are 18, a small band of Tibetans prepare to rebel against the Chinese government. The girls learn that former serf owner Zhuma has secretly shipped weapons from abroad to the rebels, but before they can report this to the PLA, Lang She kills Dawa and Nima flees into hiding. In 1959, the rebellion is put down, and Ni Wa, now a member of the PLA, returns to her hometown with a PLA work team. Under the team's leadership, the slaves all stand up, and Zhuma and Langshe are punished for their crimes. Zhaxi and Nima united.

2062. *Tears Through the Laughter (Xiao Chu Lai De Yan Lei)*

1988. Shanghai Film Studio and Jiangxi Film Studio Co-Production. Color. Letterboxed. 10 Reels. Direction: Zhang Gang. Screenplay: Zhang Gang. Cinematography: Zhang Yuanmin, Ji Hongsheng. Art Direction: Wang Renchen. Music: Wang Ming. Sound: Yu Meiqiang, Zhu Yong. Cast: Zhang Gang as Zhao Aman, Niu Beng as Director Zhong, Wu Haiyan as Bai Li

Director and actor Zhao Aman loves to do comedy, and his show "Laugh Night" is both welcomed by audiences and supported by Bai Li, an actress in his troupe. But Cultural Bureau Director Zhong is jealous because he loves Bai Li. When the Cultural Revolution starts, Zhao Aman is among those sent to a "reforming place." Zhong professes his love for Bai Li, but she refuses him. Later, those in the "reforming place" are released one by one, and only Zhao Aman still stays. After the downfall of the Gang of Four, Zhao is freed and resumes his comedy career. He forgives Director Zhong and the others who had persecuted him for political reasons. Only Bai Li will never return to him.

Teenage Factory **see** *Young Masters of the Great Leap Forward*

2063. *The Tempest (Bao Feng Zhou Yu)*

1961. Beijing Film Studio. B & W. 12 Reels. Direction: Xie Tieli. Screenplay: Lin Lan, based on the novel of the same title by Zhou Libo. Cinematography: Wu Shenghan. Art Direction: Cheng Rongyuan. Music: Li Huanzhi. Sound: Chen Yanxi. Casting: Yu Yang as Director Xiao, Gao Baocheng as Zhao Yulin, Lu Fei as Bai Yushan, Li Baiwan as Guo Quanhai, Zhao Zhiyue as Old Sun, Yan Zenghe as Old Tiantou

In 1946, in a liberated area in Northeast China, a rural land reform work team led by their Director Xiao arrives in Yuanmao Village to begin land reform among the rural people. Despotic landlord Han Laoliu and his henchman Zhang Fuying try to disrupt their work; in addition, the people do not understand the Party's land reform policy. Director Xiao exposes the enemy's conspiracy while motivating the people and developing their enthusiasm for farming. Finally, the liberated farmers in Yuanmao Village defeat the landlord's forces, and having seen the benefits of land reform, strongly support the people's war of liberation.

2064. *Temporary Dad (Lin Shi Ba Ba) (aka Interim Father)*

1992. Fujian Film Studio and Hainan Comedy Film and Television Company Ltd. Color. Letterboxed. 9 Reels. Direction: Chen Guoxing. Screenplay: Yang Xiaoxiong. Cinematography: Zhao Xiaoding. Art Direction: Zhao Zhengxue. Music: Guo Xiaohu. Sound: Guan Jian. Costume: Tong Jingqin. Makeup: Yang Wenxia. Casting: Chen Peisi as CEO Chen, Xu Ling as Yu Lin, Ye Jing as Yu Tong, Li Jiachun as the fat man, Zhao Weidong as the skinny man, Wang Yingjie as Mr. Fang

CEO Chen is a self-made man who worked his way up from a working-class background to be head of his own construction company. But hard work has left him with little time for other things in life and now at 40 he is still single. One day, he goes to a

The Tempest. **Director Xiao (Yu Yang, left) leads a rural land reform work team in a liberated area of Northeast China in 1946. 1961. Beijing Film Studio.**

shooting club and falls for one of the instructors. The lady, Yu Lin, is not immediately interested, but he sees her again when she later is hired by his company. It turns out she is a divorcee with an 11-year-old son, a fact she tries to keep secret from her co-workers. Chen takes it upon himself to find out more about Yu Lin, and in doing so meets the boy, Yu Tong. The two become good friends. The relationship between Chen and Yu develops as well, until one day a misunderstanding leads him to think she has accepted a bribe from someone seeking a contract with his company. Deeply offended, Yu Lin quits her job and leaves town. The repentant Chen regularly visits Yu Lin's son, becoming the boy's temporary dad, but neither knows exactly where she has gone. At last Yu Tong takes charge of the situation and helps Chen find Yu Lin. The three form a family at last.

2065. *A Temporary Delay in Making the Arrest (Zhan Huan Dai Bu)*

1988. Pearl River Film Studio. Color. Letterboxed. 9 Reels. Direction: Ling Qiwei. Screenplay: Ling Qiwei, Peng Yun. Cinematography:

Wang Lianping. Art Direction: Tu Benyang. Music: Du Jiangang. Sound: Wu Chengxin. Cast: Jin Xing as Yao Ke, Chen Baoguo as Xiao Yuguang, Zhao Kuier as Li Ping

Yao Ke came to Macao from the Chinese mainland a year earlier to inherit 400,000 yuan, but was swindled out of his fortune and is now heavily in debt. His lover Li Ping, manager of a Shenzhen cosmetic firm, uses the company's foreign exchange to repay Yao's debt, which gets her in considerable legal difficulty. Prosecutor Xiao Yuguang has evidence that Li Ping misused Chinese public funds in Macao, but he is hesitant to arrest her because of her previous great contributions to the company. Since Li Ping controls secret formulas for some products, his office decides to delay her arrest. The story ends with Yao Ke regaining much of his fortune and going to the prosecutors to appeal for leniency for Li Ping, who is about to go on trial.

2066. *10 Days (Shi Tian)*

1980. Guangxi Film Studio. Color. 13 Reels. Direction: Bai Cheng. Screenplay: Bai Cheng, Li Yinming. etc., Cinematography: Yang Yuming.

Art Direction: Lao Guanneng. Music: Li Yanlin. Sound: Jue Jingxiu, Li Zhuwen. Cast: Zhu Xinyun as A Feng, Han Fei as Ding Jiping, Chang Rong as Huzhai, Chen Huizhen as Lanmei, He Ling as Sister, Fang Hua as Commander Mo, Cheng Zhi as Chief of Staff Wang

Just before the liberation of Guangxi province in 1949, the Nationalist commander in the area Long Yaozu brings home a secret document from a military meeting. It is stolen by three teenagers, A Feng, Hu Zai and Lai Mei. For his laxity, the Nationalist government executes Long Yaozu and orders his son Long Jiachang, Chief of the Intelligence Branch, to recover the document within 10 days. The youngsters take the document to Uncle Nong, the undercover Communist Party Branch Secretary, who instructs them to deliver the document to Communist guerrillas in Guangxi. Uncle Nong is killed covering them when they leave the city. Government forces set up all sorts of barriers to their progress. Hu Zai is wounded, and they take him to kindly Doctor Ding Jiping who saves the boy's life. The three finally reach the rendezvous site but the guerrilla sent to meet them is shot and killed by pursuing soldiers. Lan Mei is captured, but she is rescued by the guerrilla's Communist Party liaison Huang Gang. A Feng sacrifices himself so that Hu Zai and Lan Mei escape successfully.

2067. *10 Months Pregnant (Shiyue Huaitai)*

1992. Changchun Film Studio. Color. Letterboxed. Direction: Gao Tianhong, Shou Hui. Screenplay: Wan Jie, Wu Kaiyuan. Cinematography: Li Junyan. Art Direction: Sui Zuangyuan. Music: Zhang Shigong. Cast: Zhang Yin as Zen Zhi, Xue Shujie as Darong's wife, Liu Tingrao as Liu Wurou, Zhang Feng as Lu Darong, Zhang Fan as Luer's wife

Darong's wife is a capable woman living in Ganquan Village. She already has three children, but wants one more in spite of legal restrictions. So when she again gets pregnant, she evades the local Family Planning Committee. She and her husband are happy when she has a boy, but the consequences are serious. Her husband is jailed for stealing fish from the local creek, an offense normally overlooked; one of the children becomes disabled due to lack of care; her elderly mother-in-law leaves home, blaming Darong's wife for bringing shame on the whole family. At last, Darong's

wife sees the importance of family planning, and volunteers to help the committee in its work.

2068. *10:00 on the National Holiday (Guo Qing Shi Dian Zhong)*

1956. Changchun Film Studio. B & W. 10 Reels. Direction: Wu Tian. Screenplay: Wu Tian, based on the novel "Double Bell Watch" by Lu Shi and Wen Da. Cinematography: Nie Jing. Art Direction: Zhang Jingnan. Music: Lei Zhengbang. Sound: Yuan Mingda. Cast: Yin Zhiming as Gu Qun, Zhao Lian as Ping Xiaohai, Zhao Zhiyue as Director Jin, Pu Ke as He Zhankui, Li Jie as Bai Songting, Wang Chunyin as Xiao Yu

In a Northwest China provincial capital in 1953, undercover spies He Zhankui and Bai Songting plot to blow up a public building at the next Chinese National Holiday. Their plot involves sending public security officers on a wild goose chase by mailing anonymous letters alleging the explosion will take place somewhere else. They plant the bomb with a child's wristwatch as the timer. PSB officer Gu Qun finds the actual bomb location and defuses it in time. Then he catches the spies.

2069. *Tenderness to You (Song Ni Yi Pian Wen Rou)*

1992. Beijing Film Studio. Color. Letterboxed. 9 Reels. Direction: Liu Qiuling. Screenplay: Lian Chunmin, Li Baoyuan. Cinematography: Li Yuebing. Art Direction: Yuan Chao. Music: Wang Ming. Sound: Liu Shida. Costume: Liu Jianhua, Li Fengju. Makeup: Dong Zhiqin. Cast: Peng Li as Lili, Shan Zenhong as Doudou, Liu Yajin as Shoushou, Dong Lifan as Pangpang, Xie Fang as the Woman

Doudou and Lili are regarded as an odd couple by everyone: Doudou is short and small in stature, and works as a driver; Lili is tall, lovely, and works in public relations. Despite heavy opposition from her family, and daily contact with many successful men, Lili's love for Doudou is unswerving.

2070. *The 10th Bullet Hole (Di Shi Ge Dan Kong)*

1980. Xi'an Film Studio. Color. 11 Reels. Direction: Ai Shui. Screenplay: Chong Weixi, Ai Shui. Cinematography: Cao Jinshan. Art Direction: Liu Xinghou. Music: Li Yaodong. Sound: Hong Jiahui. Cast: Cao Huiqu as Lu Hong, Bao Xun as Lu Xiaofan, Chen Lizhong as Grandma,

Yi Da as the wife, Yang Tong as Lu Xiaofan (as a child), Cao Jingyang as Uncle

After 10 years of hard labor during the Cultural Revolution, Lu Hong resumes his former post as Director of the Bingjiang City Public Security Bureau. His first case deals with a blown-up bridge, and his only son Lu Xiaofan appears to be involved. As Lu Hong reads the case file, his thoughts drift back 10 years to when Xiaofan was an innocent boy who used to touch and count the nine gunshot scars on his father's body, remnants of his war service. Now he is investigating the boy. Lu Hong's wife appeals to her husband to be lenient, as do others who sympathize with the director's situation and want him to rely on his feelings rather than policy. Determined to learn the truth, Lu Hong visits those who had known Xiaofan while his parents were exiled to the countryside. It develops that while they were gone, Xiaofan grew up in the streets without adult supervision, fell in with bad company and became a criminal. Lu Hong concludes that the evidence does not lie and sentences his son to nine years in prison. At first, Xiaofan is baffled at his father's stern judgment, but finally comes to understand Lu Hong's devotion to justice and law. As Lu Hong sees his son off to serve his sentence, the boy tearfully says, "Father, I put this tenth hole in you," to which his father replies, "Not from you, but from the Gang of Four."

2071. *Terra-cotta Warrior (Gu Jin Da Zhan Qin Yong Qing)*

1989. Canada Chinese Film Company and Hong Kong Jiamin Entertainment Company Co-Production. Color. Wide screen. 10 Reels. Direction: Cheng Xiaodong. Screenplay: Li Bihua. Cinematography: Pao Qiming. Art Direction: Xi Zhongwen. Music: Huang Dian. Sound: Zhu Qijian. Cast: Zhang Yimou as Meng Tianfang, Gong Li as Donger, Yu Rongguang as Bai Yunfei

Some 200 years B.C., the Qin Emperor orders the sacrifice of 500 virgin boys and girls to make a pill which will bring him longevity. His bodyguard Meng Tianfang falls in love with Donger, one of the girls scheduled for sacrifice. They have an affair, and for this are sentenced to be executed. Just before they die, Donger asks to kiss Meng one last time, and in doing so she passes the pill of longevity into his mouth. Many centuries pass, and Donger has been reincarnated as a ditzy movie starlet. When her Shanghai film company is on loca-

tion in northwest China, an accident awakens Meng Tianfang from his tomb. The film's leading man is actually a Japanese agent using the location filming as an excuse to link up with German agents pretending to be foreign filmmakers. Several people are killed when they get in the way of the spies, and at last Meng Tianfang bests the villains in a showdown while protecting Donger, who unfortunately dies anyway. Now it is the 1990s, and Meng Tianfang is a worker repairing the famous Terra-cotta Army of Shanxi Province. One day a group of Japanese visitors comes to the excavation site, and Meng looks up to find one of the Japanese girls smiling at him. He instantly recognizes his lover across the centuries, reincarnated once more.

2072. *Tested by Blood and Fire (Xue Yu Huo De Xi Li)*

1979. Xi'an Film Studio. Color. 10 Reels. Direction: Gao Zhiyi, Wang Zhijie. Screenplay: Zhang Wei, Chen Geng. Cinematography: Ling Xuan. Art Direction: Wang Fei, Cheng Mingzhang. Music: Xiang Yin. Sound: Che Zhiyuan. Cast: Chen Shaoze as Gao Fengchun, Wen Shujun as He Jie, Mu Huaihu as Fang Liang, Xu Zhan as Wang Zhanfei, Yu Fei as Charlie

In 1925, after Gao Fengchun and female classmate He Jie return from medical studies in England, they determine to devote their lives to helping China through medicine. They travel to Dingzhou, a mountain city where Gao had grown up, and take over a clinic run by a Western medical missionary called Charlie. The two enthusiastically turn it into a clinic for poor people. Student leader Fang Lang disagrees with them, for he believes that medicine is not going to save a China torn by warlord fighting, where the people find it hard just to live. Later, when Gao Fengchun learns that Charlie had used his religious cover to murder many Chinese, he breaks with Charlie and grows closer to Fang Liang. In a bloody counterrevolutionary massacre, Gao's hospital is destroyed. Tested by blood and fire, his dream of saving China through medical science shattered, Gao Fengchun finally realizes that intellectuals will have a future only if they join the revolution to bring down imperialists and warlords.

2073. *Textile Song (Fang Hua Qu)*

1953. Changjiang, Kunlun Film Company.

B & W. 9 Reels. Direction: Shen Fu. Screenplay: Shen Fu. Cinematography: Hu Zhenhua. Art Direction: Ding Chen and Hu Dengren. Music: Chen Gexi. Sound: Yuan Qinyu. Costume: Jiang Zhengqin. Makeup: Wang Tiebin. Cast: Qi Menshi as Meng Zhaonan, Zhong Shuhuang as Wang Kuan, Shanggua Yunzhu as Cai Azhu, Wu Yin as Abao's mother, Wang Pei as Xiao Dong, Zhang Yi as Kong Maozhang

In the days just after liberation, economic sanctions by Western nations create problems for the Baotong Textile Plant, a privately operated company in Shanghai. With the help of some Nationalist secret agents, plant owner Meng Zhaonan takes all the company's funds and flees to Hong Kong. Meanwhile, agent Kong Maozhang exploits woman textile plant worker Cai Azhuo to hurt the relationship of the workers with their union. After that, he damages the plant by setting fire to their cotton. Production is shut down, and casualties are narrowly averted. The plant's union head Wang Kuan leads the workers in overcoming the various difficulties. They resolve to use only material made in China in the future. Kong refuses to accept failure, and again tries to shut down production. In the end, the secret agents are all found out and arrested. Many workers improve their political awareness from this, and determine to help reform the capitalist side and resume normal production.

2074. *Thank You, Comrade (Tong Zhi, Gan Xie Ni)*

1978. Pearl River Film Studio. Color. 10 Reels. Direction: "Thank You Comrade" directing team, implementation director: Chen Ying. Screenplay: Li Bing, Hu Qinshu. Cinematography: Li Shengwei, Liang Xiongwei. Art Direction: Mo Renji. Music: Zhang Hong. Sound: Li Baijian. Cast: Liu Xiaoqing as Yang Jie, Zhang Zhiliang as Mr. Zhou, Xing Jitian as Mr. Fang, Wei Ming as Mr. Le, Yang Limin as Little Fatty, Gao Jianhua as Shu Sheng, Shu Yi as Yin Bijun, Liu Lihua as Yin Yuping, Zhu Shihui as Fang Xiang

A group of new workers is assigned to the East Wind environmental cleanup team just at the time upper level authorities announce that outstanding workers from this group will be selected for college attendance. This work is traditionally looked down upon by some people in society, and capitalist's wife Yin Bijun tries everything she can to stop her daughter Yuping from working there; even cleanup crew

chief Mr. Fang wants his son Fang Xiang to quit this work, although it could mean a chance to go to college. Team secretary Yang Jie had once misunderstood this work himself, but with help and education from the Party secretary and veteran workers, she correctly handles her job. When she is selected for college attendance, she decides to stay on. She also struggles with Yin Bijun's incorrect thinking and speech, and helps Yin Yuping. She also helps Fang Xiang change his thinking, and he happily stays on with his job.

2075. *That Winter (Nei Nian De Dong Tian)*

1990. Children's Film Studio. Color. Wide Screen. 9 Reels. Direction: Yu Yanfu. Screenplay: Liang Zhi, Tao Jinfeng. Cinematography: Li Tingfeng. Art Direction: Gao Guoliang, Yang Yunhui. Music: Li Yiding. Sound: Lan Fan. Cast: Che Yue as Shen Min, Feng Lei as Guo Weidong, Li Nan as Han Xiaobin, Cui Bin as Zhao Haisheng, Shi Jie as the deputy company commander

In the winter of 1969, Chinese soldiers guarding the Soviet border find an injured dog from the other side. They nurse it back to health, and the dog becomes an ambassador of goodwill between the two hostile armies on each side of the border. It at last brings them together to save a human life on the Russian side.

2076. *That's Not the Way to Go (Bu Neng Zou Nei Tiao Lu)*

1954. Unreleased. Shanghai Film Studio. B & W. 6 Reels. Direction: Ying Yunwei. Screenplay: Bao Shi, based on the novel of the same title by Li Zhun. Cinematography: Chen Minhun. Set Design: Zhang Xibai. Music: Chen Gexin. Sound: Shao Zihe. Cast: Wei Helin as Song Laoding. Lan Gu as Dong Shan, Zhao Shuyin as Xiu Lan, Liao Ruiqun as Aunt Song, Qiang Ming as Zhang Shuang, Zhang Qingfen as Zhang Shuang's wife

In the post-liberation land reform, poor farmer Zhang Shuang receives a good allocation of land, but instead of concentrating on farming focuses on speculation. As a result, he goes heavily into debt and prepares to sell the land. Liberated farmer Song Laoding tries to buy Zhang Shuang's land by exploiting Zhang's personal problems, and thereby make a sizable profit for himself. But Song's son Dongshan argues that his father should lend Zhang Shuang the money to get over his current difficulties, and then push him to work hard in the future. At first Dongshan takes the wrong approach, so he not only fails to convince his father, he also puts a stress on the father-son relationship. Later, Dongshan changes his attitude and method, recalling for Song Laoding his earlier, pre-liberation experiences. This makes him realize he must go the way of socialism. So Song Laoding lends Zhang Shuang the money originally intended for purchase of Zhang's land, enabling Zhang to get over his difficulties. Deeply moved, he vows that he will work hard at farm production in the future and catch up with the others.

2077. *Their Hope (Xi Wang)*

1977. Changchun Film Studio. Color. 14 Reels. Direction: Yu Yanfu and Xiao Guiyun. Screenplay: Zhang Tianmin. Cinematography: Wang Lei, Duan Zhenjiang. Art Direction: Wang Chong. Music: Qin Yongcheng. Sound: Hong Di, Li Zhengduo. Cast: Zhang Jinling as Ning Haiping, Zhao Fan as Yan Shuikuan, Gong Xibing as Niu Sanxi, Chi Zhiqiang as Shi Yumen, Xu Min as Xiao Xinguo, Niu Shijun as Bao Kui, Xu Guangming as Gong Liancai

Orphan Xiao Xianguo is raised from infancy by Grandma Ning in a poor fishing family. He and Grandma Ning's granddaughter Haiping grow up to become young oil field workers. When Haiping is put in charge of Unit No. 48, she makes plans to drill four new wells there. Although she has the support of Party secretary Yan Shuikuan, her plan is blocked by her supervisor Gong Liancai, who opposes anything he suspects might take some of his power. He goes so far as to arrange an incident to damage Haiping's image. Gong Liancai also labels Yan Shuikuan as a "capitalist roader." But Haiping struggles with Gong, whose followers now include Xiao Xinguo. She educates Xiao and the others with the facts, and Gong's power grab is repelled.

2078. *Their Hopes (Ta Men De Xin Yuan)*

1960. Tianma Film Studio. B & W. 11 Reels. Cinematography: Cha Xiangkang. Art Direction: Liu Pan. Music: Kang Huilin. Sound: Zhu Weigang. Three short films of women's accomplishments:

"Screws" (Luo Si Ding). Screenplay: Ye Ming, Qian Dingde. Direction: Yu Zhongying. Cast: Erlin as Wang Xiaojuan, Qiao Zhi as Yang Ling, Shi Jiufeng as Xiao Yu, Tu

Zhengping as Zhang Bingshan, Jiangshan as Master Worker Jiang, Zhang Yan as Secretary Li. Inspired by the Great Leap Forward, young woman worker Wang Xiaojuan responds to her local Party committee's campaign that "one person work like one and a half people," by reducing the time for producing screws from 14 minutes to 3, greatly improving efficiency.

"Girl Swineherd" (Yang Zhu Guniang). Direction and Screenplay collectively by the faculty of the Shanghai Film School. Cast: Yan Yongxuan, Zhong Jingwen. Wang Xiuhong, a girl swineherd in a commune, responds to the Party's call for development of swine husbandry by studying hard, accelerating her production speed and gaining advanced experience.

"Just Say You Need Me" (Zhi Yao Ni Shuo Yi Sheng Xu Yao). Direction: Jiang Junchao and Bai Yang. Screenplay: Ru Zhijuan. Cast: Zhu Manfang, Ding Tiebao. Female high school graduate Xiao Mei hopes to go to medical school but is instead assigned to a normal school, putting her personal desires in conflict with the nation's needs. Later, inspired by the school director, she gives up her individual desires and goes to the normal university.

2079. *Their Marriages (Fu Zi Hun Shi)*

1992. Nanhai Film Company & Zhejiang Film Studio Co-Production. Color. Letterboxed. 9 Reels. Direction: Situ Zhaodun, Zhu Chuanguang, Zhang Bingzhu. Screenplay: Fang Ye. Cinematography: Tian Jianmin. Art Direction: Lu Jun. Music: Jiang Yan. Sound: Wang Yunhua, Xu Huiju. Costume: Nie Yaodi. Makeup: Guan Jun, Zhang Rong. Cast: Ge You as Dayou, Ge Chunzuang as Old Zhuang, Ding Yi as Widow Zhang, Zhang Yan as Feng Xian, Mo Qi as Mo Demeng, Wu Xiaojun as A Jiao

Old Zhuang and his son Dayou have not been treated very fairly by life. Dayou's mother ran off with another man when the boy was only 13 months old, and the father never found another wife. Now Dayou is over 30, and still unmarried. At last Dayou pays 3,000 yuan to a matchmaker, who introduces him to A Jiao, a sweet country girl who seems perfect for Dayou. But it turns out A Jiao was forced out of her home and into the match. Not wanting to hold her against her will, kindly Dayou releases her from her obligation. However, by this time the girl has actually fallen for Dayou and begs to stay. All seems well until A Jiao's mother shows up: guilt-ridden over selling her daughter, she has come to take her back. Father and son stand together to show her that life's trends are irreversible, and that A Jiao now has a new life as beloved wife and daughter-in-law. The mother leaves in some embarrassment.

2080. *There Is a Coming Generation (Zi You Hou Lai Ren)*

1963. Changchun Film Studio. B & W. 10 Reels. Direction: Yu Yanfu. Screenplay: Chi Yu, Luo Jing. Cinematography: Meng Xiandi. Art Direction: Xu Wei. Music: Quan Rufeng. Sound: Wang Fei. Cast: Qi Guirong as Li Tiemei, Zhao Lian as Li Yuhe, Che Yi as Grandma Li, Han Sheng as Jiu Shan, Yin Zhiming as Patrol Director Wang, Ma Loufu as Old Man Zhang

In 1939, in a Northeast China city under Japanese occupation, lives a three generation family. Although this family is linked by common struggle and revolutionary destiny, the three generations have three different surnames. Before he can deliver a secret telegram code book to a local guerrilla troop, Li Yuhe, a communications railway worker and underground Communist Party member, is betrayed by Wang, a traitor. Also arrested are Li's mother, Grandma Li, and his daughter Tiemei. When Li bravely refuses to cooperate with the Japanese he and Grandma Li are both put to death. The daughter is released, but traitor Wang is detailed to follow her in the hopes she will lead them to the hidden code book. But the clever Tiemei fools the traitor, finds the code book and delivers it to the guerrilla troop, fulfilling the mission left behind by her father and grandmother.

2081. *There Was a Family (You Yi Jia Ren Jia)*

1951. Wenhua Film Company. B & W. 10 Reels. Direction: Sang Hu. Screenplay: Li Hongxin. Cinematography: Xu Zhiliang and Ma Lingfa. Art Direction: Wang Yuebai. Casting: Sun Jinglu as Zhong Jiayin, Shen Yang as Zhong Jiahao, Qiao Qi as Sha Daxing, Zhang Manping as Grandma, Cheng Zhi as Reverend Gao, Mao Lu as Papa Zhong, Xu Wei as Mama Zhong, Li Shouying as Sha Minxing

In 1937, the Zhong family runs a comb shop in a small town in Southeast China. The Zhongs' son Jiahao, daughter Jiayin and her high school boy friend Sha Daxing all study English with Reverend Gao, an American missionary. Gao plants poisonous thoughts with them. Later, Jiahao and Daxing go to the interior of China to join up in the anti–Japanese resistance, despite Grandma Zhong's attempts to stop them. Shortly afterwards, the Japanese invaders enter the town, and Daxing's sister Minxing is killed. Jiayin is jailed by the Japanese, but her father buys her release. Reverend Gao gets Jiayin admitted to study at a Shanghai church-run school of nursing, where she gradually develops a worship of things American. She is overjoyed to learn that Jiahao and Daxing are working as interpreters for the U.S. military. But after the Japanese surrender, Daxing brings the news that Jiahao had been murdered by American soldiers, and this changes Jiayin's attitude. She resigns her job at the American hospital, returns to her hometown with Daxing and marries him. Later, Reverend Gao tries to bribe Jiayin to persuade Daxing to stop his anti–American activities, but she refuses. The missionary then persuades the reactionary commander of the city guards to arrest Daxing. After China is liberated, Daxing is freed and the family is again united. The comb shop prospers once more. When China enters the Korean War, Jiayin volunteers to serve as a nurse in the Resist America and Aid North Korea Campaign. This time, having learned the circumstances of Jiahao's death, Grandma gives her blessing, and the whole family goes to see Jiayin off on her way to Korea.

2082. *These Things Are By No Means Insignificant (Zhe Jue Bu Shi Xiao Shi)*

1956. August First Film Studio. B & W. 8 Reels. Direction: Yan Jizhou. Screenplay: Wang Shaoyan, Yan Jizhou. Cinematography: Jiang Shi. Set Design: Xu Run. Music: Gao Ruxing. Sound: He Baoding. Cast: Zhang Aoran as the security department head, Li Hongcang as Adviser Wang, Han Mei as the housekeeper, Yan Xiaopeng as the trash hauler, Wei Qinghuai as Xiao Zhang, Fan BoTao as the photography shop manager, Guo Hua as the first reporter, Xu Peili as the second reporter, Shi Yin as Su Bing, Li Shiye as Sun Liang, Yang Jiao as Mr. Kong, Zhao Hengduo as the traitor, Sun Xianyun as Assistant Yang, Deng Jingsu as the female spy, Ming Zhofang as the hometown person, Cao Rui as the branch secretary, Li Shiyuan as Xiao Hu, Bi Xu as the cobbler

The movie consists of six short stories:

"Secret Document No. 75": Adviser Wang

is careless about security. Rushing from the house one day, he leaves a secret document with his housekeeper, who is an undercover enemy spy. Her arrest by public security officers brings Wang to his senses about the value of security.

"Little Radios": Border patrol officers arrest a spy who has snuck across the border and obtained information on Chinese army troop deployment. It turns out that "little radios" (i.e., gossip) carried the troop deployment information all over the area, till it reached a certain photography studio manager who was a covert enemy agent.

"Careless Talkers": On a train trip, a military security department chief meets two newspaper reporters who chatter rather carelessly. During the lunch break, the reporters steal some important national secrets. The department head reports the matter to the PSB, which arrests both the reporters.

"The Sentry Who Neglected His Duty": Two auto accidents occur as an urgent transport assignment is being fulfilled. It turns out that a soldier on guard had left his post to view a nearby stage performance. This allowed some spies to tamper with the trucks' tires, which caused the accidents.

"Such Love": Yang, assistant in a certain military department, is a brave man who was decorated for heroism in battle. But he is always asking others to introduce him to suitable girls, and always insists they be young, pretty and educated. At last he is introduced to what seems the perfect girl; unfortunately she turns out to be a spy sent over to the mainland by Taiwan.

"Little Confusion": Xiao Hu, guard at an army warehouse, is nicknamed "Little Confusion." One time, he falls asleep at his post (not for the first time), and spies cut the wire fence and climb in. They knock him unconscious and set a bomb to go off. At the critical moment, the inspecting platoon leader discovers and defuses the bomb just in time to save the warehouse.

2083. *They Are Growing Up (Ta Men Zai Cheng Zhang)*

1966. Haiyan Film Studio. B & W. 8 Reels. Direction: Tian Ran, Zhao Huanzhang. Screenplay: Fei Liwen. Cinematography: Peng Enli. Art Direction: Zhong Yongqin. Music: Wang Yunjie, Liang Hanguang. Sound: Liu Guangjie. Casting: Yu Guichun as Li Xiaosong, Jiang Shan as Master

Worker Zhao, Zhong Xinghuo as Zhang Ageng, Li Ming as Yang Yuhua, Jin Zhaoqu as Liu Xiaojie, Yu Zhenghuan as Ma Shaowu

"Changjiang" power plant construction site's youth group director Li Xiaosong unites people to automate a process which will speed up an installation project. Young worker Liu Xiaojie, out for personal laurels, tries to build his own machine which will compete with Li's. Li's several attempts to help Liu are rejected, because Liu thinks Li just wants to share some of the glory. On one occasion, Liu ruins an expensive pipe in an unsuccessful test of his machine, but he refuses to admit the matter. Later, after Li Xiaosong and an old worker educate him, he admits his mistakes. In the end, with Li Xiaosong's help, Liu Xiaojie successfully builds his machine.

2084. *They Are in Battle (Ta Men Zai Zhan Dou)*

1960. Unreleased. Xinjiang Film Studio. B & W. 7 Reels. Direction: Chen Gang. Screenplay: Lang Ke and Shi Hua. Cinematography: Han Gangzi, Zeng Qilu and Li Derun. Art Direction: Mu Hong and Huang Yide. Sound: Zhang Xiceng. Cast: Kong Zhaotian as Regimental Commander Cao, Zeng Zhensheng as Political Commissar Gao, Ren Zhian as Company Commander Zhang, Zhong Ruitu as the deputy company commander, Zhao Zhi as Company Commander Zhao, Jia Zijie as Mr. Men

During the wheat harvesting season, every production company of an agricultural brigade in the Xinjiang production construction regiment demands Regimental Commander Cao provide them with more workers. Not only is their request for more workers denied, they are assigned extra work to do. Regiment Commander Cao is content with what has already been achieved, putting him in conflict with Political Commissar Gao, who advocates technology upgrading in their work. Gao's plan goes through successfully, educating Cao through the realities of the situation. Cao eventually admits his errors and enthusiastically devotes himself to the effort to obtain a greater agricultural harvest.

2085. *They Are in Love (Tamen Zai Xiangai)*

1980. Beijing Film Studio. Color. 10 Reels. Direction: Qian Jiang, Zhao Yuan. Screenplay: Yang Lingyan, Wang Qi. Cinematography: Sun Cangyi. Art Direction: Hao Jingyuan. Music:

Wang Ming. Sound: Liu Shida. Cast: Zhang Ping as Chen Ao, Da Shichang as Chen Zhan, Xiao Xiong as Su Yi, Guo Xuxin as Chen Nan, Xu Yushun as Wang Hui, Qiu Ge as Chen Ping

During the Gang of Four's reign of terror, many are falsely accused and persecuted, including old military cadre Chen Ao. The injustice of this infuriates his three sons. Eldest son Chen Zhan, an eye doctor, publicly criticizes the Gang's methods as Fascist, which causes the son to be labeled a counterrevolutionary. After the Gang is defeated, he and his lover Su Yi restore their relationship, marry, and devote themselves to China's modernization. The middle son Chen Nan, disabled by a beating he received during the Cultural Revolution, perseveres in educating himself and masters three foreign languages. He falls in love with elementary school teacher Wang Hui, and they too finally get married. The third son Chen Ping became disillusioned by the violent excesses of the Cultural Revolution, and now cares only for eating, drinking and carousing. He meets and becomes involved with Zhang Lang, a similarly dissolute young woman. He comes to his senses after she dumps him, and with the help of his brothers and father, finally starts to get his life together.

2086. *They Are Not Strangers (Ta Men Bing Bu Mu Sheng)*

1982. Changchun Film Studio. Color. 11 Reels. Direction: Zhang Xinshi. Screenplay: Li Qimin, Zhang Xinshi. Cinematography: Bao Jie. Art Direction: Du Xiufeng. Music: Qun Rufeng. Sound: Wen Liangyu. Cast: Ni Ping as Xiao Jing, Li Yufeng as Zhang Dafeng, Li Shixi as Lei Mingsheng, Zhang Guixing as Zhao Tie, Qu Yun as the mother, Che Xuan as the father

Xiao Jing and Lei Mingsheng come with other educated city youth to the remote mountain village of Lihua, where Xiao Jing opens the village's first, very simple, elementary school. She and Lei Mingsheng later marry, and devote themselves to rural education. But Mingsheng is later killed in an accident, and the by-then pregnant Xiao Jing miscarries. She carries on their educational work alone. After the downfall of the Gang of Four, and Xiao Jing's father is restored to his position, she goes to Beijing to visit him. He wants her to stay, but she returns to Lihua Village to continue her work as a mountain village teacher.

2087. *They Are Young (Ta Men Zheng Nian Qing)*

1986. Xi'an Film Studio. Color. 10 Reels. Direction: Zhou Xiaowen, Fang Fang. Screenplay: Li Pingfeng. Cinematography: Zhi Lei. Art Direction: Ge Yue. Music: Zhu Shiduan. Sound: Hui Dongzhi. Cast: Hong Yuzhou as the deputy company commander, Yue Hong as Yan Pingping, Wang Gang as platoon leader, Yang Shengli as Xiao Gu

During the Sino-Vietnamese border war, a nine-man Chinese squad undertakes a mission which requires them to operate out of a mountain cave. For three months they endure such hardships as lack of food, water and sleep, operating from the cave in hours of darkness only. They hold out until relieved, but two of their number are sacrificed in the action.

2088. *The Thief of Baling (Baling Qie Zei)*

1987. Pearl River Film Studio. Color. 10 Reels Direction: Wang Yi. Screenplay: Wu Aojun, Wang Yi. Cinematography: Wu Benli. Art Direction: Zhu Jinhe. Music: Zhang Jielin. Sound: Lu Mingwen. Cast: Li Junfeng as Liu Hedong, Wang Lisha as Liu Yizhi, Zang Zhiguo as County Magistrate Wu, Xu Songyuan as Store Manager Yang, Han Haihua as Zhou Canglong, Dong Honglin as Liang Shangfei

When the Taiping Rebellion (1851–1864) collapses, Taiping officer Liu Hedong and his daughter Liu Yizhi flee and settle in the ancient city of Baling in Hunan province. There they earn their living as wood carvers. Impressed with Liu's skills, County Magistrate Wu commissions him to make a copy of a famous carved screen. After this, Wu has the real screen stolen and the copy put in its place. He then sells the original to some foreigners for 10,000 taels of gold. When the crime is discovered, Liu is arrested and thrown into jail. His daughter rescues him and then they go through a series of adventures to recover the genuine screen.

2089. *Third Class Citizens (San Deng Guo Min)*

1987. August First Film Studio. Color. 10 Reels. Direction: Huang Baoshan. Screenplay: Li Hong, Huang Baoshan. Cinematography: Chen Zhengzhong. Art Direction: Zhang Guozhen. Music: Yang Xiwu. Sound: Tang Yuanping. Cast: Zhu Daqin as Zhou Yongping, Xu Jianing as Li

Guishan, Zhao Feng as Jin Dongzheng, Zhang Yonghan as Zhou Wenbing, Wang Shuping as Wang Suyan

In the Japanese puppet state of Manchukuo the Zhou family suffers repeated mistreatment at the hands of the Japanese Army occupying Northeast China. The events in the film are viewed through the eyes of the family's 15-year-old son Zhou Yongping. His father, Zhou Wenbing, is a timid man subjected to frequent humiliations. Yongping's mother, Wang Suyan, is a hospital midwife who one day accidentally witnesses the Japanese carrying out germ warfare testing on human subjects. When the army realizes what she has learned, they order the woman and her husband arrested. For once, Zhou Wenbing makes a firm decision. He and his wife get their teenage son Zhou Yongping to safety, then calmly await their fate together.

2090. *The Third Man in Her Life (Di San Ge Nan Ren)*

1988. Shanghai Film Studio. Color. Letterboxed. 10 Reels. Direction: 10 Reels. Direction: Yu Jie. Screenplay: San Xi, Yuan Ping. Cinematography: Yu Shishan. Art Direction: Mei Kunping. Music: Cai Lu. Sound: Mei Kunping. Cast: Wu Jing as Li Jia, Wang Runshen as the Professor, Ye Zhikang as Shen Dashan, Ahdili Mijiti as Jiefu

A professor of criminology leads a group of students on a field trip to Qiasuoya, a vast and remote forested area along the northeast China border. There, the professor is invited to investigate a local murder case. The victim was forestry researcher Li Jia's husband Shen Dashan, a man recently released after serving seven years in prison. The professor and his students soon identify three suspects: Bai Hua, a dandy who had trumped up the charges on which Shen was convicted; Li Jinyu, a man who lived with Li Jia after her husband went to prison; and Jiefu, a young man of Chinese-Russian parentage who had been Li Jia's lover before her marriage. The professor's investigation eliminates Bai Hua and Li Jinyu as suspects, but both Jiefu and Li Jia confess to the murder. Then, the professor reveals the truth.

2091. *The Third Murder Victim (Di San Ge Bei Mou Sha Zhe)*

1981. Changchun Film Studio. Color. 11 Reels. Direction: Sun Sha. Screenplay: Sun Sha. Cinematography: Zhong Wenmin. Art Direction: Jin Xiwu. Music: Wang Liping. Sound: Han Weijun, Yi Wenyu. Cast: Kong Xiangyu as Fang Zhao, Liu Guanxiong as Lu Yifu, Gan Yuzhou as Qiu Erkang, Liang Danni as the girl, Jiang Jun as Yang Ding

In the early 1930s, patriotic Nationalist Army general Yang Ding is murdered in the French Concession of Shanghai. The Chinese police assign Fang Zhao to investigate. Fang Zhao is patriotic and conscientious, but finds his investigation blocked repeatedly, and before he has made a report the police announce the general was murdered by Communist agents. Fang Zhao receives a threat to drop any further investigating. He keeps probing anyway, and finally gets to the truth, but an attempt is made on his life. He is saved by the intervention of a girl named Fang Hui. She is a Communist, and is Fang Zhao's younger sister although he is unaware of that. She hates people like him who although they are patriotic still work for evil authorities. The Communist Party underground organization understands Fang Zhao, and he at last helps them get some secret documents they need, wiping away what he had done in the past.

2092. *The Third Party (Shui Shi Di San Zhe)*

1987. Beijing Film Studio. Color. 18 Reels. Direction: Dong Kena. Screenplay: Yao Yun. Cinematography: Zhen Yuyuan. Art Direction: Liu Changbao. Music: Du Mingxin. Sound: Wang Dawen. Cast: Zhang Jie as Hua Chao, Li Kechun as Sang Yucheng, Li Rong as Zhang Enshou, Yang Xiaodan as Jiajia, Liang Danni as Sang Lulu

Taught and encouraged by master painter Hua Chao, Sang Yuchen, a graduate student in the oil painting department, is accepted to study in France. Hua Chao's wife suspects something is going on between Sang and her husband, so she makes things difficult for Sang. Hua Chao's wife was his teacher's daughter, and he had married her only out of gratitude to his mentor, not because of love for the woman. Hua's wife is very bitter, and though she knows there is no love in their relationship she refuses to agree to a divorce. The appearance of the pretty and talented Sang Yuchen brings out all the wife's jealousy and hatred. When the wife begins spreading gossip about them, Hua Chao and Sang Yuchen draw

The Third Man in Her Life. 1988. Shanghai Film Studio.

together for mutual support and actually do fall in love. This love affair costs Sang a lot. Because of it, she loses her chance to study abroad and is assigned to work in a county-level cultural center. Hua Chao backs off from the relationship because of social pressure, hurting and enraging Sang by selfishness and cowardice. She gives up her illusions of love, and decides to begin a new life based on true love and art.

2093. *Third Sister Liu (Liu San Jie)*

1960. Changchun Film Studio. B & W. 11 Reels. Direction: Su Li. Screenplay: Qiao Yu, based on the classic opera of the Zhuang minority of Guangxi province. Cinematography: Guo Zhenting, Yi Zhi. Art Direction: Tong Jingwen, Zhang Qiguo. Music: Lei Zhenbang. Sound: Kang Ruixin, Han Weijun. Cast: Huang Wanqiu as Third Sister Liu, Liu Shilong as A Niu, Zhang Juguang as the old fisherman, Liang Yin as Liu Er, Zhang Wenjun as Sister Zhou, Zhang Ning as Fan

In Zhuang legend, Third Sister Liu was a Tang Dynasty (618–907) peasant girl who became a heroine among her people for her willingness to stand up to despotic landlords and

other enemies of her people. In this film, Liu takes on some pompous officials and overwhelms them with her songs and wit. Smarting from its public humiliation, the feudal government attempts to retaliate, forcing Third Sister and her lover to flee to the mountains. From there, she uses her folk songs to carry on her war against oppression.

2094. *This Case Is Not Yet Over (Ben An Mei You Jie Shu)*

1985. Shanghai Film Studio. Color. 10 Reels. Direction: Da Shibiao. Screenplay: Yang Shiwen, Shiyong. Cinematography: Cheng Shiyu. Art Direction: Lin Guoliang. Music: Xiao Yan. Sound: Yin Zhiping. Cast: Li Yuyu as Zhuo Liping, Zhou Yuyuan as He Xiaoxue, Qiu Shide as Lu Feng, Nie Yaliang as Zhong Ling, Tan Feiling as Ye Zhengqiu, Wang Aibing as Xu Minmin, Hu Siqing as Party Secretary Li Zhongmin, Liu Xiaodan as Xiao Wu

A girl named Zhuo Liping commits suicide, but before she dies she accuses a man named He Xiaoxue of having caused her to take this action. He Xiaoxue is a city foreign trade bureau cadre, and the adopted son of the city's Party Secretary. A difficult investigation

Third Sister Liu. **Third Sister Liu (Huang Wanqiu) in a happy moment with her lover A Niu (Liu Shilong). 1960. Changchun Film Studio, Guangxi Film Studio Co-Production.**

turns up evidence that He Xiaoxue had raped Zhuo, and then tried to drown her when he found she was pregnant. She survived the attack, but miscarried, leading to her decision to kill herself. But investigators find further evidence that the case is not this simple, and robbery and smuggling lie behind it.

2095. *This Is My Duty (Zhe Shi Wo Ying Gai Zuo De)*

1965. Haiyan Film Studio. B & W. 9 Reels. Direction: Zhang Tianxi. Screenplay: Li Tianji. Cinematography: Li Kui. Art Direction: Xie Muqian. Music: Xiang Yi. Sound: Ren Xinliang. Cast: Yang Zhaibao as Ding Gengbao, Li Lingjun as Liu Xiaomei, Zhou Kangyu as Liu Jun, Xu Caigeng as Wu Dalong, Shi Shugui as Li Yuzhen, Zhao Shuyin as the head nurse

Shanghai pedicab driver Ding Gengbao is devoted to serving others. At an industrial exhibition, he overhears that Fujian province's agricultural model worker Liu Xiaomei has been unsuccessfully searching for her father for more than 20 years. Ding volunteers to help her, although Liu has very little in the way of clues. With the support of his company's Party organization, Liu finds out that the father's

name was Liu Haiwu, and after many difficulties he at last finds the young woman's father. In the end, Ding is elected the representative of all Shanghai pedicab drivers, and goes to Beijing to attend the national advanced worker conference.

2096. *This Is No Misunderstanding (Zhe Bu Shi Wu Hui)*

1982. Shanghai Film Studio. Color. Letterboxed. 10 Reels. Direction: Zhao Huanzhang, Da Shibiao. Screenplay: Zhao Zhiqiang, Zhao Qinrui, Da Shibiao. Cinematography: Luo Zhensheng. Art Direction: Ju Ransheng. Music: Xu Jingxin. Sound: Wang Huimin. Cast: Huo Xiu as Zhong Qi, Chen Ye as Li Xiaoqing, Tie Niu as Jiang Weiping, Ju Naishe as Xu Zhicang, Wu Rongqin as Zhang Wei, Chi Zhongrui as Sun Shuikang

When a district disciplinary committee hears of possible business improprieties at the Four Seasons Vegetable Market, it assigns young female cadre Jiang Zhongqi to investigate the charges. The charges center around two middle managers, a man named Sun Shuikang and a woman named Li Xiaoqing. It happens that the company's general manager

Jiang Weiping is Jiang Zhongqi's brother. He is surprised when his sister briefs him on the charges, and is sure there must be some misunderstanding. When Li Xiaoqing learns of the investigator's relationship to the manager, she avoids Jiang Zhongqi, especially since Li is also Sun Shuikang's girlfriend. Jiang Zhongqi pushes ahead with her investigation, and gradually comes to the conclusion that Li Xiaoqing is an outstanding salesperson. Jiang and her brother argue about this. Li Xiaoqing is impressed with Jiang Zhongqi's commitment to justice, so she tells the investigator all she knows and agrees to assist her in her investigation. In doing so, Li uncovers a mass of evidence indicating corruption on Sun Shuikang's part. For her cooperation with Jiang, Sun angrily breaks up with Li Xiaoqing. But Jiang Weiping refuses to believe Sun is guilty of anything, and keeps him on as his chief salesperson. In the end, Sun is proven to be guilty of embezzlement and involvement in smuggling as well. This was not just a misunderstanding, but a major case of white-collar crime.

2097. *This Life of Mine (Wo Zhe Yi Bei Zi)*

1950. Wenhua Film Company. B & W. 12 Reels. Direction: Shi Hui. Screenplay: Yang Liuqing, adapted from the novelette by Lao She (1899–1966). Cinematography: Ge Weiqin and Lin Fa. Set Design: Wang Yuebai. Music: Huang Yijun. Sound: Shen Yimin, Bao Geng and Guo Liang. Costume: Qi Qiuming. Makeup: Cheng Zhi. Cast: Shi Hui as "I," Wei Helin as Old Zhao, Shen Yang as Shen Yuan, Li Wei as Hai Fu, Cheng Zhi as Hu Li, Cui Chaoming as Sun Yuan, Jiang Xiu as Master Qin, Lin Zhen as Madame Qin, Liang Ming as Sun Yuanqin, Wang Min as My Wife

Fifty years of modern Chinese history through the eyes of a Beijing policeman, known simply as "I."

At the end of the Qing Dynasty, "I" is an unemployed young man in his 20s. With an introduction from Old Zhao, a veteran policeman living in the same housing compound, "I" becomes a Qing government policeman. At that time, the Qing army and police were very corrupt, holding a virtual license to murder, burn, rape and steal, with no one daring to oppose them. Not long after, the Qing government is overthrown by Sun Yatsen's revolutionary army. "I" is assigned as the doorkeeper guarding the home of Master Qin, a high-

ranking official in the new government. But witnessing his family's luxurious lifestyle and corruption, "I" begins to lose his high hopes for the nation's future.

The "May Fourth" student movement erupts in 1919, and Master Qin is deposed. "I" is promoted to Inspector, and becomes acquainted with student movement leader Shen Yuan. A few years later, Master Qin regains power and "I" is again assigned as his doorkeeper. Master Qin's position is higher but the people are even poorer. "I" is demoted in rank and his wife dies, leaving him with a daughter and son to raise alone. Life becomes harder. When the Japanese invade China, the Nationalist government chooses to follow a policy of non-resistance, and the country is soon occupied by the Japanese. The policeman's son joins the CPC's Eighth Route Army. After that, Shen Yuan is arrested. After the Japanese are defeated, the Nationalists begin seeking out Communists and their sympathizers. "I" is jailed because of his son's service in the Eighth Route Army. In jail, "I" meets Shen Yuan, and with the latter's help, becomes more progressive in his thinking. After the liberation of Beijing, "I" finds his son and joins the revolutionary movement.

2098. *A Thousand Miles a Day (Yi Ri Qian Li)*

1958. August First Film Studio. B & W. 7 Reels. Direction: Yan Jizhou. Cinematography: Zhang Dongliang. Art Direction: Kou Honglie. Music: Gao Ruxing. Sound: Li Bojian. Three stories of progress during the Great Leap Forward:

A "Big Character Poster" (Yi Zhang Da Zi Bao). Screenplay: Zhen Hong, Ma Jixing, Li Jun and Yan Jizhou. Cast: Gu Zhonglin as Xingwang, Wu Fan as Sister Qiao, Li Huan as Mother, Li Li as the carpenter, Du Bing as Fengxian, Zhao Xuemin as the secretary. A production team in the "Forward" agricultural commune puts so much of its workforce into running a factory that there is not enough when the time arrives to fertilize the corn fields. Team leader Sister Qiao tries to make an automated spreader to save labor, but her brother Xingwang, production director, criticizes her. Sister Qiao writes a big character poster criticizing her brother's conservatism. Shortly after that, her fertilizer spreader is successfully tested, so Xingwang realizes his mistakes and writes a big character poster criticizing himself.

This Life of Mine. **Beijing policeman "I" (Shi Hui, left) finds his duties extend beyond law enforcement. 1950. Wenhua Film Studio.**

The "Great Leap's Sound Is Everywhere" (Chu Chu Yue Jin Sheng). Screenplay: Yan Jizhou. Cast: Liu Jiyun as Mr. Dong, Wang Xiaotang as Xiao Xia, Su Youlin as Old Zhang, Cu Min as a famous actor, Ha Zhgang as Han Xing, Tian Ping as the factory director. A china manufacturer runs out of fire resistant bricks just as they have to fill a large rush order. To produce in volume, they expand an automatic oven. In the rush production site they find they have run out of fire resistant bricks at a time that warehouse keeper Mr. Dong is not there. When Mr. Dong hears of this, he hurries back to the factory to handle the matter.

"On the Train" (Huocheshang). Screenplay: Li Jun. Cast: Qian Shurong as Zhu Xiulan, Li Weixing as Dawei, Xing Jitian as the writer, Zhang Chi as the factory director. "Forward" agricultural commune director Zhu Xiulan travels by train to purchase a water pump for the commune mill, but she accidentally loses her money. Her fellow passengers all donate money for her to buy the pump. Her money is found and returned to her by a janitor at one of the railway stations along the way,

but by that time there is no way to return the money to those who had donated it. So the mill installs a second pump to support the commune.

2099. *A Thousand Women Remake the Sea (Qian Nu Nao Hai)*

1958. Tianma Film Studio. B & W. 9 Reels. Direction: Tian Ran. Screenplay: Huang Shui, Jiang Sheng. Cinematography: Shen Xilin. Art Direction: Wang Yuebai. Music: Huang Zhun. Sound: Gong Jianqing. Cast: Xiang Mei as Liu Haiju, Zhang Changqian as Secretary Lu, Wang Bolun as Mr. Gui, Xu Man as the woman logistics specialist, Li Fengqi as the old crippled man, Lu Zhian as Ermei, Zhao Minqiang as Agen, Tai Keming as Ju Mu

During the Great Leap Forward campaign, Langhua and Jinxing, two fishing communes on the coast of Zhejiang province, hold a contest. Led by a young girl named Liu Haiju, a group of women from Langhua commune break with standard practice and request they be allowed to fish at sea. With the support of Party Secretary Lu she overcomes various obstacles, learns to operate a boat, and changes the traditional thinking that women are only suited for fishing from the shore. When Haiju finally leads the women to sea, they greatly improve the size of their catch and surpass their production target. At the judging, Langhua commune is declared the winner.

2100. *Three and a Half Couples and One Thief (San Dui Ban Qing Lu He Yi Ge Xiao Tou)*

1989. Changchun Film Studio. Color. Letterboxed. 10 Reels. Direction: Cui Dongsheng. Screenplay: He Guopu, Cui Dongsheng. Cinematography: Wang Jishun. Art Direction: Gong Minhui. Music: Tang Yuanru, Zhufeng. Sound: Tong Zongde. Cast: Zhang Duofu as Li Jie, Gai Lili as Wang Yan, Xu Shouqin as Director Jia

Young worker Li Jie and his girlfriend Wang Yan take a vacation trip together to Guilin Province. On the trip, a number of embarrassing incidents happen to the couple, all due to their lack of education. After they return to Shanghai, the couple want to attend night school to catch up on the formal education they lack, but find that the school they had in mind has been converted into a business, and its classroom building is now the company's warehouse.

2101. *Three Daring Daughters (Hua Zi Mei Feng Liu Zai)*

1993. Beijing Film Studio. Color. 10 Reels. Direction: Zhang Junzhao. Screenplay: Gao Xin, based on Xuan Xiaofu's original novel. Cinematography: Cai Xiaopeng. Art Direction: Li Qining. Music: Du Jiangang. Sound: Lin Lin. Costume: Chen Aimei, Tian Geng. Makeup: Shen Yueying. Cast: Jin Feng as Zhong Danong, Huang Jingshan as Mrs. Zhong, Wen Bo as Zhong Banban, Nai An as Zhong Ruirui, Ju Ying as Zhong Duoduo, Si Zhaoxin as Ding Jiyong, Li Jun as Zhao Shiwei, Jia Hongsheng as Ding Fanfu, Zhen Zhili as Shao Raode

Taiwan flower gardener Zhong Dalong has three beautiful daughters: Banban, Ruirui and Duoduo. The three young women are quite unlike in personality and character, and each pursues a love affair to a differing conclusion.

2102. *Three Eight on the Riverbank (San Ba He Bian)*

1958. Jiangnan Film Studio. B & W. 10 Reels. Direction: Huang Zhumo. Screenplay: Lu Yanzhou. Cinematography: Zhang Xiling. Art Direction: Liu Pan. Sound: Lin Bingsheng. Cast: Zhang Ruifang as Chen Shuzhen, Zhang Zhiliang as Yang Defeng, Shi Wei as Li Yin, Mao Lu as Shuzhen's father, Huang Naishuang as Shuzhen's mother, Liu Jie as Li Chaofang, Cui Zhaoming as Zhou Xialu

Anhui province peasant woman Chen Shuzhen responds to the Party's call by joining an agricultural mutual assistance group. But when she sees that it excludes some women, she drops out of the original group and with the help of political instructor Yang Defeng, forms a new group called the "Three Eight," made up of previously unorganized women. They encounter considerable difficulty in producing, but overcome all and obtain a record harvest. During the 1957 anti-rightist campaign, Chen successfully battles commune director Zhou Xialu over his wholesaling and purchasing policies. She also leads the farmers in a project to tame the river and irrigate their fields. Finally, under her leadership, a people's commune is established.

2103. *Three Family Lane (Parts 1 & 2) (San Jia Xiang)*

1982. Pearl River Film Studio. Color. 16 Reels. Direction: Wang Weiyi. Screenplay: Zen Wei, Wang Weiyi. Cinematography: Wang Yunhui. Art Direction: Li Pingye. Music: Yang Hua. Sound: Lin Guang. Cast: Ye Yayi as Chen Wenting, Rui Xuhua as Chen Wenxiong, Li Yajun as Zhou Rong, Xu Ruiping as Chen Wendi, Li Shulan as Zhou Quan, Xue Bai as Qu Tao, Lin Yunhong as He Shouren, Sun Qixin as Zhou Bing

Three families of three different classes live on a certain street in Guangzhou (Canton) in the 1920s: the He family, of the bureaucratic landlord class; the Chens, of the capitalist class; and the Zhous, a working class family. Influenced by the ideas of the "May Fourth" movement, the young people on the street all want to contribute in some way to China's rebirth and development. The film follows the many complex interactions as these young people go in different political directions. There are also several complicated love stories involved. In the end, the key figure is the Zhou family's youngest son Zhou Bing, who gradually recognizes the domineering nature of the He and Chen families. Zhou Bing becomes more committed to revolution rather than reform, and devotes himself to armed rebellion aimed at the complete overthrow of the old regime.

2104. *Three Hair Learns Business (San Mao Xue Sheng Yi)*

1958. Tianma Film Studio. B & W. 10 Reels. Direction: Huang Zuolin. Screenplay: The Shanghai People's Comedy Troupe Collective, based on an original story by Fan Haha. Cinematography: Xu Qi. Art Direction: Zhang Hancheng, Ling Lei. Music: Yun Fan. Sound: Zhu Weigang, Wu Hua. Cast: Wen Bingbing as Three Hair, Yu Xiangming as Master, Ma Qiuying as Big Sister, Liu Xiasheng as the barber, Mai Jing as the boss's wife, Nen Niang as Xiao Ying, Fan Haha as Blind Wu

Before liberation, "Three Hair," a poor child, comes from the countryside to Shanghai to find work. He locates a distant relative who turns out to be a gang leader teaching children to steal. The relative takes Three Hair in, but since the newcomer refuses to do anything harmful to others, he is kicked out. He is then accepted as a barber's apprentice, on the condition that he will first serve a fortune teller called Blind Wu. But Three Hair is badly abused there, and finally he and Xiao Ying, a little girl in service to the fortune teller, rebel and exact their revenge. The two children then flee together to seek their future.

2105. *Three Missing Persons (San Ge Shi Zhong De Ren)*

1980. August First Film Studio. Wide Screen. Color. 9 Reels. Direction: Yan Jizhou, Li Jing. Cinematography: Xue Boqin, Bai Fujin. Art Direction: Tang Shiyun. Music: Gong Zhiwei. Sound: He Baoding. Cast: Long Yishun as Jiao Jinhu, Yu Shaokang as Che Laogui, Yi Bo as Tong Xiuhua

During the Second Chinese Civil War, the Nationalists attack the Communist-held Shanganning area. As a strategic move, Communist leaders decide to temporarily abandon Yanan. When one company breaks through the Nationalist encirclement, platoon leader Jiao Jinhu, chief nurse Tong Xiuhua and food service squad leader Chen Laogui are cut off from the rest of the unit. Though badly wounded, Jiao Jinhu still takes every chance he gets to harass the enemy. Tong Xiuhua is captured, but never gives up despite being abused and tortured. Food service squad leader Chen Laogui conceals himself in the forest as a sniper. When her captors are moving Tong Xiuhua to another place, Jiao Jinhu seizes the chance to attack her escort and free her. In a counterattack on the enemy's base, the three "missing persons" meet again on the battlefield. They coordinate the Red Army's main force in a successful takeover of the enemy base. But just at the moment of victory, old veteran Chen Changgui is killed.

2106. *Three Mothers (San Ge Mu Qin)*

1959. Haiyan Film Studio. B & W. 10 Reels. Direction: Xu Sulin. Screenplay by Wu Saiwen, based on his opera of the same title. Cinematography: Zhang Guifu. Art Direction: Zong Yongqing. Music: Liu Ruyzeng. Sound: Wang Huiming. Cast: Wu Saiwen as Mrs. Zhou, Qian Aili as Wang's wife, Wang Shanqiao as Wang Zhengting, Wang Aiyu as the blind woman, Li Shoucheng as Jianhua (as a child), Lu Jusheng as Jianhua (as an adult), Bi Sha as Axiang (as a child), Tang Wen as Axiang (as an adult), Pei Zhuozhuo as Lin Ziping, Wang Xueyan as the second wife

Before liberation, construction worker Wang Zhengting is injured on the job, but has to borrow the money for his medical treatment from his boss, Lin Ziping. To repay the debt, Wang must give one of his newborn twins to Lin's second wife. She chooses the boy, Baoer. But the second wife soon commits suicide in despair over losing Boss Lin's love, and the Lin family wants to abandon Baoer. Lin's housekeeper Mrs. Zhou takes the baby home with her, planning to return him to the Wangs, but their house is destroyed in the war and she cannot find them. So she adopts Baoer, giving him the name Jianhua. A shortage of housing forces Mrs. Zhou and the boy to move to her hometown of Suzhou, where Jianhua grows up. After liberation, Jianhua joins the Chinese Army and serves in Korea. When he returns to China, he finds a job on a bridge construction site in Wuhan, where he unknowingly works alongside his father Wang Zhengting and his twin sister Axiang. One day, Mrs. Zhou comes to visit Jianhua, and seeing the Wangs there, she explains to them that he is the long-lost twin Baoer. The family is finally reunited.

2107. *Three Nameless Heroes (Wu Ming San Xia Ke)*

1992. Beijing Film Studio. Color. Letterboxed. 9 Reels. Direction: Huo Zuang. Screenplay: Yuan Lang. Cinematography: Tian Jianmin. Art Direction: Tu Juhua, Yang Yunhui. Music: Zhang Fuquan. Sound: Wang Yunhua. Costume: Dong Xiuqin. Makeup: Liu Dan. Cast: Wang Yu as Number One, Zhang Chunyan as Fifth Lotus

Blossom, Huang Degang as Number Two, Zhou Long as Number Three, Li Zhizhou as Yang Wei, Li Xuliang as Zhang Ren

In imperial China, the Yangzhou area is hit by a massive flood, depriving many people of their livelihood. Meanwhile, the governor of another region collects money from his people as gifts for the ministers in the capital, and assigns one of his officials to deliver the gift money. Three nameless heroes decide to intercept the courier and take the money for relief of the flood victims. Some bandits also want to get the money. The three nameless heroes are joined by a heroine called Fifth Lotus Blossom. A series of struggles follows, but at last justice prevails and the money is distributed among the people of Yangzhou.

2108. *Three Payees (Zhe Bei Zi Bu Qian Ni)*

1994. Changchun Film Studio. Color. Letterboxed. 9 Reels. Direction: Ge Ritai. Screenplay: Mao Jie, Mao Xiaofeng. Cinematography: Shu Li, Ba Te. Art Direction: Shen Huimin. Music: Fan Weiqiang. Sound: Meng Gang. Costume: Li Shuyan. Makeup: Liu Jiao. Cast: Hu Yajie as Ding Zhong, Xia Lixin as Xu Xuefei, Fang Zige as Lao Ma, Guo Renjin as Gai Shu, Ling Qiang as Zhang Yude, Huang Xia as Ya Dan, Xiang Xiang as Cheng Ning, Hu Lianhua as Jiang Ke, Guo Yong as Liu Erli, Di Jianqing as He Lizhang, Jing Zhenqi as Boss Zhu

A food processing plant in a certain city is on the verge of collapse due to its inability to collect debts owed to it. The plant director sends three of his employees, two men and a woman, to collect. The three try everything they can think of, including trickery, crying jags in the debtor company's office and even fighting. At last they accomplish their mission, and during the process establish friendships with several of the debtor company's employees.

2109. *Three Sad and Happy Brothers (Ku Le San Xiong Di)*

1991. Changchun Film Studio. Color. Letterboxed. 9 Reels. Direction: Wang Xuexin. Screenplay: Wang Xingdong, Wang Zhebing. Cinematography: Ning Changcheng. Art Direction: Qi Min. Music: Shi Xin, Meng Weidong. Sound: Zhang Fenglu. Cast: Yu Huadong as Lu Deng, Cui Tao as Little Zhuge, Pan Jie as Sima Gu, Guo Tao as Yage, Liu Dudu as Lu Biaobiao

Three disabled men, Lu Deng, Little

Zhuge and Yage, run a tailor shop producing special size clothing. They work very hard and their shop prospers. A man named Dai Tian comes to town and meets Lu Deng's ex-wife Sima Gu. She still owns the property the shop is located on, and leases it to Lu Deng and his friends. Dai Tian wants the property for a hotel he plans to build. He fools Sima Gu into signing the property over to him, after which he evicts the three men and closes their shop. But the three find that people really need them, and eventually they overcome their difficulties and reopen their business.

Three Swordsmen see *Saber, Sword, Smile*

2110. *Three War Buddies (San Ge Zhan You)*

1958. August First Film Studio. B & W. 9 Reels. Direction: Wang Shaoyan. Screenplay: Zhen Hong, based on the stage play of the same title. Cinematography: Li Erkang. Art Direction: Yang Wei. Music: Han Yongcang. Sound: He Baoding. Cast: Fang Hui as Lu Fengyang, Zhen Baomin as Huang Ruijiang, Liu Han as Zhou Hong, Wu Suqing as Zhou Huiyin, Wu Fan as Sister Qiu, Lan Yin as Zhou's mother

In Guangdong province, agricultural commune Director Lu Fengyang, agricultural commune Production Director Huang Ruijiang and local CPC Branch Secretary Zhou Hong are three old friends from wartime. All three had returned to their hometown after being discharged to take part in farm production. But in the new farm production situation, the three have their differences, many of them due to the arrogance and selfishness of Lu Fengyang. Lu finally realizes his errors and the three overcome the problems.

2111. *Three Women and One Dream (San Ge Nu Ren Yi Ge Meng)*

1992. Shanghai Film Studio. Color. Letterboxed. 10 Reels. Direction: Jiang Haiyang. Screenplay: Zhang Xian, Jiang Haiyang. Cinematography: Wang Tianling. Art Direction: Guo Dongcang. Costume: Zhang Lifang. Makeup: Zhu Liping. Cast: Zhen Shuang as Ning Meng, Fang Shu as Lin Bai, Wang Lan as Lan Niao

Ning Meng and Lin Bai are good friends as well as co-workers, operating a popular radio music request line. Ning Meng is a particular fan favorite, although she just reads what has been written for her by Lin Bai, who does all the writing and production planning for the program. Ning Meng answers a fan letter from a young man and agrees to meet him. They have a love affair, but when she decides to break it off, she dumps her lover rather cruelly, and manipulates her action to make it appear Lin Bai caused the breakup. Eventually, the distraught and discarded lover takes his own life. Ning Meng's selfishness and driving ambition hurt too many people, and Lin Bai finally decides her erstwhile friend must be stopped. Lin Bai begins to compete with Ning Meng, pushing herself increasingly to the forefront in the program and no longer just Ning's supporter. At last, Lin Bai wins over the audience for herself.

2112. *Three Women Dumping Their Husbands (San Nu Xiu Fu)*

1994. Guangxi Film Studio. Color. Letterboxed. 10 Reels. Direction: Luo Yuzhong. Screenplay: Wang Weiyi. Cinematography: Ning Jiakun. Art Direction: Lei Xiaolan. Music: Ma Lan. Sound: Li Yunping. Costume: Chen Aimei. Makeup: Yang Shudong, Ji Weihua. Cast: Pan Changjiang as Que Lihou, Huang Suying as the matchmaker, Geng Yi as Miss Zou, Xie Xu as the girl Li, Guli Zhaoer as the foreign wife, He Xiulan as Yichun

A sex farce about a man who marries three women, Chinese and foreign, in different dynasties and in different cultures. They all end up dumping him.

2113. *Three Years (San Nian)*

1954. Shanghai Film Studio. B & W. 10 Reels. Direction: Zhao Ming. Screenplay: Ge Qing. Cinematography: Feng Shizhi. Set Design: Huang Chong. Music: Chen Gexin. Sound: Li Liehong. Makeup: Chen Yan. Cast: Zhang Ruifang as Zhao Xiumei, Xiang Kun as Luo Xicheng, Shu Shi as Wu Yifan, Bo Li as Chen Ying, Lan Gu as Chen Caiming, Lin Zhiao as Engineer Xu

Shortly after the People's Republic is established, the Western nations apply economic sanctions on China. Luo Xicheng, a Shanghai capitalist textile mill owner, exploits the situation by withholding the wages of his workers, using the excuse that he can no longer import cotton and therefore must halt production. Meanwhile, he secretly transfers his capital to Hong Kong in preparation of expanding his textile plant there. After he leaves, the Plant Director Wu, the labor union head Zhao Xi-

umei and a worker named Chen Ying provide the leadership to the other workers in overcoming all difficulties and resuming production. One year later, Luo Xicheng suffers substantial losses in Hong Kong's capitalist market, and seeing how the Shanghai plant has developed and prospered, he returns. But his earlier illegal activities result in his being arrested and placed on trial during the "Five Anti" campaign of 1952.

2114. *Throat Cutting Sword (Duan Hou Jian)*

1988. Shanghai Film Studio. Color. Letterboxed. 11 Reels. Direction: Li Xiepu. Screenplay: Li Xiao. Cinematography: Liu Lihua. Art Direction: Zhao Xianrui. Music: Liu Yanxi. Sound: Zhou Hengliang, Xu Xiushan. Cast: Zhang Hong as Fang Zhao, Gai Lili as Hei Yanzhi, Zhang Xueao as Jin Zhihu, Wu Chunsheng as Fang Guoyi, Zhang Xiaozhong as Fu Jiangbao

In legend, after the fall of court official Li Zicheng, his close follower Ma Long kills Li's associate Fang Guoyi and steals all the treasures of the imperial court. More than 10 years later, Fang Guoyi's son Fang Zhao, now an adult, seeks to avenge his father's murder. Fang Zhao meets super kung fu expert Hei Yanzhi, and they pursue this together. But things turn out to be quite different from what Fang Zhao thought: his father Fang Guoyi turns out to be very much alive, and has devoted his life to protecting Li Zicheng. When Fang Zhao learns this, to prove he will maintain the secret intact, Fang Zhao kills himself in front of his father. The person most upset by this is his close friend Hei Yanzhi.

2115. *Thrown Together by Fate (Tian Yin)*

1987. Beijing Film Studio. Color. Widescreen. 10 Reels. Direction: Zhang Huaxun. Screenplay: Zhang Huaxun and Li Guangliang, Yang Congjie, Feng Yucuan. Cinematography: Zhang Li, Zhao Peng. Art Direction: Ma Jiesheng. Music: Lei Lei. Sound: Guan Shuxin. Cast: Zhao Xiaorui as Haniniu, Xu Shouli as Fusako Yamada, Guan Zongxiang as Hainiu's father, Zhang Chengxian as Uncle Jiang

In 1942, young Chinese fisherman Hainiu is conscripted and shipped to Japan to do forced labor. On the way he risks his life to jump overboard and escape to a desert island. He lives alone there until one day he rescues a Japanese army prostitute named Fusako

Yamada who washes up on shore. Unable to bear her life in China, she had disguised herself as a Chinese girl and tried to escape back to Japan, winding up on the island when the ship sunk. Their common fate takes Hainiu and Fusako from initial hostility to mutual understanding and at last love. Three years pass, and they have a small son they call Niuniu. However, they and their island are discovered by a group of Japanese soldiers fleeing when the imperial army collapsed. They murder Hainiu and then rape and kill Fusako. Little Niuniu sits alone on the beach crying.

2116. *Thunderstorm (Lei Yu)*

1984. Shanghai Film Studio. Color. Wide Screen. 12 Reels. Direction: Sun Daolin. Screenplay: Sun Daolin, based on the novel of the same title by Cao Yu (1910–). Cinematography: Luo Chongzhou. Art Direction: Han Shangyi, Ju Ransheng. Music: Lu Qimin. Sound: Miao Zhenyu, Feng Deyao. Cast: Sun Daolin as Zhou Puyuan, Gu Yongfei as Fan Yi, Ma Xiaowei as Zhou Ping, Hu Qingshu as Lu Gui, Liang Tongyu as Lu Dahai, Qin Yi as Lu the servant, Zhang Yu as Sifeng, Zhong Ao as Zhou Chong

In early 20th century North China lives the Zhou household, headed by Zhou Puyuan, president of a coal mining company. As a young man some 30 years earlier, Zhou Puyuan had fallen in love with Mei Siping, a servant in his family's household. The two had a son, Zhou Ping, but after the baby was born, the family had sent Mei Siping away and forced Zhou Puyuan to marry a woman of good family. Zhou Puyuan now has a new, young wife Fan Yi, but out of depression and loneliness she is having an affair with his son Zhou Ping. Working in the household is a servant named Sifeng, a girl born to Siping after she left the Zhou family home. Zhou Ping falls for her and gets her pregnant. When Mei Siping arrives and finds her daughter works for the Zhous and in the same situation she had been in 30 years before, it sets off a series of tragedies which end with the deaths of two of the principals and the spiritual destruction of the Zhou family.

Best Sound Miao Zhenyu and Feng Deyao, 1985 Golden Rooster Awards.

2117. *Tian Ci (Tian Ci)*

1983. Pearl River Film Studio. Color. 9 Reels. Direction: Yu Deshui. Screenplay: Dai Jiang. Cinematography: Ye Zhengmin, Ma Liguo. Art Direction: Zhou Chengren. Music: Zhen Qiufeng. Sound: Li Xun. Cast: Ma Chongle as Tian Chi, Hu Lingling as Mrs. Cai, Pu Chaoyin as Xia Lan, Zhang Huaizhi as A Fa

In the late 1940s, a poor farmer named Tian Ci lives in the village of Chaoshan in Guangdong province. Orphaned since early childhood, Tian Ci is a lonely but very kindly young man. On one occasion, he takes sympathy on Xia Lan, a poor little girl mistreated by a landlord, and leaves her some food gifts. For this, the landlord has him beaten nearly to death. Several years later, when he makes arrangements to meet an eligible girl, he discovers the girl is Xia Lan, but fate forces the two to separate before they can marry. A few years later, during a time when his village is flooded with refugees from a natural disaster, Tian Ci once again tries to find a wife through a matchmaker. He is cheated, however, and the woman chosen for him turns out to be Cai Ma, a middle-aged widow with a daughter. She desperately needs a man to support her, and the kind-hearted Tian Ci accepts her. They work very hard, and do have a happy family life until one day Cai Ma's "dead" husband sends her a letter asking her to come to him. Tian Ci lets her go, and raises her young daughter by himself. One day, someone introduces him to another widow. It turns out to be Xia Lan, and the two at last get together.

2118. *Tiannu (Tian Nu)*

1983. Changchun Film Studio. Color. 9 Reels. Direction: Li Qiankuan, Xiao Guiyun. Screenplay: He Mingyan. Cinematography: Wu Bengli. Art Direction: Zhong Quan. Music: Jin Xiang. Sound: Li Zhenduo. Cast: Hong Xueming as Meng Tiannu, Huang Xiaolei as Li Hua, Quan Jingzhi as Mother, Wang Qi as Meng's mother, Yi Da as Shanmei

In the winter of 1969, Shanghai girl Meng Tiannu is assigned to work in a mountainous area of Northeast China. She and a local man named Li Hua work together on developing a new, frost-resistant rice variety, and during this time they fall in love and marry. After the Gang of Four is smashed, Tiannu's mother is restored to her position, but she cannot understand her daughter's marriage. When she finds out the young couple fell in love while sharing the hard life at a remote work site, she invites her daughter to come with her family on a visit to Shanghai. Mother and daughter have a tearful and joyous reunion, and when Li Hua sees how happy his wife is to be back he insists she remain for an extended visit, while he goes back home alone. When Tiannu returns to Northeast China, she is stunned to find her husband filing for divorce. When she asks him why, he explains that he knows she will be happier in Shanghai. She tells him he is mistaken, that her heart is with him and their work together. The happily reconciled couple looks forward to the future.

2119. *Tide of Dancing Women (Wu Chao)*

1995. Beijing Film Studio, Beijing Zhuda Digital Creation Film & Television Company Co-Production. Color. Letterboxed. Direction: Shen Yue. Cinematography: Ge'ertu, Li Tao. Art Direction: Xiao Shizeng, Zhou Yisha. Cast: Wang Yanping as Lin Ruoqing, Chen Daoming as Li Junshi

In the late 1930s, beautiful Lin Ruoqin is a dancer in a Beijing dance hall. There she meets Li Junshi, scion of a wealthy family, and just returned from college abroad. The couple have little time to develop their mutual attraction, as Li is on his way to join the anti–Japanese resistance. Later, when the invaders move on Beijing, Lin flees to Shanghai where she finds work at a dance hall and becomes the toast of the town. Li Junshi comes to Shanghai on leave from the army, they get together again and fall in love. A man called Mr. Fu asks Lin to take advantage of her relationship with Li to kill a notorious Japanese collaborator called Ding Muchun. She agrees to cooperate, but the operation goes awry and Fu and her lover Li Junshi are killed along with the collaborator. Later, Lin and other dancers form a patriotic resistance movement called the "Tide of Dancing Women." After the People's Republic is established, Lin Ruoyan and other dancers are designated for reform training in new lives.

2120. *Tiger Fight (Duo Hu Lian Huan Ji)*

1990. Beijing Film Studio & Lanzhou Film Studio Co-Production with the assistance of the China Film Distribution & Exhibition Corporation. Color. 9 Reels. Wide Screen. Direction: Shi Xian. Screenplay: Zhao Wantang, Zhang Boqing. Cinematography: Rui Shuiren, Nie Zhanjun. Art Direction: Fu Delin. Music: Shi Xin. Sound: Ru Shuiren, Nie Zhanjun. Cast: Mao Hongwei as

He Zixiao, Wang Meiling as Xiuyun, Yu Chengyue as Shi Zimo, Kevin as Jonathan, Huang Fei as County Head

In 1906, Sir Charles Luckson came to China as a member of the Allied Expeditionary Force sent to quell the Boxer Rebellion. While in China, half of a bronze tiger came into Sir Charles' possession. By analyzing the text, Sir Charles learned that the other half of this priceless relic belonged to Li Biyun, a descendant of the Ming Imperial bodyguard. If the two halves could be joined, the text written on the tiger would reveal the whereabouts of a secret cache hidden by one of the last Ming emperors. After a lapse of seven years, Charles sends his son, Jonathan, to China in an attempt to locate the other half of the bronze tiger. Jonathan travels to China using the cover of a Western magic troupe. At that time, Li Has entrusted the bronze tiger to his friend Shi Zimo, who heads the Shi Family Martial Arts Academy. Shi realizes what Jonathan's real intentions are, and together with his daughter Xiuyuan and Li Biyun's son He Zixiao, he eventually seizes the other half of the tiger...

2121. *A Time of Terror (Jing Kong Shi Fen)*

1994. Beijing Film Studio, Tianshan Film Studio Co-Production. Color. Letterboxed. 9 Reels. Direction: Dong Ling. Screenplay: Gao Huanggang. Cinematography: Mulati. Art Direction: Sun Changxi. Music: Mou Hong. Sound: Du Shuyin. Costume: Wang Huiming. Makeup: Han Jianhua. Cast: Yuan Yuan as Delong, Li Ting as Meixia, Wang Rong as Li Fu, Reheman as Lu San, Wu Xin as Jin Yuntai, Tang Zheng as Xiao Yu, Jin Zhong as Jin Gui, Sang Zongzhong as Yuan Gang

Three foreign men steal a valuable pearl from a tomb, after which one of the men kills the other two. The killer, DeLong, plans to smuggle the national treasure out of China to a foreign jewelry dealer. He takes the pearl to the airport in search of a likely courier, and spotting a blind woman with a little boy, he plants the pearl in the child's toy. However, the two were only seeing someone off, not leaving themselves. DeLong follows the woman, Meixia, and her child to retrieve the pearl, and kills a woman taxi driver in the process. When the sightless Meixia becomes aware of what is going on, the pursuit becomes a battle of wits and courage between her and the killer. In the end, Meixia triumphs over the criminal and recovers the pearl for the country.

2122. *The Tin City Story (aka The Miners' Song) (Xi Cheng De Gu Shi/Guang Gong Zhi Ge)*

1959. Changchun Film Studio. B & W. 10 Reels. Direction: Zhang Xinshi. Screenplay: Mei Ding. Cinematography: Chen Minhun. Art Direction: Liu Xuerao. Music: Lei Zhenbang, Luo kegong. Sound: Huang Lijia. Cast: Ma Tianqing as Pu Gengqiang, Li Yingju as Pu Pengqiang (as a child), Liu Ren as Yang Degui, Li Baoshan as Wanzhong, Lin Na as Amei, Li Chun as Amei (as a child), Han Yan as Chen Shouting

In Yunnan province, Yi nationality teenager Pu Gengqiang is forced into slave labor in a tin mine. On one occasion, he faints from the strain of heavy labor and is almost beaten to death. He is nursed back to health by Wan Zhong and Yan Degui, two Communist Party members working undercover in the mines. When the Japanese invade China, the mine is bombed and mine owner Chen Shouting closes it and sends the workers home. After the war, Chen plans to re-open the mine, and sends his hired thugs to bring the workers back. Pu Gengqiang, now a young man with a wife, flees rather than go back, but his mother is kicked to death protecting her son's flight. Pu reaches a small town where he meets up again with Wan Zhong, who helps him get a paid job in the mine there. Under Wan's tutelage, Pu becomes an enthusiastic participant in the workers' movement. During a strike, the capitalists murder their old friend Yang Degui, so Wan and Pu join a Communist guerrilla force which wipes out the capitalists, including Chen Shouting. After Liberation, Pu Gengqiang and his wife are reunited.

2123. *To Be Taken In (Shang Yi Dang)*

1992. Fujian Film Studio. Color. Letterboxed. 9 Reels. Direction: He Qun and Liu Baolin. Screenplay: Zhang Xiaolong and Wang Hong, based on the novel "Our Recollections of Youth" by Liang Man. Cinematography: Yu Xiaojun, Zhang Yuan, Yin Yan. Art Direction: Lin Zhihan, Feng Lei. Music: Zhang Shaotong, Liu Lifei, Ma Ding. Sound: Wu Ling, Xu Gang. Costume: Zhang Weimin. Makeup: Zhou Qin. Cast: Ge You as Liu Shan, Ju Xue as Zhen Zhen, Geng Ge as Yang Meng, Li Wenling as Xu Jie, Zhu Hongjia as Gong Shiwei, Kang Xun as Liu Yi, Guan Sheng as Zhou Ling, Deng Wei as Lei Han

Liu Shan's parents go overseas, and when they gain permission to stay there permanently, they begin pressuring their son to join them, but he keeps stalling them. To help out a friend, Liu accepts a temporary contract position as a high school teacher. He has an wonderful experience at the school: his students love him because of his sincerity and openness. However, his girl friend Yang Meng breaks off with him because of his lack of enthusiasm for going abroad. Liu asks his parents to grant him another year's stay in China, but then the school informs him his contract will not be renewed.

2124. *To Die Like a Man (Parts 1 & 2) (Huan Le Ying Xiong) (Part 2 also released as "The Dead and the Living") (Yin Yang Jie)*

1988. Fujian Film Studio. Color. 18 Reels. Wide Screen. Direction: Wu Ziniu. Screenplay: Sima Xiaojia, based on the novel "Stormy Tong River" by Sima Wensen. Cinematography: Yang Wei, Liu Junyun. Art Direction: Tang Peijun, Zhao Shaoping. Music: Shi Wanchun. Sound: Chen Bingkang. Cast: Tao Zeru as Cai Laoliu, Xu Shouli as Yusuan, Shen Junyi as Xu Sanduo, Yang Shaohua as Xu Xiantong, Tu Men as Xu Datou

In the early 1930s, underground Communist Cai Laoliu, who has been living abroad for many years, returns to Fujian province to reunite with his wife Yusuan. When he arrives and finds that she now has a 5-year-old daughter, he angrily destroys their marriage bed. There are other hatreds in that part of China: rivalry between the villages of Lower Mu and Upper Mu has often erupted into violence. When Major Lin Xiongmo of the Nationalist Army takes up his post as Garrison Commander, Cai Laoliu learns that the Major's objective is to keep the two villages from ever getting together. So Cai persuades Lower Mu headman Xu Sanduo to negotiate peace with Upper Mu. But Cai is killed by the Nationalist authorities when his own father informs on him. The grief-stricken Yusuan buries her husband and then burns down their house. Outraged at the killing of his friend, Xu Sanduo goes to the nearby town and engages in a shooting spree, after which he is arrested and jailed by Xu Xiantong, the head of Upper Mu

Village. After the prisoner calms down, he is set free and both sides finally agree to negotiate peace on the day of the Mid-Autumn Festival. However, a mysterious fortune-teller appears and convinces Xu Xiantong's dim-witted foster son Xu Datou to murder his father and sister, then pin the blame on Xu Sanduo of Lower Mu. When the feud between the two villages flares up again, the Nationalist commander seizes the opportunity to move against both villages.

Best Director Wu Ziniu, 1989 Golden Rooster Awards.

Best Actor Tao Zeru, 1989 Golden Rooster Awards.

Best Actress Xu Shouli, 1989 Golden Rooster Awards.

Best Supporting Actor Shen Junyi, 1989 Hundred Flowers Awards.

2125. *To Live (Huo Zhe)*

1993. Era Intl. (H.K.) in association with Shanghai Film Studio. Color. 125 minutes. Direction: Zhang Yimou. Screenplay: Yu Hua, Lu Wei, based on the novel "Lifetimes" by Yu Hua (1960–). Cinematography: Lu Yue. Art Direction: Cao Jiuping. Music: Zhao Jiping. Sound (Dolby): Tao Jing. Cast: Ge You as Fugui, Gong Li as Jiazhen, Niu Ben as Town Chief, Guo Tao as Chunsheng, Jiang Wu as Erxi, Ni Dahong as Long'er, Liu Tianchi as Fengxia, as an adult, Deng Fei as Youqing

Modern Chinese history as seen through the life of one Chinese family. In China in the late 1940s, Fugui, scion of a family of wealth and privilege, gambles away his ancestral home. Leaving his wife and two children, he goes on the road to make a living as a traveling puppeteer, but his performing troupe is conscripted into the Nationalist Army during the Civil War. Fugui is captured by the Communists, who take him into service as a puppeteer. After liberation he returns to his native village a respected Red Army veteran, just in time to see the gambler who won his home executed as a capitalist. Fugui and his wife Jiazhen settle down to family life under communism. But in 1958, their son is killed by an auto driven by Fugui's best friend; both driver and victim were exhausted from excessively long hours of work in the Great Leap Forward campaign to rapidly industrialize the nation. During the Cultural Revolution, their daughter marries a young worker, and Fugui and Jiazhen soon look forward to being grandpar-

ents. But when the baby arrives, the new mother has complications, and the Red Guards running the hospital are lost as to how to help. In the end, the now-elderly grandparents take their grandson to decorate the graves of his mama and uncle.

Best Foreign Film, British Film Academy, 1994

Grand Jury Prize, Cannes Film Festival, 1994

Best Actor, Ge You, Cannes Film Festival, 1994

2126. *To Sea (Xiang Hai Yang)*

1959. Haiyan Film Studio. B & W. 9 Reels. Direction: Lin Yang. Screenplay: Cheng Jingshan, Zhang Daoya, Wu Wen, Tang Jian, Lin Yang. Cinematography: Cao Weiye. Art Direction: Lin Yongqing. Music: Gao Tian. Sound: Chen Jingrong. Makeup: Wang Hanyong. Cast: Wen Xiying as Wang Ping, Gao Bo as Chen Zhizhong, Liu Fei as Ma Guohua, Sun Yongping as Xio Liu, Li Qizhen as Li Bingzheng, Mao Lu as Mr. He

In the fall of 1949, to build a strong navy as rapidly as possible, China's new Communist government assigns many of its best army commanders to naval duty. Wang Ping, former commander of an artillery regiment, is assigned to the warship "Anger" as political commissar. Ship's captain Chen Zhizhong, graduate of the British Royal Naval Academy, had served as executive officer on a Nationalist warship, but left when passed over for promotion to captain. After liberation he joined the people's navy. In training sailors, Chen uses traditional methods. When Wang Ping finds that these training methods are unsuitable to the Party's principles for building the navy rapidly, he suggest the sailors be given shipboard experience along with their studies. Chen believes this too risky, so Chen and Wang argue about it. Finally, after experiencing many setbacks, Chen changes his thinking in the face of reality, and agrees to adopt new training methods which greatly improve efficiency. The first time the "Anger" puts to sea, it encounters the Nationalist warship Captain Chen had served on before, and routs it completely.

2127. *Toast, Woman Soldiers (Gan Bei, Nu Bing Men......)*

1985. Beijing Film Studio. Color. 10 Reels. Direction: Du Yu. Screenplay: Cheng Ping, Long

To Die Like a Man. Xu Sanduo (Shen Junyi, left) and Yusuan (Xu Shouli). 1988. Fujian Film Studio.

Qinling. Cinematography: Sun Cangyi. Art Direction: Mao Kezhan. Music: Ai Liqun. Sound: Zhang Zhizhong. Cast: Liu Jia as Xue Ye, Li Nailun as Lu Juanzhen, Wu Dan as Qiu Xiaofeng, Li Qihou as Huang Yang, Chen Qin as Xue Lian

To get away from an unhappy home life and an abusive stepmother, Beijing girl Xue Ye enlists in the army in 1973 and is assigned to a telecommunications unit. On a field assignment, she rescues a small boy, Xia Xia, from drowning. She meets the boy's father Huang Yang, a music school teacher deserted by the boy's mother. Their mutual attraction soon blossoms into romance. Trouble starts when her stepsister is assigned to her unit. Jealous when Xue Ye receives a promotion, the stepsister spreads some vicious rumors about Xue Ye and the teacher, rumors which lead eventually to the army command ordering that Xue Ye be given an early discharge. She takes Xia Xia with her and cares for him despite the gossip of others. Years pass, and in 1983 her former army comrades gather at the Great Wall to celebrate Xue Ye's finally getting married to Huang Yang. Although happy now, Xue Ye misses military life very much.

2128. *Today Is My Day Off (Jin Tian Wo Xiu Xi)*

1959. Haiyan Film Studio. B & W. 9 Reels. Direction: Lu Ren. Screenplay: Li Tianji. Cinematography: Zhang Guifu. Art Direction: Zhang Xibai. Music: Shi Yongkang. Sound: Zhou Hengliang. Cast: Zong Xinghuo as Ma Tianmin, Ma Ji as Yao Meizhen, Li Baoluo as an old farmer, Shangguan Yunzhu as the chief physician, Wang Sujiang as the team leader, Shi Yuan as Luo Ailan, Zhao Shuyin as Liu Ping, Qiang Ming as Director Yu, Chen Shu as the barber, Li Huanqing as Wang Xiuling, Gao Zheng as Liu Qi

It is policeman Ma Tianmin's day off, and his chief's wife Yao Meizhen has fixed him up with Liu Ping, a young woman she knows. On his way to keep the date, Ma Tianmin helps an old farmer rescue one of his little pigs which has fallen into a stream, he helps a man get his sick children to a hospital emergency ward, and returns a wallet and train ticket to the person who lost them. Since he stopped to do all these things, he misses the time of the date, and Liu Ping's home is dark when he arrives. Miffed at being stood up, the young woman treats him coldly. But as it turns out, the old farmer he stopped to help was Liu Ping's father, who praises the young man very highly. When Liu Ping finally learns that Ma Tianmin's kindness and consideration for others caused him to be late, her opinion of him improves considerably.

2129. *Tonight There Will Be a Snowstorm (Jin Ye You Bao Feng Yu)*

1984. Changchun Film Studio. Color. Wide Screen. 10 Reels. Direction: Sun Yu. Screenplay: Xiao Lijun, Dai Zhiqi, Sun Yu. Cinematography: Zhong Wenmin. Art Direction: Ye Jiren. Music: Wu Damin. Sound: Chen Wenyuan, Fu Lingge. Cast: Chen Daomin as Cao Tieqiang, Yu Li as Pei Xiaoyun, Liu Cangwei as Can Shuwen, Han Guangping as Zhen Yuru, Dan Weihong as Liu Maike

In the North China border region of Beidahuang, in the winter of 1979, young woman soldier Pei Xiaoyun proudly goes to her first guard duty. A major winter storm is due to hit the area that same night. There is much dissension back at the barracks: with the recent downfall of the Gang of Four, intellectuals who had been sent to the rural areas during the Cultural Revolution are now flooding back to China's cities, and many of Pei Xiaoyun's comrades want to go home as well. Most of the troops at Beidahuang are educated young people assigned to doing construction work for the military. The regimental commander at Beidahuang has to keep them for a while longer, as they cannot all return at the same time. As the night wears on, the dissidents argue and bicker with their officers and with each other. In addition, Mess Sergeant Liu Maike's wife is about to give birth. One of the group tries to rob the installation's bank, and when Liu tries to prevent this he is fatally stabbed. Before dying, he shoots and kills the robber. Just at that moment his wife gives birth to a son. The storm hits, and then a fire breaks out in a warehouse. When the fire is out, they recall that in the confusion the guard was unchanged. Pei Xiaoyun is found dead in the snow. The next morning, with the storm past, all is calm again. Chastened by it all, Cao Tieqiang and Can Shuwen decide to relinquish their right to return, and move to another construction assignment.

2130. *Top (Luo Xuan)*

1981. August First Film Studio. Color. Letterboxed. 9 Reels. Direction: Bai Fujin. Screenplay: Huang Ying. Cinematography: Bai Fujin, Wang Jianguo. Art Direction: Cui Denggao. Music: Li Weicai. Sound: Song Tianpei. Cast: Liu Linian as Liang Dapeng, Zhao Xiuling as Zhang Lei, Sun Jitang as Gao Ermin, Gu Lan as Director Chen, Zhao Ruping as Director Shi

In the summer of 1977, missile design engineer Zhang Lei returns to her beloved job after having to spend several years in the countryside. While happy to be back, she is upset that work has stopped on the "Miracle Arrow No. 5" missile project and is able to get it started again. She is also not pleased that her former lover Liang Dapeng is in charge of missile testing, for she blames him for the false accusations which got her in trouble 10 years before. The two try to establish a working relationship which will not damage the work, and in time Zhang Lei finds out Liang Dapeng was an innocent person, not the one who ruined her. Meanwhile, various other forces are working to get the missile project halted again, but Zhang Lei is able to overcome them. The project is successful, and she and Liang Dapeng get together again.

2131. *Top Secret (Jue Mi Xing Dong)*

1992. Guangxi Film Studio. Color. Letterboxed. 9 Reels. Direction: Xu Cangling, Lu Dongqin. Screenplay: Gong Sida, Luo Bangwu, Pao Xueqian. Cinematography: Lu Dongqin. Art Direction: Zhang Yafang. Music: Jin Fuzhai. Sound: Han Weijun. Costume: Mei Ling. Makeup: Dang Dongdong. Cast: Mao Yongmin as Liu Daha, Sun Jihong as Jin Ping, Shen Fa as Ma Tai, Xu Guanghe as the short man, Wang Wei as the tall woman

Yuzhou Chemical Plant Director Ma Tai orders his driver Liu Daha and his secretary Jin Ping to quietly move a truckload of waste out to the suburbs and dump it there. At the same time, another man and woman are driving an identical truck to the suburbs as part of a drug deal. As each couple carries out their covert mission, they wind up exchanging trucks by mistake. This sets off a series of misadventures which ends with police apprehending the drug dealers.

2132. *The Torrent (Ji Liu)*

1960. Haiyan Film Studio. B & W. 11 Reels. Direction: Qiangming. Screenplay: Fei Liwen, Qiangming. Cinematography: Chen Zhengxiang. Art Direction: Zhang Wanhong. Music: Xiao Leng, Zhang Linghao, Yin Handuan, Liang

Liang. Cast: Jiang Jun as Tian Fang, Gao Zheng as Liang Zhiping, Jiang Tianliu as Wu Jian, Li Ming as Wang Qun, Li Yong as Zhu Dongsheng, Zhao Shuyin as Tian's mother

In the fall of 1958, production is growing so rapidly at a machine plant under the Shanghai No. 2 Industrial Bureau that it keeps running out of raw materials. Bureau director Tian Fang suggests a technology upgrade could resolve the problem, but some other leaders disagree. Tian sticks to his opinion, however, and does not give up despite some initial failures. Finally, all technological renovation is accomplished successfully, and everyone improved their understanding.

2133. *The Torrential Red River (Hong He Ji Lang)*

1963. Beijing Film Studio. B & W. 11 Reels. Direction: Wei Rong. Screenplay: Liu Wanren, Cheng Shirong and Wu Yi. Cinematography: Chen Guoliang. Art Direction: Chen Yiyun. Music: Ma Ke. Sound: Liu Shida. Cast: Li Minjie as Zhang Tiewa, Yang Jianye as Gao Feihu, Qiu Yuzhen as Zhang Xiangnu, Lu Fei as Wang Guodong, Chun Li as Uncle Liu, Guo Shutian as Yang the carpenter

During the Chinese Civil War, Red Army platoon leader Zhang Tiewa and his comrade Gao Feihu are assigned to return to their hometown to foment revolutionary guerrilla warfare activities among the people. While crossing the Red River by ferry, they are spotted by Nationalist Army Commander Yao Deyuan, which places them in danger. They are rescued by an elderly boatman called Uncle Liu. Later, Yao has Zhang Tiewa's mother and sister Xiangnu arrested. Tiewa and Feihu kill Yao's father-in-law, a landlord, and rescue Tiewa's mother and sister. They raise a guerrilla force to fight the Nationalist forces in the area. Feihu and Xianghu fall in love and marry. However, the guerrillas suffer disaster when their chief courier is intercepted and captured by the enemy, which leads to the almost total annihilation of Tiewa's troop. Learning from this, Tiewa changes his tactics, and in the end overcomes the enemy forces.

2134. *The Tough Group (Cang Hai Xiong Feng)*

1992. Pearl River Film Studio. Color. Letterboxed. 10 Reels. Direction: Wu Houxing. Screenplay: Du Xiaojuan. Cinematography: Zhao Jiajie, Zhang Xijun. Art Direction: Zhang Ruo. Music:

Xu Zhaoji. Sound: Feng Lunsheng. Costume: Hu Hailiang, Liang Lijuan. Makeup: Wu Zhixin. Cast: Chen Rui as Liang Hai, Wang Haiyan as Shen Qing, Hong Yuzhou as Zhen Dachao, Sun Ao as Zhao Ali, Ma Yuliang as Pan Fei, Qi Mengshi as Su Dingcheng, Zhao Xiuli as Su Shan

Pan Fei, CEO of the Chinese South Sea Oil Company, and woman geologist Su Shan arrive for an inspection visit to the No. 1 oil drilling platform, China's first experiment with offshore drilling. It is a big success, and later the very excited Pan begins to reflect on the early beginnings of South Sea exploration. China's oil recovery workers, including his good friend Liang Hai, learn from foreign workers. National pride pushes the Chinese to work hard, and their devotion wins the praise and respect of American project manager Anderson. However, when a typhoon hits, it brings disaster to the project, and the deaths of 61 workers from 9 nations. Among the dead are 35 Chinese, including Liang Hai.

2135. *Tour to "Next Time Departing" Port ("Xia Chi Kai Chuan" Gang You Ji)*

1984. Beijing Film Studio. Color. Letterboxed. Direction: Qin Zhiyu. Screenplay: Qin Zhiyu. Cinematography: Lu Le, Sun Cheng. Art Direction: Yang Yuhe. Music: Wang Xiling. Sound: Lan Fan. Cast: Qin Yi as Tang Xiaoxi, Shen Chunxiang as Xiao Xiong, Meng Jia as the Wood Man, Yu Meng as the Cloth Girl, Xu Huan as Xiao Mei, Zhang Yan as Mother

Tang Xiaoxi is a bright and personable child, but has no sense of the importance of doing things on time. His favorite expression is "I'll do it next time." One day he falls asleep and in a dream has a scary adventure in which he gets himself into a lot of trouble through procrastinating. When he awakens he realizes his mistake in not paying attention to time.

2136. *Track of the Wolf (Lang Ji)*

1986. Inner Mongolia Film Studio. Color. 9 Reels. Direction: Sun Zhiqiang. Screenplay: Tian Li, Xu Jingyang, Xu Shouzhi. Cinematography: Geritu. Art Direction: Shen Minquan, Tong Yonggang. Music: Chuhua Buhe. Sound: Buren. Cast: Ailiya as Ailiya, Zhao Guohua as Chen Fei, Pan Mingxiang as Director Bao, Liu Lijun as Pan Na, Liu Yancheng as Zhen Xianmin

In Qinshan City, a development company's warehouse is broken into and robbed, and one of the company's secretaries vanishes without a trace. Assigned to the case are the male-female detective team of Chen Fei and Ailiya, partners as well as lovers. They make progress in their investigation despite some bumbling errors made by Chen. At last, though, they succeed in identifying and arresting the son of Mayor Zhen Xianmin as the head of the gang that pulled the robbery. But when Ailiya returns to her office she finds Chen Fei dead, a suicide. His suicide note tells her that he was also one of the gang, a fact that would come out soon, and that his apparent errors were really attempts to prevent her finding the truth.

2137. *Tracks of the Explorers (Kai Tuo Zhe De Zhu Ji)*

1983. Beijing Film Studio. Color. 10 Reels. Direction: Su Fei. Screenplay: Song Rixun, Du Yizuang, Su Fei. Cinematography: Du Yizuang. Art Direction: Yu Yiru, Na Yutai. Music: Wang Ming. Sound: Wang Fuan. Cast: Jiao Huang as Xin Qimin, Wang Hui as Wei Daxiong, Guo Weiling as Li Zhen, Yu Yang as Guan Gengrong, Bao Xun as Liu Jun, Wang Yan as Wang Ling

During the Cultural Revolution, agriculture expert Xin Qimin is sent to work in the desert for having dared to speak the truth. Now, 18 years later, his life is very hard but he has devoted himself to developing farmland in the desert. The government sends a woman named Li Zhen to investigate some things about the desert operation they find strange, and there she meets Xin Qimin unexpectedly. It is a surprise for both, as they had been lovers in college, but politics had torn them apart. Xin is still single, and still loves Li Zhen. The director of the desert development site, Wei Daxiong, was also one of Li's college classmates, and he has taken an entirely different path. Wei knows how to deal with every political situation and has juggled the farmland's books to fit its model image. Xin presents Wei his evidence that the figures are false, setting up a confrontation between the two…

2138. *Tragedy on the Execution Ground (Lao Shao Ye Meng Shang Fa Chang)*

1989. Changchun Film Studio. Color. 10 Reels. Wide Screen. Direction: Jin Tao. Screenplay: Zhou Zhentian. Cinematography: Zhong Wenming. Art Direction: Yang Baocheng. Music: Yang Yilun. Sound: Gu Xiaolian. Cast: Li Youbin as Scholar Qiang, Hao Yan as Yanqiu, Li Daqiang as Jin the Crab, Liu Yan as Erhenzi

In 1871, anti-foreign riots break out in the city of Tianjin. Some foreign priests are killed and their church burned. The perpetrator escapes. To appease the outraged foreign governments which hold concessions in China, the Qing Government dispatches an imperial envoy to Tianjin to investigate the case. After considerable negotiation, the foreign embassies and the imperial envoy decide that the Qing Government must execute 16 criminals on October 19. But execute who, since no criminals can be found? With no way out of the situation, the imperial envoy and the governor of Tianjin have the idea of asking for volunteers to die for 200 taels of silver each. The scheme works, and the rest of the film focuses on the voluntary sacrificial lambs: there is a filial son who chooses to sell his life to pay for his father's funeral; a scholar who dreams of becoming a famous martyr; a Taoist who believes such a death will assure him a place in heaven… On the appointed date, the 16 await their execution, and, dressed as heroes, walk to the execution ground. There, the people applaud them and see them off with ceremonial wine. The 16 heroes go to their deaths unflinchingly, playing out a ridiculous and regrettable tragedy.

2139. *A Tragic Tale of the Grasslands (Da Mo En Chou)*

1992. Youth Film Studio. Color. Letterboxed. 9 Reels. Direction: Xu Tongjun. Screenplay: Li Ning, Yu Yonghe. Cinematography: Zhang Huijun. Art Direction: Zhou Dengfu. Music: Fu Lin. Sound: Zhang Yaling. Costume: Xu Xianping. Makeup: Guo Shuyi. Cast: Xing Mingshan as Menghe, Qi Yan as Longxia, Aladan Zuola as Gangema, Daoerji Sangye as Baha, Wang Chi as Zhamu, Ererdeng Boergan as Boyin

Menghe, a young man from the Mongolian prairie, is in Beijing with his father Boyin on business. Meanwhile, back home his fiancee Gangema is being sexually harassed by local aristocrat Baha. In their struggle, Gangema is able to flee, but her home burned down and her mother killed. Meanwhile, Baha sends several thugs to Beijing to eliminate Menghe. The young man survives the attack, but his father Boyin is killed. Aided by a woman called Longxia, the young couple get together, battle Baha and his thugs and succeed in killing the villain.

2140. *Train Number 12 (Shi Er Ci Lie Che)*

1960. August First Film Studio. B & W. 8 Reels. Direction: Hao Guang. Screenplay: Ding Zhiling and Zhen Hong, based on the stage play of the same title. Cinematography: Chen Jun. Art Direction: Zhang Zheng, Shi Lei. Music: Wu Zhuqiang. Sound: Li Lin. Cast: Liu Xiujie as Sun Mingyuan, Li Mingqi as Xiao Ye, Zhang Yingming as Xiao Yang, Jin Lanying as Xiao Li, Chen Xiuying as Xiao Jin, Jing Fuyou as Mr. Zhen, Sun Jie as Uncle Luo, Tong Xucheng as Station Director Sun, Zhang Xuefu as Liu Mantang, Zhao Guang as Party Secretary Le, Wu Guodong as the driver

Train Number 12 from Shenyang to Beijing is blocked by a flash flood in the mountains. The train crew chief, a young woman named Sun Mingyuan, joins forces with a PLA senior colonel among the passengers to organize and lead the train crew and passengers in overcoming their difficulties. The passengers take care of each other, sharing their limited food and caring for the children, elderly and sick people on board. Finally, railway policemen Mr. Zhen risks his life to cross the flooded area and make contact with a nearby people's commune. With the commune people's help, the train finally arrives safely in Beijing.

2141. *A Train Through the Flames of War (Feng Huo Lie Che)*

1960. Changchun Film Studio. B & W. Wide & Narrow Screens. 10 Reels. Direction: Zhu Wenshun. Screenplay: Zhao Lepu. Cinematography: Bao Jie, Li Huailu. Art Direction: Liu Xuerao. Music: Lou Zhanghou. Sound: Huang Lijia. Cast: Li Yalin as Liu Feng, Shi Kefu as Kim Wanji, Liu Ru as Li Changge, Yang Huang as Miao Jingchun, Ren Weimin as Little Fat, Zhang Jianyou as Xiao Guo

Early in the Korean War, train driver Liu Feng accepts the assignment of shipping urgently needed military supplies to the frontlines. Aided by Korean railroad instructor Kim Wanji and other Koreans, he passes through heavy American shelling and barricades and delivers the goods to their destination. At one point he is shot while making some engine repairs, but is saved by some Koreans. Finally, after Liu and Kim have accomplished their mission and returned to China, Kim is reunited with the mother he has not seen for a long time.

2142. *The Traitor (Pan Guo Zhe)*

1980. Xi'an Film Studio. Color. 9 Reels. Direction: Zhang Qicang. Screenplay: Ji Xing, Ji Rao. Cinematography: Niu Han. Art Direction: Cheng Minzhang. Music: Wei Ruixiang. Sound: Xiong Huajuan. Cast: Ma Jingwu as Niu Yusheng, Yu Ping as Tian Fang, Na Renhua as Tian Tian, Shen Guanchu as Li Jun

In the summer of 1975, an invasion of snakes threatens the area around the Southwest China border. Niu Yusheng, a returned overseas Chinese, leads an exploration team to the area. When they investigate the site, Niu Yusheng concludes there is a black cobra in the area, and its poison is precisely the material he needs for making a new medicine for treating snakebite. He instructs the team to search specifically for this snake. One member of his team, Li Jun, has been assigned "special duty," euphemism for keeping an eye on Niu Yusheng. Li Jun's lover Tian Tian, the team's guide, is an innocent and vivacious girl who greatly admires the team leader, and is very unhappy with Li Jun's behavior. Later, as Niu tries to catch the black cobra, the snake shoots poison into his eyes and he is taken to a hospital. His doctor turns out to be Tian Fang, Niu Yusheng's ex-wife, who 19 years earlier had been forced by political pressure to take their baby daughter and leave him. Tian Fang tells him that Tian Tian is their daughter. Later, when Tian Tian is bitten by the cobra, Niu Yusheng saves her life with his new medicine. But the family reunion is shortlived, for Li Jun receives an order to arrest Niu Yusheng.

2143. *Transnational Robbery (Kua Jie Da Jie An)*

1991. Xiaoxiang Film Studio. Color. Letterboxed. 9 Reels. Direction: Hu Bing and Yu Liping. Screenplay: Hu Bing. Cinematography: Liu Junyun. Art Direction: Na Shufeng. Music: Zhen Qiufeng. Sound: Huang Siye. Costume: Long Xiaoping. Makeup: Yi Xiaoxiao. Cast: Wang Fuyou as Gan Guyan, Zhao Min as Cai Li, Wang Chunli as Ding Runchun, Zhang Huibo as Ai Demin, Zhao Xiuli as Ou Haiyun, Wei Luping as An Huaqi, Zhang Ping as Bao Kunzheng

In a Special Economic Zone in South China, criminal Bao Kunsheng deceives migrant worker Cai Li into helping him in a robbery which quickly escalates into murder. Bao and his confederate Ai Demin pretend to be overseas Chinese businessmen to gain access to an art auction. They hold up the auction, steal a priceless gold Buddha and escape in a hail of bullets. But their plans go awry when the duped Cai Li is not killed, as they had planned. They go back to kill the young worker, but he eludes them. So police and gunmen are both searching for Cai Li.

2144. *Traveling Through the Storm (Feng Yu Li Cheng)*

1978. Beijing Film Studio. Color. 11 Reels. Direction: Cui Wei. Screenplay: Cui Wei, Yu Shan. Cinematography: Nie Jing. Art Direction: Tu Juhua. Music: Lu Yi. Sound: Wang Yunhua, Lai Qijian. Cast: Gao Weiqi as Lu Yunzhi, Mu Huaihu as Tian Geng, Wang Bingyu as Yan Kunyu, Liu Zongyou as Han Tie, Pao Huiping as Li Tonghua, Shi Xi as Wang Dongliang, Chi Jianhua as Yao Xingbang

In the spring of 1975, to assure normal railway transport, the Sangluo section of the Zhongzhou Railway sets up an equipment inspection and maintenance team headed by Lu Yunzhi, director of the their revolutionary committee. The teams undertake to walk the entire 250 kilometers of railway line checking the equipment. Yao Xingbang and other followers of the "Gang of Four" fear that the railway workers' effort will endanger their conspiracy to "stabilize Shanghai, disrupt China," so Yao arranges that all sorts of difficulties be thrown in the inspectors' path. He even sends bodyguards to abduct Lu Yunzhi. With the aid of railway maintenance workers and the people, Lu Yunzhi is rescued, and the inspection team finally succeeds in reaching its destination at the end of the line.

2145. *Treasure (Gui Bao)*

1983. Emei Film Studio. Color. 9 Reels. Direction: Li Jiefeng. Screenplay: Sun Jingrui. Cinematography: Sun Guoliang, Zhang Wenzhu. Art Direction: Yan Dingfu. Music: Gong Zhiwei. Sound: Hua Yuezhu. Cast: Feng Qinling as Pan Meiyun, Zhen Jiasheng as Wang Mindao, Zhou Chu as Pan Wenda, Niu Qian as Han Shouren, Xu Haiyan as Sun Jiajun, Qu Zhi as Zhang Dewu, Huang Kai as Jianglan

In the 18th century, the Manchu court spends a huge quantity of gold to make a set of gold musical bells. When the Manchu government is overthrown in 1912, corrupt officials use these bells as collateral to secure a loan from the Chuangye Bank; when they default on payment the bells become bank property. Bank manager Pan Wenda instructs his son-in-law Yang Jianglan to take care of them. The story centers on how Yang, an honest and patriotic young man, struggles over the years to protect the bells and prevent their falling into the hands of either the Japanese or the Nationalist government. When the People's Republic is founded, Yang turns over to the new Communist government the bells he has protected for over four decades.

2146. *The Treasure Cave in the Desert (Sha Mo Bao Ku)*

1981. Changchun Film Studio. Color. 10 Reels. Direction: Qin Basheng. Screenplay: Zhu Ma, Xiang Chu. Cinematography: Li Fengming. Art Direction: Liang Shukui, Ju Lutian. Music: Wu Damin. Sound: Liu Xingfu. Cast: Zhao Jiaqiu as Gao Yizhi, Wang Yi as He Xiangfeng, Wang Zhihua as Zhang Fengya, Kang Baomin as Li Ou, Xu Meina as Yang Na

A true story. In 1941, successful artist Gao Yizhi sells everything he owns to collect funds for an exploration trip to the Dunhuang caves with his colleagues He Xiangfeng and Zhang Fengya and students Li Ou and Yang Na. At first, the local people who protect the national treasures at Dunhuang are suspicious of the newcomers, but gradually begin to understand and help in their work of collecting samples of wall paintings and colored sculptures. Gao and the others work hard under extremely harsh circumstances, gathering what they can while causing the smallest possible damage to the caves. To publicize the findings as widely as possible, Gao Yizhi holds an exhibition of many of the artworks in Chongqing, which draws people from all classes of society. A profiteering businessman gives Gao some trouble, but he overcomes this with the support of honest people who want the treasures kept for the people. Gao's exhibition is a great success and he returns to the mountains with the funds he has collected to continue the work. His arrives to find that his long-time love He Xiangfeng, who had remained in Dunhuang, is very ill. She dies, and Gao Yizhi and the local people bury her at the archaeological site. Gao Yizhi vows to devote the rest of his life to protecting China's national treasures in the Dunhuang caves.

2147. *Trendy Girl (Xin Chao Gu Niang)*

1991. Shenzhen Film Company. Color.

Letterboxed. 9 Reels. Direction: Liu Guoquan. Screenplay: Li Ning and Xiao Zengjian. Cinematography: Ge Ritu. Art Direction: Li Hong. Music: Wang Ming. Costume: Liu Huiping. Makeup: Wu Guihua. Cast: Yuan Li as Lin Chunping, Liang Tian as Yang Ding, Chen Yude as Yan Wenjie, Ding Yi as Li Jing

Bright and capable mountain girl Lin Chunping rejects an arranged marriage and leaves her hometown. In the city, she fails to find her uncle who lives there, but she does become acquainted with Yang Ding, a girl who works as a taxi driver. Yang's parents help Lin get a job as a storehouse keeper in a fireworks plant. The plant is operating in the red, but Lin finds ways they can improve the situation. She is soon moved into management, and the plant prospers. Her love life starts looking up as well.

2148. *Trials of a Long Journey (Wan Li Zheng Tu)*

1977. Beijing Film Studio. Color. 11 Reels. Direction: Yu Yang. Screenplay: Han Chunling and Jia Menglei. Cinematography: Zhang Qinhua. Art Direction: Yang Yuhe, Lu Zhicang. Music: Interns of the Central No. 57 Art Institution Music School's Composing Department. Sound: Fu Yinjie. Cast: Da Shichang as Chang Dajin, Meng Qinliang as Zhao Hu, Yu Zhi as Lu Fang, Gu Yuqing as Guo Erfeng, Wang Bingyu as Zhou Yunpeng, Mei Zhaohua as Cai Xiaochuang, Wang Qiuying as Cai Degui, Chen Zhijian as Hu Qi

In the "Agriculture Must Learn from Dazhai" campaign, bus transport Unit No.9's deputy director Chang Dajin proposes a plan to "assist agriculture through bus deliveries," which is supported by transport leadership and employees and welcomed by the farmers. However, his arrogant supervisor, Unit No.9's director Zhao Hu is unenlightened as to the importance of helping agriculture, so he is not enthusiastic. One of Unit No. 9's employees, Cai Degui, runs an unauthorized transport business with counterrevolutionary Hu Qi, so they hate this movement. With Chang Dajin's help, Zhao Hu begins to gain awareness. When Cai and Hu try to set fire to a wood bridge, blocking the way of the transport unit in delivering goods to a rural reservoir endangered by flooding, they are caught by the commune's militia brigade.

2149. *Trip to Tianshan Mountain (Tian Shan Xing)*

1982. August First Film Studio. Color. 10 Reels. Direction: Jing Mukui. Screenplay: Li Bingkui. Cinematography: Huang Fuxing. Art Direction: Ni Shaohua. Music: Fu Gengcheng. Sound: Guo Yisheng. Cast: Yan Shikui as Zhen Zhitong, Zhao Na as Li Qian, Li Xuejian as Yu Haizhou, Song Chunli as Lu Yingxian, Yun Chunmian as Regimental Commander Xue

High school students Zhen Zhitong and his girlfriend Li Qian volunteer to work in the countryside during the Cultural Revolution. After the initial enthusiasm wears off and the realities of harsh rural life sinks in, Li Qian uses connections to return to Beijing. When Zhen is admitted to an army engineering school in Beijing, the two resume their relationship, and their friendship develops into love. Li Qian wants them to marry and settle in the city, but Zhen Zhitong wants to return and resume his work at Tianshan Mountain. He struggles with the dilemma, but at last goes back. He misses Li terribly. She later visits him while on a business trip, and is shocked to find how much the people of this area are sacrificing to build the nation. Zhen appeals to Li to stay with him in the mountains, but she is reluctant to go back to that kind of life. Li has reached a crossroads in her life…

2150. *Troop Commander (Dai Bing De Ren)*

1964. August First Film Studio. B & W. 11 Reels. Direction: Yan Jizhou. Screenplay: Xiao Yu and Yan Jizhou, based on the stage play of the same title by Xiao Yu. Cinematography: Zhang Dongliang, Cao Jingyun. Art Direction: Shang Rongguang. Music: Yan Ke. Sound: He Baoding. Cast: Hong Wansheng as Xiao Guo, Huo Deji as Niu Fushan, Zhang Hengli as Xiao Yihu, Hu Qufei as Qu Xiaolong, Li Jiufang as Jiang Defa, Gao Baocheng as Lin Zhiyong

New recruit Qu Xiaolong does not behave well in his first assignment, and his platoon leader Jin Dahong does little to encourage the newcomer to change. Even criticism from company commander Lin Zhiyong does little to change things. What does change Xiaolong's attitude is his meeting Niu Fushan, a veteran who had once saved the lives of Xiaolong's parents and had been seriously wounded in liberating their village. Xiao Long vows to emulate this veteran and become a good soldier by training and working hard. His change also has a good influence on platoon leader Jin Da-hong.

2151. *The Trouble-shooters (Wan Zhu)*

1988. Emei Film Studio. Color. 10 Reels. Letterboxed. Direction: Mi Jiashan. Screenplay: Wang Shuo, Mi Jiashan. Cinematography: Wang Xiaolie. Art Direction: Gan Shaocheng. Music: Xie Jun. Sound: Luo Guohua. Cast: Zhang Guoli as Yu Guan, Pan Hong as Ding Xiaolu, Ge You as Yang Zhong, Liang Tian as Ma Qing, Sun Fengying as Lin Pei, Ma Xiaoqing as Liu Meiping

A strange story which combines comedy, farce, black humor and the rapid-paced Chinese comic dialogues called "crosstalk." It tells of a group of young people who set up the 3-T Company, an enterprise intended to "alleviate depression, resolve problems and take responsibility for other persons." Through a series of comic incidents, the unusual company dispenses pleasure, anger, sorrow and joy, just about all of life's sweet and bitter experiences.

2152. *Troubled Daughters-in-Law (Xi Fu Men De Xin Shi)*

1983. Shandong Film Studio. Color. 10 Reels. Direction: Jia Shihong. Screenplay: Dai Lu. Cinematography: Chen Ruijun and Sun Guochuan. Art Direction: Sun Yunjiu and Han Zhilu. Music: Li Weicai. Sound: He Baoding and Wang Honggao. Cast: Wang Lue as Jin Feng, Hou Yuling as Yu Fen, Liu Fang as Yin Ling, Liu Hongkun as Yu Chuanhai, Li Chixiu as Chuan Shan, Yu Yong as Chuan Jiang, Dong Weimin as Da Shunzi, Zhang Zhenliang as Mao Chen, Yu Lingling as Qiao Ye

After the 3rd Plenary Session of the 11th Party Congress, the Taohuayu Production Unit grows steadily more prosperous. More people can afford to get married, and naturally the birth rate increases. With so many people wanting to have more than one child, the unit's director Yu Chuanhai ignores the government's family planning policy. Even his own wife Jin Feng wants a second child. This neglect of the policy troubles Yin Ling and several other young wives who work at the commune's family planning office. They patiently explain the policy and help others to understand the reasons behind it. In time, even Jin Feng changes her thinking.

2153. *The Troubled Family (Fan Nao Jia Ting)*

1992. Changchun Film Studio. Color. Letterboxed. 9 Reels. Direction: Zhao Weiheng. Screenplay: Li Qiuyan. Cinematography: Qian Damin. Art Direction: Liu Hong. Music: Chen Chunguang. Sound: Sheng Hongtao. Costume: Zhao Jing, Wang Dandan. Makeup: Yan Zhenrong, Wang Xiaoqiong. Cast: You Yong as Erzhu, Chun Li as Master Worker Zhen, Tao Yuling as Zhen's mother, Jin Meng as Xiaofeng, Xu Ling as Shanshan, Wu Mian as Shen Yan

Old worker Mr. Zhen has always been a kindly, honest and hardworking man. But now he is deeply troubled by the strange behavior of his children: his eldest son Dajian quits his government-guaranteed job to open a restaurant; his younger son Erzhu rejects the traditional girl from the countryside selected for him by his parents as appropriate for his status; and daughter Xiao Feng has no job and just stays at home. Through the young people's separate stories, we see some of the evolution of Chinese society and how families are changing with it. Erzhu falls in love with Shen Yan, doctor at the construction site where he works; Xiaofeng becomes a finalist for an on-camera job at a TV station; but Dajian becomes involved in some shady business dealings.

2154. *Troubled Marriage (Qi Hun Guai Shi)*

1991. Youth Film Studio. Color. Letterboxed. 9 Reels. Direction: Jiang Shixiong, Screenplay: Bao Suibing, Cinematography: Li Tingzheng, Art Direction: Liu Shi, Music: Yang Nailin, Cast: Jin Jinglan as He Xian's mother, Zhang Shuangli as Huang Tianbang, Fu Lai as Cai Wei, Yun Yuchun as Fulai's mother, Wang Fuer as Juhua, Li Weijian as Tie Niu, Zhang Peiyu as Shui Xiu

2155. *A Truck Convoy Passing Through Town (Che Dui Chong Cheng Shi Jing Guo)*

1987. Shanghai Film Studio. Color. 10 Reels. Direction: Lu Ping. Screenplay: Xiong Yu, Luo Xing. Cinematography: Cai Zhengchang. Art Direction: Xue Jianna. Music: Lu Qimin. Sound: Xie Guojie, Xu Xiushan. Cast: Ren Guangzhi as Liu Ping, Hong Rong as Liu's wife, Liu Xiaomin as Youwa, Wu Dan as the woman driver, Zhu Baojun as White Face, Zhu Danhu as Dandan

A petroleum prospecting team stops overnight in a certain city on its way to a remote area. Team leader Liu Ping stops to visit his wife and son, who live in that city. His wife is an accomplished architect, and tries again to persuade him to give up roaming around the country prospecting and settle down again in the city. The couple passes the night with mixed feelings. The film also tells the different stories of other team members: young worker Youwa, Dr. Xiao Baolian, and others. The next morning the team leaves the city, each of its members having renewed confidence in the path they have chosen.

2156. The True and False Comedy Master (Zhen Jia You Mu Da Shi)

1994. Changchun Film Studio. Color. Letter-boxed. 9 Reels. Direction: Liu Erwei. Screenplay: Ding Mu. Cinematography: Gao Hongbao. Art Direction: Guo Tingsheng. Music: Ke Xin. Sound: Zhang Qingjiang. Costume: Ge Junjie. Makeup: Lei Longlong. Cast: Gong Hanlin as Xiao Guan, Li Yinqiu as Wen Jiayu, Zhan Jinbo as Wu Dayong, Chen Kaihui as Yu Chunna, Li Daqiang as fat head, Wang Jinglun as Xiao Hu, Fu Hong as Zhong Ling, Song Muge as Guoguo, Zhao Naixun as Yangguang

In a certain city live two men who are exactly identical in appearance. This situation is complicated by the fact they share the same name, Xiao Kou. One is a show business celebrity, the other a teacher. Although the two have never met, and have nothing to do with each other, the celebrity's fans mistake Xiao Kou the teacher for Xiao Kou the star, which leads to a series of humorous misunderstandings and incidents. This all reaches a climax when the star's director drags the teacher on stage to perform, and his ineptitude proves an embarrassment to everyone. At last, both Xiao Kous show up on stage together, and shake hands. The audience gives them a standing ovation when they finally understand the situation.

2157. The True Hearted (Xin Xiang)

1991. Pearl River Film Studio. Color. 10 Reels. Letterboxed. Direction: Sun Zhou. Screenplay: Miao Yue, Sun Zhou. Cinematography: Yao Li. Art Direction: Shi Haiying. Music: Zhao Jiping. Sound: Deng Qinghua, Feng Jingsheng, Lu Hong. Cast: Fei Yang as Jingjing, Zhu Xu as Grandfather, Wang Yumei as Aunt Lian, Fu Lili

as Jingjing's mother, Qian Yifei as old Taiwanese man, Zhang Shen as Tong Ling, Cao Zheng as the director, Luo Xueying as the school principal, Li Guangneng as A Kun

When Jingjing's parents get divorced, he has to move to his maternal grandfather's to live for a time. His grandfather, whom he has never met before, lives alone. Both feel like strangers, and so a series of conflicts emerge. Jingjing meets his grandfather's friend Aunt Lian, a woman who has lived alone since her husband left for Taiwan decades ago. She and Jingjing's grandfather have a loving relationship, much like that of a married couple, and they rely on each other for survival. Their tranquil life is interrupted by a letter from Aunt Lian's husband in Taiwan, who intends to return to mainland China to join Lian. Although she loves grandfather, Aunt Lian feels that honor and loyalty demand she accept reunification with her husband and she must make the psychological adjustment. But then word comes that the husband has died just before embarking on the trip. This second shock proves too much for Aunt Lian and she dies too. In order to give Aunt Lian a decent burial, grandfather has to sell all the costumes and other paraphernalia he used when he was a Beijing Opera star. To help grandfather raise the cash for the funeral, Jingjing goes to the docks to sing as a street performer.

Best Cinematography Yao Li, 1992 Golden Rooster Awards.

Best Sound Deng Qinghua, Feng Jingsheng and Lu Hong, 1992 Golden Rooster Awards.

2158. The True Story of A Q (A Q Zheng Zhuan)

1981. Shanghai Film Studio. Color. Wide Screen. 12 Reels. Direction: Ling Fan. Screenplay: Chen Baichen, based on the story by Lu Xun (1881-1936). Cinematography: Chen Zhengxiang. Art Direction: Ge Shicheng, Zhao Yixuan. Music: Wang Yunjie. Sound: Liu Guangjie. Costume: Cao Yingping. Cast: Yan Shunkai as A Q, Li Wei as Master Zhao, Wang Suya as Lady Wu, Zhang Youyun as the Little Nun, Bao Fumin as the son

Near the end of the Qing (Manchu) Dynasty, A Q works as a temporary day laborer. He has nothing: no social status, no money, not even a surname. He is looked down upon by everyone in spite of his willingness to work hard. Finding no work in the countryside, in

The True Hearted. After his parents' divorce, troubled Jingjing (Fei Yang, left) moves to his grandfather's home and finds a new playmate. 1991. Pearl River Film Studio.

order to survive he goes to the city to do hard labor in the household of Scholar Bai, where he is punished for making an honest comment. Later on, when he is really desperate for work, he steals some used clothes and sells them; then, feeling he is "rich," he returns to his home village. However, this temporary prosperity is soon over, and he remains in poverty. In 1911, the Manchus are overthrown, and A Q becomes very excited over the idea of revolution, claiming to be a revolutionary. But no one takes him seriously in this either. Later, he is falsely accused of robbery by local landlord Master Zhao and his son. When questioned about his innocence or guilt, A Q boasts once too often about his false exploits, and he is convicted and executed.

Best Actor Yan Shunkai, 1983 Hundred Flowers Awards.

Best Costume Cao Yingping, 1982 Golden Rooster Awards.

2159. *Truly Great People of This Generation (Feng Liu Ren Wu Shu Jin Zhao)*

1960. Tianma Film Studio and Hai Yan Film Studio Co-Production. Color. 10 Reels. Direction: Zhao Ming, Jiang Junchao and Yu Zhongying. Screenplay: Fei Liwen and Ai Mingzhi. Cinematography: Shi Fengqi and Zhang Xiling. Art Direction: Lu Jingguang. Music: Ji Ming, Zhang Linyi and Yang Zhezheng. Sound: Yuan Qingyu and Lu Jinsong. Cast: Zhao Dan as Gao Hailin, Qi Heng as Fang Qiang, Zhang Fa as Master Worker Song Aixiang, Bai Mu as Master Worker Zhang, Wang Danfeng as Song Fenglan, Li Nong as Qian Wentao

Shanghai Hongguang Scientific Instrument Plant worker Gao Hailin is opposed by his supervisor, conservative master worker Song Aixiang when he begins research on a sophisticated instrument — a high voltage power bridge. With support from the plant's Party secretary Fang Qiang and other workers, he overcomes many difficulties and finally produces working drawings of the bridge. Over 300 tests of the device fail, shaking his confidence. But Secretary Fang educates him from his own revolutionary experience, and with renewed determination Gao finally succeeds.

2160. *Tunnel Warfare (Di Dao Zhan)*

1965. August First Film Studio. B & W. 10 Reels. Direction: Ren Xudong. Screenplay: Ren Xudong, Pan Yunshan, Wang Junyi and Xu Guoteng. Cinematography: Yang Guangyuan. Art Direction: Shang Rongguang, Fang Xuzhi. Music: Fu Gengcheng. Sound: Hou Shenkang. Cast: Zhu Longguang as Gao Chunbao, Wang Bingyu as Gao Laozhong, Zhang Yongshou as Zhao Pingyuan, Zhu Qi as Company Commander Cui, Liu Xiujie as Lin Xia, Han Guodong as Da Kang

In 1942, when the Japanese invaders launch their "big sweep" of China, they build bases throughout China from which to control the countryside and cities. In Hebei province, the people of Gangjia Village, led by Party Secretary Gao Laozhong and local militia director Gao Chunbao, dig a network of caves with multiple entrances as a sanctuary for villages in case of attack. When the Japanese launch a surprise raid on the village, the Chinese are saved only by Party Secretary Gao Laozhong, who sacrifices his own life to warn the village. Gao Chunbao and new Party Secretary Lin Xia study Chairman Mao's "On Protracted War." Applying the experiences and lessons of their earlier use of the tunnels, they convert the original network from just a hiding place to a place for carrying out offensive operations. The following summer, before the Japanese launch a second attack, the villagers use the new network of tunnels to wipe out Japanese agents who have come ahead of the attack, which results in the enemy suffering serious losses due to a lack of coordination from within. The villagers continue improving their network, and finally are able to coordinate an attack on the Japanese base at Hefengkou by the Eighth Route Army and a guerrilla troop, wiping out the Japanese base and killing the commander who had led the original attack on Gangjia Village.

2161. *Turn Around and Smile (Hui Tou Yi Xiao)*

1981. Pearl River Film Studio. Color. 10 Reels. Direction: Zhang Liang. Screenplay: Zhou Jie. Cinematography: Li Zhexian. Art Direction: Wang Huixun. Music: Li Weicai. Sound: Lin Guoqiang. Cast: Gao Baocheng as Director Gu, Li Shixi as Xin Minliang, Yin Shiqing as Sister Hua, Li Tingxiu as Wang De, Zhao Chunchang as Feng Xi, Xing Mali as Gao Fu

The story is set in 1977, a time of transition in the Chinese economy. In a poor mountainous region of China, the Shibawan Manufacturing Plant has a reputation for efficiency and productivity, but is actually quite the opposite, largely because Managing Director Gu believes that every directive from above, every policy and procedure, must be followed to the letter. He deals harshly with anyone doing or suggesting anything that smacks of capitalism. Inspired by the 3rd Plenary Session of the 11th Party Congress, which urged the Chinese people to be more liberal in their thinking, some younger and more ambitious people in the plant start to apply new ideas to production. This is not easy to do in Shibawan. Director Gu tries hard to adjust to the new policy, but always feels uneasy, that everything is changing too rapidly for him to catch up.

2162. *Turning Bad Luck into Good (Feng Xiong Hua Ji)*

1989. Guangxi Film Studio. Color. Letterboxed. 10 Reels. Direction: Yan Gong, Jiang Yaozen. Screenplay: Li Tianji. Cinematography: Meng Xiongqiang. Art Direction: Jin Bohao, Lei Xiaolan. Music: Li Yanlin. Sound: Li Zuwen. Cast: Hao Guang as Fan Jing, Fang Hua as Guijingcang, Xu Shouqin as Xu Wenbing, Xu Fenglan as Peipei

Towards the end of World War II, Japanese soldiers mistake a simple village schoolteacher for a Chinese guerrilla fighter. This leads to a succession of seriocomic adventures in which the innocent man is pursued across China by the Japanese on one hand, and applauded as a hero of the resistance by the Chinese on the other, when all he really wants is to survive.

2163. *Twilight Star (Qi Ming Xing)*

1992. Tianjin Film Studio and Youth Film Studio Co-Production. Color. 11 Reels. Direction: Xie Jin. Screenplay: Hang Ying. Cinematography: Lu Junfu and Gao Gengrong. Art Direction: Sun Zhendong. Music: Yao Shengchang. Sound: Liu Xiaochuan. Costume: Zhang Jing, Li Qi. Makeup: Xie Weiming, Zhang Huiling. Cast: Liu Yang as Chengcheng, Li Ming as Niuniu, Liu Zifeng as Xie Changgeng, Zhang Xin as Shi Tie

Nine-year-old Xie Chengcheng is a retarded child who lost his mother a few years ago. Since he cannot go to school, or take care of himself, he has to be locked up whenever his father goes out. His father Xie Changgeng, just 40, learns he has lung cancer. He takes out all his savings and takes his son to a park playground for one last fun time. He plans to kill the boy, then take his own life afterwards. But he is unsuccessful, and his factory labor union chief puts Xie into the hospital; meanwhile, the district civil affairs department arranges for Chengcheng to go to a school for retarded children. He learns many things there. Eventually, his father becomes ill again and has to return to the hospital. But this time he is happy and peaceful inside, when his growing son sends him a loving gift the boy made in school.

2164. *Twin Brothers (Xiao Gui Jing Ling)*

1992. Shenzhen Film Studio. Color. Letterboxed. 8 Reels. Direction: Wen Lumin. Screenplay: Teng Hua, Liang Dewu, Wen Lumin. Cinematography: Xu Jiansheng. Art Direction: Huo Tingxiao. Music: Guo Wenjing. Sound: Zhang Lei. Costume: Liu Yanping. Makeup: Zhu Jian. Cast: Wang Yi as Yang Tian, Sun Yue as Chen Mu, Yue Hong as Chen Yue, Tan Zongrao as Yang Cheng

Eleven-year-old Yang Tian lives with his divorced father Yang Cheng, a software designer. The father designs a software package which has considerable commercial potential, but it is stolen. About this time, Yang Tian goes to a children's activity, where he meets a boy named Chen Mu, visiting from another city. To their mutual surprise, the two boys look exactly alike. They become good friends, but afterwards they get on each other's train by mistake. It turns out the two are twin brothers, each living with one parent. They join forces to bring their parents back together again, and in the process find the man who stole their father's design.

2165. *Twins Come in Pairs (Ta Lia He Ta Lia)*

1979. Shanghai Film Studio. Color. 10 Reels. Direction: Sang Hu. Screenplay: Wang Lian, Sang Hu, Fu Jinggong. Cinematography: Qiu Yiren. Art Direction: Liu Pan, Li Runzhi, Music: Xu Jingxin. Sound: Zhu Weigang, Jin Fugeng. Cast: Gao Yin as Gu Yuanyuan and Gu Fangfang, Mao Yongming as Yang Dalin and Yang Xiaoling, Han Fei as Mr. Gu, Sun Jinglu as Mother Yang, Zhong Xinghuo as Father Yang, Shi Jiufeng as the TV reporter, Li Qing as Lingdi, Cheng Zhi as the houseguest

Gu Fangfang and Gu Yuanyuan are twin sisters while Yang Dalin and Yang Xiaolin are twin brothers. Yuanyuan's girlfriend Lingdi introduces Yang Xiaolin to Yuanyuan as a potential boyfriend. Meanwhile, Yang Dalin, a scientific researcher, seeks out Gu Fangfang, for he hears that her own research may be of importance to his. The two sets of twins' identical appearance creates a series of comic misunderstandings. Dalin and Fangfang, both devoted to their work, fall in love with each other as well. However, the course of true love is not so smooth for Xiaolin and Yuanyuan: although attractive and intelligent, they are also selfish and undisciplined, and quarrel over practically everything. Finally, with the help of their siblings and the pressures of social trends, Xiaolin and Yuanyuan realize their imperfections and start to work on their careers and their relationship.

2166. *Two A.M. (Wu Ye Liang Dian)*

1987. Shanghai Film Studio. Color. 10 Reels. Direction: Bao Zhifang. Screenplay: Hu Huiying, Zhao Zhiqiang, Shen Yaoting. Cinematography: Zhou Zaiyuan. Art Direction: Chen Shaomian. Music: Liu Yanxi. Sound: Zhu Weigang, Zhao Jianzhong. Cast: Yan Xiaoping as Xiao Qi, Wang Shikui as Cao Dongming, Zhang Min as Fang Yaping, Mai Wenyan as Yang Ni

Fang Yaping and her mother live in an old, Western-style house in Shanghai. Yaping had been a textile worker, but poor health forced her into premature retirement. The same condition has in the past prevented her from marrying. Then she meets Dr. Cao Dongming, who subjects the spinster to a whirlwind courtship. They marry, but to her surprise her new husband insists they live in the Fangs' old and somewhat run-down home rather than his modern and more attractive one. She is also puzzled by his secretive and at times strange behavior, and soon discovers he is seeing another woman. She files for divorce. Yaping and her mother are surprised by the sudden appearance of Yaping's father, who disappeared more than 30 years earlier. While he tells his wife and daughter he has been overseas for most of that time, he gives little detail about his activities. Before he leaves, he shows them a safe hidden in the sitting room. He tells them it contains 100 taels of gold; it is theirs, but they can only open the safe at 2 a.m. After this, strange things begin to happen and the gloomy old house shows periodic signs of being haunted. When her mother dies suddenly, Yaping begins to fear her own life is in danger. She gets help when a young woman lawyer named Xiao Qi shows up investigating Fang Yaping's divorce petition. Together the two women trace and unravel a complex web of intrigue.

Two Brands **see** *Spring Orchid, Fall Chrysanthemum*

2167. *Two Empress Dowagers (Liang Gong Huang Tai Hou)*

1987. Changchun Film Studio. Color. 11 Reels. Direction: Wang Xuexin. Screenplay: Yang Chunbing. Cinematography: Wang Qimin. Art Direction: Ju Lutian. Music: Chen Shouqian. Sound: Li Zhenduo. Cast: Fang Shu as Cixi, Liu Dong as Cian, Zhang Weike as An Dehai, Wang Zhiwen as Emperor Tongzhi

In 1861, Prince Yixin convinces the Empress Dowager Cixi and the Empress Dowager Ci'an to stage a coup d'etat, putting to death eight ministers who had held power. From that point on the two women took over China's state affairs. To satisfy her desire to hold all power, the Empress Dowager Cixi, beautiful and charming, yet cruel and astute, kept adding to her power. At last she was strong enough to have the Empress Dowager Cian killed and the entire country under her autocratic rule. At that point China entered one of the darkest periods of its history.

2168. *Two Families (Liang Jia Ren)*

1963. Changchun Film Studio. B & W. 8 Reels. Direction: Yuan Naicheng. Screenplay: Lin Mocheng, based on the novel, "The Bridge" by Liu Pengde. Cinematography: Gu Wenhou. Art Direction: Li Fan. Music: Lei Zhengbang. Sound: Hong Di. Cast: Fang Hua as Gao Zhengguo, Wang Jianhua as Lady Gao, Chen Xuejie as Erzhu, Wang Tingsheng as Chen Weibang, Huang Ling as Mrs. Chen, Huo Deji as Xiao Hai

Before liberation, Gao Zhengguo and Chen Weibang were both impoverished farmers. After liberation and land reform, and the resultant improvement in their living standards, Gao Zhengguo becomes personally ambitious. He wants to engage in private production activities such as hiring farm laborers, buying more land, storing grains, etc. The farmer's association cautions him to avoid

going down the former capitalist road. His daughter Erzhu quarrels with him over this issue, and he has a falling out with his old friend Chen Weibang. Li Chun, another farmer who had engaged in individual production, suffered severe losses, which made him decided to join the commune, but his wife still sells land without telling him. When she realizes she has done wrong, she is terribly worried and commits suicide. After witnessing Li Chun's family tragedy, Gao Zhengguo decides to join in agricultural cooperation. The Gao and Chen households recover their former close relationship.

2169. *Two Families' Happiness (Liang Jia Chun)*

1951. Changjiang Film Studio. B & W. 10 Reels. Directors: Ju Baiyin and Xiu Bingduo. Screenplay: Li Hongxin, based on Gu Yu's novel, "Forced Bonding Cannot Be Sweet." Cinematography: Li Fengzhi. Cast: Wang Longji as Xiao Yong, Qing Yi as Zhui Er, Shi Hanwei as the Village Secretary, He Jianfei as the Village Head, Gao Bo as Big Kang, Wang Renmei as the Women's Committee Director, Dai Yun as Xiao Yong's mother, Jiang Rui as Zhui Er's father, Zhou Min as Zhui Er's mother

After land reform is implemented in a village in North China, model student Zhui Er and model worker Big Kang fall in love, However, Zhui Er's father is very traditional in his outlook, and regards his daughter's dating and subsequent romance as something disgraceful. He arranges instead for his 20-year-old daughter to marry Xiao Yong, the 9-year-old son of an old friend, to repay a favor from years before, After Zhui Er is married into Xiao Yong's family, she of course has no affection for the boy, but longs for her former lover Big Kang. As time passes, her health begins to fail. Xiao Yong, mocked by his classmates for all this, refuses to go to school. Finally, the director of the village women's committee intercedes, and through her persuasive work with both families, Zhui Er's father comes to realize his mistake and Xiao Yong's mother agrees to letting her son divorce. Zhui Er and Big Kang are happily married.

2170. *Two Fugitive Girls (Yue Yu Nu Qiu)*

1992. Guangxi Film Studio. Color. Letterboxed. 10 Reels. Direction: Jiang Shusheng, Jiang

Yaozen. Screenplay: Han Zhijun. Cinematography: Liu Baogui. Art Direction: Liu Weixin. Music: Liu Xijin. Sound: Lin Lin. Costume: Mei Ling, Tian Geng. Makeup: Shen Yueying, Liu Yan. Cast: Tu Ruyin as Ding Lan, Xiao Yang as Pang Yong, Wang Jinghua as Wei Cuicui, Liu Dong as Shen Jing, Sun Weimin as Wei Kai, Zhou Liangliang as Cuicui's mother

Ding Lan and Wei Cuicui break out of a woman's prison. As the search for them goes on, Chief Investigator Pang Yong carefully studies the two young women's files, and finds some suspicious points in their cases. Ding Lan had been an accountant for the Tongda Trading Group, and Wei Cuicui a worker at the company's credit union. It turns out they had both been framed for the crimes of company director Hu. The two fugitives go to Hu's place, where they obtain evidence which clears them and proves Hu's guilt, then they return to the prison.

2171. *Two Generations (Liang Dai Ren)*

1960. Xinjiang Film Studio. B & W. 9 Reels. Direction: Chen Gang and Ou Fan. Screenplay: Hong Liu, Ren Mo and Rehamu Hasimufu. Cinematography: Liu Jingtang and Zeng Qilu. Art Direction: Li Zhongzhi. Sound: Zhang Xiceng. Cast: Jiang Suying as Meng Ying, Maimaiti Xiripu as Aili, Zeng Zhensheng as Zhao Bing, Su Han as Alamuhan, Gao Yan as Aximu, Tuouti Aizezi as Director Maimaiti

In the Xinjiang Uighur Autonomous Region prior to liberation, young Communist couple Meng Ying and Zhao Bing are arrested by local tyrant Sheng Shicai. Zhao Bing, the husband, is killed and their infant son rescued by a Uighur nationality man. Eighteen years later, the widowed Meng Ying returns to Xinjiang as the new Party Secretary at the Lanzhou-Xinjiang railway construction site. During the construction, bulldozer operator Aili suggests a new approach but is opposed by undercover reactionaries Wang Dong and Director Maimaiti. Meng Ying supports Aili's idea, and decides to let him first go explore the mountain. At this time, Aili's grandfather, commune director Aximu arrives and demands Meng Ying assign someone else to take on this risky job since Aili is Meng's son he had rescued years before. However, Meng is still determined to give the assignment to Aili. The construction is eventually successful, and mother and son are happily reunited.

2172. *Two Girls (Liang Ge Shao Nu)*

1984. Henan Film Studio. Color. 10 Reels. Direction: Yang Yanjing. Screenplay: Liu Wenmiao, Gong Longxiang, Wan Boao, Guo Qilong. Cinematography: Cai Zhengchang, Song Chunjing. Art Direction: Sun Lin. Music: Xu Jingxin. Sound: Lin Bingsheng, Cui Weimin. Cast: Zhao Jing as Lili, Liu Zhifeng as Doctor Wu, Wei Guochun as Zhiqiang, Zhang Hongli as Sister, Zhao Jing as Shuping, Liu Zhifeng as Zhen Wang

In the first of two unconnected stories, kindly Doctor Wu finds a girl has fainted in front of his house. He brings her into his home and restores her to health. She ingratiates herself into his life, and the two are married. He does not know that the young woman arranged her "collapse" to meet him and marry him for his money. Later, when Doctor Wu goes on a trip and word comes he has been injured, she is very happy at the news.

In the second story, a naive young girl named Shuping is seduced by a young man she has known only briefly. When she finds herself pregnant, Shuping goes to the address he gave her, and finds he has disappeared. Shuping attempts suicide, but is saved by Zhen Wang, a man passing by. He counsels her, and helps her find the courage to go on living.

2173. *Two Heroes' Meeting (Parts 1 & 2) (Shuang Xiong Hui)*

1984. Beijing Film Studio. Color. Wide Screen. 18 Reels. Direction: Chen Huaai. Screenplay: Li Zhun. Cinematography: Nie Jing. Art Direction: Qin Wei, Wang Jixian, Tu Juhua. Music: Du Mingxin. Sound: Liu Shida. Cast: Xu Huanshan as Li Zicheng, Yang Zhaibao as Zhang Xianzhong, Wang Hui as Hao Yaoqi, Zhi Yitong as Xu Mingxian, Xin Jing as Lin Mingqiu

In 1638, a decade of peasant revolts is drawing to a close. Suppression by troops of the decadent Ming government and squabbling among the various peasant groups has left only Li Zicheng's rebels still holding out. His force is surrounded and wiped out by the government troops, but Li is able to flee into the Shangluo Mountains. There, he decides to look for former rebel Zhang Xianzhong. Zhang had surrendered earlier and although pardoned because of ill health he is still not trusted by the government. Li Zicheng meets Zhang at the town of Gucheng and urges Zhang to rebel again. Zhang is interested, but he fears that he and Li will end up in a power struggle once the rebellion is under way, so the negotiations break off without an agreement. Li Zicheng does not give up, but calmly and amiably continues his persuasive efforts. At last, the two forge an alliance against the Ming regime, and one year later succeed in over-throwing it.

2174. *Two Knights and a Woman (Die Xue Jin Lan)*

1992. Tianshan Film Studio. Color. Letter-boxed. 9 Reels. Direction: Sun Sha. Screenplay: Li Yawei. Cinematography: Meng Xianddi, Wen Jiwu. Art Direction: Yang Baocheng, Feng Zhenghuan. Music: Yang Yilun. Sound: Liu Qun, Zhao Xudong. Costume: Qi Chunzhi, Ma Jun. Makeup: Yang Shudong, Ji Weihua. Cast: Shen Junyi as Ji Zhengtian, Yu Hui as Qi Man-ling, Guo Bichuan as Fu Qinquan, Sun Shubing as Hu Weihan, Chen Yongxia as Fu Qinqin, Liu Qinsheng as Zhen Renmei

2175. *Two Little Soccer Teams (Liang Ge Xiao Zhu Qiu Dui)*

1956. Shanghai Film Studio. B & W. 9 Reels. Direction: Liu Qiong. Screenplay: Liang Yanjing. Cinematography: Cha Xiangkang, Lu Junfu. Art Direction: Zhang Xibai. Music: Li Yinhai. Sound: Chen Jingrong. Cast: Zhao Mao as Wang Li, Qiang Ming as the traffic policeman, Liu Xi-anwen as Zhu Ru, Han Fei as Xu Da, Wang Pei as Wu Wenxin, Zhang Huaqiang as Zhou Bing

Wang Li, Zhou Bing and Li Ming are three good friends, all key players on their school's soccer team. After Wang Li is named captain of the senior class team, he becomes very arro-gant. No longer a team player, he uses each game as a showcase for his own ability, and offers no help to his teammates. Junior class player Li Ming, on the other hand, is sincere and modest, a team player who helps others. The junior class team does very well. When the intramural soccer contest is played, Wang Li's attempt to put on a one-man show results in a loss for his senior team and an injury to his friend Li Ming. With help from his teach-ers, parents and classmates, Wang Li realizes his mistakes and finally became an excellent school soccer team member. The three friends become even closer as a result.

2176. *Two Pairs of Halves (Liang Dui Ban)*

1986. Xi'an Film Studio. Color. 9 Reels. Di-rection: Wang Zhijie. Screenplay: Wang Zhijie, Ni Yunhong. Cinematography: Duan Deren, Li Jianzhen. Art Direction: Hu Qiangsheng, Wang Yingbing. Music: Xiang Yin. Sound: Hong Jiahui. Cast: Aodeng Gaowa as Qiumei, Tan Xin as Jin Gui, Chen Hongmei as Wang Chunlan, Ma Ling as Lady Yang, Ge Zhijun as Wu Laoshan

Lady Yang and Wu Laoshan strike an agreement to pair up their daughters and sons, and that someday their families will be interre-lated through these marriages. When the time comes years later to carry out the agreed-to arrangement, the children predictably balk and choose their own partners.

2177. *Two Patrol Soldiers (Liang Ge Xun Luo Bing)*

1958. Jiangnan Film Studio. B & W. 9 Reels. Direction: Fang Huang. Screenplay: Ji Kang, Gong Pu. Cinematography: Xian Yu. Art Direc-tion: Liu Pan, Li Pingye. Music: Gao Tian. Sound: Lin Bingsheng. Cast: Bai Mu as Ma Changgeng, Feng Xiao as Xiao Yan, Er Lin as Mi Xia, Liu Fei as Yan Guang, Sun Jinglu as Yixian, Lan Gu as Wu Dahai, Fu Botang as Yang Guocai, Li Baoluo as Old Song

Two soldiers stationed along the South China border, the veteran Ma Changgeng and young recruit Xiao Yan, are good friends as well as comrades-in-arms. One night while they are on patrol, Ma Changgeng's careless-ness in smoking allows some enemy agents to cross the border into China. The agents are later tracked down and killed, but when Xiao Yan criticizes Ma, the veteran refuses to accept it, and the two break off their friendship over the incident. Another time, some enemy agents are air-dropped into China, and Ma again fails in his duty by passing on agent Yang Guocai, disguised as an old woman. Ma Changgeng is punished for this, and reassigned to work as a cook's helper. With the help of veteran cook Old Song and others, he comes to realize his errors. Later, Ma redeems himself by helping Xiao Yan coordinate the border troops in tracking down Yang Guocai. The two become friends again.

2178. *Two Virtuous Women (Zhen Nu)*

1987. Beijing Film Studio. Color. 10 Reels.

Direction: Huang Jianzhong. Screenplay: Gu Hua (1942–), based on his novel of the same title. Cinematography: Chen Youqun. Art Direction: Yu Fengming. Music: Si Wanchun. Sound: Zhen Chunyu. Cast: Gu Yan as Guihua, Fu Yiwei as Qingyu, He Wei as Che Ganzhi, Li Baotian as Wu Laoda, Li Dan as Shanshao

Qingyu and Guihua are two young women who live in different times, but both suffer the trauma of traditional Chinese morality. Qingyu is an innocent Qing Dynasty maiden of only 18. After her husband dies an early death, she is forced to remain a widow. For the rest of her life she chants scriptures daily and abstains from eating meat, her only companions an oil lamp and a small dog. In her self-realization process, Qingyu gradually becomes aware of the evils of feudal ethics, and in the end dies for love, nursing her hatred. The time shifts to present-day rural China. Guihua is an innkeeper, young, beautiful and hardworking. Her husband is a truck driver, an abusive man named Wu Laoda. After suffering all she can bear of her husband's maltreatment, Guihua asks for a divorce. Because of this action, she is subjected to constant insults and abuse from their neighbors, and almost buried alive.

Two Virtuous Women. Qingyu (Fu Yiwei) is a victim of traditional Chinese morality, forced to remain a widow after her husband dies. 1987. Beijing Film Studio.

2179. *The Two You Sisters in the Red Mansion (Hong Lou Er You)*

1951. Guotai Film Studio. B & W. 12 reels. Direction: Yang Xiaozong. Screenplay: Yang Xiaozhong, based on Chen Linxi's original adaptation of the classic novel, "A Dream of Red Mansions" (Hong Lou Meng) by Cao Xueqin (1717–1763). Cinematography: Zhu Jing. Cast: Yan Huizhu as Third Sister You, Lin Muyu as Second Sister You, Jin Chuan as Liu Xianglian, Li Baoshou as Jia Zhen, Zhou Chu as Jia Lian, Lu Shan as Wang Xifeng, Kang Zou as Jia Rong

During the era when the Qing (Manchu) Dynasty was at the height of its brilliance and power (1662–1796), the two You sisters arrive with their mother for a wedding celebration at the Jia family's mansion. Their beauty quickly draws the attention of their distant cousin, the Jia family's playboy son, Jia Zhen. He sets out to seduce them, making use of their poor family background. Third Sister You is a strong young woman, not beguiled by wealth or power; her love is Liu Xianglian, an opera performer of low class origins. Second Sister You is weaker: she is seduced by Jia Zhen, then later secretly married to his younger brother Jia Lian as a second wife. To avoid Jia Zhen's per-

sistent blandishments, Third Sister You returns to her countryside home and sees Liu Xianglian again. She sends him a sword as a symbol of their betrothal. Soon after, Jia Lian's first wife Wang Xifeng discovers her husband's secret marriage to Second Sister You; she takes Second Sister You into her home, but bullies and mistreats her when Jia Lian leaves on a trip. She also gives the second wife some medicine which aborts her baby. After Jia Lian returns, she does not allow Second Sister to see him. By this time, Jia Lian has taken a new lover and abandons Second Sister. Upset and remorseful, Second Sister commits suicide. When her sister learns of this, she returns to the Jia mansion to confront the family. But Jia Zhen spreads rumors about her to destroy her reputation. The rumors reach the ears of Liu Xianglian, causing him to break their engagement. Third Sister You commits suicide over this. When Xianglian learns the truth, he is overcome with regret and flees, vowing he will avenge Third Sister someday.

2180. *Two Young Eighth Route Army Soldiers (Liang Ge Xiao Ba Lu)*

1978. Changchun Film Studio. Color. 10 Reels. Direction: Zhu Wenshun. Screenplay: Li Xintian. Cinematography: Zhang Songping. Art Direction: Tong Jingwen, Wu Qiwen. Music: Zang Dongsheng, Zhang Jingyuan. Sound: Liu Yushan. Cast: Ma Ren as Sun Daxing, Li Jianjun as Wu Jianhua ("Little Wu"), Shi Kefu as Jin Xiwu, Li Ying as Jin's wife, Li Wenwei as Grandpa Liu, Liu Huimin as Grandma Liu

In 1943, Daxing and Little Wu, two young Eighth Route Army soldiers, are wounded. Underground Party member Jin Xiwu arranges for them to recover in the home of his in-laws, Grandpa and Grandma Liu. Their town, Liu Ji, is under Japanese occupation. Jin and the Lius learn that the Japanese plan an attack on the Eighth Route Army's base, so they prepare to notify the Communist forces. However, Daxing and Little Wu act on their own and burn down the enemy's grain storage, disrupting the Party organization's plans, subjecting them to Party criticism. Jin later gives the youngsters a second chance by sending them to scout the enemy's defense. The two risk their lives to deliver information to the Eighth Route base. The Japanese are driven from Liu Ji, and Daxing and Little Wu return to the army.

2181. *An Unbending Woman (Jue Jiang De Nu Ren)*

1983. Fujian Film Studio. Color. 10 Reels. Direction: Da Qi. Screenplay: Zhou Weizhi. Cinematography: Cai Naide, Lin Bingkun. Art Direction: Chen Xiaoxia. Music: Zhang Shaotong. Sound: Wu Hua, Liu Jijie. Cast: Qin Yi as Meng Hua, Da Qi as Xing Dawei, Min Zhi as Zhang Peiwen, Tu Lan as Cao Wu

At the end of the Cultural Revolution, chemical engineer Meng Hua returns from the countryside to her former unit, the Shanjiang City Chemical Plant, where she is now Chief Engineer. Although she suffered much during those years in exile, including the loss of her husband, she has lost no enthusiasm for her work. In the process of installing new, imported equipment, she reaches the conclusion that the management system is backward and inappropriate for modernization of the chemical industry. She lobbies for a change which will put a new, professionally competent director in place, and nominates herself for the job.

2182. *Unconventional Small Station (Feng Liu Xiao Zhan)*

1988. Xiaoxiang Film Studio. Color. Letterboxed. 9 Reels. Direction: Chen Lu. Screenplay: Jiang Xun, Xiao Wen. Cinematography: Yu Li Ping. Art Direction: Xiong Jianhua. Music: Ji Xiping, Chen Lang. Sound: Liu Yishen. Cast: Zhu Yurong as Station Director Yao, Wang Guoqiang as Zhang Zhang

As economic reforms take hold in China, the volume of goods transported in the countryside grows dramatically. One state-owned transport station cannot meet the demand. Although Station Director Yao works very hard, her conservative approach results in a declining situation and lower employee income. Contrasted with this is a nearby privately owned transport station which farmer Zhang Zhang started with just a tractor; it is booming. In order to improve the situation, Yao decides to sell an old truck and then use the money as a bonus for employees. Zhang Zhang signs a contract with Yao and purchases the truck. However, the situation at Yao's station continues to fail and she herself is removed from her post due to certain irregularities in selling the truck. Zhang Zhang is invited to run the state-owned station because of his capability. Zhang goes to Yao and sincerely points out the reasons for her failure; he then invites her to be his partner. Yao examines everything she did before and draws a lesson from it. The two now work together.

2183. *Unconventional Woman Detective (Feng Liu Nu Tan)*

1988. Shanghai Film Studio & Zhejiang Film Studio Jointly. Color. Letterboxed. 9 Reels. Direction: Li Xin. Screenplay: Li Xin. Cinematography: Zhang Dongdong. Art Direction: Lu Jun, Wang Jianjun. Music: Li Lifu. Sound: Zhang Hua, Guo Qiang. Cast: Wu Dan as Wu Bing, Lu Jun as Tengye Tailang

PSB inspector Qi Haimin, who had been investigating a case of people being sold abroad, is found shot to death. The murder investigation is assigned to woman investigator Wu Bing. With the help of Interpol detective Tengye Tailang, Wu Bing finds that a language school is really a front for the illegal kidnapping and people-smuggling activities. At last, however, her investigation also finds that Tengye Tailang is the actual killer. When cornered, the killer chooses to leap from a building and commit suicide. The case is closed.

2184. *An Unconventional Woman Spy (Feng Liu Nu Die)*

1989. Beijing Film Studio and Hainan International Film and Television Company Co-Production. Color. Wide Screen. 10 Reels. Direction: Du Yu. Screenplay: Liu Xi. Cinematography: Chen Youqun, Cheng Zhong. Art Direction: Mo Kezhan, Ma Zhaoren. Music: Ai Liqun. Sound: Zhang Zhizhong. Cast: Fu Yiwei as Chuandao Fangzi, Wusong Xiaozhang as Chuandao Liangsuo, Li Rentang as Prince Su, Jirri Gele as Ganzhuer Zhabu, Gao Du as Xiaocai Qincui, Xu Zhanshan as Yanho, Shen Guanchu as Jiaheng, Zhang Jianmin as Shengshan, Yang Yannan as Heiganzi

The true story of Jin Bihui, born the daughter of Manchu Prince Su toward the end of the Qing Dynasty. When the empire collapses, the Prince sends his six-year-old daughter to Japan to be raised. She is given a Japanese name and education, and is trained from childhood in the techniques of espionage. After she grows up, Jin returns to China as a spy, and is directly involved with many of the war crimes committed in China by the Japanese. After World War II ends, she is imprisoned in China, and in 1948 is executed as a war criminal at the age of 42.

2185. *Under the Bridge (Da Qiao Xia Mian)*

1983. Shanghai Film Studio. Color. 11 Reels. Direction: Bai Cheng. Screenplay: Bai Cheng, Ling Qiwei, Zhu Dian, Zhen Binghui. Cinematography: Qiu Yiren. Art Direction: Jin Qifeng. Music: Liu Yanxi. Sound: Feng Deyao. Cast: Gong Xue as Qin Nan, Zhang Tielin as Gao Zhihua, Wang Ping as Gao's mother, Yin Xin as Xiao Yun, Fang Chao as Dongdong

Soon after an educated young woman named Qin Nan is permitted to return to her urban home from the countryside, she meets a young man named Gao Zhihua who has had a similar experience in life. The two fall in love. Gao Zhihua's mother is particularly impressed with her son's choice, and she hopes the two will marry. But Qin Nan has a secret past: during her time in the countryside, she had an affair which left her with a small son called Dongdong. After much soul-searching, she decides to be open about her past, and brings Dongdong to live with her in the city. This is shattering to the Gao family, and the mother makes clear its unacceptability. Gao Zhihua is also shocked at the revelation, but he decides

that his personal happiness demands a break with tradition. He asks Qin Nan to marry him and build a new life together with her child.

Best Actress Gong Xue, 1984 Golden Rooster Awards.

Best Actress Gong Xue, 1984 Hundred Flowers Awards.

2186. *Under the White Poplar Tree (Bai Yang Shu Xia)*

1983. Guangxi Film Studio. Color. 9 Reels. Direction: Ba Hong, Xing Rong. Screenplay: Peng Mingyan. Cinematography: Wen Zhixian. Art Direction: Cheng Rongyuan. Music: Su Tie. Sound: Li Zhuwen. Cast: Xia Liyan as Jiang Hong, Jia Liu as Mr. Fu, Wu Yi as Mrs. Fu, Zhang Yan as Old Mr. Xue, Wang Wei as Xue Guangming, Huang Huanfeng as Fu Gang, Wang Benzhou as Fu Qiang, Yu Sheng as Zhang Fang

A girl named Jiang Hong and two boys named Xue Guangming and Fu Gang are three close friends sent down from the city to work on a farm. There, Jiang Hong and Fu Gang fall in love, so when Fu Gang has the opportunity to return to the city he gives it to Xue Guangming, allowing Xue to care for his aging parents. Fu Gang later enters the army but dies in service. After she returns to the city, Jiang Hong gets together with Xue Guangming and the two marry. Fu Gang's younger brother Fu Qiang is devoted to his job, and his parents help out by doing his family housework. However, when Fu Qiang's mother falls ill, Fu Qiang's wife Zhang Fang uses all sorts of excuses to keep the family from spending anything on her mother-in-law's treatment. A family argument erupts, and Zhang Fang leaves home despite Jiang Hong's attempts to dissuade her. At New Year's Eve, the entire family thinks of Zhang Fang and how much they miss her. Alone on the holiday, Zhang Fang recalls the good family life she left, and weeps quietly.

2187. *Undercover Investigation in the Golden Triangle (Mi Chuang Jin San Jiao)*

1988. Youth Film Studio. Color. Letterboxed. 9 Reels. Direction: Zhen Dongtian. Screenplay: Xiao Jian, Zhan Xiangchi, Zhen Dongtian. Cinematography: Qu Jianwei. Art Direction: Wang Yanjing. Music: Hao Jian, Dong Liqiang. Sound: Huang Yingxia. Cast: Zhang Fang as Mr. Dai,

Xue Yong as Huang Lin, Zhao Jianwen as Bai Hu, Wang Rui as Black Cat

A Hong Kong drug organization sends some of its people into Southeast Asia's "Golden Triangle" region to seek out a new channel for their drug traffic. Beijing authorities assign undercover agent "09" to infiltrate the organization and counter their actions. "09," whose real name is Bai Hu, is successful in infiltrating the gang, and after surviving a series of risky adventures and narrow escapes, he accomplishes the initial phase of his mission and is assigned to continue his mission in Hong Kong.

2188. *The Undercover Vanguard (Dixia Jianbing)*

1957. Changchun Film Studio. B & W. 10 Reels. Direction: Wu Zhaodi. Screenplay: Liu Zhixiang. Cinematography: Chen Minhun. Art Direction: Dong Ping. Music: Li Ning. Sound: Jiang Junfeng. Cast: Pu Ke as Tao Gan. Li Lin as Zhou Zhifu, Zhang Yuan as Sun Ying, Chen Rubing as Ai Yongbo, Zhang Juguang as Song Xin, Li Mengrao as Director Tian

Shortly before the liberation of Beiping (now Beijing), Communist "Red Pine Team" cell leader Tao Gan assumes the cover name and identity of a trading company manager. His objective is to acquire a key item of information, specifically the date that U.S. military advisors want the Nationalist 6th Army Division withdrawn from the Beiping area and relocated to a less vulnerable position. The information is to be transmitted to the Nationalists via agent Zhou Zhifu. Tao Gan makes Zhou Zhifu's acquaintance, but the latter is too sophisticated to divulge anything worthwhile, and repeatedly thwarts the Communist's best efforts with false clues. Tao is able to replace Zhou's assistant with his own man, Ai Yongbo. Ai Yongbo learns the withdrawal date and relays it to Tao Gan, but Ai soon does something to arouse Zhou Zhifu's suspicion, and Zhou puts out the false story that the withdrawal has been postponed. To confirm this information, Tao Gan takes the risk of meeting Ai Yongbo, and as a result he decides the postponement story is false. As they leave their meeting place, Zhou and his agents spring the trap. Ai Yongbo sacrifices himself so that Tao Gan can get away and deliver the information to the Communist forces. The Nationalists withdraw on the scheduled date, but the Communists, acting on Tao's information,

ambush the 6th Division and wipe it out entirely.

2189. *Undercover Young Pioneers (Di Xia Shao Xian Dui)*

1959. Tianma Film Studio. B & W. 10 Reels. Direction: Gao Heng. Screenplay: Xi Lide, based on a stage play originally produced by the China Welfare Association's Children's Art Theater. Cinematography: Luo Jizhi. Art Direction: Lu Jingguang. Music: Chen Mingzhi, Chang Xhouzong. Sound: Zhou Yunling. Cast: Liu Angu as Jiang Dacheng, Jiang Zhiqiang as Lu Xiaoke, Gu Guoyi as Chen Yuzhen, Kang Ansheng as He Guisheng, Yao Jinshi as Wu Guangen, Lin Bin as Teacher Yang, Zheng Min as Principal Zhu, Zhang Xiaofen as Mother Jiang, Jiang Shan as the doorkeeper

On the eve of the liberation of Shanghai, Jiang Dacheng, Chen Yuzhen and Lu Xiaoke are members of a covert Young Pioneers group in their high school. Under the guidance of Teacher Yang, they edit an underground student newspaper and distribute handbills which expose the corrupt Nationalist government and urge the people to revolutionary struggle. They arouse the suspicions of government agent Inspector Wu and school principal Zhu, but Teacher Yang covers them himself. Finally, the finger of suspicion points to Yang as the instigator, and agents are sent to arrest him. But the students help their teacher escape to safety. After the liberation of Shanghai, the underground Young Pioneers hold a formal ceremony of joining the organization.

2190. *The Underground Transport Route (Di Xia Hang Xian)*

1959. Tianma Film Studio. B & W. 11 Reels. Direction: Gu Eryi. Screenplay: Zuo Qing, He Zepei, Wang Pengnian. Cinematography: Cha Xiangkang. Art Direction: Wang Yuebai. Music: Wang Yi. Sound: Gong Lianqing. Makeup: Li Ping. Cast: Zhong Shuhuang as Lin Shengguan, Qi Heng as Chen Awang, Shi Jiufeng as Jiang Caide, Jiang Shan as Staff Officer Wei, Wang Qi as the branch director, Lin Bin as Shengguan's wife, Zhou Yiqin as Xiao Yu, Yu Fei as Captain Yang

In 1947, Lin Shengguan is the pilot of a river boat in Fujian province by day, and a CPC undercover agent at night. With his comrade Jiang Caidi, he devises an secret route for running guns to a Communist guerrilla base. On one of their nighttime trips, they are followed by a government agent, but Shengguan kills the agent before he can report their activities. An old pilot named Chen Awang witnesses this. Government agents have a priest pressure Awang, a Christian, to tell them all he knows. After an ideological struggle, Awang decides not to tell them the truth. Soon after, Shengguan accepts another gunrunning mission, and is followed by two government boats. When Shengguan arrives at the rendezvous site, a guerrilla troop dressed as government security forces begins to unload all the weapons as the government boats draw close. Just as the pursuers arrive, Old Awang takes control of Shengguan's boat and drives it into the pursuing ships, dying with the enemy and saving the mission.

2191. *The Uneasy Journey (Bu Ping Jing De Lu Cheng)*

1983. Shanghai Film Studio. Color. 10 Reels. Direction: Tang Huada. Screenplay: Li Pingfen, Lu Wei, Yu Bengzheng Cinematography: Luo Jisheng. Art Direction: Wu Weifei. Music: Xu Jingxin. Sound: Dong Jujing. Cast: Gao Bo as Fang Yizhi, He Ling as Fang Jisheng, You Jia as Ding Lan, Ye Zhikang as Zhang Guoqiang, Chen Ye as Fang Juan, Zhou Guobing as Fang Rongsheng

When a city's Party Secretary Fang Yizhi retires, he decides to take advantage of a policy dictating that people separated from their children during the Cultural Revolution may upon retirement bring one child back to live with them in the city. Fang has four grown children scattered throughout China; which will he choose? To help him decide which of his children most need relocation, Fang travels on a visit to each. He first visits his eldest son Fang Jisheng, who is shocked to learn his father is retiring, for he feels this will be detrimental to his own interests. Fang Yizhi decides his son has grown so selfish he does not deserve to be brought back. His daughter Fang Juan had a rocky marriage in the past. On this visit, although he does not meet her himself, he finds her home a happy and warm one, so he feels comfortable leaving her there. On his way to visit his second son, Fang Yizhi finds that his youngest, geologist Fang Rongsheng, is away at a new prospecting site. Fang Yizhi is happy with the youngest son's situation, and proceeds to visit Fang Rongsheng, his second son. Rong works at a leper colony hospital hidden deep in the mountains. He tells his father that he is

devoted to the place and to his work, and does not want to leave. Satisfied with this child's situation as well, Fang Yizhi returns home by himself.

2192. *The Unexpected Passion (Zao Yu Ji Qing)*

1990. Beijing Film Studio. Color. 9 Reels. Wide Screen. Direction: Xiao Gang. Screenplay: Zheng Xiaolong, Feng Xiaogang. Cinematography: Zeng Nianping. Art Direction: Huo Jianqi. Music: Lei Lei. Sound: Li Bojiang, Guan Jian. Cast: Yuan Yuan as Liu He, Lu Liping as Liang Xiaoqing

Liu He is an extra at a film studio. Poor, and not particularly attractive, he has no success in love. By chance he meets Dr. Liang Xiaoqing, a young woman suffering from terminal cancer. An ill fate has brought them together, but passion blossoms soon between them. The determined young man's tenderness brings joy to the heart of a dying young girl. They are to share three months of romance.

2193. *Unfalling Horizon (Bu Cheng De Di Ping Xian)*

1987. Emei Film Studio. Color. 10 Reels. Direction: Mi Jiashan, Han Shanping. Screenplay: Ge Guangjian, Jiang Huansun. Cinematography: Luo Xun, Rao Ren. Art Direction: Wang Longsheng. Sound: Li Jian. Cast: Wang Zhenrong as Zhou Liang, Wu Jian as Zhou Liang, Sun Fengyin as Yuxiu, Yi Hongwei as Chen Xiaogui, Dong Danunjun as Wang Lianshan

As he prepares for the ceremony honoring him on his retirement, PLA Deputy Commander Zhou Liang looks back over his career, particularly his early days in the Red Army on the Long March. He had been a bandit before joining the Red Army, and actually enlisted because it would afford him greater opportunities to make money by stealing. The story tells how Zhou is gradually changed by his experiences on the Long March, particularly his assignment to a special squad entrusted with protecting a large sack of money and transporting it to the main Red Army force. At first, he plans to steal the money and desert, but as his comrades are killed one by one protecting it, he becomes dedicated to the mission and to the revolution. At last, the sole survivor from the squad, he arrives at the main force's camp and turns in the money.

2194. *An Unfinished Chess Game (Yi Pan Mei You Xia Wan De Qi)*

1982. Beijing Film Studio & Japan Dongguangdejian Film Studio Co-Production. Color. 10 Reels. Direction: Zuoteng Chunmi and Duan Jishun. Screenplay: Li Hongzhou, Ge Kangtong, Dayejinzhi, Anpeichelang and Shengboshinan. Cinematography: Anteng Zhuangping and Luo Dean. Art Direction: Muchunweifu and Xiao Bing. Music: Lin Guang and Jiang Dingxian. Sound: Qiaobeng Wenxiong, Lu Xiancang. Cast: Sun Daolin as Kuang Yishan, Du Peng as Guan Xiaozhou, Shen Guanchun as A Min, Shanguo Liantailang as Songbo Lingzhuo, Shantian Jiazhi as Ren

When the famous Japanese chess player Songbo Lingzhuo is invited to China in the 1920s, "South China's Chess King" Kuang Yishan accepts an invitation to meet him, and brings along his eight-year-old son Amin. Kuang and Songbo greatly admire each other's skill, and the Japanese notes that little Amin shows real aptitude for the game as well. The two masters start a game, but the deteriorating political situation between their countries interrupts it. Kuang Yishan trains Amin to play chess, and later sends the youngster to Japan to study with Songbo. Amin lives with the Japanese master's family, and eventually marries and has a baby girl with Songbo's daughter Ba. Amin attains the highest chess ranking in Japan, but his refusal to become a Japanese citizen leads to his murder during the war. His death drives his wife Ba insane. When World War II ends, Kuang Yishan goes to Japan to look for his son Amin but learns he is dead. In 1949, the PRC is established and Kuang Yishan begins a new life. He decides to train a new generation of Chinese chess players. In 1956, Songbo is part of a Japanese chess delegation visiting China, and he brings Amin's daughter along to visit Kuang Yishan. He also brings Amin's ashes to Kuang Yishan and his wife. Then the two old friends, having gone through so many ups and downs in their lives, finally sit down to finish the chess game they had started 30 years before. (Note: the chess game referred to is the Asian version called "Weiqi" in China and "Go" in Japan.)

2195. *An Unfinished Comedy (Wei Wan Cheng De Xi Ju)*

1957. Changchun Film Studio. B & W. 8 Reels. Direction: Lu Ban. Screenplay: Luo Tai and Lu Ban. Cinematography: Zhang Hui. Art Direction: Xu Wei. Music: Ma Lin and Zhang Yutian. Sound: Zhang Jianping. Cast: Fang Hua as Yi Bingzhi (The Critic), Su Manyi as Lan Yan, Chen Zong as Director Li, Ning Jiaping as Mother, Zhang Qingzhen as Little Sister, Bai Mei as the Oldest Son's Wife

Two nationally famous comic actors make a study visit to the Changchun Film Studio, where they watch three comedies. The first story satirizes a leading cadre manager named Zhu who loves taking it easy and hates to work. The second satirizes people who indulge in boasting and overstatement. The third satirizes two brothers who abandon their elderly mother. The critic accompanying the two criticizes the three comedies and puts labels on them.

2196. *The Unfinished Diary (Wei Wan Cheng De Ri Ji)*

1991. Children's Film Studio. Color. 8 Reels. Direction: Huang Jun. Screenplay: Xia Youzhi. Cinematography: Xie Ping. Art Direction: Zhang Yikuan. Music: Liu Weiyi. Sound: Lan Fan. Costume: Liu Yun. Makeup: Sun Bing. Cast: Zhang Ning as Lai Ning, Zhu Jiang as Xu Zi, Yi Han as Wang Jiang, Du Jiangning as Father, Gao Chengjun as Mother, Zhou Ayi as Little Sister

A morality play for teenagers and children, told through a series of stories about the life and good works of Lai Ning, a Chinese teenage role model.

2197. *Unforgettable Battle (Nan Wang De Zhan Dou)*

1976. Shanghai Film Studio. Color. 12 Reels. Direction: Tang Xiaodan, Tian Ran. Screenplay: Collective, recorded by Sun Jingrui and based on his novel of the same title. Cinematography: Xu Qi, Ma Linfa, Zhu Yongde. Art Direction: Ding Cheng. Music: Xu Jingxin. Cast: Da Shichang as Tian Wenzhong, Zhou Guobing as Zhao Dongsheng, Ma Cangyu as Li Guangmin, Chen Ye as Fan Kejun, Zhang Yunli as Qin Laogang, Xu Bu as Sun Xiongfei, Bai Mu as Chen Futang

In 1949, after the PLA liberates the city of Fuguo in southeast China, the Nationalists give secret agent Chen Futang an undercover assignment as a grain store manager. His mission is to gain control of the city's grain supply and use it subvert the new Communist administration. PLA administrative grain purchase work team director Tian Wenzhong brings a work team into the grain producing area, and organizes the people to battle the conspiracy. After a series of battles with undercover agents, traitors and bandits, Tian and his team smash their enemy's conspiracy, and catch both Chen Futang and the bandits' chief.

2198. *Unforgettable High School Days (Nan Wang De Zhong Xue Shi Guang)*

1986. Changchun Film Studio. Color. 10 Reels. Direction: Yu Zhongxiao, Lu Jianhua. Screenplay: Dai Lu, Lu Jianhua. Cinematography: Feng Bingyong. Art Direction: Gao Guoliang. Music: Wang Ming. Sound: Dong Baosheng. Cast: Luo Gang as Zhou Yi, Yang Liyi as Wang Xiaohui, Gu Ying as Wang Daguang, Huang Jingtang as Guan Ming, Chen Wei as Lin Chunmei

Zhou Yi is an excellent student at Huanghai High School. His dream is to gain admission to one of China's "key" universities. His neighbor, a girl student named Wang Xiaohui, studies very hard. The story deals with the problems of these young people as they work toward their educational goals. At last, all are admitted to college except Zhou Yi, who gives up his chance to take the exams for family reasons. He vows to make a strong effort to gain a college education on his own at an open university.

2199. *Unfortunate Women (Bei Tun Chi De Nu Zi)*

1988. Tianshan Film Studio and Lanzhou Film Studio Co-Production. Color. Letterboxed. 9 Reels. Direction: Fan Minren. Screenplay: Zhang Fang. Cinematography: Zhang Xiaoguang. Art Direction: Wang Chuncheng. Music: Guan Tianzi. Sound: Wang Jie, Xiong Huajuan. Cast: Liu Peiqin as Lin Gengsheng, Xu Ning as Ye Nu, Chen Jing as Yingzhen, Hu Xiaoguang as Hu Dali

Lin Gengsheng, a scientist at a desert research institute, makes an exploratory trip to a very remote part of the desert to complete a project. He becomes acquainted with Ye Nu, a local girl, who tells him of a nearby "ghost town," which local custom forbids outsiders from entering. Curious, Lin approaches the town, and a sudden sandstorm forces him to seek sanctuary there. This angers the local people, who also blame Ye Nu for telling him of it. In addition to Ye Nu's story, a subplot

concerns her friend Yingzhen, struggling to avoid an arranged marriage. Both women come to tragic ends, as Yingzhen commits suicide and Ye Nu loses her mind from the combination of her people's criticism, her friend's death and Lin Gengsheng's sudden decision to leave.

2200. *Unique Skill Of Cangzhou (Cang Zhou Jue Zhao)*

1991. Changchun Film Studio. Color. Letterboxed. 9 Reels. Direction: Xu Shutian, Screenplay: An Shihua, Cinematography: Meng Xiandi, Zhang Dingyu, Art Direction: Tian Feng, Music: Deng Erbo, Sound: Dong Baosheng, Cast: Zhang Xucheng, An Yaping, Chao Ping, Zhang Zhaobei

In modern Cangzhou, known historically as the home of Chinese kung fu, famed martial arts expert Wu Lengtian keeps in his home a book which details many kung fu secrets. The film follows his struggles to retain possession of the book, sought by many different people with different motives.

2201. *Uniting Against the Invaders (Kang Bao Sheng Si Lian)*

1992. Yunnan Minority Film Studio. Color. Letterboxed. 9 Reels. Direction: Qiu Lili, Xiao Feng. Screenplay: Ni Feng. Cinematography: Ning Jiakun, Li Erjing. Art Direction: Li Zhengxin, Xu Shaojun. Music: Guo Wenjing. Sound: Ouyang Feng. Costume: Shi Ping, Zhao Qiongxian. Makeup; Duan Hong, Guan Jun. Cast: Huang Guoqiang as Dagelai, Li Yunjuan as Ye Qia, Yang Minsheng as Le Jiawang, He Meiping as Bolipa, Dani Yaer as Chilunde

In the mid–19th century, Dagelai and Ye Qia, a young Suli nationality couple, find their wedding interrupted by the arrival of soldiers commanded by local leader Le Jiawang. They try to arrest Dagelai, but he resists and in doing so falls into the river, assumed drowned. Two years later, the young man shows up again in his hometown under another name. At this time, the British troops invade China, and Dagelai makes common cause with his old nemesis Le Jiawang to repel the invaders. Ye Qia, however, has been converted to Christianity and sides with the British in the struggle. She realizes her mistake too late, and is killed in the fighting. Dagelai is able to kill the British commander.

2202. *Unlimited Potential (Wu Qiong De Qian Li)*

1954. Northeast Film Studio. B & W. 10 Reels. Direction: Xu Ke. Screenplay: Yu Min. Cinematography: Wang Chunquan. Art Direction: Zhang Jingnan. Music: Su Min. Sound: Huang Lijia. Cast: Xie Tian as Meng Changyou, Chen Ge as Secretary Liu, Wei Yuping as the Factory Director, Yi Yiqing as Engineer Ding, Lu Fei as Jin Ming, Fang Hui as Big Li

In the early years after liberation, the outmoded facilities in a small Northeast China steel mill keep the workers from doing their jobs well. In addition, the workers have little job security. The director of the inventory department proposes a facility upgrade based on his two years of studying problems. Engineer Ding, who goes strictly by the book in everything, believes the risks are too great; the bureaucratic plant director is also opposed. Only the mill's Party Secretary Liu supports Meng Changyou's suggestion. The first test fails due to a flawed design, but with Engineer Ding finally seeing the light and helping, Meng Changyou overcomes the difficulties and devises a new method. With the steelmaking process automated and mechanized, working conditions improve and production is more efficient.

2203. *An Unlucky Married Man (Hun Wai Lian Zhe De Qi Yu)*

1994. Changchun Film Studio. Color. Letterboxed. 9 Reels. Direction: Zhang Zhongwei. Screenplay: Zhang Zhongwei, Wang Xiaolian. Cinematography: Qian Daming. Art Direction: Wang Di. Music: Guo Xiaotian. Sound: Sheng Hongtao, Yuan Xuefeng. Costume: Bai Lu. Makeup: Yan Zhenrong. Cast: Gong Hanlin as Zhou Changchou, Jin Zhu as Zhao Ling, Chao Xiao as Wang Shengli, Zhao Xintian as Yingzi, Zhan Jingbo as the fat man, Zhang Zhongwei as the Chief of Detectives, Guo Yifeng as Liu Huan

When his wife Zhao Ling becomes pregnant, bored clothing store owner Zhou Cangshou, starts an affair with a girl named Yingzi. One evening he arrives at her home to pick her up for a date, and finds her dead, an apparent murder victim. Frightened, he flees without reporting the incident. He starts receiving phone calls from a man wanting to blackmail him. He starts making payments to the blackmailer. His increasingly irrational behavior is noticed by his wife and customers. Then one day, on the street, he sees the supposedly dead Yingzi.

Shocked, he starts his own investigation and at last finds the girl's "murder" was a hoax, set up by Yingzi and her partner, a man named Wang. Zhou at last breaks down and tells his wife, who convinces him they should go to the police. The blackmailers are arrested, but the stress of it all has deranged Zhou Cangshou's mind.

2204. *Unquiet Days (Bu Ping Jing De Ri Zi)*

1978. Pearl River Film Studio. B & W. 10 Reels. Direction: Yu Deshui. Screenplay: Xie Min. Cinematography: Huang Yonghu. Art Direction: Zhou Chenren. Music: Liang Lizhu. Sound: Jiang Shaoqi. Cast: Tian Dan as Chen Chishui, Zhang Jie as Gao Peng, Jian Ruichao as Meng Guang, Yu Xiamei as Hai Hua, Wang Zhifang as Li Ying, Zhang Lianfu as Tian Geng

After Mao Zedong's death in 1976, a large provincial oil refinery vigorously develops its production under the leadership of plant Party Secretary Chen Chishui. Provincial Party Secretary Xiang Chunsheng decides the lessons of this plant's experience should be spread throughout the province. However, the provincial revolutionary committee Deputy Director Cui Hanjie, supported by the Central Party Deputy Chairman Wang Hongwen, one of the "Gang of Four" try to disrupt production. They attempt a power grab by attacking Chen Chishui and Xiang Chunsheng. Chen and Xiang firmly oppose them. Just as the struggle reaches its most intense period, news arrives that the Gang of Four has been defeated.

2205. *Unrequited Love (Re Lian)*

1989. Emei Film Studio. Color. 10 Reels. Letterboxed. Direction: Lu Xiaoya. Screenplay: Lu Xiaoya. Cinematography: Li Baoqi. Art Direction: Gan Shaocheng. Music: Lei Lei. Sound: Luo Guohua, Shen Jinghua. Cast: Li Kechun as Wen Jiefei, Lu Xiaohe as Fan Jiyuan, Xiong Dahua as Zhang Shu

Following its upgrading to provincial status in the 1980s, Hainan Island developed rapidly, and is now China's largest special economic zone. Wen Jiefei, a graduate from a teacher's college on the mainland, comes to the island with her hopes and dreams, just like hundreds of thousands of other young people. After several unsatisfactory jobs, she at last finds work teaching. For a time she dates her old classmate and colleague Zhang Xu, a middle school teacher, but then rich peasant entrepreneur Fan Jiyuan enters her life and they begin a serious romance. Zhang Xu leaves the island when his dreams turn sour, his love for Wen unrequited and his teaching undervalued by Hainan's money-obsessed society. Wen Jiefei marries Fan, but soon becomes aware there is a sizable educational and cultural gap between them. They have a son, but the birth only seems to make her more confused and unhappy.

2206. *Unsolved Case No. 9 (Di Jiu Hao Xuan An)*

1990. Beijing Film Studio. Color. Wide Screen. 9 Reels. Direction: Liu Guoquan. Screenplay: Hu Bing. Cinematography: Guan Qingwu. Art Direction: Liu Changbao. Music: Fu Lin. Sound: Li Bojiang. Cast: Li Rentang as Ni Chunqiu, Chen Yude as Du Guanjun, Wang Yongge as Liang Guang

Ni Chunqiu, head of a TV manufacturing plant, arouses the suspicions of Du Guangjun, another company's executive. Du notes that Ni gives repeated and apparently unwarranted favoritism to the head of a third company, a man named Liang. Curious, Du starts his own private investigation of the relationship between Ni and Liang. Liang had once been Ni's driver, but now heads his own company. Du's probe leads him to Liang's mistress, but he finds her dead of poisoning, along with a foreign man who turns out to have been her secret lover. The official investigation begins, with Du turning over to detectives what he has learned. It turns out that Liang had been blackmailing Ni for years, and the murder victims were poisoned by mistake, by drinking liquor intended for the blackmailer.

2207. *An Unusual Experience in a Wandering Life (Piao Po Qi Yu)*

1983. Shanghai Film Studio. Color. 11 Reels. Direction: Yu Bengzheng. Screenplay: Ji Xing, Xian Zhiliang. Cinematography: Peng Enli. Art Direction: Yang Shaolu. Sound: Li Bingkui. Cast: Wang Sihuai as the intellectual, Xue Shujie as Wildcat, Li Wei as Duo Bazhi, Liu Xingyi as Bai Fei, Ming Zenhong as Xiao Heiniu

In 1935, an impoverished young intellectual wanders through Southwest China. One day he faints from lack of food, and wakes to find himself in the camp of a band of robbers. The bandit chief wants him to join them, and although the young man is unwilling they force him to stay. He desperately wants to leave, but he is too frightened of the chief to say anything. In time he becomes acquainted with the chief's daughter, a girl called Wildcat, and she tells him of their background. At one time her family had been an ordinary, hard-working farm family, but after her mother was raped by a local landlord the father had killed him. This forced him into a life of crime. The young man is shocked to hear this, and now understands the chief a bit better. He decides that if he just says good-bye and leaves the chief may let him go. But that night their camp is raided, and although they drive off their attackers the chief is killed. Wildcat buries her father, then leads the band away to establish a camp elsewhere. The young man watches them go, hoping they will find a better life somewhere.

2208. *Unwanted Daughter (Duo Ci Yi Nu)*

1990. Xi'an Film Studio. Color. Wide Screen. 9 Reels. Direction: Zhang Gang. Screenplay: Zhang Gang. Cinematography: Zhang Jian. Art Direction: Wang Renqin. Music: Wang Ming. Cast: Ni Yuanyuan as Qiuqiu, Xue Shujie as Pan Yulan, Niu Beng as Zhong Liangjian

Little Qiuqiu's parents were divorced when she was only six years old. Her mother Pan Yulan remarries, but Qiuqiu's stepfather dislikes the girl and refuses to accept her. Her father Fan Aman also believes Qiuqiu is an obstacle to his getting remarried, so arranges for her to be sent to the countryside to live with her grandfather. Qiuqiu realizes nobody wants her, so she runs away from home. The little girl's plight arouses many people's sympathy, and even her father's lover changes her mind. She and Fan Aman find Qiuqiu and bring her home with them, to build a new family together.

2209. *An Unwelcome Lady (Hong Chen)*

1994. Beijing Film Studio. Color. Letterboxed. 12 Reels. Direction: Gu Rong. Screenplay: Huo Da, Wang Weizhen, based on their novel of the same title. Cinematography: Qian Tao. Art Direction: Shi Jianquan. Music: Ma Ding. Sound: Tong Jun, Shen Dong. Costume: Zhao Ruhua, Liu Jicheng, Lu Wenfang. Makeup: Hao Xia, Zhao Jie. Cast: Xu Songzi as Dezi's wife,

Tao Zeru as Dezi, Xu Lei as Sun Guizhen, Chen Baoguo as Ma Sansheng, Liu Jian as Doctor Liang, Feng Lei as Crazy Shun'er, Ma Enran as Crazy Shun'er's uncle, Xiao Chi as Liang's mother, Yu Lingda as Heizi

In Beijing in the early 1960s, pedicab driver Dezi meets and marries a very attractive woman. Their life together is happy except that she cannot bear children. When it is learned that Dezi's wife had formerly been a prostitute, their neighborhood administrative director Sun Guizhen makes trouble for the woman and humiliates her. Sun herself is a hypocrite, a woman having an affair with the brother of her late husband, a man she claims was a martyr to the revolution although no one can verify that. When the Cultural Revolution starts in 1966, Dezi's wife is pulled out and sent down to the countryside for remedial labor. She is later permitted to return, but the humiliation from Sun and others continues, even for a long time after Mao Zedong dies. After the Cultural Revolution years are past, Dezi starts to complain that marrying her has messed up his life and joins the neighbors in discriminating against her. With the one person she relied on having rejected her, Dezi's wife kills herself with an overdose of sleeping pills.

2210. *Urban Gunman (Du Shi Qiang Shou)*

1992. Beijing Film Studio. Color. Letterboxed. 9 Reels. Direction: Hu Mei. Screenplay: Liu Shugang, Shen Jimin. Cinematography: Yan Junsheng, Liu Ping. Art Direction: Yang Wan. Music: Shan Bao. Sound: Zhang Baojian. Costume: Zhang Yongyi. Makeup: Guo Jingxia. Cast: Shi Ke as Hao Ying, Liang Guoqing as Qi Xiaochuan (Hao Nan), Yan Gang as Gan Dayong, Zong Ping as Zhao Kailiang, Pan Jie as Yi Yiling, Xia Zongxue as Bai Xuanfeng, Zhou Qi as Qi Tianlong

On his deathbed, Hong Kong triad boss Qi Tianlong tells his nephew Qi Xiaochuan that the latter's father was killed by Gan Dayong, a mainland chief of detectives. His dying wish is that Tianlong kill the policeman. The nephew goes to the mainland and begins stalking his quarry, but soon begins picking up clues which lead him to something disturbing: it seems that the policeman is the gangster's natural father, and had been abducted by Qi Tianlong when a very small child. When he finally confronts Gan, the officer presents him with evi-

dence of this, but after a life of violent crime such a revelation is too much for Qi Xiaochuan to bear: he rejects it all, and in a rage determines to blow up a factory. Gan Dayong then goes to his daughter Hao Ying and tells her the truth about her own background: that she was the daughter of Qi Tianlong, left behind by him when he abducted Gan's own son. He sends her to stop Qi Xiaochuan, and in a final shootout, she kills the Hong Kong gunman.

2211. *Urban Masquerade Party (Cheng Shi Jia Mian Wu Hui)*

1986. Changchun Film Studio. Color. 10 Reels. Direction: Song Jiangbo. Screenplay: Qin Peichun, Cui Jingsheng. Cinematographer: Lei Xianle. Art Direction: Gong Minhui. Music: Liu Xijin. Sound: Gu Xiaolian, Cao Feng. Cast: Lu Liang as Luo Han, Zhang Yi as Tang Xiaoyun, Chen Xiaoxuan as Su Yan, Zhou Yue as Ping Fen

In Shanghai, Luo Han's romance with bank teller Ping Fen is going nowhere due to her mother's objections to Luo Han's occupation as a plumber. In frustration, Luo Han decides to get away and go on a trip. On the train, he meets Tang Xiaoyun, an unhappy young woman who dreams of being a writer but is becoming suicidal from constant rejection of her magazine submissions. Luo Han decides to help her in his own way: he pretends to be Su Yan, a magazine editor. They begin to correspond, and he offers helpful commentary on her poems. At last, with his help, she succeeds in getting one of her poems published, and her confidence is restored. Luo Han's experience has matured him as well, and at last he and Ping Fen get together.

2212. *Urban Monk (Du Shi He Shang)*

1991. Beijing Film Studio. Color. Letterboxed. 9 Reels. Direction: Huo Zhuang. Screenplay: Gui Yuqin. Cinematography: Shao Aole, Tian Jianmin. Art Direction: Yang Wan, Shu Gang. Music: Zhang Fuquan. Sound: Wang Yunhua. Cast: Xu Shaohua as Liao Yuan, Zhao Lijuan as Jin Meimei, Dong Ping as Liu Qianying, Zhang Xucheng as Zhang Deshuo, Han Xiaolei as Manager Jin

In a certain large city, hotel guests begin demanding vegetarian dishes on the menu. So the manager invites the monk Liao Yuan, famed for his meatless cuisine, to oversee this part of the hotel's food preparation. The monk accepts, but when he arrives he at first finds city life somewhat overwhelming. Hotel singer Lin Qianying befriends the monk and helps make the transition a bit easier for him. She owns a priceless antique, which martial arts coach Zhang Deshuo has long planned to get away from her. When Zhang learns the singer's new friend is also a martial artist, one with super skills, he sees the monk as an obstacle and decides to move fast. Zhang breaks into Lin's home and takes the treasure. Although Liao Yuan's beliefs hold that monks should not interfere in the more worldly society, his natural instinct to help the weak and punish wrongdoing makes him go to battle with Zhang and his followers and defeat them. When his contract term expires, the monk returns to his simple temple life, but everyone at the hotel knows they will miss him very much.

2213. Urban Village (Du Shi Li De Chun Zuang)

1982. Xi'an Film Studio. Color. 11 Reels. Direction: Teng Wenji. Screenplay: Liang Xingmin, Qin Peichun. Cinematography: Zhu Dingyu, Wang Xiangshan. Art Direction: Cheng Minzhang. Music: Xu Jingxin. Sound: Dang Chunzhu. Cast: Yin Tingru as Ding Xiaoya, Wei Guochun as Du Hai, Zhao Youliang as Shu Liang, Huang Yijuan as Shu Xiuyun, Li Ping as Zhu Lifang

Shanghai shipyard worker Ding Xiaoya is happy when she is elected a model worker in her unit, but soon finds that her new status has isolated her from fellow workers. In fact, the only two people not invited to their colleague Zhu Lifang's wedding are her and a man named Du Hai, who has a past criminal record. Everyone's coolness to the two make them very lonely. One day, Ding Xiaoya is given a high-altitude assignment though she is ill. She falls and is injured, which makes people like Zhu Lifang realize how unfairly Ding has been treated. When a fire breaks out in the workers' dormitory, Du Hai is one of those who rescue many others. But when Zhu Lifang returns to his quarters and finds some of his possessions missing, he accuses Du, because of Du's past record. Du Hai's name is at last cleared, and he and Ding Xiaoya fall in love.

2214. Vagabond Miraculous Troupe (Jiang Hu Qi Bing)

1990. Xi'an Film Studio & Hong Kong Changhe Film Company Co-Production. Color. 9 Reels. Direction: Zhang Che. Screenplay: Zhang Che. Cinematography: Jie Delin. Art Direction: Wang Yingbing. Music: Deng Shaolin. Sound: Zhou Guozhong. Cast: Jia Yongquan as Xiao Jun, Du Yumin as Si Zhi, Dong Zhihua as Mu Yiqi

During the Tang Dynasty (618–907), the King of Gaoli sends one of his country's national treasures, the "blood horse" to the Tang emperor as tribute. However, the horse is stolen on route by four famous Southeast China bandits. The film tells of various elements of society all battling over the treasure.

2215. The Vanished High School Girl (Shi Zong De Nu Zhong Xue Sheng)

1986. Shanghai Film Studio. Color. 10 Reels. Direction: Shi Shujun. Screenplay: Shi Shujun. Cinematography: Zhao Junhong. Art Direction: Dong Jingsheng. Music: Xu Jingxin. Sound: Ni Zheng. Cast: Liu Yu as Wang Jia, Qian Yongfu as Father, Zhang Wenrong as Mother

Junior high school student Wang Jia is a girl just starting to have an interest in boys. She develops a serious crush on an older boy, a music student with a lovely singing voice. Her infatuation with the boy disrupts her life: she sleeps poorly, becomes alienated from her classmates, neglects her studies, and indeed finds it hard to do anything. When Wang Jia finally is able to summon enough courage to tell the boy how she feels, she is devastated to learn he already has a girl friend. When she tells her mother about it, instead of extending sympathy and understanding her mother harshly criticizes the girl and grounds her indefinitely. Hurt and angry, Wang Jia runs away from home. Her father sets out to look for her, searching from city to city. As he seeks his daughter, the father comes to realize the need teenagers have for care and understanding.

2216. The Vanished Woman (Xiao Shi De Nu Ren)

1992. Fujian Film Studio. Color. Letterboxed. 9 Reels. Direction: He Qun, Liu Baolin. Screenplay: Fu Xuen, He Qun, based on the novel by Wang Shuo (1958–). Cinematography:

Yin Yan, Zhang Yuan, Yu Xiaojun. Art Direction: Lin Zhihan, Feng Lei. Music: Ma Ding. Sound: Chao Jun. Costume: Zhang Weimin. Makeup: Zhou Qin, Xing Jiang. Cast: Ge You as Dan Liren, You Yong as Li Jianping, Geng Ge as Qu Li, Ju Xue as Lin Mei, Er Yang as Ren Baihai

One winter's night in North China, a woman's headless corpse is found beneath the ice of a skating pond. From a list of more than 100 missing persons, investigators Dan Liren and Qu Li conclude the victim was Liu Lizhu, a restaurant worker. By tracking the clues they at last prove the killer to be Li Jianping, well-known in arts and entertainment circles as a notorious seducer of young women. Their evidence convicts Li, who receives the death sentence.

2217. *The Vast Ganshui River (Ganshui Cangmang)*

1979. Changchun Film Studio. Color. 12 Reels. Direction: Jiang Shusheng. Screenplay: Yan Xue. Cinematography: Chen Chang'an, Zhao Yue. Art Direction: Huang Zhaohui. Music: Quan Rufeng. Sound: Zhang Fenglu. Cast: Li Chengbing as Chen Zhanjiang, Wang Zhigang as Fang Liang, Liang Yin as Mr. Wu, Yang Jianye as Regimental Commander Luo, Lin Qiang as Li Hu, Yu Yanping as Xu Hai

In 1934, Red Army Regimental Commander Chen Zhanjiang witnesses the tragic results of the military's following the optimistic line of Communist leader Wang Min. He and Political Commissar Fang Liang petition the Communists' provisional central government to abandon Wang Min's policies. Not only is their request denied, Chen is dismissed from his command and assigned to go behind enemy lines as a covert agent. Behind the lines, Chen organizes a guerrilla troop which uses a flexible guerrilla strategy, counter to official strategy. But his political troubles do not end: followers of Wang Min attack his strategy and accuse him of treason. He is sentenced to be executed, but just before the sentence can be carried out, Fang Liang arrives with the news that Mao Zedong has regained control of the Party leadership and Wang Min has been deposed. Chen is exonerated.

2218. *Vast Oceans and Skies (Hai Kuo Tian Kong)*

1958. August First Film Studio. B & W. 10 Reels. Direction: Li Sutian. Cinematography: Kou Jiwen. Art Direction: Wang Wei. Music: Li Weicai. Sound: Li Yan.

Three stories of the Chinese armed forces during the Great Leap Forward:

"Overjoyed" (Xi Chu Wang Wai). Screenplay: Lin Yinwu and Chan Wen. Cast: Zhao Xuemin as Li Zhenhai, Zhou Zou as Director He, Liu Jiang as Director Gao, Chen Bo as the Vice Commander, Tian Ping as the warship's Political Commissar, Xing Jitian as Minister Liu. Li Zhenhui, director of a fishing commune in a coastal city, goes to many boat manufacturers trying to order 10 mechanically operated fishing boats, but none can fulfill his needs. Later, he visits the warship he once served on, and is deeply moved when he sees how the sailors are achieving the Great Leap Forward's aims. Finally, with the assistance of the navy and the boat manufacturers, Li resolves his ordering problem.

"Masters of the Skies" (Tian Kong De Zhu Ren). Screenplay: Yang Zhaolin, Ai Yang. Cast: Wang Yi as Xin Zhitao, Wei Liangyan, as Liu Xinyuan, Zhao Song as Old Liu, Chen Yao as the Political Commissar, Guo Xianzong as Xu Pusheng, Liangdian as Wang Zhongyu. A naval aviation weather broadcasting station accurately forecasts the weather, assuring flight safety. In an air battle, they shoot down a Nationalist reconnaissance plane flying at more than 10,000 meters, protecting China's air sovereignty and becoming real masters of the air.

"Collective Honor" (Jiti De Rongyu). Screenplay: Ai Yang, Chan Wen. Cast: Wang Xingang as Zhao Yulin, Ha Zhigang as Wang Yiqun, Luo Zhengpei as Liao Jicang, Wu Xixia as the warship's Political Commissar, Liu Bingzhang as the Captain, Li Chunhua as the Gunnery Chief. Inspired by the Great Leap Forward, instructors and sailors on a naval warship work hard and skillfully. With each department cooperating closely, they accomplish a perfect score of 100% in their gunnery practice at sea.

2219. *Vengeful Lady (Fu Chou Nu Lang)*

1988. Beijing Film Studio. Color. 10 Reels. Direction: Xu Lei. Screenplay: Wang Jing. Cinematography: Li Yuebing, Li Shanlin. Art Direction: Yang Yunhui. Music: Li Lifu. Sound: Zhang Ye. Cast: Shen Junyi as Xu Shuhuai, Wang Zhixia as Shi Qin, Niu Piao as Wang Shaojun, Wu Lijie as Huang Fang, Yang Mei as Du Xiaoli, Liu Xiaoli as Liu Ying, Liang Bing as Yun Ying, Wang Zhixia as Chou Jingru

On his return from a business trip, successful

executive Wang Shaojun notices a woman in a black raincoat following him to his home. Later, at a dance hall, an attempt is made on his life. He survives, and tells investigator Xu Shuhuai he is certain the lady in the black raincoat tried to kill him, and that he believes she is his former lover Shi Qin. Investigating further, Xu Shuhuai finds that Wang Shaojun has had many relationships with many women. When he questions them, three of these women claim they made the murder attempt. At last, the real killer is identified as another person altogether: while she was the woman in the black raincoat, she is actually Shi Qin's twin sister Chou Jingru. Chou Jingru arrives to turn herself in.

2220. *Victory for the People of Inner Mongolia (Nei Meng Gu Ren Min De Sheng Li)*

1950. Northeast Film Studio. B & W. 12 Reels. Direction: Gan Xuewei. Screenplay: Wang Zhengzhi. Cinematography: Du Yu and Li Guanghui. Art Direction and Assistant Direction: Li Enjie. Music: Xu Huicai and Li Xi, Sound: Sui Xizhong. Costume: Zhang Zhenying. Makeup: Bi Zepu. Cast: Yu Chun as Su He, Bai Dafang as Master Daoerji, En Hesen as Dundebu, Fang Hua as Mr. Yang, Guangbu Daoerji as Menghe Bateer, Zhang Ping as Minister Buhe, Sun Xi as Tusula Geqi

Yang, a secret agent in the employ of the U.S. and the Chinese Nationalists, is assigned to Inner Mongolia, where he links up with Tusula Geqi, a Mongolian anti–Communist. At the same time, Menghe Bateer and Su He are sent to this region by the Communist Party, to do organizational work. Caught in the middle is a Mongolian horseman named Dundebu who at first believes the Nationalist agents, but converts after witnessing a succession of good works by the Communists and after his friend Meng is murdered by the Nationalist agents. Soon after, Nationalist troops invade the region, but are turned back by a joint Mongolian-Chinese Communist force. Yang and Tusula Geqi are captured, and in the end Dundebu joins the Communist army.

2221. *Village in Reform (Shao Dong De Xiang Feng)*

1991. Pearl River Film Studio. Color. Letterboxed. 10 Reels. Direction: Wang Jing, Li Shu, Xu Weihua. Screenplay: Jin Haitao. Cinematog-

raphy: Li Xiaolin, Shao Yiyun. Art Direction: Zhang Zhichu. Music: Chen Taizhao. Sound: Wu Hongtao. Cast: Ni Xuehua, Chen Rui, Pu Chaoying, Meng Weimin, Pan Yu

The winds of reform sweep through a small town in West Hunan. Kindly and hardworking peasant woman Liu Yue takes the lead in operating a brickmaking factory, and becomes prosperous as a result. Another woman, Yuxin, returns to the village after the breakup of her marriage in the city, and opens a public bath. Liu Yue's husband borrows money from Yuxin to open a karaoke dance hall, and also begins an affair with her. When Liu Yue learns the truth, she leaves her husband.

2222. *Visions from a Jail Cell (Mo Ku Zhong De Huan Xiang)*

1986. Emei Film Studio. Color. 10 Reels. Direction: Wang Jixing. Screenplay: Zhou Mi, Fu Xiaomin. Cinematography: Qiang Jun, Du Xiaoshi. Art Direction: Wu Xujing, Gao Xinchun. Music: Ju Xiaosong. Sound: Wang Guangzhong, Liu Renhua. Cast: Xia Jing as Little Luobotou, Wang Chunzi as the girl, Sun Chun as the prison warden, Zhang Guohui as the general, Qi Mengshi as the crazy man, Xiu Jingshuang as Mama

Little Luobotou ("Radish") is the son of revolutionaries, and was born in a Nationalist prison, where he still lives with his mother. The only world he has known in his young life is a narrow, limited cell, and a sky he sees only through a high ceiling window. His only friends are some other prisoners, and a teenage girl also imprisoned because of her family's activities. When he reaches school age, he begs his mother to send him to school, something she cannot do. But other prisoners sympathize, and start a hunger strike in an effort to get him the opportunity. Little Luobotou dreams that this will get him to school, but it only results in his mother's execution. When the little boy reaches age 9, he and the girl are permitted for the first time to leave the prison for awhile. As they are running and playing in a field, a bored soldier decides to use them for live target practice and kills the two children.

2223. *A Visit from a Dead Man (Yi Ge Shi Zhe Dui Sheng Zhe De Fang Wen)*

1987. Beijing Film Studio. Color. 10 Reels. Direction: Huang Jianzhong. Screenplay: Liu Shugang. Cinematography: Zhao Fei. Art

Direction: Shi Jiandu. Music: Ju Xiaosong. Sound: Zhen Chunyu. Cast: Chang Lantian as Ye Xiaoxiao, Lin Fangbing as Tang Tiantian

A young man named Ye Xiaoxiao witnesses a robbery being committed on a bus and intervenes to catch the thief. But the robber intimidates his victim into refusing to admit the theft took place. The robber is released, then beats Xiaoxiao to death. The young man's ghost begins visiting live people, but he finds that no one is aware of what actually happened, or the circumstances which led to his death. He is very hurt and lonely, feeling that his sacrifice was in vain. But his girlfriend Tiantian begins having dreams about what happened, and follows up on the clues these dreams give her. At last, her investigation leads to the truth and to the apprehension of Xiaoxiao's killer. His sacrifice is acknowledged, and he is honored with posthumous Communist Party membership.

2224. *Visit the Fort with Arms (Qiang Fang Yao Sai)*

1991. Changchun Film Studio. Color. Letterboxed. 10 Reels. Direction: Hua Ke. Screenplay: Wang Rongchun and Pei Ming. Cinematography: Wang Changning. Art Direction: Wei Hongyu. Music: Liu Weiguang. Sound: Tong Zongde, Yang Yuedong. Cast: Du Zhengqin as Xia Houliang, Shen Huifeng as Qing Shuzhen, Li Wei as Captain Lan, Ma Shuchao as Staff Officer Tian, Liu Zhibing as Officer Xin

In 1949, on the eve of liberation, a final battle is shaping up for the military port of Qudao in Xiamen, on the Southwest China coast. An agent infiltrates Nationalist intelligence headquarters and coordinates the PLA's taking of this key port.

2225. *The Visitor on Ice Mountain (Bing Shan Shang De Lai Ke)*

1963. Changchun Film Studio. B & W. 10 Reels. Direction: Zhao Xinshui. Screenplay: Bai Xin. Cinematography: Zhang Yi. Art Direction: Shi Weijun. Music: Lei Zhengbang. Sound: Lin Bingcheng. Cast: Liang Yin as Platoon Leader Yang, Abudu Limiti as Amier, Gu Shuyin as the fake Gulandanmu, Enhesheng as Ni Yazhi, Tuerdimusha as Relipu, Ma Loufu as Amanbayi

In 1951, a band of gangsters and spies plan to infiltrate China through the mountains of Xinjiang. Bandit chieftain Amanbayi exploits the fact that border guard Amier had years before loved a girl named Gulandanmu by send-

ing a woman spy to pretend she is Gulandanmu, and through her gain information from Amier concerning the border defenses. The Chinese border guards' platoon leader Yang sees through the conspiracy, and in this way gains information about the enemy. After this initial failure, the enemy sends the real Gulandanmu, who was bitter over the way she had been treated by her native village. But Yang turns her to working for the Chinese, and captures all the bandits and spies. He also reunites the lovers Gulandanmu and Amier, who had been unhappily separated for eight long years.

2226. *Vital Lover (Can Ku De Qing Ren)*

1986. Emei Film Studio. Color. 9 Reels. Direction: Yin Xianglin. Screenplay: Qian Daoyuan. Cinematography: Li Dagui. Art Direction: Xia Zhengqiu. Music: Tang Qinshi. Sound: Lin Bingcheng. Cast: Sun Chun as Xiao Yuan, Fu Lili as Shen Yafei, Wang Shuren as Mu Chunlin, Wang Mingzhi as Jin Feng, Zhang Qi as Xiao Rui

A huge, modern theater is to be built, and competitive bidding starts for design of its decorative lighting. Deputy managers from two companies compete fiercely for the contract: Caihong Company's Xiao Yuan, and his former lover, Xuanqiu Company's Shen Yafei. Shen is a single-minded and determined woman who puts nothing before her devotion to business. She even stoops to dirty tricks and cheating in the process, such as stealing a copy of the Caihong Company's light design and trying to destroy its new design production. At last, although the Caihong Company offers the better design, Shen Yafei wins.

2227. *A Voice from the Heart (Xin Xuan)*

1981. Shanghai Film Studio. Color. Letterboxed. 10 Reels. Direction: Lin Zhiao, Xu Jihong. Screenplay: Yan Geqin. Cinematography: Luo Zhensheng, Zhao Junhong. Art Direction: Chen Chudian. Music: Yang Yu. Sound: Luo Zhensheng, Zhao Junhong. Cast: Yu Ping as Mrs. Ni, Bao Xun as Li Xiaofeng, Gao Bo as the husband, Hu Yiyi as Xiao Qin

On a Korean battlefield in 1951, an elderly Korean lady rescues and cares for a badly wounded Chinese Army musician named Li Xiaofeng. After regaining consciousness, Li

Xiaofeng is extremely upset to find he can no longer see. Although neither can understand the other's language, the Korean lady knows a tune called the "No Character Song" that breaks down their language barrier, and Li Xiaofeng composes violin music for the song. Meanwhile, Xiaofeng's sister Xiao Jing and other members of the army performance troupe have been looking everywhere for Li Xiaofeng. They find him just as their unit is about to move out, and in the rush to leave Li Xiaofeng has no time to say goodbye to the old woman, just leave a note. Li Xiaofeng later regains his sight in the hospital, and returns with some fellow soldiers to see the old woman. The village is apparently deserted, but before turning to go Li Xiaofeng plays the "No Character Song" on his violin. From out of the rubble the old lady comes out to greet them.

2228. *Volley Ball Flower (Pai Qiu Zhi Hua)*

1980. Changchun Film Studio. Color. 9 Reels. Direction: Lu Jianhua. Screenplay: Lu Jianhua. Cinematography: Fang Weiche, Jia Shouxing. Art Direction: Liang Shukui, Ye Jiren. Music: Quan Rufeng. Sound: Han Weijun. Cast: Guo Zhengqin as Wu Zhengya, Guo Yuntai as Director Shang, Huang Daliang as Tian Dali, Cui Muyan as Lin Xue, Gao Fang as Doctor Li, Guo Ming as Wu Lingling

Nanhai City women's volleyball coach Wu Zhengya has rich technical, tactical and physical training experiences from his many years' of training, and has a national reputation for excellence. Wu's success leads to a head coaching job in North China for his assistant Tian Dali. In his new job, Tian discovers a good female athlete named Ling Xue, and after strict training she becomes a player with a bright future. Ling Xue grows very fond of Tian's five-year-old daughter Tian Xiaoli, leading to Ling and Tian Dali falling in love. However, Tian Dali sends her to Nanhai City to work with his mentor Wu because he believes it will be better for her future. During the Cultural Revolution, Tian Dali and Wu are both criticized and ousted from their jobs. After things return to normal, Wu is again named a head coach, and wants to restore the spirit of women's volleyball which had been lost during the Gang of Four era. However, what he hopes to achieve is misunderstood by his own daughter, woman volleyball player Wu Lingling. Later, through patient teaching by Wu Zhengya and his wife,

Wu Lingling devotes herself to harsh training. Finally, Tian Dali who had been in oblivion for many years comes "back to life." It turns out that he had been protected by some honest people, who hid him in remote places. When Tian learns that Ling Xue is still waiting and hoping for his return, he hurries to meet her.

2229. *Volunteer Anti-Japanese Heroes (Tie Xue Qun Ying)*

1991. Changchun Film Studio. Color. Letterboxed. 9 Reels. Direction: Zhou Wei, Screenplay: Zhao Ruosheng, Zhang Jiongqiang, Cinematography: Yu Bing, Art Direction: Xu Zhenkun, Music; Chen Shouqian, Sound: Wang Baosheng, Xing Guocang, Cast: Zhang Jingsheng, He Qiang, Wang Gang, Chen Jimin

After the Mukden Incident of September 18th, 1931, when the Japanese began their forcible occupation of Northeast China, the Volunteer Army opposing the aggressors sends an eight-man special team into Japanese-held territory. There, they blow up a Japanese arms warehouse and become a symbol of resistance for all the Chinese people in the struggle to come.

2230. *Waiting (Deng)*

1983. Changchun Film Studio. Color. 10 Reels. Direction: Wang Anda. Screenplay: Lu Qi. Cinematography: Wang Jishun. Art Direction: Wu Houxing. Music: Si Wanchun. Sound: Dong Baosheng. Cast: Long Liling as Shuyun, Sun Qixin as Xiaolin, Song Yining as Lanyin, Wang Dong as Youtian

During the Cultural Revolution, a young man named Xiaolin is sent down to the countryside from the city after his father is branded a "capitalist" and ousted from his official position. When he arrives, he finds his political status leads nearly everyone to shun him. The lone exception is Shuyun, an innocent and good-hearted peasant girl. With her encouragement, Xiaolin gradually comes to love the land and the rigorous life of the countryside, and in time he and Shuyun fall in love. Then a letter arrives from his father telling Xiaolin his father is restored to his old post, and the boy should return immediately to the city. Xiaolin decides to return and resume his education, and gradually convince his parents to accept his peasant girl friend. Shuyun promises to wait for him. Years pass, and while Shuyun continues to wait, Xiaolin makes little progress with his parents, who regard their son's romance as puppy love infatuation that will soon pass. As college graduation approaches, Xiaolin makes one final effort to change their minds. A bitter argument ensues, after which Xiaolin walks out, determined to return to the countryside where Shuyun still patiently waits for him.

2231. *Waiting for Spring (Wang Chun Feng)*

1987. Beijing Film Studio & Hong Kong Jun Yeh Films, Ltd. Co-Production. Color. Widescreen. 10 Reels. Direction: Xie Yuchen. Screenplay: Xie Yuchen, Li Ziwei. Cinematography: Yang Wenqing. Art Direction: Fu Delin, Zhen Huiwen. Music: Ma Ding. Sound: Wang Ming. Cast: Tong Fei as Lin Chenhui, Wang Hui as Lin Tongren, Yin Xin as Li Xiulan, Wu Lanhui as Lin Weiguo, Cao Duo as Hou Junzheng, Yu Shaokang as the elderly overseas Chinese

When war erupts between China and Japan, Lin Tongren's son Lin Chenhui has to leave his studies in Japan and return to his home in Taiwan, at the time part of the Japanese Empire. At the family gathering to welcome his return, the festive mood is broken when a Japanese officer crashes the party and insults the family. When Chenhui and his fiancee Li Xiulan get married, his jealous brother Weiguo helps the Japanese imprison Chenhui in order to get his wife. Xiulan refuses to marry Weiguo and when he makes physical advances she kills him then escapes with the help of a waitress to go into hiding. Liu Chenhui is released from prison to serve in the Japanese Army in the Philippines. After the war, he finally returns home and finds Xiulan. As the sun sets, Chenhui, Xiulan and her mother take a stroll in a gentle breeze which reminds them of the approach of spring.

2232. *Waitress (Duan Pan Zi De Gu Niang)*

1981. Youth Film Studio. Color. 8 Reels. Direction: Ma Jingwu, Liu Sibing. Screenplay: Li Ranran. Cinematography: Meng Haifeng, Gu Wenkai. Art Direction: Wang Xinglai, Liu Guangen. Music: Ma Ding, Huang Yuan. Sound: Wang Yunhua, Mu Xiaocheng. Cast: Guo Jin as Xiao Fanzi, Yang Xiaodan as Zhang Zhi, Yuan Munu as Tong Yin, Lu Xiaogang as Xiao Gu

Xiao Fanzi is unhappy with her job as a waitress. She often daydreams of becoming an actress, a doctor, or some other profession. When reality intrudes on her dreams, it makes her mad, and she takes out her anger on her customers. Xiao Fanzi's friend Zhang Zhi encourages her to study a foreign language and brings her a radio, but not only is Xiao Fanzi not interested in studying, she also fails to understand why another waitress named Tong Ying is doing so. Xiao Fanzi begins to date Xiao Gu, a young man with no ambition at all. But after experiencing a series of setbacks, Xiao Fanzi finally realizes Xiao Gu is not a respectable young man, and Zhang Zhi is the perfect man for her. But before she has a chance to tell him how she feels, she discovers he already has a steady girlfriend: her co-worker Tong Ying, whose studies have gained her admission to evening university. Xiao Fanzi now starts to think seriously about her life and future.

2233. *Wake Up, Mom (Xing Lai Ba, Ma Ma)*

1986. Inner Mongolia Film Studio. Color. 9 Reels. Direction: He Ye, Nayintai. Screenplay: Yi Baderonggui. Cinematography: Geritu. Art Direction: Ruan Qinbo. Music: Shuirubu. Sound: Huhe. Cast: Ai Liya as Nala, Wulan Baoyin as A Sier, Daoerji as Danba, Liu Kui as Hada

College professor Asier notes that Sharala, one of his female students, has been absent from class. He knows she is the daughter of Nala, a girl he had known in high school. Asier recalls that Nala had also aspired to college, but just before the entrance exams her brother had dragged her home, for he wanted her to leave school and get married. Now many years have passed, and Asier fears that history is being repeated. Asier and others go to Nala and persuade her to let her daughter go on to college.

2234. *Walk Ahead of the War (Zou Zai Zhan Zheng Qian Mian)*

1978. August First Film Studio. Color. 11 Reels. Direction: Hao Guang, Wei Long. Screenplay: Li Pingfeng, Lu Wei, Xu Qindong, Yang Tao. Cinematography: Yang Zhaoren, Gao Jiuling. Art Direction: Zhang Guozhen, Li Jiayan. Music: Fu Gengcheng. Sound: He Baoding. Cast: Li Muran as Yan He, Li Longying as Yan He (as a youth), Tang Guoqiang as Li Tiecheng, Zhang Shaoli as the reporter, Gao Yang as Yang Jian, Wang Tongle as the deputy company commander

On a summer night in 1975, the "Red Fourth," a tank company honored for its record in battle, suffers a serious training accident. The accident is due to the unit's training being constantly disrupted by Lin Biao and the "Gang of Four" over a long period of time. The unit's lowered efficiency greatly disturbs their deputy commander Yan He, so he personally supervises all training from that point on. This concerns the Gang of Four, so they send reporter Wei Xianyuan on special assignment to cause as much ideological confusion among the military as possible. But Yan He and "Red Fourth" commander Li Tiecheng adhere to their goal of improving their troops' training, and directly oppose the Gang's stooge. With support from the Central Military Committee, the officers and men break through the various obstacles in their path and successfully hold large-scale maneuvers to celebrate the 40th anniversary of the Long March.

2235. *Walking into a Group of Elephants (Zhou Jing Xiang Qun)*

1989. Children's Film Studio. Color. Letterboxed. 9 Reels. Direction: Luo Xiaoling. Screenplay: Yan Tingting. Cinematography: Liu Fengdi. Art Direction: Ma Gaiwa. Music: Liu Weiguang. Sound: Zhen Chunyu. Cast: Ma Jia as Shabei, Huang Wen as Boss Jin, Fei Kunwu as Maomao, Yu Xiaojun as Gougou

An elderly Ainu nationality man discovers a cave full of stolen antiques hidden in the forest, but is murdered before he can report his find to the police. He is able to leave his granddaughter Shabei a line from an Ainu folk song which provides a clue to the antiques' location. Boss Jin, a shady antiques dealer, lures the girl into town so he can get the clue from her. Others get involved, including a search team led by Professor Chen, accompanied by his police officer daughter. At last the antiques are found and returned to the nation.

2236. *Walking Through Misty Valley (Zou Guo Mi Hun Gu)*

1987. Changchun Film Studio. Color. 10 Reels. Direction: Liu Wenyu. Screenplay: Sheng Manzhu, Jia Lixian. Cinematography: Sun Hui, Zhang Shaoge. Art Direction: Gao Tinglun. Music: Fan Weiqiang. Sound: Wang Lin. Cast: Wang Xinjian as Liu Jiliang, Li Xiaowen as Lin Yueqi

Young painter Liu Jiliang and his fiancee Lin Yueqi go to a forest to paint but lose their way and walk into a misty and confusing val-

ley. There, they meet three other people: a fugitive Ye Maozhi, salesman Xiao Fanzhi and local product buyer Sun Cangde. The five make their way together, suddenly Lin Yueqi finds a large patch of ginseng. Everyone except Lin wants this precious, and potentially lucrative, find. After a bloody fight ensues, Liu Jiliang takes possession of the ginseng. He abandons the sick Lin in the forest, and runs off with his treasure. At last, PSB officers find Lin Yueqi and set off in pursuit of Liu. Suddenly, Liu Jiliang awakens to find it was all a strange dream.

2237. *Wallet (Pi Bao)*

1956. Changchun Film Studio. B & W. 4 Reels. Direction: Wang Lan. Screenplay: Tian Ye, based on the novel "Father Liu Shihai's Wallet" by Bai Xiaowen. Cinematography: Li Guanghui. Art Direction: Tong Jinwen. Music: Quan Rufeng. Sound: Jue Jinxiu. Cast: Su Liqun as Liu Shihai, Ouyang Mingde as Zhang Aimin, Wang Guangru as Qian Peiyin, Che Xuan as Researcher Liu, Zhang Fengxiang as Director Liu, Zhang Juguang as Director Zhao

A researcher in a major scientific institution loses his wallet containing classified information. Three Young Pioneers, the researcher's son Liu Shihai and his friends Zhang Aimin and Qian Peiyin, determine to find it. During their search for the wallet, chubby little Zhang Aimin loses his patience and quarrels with Liu Shihai. They find and follow some clues which lead them to discover the wallet was stolen by a man named Wang, an office clerk in the institution. They also find Wang to be a spy, so they coordinate his arrest and recover the wallet.

2238. *The Wanderer and the Swan (Liu Lang Han Yu Tian Er)*

1985. Guangxi Film Studio. Color. 9 Reels. Direction: Wu Yinxun. Screenplay: Chen Wu. Cinematography: Zhu Dingyuan. Art Direction: Si Xun. Music: Yang Shaoyi. Sound: Han Weijun. Cast: Li Baotian as Mozhuoer, Wu Dan as Xinghua, Qian Zhangang as Ding Zhaohua, Liang Qinggang as Chun Liu, Li Zhonghua as Tian Di, He Zhuping as Taohua

A tramp called "Mozhuoer" (a cloth used for cleaning tables) makes his living as a restaurant busboy. Years before, he had left his native township in Guangxi when the political line of the day forced him to abandon his chosen field of raising fish. Years of drifting and a menial occupation have given him some bad habits, such as laziness and a tendency to brag. One day, he accidentally meets his old friend Chun Liu and his wife. Chun Liu had remained in their home town and became fairly prosperous raising fish when the reforms came in. They persuade the tramp to return with them. Back home, he renews an acquaintance with Chun Liu's younger sister Xinghua, an attractive young woman who had been abandoned by her former lover when she became pregnant. She attempted suicide, and at that time Mozhuoer had intervened to save her life. He later gave her comfort and the will to go on in life. Xinghua believes in Mozhuoer, and is convinced he can overcome his shortcomings and become respectable again. Although only she and the Chun couple think he can do it, Mozhuoer becomes successful at breeding baby fish. He and Xinghua look forward to the future together.

Women's Association Best Actress Award to Wu Dan, 9th International Film Festival.

2239. *Wanderers (Lang Ren)*

1988. Tianshan Film Studio. Color. Letterboxed. 9 Reels. Direction: Li Wei. Screenplay: Abulimiti Yiwusiahbuliti Muhanmude. Cinematography: Baihaiti. Art Direction: Xierzhati. Music: Nusilaiti. Sound: Mayinuer. Cast: Shadike as Kadeer, Huerxide as Zuhala

After the revolution of 1911 which overthrew the Qing Dynasty government and established the Republic of China, an expatriate Uighur artist colony decides to return to China from overseas. By accident, they receive a secret order from a "Commander Zhang" ordering the assassination of a former government minister. From then on, the artists suffer a series of persecutions from their refusal to turn over the order. At last, they leave and begin a nomadic existence in the Gobi Desert.

2240. *Wang Rilian (Wang Ri Lian)*

1986. August First Film Studio. Color. Widescreen. 9 Reels. Direction: Wei Linyu. Screenplay: Xu Guangyao. Cinematography: Wei Linyu. Art Direction: Li Jian. Music: Ye Xiaogang. Sound: Zhu Junshan. Cast: Pu Chaoying as Wang Rilian, Wu Ruofu as Dasan, Zhang Zhijian as the pharmaceutical expert

On the plains of central Hebei province during World War Two, many unsung men and women make heroic sacrifices for the anti-Japanese effort. One of these is Wang Rilian, an intelligent, beautiful and courageous country girl. Her husband Dasan is a liaison, delivering messages between local guerrillas and the Eighth Route Army. Rilian's contribution is as a guide, escorting passing Chinese comrades through her rural area to their destinations. One stormy night, she takes on her most difficult mission, escorting a pharmaceutical expert through the Japanese lines and into Chinese-held territory. The trek is arduous, but at last they arrive safely at their destination. But the mission has tragic results for Rilian, as her husband Dasan is killed covering them.

2241. *Wanted Circular (Tong Ji Ling)*

1984. Guangxi Film Studio. Color. 9 Reels. Direction: Jin Shuqi. Screenplay: Hu Bing. Cinematography: Lu Dongqin. Art Direction: An Ping. Music: Yang Shaoyi. Sound: Li Zhuwen. Cast: Xiao Gancen as You Mencai, Wang Xueqin as Tang Junfeng, Tan Zhizhong as Zhen Bangjie, Cui Zhi as Hao Yong, Sun Luwei as Bai Fei, Xu Zhiqun as Bai Yan

Prisoner You Mencai escapes from the officers taking him to a local hospital for treatment. Shortly thereafter, a store cashier is murdered during a robbery. Chief Investigator Tang Junfeng concludes that these two crimes are related. His investigation takes many intricate plot turns, but at last the evidence leads to a local grocer named Bai Fei. Bai and wife attempt to flee, but are killed in the attempt.

2242. *War Against Drugs (Ji Du Zhan)*

1991. Emei Film Studio. Color. Letterboxed. 10 Reels. Direction: Tai Gang. Screenplay: Qian Daoyuan. Cinematography: Li Erkang and Fu Wei. Art Direction: Xia Zhiqiu. Music: Xiao Gang. Sound: Qiu Su. Cast: Cai Hongxiang as Mu Banglie, Liu Xin as Lu Xiaoyu, Zhao Liang as Da Luo, Deng Qian as sister Ou, Li Yunliang as Xiao Zhu, Liu Yan as Jiao Lan, Xu Liankai as boss Nan, Tai Gang as Boss Xi

Senior police officer Mou Banglie is sent by the Ministry of Public Security against a Hong Kong drug dealing organization. The drug ring, headed by an expert on China called "Carlos," wants to create a drug delivery channel from the golden triangle through China then on to Europe and America. Mou Banglie arrives in South China and begins working with his veteran former partner Ma Wenshou and several younger police officers. They at last succeed in outwitting the tricky Carlos and smash his plan.

2243. *War Interlude (Zhan Zheng Cha Qu)*

1987. Children's Film Studio. Color. 10 Reels. Direction: Zhang Yuqiang. Screenplay: Xu Zhiheng. Cinematography: Yan Junsheng, Du Yimin. Art Direction: Xiao Bing, Xia Nan. Music: Jin Xiang. Sound: Zhang Zhizhong. Cast: Zhang Bing as Xiujiu, Gao Caixia as Yunfeng, Jin Yan as Yuzhen, Zhang Xu as Chouwa

In the summer of 1941, a detachment of the Eighth Route Army breaks out of a Japanese encirclement after some fierce fighting. Xiuju, a young girl working as a Chinese liaison, is sent on various missions to contact other units of the Eighth Route Army. She matures from a little girl to a seasoned soldier.

2244. *The War of Divorce (Li Hun Da Zhan)*

1992. Beijing Film Studio. Color. Letterboxed. 10 Reels. Direction: Chen Guoxing. Screenplay: Ma Junji, Chen Guoxing. Cinematography: Zhao Xiaoding. Art Direction: Song Zhenshan, Yang Hong. Music: Gao Erdi. Costume: Liu Huiping. Makeup: Cui Fa. Cast: Ge You as Da Ming, Ma Xiaoqing as Xiao Feng, Hou Yaohua as Liu Yishou, Cai Ming as Yinzi

Xiao Feng is a taxi driver, her husband Da Ming a trumpet player in a hotel's house band. Their relationship is quite amicable, but Xiao Feng has grown restless and dissatisfied with their marriage, craving more excitement. So she asks for a divorce. Because of a legal technicality, they cannot divorce easily and have to remain together indefinitely. This forces them to the realization that they still love each other and gives them a new understanding of their marriage and of life.

2245. *War of the Century (Shi Ji Zhi Zhan)*

1992. Inner Mongolia Film Studio. Color. Wide Screen. 9 Reels. Direction: Qin Wubo, Zhang Yuanlong. Screenplay: A Buer, Shange. Cinematography: Lin Jian. Art Direction: Dong Yonggang. Sound: Ao Si. Costume: Narina, Cui Xiaohong. Makeup: Su Hong, Ma Xiaoyun. Cast: Li Yunjuan as Gaowa, Liu Guizhu as Liu Yulan, Jin Xing as Coach Xie

Gaowa is an excellent judoist. She wins a world championship gold medal for China, but is severely injured during the final match. The Asian Games are coming up and the selection committee has a dilemma as to who they should send to represent China: Gao Wa, the world's best but still recovering; or Liu Yulan, less experienced but younger and healthier. The film centers around the committee's struggle to reach a collective decision. At last, they select Liu Yulan, and Gao Wa unselfishlessly accompanies Liu Yulan as her teammate and counselor. At the Asian Games, Liu defeats a Japanese participant and wins the gold medal.

2246. *War Sends the Women Away (Zhan Zheng Rang Nu Ren Zou Kai)*

1987. Shanghai Film Studio. Color. 10 Reels. Direction: Zuang Hongsheng. Screenplay: Guo Jingting. Cinematography: Shen Miaorong. Art Direction: Lu Xuehan. Music: Liu Yanxi. Sound: Lu Xuehan. Cast: Chen Jianfei as Xu Lei, Na Renhua as Lan Yuzhi, Feng Enhe as Jiao Yongtai, Li Li as Fengyin, Wang Yuxiao as Zhang Dazuang, Wu Jing as Liao Yonghui

Just before Spring Festival, the personnel at a PLA base joyfully begin receiving visits from their families, who have traveled to the base from all over China. Suddenly, orders arrive putting the entire base on alert, and the visitors are ordered to leave within two days. Through the experiences of several affected families, the film shows the hardship and sacrifice borne by people in the military.

2247. *Ward No. 16 (Shi Liu Hao Bing Hao)*

1983. Changchun Film Studio. Color. 10 Reels. Direction: Zhang Yuan, Yu Yanfu. Screenplay: Qiao Xuezhu. Cinematography: Wang Jishun. Art Direction: Shi Weijun. Music: Wu Damin. Sound: Chen Wenyuan. Cast: Li Ling as Chang Ling, Song Xiaoyiny as Liu Chunhua, Feng Enhe as Chen Zhongnan, Fang Hui as Sang Qinqin, Fang Xiaoqing as Tian Jingjun

Chang Ling, Tian Jingyun and Sang Qinqin are three women patients sharing the same ward in a hospital specializing in lung ailments. All are very depressed until one day, a new patient arrives, a young teacher from the countryside named Liu Chunhua. The newcomer has the sort of sunny, cheerful personality that perks up everyone's spirits. She is particularly helpful to Chang Ling, who has a great deal of difficulty coping with her disease and despairs of ever resuming a normal existence. Liu Chunhua inspires Chang Ling to have a new attitude and look forward to life with hope and confidence. Chang Ling later finds out that her disease is quite ordinary and curable, but Liu Chunhua has lung cancer. Even though her illness is terminal, the young teacher's only concerns are for her students back in the countryside and for her supportive and loving husband Chen Zhongnan. Liu Chunhua quietly passes away, but her spirit remains with her roommates. Chang Ling decides to return to the countryside with Chen Zhongnan and take over Liu's work.

Best Picture, 1984 Hundred Flowers Awards.

Best Supporting Actress Song Xiaoying, 1984 Golden Rooster Awards.

2248. Warriors in a Clear Blue Sky (Bi Kong Xiong Shi)

1961. August First Film Studio. B & W. 8 Reels. Direction: Yuan Xian. Screenplay: Zeng Xiangle and Xiao Mingzhen. Cinematography: Chen Ruijun. Art Direction: Zhang Zheng. Music: Yan Ke. Sound: Kou Shenkang. Cast: Zhao Ruping as Lin Dahai, Zhang Lianfu as the company commander, Hu Xiaoguang as the political commissar, Zhang Liang as Li Erwa, Wang Xinjian as Liu Shengjun, Wang Yi as Zhou Ming

When peasant Lin Dahai joins the army he is assigned to the paratroops. He is disappointed about his assignment, and it affects his training. At one point he fails to jump during a practice jump, and is reprimanded. One night he leaves his guard post without permission to answer a call of nature, and is again disciplined by his company commander. In time, he makes progress with the patient help of the political commissar. When Dahai's hometown suffers a disastrous flood, he begs and receives permission to go home and help in the relief mission. From then on, Lin Dahai progresses rapidly and becomes an excellent PLA parachutist.

2249. Warriors of China (Zhong Guo Yong Shi)

1990. Changchun Film Studio. Color. 9 Reels. Wide Screen. Direction: Wang Xuexin. Screenplay: Liu Yiran, Yu Yonghe. Cinematography: Ning Changcheng, Li Sen. Art Direction: Cui Yongquan, Xiao Shizeng. Music: Xiao Chen.

Sound: Xing Guocang. Cast: Du Zhenqing as "Black Lion," Xing Minshan as "Wolf," Li Yunjuan as "Snake," Zheng Rong as Zhang Yu

One day, a terrorist group attacks a nuclear power station in an unnamed country. This leads to a serious nuclear leak causing fall-out to spread over a host of other countries. Zhang Yu, a Chinese nuclear pollution expert in anti-nuclear chemicals, sets out for the disaster area to assess the damage. But on the way he is kidnapped by the terrorists headed by a man known as "Wolf." The terrorists plan to exchange the scientist for members of their group currently serving prison sentences. To safeguard world peace and carry out international obligations, the Chinese government dispatches a special services unit headed by "Black Lion" and "Snake" to rescue Zhang Yu.

2250. The Warrior's Tragedy (Bian Cheng Lang Zi)

1993. Inner Mongolia Film Studio & Hong Kong Xunqi Film Studio and Taiwan Longxiang Film Making Corp. Co-Production. Color. Letterboxed. Direction: Chen Xunqi (Frankie Chan). Screenplay: Chen Xunqi, based on a novel by Gu Long. Cinematography: Wu Rongjie. Art Direction: Yang Yuhe. Music: Dao Erji. Costume: Liu Yingzi, Shi Yulan, An Aliguna, Xiao Hong. Makeup: Wang Xizhong, Su Hong, Ma Suying, Zhang Yuming, Chao Ying. Cast: Di Long as Fu Hongxue, Chen Xunqi (Frankie Chan) as Ye Kai, Xu Huanshan as Ma Kongqun, Chen Yulian as Shen Shanniang, Peng Jieyin as Ma Fangling, Xu Ling as Cui Nong, Yuan Yongyi (Anita Yuen) as Ding Lingling, Zhang Zhilin (Julian Cheung) as Lu Xiaojia, Luo Jialiang as Murong Mingzhu, Feng Kean as Xiao Bieli, Wang Luyao as Ding Baiyun

At the foot of Snowy Mountain, Fu Hongxue, son of the famous martial artist Bai Tianyu, is ordered by his mother Bai Feng to kill her longtime enemy Ma Kongqun. Baifeng's younger sister has lived with Ma Kongqun for years, and this creates problems for Fu.

2251. The Watch (aka An Orphan on the Streets) (Biao)

1949. Wenhua Film Company. B & W. 11 reels. Direction: Zuo Lin. Screenplay: Zuo Lin, adapted from the novel by the Russian writer L.Pandeleev. Cinematography: Xu Qi. Cast: Zhao Qian Sun as Xiao Niu, Chen Zhi as Yin Xiao Cheng, Sheng Yang as Lei Cunhua, Yu

Zhongying as Old Wan, Tian Zhengdong as Hu Dekui, Cui Chaoming as the investigating officer, Zhou Ruide as Little Fatty

A homeless Shanghai orphan is sent to reform school, where he keeps secret the fact that he still possesses a watch he stole just before his arrest on other charges. The school's corrupt director learns of the watch and uses it to blackmail the boy into still more criminal activity. But when the orphan hears of the serious economic hardship his theft has brought to the shop owner and his family, the youngster repents, confesses all his crimes and exposes those of the director.

2252. *Water (Shui)*

1957. August First Film Studio. B & W. 6 Reels. Direction: Hua Chun, Shi Wenzi. Screenplay: Chen Zongfeng. Cinematography: Chen Ruijun. Art Direction: Li Xinmo. Music: Li Weicai. Sound: Kou Shenkang. Cast: Yu Shaokang as Doctor Liu, Jia Xinghui as Liu Xiuqing, Wang Lianhai as Sun Jipu, Wang Dianyu as the political instructor, Wang Dieqing as an old Muslim man, Pao Mengmei as a Muslim woman

In the summer of 1947, a PLA field hospital staff crossing a desert in transit to another assignment is threatened with enemy attack and a shortage of water. Aided by an elderly Muslim man, they resolve their water shortage. When they run short of emergency medicine, the old man promises to give them some restorative waters which he had set aside to treat his ailing grandson. When the pursuing enemy force captures one of the wounded, the old man hides Doctor Liu in his home while the doctor successfully treats the grandson. The old man then gives the enemy troops some drugged water, which incapacitates them while the doctor takes their weapons and frees the captured PLA soldier. The staff then proceeds on their transfer assignment.

2253. *Water Bird Action (Shui Niao Xing Dong)*

1986. Fujian Film Studio. Color. 9 Reels. Direction: Luo Guanqun. Screenplay: Xie Guangning. Cinematography: Qiao Jicang, Yang Ming. Art Direction: Liu Jiahuan. Music: Liu Yanxi. Sound: Zhu Wenzhong. Cast: Zhou Yuyuan as Shanben Yinmin, Liu Wei as Ouyang Peng, Zhang Jiumei as Lingzhi

In the summer of 1934, the Japanese high command plans to create an incident in China which will give them the excuse for an inva-sion. On June 9th they announce the disappearance of one of their diplomats stationed in Nanjing, and give the Chinese government a deadline for finding him. Two of the Nanjing Police Department's top detectives scour the city and find the missing man before the deadline expires.

2254. *Water Dropping Guanyin (Di Shui Guan Yin)*

1984. Shanghai Film Studio. Color. Letterboxed. 10 Reels. Direction: Song Chong. Screenplay: Zhou Danya, Kang Xu. Cinematography: Zhang Yuanmin. Art Direction: Xue Jianna, Music: Huang Zhun. Sound: Liu Guangjie. Cast: Qian Yongfu as Li Zhenhua, Guo Jin as Yili, Zhang Zhihua as Zhang Ping, Yisulahan as Yila, Wang Shaoguang as Boss Jiao, Feng Qi as Manager Yang, Ma Guanyin as Qian Shouan

Operating on the orders of a covert spymaster known only as "Guan Yin," a spy working for a foreign power steals China's secret "F-3" defense plans from a base in South China, and attempts to take it out of the country. The PSB director sends his best investigators, Li Zhenhua and Zhang Ping, to intercept the spy and recover the plans. In doing so, they obtain a vital clue as to the identity of "Guan Yin," sought by the PSB for over 20 years. They flush out "Guan Yin," but he turns out not to be the top spy in China. To root out the true spymaster, Li and Zhang must themselves assume cover identities.

2255. *Waves of Anger (Nu Chao)*

1963. August First Film Studio. B & W. 11 Reels. Direction: Shi Wenzhi. Screenplay: Wu Zhili, Wei Yang, Zhen Hong. Cinematography: Yang Zhaoren. Art Direction: Liu Qian, Ren Huixing. Music: Gong Zhiwei. Sound: Guo Dazheng. Cast: Zhang Ping as Qiu Jin, Zhou Fengshan as Luo Dacheng, Guan Shuzhen as Su's wife, Liu Bingzhang as Su, Ju Chunhua as Ma's grandfather, Huang Huanguang as Ma Changsheng, Hu Xiaoguang as Wang Huaizhi

In 1927, after Chiang Kaishek broke up the Communist-Nationalist coalition and began the slaughter of leftists, one of those arrested is Qiu Jin, chairman of a farmers' association in Hunan province. While he is able to survive the massacre, he is seriously wounded in the fighting. Rescued and restored to health with the aid of Luo Dacheng, a special liaison assigned to his county, Qiu Jin again raises a farmers' militia to fight the Nationalist government. But poor leadership by Wang Huaizhi, a special liaison from the central Party authorities, results in serious losses to the revolutionaries. Luo Dacheng is killed in battle, and Wang Huaizhi is also killed by the enemy. Qiu Jin at last organizes and leads a farmers' militia which becomes part of the Communist forces under Mao Zedong.

2256. The Way They Were (Yi Luo Huang Yuan De Ai)

1994. Tianshan Film Studio. Color. Letterboxed. 9 Reels. Direction: Jin Lini. Screenplay: Nie Xin. Cinematography: Zhao Peng. Art Direction: Ma Shaoxian. Music: Gao Erdi. Sound: Wu Xuezhong. Costume: Jiang Yanen, Zhang Xiurong. Makeup: Xiaojie. Cast: Song Jia as Wenxiu, Chen Xiguang as Ji Gang, Li Xinming as Wu Qi, Jiang Mengling as Qiu Shao, Wang Tianxiang as Yangyang (as a child), Wang Xufeng as Yangyang (as a young man), Zhang Han as Cuicui, Wang Yong as Liang Hai, Zhang Chunhua as Chunhua, Ma Xin as Xiao Ding

In the early 1950s, a group of women criminals including a girl named Wenxiu are assigned as part of their rehabilitation to work at a land development base previously populated only by men. One of the men, Ji Gang, soon falls in love with Wenxiu, and she gets pregnant. But when Ji Gang learns that Wenxiu's crime had been prostitution, he cannot bear the pressure and marries another woman. Wu Qi, a kindly older man, takes Wenxiu in and marries her, after which she bears Ji Gang's son, Yangyang. Wu Qi is killed in a work accident, and Ji Gang's wife leaves him when she learns he still loves Wenxiu. But Wenxiu not only refuses to reconcile with Ji Gang, she will not let him do anything for their son. Years later, when Yangyang leaves for college, the two now-middle-aged parents make up their past differences, but Ji Gang passes away before Yangyang can acknowledge the old man as his father.

2257. We Are the World (Wo Men Shi Shi Jie)

1988. Xi'an Film Studio. Color. Letterboxed. 9 Reels. Direction: Fang Fang, He Yuan. Screenplay: Zhang Xianliang. Cinematography: Zi Lei, Zhao Lei. Art Direction: Tong Huamiao. Music: Tao Long. Sound: Li Lanhua. Cast: Wang Gang as County Director Ma, Zefu Benahwei as Mr. Beierman

In 1940, Northwest China suffers the worst drought in the area's history, and everyone prays for rain. A foreign priest arrives from more than 1,000 miles distant to lead the people in prayers, and a drenching rain occurs shortly thereafter. A young shepherd becomes the first friend of the priest. Forty years have passed, and in the same area that young boy is now a middle-aged man, County Director Ma. Ma leads his people in building a water conservancy project, but their poverty and the harsh natural conditions of the area work against them. He hears that the United Nations Food and Agriculture Association will provide help to the area. Six years later, a UN officer Mr. Beierman comes to inspect the construction, and while he is happy about the changes that have taken place, he also finds that Ma's contractual violations force him to dismiss Ma from his position. On his way back home, Ma dies on the land. An elderly foreign man stands in front of Ma's tomb, having come for a last visit with the first Chinese friend he made nearly a half century ago.

2258. We Belong to One Generation (Wo Men Shi Yi Dai Ren)

1960. Changchun Film Studio. B & W. 10 Reels. Direction: De Guangbudaoerji. Screenplay: Li Jianrao. Cinematography: Bao Jie. Art Direction: Liu Jinnai. Music: Lou Zhanghou. Sound: Huang Lijia. Cast: Pu Ke as Liu Tingdong, Guo Zhenqing as Zhao Zhengcang, Ma Loufu as the Party Secretary, Sheng Linzhong as the factory director, Zhang Hui as Zheng Zhixiu, Xu Bukui as Zhao Zhengcang (as a child)

A machine factory's Party committee gives the job of training a group of new apprentices to veteran worker Liu Tingdong. New apprentice Li Tiezhu, from the countryside, has frequent disagreements with fellow new apprentice Xia Quan who comes from a small business background. Under Liu Tingdong's tutelage, Li, Xia and others all go on to new job assignments.

2259. We Belong to the Eighth Route Army (Wo Men Shi Ba Lu Jun)

1978. August First Film Studio. Color. 12 Reels. Direction: Wang Ping. Screenplay: Li Bai, Dong Xiaohua, Li Changhua. Cinematography: Cao Jingyun, Cai Jiwei. Art Direction: Ren Huixing, Fei Lanxin, Zhang Zheng. Music: Gong Zhiwei. Sound: Shi Pingyi. Cast: Ma Cangyu as

Zhao Changlong, Gao Baocheng as Zhou Weihu, Zhen Qianlong as Yang Xueren, Lan Faqin as Wei Dazhang, Zhu Kexin as Du Li

In 1941, the darkest period for the resistance, Japanese troops and Nationalist collaborators launch a massive assault on the provinces of Shaanxi, Gansu and Ningxia, held by the Communists. An Eighth Route Army charcoal-making team led by Zhao Changlong leaves its Yan'an base and goes deep into the mountains to dig a cave and make charcoal. Not all of the group is happy about this: young soldier Wei Dazhang cannot see the importance of charcoal-making to the war, and longs to be in combat; Zhao's deputy Yang Xueren is an individualist, still doing things the way the old warlord soldiers did. Zhao Changlong and Head Nurse Du Li set examples by their own conduct and bring them together to overcome the many physical and ideological difficulties. They finally unite the small team, and all unselfishlessly devote themselves to the work.

2260. *We Don't Understand Love the First Time (Chu Lian Shi, Wo Men Bu Dong Ai Qing)*

1987. Changchun Film Studio. Color. 9 Reels. Direction: Zhu Wenshun, Chen Xuejie. Screenplay: Fei Min. Cinematography: Duan Zhengjiang. Art Direction: Liu Xuerao. Music: Chen Shouqian. Sound: Wang Lin. Cast: Guo Xuxin as Zhou Hang, Wang Hui as Chen Wanxia, Pang Ming as Mu Yin, Liu Wei as Zhang Dashun

A group of young cleaning workers are angry and resentful that people look down upon the work they do. In addition, they have trouble finding girlfriends. One of them, handsome Zhou Hang, vows he will gain some respect for his fellows by finding a beautiful girl to be his wife. He meets Chen Wanxia, a girl who works in an instrument factory, and passes himself off as a college graduate. They fall in love and Wanxia becomes pregnant, but they break up because she realizes she wants to have a better future than he can provide. The woman manager of a clothing store has loved Zhou in secret. She helps Zhou Hang out of his painful situation and supports him financially to study fashion design. Zhou Hang at last become a part-time clothes designer. At a fashion show, Zhou Hang's products are well-received. He finds Wanxia, now a college student, is one of those in the audience applauding.

2261. *We Met Him Before (Ta, Wo Men Jian Guo)*

1985. Xi'an Film Studio. Color. 3-D. 6 Reels. Direction: An Qinyun, Chen Xingzhong. Screenplay: Chen Xingzhong, An Qingyun. Cinematography: Yan Zhijie. Art Direction: Liu Xinghou. Music: Zhao Jiping. Sound: Chen Li. Cast: Dai Shulin as Zhang Xiaosan, Rong Xia as Shen Xiaocong

Acrobatic performer Zhang Xiaoshan is 30 and still does not have a girlfriend. He is introduced to daycare worker Shen Xiaocong and make a date to meet in the park the following Sunday. However, he fails to meet her on time because he keeps stopping on the way to assist others. Although he is misunderstood, once people see the purity of his motives, all misunderstanding passes. Shen Xiaochong falls in love with him.

2262. *Wedding (Hun Li)*

1979. Beijing Film Studio. Color. 10 Reels. Direction: Duan Jishun. Screenplay: Hang Ying, Duan Jishun, Yin Zhiming. Cinematography: Zhang Shiwei. Art Direction: Wang Yi. Music: Wang Yanqiao. Sound: Zhang Baojian. Cast: Liu Xiaoqing as Sheng Ming, Zhang Lianwen as Yue Zhipeng, Zhu Yurong as Sheng Jie, Xu Ming as Gao Yu, Zhang Yuyu as Sheng Nan, Liu Yanli as Wang Dalong

In the spring of 1975, young technician Yue Zhipeng goes from Beijing to a national key construction site where his girlfriend Sheng Ming works as well. Yue Zhipeng and Sheng Ming are in charge of the design work. While Yue Zhipeng and the workers work their hardest, the "Gang of Four" plans to destroy their work. Just at that time, Premier Zhou Enlai dies, and because Yue Zhipeng writes a letter to the central government critical of the disruption to their work caused by the Gang, order are given to get him for this. Sheng Ming senses that Yue's future is uncertain, so she decides the two will marry immediately. On the day that the Gang's henchman Gao Yu arrives to arrest Yue Zhipeng, he and Sheng Ming are being married to funeral music.

2263. *The Wedding Night Murder Case (Liang Xiao Xue An)*

1988. Beijing Film Studio. Color. 9 Reels. Direction: Yu Zhongyi. Screenplay: Yu Zhongyi, Sun Fengqing. Cinematography: Gao Lixian. Art Direction: Ma Zhaoren. Music: Xu Jingqin.

Sound: Zhang Zhian, Cast: Guan Zongxiang as Niu Pin, Jiang Hong as Liu Chunxiu, Huang Ailing as Yang Qiaoyu, Jin Hong as Duan Zhenju, Huang He as Chonger, Hu Jianbing as Liu Xifa

Niu Pin, a detective in trouble with his supervisors, and in fact recently demoted, is assigned to look into a murder case. The victim is the daughter of a local official, stabbed to death on her wedding night. Chonger's mother Yang Qiaoyu is convinced her daughter was murdered by her groom Zhou Qiling, but his parents are just as impassioned in defense of their son. Determined to reinstate himself by getting to the bottom of things, Niu Pin doggedly pursues the few clues. At last, it turns out that Zhou Qiling had been an adopted child, given up at birth by his real mother Liu Chunxiu. She had gone to see and congratulate her son on his wedding night, but she and Chonger had gotten into an argument. The angry bride had taken a pair of scissors with which to attack Chunxiu, but had fallen and killed herself, a case of accidental suicide.

2264. *Wedding on the Execution Ground (Xing Chang Shang De Hun Li)*

1980. Changchun Film Studio. Color. 12 Reels. Direction: Guang Budaoerji, Cai Yuanyuan. Screenplay: Zhang Yisheng, Cai Yuanyuan, Zhao Yurong. Cinematography: Li Huailu, Zhang Xiaoqiu. Art Direction: Li Wenguang. Music: Yan Ke. Sound: Hong Di. Cast: Song Xiaoyin as Chen Tiejun, Li Qimin as Zhou Wenyong, Guan Changzhu as Director Lu

In February 1928, the commander-in-chief of the Guangzhou workers' rebellion Zhou Wenyong and Guangdong Women's Association worker Chen Tiejun are imprisoned and sentenced to death. Comrades devise a plan to rescue them, but they reject it because it could result in huge losses. When Zhou Wenyong and Chen Tiejun are assigned to the work of organizing the rebellion they at first pretend to be a couple; Guangzhou at the time is full of spies, and the couple's marital status is called into question. As they experience so much together, sharing joy and sorrow, victory and defeat, they gradually develop trust, respect and caring for each other. However, the Guangzhou rebellion fails, and they both are jailed. Prison does not shake their beliefs or their love. On the execution ground, they ask to be married on the spot, after which they are both put to death.

2265. *The Weddings (Gao Peng Man Zhuo)*

1991. Changchun Film Studio. Color. 9 Reels. Letterboxed. Direction: Wang Fengkui. Screenplay: Fei Ming, Wang Fengkui, Cinematography: Zhang Zhongwei. Art Direction: Ju Lutian. Music: Gao Erdi. Sound: Ju Lutian. Cast: Li Zhiyu as Nian Wangqiu, Chen Xiaoyi as the Bride, Xie Yuan as Dakuan, Ma Ling as Baoling, Xu Zhongquan as Bureau Head Yan

A comedy centering on three households living in one of the single-story housing courtyards common in Chinese cities: the family of Yan, a bureaucrat recently promoted to Minister of Railways; Dakuan and Baoling, a self-employed young couple living together though unmarried; and Nian Wangqiu, a bachelor teacher. Teacher Nian is due to get new housing, so Yan wants to jump the queue by getting his youngest son to marry quickly. Housing priorities are determined by applicants' marital status. Yan's action angers the others. In order to recover the apartment that the teacher should have received, Dakuan and Baoling decide to stage a wedding for Nian. Then they decide to get married as well. The next day, the courtyard is a busy place, with three wedding ceremonies being held simultaneously, TV crews on the scene covering the event, and a procession of Nian's students coming to offer congratulations. Nian's stand-in "bride" turns out to have actually fallen in love with him. But Minister Yan's new daughter-in-law walks out on her ceremony to look for her former lover...

2266. *Weekend Love Corner (Zhou Mo Lian Ai Jiao)*

1991. Changchun Film Studio. Color. Letterboxed. 9 Reels. Direction: Wang Fengkui, Gu Jing. Screenplay: Peng Mingyan, Han Zhijun. Cinematography: Liu Fengdi, Li Li. Art Direction: Guo Yansheng, Zhang Yi. Music: Gao Erdi. Cast: Liu Xiaolingtong as Du Dachuan, Fu Yiwei as Wu Xiaolan, Yan Qin as Bailing Niao, Fang Qinzhuo as Li Yueping

In a Beijing "dating corner," young and handsome Du Dachuan meets government clerk Wu Xiaolan. Although he is a construction worker, Dachuan passes himself off as a college professor. Dachuan's buddy Guo Xiaoxing did go to college, but he is so homely no girl is interested in him. A third couple is Huang Ming, a single older woman, and Dachuan's middle-aged and divorced cousin.

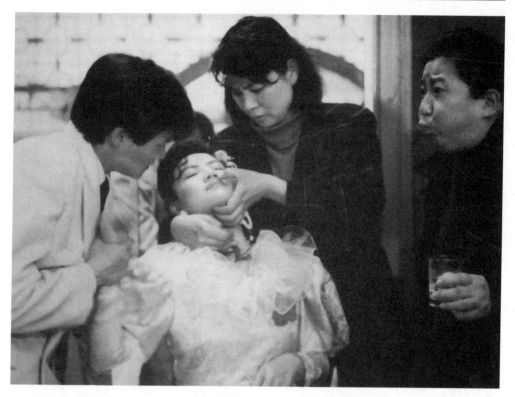

The Weddings. **A madcap situation at one of the three weddings in the story. 1991. Changchun Film Studio.**

Eventually, these people all find true love with someone.

2267. *Weekend Lover (Zhou Mo Qing Ren)*

1993. Fujian Film Studio & Hainan Xinghai Fixed Asset Company Ltd. Co-Production. Color. Letterboxed. 96 minutes. Direction: Lou Ye. Screenplay: Xu Qin. Cinematography: Zhang Xigui. Art Direction: Li Jixian. Music: Zhang Shaotong. Sound: Lu Jiajun. Cast: Wang Zhiwen as La La, Ma Xiaoqing as Li Xin, Jia Hongsheng as A Xi, Nai An as Chen Chen, Wang Xiaoshuai as Zhang Chi, Wu Tao as A Kai

Teenager A Xi is sent to prison for nine years for killing another youngster. When he is released, he looks up his old girlfriend Li Xin, and finds her now involved with another young man La La. Determined to regain his lost love, A Xi begins stalking the two, showing up and confronting them when they least expect it. The tension builds to a confrontation between the two rival suitors.

2268. *Weeping at Suzhou (Lei Sha Gu Su)*

1985. Beijing Film Studio. Color. 10 Reels. Direction: Chen Fangqian. Screenplay: Zhang Shuliang, Chen Fangqian. Cinematography: Li Yuebing. Art Direction: Li Gengcheng. Music: Hu Weili. Sound: Liu Shida. Cast: Bai Ling as Wang Lianjuan, Shen Guanchu as Zhang Qinyun, Cai Min as Xiao Ling, Wu Qianqian as Jiang Suqing, Li Mengrao as the Suzhou administrator

In the Ming Dynasty, Wuxi County admininstrator's daughter Wang Lianjuan has an unhappy life. In addition to a lack of love in her family, she is abused by her stepmother. Her only solace is her relationship with Zhang Qinyun, son of the Suzhou administrator. When she gets pregnant, Zhang loses all interest in her, and marries the daughter of his father's superior, senior administrator Jiang Suqing. When Wang Lianjuan goes to Zhang for help, he tries to poison her. She survives his attempt on her life, but is so disheartened that after the baby is born she gives up and dies anyway. Jiang Suqing's father, an honest administrator dedicated to justice, has his son-in-law executed, then adopts the baby boy himself.

2269. *The Wei River's New Song (Wei Shui Xin Ge)*

1977. Xi'an Film Studio. Color. 9 Reels. Direction: Liu Bing. Screenplay: Chen Zhongshi. Cinematography: Lin Jing. Art Direction: Wang Fei. Music: Li Yaodong. Sound: Hua Juan. Cast: Li Antai as Liu Donghai, Ding Weiming as Donghai's mother, Cheng Yi as Li Jianshan, Yang Youhuan as Man Tun, Chun Li as Liu Tianyin, Wang Yinlin as Tianyin's wife, Tan Tuo as Liu Jingzai

After being appointed Party Secretary of the Liu Family Bridge Unit 1973, young Liu Donghai stresses the "agriculture must learn from Dazhai" movement, but his campaign is hampered by former landlord Liu Jingzai in league with some local counterrevolutionaries. Liu Jingzai also attempts to affect the friendship of Liu Donghai with unit director Liu Tianyin and Liu Donghai's relationship, aiming to break up their "three associations" leadership group. Liu criticizes the neocapitalists, and smashes their conspiracy. His efforts to make "agriculture learn from Dazai" is successful.

2270. *Well (Jing)*

1987. Emei Film Studio. Color. 10 Reels. Direction: Li Yalin. Screenplay: Zhang Xian. Cinematography: Li Baoqi, Pan Jing. Art Direction: Chen Desheng. Music: Tang Qinshi. Sound: Luo Guohua. Cast: Pan Hong as Xu Lisha, Li Zhiyu as Zhu Shiyi, Lin Daxing as Tong Shaoshan, He Xiaoshu as Zhu's mother

When young and beautiful Xu Lisha graduates from college at the outset of the Cultural Revolution, her family's capitalist background gets her assigned to menial work washing bottles. Minor bureaucrat Zhu Shiyi finds her attractive and offers her marriage, which also offers some measure of political protection. But once they are married, Zhu and his mother totally change their treatment of the young woman, treating her as little more than their household slave. When the Cultural Revolution is over, Xu Lisha secures a position in the chemical engineering field she trained for, and in time she and her assistant Tong Shaoshan develop a new drug which is very successful. Zhu Shiyi, whose own status is now quite low, grows jealous of his wife's success. He starts to spread rumors about his wife's rela-

tionship with her assistant, driving her to ask for a divorce. But when she professes her love to Tong Shaoshan, he rejects her as he cannot bear the societal pressure. Xu Lisha's hopes for a normal life are at an end, and she is on the verge of a mental breakdown.

Best Actress Pan Hong, 1988 Golden Rooster Awards.

Best Picture, 2nd Class and Best Actress Pan Hong, 19th Taormina Film Festival.

2271. *A Well Off Household (Xiao Kang Ren Jia)*

1958. Haiyan Film Studio. B & W. 9 Reels. Direction: Xu Tao. Screenplay: Li Zhun. Cinematography: Qiu Yiren. Art Direction: Yao Mingzhong. Music: Wang Yunjie. Sound: Lu Zongbo. Makeup: Yao Yongfu. Cast: Han Fei as Wang Xiaoan, Ma Ji as "Know-It-All," Hong Xia as Liu Chunnu, Xia Tian as Wang Xiang, Jiang Rui as Uncle, Li Lingjun as Narcissus

After production activist Liu Chunnu marries young farmer Wang Xiaoan, she joins enthusiastically in the work of the commune, but dislikes working in the family's orchard. This displeases her mother-in-law, who everyone refers to as "Know-It-All." When a grain wholesaling campaign is adopted, the mother-in-law and father-in-law Wang Xiang are conservative in their thinking, and plan to avoid having to sell their surplus to the state. Xiaoan meekly gives in to his parents. In addition, "Know-It-All" stirs up disagreements between the young couple. At first Chunnu worries about her relationship with her in-laws, but with the support and encouragement of the commune director she first wins over her husband, who then denounces his parents at a public meeting. This wakes up the older couple to their errors, and they not only agree to sell their surplus to the state, they help persuade their relatives to do so as well.

2272. *What Are You Thinking? (Ni Zai Xiang She Me)*

1983. Pearl River Film Studio. Color. 11 Reels. Direction: Wang Ti, Chen Ying, Xing Jitian. Screenplay: Gu Xiaoyan. Cinematography: Xie Yongyi, Bai Yunsheng. Art Direction: Li Wenguang. Music: Yang Shuzheng. Sound: Den Qinhua. Cast: Liang Yin as Ma Changqing, Wang Yuzhang as Liu Guoqing, Wang Fangbo as Ding Wancai, Liu Yuhua as Gao Liansheng, Jin Yikang as Xiao Xiao, Zhang Nan as Xiao Shuangzhi

In the 1970s, just before the Gang of Four's downfall, Party Secretary Ma Changqing moves to his new position at the Hongshe Mine, accompanied by his wife and daughter. He finds things in total disorder. For one thing, the house assigned to him is already occupied by a young newlywed couple. Through their spokesperson Liu Guoqing, other young miners resent his instructional methods, particularly his frequent comparisons of the bitter life of old China with the life of today. One rainy night, when another young couple's roof leaks badly, he helps repair it in the rain, which gives the young workers a better impression of him. They talk with him and express their hopes for the mine, and their desire for the Party's trust and support. Ma Changqing now trusts Liu Guoqing to help him unite the young workers he will bring up under the Party's leadership.

2273. What Price Survival (Zhan Hu Tu Long)

1994. Changchun Film Studio, Hong Kong Yindao Film Studio. Color. Letterboxed. 9 Reels. Direction: Li Rengang. Screenplay: Chen Zhaoxiang. Cinematography: Zhang Dongliang. Art Direction: Wang Yuwei, Zhang Zhongtian. Costume: Li Jingping, Wang Xiyou, Chen Xiaoling. Makeup: Liu Bingkui, Jin Wansheng, Pan Li. Cast: Liu Songren, Jiang Dawei, Xu Shaoqiang, Wu Xingguo, Yang Caini, Gao Jie

Around the beginning of the Republic of China (c1912), two very competitive friends, Wang Jingguo and Bai Fuguo, become enemies. Wang beats Bai and takes Bai's baby son Bai Ning, although Wang loses an arm in the process. Twenty years pass, during which Wang trains the boy to grow up and someday kill Bai Fuguo. Bai Ning also falls in love with Wang's daughter Xiao Lian. The inevitable tragedy happens at last: Bai Ning finds Bai Fuguo and kills him as he was conditioned to do. But Bai Fuguo does not die immediately, and is able to pass a note to his son telling him the whole truth, that the man he has just killed was his own father. Deeply depressed, he vows to fight no more. Meanwhile, Wang Jingguo plans to kill Bai Ning. Bai Ning and Xiao Lian marry, and leave together. When Wang catches up to them, rather than fight, Bai Ning chooses to cut off one of his own arms to settle the score.

2274. Wheels Rolling (Che Lun Gun Gun)

1975. Changchun Film Studio. Color. 10 Reels. Direction: Yi Yiqin. Screenplay: Xue Shouxian. Cinematography: Wu Guojiang. Art Direction: Li Junjie. Music: Chen Min. Cast: Da Qi as Geng Dongshan, Lu Yalin as Geng Chunmei, Ye Zhikang as Lei Ming, Zhao Dengfeng as Guo Diankun, Li Yalin as the Political Commissar, Song Xuejuan as He's wife, Li Jie as Zhen Zicheng

In the winter of 1948, civilians organize a small transport team in the Jiaodong liberated area, to deliver food to PLA units in the frontlines. Led by veteran civilian worker Geng Dongshan and his adopted daughter, political supervisor Geng Chunmei, their main obstacle is a bandit gang headed by landlord Zhen Zicheng. After victory in the battle of Huaihai, Chunmei meets her long lost brother. At this time, Chairman Mao call for "Carrying the revolution to the end." Geng then brings the civilian workers to participate more directly in fighting. During one encounter, Geng and his daughter kill Zhen Zilong. Through the people's efforts, the PLA occupies Nanjing, receiving a great victory in the revolutionary war.

2275. The Wheels' Song (Chen Lun Si Chong Zou)

1984. Shanghai Film Studio. Color. Letterboxed. 9 Reels. Direction: Zhang Junxiang, Li Xiepu. Screenplay: Pan Xiaoju, Renke. Cinematography: Ju Jiazhen. Art Direction: Zhang Bingjian. Music: Xu Jingxin. Sound: Ren Daming. Cast: Liu Xingyi as Shen Xin, Ai Liya as Gesang Lamu, Li Wei as Nima Chiren, Li Zhen as Wang Xiaoduo

A military vehicle travels down a Tibetan highway, carrying PLA platoon leader Shen Xin and new recruit Wang Xiaoduo. They meet and give a ride to Gesang Lamu, a Tibetan girl returning home after having just graduated from Beijing Medical School. On the road, the trio find a very ill Tibetan hunter named Nima Chiren. But they also find he is smuggling organs taken from endangered animal species, a violation of Chinese law. Shen Xin interrogates the man, and it soon develops that Shen Xin's father had been killed on the very highway they are now traveling. The young soldier volunteered for Tibetan service out of his great concern for the land and its people, and his desire to help them out of poverty.

2276. *When All the Leaves Turn Red (Deng Dao Man Shan Hong Ye Shi)*

1980. Shanghai Film Studio. Color. 10 Reels. Direction: Tang Huada, Yu Bengzheng. Screenplay: Gao Xing, Luo Zhimin. Cinematography: Shen Xilin. Art Direction: Han Shangyi, Yan Cangming, Chen Shaomian. Music: Xiang Yi. Sound: Zhou Hengliang. Cast: Wu Haiyan as Yang Yin, Ding Jiayuan as Yang Min, He Lin as Zhang Laishui, Gao Yin as Wu Suqing, Ma Guanyin as Fei Guangbing

In order to experience shipboard life first hand for an upcoming movie, some film actors and actresses go on a voyage. Actress Wu Suqing falls in love with Fei Guangbing, one of the ship's attendants, but they have a disagreement over Fei's job. Third Mate Yang Yin has romantic problems with her lover Yang Min, and when Yang Min is killed changing a failed navigation beacon, she finds a letter to her he left behind. First Mate Zhang Lianshui also loves Yang Yin, but she still grieves for her dead lover. Through Yang Yin and Yang Min's great love, Wu Suqing and Fei Guangbing begin to get their own relationship straightened out. Zhang Lianshui still loves Yang Yin…

2277. *When the Grapes Mature (Pu Tao Shu Liao De Shi Hou)*

1952. Northeast Film Studio. B & W. 9 Reels. Direction: Wang Jiayi. Screenplay: Sun Qian. Cinematography: Wang Chunquan. Art Direction: Liu Xuerao. Music: Zhang Guocang. Sound: Lin Bingcheng. Cast: Du Defu as Ding Laogui, Ouyang Ruqiu as Old Lady Zhou, Li Baiwan as Ding Shuangxi, Liu Yi as Zhou Honge, Liu Yanjin as Hu Zhenzhen, Yu Yang as Gong Yuquan

In 1951, Nansha Village's grape harvest is exploited by a speculator trying to lower the purchase price. Since the local cooperative is only concerned with its members' living necessities and not their business problems, the members lose their enthusiasm for production. Old Mrs. Zhou wants to sell her grapes quickly, to purchase watering equipment and to pay for her daughter Honge's wedding to Ding Shuangxi, son of co-op director Ding Laogui. However, the father is opposed to any such new involvement for the co-op, and his refusal to buy her grapes creates hard feelings between the two families. In anger, Mrs. Zhou agrees to sell her grapes to speculator Diao Jing, but is persuaded by worker Gong Yuquan to hold off on this while the Communist Party authorities consider the matter. The village party branch committee reports the situation to the county committee. The county committee and county associated union then instruct the cooperative that it must market local special products for its members. Gong Yuquan also brings the members the good news that a winery will soon start production locally, defeating the speculator by providing an alternative sales outlet for grapes. At a local temple meeting, Old Mrs. Zhou sells her grapes to the co-op under the leadership of Ding Laogui, and voluntarily donates the money to the Resist America and Aid North Korea Campaign. She and Ding are friends once again, and the two young lovers look forward to their marriage.

2278. *When Will the Sky Turn Bright (Wen Tian He Shi Ming)*

1988. Beijing Film Studio. Color. 10 Reels. Direction: Ma Erlu, Wang Biao. Screenplay: Yue Ye. Cinematography: Tu Jiakuan. Art Direction: Duan Zhengzhong. Music: Dong Kui. Sound: Fu Yinjie. Cast: Yan Xiang as Guo Moruo, Su Lin as Zhou Enlai

Writer and intellectual Guo Moruo's left-wing politics have forced him to stay in Japan to escape government persecution, but when the Japanese invade China, he returns to do his part in the resistance effort. He writes and produces a drama titled "Qu Yuan" which uses a famous historical figure as a metaphor for China's contemporary political situation. The play is hugely popular throughout China, but angers Chiang Kaishek, who then creates what becomes known as the "Wannan Incident": the dramatic company performs the play in various places, and at one, Chiang's troops stop the performance and arrest the company. But the people protest so strongly that the army is forced to let them go.

2279. *Where Is the Visitor From (Ke Chong He Lai)*

1980. Changchun Film Studio. Color. 11 Reels. Direction: Guangbu Daoerji. Screenplay: Guo Weiqiang. Cinematography: Zhang Xiaoqiu. Art Direction: Liu Sheng. Music: Lei Yusheng. Sound: Yu Kaizhang, Wang Wenfu. Cast: Du Xiongwen as Feng Guozhu, Xue Li as Maigelike, Kai Ti as Catherine, Ni Pu as

Aosiboge, Kelifu as Daerman, Xu Guangmin as Lin Jingcai

In the 1970s, Chinese and international businessmen come to Guangzhou for a trade fair. Among those arriving at the Huangcheng Hotel are European Amalgamated Minerals Company President Maigelike and his secretary Catherine and Hong Kong businessmen Lin Jingcai and Cao Jingsan. After the welcoming reception, Maigelike finds that someone has opened the briefcase in his office, and his notebook containing important economic information is missing. He reports this to Chinese foreign affairs officer Feng Guozhu and asks for assistance. After losing the notebook, Maigelike continues receiving instructions by fax, but these instructions unnerve him and distract him from concluding contracts with the Chinese. He is so uncertain that he calls his board of directors and learns that the board had sent him no instructions since he had arrived in Hong Kong. It turns out that Aosiboge, a spy for the Soviet KGB, had gained Catherine's trust, collected information from her concerning her boss's business situation and then sent the false instructions.

2280. *Whirlwind (Tao Se Xuan Feng)*

1992. Xiaoxiang Film Studio. Color. Letterboxed. 9 Reels. Direction: Liu Yuefei. Screenplay: Cheng Keng. Cinematography: Li Xiaoping. Art Direction: Li Shu. Music: Xu Jingxin. Sound: Huang Siye, Wang Zhihong. Costume: Li Huiming, Lin Heming. Makeup: Feng Xiaoqing. Cast: Jin Di as Gan Qiang, Xu Lei as A Mian, Han Qing as Gan Ge, Li Qingqing as Su Lin

Amian is abandoned by her husband during the Cultural Revolution. She is raising their son alone when she meets a widowed policeman with two daughters. They merge families. One of the girls also joins the police when she grows up. The father is murdered while investigating a drug case. Five years later, the police track down the killer, and the daughter shoots him to death, only then finding out he is her own stepbrother. The girls are very upset and comforting to Amian over this turn of events, but are unaware she is the actual boss of the drug ring. When her stepdaughter's investigation is getting too close to the truth, Amian arranges for her other stepdaughter to be kidnapped, but the plot fails. The police surround the drug ring's factory. Amian plants explosives, locks herself in the room where her son died, and blows up the building.

2281. *Whirlwind Boy (Xuan Feng Xiao Zi)*

1994. Pearl River Film Company, Taiwan Changhong Film Corporation, Ltd. Co-Production. Color. Letterboxed. 9 Reels. Direction: Pi Jitao. Screenplay: Ye Yunqiao. Cinematography: Chen Rongshu. Art Direction: Zhang Jiping. Cast: Lin Zhiying as Si Mao, Chen Xiaolong as She Xiaolong, Xu Haoying as Zhenzhu, Xu Ruoxuan as Ann

A teenage love triangle in Hong Kong. A boy has a serious crush on one girl, unaware that another girl cares for him. He at last wakes up and realizes the other girl is really the one for him.

2282. *The White Dragon Horse (Bai Ma Long)*

1981. Pearl River Film Studio. Color. 8 Reels. Direction: Huang Shu, Huang Dantong. Screenplay: Huang Shu, Kong Liang. Cinematography: Wu Yukun, Zeng Jing. Art Direction: Qin Hongyi. Music: Lu Qimin, Huang Zhun. Sound: Li Xun. Cast: Xu Ping as Dandan, Han Sudong as Dongdong, Li Jiayang as Grandpa

One spring day, in a part of South China held by the Red Army, a brother and sister named Dandan and Dongdong are playing. Suddenly everything is thrown into chaos by an enemy attack: the Red Army retreats, and many civilian refugees take flight. In the retreat, Dandan and Dongdong become lost. They find the Red Army commander's white dragon horse which had run off when its wounded rider had fallen off. The children treat the horse's injuries, and when the horse later recovers it carries them back to the Red Army main force.

2283. *White Dragon Sword (Bai Long Jian)*

1986. Hebei Film Studio. Color. Wide Screen. 9 Reels. Direction: Tian Jinfu. Cinematography: Cao He. Art Direction: Yang Wan. Music: Wang Ming. Sound: Zhang Jiake. Cast: Liu Xiaohong as Liu Lan, Ji Qiling as Du Baojie, Ma Zheng as Zhao Rongda, Wang Shuqin as Mother Wang

Oppressed common people battle their Qing rulers in the early years of the 19th Century.

2284. *The White-Haired Girl (Bai Mao Nu)*

1950. North-East Film Studio. B & W. 13 Reels. Directors: Wang Bin and Shui Hua. Screenplay: Shui Hua, Wang Bin and Yang Runshen, adapted from a traditional Chinese folk opera. Cinematography: Qian Jiang. Set Design: Lu Gan. Sound: Sha Yuan. Music: Qu Wei, Zhang Lu and Ma Ke. Music performed by the Eastern Film Orchestra. Singers: Wang Kun, Meng Yu, Zhang Ping and Li Yaodong. Costume: Wang Leng. Makeup: Sun Yuemei. Cast: Tian Hua as Xi Er, Li Baifang as Wang Dachun, Chen Qiang as Huang Shiren

The White-Haired Girl. Years of living in the mountains like an animal have turned the hair of Xi Er (Tian Hua) completely white. 1950. Northeast Film Studio.

In a remote mountain village in Northeast China, the gentle romance of Xi Er, daughter of a tenant farmer, and Wang Dachun, a young farmer, is shattered by a cruel landlord, Huang Shiren. Lusting for the girl, Huang pressures her father to sell his daughter to settle his debts, then forces the father to commit suicide. Xi Er is forcibly taken to Huang's home, where she is raped by the landlord. After an unsuccessful attempt at rescuing her, Dachun is forced to flee from the area and seek refuge with the Red Army. Xi Er eventually escapes from Huang's house, and hides herself in the mountains. For a long time she lives there like an animal, and eventually her hair turns white. Consequently, a rural legend grows of a white-haired, female spirit haunting the mountains. Huang uses this legend to keep the peasants terrified. Two years later, Dachun returns with his military unit to his native village to lead the peasants in their fight for emancipation, but finds his work obstructed by the legend. In order to disprove the superstition, Dachun goes deep into the mountains in search of this white-haired spirit, and discovers she was originally his Xi Er. After the secret of the white-haired spirit is revealed, the peasants turn on Huang Shiren, and expose the landlord's many crimes. Xi Er returns to the village to take part in its work, her hair gradually becomes black again, and she and Dachun marry and pass their lives happily. Remade in 1970 as a TV movie, with several plot alterations, including a new ending more politically correct for Cultural Revolution fanaticism.

2285. *White Lotus (Bai Lian Hua)*

1980. Shanghai Film Studio. Color. Wide Screen. 11 Reels. Direction: Zhong Shuhuang, Sun Yongping. Screenplay: Xie Hong, Zhang Huaxun. Cinematography: Yin Fukang, Zhen Hong. Art Direction: Zhang Wanhong, Wu Tianci. Music: Xiao Yan. Sound: Wang Huimin. Cast: Wu Haiyan as Bai Lianhua, Gong Xibing as Xiao Lie, Xu Bu as Peng Bingqin, Wang Hui as Uncle Ma, Yu Guichun as Ma Hou

Bai Lianhua heads a farmers' self-defense troop. She meets Red Army regimental commander Xiao Lie and is persuaded to bring her forces into the Red Army, in a joint effort to deal with despot Gao Jingxuan's son, enemy division commander Gao Zhankui. Bai Lianhua joins the Red Army and soon marries Xiao Lie. However, Bai's troops are not regulars, and their lack of professionalism soon begins causing problems after they are part of the better-organized Red Army. Bai Lianhua argues with Political Commissar Peng Bingqin, while Gao Zhankui creates an incident which makes Bai Lianhua look like a spy. Peng Bingqin arrests Bai Lianhua. Because of Peng's biased view of Bai and the enemy's machinations, Bai Lianhua goes to Gao Zhankui's base, planning to capture him and prove she is innocent of the false accusations. But Bai Lianhua is detected and pursued by enemy troops. Trapped, she hurls herself from a high cliff.

2286. *Who Does He Love? (Ta Ai Shui)*

1980. Pearl River Film Studio. Color. 9 Reels.

Direction: Xian Biying. Screenplay: Bi Bicheng. Cinematography: Liang Xiongwei, Bai Yunsheng. Art Direction: Ye Jialiang, Chen Shuwen. Music: Ding Jialing, Jin Youzhong. Sound: Lu Minwen. Cast: Pan Zhiyuan as Yang Ming, Che Xiuqin as Xiao Ying, Ye Nan as Ning Yan, He Qianrong as Dong Lin

In the mid–1970s, individualistic young worker Yang Min plans to work his way up the bureaucratic ladder by currying the favor of Ning Qiao, director of a cultural bureau's revolutionary committee, and by dating Ning Qiao's daughter Ning Yan. In 1975, Ning Qiao is removed from his position and is replaced by Xiao Yi, the man who had held the position before the Cultural Revolution. Yang Ming immediately abandons his courtship of Ning Yan, and turns to Xiao Yi's daughter Xiao Ying. Despite her father's warnings about the young man, Xiao Ying falls for him. The following year, when a new political campaign called "attacking the rightist wind" starts, Yang Ming sells out Xiao Yi, drops Xiao Ying and turns once more to backing Ning Qiao again. Xiao Ying at last comes to realize the difficulty of recognizing a person's true nature.

2287. Who Has Been Abandoned (Shui Shi Bei Paoqi De Ren)

1958. Haiyan Film Studio. B & W. 8 Reels. Direction: Huang Zhumo. Screenplay: Sun Qian. Cinematography: Cao Weiye. Art Direction: Hu Dengren. Music: Ji Ming. Sound: Zhou Yunling. Makeup: Zhou Menglei. Cast: Li Wei as Yu Shude, Zhao Shuyin as Yang Yumei, Hong Xia as Chen Zuoqing, Tian Nu as Xiao Wang, Zong Xinghuo as Zhou Libeng, Su Yin as Guizhi

At a New Year's Eve office party in an unnamed city, Yu Shude, director of a government agency, seduces young and innocent office worker Chen Zuoqing. She loves him and enters into a serious affair, unaware that he has a wife and two children in the countryside. Having not heard from him for some time, Yu Shude's wife Yang Yumei writes a letter which is discovered by Chen Zuoqing, by now pregnant, and the girl realizes she has been deceived. She threatens to expose him, and in order to protect his reputation and position, Yu Shude asks his wife for a divorce. Yang Yumei had forgiven him for past transgressions during their more than 10 years of marriage, but this time she realizes how rotten he is, and she agrees to the divorce. Finally Chen Zuoqing, with counseling from the Communist

Party organization, realizes her mistakes and takes Yu Shude to court. He ends up losing everything and everyone who ever loved him.

2288. Who Is the Murderer? (Shui Shi Xiong Shou)

1956. Shanghai Film Studio. B & W. 7 Reels. Direction: Fang Huang. Screenplay: Sun Qian, based on the novel of the same title by Gao Kun. Cinematography: Yao Shiquan. Set Design: He Ruiji, Fu Shuzhen. Music: Zhou Xianruo. Sound: Zhou Hengliang. Cast: Shu Yi as Guo Xiuer, Langu as Tian Dahu, Bai Mu as Zhang Wanshou, Jiang Rui as Zhang Dengshan, Gao Xiaoou as Tian Yunqin, Su Yu as Yun Qin's wife

During the wheat harvesting season, Baiyangshu Agricultural Cooperative's Director Zhang Dengshan quarrels with No. 2 production team's director Tian Dahu over a harvest-related issue. Right after that, Zhang Dengshan is found dead from poisoning. Zhang Dengshan's nephew Zhang Wangshou decides the murder is connected with the victim's argument with Tian Dahu, and suggests that Tian is the killer. Many agree with him that Tian should be charged. Investigators undertake a painstaking analysis of the evidence, and find that Zhang Wangshou is a spy conspiring with a rich farmer named Tian Yunqin to destroy the co-op's work and drive up his farm prices. He killed his uncle to keep him from exposing the scheme. Zhang tries to run but is stopped by co-op members, led by Tian Dahu's fiancee Guo Xiuer.

2289. Whoever Wears This Flower (Shui Daizhe Duo Hua)

1979. Changchun Film Studio. Color. 10 Reels. Direction: Hua Ke. Screenplay: Fang Youliang. Cinematography: Shu Xiaoyan, Tang Yunsheng. Art Direction: Jin Bohao, Ye Jiren. Music: Lou Zhanghou. Sound: Yuan Minda, Wang Wencang. Cast: Shi Shugui as Feng Puyin, Zhao Jiayan as Ma Da, Guo Yuntai as Supervisor Gao, Jiang Tong as Su Tieling, Yi Fuwen as Pei Jie

In 1962, an oil field conducts a large scale evaluation of its logistics service. Feng Puyin, the woman in charge of the oil field's sewing and tailoring shop, brings in the family members of oil field workers and shows them how they can serve by recycling old materials and be thrifty. Her husband, human services director Ma Da, thinks that thrift is unnecessary. But oil field supervisor Gao supports her efforts, and appoints her deputy director of the inspection team. Feng Puyin's woman workers upgrade their technology to develop and expand the shop while spending less, but Ma Da's love of spending money hampers their work. He even plans to tear down their old shop building and replace it with a new one. At the meeting to review his plan, Ma Da makes what he thinks is a wonderful presentation, but Supervisor Gao criticizes his pattern of excessive spending. The women workers at the sewing shop are all given red flowers as a symbol of their contributions.

2290. *Why Was I Born? (Wei She Me Sheng Wo)*

1984. Emei Film Studio. Color. 10 Reels. Direction: Li Yalin, Yan Wenfan. Screenplay: Yao Yun. Cinematography: Li Baoqi. Art Direction: Chen Desheng. Music: Tao Jiazhou. Sound: Zhang Jianping. Cast: Ji Chengmu as Chen Songsong, Lei Ming as Chen You, Fang Qinzhuo as Qin Yujuan, Li Zonghua as Teacher Fang, Shi Ling as Mr. Wang

Chen Songsong is a young boy living with his train driver father after his parents' divorce. The father's work keeps him away from home a lot, so Songsong is very lonely. Once, when he goes to visit his mother, his father beats him for disobeying a command to have nothing to do with her. When the father starts dating another woman, Songsong's feelings of loneliness and neglect grow even worse and start to affect his behavior in school and his relations with other children. Able to bear it no longer, Songsong at last goes to see his mother again, and finds she has remarried a man with a daughter. Seeing her new family has no room for him, the distraught Songsong runs out into a heavy rainstorm and gets soaked. He falls ill and dies.

2291. *Widow Village (Gua Fu Cun)*

1988. Pearl River Film Studio and Hong Kong Sil-Metropole Organization Co-Production. Color. 9 Reels. Wide Screen. Direction: Wang Jin. Screenplay: Chen Lizhou, Wang Yan. Cinematography: Zhao Xiaoshi. Art Direction: Zhao Qingqiang. Music: Cheng Dazhao. Sound: Deng Qinhua. Cast: Liang Yujin as Duomei, Yu Li as A Lai, Hao Jialing as Sister Ting, Tao Zeru as Side, Xie Yuan as A Tai

In the southern part of Fujian province, a remote fishing village has for some years been called "Widow Village," because it is inhabited solely by women and children. The men of the village were all lost at sea in a violent typhoon. Enduring many hardships, the widows raise their children alone and encourage them to marry early. The village also has a strange marriage custom which stipulates that after their marriage girls may visit their husbands' families only on three family holidays a year, and then only at night. They are also forbidden from having children. Those who violate these customs are disgraced and drowned in the ocean. These oppressive and bizarre marriage customs bring considerable suffering to the village's young couples: Sister Ting and her husband Wanfu have been married for over 10 years but are still childless; Duomei and Side became lovers at first sight, but in four years of marriage have yet to sleep together; A Lai and A Tai have been married for just over a year, but dare not live together. They are slowly starting to gain the courage to resist these strange customs, when a further complication arises: the young husbands are all conscripted into the army, changing the village once more into "Widow Village."

Golden Panda Award, 6th Montpellier Film Festival.

2292. *A Wifeless Family (Guang Gun Zhi Jia)*

1988. Tianshan Film Studio. Color. 9 Reels. Letterboxed. Direction: Tu Yigong. Screenplay: Maimaiti Yiming. Cinematography: Ni Jiati, Mu Lati. Art Direction: Ah Dixia, Ya Sen. Music: Yi Kemu. Sound: Aierkeng. Cast: Wu Ger as Ka Der, Maimaiti Xilifu as Tuerdi, Ju Laiti as Na Der

A situation comedy of love affairs and mismatches that takes an affectionate look at Uighur life in Xinjiang. The central characters are Tuerdi, a retired worker, and his three grown sons. They lead quiet lives, but their neighbors call them the "wifeless family," because the three sons seem to have trouble getting suitably married.

2293. *A Wife's Letter (Qi Zi De Xin)*

1983. Shanghai Film Studio. Color. Direction: Yang Lanru. Screenplay: Lu Yanzhou. Cinematography: Zhen Xuan. Art Direction: Zhen Changfu. Music: Gao Tian. Sound: Zhen Xuan. Cast: Sheng Yaren as Xu Zhuqin, Wang Zhigang as Ding Feng

Ding Feng is a capable and successful Party

Secretary, while his wife Xu Zhuqin has her own professional career. They have two lovely children. Now, in middle age, they should be happy, but Xu Zhuqin is not happy at all. She had loved her original career in scientific research, but had been forced out of that job during the Cultural Revolution. When times returned to normal, she was assigned to a political job at the prefectural Party Committee, but had to leave her job again when her upwardly mobile husband was transferred. Leaving her original career has been very painful for her, and now she has the chance to return to it, doing research on seafood products. Her husband cannot understand her wanting to leave. She writes her husband a letter explaining her feelings, and after reading it Ding Feng at last understands. He accepts and supports his wife's decision.

2294. *Wild Canton Dragon (Shen Gang Kuang Long)*

1989. Pearl River Film Studio and Hong Kong Zibao Film Company Co-Production. Color. Letterboxed. 9 Reels. Direction: Hong Feng. Screenplay: Hong Feng, Fu Sixin, Luo Shumin. Cinematography: Peng Junwei. Art Direction: Zhu Jinhe. Music: Huang Zhixiong. Cast: Mo Zhijiang as Lao Jiaqi, Zhang Qi as Bai Jinlong, Xu Dongfang as Hong Weihua, Dong Yanbo as Kong Lishan

2295. *Wild Mountains (Ye Shan)*

1985. Xi'an Film Studio. Color. 10 Reels. Direction: Yan Xueshu. Screenplay: Yan Xueshu, Zhu Zi. Cinematography: Mi Jiaqin. Art Direction: Li Xingzhen. Music: Xu Youfu. Sound: Li Lanhua. Costume: Ma Liping. Cast: Du Yuan as Hehe, Yue Hong as Guilan, Xin Ming as Huihui, Xu Shouli as Qiurong, Tan Xihe as Ershui

The story focuses on two families living in the village of Jiwowa, deep in the Qinling Mountains. In one, husband Huihui is satisfied with his basic living conditions but unhappy with his wife Guilan's infertility. In the other, husband Hehe is dissatisfied with farming, and is constantly trying other means of earning a living, such as fishing, making tofu, etc. None of these are successful. His wife Qiurong cannot bear this any more and divorces him. The childless Huihui and Guilan eventually divorce as well, after which Huihui marries Qiurong, giving him the lifestyle of his dreams. The public gossip really starts humming when Guilan courageously marries Hehe. Unlike his first wife, Guilan strongly supports Hehe's efforts to do something different. With her encouragement, he at last succeeds, then brings such new equipment as a tractor and a noodle maker into their village. Hehe and Guilan now have a household envied by all the rest of the villagers, while Huihui and Qiurong still farm with old-fashioned hand tools.

Best Picture, 1986 Golden Rooster Awards.

Best Director Yan Xueshu, 1986 Golden Rooster Awards.

Best Actress Yue Hong, 1986 Golden Rooster Awards.

Best Supporting Actor Xin Ming, 1986 Golden Rooster Awards.

Best Sound Li Lanhua, 1986 Golden Rooster Awards.

Best Costume Ma Liping, 1986 Golden Rooster Awards.

Grand Prix, 8th Nantes Tri-Continental Film Festival.

2296. *Wildman (Ye Ren)*

1985. Xiaoxiang Film Studio. Color. 9 Reels. Direction: Hu Shue. Screenplay: Zhao Yongen. Cinematography: Wang Kekuan. Art Direction: Li Runzhang. Music: Wei Jingshu. Sound: Liu Feng. Cast: Hong Yuzhou as Tan De, Ha Xiaoyao as Meng Qi, Zhang Zhiqiang as He Cai, Qian Jiahua as Gu Chuan, Shang Lihua as Ni Qing

A research institute organizes an expedition to search a mountainous region for a "wildman" believed living there in the wilds. On an earlier, ill-fated expedition, Professor Ni was murdered, supposedly by his daughter's lover Meng Qi. Meng Qi disappeared, and was never seen again. Some expedition members, like their strange guide Tan De, are veterans of the first trip, while some are new, like young driver He Cai. When the expedition reaches the target area, Ni's daughter Ni Qing spots the wildman one day, and follows him. She discovers the "wildman" is really Meng Qi. He tells her that Tan De had murdered the professor by pushing him from a cliff; when Meng reached Ni to help him, the older man died, and since it appeared Meng had killed him, and Meng fled in panic. At this point, Tan De appears and tries to kill both Meng and Ni Qing. But He Cai shows up and, revealing his true identity as an undercover detective, arrests Tan De. Ni Qing and Meng Qi are reunited.

Top: Widow Village. The women of Widow Village suffer bitterly under oppressive and bizarre marriage customs. 1988. Pearl River Film Studio, Hong Kong Sil-Metropole Organization Co-Production. *Bottom: A Wifeless Family.* The contented bachelors of the title. 1988. Tianshan Film Studio.

2297. *The Wild West (Xi Bu Huang Ye)*

1992. Inner Mongolia Film Studio. Color. Letterboxed. 10 Reels. Direction: Zhan Xiangzhi. Screenplay: Zhan Xiangzhi. Cinematography: Ge Ritu. Art Direction: Tong Yonggang. Music: Guo Zhijie. Sound: Ao Si. Costume: Hong Xiuyan. Makeup: Su Hong. Cast: Gong Youchun as Xiao Xue, Ning Cai as Ma Guangzong, Wang Xiaolei as Ma Yaozhu, You Fengrong as Xiao Chensi

During the Republican period of Chinese history (1911–1949), an evil man named Ma Yaozhu takes over a town in the far western desert of China. He appoints himself mayor and runs the town as his own private fiefdom. He had abandoned his own wife and baby son years before, and after becoming wealthy and powerful, killed a man and forced the man's widow Xiao Chensi to become his mistress. Now, his son Ma Guangzong is grown up and comes to the town seeking revenge. Also showing up seeking vengeance is Xiao Chensi's daughter Xueniang. Much gunfighting ensues between the newcomers and Ma Yaozhu's henchmen, but at last the villain is slain and the town freed from his tyranny.

2298. *Wild Wolf Valley (Ye Lang Gu)*

1989. Beijing Film Studio. Color. Letterboxed. 9 Reels. Direction: Shi Xian, Cheng Dexin. Screenplay: Feng Lingzhi. Cinematography: Wang Zhaoling. Art Direction: Ning Lanxin, Yuan Chao. Music: Zhao Jiping. Sound: Lan Fan. Cast: Gu Zhi as Zhang Duanhun, Tan Mindi as Guoguo, Xie Gang as Hua Mianlang

Terrorized by a pack of wolves led by a wolf called Qiaole, villagers hire a famed hunter named Zhang Duanhun to defend them from the animals. Zhang sets traps and catches three wolf cubs. His daughter Guoguo plays with and cares for the cubs, grows fond of them and at last sets them free. One year later, Zhang and Guoguo are attacked by wolves, and while Qiaole and his now-adult cubs kill the hunter they let Guoguo live. She swears to avenge her father, and enlists the help of another hunter named Hua Mianlang. At last, Hua's team of hunters surrounds the pack in a valley. Guoguo shoots one of Qiaole's three cubs, but then loses her nerve to do any more. Hua kills the other two, but Qiaole kills Hua Mianlang. Soon after this, people are surprised to find a grave where the three wolves have been buried, and Guoguo is

found dead, a suicide, in front of Hua Mianlang's tomb.

2299. *Will a Miracle Occur? (Qi Ji Hui Fa Sheng Ma?)*

1982. Shanghai Film Studio. Color. 11 Reels. Direction: Xu Suling, Sha Jie. Screenplay: Meng Shenghui, Chen Weiruo, Guo Zemin. Cinematography: Chen Ling, Cai Guangeng. Art Direction: Zhang Wanhong. Music: Liu Yanxi. Sound: Wu Jianghai, Wang Shu. Cast: Xiang Mei as Zhang Yulei, Wang Bing as Cao Lixiong, Zhao Jing as Cao Zhen, Lou Jicheng as Sun Haitao, Wu Yunfang as Li Yu, Zhu Yuwen as Lin Shuxian

Zhang Yulei, Li Yu and Lin Shuxian are female college journalism students. The film follows their lives after graduation. Zhang Yulei marries co-worker Cao Lixiong and gives up her cherished career to support him. He rises to become the associate editor of a major newspaper, while their daughter Cao Jing becomes a prominent stage actress. The family is close-knit and prosperous, but Zhang Yulie wants to resume her career. Her husband Cao Lixiong will not even consider it. He does all he can to stop her, but in the end she wins out and makes significant contributions in journalism. Even her husband Cao Lixiong comes to appreciate her talent. Li Yu and her journalist husband Sun Haitao are both devoted to their careers, and although her health is very bad Li Yu never gives up her own writing or her support of her husband, even to the end of her life. In contrast with these two couples, Lin Suxian lacks ambition and chooses to rely totally on her husband. When he dies, she has nothing left, not even the spirit to go on.

2300. *Willow in the Spring Breeze (Chun Feng Yang Liu)*

1959. (Unreleased) Tianma Film Studio. B & W. 8 Reels. Direction: Chen Fan. Screenplay: Wang Zhiqiang and Zhou Jie. Cinematography: Shi Fengqi. Art Direction: He Ruiji. Music: Zhang Linyi. Sound: Huang Dongping. Cast not credited

In the early spring of 1956, a medical team is sent to a rural county in South China which has had an outbreak of blood fluke, to treat the victims and prevent its further spread. Deputy Director Yuan, a technical expert, advocates a conventional method of killing the oncomelania which hosts the blood fluke, but using it only results in poisoning some cattle. Two blood fluke victims, Yanshou and Yougeng, have been sent home as untreatable by the county clinic, so Director Tian goes to visit them and see what he can do to help them. He and doctor Yang decide that the source of the problem is water used for irrigating fields has been contaminated during the construction of a water conservancy project. They suggest a plan which will use both local and central government methods to kill the oncomelania. With the support of the county Party secretary, they finally succeed in eradicating the oncomelania. Yanshou and Yougeng's blood fluke is also cured. Deputy Director Yuan learns some new ways of doing things.

2301. *Wind and Snow on Dabie Mountain (Feng Xue Dabie Shan)*

1961. Anhui Film Studio. B & W. 10 Reels. Direction: Huang Zumo. Screenplay: Chen Dengke and Lu Yanzhou. Cinematography: Zhang Baozhi and Xu Bing. Art Direction: Shen Weishan and Lu Yujia. Music: Han Yongcang. Sound: Shen Yimin and Cha Fuguo. Cast: Lei Ping as Wu Hongying, Ding Yihong as Lin Tianxiang, Duan Baoxin as Zhen Chongyi, Zhang Ming as Xiuzhen, Liu Han as Zhen Yunling, Yi Da as Lin Xiaofang

In 1929, Lin Tianxiang, a young farmer from the Dabie Mountains and his wife Xiuzhen come under the influence of undercover Party members Zhen Chongyi and his wife Wu Hongying. In 1935, Zhen is killed in battle, and the Lins take Zhen's son Yunlong along with them on the Red Army's Long March to Yan'an in North Shanxi. Lin is transferred to another part of China and Xiuzhen is later killed in another battle. Hongying remains behind to work at the Yan'an base. She also raises the Lins' daughter Xiao Fang, and is wounded protecting the girl during an attack. In 1947, Lin and Yunlong return to their hometown. By that time, Lin has become a PLA division commander, Yun Long is a company political commissar and Xiao Fang works for the PLA. However, during war time, they do not recognize each other. On the day the People's Republic of China is founded, they meet at Beijing's Gate of Heavenly Peace.

2302. *The Wind Blows from the East (Feng Cong Dong Fang Lai)*

1959. Co-Production of the Changchun Film Studio and Moscow Film Studio. Color. (Wide Screen). Wide 11 Reels, Narrow 10 Reels. Direction: E. Jigan, Gan Xuewei. Screenplay: B Kerefunikuofu, Lin Shan, E Jigan, Gan Xuewei. Direction: E Jierbeiershitan, Shi Lianxing. Cinematography: A Gelichate, Baojie. Art Direction: Jixieliaofu, Wang Tao. Music: Keliukefu, Li Huanzhi. Cast: M Kangtelaqiyefu as Lenin, Tian Fang as Wang Demin, N Jimitelieyefu as Mateweiyefu, Lin Zhiao as Secretary Chen, C Guoji as Shiweiliuofu, N Kangte Lajiyewa as Ye Linna

Construction site director Wang Demin and Soviet Union expert Mateweiyefu recall their past experiences together. During the October revolution, Wang Demin was almost killed by White Russians in the Soviet Union, but was rescued by Mateweiyefu. The two then join the Soviet Red Army together. They later did Saturday volunteer work together and are received by Lenin. A few years later, the two meet at a China hydropower station construction site. Wang Demin's son Wang Xiao is a student in the Soviet Union, and he and his Russian classmate Kalina journey together to visit their parents at the construction site (Kalina's mother works at the same hydropower station site), but they run into danger on the way, and are saved by fishermen. Through the joint efforts of the Chinese and Soviet experts and workers, they finally conquer the flood and build the hydropower station.

2303. *Winding Mountain Road (Shan Ru Wan Wan)*

1982. Xi'an Film Studio. Color. 9 Reels. Direction: Zhang Qicang. Screenplay: Xie Fengsong, Liang Xing. Cinematography: Lin Jing. Art Direction: Cheng Minzhang, Zhang Xiaohui. Music: Li Yaodong. Sound: Dang Chunzhu. Cast: Wang Yan as Jin Zhu, Zhao Chunmin as Ermeng, Li Fengxu as Fengyue, Bi Fusheng as Second Uncle, Liu Lu as Huanhuan

In a mountainous part of South China, mine worker Wang Dameng is killed in a mine accident. His wife Jin Zhu gives her late husband's brother Ermeng the opportunity to take over Dameng's old job. Despite the poverty and hard life she and her daughter Huanhuan must endure, Jin Zhu helps Ermeng and his fiancee Fengyue in any way she can. Ermeng comes to realize that he and Fengyue really have little in common; he finds his sister-in-law's personality and kindheartedness more attractive, and decides he wants to marry her instead. This goes strongly against the conventions of the time. Jin Zhu thinks it would be improper for a widow to marry a bachelor brother-in-law, so she tries to get Ermeng and Fengyue back together. When another accident severely injures Ermeng, and it looks as if he will be permanently disabled, Fengyue breaks off their relationship. Jin Zhu decides she and Ermeng should get together after all.

2304. *A Window on America (Mei Guo Zhi Chuang)*

1952. Wenhua Film Company. B & W. 11 Reels. Direction: Zuo Lin, Shi Hui, Ye Ming. Screenplay: Zuo Lin, based on an original work by Dihaolu China. Cinematography: Xu Yi, Zhang Xiling. Cast: Yu Fei, Shi Hui, Lin Zhen, Chen Xu

An American worker, unemployed and about to be drafted to fight in Korea, commits suicide by jumping from a window in a tall building. From this incident the building's owner comes to see the true colors of a speculator he had been doing business with, and cancels the "slave" contract he had signed earlier.

2305. *Wing to Wing Through the Sky (Chang Kong Bi Yi)*

1958. August First Film Studio. B & W. 10 Reels. Direction: Wang Bing, Li Shutian. Screenplay: Zhu Danxi, Li Jing. Cinematography: Liu Ying, Kou Jiwen. Art Direction: Mai Yi. Music: Li Weicai. Sound: Kou Shenkang. Cast: Cao Huiqu as Zhang Hu, Yang Huang as Yang Hua and Xiao Guo, Wang Runsheng as Division Commander Fang, Hu Xu as Political Commissar Li, Wang Ren as Wang Zhong, Zhang Fusheng as Zhang Wen

In Korea, Volunteer Air Force pilot Zhang Hu is at first reluctant to fly in the subordinate wing position. In his first air battle, he goes off on a solo attack to seek personal glory, contrary to his group commander's orders. As a result, he is pursued by enemy aircraft and his group's lead plane is damaged rescuing him. With help from his leaders and comrades, he overcomes his desire for personal glory and in the next air battle he screens the lead plane in downing an enemy aircraft. Later, although wounded, he intercepts and shoots down an enemy plane attempting to bomb a bridge. He is decorated for this, and promoted to lead plane. In the end he is reunited with his lost love, Volunteer Army nurse Yang Hua, from whom he had parted five years previously.

2306. *With Sugar (Gei Ka Fei Jia Dian Tang)*

1987. Pearl River Film Studio. Color. 9 Reels. Direction: Sun Zhou. Screenplay: Zhen Hua. Cinematography: Zhen Hua, Wang Suiguang. Art Direction: Tu Bengyang. Music: Zhu Shirui. Sound: Feng Lunsheng. Cast: Chen Rui as Gang Zai, Li Fengxu as Lin Xia, Peng Lizhi as Fats, Du Ying as Little Brother

Gang Zai, a self-employed commercial photographer, is something of a ringleader among a group of ambitious young people in the prosperous city of Guangzhou. Lin Xia, a cobbler, arrives from Zhejiang province in east China, and from the moment Gang Zai frames her in his camera lens he is struck by her fresh innocence. He falls in love with her. Although she is initially unsure about the young man's flippant and carefree manner, Lin Xia is so taken with Gang Zhai's expressions of love that she finally gives in. Their romance is a rocky one, however, and finally Lin Xia returns home to think things over. When she arrives there, her mother forces her to marry someone she doesn't want so her brother can marry the man's sister. Gang Zhai is left alone and confused.

2307. *The Wolf and the Angel (E Lang Yu Tian Shi)*

1990. Chinese Film Company & Hong Kong Zhenye Film Company Ltd. Co-Production. Color. Wide Screen. 10 Reels. Direction: Xie Yucheng. Screenplay: Zhang Longguang, Chen Yanmin. Cinematography: Zhao Xiaoding. Art Direction: Tu Juhua. Music: Ma Ding, Zhen Jingyi. Sound: Xie Guojie. Cast: Hu Jun as Zhu Ge, Yan Qin as Lin Anqi, Huang Guoqiang as Zhong Guoren, Lu Zhi as Zhao Deshan

In Taiwan, Taipei city councilman Zhu Ge is also a ruthless mobster. He desires night club singer Lin Anqi, and attempts to force himself on her when she rejects him. Police officer Zhong Guoren intervenes to help her. But Zhu Ge doesn't give up, and later rapes Lin. When he learns of this, Zhong angrily goes to Zhu's headquarters and kills the gangster. But Zhu's cohorts retaliate by killing Lin

Anqi. Zhong launches a one-man war against the gang, and in a final battle he blows up the gang and himself.

2308. *Wolf Dog Adventure (Lang Quan Li Xian Ji)*

1985. Changchun Film Studio. Color. 10 Reels. Direction: Zhang Hui. Screenplay: Wang Zhebing, Wang Xingdong. Cinematography: Yang Penghui. Art Direction: Shi Weijun. Music: Zhu Zhongtang. Sound: Wang Wenfu. Cast: Liu Wentao as Zhang Mazha, Tian Bo as Erhu, Wang Qinbei as Yuan Mei, Shi Rong as Zhang Ju, Liu Tingyao as Duan Fei, Zhang Zhizhong as Niu Wu

In rural northeast China, elementary school students Mazha and Erhu live next to a PSB dog training base. The boys greatly admire one particular dog, and at last succeed in luring him out to breed with their female dog Shanhu. Shanhu has two fine puppies, "Gongzhi" and "Langya." They train the two dogs, and in a later action against a robbery gang the two dogs assist the PSB in apprehending the criminals. "Gongzhi" is killed in the action, and the boys donate "Langya" to the PSB training base.

2309. *A Wolf Enters the House (Cai Lang Ru Shi)*

1991. Xi'an Film Studio. Color. Letterboxed. 9 Reels. Direction: Qiang Xiaolu. Screenplay: Qiang Xiaolu. Cinematography: Song Chao. Art Direction: Cheng Minzhang. Cast: Liang Danni as the woman, Feng Yuanzheng as the big guy, Wei Qin as the child

2310. *Wolf Smoke (Lang Yan)*

1990. Changchun Film Studio & Hong Kong Sifang Film Company Ltd. Co-Production. Color. Wide Screen. 9 Reels. Direction: Han Baozhang, He Minxiao. Screenplay: Cheng Gang. Cinematography: Chen Zhongyuan. Art Direction: Xu Zhengkun. Music: Lei Lei. Sound: Tong Zongde. Cast: Bai Ying as Da Qinlong, Jing Feng as Zhao Minxuan, Shi Zhongtian as Wu Lianqin, Zhang Fuyin as Bai Wei

In Northeast China during World War II, a legendary "greenwoods bandit" called the "Big Green Dragon" wages a personal guerrilla war against the Japanese. At one point, he helps a small town which was being brutalized by Japanese troops. A local official, Zhao Minxuan, plans to entertain the guerrilla

fighter as a way of showing gratitude. But the town's police chief Wu Lianqin, a secret Japanese collaborator, plans to use the occasion to catch the "Dragon." Wu lures the Dragon's close friend Shi Zhier into betraying him for Bai Wei, a woman Shi desires. The Dragon and some of his followers are killed. Overcome with remorse for what he has done, Shi has Bai Wei help him kill Wu, after which Shi kills himself.

2311. *Woman Bandit in a Blue Shirt (Lan Shan Nu Fei)*

1989. Yunnan Film Studio. Color. Wide Screen. 9 Reels. Direction: Huangpu Keren. Screenplay: Zhang Xiaojing, Ma Ming. Cinematography: Ning Jiakun, Tian Jianmin. Art Direction: Zu Shaoxian. Music: Guo Xiaodi. Sound: Yao Guoqiang, Chen Baolin. Cast: Chen Wei as Baozhu, Zhang Guangbei as Dongfang Hong

Shortly after the Manchu Dynasty is overthrown in 1912, a valuable painting called the "Eight Horses" disappears from the Imperial Palace. A female bandit called Baozhu, who always wears a blue shirt, sets out with her elder sister Xiao Juan to look for it. The two women bandits are in a race to find the picture before the police, led by Chief of Detectives Dongfang Hong. Both women are actually in love with Hong, but he is only interested in Baozhu. Xiao Juan at last finds the painting, but is killed. Baozhu is so upset that she decides to let the police keep the painting, and she sets out to avenge her sister. The picture is stolen again, and the story continues.

2312. *Woman Basketball Player No.5 (Nu Lan Wu Hao)*

1957. Tianma Film Studio. Color. Direction: Xie Jin. Screenplay: Xie Jin. Cinematography: Huang Shaofeng, Shen Xilin. Music: Huang Zhun. Sound: Lu Zhongbo. Art Direction: Wang Yuebai. Cast: Liu Qiong as Tian Zhenghua, Qin Yi as Lin Jie, Cao Qiwei as Lin Xiaojie, Yu Mingde as Lao Meng

Before liberation, basketball player Tian Zhenghua is in love with Lin Jie, daughter of the team owner. Before a game with some foreign soldiers, the owner accepts a bribe to have his team throw the game, but out of national pride, Tian Zhenghua refuses to go along, and the Chinese team wins. In retaliation for this, Tian is beaten up and severely injured, and the

Woman Basketball Player No. 5. **After 18 years, Coach Tian Zhenghua (Liu Qiong, second left), meets his former lover Lin Jie (Qin Yi, right) when she comes to see her daughter Lin Xiaojie (Cao Qiwei, third left). 1957. Tianma Film Studio.**

daughter is forced into a marriage with one of the owner's wealthy cronies. Eighteen years pass, and Tian has become the coach of the Shanghai Women's basketball team. Lin Jie now has a daughter Lin Xiaojie, a basketball player with great potential, but the influence of her family and friends have instilled in her a bad attitude regarding sports, which Coach Tian works patiently to correct. Lin Xiaojie is badly injured in a game, and Tian Zhenghua and Lin Jie meet again while visiting the injured girl. They talk, clear up their misunderstandings and reconcile. The story concludes with Lin Xiaojie's selection to China's National Team.

2313. *The Woman Bureau Chief's Boyfriend (Nu Ju Zhang De Nan Peng You)*

1986. Shanghai Film Studio. Color. 10 Reels. Direction: Sang Hu. Screenplay: Wang Lian, Sang Hu, Li Yizhong. Cinematography: Qiu Yiren, Sun Yeling. Art Direction: Pu Jingsun. Music: Lu Qimin, Cai Lu. Sound: Lu Xuehan. Cast: Guo Kaimin as Ding Dasheng, Chen Yanhua as Zhou Qing, Wang Suya as Ding's mother,

Zhang Ming as Huijuan, Yan Shunkai as Cui Hailong, Liu Changwei as Xiao Wang, Huang Yijuan as Zhang Jindi

Her excellent work record as a letter carrier brings Zhou Qing a promotion to deputy director of a branch postal station. This upsets her conservative boyfriend Ding Dasheng, for now she outranks him in status. Ding's mother takes advantage of this to introduce her son to Zhang Jindi, a girl interested solely in money. Ding Dasheng realizes he has been wrong when a con man cheats Dasheng by convincing him he is ignorant and uneducated. He breaks off with the golddigging Zhang and reconciles with Zhou Qing.

2314. *A Woman Commando (Nu Zi Bie Dong Dui)*

1989. Pearl River Film Studio. Color. 9 Reels. Letterboxed. Direction: Jin Zuoxin, Wang Liangping. Screenplay: Si Huang, Guang Yue. Cinematography: Wang Lianping. Art Direction: Zhu Jinhe, Xiao Aili. Music: Du Jiangang. Sound: Zhu Jinhe, Xiao Aili. Cast: Liu Wei as Military Officer Yang, He Qing as Lin Manyun, Zhu

Yaying as Feifei, Zhang Yuekai as Song Baoxian, Wang Xiaozhong as Wang Yaoweng

During the War of Resistance against Japan, eight exiled young girls sit for military school entrance examinations. They come from different backgrounds and have different experiences, but all are fired with patriotic enthusiasm. But they find themselves tricked into becoming woman commandos. Put through the most rigorous training, the girls suffer many hardships and difficulties, but graduate as brave and skilled killers. Their assignment is actually a suicide mission, to assassinate Japanese officials and their Chinese collaborators. They have practically no chance of coming out alive, and six of them die in vain. The cruel reality makes their two surviving comrades realize that resisting the Japanese aggressors and saving their nation involves another course of action. Early one morning, they desert the army and start the long trek north to join Communist forces at Yan'an.

2315. *Woman Commune Director (Nu She Zhang)*

1958. Changchun Film Studio. B & W. 10 Reels. Direction: Fang Ying. Screenplay: Hu Su, Fang Ying. Cinematography: Ge Weiqing. Set Design: Wang Guizhi. Music: Lei Zhengbang. Sound: Hong Di. Cast: Qi Ruyan as Song Chunliang, Zhang Yun as Wu Laorui, Gu Qian as Zhao Quanyou, Li Jie as Zhao Mingde, Yu Wenzong as Liu Shousheng, Liang Yin as Bai Shuangli

In 1952, at a North China agricultural commune, accountant Liu Shousheng embezzles the commune's funds. This gives Wu Laorui, an older commune member who had never liked the idea, an excuse to drop out. Liu Shousheng's wife, commune director Song Chunliang, detests her husband's criminal actions, but his mother pleads with her daughter-in-law to intercede on his behalf with the commune. Although she loves her husband, she still testifies against him in court for the good of the entire commune membership. Liu Shousheng is sent for reform through labor, and is later released early for good behavior. Sometime after his return, the commune is granted a loan for a hydropower project, and on Song Chunliang's recommendation, Shousheng is sent to pick up the money, which raises the suspicion of the membership. However, he returns with all the money, so the people trust his wife more than ever.

2316. *Woman Demon Human (Ren Gui Qing)*

1987. Shanghai Film Studio. Color. 11 Reels. Direction: Huang Shuqin. Screenplay: Huang Shuqin, Li Ziyu, Song Rixun. Cinematography: Xia Lixing, Ji Hongsheng. Art Direction: Zhen Changfu. Music: Yang Mao. Sound: Ge Weijia. Cast: Pei Yanling as Zhong Dao, Xu Shouli as Qiu Yun, Li Baotian as Father, Wang Changjun as Mother, Ji Qiling as Teacher Zhang, Wang Feifei as Qiu Yun (as a child), Gong Ling as Qiu Yun (as a teenager)

Qiu Yun is a famous actress in the Kunqu school of Chinese opera. She specializes in male roles, and attains her greatest success in the title role in "Zhong Kui Marries Off His Sister." Zhong Kui is a mythic Chinese character who after his death returned to earth as a benevolent ghost determined to rid the world of demons. His exploits were portrayed in several operas, and in this one he works to marry off his sister. Although she is a success, Qiu Yun has experienced many frustrations in her life. She loved performing from an early age, but interpreted the facts surrounding her mother's elopement to mean that actresses who played women's roles had a very low social position. Because of this, she herself determined early in her career to play only male roles and to live her own life as much like a man as possible. Her career successes do not bring her personal happiness, however. Instead, they generate gossip and slander in the newspapers. All in all, Qiu has lost her womanhood without gaining the freedom men enjoy. More and more she comes to rely on the character of Zhong Kui to keep her going.

Best Screenplay Huang Shuqin, Li Ziyu and Song Rixun, 1988 Golden Rooster Awards.

Best Supporting Actor Li Baotian, 1988 Golden Rooster Awards.

Best Picture, Golden Bird Award, 5th Rio de Janeiro International Film, TV & Video Festival.

Public Grand Prix, 11 Women Directors Film Festival.

2317. *Woman Detective Bao Gaiding (Nu Shen Tan Bao Gai Ding)*

1989. Beijing Film Studio. Color. Letterboxed. 9 Reels. Direction: Xu Qingdong. Screenplay: Fu Xuwen. Cinematography: Zhou Jixun. Art Direction: Chen Jiyun, Yang Zhanjia. Music: Wang Ming. Sound: Liu Shida. Cast: Gong Youchun as Yu Xiaoning, Shen Junyi as Zuo Lin,

Qian Yongfu as Tao Jianfei, Ma Xiaoqing as Xiao Shaobing

Policewoman Yu Xiaoning, who underworld figures call "Bao Gaiding" (a play on the characters in her name), graduates from investigative training and is assigned to homicide. As she starts her first investigation, her boyfriend Zuo Lin, an excellent policeman, begins avoiding her. Her first case involves the murder of a young woman who was frequently seen with mob figures. Bao learns the victim had the nickname "Black Rose"; she traces this clue through the underworld, and eventually the trail leads her to Zuo Lin. It turns out that the dead girl was Zuo Lin's sister, and he had killed her in an argument about her consorting with gangsters. As detectives close in on him, Zuo Lin finds Tao Jianfei, the crime boss who led his sister into the life that proved her undoing. The policeman kills the crime boss, then himself.

2318. *A Woman for Two* (*Chun Tao*)

1988. China Nanhai Films Ltd. and Liaoning Film Studio Co-Production. Color. 9 Reels. Wide Screen. Direction: Ling Zifeng. Screenplay: Han Lanfang, based on an original story by Xu Dishan. Cinematography: Liang Ziyong. Art Direction: Xia Rujin. Sound: Wang Yunhua. Cast: Liu Xiaoqing as Chuntao, Jiang Wen as Liu Xianggao, Cao Qianming as Li Mao

On their wedding night, Chuntao and her husband are attacked by a group of bandits. They become separated during the fight, and she cannot find him the next day. Chuntao goes on to Beijing alone, where she supports herself by collecting garbage. On the way to the city she had met a man named Liu Xianggao, and she now moves in to live with him. All goes well until a few years later, when her husband Li Mao, now a legless beggar, suddenly turns up. Chuntao feels she must take him back so they set up a family consisting of two men and a woman. At last, Liu Xianggao leaves and Li Mao hangs himself. In the end, the three people are reunited supernaturally.

Best Picture, 1989 Hundred Flowers Awards.

Best Actor Jiang Wen, 1989 Hundred Flowers Awards.

Best Actress Liu Xiaoqing, 1989 Hundred Flowers Awards.

2319. *A Woman from North Shaanxi* (*Shan Bei Da Shao*)

1991. Xi'an Film Studio. Color. 9 Reels. Letterboxed. Direction: Yang Fengliang, Zhou Youchao. Screenplay: Zhang Yingwen, Yang Zhengguang. Cinematography: Zhang Xiaoguang. Art Direction: Liu Yichuan. Music: Zhao Jiping. Sound: Guang Changning. Cast: Luo Yan as the Woman, Jia Hongsheng as Jin Dayi, Cao Jingyang as Ha the Beard

In Northern Shaanxi Province in the closing days of the Chinese Civil War, the PLA encounters the fleeing cavalry of Nationalist warlord general Ma Bufang. In the fierce fighting, the PLA captures Jin Dayi, a member of Ma's cavalry. The local government of North Shaanxi puts Jin Dayi in the custody of a peasant household while his wounds heal. The woman of the household takes care of Jin, caring for him kindly and carefully, and even learns to tolerate his worst habits. Jin Dayi recovers and prepares to return home, when the warlord intrudes in his life once again. The villagers are transporting grain when some of Ma's men ambush them. Jin makes a stand and repays the woman for the kindness she showed him.

2320. *Woman Hairdresser* (*Nu Li Fa Shi*)

1962. Tianma Film Studio. B & W. Direction: Ding Ran. Screenplay by Qian Dingde and Ding Ran, adapted from the stage play of the same name. Cinematography: Sheng Xiling. Art Direction: He Ruiji. Music: Yang Suzheng. Sound: Zhu Weigang. Cast: Wang Danfeng as Hua Jiafang, Han Fei as Director Jia, Gu Yelu as Mr. Zhao, Xie Yibing as Mrs. Zhao, Gao Cui as Elder Sister, Ma Ji as Teacher Hua, Gao Xiaoou as an old worker, Shi Ling as a middle-aged customer, Yang Gongmin as the reporter, Jiang Yifang and Luo Yutao as women hairdressers

Hua Jiafang, an urban housewife, longs to study hair dressing, but her husband — department head in a state-owned company — objects strongly, for he regards service work as demeaning. Taking advantage of her husband's extended absence on a business trip, she covertly takes a course in hair dressing, gets a job, and soon becomes quite skilled at her trade. After her husband returns, she still goes to work, but leads him to believe she is an elementary school teacher. She eventually proves so talented that her fame spreads, and a great demand arises for her services. One day her

A Woman for Two. Several years after Chuntao (Liu Xiaoqing) has given her husband Li Mao (Cao Qianming) up for dead, he unexpectedly reappears, a legless beggar. 1988. China Nanhai Film Ltd., Liaoning Film Studio Co-Production.

husband shows up demanding his hair be cut by the famous Barber No. 3 he has heard so much about. For some time she stalls him by disguising herself and taking advantage of his extreme nearsightedness, and he is quite vocal in his praise. Eventually the masquerade is uncovered. But Hua's husband has praised her so highly in public that he is too embarrassed to admit he was fooled, so he has to publicly support her work and change his attitude regarding women in service occupations.

2321. *Woman Hero (Jin Guo Ying Lie)*

1985. Emei Film Studio. Color. 9 Reels. Direction: Li Jiefeng. Screenplay: Rao Qu, Yuan Xianan. Cinematography: Sun Guoliang. Art Direction: Xia Xinqiu. Music: Mu Hong, Yu Yu. Sound: Hua Yuezhu. Cast: Fu Lili as Bai Luping, Liu Boying as Zhen Shi, Lou Jicheng as Ge Lie, Weng Ru as Ye Liang, Sun Hong as He Min, Qiang Meidi as Lu Youwen

In the fall of 1940, in China's wartime capital of Chongqing, a series of intelligence leaks infuriates Nationalist spy chief Ge Lie. He orders the arrest of six Nationalist Army telecommunications workers and a mysterious woman named Bai Luping. Five years later, they are all secretly put to death. For years, the incident baffled many in the CPC and the PLA. Who were these people? Were they revolutionary martyrs? In the early 1980s, the Sichuan provincial committee assigns researchers to probe the matter and interview some people familiar with the case who are still living. After gathering many documents and holding interviews, this bit of history is cleared up. Bai Luping's name was originally Lu Junqin, the daughter of Sichuan army division commander Lu Youwen. But Lu Junqin hates her reactionary family and joins the CPC to devote herself to the anti–Japanese struggle. She later was entrusted by the CPC underground organization with infiltrating Nationalist headquarters as Bai Luping. She and the others accomplished much for the Communist revolution before being arrested and subsequently executed by the Nationalists in the summer of 1945.

2322. *Woman Hero Lu Siniang (Feng Cheng Nu Xia Lu Si Niang)*

1988. Changchun Film Studio. Color. 10 Reels. Direction: Gao Tianhong. Screenplay: Ru Cheng, Ya Li. Cinematography: Wang Erjiang, Ning Changcheng. Art Direction: Gao Guoliang. Music: Lei Yusheng. Sound: Dong Baosheng, Luo Huailun. Cast: Chen Yongxia as Lu Siniang, Wang Zhicheng as Chou Ying, Gao Hongping as Sister Wei, Zhang Dehui as Wang Xian

Although distinguished scholar Lu Liuliang is very loyal to the Qing government, cruel Emperor Yongzheng still has Lu and his family put to death. The sole survivor is his daughter Lu Siniang. She uses her super kongfu skills to kill Yongzheng. Afterwards, she and her niece Sister Wei, her adopted son Wang Xian, and an orphan boy named Chou Ying live in a small town called Penglai. Over 10 years go by, and the boys have grown up. One day by chance Chou Ying finds Ma Long, the man who killed his parents. With the help of Lu Siniang, Sister Wei and Wang Xian, Chou Ying also avenges his parents.

2323. *Woman Killer (Niu Chi Ke)*

1988. August First Film Studio. Color. Wide Screen. 10 Reels. Direction: Cai Jiwei. Screenplay: Jiang Puli, Wu Zhiniu. Cinematography: Zhang Chi. Art Direction: Ren Huixing. Music: Li Weicai. Sound: Zen Minzhe. Cast: Yue Hong as Xu Yuenan, Sun Feiu as Chen Quanguang

The story takes place during the warlord era of 1925 to 1935. Xu Yuenan's father Xu Songping is a famous military leader. He is defeated by Southeast Allied Troop Commander Chen Quanguang, who humiliates Xu Songping by putting him on public exhibition. Xu Yuenan determines to avenge her father, and hires a bandit to kill Chen Quanguang. The attempt fails, and she turns to a relative for help, but is rejected. She then places her hopes in sympathetic officer Wang Qinghong and marries him. But once Wang becomes her husband, he puts aside all thoughts of revenge. At last, she kills Chen Quanguang by herself, and under the pressure of many people in China, Xu Yuenan is released.

2324. *Woman Killer (Nu Sha Shou)*

1992. Tianshan Film Studio. Color. Letterboxed. 9 Reels. Direction: Lei Xianhe. Screenplay: Jia Ruo, Sheng Manmei. Cinematography: Meng Xiandi, Wen Hongwu. Art Direction: Gan Jun. Music: Chen Chunguang. Sound: Zhang Qingjiang, Yang Yuedong. Costume: Zhang Shufang. Makeup: Ji Weihua, Dan Xiangsuo. Cast: Si Yi as Muyu, Si Yi as Jier, Wei Zi as Shang Xia, Tao Hong as Ding Rongrong, Du Peng as Zhou Longfei

The corrupt president of a multinational corporation seeks to eliminate his business rival Zhou Longfei by having him killed. He hopes thereby to have the China market for their product all to himself. He sends Hong Kong model Jier, really a contract killer, to the mainland to implement the plan. When Zhou Longfei comes to the mainland for a business conference, policeman Shang Xia and policewoman Ding Rongrong are assigned to protect him. Jier had been a policewoman at one time, but a head injury caused a loss of memory which was exploited by the mob. Zhou Longfei is protected, signs his contract and returns to Hong Kong. But when he arrives at the Hong Kong airport and is happy to see his son coming to meet him, his joy turns to shock when his son suddenly pulls a gun on him.

2325. *Woman Living Buddha (Nu Huo Fuo)*

1986. Beijing Film Studio. Color. 15 Reels. Direction: Li Wei. Screenplay: Qin Wenyu. Cinematography: Yan Junsheng. Art Direction: Liu Wentao, Yang Wan. Music: Bianduo Baidenglangji. Sound: Zhen Chunyu, Guan Shuxin. Cast: Pubu Zuoma as Jizhun Sangmu, Zhaxi Dunzhu as Gang Qiongsai, Zuoma as Zhuga, Duo Ji as Bai Ma

The time of this story is from the spring of 1958 to the winter of 1959. At that time, Tibetan revolutionaries are planning to leave Tibet for India and there to organize a movement to separate from China. They visit the woman Living Buddha to persuade her to join them in leaving the country. At the same time, the CPC is trying to get her to stay in Tibet. She at last decides to go with the separatists. They experience many hardships on the journey but at last arrive in India. There, she finds herself subjected to pressures to join the Tibetan independence movement. The Living Buddha's crown is stolen, and she witnesses the squalid conditions of others who came before her. She decides against joining the independence movement, and returns to China.

2326. *Woman Mayor's Private Life (Nu Shi Zhang De Si Ren Sheng Huo)*

1987. Shanghai Film Studio. Color. 10 Reels. Direction: Yang Yanjing, Screenplay: Xu Yinghua, Cinematography: Shen Miaorong, Sun Yeling, Art Direction: Chen Chudian, Music: Xu Jingxin, Sound: Ren Daming, Cast: Zhang Weixin as Mayor Gu, Liu Zhifeng as Chen Zhiping, Wang Jiayi as Longlong

2327. *Woman Melon Garden Guard (Gua Peng Nu Jie)*

1985. Pearl River Film Studio. Color. Wide Screen. 10 Reels. Direction: Wang Yi. Screenplay: Wu Peimin, Yang Jifu, Yu Li and Huang Shanfei, based on the novelette of the same title by Liu Shaotang (1936–). Cinematography: Li Zhexian. Art Direction: Ye Jialiang. Music: Liu Zhuang and Liu Wei. Sound: Lu Mingwen. Cast: Lin Quan as Meizi, Zhang Jiumei as Hua Sanchun, Xu Dongfang as Wu Lian, Yan Bide as Hua Zijin, Niu Shijun as Liu Shaoqing

In the 1930s, in Liuxiang Village on the banks of the Yunhe River, widowed melon planter Liu Shaoqing lives with his daughter Meizi, a skilled kongfu fighter. She is very fond of village teacher Wu Lian, but when she learns he is in love with beautiful village girl Hua Sanchun, Meizi helps them get married. When the Japanese invade China, Wu Lian leaves to join the underground resistance, and after he leaves, Meizi saves Sanchun's life at the risk of her own. Sanchun is the daughter of local despot Hua Zijin, but broke with her family to marry Wu. Sanchun and her father have a final shootout in which each kills the other. The Yunhe continues flowing as it always has, and Meizi will start a new life.

2328. *Woman Military Instructor's Report (Niu Jiao Guan De Bao Gao)*

1988. August First Film Studio. Color. 10 Reels. Direction: Li Jun. Screenplay: Li Jun, Zhang Xiaoran. Cinematography: Wu Feifei. Art Direction: Li Jian. Music: Du Xingcheng. Sound: Shen Guorui. Cast: Han Yueqiao as Liang Yaya, Wu Gang as Chen Chi, Du Yuan as He Yiqiang, Pan Xiaozhi as Yang Jingyi

Military school instructor Liang Yaya goes to a south China city to see how the school's graduates are doing in military service. She first finds He Yiqiang, a recent graduate who has now become a platoon leader. Then she interviews Yang Jingyi, now a military court lawyer. The third she talks to is political propaganda officer Liu Yu, who has been quite successful in training the women's military band. Liang Yaya's last interview is with graduate Chen Chi, who graduated at the same time she did, and who for a time was her lover. Now he is an artillery brigade commander.

2329. *A Woman Obsessed by Love (Chi Qing Nu Zhi)*

1992. Beijing Film Studio. Color. Letterboxed. 9 Reels. Direction: Liu Guoquan. Screenplay: Li Baolin. Cinematography: Ru Shuiren. Art Direction: Zhang Jianfang. Music: Fu Lin. Sound: Wang Dawen. Costume: Liu Huiping. Makeup: Hao Xia. Cast: Sun Song as Xiao Tong, Xin Ying as Ding Shan, Zhou Lijing as Lin Kuan, Ju Ying as He Xiaohong, Han Ying as the wet nurse

When word arrives that her husband Lin Kuan has been killed in an auto accident overseas, musical performer Ding Shan has a mental breakdown. In reality, Lin is alive, and faked his own death as part of a scheme to swindle an elderly woman overseas. He then returns to China, and disguised as an old man, sets out to kill his wife. Meanwhile, the overseas woman's son Xiao Tong also comes to China to visit his mother's family. When he finds that Lin is there as well, he and a young woman named He Xiaohong apprehend the swindler and bring him to justice. Xiao Tong and He Xiaohong fall in love during the operation.

2330. *A Woman Pianist's Story (Gui Ge Qing Yuan)*

1990. Shanghai Film Studio and France Aifeier Film Company, Beiersite Film Company, Second Television Station, Canadian International Film Company Co-Production. Color. Wide Screen. 10 Reels. Direction: Zhang Nuanqin, Da Shibiao. Screenplay: Yakedaofuman, Zhang Nuanqin, Makesi Feixieer, Daweide Miluo. Cinematography: J.C. Lalie, Zhang Yuanmin. Art Direction: Ju Ransheng. Cast: Qin Yi as Qingli, Chen Jie as Qingli (as a child), Jiang Wen as Huiyi, Zhou Yemang as Chen Youhuang

From girlhood, Qingli loved the piano. She becomes a brilliant student at music school in Shanghai, and her father Huiyi agrees that upon graduation she can pursue further study in Paris. However, the rest of the family persuades her father to change his mind and instead arrange a marriage for her to Chen Youhuang, son of wealthy businessman Chen Shuyi. This destroys the father-daughter relationship. The marriage does turn out well, however, Qingli and Youhuang do come to love each other after the marriage, and she continues practicing piano and attending concerts. She continues to have no contact with her father, however. When her husband dies, Qingli leaves Shanghai and moves to Hong Kong. Many years later, she is a concert pianist living in Paris, and begins to wonder about her father, whom she has neither seen nor spoken to in 30 years. One evening she is performing at a concert hall, and her father unexpectedly appears...

2331. *Woman Police Officer (Nu Jing Guan Ri Ji)*

1991. Changchun Film Studio. Color. Letterboxed. 9 Reels. Direction: Xue Yandong. Screenplay: Jiang Dian. Cinematography: Liu Fengdi, Li Li. Art Direction: Liu Hong. Music: Yang Yilun. Sound: Huang Yongqing, Sheng Hongtao. Cast: Wang Xu as Meng Xueyu, Jia Xinguan as Tang Kun, Qu Yan as Guo Aizhu, Wang Luyao as Maomao, Li Junhai as Lao Ba

Chief of detectives Guo Min learns of an upcoming major drug deal. He assigns principal responsibility for the case to veteran woman officer Meng Xueyu. But things don't go as planned, the criminals get away and Guo Min is killed. Blaming herself, Meng Xueyu volunteers to travel to South China in the guise of "Boss Jin" and infiltrates the drug ring. Her late boss's sister Guo Aizhu is public relations officer for the Yatai Pharmaceutical Company, and uses her position to provide a cover for Meng Xueyu. But the head of the drug dealers is very clever and soon identifies "Jin" as an undercover cop. Her life endangered, Meng soon comes to battle with the drug ring sooner than she planned. She cracks the case, however, killing the drug lord in the process. She returns home to learn that her boyfriend, not knowing where she was, has accepted an offer to study abroad and is leaving that same day. She rushes to the airport, but gets there after the plane has just taken off.

2332. *Woman Prisoners-Rocks-Black Mountain Forest (Nu Fan-Yao Gun-Hei Shan Lin)*

1993. Emei Film Studio. Color. Letterboxed.

Direction: Liu Mushan. Screenplay: Guo Shaogui. Cinematography: Fu Wei. Art Direction: Chen Desheng. Music: Wang Hong. Cast: Zhang Guangbei as Lin Shan, Chen Jing as Li Na, Fan Chunxia as Yao Cuifang, Han Haihua as "Wild Pig," Wu Jian as Lao Gun

In the early 1980s, the residents of a mountain village have two new neighbors. Two women, Li Na and Yao Cuifang, break out of a labor reform camp where they had been sentenced for prostitution, and come to the mountain village to hide out. Their dissolute natures soon clash with the traditional mores of the villagers, but in time the local people's hard work, decency and simple pleasures converts the two women. The women gain the ability to distinguish right from wrong, and decide to go back to the labor reform camp.

Woman Sesame Oil Maker see *Women from the Lake of Scented Souls*

2333. *A Woman Singer Roaming the World (Tian Ya Ge Nu)*

1995. Shandong Film Studio. Color. Letterboxed. Direction: Liu Guoquan. Screenplay: Hua Ershi. Cinematography: Li Dawei. Art Direction: Zhang Yafang. Cast: He Saifei as Ajun, Sun Song as Xiao Chen, Li Yuanyuan as Ayun, Jin Ming as Xiao Ming

Three sisters, Ayun, Ajun and Xiaoming, come to Shanghai to earn a living about the time the Japanese invade China. Xiaoming is blind, and to earn the money needed to restore her vision, Ayun becomes a prostitute. The only friends the sisters have are the denizens of a tea house, people from the lowest elements of society. One of these, Xiao Chen, writes a song called "Four Seasons," which Ajun sings in a tea house. Shanghai's top triad head Lu Jinxing hears her sing and lusts for her, which greatly concerns her friends. Later, Ayun is killed by another gangster. Then Ajun disappears. Actually, she has gone secretly to Hong Kong to pursue a singing career. Ten years later, she is a top singer in Hong Kong and Southeast Asia. Ajun returns to Shanghai, and she and Xiao Chen plan to marry. But the years of hard work and stress have taken their toll, and Ajun collapses.

2334. *Woman Soldier's Song (Nu Bing Yuan Wu Qu)*

1986. Changchun Film Studio. Color. 11

Reels. Direction: Chen Jialin, Sun Qinguo, Screenplay: Jiang Sheng, Cinematography: Zhong Wenmin, Art Direction: Jin Xiwu, Music; Jin Fuzhai, Sound: Zhang Fenglu, Cast: Wang Liyun as Ji Xian, Fu Yiwei as Pan Fanfan, Wu Lijie as Lin Ying, Zhang Liping as He Ya'nan, Dong Bingshun as Xu Jie, Song Yongkun as Deputy Commander Pan

Two women, both of them veteran PLA medical personnel, meet on a train and begin to reminisce about their early army days in wartime. Besides these two women, Ji Xian and Lin Ying, there were two other girls named Pan Fanfan, daughter of a high-ranking officer, and He Yanan, a college graduate. At first the four did not get along, but as they matured on the battlefield they became close friends, although at last He Ya'nan dies in battle.

2335. Woman Star of the "Macho Man Dance Hall" (Nan Zi Han Wu Ting De Nu Ming Xing)

1990. Tianshan Film Studio. Color. Wide Screen. 10 Reels. Direction: Guang Chunlan. Screenplay: Duan Baoshan, Guang Chunlan. Cinematography: Qi Xing. Art Direction: Xieerzhati. Music: Liu Gang, Nusilaiti Waerding. Sound: Aierken Bawudong, Cast: Reheman as Baikeli, Dilinuer as Guli, Mulading as Bulizi

Searching for a fresh, new face to play the female lead in the film "Secret Lover," deputy studio head Baikeli finds young housekeeper Guli working in the home of a studio artist. He casts her in the lead role, and as part of their preparation he, Guli and screenwriter Mulading travel to Xinjiang to experience life there. They have a series of humorous incidents during their stay with the local people, and when the time comes to return Baikeli announces the film's title will be changed to "Gifted Comedy Star of West China."

2336. Woman Swimmer (Mei Ren Yu)

1986. Pearl River Film Studio. Color. 3-D. 7 Reels. Direction: Lu Yu, Zhang Rongren, Er Lin. Screenplay: Yang Yinzhang, Zhu Ma. Cinematography: Zhou Jianhui. Art Direction: Man Qinhai. Music: Zhang Hong. Sound: Wu Chengxin. Cast: Hu Jingjing as Zhao Meiyin, Xu Ming as Wang Jianqi, Lu Jie as Yixiu Meizhi, Zhou Wenqiong as Wang Lili

2337. Woman-Taxi-Woman (Nu Ren Taxi Nu Ren)

1991. Beijing Film Studio. Color. 9 Reels. Letterboxed. Direction: Wang Junzheng. Screenplay: Qiao Xuezhu. Cinematography: Li Yuexia. Art Direction: Chen Xiaoxia. Music: Chen Yuanlin. Sound: Ren Shanpu. Cast: Ding Jiali as Zhang Gaixiu, Pan Hong as Qin Yao, Ge You as Gaixiu's husband, Wang Bing as the director, Yan Meiyi as the director's wife, Liu Qiong as the old man

A minor traffic accident involving two women takes them from initial hostility to acquaintance and then close friendship. The women, taxi driver Zhang Gaixiu and scientist Qin Yao, are as different as one could imagine: a down-to-earth blue collar type with a solid marriage, and a career-driven yuppie with a succession of unsuccessful romances. But over time each finds and appreciates the worth and admirable characteristics of the other, to their mutual benefit and personal growth.

2338. A Woman's Destiny (Yi Ge Nu Ren De Ming Yun)

1984. Xiaoxiang Film Studio. Color. Wide Screen. 10 Reels. Direction: Yuan Ye, Zhang Jinbiao. Screenplay: Fan Zhou, Zuo Xin, Wang Yayuan and Ding Xufeng, based on the novel "Star" by Ye Zi. Cinematography: Ding Xiaodong. Art Direction: Li Runzhang. Music: Lu Yuan. Sound: Ning Yuqin. Cast: Yin Xin as Meichun, Gao Weimin as Chen Derong, Wang Bozhao as Huang Liqiu, Dai Dawei as Cuconba

In the early 1920s, hard-working farm woman Meichun carries on despite being burdened with a shiftless and abusive husband, Chen Derong. But when he gambles away their prize hen, it becomes too much for her to bear and she leaves him. In the summer of 1926, a great wave of revolutionary fervor sweeps China, and many outsiders come to the rural areas as organizers. One of these is an idealistic young man named Huang Liqiu, with whom Meichun falls in love. They soon marry, and the following year have a son. But in that same year Chiang Kaishek turns on the Communists, and Huang Liqiu is among those killed. Meichun decides she must be content with the memories of that brief interlude of happiness, and returns to Chen Derong in order to provide a home and father for her baby. But Chen is more abusive than ever, so she leaves for good.

2339. *Woman's Power (Nu Ren De Li Liang)*

1985. Changchun Film Studio. Color. 10 Reels. Direction: Jiang Shusheng, Zhao Shi. Screenplay: Xue Ke. Cinematography: Zhang Songping. Art Direction: Shi Weiun. Music: Liu Xijin. Sound: Tong Zongde. Cast: Lin Daxin as Zhou Lusheng, Li Kechun as Li Sha, Zhao Yan as Geng Cang, Yi Ga as Luo Xiaoguang, Chen Jidong as Han Chunguang

The Zhushan City Chemical Plant is in serious crisis, with too much inventory in storage and the company existing on borrowed money. The director resigns and Deputy Director Geng Cang has no idea what to do about the situation. One assistant engineer, a 29-year-old woman named Li Sha, presents some suggestions to provincial authorities. The provincial party committee secretary is so impressed he names her director. Most of the plant's employees refuse to cooperate with Li Sha because of her age and gender, but she overcomes the many difficulties and eventually gains everyone's respect and support.

2340. *A Woman's Story (Nu Ren De Gu Shi)*

1987. Shanghai Film Studio. Color. 10 Reels. Direction: Peng Xiaolian. Screenplay: Xiao Mao. Cinematography: Liu Lihua. Art Direction: Zhou Xinren. Music: Yang Mao. Sound: Tu Minde. Cast: Zhang Wenrong as Mother Laizi, Zhang Ming as Xiao Feng, Song Ruhui as Jin Xiang

Mother Laizi, Xiao Feng and Jin Xiang are all hardworking natives of a poor village in the shadow of the Great Wall. All her life, Mother Laizi has worked hard to support her family, never thinking of herself. Xiao Feng lives with her elderly mother and four sisters, and local villagers look down on them because there are no men in their family. Jin Xiang was almost victimized by the traditional rural practice of arranged marriages, but has managed to escape her fate. The three women decide to start a small business together, buying yarn on credit in cities and small towns and then selling it in the countryside. In their travels they have many new experiences. The film tells about the lives of these three women, and against this background reveals how reforms are changing the lives and attitudes of women in China's countryside.

Jury's Special Nomination Award, 12th Clermont International Women's Festival.

2341. *A Woman's Street (Nu Ren Jie)*

1989. Pearl River Film Studio. Color. 10 Reels. Letterboxed. Direction: Zhang Liang. Screenplay: Hong Santai, Zhang Liang. Cinematography: Han Xingyuan. Art Direction: Guan Yu. Music: Wang Wenguang. Cast: Chen Ling as Ouyang Suihong, Mao Haitong as Bai Yan, Huang Pingshan as He Weixiong, Liu Pei as Cheng Liying, Li Ying as Fu Xiaolian, Lu Mimi as Zhao Qiaozhen, Lu Dou as A Kun, Huang Weixiang as A Kun's wife, Kong Xianzhu as Suihong's father

A light romantic comedy. Two young women, intelligent and pretty Ouyang Suihong and young and energetic Bai Yan, are private traders in clothes in the same bustling street. Nothing is completely smooth for the two, either in their business or their love affairs, with profit and loss in both.

2342. *Women Are Human Too (Nu Ren Ye Shi Ren)*

1992. Guangxi Film Studio. Color. Letterboxed. 9 Reels. Direction: Lu Jianhua, Yu Zhongxiao. Cinematography: Chen Chang'an. Art Direction: Liang Shukui. Music: Wang Ming, Wu Chaofan. Cast: Zhang Jinling as Gao Jinfeng, Liang Qingang as Zhang Shangeng, Chen Yude as Zhang Daqiang, Jin Yi as Li Suyun, He Wei as Sun Laoshan, Liu Lili as Zhen Shanmei

After three daughters, farmer Zhang Daqiang forces his wife Li Suyun to have another baby, although her doctor has warned she has a weak heart. Their neighbor Zhen Shanmei also wants a son. When Gao Jinfeng is named head of the village family planning committee he struggles with these people's traditional thinking. The strain of pregnancy at last proves fatal for Suyun, which wakes people up. The village people begin to comply with the family planning policy.

2343. *Women Avengers (Fu Chou De Nu Ren)*

1992. Pearl River Film Studio. Color. Letterboxed. 10 Reels. Direction: Wang Wei. Screenplay: Xiao Jian. Cinematography: Zhen Kangzhen. Art Direction: Zhu Jinhe. Music: Fang Xiaoming. Sound: Lu Mingwen. Costume: Liang Shufang. Makeup: Wen Huiying, Yao Hu. Cast: Yuan Xingzhe as Li Qingzhu, Liu Jiaoxin as Jingshang Anfu, Pu Chaoyin as Jin Qinghua, Mao Haitong as Fu Chunfeng

Early in 1945 as he confronts certain defeat, the Japanese commander on the South

China Sea coast, Shojo Gampu loses control of his troops and himself. He orders the execution of several dozen local men. Their widows, led by a brave woman named Li Qingzhu, swear to have their revenge. They are joined by Fu Chunfeng and several other high school girls raped by Shojo's troops. The women organize a guerrilla troop to carry out sabotage and assassinations of Japanese soldiers. To counter them, Shojo forces a Korean "comfort woman" to organize an all-woman anti-guerrilla unit. But ultimately Li and Feng's strong anti-Japanese brigade succeeds in overcoming Shojo's demoralized troops at the battle of Moon River, and kill the Japanese commander.

2344. *Women Flowers (Nu Ren Hua)*

1994. Pearl River Film Company. Color. Letterboxed. 10 Reels. Direction: Wang Jing. Screenplay: Wang Jing, adapted from Su Fanggui's novel "Story of Adopted Sisters." Art Direction: Zhao Guoliang, Xu Xiaoli. Music: Cheng Dazhao. Sound: Feng Lunsheng, Zhu Weijiang. Costume: Wang Jizhu, Wei Qun. Makeup: Zuo Nannan, Liu Xiuming. Cast: Pu Chaoying as Shang Meiju, Yuan Li as Yanzhi, Liu Wei as A Di, Zhu Hongbo as A Fu, Zhou Yan as A Qin, Xie Ling as A Ying, Xu Xiaodan as A Hui, Gao Changlin as A Lin

In the Pearl River delta region early in the 20th century, some women who have decided to remain spinsters adopt several young, pretty girls and raise them to be elegant in manner and attractive to men. Their aim is to sell these girls when grown to wealthy and powerful men as concubines. One of the women is Shang Meiju: being jilted by a lover has left her in a mental state to strictly adhere to the other women's rules, such as abstaining from sex with a man. However, she does have an affair with A Ying, a strong and domineering woman. Another woman, A Di, has an affair with a man, A Fu, and the others make her life miserable as a result. A fourth woman, A Qing, commits suicide when she finds herself pregnant. Yanzhi is one of the girls adopted by Shang Meiju; when she learns this woman she thought was her loving adoptive mother actually plans to sell her as if she were an object, she kills herself in front of Shang. Shang Meiju at last goes insane and is taken away. No one is happier at this than another one of her adoptees Xiuling, who will now be free to marry.

2345. *Women from the Lake of Scented Souls (aka Woman Sesame Oil Maker) (Xiang Hun Nu)*

1992. Changchun Film Studio and Tianjin Film Studio Co-Production. Color. Letterboxed. 10 Reels. Direction and Screenplay: Xie Fei. Cinematography: Pao Xiaoran. Art Direction: Ma Huiwu and Wang Jie. Music: Wang Liping. Sound: Liu Xiaochuan. Costume: Zhang Jing, Wei Lianxiang. Makeup: Zhang Huiling. Cast: Siqin Gaowa as Xianger Shen, Lei Gesheng as Fuer Shu, Wu Yujuan as Huanhuan, Chen Baoguo as Ren Zhongshi, Ye Lingliang as Lao Wenai, Hu Xiaoguang as Dunzi

In a mountain village, Xianger Shen operates a successful business making and selling sesame oil. Her personal life is unhappy, however: her husband Fuer, a much older man to whom she was married at the age of seven, does little but take it easy by day and get drunk at night, a lazy and abusive burden. In addition, their only child Dunzi is an epileptic, legally barred from marrying. Desperate for a woman, he is becoming a problem for the local girls he harasses, particularly one pretty girl named Huanhuan. Xianger's only comfort are her occasional trysts with Ren Zhongshi, a Beijing driver whose work regularly brings him to her village. A Japanese businesswoman comes to Xianger's village to meet the maker of this renowned sesame oil, which her company wants to import to Japan. Xianger is brought to Beijing to talk contract, and while there she calls Ren Zhongshi, only to find her lover is a married man with a family. When the business talks conclude, the saddened Xianger returns to her village. She determines to find Dunzi a wife, and her son begs her for Huanhuan. By exploiting a loophole in the law, she offers to pay off the heavy debts of Huanhuan's family if their daughter will marry Dunzi. The family readily agrees, and the couple are wed. But on their wedding night Dunzi tries to kill Huanhuan while having a seizure. Huanhuan also tells Xianger that Dunzi is impotent. The girl declines Xianger's offer to let her out of the marriage, for as she says, no other man will have her now. Too late, Xianger realizes that she has deprived the girl of the love she deserves, and has trapped her in the same loveless existence in which Xianger finds herself.

Golden Bear Award, 43rd Berlin International Film Festival.

2346. *Women Locomotive Drivers (Nu Si Ji)*

1951. Shanghai Film Studio. B & W. 9 Reels. Direction: Xian Qun. Screenplay: Ge Qing, based on the true story of China's first woman train driver. Cinematography: Luo Jizhi. Zhang Hongkang. Art Direction: Han Xin and Chen Bosheng. Music: Ge Yan. Sound: Miao Zhenyu. Costume: Wu Zutong. Cast: Su Xiuwen as Sun Guilan, Ke Gang as Zhou Suying, Zhao Suyin as Feng Xiaomei, Ling Zhihao as Gao Furong, Qiang Ming as Xie Daofu, Su Hui as Master Worker Lu

After the liberation of Northeast China, the Dalian Section of the China Changchun Railway begins training its first group of women locomotive drivers. Their instructor Master Worker Lu believes this is strictly man's work, and doubts women can be taught to do it. Sun Guilan is poorly educated, and has particular difficulties learning, but makes rapid progress after the local Party branch sends the enthusiastic Xiao Zhang to help her. Sun's chief rival is Feng Xiaomei, a better-educated young woman who looks down upon Sun Guilan. Feng challenges Sun to a contest in train inspection examination. Sun agrees to a collective contest which will help all the students. Sun's group wins, largely because Feng's concern only for her personal record holds her group back. In the final test, controlling the train, Feng proudly drives the train, but when she suddenly encounters a mule cart on the track she does not know what to do. Fortunately, Sun keeps her head and brings the train to a halt, avoiding an accident. Feng Xiaomei is very moved, and realizes her error in pursuing individualism. Master Worker Lu also overcomes his lack of respect for women. Under the leadership of the CPC, and with the help of Soviet specialists, the women students finally master the skill and become the first group of Chinese women railway engineers.

2347. *The Women of Yellow Earth Hill (Huang Tu Po De Po Yi Men)*

1988. Beijing Film Studio. Color. 10 Reels. Direction: Dong Kena. Screenplay: Ma Feng, Sun Qian. Cinematography: Yan Junsheng. Art Direction: Wang Jixian. Music: Lu Zhulong. Sound: Wang Dawen. Cast: Li Kechun as Luye, Zhao Zhiyue as Old Man Le, Jin Feng as Village Director Yuan, Li Zonglun as Datong

Huangtupo is a mountain village of only about 40 to 50 households. After the 3rd Plenary Session of the 11th Party Congress, collective property is allocated to each household on a contracted responsibility basis. After the Spring Festival, the younger, stronger workers all leave home to find jobs, and only women are left to tend the deteriorating fields. Luye talks it over with her in-laws, and using 5,000 yuan earned by her husband, she buys a tractor and contracts all the farmland. She then organizes the women into a collective contractual union. The women's hard work realizes a big harvest, and when grain sales become a problem they overcome it by founding a small food processing plant.

2348. *Women Pilots (Nu Fei Xing Yuan)*

1966. Beijing Film Studio. Color. 12 Reels. Direction: Cheng Ying, Dong Kena. Screenplay: Feng Deying. Cinematography: Gao Hongtao. Art Direction: Yu Yiru. Music: Huang He, Ding Jiaqi. Sound: Liu Shida. Casting: Xu Yan as Lin Xuezheng, Li Lingxiu as Yang Qiaomei, Chen Zhurong as Xiang Fei, Ha Zhigang as Political Commissar Wang, Zhao Zhengtao as Yang De, Liu Diancheng as Guo Huaxiang

Some of the new students at a school for air force pilots are Lin Xuezheng, the daughter of a revolutionary martyr, Yang Qiaomei, a peasant girl who had once been sold as a child bride in the old society, and high school student Xiang Fei, the daughter of a teacher. Lin Xuezheng and Yang Qiaomei have little formal education, and have difficulty studying aviation theory. Although Xiang Fei's higher educational level enables her to do well at theory, her progress is hampered by capitalistic thoughts. The pilot school's political commissar Wang, a veteran of the Long March, devotes personal attention to each student, dealing with each one's individual situation. Yang Qiaomei studies Chairman Mao's writings and becomes the first to solo; Lin Xuezheng strengthens her legs through strict physical training, and finally overcomes her shortcomings. Finally, with education by the Party organization and the help of her comrades, Xiang Fei also solos successfully.

2349. *Women Soldiers (Nu Bing)*

1981. August First Film Studio. Color. 10 Reels. Direction: Hao Guang. Screenplay: Li Bai, Dong Xiaohua. Cinematography: Chen Ruijun. Art Direction: Shi Pingyi. Music: Gong Zhiwei.

Sound: Zhang Zheng, Cui Denggao. Cast: Ni Ping as Zhou Yiyan, Wang Lihua as Gao Shier, Xu Jinjin as Yu Jie

In 1947, three women members of a PLA performance troupe lose contact with the army. They are the troupe's deputy director Zhou Yiyan and new recruits Yu Jie and Gao Shier, who looks like a young boy. They rush to catch up with their unit, but when they arrive find that the Nationalist Army now occupies that area. The enemy spots them, but they are successful in getting away. One night, they happen to run into a PLA rear guard unit, and although they are nearly exhausted put on a show for the troops anyway. After that, the soldiers receive an emergency order to pull out, but they cannot take the three women along. So they have to continue their search for the main force. On the way, Yu Jie falls ill, and Gao Shier runs into a band of Nationalist soldiers. Luckily, they take her to be a local boy and make her guide them to the nearby town of Linhe. Yu Jie follows while Zhou Yi goes to borrow a mule. When she returns, the others are gone, so she hurries to Linhe. She arrives to find that the PLA has wiped out the enemy there and now occupies the town. All three are safely back with their unit.

2350. *Women's Diving Team Member (Nu Tiao Shui Dui Yuan)*

1964. Changchun Film Studio. Color. 10 Reels. Direction: Liu Guoquan. Screenplay: Geng Geng. Cinematography: Wu Guojiang. Art Direction: Liu Jinnai. Music: Quan Rufeng. Sound: Yuan Mingda. Cast: Zhang Kejing as Chen Xiaohong, Zeng Shaomei as Huang Guilan, Wang Yinpu as Wang Zhengqian, Li Zhengde as Zhou Bing, Zhen Deqian as Gao Limei, Dong Xili as Lin Zhiqing

High school student Chen Xiaohong learns to dive for recreation, but with the help of her coach Wang Zhengqian and her teammates Gao Limei and Huang Guilan, she becomes the national junior girls' diving champion. Later, ambitious new coach Zhou Bing, thinking her further success will reflect favorably on him, lays out a much-too-advanced training plan for Xiaohong. Just a month later, he enters her in the national seniors contest, but Xiaohong receives a 0 score for impractically trying a dive with a very high degree of difficulty, which she fails miserably. While she improves steadily after that with help from her coach and teammates, the psychological effect of her

failure prevents her from doing that one particular dive. Then one day on a school outing, a child falls into the water, and Xiaohong dives from a 10-meter high cliff to save him, by chance performing that particular dive in doing so. Having broken through her mental block, Xiaohong and her teammates Gao Limei and Huang Guilan all receive high marks in the next national competition.

2351. *Women's Drug Rehabilitation Centre (Niu Zi Jie Du Suo)*

1992. Pearl River Film Studio. Color. Letterboxed. 10 Reels. Direction: Wang Jing, He Qun. Screenplay: Lin Fan. Cinematography: Yang Weidong. Art Direction: Song Weidong. Costume: Wang Jizhu, Fan Shunhua. Makeup: Li Yuxiang, Zuo Nannan. Cast: Zhao Kuier as Lu Hong, Pu Chaoyin as Lin Fangfei, Jin Di as A Qing, Ju Xue as Luo Tongtong, Ru Ping as Li Juan, Chen Rui as Zhou Jian, Li Yusheng as Liu Wei

Two Hong Kong triads battle over a drug supply shipped to the Chinese interior. Clues point to a woman called "Qi Mei" as the key person in the drug traffic, so chief investigator Zhou Jian and his assistant Liu Wei decide to begin their investigation at the Women's Drug Treatment Center. Meanwhile, one of the triads sends a man to the same place in the guise of a reporter, also looking for her. At last, the two triads have a violent confrontation over Qi Mei, but they fall into a police trap and are caught.

2352. *Women's Valley (Nu Er Gu)*

1995. Xie Jin-Hengtong Film & Television Corp. Ltd., Zhejiang Film Studio Co-Production. Color. Letterboxed. Direction: Xie Jin. Screenplay: Zhou Jianping. Cinematography: Shen Miaorong. Art Direction: Mei Kunping. Music: Jin Fuzai. Cast: Li Cuiyun, Ma Lingyan, Zhao Na'na, Zhao Wei, Lu Zhenping, Liao Dongyan, Dubian Meisui, Wang Dongqing, Zhen Rongrong

In a women's prison in a valley, several women of varying backgrounds come to serve their sentences and perhaps get their lives turned around. Naive Feifei has confessed to crimes actually committed by her husband; after she is behind bars, he abandons her. Jinger was a hospital worker with a terminally ill husband; to ease his suffering, she stole precious pain-killers. Qiuzhi was imprisoned as a sex offender; her father committed the same offense but was never caught. Prison warden You devotes herself to helping the women in her charge and helping them find new lives. The film follows these three prisoners after their release. Feifei comes to her senses about her husband, and after her release becomes a very successful businesswoman. Jinger returns to the hospital and after one year has reimbursed it for all she took, after which she resigns to become a nun. Qiuzhi meets and marries a self-employed businessman.

2353. Women's World (Nu Xing Shi Jie)

1991. Xiaoxiang Film Studio. Color. 10 Reels. Letterboxed. Direction: Dong Kena. Screenplay: Zhao Baohua, Han Zhijun. Cinematography: Li Xiaoping, Zhang Yuefu. Art Direction: Tan Shengshan. Music: Zou Ye. Sound: Liu Yishen, Song Wei. Cast: Bai Han as Li Qing, Chen Xigang as Peng Enliang, Ding Yi as Lu Yun, Liu Jihong as Xia Mengfan, Li Jing as Feng Xuan, Wu Ying as Tao Tianyi

The lives and loves of three middle-aged Chinese women. Li Qing is chief reporter at the Consumer Times, Lu Yun is a member of the Women's Rights Department of the Women's Association, while Tao Tianyi is a violinist with the Film Orchestra. The three have been good friends since school, but all have had different life experiences. Li's husband is a factory manager, who loves his wife. But with both very involved in their separate careers, they have little time together and problems begin to crop up in their marriage. Lu is tough on her husband, who she believes would never betray her. She fails to realize that he is still in love with the violinist Tao, his girlfriend 20 years ago before he married Lu.

2354. Wonder Boy (Pi Li Bei Bei)

1988. Children's Film Studio. Color. 9 Reels. Direction: Song Chong, Wen Luming. Screenplay: Zhang Zhilu. Cinematography: Wang Jiuwen. Art Direction: Feng Xiaoning. Music: Xu Jingxin. Sound: Ren Daming. Cast: Zhang Jing as Liu Beibei, Wang Ying as Yang Weiwei, Zhang Yi as Liu Chang

As a UFO streaks across the silent city sky one evening, a child is born in the local hospital. He is named Beibei. Because Beibei's hands emit an electric charge, he cannot get as close to his parents and other children as he would like, but he does not want to tell anyone his secret. After Beibei helps an old blind man recover his sight, a scientific research institute takes Beibei into custody for tests. The little boy escapes with the help of his classmates, Weiwei, Jinfeng and Jingjing. The four children run to the Great Wall and call out to Beibei's maker. As a result, Beibei loses his special power, but is happy because he can now walk hand in hand with his friends.

2355. Wonderful Romance (Qi Yuan Qiao Pei)

1990. Changchun Film Studio. Color. Wide Screen. 9 Reels. Direction: Wang Yabiao. Screenplay: Wang Bingquan. Cinematographer: Chen Chang'an, Wang Jian. Art Direction: Ju Lutian. Music: Zhu Zhongtang. Sound: Gu Xiaolian. Cast: Yi Guohua as Hu Yan, Han Ping as Liu Fengyun, Zhang Xiqian as Wu Lian, Wu Kejian as Tu Biao

Outstanding scholar Hu Yan is engaged to Liu Fengyun, daughter of the magistrate of Yangzhou. On the way to fulfill his duty and marry this girl he has never met, he mistakenly boards the wrong boat and meets another girl with whom he immediately falls in love. After some difficulties, the two are married. Meanwhile in Yangzhou, another scholar named Wu Lian is taken by Miss Liu to be her fiance. They fall in love and get married as well.

2356. A Wood House Covered by Green Vines (Pa Man Qin Teng De Xiao Wu)

1984. Emei Film Studio. Color. 10 Reels. Direction: Xiang Ling. Screenplay: Chen Dunde, Gu Hua. Cinematography: Li Erkang. Art Direction: Xia Zhengqiu. Music: Tian Liantao. Sound: Lin Bingcheng. Cast: Wang Yan as Pan Qinqin, Li Shixi as Li Xinfu, Lei Luosheng as Wang Mutong, Zhang Tao as Xiao Tong, Hong Fang as Xiao Qin

During the Cultural Revolution, educated city youth Li Xinfu is sent to a forest region to work. When he stops some people from overcutting precious timber, he is accused of "preventing production" and reassigned. He frequently clashes with his new supervisor Wang Mutong, who resents the young man's arrival. Li Xinfu repeatedly warns Wang of the dangers of forest fires, but when one finally does occur, Li is the one accused and sent to prison for negligence. After the downfall of the Gang of Four, Li Xinfu is released, and returns to the forest. This time, his reports are heeded.

2357. *Wooden House (Mu Wu)*

1984. Beijing Film Studio. Color. Letter-boxed. 10 Reels. Direction: Shi Yifu, Li Xin. Screenplay: Zhang Tianmin, Zhang Xiaotian. Cinematography: Wu Shenghan, Wang Zhaoling, Hu Jihe. Art Direction: Liang Shukui, Yi Hongyuan. Music: Jin Xiang. Sound: Ning Menghua. Cast: Jin Ange as Zhong Shi, Zhai Junjie as Pu Jianqiu, Dong Ji as Yi Laoda, Lu Guilan as the wife, Zhu Longguang as Lu Yuan, Bai Zhidi as Xian Ping

The lives and enduring friendships of four men over a period of 43 years, starting with their youthful experiences during World War II, through the revolutionary war that followed, and through China's modern political struggles. A subplot concerns their relationship with a boatman named Yi Laoda and his family. After the Cultural Revolution, the four meet again at a large water conservancy project and decide to go together to visit Yi Laoda.

2358. *The Wooden Man's Bride (Wu Kui)*

1993. Xi'an Film Studio and Taiwan Long Shong Intl. Color. Letterboxed. 11 reels. Direction: Huang Jianxin. Screenplay: Yang Zhengguang, based on the novel by Jia Ping'ao. Cinematography: Zhang Xiaoguang. Art Direction: Teng Jie. Music: Zhang Dalong. Sound (Dolby): Yan Jun. Costume: Du Longxi. Makeup: Cheng Yin and Sun Wei. Cast: Chang Shih as Wu Kui, Wang Lan as the Young Mistress, Gu Baoming as Wu Kui's Brother, Wang Yumei as Madame Liu, Wang Fuli as Sister Ma, Kao Mingjun as Chief Tang

In remote and desolate Northwest China in the 1920s, bandits attack a wedding procession carrying a bride-to-be across the desert to her arranged marriage. One of the sedan bearers, a simple man named Wu Kui, fights bravely to defend the bride, but she is abducted anyway. When word of the incident reaches the intended groom, he accidentally kills himself rushing to save her. The courageous and headstrong Wu Kui invades the bandits' lair, so impressing the bandit chieftain that Wu and the woman are released. When she reaches her late fiance's family mansion, his mother subjects the girl to a humiliating virginity check, after which the mother, Madame Liu, marries the girl to a carved wooden statue, with an admonition that the girl remain faithful forever to this stand-in for the dead man. The girl tries to escape, but is caught and punished each time. Wu Kui is her only friend in the household, and in this time leads to romance. When the cruel Madame Liu catches them in the act, she drives Wu from the house and has the girl crippled to prevent her escaping or being unfaithful again to her wooden mate. Kui goes to the bandits once more to beg their help, but finds they have all been wiped out. He goes off to recruit his own band, and returns to the mansion a year later at their head. He orders the cruel Madame Liu hanged, then carries off his bride, hobbled but free at last.

2359. *Woodwind Instrument's Sound in the Wind (Feng Cui Suo Na Sheng)*

1983. Xiaoxiang Film Studio. Color. 10 Reels. Direction: Ling Zhi. Screenplay: Han Shaogong. Cinematography: Wang Kekuan. Art Direction: Xia Rujin. Music: Wang Ming. Sound: Ning Yuqin. Cast: Li Jun as Erxiang, Jin Xing as Deqi, Zhao Runfeng as Decheng, Zhao Shulan as Lady Jin Lan, Zhang Yanli as Yuhuan, Yang Zichun as Hanwen's father

After peasant girl Erxiang marries Dacheng, a boy from a neighboring village, she finds that her new husband is selfish and obsessed with making money. In contrast, his deaf younger brother Deqi is a sweet boy more interested in helping others than in material pursuits. Dacheng says that someone so concerned for others is stupid, and when Erxiang helps a neighbor by baby-sitting, her husband mocks her as well. Dacheng later resumes an involvement with an old girl friend, and then falsely accuses Erxiang of having an affair with his brother. Their marriage breaks up, but Erxiang finds that her only concern is for Daqi, who cannot take care of himself. One day while working on a raft, Daqi has a fatal accident. Everyone, especially Erxiang, misses him very much.

2360. *Working Girls in the SEZ (Te Qu Da Gong Mei)*

1990. Pearl River Film Production Corporation. Color. 10 Reels. Wide Screen. Direction: Zhang Liang. Screenplay: Wang Jingzhu, Zhang Liang. Cinematography: Yan Xuzhong. Art Direction: Zhang Zhichu. Music: Zhang Hong. Sound: Huang Minguang. Cast: Liu Shuang as Li Tingmei, Liu Yanjun as Li Sixi, Wang Qian as Xing Zi, Sun Qixin as Jiang Hao,, Zhang Yongxia as Cai Yun

A group of young women from an impoverished mountain area come to one of China's special economic zones to work in a factory. Their motives for coming to the SEZ vary, some wanting to learn about the modern world outside of their villages, discover themselves as individuals, pursue new lifestyles, learn skills they can take back home, etc. They also have to cope with the temptations of money and urban loneliness. While focusing on the girls' several stories, the film is really a hymn of praise to the special economic zones and what they have brought to China economically.

2361. *The World Bright Again (Da Di Chong Guang)*

1950. Shanghai Film Studio. B & W. 10 Reels. Direction: Xu Tao. Screenplay: Yuan Yunfan. Cinematography: Feng Sizhi, Qiu Ge. Art Direction: Wang Changcheng. Music: Zhu Jianer. Sound: Lin Bingsheng, Wang Xingzhou. Costume: Han Mingde, Zhang Jingcheng. Makeup: Zhang Yingmei. Cast: Pan Wengzhan as Zhou Qiang, Jin Yan as Old Shen, Zhang Zhen as Yang Yuwen, Xiang Kun as Chen Guangsheng, Tian Ran as Guo Zhiying, Wang Qi as Sun Erhu

In August 1945, after the Japanese surrender, Nationalist forces violate the Nationalist-Communist cease-fire and launch an attack on the Communist New Fourth Army, which had been pulling out of East China as part of the agreement. During the attack, several of the Communists are taken prisoner while covering the transfer of wounded. With the help of some local people, they flee into the mountains, and most of them survive there until they connect with the CPC underground, organize a people's military force, and establish a mountain base to wage guerrilla warfare against the enemy. In 1949, a massive PLA force successfully crosses the Changjiang River, and the guerrillas finally link up with their own army.

2362. *The World's Number One Sword (Tian Xia Di Yi Jian)*

1988. Changchun Film Studio. Color. 9 Reels. Direction: Zhao Xinshui, Wang Wenzhi. Screenplay: Ni Feng. Cinematography: Yu Bing. Art Direction: Xu Zhenkun. Music: Liu Xijin. Sound: Yu Kaizhang, Liao Yongliang. Cast: Kou Zhanwen as the Number One Sword, Lu Nan as the female Number One Sword, Shi Chongren as Qing Yi, Ge Dianyu as Lu Ta, Peng Guizhou as Kong Jiexiong

In the 1660s, after the Sanfan Rebellion is put down, a group of fleeing rebels led by Kong Jiexiong makes its way to the Luzhou area of Yunnan province. There, they make alliance with Lu Ta, local Bayi nationality chieftain, to set up an independent kingdom. This angers Chinese Emperor Kangxi, who dispatches senior court official Qing Yi to the Luzhu area to arrange the suppression of this new effort at separation. Qing Yi contacts and organizes some local fighters, including a man and woman each known as "Number One Sword." After a series of life-and-death battles, the separatist conspiracy is smashed.

2363. *Worry Amidst Happiness (Chou Mei Xiao Lian)*

1984. Jiangxi Film Studio. Color. Direction: Zhang Gang. Screenplay: Zhang Gang, Mao Bingquan. Cinematography: Tang Yulin. Art Direction: Zhao Yixian. Music: Jie Cheli, Zhou Bo. Sound: Yu Meiqiang. Cast: Cheng Zhi as He Aman, Wang Qingbao as Zhenzhen, Zhu Manfang as Liu Yufeng, Hua Minwei as Guan Mugeng, Chen Xi as Director Liu, Luo Yunhan as Xiong Afu

In the period just after the 3rd Plenary Session of the 11th Party Congress, Xiong Afu goes to the market to sell his grain, accompanied by his son Guan Mugeng and the latter's arranged fiancee Zhenzhen. When they arrive, they find that so many people are waiting to sell grain that the warehouses are full. He Aman, Director of Grain Purchasing, has an idea for expanding and renovating his work unit's warehouse so it can hold more grain. In participating in the renovation work, Mugeng and Zhenzhen really fall in love.

2364. *Wreathed in Smiles (aka Flowers Meet the Spring Rain) (Xiao Zhu Yan Kai/Hua Lian Chunyu)*

1959. Changchun Film Studio and Haerbin Film Studio joint produced. Color. 12 Reels. Direction: Yu Yanfu. Screenplay: Cong Sheng. Cinematography: Wu Guojiang. Art Direction: Wang Xingwen. Music: Lei Zhenbang. Sound: Wang Fei. Cast: Zhang Yuan as He Huiyin, Ren Yi as Ding Guocai, Huang Ling as Hu Guizhen, Ye Linlang as Wang Liyun, Jin Di as Luo Yuhua, Li Sufeng as Gao Caifeng

Some construction workers' wives respond enthusiastically to the Party's call, and go out of their homes to take part in social work. This proves very controversial, as some people think that a woman's place is in the home, serving her husband and caring for their children. Many family arguments erupt over this. Neighborhood group leader He Huiying patiently undertakes the ideological work necessary to improve the situation. In the end, working outside the home bolsters the housewives' self-image as well as improving their social status.

2365. *Wu Lang's Story (Wu Lang Ba Gua Gun)*

1990. Emei Film Studio & Hong Kong Hezhong Film Company Co-Production. Color. Wide Screen. 9 Reels. Direction: Du Guowu. Screenplay: Du Wenbo. Cinematography: Du Xiaosi. Art Direction: Lin Qi. Cast: Liang Xiaolong as Wulang, Huang Zhaoshi as Ruo Lan

In the early years of the Northern Song dynasty (late 10th century A.D.), the Kingdom of Liao invades the Song. In a battle at Jinsha Beach, Song General Yang Jiye's army is almost wiped out, his two sons being the only survivors. One son, Wulang, is badly wounded but makes it to a temple to seek sanctuary. After recovering, Wulang decides to become a monk. He proves such an apt student that the master monk designates Wulang as his eventual successor. This angers the previous heir apparent, who leaves the temple and joins the Liao. After Wulang becomes the master monk, he teaches kung fu to the rest of the monks, then leads a counter-attack which defeats the Liao.

2366. *Wu Ni (Wu Ni)*

1992. Inner Mongolia Film Studio. Color. Wide Screen. 3-D. Direction: Zhang Yuqiang, Geng Deng. Screenplay: Qing Wubo, Bade Ronggui, Chen Da, Zhang Yuqiang. Cinematography: Huang Xinyi, Ge Lisheng. Art Direction: Ao Lige. Sound: Hu Bing. Cast: Zhang Yan as Wu Ni, Che Lulu as Wu Ni (as a child), Jiang Baoying as Mother, Ba Teer as Geerdi, Cha Gan as Nuo Ming

A Japanese orphan girl is adopted by a Mongolian family and renamed Wu Ni. She grows up, goes to college and becomes a teacher, then returns to her prairie home to teach elementary school. She marries a Mongolian man, but he dies during the Cultural Revolution. She grows weak from overwork and hardship, but is unflagging in her dedication to educating children. Her family and students are all devoted to her. At last she goes to Japan to visit her relatives there, but decides that China is the land she loves, so she returns.

2367. *Wudang (Wu Dang)*

1983. Changchun Film Studio. Color. 10 Reels. Direction: Sun Sha. Screenplay: Xie Wenli. Cinematography: Han Dongxia. Art Direction: Gong Minhui. Music: Wang Ming. Sound: Yuan Minda. Cast: Lin Quan as Chen Xuejiao, Zhao Changjun as Sima Jian, Li Yuwen as Wu Yunlong, Ma Zhenbang as Nanshan, Tang Yali as Wu Jinjin, Wang Xiaozhong as Chen Wei

In the late 19th century, the corrupt Manchu government brings many foreign martial artists to China to display their skills. In the city of Zhongzhou, five Japanese martial artists challenge all Chinese to fight them. They believe their repeated humiliating triumphs over Chinese fighters prove their nation's natural superiority. Chen Wei, a specialist in the "Wudang" school of fighting, accepts the challenge in order to defend Chinese national pride. However, he is killed during the contest with a hidden weapon. Later, his colleague Wu Yunlong dies in the same way. Chen's daughter Chen Xuejiao goes to the Nanshan Temple to study martial arts, and the master monk there tells her his pupil Sima Jian is her best choice as a partner to fight the Japanese. In the end they win the battle, but Sima Jian is badly injured and Chen Xuejiao must see that he gets to a safe place to recuperate.

2368. *Xia Minghan (Xia Ming Han)*

1985. August First Film Studio. Color. Letterboxed. 9 Reels. Direction: Jia Shihong. Screenplay: Ju Yinchun, Chen Xinhua. Cinematography: Zhang Dongliang. Art Direction: Liu Fan. Music: Wang Zhulin. Sound: Li Qinheng. Cast: Wu Gang as Xia Minghan, Yu Li as Zheng Jiajun, Ji Ping as Xia Mingzhen

The story of Xia Minghan, a leading Communist figure of the 1920s. Xia is born into a family of feudal administrators, but leaves school and breaks with his family during the May 4th Movement. He becomes a revolutionary and joins the Communist Party, rising to become one of the CPC's top grass-roots organizers. In 1927, when Chiang Kaishek turns on the Communists, the CPC's Hunan Committee decides to organize a rebellion in that province, and Xia is sent to organize in the Changsha area. But the Nationalist government has Xia on its black list, and arrests him. Xia resists all efforts to get him to betray the revolution, and is executed in the spring of 1928.

2369. *Xi'an Incident (Parts 1 & 2) (Xi An Shi Bian)*

1981. Xi'an Film Studio. Color. 19 Reels. Direction: Cheng Yin. Screenplay: Zhen Zhong, Cheng Yin. Cinematography: Gao Hongtao, Zhen Yiyuan, Chen Wancai. Art Direction: Zhang Zhien, Lu Guangcai. Music: Li Yaodong. Sound: Hong Jiahui, Dang Chunzhu. Makeup: Wang Xizhong, Li Ende. Cast: Jin Ange as Zhang Xueliang, Xin Jing as Yang Hucheng, Wang Tiecheng as Zhou Enlai, Sun Feihu as Chiang Kaishek, Xiu Zongdi as He Yinqin, Zhu Kexin as Song Meiling (Madame Chiang)

On December 12, 1935, Chiang Kaishek is in Xi'an on an inspection visit. At that time two Nationalist Army generals, Northeast Army commander Zhang Xueliang and Northwest Army commander Yang Hucheng, lead their troops in rebellion against Chiang and place him under house arrest. Their aim is to force Chiang to agree to drop his campaign against the Communists and make common cause in resisting the Japanese invasion of China. After the Xi'an rebellion, the Chinese political situation becomes very complex. In Nanjing, China's collaborationist President Wang Jingwei wants to bomb Xi'an, feeling that taking this action will enhance his own political standing. The Chinese Communists send a delegation to Xi'an headed by Zhou Enlai. Their objective is to get Chiang to resist the Japanese and prevent the outbreak of civil war. The Communists persuade Generals Zhang and Yang to sit down and negotiate. Serious three-way negotiations are held involving the CPC representatives, the rebel generals and Chiang's people, which include his wife, Song Meiling. They finally reach a peaceful resolution, with Chiang agreeing to cooperate with the Communists in a united anti-Japanese front. The "Xi'an Incident" was a great turning point in modern Chinese history.

Best Director Cheng Yin, 1982 Golden Rooster Awards.

Best Supporting Actor Sun Feihu, 1982 Golden Rooster Awards.

Best Makeup Wang Xizhong and Li Ende, 1982 Golden Rooster Awards.

2370. *Xi'an Massacre (Xi An Sha Lu)*

1989. Xi'an Film Studio and Hong Kong Changhe Film Company jointly. Color. Letterboxed. 9 Reels. Direction: Zhang Che. Screenplay: Zhang Che. Cinematography: Chen Wancai, Ma Delin. Art Direction: Liu Xinghou. Music: Deng Xiaolin. Cast: Jia Yongquan as Ma Tengyun, Xu Zhijian as Qu Datong, Du Yumin as Tang Zhankui, Dong Zhihua as He Yuanxin, Zhou Long as Fu Tianhao

In Xi'an in 1924, a young woman named Xiao Cui is killed during a holdup by a gangster named Tang Zhankui. It turns out she was the fiancee of Ma Tengyun, Chief of Detectives on the Xi'an police. Ma pretends to assign the case to his deputy He Yuanxin, while he himself secretly allies with underworld figure Qu Datong, hoping that Qu will lead him to Tang, so Ma can have personal vengeance. As the investigation proceeds, He Yuanxin begins to suspect Ma, and a struggle develops between the two detectives. Qu Datong sets its up so that He Yuanxin kills Ma Tengyun, then traps He. But He is able to flee, and kills Qu's brother and father. To protect the legal system, he turns himself in.

2371. *Xian Xinghai (Xian Xing Hai)*

1995. Pearl River Film Company. Color. Letterboxed. Direction and Screenplay: Wang Hengli. Cinematography: Wang Hengli, Huang Xiaoxin, Chang Yu. Art Direction: Zhang Yan. Music: Cheng Dazhao. Cast: Zhang Zhizhong as Xian Xinghai, Hasi Gaowa as Qian Yunling, Xia Heping as Guang Weiran, Hua Mingwei as Zhang Shu

A film biography of Chinese composer Xian Xinghai. Born in Macao in 1905, he goes to France to study music in spite of impoverished circumstances. In France he writes his first great work, "Wings." In 1935, Xian returns to China and devotes himself to writing patriotic songs for the cause of national salvation. He later goes to the Chinese Communist base at Yan'an, where he composes his masterpiece, "Yellow River Chorus." Xian Xinghai dies in Moscow in 1945.

2372. *Xiangma County Administrator (Xiang Ma Xian Zhang)*

1986. Changchun Film Studio. Color. 9 Reels. Direction: Li Hua. Screenplay: Qian Daoyuan. Cinematography: Meng Xiandi. Art Direction: Guo Tingsheng, Liang Xianchuan. Music: Yang Yang. Sound: Liu Xingfu. Cast: Li Xianggang as Zhang Dachuan, Lin Daxing as Wen Siye, Ma Junqing as Yang Bagu, Ren

Weimin as Huang Tianbang, Zhang Fenglai as Director Zhu, Sun Minlan as Juxiang

In 1929, Zhang Dachuan is a "greenwoods bandit" in Sichuan. Wherever he and his band may travel in the province, the local police can never catch them, even when they try. When Zhang brings his band into one particular county, the fearful county administrator takes flight, leaving the county government vacant. At his people's urging, Zhang Dachuan spends some money and buys the title of county administrator for himself. He decides to govern in the people's interests, something hitherto unknown here, and punishes all the local despots. He and his wife decide that while government work is satisfying it is also unprofitable. So they decide to run the county by day and indulge in banditry by night. It all comes to an end when the national government sends troops into Sichuan to suppress all bandits. Zhang's wife is killed, and he is captured and executed.

2373. *Xiangsi Woman's Hotel (Xiang Si Nu Zhi Ke Dian)*

1985. Beijing Film Studio. Color. 10 Reels. Direction: Dong Kena. Screenplay: Ye Dan. Cinematography: Zhang Shiwei. Art Direction: Duan Zhengzhong. Music: Hu Weili. Sound: Ning Menghua, Wang Dawen. Cast: Zhang Xiaolei as Zhang Guanyin, Zhong Xinghuo as Zhao Xing, Liu Yu as Qiao Shanla, Zhang Chao as Qi Nansheng, Wu Dan as Wu Xiang

In the town of Xiansi, in a remote area of south China, the local hotel is reorganized as a part of general reforms. The incompetent former staff is dismissed, and a woman accountant named Zhang Guanyin appointed hotel manager. She institutes a program of customer service and other reform measures, and the hotel becomes the preferred stopping place for drivers passing through Xiansi. But former manager Qiao Shanla and the other dismissed hotel staff band together to make trouble for Zhang. She does have support from others, however, including a man named Qi Nansheng, who she marries. At last, Zhang Guanyin decides the pressures from the network of opposition are not worth it, and with mixed feelings she leaves Xiansi.

2374. *Xiao Hai (Xiao Hai)*

1981. Xiaoxiang Film Studio. Color. 10 Reels. Direction: Duan Bing. Screenplay: Chong Zhejia, Fu Qifeng. Cinematography: Wang Kekuan. Art Direction: Rao Weiquan. Music: Wang Ming. Sound: Yan Ji. Cast: Tong Qingwei as Yue Xiaohai, Zhang Yan as Yue Xiaoyan, Yao Jiwen as Xiao Linzhi, Liu Haibo as Ke Dawei, Wang Zhigang as Yue Shihai, Tang Qun as Xiao Hai's mother

Fifth grade student Yue Xiaohai and his little sister Yue Xiaoyan become very interested in model airplanes. Xiaohai applies himself to learning all he can about airplanes, but his teacher and mother both fear this interest will affect his regular studies, so they give him no encouragement. But Xiaohai's father Yue Shihai supports his son, even saving his own spending money to purchase reference materials for the boy. At last, when Xiaohai's mother sees that Xiaohai's grades are good, that he has not neglected his studies for his hobby, she also gives her support. Through this off campus program, Xiaohai makes many new friends.

2375. *Xiaoer Bulake (Xiao Er Bu La Ke)*

1984. Shanghai Film Studio. Color. Letterboxed. 10 Reels. Direction: Tang Xiaodan, Bao Qicheng. Screenplay: Yang Renshan. Cinematography: Ren Zhixin. Art Direction: Zhang Wanhong, Qin Bosong. Music: Xu Jingxin. Sound: Yang Liangkun. Cast: Zhou Lijing as Li Shiyin, Zhang Weixin as Qiaozhen, Zhu Ling as Ye Juan, Wu Xiqian as Mr. Xu

In 1960, 17-year-old Li Shiyin comes to Xinjiang to seek work. He meets Mr. Xu, an old driver who helps Li find work as a driver as well. At the start of the Cultural Revolution, he marries an educated girl named Qiaozhen. It turns out she already has a lover and married Li Shiyin, an ordinary worker, as that was a way for educated people to avoid political persecution. The kindly Li Shiyin allows her to go off with her lover. Seven years pass, and Li meets Ye Juan, a young mother with a sick child. He helps her get the boy to the hospital, and afterwards learns her story. An educated young woman from Shanghai, she had been sent to Xinjiang during the Cultural Revolution. There she had been sexually harassed and exploited for years by her supervisor, and her son was the result of that humiliating experience. But she has never given up hope. The two find that their unhappy experiences draw them close together, and the two decide to start a new life together.

2376. *Xiaoxue (Xiao Xue)*

1991. Changchun Film Studio. Color. 9 Reels. Letterboxed. Direction: Qi Jian. Screenplay: Qi Jian, Jiang Ling. Cinematography: Zhang Zhongwei, Liu Taitian. Art Direction: Qi Ming. Music: Zhang Weijing. Sound: Luo Huailun, Gu Kejian. Cast: Wang Xueqi as Du Jian, Niu Meng as Xiaoxue, Xiao Xiong as Chi Yuan, Zhu Lin as Ou Lu

Xiaoxue is a little girl who loves to dance. Her teacher in the Children's Palace discovers her dancing talent and enrolls her in dancing classes. But Xiaoxue's father strongly opposes the teacher's decision, because Xiaoxue's mother was a dancer and left for France when her child was very young. Xiao Xue goes to the airport in search of her mother. When her father finds her in the rain, she has passed out. Because of a high fever and exposure, the little girl becomes deaf. Her mother returns from abroad and wants to take her daughter to France for medical treatment. But she is stopped by Xiao Xue's father, who tries every possible means to perk up his daughter's spirits and will to go on. With the care of her father and teachers, Xiao Xue is finally able to perform a joyous dance at the Beijing Children's Dance Competition.

2377. *Xiazai Catches the Thieves (Xia Zai Qing Dao Ji)*

1988. Children's Film Studio. Color. 9 Reels. Direction: Zhang Yuqiang. Screenplay: Lin Xiping. Cinematography: Li Tingshu. Art Direction: Guo Juhai. Music: Mei Hongfu, Jin Min. Sound: Zhen Chunyu. Cast: Long Lan as Xiazai, Peng Yi as Feizai

A teenager named Xiazai leaves his small town and travels to the city, taking with him over 1,000 yuan with which to buy an electronic music instrument. When he arrives, he meets his old friend Feizai and they decide to have lunch together. While they are engrossed in conversation, some thieves steal Xiazai's bag and all his money. The two boys begin a search for the money, and after various adventures recover the bag, only to discover it now contains over 20,000 yuan. They bury the money, then find the thieves are after them, as the bag's contents are all the loot from a series of robberies. The thieves overtake and catch the boys, but they are saved at the last moment by a man called Lao Liu, a PSB detective under cover as a gang member.

2378. *Ximen Area Police Station Story (Xi Men Jing Shi)*

1994. Jiangxi Film Studio, Fujian Film Company Co-production. Color. Letterboxed. 10 Reels. Direction: Huang Jun. Screenplay: Li Mengxue, Huang Jun, Liu Aodong. Cinematography: Yu Xiaojun. Art Direction: Gan Zongrong. Music: Dong Weijie. Sound: Zhang Shubing. Costume: Yao Xiaohong. Makeup: Lu Aihua. Cast: Niu Zhenhua as the director, Huang Siwei as Yang Hua, Zhu Jie as Xia Yun, Yang Haiquan as A Mu, Huang Zongluo as Uncle, Jin Shunzi as Fang Xinxin

A family named Yang is instrumental in the capture and conviction of a criminal, Amu. During his years behind bars, Amu plots his revenge against the family, and upon his release, he starts by killing Yang Hong, husband of Amu's ex-girl friend. The Chief of the Ximen Police Station, An Dong, quickly sees what is going on, and concludes the most likely next victim will be the murdered man's brother Yang Hua. He puts together a plan to protect Yang Hua and trap the killer. But Amu counters by abducting An Dong's pregnant wife Xiao Yun, very close to going into labor. When the police corner Amu with his hostage, An Dong uses his sharpshooting skills to kill the criminal with a single, accurately placed shot.

2379. *The Ximens (Xi Men Jia Zhu)*

1989. Changchun Film Studio. Color. 10 Reels. Letterboxed. Direction: Sun Sha. Screenplay: Du Lijuan. Cinematography: Liu Jiankui. Art Direction: Yang Baocheng. Music: Xu Zhijun. Sound: Yi Wenyu. Cast: Zhang Yechuan as Heijian, Liu Yubin as Ximen Guotai, Qiang Yin as the Wife, Gu Yunping as the Concubine

The Ximen clan is a feudal Chinese family that has held hereditary privileges for many generations. Clan member Ximen Guotai kills his elder brother and sister-in-law and usurps the peerage. Guotai has two sons, Ximen Sen by his wife and Ximen Liu by his concubine. The two brothers bitterly compete for the peerage, with each backed strongly by his mother. The family conflict spreads to the wife and concubine, then to the other family members. Eventually Ximen Guotai and his wife have a falling out, the quarrel takes a tragic turn, and eventually the powerful family sinks further into decline and at last is destroyed by internecine feuding.

2380. *A Xinjiang Boy in Guangzhou (Guang Zhou Lai Le Xin Jiang Wa)*

1994. Pearl River Film Company. Color. Letterboxed. 9 Reels. Direction: Wang Jing. Screenplay: Yu Li, Wu Houxing, Li Yunwei, Jiang Xiaochuan. Cinematography: He Yongjian, Wang Yuandong. Art Direction: Zhao Guoliang, Xier Zhaoti Yakefu. Music: Chen Dazhao. Sound: Feng Lunsheng, Zhu Weijiang. Costume: Liang Shufang. Makeup: Zuo Nannan. Cast: Nabijiang Abududa as A Budu, Zhang Liwei as Situ Jie, Huang Jingshang as Liao Apo, Muyasaier Tuheti as Mother, Zhang Xiaoying as Aunt Lu, Lin Tao as Liao Agong

On a train trip to Guangzhou, six-year-old Uighur boy Abudu becomes separated from his older brother. After arriving, the little boy is picked up by two hoodlums who try to get the child to help them steal. But Abudu is honest, and persists in messing up each theft attempt. In time, an elderly couple take the boy home with them, then write a letter to the local daily newspaper asking for help. Abudu's situation gets a great deal of attention, and at last his mother comes to get him.

2381. *The Xu Family Inheritance Case (Xu Shi Yi Chan An)*

1989. Fujian Film Studio. Color. Letterboxed. 9 Reels. Director: Mi Jiashan. Screenplay: Qi Jian. Cinematography: Zhong Xingzhuo, Wang Shen. Art Direction: Liu Nanyang. Music: Li Lifu. Sound: Mi Wenzhong. Cast: Li Ruping as Yuan Yifang, Chen Maya as Sang Lu, Li Geng as the bold man, Zhang Guoli as Xiang Huan, Zuo Ling as Qiao Ke, Hou Yaohua as Chen Qiushuang

In Hong Kong, trading company executive Yuan Yifang and his female cousin Sang Lu are notified that her father on the mainland has left his considerable fortune to Yuan and Sang jointly. They travel to the mainland to claim it, but both are murdered shortly after they arrive. Investigators find there are really two cases here, separate but related: the murders were committed by underworld figures in the employ of Yuan's boss, company CEO Chen Qiushuang, for reasons unconnected to the inheritance. The latter case is complicated by the arrival from overseas of another woman named Sang, who claims she is the true legatee and that she never had a sister named Sang Lu. In the end, the investigators get it all straightened out, and the inheritance goes to Yuan Yifang's daughter back in Hong Kong.

2382. *Xue Lang (Xue Lang)*

1989. Youth Film Studio. Color. Letterboxed. 9 Reels. Direction: Zhan Xiangchi. Screenplay: Jiang Ao. Cinematography: Zhang Chi. Art Direction: Li Yongxin. Music: Guo Xiaodi. Sound: Wang Dawen. Cast: Hasibageng as Xue Lang, Qinaritu as Badouyan, Gao Baobao as Guoergule

While serving a prison term for horse stealing, Xue Lang rescues some horses belonging to the PLA, so is given an early release. When he returns to his native prairie, his old crony Badouyan asks Xue Lang to join him in rustling once more. Xue Lang refuses, as he wants to make an effort to go straight. The two become enemies after that. Xue Lang starts a search for Guoergule, the girl he loved and longed for while in prison. When he at last locates her, he finds she has become a prostitute, so he leaves. Eventually, he and Badouyan have a showdown in the desert, which neither survives. Guoergule has followed Xue Lang into the desert, and dies with him.

2383. *The Xueqing Horse (Xue Qing Ma)*

1979. Shanghai Film Studio. Color. 9 Reels. Direction: Yu Zhongyin. Screenplay: Meng Haipeng. Cinematography: Lu Junfu. Art Direction: Zhang Wanhong. Music: Yang Mao. Sound: Wang Huimin. Cast: Nabijian as the strange man, Ye Zhikang as Geng Liancheng, Huerxide as Ayixia, Muhataer as Aibaidula, Walimula as the father, Mayila as the mother, Ma Minyi as the regimental commander, Mulanlifu as Bayijian

Shortly after the liberation of Tibet, a PLA cavalry unit pursuing bandits comes to a village called Aiershang. A strange person interferes with their activities. The unit's chief investigator Geng Liancheng finds that the man is called Yeerha Nati. Five years before, a Chinese businessman gave him a pony, which in a few years grew up to the famous "Xueqing" horse, winner of many races. This so angers local herd owner Bayijian that he forces Yeerha Nati to leave his hometown and move to Aiershang. Yeerha Nati's lover Ayixia is then abducted by Bayijian and his parents are killed. Yeerha Nati's attempt at revenge fails, and he is wounded. He offers to lead the PLA to the bandits' headquarters and the regimental commander orders Geng to follow this strange man. In the battle, Yeerha kills Bayijian, but the herd owner first kills the Xueqing horse. Yeerha Nati is very upset about it, as is the regimental commander: it turns out he was the Chinese businessman who had stayed at the home of Yeerha Nati's parents five years earlier and had sent him the pony as a gift. Yeerha joins the PLA, and Ayixia sees him off.

2384. *Xumao and His Daughters (Xu Mao He Ta De Nu Er Men)*

1981. Beijing Film Studio. Color. 10 Reels. Direction: Wang Yan. Screenplay: Wang Yan, based on the novel by Zhou Keqin (1936–). Cinematography: Zou Jixun. Art Direction: Chen Yiyun, Kang Ling. Music: Xiang Yi. Sound: Lan Fuan. Cast: Li Xiuming as Xu Xiuyun, Zhang Jinling as Qiuyun, Li Wei as Xu Mao, Lu Guilan as Yan Shaochun, Yang Zhaibao as Jin Dongshui, Zhang Lianwen as Zhen Bairu

In west Sichuan province in the winter of 1975, Xu Xiuyun, divorced fourth daughter of elderly Xu Mao, refuses the marriage arranged for her by her third sister Qiuyun, and chooses not to remarry. Xiuyun is the loving adoptive mother of her deceased eldest sister's child, and out of concern for the eldest sister's husband Jin Dongshui helps care for him as well. When the country assigns a work team under Yan Shaochun to help rebuild the village, it brings the local people their first real hope of stability and economic prosperity. Zhen Bairu, the production team's deputy Party Secretary and Xiuyun's ex-husband, had divorced her because he thought it would further his career to be free of her. Now, when he senses a change in the political atmosphere, Zhen rushes to see Xu Mao to petition for remarriage to Xiuyun but she ignores and refuses him. So Zhen Bairu begins spreading rumors that Xu Xiuyun and Jin Dongshui are having an illicit affair. So many people, including her father and the work team, misunderstand her relationship with Jin Dongshui that Xiuyun attempts suicide. Jin Dongshui saves her, however, and gives her renewed confidence and courage about her life. After investigating the matter, Yan Shaochun fires Zhen Bairu and restores Jin Dongshui to his position as production team Party Secretary. With Yan Shaochun's help, Xu Mao finally agrees to Xu Xiuyun marrying Jin Dongshui. However, the "attack the rightist wind" political campaign soon begins, and the work team is forced to withdraw from the village. Zhen Bairu starts a new rise to power. As Yan Shaochun leaves, Xu Xiuyun tells him that after this she will fear nothing, but will work to win a bright future for the people of her village.

Best Actress Li Xiuming, 1982 Golden Rooster Awards.
Best Actress Li Xiuming, 1982 Hundred Flowers Awards.
Best Cinematographer Zou Jixun, 1982 Golden Rooster Awards.

2385. *Xumao and His Daughters (Xu Mao He Ta De Nu Er Men)*

1981. August First Film Studio. Color. 9 Reels. Direction: Li Jun. Screenplay: Zhou Keqin, Xiao Mu, based on Zhou's novel. Cinematography: Yang Guangyuan. Art Direction: Zhen Minzhe. Music: Yan Ke. Sound: Li Jian. Cast: Jia Liu as Xu Mao, Tian Hua as Yan Shaochun, Wang Fuli as Fourth Daughter, Zhou Hong as Seventh Daughter, Zhao Na as Ninth Daughter, Xu Guangmin as Zhen Bairu

An old man named Xu Mao has led a life of almost constant sorrow. After his wife dies. leaving him a middle-aged man with nine daughters, the Cultural Revolution brings a series of disasters which follow the family like a curse. His fourth daughter is carried off and forced to marry a man named Zhen Bairu, and although she is able to divorce him a few years later, father and daughter both suffer severe emotional and psychological damage. The eldest daughter dies after her husband is falsely accused and taken away. When a work team comes to the village, its head Yan Shaochun sees the cold feelings the village people have for the Party. She investigates the cause of this hostility and finds that all have suffered, though none so much as Xu Mao. The work team sets about helping people like Xu Mao regain their will to go on, and he in turn gains confidence from the people. When the political atmosphere changes, the team has to leave, but the village people sincerely hope they will return someday.

2386. *Yamaha Fish Stall (Ya Ma Ha Yu Dang)*

1984. Pearl River Film Studio. Color. Letterboxed. 10 Reels. Direction: Zhang Liang. Screenplay: Zhang Yiwu, Huang Jinghong. Cinematography: Han Xingyuan, Wang Hengli. Art Direction: Zhang Zhichu. Music: Chen Qixiong. Sound: Lin Guoqinag. Cast: Zhang Tianxi as A Long, Xu Ruiping as Kui Mei, Yang Liyi as Zhuzhu, Li Zhiqiang as Haizi, Huang Mianshang as Mother, Shi Jian as Uncle Kui

When young A Long is released from a reformatory, he wants to go straight. With money borrowed from friends, A Long, his girl friend Zhuzhu and best friend Haizi start a fish shop. But A Long's caring only for money leads to the business's failure and the breakup of the three friends' relationship. Neighborhood Association leader Kui Mei helps A Long see his mistakes, and come to realize money is not enough, one must strive to be a good person as well. He reconciles with Zhuzhu, and they decide to give business another try.

Best Art Direction Zhang Zhichu, 1985 Golden Rooster Awards.

2387. *The Yan'an Guerrilla Troop (Yan'an You Ji Dui)*

1961. Xi'an Film Studio. B & W. 10 Reels. Direction: Jiang Yingzong. Screenplay: Collective, recorded by Zhong Jiming. Cinematography: Cao Jinshan. Art Direction: Zhang Jingnan. Music: Xu Youfu. Sound: Hong Jiahui. Cast: Zheng Danian as Secretary Zhou, Yi Donglin as Troop Director Chen, Li Shirong as Deputy Director Yang, Cheng Senlin as Cao Wenhu, Cheng Yi as Zhao Degui, Sun Xuewen as Xiao Liu

In 1947, a Nationalist general launches a major attack on the Shanganning liberated area, forcing the PLA to retreat. After the withdrawal the people of Yan'an organize a guerrilla band to harass the enemy. One of their guerrilla actions was to capture the airplane delivering food supplies to the Nationalist force. This results in a Nationalist move to seize the local farmers' fall harvest, but the guerrillas foil the attempt.

2388. *The Yang Clan's Woman Commander (Yang Men Niu Jiang)*

1960. Beijing Film Studio. Color. 15 Reels. Direction: Cui Wei, Chen Huaikai. Screenplay: Fan Junhong and Lu Ruimin. Cinematography: Nie Jing. Art Direction: Qing Wei. Sound: Chen Yanxi. Cast: Wang Jinghua as Grand Master Yu, Yang Qiuling as Mu Guiying, Liang Youlian as Yang Wenguang, Guo Jinghua as Qi Niang, Wang Wangshu as Master Cai, Yang Suqing as Da Niang

During the Northern Song Dynasty (960–1127), the Kingdom of Western Xia invades China and in the ensuing battle, Song commander Yang Zongbao is killed. Grand Master Yu at the age of 100 leads the Yang clan's women soldiers to the border to resist the enemy and protect the country. Yang Zongbao's son Yang Wenguang accompanies them despite his youth and his being the sole surviving child of his family. The Yang army is finally victorious.

2389. *The Yang Family's Generals (Yang Jia Jiang)*

1984. Henan Provincial Performance Company & Hong Kong Nanhai Company Co-Production. Color. 10 Reels. Direction: Chen Zuo. Screenplay: Qun Li. Cinematography: Yang Jun. Art Direction: Zhang Xiujiang, Zhao Guichun. Music: Wang Jixiao, An Zhiyu. Cast: Nie Jianguo as Yang Wulang, Xu Qinxiang as Yeluqi

In a bloody battle between the armies of the Song and Liao, the Song troops fight bravely under their leader General Yang Wulang. But his superior, General Pan Renmei, betrays the Song troops by ordering a withdrawal that would put them in a very unfavorable position. General Yang Ye disobeys and encourages his troops to carry on and fight to the last man. For this, Pan Renmei conspires to betray Yang Ye. His troops surround Yang Ye at the Suwu Temple, where Yang commits suicide. Yang Wulang continues fighting, and at last he stabilizes the border and catches Pan Renmei.

2390. *Yang Guifei (Yang Gui Fei)*

1992. Guangxi Film Studio. Color. Letterboxed. 15 Reels. Direction: Chen Jialin. Screenplay: Bai Hua, Tian Qin, Zhang Xian and Guohong Weixiong (Japan). Art Direction: Jin Xiwu, Lu Qi and Zhao Jun. Music: Wang Xian, Yao Shengchang. Sound: Liu Shida. Costume: Li Jianqun. Makeup: Yang Shudong, Jiang Xiaoqun. Cast: Zhou Jie as Yang Yuhuan, Zhang Ying as Yang Yuhuan as a child, Liu Wenzhi as Emperor Xuan Zong, Li Ruping as Gao Lishi, Pu Chunxi as Shouwang Mao, Li Jianqun as Wu Huifei, Chen Yunru as Zhang Liangying, Lin Daxing as Zhongwang Heng, Cheng Wenkuan as Yang Guozhong

During the reign of the Tang Emperor Xuan Zong, young and beautiful Yang Yuhuan is married to the emperor's son, Prince Mao. When the empress dies, Xuan Zong gives Yuhuan the title of Princess and takes her for himself. Yang Yuhuan and Xuan Zong love each other very much, and he soon promotes all her relatives. In 755, General An Lushan, commander of the emperor's border forces, starts a rebellion which is disastrous for China. Xuanzong takes Yang Yuhuan and the rest of his entourage and flees the capital. Later, honest General Chen Xuanli discusses the situation with the emperor's son Li Heng, and they agree that Yang Yuhuan's brother Yang Guozhong must die, as he has been in league with the rebels. His death creates a perilous situation for them, so they decide Yang Yuhuan must die as well. Yang Yuhuan realizes she cannot avoid her fate, so she tells the now 72-year-old Emperor Xuan Zong he must go on without her, after which she commits suicide.

Best Art Direction Jin Xiwu, Lu Qi and Zhao Jun, 1993 Golden Rooster Awards.

Best Costume Li Jianqun, 1993 Golden Rooster Awards.

Best Picture, 1993 Hundred Flowers Awards.

2391. *Yang Kaihui (Yang Kai Hui)*

1995. Beijing Film Studio. Color. Letterboxed. Direction: Qin Zhiyu. Screenplay: Zhang Xuan, Qin Zhiyu. Cinematography: Tu Jiakuan, Ru Shuiren. Art Direction: Ma Gaiwa. Music: Ma Ding. Cast: Chang Yuan as Yang Kaihui, Wang Ying

Yang Kaihui was Mao Zedong's first wife, a revolutionary and Communist Party member who was killed by the Nationalist police in October, 1930. Kaihui, daughter of Mao's teacher Yang Cangji, first meets the young revolutionary when she is just 14. Later, in Beijing, she and Mao fall in love, and he influences her to join the revolution. After Chiang Kaishek turns on the Communists, Yang Kaihui is arrested. She rejects a government offer of clemency in exchange for a public denunciation of Mao, and is executed at the age of 29, leaving her husband and three young sons.

2392. *Yanzhi (Yan Zhi)*

1980. Zhejiang Film Studio. Color. Wide Screen. 10 Reels. Direction: Wu Peirong, Jin Shan. Screenplay: Shuang Ge, Wei Er. Cinematography: Zhou Rongzheng. Cast: Zhu Biyun as Yanzhi, Xia Jiangnan as Er Qiuji, Zhang Zhimin as Wu Nandai, Ping Fan

In the town of Dongcang, veterinarian Bian Shan's beautiful daughter Yanzhi is in love with scholar Er Qiuji but her father opposes the relationship. One morning, Bian Shan is found murdered, one of his daughter's embroidered shoes clutched in his hand. Dongcang magistrate Zhang Hong jails the young lovers for the murder, but two of Er

Qiuji's friends, Shu Jie and Wu Nandai, petition the court to investigate the case further. The case is given to a new magistrate, but he concludes that Shu Jie is the murderer. He releases Er Qiuji and Yanzhi and sentences Shu Jie to death. The case is at last resolved by Zhang Hong's old mentor Yu Shan; assisted by Wu Nandai, he finds out the real killer is the playboy Mao Da. Er Qiuji and Yanzhi, Shu Jie and his lover Wang Chunlan, are now all cleared and able to marry.

2393. *Yaya (Ya Ya)*

1979. Changchun Film Studio. Color. 12 Reels. Direction: Sun Yu. Screenplay: Liu Ke. Cinematography: Meng Xiandi, Han Dongxia. Art Direction: Liu Jinnai, Liang Shukui. Music: Si Wanchun, Zhou Minde. Sound: Kang Ruixin. Cast: Song Xiaoyin as Yaya (mother and grown daughter), Gu Duo as Yaya (as a child), Ruan Fujiang as Luosang, Zhang Lun as Gabo, Pubuchiren as Suolangwangdui, Dunzhupingchuo as the old man, Qiongda as Tudeng

In 1935, in a serf owner's manor in Tibet, Tibetan girl Yaya is in love with Luosang, a young carpenter. When the two marry, the Master Gabo drives Luosang from the manor. The following year, Yaya gives birth to a daughter, but Luosang disappears, and Yaya never sees him again. Yaya dies. Fifteen years later, Luosang, now a PLA deputy divisional commander, leads an army into Tibet. He learns of his wife's death, and that their daughter, age four at the time, had been sold to a tribe called the Jimi, who had renamed the girl Yaya. He learns that Yaya now runs a military supply depot. Gabo, now the head of an anti-Communist rebel force, tries to destroy the depot, but Yaya leads a brigade of liberated serfs to resist Gabo's forces. With help from the PLA, Yaya's force puts down the rebellion. Yaya is at last reunited with her father Luosang.

2394. *Ye Hena (Ye He Na)*

1982. Kunming Film Studio. Color. Letterboxed. 10 Reels. Direction: Chen Zhenghong. Screenplay: Luo Shui, Li Junlong. Cinematography: Liao Jiaxiang. Art Direction: Li Zhengxin, Xu Kaicheng. Music: Jin Fuzhai. Sound: Jia Xianjie. Cast: Di Xiaohui as Ye Hena, Chen Jianfei as Lu Nanping, Lu Xiaohe as Aiga, Liu Xin as Aibo Leke

In the Washan Mountain region along China's southwest border, a PLA soldier is killed rescuing a Wa nationality orphan girl named Ye Hena. Years later, the soldier's son Lu Nanping is assigned to the region as part of the border patrol and is warmly welcomed by the local people, who still remember his father's sacrifice. Ye Hena has become an enthusiast for the region's construction. The elderly commune director introduces them, hoping they will someday marry. But the Cultural Revolution intervenes, Lu Nanping is falsely accused, and Ye Hena is persecuted. She flees into the mountains to get away from the political attacks on her. Commune director's son Aiga secretly helps and protects her while she is in hiding, and the two of them build up a strong mutual affection during this time. Aiga is later attacked by gangsters who abduct him across the border to work for them. After the 3rd Plenary Session of the 11th Party Congress, Lu Nanping and Ye Hena are able to return to the area, and the local people resume their hope the two will at last get together. Aiga is sent back by the foreign gangsters to detect the situation there, and he meets with Ye Hena, now part of the anti-gangster civil guard. She persuades Aiga to return and help rebuild the country. Ye Hena and Aiga are reunited.

2395. *Ye Jianying in Guangzhou (Chi Zha Pu Zhou Ye Jian Ying)*

1994. Guangxi Film Studio. Color. Letterboxed. 10 Reels. Direction: Xiao Lang, Qiu Lili. Screenplay: Zhang Yiping. Cinematography: Ru Shuiren, Ning Jiakun. Art Direction: Chen Xiaoxia, Zhang Wenqi. Music: Zou Ye. Sound: Wang Yunhua. Costume: Yang Yuling, Li Xiuming. Makeup: Guan Jun, Zhang Rong. Cast: Chen Rui as Ye Jianying (as a youth), Zhang Yunli as Ye Jianying (as an old man), Mao Haitong as Lin Cui, Huang Guoqiang as Zhen Jiesheng, Liu Peiqi as Huang Ying, Jiang Gengcheng as Zhang Xueling

Biographical film about the early revolutionary activities of Ye Jianying, a Communist Party organizer in the Puzhou area of Guangzhou Province in the early 1920s.

2396. *Yellow Earth (Huang Tu Di)*

1984. Guangxi Film Studio. Color. 10 Reels. Direction: Chen Kaige. Screenplay: Zhang Zhiliang. Cinematography: Zhang Yimou. Art Direction: He Qun. Music: Zhao Jiping. Sound: Lin Lin. Costume: Tian Geng, Chen Bona. Makeup: He Hong. Cast: Wang Xueyin as Gu Qing, Xue

Bai as Cui Qiao, Tan Wang as Father, Liu Qiang as the Younger Brother

In 1939, Eighth Route Army soldier Gu Qing comes to a village in northern Shaanxi province to collect folk songs for the army to possibly adapt for campaign songs. He stays with one of the poorest families in the village, consisting of a widower, his 12-year-old daughter and son. Gu Qing helps them in the fields and they teach him songs. He tells them stories of the revolution, and how the women in the army are taught to read and can marry who they choose. This especially appeals to the daughter, Cui Qiao, who fears she will meet the same fate of so many young village girls, the overworked and abused wives of much older men. Her worst fears are realized when she turns 13 and her father betroths her to marry a middle-aged man. When the soldier leaves, she asks him to take her with him to Yan'an, without telling him about her scheduled marriage. Gu Qing has to decline her request, saying it would be against regulations. He promises to make application for her, however, and to return in the spring. She is married to the older man, but then decides to leave and join the army herself. She apparently drowns while crossing the Yellow River. The following spring, the soldier returns to the village and finds all the male residents conducting a rain dance, doing things as they have always been done.

Best Cinematography Zhang Yimou, 1985 Golden Rooster Awards.

2397. *Yellow Flowers on the Battlefield (Zhan Di Huang Hua)*

1977. Beijing Film Studio. Color. 10 Reels. Direction: Ma Erlu. Screenplay: Dunde Sier and Zhang Changgong. Cinematography: Sun Cangyi. Art Direction: Chen Zhaomin. Music: Moer Jihu, Tuli Guer. Sound: Sun Yumin, Wang Jinxiang. Cast: Siqin Bilige as Maxi Batu, Sharen Gaowa as Shandan, Si Qing as Wuren Saihan, Tai Heping as Li Yong, De Geji as Mai Lisu, Gao Linghua as Zhao Jing, An Zhenzheng as Qi Shuhong

In 1959, in a commune in Inner Mongolia, a dispute erupts over control of local art, and the direction it should take. Qi Shuhong, a policeman in the old society with a new identity as a veteran artist, advocates a reactionary approach, and does succeed in persuading some people. He is opposed, successfully, by young Maxi Batu, a performer in the Wulan

Muqi Acting Trouple. In the end, the Wulan Muqi troupe is singled out for praise by Chairman Mao and Premier Zhou, and the troupe becomes a model for acting troupes throughout China.

2398. *Yellow Ghosts at Night (Ye Mu Xia De Huang Se You Ling)*

1989. Shanghai Film Studio. Color. Letterboxed. 10 Reels. Direction: Da Sibiao. Screenplay: Zhao Zhiqiang, Hu Huiying. Cinematography: Cheng Shiyu. Art Direction: Dong Chongxiang. Music: Liu Yanxi. Sound: Gong Dejun. Cast: Shen Ming as Ouyang Mei, Qi Minyuan as Gu Wenbing, Duan Shiping as Dali, Tan Yang as Pan Jianping, Xia Jun as Lanling

To smash the growing traffic in illegal pornographic videos, the PSB assigns female officer Ouyang Mei to undercover work at the major hotel which is a focus of the activity. She and a fellow officer infiltrate and smash the pornography ring. A subplot deals with the fate of Dali, a young girl enticed into prostitution by watching too many pornographic movies. When she learns she has contracted venereal disease, she burns herself to death.

2399. *Yellow House (Huang Se Bie Shu)*

1987. Inner Mongolia Film Studio. Color. Letterboxed. 9 Reels. Direction: Chen Da, Qin Wubo. Screenplay: Lu Zhirong. Cinematography: Du Rong, Ge Lisheng. Art Direction: Tong Yonggang. Music: Chulun Buhe. Sound: Buren Bayaer. Cast: Liao Xueqiu as Yu Ping, Zhang Shan as Hubitai, Baoyin Hexige as Zhao Lu, Naren Gaowa as Narisha, Pan Hexiang as Sha Zhou, Pan Ying as A Runa, Yu Lesi as Bateer

In the vast grazing area along the Chinese-Mongolian border, a young girl named Yu Ping escapes from a labor reform camp and hides in a Russian-style old wooden house. The owner, Hubitai, gives her sanctuary as an act of kindness. But little things start to arouse his suspicions of Yu Ping. It turns out that Yu Ping has lost all her relatives except her son Jingjing, who was given to someone else to raise when his mother was sent to the camp. Yu Ping has lost all her confidence in life, and now she just wants to see her son one last time. Eventually, Yu Ping gets to see her son, now adopted by Hubitai's good friend Zhaolu and his wife. After she has seen him, the police arrive to take Yu Ping away.

2400. *Yellow River Teenager (Huang He Shao Nian)*

1975. Changchun Film Studio. Color. 9 Reels. Direction: Lu Jianhua, Li Guanghui. Screenplay: Yan Yi. Cinematography: Li Guanghui, Xu Shouzen. Art Direction: Li Wenguang, Dong Ping. Music: Chang Sumin, Zhang Chun. Cast: Liu Jizhong as Zhao Zhiyan, Li Junhai as Zhang Ge, Shi Kefu as Chen Yongtao, Ma Ren as Liu Quan, Cheng Mei as Liu Ni, Sui Guifeng as Liu's wife

During the anti–Japanese resistance, teenager Zhao Zhiyan joins an anti–Japanese guerrilla troop, and is assigned duty as a courier and as a guard of the troop's children. When the Chinese plan to attack an enemy force in a nearby town, Zhao is given the mission of delivering relevant letters to the head of the guerrilla troop. On the way, Zhao is arrested by the enemy. But he does not panic, escapes, and accomplishes his mission with the help of various others he meets along the way. When the battle begins, Zhao successfully coordinates the guerrillas' actions from within the town.

2401. *The Yellow River Turns Around Here (Huang He Zai Zhe Li Guai Le Ge Wan)*

1986. Xi'an Film Studio. Color. 10 Reels. Direction: Jin Yin. Screenplay: Tian Dongzhao, Luo Xianbao. Cinematography: Zhao Haifu, Nie Tiemao. Art Direction: Liu Xinghou. Music: Zhao Jiping. Sound: Che Zhiyuan. Cast: Feng Enhe as Zhao Da, Yang Xiaojun as Goudan, Huang Ailing as Qingqing, Wu Qianqian as Shen Yulan, Wang Xiangrong as Shuangxi, Cai Hongxiang as the lame man

In 1969 at a place near the Yellow River, poor farmer Zhao Da is still single at the age of 30. He loves Goudan, a kind and pretty girl from a neighboring village, but Cultural Revolution persecution drives her to suicide. To satisfy his mother's wishes, Zhao Da agrees to be "married" to a young girl who had just died. Later, his love life seems to be picking up when he meets a woman named Yu Lan. They agree to marry, but then he learns she is the natural mother of the dead girl he "married" earlier. Zhao Da does not know what to do...

2402. *Yellow Sand and Green Waves (Huang Sha Lu Lang)*

1965. Haiyan Film Studio. Color. 12 Reels.

Direction: Jiang Yusheng. Screenplay: Wang Yuhu. Cinematography: Luo Chongzhou. Art Direction: Hu Zhuoyun. Music: Gao Tian, Kuerban Yibulayin. Sound: Chen Jingrong. Cast: Ailiman Abudula as Botamuhan, Maimaiti Xielipu as Hasimu, Tuerxun Tuohuti as Mushayaxing, Abudu Reheman as Halike, Younusi Abiti as Hashan director, Niyazi Muming as Saiyiti

In Xinjiang, Botamuhan, the deputy director of an agricultural commune is enthusiastic about planting wheat in some nearby undeveloped land. He is opposed by commune director Hasimu, who wants to put their resources into by-product production, which is more profitable. But Botamuhan pushes ahead and plants the wheat. Eventually he is proven correct in the matter.

2403. *Yimeng Mountain People (Yi Meng Shan Ren)*

1992. Shanghai Film Studio. Color. Letterboxed. Stereo. 10 Reels. Direction: Zhao Huanzhang. Screenplay: Fang Yihua. Cinematography: Can Lianguo. Art Direction: Shen Lide. Music: Yang Shaolu. Cast: Nai She as Wei Chunhou, Zhang Zhihua as Song Qinlan, Chen Yude as Yang Jingcai, Dai Zhaoan as Zhang Dahan, Wang Qin as Wei Chunfang, Zhu Ming as Xu Dashan

The area around Yimeng Mountain, at one time a major revolutionary region, is still quite poor. Newly installed Party Secretary Wei Chunhou proposes building a power line and a road to make the area more productive and raise the people's income. Most of the people in the area respond enthusiastically although a few traditionalists are negative. Wei puts himself squarely in the middle of the controversy by putting up his own money to get the project under way. In the end, the people move forward to prosperity.

2404. *You Are Not 16 (Ni Mei You Shi Liu Sui)*

1994. Emei Film Studio. Color. Letterboxed. 9 Reels. Direction: Mi Jiashan. Screenplay: Miao Yue. Cinematography: Zhong Xingzuo. Art Direction: Zhang Guojun. Music: Li Lifu. Sound: Li Jian. Costume: Liu Huifang. Makeup: Yang Maorong. Cast: Mao Qi as Yang Wande, Gong Peibi as A Li, Lin Guoqi as Cai Youhe, Zhang Guoli as teacher Xiao Lin, Xu Wendun as Chen Jinfa, Zhang Ruyu as Cai Xiaomei, Mou Yi as A Hui

A heavy rain causes the roof to collapse on a middle school classroom, and several students are killed. School principal Yang Wande is blamed, and beaten by the children's parents. Everything in the school is in a state of disrepair or inoperable, but this is in an impoverished area, and there is no money. Yang quietly bears the criticism, but does all he can to get the school reopened and get all the students to come back. But many students have quit to go to work, and there are only about 300 of them left. The film ends on a hopeful note as one bright and capable girl student passes up her chance to move to Hong Kong in order to stay on and teach younger children.

2405. *Young Couples (Yuan Yang Lou)*

1987. Youth Film Studio. Color. 14 Reels. Direction: Zhen Dongtian. Screenplay: Wang Peigong. Cinematography: Gu Wenkai, Qu Jianwei. Art Direction: Liu Ying. Sound: Zhang Ruikun, Li Bojiang. Cast: Tian Shaojun and Ji Ling as the first couple, He Wei and Fang Hui as the second couple, Guo Kaimin and Song Chunli as the third couple, Zhao Yue and Liu Jian as the fourth couple, Song Xiaoying and Zhao Fuyu as the fifth couple, Xiao Xiong and Liu Xingye as the sixth couple, Guo Xuxin as the building caretaker, Zhao Jing as the girl

New things emerge systematically in the urban modernization process. In Beijing, an apartment building is constructed specifically for young newlyweds. Local residents affectionately call it the "love nest." The film tells the stories of six different young couples living in the building, a worker couple, a graduate student couple, two artists, etc., from their romances and weddings, through their marital problems and family life.

2406. *Young Erhei's Marriage (Xiao Erhei Jiehun)*

1964. Beijing Film Studio. B & W. 9 Reels. Direction: Gan Xuewei, Shi Yifu. Screenplay: Gan Xuewei and Shi Yifu, based on the novel of the same title by Zhao Shuli (1905?–). Cinematography: Meng Qinpeng. Art Direction: Chi Ning, Xiao Bing. Music: Qiao Gu. Sound: Lu Xiancang. Cast: Yu Ping as Xiao Qing, Yang Jianye as Young Erhei, Zhao Zhiyue as Er Zhuge, Zhou Ting as San Xiangu, Ge Chunzhuang as Jin Wang, Guo Jun as Yu Fu, Li Baifang as the district director, Yu Zhaokang as the village head

During World War II, in a recently liberated village in Shanxi, militia commander

Erhei and women's auxiliary member Xiao Qing fall in love and want to marry. Erhei's father Er Zhuge, a very superstitious man, objects because he believes the two have mismatched fortunes. Others, including the village military committee director Jin Wang and his brother, object to the relationship because they worry about the effect it might have on village political power. Some villagers make personal attacks on Erhei, and some traditionalists, including her mother, criticize Xiao Qing for wanting to choose her own spouse. However, the village director is able to stop all these attacks. With his support, Erhei investigates some strange circumstances and finds evidence of criminal activities by the Jin brothers. He is finally able to convince the district director of the brothers' crimes, and they are arrested. The district director then convinces Er Zhuge and Xiao Qing's mother San Xiangu that the two lovers should be allowed to marry of their own free will.

2407. *Young Friends (Nian Qing De Peng You)*

1981. Emei Film Studio. B & W. 10 Reels. Direction: Jia Mu, Zhang Xihe. Screenplay: Yang Yinzhang, Qian Daoyuan, Jia Mu, Liu Zhigang. Cinematography: Li Dagui, Zhang Huaming. Art Direction: Xie Huibing. Music: Tian Feng. Sound: Zhang Jianping, Peng Wenguang. Cast: Zhou Lijin as Zhen Bing, Fang Shu as Zhao Zhengzheng, Wang Wei as Zhao Lili, Zhu Xiaoming as Ma Lin, Su Guiming as Liu Xiaojia, Zhang Tielin as He Jianwu

In the spring of 1979, war erupts on the Sino-Vietnamese border. When transportation platoon leader Zhen Bing goes to a local hospital to say goodbye to his fiancee, Doctor Zhao Lili, the two argue about his volunteering to leave her and join the conflict, so Zhen Bing goes to the front with an uneasy mind. At the front, Zhen Bing unexpectedly meets her sister Zhao Zhenzhen, an army medic. The two lose many of their comrades in the fighting, nurse Liu Xiaojie, truck driver He Jianwu and others. Zhen Bing suppresses the pain of losing friends and the pain of his love life, and devotes himself to the fighting. As the war progresses, Zhao Zhenzhen finds her admiration and affection for him growing, and she writes many letters to her sister describing the man she has come to love. When the war ends, the Chinese border army returns, and Zhao Zhenzhen happily meets her sister Zhao Lili.

When Zhao Lili realizes the man her sister loves is Zhen Bing, she is very ashamed of herself. Zhao Lili realizes she has been selfish and decides to join a medical team on the border. Zhao Zhenzhen returns home and learns that Zhen Bing is the man her sister had hurt earlier. She goes to find Zhen Bing, but he has left to visit his lost comrade He Jianwu's mother in North China.

2408. *Young Huang Feihong (Yi Xia Huang Fei Hong) (orig. title: Shao Nian Huang Fei Hong)*

1992. Shanghai Film Studio and Hong Kong Yingfeng Film Company Co-Production. Color. Letterboxed. 9 Reels. Direction: Li Zhao. Screenplay: Situ An, Huang Shoukang, Li Zhao. Cinematography: Yang Geliang. Art Direction: Xu Songlin. Music: Cheng Jingrong. Costume: Zhang Jufang, Zhang Xuelin. Makeup: Wang Zhengrong. Cast: Qian Jiale as Huang Feihong (Cantonese: Wong Fei Hung), Lin Zhengyin as Shibingwei, Wu Xueen as Yingzi, Sun Guoming as Hatieer, Huang Shaopeng as Huang Lingying

In the mid–19th century, kung fu master Huang Lingying is admired and respected by the people of Guangzhou, who he has helped many times. More than a decade before, Huang had run a certain Japanese out of town, and now the man has returned seeking revenge. When the Japanese finds that his adversary has died during his absence, he challenges Huang's son Huang Feihong instead. But the challenger's sister has fallen for Huang Feihong and tries to intercede, fearing someone will be seriously hurt or killed. At last, the two men meet and fight. Huang is the winner, and teaches the Japanese a lesson in the process. The defeated man thinks things over and decides to become a monk.

2409. *Young Man Lu Ban (Qing Nian Lu Ban)*

1964. Beijing Film Studio. B & W. 9 Reels. Direction: Shi Daqian. Screenplay: Shi Daqian. Cinematography: Yu Zhengyu, Xu Xiaoxian. Art Direction: Zhang Xiande. Music: Su Ming. Sound: Liu Shida. Cast: Bi Jiancang as Li Shanbei, Li Changle as Qin Shuzhen, Wang Ban as Master Worker Gao, Zhang Zhang as technician Han, Zhang Ying as Secretary Chen, Fang Hui as Director Liu

Young construction worker Li Shanbei has a poor background, and very little education.

He meets Qiu Shuzhen, a young woman technician recently graduated from college. She looks down upon him at first, thinking him stupid. But when she learns of his difficult past, she is impressed by his ambition and intelligence, and helps Shanbei study. The two become friends and gradually fall in love. After three years, Shanbei significantly improves his educational level, and successfully revises a backward process at his work.

2410. *Young Masters of the Great Leap Forward (Da Yue Jin Zhong De Xiao Zhu Ren)*

1958. Tianma Film Studio. B & W. 3 Reels. Four stories of young people involved in the Great Leap Forward campaign of the late fifties:

"Service" (Fuwu). Direction: Xie Jin. Screenplay: Qing Yi. Cinematography: Luo Jizhi. During the campaign, members of the Young Pioneers do volunteer work in a book store. They take care of customers from everywhere, recommend new books to customers, and lend umbrellas to customers when it rains.

"The Little Weather Station" (Xiao Qi Xiang Tai). Direction: Xie Jin. Screenplay: Ding Ran. Cinematography: Luo Jizhi. Science-loving youngsters establish a meteorology study group and set up a small weather forecasting station to report weather conditions to their classmates. They are wrong a few times and are criticized for it by their friends. But they do not give up, for they know they are doing meaningful work in support of the agricultural Great Leap Forward.

"Cultural Pioneers" (Wen Hua Xian Feng). Direction: Yang Xiaozong. Screenplay: Yin Zhi. Cinematography: Peng Engli. Children in a suburban area zealously join in the work of the campaign by tackling illiteracy in the countryside. In just eight days they teach more than 800 illiterates to read.

"Teenage Factory" (Shao Nian Gong Chang). Direction: Zhang Tianci. Cinematography: Lu Junfu. During the busy planting season, seven high school students build a fertilizer plant to help resolve a fertilizer shortage. They help a farm commune get over its major difficulty and are praised by the commune director.

2411. *Young Master's Suffering Experience (Shao Ye De Mo Nan)*

1987. Shanghai Film Studio. Color. 14 Reels.

Direction: Wu Gongyi, Zhang Jianya. Screenplay: Ai Minzhi, Siminshan, Hansi Xiaogete. Cinematography: Xia Lixing. Art Direction: Qiu Yuan. Music: Ju Xiaosong. Sound: Feng Deyao. Cast: Chen Peisi as Jin Fu, Zhao Jialing as Lianhua, Li Wei as Wang Zhe, Luerfu Hubo as Weilian

In Shanghai in the 1920s, Jin Chun'ao dies, stipulating in his will that his playboy son Jin Fu should marry his fiancee Lianhua as soon as possible, and if this is done the couple will inherit a fortune the old man has deposited in a California bank. Shortly after this, a letter comes from America informing them that the bank in California has closed, and the fortune is lost. Jin Fu declares bankruptcy. In order to help her lover, Lianhua gives him a sum of money she borrows using her house as collateral. Jin Fu is so moved by this that he decides to do something for her. He uses the money to take out a large life insurance policy on himself, naming Lianhua as beneficiary; his plan is to commit suicide, so she will be rich. The movie follows his comically unsuccessful attempts to kill himself, some thwarted by his own bungling, some by intervention from the insurance company, which suspects what he plans to do. At last Lianhua convinces Jin Fu he will be better off starting a new life with her.

2412. *Young Men's Story (Ge Men Zhe Teng Ji)*

1983. Emei Film Studio. Color. 9 Reels. Direction: Zhang Qi, Li Yalin. Screenplay: Zhong Jieyin, Hou Yeping. Cinematography: Li Baoqi. Art Direction: Chen Desheng. Music: Wang Ming. Sound: Zhang Jianping. Cast: Sha Jingcang as Niu Baoshan, Ding Xiaoyi as Factory Director Ding, Zhang Yin as Yu Minli, Diao Xiaoyun as Mu Yanyan, Li Yunjie as Zhang Pei, Liu Mumei as Hou Xiaocheng

Niu Baoshan, head of the decorating unit for a construction company, signs a contract to do some unauthorized work on the Nancheng Mansion, and receives an advance of 1,000 yuan. Youth Secretary Yu Minli is particularly upset at the deal. While Niu realizes the contracting agent he dealt with is not at all what he presents himself to be, and that such sub rosa agreements are illegal, he figures a contract is a contract, and nothing can be done about it. When Factory Director Ding arrives at the construction site, he sharply criticizes the contracting agent's actions, and announces to the workers a newly approved reform plan which will implement fixed volume processing for their unit. Also, if they complete their regular work ahead of schedule, they can get overtime pay for work on the Nanchang Mansion. The workers draw new hope from his words.

2413. *Young Peng Dehuai (Shao Nian Peng De Huai)*

1985. Children Film Studio. Color. Letterboxed. 8 Reels. Direction: Ma Bingyu. Screenplay: Ding Rongyan. Cinematography: Sun Cangyi. Art Direction: Shi Jiandu. Music: Yang Xiwu. Sound: Wu Ling. Cast: Li Hailang as Peng Dehuai (as a youth), Guo Hanlan as Peng's mother, Mei Rongqing as Grandpa, Zhou Guangda as Father, Li Shunan as Uncle, Yang Yanqiang as Luo Man, Fu Dalong as Peng Dehuai (as a child)

The early years of the man who became one of China's great revolutionary generals and the PRC's first Minister of National Defense. Peng Dehuai's childhood is spent in a mountain village in the Xiangtan area of Hunan province during the early years of the Republic of China. Blessed with both physical strength and intelligence, Peng becomes his family's main means of support after his mother dies and his father's health fails. His elderly grandfather decides to leave the family and live out his days as a beggar, rather than add to the family's burdens. When a local despot tries to bully Peng and his young friends in the village, they oppose him. For this, Peng Dehuai is forced to leave the village and go to work as a laborer in a nearby coal mine. When the village is later faced with possible famine, Peng leads the villagers in breaking into the landlord's grain warehouse. This gets 15-year-old Peng Dehua put on the list of most-wanted fugitives. He leaves his hometown for good, and sets out on a new, revolutionary road.

Children's Film Award, 15th International Film Festival of Figueira da Foz.

2414. *The Young People in Our Village (Part 1) (Wo Men Cun Li De Nian Qing Ren)*

1959. Changchun Film Studio. Color. 11 Reels. Direction: Su Li. Screenplay: Ma Feng. Cinematography: Guo Zhenting. Art Direction: Dong Ping. Music: Zhang Dicang. Sound: Jiang Junfeng. Cast: Li Yalin as Gao Zhanwu, Liang Yin as Cao Maolin, Jin Di as Kong Suzhen, Yang Huang as Liu Xiaocui, Liu Zengqing as Li Keming, Sun Yu as Wang Ergou

Gao Zhanwu returns from his army service determined to improve the lives of the people in his native village in the mountains. He leads a group of young people in completing in two months an irrigation project which was originally planned to take two years. One of his workers, a young farmer named Cao Maolin, falls for a high school graduate named Kong Suzhen, but being too shy to express his feelings for her he asks Gao Zhanwu to talk to her for him. Gao Zhanwu also loves Kong Suzhen, but when he learns of Maolin's love for Suzhen, he decides to help. Kong Suzhen really loves Gao Zhanwu, so Gao's repeated urgings of Cao Maolin's suit disappoint her greatly. But Cao Maolin eventually finds true love with another girl, Liu Xiaocui, leaving Gao Zhanwu free to express his true feelings to Kong Suzhen.

2415. *The Young People in Our Village, (Part 2) (Wo Men Cun Li De Nian Qing Ren)*

1963. Changchun Film Studio. Color. 10 Reels. Direction: Su Li, Yi Yiqing. Screenplay: Ma Feng, Cinematography: Guo Zhenting. Art Direction: Tong Jingwen. Music: Zhang Dicang. Sound: Jue Jingxiu. Cast: Li Yalin as Gao Zhanwu, Jin Di as Kong Suzhen, Liang Yin as Cao Maolin, Song Xuejuan as Xiaocui, Liu Zengqing as Li Keming, Lu Guilan as Feng Qiaoying

Deputy agricultural production group director Gao Zhanwu leads the young people of Kongjia village in changing their hometown's image. He suggests building a small hydropower station in the village, but the conservative old commune director is opposed, as he thinks it an impossible task. However, commune Party Secretary Zhao supports the young people's suggestion, and assigns project responsibility to Gao. As they work together on drawing up the project blueprints, two of the young people, Li Keming and Feng Qiaoying, fall in love. Under Gao Zhanwu's leadership, the village young people not only build the power station, but also send Kong Suzhen and Li Keming to help a neighboring village construct their own power station. Kongjia Village's young people make further progress in working, studying, friendship and romance.

The Young People in Our Village (Part 1). The young people take a happy break from village construction. 1959. Changchun Film Studio.

2416. *Young People with Big Ambitions (Ren Xiao Zhi Da)*

1959. Zhejiang Film Studio. B & W. 7 Reels. Direction: Shi Xing, Wu Xiangzhi. Screenplay: Huang Jieji, Zhong Puping. Cinematography: Guo Xianghui, Chen Ling. Art Direction: Xu Keji. Music: Chen Xianyu. Sound: Ren Xinliang. Cast not credited

In 1958, a group of elementary school students plant an experimental field under the supervision of their teacher and the agricultural commune secretary. They do not fear hard work, dare to be bold in thought and action, and realize a large harvest from the experimental field. One of their number who is lazy and given to playing pranks corrects his mistakes and joins the Young Pioneers.

2417. *Young Prisoners of War (Shao Nian Zhan Fu)*

1989. Children's Film Studio. Color. 9 Reels. Letterboxed. Direction: Du Yuzhuang. Screenplay: Cao Wenhan, Wang Xingdong. Cinematography: Du Yuzhuang, Zi Yan, Xie Ping. Art Direction: Wang Jixian. Music: Niu Chang.

Sound: Lan Fan. Cast: Che Yue as Ouyang Shi, Zi Jiang as Gameng, Hang Haibo as Xiao Bajin, Song Jingjiao as Xue Meizi, Basen as the Regimental Commander, Ge Batuqinggele as the Company Commander

The story opens in March, 1937, on the corpse-strewn Gansu Corridor, where a ragged group of young Red Army prisoners of war staggers through the vast Gobi Desert on their way to imprisonment. Escorting them are cavalrymen of the Ma Clan, a warlord army allied with the Nationalists, a twisted collection of people responsible for many deaths. Several months later, the "Xi'an Incident" occurs, and a new period of Nationalist-Communist collaboration begins. The regimental commander of the Ma Clan tries to reorganize the young POWs into his own Children's Battalion, but they resist this. Timid Tang Baoyuan and Xiao Bajin are forced to wear army uniforms. Meanwhile, back in the POW camp, Ouyang Shi, the head of the Young Pioneers Battalion of the Red Army, helps Gameng and Xiao Bajin escape from the camp. But on their way to link with the main force of the Red Army, Xiao Bajin dies, and Gameng is captured. A series of

The Young People in Our Village (Part 2). Kong Suzhen (Jin Di) works as an electrician on the power station project. 1963. Changchun Film Studio.

Haidong as Teacher Zheng, Zhu Jiewen as Doudou, Han Jianrong as Chen Guyuan, Liu Changwei as the TV director, Tie Datong as Doudou's grandmother

Junior high school student Ge Lan is blessed with a beautiful singing voice. With careful training from her teacher Ye Xiulian, she takes first prize in the city's student singing competition. The city's Youth Arts Development Center head Chen Guyuan also is taken with the young girl's voice, and gets her heavily involved in recording tapes and making frequent stage performances. This soon has a negative effect on Ge Lan's school work, but her mother likes the money so much she withdraws her daughter from school. Frequent performing and having to sing inappropriate songs eventually make Ge Lan ill, and she loses her voice. Teacher Ye visits her and encourages her to return to a normal schoolgirl's life. With his and her classmates' help, Ge Lan returns to school and her voice soon returns.

violent incidents, in which Ouyang Shi is killed, leads the young POWs to try and break out of the camp again, but Tang Baoyuan is left behind.

2418. *Young Singing Star (Xiao Ge Xing)*

1986. Children's Film Studio. Color. Letterboxed. 9 Reels. Direction: Wu Zhennian. Screenplay: Pan Borong, Wu Zhennian. Cinematography: Shen Jie, Luo Yong. Art Direction: Xiao Feng. Music: Jin Fuzhai. Sound: Ren Daming, Qian Youlan. Cast: Dong Xiaoxia as Ge Lan, Wang Ping as Ye Xiulian, Song Guanghua as Ge Lan's mother, Li Lianyi as Ge Lan's father, Hu

2419. *Young Soldiers in Field Officers' Uniforms (Chuan Xiao Guan Gu De Xiao Bing)*

1985. Beijing Film Studio. Color. 9 Reels. Direction: Yuan Yuehua. Screenplay: Zhang Zhenxin. Cinematography: Chen Youqun, Hu Jihe. Art Direction: Ma Zhoren. Music: Ai Liqun. Sound: Zhang Jiake. Cast: Tang Xi as Xu Eleven, Yu Jia as Fat Yin, Mei Hong as Yu Xiaofei, Wang Shuang as Xia Anan, Wang Yuzhang as Chen Huashan, Yu Shaokang as Qi Agong

A military performing arts unit's acrobatic troupe numbers a few young members among its performers. To give the youngsters a taste of the military life ahead of the troupe, division headquarters decides to send them for military training, although they are underage for actual military service. At first, the young people treat the whole thing as a joke, leading to a number of embarrassing incidents in training. But in time they come to understand how the strict training can help them improve their art. When their training is finished, the young people all find they have grown fond of military life.

2420. Young Sword Hero (Shen Zhou Xiao Jian Xia)

1989. Guangxi Film Studio & Japan Fuji Company Co-Production. Color. Letterboxed. 9 Reels. Direction: Luo Yuzhong, Gaosu Canghong. Screenplay: Mao Zhengshan, Gaosu Canghong, Luchun Qinxiang. Cinematography: Feng Baogui, Tianduan Jinzhong. Art Direction: Chen Yaogong. Music: Li Yanlin. Sound: Li Yunping. Cast: Wang Demin as Minwei, Gong Lifeng as Yingwan, Guan Binghua as Yuean, Gao Wei as Wuwan, Zhang Zhihong as Mingzhu, Zhang Yuan as Mingde

A tale of revenge, set about 400 years ago in the forested Tianshanbao area of southwest China. When their home is attacked, the son and daughter of a wrongly persecuted and slain village head are borne to safety by their father's housekeeper. The children return 10 years later to avenge their father.

2421. The Young Woman and the Thief (Shao Nu He Xiao Tou)

1985. Henan Film Studio. Color. 6 Reels. Direction: Yang Yanjing. Screenplay: Liu Wenmiao, Gong Longxiang, Wan Baiao. Cinematography: Cai Zhengchang. Art Direction: Sun Lin. Music: Xu Jingxin. Sound: Cui Weimin. Cast: Zhao Jing as Xiao Jing, Yuan Yuan as Xiao Wang

Xiao Wang keeps trying to put his past as a street tough behind him, but his old buddies keep making it hard for him to go straight. A young woman teacher he meets encourages him to keep trying and to get a regular job. He does so, and turns out to be an excellent worker. The teacher and the ex-thief fall in love, but one day when they are out for a walk they see a small child fall into some water. Without hesitating, Xiao Wang jumps in to rescue the tot, and although the child is saved Xiao Wang is drowned, leaving Xiao Jing in deep sorrow.

2422. The Younger Generation (Nian Qing De Yi Dai)

1965. Tianma Film Studio. B & W. 12 Reels. Direction: Zhao Ming. Screenplay: Chen Yun and Zhao Ming, based on the stage play of the same title by Chen Yun. Cinematography: Shi Fengqi. Art Direction: Wei Yuzhen, Li Jingui. Music: Xiao Yan. Sound: Gong Zhenming. Cast: Yang Zhaibao as Xiao Jiye, Da Shichang as Lin Yusheng, Cao Lei as Lin Lan, Zhu Manfang as Xia Qianru, Wun Xiying as Lin Jian, Sha Li as Grandma Xiao

Shanghai Geology Institute graduates Xiao Jiye and Lin Yusheng are assigned to work in a geological prospecting team in West China's remote Qinghai province. After half a year, Lin falls ill and returns to Shanghai for treatment. Xiao Jiye's team discovers a new mine, after which he is assigned to return to Shanghai to make a proposal for exploiting it and at the same time look into the situation concerning Lin, who has still not returned. In Shanghai, Xiao finds that Lin Yusheng had falsified his medical history so that he could remain in Shanghai and avoid returning to the harsh working environment of Qinghai. After Xiao earnestly criticizes Lin's errors, Lin realizes he is wrong and agrees to return to Qinghai with Xiao. In addition, the mining proposal is approved.

2423. The Younger Generation (Nian Qing De Yi Dai)

1976. Shanghai Film Studio. Color. 9 Reels. Direction: Ling Zhiao, Zhang Huijun. Screenplay: Chen Yun and Shi Fangyu, based on the stage play of the same title by Chen Yun. Cinematography: Chen Zhengxiang, Cao Weiye. Art Direction: Huang Jianfeng. Music: Guo Yuchun, Xiao Peiyan. Cast: Bi Jiancang as Xiao Jiye, Zhang Ruifang as Grandma Xiao, Li Yan as Lin Jian, Xiao Chi as Xia Shujuan, Li Xiumin as Lin Lan, Hong Rong as Xia Qianru, Da Wuchang as Lin Yusheng

This is a remake of the Tianma Film Studio's 1965 film of the same title.

2424. The Younger Generation (Xiao Zi Bei)

1979. Changchun Film Studio. Color. 9 Reels. Direction: Wang Jiayi, Luo Tai. Screenplay: Si Mingshan, Wu Benwu, Zhou Yang, Sun Xiongfei. Cinematography: Wu Guojiang, Zhao Yue. Art Direction: Wang Jiru, Jing Xiwu. Music: Lei Zhengbang. Sound: Kang Ruixin. Cast: Chen Yixin as Xiao Qing, Wang Weiping as Xiao Ge, Chi Zhiqiang as Xiao Huang, Yu Yanping as Xiao Bai, Zhang Mingming as Xiao Hong, Wang Qingbao as Xiao Lan, Lin Bin as Mama

Xiao Ge, a young worker at the Shanghai Heping Restaurant, loves studying science and technology. His constantly talking about his interest attracts the attention of his fellow passengers on the No. 003 bus everyday, as well as bus attendants Xiao Qing and Xiao Huang and bus driver Xiao Hong. One day, Xiao Qing happens to find a picture of Xiao Ge on the bus and pockets it, thinking to return it to him later. At home, her mother finds the picture and, mistakenly thinking the young man in the picture is her daughter's boyfriend, decides to have his background investigated. Meanwhile, Xiao Ge has been designing an automatic stop announcement device for the attendants, and Xiao Qing helps him. When Xiao Qing's mother learns that Xiao Ge is a baker in a restaurant, she is reluctant to accept him as her daughter's suitor. The story ends happily, with Xiao Ge and Xiao Qing falling in love, and with the support of Xiao Huang, Xiao Bai and transit policeman Xiao Lian, the announcement device is installed at each Shanghai station.

2425. *Your Smile (Ni De Wei Xiao)*

1986. Beijing Film Studio. Color. 10 Reels. Direction: Ma Bingyu. Screenplay: Zhang Tianmin. Cinematography: Sun Changyi. Art Direction: Duan Zhenzhong. Music: Zhao Jiping, Zhang Qingxiang. Sound: Wu Ling. Cast: Yu Lan as Chen Airan, Yuan Zhiyuan as Song Shangqing, Zhen Baomin as Jin Ye, Wei Guochun as Teacher Li, Jean Johnson as Louise, Yuan Yuan as Yuan Ada

Female tour guide Chen Airan loves her job and is very popular with her clients. The film relates the individual stories of some of these (an overseas Chinese businessman, a lonely Japanese man, two young Chinese living abroad). A common thread is the development of Chen Airan's own romantic involvements. She loves a teacher named Li, but then her best friend Louise, a foreign girl, confides that she herself has fallen for the young teacher.

2426. *Youth (Qing Chun)*

1977. Shanghai Film Studio. Color. Letterboxed. 12 Reels. Direction: Xie Jin. Screenplay: Li Yunliang, Wang Lian. Cinematography: Shen Xilin, Ju Jiazheng. Art Direction: Hu Dengren, Yan Cangming. Music: Ge Yan. Sound: Zhu Weigang. Cast: Chen Chong as Ya Mei, Yu Ping as Xiang Hui, Wang Xiyan as Cai Fangcheng,

Yuan Yue as the Commander, Zhang Yu as Jin Ayan, Gu Yuqing as Ling Xue

Ya Mei, a deaf mute for 13 years, has both her senses restored by a PLA medical team. She enlists, and is assigned to communications work. In a test, Ya Mei makes an error in answering the telephone, which leads deputy regimental commander Cai Fangcheng to conclude she is unsuitable for this type of work, and try to get her reassigned. Meanwhile, Red Army soldier Xiang Hui, a wounded war veteran, takes a turn for the worse physically which requires her evacuation to Beijing for treatment. Although she is suffering badly, Xiang Hui's vigorous revolutionary will inspires Ya Mei and other soldiers, and invigorates Cai Fangcheng's revolutionary spirit, which had been flagging of late. His new attitude leads Cai to begin mentoring Ya Mei, and with his help and training she becomes an outstanding communications specialist and a Party member.

2427. *Youth at a Construction Site (Gong Di Qing Nian)*

1958. Changchun Film Studio. B & W. 9 Reels. Direction: Wu Zhaodi. Screenplay: Yu Ming. Cinematography: Liu Yongzhen. Art Direction: Tong Jingwen. Music: Che Min. Sound: Jue Jingxiu. Cast: Ying Zhiming as Shang Yue, Ren Yi as Bai Fu, Li Mengrao as Mu Qing, Pan Demin as Wun Guomao, Wu Bike as Jing Chunrong, Ma Shida as Jin Peilei

At a construction site, young technician Shang Yue repeatedly suggests mechanization plans which are impractical. The site is badly damaged by a violent storm, and he is once again encouraged to redesign his plan. His efforts are also deterred by opposition from conservative site director Bai Fu and his own unhappy love affair. But with the criticisms and help of other leaders and workers, he finally comes up with a successful mechanization plan which greatly improves efficiency and leads to the mission being accomplished ahead of schedule.

2428. *Youth in the Flames of War (Zhan Huo Zhong De Qing Chun)*

1959. Changchun Film Studio. B & W. 10 Reels. 10 Reels. Direction: Wang Yan. Screenplay: Lu Zhuguo and Wang Yan, based on the novel of the same title by Lu Zhuguo. Cinematography:

Wang Qiming. Set Design: Sun Shixiang. Music: Zhang Dicang. Sound: Chen Wenyuan. Cast: Wang Suya as Gao Shan, Pang Xueqing as Lei Zhenlin, Lin Nong as the Regimental Commander, Zhang Hui as the Company Commander, Ma Shida as the Squad Leader

In 1947, to avenge her father's death in the Civil War, a girl named Gao Shan disguises herself as a young man and joins the PLA. She is soon named deputy platoon leader of the "Sharp Knife" platoon, a crack outfit. Platoon leader Lei Zhenlin lacks respect for his deputy, due to the latter's small stature, and gives Gao Shan assignments only reluctantly. But Gao Shan always completes every mission successfully. The two argue about tactics on the eve of an attack on enemy headquarters. The next day, Lei's recklessness gets him in a tough spot, and Gao is wounded rescuing him. When Lei goes to visit his deputy in the hospital, he finds out Gao is a woman, and is deeply moved. During the push to final victory, Lei Zhenlin gives his command sword to Gao as a memento. Gao Shan watches Lei Zhenlin's figure disappear in the distance.

2429. *Youth Is Like a Flame (Qing Chun Si Huo)*

1976. Beijing Film Studio. Color. 12 Reels. Direction: Dong Kena. Screenplay: the Maansan City Cultural Bureau's Writing Team. Cinematography: Xu Xiaoxian. Art Direction: Hao Guoxin, Mo Kezhan. Music: Tian Feng. Sound: Zhang Jiake. Cast: Yang Yaqin as Liang Dongxia, Xin Jing as Mr. Ding, Lu Fei as Chen Ao, Zhao Kuier as Li Sanhong, Li Shijiang as Li Sanhu, Chen Mimi as Feng Xue, Li Shujun as Yu Chongwu

In 1971, Liang Dongxia, a young electrician at the South China Steel Company's steel rolling plant, forms a team to automate the steel rolling machine. The revolutionary committee director does not support the workers' efforts, relying instead on Design office director Yu Chongwu. The Bureau of Metals Party secretary encourages Liang's team to take over a part of the plant known as the "capitalist class conventionally occupied area." Yu Chongwu then change his tactics and tries to stop the automation efforts by corrupting young worker Gao Lei, who has dreams of becoming famous, encouraging Gao Lei to set up another team to compete with Liang's. Yu steals calculations from Liang's team for Gao, but at a mass meeting Liang Dongxia discloses

Yu Chongwu's theft and criticizes the incorrect line of the revolutionary committee director. Gao Lei is also educated from this.

2430. *Youth Karaoke (Qing Chun Ka La Ou K)*

1991. Changchun Film Studio. Color. 10 Reels. Letterboxed. Direction: Wang Xuexin. Screenplay: Hai Nan. Cinematography: Ning Changcheng. Art Direction: Zhang Yan. Music: Dong Lin. Sound: Zhang Fenglu, Zhang Hngguang. Cast: Tao Jin as Tao Jing, Shen Danping as Dan Qing, Ma Tianfang as Jin Fan, Fang Qingzi as Yanyan, Pan Jie as Mimi, Mu Huaihu as Xu Zhanshan, Cai Wenyan as Zhu Hong, Liang Danni as A Hui, Zhang Huizhong as Wan Jiale

Tao Jing, editor of the magazine "New Dance," places a personal ad on television and in the newspapers seeking a prospective bride for his close friend Jin Fan, first mate of an oceangoing freighter. They choose three women from the thousands who reply — graduate student Zhu Hong, painter Dan Qing and fashion model Mimi. Complications ensue, as the two friends become entangled in an intricate web of former girlfriends and old friends, but everything in this comedy turns out happily in the end.

2431. *Youth on Water (Shui Shang Chun Qiu)*

1959. Beijing Film Studio. Color. 10 Reels. Direction: Xie Tie. Screenplay: Yue Ye, Zhou Zheng, Xie Tie, Zu Xifan. Cinematography: Chen Guoliang. Art Direction: Zhen Yiyun, Mo Renyi. Music: Su Xia. Sound: Lu Xiancang, Wang Junhua. Cast: Su Shi as Hua Zhenlong, Yu Yang as Hua Xiaolong, Luo Guoliang as Li Zhiyun, Su Mai as Jiang Yuling, Wang Yingfu as Zhou Huiliang, Liang Yansheng as Coach Zhang

In old China before liberation, Master Huaqi, a merchant, discovers young fisherman Hua Zhenlong to be a talented swimmer. Huaqi cons the young man into entering an international swimming meet in the Tianjin Colonial Governance Zone by appealing to his patriotism, claiming his participation will honor China. Actually, the merchant plans to bet heavily on the young man. Hua Zhenlong's superior speed and skill wins the championship, which angers some foreign gamblers. They hire thugs to beat up Hua, but some college students help him escape danger. After World War II, Hua resumes his swimming

Youth Karaoke. **Dance magazine editor Tao Jing (Tao Jin, left) meets painter Dan Qing (Shen Danping). 1991. Changchun Film Studio.**

career, and enters a major meet. However, he is prevented from competing by the local chief of police, whose son is also an entrant. After liberation, Hua Zhenlong becomes the coach at an amateur swimming school, and trains his son Hua Xiaolong to be a championship swimmer who sets a new world record.

2432. *The Yue Family's Young General (Yue Jia Xiao Jiang)*

1984. Zongyi Film Company. Color. Wide Screen. 9 Reels. Direction: Wang Zhiyu. Screenplay: Bi Bicheng, Wang Zhiyu. Cinematography: Yang Wenliang. Art Direction: Si Qiping. Music: Xu Jingxin. Sound: Zhou Hengliang. Cast: Xun Feng as Yue Yun, Zhang Xiling as Ying Lingzhi, Zhang Chengzhong as Jin Danzhi, Liu Weimin as Niu Tong, Sun Huaman as Grandma, Shen Wei as Yue Zheng, Wei Wei as Yue Ting

In 1127, the king of the country of Nuzhen invades middle China and his troops kidnap two members of the Southern Song imperial family. General Yue Fei leads the defenders, and the Nuzhen commander attacks Yue Fei's home and kidnaps the General's mother to force a surrender. Yue Fei's son Yue Yun goes to the battlefield, and with his grandmother's support and encouragement helps turn the tide and protect the country.

2433. *Yue Opera Actress (Feng Yu Xiang Si Yan)*

1991. Shanghai Film Studio. Color. Letterboxed. 10 Reels. Direction: Shen Yaoting. Screenplay: Gu Songsi. Cinematography: Si Junping. Art Direction: Qin Baisong. Music: Yang Shaoxiang. Sound: Xu Xiushan. Cast: Mao Shanyu as Zu Yunyan, Hu Dagang as Wei Liangren, Wei Guochun as Shao Wang, Wang Weiping as Yang Shuifa, Xu Jun as Xiao Wang, Hong Rong as Wei's mother, Wu Yunfang as Shao's mother

During World War II, Zu Yunyan, famed for her performances in the Yue school of opera, is visiting a mountain area when she happens upon a badly injured Chinese pilot. Knowing the Japanese are searching for him, she hides him in a cave and cares for him. They marry a few months later. The pilot, Shao Wang, eventually returns to duty, and Zu Yunyan gives birth to their son. Life is particularly difficult for her after that, although she receives considerable assistance from her former opera colleague Wei Liangren. Zu later moves to Shanghai to live with Shao Wang's elderly and infirm mother, where she spends five years waiting. She experiences hardship and want, along with the persecution of a Chinese traitor. At last, at war's end, Shao Wang returns as a high-ranking officer. The couple

Youth on Water. 1959. Beijing Film Studio.

have one more heartbreaking misunderstanding before reuniting for good.

2434. *Yue Yue (Yue Yue)*

1986. Beijing Film Studio. Color. 10 Reels. Direction: Qiqing Gaowa. Screenplay: A Cheng. Cinematography: Ru Shuiren. Art Direction: Men Yufeng. Music: Zhao Jiping. Sound: Zhang Hua. Cast: Bai Ling as Wang Xiaoyue, Huang Xiaolei as Menmen, Sun Xiangguang as Caicai, Li Wei as Father

Wang Xiaoyue, called "Yue Yue," and her father contract for a small plot of land and a boat. Her parents arrange an engagement for her with Caicai, honest but very traditional and conservative. Menmen, a nice young man more inclined to arts than to farming, likes Yue Yue a lot. She and Caicai at last become formally engaged, but Menmen refuses to give up. He buys Yue Yue an attractive jacket, angering Caicai, who confronts Menmen. Yue Yue hopes the man she eventually marries will be a combination of Menmen and Caicai.

2435. *Yunnan Story (Yun Nan Gu Shi)*

1993. Taiwan Zhongsheng Company, Taiwan Golden Tripod Film and Television Company and Beijing Film Studio Co-Production. Color. Wide Screen. 10 Reels. Direction: Zhang Nuanqin. Screenplay: Xu Tiansheng, Xie Ting. Cinematography: Wang Xiaolie. Art Direction: Shu Gang. Music: Lin Weizhe, Li Xinyun. Sound: Li Bojiang. Costume: Dong Xiuqin. Makeup: Xia Juan. Cast: Lu Xiuling as Shu Zhi, Lin Jianhua as Xia Luo, Pu Chunxi as Ge Sha

When the Japanese are defeated in World War II, a young Japanese woman is separated from her family and stranded in China. She attempts suicide, but is stopped by a young Chinese army officer. They get married, although he is dismissed from the service for doing so. He takes his bride back to his home province of Yunnan, to the remote mountain village of his family. He soon falls ill and dies, and his younger brother takes care of the woman. They later marry and have a son. The woman finds a role in the village, helping the people improve their birthing methods and child care. During the Cultural Revolution she is accused of being a Japanese spy and persecuted. When China adopts the policy of reform and opening to the outside, she re-establishes her connection with her family in Japan, and at last gives in to their urgings to visit. She feels alienated there, however, and realizes that

Yunnan is her home. She returns to Yunnan and happily sees her husband waiting to welcome her, carrying their small grandson.

2436. *The Zhang Family's Daughter-in-Law (Zhang Jia Shao Nai Nai)*

1985. Shanghai Film Studio. Color. 10 Reels. Direction: Ye Ming. Screenplay: Ye Ming. Cinematography: Cha Xiangkang. Art Direction: Xie Muqian. Music: Yang Mao. Sound: Lu Xuehan, Lu Jinsong. Cast: Li Lan as Ouyang Ruili, Lu Liping as Wenying, Wang Weiping as Wenyao, Sun Jian as Wenguang, Bai Mu as Father-in-Law

The Zhang family's long history of engaging in business brings them under attack during the Cultural Revolution, resulting in their being stripped of their possessions and livelihood. Daughter-in-law Ouyang Ruili had grown used to comfort, but now she assumes the burden of making a living for the family. She works very hard to support everyone. After the 11th Party Congress, all the family's property is returned. Ruili's father-in-law divides his fortune among his three children, and gives a half-share to Ruili for her ten years of hard work on the family's behalf. The family once again enjoys luxury and privilege, but they rapidly begin to lose the mutual understanding and help they had during the difficult years. The Zhang family's daughter begins to quarrel with Ruili, and eventually Ruili and her husband are forced to move out of the family home. Recalling the years she earned a living by menial and simple labor, Ruili decides she will create her own family's future through hard work, and not by having anything given to them.

2437. *Zhang Heng (Zhang Heng)*

1983. Shanghai Film Studio. Color. 10 Reels. Direction: Huang Zhumo. Screenplay: Yu Li. Cinematography: Ma Linfa, Ren Zhixin. Art Direction: Chen Shaomian. Music: Xiao Yan. Sound: Lin Bingsheng. Cast: Xu Huanshan as Zhang Heng, Gao Bo as Heng Zheng, Qin Yi as Heng's wife, Zhu Jianmin as Cui Yuan, Xiao Xiong as Heng Er, Gong Xue as Lanzhu

During the Eastern Han Dynasty (25–220 A.D.), China is struck with a series of devastating earthquakes, and many believe the imperial court's extreme corruption is the cause. Although religious ceremonies are the most popular way of dealing with natural disasters, scientist Zhang Heng devotes his life to designing instruments for predicting earthquakes. He encounters considerable opposition from those who believe his approach sacrilegious, but he at last succeeds. However, his life takes a tragic outcome when he loses his fiancee and his official post. Zhang Heng is still respected as one of China's greatest early scientists.

2438. *Zhao Baiwan's Dream (Zhao Bai Wan Meng Huan Qu)*

1991. Changchun Film Studio. Color. Letterboxed. 9 Reels. Direction: Lu Shaolian. Screenplay: Fang Yihua. Cinematography: Yang Penghui, Yu Zhenghai. Art Direction: Liu Sheng. Music: Wang Meng. Sound: Wang Baosheng and Wang Qinchao. Cast: Xu Zhongquan as Zhao Baiwan, Liu Wei as Yang Xiaobo, Liang Tian as Zhao Fengdeng, Zhang Xiaoling as Wu Sujuan, Zhang Shuming as Dai Bing

Ambitious township entrepreneur Zhao Baiwan wants his son Fengdeng to marry Luo Shanshan, daughter of the city's commerce director. But Shanshan, a college graduate, wants an educated husband and Fengdeng is illiterate. So Zhao Baiwan arranges for Yang, a self-educated driver who loves literature, to go to school and earn a diploma in Fengdeng's name. They plan to use that to win Shanshan. Two years later, the driver returns with a diploma and a novel published in Fengdeng's name. Suddenly Zhao Fengdeng is a famous writer, and the media flocks to interview him. He makes many foolish mistakes trying to carry off his dual role. At last, Shanshan falls in love with the driver.

2439. *Zhao Qian Sun Li (Zhao Qian Sun Li)*

1982. Emei Film Studio. 9 Reels. Direction: Liu Zhinong. Screenplay: Li Shu, Li Pei, Pang Jiasheng. Cinematography: Zhang Jiwu. Art Direction: Xie Huibing. Music: Tao Jiazhou, He Min. Sound: Hua Yuezhu. Cast: Sun Bing as Qian Guangrong, Li Kechun as Zhao Chunmei, Yan Cheng as Li Erniang, Ao Lu as Sun Dongsheng, Wun Xianqiao as Li Wanle, Hu Fumin as Li Wanping

Qian Guangrong is an honest, kindly and capable production team director, but in 1958 he is falsely accused and forced to break off his romantic relationship with Li Erniang. He remains a bachelor, but in time adopts a son named Sun Dongsheng. Li Erniang has to

Zhao Yiman. Zhao Yiman (Shi Lianxing), a woman hero of the Northeast China Volunteer Army. 1950. Northeast Film Studio.

marry another man, and they also have a son, but when her husband dies she must raise the boy alone. The son grows up and becomes engaged to a strong and capable young woman named Zhao Chunmei, but he is accidentally killed the night before their wedding. His fiancee chooses to stay on and live with Li Erniang. The story ends with a double wedding: Qian Guangrong and Li Erniang, Sun Dongsheng and Zhao Chunmei, one family with two different surnames.

2440. *Zhao Yiman (Zhao Yiman)*

1950. Northeast Film Studio. B & W. 10 Reels. Direction: Sha Meng. Screenplay: Yu Ming. Cinematography Supervisor: Wu Weiyun. Cinematography: Bao Jie. Set Design: Qin Wei. Music: Zhang Dicang. Sound: Jue Jingxiu. Costume: Wang Leng. Cast: Shi Lianxing as Zhao Yiman, Zhang Ping as Mr. Cao, Zhang Ying as Zhang Qiang, Wang Yan as Regimental Commander Wang, Ouyang Ruqiu as Aunt Lu, Liu Ru as Uncle Lu

In 1933, CPC member Zhao Yiman and her husband Mr. Cao lead a strike in Japanese-occupied Harbin in Northeast China. Al-

though the strike is successful, Mr. Cao is arrested. Zhao Yiman moves to the countryside to organize people in support of the Volunteer Army. She later becomes leader of an anti-Japanese guerrilla force. Soon thereafter, she learns her husband has died in prison at the hands of his captors. Zhao Yiman continues leading her forces, taking out her sorrow on the battlefield. In the winter of 1935, a large Japanese force surrounds the Chinese volunteers camp, and during their breakout Zhao Yiman is seriously wounded and taken prisoner. In jail, she is subjected to torture but continues to resist. She escapes but is recaptured and returned to prison. This time, she dies heroically in captivity.

2441. *Zhenzhen's Beauty Parlor (Zhen Zhen De Fa Wu)*

1986. Youth Film Studio. Color. 10 Reels. Direction: Xu Tongjun. Screenplay: Xia Lan. Cinematography: Liao Jiaxiang. Art Direction: Liu Ying. Music: Ma Ding. Sound: Zhang Yaling. Cast: Kuang Ping as Zhenzhen, Yin Guohu as A Ming, Zhao Ming as Cai Xiang, Zhou Hong as Huang Ling, Yan Qing as Miaomiao

Zhou Enlai (Parts 1 & 2). During the last days of his life, Chinese Premier Zhou Enlai (Wang Tiecheng) carries on working from his hospital bed, as his wife Deng Yingchao (Zhen Xiaojuan) lends support. 1991. Guangxi Film Studio.

On a little Beijing street connecting Beihai Park and Jingshan Park, reform is taking hold. Self-employed laborer Zhenzhen opens a beauty parlor, and invites A Ming, a young man from Guangzhou, to be her chief hairdresser. The business is hugely successful at first, but soon Zhenzhen finds herself locked in a competitive struggle when the Meimei Beauty Parlor opens across the street. Worse, the competing parlor is partly owned by Cai Xiang, a young oil-cake maker who used to be Zhenzhen's boyfriend. The two still care for each other, but Cai Xiang has an affair with Huang Ling, a cigarette vendor, who falls madly in love with him. Then Cai Xiang's sister Miaomiao shows up. Determined to learn hairdressing from A Ming, she spends nearly all her time hanging around Zhenzhen's parlor. As time passes, Zhenzhen and A Ming gradually fall in love. But then A Ming's girlfriend shows up from Guangzhou to complicate matters.

2442. *Zhou Enlai (Parts 1 & 2)* (*Zhou En Lai*)

1991. Guangxi Film Studio and China Film Export & Import Corporation. Color. 16 Reels. Wide Screen. Direction: Ding Yinnan. Screenplay: Song Jialing, Ding Yinnan, Liu Simin. Cinematography: Yu Xiaoqun, Lei Jiaming. Art Direction: Li Wenguang. Music: Cheng Dachao. Sound: Lin Guang, Huang Minguang. Makeup: Yan Bijun, Wang Xizhong. Cast: Wang Tiecheng as Zhou Enlai, Zhen Xiaojuan as Deng Yingchao, Jin Jiefang as the head bodyguard, Shen Liang as Doctor Wu, Zhang Keyao as Mao Zedong, Guo Fazeng as Liu Shaoqi, Liu Huaizheng as Zhu De, Bi Geng as Chen Yun, Lu Qi as Deng Xiaoping, Zhang Yunli as Chen Yi, Gao Changli as He Long, Zhen Rong as Dong Biwu, Liu Simin as Liao Chengzhi, Wang Huaiwen as Luo Qingchang, Gu Bangjun as Xiong Xianghui

A long, epic film, set basically during the Cultural Revolution decade (1966–1976), but actually reviewing modern Chinese history: the Great Revolution, the Northern Expedition, the Long March, the War of Resistance Against Japan, the War of Liberation and the founding of New China. Set against this is the life of Zhou Enlai. During the nightmarish Cultural Revolution years, Zhou Enlai provides sanctuary in his own home to a man and his wife persecuted by Red Guards, and protects Communist Party figure Chen Yi at a denunciation meeting. Towards the end of the Cultural Revolution, Lin Biao and his son Lin Liguo attempt to stage a coup d'etat and murder Chairman Mao Zedong, but are unsuccessful and flee in panic after their failure. Their plane finally crashes in Mongolia. Mao's wife Jiang Qing and her clique, the "Gang of Four," at first collude with Lin Biao, and then make a power grab of their own. At last, Zhou is instrumental in arranging Richard Nixon's face-to-face meeting with Mao Zedong.

Best Actor Wang Tiecheng, 1992 Golden Rooster Awards.

Best Actor Wang Tiecheng, 1992 Hundred Flowers Awards.

Best Makeup Yan Bijun and Wang Xizhong, 1992 Golden Rooster Awards.

Best Picture, 1992 Hundred Flowers Awards.

2443. *Zhu De and Agnes Smedley (Zhu De He Shi Mo Te Lai)*

1985. August First Film Studio. Color. 9 Reels. Direction: Li Jun. Screenplay: Li Hua. Cinematography: Wei Linyu. Art Direction: Li Jian. Music: Shi Feng. Sound: Li Lin. Cast: Liu Huaizheng as Zhu De, Elizabeth Gunamei as Agnes Smedley, Li Hongwei as Liu Xian, Li Peiying as Kang Keqing

American journalist Agnes Smedley arrives in China in 1928. She wants to go to Yan'an and meet legendary Chinese General Zhu De, but this desire is unfulfilled until 1937. When the anti–Japanese War breaks out, General Zhu De leads the Eighth Route Army to North China, and Smedley travels with the army, reporting the Red Army's resistance efforts to the world. She also writes *The Great Road*, a book which becomes the standard English-language biography of Zhu. After the PRC is established in 1949, her enthusiastic support of the new regime subjects her to severe personal attacks in her home country, so Agnes Smedley leaves the U.S. and moves to London. After Smedley's death, in accordance with her wishes, her ashes are placed in Beijing's Babaoshan Cemetery. Zhu De writes the epitaph for her memorial.

2444. *Zuo Wenjun and Sima Xiangru (Zuo Wen Jun He Si Ma Xiang Ru)*

1984. Emei Film Studio. Color. 10 Reels. Direction: Zen Weizhi. Screenplay: Chen Zeyuan, Tao Kaiming, Yang Chengle, Xiang Xincheng, Zhao Xuebing. Cinematography: Zhang Jiwu. Art Direction: Yan Dingfu. Music: Yu Linqin. Sound: Lin Bingcheng, Luo Guocheng. Cast: Wu Qianqian as Zuo Wenjun, Jin Hong as Sima Xiangru, Fei Anqi as Zuo Wangsun, Gu Xiaoqing as A Yi, Li Alin as Muguo, Chen Lei as Wang Ji, Sui Diexin as Chen Zhen

In the early Han Dynasty (ca200 B.C.), wealthy merchant Zuo Wangsun marries his daughter Wenjun to a man who soon dies, leaving Wenjun a widow at 17. She later meets and falls in love with the scholar Sima Xiangru. But when the young man goes to her father to ask for Wenjun's hand, Zuo Wangsun refuses, for he wants his daughter to marry fellow merchant Chen Zhen. Zuo Wenjun tells Sima Xiangru to write a memorial to the throne setting forth a plan for the governance of Southwest China. The emperor is so pleased with the plan he bestows favored status on the scholar, which enables the two lovers to get together.

Glossary

Anti-Japanese War The Chinese resistance prior to the start of World War II.

Beiping Official name of Beijing during the period 1928–1949, when the capital of the Republic of China was located at Nanjing.

cadre Person holding a position of some responsibility, usually administrative, in either the Communist Party or the government at any level.

Chiang Kaishek (1887–1975). Chinese general and politician. Commander of the Nationalist armed forces from the 1920s until the final defeat in 1949. President of the Republic of China on the mainland 1948–49, and on Taiwan 1950–75. Name romanized as Jiang Jieshi in the PRC.

commune The highest level and largest administrative and collective unit in rural China from 1958 to the early 1980s. Communes were divided into production brigades which were in turn divided into production teams (*q.v.*). After 1985, these were replaced by townships and villages (*q.v.*).

CPC the Chinese Communist Party. Also referred to as "the Party."

Cultural Revolution Although the term appeared in CPC literature as early as 1940, the expression as used here means the Great Proletarian Cultural Revolution, a political campaign initiated by Mao Zedong in August 1966 to re-ignite the fires of revolution among the masses. (See Introduction.) Sometimes referred to by Chinese writers as "the 10 years of chaos," the Cultural Revolution decade (1966–76) is often divided into three phases: 1966–69, the era of Red Guard militance; 1969–71, the rise and fall of Lin Biao, Mao's one-time heir apparent; and 1971–76, when the Gang of Four (*q.v.*) was at the zenith of its power. The Gang's arrest in October 1976 was later officially designated as the end of the Cultural Revolution. Many of the movies of the 1980s deal with the third phase, and the first phase began appearing as a theme in films of the 1990s.

Eighth Route Army The main Chinese Communist army, forerunner of the PLA (*q.v.*).

Eleventh Party Congress The August 1977 congress which announced the policies of opening and reform, turning China from a highly centralized economy to a market-oriented one.

Gang of Four Four leading radical figures, led by Mao Zedong's widow Jiang Qing, who dominated China politically during the Cultural Revolution (*q.v.*) decade of 1966–76.

Great Leap Forward An economic campaign, initiated in 1958, designed to spur industrial and agricultural production to the world's standard of development after the cutoff of Soviet aid.

Great Proletarian Cultural Revolution See: Cultural Revolution.

greenwoods bandits In Chinese history and literature, "greenwoods" bandits or "brothers of the green woods" were honest men forced into banditry by evil officials or an oppressive government. Their image in China was similar to that of Robin Hood and his Merry Men in the West.

Han or **Han Chinese** The ethnic majority of Chinese, some 93 percent of the population.

liberation term used by the CPC to refer to their taking power in a particular area. Also refers to the establishment of the People's Republic in 1949.

Long March the Red Army's 8,000-mile (12,500 km) retreat from the Nationalists' "extermination campaigns." The epic journey took a full year and was survived by fewer than a third of those who set out. A hallowed landmark in Chinese Communist history.

Manchu The native Mongolian race of Manchuria (now Northeast China), which conquered and ruled China from 1644–1912 as the Qing (Ch'ing) Dynasty.

Manchukuo Former country (1931–1945), established in Northeast China as a Japanese puppet state.

Mao Zedong (1893–1976) Communist Chinese leader during the years of revolution, and after the founding of the PRC, Chairman of the Party, the number one position in the government. Name often romanized as Mao Tse-tung in the West.

Nationalist Party The ruling political party in China from the establishment of the Republic of China in 1912 until the Communist victory in 1949, when the Nationalist government evacuated to Taiwan.

overseas Chinese Term used to refer to a person of Chinese origin, regardless of citizenship, who lives abroad on a permanent basis.

Party Secretary Politically responsible position, at every level of government under the Communist Party.

PLA The People's Liberation Army, the armed forces of the People's Republic of China. The PLA encompasses all of China's military, including its air and naval forces.

PRC People's Republic of China.

production team The lowest level of administrative unit in rural China from 1958 to the early 1980s. The team usually owned the majority of a commune's land and distributed its members' income. Replaced by villages (*q.v.*).

PSB Public Security Bureau.

SEZ Special Economic Zone. Beginning in 1979, China established small areas along the coast intended to promote economic development and raise the level of technology by luring foreign investment with preferential policies and facilities.

Sun Yatsen (1866–1925) Father of the Chinese revolution and founder of the Nationalist Party and the Republic of China. Name romanized as Sun Zhongshan in the PRC.

Taiping Rebellion A people's uprising against the Qing (Manchu) government in the mid–19th century.

village Administratively, the lowest level such unit in rural China, replacing the production brigade and production team.

Volunteer Army A coalition guerrilla army, drawn largely from bandits, peasants and Chinese soldiers who deserted in protest of their government's refusal to resist the Japanese invasion of Northeast China and its establishment of the puppet state of Manchukuo.

War of Liberation The Communist-Nationalist Civil War of 1947–49.

Yan'an City in Northern Shanxi province in North China. The Chinese Red Army retreated here on the Long March (*q.v.*) of 1934–35 and made Yan'an its headquarters for the next 10 years.

yuan The Chinese monetary unit.

Yuan Shikai (1859–1916) General who played a key role in the overthrow of the Qing Dynasty. President from 1913–16. Civil war erupted when he attempted to have himself declared Emperor.

Zhou Enlai (1898–1976) CPC politician and statesman. After liberation, served as Premier, the number two position in the PRC government. Name often romanized as Chou En-lai in the West.

Sources

As I stated in the introduction, Chinese sources for research on motion pictures are abundant, the period 1949–1979 remarkably so: after 1979 there was a flood of publication in China commemorating the first 30 years of the Communist regime, and reviewing the nation's achievements in many fields, including the performing arts. This makes it more likely that any historical work concentrating on this period will be solidly researched. The first and last books listed are representative of this deluge, and were indispensable to the compilation of this work. The next likely such outpouring is expected at or shortly after the turn of the century, as the PRC looks back on its first half-century.

While it would be impossible to list here all Chinese publications on the subject since 1949, or even those that update the principal references, I have included all works I used in the compilation of this filmography as well as many others which I have examined and believe would be useful to film historians. I have emphasized reference works and secondary sources that provide further guides to research.

The translated title for each entry is in most cases my own; exceptions are made for those publications which carry an English language title as well as the Chinese. In these instances the English title is given in quotation marks.

BOOKS

Chen Huangmei, ed. *Dangdai zhongguo dianying* ("Contemporary Chinese Film"). 2v. Beijing: China Social Science Press, 1989. An overview of developments since 1949. Volume 1 deals with feature films, with Volume 2 covering other types of film, e.g., news, educational, scientific, etc.

Cheng Jihua, ed. *Zhongguo dianying fazhan shi* (History of the Development of Chinese Film). 2v. 1963. Reprint. Beijing: China Film Press, 1980. The most comprehensive Chinese work on the subject, covering from the beginnings to 1949.

China Film Association, ed. *Zhongguo dianying jia liezhuan* ("Biographies of Chinese Film Artists"). Beijing: China Film Press, 1991.

_____. *Zhongguo dianying jinjijiang wenji* (A Collection of the Golden Rooster Prize Essays). Beijing: China Film Press, 1983. Essays discussing prize-winning films and filmmakers.

Mei Duo. *Mei Duo dianying pinglun ji* (Mei Duo's Critical Essays on Films). Chengdu: Sichuan Literature and Art Press, 1985. Collection of articles by a noted film critic.

Quangguo Baokan Dianying Wenzhang Mulu Suoyin (Bibliographic Index of National Motion Picture Periodical Literature, 1949–1979). Beijing: China Motion Picture Publishing House, 1983. Jointly compiled by the Beijing Library and the China Filmmakers Association, this work indexes approximately 30,000 articles and film reviews from 62 PRC newspapers and 108 magazines. Coverage is not limited to Chinese films, but includes foreign developments as well. Arrangement is by the Beijing Library's classification scheme, and an appendix lists entries chronologically within periodical title.

Yang Sheng et al., eds. *Zhongguo dianying yanyuan bairen zhuan* ("Biographies of a Hundred Chinese Film Stars"). Wuhan: Changjiang Literature and Art Press, 1984.

Yang Wenming and Xie Xizhang, eds. *Zhongguo dianying mingxing lu* ("Chinese Film Stars"). Beijing: Xuewan Press, 1990.

Zhongguo da baike quanshu dianying (China Encyclopaedia: Motion Pictures). Beijing, Shanghai: China Encyclopaedia Publishing House, 1991. Not so comprehensive as the next entry. Includes foreign motion picture developments as well as Chinese.

Zhongguo dianying da cidian ("China Cinema Encyclopaedia"). Shanghai: Shanghai Dictionary Publishing House, 1995. Massive work covering all aspects of Chinese film, historical and contemporary. Particularly valuable for illustrated biographies and brief articles about notable films, film studios, film publications, from all historical periods.

Zhongguo Yingpian Dadian: gushi pian, xiqu pian, 1977–1994 ("Encyclopaedia of Chinese Films": feature films, opera films, 1977–1994). Beijing: China Motion Picture Publishing House, 1995. Jointly compiled by the China Film Art Research Center and the China Motion Picture Information Library. Published to commemorate the 100th anniversary of the motion picture, this is the most comprehensive resource for the era covered although I found a number of films excluded for reasons unexplained, probably political.

Zhongguo Yishu Yingpian Bianmu, 1949–1979 (Catalog of Chinese Feature Films, 1949–1979). 2v. Beijing: Culture and Art Publishing House, 1981. Jointly compiled by the Chinese Film Archive and the Film Research Institute of the Chinese Academy of Art, this filmography is *the* source of basic information on films in the era covered. In addition to feature films, it includes detailed credits and synopses for filmed stage operas, documentaries and animated films. The arrangement is chronological.

PERIODICALS (available outside of China)

Dangdai Dianying ("Contemporary Cinema"). Beijing: China Film Art Research Center, 1984–   . Bi-Monthly. Scholarly journal carrying commentaries on the work of noted directors and performers, historical articles and film appreciation.

Dazhong Dianying ("Popular Cinema"). Beijing: Chinese Film Artists Association, 1950–   , title changed from *Renmin Dianying* (People's Cinema) in 1979. Monthly. The most widely read Chinese film magazine, with a circulation of more than 100 million. Content includes commentary on many current and some classic Chinese and foreign films, personality profiles, news of the Chinese (including Hong Kong and Taiwan) and foreign film communities, etc. Annually conducts a readers' poll wich determines winners of the "Hundred Flowers" film awards.

Dianying Chuangzuo ("Cinematic Creation"). Beijing Film Academy, 1958–   . Bi-Monthly. Aimed at motion picture fans and film industry workers alike, regular features of this journal include: excerpts from film scripts; reports on the activities of filmmakers, including their first-person accounts; theories of filmmaking; discussions of film personalities of the past; selected news items, etc.

Dianying Gushi ("Film Stories"). Shanghai Yunglo Company, Ltd., 1952– . Monthly. A profusely illustrated, high-level popularization, each issue provides credits and synopses for recent Chinese feature film releases as well as foreign films released in China, profiles of current and past Chinese and foreign film personalities, and commentary on various social, legal and political developments which can affect China's film industry. A valuable regular feature of the magazine are its lists of data compiled from widely scattered sources, e.g., Chinese films appearing at international film festivals.

Dianying Huakan (Film Pictorial). Xi'an: Shaanxi Film Company. 1985– . Monthly. Announces new films from the Xi'an, Emei, Zhujiang, August First, Xiaoxiang, Guangxi and Tianshan Film Studios. Does not carry the news and profile columns usually found in other periodicals.

Dianying Shijie (Film World). Changchun Film Studio. 1958– . Monthly. Articles on virtually every aspect of domestic and foreign motion pictures and their creation, with particular attention to those produced by the Changchun Film Studio.

Dianying Xinzuo ("New Films"). Shanghai Film Artists Association. 1979– . Bi-Monthly. A journal of theoretical research, criticism and articles on filmmaking. Regularly includes scripts and synopses, interviews and discussions with filmmakers, criticism, profiles, etc.

Dianying Yishu (Film Art). Beijing: China Film Artists Association. 1956– , title changed from *Zhongguo Dianying* (Chinese Cinema) in 1959. Bi-Monthly. The Association's professional journal. Contents include papers on motion picture screenwriting, directing, acting, cinematography, sound recording and other technical aspects of filmmaking, as well as research papers on movie history and contemporary foreign films.

Juying Yuebao ("Stage and Screen"). Nanjing: Jiangsu Hall of Culture. 1959– . Monthly. General articles on stage, screen and TV productions. Articles tend to be theoretical or critical.

Shangying Huabao ("Shanghai Film"). Shanghai Film Studio. 1956– . Monthly. The emphasis here is on discussion and popularization of films from Shanghai's studios, i.e., the Shanghai Film Studio, Shanghai Animated Film Studio, Shanghai Scientific and Educational Film Studio and the Shanghai Film Translation and Dubbing Studio. Also some discussion of foreign films and film artists.

Zhongguo Dianying Nianjian ("China Film Yearbook"). Beijing: China Motion Picture Publishing House, 1982– . This annual publication has been the ultimate authority for PRC film developments ever since its inception. In addition to numerous articles on a wide range of contemporary and historical topics, each large volume contains a filmography with credits and lengthy plot summaries of every feature film produced in China during the previous year. Publication was on a very regular basis until the 1992 volume, covering 1991 developments. Publication has been very slow since then: the 1993 volume carries a 1993 imprint, but actually came out in early 1996.

Zhongguo Yinmu (China Screen). Beijing: China Film Export and Import Corporation. 1958-1966; 1980– . Quarterly. Chinese language version of *China Screen*, which ceased in 1994. Unlike the English version, also covers Western releases in the PRC.

Index

This book uses Pinyin romanization for the spelling of Chinese names. This system presents a problem in indexing because distinctly different Chinese names may appear similar, even identical, when romanized. For example, four individuals with four different Chinese names are all listed as "Zhang Yuan" in this book.

Moreover, it is not uncommon for two or more members of the Chinese movie community to work under the same name. As an example, this book lists two directors named Xu Ke: the modern Hong Kong–based filmmaker known to Western fans of martial arts movies as Tsui Hark, and a namesake who was active in the 1940s.

To differentiate between similar names (and thus make the index more useful for the reader), I have adopted the following:

—"**a**" and "**d**" establish whether a credit is for acting or directing.

—"**f**" and "**m**" are used to distinguish female and male performers having identical names, except in the few cases where I was unable to determine gender with certainty.

— when two or more persons of the same sex have the same name, I have indicated the decade(s) in which each was most active. In the few cases where a juvenile actor was active in the same decade as an adult namesake, I have added a **j** to the juvenile's entry.

— where possible, cross-references are provided for Hong Kong or Western-based filmmakers known outside of China by other names.

References are to entry numbers.